MW01233394

Teacher's Edition Author
JOSEPH H. DEMPSEY
Classroom Teacher, Morris School District, Morristown, New Jersey

Student's Text Authors
HERBERT J. BASS
Professor of History, Temple University

GEORGE A. BILLIAS
Professor of History, Clark University

EMMA JONES LAPSANSKY
Assistant Professor of History, Temple University

SILVER BURDETT COMPANY
MORRISTOWN, NEW JERSEY
Glenview, Illinois Palo Alto Dallas Atlanta

Program Contributors

CONSULTANT

Beth Millstein, History Teacher
Adlai Stevenson High School, New York, New York

END-OF-CHAPTER-MATERIAL AUTHOR AND CRITIC READER

Clara W. Mason, History Teacher
Jonathan Dayton Regional High School
Springfield, New Jersey

CRITIC READERS

Charles A. Loparo, Assistant Superintendent
Brecksville-Broadview Heights, Ohio, School System

Norma Norton, Principal
Auburn, Alabama, School System

Nobuo Watanabe, Coordinator of Social Studies
Superintendent of Schools Office
Contra Costa County, California

Oscar Zepeda, History Teacher
Del Valle, Texas, High School

Acknowledgments

Page 89: Excerpt from *A History of the English-Speaking Peoples*, Vol. 3, *The Age of Revolution* by Winston Churchill. Copyright 1957 Dodd, Mead & Company. Reprinted by permission of Dodd, Mead & Company and The Canadian Publishers, McClelland and Stewart Limited, Toronto. Page 259: Excerpt from *Alistair Cooke's America* by Alistair Cooke. Copyright © 1973 Alfred A. Knopf, Inc. Reprinted by permission. Page 398: Excerpt from *The Immigrant in American History* by Marcus Lee Hansen. Copyright 1940 by the President and Fellows of Harvard College. Reprinted by permission. Page 478–479: Excerpt from *The Diary of George Templeton Strong* edited by Allan Nevins and Milton H. Thomas. Copyright 1952 by Macmillan Publishing Co., Inc. Reprinted by permission.

 ISBN 0-382-02454-0

Contents

About the Authors and Consultant

HERBERT J. BASS Dr. Bass is Professor of History and Chairman of the History Department at Temple University in Philadelphia, Pennsylvania. His teaching career spans more than twenty years and includes teaching at Clark University and the University of Maine. His special area of study is late-nineteenth- and twentieth-century America. Dr. Bass is the author of *America's Entry into World War I*, editor of *The State of American History*, and co-editor of *Readings in American History*. In addition, he has written articles and reviews for professional journals and has taught summer NDEA institutes in which new materials were created for the teaching of history in high schools. He is a member of the American Historical Association and the Organization of American Historians.

GEORGE A. BILLIAS Dr. Billias is Professor of American History at Clark University in Worcester, Massachusetts. He has also taught at the University of Maine and has served as National Defense Historian for the U.S. Air Force. In his twenty-four years of college teaching, he has specialized in American military, legal, and constitutional history. Dr. Billias has been co-editor of and a contributor to a number of history books, including *Interpretations of American History: Patterns and Perspectives*, and has written many articles for historical journals. He has won numerous academic honors, including a Guggenheim Fellowship, and is a member of the Institute of Early American History and Culture and the American Historical Association.

EMMA JONES LAPSANSKY Dr. Lapsansky is Assistant Professor of History at Temple University in Philadelphia, Pennsylvania. Formerly she taught at Moore College of Art and at the University of Pennsylvania. In her nine years of teaching at the college level, Dr. Lapsansky has specialized in American social history and Afro-American history. Her writings include a research report titled "Before the Model City: An Historical Exploration of the Negro in North Philadelphia." Among the professional organizations Dr. Lapsansky belongs to are the American Historical Association, Organization of American Historians, and the Association for the Study of Afro-American Life and History.

JOSEPH H. DEMPSEY Mr. Dempsey has been teaching in the Morris School District, Morristown, New Jersey, for nineteen years. He originated, designed, and implemented the Academic Advancement Program, which was funded by the U.S. Office of Education. The program, successfully replicated in over twenty other school districts, received the Education Pacesetter Award from the President's Council on Education. Mr. Dempsey has served as Executive Director for the Morris County Council of Education Associations and participates in numerous educational and professional organizations, including the National Council for the Social Studies.

CLARA W. MASON Mrs. Mason teaches history at Jonathan Dayton Regional High School in Springfield, New Jersey. Her teaching career covers thirty years and includes experience in teaching a wide variety of history and social studies courses at the high school level. She has participated in summer workshops in American history and government and serves as a cooperating teacher for student teachers from five area colleges and universities.

BETH MILLSTEIN Ms. Millstein is Assistant Chairperson in the Social Studies Department at Adlai Stevenson High School in the Bronx, New York, and is responsible for a women's studies program. She is co-author of a high school and junior college text entitled *We, the American Women: A Documentary History*. Ms. Millstein has taught the full spectrum of high school social studies courses in her ten-year career. She is a member of the Executive Board of the Association of Teachers of Social Studies for New York City.

About the Book

In writing this book we had two chief aims. One was to invite the readers to explore with us that perennially relevant and intriguing question, What makes Americans American? Our plan was to focus on a number of those beliefs and attributes that are, if not unique to Americans, at least characteristic of us—beliefs such as those in limited government and in progress, attributes such as ethnic diversity and mobility. Then in each unit we would range through our history explaining how each characteristic came to be associated with the very essence of Americanness. We make no claim to inclusiveness: surely the relatively few characteristics that we could single out for exploration in a book such as this do not exhaust the list of American characteristics; and a brief list drawn up by other historians might well not match our own. But just as certainly, the topics we have focused on are among the most important, and an understanding of them goes far toward understanding what Americanness means.

Our second chief aim was to tell the full story of America's history in all its rich detail. By allowing America's majestic development from frontier settlements to world power to unfold on these pages, we believed we could contribute to an appreciation both of America's past and of history in general.

At an early point in our planning, we frankly wondered if it would be possible to accomplish both these aims in the same book. The main obstacle seemed to be one of clashing organizational demands. To explore American characteristics and their historical roots seemed to demand a topical approach; to tell the story of America required a chronological one. As historians who appreciate that time and sequence are the very essence of history, we believed it necessary to retain a chronological organization.

Our concern proved groundless, for the conflict turned out to be no conflict at all. We have dealt with all the familiar—and many not-so-familiar—events, persons, and forces in American history within an overall chronological organization. At the same time, each unit, after an introduction that establishes the continued vitality of one of those beliefs or attributes we have identified as characteristically American, explains how it came to be so. Thus, for example, the unit on the colonial era includes all the major developments of the period that any good text is expected to cover. But the unit also attempts to explain how the very conditions of existence in the New World led to the enduring association of the idea of opportunity with America. Similarly, the second unit deals with the history of the American Revolution—probably in greater depth, in fact, than most high school histories do. But it also leads the readers to an understanding of the way in which this formative event in our life as a people has shaped the way Americans view revolutions in our own world. And so on, with each succeeding unit. Whenever possible, we have tried to lead our readers to these larger understandings through techniques that make them active rather than passive learners.

How well we have succeeded must be judged by others. To the extent that we have, however, we will have helped our readers better understand who they are and how they got to be that way. And if we have done that, we can take satisfaction in having achieved one of the most important ends of history. For good history does not merely chronicle the past; it informs the present.

Herbert J. Bass George A. Billias Emma Jones Lapsansky

Features of the Student's Text

A

★1★

George Washington
1732–1799

Born in VIRGINIA
In Office 1789–1797
Party NONE

Elected and reelected by unanimous electoral vote. Helped erect government departments, agencies, and courts. Advised the United States to stay clear of permanent foreign alliances.

★ ★ ★ ★ ★ ★ ★ ★

B

Hero . . . and Traitor

Every war produces heroes and traitors. The Revolutionary War was no exception. In the careers of Nathan Hale and Benedict Arnold, one can see a clear example of this pattern.

Nathan Hale was born in Connecticut and attended Yale College. He was teaching school when war broke out, but en-

C

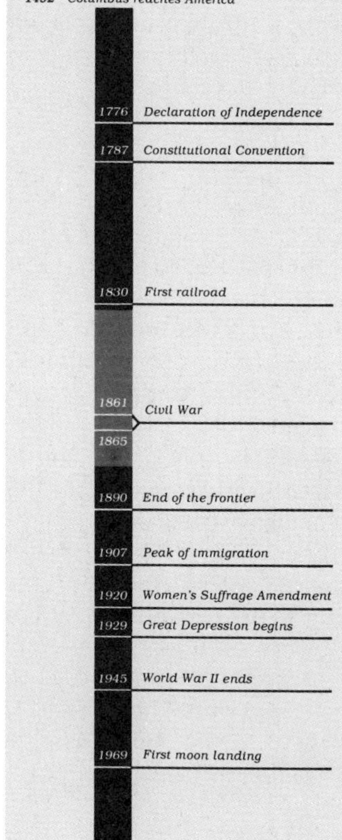

D

CHECKUP

1. How did relations change between the United States and the Soviet Union during the 1950s?
2. What part did America play in the war in the Middle East in 1956?
3. In what two ways did the United States become involved with events in Cuba during Kennedy's administration?

E

Key Facts from Chapter 14

1. The term *manifest destiny* became popular during the 1840s as an expression of the expansionist goals of the United States.
2. Texas became independent of Mexico in 1836 and joined the United States in 1845.

F

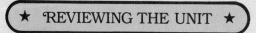

★ REVIEWING THE CHAPTER ★

People, Places, and Events

Navigation Acts *P. 82*
French and Indian War *P. 85*
Stamp Act *P. 87*
Conspiracy theory *P. 88*
Stamp Act Congress *P. 90*

who sided with the British.) What arguments might you use to win him or her away from the Loyalist cause?

Chapter Test

On a separate piece of paper, write **T** *if the statement is true and* **F** *if the statement is*

G

★ REVIEWING THE UNIT ★

Skills Development: Creating a Time Line

In your study of American history, you have learned about many of the important events that have helped to shape the nation. Some of those events are shown in the chronological listing that follows.

1954 *Brown* v. *Board of Education of Topeka, Kansas*
1955 Martin Luther King, Jr., led Montgomery, Alabama, boycott
1965 Voting Rights Act

H

Webster's American Language

The burst of nationalism that America experienced after the War of 1812 expressed itself in many different forms. One way was through changes in language suggested by Noah Webster, a native of Connecticut. Soon after the Revolutionary War, Webster, a graduate of Yale College, had written, "America must be as independent in *literature* as she is in *politics* . . ." He wanted to form a national "American" language that would be distinct from English. He was convinced the first step toward achieving America's literary indepen-

Features of the Student's Text

Our American Heritage consists of thirty-six chapters organized into ten units. The basic text is enhanced by some 450 illustrations, more than 60 maps, and a variety of charts, graphs, and tables.

A

The Presidents. At appropriate places throughout the book are special boxes on the Presidents of the United States. Each box includes a portrait together with factual information on the President and his administration.

B, H

Special-interest materials. Interspersed throughout the text is a variety of materials to complement the basic narrative. The "Sidelights on History" deal with outstanding people and significant events and developments in American history. The materials called "America Expresses Itself" focus on some of the responses of Americans to events and developments of the times in which they lived. The features "Inventions that Changed the Face of America" look at the far-reaching effects of certain technological changes.

C

Time lines. At the beginning of each unit is a time line, common to all units, that shows some of the major events in American history. The time period covered in a unit is set off in a distinctive color. At the end of each unit is another time line, this one focusing on the period covered in the unit.

D

Checkup questions. Each chapter is divided into two to four lessons. At the end of each lesson are questions labeled Checkup. These questions, covering the main points of the lesson, may be used in a variety of ways. The students may use them to check their grasp of the material. The teacher may wish to use these questions for class discussion or written homework.

E

Key facts. At the end of each chapter is a list of the most important facts presented in that chapter. The list may be used in reviewing the chapter, or the teacher may wish to have students read this prior to reading the chapter as a means of getting the main points in mind.

F

Chapter review. At the end of each chapter is a page titled "Reviewing the Chapter." It consists of three elements.

(1) "People, Places, and Events" is a selective listing of important names and terms within the chapter. Each name or term includes a page reference, showing where it first appeared.

(2) "Review Questions" consists of a series of questions covering all lessons in the chapter. These are usually factual questions and generally have a different thrust from the Checkup questions in the body of the chapter. The answers to "Review Questions" are included in the margin of the page in the Teacher's Edition.

(3) "Chapter Test" is the final element of the chapter review page. The test usually takes one of the following forms: true-false, multiple choice, matching, or fill-in. Since the test centers on the subject matter covered in the two preceding sections of the page, it can be used to best effect after those sections have been completed. The test answers may be found in the Teacher's Edition, on the appropriate page.

G

Unit review. At the end of each unit are two pages titled "Reviewing the Unit."

(1) The first page consists of a unit summary and time line. As we said earlier, the time line at the end of the unit focuses on the specific period that the unit covers. In reviewing the unit, the summary and time line may be used separately or in conjunction.

(2) The second end-of-unit page is devoted to skills development. An exercise highlighting the theme of the unit aims to develop a specific social-studies skill. The following skills are among those that are developed.

Creating a Time Line
Reading a Map
Interpreting a Map
Gathering Source Material
Analyzing Source Material
Interpreting Graphs
Interpreting a Table
Interpreting Cartoons

Features of the Teacher's Edition

Each chapter of the Student's Text is divided into teaching lessons. The approximate number of days to be devoted to a lesson is stated at the beginning of the lesson. All the basic material needed to teach a lesson is conveniently located in the Teacher's Edition margins of the text pages. The material is organized in the following categories.

Background Information
Performance Objectives
Famous People
Vocabulary
Activities

A brief explanation of each of these categories follows.

Performance Objectives. These are statements of what the student can be expected to do with the content of the chapter after he or she has read and studied it. The performance objectives are stated in terms of demonstrable or observable student behavior. They have been written with the following questions in mind: What should the student be able to do? Under what conditions should he or she be able to do it? How will he or she do it? How will the teacher know when the student has done it?

Famous People. This is a listing of people who have played significant roles in history and whose names appear in the lesson. The teacher may wish to have the class do oral or written reports on these individuals.

Vocabulary. This section includes a listing of key words and terms that appear in the lesson. The teacher may wish to review this list with the students in the classroom or may prefer to use it as the basis for homework assignments.

This is a reduction of the actual pages in the Teacher's Edition.

LESSON 2 *(2 days)*

Performance Objectives

1. To describe in writing the working conditions prevalent in most factories in the latter half of the nineteenth century.
2. To list and explain the major advances and setbacks enjoyed and suffered by organized labor from the 1850s to 1900.

Famous People

Terence V. Powderly, Samuel Gompers, Eugene V. Debs

Vocabulary

Laissez faire, Sherman Anti-Trust Act, *Progress and Poverty,* "needle trades," collective bargaining, National Labor Union (NLU), Knights of Labor, Haymarket Riot, anarchists, American Federation of Labor, yellow dog contract, blacklist, injunction, Homestead Strike, Pullman Strike

From Rags to Riches

The dream of success in terms of personal progress was a persistent theme in American novels during the period after the Civil War. An almost endless stream of books encouraged boys to feel that they could go from rags to riches. With a few variations, those books told the same tale: how a poor youth of noble character overcame setbacks to achieve worldly success.

One author who made a career of writing such books was Horatio Alger. The son of a Massachusetts clergyman, he became a minister himself because his father insisted on it. But in 1866 he left the pulpit, settled in New York, and began his writing career. His books—such as *Luck and Pluck* and *Tattered Tom*—dealt with penniless lads who rose to fame and fortune. Alger's novels made the moral that in America, success could come to anyone who worked hard, had courage, was of good character, and was blessed with good luck. Alger wrote 130 books all on this same theme, and more than 20 million copies were sold.

Girls were also provided with success stories, but such stories for girls focused on home and family rather than on the business world. Martha Finley was to girls what Horatio Alger was to boys. Thousands of girls followed the trials of Elise Dinsmore, the pure-in-heart heroine in a number of Martha Finley's novels.

About 1900, a new kind of popular literature—the dime novel—appeared. Printed on cheap paper in magazine form, the dime novel offered stories with such titles as "From Bootblack to Senator" and "Winning the Dollars."

For more than half a century, the success stories of Horatio Alger, Martha Finley, and others were read by countless boys and girls. Those novels shaped the views of a great many Americans about personal progress and success.

This dust cover from a book by Horatio Alger indicates the rags-to-riches theme of that writer's stories. The penniless newsboy will surely go on to win fame and fortune through perseverance, courage, and a bit of luck.

510

Activities. In each lesson, a number of activities are suggested for use with the text. The activities are designed to add to the students' knowledge as well as to help develop skills. The activities vary from lesson to lesson, depending on the nature of the content and the purpose of the lesson.

There may be more activities than you will care to use for a particular lesson. *It is not necessary to carry out all of the activities.* Select those that seem most appropriate for your class. Feel free to alter them if you wish. For example, you may feel that a discussion is a more effective way to develop a topic than is a suggested written report. Or you may believe that on a particular issue your class will benefit more from a debate than from a film.

Each activity has a descriptive heading. Among the kinds of activities are the following.

Reading for Information
Creative Writing
Using a Map
Research
Oral Report
Discussion
Debate
Films
Guest Speaker
Thought Provoker

Before your class begins its study of a unit, you may find it desirable to read the material in the margins of the text pages. You will then be able to assign activities ahead of time, so that students will have them completed at the time the lesson is being studied.

Background Information. This material is intended to enrich and extend the text as well as the illustrations. Background information is supplied for all chapter opening pictures. This information, when used to gain the interest of the students, can be an effective motivating device for the study of the lesson.

LESSON 2

The Cost of Progress

By no means did all Americans agree with the justifications of social Darwinism. They pointed out that most of those who talked of *laissez faire*, that is, no government interference, in fact sought and received government aid. Such aid included high tariffs and land grants from the federal government and tax breaks from local ones. Those who talked about the need for competition were often the same ones who did whatever they could to prevent it. Indeed, they often acted illegally to avoid it.

Critics of big business. Some Americans did not accept the idea that government should never interfere, nor that business consolidations were natural, necessary, and good. They demanded a law to outlaw trusts and other such combinations. In 1890, Congress responded with the Sherman Anti-Trust Act. This law declared that combinations that restrained trade in interstate commerce were illegal. Little came of the law for a number of years as court decisions sharply limited its use.

Many people also rejected the social Darwinist view that progress could only come through the elimination of the weak by the strong. In *Progress and Poverty* (1879) Henry George, a newspaper writer, reformer, and self-taught economist spoke for many when he wrote:

> So long as all the increased wealth which modern progress brings goes but to build up great fortunes to increase luxury and make sharper the contrast between the House of Have and the House of Want, progress is not real and cannot be permanent.

It was in the cities that the contrast between the House of Have and the House of Want was most striking. Just blocks from Charles Schwab's mansion was the shantytown in which the Irish immigrant poor lived in crude huts of wood and cardboard. Some blocks farther away were neighborhoods whose very names—Hell's Kitchen and Bandit's Roost—told of the desperate conditions of life there. It is doubtful that these people saw millionaires as the same "bargain" for society that William Graham Sumner did.

The workers' lot. The working conditions in America's mills, factories, and mines had hardly improved over what they had been before the Civil War. As late as 1900, the average workweek was 58 hours. In the steel industry, it was 72 hours. Women made up 20 percent of the work force in manufacturing. They generally received less pay than men, although they worked the same long hours. Women made up the largest part of the work force in the "needle trades," making dresses and other clothing.

Children made up another important part of the work force. In 1890, 600,000 boys and girls between ten and fourteen years of age were working 10 to 12 hours a day in factories and mines. Even younger children worked the 12-hour night shift in some southern cotton mills. A nineteenth-century reformer named Sarah Cleghorn captured the unfairness of child labor in these bitter lines.

> The golf links lie so near the mill
> That almost every day
> The laboring children can look out
> And see the men at play.

511

Activities

1. ESSAY After students hare read the lesson, have them write brief essays describing wages and working conditions in American industry during this period. They should try to show why people would consider joining unions.

2. USING A CHART Today's unions are much different from the first unions. The direction of change can be seen between the time of the NLU and the AF of L. Have students construct a chart showing similarities and differences between the NLU, the Knights of Labor, and the AF of L. The categories might include Leaders, Membership (who belonged), Goals, and Accomplishments. All the information can be found in or inferred from the text, except that William Sylvis was the leader of the NLU. For a more complex exercise, have students decide what categories to use.

Background Information

1. SHERMAN ANTI-TRUST ACT In its early years this act was used primarily in the opposition of labor unions and thus actually helped the businesses it was designed to limit. The courts ruled that labor unions were organizations that worked "in restraint of trade" and thus were prohibited by the law under the commerce section of the Constitution. The leaders of the unions were served injunctions by the court to stop striking or even to stop organizing the workers. If they refused, they could be sent to jail for contempt of court. The Norris-LaGuardia Anti-Injunction Act, the Wagner Act, and changing court opinions ended this practice by the 1940s.

Books and Other Media

UNIT ONE

Books For Teachers and Students

America. Alistair Cooke. Alfred A. Knopf, Inc.

The American Story. Earl Schenck Miers, ed. Channel Press.

European Discovery of America. Samuel Eliot Morison. Oxford University Press, Inc. (1)*

Films (16mm)

European Expansion: Its Influence on Man. McGraw-Hill Films. 19 min., color. (1)

First Americans, Parts I & II. NBC Films. Part I 20 min; Part II 32 min., color. (4)

Religious Freedom in America's Beginnings. Coronet Films. 14 min., color. (2)

Filmstrips

Colonial America. American Heritage Publishing Co. Series of 5 filmstrips, color, sound. (3)

Discovery and Exploration. American Heritage Publishing Co. Series of 5 filmstrips, color, sound. (1)

UNIT TWO

Books for Teachers and Students

Benjamin Franklin. Carl Van Doren. The Viking Press, Inc. (6)

The War of the Revolution, Vols. I & II. Christopher Ward. Macmillan, Inc. (2–3)

Films (16mm)

The American Revolution, Part I: The Course of Liberty. Robert Saudek Associates, Inc. 25 min., color. (5)

The American Revolution, Part II: The Impossible War. Robert Saudek Associates, Inc. 25 min., color. (6)

Filmstrips

The American Revolution—Roots of Rebellion. Globe Filmstrips. Series of 6 filmstrips, color, sound. (5–6)

The Loyalists in the American Revolution. Multi-Media Productions. 1 filmstrip, color, sound. (7)

UNIT THREE

Books for Teachers and Students

The Great Rehearsal: The Story of the Making and Ratifying of the Constitution of the United States. Carl Van Doren. The Viking Press. (9)

Jefferson and His Time. Dumas Malone. Little, Brown and Company (9–10)

The Way Our People Lived: An Intimate American History. William E. Woodward. Washington Square Press. (11)

*Refers to the chapter or chapters for which this material is particularly appropriate.

Films (16mm)

Constitution: One Nation, Parts I & II. Ford Foundation TV Workshop. 30 min., b & w. (9)

Thomas Jefferson. Handel Film Corporation. 34 min., color. (10)

A Time to Grow: The Louisiana Territory. Teaching Film Custodians. 20 min., b & w. (11)

Filmstrips

The Constitution: The Compromise That Made a Nation. Learning Corporation of America. Series of 2 filmstrips, color, sound. (9)

Mr. Madison's War. Multi-Media Productions. 1 filmstrip, color, sound. (11)

UNIT FOUR

Books for Teachers and Students

The Age of Jackson. Arthur M. Schlesinger, Jr. Little, Brown and Company. (13)

America Moves West. Robert E. Riegel and Robert G. Athearn. The Dryden Press, Inc. (12–14)

Democracy in America, Vols. I & II. Alexis de Tocqueville. Vintage Books. (12)

John Quincy Adams and the Foundations of American Foreign Policy. Samuel Flagg Bemis. Alfred A. Knopf, Inc. (13)

Films (16mm)

Andrew Jackson at the Hermitage. Coronet Films. 16 min., color. (13)

Canals: Towpaths West. Indiana University, Audio-Visual Center. 17 min., color. (12)

The Man Who Took a Chance: Eli Whitney. Teaching Film Custodians. 20 min., b & w. (12)

Texas and the Mexican War. Encyclopaedia Britannica Films. 16 min., color. (14)

Filmstrips

The American Frontier as the Camera Saw It. Imperial Film Co. Series of 4 filmstrips, sound. (12–14)

The Jackson Years: The New Americans. Learning Corporation of America. Series of 2 filmstrips, color, sound. (13)

Manifest Destiny. Multi-Media Productions. Series of 2 filmstrips, color, sound. (14)

UNIT FIVE

Books for Teachers and Students

Abraham Lincoln: The War Years. Carl Sandburg. Harcourt Brace Jovanovich, Inc. (17)

Eyewitness: The Negro in American History. William Loren Katz. Pitman Publishing Corporation. (15)

A Stillness at Appomattox. Bruce Catton. Doubleday & Company, Inc. (17)

Films (16 mm)

Background of the Civil War. Film Associates of California. 20 min., color. (17)

Black History: Lost, Stolen or Strayed. CBS Films. 53 min., color. (15)

The Civil War: Postwar Period. Coronet Films. 16 min., color. (18)

Heritage of Slavery. CBS Films. 56 min., color. (15)

Johnson and Reconstruction. MGM Films. 36 min., b&w. (18)

Filmstrips

The Civil War. American Heritage Publishing Co. Series of 5 filmstrips, color, sound.

Slavery. Zenger Productions. Series of 2 filmstrips, color, sound.

The Years of the Reconstruction: 1865–1877. McGraw-Hill Films. Series of 2 filmstrips, color, sound. (18)

UNIT SIX

Books for Teachers and Students

Beyond the Melting Pot. Nathan Glazer and Daniel P. Moynihan. The M.I.T. Press. (19–22)

The Uprooted. Oscar Handlin. Little, Brown and Company. (19–22)

Films (16 mm)

The Immigrant Experience: The Long, Long Journey. Learning Corporation of America. 28 min., color. (21)

Immigration in the 19th Century. David Wolper Productions, Inc. 12 min., b&w. (19)

Immigration in the 20th Century. David Wolper Productions, Inc. 13 min., b&w. (20)

Filmstrips

America, The Melting Pot: Myth or Reality. Current Affairs Films. 1 filmstrip, color, sound. (21)

Out Multi-Ethnic Heritage. Educational Activities. Series of 5 filmstrips, color, sound. (22)

UNIT SEVEN

Books for Teachers and Students

The Age of Enterprise: A Social History of Industrial America. Thomas C. Cochran and William Miller. Harper & Row, Publishers, (23–26)

America As a Civilization. Max Lerner. Simon and Schuster, Inc. (25)

The Americans: The Democratic Experience. Daniel J. Boorstin. Random House, Inc. (23–25)

The Good Years: From 1900 to the First World War. Walter Lord. Harper Brothers. (25)

The World of the American Indian. National Geographic Society. (24)

Films (16mm)

America Becomes an Industrial Nation. McGraw-Hill Films. 25 min., color. (23)

The Automotive American. National Educational Television. 29 min., b&w. (25)

Eyeball Witnesses. National Educational Television. 30 min., b&w. (24)

The Industrial Revolution: Beginnings in the United States. Encyclopaedia Britannica Films. 25 min., color. (23)

The Real West. NBC Films. 51 min., b&w. (24)

This Union Cause. Contemporary Films, Inc. 23 min., color. (25)

Toward the Gilded Age. NBC Films. 25 min., color. (25)

The Twenties. McGraw-Hill Films. 25 min., color. (26)

Filmstrips

The Great Depression: 1929–1939. Guidance Associates. Series of 2 filmstrips, color, sound. (26)

Inventions and Technology That Shaped America, Part I: Colonial Times to Civil War. Learning Corporation of America. Series of 6 filmstrips, color, sound. (24)

The Rise of the Industrial Giants. McGraw-Hill Films. Series of 2 filmstrips, color, sound. (23)

UNIT EIGHT

Books for Teachers and Students

The American People in the Twentieth Century. Oscar Handlin. Beacon Press. (29–30)

Cities in American Life. Richard C. Wade, ed. Houghton Mifflin Company. (29)

The Other America. Michael Harrington. Macmillan, Inc. (30)

Films (16mm)

The New Deal. McGraw-Hill Films. 25 min., color. (30)

The Progressives. McGraw-Hill Films. 25 min., color. (29)

Trusts and Trust Busters. McGraw-Hill Films. 25 min., color. (29)

Filmstrips

America in the 1890's. Coronet Films. A multi-media kit: 1 filmstrip, color, sound; 4 duplicating masters. (29)

The Reckless Years: 1919–1929. Guidancy Associates. Series of 2 filmstrips, color, sound. (29)

UNIT NINE

Books for Teachers and Students

The Origins of the World War. Sidney Bradshaw Fay. Macmillan, Inc. (32)

The Path Between the Seas: The Creation of the Panama Canal: 1870–1914. David McCullough. Simon and Schuster, Inc. (31)

Roosevelt: The Soldier of Freedom. James McGregor Burns. Harcourt Brace Jovanovich, Inc. (33)

The Splendid Little War. Frank Freidel. Bramhall House. (31)

Films (16mm)

The Great War. NBC Films. 52 min., b&w. (32)

Growth of American Foreign Policy. McGraw-Hill Films. 20 min., b&w. (31)

Home Front, 1917–1919: War Transforms American Life. CBS Films. 17 min., b&w. (32)

The Second World War: Prelude to Conflict. Encyclopaedia Britannica Films. 29 min., b&w. (33)

The Second World War: Triumph of the Axis. Encyclopaedia Britannica Films. 24 min., b&w. (33)

Wilson's Fight for Peace. CBS Films. 26 min., b&w. (32)

Filmstrips

The United States Becomes a World Power. McGraw-Hill Films. Series of 2 filmstrips, color, sound. (31)

World War II. American Heritage Publishing Co. Series of 5 filmstrips, color, sound. (32)

UNIT TEN

Books for Teachers and Students

Breach of Faith: The Fall of Richard Nixon. Theodore H. White. Reader's Digest Press. (Atheneum Publishers) (36)

A History of the Cold War. John Lukacs. Doubleday & Co., Inc. (Anchor Books) (34)

Lyndon Johnson and the American Dream. Doris Kearns. Harper & Row, Publishers. (36)

Meeting at Potsdam. Charles L. Mee, Jr. M. Evans & Co., Inc. (34)

Mexican Americans. Joan W. Moore. Prentice-Hall, Inc. (36)

A Pictorial History of Women in America. Ruth Warren. Crown Publishers, Inc. (36)

We, the American Women: A Documentary History. Beth Millstein and Jeanne Bodin. Science Research Associates, Inc. (36)

Films (16mm)

The Age of Kennedy: The Presidency. NBC Films. 53 min., b&w. (36)

Germany After the Fall. National Educational Television. 58 min., b&w. (34)

Modern Women: The Uneasy Life. National Educational Television. 60 min., b&w. (35)

The Negro and the American Promise. National Educational Television. 59 min., b&w. (35)

The Truman Years. Teaching Film Custodians. 19 min., b&w. (34)

The Warren Years: The Great Decisions. National Educational Television. 24 min., b&w. (35)

Filmstrips

The 1950s. Social Studies School Service. Series of 6 filmstrips, color, sound. (34–35)

The 1960s. Social Studies School Service. Series of 6 filmstrips, color, sound. (34–35)

The 1970s. Social Studies School Service. Series of 6 filmstrips, color, sound. (35–36)

Professional Books for Teachers

Banks, James A., ed. *Curriculum Guidelines for Multiethnic Education.* Washington, D.C.: National Council for the Social Studies, 1976.

Barr, Robert D., James L. Barth, S. Samuel Shermis. *Defining the Social Studies.* Washington, D.C.: National Council for the Social Studies, 1977.

Bloom, Benjamin S. *Human Characteristics and School Learning.* New York: McGraw-Hill Book Company, 1976.

Broudy, Harry S. *The Real World of the Public Schools.* New York: Harcourt Brace Jovanovich, Inc., 1972.

Cremin, Lawrence A. *Public Education.* New York: Basic Books, Inc., Publishers, 1976.

Fair, Jean and Fannie R. Shaftel, eds. *Effective Thinking in the Social Studies.* Washington, D.C.: National Council for the Social Studies, 1967.

Mager, Robert F. and Peter Pipe. *Analyzing Performance Problems.* Belmont, California: Fearon Publishers, 1970.

Muessig, Raymond H., ed. *Controversial Issues in the Social Studies: A Contemporary Perspective.* Washington, D.C.: National Council for the Social Studies, 1975.

Shaver, James P., ed. *Building Rationales for Citizenship Education.* Washington, D.C.: National Council for the Social Studies, 1977.

Tests

On pages T13–T32 are tests for each unit in the book. Teachers should feel free to duplicate the tests or, if they prefer to make their own tests, to select those items that they deem appropriate for their students. Each test consists of three parts. Part A and Part B are made up of objective types of questions—true-false, multiple choice, fill-in, and so forth. In general, Part B is more difficult than Part A, and the grading system should reflect that difference. Part C consists of essay questions geared to the chapters in the unit. Be sure to give students specific directions for answering the essay questions. You may wish to use the questions separately, possibly as written assignments for homework or in the classroom.

UNIT 1 TEST

PART A *In the margin at the left of the number, write* **T** *if the statement is true or* **F** *if the statement is false.*

1. The first Americans came from Central Europe.
2. Spain was the first European country to make large land claims in America.
3. The Spaniards explored Central America.
4. The English were the first Europeans to explore the Great Lakes and the Mississippi River.
5. The English explorers concentrated their efforts on North America.
6. In the 1500s, Spain was the richest country in the world because of its manufacturing.
7. The defeat of the Spanish Armada made England the leading sea power in the world.
8. The greatest attraction for settlers in the New World was the abundance of land.
9. The enclosure movement in England encouraged tenant farmers to go to America.
10. St. Augustine was the first city founded in what would become the United States.
11. The Puritans wanted to establish a community based on common ownership of all property.
12. William Penn started a colony primarily for Catholics.
13. By 1776, English was the language of almost every colonist.
14. In the English language, the term *black* implied "evil" or "inferiority" even before Africans were imported as slaves.
15. Traffic in slaves was part of a three-cornered trade system between America (including the West Indies), Africa, and Europe.
16. In general, the colonists felt that the Indians were less than human.
17. The colonies were self-sufficient and therefore did not trade much with other countries.
18. Skilled workers had better living and working conditions in Europe than in America.
19. The case of John Peter Zenger established the principle of freedom of religion.
20. Colonial legislatures and governors were elected by the colonists.

PART B *For each sentence, circle the letter of the best ending.*

1. The first document leading toward religious freedom in the colonies was the **(a)** Maryland Toleration Act, **(b)** Mayflower Compact, **(c)** Great Awakening, **(d)** Articles of Confederation.
2. In Jamestown, the problem of labor shortages was solved by **(a)** instituting the headright system, **(b)** encouraging women to settle there, **(c)** offering land to indentured servants, **(d)** all the above.
3. The increase in slaves in the late 1600s was mainly for the purpose of **(a)** providing more workers in the mines, **(b)** producing more tobacco and rice, **(c)** supplying more house servants, **(d)** providing more Indian fighters.
4. Social mobility refers to a person's ability to **(a)** rise in rank, **(b)** move from place to place, **(c)** move from job to job, **(d)** interact with other people.
5. The major factor that made a colony grow quickly or slowly was **(a)** the country that originally owned it, **(b)** the method of government, **(c)** the way the land was distributed, **(d)** the religion of the settlers.
6. The early explorers of America were looking for all the following *except* **(a)** a faster way to the East, **(b)** gold, **(c)** places to settle themselves, **(d)** trading locations.
7. All the following are reasons that specific colonies were founded *except* **(a)** profit, **(b)** industrial sites, **(c)** religious freedom, **(d)** a place for debtors.
8. The English government established colonies for all the following reasons *except* **(a)** increasing trade, **(b)** weakening the power of the king, **(c)** creating jobs, **(d)** providing land for its citizens.
9. Jamestown had problems in its early years for all the following reasons *except* **(a)** a high death rate, **(b)** food shortages, **(c)** company ownership of the land, **(d)** a population with too many farmers.
10. All the following were requirements for voting in the colonies *except* **(a)** being a white male, **(b)** being over 21, **(c)** owning a certain amount of property, **(d)** never having been an indentured servant.

PART C *Your teacher will give you directions for answering these essay questions.*

Chapter 1 • "America, you have it better." Was Goethe's statement a reality, or a dream? Support your answer with references to America's physical resources as well as the experiences of people who came to America.

Chapter 2 • What were the similarities and differences between the Northern, Middle, and Southern colonies?

Chapter 3 • Describe the condition of women in the colonies. Why, do you think, did they have more rights and opportunities than women in Europe had?

Chapter 4 • Why was social mobility greater in the colonies than in Europe? Who was excluded from this upward social movement, and why?

ANSWERS

PART A

1. F	**6.** F	**11.** F	**16.** T
2. T	**7.** T	**12.** F	**17.** F
3. T	**8.** T	**13.** F	**18.** F
4. F	**9.** T	**14.** T	**19.** F
5. T	**10.** T	**15.** T	**20.** F

PART B

1. a	**6.** c
2. d	**7.** b
3. b	**8.** b
4. a	**9.** d
5. c	**10.** d

UNIT 2 TEST

PART A *Match the name or term in the first section with its descriptive word or phrase in the second section. Write the correct letter at the left of the number.*

1. Writ of assistance
2. Stamp Act
3. Quartering Act
4. Townshend Act
5. Boston Tea Party
6. Privateers
7. Guerilla warfare
8. Mercenaries
9. Nathan Hale
10. Committees of Correspondence
11. Yorktown
12. Fort Ticonderoga
13. Saratoga
14. Lexington and Concord
15. Trenton and Princeton
16. Sam Adams
17. George Washington
18. Tom Paine
19. John Paul Jones
20. Benedict Arnold

a. Hit-and-run military tactics
b. Tax on certain imported goods
c. Traitor during the Revolution
d. Commander in chief of the Continental Army
e. Resulted in the closing of Boston Harbor
f. Sons of Liberty leader from Boston
g. Law allowing troops to live in certain buildings
h. Helped organize opposition to British in the various colonies
i. Tax on newspapers, pamphlets, and legal documents
j. First battles of Revolutionary War
k. Naval hero of Revolution
l. Search warrant requiring no court permission
m. Used to attack British shipping
n. An executed American spy
o. Winter victories that raised Patriots' morale
p. Guns captured here helped free Boston
q. Author of *Common Sense*
r. Site of British surrender ending the war
s. Hired foreign soldiers
t. American victory that brought France into the war as an ally

PART B *Write in the blank the name or term needed to complete the sentence. Some answers may require more than one word.*

1. The ______ War ended French claims on the continent of North America.
2. Loyalists were colonists who favored the ______ side during the war.
3. In 1770, the first bloodshed resulting from colonial opposition to the British was called the ______.
4. The various state ______ became the basic units for the Continental Army.
5. The Marquis de Lafayette and Casimir Pulaski were examples of ______ who aided the Continental Army.
6. The Continental Army was held together by the personality and appearance of ______.
7. Deborah Sampson Gannet was one example of the women who ______ during the Revolution.
8. For most of the war, the ______ army was the attacker.
9. ______ was the British general whose surrender marked the end of the fighting.
10. The Treaty of ______ in 1783 officially recognized the United States and outlined its borders.
11. At the ______, delegates from the colonies wrote and later approved the Declaration of Independence.
12. The Declaration of Independence states that government is based on the consent of the ______.
13. The largest part of the Declaration of Independence was the list of complaints against ______.
14. Despite the loss of farm laborers to the army or militias during the war, crop production remained high because of the work of ______.
15. Before the war was over, such rights as trial by jury, freedom of the press, and freedom of religion were guaranteed by ______.
16. The new governments set up during the war limited ______ to white, male property owners.

17. The conspiracy theory claimed that British officials were trying to take away American ________.

18. The term ________, which had been an insult before the war, became a source of pride after the war.

19. Americans and some others felt that the Revolution should be a ________ for other people who wanted freedom.

20. When other revolutions occurred, Americans judged them on the basis of how similiar their ________ were to those of the American Revolution.

PART C *Your teacher will give you directions for answering these essay questions.*

Chapter 5 • Prior to 1763, the American Revolution was inconceivable to most Americans; by 1775 it seemed inevitable. Identify events and ideas that account for this change in attitudes. Identify the point when you think war became unavoidable.

Chapter 6 • Using the copy of the Declaration of Independence on pages 108–112, answer the following questions. If, in fact, the fighting had already started and each colony had started writing independent constitutions, what was the purpose of the Declaration of Independence? How was that purpose reflected in the organization and wording of the document?

Chapter 7 • The United States was incredibly lucky to win the Revolutionary War. Support this statement by explaining how each of the following factors could have affected the outcome of the war if events had turned out differently: **(a)** foreign allies, **(b)** Loyalists, **(c)** money, **(d)** British strategy and generals, **(e)** localism.

Chapter 8 • A revolution is generally defined as a complete and dramatic change. Using this definition, some people contend that the American Revolution was really not a revolution. Present an argument defending or attacking this idea.

ANSWERS

PART A

1. l	5. e	9. n	13. t	17. d
2. i	6. m	10. h	14. j	18. q
3. g	7. a	11. r	15. o	19. k
4. b	8. s	12. p	16. f	20. c

PART B

1. French and Indian
2. British
3. Boston Massacre
4. militias
5. foreigners
6. George Washington
7. fought
8. British
9. Cornwallis
10. Paris
11. (Second) Continental Congress
12. governed
13. King George III
14. women
15. state constitutions
16. voting (suffrage)
17. liberty
18. Yankee
19. model
20. goals

UNIT 3 TEST

PART A *For each sentence, circle the letter of the best ending.*

1. A major characteristic of the federal system is the United States government's **(a)** complete power over states and individuals, **(b)** complete lack of power over states and individuals, **(c)** limited power over states and individuals.

2. One of the landmarks of self-government in America is the agreement to work for "just and equal laws," as expressed in **(a)** the Mayflower Compact, **(b)** the Articles of Confederation, **(c)** the Northwest Ordinance.

3. Noah Webster is remembered for his work in developing **(a)** the federal system of government, **(b)** the Whig party, **(c)** the American language.

4. The Louisiana Purchase in 1803 **(a)** was opposed by President Jefferson, **(b)** doubled the size of the country, **(c)** weakened the power of the central government.

5. The War of 1812 ended **(a)** in a clear-cut American victory, **(b)** in an unimportant American defeat, **(c)** without either side winning.

6. Immediately after the War of 1812, the United States **(a)** saw an outburst of intense party strife **(b)** looked forward to a calm, prosperous future, **(c)** fell into an economic depression.

7. During the French Revolution and the European wars that followed, President Washington followed a policy of **(a)** neutrality, **(b)** favoring France, **(c)** favoring the British.

8. Alexander Hamilton favored rule by **(a)** the upper class, **(b)** all the people, **(c)** farmers and semiskilled workers.

9. The Democratic-Republican political party was started by **(a)** Alexander Hamilton and John Adams, **(b)** James Madison and Thomas Jefferson, **(c)** Henry Clay and Andrew Jackson.

10. The XYZ Affair was part of a conflict with **(a)** France, **(b)** Britain, **(c)** Mexico.

11. Presidents Jefferson, Madison, and Monroe were known as the **(a)** War Hawks, **(b)** Virginia Dynasty, **(c)** Federalist Three

12. The part of Jefferson's program that best reflected his support of the Bill of Rights was his **(a)** attempt to throw out the Federalist judges, **(b)** sending ships to fight the Barbary pirates, **(c)** allowing the Alien and Sedition Acts to end.

13. The major weakness of the Articles of Confederation concerned **(a)** the balance of power between the state and central governments, **(b)** the government of territories and the formation of new states, **(c)** the control of foreign affairs.

14. The Northwest Ordinance established a method **(a)** for slavery to be established in the territories, **(b)** for territories to become states, **(c)** for the United States to claim new land.

15. One issue that the Constitutional Convention wanted to avoid was **(a)** slavery, **(b)** tariffs, **(c)** the printing of money.

16. The desire to make the central government stronger than the state governments was written into the Constitution in the **(a)** Bill of Rights, **(b)** preamble, **(c)** supremacy clause.

17. The system of limiting the power of each branch of government is called **(a)** the judicial system, **(b)** checks and balances, **(c)** the supremacy clause.

18. The Great Compromise between large and small states at the Constitutional Convention resulted in the decision to have **(a)** a Vice President, **(b)** a bicameral legislature, **(c)** the indirect election of the President.

19. The case of *Marbury* v. *Madison* added to the power of **(a)** the Republicans, **(b)** the Supreme Court, **(c)** the President.

20. One reason for Anti-Federalist opposition to the Constitution was that **(a)** it did not make the central government strong enough, **(b)** it provided for the separation of powers, **(c)** it lacked a Bill of Rights.

PART B *In the following pairs of phrases, one phrase is the cause, and the other is the effect. In each pair, circle the letter of the phrase that is the* cause.

1. **a.** Tie between Aaron Burr and Thomas Jefferson in election of 1800
   b. Twelfth Amendment, changing electoral system
2. **a.** U.S. opposition to paying bribes to pirates
   b. War with Tripoli
3. **a.** British decision to stop War of 1812
   b. U.S. naval control of Great Lakes
4. **a.** Western support for War of 1812
   b. Desire for land in Canada
5. **a.** British impressment of U.S. sailors
   b. Embargo Act
6. **a.** Indirect election of President
   b. Distrust of common people
7. **a.** Formation of Democratic-Republican party
   b. Opposition to Federalist programs
8. **a.** Alien and Sedition Acts
   b. Kentucky and Virginia Resolutions
9. **a.** Belief in strong state government
   b. Weaknesses in the Articles of Confederation
10. **a.** Federalists' fear of immigrants joining the Democratic-Republican party
    b. Passage of Naturalization Act

PART C *Your teacher will give you directions for answering these essay questions.*

Chapter 9 • Explain the necessity of compromise in writing the Constitution. List and explain three issues that were settled by compromises.

Chapter 10 • Thomas Jefferson and Alexander Hamilton represented the range of political opinion in their time. Explain how they were alike and how they were different in their thinking. Be sure to touch upon *at least* the following items: **(a)** the ideal citizen, **(b)** the tariff, **(c)** the power of the central government, **(d)** the national bank.

Chapter 11 • The results of the War of 1812 had nothing to do with the causes. Attack or defend this statement. In doing so, identify the causes and results of the war and tell who supported the war and why they did. Also explain the overall effect of the war on the country.

ANSWERS

PART A

1. c	**6.** b	**11.** b	**16.** c
2. a	**7.** a	**12.** c	**17.** b
3. c	**8.** a	**13.** a	**18.** b
4. b	**9.** b	**14.** b	**19.** c
5. c	**10.** a	**15.** a	**20.** c

PART B

1. a	**6.** b
2. a	**7.** b
3. b	**8.** a
4. b	**9.** a
5. a	**10.** a

UNIT 4 TEST

PART A *Match the name or term in the first section with its descriptive word or phrase in the second section. Write the correct letter at the left of the number.*

1. John Quincy Adams
2. Daniel Boone
3. John C. Calhoun
4. Henry Clay
5. John C. Fremont
6. William H. Harrison
7. Sam Houston
8. Andrew Jackson
9. James K. Polk
10. Winfield Scott
11. Brigham Young
12. Nullification
13. Rendezvous
14. Sectionalism
15. Spoils system
16. Trail of Tears
17. Canals
18. Cotton gin
19. Railroads
20. Steamboat

a. Giving government jobs to political friends
b. Indian removal to the West
c. Extended water transportation to areas with no rivers
d. Meeting of trappers and traders
e. Linked major cities to farmlands
f. Spoke for states' rights
g. Made river transportation two way
h. Spoke for the common man
i. Favoring one part of the country over another
j. Responsible for several important compromises
k. President responsible for Mexican War
l. "Tippecanoe and Tyler, too!"
m. President of Lone Star Republic
n. Assured South of a very profitable crop
o. Opposed by Congress throughout Presidency
p. Declaring federal laws invalid within a state
q. Most famous pioneer
r. Leader of Mormons in Utah
s. Captured Mexico City in Mexican War
t. Leader of revolt in California

PART B *Write T at the left of the number if the statement is true. If the statement is false, change the underlined word or words to make the statement true. Write your change at the end of the statement.*

1. <u>Ratification</u> is the idea that the United States would eventually control all the land from the Atlantic to the Pacific.

2. <u>The Rocky Mountains</u> were the first temporary barrier to United States expansion.

3. <u>Hunters and trappers</u> were generally the first whites to go into a new territory.

4. The transportation revolution affected trade by making it <u>more expensive</u>.

5. Canals were used most frequently in the <u>Southwestern</u> states.

6. In the 1800s, the <u>West</u> was the section that was most interested in states' rights.

7. In the election of 1824, John Quincy Adams won the election in the House of Representatives even though <u>Henry Clay</u> had more electoral votes.

8. In 1825, Oklahoma was made part of a <u>guaranteed territory</u> for the Indians.

9. The election of 1828, when Andrew Jackson defeated <u>John C. Calhoun</u>, marked the split of the Republican party into two parties.

10. The election of Andrew Jackson indicated the rise of the <u>South</u> as a new factor in the sectional conflict.

11. By the 1830s the United States in general had become <u>less</u> democratic in terms of property and religious requirements for holding office.

12. <u>The Tariff of 1828</u> caused South Carolina to claim a sovereign right to declare federal laws unconstitutional.

13. The nullification crisis ended when Congress <u>raised</u> the tariff and South Carolina backed down.

14. President Jackson's land distribution policies contributed to the Panic of 1837 and the depression that followed.

15. President Jackson supported the idea of a national bank.

16. Western banks in general were very tight with loans and printed a lot of paper money.

17. According to the treaty of Guadalupe Hidalgo, the United States annexed New Mexico and northern California.

18. The United States almost went to war with Spain over the Oregon Territory.

19. When William H. Harrison died, Martin Van Buren became President.

20. The mobility of Americans has contributed to their feeling that they can improve their lot.

PART C *Your teacher will give you directions for answering these essay questions.*

Chapter 12 • The removal or elimination of the native Indian populations was an inevitable consequence of white America's growth. Attack or defend this statement, citing specific events and the attitudes of the people involved.

Chapter 13 • Explain the view of each section (North, South, West) on the following issues: **(a)** tariff, **(b)** slavery, **(c)** government land policies, **(d)** policy toward Indians, **(e)** internal improvements, **(f)** banking. How would the disagreements lead to states' rights arguments? How did Congress try to reconcile these differences?

Chapter 14 • How did the United States fulfill its manifest destiny between the years 1830 and 1850? Identify the countries involved, the methods employed, and the ideas behind manifest destiny.

ANSWERS

PART A

1.	o	**11.**	r
2.	q	**12.**	p
3.	f	**13.**	d
4.	j	**14.**	i
5.	t	**15.**	a
6.	l	**16.**	b
7.	m	**17.**	c
8.	h	**18.**	n
9.	k	**19.**	e
10.	s	**20.**	g

PART B

1.	Manifest destiny	**11.**	more
2.	The Appalachians	**12.**	T
3.	T	**13.**	lowered
4.	less expensive	**14.**	banking
5.	Northeastern	**15.**	opposed
6.	South	**16.**	loose
7.	Andrew Jackson	**17.**	T
8.	T	**18.**	Britain
9.	John Q. Adams	**19.**	J. Tyler
10.	West	**20.**	T

UNIT 5 TEST

PART A *In each blank, write the name or term needed to complete the sentence.*

1. Whipping was the most commonly accepted form of punishment for ________.
2. In the 1830s, people who favored immediate freedom for slaves were known as ________.
3. The idea of ending American slavery by settling freed slaves in Africa was called ________.
4. Harriet Tubman was famous for her leadership of the ________.
5. A former slave who became a leading abolitionist and author was ________.
6. The fighting between proslavery and antislavery forces in the territories was most bitter and widespread in the territory of ________.
7. The Supreme Court decision stating that slaves were property and therefore could be taken into territories was put forth in the case of ________.
8. The widely read antislavery novel by Harriet Beecher Stowe was called ________.
9. The fighting in the Civil War officially started with the South's attack on ________.
10. Both battles of Bull Run resulted in Union ________.
11. General Lee's invasion of the North was turned back in the battle of ________.
12. Lincoln's search for an aggressive, effective general ended with his appointment of ________.
13. The side that was favored with better military leadership in the Civil War was the ________.
14. The Confederacy's chances for success were based largely on England's and the North's economic need for ________.
15. Unlike the United States Constitution, the Confederate Constitution acknowledged the sovereignty of the ________.
16. Jefferson Davis was the Confederacy's ________.
17. The Reconstruction plan that would have quickly and easily reunited the South and the North was first put forth by ________.
18. Thaddeus Stevens and Charles Sumner were the leaders of the group known as ________.
19. The President who was impeached but not convicted by the Senate was ________.
20. Many Northerners who went to the South after the Civil War were labelled by hostile Southerners as ________.
21. The most widespread organization designed to prevent blacks from obtaining or using their rights was the ________.
22. In the early 1900s, the black leader who said that blacks should advance economically rather than socially or politically was ________.
23. During this same period, the speaker for blacks who believed in demanding full political, social, and civil rights was ________.
24. The Supreme Court case of *Plessy* v. *Ferguson* legally justified the "separate but equal" laws known as ________.
25. In the Compromise of 1877, the Republicans traded the withdrawal of federal troops from the South for acceptance by the Democrats of the election of President ________.

PART B *For each sentence, circle the letter of the best ending.*

1. Slaves resisted their condition by **(a)** running away, **(b)** working very slowly, **(c)** injuring themselves, **(d)** all of the above.
2. As the abolitionists became more outspoken and active, the South responded by **(a)** admitting that slavery should end, **(b)** ignoring the abolitionists, **(c)** giving slaves more rights, **(d)** none of the above.
3. The Compromise of 1850 **(a)** admitted California as a free state, **(b)** kept slavery out of the Mexican Cession, **(c)** allowed Congress to control slave trading among the states, **(d)** all of the above.
4. The Lincoln-Douglas debates resulted in **(a)** Douglas being reelected to the Senate from Illinois, **(b)** Lincoln gaining a national reputation for opposing slavery in the territories, **(c)** the South being upset by the Freeport Doctrine, which showed how antislavery forces could avoid the effect of the Dred Scott decision, **(d)** all of the above.

5. John Brown's raid at Harpers Ferry was seen in the South as **(a)** a symbol of Southern resistance, **(b)** a sign of Northern interference, **(c)** the beginning of a widespread slave revolt, **(d)** all of the above.

6. On the issues of slavery and secession, President Lincoln took the stand that he would allow **(a)** slavery but not secession from the Union, **(b)** secession but not slavery, **(c)** neither slavery nor secession, **(d)** none of the above.

7. The draft law of 1863 was opposed by many Northerners because **(a)** only blacks were drafted, **(b)** for $300 a drafted person could avoid military service, **(c)** it caused rioting in Richmond, **(d)** all of the above.

8. Once they had control of Congress, the Radical Republicans tried to curb the other branches of government by **(a)** limiting the kinds of cases the Supreme Court could hear, **(b)** limiting the President's control of the army, **(c)** limiting the President's right to remove his advisors, **(d)** all of the above.

9. After the Civil War, most black politicians in the South believed that they could not obtain their demands by themselves, so they cooperated with **(a)** the poor white sharecroppers, **(b)** the upperclass planters, **(c)** the middle-class independent farmers, **(d)** all of the above.

10. The sharecropping and crop-lien systems hurt the South by **(a)** continuing the one-crop agricultural economy, **(b)** allowing freedmen to buy land, **(c)** providing a credit system when cash was unavailable, **(d)** none of the above.

PART C *Your teacher will give you directions for answering these essay questions.*

Chapter 15 • In 1787 many people thought slavery would die out on its own. Write an essay giving the reasons people thought it would die out and explaining why it did not.

Chapter 16 • Explain how each type of person named below would have felt about slavery before 1860. What kinds of programs and ideas of the time might each have supported? Try to show the differences of opinion between **(a)** a free black, **(b)** a Northern abolitionist, **(c)** a Southern planter, **(d)** a Southern lower-class white, and **(e)** a Northern middle-class white.

Chapter 17 • What were the advantages of the North and of the South at the start of the Civil War? Which factors do you think were the most important in the eventual Northern victory? Be sure to defend your choices.

Chapter 18 • Outline the rise and decline of black civil rights from the Civil War through the early 1900s. Indicate what groups and laws favored increasing equality and what groups and laws limited equality.

ANSWERS

PART A

1. slaves
2. abolitionists
3. colonization
4. underground railroad
5. Frederick Douglass
6. Kansas
7. Dred Scott
8. *Uncle Tom's Cabin*
9. Fort Sumter
10. defeats
11. Gettysburg
12. U. S. Grant
13. South
14. cotton
15. states
16. President
17. Abraham Lincoln
18. Radical Republicans
19. Andrew Johnson
20. carpetbaggers
21. Ku Klux Klan
22. Booker T. Washington
23. W. E. B. Du Bois
24. Jim Crow
25. Rutherford B. Hayes

PART B

1. d
2. d
3. a
4. d
5. b
6. a
7. b
8. d
9. b
10. a

UNIT 6 TEST

PART A *In the margin at the left of the number, write **T** if the statement is true or **F** if the statement is false.*

1. In immigrant families, assimilation into American life was easier for young people than for their parents.
2. The publication in America of foreign-language newspapers was useful for the Americanization of immigrants as well as for helping them stay aware of ethnic interests.
3. German Americans as well as Japanese Americans were relocated during World War II.
4. Since World War II, most American immigrants have come from the Western Hemisphere.
5. One of the first things that immigrants to America dropped was their native-language churches.
6. The immigration law of 1965 was designed to end the inequities of the quota system.
7. Anti-Semitism is prejudice or discrimination against Jewish people.
8. The immigration act of 1924 was designed to favor the New Immigration.
9. Working outside the home caused many immigrant women to question the traditional roles that their mothers had always accepted.
10. Opinions differ on whether ethnicity will continue or eventually die out in America.
11. Ellis Island and Castle Garden were centers for relocating Japanese Americans during World War II.
12. The physical examination for immigrants was only a formality, since everyone passed.
13. People sometimes left their European village in a group to go to America together.
14. The dominant-culture theory of assimilation said that immigrants should learn the language, customs, and values of America gradually, while also keeping their previous culture.
15. Ethnicity refers to the absorption of the dominant culture of a country.
16. Some immigrants planned on working to save money and then returning to their own country.
17. Skilled workers were less welcome as immigrants than unskilled workers, since the skilled worker was more likely to take someone else's job.
18. English-speaking immigrants were assimilated more quickly into American culture.
19. The first wave of immigrants came mostly from Northern and Western Europe.
20. In the United States today, ethnic pride and awareness are declining.

PART B *Write in the blank the name or term needed to complete the sentence.*

1. People who share a common culture, origin, religion, or race are often called an ________ group.
2. The technological shipping innovation that speeded and increased immigration in the late 1800s was the ________.
3. The failure of the potato crop in ________ during the 1840s accounted for a huge growth in immigration from that country.
4. The pogroms, or persecutions of the ________, encouraged emigration from Russia.
5. Writings from friends and relatives about opportunities in the United States were passed around Europe and became known as the ________.
6. The New Immigration was from ________ and ________ Europe.
7. Most of the people of the ________ Immigration settled in cities.
8. The term for opposition to foreign immigration and influence is ________.
9. In the early 1900s, resistance to immigration was often tied to the concept of ________, which associated certain characteristics with certain groups.
10. Historically, on the West Coast, discrimination centered on people from ________ and ________.
11. The fear that Communists would emigrate to America to spread revolution was known as the ________ of 1919–1921.

12. The ________ could be particularly upset by their relocation during World War II, since it violated their rights as natural-born American citizens.

13. In order to speed assimilation among immigrants, patriotic societies and businesses started ________ programs to teach about government and society in the United States.

14. The key to assimilation of American culture was learning the ________, which was usually done in schools by the children of the immigrants.

15. Social reformers, one of whom was ________ of Hull House, aided the immigrant poor, especially in the cities.

16. Around Miami, immigrants from ________ have been very successful because they have used their middle-class skills in American businesses.

17. People of recent immigrant group, who were American citizens before they came to New York and other states, are the ________.

18. The largest minority group in the Southwestern United States is made up of ________.

19. The theory of immigration that claims that in America all cultures were blended into one new one is called the ________ theory.

20. The term ________ refers to the theory that immigrant groups have assimilated American ideas but have also kept certain aspects of their own cultures.

PART C *Your teacher will give you directions for answering these essay questions.*

Chapter 19 • Identify the "push" and "pull" factors that caused emigration to America. Once the immigrants had arrived, what factors determined how successful they were likely to be?

Chapter 20 • What was "new" about the New Immigration? What was the effect of the New Immigration on America?

Chapter 21 • America wanted immigration but it did not want immigrants. Explain America's two opinions about immigration, and show how these opinions have been expressed in actions and feelings from the 1850s to the present.

Chapter 22 • How did immigrants respond to the experience of immigration? Identify ways in which the immigrants accepted assimilation and ways in which they resisted it.

ANSWERS

PART A

1. T	**5.** F	**9.** T	**13.** T	**17.** F
2. T	**6.** T	**10.** T	**14.** F	**18.** T
3. F	**7.** T	**11.** F	**15.** F	**19.** T
4. T	**8.** F	**12.** F	**16.** T	**20.** F

PART B

1. ethnic
2. steamboat
3. Ireland
4. Jews
5. American Letters
6. southern, eastern
7. New
8. nativism
9. race
10. China, Japan
11. "Red" scare
12. Nisei (Japanese Americans)
13. Americanization
14. language
15. Jane Addams
16. Cuba
17. Puerto Ricans
18. Mexican Americans
19. melting pot
20. cultural pluralism

UNIT 7 TEST

PART A *For each sentence, circle the letter of the best ending.*

1. The effect of the War of 1812 on American manufacturing was to **(a)** hurt it by stopping trade with Great Britain, **(b)** help it by forcing American industries to grow, **(c)** hurt it by taking away money that would have been invested, **(d)** help it by lowering taxes.

2. Ralph Waldo Emerson worried about America's **(a)** increasing use of machines, **(b)** rising prices of goods, **(c)** increasing materialism, **(d)** all of the above.

3. Corporations boomed in the 1850s because **(a)** they raised less money, **(b)** they were only chartered for a limited time, **(c)** investors had limited liability, **(d)** all of the above.

4. One feature of the American system of manufacturing was Eli Whitney's idea of **(a)** the assembly line, **(b)** the automated factory, **(c)** interchangeable parts, **(d)** the eight-hour work day.

5. The first American textile mills were centered in **(a)** the Southeast, **(b)** the Northwest, **(c)** the Northeast, **(d)** the Southwest.

6. Open-range cattle ranching ended when **(a)** the government closed the range, **(b)** prices for cattle went up, **(c)** severe weather killed most of the range cattle, **(d)** all of the above.

7. The Sioux Indians lost the rights to the Black Hills reservation after **(a)** they attacked a white settlement, **(b)** gold was discovered there, **(c)** their population declined too much, **(d)** they moved to Oklahoma.

8. The farmers of the Great Plains had to face the problem of **(a)** too few trees, **(b)** little rain, **(c)** loneliness, **(d)** all of the above.

9. The end of Indian resistance on the Great Plains was ensured when **(a)** Sioux were defeated near the Little Bighorn River, **(b)** the Indians were offered reservations, **(c)** the buffalo herd was destroyed, **(d)** the Seminoles were defeated.

10. The American cowboy was modeled after cowboys in **(a)** Spain, **(b)** North Africa, **(c)** Mexico, **(d)** none of the above.

11. In the 1870s the Centennial Exposition symbolized America's optimism about industry, while America's industrial problems were symbolized by **(a)** the Prohibition amendment, **(b)** the Pullman railroad strike, **(c)** the Homestead Act, **(d)** the Freedmen's Bureau.

12. The government's attitude toward industrialization in the late 1800s was best shown in its **(a)** subsidies to the railroads, **(b)** passage of low tariffs, **(c)** passage of the Sherman Anti-Trust Act, **(d)** support of labor unions.

13. A wealthy business leader whose wealth was based on oil was **(a)** John D. Rockefeller, **(b)** Albert T. Fall, **(c)** Gustavus Swift, **(d)** Andrew Carnegie.

14. As weapons against the early unions, owners used **(a)** blacklists, **(b)** "yellow dog" contracts, **(c)** court injunctions, **(d)** all of the above.

15. "America as a consumer society" refers to the idea that **(a)** industry grew in the early 1900s, **(b)** production was much greater than consumption, **(c)** Americans began buying more wisely, **(d)** none of the above.

16. The Homestead and Pullman strikes were examples of strikes in which **(a)** the unions won their demands, **(b)** violence took place, **(c)** the government sided with the unions, **(d)** boycotts were effective.

17. The theory that justified the vast wealth of certain industrialists was known as **(a)** the conspiracy theory, **(b)** social Darwinism, **(c)** vertical integration, **(d)** none of the above.

18. American industrial output first surpassed agricultural output in **(a)** the 1840s, **(b)** the 1860s, **(c)** the 1890s, **(d)** the 1920s.

19. A trust was **(a)** a government organization to help the unemployed, **(b)** a form of business consolidation, **(c)** an early labor union, **(d)** a bank loan.

20. A court case that symbolized the fear of radical political ideas was **(a)** the Sacco-Vanzetti case, **(b)** the Scopes trial, **(c)** the Teapot Dome trial, **(d)** the Johnson impeachment.

21. During the 1920s, the government gave the greatest aid to **(a)** the factory worker, **(b)** the farmer, **(c)** the business person, **(d)** the soldier.

22. The cause of the Great Depression was that **(a)** industry's ability to produce goods was greater than the country's ability to consume them, **(b)** wages rose faster than prices, **(c)** farmers were making too much money, **(d)** inflation reduced the value of the dollar.

23. The flapper symbolized **(a)** a more independent woman, **(b)** a return to the values of earlier times, **(c)** the effect of the Great Depression, **(d)** the woman factory worker.

24. The widespread effect of business on life in America in the 1920s was best shown by **(a)** the airlines industry, **(b)** the plastics industry, **(c)** the automobile industry, **(d)** the television industry.

25. A criticism of the "scientific management" of factories was that it **(a)** wasted the company's money, **(b)** was too scientific, **(c)** treated workers like machines, **(d)** lowered production.

PART B *For each set of events, number the items in the order in which they occurred.*

1. _____ Samuel Slater's cotton mill built
   _____ Textile-mill town of Lowell started
   _____ National Trades Union founded
2. _____ Copper mining more important than mining of gold or silver
   _____ California gold rush
   _____ "Pike's Peak or Bust" and Comstock Lode
3. _____ "Battle" of Wounded Knee
   _____ George Custer and Little Bighorn
   _____ Colonel Chivington's attack
4. _____ Dawes Act
   _____ Reservations established in Oklahoma and the Dakotas
   _____ Indian Reorganization Act
5. _____ Knights of Labor founded
   _____ American Federation of Labor founded
   _____ National Labor Union founded
6. _____ Transcontinental railroad completed
   _____ John D. Rockefeller controls oil industry
   _____ Sherman Anti-Trust Act passed
7. _____ Calvin Coolidge elected President
   _____ Herbert Hoover elected President
   _____ Warren G. Harding elected President
8. _____ Harding administration scandals
   _____ Stock market crash
   _____ "Red" scare
9. _____ American Federation of Labor started
   _____ Prohibition started
   _____ Great Depression began
10. _____ Pullman Strike
    _____ Homestead Act
    _____ Reaper invented

PART C *Your teacher will give you directions for answering these essay questions.*

Chapter 23 • By 1860, what was America's definition of progress? How did this idea affect the development of industry in the United States?

Chapter 24 • Outline the changes that occurred in the American West during the nineteenth century. Include the groups involved, technological developments, and the roles of the government in these changes.

Chapter 25 • What factors were responsible for the remarkable growth of American industry from the Civil War to the 1900s?

Chapter 26 • The New Era of the 1920s was supposed to be the beginning of prosperity for all. Identify those people who benefited from the New Era and those who did not. Explain how these others were excluded and how their exclusions contributed to the end of the New Era.

ANSWERS

PART A

1. b	**6.** c	**11.** b	**16.** b	**21.** c
2. c	**7.** b	**12.** a	**17.** b	**22.** a
3. c	**8.** d	**13.** a	**18.** c	**23.** a
4. c	**9.** c	**14.** d	**19.** b	**24.** c
5. c	**10.** c	**15.** d	**20.** a	**25.** c

PART B (Date added for teacher's use.)

1. 1 (1788)
2 (late 1820s)
3 (1834)

2. 3 (1900)
1 (1848)
2 (1858–59)

3. 3 (1890)
2 (1876)
1 (1864)

4. 2 (1887)
1 (1860s)
3 (1934)

5. 2 (1869)
3 (1881)
1 (1866)

6. 1 (1869)
2 (1879)
3 (1890)

7. 2 (1924)
3 (1928)
1 (1920)

8. 2 (1922–24)
3 (1929)
1 (1919–21)

9. 1 (1881)
2 (1920)
3 (1929)

10. 3 (1894)
2 (1862)
1 (1834)

UNIT 8 TEST

PART A *Match each name in the first section (1–10) with the correct description in the section that follows (a–j). Write the correct letter at the left of each number.*

1. William Jennings Bryan
2. William McKinley
3. Elizabeth Blackwell
4. Theodore Roosevelt
5. Franklin Roosevelt
6. Herbert Hoover
7. Dorothea Dix
8. Lincoln Steffens
9. Woodrow Wilson
10. Horace Mann

a. Democratic President of the progressive era
b. Muckraker concerned with political corruption
c. First female medical doctor in the United States
d. Concerned with treatment of the insane
e. Campaigned for free public education
f. Democratic candidate for President in 1896
g. First "modern" President
h. "New Deal" President
i. President when Great Depression started
j. Republican candidate for President in 1896

Match each name in the group below (11–25) with the correct description in the list that follows (k–y). Write the correct letter at the left of each number.

11. Seneca Falls Convention
12. Federal Deposit Insurance Corporation
13. Commission form of government
14. Direct election of Senators
15. Free silver at 16 to 1
16. Temperance movement
17. Utopian communities
18. Social Security Act
19. Works Progress Administration
20. Garfield's assassination
21. Hepburn Act
22. Wagner Act
23. Woman suffrage
24. Henry George's *Progress and Poverty*
25. The Grange

k. Protected an individual's money in a bank
l. Weakened political power of state legislatures
m. Attempted to increase the money supply
n. Created jobs for many kinds of workers
o. Designed to reform city politics
p. First organized statement of women's grievances
q. Aimed to bring about Prohibition
r. Increased power of ICC to regulate railroad rates
s. Gave workers the right to form unions
t. Attempted to develop new ways of living
u. Social organization that turned to protest
v. Proposed the Single Tax
w. Nineteenth Amendment
x. Old-age pensions and unemployment benefits
y. Won support for civil service reform

PART B *For each sentence, circle the letter of* ***each*** *possible correct ending. There can be more than one correct answer. Circle all correct answers.*

1. American reform interests have been encouraged by **(a)** the Declaration of Independence, **(b)** big business, **(c)** religion, **(d)** political party machines.

2. Prior to 1860, various reformers were interested in **(a)** the treatment of the insane, **(b)** the peace movement, **(c)** temperance, **(d)** women's rights.

3. The Pendleton Act **(a)** set up the Civil Service Commission, **(b)** was a New Deal measure, **(c)** dealt with farm problems, **(d)** tried to reform patronage and spoils systems.

4. After the Civil War, farmers' problems included **(a)** the reliance on cash crops, **(b)** high tariffs, **(c)** underproduction of crops, **(d)** isolation.

5. Solutions to the farmers' problems in the 1890s were sought by **(a)** the Republican party, **(b)** the Grange, **(c)** the farmers' Alliances, **(d)** the Populist party.

6. William Jennings Bryan lost the election of 1896 because **(a)** the Populists ran their own candidate, **(b)** urban workers did not support him, **(c)** many people feared free silver would bring higher prices, **(d)** Bryan was not a good public speaker.

7. Problems that the progressives were concerned with included **(a)** child labor, **(b)** living conditions in the cities, **(c)** corruption in government, **(d)** woman suffrage.

8. The candidates for President in the election of 1912 were **(a)** William H. Taft, **(b)** Theodore Roosevelt, **(c)** Eugene Debs, **(d)** Woodrow Wilson.

9. President Theodore Roosevelt favored government action to **(a)** regulate industry, **(b)** protect consumers, **(c)** make natural resources easily available to private industry, **(d)** break strikes.

10. The New Deal **(a)** solved the problems of the depression, **(b)** expanded governmental authority, **(c)** was unsuccessful in aiding the banks, **(d)** established the welfare state.

PART C *Your teacher will give you directions for answering these essay questions.*

Chapter 27 • What factors served to encourage and limit the reform movement in the United States?

Chapter 28 • Outline the Omaha Platform. How were these ideas going to solve the farmer's problems? Who else was the Omaha Platform supposed to attract?

Chapter 29 • What problems were the progressives concerned with? Who did they expect to solve the problems, and how successful were the solutions?

Chapter 30 • The New Deal had something for everyone. Support this statement by showing what the New Deal offered each of the following groups: **(a)** farmers, **(b)** people in business, **(c)** factory workers, **(d)** young people, **(e)** the unemployed.

ANSWERS

PART A

1. f	**6.** i	**11.** p	**16.** q	**21.** r
2. j	**7.** d	**12.** k	**17.** t	**22.** s
3. c	**8.** b	**13.** o	**18.** x	**23.** w
4. g	**9.** a	**14.** l	**19.** n	**24.** v
5. h	**10.** e	**15.** m	**20.** y	**25.** u

PART B

1. a,c	**6.** b,c
2. a,b,c,d	**7.** a,b,c,d
3. a,d	**8.** a,b,c,d
4. a,b,d	**9.** a,b
5. b,c,d	**10.** b,d

UNIT 9 TEST

PART A *In the margin at the left of the number, write **T** if the statement is true or **F** if the statement is false.*

1. George Washington recommended a policy of international involvement.
2. The Imperialists claimed that America needed new markets for its industrial output.
3. Theodore Roosevelt was an isolationist concerning relations with Spain.
4. More Americans died of disease in the Spanish-American War than died from the fighting.
5. After opposing Spain's tactics in Cuba, the United States used many of the same tactics in the Philippines.
6. German submarine warfare was a major cause for the United States to enter World War I.
7. The American entrance into World War I was unimportant, since the war was almost over.
8. Wilson's idea of an association to keep world peace was missing from the Treaty of Versailles.
9. Wilson's Fourteen Points were accepted by the other Allies as their war goals.
10. Henry Cabot Lodge was a leader of the reservationists who opposed the League of Nations.
11. If Wilson had been willing to accept a compromise, the Treaty of Versailles might have been approved in the Senate.
12. In 1926 the United States finally joined the League of Nations.
13. The major Axis powers in World War II were Japan, Germany, and Italy.
14. England and France were unprepared for World War II.
15. Even before Pearl Harbor, Roosevelt pushed for aid for the Allies.
16. During World War II, America's industrial output failed to expand to meet Allied needs.
17. Once Japanese expansion in World War II was halted, the Allies had little trouble forcing the Japanese back to their home island.
18. World War II expanded job opportunities for women and minority groups.
19. Plans for the United Nations were begun even before World War II ended.
20. During both world wars, the powers of the government were greatly expanded.

PART B *The United States has almost always had two conflicting trends in its foreign policy. One is toward isolating itself from world involvement, and the other is toward intervening in international affairs. At the left of the number, label the item as primarily following the trend toward isolationism **(ISO)** or internationalism **(INT)**.*

1. President Washington's Farewell Address
2. Monroe Doctrine
3. Josiah Strong's *Our Country*
4. Open Door Policy
5. Yellow journalism
6. Spanish-American War
7. Decision to keep the Philippine Islands
8. Hay–Bunau–Varilla Treaty, obtaining canal
9. Roosevelt's Corollary to Monroe Doctrine
10. Wilson's Fourteen Points
11. General John Pershing's A.E.F.
12. The irreconcilables
13. Rejection of the Treaty of Versailles
14. Washington Conference of 1921–1922
15. Kellogg-Briand Pact, outlawing war
16. Presidential recommendations to join World Court
17. Neutrality Acts of 1935–1937
18. Fortress America
19. Military aid to the Soviet Union during World War II
20. Signing United Nations charter

PART C *Your teacher will give you directions for answering these essay questions.*

Chapter 31 • In the late 1800s and early 1900s, what were the arguments for and against America becoming an imperialistic power? How successful were America's attempts to build an empire?

Chapter 32 • What were the major ideas of Wilson's Fourteen Points? How did they compare with those in the final Treaty of Versailles? What reasons can you give for the differences?

Chapter 33 • After World War II, many Americans felt that America's isolationism had contributed to causing the war. How might they justify that argument? What efforts did America make during and after World War II to avoid this problem in the future?

ANSWERS

PART A

1. F	**5.** T	**9.** F	**13.** T	**17.** F
2. T	**6.** T	**10.** T	**14.** T	**18.** T
3. F	**7.** F	**11.** T	**15.** T	**19.** T
4. T	**8.** F	**12.** F	**16.** F	**20.** T

PART B

1. ISO	**5.** INT	**9.** INT	**13.** ISO	**17.** ISO
2. ISO	**6.** INT	**10.** INT	**14.** INT	**18.** ISO
3. INT	**7.** INT	**11.** INT	**15.** INT	**19.** INT
4. INT	**8.** INT	**12.** ISO	**16.** INT	**20.** INT

UNIT 10 TEST

PART A *Write in the blank the name or term needed to complete the sentence. Some answers may require more than one word.*

1. After World War II, veterans were aided by benefits provided under the ______.
2. In the election of 1948, the unexpected winner for President was ______.
3. Accusing people of being Communists without providing proof was known as ______.
4. The successful launching of ______ caused many Americans to think America had been surpassed in scientific knowledge by the Soviet Union.
5. The Supreme Court in *Brown* v. *Board of Education of Topeka, Kansas,* declared unconstitutional facilities that were "______."
6. The civil rights leader known for nonviolent tactics was ______.
7. By the late 1970s, conditions for black Americans had improved considerably, except for those blacks still living in the ______.
8. Alcatraz Island (1969) and Wounded Knee, South Dakota, (1973) were scenes of protests by ______.
9. Cesar Chavez, the Chicano leader, became famous for organizing a union for ______.
10. Equality of opportunity, the elimination of role stereotyping, and consciousness raising are all interests of the ______.
11. The phrase designating John F. Kennedy's program of social legislation was the ______.
12. Growing opposition to the war in Vietnam led to the decision of President ______ not to seek reelection.
13. The "unelected" President who helped to restore confidence in his office was ______.
14. After World War II, the group of new countries that did not ally themselves with the Soviet Union or the United States became known as ______.
15. After World War II, the United States program of economic aid to Europe was known as the ______ Plan.
16. The United States reaction to postwar expansionism by the Soviet Union was known as the policy of ______.
17. The military alliance committing the United States to defend Western Europe is known as ______.
18. Communist Chinese troops first fought Americans in ______.
19. The idea that if one country in Southeast Asia fell to communism, others would follow was known as the ______ theory.
20. Meetings between the leaders of the Soviet Union and the United States were called ______ conferences.
21. The Bay of Pigs was the site of a United States-aided invasion of ______.
22. In setting up missile sites, Cuba received help from ______.
23. One of the most surprising foreign-policy decisions of President Nixon led to his trip to ______.
24. The easing of tensions between the Soviet Union and the United States was called ______.
25. The shift toward human rights and arms control was a mark of the foreign policy of ______.

PART B *Using the letters* **(a–e)** *in the list below, label the numbered terms or events that follow according to the presidential eras in which they belong. Notice that several Presidents are paired, since the second completed the other's term. Write the correct letter at the left of the number.*

a. Roosevelt-Truman
b. Eisenhower
c. Kennedy-Johnson
d. Nixon-Ford
e. Carter

1. Henry Kissinger as secretary of state
2. Cuban missile crisis
3. Ghetto riots in Los Angeles (Watts) and Newark
4. Civil Rights Act passed
5. Removal of General MacArthur
6. Emphasis on human rights in foreign policy
7. Bay of Pigs invasion
8. Containment policy adopted
9. *Brown* v. *Board of Education of Topeka, Kansas*
10. McCarthyism started
11. War on poverty
12. National Organization for Women (NOW)

13. Vice President resigns
14. U-2 spy-plane incident
15. Watergate break-in
16. Last American troops leave Vietnam
17. Martin Luther King, Jr., assassinated
18. Khrushchev visits United States
19. First military advisers to Vietnam
20. Marshall Plan started

PART C *Your teacher will give you directions for answering these essay questions.*

Chapter 34 • Briefly outline the United States opposition to communism from the end of World War II to the present. How have America's policies changed over the years? How do you explain the changes?

Chapter 35 • The 1950s was an era of confidence and stability in America. Attack or defend this statement by referring to specific events and attitudes of the period.

Chapter 36 • The 1960s and 1970s are usually shown as a period of violent protest, corruption, and failure in American politics and policies. For this essay, present an argument supporting the opposite point of view by showing a positive interpretation of this period.

ANSWERS

PART A

1. GI Bill of Rights
2. Harry S. Truman
3. McCarthyism
4. *Sputnik*
5. separate but equal
6. Martin Luther King, Jr.
7. ghettoes
8. Indians
9. farm workers
10. women's movement
11. New Frontier
12. Lyndon Johnson
13. Gerald Ford
14. the third world
15. Marshall
16. containment
17. NATO (North Atlantic Treaty Organization)
18. Korea
19. domino
20. summit
21. Cuba
22. the Soviet Union
23. China
24. détente
25. President Carter

PART B

1. d	**5.** a	**9.** b	**13.** d	**17.** c
2. c	**6.** e	**10.** a	**14.** b	**18.** b
3. c	**7.** c	**11.** c	**15.** d	**19.** b
4. c	**8.** a	**12.** c	**16.** d	**20.** a

OUR
AMERICAN
HERITAGE

CONSULTANT

Beth Millstein, History Teacher
Adlai Stevenson High School, New York, New York

END-OF-CHAPTER-MATERIAL AUTHOR AND CRITIC READER

Clara W. Mason, History Teacher
Jonathan Dayton Regional High School
Springfield, New Jersey

CRITIC READERS

Charles A. Loparo, Assistant Superintendent
Brecksville-Broadview Heights, Ohio, School System

Norma Norton, Principal
Auburn, Alabama, School System

Nobuo Watanabe, Coordinator of Social Studies
Superintendent of Schools Office
Contra Costa County, California

Oscar Zepeda, History Teacher
Del Valle, Texas, High School

TEACHER'S EDITION AUTHOR

Joseph H. Dempsey, Classroom Teacher
Morris School District, Morristown, New Jersey

OUR AMERICAN HERITAGE

HERBERT J. BASS
Professor of History • Temple University

GEORGE A. BILLIAS
Professor of History • Clark University

EMMA JONES LAPSANSKY
Assistant Professor of History • Temple University

SILVER BURDETT COMPANY
MORRISTOWN, NEW JERSEY
GLENVIEW, ILLINOIS   PALO ALTO
DALLAS   ATLANTA

ACKNOWLEDGMENTS

Page 4: Excerpt from "The New Immigrants: Still the Promised Land." Reprinted by permission from *TIME, The Weekly Newsmagazine;* Copyright Time Inc. 1976. Page 64: Excerpt from *White over Black: American Attitudes Toward the Negro, 1550–1812* by Winthrop D. Jordon. Reprinted by permission of The University of North Carolina Press and the Institute of Early American History and Culture. Page 84: Excerpt from *The American Historical Review*, January 1926, p. 231, by Charles M. Andrews. Reprinted by permission. Page 146: Excerpt from "The American Revolution and the World" by Gordon Wood from *Brown Alumni Monthly*, July–August 1976, p. 26. © Gordon Wood. Reprinted by permission. Page 244: George W. Pierson, *The Moving American* (New York: Alfred A. Knopf, 1973), pp. 7–8. Page 245: Poem "Daniel Boone" by Stephen Vincent Benét. From *A Book of Americans* by Rosemary and Stephen Vincent Benét. Holt, Rinehart and Winston, Inc. Copyright 1933 by Rosemary and Stephen Vincent Benét. Copright renewed © 1961 by Rosemary Carr Benét. Reprinted by permission of Brandt & Brandt. Page 248: Excerpts from *Westward Expansion: A History of the American Frontier* by Ray A. Billington. Copyright 1974 Macmillan Publishing Co., Inc. Reprinted by permission. Page 395: Excerpt from *Why Can't They Be Like Us?: AMERICA'S WHITE ETHNIC GROUPS* by Andrew M. Greeley. Copyright © 1970, 1971 by Andrew M. Greeley. Reprinted by permission of the publishers, E. P. Dutton. Pages 404–405: Excerpts from Alan Conway, *The Welsh in America.* The University of Minnesota Press, Minneapolis. © Copyright 1961 University of Minnesota. Page 405: Excerpts from Theodore C. Blegen, *Land of Their Choice*, University of Minnesota Press, Minneapolis, © Copyright 1955 by the University of Minnesota. Page 417: Emily Balch, *Our Slavic Fellow Citizens* (New York: Charities Publication Committee). © 1910 by Emily Greene Balch. Page 417: Excerpts adapted from pp. 18–19 and 20–21 of *The Promised Land* by Mary Antin. Copyright 1912 by Houghton Mifflin Company. Copyright 1940 by Mary Antin. Reprinted by permission of Houghton Mifflin Company. Page 421: Excerpt from *The Autobiography of Theodore Roosevelt.* Copyright 1913 Charles Scribner's Sons. Reprinted by permission of Charles Scribner's Sons. Page 421: Excerpt from *Laughing in the Jungle* by Louis Adamic, p. 19. © 1932 by Louis Adamic. Reprinted by permission of Harper & Row, Publishers, Inc. Page 422: Excerpt from "When the Boss Went Too Far" by Cesidio Simboli from *World Outlook*, October 1917. Reprinted by permission. Page 430: Excerpt from *American Immigration* by Maldwyn Jones, p. 124. © 1960 by University of Chicago Press. Reprinted by permission. Page 442: Excerpt from *The Great Betrayal* by Audrie Girdner and Anne Loftis. Copyright © 1969 by Audrie Girdner and Anne Loftis. Reprinted by permission of Macmillan Publishing Co., Inc. Page 447: Excerpt from *An American in the Making* by Marcus Ravage, pp. 60–61. © 1917 by Harper and Bros. Reprinted by permission of Harper & Row, Publishers, Inc. Page 448: Carl Schurz, *The Reminiscences of Carl Schurz* (New York: The McClure Co., 1908), Vol. 3, pp. 257–258. Page 450: Excerpt from "Evil and the American Ethos" by Robert Bellah in *Sanctions for Evil*, N. Sanford and C. Comstock, eds. © by Jossey-Bass 1971. Reprinted by permission. Page 450: Excerpt from *The Soul of an Immigrant* by Constantine M. Panunzio. Reprinted by permission of Perina Panunzio. Page 452: Excerpt from *Love and Pasta* by Joe Vergara, pp. 4–5. © 1968 Joseph R. Vergara. Reprinted by permission of Harper & Row, Publishers, Inc. Page 452: Excerpt from *The Odyssey of a Wop* by John Fante, September 1933. Reprinted by permission of *American Mercury*, Torrance, California 90505. Page 452: Excerpt adapted from *What Makes Sammy Run?* by Budd Schulberg, pp. 237–238. Reprinted by permission of Barbara Schulberg. Page 453: Excerpt from "Single or Triple Melting Pot? Intermarriage in New Haven, 1870–1950" by Ruby J. Reeves Kennedy, *American Journal of Sociology*, Vol. 58 (1952), p. 56. Reprinted by permission of The University of Chicago Press. Page 456: Excerpt from *Ethnic Americans* by Leonard Dinnerstein and David Reimers. Reprinted by permission of Harper & Row, Publishers, Inc. Page 558: Excerpt from *Ante-Bellum Reform* by David B. Davis. Copyright © David Brion Davis 1967. Reprinted by permission of Harper & Row, Publishers, Inc. Page 740: Excerpt from speech of Martin Luther King, Jr., entered in *Congressional Record*, September 3, 1963. Page 742: Excerpt from *Stride Toward Freedom* by Martin Luther King, Jr. Reprinted by permission of Harper & Row, Publishers, Inc.

ISBN 0-382-02451-6

CONTENTS

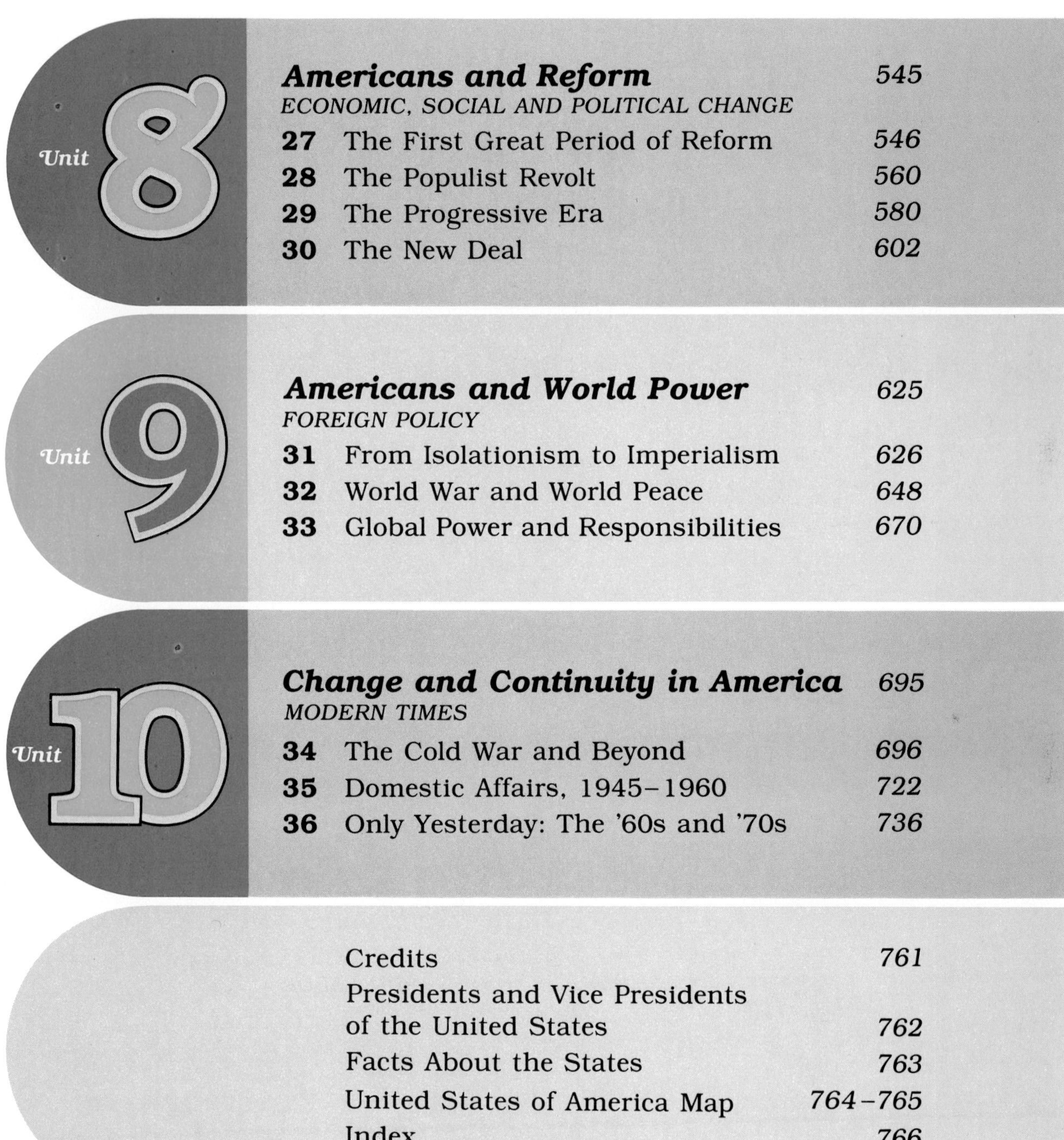

Maps, Charts, Tables, and Special-Interest Materials

MAPS

CHARTS AND TABLES

SPECIAL-INTEREST MATERIALS

Unit 1

Americans and Opportunity

THE COLONIAL PERIOD

Background Information

1. PICTURE When the first explorers reached the shores of North America, they found a vast and untouched wilderness. Only a handful of Indians inhabited the forests and plains of this great continent. This photograph of Mt. Hood, in northern Washington, symbolizes both the beauty and the wildness of the New World that greeted the early adventurers. It was a land filled with promise.

CHAPTER 1
THE PROMISE OF AMERICA

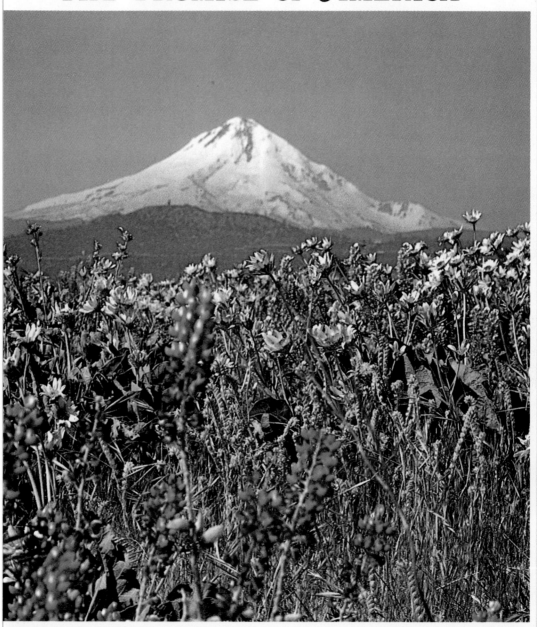

LESSON 1

IN THE YEAR 1516, an Englishman named Sir Thomas More wrote a book called *Utopia*. The book was about a society that Sir Thomas created in his imagination. His Utopians lived amidst plenty. Everyone had an opportunity to live a good and happy life. They enjoyed liberty and freedom of thought. They were considerate of each other's rights and were careful not to offend one another's beliefs. A peace-loving people, they went to war only in self-defense. Ever since More wrote this book, the words *Utopia* and *utopian* have come to mean perfect or ideal.

Since Utopia was a product of Sir Thomas More's imagination, he was free to place it anywhere on earth. The spot he chose was an imaginary island off the American coast. Europeans had learned of America's existence a few years earlier through the voyages of Christopher Columbus. They saw it as an untouched wilderness, a place where one could start afresh, free from injustices of the Old World lands. To Sir Thomas More, America was the natural setting for his perfect society.

Two hundred sixty-six years later, in 1782, a French immigrant to America, Michel Guillaume Jean de Crèvecoeur, wrote a volume of essays called *Letters from an American Farmer*. Crèvecoeur and his American-born wife had settled on a farm in Orange County, New York. In one essay Crèvecoeur explained how America changed immigrants. We have changed a few words and shortened his paragraph to make his meaning clearer.

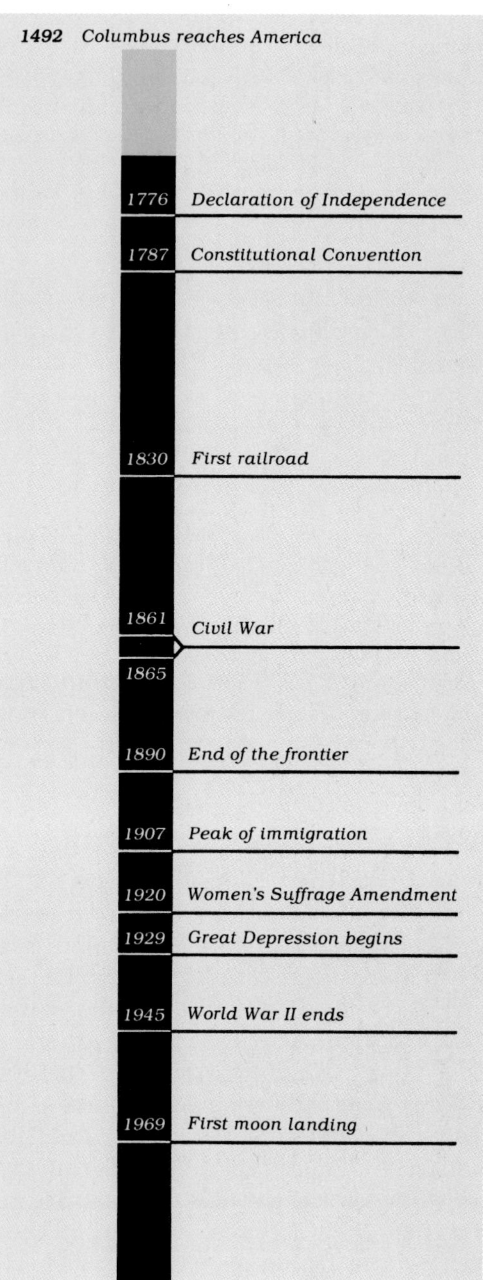

LESSON 1 *(1 to 2 days)*

Performance Objectives

1. To demonstrate an understanding of the idea of America as a land of opportunity by finding evidence to support this theme in the lesson. **2.** To explain orally or in writing three main motives that encouraged Columbus and other Europeans to explore the New World. **3.** To identify on an outline map those parts of the New World claimed for **(a)** Spain, **(b)** Portugal, **(c)** France, **(d)** England, **(e)** Holland, and **(f)** Sweden and Finland.

Famous People

Sir Thomas More, Crèvecoeur, Goethe, Christopher Columbus, John Cabot, John Verranzano, Jacques Cartier, Pedro Cabral, Ponce de León, De Soto, Coronado, Cortes, Pizarro, Henry Hudson

Vocabulary

Utopia, Hispaniola, "gold, glory, and God," St. Augustine, Aztecs, Incas, New Amsterdam

Activities

1. INTRODUCING THE UNIT The central theme of this unit is that America has offered opportunities (albeit sometimes quite limited) to the people who came to this country.

As a motivational activity, develop a discussion around the possibility of starting space colonies sometime in the future. The questions below could be used as starting points, but allow the students' responses to show the direction of the discussion. Try to encourage participation by asking questions where almost any answer is "correct."

Suggested questions: Suppose there were a company starting a space colony. **(a)** How many of you would consider joining this venture? Why or why not? **(b)** What would make the idea interesting to you? What would be unattractive about the idea? **(c)** What kinds of people would probably want to join this venture? Why? **(d)** Who would be the leaders of the colony? What type of political and social structure might the colony have? **(e)** If particular groups in society could form their own colonies, which groups do you think would be interested in going off on their own? Why? **(f)** What kind of relations do you think the colonies would establish with earth? With each other? What problems would possibly develop?

After taking this discussion as far as you want it to go, compare the space colony situation with that of explorers coming to America. Either similarities or differences are useful for discussion.

> In this great American asylum, the poor of Europe have by some means met together. Can wretches who wander about, who work and starve, call England or any other kingdom their country? No! But in America, everything makes them new people; new laws, a new mode of living, a new social system. In Europe they were as so many useless plants, . . . they withered, and were mowed down by want, hunger, and war; but now in America they have taken roots and flourished.

In 1976, almost two hundred years after Crèvecoeur, Bit Chuen Wu, a twenty-three-year-old Chinese immigrant, became part owner of a small restaurant in Palo Alto, California. After several weeks in his new business, Wu looked back on his life in America.

> Since I am in America, I have time only for work, just go home and watch TV, then go to sleep. I am too tired to read newspaper. I have no time to meet girls. I do the kitchen work. I wait on tables. But it is o.k. In Hong Kong I never get a chance to save money and become my own boss. It is very good to be your own boss. You get the profits.

A Country Where Everything Was Possible

The writings and remarks of Sir Thomas More, Crèvecoeur, and Bit Chuen Wu span more than four and a half centuries. Still, a common theme runs through them. It is the idea of America as a land of opportunity. Opportunity did not mean the same to all three. Reread the words of Crèvecoeur and Bit Chuen Wu, for instance. You will quickly see what some of the differences are. But whether their interest was in peace, plenty, and freedom, or a place where broken men and women could start again, or a land where one could become one's own boss, all three of these people saw America as the country where everything was possible.

For nearly four hundred years, people the world over have seen these same opportunities in America. Goethe, the great German poet, summed it up: *Amerika, du hast besser,* "America, you have it better." More than forty million people over the years have been led by that belief to leave their native lands for America. Probably most people in the world still share Goethe's view.

To most Americans today it is clear that not everyone has shared in this opportunity equally. Too often minorities have not. Nor have the poor. Yet it is also true that many millions, including members of racial and religious minorities, have found in America a chance to be what they wanted to be. They have found opportunities to make of themselves and their lives what they can.

The idea of America as a land of opportunity continues to have a strong hold on our minds today. In 1976—200 years after this country was born—a group of college freshmen were asked to rank the traits they thought were most clearly American. The majority placed Opportunity near the top of their lists.

America's abundance. How did it happen that America came to be so identified with the idea of opportunity? The place to start looking for the answer to this question is in the very beginnings of our history. For the idea of America as a land of opportunity, as More's *Utopia* suggests, is as old as America itself.

That idea in turn was connected with America's abundance—its rich soil, thick forests, and large deposits of metals and minerals.

From the time Europeans first became aware of the New World, they thought of it as the land of plenty. Read, for example, one of Columbus's first reports of the New World. In it he is describing the island of Hispaniola in the Caribbean Sea. Columbus believed he had landed in Asia, on islands then known as the Indies (today the East Indies). That is why he called the people Indians. Note how the picture of a land of plenty runs through Columbus's report.

> This island and all the others are very fertile. . . . Its lands are filled with trees of a thousand kinds. . . . there are very large tracts of cultivable lands, and there is honey, and there are birds of many kinds, and fruits in great diversity. In the interior are mines of metals, and the population is without number.

In this drawing from a French book of 1584, Christopher Columbus holds an astrolabe, a navigational device for measuring the angle between the horizon and the stars or planets.

Columbus's voyage. Christopher Columbus, an Italian by birth, was sailing under the flag of Spain when he sighted land in the Western Hemisphere on October 12, 1492. At that time, Spain and a number of other European nations were seeking new trade routes to the Indies. There they could get beautiful silks, shining jewels, and such spices as pepper and cloves.

Trade with the Far East at that time was slow, dangerous, and costly. The trade routes between Europe and Eastern Asia ran for hundreds of miles—across deserts and through mountain passes—in regions where bandits lay in wait. For these varied reasons, Europeans dreamed of finding a water route to the Far East. A water route would increase trade and bring riches to the nation that discovered it.

Columbus had long believed he could reach the Far East by sailing west from Europe. After many years he had finally persuaded the King and Queen of Spain to back him with ships and money. Columbus did not know, of course, that a great land mass blocked his way. The stories of earlier seafarers going to the Western Hemisphere had been lost or forgotten (see page 8).

2. LISTENING FOR INFORMATION You may wish to read to your students the selection from *Utopia* in *The Western Tradition: From the Renaissance to the Atomic Age* by Eugen Weber (Boston: D. C. Heath, 1965). A summary of More's *Utopia* appears on page 1418 in *The People's Almanac* by David Wallechinsky and Irving Wallace (Garden City, N.Y.: Doubleday, 1975).

Background Information

2. CRUSADES The series of wars that we call the Crusades began about 1100 and lasted until almost 1300. Christians and Moslems had been in conflict before the Crusades and continued in conflict for many years afterward. The word *crusade* has its root in the Latin word for cross, *crux.* Those who joined a crusade sewed strips of cloth in the shape of a cross to their clothing. People who "took the cross" became crusaders and were to be aided by other Christians along the way to the Holy Land. While the Crusades certainly had a basis in religious faith, they also served to increase European territory and wealth. There were four major crusades. The first was a victory for the Christians; they managed to capture and hold Jerusalem. The Second Crusade was a victory for the Moslems. The Third Crusade was a standoff. The winner of the Fourth Crusade was Venice, which was able to gain trade advantages in Byzantium. These crusaders never reached the Holy Land.

3. THOUGHT PROVOKER *The Great Frontier* by Walter Prescott Webb (Austin: University of Texas Press, 1964) is a classic in historical theory. In this book, Professor Webb implies that the Age of Exploration came about because of the increasing strain of population on the available land. In fifteenth-century Europe, which he calls "the Metropolis," there were 3.75 million square miles of land for 90 million people, or a "land–man ratio of 1:24." The vastness of the New World increased the ratio to 1:4.8 by the year 1650. Professor Webb describes the next 300-year period of expansion to fill this new land as a "boom" period and says that, compared with other historical ages, it was abnormal. Webb adds that if Europe in 1500 was $\frac{L}{M} = 24$, then with the addition of land from the New World, $\frac{L}{M} = 24 + x$ acres. However, as population increased, the x factor decreased, to the point where it became a minus x by 1930. The history your students will study in this text will tell how this new land was explored, settled, tamed, apportioned, fought over, cultivated, developed, and subdivided. Something for your students to think about is Webb's warning: "If population goes on increasing, the time will inevitably come when the land portion for each person is too small to furnish an independent subsistence. . . . Judges will then conclude that land has become more valuable than people." Ask your students for their reactions to Professor Webb's ideas.

4. RESEARCH/ORAL REPORTS Assign some of your students to present brief reports on the following explorers: Cabot, Verrazano, Cartier, Cabral, Ponce de Léon, De Soto, Coronado, Cortes, Pizarro, and Henry Hudson.

SOME EXPLORERS OF AMERICA

Francisco de Coronado, was a Spanish noblemen who explored the American Southwest in 1540 and 1541. Searching for gold, he led his expedition as far east as Kansas. His men were the first Europeans to see the Grand Canyon.

Juan Ponce de León, a Spaniard, landed in 1513 in what is now Florida. There he sought in vain for a legendary spring called the Fountain of Youth. He conquered the island of Puerto Rico and served as its governor.

Henry Hudson, an English sea captain, made four voyages to America between 1607 and 1611. He explored the river and the bay that now carry his name, but he failed to find what he was seeking—a northern sea route to Asia.

John Cabot, an Italian sea captain sailing under the flag of England, reached the coast of North America in 1497, probably in what is now eastern Canada. His voyage gave England its claim to the mainland of North America.

Robert Sieur de La Salle of France became a fur trader in Canada. In 1682 he explored the Mississippi to its mouth and claimed the entire region for France. On a later expedition, he was assassinated by one of his own men.

Gold, glory, and God. Columbus made four voyages to the New World, but he never realized what he had done. He died thinking he had found an all-water route to the islands of the Far East.

Only slowly did the truth dawn on Europeans. As it did, America captured their imagination. Every European country that could do so hurried to claim part of the New World. John Cabot, an Italian captain like Columbus, explored the northeastern part of North America for England. John Verrazano and Jacques Cartier sailed along the eastern coast of North America and claimed it for the King of France. Spanish adventurers pushed into Central and South America. And Pedro Cabral took possession of what we now call Brazil for Portugal.

The explorers who followed Columbus, and the kings and queens who sent them forth, were all motivated by the same three things. They sought, first of all, gold. By custom, the king would receive one fifth of all gold found, but the explorers could keep the rest. They also hoped to bring glory to their country and king. And, in that deeply religious age, they wanted to carry the Christian religion to other peoples in the world. Gold, glory, and God, then, inspired the search for new lands.

Columbus himself well illustrates the point. He hoped to find gold—recall his reference to "mines of metals" in his report about Hispaniola. He also hoped to find an all-water route to Asia, a deed that would bring glory to him personally and to the King and Queen of Spain. And he wanted to convert the Indians to Christianity. Columbus sometimes signed his name *Christo Ferens*, "Christ Bearer," showing his desire to carry the name of Christ to non-Christian peoples. In fact, he even planned to use part of the riches he might find to pay for a new Christian crusade to the Holy Land.

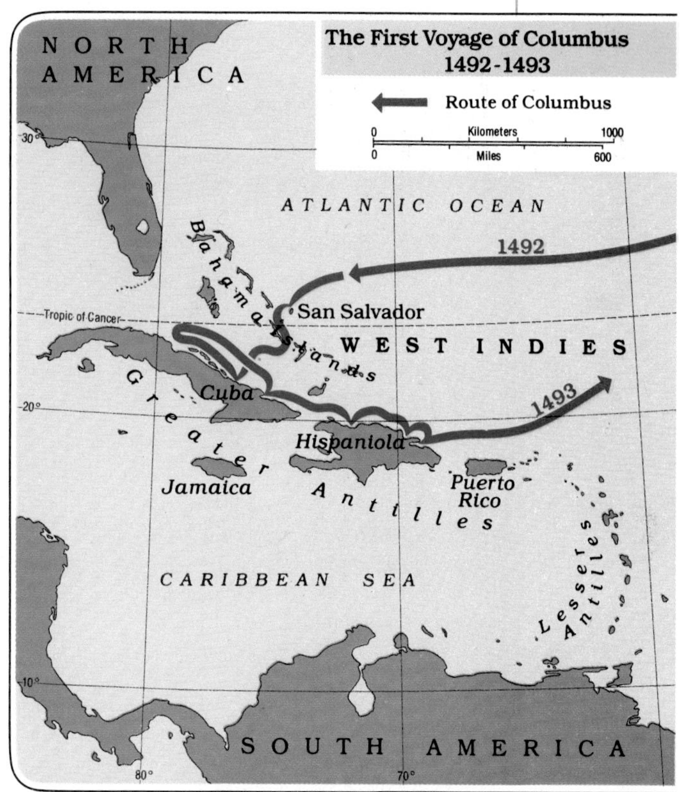

What chain of islands of the West Indies did Columbus first sight? What major islands did he sail along? Did he sight the coast of what is today the United States?

Explorers and conquerers. Spain was the nation that followed up Columbus's voyages most quickly. During the 1500s the Spanish explorers expanded their

Continued on page 9

5. **USING A MAP** On an outline map of the Western Hemisphere, have the students do the following.
a. Label the areas claimed by those European nations mentioned in Performance Objective 3.
b. Show the routes of the explorers named in the lesson, using the maps in the chapter as guides.

If necessary, remind the students to include a map key.

6. **DISCUSSION** Ask students to cite opportunities—real or imagined—that America has been credited with offering people during the past three centuries. Which opportunities were actually available? Are they still available? Or does the United States offer different opportunities today? Encourage students to find and share newspaper articles that support their ideas in this discussion.

Who Discovered America?

When the discovery of America is mentioned, most people think of Columbus and the date 1492. The fact is that men and women reached America long before Columbus. The first discoverers of America were the people we know as Indians. They came from Siberia, across what is now the Bering Strait, into North America at least 25,000 years ago.

Can we say that Columbus was the first *European* to touch American shores? Once again, others came before him. A Norse explorer named Leif Ericson reached the North American coast around the year 1000. Sailing west from Greenland, Ericson and his companions landed on a shore they called Vinland. This may have been Newfoundland.

Still other people from the Eastern Hemisphere may have reached America long before Columbus. Claims have been made that Celts, Carthaginians, and Phoenicians explored North America as early as 800 B.C. It is known that French fishermen sailed to the waters off Newfoundland at an early date and dried their catch on shore. In the ninth century, Scandinavians occupied Iceland and drove out Irish colonists living there. These Irish wanderers were bold and skillful sailors in their skin-covered boats. Might the Irish, then, have been the first to reach America?

Scholars have put forth still different ideas about the early comers to America. Some think Africans reached the New World in very early times. And it is believed by some that an inscription found in Brazil shows that a boatload of Jews or Phoenicians sailed to America from the Red Sea as early as the sixth century B.C. Several archaeologists have argued that Japanese fishing boats, Chinese junks, and Polynesian outrigger canoes brought people across the Pacific to America in the distant past.

If some—or all—of these peoples did reach America before 1492, why does Columbus's name loom so large in American history? The answer is that it was Columbus's rediscovery of America—after earlier voyages had been forgotten—that resulted in lasting contact with the rest of the world.

It took many hundreds of years for people to advance along the migration routes shown below.

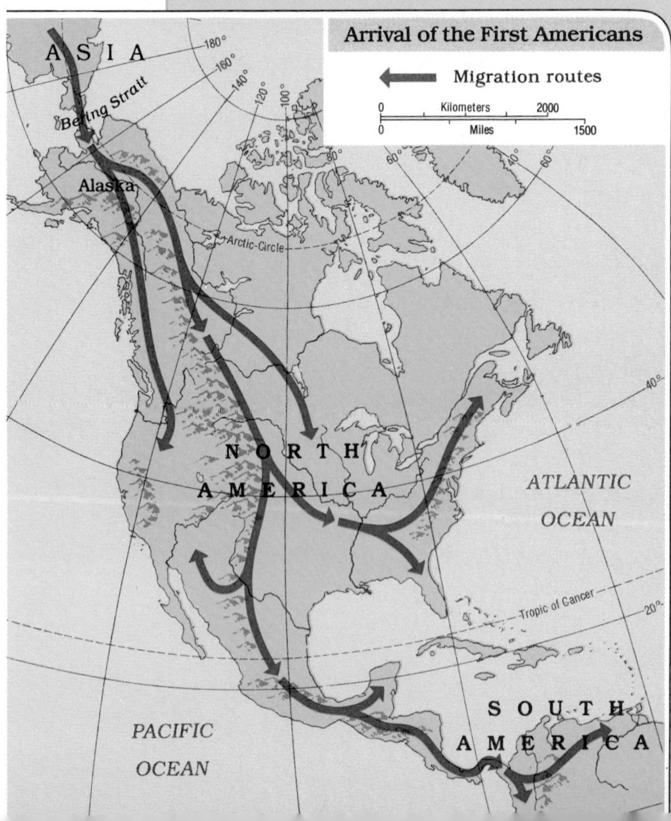

claims to the lands in and around the Caribbean Sea and the Gulf of Mexico. Those claims included most of what are today the southern and western parts of the United States.

Ponce de León, De Soto, and Coronado explored lands extending from Florida to the Grand Canyon in Arizona. In 1565 in Florida the Spaniards founded St. Augustine. It is today the oldest city in the United States.

The Spaniards' main attention, however, centered on lands farther to the south. There they discovered two rich Indian civilizations—those of the Aztecs of Mexico and the Incas of Peru. The Spanish invaders were led by Cortes in Mexico and by Pizarro in Peru. Using guns and horses, they overcame the Indians. They seized the Indians' gold and silver and forced them to dig for more in the mines. The treasure taken from the Aztecs and Incas made Spain in the 1500s the richest nation in the world.

In the race to discover and claim new lands, Portugal was next to Spain. A nation of great sailors and navigators, Portugal claimed Brazil in South America and created a vast empire in Asia and Africa.

In the late 1500s and 1600s, other European countries plunged into the race for colonies. Because the Spaniards were already well established in South and Central America, the latecomers centered their attention on North America. The French founded several settlements in eastern Canada, beginning in 1608. Holland, following up the voyages of Henry Hudson on the river that now bears his name, founded a colony in North America. It was called New Netherland. The colony's main settlement, named New Amsterdam, was founded in 1624 where New York City stands today. And a small group of Swedes and Finns founded a colony, New Sweden, on the Delaware River.

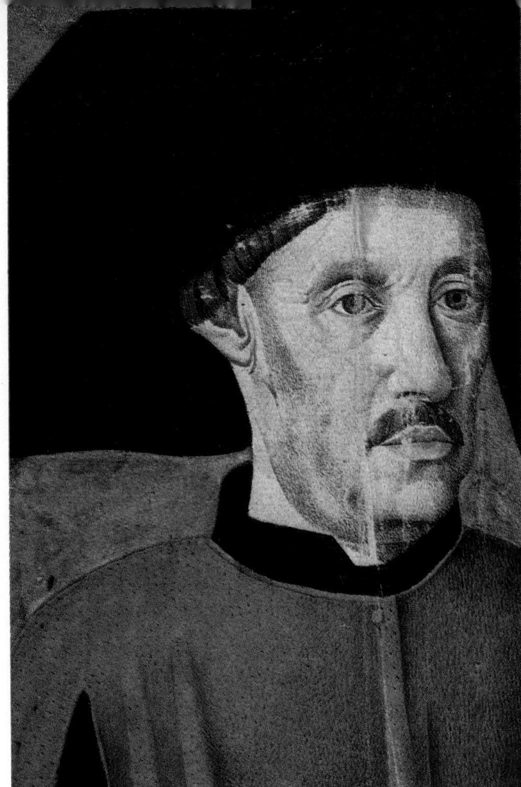

Prince Henry of Portugal enlisted the aid of scholars, mapmakers, and sea captains to advance the study of geography and navigation. His efforts ushered in the Age of Exploration.

CHECKUP

1. In what respects did the feelings of Sir Thomas More, Crèvecoeur, and Bit Chuen Wu about America differ? How were their feelings alike?
2. What was Columbus seeking when he sighted land in the Western Hemisphere?
3. What parts of the New World did Spain explore and lay claim to? Where did other European countries make claims?

7. ESSAY After the students have read the lesson, ask them to write essays explaining the significance of "gold, glory, and God" as motivating forces in the exploration of the New World.

This activity provides an opportunity for you to assess the students' ability to write a well-developed paragraph. If a number of students are having difficulty, perhaps you would want to review with them the essentials of paragraph construction.

Background Information

3. HORSES IN THE NEW WORLD The first horses were brought to the New World in 1519 by Cortes. He had sixteen horses and a colt born on the ship that brought them. In time, the Spaniards brought other horses to the New World to help in their explorations of the vast land. They raised horses on unfenced ranges, and it was natural that some of the stock horses strayed from the haciendas. In addition, some horses were lost on long journeys of exploration. These lost and strayed animals were called mesteños—mustangs—from the Spanish word meaning strayed, or ownerless, animals. For 24 years after the landing of Cortes, a royal edict prohibited an Indian's riding a horse. However, as the number of mustangs multiplied, the Indians learned to capture and master them.

With the development of ranching, mustangs were regarded as a nuisance and were killed off. Today's wild horses of Arizona, Wyoming, and other Western states are not of the unmixed Spanish breed, nor are the wild horses along the Carolina seaboard.

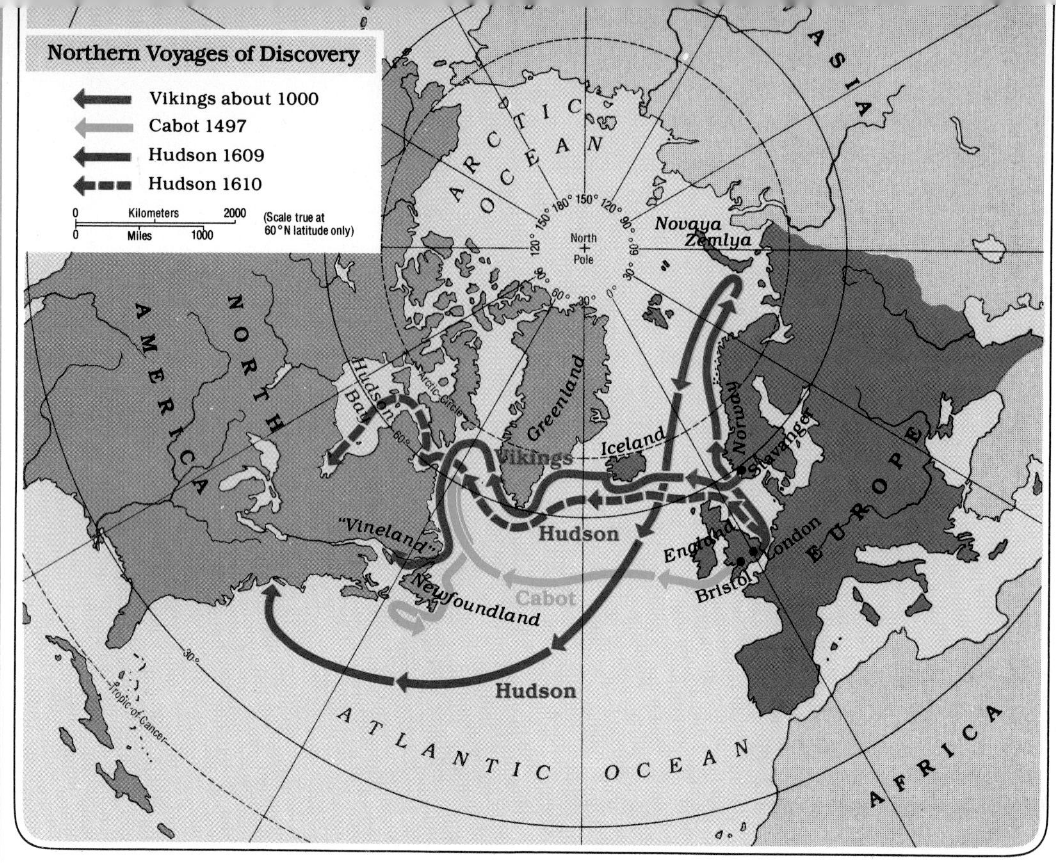
Northern Voyages of Discovery
Vikings about 1000
Cabot 1497
Hudson 1609
Hudson 1610
Kilometers
Miles
(Scale true at 60°N latitude only)
ARCTIC OCEAN
North Pole
ASIA
Novaya Zemlya
NORTH AMERICA
Hudson Bay
Arctic Circle
Greenland
Iceland
Norway
Stavanger
Vikings
Hudson
"Vineland"
Newfoundland
Cabot
England
London
Bristol
EUROPE
Hudson
Tropic of Cancer
ATLANTIC OCEAN
AFRICA

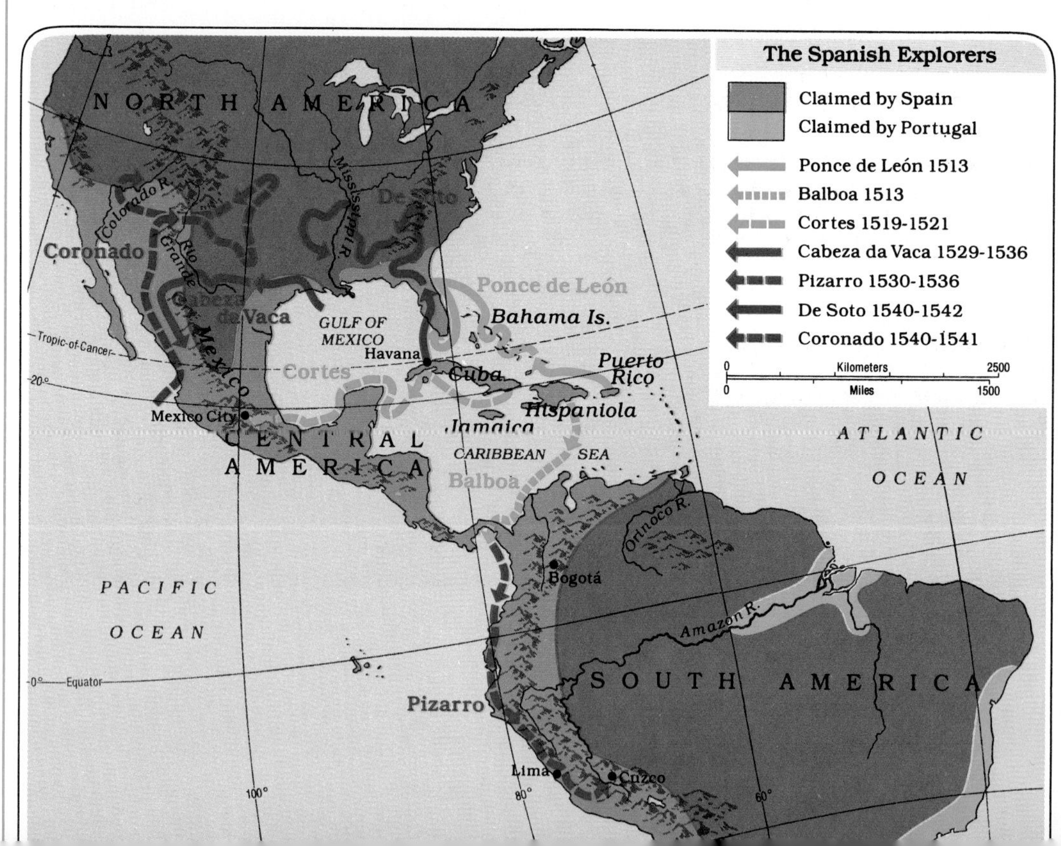
The Spanish Explorers
Claimed by Spain
Claimed by Portugal
Ponce de León 1513
Balboa 1513
Cortes 1519-1521
Cabeza da Vaca 1529-1536
Pizarro 1530-1536
De Soto 1540-1542
Coronado 1540-1541
Kilometers
Miles
NORTH AMERICA
Colorado R.
Rio Grande
Mississippi R.
De Soto
Coronado
Cabeza de Vaca
Ponce de León
Bahama Is.
GULF OF MEXICO
Havana
Tropic of Cancer
Mexico
Cortes
Cuba
Puerto Rico
Hispaniola
Mexico City
Jamaica
CENTRAL AMERICA
CARIBBEAN SEA
Balboa
ATLANTIC OCEAN
Orinoco R.
Bogotá
PACIFIC OCEAN
Amazon R.
Equator
SOUTH AMERICA
Pizarro
Lima
Cuzco

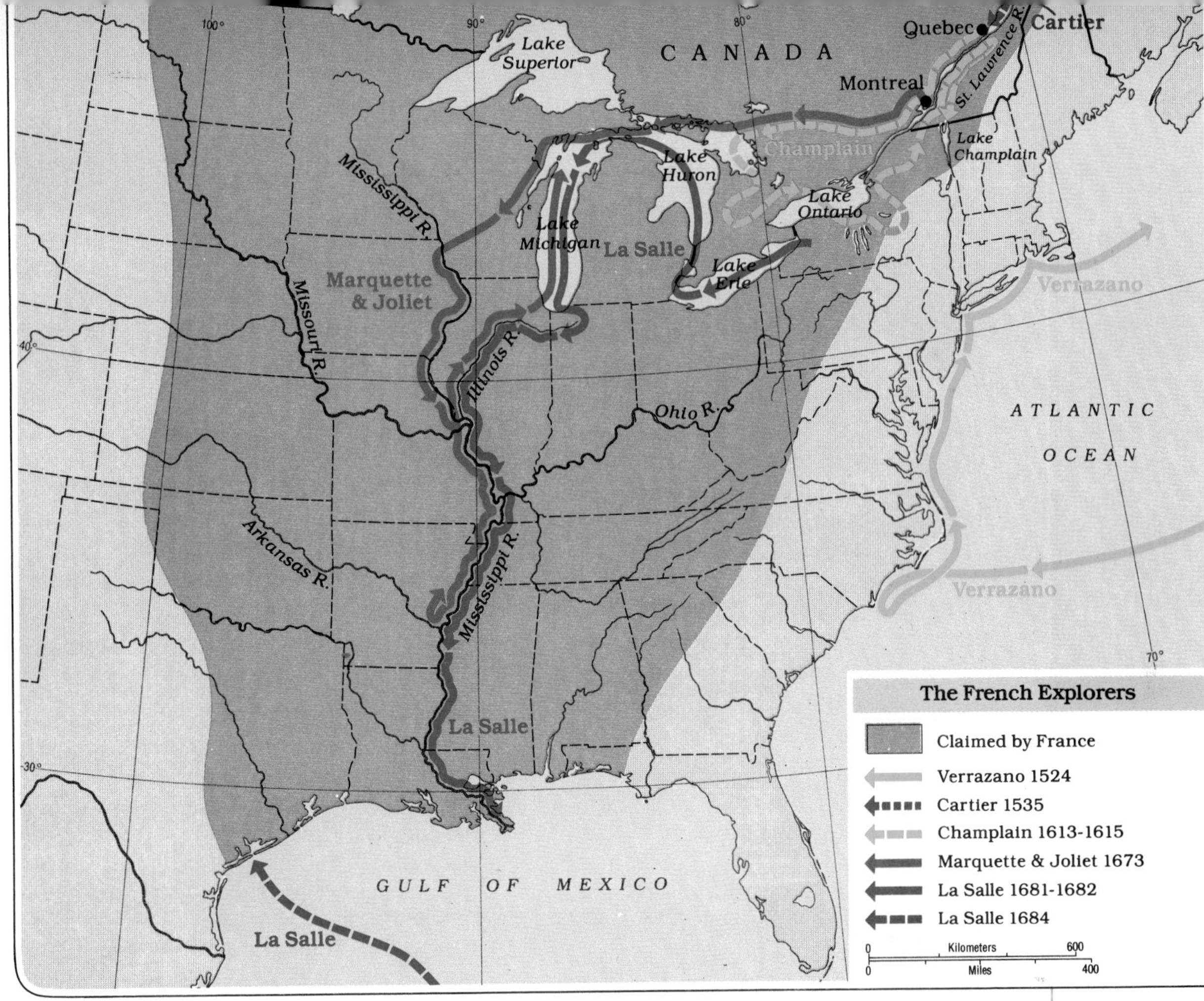

(Upper left) The first European explorers of the northeastern coast of North America are believed to have been the Vikings. The remains of a Viking settlement have been unearthed in northern Newfoundland. John Cabot and Henry Hudson, both sailing under the English flag, also explored this northern coastline. England's claims to North America were based on the exploration of Cabot.

(Lower left) During the first half of the sixteenth century, Spanish explorers ranged through New World lands from Kansas to Peru. Of those whose routes are shown on this map, Cabeza de Vaca may have had the most amazing journey. Shipwrecked off the Texas coast, he and a few companions wandered for eight years through the countryside of northern Mexico before reaching a Spanish settlement.

(Above) The French centered their exploration efforts on the St. Lawrence River, the Great Lakes, and the Mississippi River. However, Verrazano, an Italian sailing under the French flag, explored the Atlantic coast from Massachusetts to the Carolinas. Verrazano is believed to have been the first European to sail into the waters of New York Bay.

LESSON 2 *(1 to 2 days)*

Performance Objectives

1. After outlining this lesson, to write a summary describing the appeal of America to rulers, adventurers, merchants, the clergy, and ordinary people. **2.** To distinguish between fact and opinion and to identify, orally or in writing, several examples of each as found in the source material quoted in this lesson.

Famous People

Queen Elizabeth, Richard Hakluyt, King Philip, Sir George Peckham, Sir Walter Raleigh, James I

Vocabulary

Joint stock company, shares, investors, enclosure movement, charter

Activities

1. LISTENING FOR INFORMATION You may wish to read more to your class from Hakluyt's *Divers Voyages Touching the Discovery of America.* An excerpt is included in *The Western Tradition: From the Renaissance to the Atomic Age* by Eugen Weber (Boston: D. C. Heath, 1965). In the same book there is an interesting letter from Paolo Toscanelli, a Florentine scientist and astronomer, to Christopher Columbus.

LESSON 2

England and the Race for Colonies

It was England, one of the last nations to enter the race for colonies, that was to leave the greatest mark on North America. During the middle part of the sixteenth century, while Spain was gobbling up much of South and Central America,England was tied up with religious and political quarrels at home. But with the reign of Queen Elizabeth, from 1558 to 1603, many of these problems were settled.

An expanding trade. During these years, trade brought prosperity to England. English merchants enjoyed a growing trade in wool with European countries across the English Channel. They also reached out for trade with distant lands. The expense and risk of such trade in those days was too great for any one person. But English merchants came up with an idea for pooling their money and sharing the risks. This idea was the *joint stock company*.

Merchants would buy "shares," or "stock," in the company at so much per share. If there was a loss—for example, if a company's ship sank—the merchants would lose what they had put in, but no more. Profits would be divided according to the number of shares each person held. By the late 1500s, English merchants were using the joint stock company to promote trade with places as far away as Russia and India.

Reasons for colonizing. As England became more prosperous, a number of persons became interested in founding colonies. Through their writings, they tried to convince others that colonies would be a good thing for England. One of these writers was a clergyman named Richard Hakluyt. Earlier we summed up the motives of European explorers and rulers in three words—God, gold, and glory. When you read the following piece written by Hakluyt, try to find the sentences in which he appeals to each of these motives. To do this you will need two additional facts. First, England was a Protestant country and the deadly enemy of Catholic Spain. Second, once a year King Philip of Spain sent a fleet to carry gold and silver from the New World to Spain. We have changed some words in order to make Hakluyt's meaning clearer.

> Planting an English colony would keep the Spanish from taking all of America. From America, England could get trees for masts and such naval supplies as pitch, hemp, and tar. With the best ship builders in the world and with an ample supply of brave young men, presently unemployed, to man its vessels, how easy will it be for our navy to keep the Spanish navy from making its yearly voyage to Spain with gold and silver. Planting a colony in America would also promote the Protestant religion. Too, it would provide a place where the many unemployed in England could grow up under better conditions than at present.

Another Englishman who wrote in favor of colonizing in America was Sir George Peckham. In fact, Peckham invested money in a company that tried to plant a colony in Newfoundland as early as 1583. He gave these reasons why England should encourage the founding of colonies in America.

> . . . it is well known that all [Indians] . . . take [great] delight in any garment no matter how simple. . . . What a market

After the great Spanish fleet, called the Armada, was routed by the English in 1588, England became a major power in the race for colonies in the New World.

for our English clothes will result from this, and what a great benefit to all those engaged in making and selling clothes.

Our country will be generally benefitted, moreover, because a great many unemployed who are . . . burdens [in England] will be put to work in America. . . .

And then Peckham sums up (again, words have been changed slightly):

Then shall Her Majesty's empire be enlarged. Idleness will be banished from the country, depressed towns will be revived, many poor and needy persons will be helped and the Indians taught to know Christ.

Which of the arguments that Hakluyt used do you find repeated by Peckham? What new reasons for colonizing does Peckham add?

Attracting investors. Queen Elizabeth could not afford to finance colonies as did the King of Spain. Instead, she made contracts with private individuals and companies to plant colonies for England. What possible gains attracted them to risk their money in such chancy ventures? Again, we can turn to Sir George Peckham for part of the answer. In the same pamphlet from which we quoted above, Peckham addresses a paragraph to the persons he is trying to interest in investing:

Now, to the merchants who are disposed to support worthy projects I will say . . . that in that part of America are found the most wholesome and best climate, the most fertile soil, and all those products for which

2. OUTLINING/ESSAY The skill of outlining will prove valuable to the students throughout their school years. Present the form of a topic outline, drawing the following breakdown on the chalkboard.

I. *(Main topic)*
 A. *(Subtopics of I)*
 B.
  1. *(Subtopics of B)*
  2.
   a. *(Subtopics of 2)*
   b.

Explain that the outline shows the order of the various topics, the relative importance of each, and the relationship between the various parts. The headings are given in brief phrases, clauses, or single words, and are numbered and lettered consistently, as in the example. If you need more information about a topic outline, perhaps the English teachers would have appropriate material. A suggested reference text is *English Grammar and Composition: Fourth Course* by John E. Warriner and Francis Griffith (New York: Harcourt Brace Jovanovich, Inc., 1973).

Point out to your students that the chief value of an outline is to help in planning a talk or paper. Then assign Lesson 2 for reading and outlining. Tell the students that they will be expected to use their outlines to write an essay.

After they have completed their outlines, go over and discuss the material briefly to be sure that students have the essential information arranged in a proper topic outline. Then assign them to write an essay as described in Performance Objective 1.

Background Information

SIR WALTER RALEIGH (1552?–1618) Raleigh was a soldier, explorer, historian, and entrepreneur. He first became involved with the New World in 1578, when he went on a voyage that combined exploration with harassment of Spanish treasure ships. This voyage sparked Raleigh's interest in exploration. He felt strongly that England should take advantage of its claim (established by John Cabot) to a portion of the New World, and he spent a fortune trying to establish a colony. Each attempt failed, although the settlers he sent did manage to explore coastal territory from North Carolina to Florida. Raleigh named the area Virginia in honor of Queen Elizabeth, known as the Virgin Queen. Although he was unsuccessful in efforts to find gold on his explorations, Raleigh did find the potato, and introduced its cultivation on his estate in Ireland.

During the reign of Elizabeth, Raleigh enjoyed, for the most part, a favored standing at court. Upon Elizabeth's death in 1603, James I ascended the throne and Raleigh found himself in disfavor. James I accused Raleigh of treason and had him imprisoned in the Tower of London for twelve years. During that time Raleigh wrote his *History of the World.* When Raleigh was released, James I sent him on a mission in search of gold in South America under orders not to fight with the Spaniards. But Raleigh's expedition did attack the Spaniards, and when Raleigh returned to England, King James had him reimprisoned and eventually executed for disobeying orders.

we now have to make dangerous voyages to Barbary, Spain, Portugal, France, Italy, Moscovy, and Eastland.

What does Peckham think will attract merchants to invest in colonies? Add to these the hope of finding gold and silver, and you can see why some men might risk their money to found a colony.

Several Englishmen, including Sir Walter Raleigh and Sir George Peckham, did try to found colonies in North America before 1600. All of them failed, and lost small fortunes in the attempts. Their experiences showed that colonizing was too expensive for individuals, or even for small groups. When the English finally succeeded in planting a colony in Virginia, it was through a joint stock company.

Attracting settlers. One can understand why kings and queens, adventurers and investors, might want colonies in the New World. But why should the ordinary people of England want to leave home to live there?

A part of the answer is in the writings of Richard Hakluyt and Sir George Peckham that you read earlier. What is the economic condition that they describe at that time in England? If you cannot recall, turn to pages 12 and 13 and reread what they wrote.

The condition that Hakluyt and Peckham describe was connected with the wool trade you read about earlier. As the demand for wool increased, England's large landowners saw that they could make more money by raising sheep on their land than by renting the land out in small lots to farm families, as they had been doing. The changeover from farming to sheep raising was called the *enclosure* movement, because the owners *enclosed,* or fenced in, their fields. Thousands who had formerly farmed were thrown off the land by the enclosure movement. They roamed the roads looking for work. People in this condition might well be interested in trying for a new life in the New World—especially if it was all that Peckham said it was.

An advertisement of the Virginia Company of London gives some further clues as to why common people might

In the early 1600s, a variety of books and leaflets were printed in England to attract settlers to Virginia. The opening page of one such book is shown below.

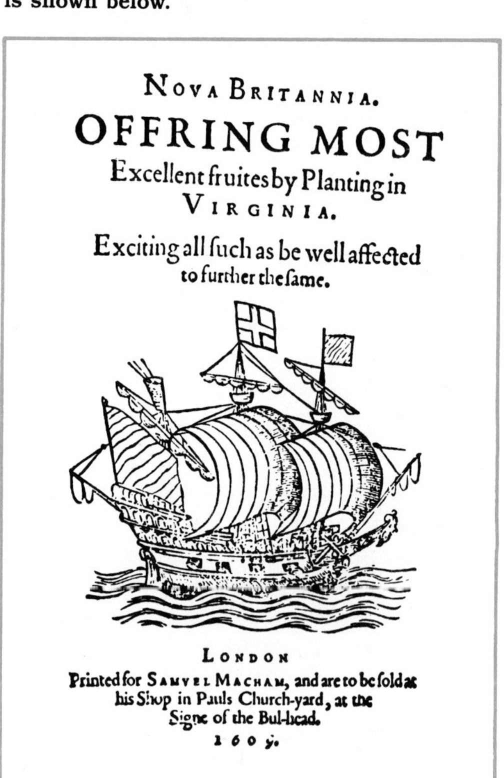

NOVA BRITANNIA.

OFFRING MOST

Excellent fruites by Planting in

VIRGINIA.

Exciting all ſuch as be well affected to further the ſame.

LONDON

Printed for SAMVEL MACHAM, and are to be ſold at his Shop in Pauls Church-yard, at the Signe of the Bul-head.

1609.

In the early seventeenth century, the changeover from farming to sheepraising on the large estates of England forced many farm families off the land and encouraged emigration to America.

decide to become colonists. The Virginia Company was a joint stock company formed by a small group of merchants and gentlemen in London. In 1606, James I, the new King of England, gave the company a *charter,* or contract, to found a colony in America.

Following is one of the leaflets that the company handed out on the streets in several English cities. As you read it, ask yourself these questions: To whom is this advertisement addressed? What attractions does it offer one to become a colonist?

This notice is published to announce the expedition to all workmen of whatever occupation—blacksmiths, carpenters, barrelmakers, ship builders, wood workers, and all work with any kind of metal, brickmakers, architects, bakers, weavers, shoemakers, sawers of lumber, spinners of wool, and all others, both men and women, of any occupation—who wish to join this voyage for colonizing the country. . . . They will be listed as investors in this voyage to Virginia, where they will have houses to live in, vegetable gardens and orchards, and food and clothing provided by the Company. Besides, they will receive a share in all the products and profits that may result from their labor, each in proportion; and they will also receive a share of the land that is to be divided, for themselves and their heirs forever.

3. FILMS *The English and Dutch Explorers* (11 minutes, color; Encyclopaedia Britannica Films, Inc.). *Sir Francis Drake—Rise of English Sea Power* (33 minutes, b&w; Encyclopaedia Britannica Films, Inc.). *European Expansion: Its Influence on Man,* History of Man series (19 minutes, color; Jules Power International Production and McGraw-Hill Text Film Division for ABC). The latter film analyzes several motives for the rise of exploration and colonization.

The films are available for rental from the Audio-Visual Center, Indiana University, Bloomington, Ind. 47401, or other film depositories.

4. DISCUSSION Discuss with your students the terms *fact* and *opinion.* Be sure they understand that a fact may be a statement that can be established as true; an opinion may be a belief founded on probable evidence. Ask students to analyze the quoted source material in this lesson and to list several facts and several opinions given there that would attract a person in England to become a colonist in America. Encourage students to discuss their answers with the rest of the class.

5. POSTERS Have your students work in small groups to create posters aimed at enticing investors to support a colonizing adventure in the New World. Suggest that they use a modern advertising approach, perhaps modeling their posters on ads they have seen in magazines or on TV.

Answers To Review Questions

1. Sir Thomas More saw America as an untouched wilderness, a place where one could start afresh, free from injustices of the Old World. Crèvecoeur believed America was a land where broken men and women could start life again and flourish. Bit Chuen Wu found that America was a land where one could save money and become one's own boss.

2. Rich soil, thick forests, and large deposits of metals and minerals.

3. Existing routes were slow, dangerous, and costly. Deserts, mountains, bandits, and hostile Turks blocked the trade routes between Europe and Eastern Asia. For these reasons, Europeans dreamed of finding a water route to the Far East.

4. Spain became wealthy by seizing gold and silver from two rich Indian civilizations—those of the Aztecs of Mexico and the Incas of Peru.

5. France, Holland, Sweden, and England

6. **(a)** to get from the New World raw materials, such as lumber and naval stores, with which to build a navy and stop the Spanish treasure ships; **(b)** to promote the Protestant religion; **(c)** to provide a place for the many unemployed in England to live under better conditions; **(d)** to expand trade by providing a market for English goods; and **(e)** to enlarge the English empire (Students may suggest additional answers that are reasonable and acceptable.)

The importance of land. You may have noted one theme that runs through nearly all the writings aimed at interesting investors, "gentlemen," and ordinary people in the New World. Write as they may about riches and precious metals, all of them sooner or later come to the idea of land—abundant land.

To understand why that theme would have such an appeal, you need to understand the importance of land in the England of that day. Land was the greatest source of wealth and income in sixteenth- and seventeenth-century England. It was also the yardstick by which one's importance was measured. Generally speaking, the more land one owned, the more important one was. That is why rich merchants bought large landed estates. Owning a large amount of land marked one as a member of the upper class. Since family land was usually inherited by the oldest son, younger sons had to look elsewhere for land of their own. Even at the bottom of the social ladder, land was important. Independent, small farmers who owned land had a higher standing and more rights than those who farmed on rented land.

Between 1540 and 1640, England's population doubled. In a country where land was so important, there simply was not enough of it to go around. And being scarce, land became all the more costly.

Something for everyone. Thus America offered something for everyone. For rulers and adventurers, gold and glory; for merchants, markets and raw materials; for the deeply religious, an opportunity to spread Christianity; and for all alike, land. By the early 1600s, England was ready to enter the race to found colonies in the New World.

CHECKUP

1. Why was the joint stock company effective in promoting England's trade?
2. What arguments were put forth by those who favored the planting of English colonies in the New World?
3. Why might people in England want to leave their homeland and become colonists in America?

Key Facts from Chapter 1

1. Those who have come to America from earliest times onward have seen it as a land of opportunity.
2. The picture of America as a land of opportunity is closely related to its abundance of natural resources, especially land.
3. The first discoverers of America were the people that Columbus called Indians.
4. Columbus's voyage in 1492 was important because it ushered in an era of New World exploration and colonization.
5. The three-fold aim of the European explorers of America was to find gold, to win glory, and to spread the Christian religion.

★ REVIEWING THE CHAPTER ★

People, Places, and Events

Utopia *P. 3*
Christopher Columbus *P. 5*
John Cabot *P. 7*
John Verrazano *P. 7*
Jacques Cartier *P. 7*
Pedro Cabral *P. 7*
Ponce de León *P. 9*
De Soto *P. 9*
Coronado *P. 9*
St. Augustine *P. 9*
Cortes *P. 9*
Pizarro *P. 9*
Henry Hudson *P. 9*
Richard Hakluyt *P. 12*
Sir George Peckham *P. 12*
Enclosure movement *P. 14*

Review Questions

1. In what ways did each of the following people see America as a land of opportunity: Sir Thomas More, Crèvecoeur, and Bit Chuen Wu? *Pp. 3–4* Les. 1

2. What three natural resources contributed to the idea of America as a land of plenty? *P. 5* Les. 1

3. Why were Europeans interested in finding new trade routes to the Far East? *P. 5* Les. 1

4. How did Spain become the world's richest nation in the 1500s? *P. 9* Les. 1

5. Which nations established claims on North America? *P. 9* Les. 1

6. List five reasons why England became interested in founding colonies in the New World. *Pp. 12–13* Les. 2

7. Why might the ordinary English person, especially the farmer, have been willing to leave England and settle in the New World? *Pp. 14–16* Les. 2

Chapter Test

Complete each sentence by writing the correct answer on a separate piece of paper.

1. Sir Thomas More located Utopia (off the coast of America, on the lost continent of Atlantis).

2. For hundreds of years, America has been identified with the idea of (hard times, opportunity).

3. European merchants dreamed of finding a (land, water) route to the Far East.

4. The motives that led Europeans to explore the New World can be summed up as (gold, glory, and God; liberty, equality, and fraternity).

5. Spanish claims in the New World include most of what are today the (southern and western, northern and eastern) parts of the United States.

6. Most of North America was eventually claimed by explorers from (France and England, Norway and Italy).

7. In order to share the financial risks of founding a colony, English merchants organized (royal companies, joint stock companies).

8. The enclosure movement encouraged many English (farmers, factory workers) to move to the New World.

9. In order to establish a new settlement, the English colonists needed a (letter, charter) from the English ruler.

10. In sixteenth- and seventeenth-century England, a person's importance was measured by his or her ownership of (ships, land).

7. Unemployment was high among the working class in England. As a result of the enclosure movement, thousands of small farmers were thrown off the land, and they, too, roamed the roads looking for work. People in that condition might well have been interested in trying for a new life in the New World. The promise of abundant land in America was especially attractive to the ordinary people. In sixteenth- and seventeenth-century England, land was the yardstick by which one's importance was measured. Even those at the bottom of the social scale could hope to own land in the New World.

Background Information

1. PICTURE This painting by artist Edward Hicks (1780–1849) shows William Penn making his famous treaty with the Indians in 1682. Hicks painted this theme several times, so there are copies in different museums. This one is from the Abby Aldrich Rockefeller Folk Art Collection at Colonial Williamsburg. The painting shown here was often repeated, in miniature size, in the background of "The Peaceable Kingdom," an art work that Hicks painted about one hundred times during his career.

William Penn's dealings with the Indians is one of the brightest pages in his political record. Even before his own arrival in Pennsylvania he sent the Indians a message of friendship: "I have great Love and Regard towards you, and I desire to win and gain your Love and Friendship by a Kind, Just and Peaceable Life." In his negotiations with the Indians, Penn made every effort to satisfy them. He explained that he wished to live with them "in peace and friendship," that he and his followers "met them unarmed because their religion forbade the use of hostile weapons," and that "they come not to injure others but to do good." The Indians responded by remaining deeply loyal to Penn and giving his name loving respect.

CHAPTER 2

THE ENGLISH COLONIES

LESSON 1

IN LATE DECEMBER 1606, three ships with 120 men and boys set sail from England for America. Four months later the ships entered Chesapeake Bay, and the passengers put ashore on a swampy peninsula a few miles up the James River. So was founded Jamestown, England's first permanent colony in the New World.

The Jamestown Colony

The leader of the Jamestown colony was called a governor, but he was really more like a manager in charge of a business. He took his orders from the investors back in England. And they left no doubt, from the very first orders, that his job was to produce a profit. The governor was to divide the settlers into three groups of 40 each. The first group was to build a storehouse for food and a fort to protect against Indian attack. The second would grow food. The third group of settlers would get on with the business of making a profit for the London investors. They were to explore the rivers, looking for the dreamed-of water route to the Far East. And when they came upon a spot where it was felt there might be minerals, half of them were to dig for gold.

To help in this effort, the Virginia Company sent over two goldsmiths, two refiners, and several jewelers. They came in the second shipload of settlers, arriving on New Year's Day, 1608. At the same time, the colony's settlers were supposed to enter into trade with the Indians for furs and food.

Hard times. The first several years of the Virginia colony went badly. The death rate was very high, mainly because of sickness and disease. Sixteen of the original 120 had died aboard ship. Of the remaining 104, 51 died before the second group arrived. The death rate among the second group was equally high.

Further, the colony failed to raise enough food to feed itself. There were several reasons for this. One was that the men wasted time chasing after gold, which they never found, rather than raising food crops. Another reason was that over half of the first group of settlers and a third of the second were "gentlemen." People in the "gentlemen" class did not work with their hands in England, and they clearly didn't plan to do so in Virginia.

Still another reason for the food shortage had to do with the ownership of land. The advertisement had read, "They will also receive a share of land that is divided, for themselves and their heirs forever." But in Virginia the settlers learned that this would not happen for many years. In the meantime, the company owned all the land. Since everyone was fed from the common storehouse, regardless of how much or how little he worked, there developed an attitude of "let the other fellow do it."

In 1608 Captain John Smith became the leader of the governing group. He knew that the colony could not keep depending on investors in London for food. Instead of foolishly hunting for gold, Virginians would have to cut

LESSON 1 *(1 to 2 days)*

Performance Objectives

1. To demonstrate a knowledge of the history of the Jamestown settlement by writing a paragraph that describes the important developments between 1607 and 1624. **2.** To create a ten-question recall test from the information contained in the lesson.

Famous People

Captain John Smith, John Rolfe

Vocabulary

Jamestown, Virginia Company, "gentlemen," headright system, indentured servants

Activities

1. FILMS *Elizabeth: The Queen Who Shaped an Age,* Western Civilization: Majesty and Madness series (27 minutes, color; John Secondari Productions). *Jamestown Colony, 1607 through 1620,* (17 minutes, color; Coronet Films). *Jamestown–The First English Settlement in America* (22 minutes, b&w; Encyclopaedia Britannica Films, Inc.).

2. DISCUSSION Samuel Eliot Morison states that an Indian needed twenty times as much land to live on as an English colonist needed. Discuss this statement with your students, and ask them to give possible reasons why Morrison made that statement.

3. LISTENING FOR INFORMATION If you can obtain a copy of *The American Story: The Age of Exploration to the Age of Atom* edited by E. S. Miers (Great Neck, N.Y.: Channel Press, 1956), share with the class "Experiment in Colonization" by Louis B. Wright. It tells the story of what befell the bold adventurers who first arrived in Virginia. You may want to keep *The American Story* on hand for use throughout the year. This book contains many essays by some of the best American historians, and students find the writings most interesting.

Also read the first three pages of "The Mayflower," Chapter 12 in Winston Churchill's *The New World,* Vol. 2 of *A History of the English-Speaking Peoples* (New York: Dodd, Mead, 1956). These pages deal with the background and settlement of the Jamestown colony. The remainder of the chapter will be used in Lesson 2.

Captain John Smith not only provided leadership at Jamestown but also explored the coast of the region which he named *New England.*

trees, clear fields, and till the soil. That meant everyone. Smith ordered: "He that will not work shall not eat."

But in 1609 Smith returned to England. The following winter was the worst time yet for the colony. Food ran out, and settlers fell victim to illness. Of the 600 men who had come to Virginia from England, there were but 60 alive by the spring of 1610. These survivors were preparing to give up and leave for England when a fleet arrived with supplies and new settlers.

Land and tobacco. During the next few years two important developments changed the future of the Virginia colony. One concerned land. Beginning in 1614 the company allotted three acres (1.2 ha) practically rent free to those who had lived in the colony for seven years. Except for a small amount of corn that settlers had to give to the warehouse, whatever food was grown on the land remained theirs. By 1616 a majority of the colonists were living on land that they could call their own.

In a history of the Virginia colony that Captain John Smith wrote in 1624, he describes what followed:

> When our people were fed out of the common store, and labored jointly together, glad was he who could slip [away] from his labor, or [sleep] over his task . . . the most honest among them would hardly [work] so much . . . in a week, as now for themselves they will do in a day.

The second important development had to do with Virginia's economy. The London investors had hoped that Virgina could produce something that could be sold at a profit. During the first few years of the settlement, the company had sent over gold refiners, glassblowers, winemakers, and silk growers. Their efforts had been for nothing.

What finally saved the colony was not gold or wine or silk, but a humble weed—tobacco. Virginia Indians had long grown a bitter-tasting type of tobacco. In 1612 John Rolfe, one of the colonists, experimented with seeds of a milder tobacco, grown in the West Indies. Virginia's climate and soil turned out to be ideal for this new crop. In England smoking had become something of a craze about 30 years earlier, and tobacco brought high prices. Within a few years everyone in the colony was raising it on every available piece of land—even in the streets of Jamestown.

By 1619 England was receiving over 40,000 pounds (18,000 kg) of tobacco every year from Virginia, more than from any other place in the world. Ten years later, Virginia sent thirty times as much. Virginia at last had a crop that could bring it prosperity.

The headright system. The crying need now was for laborers to raise the tobacco. The Virginia Company tried many ways to get people to America. It sent over orphaned children. It tried to attract people who were willing to work for the company on the same terms as earlier settlers. It advertised for women who wished to find husbands—until then only a few already married women had come to Virginia.

There was one magnet, however, that could draw people to the New World more than any other. That was the opportunity to own land. The company had taken one step in that direction in 1614. In 1618 it went all the way with the *headright system.* A gift of land, usually 50 to 100 acres (20 to 40 ha), was given to any person in England

THE METRIC SYSTEM

In the text at the top of page 20, you will see the words "three acres (1.2 ha)." This means that 1.2 ha, or hectares, is about the same as three acres. A hectare is a unit of measure in the metric system.

The metric system for measuring area, distance, weight, capacity, and temperature is in use in all major countries except the United States. Plans are being made to "go metric" here also.

To prepare you for this change, both U.S. and metric measurements are given in this book. Each U.S. measurement in this book is followed by the metric measurement that is about equal to it. Acres are changed to hectares (ha), inches to centimeters (cm), feet or yards to meters (m), miles to kilometers (km), pounds to kilograms (kg), quarts to liters (l), and degrees Fahrenheit (°F) to degrees Celsius (°C).

The first task of the English colonists at Jamestown in 1607 was to build shelters and a fort.

4. ESSAY After the students have read Lesson 1, ask each student to write a descriptive paragraph about the history of the Jamestown settlement, including information on the following points.

a. The purpose of the settlement

b. Who the settlers were (background, training, etc.)

c. Problems encountered and how they were solved

d. Lessons that were learned that were helpful to later colonists

5. TESTING After the students have read Lesson 1, have them each make up a ten-question recall test and then exchange tests with another student.

6. RESEARCH/ORAL REPORT Assign one or two students to investigate and report on one of the great mysteries of American history—the fate of the members of the Lost Colony. The name was given to an early settlement on Roanoke Island, off what is today North Carolina. The colony is called *lost* because no one has ever discovered what happened to it.

Background Information

2. THE FIRST STRIKE On September 17, 1962, the Attorney General of the United States, Robert F. Kennedy, spoke before the Polish Roman Catholic Union Convention in Baltimore, Maryland. The following is quoted from that speech.

"Although Poland is a much older nation than the United States, our destinies have been closely and profitably intertwined.

"A few years after its founding, Jamestown, the first permanent settlement in America, was in trouble. The gentlemen adventurers who formed Captain John Smith's company had little taste for the hard task of building a colony in a hostile wilderness. They were most interested in vain searches for gold than in clearing stubborn forests or ploughing fields.

"Smith sent to London for help. He asked for men who would work and who had the skills necessary to create a civilization in the wilderness.

"The next ship brought help. Not more gentlemen seeking a quick fortune, but six skilled craftsmen—Lowicki, Stefanski, Mata, Bogdan, Zrencia and Sadioski.

"These first six Poles in the New World went to work. They established a glass furnace—the first industry in America—and helped the colony to start a soap works and a saw mill. John Smith credited their example of skill and industry with saving Jamestown.

"A few years later, when the colony was to elect the first representative legislature in America, the governor ruled that only those born in England could vote. The Poles promptly put down their tools and proclaimed, 'No vote, no work.' The governor relented and the annals of the Jamestown colony for 1619 note that Poles were extended the full right accorded other settlers.

"It is not surprising that this first strike in America was by Poles and that it was staged in the name of freedom."

Jamestown, the first permanent English settlement in America, was located on swampy ground beside the James River in Virginia. Inside the stockade, at left, were a church, storehouse, and dwellings.

who would move to Virginia. Instead of having to work for the company for seven years, a landless Englishman could become an instant landowner. A settler could get another 50 acres (20 ha) free by paying the transportation of some other person to Virginia. *Indentured servants*—persons who agreed to work for a number of years for whoever would pay their passage to America—would also get a headright of 50 free acres at the end of their term of service.

Fifty acres! This was more land than many an Englishman dared dream of owning in a lifetime. With this change in land policy, the stream of settlers grew rapidly. The headright system enabled many to acquire huge estates by paying the fare of other persons, perhaps indentured servants, to the colony. And servants were willing to come because they could look forward to the time when they, too, might own land in Virginia.

In the years from 1619 to 1624, 4,500 settlers came to Virginia, and the colony was safely established.

A promise fulfilled. Thus for many of the Virginia colonists, the promise of opportunity in America was fulfilled. Near the end of his history of Virginia, Captain John Smith explains the appeal of America in these words:

> What man who is poor . . . can desire more contentment than to walk over and plant the land he has obtained by risking his life? . . . Here nature and liberty give us freely that which we lack or have to pay dearly for in England. What pleasure can be greater than to grow tired from . . . planting vines, fruits, or vegetables, from working their own mines, fields, gardens, orchards, buildings, ships, and other works?

Two final notes on the Virginia colony. First, in 1619 a new and unexpected supply of labor arrived in Virginia. A Dutch ship carrying a cargo of twenty black Africans landed in Jamestown. Thus began one of the most tragic chapters in American history. You will read about what followed later in this unit.

Second, while Virginia settlers became prosperous, the Virginia Company never did. Once colonists owned their own land, profits from tobacco growing went mostly to them. What little the company received was made on selling the crop in England for the planters. In 1624 King James took over the colony, thus ending the company's role.

CHECKUP

1. Why did things go badly for the Jamestown colony in its first years?
2. What two developments changed the colony's future for the better?
3. Describe the headright system. What effect did it have on Virginia's growth?

LESSON 2

The New England Colonies

To a number of English people, America represented an opportunity of quite a different kind. This was the opportunity to worship God as they chose.

During the Protestant Reformation, in the 1500s, King Henry VIII broke away from the Roman Catholic church and established the Church of England, placing himself at its head. His action left the English people divided for more than a century.

The majority of the English accepted the Church of England, or the Anglican church, as it was called. On one side of them stood those who remained Roman Catholics and refused to recognize the Anglican church as the new national faith. On the other side were the Protestants who wanted the Anglican church to move much further away from the Roman Catholic church. Faced with dissent on both sides, English monarchs persecuted both Catholics and extreme Protestants.

The Puritans. The more extreme English Protestants were called Puritans, because they wanted to "purify" the Anglican church by removing all Catholic influences. Thus they wanted to do away with priests' robes and most rituals. They felt there should be no religious statues, stained-glass windows, and music during services. Such things, the Puritans said, came between the people and their worship of God. They also thought that each local congregation should govern itself, and so wished to do away with bishops, a holdover from Catholicism.

Most Puritans had no wish to leave the Anglican church. A small minority, however, saw no hope of reforming the church from within and left it. These Separatists formed their own congregations and proceeded to hold their own religious services.

King James I, who came to power in 1603, did not take kindly to the Puritans, whether Separatists or not. As king, remember, James was not only the ruler of England but also the head of the Anglican church. To defy the church was also to defy him. James therefore ordered the Puritans to get in line or he would "harry [drive] them out of the land." When the Puritans refused, James was as good as his word.

LESSON 2 *(1 to 2 days)*

Performance Objectives

1. To explain, orally or in writing, the similarities and differences between the Puritans and the Pilgrims, especially as those differences related to the founding of the several American colonies. **2.** To demonstrate a knowledge of the settlement of the New England colonies by constructing a chart showing the important facts about each colony.

Famous People

King Henry VIII, King Charles I, John Winthrop, Roger Williams, Anne Hutchinson, Reverend Thomas Hooker, John Davenport, Theophilus Eaton

Vocabulary

Protestant Reformation, Anglicans, Catholics, Puritans, Separatists, Pilgrims, *Mayflower,* Plymouth, Massachusetts Bay Colony, commonwealth, Providence, New Haven, Province of Maine

Activities

1. **FILMS** *English and Dutch Colonization in the New World* (11 minutes, color; Coronet Films). *The Pilgrim Adventure,* Saga of Western Man series (52 minutes, color; American Broadcasting Company). *Religious Freedom in America's Beginnings* (14 minutes, color; Coronet Films). *Roger Williams—Founder of Rhode Island* (28 minutes, b&w; Encyclopaedia Britannica Films, Inc.). A thorough understanding of the colonization movement requires a good understanding of seventeeth-century English history. A film that provides such an understanding is *Puritan Revolution—Cromwell and the Rise of Parliamentary Democracy,* Western Civilization: Majesty and Madness series (33 minutes, color; Learning Corporation of America).

The Pilgrims. Fearing arrest, a small band of Separatists, later known as Pilgrims, fled to Holland in 1609. There they had complete religious freedom and they prospered. The Pilgrims worried, however, lest their children take on Dutch ways and forget their English heritage. After ten years, therefore, they decided to leave Holland for America.

One of their leaders got permission to plant a colony on the territory of the Virginia Company. A group of London merchants financed them. The Pilgrims planned to set up a trading post and fishing settlement. All the capital and profits were to be placed in a common pool for seven years, by which time they hoped to pay off their debt to their London backers.

On September 16, 1620, the *Mayflower,* a leaky vessel of 180 tons (160 t), left England bound for America. Of the 101 passengers aboard, there were 35 Pilgrims from Holland and 52 other Separatists from England. Many of those who were not Pilgrims were going to America more for the opportunity to get land or work there than for religious reasons.

The Plymouth colony. Blown off course, the *Mayflower* arrived at Cape Cod, outside the territory of the Virginia Company, in early November. Nevertheless,

After a voyage of 64 days, the Pilgrims landed on Cape Cod in November 1620. They came ashore, sent out an exploring party, heated water and washed clothes, and then sailed on to the site of Plymouth.

the Pilgrims decided to settle at what is now Plymouth, Massachusetts.

Through the harsh winter that followed, the Pilgrims struggled to keep their tiny colony alive. The first year was as desperate as that in Jamestown. By spring, 44 people had died. Only after several hard years did the Plymouth colony establish itself. Discouraged by the colony's inability to make a profit, the London backers stopped sending supplies in 1624. Three years later the partnership between the merchants and Pilgrims ended, and the colony was on its own.

Plymouth grew slowly. By 1648 it had managed to pay off its debt to the London merchants, but it never really prospered. In 1691 it was absorbed by its larger neighbor, the Massachusetts Bay Colony. Still, Plymouth was the first colony to realize the opportunity that America gave to those seeking religious freedom. Its example influenced thousands of later settlers.

Massachusetts Bay Colony. One group of non-Separatist Puritans and their leader, a lawyer named John Winthrop, watched the Pilgrim experiment with great interest. When it became clear that the new king, Charles I, would reintroduce certain Catholic practices, these Puritans also decided to move to America. There they would be able to lead Christian lives according to the rules of conduct in the Bible. Their community would be a model of godliness. It would, they were sure, win the admiration and imitation of all England.

In 1629 these Puritans formed a joint stock company, called the Massachusetts Bay Company, and elected Winthrop governor. During the next six months, 1,000 men, women, and children left to take up life in the wilderness of New England.

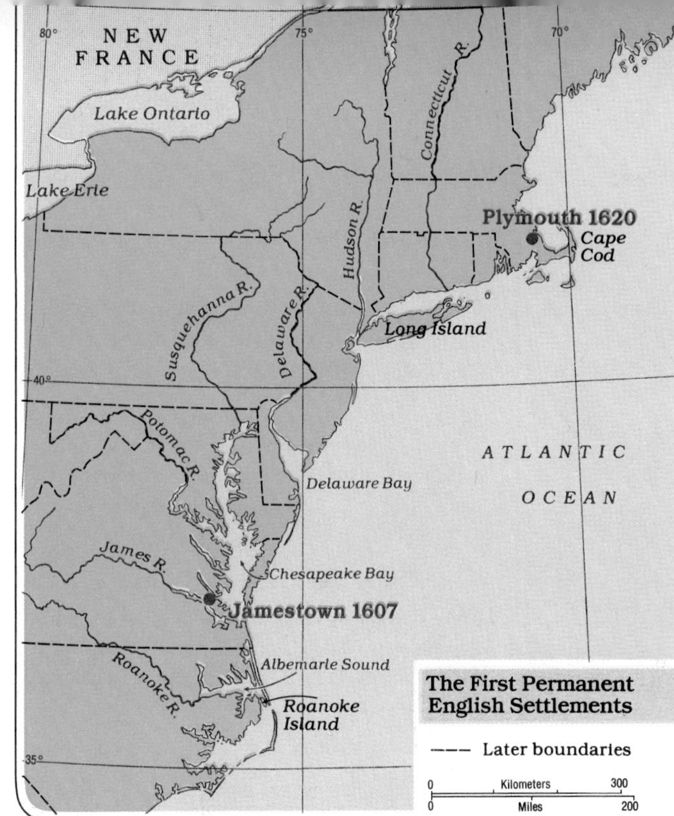

The first permanent English settlements were at Jamestown and Plymouth, but other English settlements had been attempted earlier. One was at Roanoke Island where, in 1587, a colony of about 150 people was set up. When a ship put in there in 1590, the settlers had disappeared. No one knows what happened to the Lost Colony.

The question of motive. What you have read so far would lead you to conclude that John Winthrop had a simple, single motive in going to America. Yet Winthrop may have had another reason. He had several sons, and in England it was common practice for a father to give his sons half his property when they came of age, usually at twenty-one. Three of

2. DISCUSSION The Time-Life book *The World's Great Religions* (New York: Time Inc., 1957) has an excellent description of the religious furor that took place in England in the fifteenth and sixteenth centuries. It includes a chart, on pages 204–205, that serves as a good introduction to a discussion of the religious differences that helped cause the colonization movement.

3. USING A CHART Ask the students to write these column headings on their papers: Colony, Date Founded, Founder, and Reason for Settlement. Then, after students have read the lesson text, have them complete their charts. You may wish to ask certain students in the class to assist other students with this activity.

After students have completed their charts, ask them to use the information to discuss the similarities and differences among the colonies.

4. LISTENING FOR INFORMATION Share with the class the remainder of Chapter 12 in Churchill's *The New World,* begun in Lesson 1. George F. Willison's essay in *The American Story* (see Lesson 1) will also be of interest to the students. You may wish to ask a few of the better readers in the class to present this additional material.

Winthrop's sons had recently come of age. In his journal, Winthrop remarks that he has given away half of his estate to his sons and could no longer live as well as he had before. He asks (again, wording has been changed to make his meaning clearer):

> Why, then, should I continue to stay in England (where an acre of land costs as much as a hundred acres in America) at a time when that whole rich continent lies unused?

What may have been Winthrop's other motive for going to America? Which motive do you think was more important, this one or the religious motive?

Why did it happen? The last question points up a major problem we always face in understanding both the past and present. The hardest thing to know is not *what* happened but *why* it happened; not *what* people did but *why* they did it. In other words, the causes of events and the motives of people are the most difficult things to know for certain.

Sometimes we can be fairly sure that several motives were, or are, present. But then it is difficult to be sure which was the most important. Earlier in this unit you read that the explorers were motivated by God, gold, and glory. True enough. But which of these three was most important in their minds? Would any one of them have been motive enough to explore if the other two had been absent? And if so, would the same motive have been the most important one for each of the explorers? In trying to answer such questions, we must not assume too quickly that what would be the most important to us was, or is, most important to others. That is especially true when we are dealing with the motives of people of an earlier age or a different culture.

At times, we can be fairly confident that we understand people's motives. The motives of the 35 Pilgrims who left Holland for America, for example, are quite clear. More often, we are left with uncertainty.

Which motive was the most important in leading John Winthrop and his fellow Puritans to come to America? Most probably it was the religious one. But would Winthrop and others have come to America even if the religious motive had not been present? That we can never know for sure. The entry in Winthrop's journal makes it clear that he had mixed motives, and this was true in the case of many other settlers.

The Puritan settlements. Winthrop's group spent its first winter in the Massachusetts Bay Colony in a settlement called Salem. In 1630 they founded Boston, which became the colony's capital. Soon they started other communities nearby.

Although founded as a trading company, the Massachusetts Bay Colony quickly changed into a self-governing commonwealth. Laws were based on the Bible and Puritan belief. All members were required to attend church. The clergy and the elected officials were to be obeyed without question, for it was believed they held their authority from God. This was a tight community of true believers. Strangers were not welcome, nor was disagreement allowed.

Massachusetts grew rapidly. Between 1633 and 1643, about 20,000 persons came. Did all of them come for religious reasons? It is true that religious persecution in England had become worse during this time. But only about 4,000 of those who came were members of Puritan churches in England. That suggests that a good many of the 20,000 were drawn to America at least partly by the same kinds of opportunity that drew settlers to Jamestown—the chance for land and jobs and the hope of improving their lives.

Rhode Island. The strictness of the Massachusetts Puritan leaders led to the founding of the colony of Rhode Island. Roger Williams was a young minister in Massachusetts Bay. Winthrop and others thought his religious ideas were dangerous. Williams believed, among other things, that the government should have no authority over the people in matters of religion. He also argued that the land on which the Bay Colony was located still belonged to the Indians, since the English settlers had never purchased it from them.

Fearing that such ideas might lead to a revolt against their authority, the Puritan leaders brought Williams to trial. They convicted him and ordered him banished in 1635. Warned by friends that he was going to be shipped back to England, Williams fled into Indian country. For fourteen weeks he lived in the wintry wilderness, kept alive by the Narragansett Indians who gave him food and shelter. In the spring of 1636, Williams started his own settlement at Providence.

Two years later, the Puritan leaders ordered out Anne Hutchinson, another dissenter. Anne Hutchinson had been holding meetings in her home to discuss church sermons. She soon began to preach that people would find God's guidance through an inner light rather than from the sermons of a minister. Such ideas were too much for the Puritan clergy. They also criticized Anne for stepping out of her "proper" place as an obedient Puritan wife and mother and doing things that only men should do. Hutchinson was tried, found guilty, and driven from the colony. She settled in

Anne Hutchinson, whose religious views were not acceptable to the Puritan rulers of Massachusetts Bay, was brought to trial, found guilty, and forced to leave the colony for Rhode Island.

5. USING A MAP Provide copies of an outline map of the eastern United States. Then have the students draw in and label the New England colonies and their capital cities and important geographical features, using as a guide the maps "The New England Colonies" (see page 28) and "The English Colonies" (see page 51). Students should include Massachusetts, Rhode Island, Connecticut, and New Hampshire; the cities of Portsmouth, Boston, Providence, Newport, Hartford, and New Haven; such geographical features as the Connecticut River and the Atlantic Ocean.

Ask the students to keep their maps because they will be adding to them in Lesson 3.

Note: You students will soon be thinking about college applications. You might like to have them list the names, dates, and locations of colleges and universities that are found in the New England area. *The World Almanac* would be of help; so, too, would *Barron's Profiles of American Colleges.*

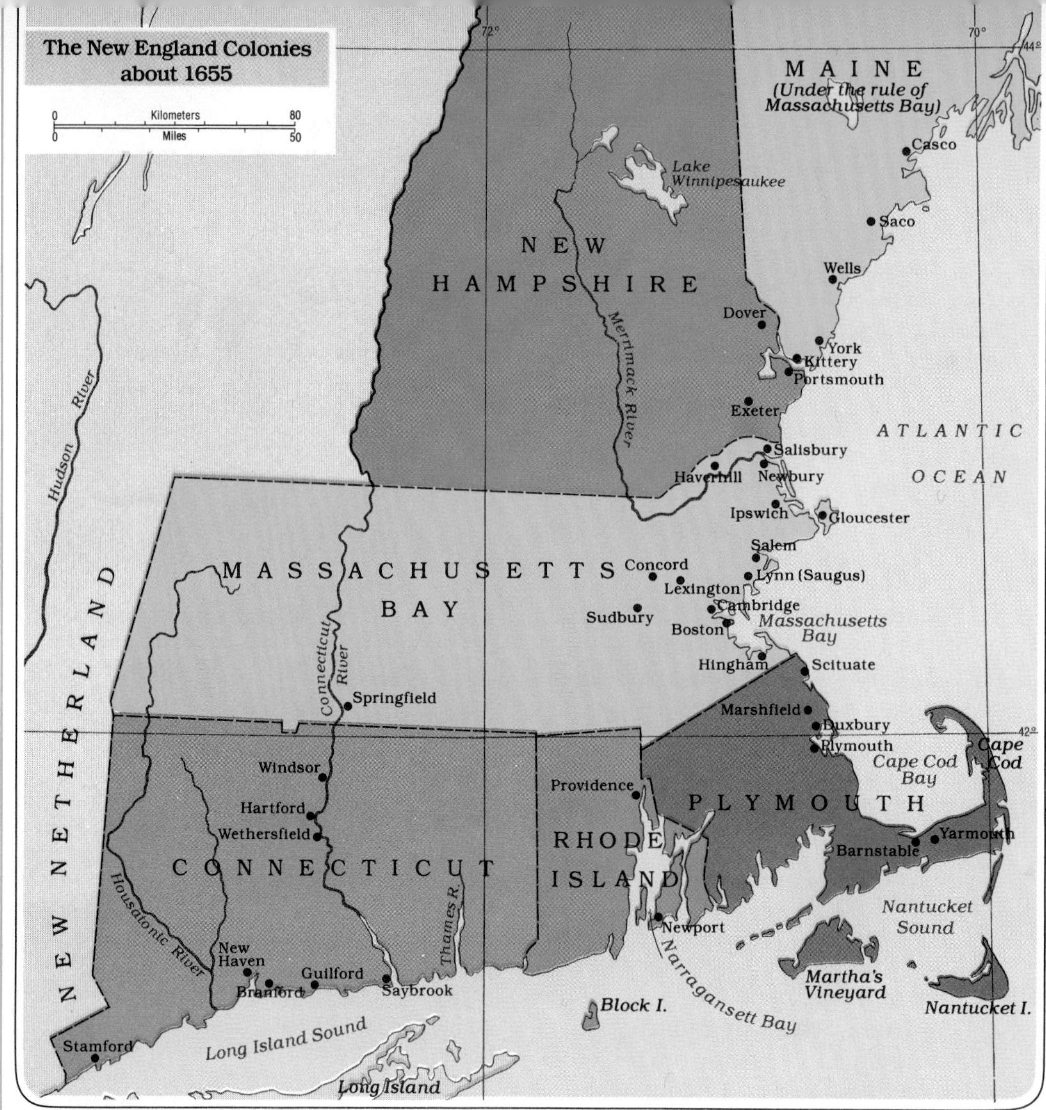

The Great Migration of the 1630s saw more than 20,000 people emigrate to New England. Numerous settlements were made. On the map note the boundary between Massachusetts Bay and Plymouth colonies. It was in effect until 1690, when Plymouth became a part of Massachusetts Bay Colony.

Narragansett, not far from Providence. Later, other religious dissenters founded communities in the area.

In 1663 the King of England combined all of these settlements into the colony of Rhode Island. The colony's charter guaranteed religious freedom to all.

Connecticut, New Hampshire, and Maine. Three other New England colonies were formed under quite different circumstances. In 1635 and 1636, whole congregations left Massachusetts for the rich Connecticut Valley. Unlike Williams and Hutchinson, these people had no quarrel with religious leaders in

Massachusetts. They simply were seeking better farmlands.

One congregation, led by the Reverend Thomas Hooker, set up several communities along the Connecticut River. Another Massachusetts group, headed by John Davenport and Theophilus Eaton, started a colony in New Haven. In 1662 Connecticut received a royal charter that set up a government for all settlements in that region.

Other colonists from Massachusetts Bay moved to the north. A number of small fishing villages and fur trading posts already existed there. Massachusetts claimed all this territory, but in 1679 the residents in one part of it got their own charter from the king. They founded the colony of New Hampshire. The other area, known as the Province of Maine, was to remain a part of Massachusetts until 1820.

CHECKUP

1. Why was the Plymouth colony founded?
2. How did the Pilgrims and the Puritans differ? How were they alike?
3. Who were the first colonists in Rhode Island and Connecticut? Why did they move there from Massachusetts?

LESSON 3

The Middle and Southern Colonies

In 1624 Captain John Smith, in his history of Virginia, gave the following advice to those who wished to plant colonies in America. Again we have changed the wording slightly:

> Do not rely too much on renting, dividing, or selling lands for your own profit. And do not impose too much on ordinary settlers, either by requiring them to pay too much of their produce into your common storehouse or by any heavy tax for the sake of your immediate profit. But give every man as much land as he can farm freely without limitation, paying you half his produce or upon some other terms. And at the end of five or six years let him have twenty, thirty, or forty, or a hundred acres for every acre he has cultivated, for himself and his heirs forever. . . .
>
> In such a colony a servant who will work can within four or five years live as well there as his master did here in England. For where so much land lies unused in America, a man would be mad to start by buying or renting or paying very much for it.

Smith understood that without the labor of ordinary people, no colony could succeed. He also understood that the promise of free land, more than anything else would bring these people to America.

The wisdom of Smith is clear to us today. Oddly, later colonial promoters did not follow his lead at first. They each had their own goals and their own ideas of how to succeed. Some wanted to keep most of the land for themselves and rule like a king over those who worked it. In the end, however, most of them had to return to John Smith's blueprint for success.

Maryland. The founding of Maryland is a case in point. Sir George Calvert, a wealthy friend of the king, wanted a colony of his own. Owning a colony could bring wealth and status, but Calvert also had another reason. A recent convert to Catholicism, he sought a haven for his fellow Catholics, who were still being persecuted in England.

In 1632 King Charles I gave Calvert a large area of land, naming it Maryland in

LESSON 3 *(1 to 2 days)*

Performance Objectives

1. To show on an outline map the original thirteen colonies and their capitals. **2.** To demonstrate a knowledge of the settlement of the middle and southern colonies by constructing a chart showing the important facts about each colony.

Famous People

Sir George Calvert, Cecilius Calvert, King Charles II, Duke of York, Lord John Berkeley, Sir George Carteret, William Penn, Francis Pastorius, James Oglethorpe

Vocabulary

Baronies, quitrent, Toleration Act, plantations, pay crop, proprietors, Society of Friends, Quakers, debtors, indigo, Scotch-Irish, Presbyterians, Huguenots

Activities

1. FILM *Colonial Expansion of European Nations* (13 minutes, color; Coronet Films) shows some of the social and cultural conditions in Europe during the sixteenth century that led to colonial expansion in various parts of the world. The film is available for rental from the Audio-Visual Center, Indiana University, Bloomington, Ind. 47401, or other film depositories.

Background Information

1. NEW NETHERLAND The Dutch based their claim to land in the New World on the voyage of Henry Hudson. The New Netherland colony included parts of what are now Connecticut, Delaware, New Jersey, and New York. The economic basis for the colony was the fur trade. Thirty families settled at the mouth of the Hudson River in 1624. Peter Minuit bought Manhattan Island from the Indians in 1626 and the first permanent settlement—New Amsterdam—was founded. Trading posts were established near present-day Trenton, New Jersey; Hartford, Connecticut; and Albany, New York, up the Hudson River. Discontent among the Dutch settlers with their governors and the Dutch West India Company, which ran the colony, made it easy for the English to take over New Netherland in 1664. The English named the colony New York in honor of the Duke of York, brother of the English king.

As a Dutch colony, New Netherland attracted many different peoples because the Dutch practiced religious toleration. The first Jewish community in North America was in New Amsterdam. The Jews had fled religious persecution in Spain and Portugal and their colonies. Other peoples to settle in New Amsterdam included Swedes, Huguenots (French Protestants), English, Africans, and Spaniards.

In 1752, Baltimore was a fishing and farming village of 100 people. Its name came from the title of Maryland's founders, George and Cecilius Calvert, the first and second Lord Baltimore.

honor of his queen. Calvert would rule and do with the land as he wished. George Calvert died that year, and the grant of land was given to his son Cecilius Calvert, who carried out his father's plan.

That plan was to divide the land into a few great estates, called *baronies.* Each owner would bring over peasants to live under his rule and work the land. Calvert's profits would come from an annual fee, called a *quitrent,* that the landholders would pay him.

The plan never worked. Calvert did give out a number of large estates, but the owners found it hard to attract people to work them. And for good reason. Why should one go to Maryland to live as a peasant on someone else's land when Virginia offered free land under the headright system?

To attract more settlers, Calvert adopted the same idea of giving free land to those who paid their own way over. A husband and wife were promised 100 acres (40 ha) each, with 100 acres more for each servant they brought, and 50 acres (20 ha) for each child under sixteen. To anyone who brought over five men between the ages of sixteen and fifty, Calvert gave 2,000 acres (800 ha).

Calvert soon had to give up on his dream of making Maryland a haven for Catholics. Landowners wanted workers too much to be fussy about their religion. They accepted Protestants as well as

Catholics. Soon Protestants outnumbered Catholics in the colony.

The two groups quarreled bitterly. To put an end to this trouble, Calvert urged the legislature to pass the Toleration Act in 1649. This law was hardly tolerant by today's standards. It granted religious freedom to all Christians, but atheists, Jews, and other non-Christians who entered Maryland could be put to death. Even with these restrictions, the act was an important step toward greater religious liberty.

With these changes, Maryland began to grow. In many ways it was like Virginia. It was a land of many small farmers and an increasing number of large plantations. And as in Virginia, the major crop was tobacco.

The Carolinas. The story of the Carolina colony was similar to that of Maryland. In 1663 King Charles II gave a large tract of land to eight of his supporters. Like Cecilius Calvert, these men had grand ideas of setting up great estates and running their colony entirely for their own profit. In their plan, they and their descendants would own the land forever and rule its inhabitants.

The Carolina proprietors, like Calvert in Maryland, very quickly had to adopt the advice that John Smith had given forty years earlier. To attract settlers, they offered a headright of 100 acres (40 ha) for each settler, with additional land for each servant who was brought over.

Carolina gradually developed into two separate parts that were quite different from one another. The southern part was a land of large plantations, worked mostly by slave labor. Rice was the main *pay crop*— that is, the crop to sell. The northern region was settled mostly by small farmers. They raised tobacco, and, for the most part, they worked their own land without the use of slaves. Their trade was mainly with Virginia. In 1729, the two sections were split into the separate colonies of South Carolina and North Carolina.

New York. You will recall that New York was originally the Dutch colony of New Netherland. Britain seized it in 1664 in a war with Holland. The English king, Charles II, gave his brother, the Duke of York, the former Dutch colony as well as everything else between Maryland and Canada—excepting Pennsylvania—that had not already been given away. The Duke was to be the absolute ruler and

In its style of architecture and in its general appearance, the city of New York reminded visitors in colonial times that, until 1664, it had been New Amsterdam, a Dutch settlement.

2. USING A MAP This activity is a continuation of Activity 5 in Lesson 2. Have the students draw in and label the middle and southern colonies and their capital cities and important geographical features, using as a guide the map "The English Colonies" (see page 51). Students should include those geographical features as shown on the text map. After students have completed the map work, you may wish to have them each write five questions that can be answered from the information shown on their maps. Then ask volunteers to read their questions; have the rest of the students find the correct answers by using their own outline maps.

Note: If the locating of colleges was successful and/or useful in Lesson 2, repeat the activity for the middle and southern colonies.

3. USING A CHART Ask your students to write these column headings on their papers: Colony, Date Founded, Founder, and Reason for Settlement. Then, after students have read the lesson text, have them complete their charts and use the information to discuss the similarities and differences among the colonies.

owner of New York. He could set up any kind of government he wanted. He could keep, sell, or rent the unoccupied lands.

A large group of non-English Europeans, mostly Dutch, were already living in New York when the English took it over. Wisely, the Duke put a governor in charge with orders to treat the conquered Dutch with "humanity and gentleness." He did not try to force upon them any change in language, religion, or customs. The colony was large enough for all.

To build up the English population, the governor gave large amounts of land on Long Island to friends. They in return sold the land in small pieces at low prices. New York did not adopt the headright system, and this colony grew more slowly than several of those that did.

New Jersey. One of the first things the Duke of York did when he got his huge land grant was to give a large slice of it to two friends, Lord John Berkeley and Sir George Carteret. That piece, lying between the Hudson and Delaware rivers, became New Jersey. The old colony of New Sweden, as well as settlements of Dutch, Finns, and English, already existed in this area.

Berkeley and Carteret advertised in England for settlers. They also gave part of their land to other proprietors. But like New York, New Jersey grew slowly.

Pennsylvania. The colonizer who best understood the appeal of America to ordinary people was William Penn. Penn was a member of a religious group called the Society of Friends, also known as the Quakers. Penn longed for a place where this much-persecuted group could follow its ways in peace. King Charles II owed a large sum of money to Penn's father. When the father died, Penn persuaded the King in 1681 to pay off the debt with land in America. He called it Pennsylvania, meaning "Penn's woods."

Penn intended his colony to be both a religious haven and a good business. He invited all persons who wanted religious freedom to come. This meant not only Quakers in England but all other groups who were being persecuted in Europe. The colony would govern itself, and there would be complete political and religious freedom.

These promises and a description of the fine soil and climate Penn put into a pamphlet he called *Some Account of the Province of Pennsylvania.* Shrewdly, Penn translated the pamphlet into French, Dutch, and German and distributed it widely in Europe. He aimed his appeal to those who might buy or rent land as well as to those who would come as servants. Each newcomer who paid the way over would receive 50 acres (20 ha) free. One could buy larger lots very cheaply—5,000 acres (2,000 ha) for just 100 pounds. Small plots could be rented for as little as a penny an acre. Indentured servants were promised 50 acres on completion of their service.

How did Penn expect to make his colony profitable? Francis Pastorius, who was a German minister, led one of the early groups that settled in Pennsylvania. In a report home, he explained:

> Our Governor, William Penn, intends to establish and encourage the growing and manufactory of woolens; to introduce the cultivation of the vine, for which this country is peculiarly adapted, so that our Company had better send us a quantity of

Continued on page 34

Indentured Servants

What would you do if you wanted to come to America from England to settle and did not have the money to pay the passage? You would have done what thousands of settlers like Robert, below, did: you would sign on as an indentured servant. This meant signing a contract, or an indenture, promising to work for a number of years to repay the passage money. Here is a copy of Robert's indenture, in 1619.

> The said Robert does hereby [contract] faithfully to serve the said Sir William, Richard, George and John for three years from the day of his landing [in] Virginia, there to be employed in the lawful and reasonable works and labors . . . and to be obedient to such governors . . . as they shall from time to time appoint and set over him. In consideration thereof, the said Sir William, Richard, George and John do covenant to transport him . . . with all convenient speed into the said land of Virginia at their costs and charges . . . and to maintain him with [food and clothing] . . . and in the end of the said term to make him a free man . . . and to grant said Robert thirty acres of land.

During Robert's three-year term of service, he was not a free man. He could work only for his masters or anyone they asked him to work for. Robert was not free to leave the place where he was employed, nor could he marry without the consent of his masters. In return for his labor, as noted, his masters were to pay his transportation to Virginia and to provide him with food and clothing.

After Robert had served his three years, he would become a free man and would be released from his contract. He would be given what were known as "freedom dues"—in this case, 30 acres (12 ha)—to allow him to set himself up as an independent farmer.

Both men and women came over as indentured servants. Some found their masters treated them kindly; others were treated cruelly. But whether the treatment was kind or cruel, many persons like Robert took this opportunity to get to America.

In exchange for passage to America, many Europeans bound themselves to labor for a definite period, often three to five years. They often served as farm workers, especially in the Middle Colonies.

Background Information

2. NEW SWEDEN The first Swedish settlers came to the Delaware region in 1638. They called their colony New Sweden. They built Fort Christina near present-day Wilmington. As new settlers came from Sweden and Finland, the colony expanded. The Dutch in New Amsterdam felt that New Sweden was in their territory. In 1651, Peter Stuyvesant sent a force of men to build and settle Fort Casmir, which was near what is now New Castle, Delaware. Fort Casmir fell to the Swedes in 1654. But one year later the Dutch were able to subdue the Swedish colonists, and they made all New Sweden part of the Dutch colony.

Museum of Fine Arts, Boston

The Quakers, shown here at one of their meetings, were among Pennsylvania's first settlers.

> wine-barrels and vats of various sorts, also all kinds of farming and gardening implements. . . .

The land that Pastorius bought lay north of Philadelphia. Others bought land farther west, and Pennsylvania prospered.

Delaware. The history of Delaware is closely connected with that of Pennsylvania. The colony had passed through the hands of the Swedes and Dutch before the English took it over along with New York in 1664. In 1682 Delaware was granted to William Penn along with Pennsylvania. For the next 22 years, the two colonies had the same governor and legislature. After 1704, Delaware was allowed its own legislature.

Most of the settlers were small farmers, who worked their land without either indentured servants or slaves. A policy of religious toleration helped the small colony to grow rapidly.

Georgia. Georgia was the last of the thirteen colonies to be settled. Although the main reasons for its founding were different from those for all the other colonies, Georgia illustrates the idea of America as opportunity as much as they.

In England in the 1700s, persons who could not pay their debts were put in jail. They stayed there until family or friends paid those debts or until they somehow worked their way out. Many never did, and died in jail.

James Oglethorpe, an English reformer and soldier, was moved by their condition. One of his own close friends had died in debtor's prison. Oglethorpe came up with the idea of a colony where such prisoners could get a new start in life. He also pointed out to the king that the colony might serve as a military barrier against the Spanish, who then owned Florida. In 1732 the King gave Oglethorpe and twenty trustees a charter. The following year, the first group of settlers arrived in Georgia, the colony that gave the unfortunate a second chance.

During its first 20 years, Georgia grew slowly. Few were attracted to a colony where they might have to face military attacks by the Spanish as well as malaria. While everyone was given 50 acres (20 ha) free and tools, no one was allowed to own more. Slavery was also prohibited. Contrary to Oglethorpe's plans, the majority of early settlers were neither debtors nor English. A large number came from Austria, Switzerland, and Germany.

After 1752, slavery was allowed, and settlers were permitted to acquire more than 50 acres. This gave rise to plantations, on which were grown rice and indigo, a plant from which was made a blue dye for coloring cloth. But by 1760 Georgia's population was still only 9,000, a third of whom were slaves. It remained the smallest of the thirteen colonies as measured by population.

A babble of languages. Until about 1700, although there were pockets of non-English people here and there, colonial society was mainly English. England was the main source of immigration, and English was spoken nearly everywhere.

Beginning in the 1700s, that sameness ended. The New England colonies remained mainly English all through the colonial period. But by 1776, in the colonies from New York south, half the population was non-English. Germans, Scots, Scotch-Irish, Swiss, Africans, and French had come streaming into America, many as indentured servants. Soon a babble of languages was heard up and down the land.

For most of these people, as for the English, America meant opportunity and free or cheap land. But for many, it was not simply a wish to do something better that led them to emigrate from the Old World. It was the desperate need to leave something worse.

We know this because of the years in which each group of immigrants arrived. Immigrants came to America in a series of waves between 1700 and 1776. Each wave came at a time of serious problems for that group in its homeland. Sometimes the problems were economic, like famine. Sometimes there was political persecution, and sometimes religious. Often several of these problems occurred at once.

The Scotch-Irish. An example of a people beset by several problems was the Scotch-Irish. These people were Scots whom the British king moved to northern Ireland to keep down the restless Irish in the early 1600s. The Scotch-

4. DISCUSSION Two years before the *Mayflower* sailed for America, an English Separatist received a charter for a Virginia plantation, and with 180 others, sailed for America. However, on the voyage, 130 of those people died aboard the crowded, unsanitary ship. Word of the tragedy must have discouraged many potential colonists, yet many others came on later trips.

Discuss with your students the following questions: Would "gold, glory, and God" have been enough motivation for you to take such a risk? What other possible motives might these colonists have had to come to the New World?

5. CREATIVE WRITING Ask your students to imagine that they are prospective colonists aboard the first ships to reach North America. They have no frame of government, no plan of organization, no laws or rules. Ask students to come to a written agreement—no longer than 300 words—that would be the basis for their life in the New World.

Divide students into small groups and have each group elect a secretary to record their ideas. After each group has written its plan of organization, encourage a class discussion of these thoughts and ideas. Are certain ideas common to all groups? How does each group deal with the concept of authority?

When the students have completed this activity, read to them the Mayflower Compact, which may be found in Commager's *Documents of American History*.

Answers To Review Questions

1. For the first several years Jamestown seemed doomed to failure for the following reasons: **(a)** the London Company wanted a quick profit from the colony; **(b)** the colony failed to raise enough food to feed itself because many settlers either chased after gold or were from the "gentlemen" class and did not have necessary skills; and **(c)** there was no private ownership of land, which gave rise to an attitude of "let the other person do it." Two important developments prevented Jamestown from failing: **(a)** the division of land so that a majority of the colonists call their own, and **(b)** the successful cultivation of tobacco.
2. A Puritan wished to purify the Anglican church of its Catholic practices. A Separatist, however, wished to break away from the Anglican church because of its Catholic practices.
3. The Plymouth colony, settled by the Pilgrims, and the Massachusetts Bay Colony, founded by the Puritans, ultimately became Massachusetts. Massachusetts was a self-governing commonwealth. Laws were based on the Bible and Puritan belief. All members were required to attend church. The clergy and elected officials were to be obeyed without question.

Irish were Presbyterians in religion. They soon felt discriminated against by the Anglican church. English landlords also caused resentment by raising the rents. On the heels of this came crop failures in 1716 and 1717. In the next fifty years, 250,000 Scotch-Irish left for America. Most of them settled in the middle and southern colonies.

The story was similar in other lands. Skilled workers left Switzerland for America when unemployment struck in the early 1730s. From France came the Huguenots—Protestants persecuted in a Catholic land. From Ireland came Catholics—persecuted by their Protestant English rulers. And from the many German provinces came thousands who were fleeing religious persecution, frequent wars, and hard times.

The stamp of England. Little more than a hundred years after its first shaky settlement at Jamestown, the English firmly controlled the Atlantic coast of North America from Canada to Georgia. They also owned sugar-rich islands in the Caribbean Sea. Even though the population had come from many lands, the stamp of England was on most of North America. English was the language of the government and of two thirds of the people. Settlers lived under the laws of England, and of local governments, modeled on England's. They used goods bought from England, and they accepted English institutions.

This did not mean, however, that life in the colonies was no different from life in England. Most colonists had originally planned to reproduce their European ways of life in the New World setting, and to some extent, they succeeded. But the special conditions in America brought about changes from the beginning. In the next chapter, you will look at a few of those changes.

CHECKUP

1. What thing did the founders of the colonies soon find was most important in attracting settlers?
2. How did Calvert, Penn, and Oglethorpe differ in their approaches to setting up colonies?
3. How did the Old World backgrounds of settlers in the middle and southern colonies differ from the backgrounds of those in the New England colonies?

Key Facts from Chapter 2

1. The first permanent English colony in America was established at Jamestown, Virginia, in 1607.
2. The desire to worship in their own way and to own land were among the reasons why Europeans settled in America in colonial times.
3. The Maryland Toleration Act of 1649 was, despite limitations, an important step toward religious liberty.
4. Until about 1700, colonial society was mostly English; after that time, there were increasing numbers of other nationalities.

★ REVIEWING THE CHAPTER ★

People, Places, and Events

Jamestown *P. 19*
John Smith *P. 19*
Mayflower *P. 24*
Plymouth colony *P. 24*
Massachusetts Bay Colony *P. 25*
John Winthrop *P. 25*
Roger Williams *P. 27*
Anne Hutchinson *P. 27*
Sir George Calvert *P. 29*
Toleration Act, 1649 *P. 31*
Lord John Berkeley *P. 32*
Sir George Carteret *P. 32*
William Penn *P. 32*
James Oglethorpe *P. 35*

Review Questions

1. Explain why early Jamestown seemed destined to fail. Why didn't it fail? *P. 19* Les. 1
2. Who were the Puritans? What was the difference between a Puritan and a Separatist? *P. 23* Les. 2
3. Which two settlements united to become the colony of Massachusetts? Explain how Massachusetts was governed. *Pp. 25–26* Les. 2
4. Why did Calvert have to give up his dream of making Maryland a refuge for Catholics? *Pp. 30–31* Les. 3
5. How did the economic growth of the Carolina colony cause it to develop into two separate parts? *P. 31* Les. 3
6. Why was William Penn so successful in founding Pennsylvania? *P. 32* Les. 3
7. How does the founding of Georgia illustrate the idea of America as a land of opportunity? *P. 34* Les. 3
8. Why did people from countries other than England settle in the English colonies? *P. 35* Les. 3

Chapter Test

Complete the chart on the English colonies by filling in each blank space with the correct answer. Write your answers on a separate piece of paper.

	Name of colony	Founder or leader	Reason for settlement
1.	Jamestown	John Smith	Profit
2.	Plymouth	Pilgrims	Religious freedom
3.	Massachusetts Bay	John Winthrop	Religious freedom
4.	Rhode Island	Roger Williams Anne Hutchinson	Religious freedom
5.	Maryland	Calvert	Religious freedom
6.	New York	Duke of York	Profit
7.	New Jersey	Carteret, Berkeley	Profit
8.	Pennsylvania	William Penn	Religious freedom
9.	Delaware	William Penn	Religious freedom, profit
10.	Georgia	James Oglethorpe	Refuge for debtors

4. Originally, Calvert divided the land into a few great estates owned by friends. Each owner would bring over peasants to live on and work the land. However, the owners had difficulty attracting people to work for them because free land was available elsewhere. To attract more settlers, then, Calvert agreed to give free land to those who paid their own way to Maryland. Landowners wanted workers too much to care about their religion, so they accepted Protestants as well as Catholics.
5. The southern part had large plantations, worked mostly by slave labor. In the northern section, small farmers raised tobacco without the use of slaves. Eventually, the two sections were split into two separate colonies.
6. Penn promised that the colony would govern itself and that there would be complete religious and political freedom. He encouraged the establishment of businesses, which helped to make his colony profitable. He also made it easy for settlers to acquire land.
7. Georgia was founded as a refuge for debtors in the hope that they could get a new start in life.
8. Each group of immigrants had a serious problem confronting them in their homeland. Sometimes the problem was famine, political or religious persecution, or a combination. In addition, immigrants were attracted by the same things that had attracted English settlers—opportunity for political and religious freedom and free or cheap land.

Background Information

1. PICTURE Shown here is a detail from a mural painted over the mantelpiece at the home of Martin Van Bergen of Leeds, New York. The artist is unknown. From the mural, painted about 1735, one can catch a glimpse of a particular life-style enjoyed by a few people in colonial America. The Catskill Mountains are shown in the background. This painting is at the museum of the New York State Historical Association in Cooperstown.

REALIZING THE PROMISE

LESSON 1

IN VIRGINIA, land free and labor scarce
In England, land scarce and labor plenty

So went two lines of an English poem of 1647. Those two lines explain much about colonial America. You have already seen the connection between them and the decision of thousands to leave England for America. And you will remember how they are related to both indentured service and slavery. In this chapter you will see how these two lines also help explain many other things—religion and government in the English colonies, the shape of the colonial economy, the position of workers, and the position of women.

Religion and Government

The seventeenth and eighteenth centuries were an age of strong religious beliefs and intolerance. Even those who sought religious freedom for themselves were very quick to deny it to others. You will recall how the Puritans of Massachusetts dealt with dissenters, such as Roger Williams and Anne Hutchinson. They also persecuted Quakers, and even condemned them to death for not following Puritan laws. Needless to say, Catholics and Jews were few in Massachusetts for many years.

Freedom of religion. But the future did not belong to intolerant people like the Puritans. It belonged instead to people like Roger Williams and William Penn who practiced freedom of religion in their colonies.

Religious toleration did not come all at once in America. It grew gradually, and even by the time of the American Revolution it was not complete. Toleration gained for two reasons. One was that people like Penn sincerely believed in religious freedom and promoted it. The second was the ever important fact of labor shortage in America. Colonizers quickly discovered that a promise of religious freedom increased their chances of attracting settlers. You will recall that when Catholic landowners in Maryland needed people to work the land, they gladly settled for Protestant farmers. Three years after the founding of Carolina, the proprietors included the following as the first point in their advertisement for settlers: "Full and free liberty of conscience is granted to all, so that no man is to be molested or questioned concerning matters of religious concern." The owners of New Jersey also assured everyone of freedom of conscience.

Thus in several colonies there were people of many religions. A traveler to Philadelphia in the eighteenth century was surprised at the number of different religions he found in the tavern where he stayed. At his table sat "Roman Catholics, Church men, Presbyterians, Quakers, Newlightmen, Methodists, Seventh Day men, Moravians, Anabaptists, and one Jew." In New York City in the 1750s, one observer counted two Anglican churches, two Lutheran, and one Quaker meetinghouse. A similar distribution existed in the neighboring colony of New Jersey.

Continued on page 41

LESSON 1 *(2 days)*

Performance Objectives

1. To explain in a descriptive paragraph the differences between the three kinds of colonial governments—royal, proprietary, and corporate—and to name the colonies that had each type. **2.** To state why religious freedom, while not perfect, was much greater in the colonies than in England. **3.** To cite two reasons for the development of legislatures and to differentiate between the functions of the two houses by writing a newspaper article.

Famous Person

Governor Thomas Hutchinson

Vocabulary

The Great Awakening, hereditary aristocracy, assembly, legislature, House of Burgesses, council, veto, proprietary, royal, and corporate colonies

Puritanism

John Winthrop, governor of Massachusetts Bay, symbolized the spirit of Puritanism that resulted in New England's successful settlement. Like most Puritans, he came to America to practice his own idea of a "Godly life." What Winthrop hoped to do was to establish a much more perfect Christian community than England had ever known. If the Puritans of New England succeeded, then, Winthrop believed, the inhabitants of Old England would follow their example. For this reason he wrote, just before landing in Massachusetts in 1630, that his colony would be "as a City set on a Hill, the eyes of all people . . . upon us."

What Winthrop and the other Puritans did in Massachusetts influenced all of American history. As one great scholar wrote, "Without some understanding of Puritanism . . . there is no understanding of America." When the descendants of New England settlers migrated westward, they carried Puritan attitudes with them clear across the continent.

What were these Puritan traits, and how have they influenced America? The Puritans believed first of all in the idea of a mission in history. Just as the Puritans believed Massachusetts should become a "City set on a Hill," so most Americans have believed their country has some larger role to play in human history and that it should set an example for other nations. Puritans believed deeply in religion and morality. Many historians feel that America's religious history and moral attitudes as a people are connected to what happened in early New England. The Puritans had a great respect for learning. The American emphasis on education, scholars feel, can be traced back to these seventeenth-century origins. In their business life, the Puritans believed in hard work, constant activity, and thrift. Many Americans in the nineteenth and twentieth centuries have shared a belief in these same values. Finally, the Puritans believed in constitutionalism and limited government—ideals that Americans have cherished.

Thus, America's cultural heritage and national character may be said to have their roots in the Puritan tradition of John Winthrop and other founders of New England.

The *New England Primer*, reflecting Puritan values, was long used in American schools.

The Great Awakening. In the 1730s and 1740s, a series of great religious revivals swept the colonies. Called the Great Awakening, the revivals split many Protestant churches in two. The religious meetings attracted thousands of people from the lower classes of society. One effect was to spread democratic ideas in religion.

All of this does not mean that religious toleration was complete. You will recall that the Toleration Act of 1649 in Maryland was not extremely tolerant. In many colonies, Catholics and Jews could not hold office, and often could not vote. In some, however, such barriers were dropped in practice. Even with the restrictions that remained, there was greater religious freedom in colonial America than in England, and much greater freedom than in most other parts of Europe.

A role in government. In the same pamphlet in which they promised religious liberty to settlers, the founders of Carolina made another promise to induce people to move there.

> A governor and council are to be appointed among the settlers, to carry out the laws of the assembly, but the governor *is to rule but three years, and then learn to obey.* The governor has no power to lay any tax or to make or repeal any law without the consent of the settlers in their assembly. . . The settlers are to choose annually from among themselves a certain number of men, apportioned as they wish, to constitute with the governor and his council the general assembly, which shall have the sole power of making laws and laying taxes for the common good when need shall require.

The authors of this promise in 1666 were the same lord proprietors who originally planned for Carolina to be ruled by a hereditary aristocracy. It is safe to assume, therefore, that they thought it was either desirable or necessary to promise settlers a role in government.

By the time the founders of Carolina made this promise, a number of colonies already had assemblies, or legislatures. Virginia was the first. The Virginia company's charter of 1606 said that the settlers would have the same liberties "as if they had been living and born in England." In its early years, however, the company had treated the settlers as employees. They had no say at all in the running of the colony.

To attract settlers, the company made several important changes in 1618. The most important, you will recall, had to do with land. Another change gave settlers the right to elect representatives to an assembly. Along with the governor and his council, this body would make laws for the colony. The House of Burgesses, as the assembly was called, met for the first time in 1619. It was the first representative legislature in the English colonies.

There had been an assembly in the Massachusetts Bay Colony since 1634. Five years later Connecticut drew up a constitution calling for the election of a governor and a two-house legislature. Rhode Island followed suit in 1647. Even in Maryland, where Calvert had planned to rule like a lord, an elected legislature was soon set up.

Why legislatures developed. Why did legislatures develop in Britain's North American colonies? The reasons are

Continued on page 43

Activities

1. **FILMS** *English Influences in the United States,* Cultural Influence series (11 minutes, color; Coronet Films). *The Splendid Dream: William Penn* (19 minutes, b&w; Teaching Film Custodians). The film *Courage in Connecticut: The Protection of Democracy, 1687* (19 minutes, b&w; Teaching Film Custodians) focuses on the crises in Connecticut over the power of the royal governor versus the colonists. *Minorities: In the Name of Religion* (16 minutes, color; Coronet Films) discusses religious groups in America and the conflicting influences of religious toleration and religious discrimination.

2. **LISTENING FOR INFORMATION** Read to your students "A Red Sinking Sun" in *The American Story: The Age of Exploration to the Age of the Atom* edited by E. S. Miers (Great Neck, N.Y.: Channel Press, 1956). This essay on Bacon's Rebellion was written by Thomas Jefferson Wertenbaker, a distinguished American historian. Also read (from the same book) Carl Bridenbaugh's "William Penn, Founder of Colonies."

3. READING FOR INFORMATION/ESSAY Have your students read the Sidelight on History "How the Colonies Were First Governed," page 42. Then have them write descriptive paragraphs explaining the three kinds of colonial government—royal, proprietary, and corporate—and naming the colonies that had each type.

How the Colonies Were First Governed

The thirteen original colonies represented three different kinds of government—proprietary, royal, and corporate. Each was similar in that it had a governor, a legislature, and some form of court system. The chief difference in the three types of colonial government lay in the method of selecting a governor. In the proprietary colonies the governor was selected by the proprietor, with the approval of the king. In the royal colonies he was appointed by the king alone. And in the corporate colonies the governor was elected directly or indirectly by the voters.

Maryland was a prime example of a proprietary colony. Control of the colony lay in the hands of the proprietor, Lord Baltimore, who had the power to govern and held title to the land both by virtue of a charter granted by the king. Lord Baltimore was to Maryland what the English king was to England. Baltimore appointed the governor and delegated to him the power to govern. Many colonies, like the Carolinas, began as proprietary colonies but then became royal colonies. By the end of the colonial period, only three colonies—Maryland, Pennsylvania, and Delaware—remained proprietary colonies.

In the royal colonies, the king appointed the governor and was able thereby to keep closer control. Several colonies, like Massachusetts Bay, started out as charter provinces, in which a charter to colonize was granted to a private company. Others, like New Jersey, were proprietary colonies for a time. But the trend after the 1680s was toward changing proprietary and charter colonies into royal colonies. By the end of the colonial period, eight of the provinces were royal colonies: New Hampshire, Massachusetts, New York, New Jersey, Virginia, North Carolina, South Carolina, and Georgia.

Corporate colonies were those with the greatest degree of self-rule. They were operated under a charter held by the colonists. Only two of the thirteen colonies—Rhode Island and Connecticut—were corporate colonies.

As Maryland's proprietor, Cecilius Calvert, the second Lord Baltimore, had far-reaching powers under a charter granted by the English king.

slightly different for each colony, but in general they boil down to two. First, English people were used to the idea that laws should be made by an elected legislature. One of the "rights of Englishmen" was the right to have their laws, especially tax laws, made by a body that represented them. It was natural that English settlers in North America would want the same rights. In their minds they were simply English people who happened to be living overseas.

The second reason was a very practical one. The American colonies were 3,000 miles (4,800 km) from England. Conditions in the colonies were different from those in England. Parliament, sitting in London, could not understand the problems of a wilderness settlement in Virginia or New England and make wise laws to deal with them.

Council and assembly. In some colonies, such as Carolina and Virginia, promoters freely gave settlers the right to have a legislature. In others, the right was won only after a long struggle. But by 1700, every colony had its own legislature. Most legislatures were made up of two houses. One was generally called the *council*, or *governor's council*. Its members were usually appointed by the governor, with the king's approval. The governor appointed men who would support him and the interests of the empire as a whole.

In most colonies the council was made up of the wealthiest and most important people. Often it was controlled by a few families. In Virginia, for example, almost a third of all the councillors appointed between 1680 and 1775 came from just nine families. In South Carolina, a fourth of the councillors between 1729 and 1775 came from just seven families. In New York, twenty-five of the twenty-eight appointed between 1750 and 1776 came from great landowning families.

The other house was usually called the *assembly*. Its members were elected by the colonists. The assembly had a part in making all laws. Its most important power was the power to lay taxes. No tax could be passed without its consent.

The governor was appointed either by the king or the proprietors. In only two colonies, Connecticut and Rhode Island, was he elected. But in all colonies the governor had sweeping powers. He had the right to call the legislature to meet, and he could also order it to adjourn. He could *veto*, or disapprove, laws passed by the assembly. He also could appoint many other officials in the colony, and often could make large gifts of land to favorites. The governor used both the appointments and the gifts to build up support for himself.

The right to vote. Colonists voted for their representatives to the assembly, but not all colonists had the right to vote. Voters had to be white, male, twenty-one or over, and had to own a certain amount of property. At one time or another, Catholics were not allowed to vote in five of the colonies, and Jews were not allowed to vote in four. With few exceptions, women could not vote. Indians and blacks could not vote at all.

Still, a very large number of colonists had the right to vote. Land was so cheap that most colonists could meet the property requirement. In every colony, at least 50 percent of the white adult males could vote. In Massachusetts, between

4. RESEARCH/ORAL REPORT For an example of how a colony formed its government, have some of your students study the "Fundamental Orders of Connecticut," which may be found in *Documents of American History* edited by Henry Steele Commager (New York: Appleton-Century-Crofts). Ask the students to make a diagram of the government so described and to be prepared to explain it to the rest of the class.

5. CREATIVE WRITING After the students have read the lesson, assign them to write newspaper articles about the conflict that developed in colonial government between the governor and the assembly. Have students include the following facts as background material for the articles: the two reasons for the development of the legislatures and the differences in the functions of the two houses. Urge students to be imaginative in their creation of the news stories, but also caution them to use as much factual information as possible.

6. **RESEARCH/ORAL REPORTS** In the American colonies, five systems of theology were widely accepted.
a. Calvinism (Presbyterians, Huguenots, and Dutch Reformed)
b. Federal and Covenant (Puritan Congregationalists of New England)
c. Arminianism (the Church of England, which followed the ideas of the Dutch theologian Arminius)
d. Antinomianism (the followers of Anne Hutchinson and the Quakers)
e. Catholicism
Assign students to examine each of the systems, and have them report to the class why religious toleration was a difficult goal. Then ask one student to state why religious freedom in the colonies, while not perfect, was much greater than in England.

7. **ROLE-PLAYING** Walter Prescott Webb, in his *The Great Frontier* (Austin: University of Texas Press, 1964), wrote that after the exploration and settlement of the New World, these pertinent questions had to be asked:
a. How big is the new land?
b. Who lives in it?
c. What is it worth? What is it good for? What can we get out of it?

The history of our country is the attempt to answer those questions. Ask your students to imagine that they are members of a colonial legislature. Have them devise ways in which those questions might be answered peaceably.

80 and 90 percent could. Governor Thomas Hutchinson, who favored limiting the right to vote, once said in disgust that in Massachusetts "everything in the shape of a man could vote."

Assembly versus governor. The assembly, or lower house, spoke for the interests of the colonists who elected its members. The governor and council, on the other hand, spoke for the interests of the king and Parliament. Often these two interests came into conflict. As a result, in many colonies there were struggles between assembly and governor.

These struggles pointed up the fact that the colonists lived under two sets of laws. One came from their own legislatures. The other was the laws and rules that Parliament made for them. Such laws governed trade, for example. During the first half of the 1600s, Parliament didn't make many laws for the colonies. Later, when it did make laws, it did very little to enforce them. So for most of the colonial period, the colonies had a great deal of freedom in running their own affairs.

When an argument between an assembly and a governor did take place, it usually concerned the right of self-government. In such a dispute, the chief weapon an assembly had was control over the spending of the colony's tax money. In many colonies, the assembly also paid the governor's salary. On a few occasions an assembly tried to reduce the governor's salary or even withhold it altogether, in order to bring him into line. These conflicts between assembly and governor became more frequent and more serious in the years just before the American Revolution.

CHECKUP

1. Why, as time went on, did religious toleration increase in the colonies?
2. Why did legislatures develop in the colonies? How did the two houses of most legislatures differ?
3. Who were the voters in the colonies? Who could not vote?

LESSON 2

The Colonial Economy

Nine tenths of all Americans farmed for a living. True to the promise of America, the large majority of them owned their own land, either through purchase or headright. There was another very large class of small farm owners, however, who did not get their land in either of those ways. These persons were called *squatters*. They simply moved out to the edge of settlement, or the frontier, cleared a piece of land, and farmed it without buying it or otherwise getting a legal claim to it. Some of these frontier people were new immigrants who had headed straight for the backcountry. Some were sons and daughters of farmers from older communities where the best lands were already taken. And some were simply restless people, always moving on—people who felt crowded if there was another farmhouse in sight of their own dwelling.

Squatters lived in the backcountry of every colony. In Pennsylvania alone there were about 100,000 squatters by 1726. Having settled and improved the land, squatters felt it was rightfully theirs. Often, in time, it did become theirs. But in the meantime, squatting led to fights and lawsuits between those who lived on the land and those who legally owned it.

Geographic mobility. Benjamin Rush, a Philadelphia doctor, traveled through Pennsylvania's backcountry in the eighteenth century. Describing the squatter he wrote: "The first settler in the woods is generally a man who has outlived his credit or fortune in the [settled] parts of the state." Rush was pointing out something important about life in America. That is the ease and freedom with which people moved from place to place. It was far different in European countries, where land was scarce. There most people remained fixed in one place all their lives.

The ability to move from place to place is called *geographic mobility*. A society in which it is easy to move about, as it was in colonial America, is said to be geographically mobile. Geographic mobility is closely connected to opportunity. Do you see how? Rush's description gives you a strong clue.

Farming in the South. Because of climate and geography, farming differed from one part of the country to another. The South was a region mainly of large plantations and small farms. Plantations sometimes ranged from 1,000 to 6,000 acres (400 to 2,400 ha), and sometimes more. They specialized in raising pay crops. In Maryland, Virginia, and North Carolina, the pay crop was tobacco. Rice and indigo were the pay crops of South Carolina and Georgia. Until the 1680s, much of the work on these plantations was done by white indentured servants. After that date, it was performed more and more by black slaves.

Most plantations were located along the South's many rivers. Each had its own dock. Tobacco and other crops could be loaded directly onto the ships that would carry them to England and other lands.

Large plantations provided for almost all their own needs. George Washington's Mount Vernon is a good example. To feed his slaves, Washington raised wheat, cattle, and hogs, and set up nets in the Potomac River to catch fish. Slave blacksmiths, carpenters, and bricklayers made all the materials for the buildings. Cider and liquor were stored in barrels made on the plantation. Wheat was ground into flour in a mill on the plantation. There was also a weaving shed, where wool and flax, a plant fiber, were turned into material for clothing for the slaves.

Virginia planters oversee the loading of casks of tobacco on a ship bound for England. The rich soil and the long growing season in Virginia made tobacco farming a profitable activity.

LESSON 2 *(1 to 2 days)*

Performance Objectives

1. To contrast farming in the North with farming in the South by listing at least three differences. **2.** To describe the trade patterns that developed in colonial America by drawing and labeling a map. **3.** To describe orally or in writing the status of women in colonial America.

Famous People

Martha Custis, John Peter Zenger

Vocabulary

Squatters, geographic mobility, "bread colonies," triangular trade, dowries

Activities

1. MOCK TRIAL In Book II, Chapter V, of *Two Treatises of Government,* John Locke, discussing property, wrote, "God, who hath given the world to men in common, hath also given them reason to make use of it to the best advantage of life and convenience. . . . Though the earth and all inferior creatures be common to all men, yet every man has a 'property' in his own 'person.' . . . The 'labour' of his body and the 'work' of his hands, we may say are properly his. Whatsoever, then, he removes out of the state that Nature hath provided and left it in, he hath mixed his labour with it, and joined to it something that is his own, and thereby makes it his property."

In light of Locke's theory on property, ask your students to hold a trial to determine the guilt or innocence of a squatter who has settled in western Pennsylvania on unexplored land—but land that has been given by the king to an English nobleman. The squatter is charged with tresspass and theft. If the students find the squatter innocent, ask them to hold another trial, one in which the claimant is an Indian.

Plantation owners like Washington dominated southern life, but there were possibly nine or ten times more small farm owners. Most southern farms were between 100 and 200 acres (40 and 80 ha); some were smaller. Many were acquired through headrights. Some were located between the large plantations, near the coastal areas. Others were further inland, along the backcountry.

Most small farmers raised enough food for their own needs and also raised a small pay crop besides. Usually that crop was tobacco. Small farmers probably raised more than half the tobacco grown in the South. They sold or exchanged it for farming tools, salt, and other needed items. Usually they farmed the land themselves, without the help of slaves or indentured servants.

Farming in the North. Except for a few large estates, the lands in New England and the middle colonies were owned and worked by small farmers. In New England, where the soil was rocky and the growing season short, farming was less profitable than it was elsewhere. Most New England farms were also smaller, running between 70 and 100 acres (28 and 40 ha). The main crop was corn, which was eaten by both humans and animals.

The labor force was the family. Husbands, wives, and children—and here and there an occasional hired hand—worked together to gain a living from the sometimes unwilling soil. On farms this small, there was little demand for indentured servants. Most farm families succeeded in raising enough for their own needs, with a little left over for sale. In the evenings family members made their own household furnishings and farming tools.

In contrast to New England, the soil and climate of the middle colonies—New York, New Jersey, and Pennsylvania—were ideal for farming. Farms in this region were larger than in New England, generally between 150 and 200 acres (60 and 80 ha). The following account by one farmer describes farming in the middle colonies.

> My farm gave me and my whole family a good living on the products of it; and left me, one year, with . . . one hundred and fifty silver dollars, for I never spent more than ten dollars a year, which went for salt, nails, and the like. Nothing to wear, eat, or drink, was purchased, as my farm provided all. With this saving, I put money to interest, bought cattle, fatted and sold them, and made great profit.

Some of the wheat and corn that farmers like this one grew for sale fed residents of cities, such as Philadelphia and New York. Because England grew enough wheat and corn for its own needs, the rest of it was shipped to the West Indies and to countries in southern Europe. Since the middle colonies were the main producers of food for export, they came to be known as the "bread colonies."

Because farms in the middle colonies were large, there was a great need for labor. Farmers in this region relied heavily on indentured servants. Many came voluntarily, happy to sell several years of their labor for passage to America. Others did not come voluntarily. Some of those were orphan children sent by the English government, which did not wish to support them. Others were children sent by parents who were

2. **FILMS** *Colonial America in the Eighteenth Century* (17 minutes, color; McGraw-Hill Text Film Division). *Colonial Printer* (26 minutes, color; Colonial Williamsburg, Inc.). *Home Life* (21 minutes, color; Eastman Kodak Company and Colonial Williamsburg, Inc.). These films are available for rental from the Audio-Visual Center of Indiana University, Bloomington, Ind. 47401, or from other film depositories.

New England fishermen lay their catch out to dry. Dried fish was a major article in colonial trade.

too poor to raise them. British judges sometimes sentenced convicts to forced labor in America. All told, somewhere between 60 percent and 75 percent of white immigrants before the Revolution were indentured servants. The majority of these wound up in Pennsylvania and the other middle colonies.

In addition, farm owners hired workers for wages. How did such hired workers fare? The following account by one farm owner tells us something about their condition.

> As to labor and laborers . . . you must give them what they ask: three shillings per day in common wages and five or six shillings in harvest. They must be at your table and feed . . . on the best you have.

Do you see any connection between this farmer's complaint and the two lines of the old English poem at the beginning of this chapter?

Trade and commerce. While more than 90 percent of the people lived on farms or in farming villages, 10 percent did not. The rise of cities added another side to the opportunity of America. For one thing, the trade and commerce of the cities was next only to farming in importance in the colonial economy. For another, the cities provided a good living for skilled and unskilled workers, merchants, and seamen.

Much of the commerce was among the thirteen colonies themselves. Fish and

3. USING A MAP After your students have read the lesson and carefully studied the map of trade routes on page 49, have them sketch in those routes on outline maps of the world. At the completion of the map work, briefly discuss the different triangular routes that can be traced out on their maps.

4. LISTENING FOR INFORMATION You may wish to read to the class, or play a tape that you have prerecorded, sharing the section "A Paradise for Women" in Carl N. Degler's *Out of Our Past: The Forces That Shaped America* (New York: Harper & Row, 1970).

meat from New England and wheat, flour, and iron goods from the middle colonies were shipped to the plantations of the South. Payment was made either in cash or in crops—tobacco or rice—that were then sold in other markets, either in the North or in Europe.

Colonial merchants carried on an active trade with the West Indies and southern Europe. West Indian planters exchanged sugar, molasses, and gold and silver coins for the fish, meat, and grains they needed to feed their slaves. The coins were especially welcome because the American colonies were always short of currency. Fish were also in great demand in the Catholic countries of southern Europe, where Catholics were forbidden to eat meat on Fridays and various holy days. Northern merchants also shipped grain, meat, and lumber to these countries. In payment, they received wine, and fruits, and sometimes silver and gold coins.

England was one of America's main markets. Although England did not need the products of northern farms and fisheries, northern merchants had an active trade carrying the South's rice and tobacco to England. They also carried to that country sugar and molasses they had received in the West Indies. These goods were exchanged for such manufactured goods as cloth, furniture, and finished iron products.

You may have noticed that some of the trade of the colonists was triangular, or three-cornered. That is, it involved northern ports, southern ports, and the West Indies; or northern ports, the West Indies, and England. There was another triangular trade in which a few colonial merchants were involved. That was the slave trade. A ship captain might carry rum from his home port of Bristol or Newport, Rhode Island, to the Guinea Coast of Africa. There he exchanged the rum for slaves, at the rate of about 100 gallons (380 liters) for a young male. With his human cargo, the captain set sail for the West Indies, where he sold the slaves for money and molasses. From there it was home to Rhode Island. In dozens of small distilleries the molasses was made into rum, which would be taken by other ships to Africa, and so on.

Jobs for all. The shipping and shipbuilding industries provided numerous jobs. In 1760, between 300 and 400 ships were built in New England towns. That meant a demand for shipbuilders and carpenters, ropemakers and sailmakers, captains and sailors. It also meant work for unskilled dockworkers who loaded and unloaded ships.

As city populations grew, so did the demand for skilled workers of all kinds. Many left crowded English cities for American towns, where their skills as shoemakers, bakers, and printers brought higher wages. Occasionally a town even offered skilled workers land, a house, and a guaranteed amount of work if they would settle there. Wages paid to skilled and unskilled workers in America were two to three times higher than those paid in England. Once again, the two lines of the poem on page 39 give you the reason.

Other colonists made a living from what a generous Nature gave. The sea provided a living for New England fishermen. Forests yielded lumber and such forest products as pitch, tar and turpentine, used by shipbuilders in

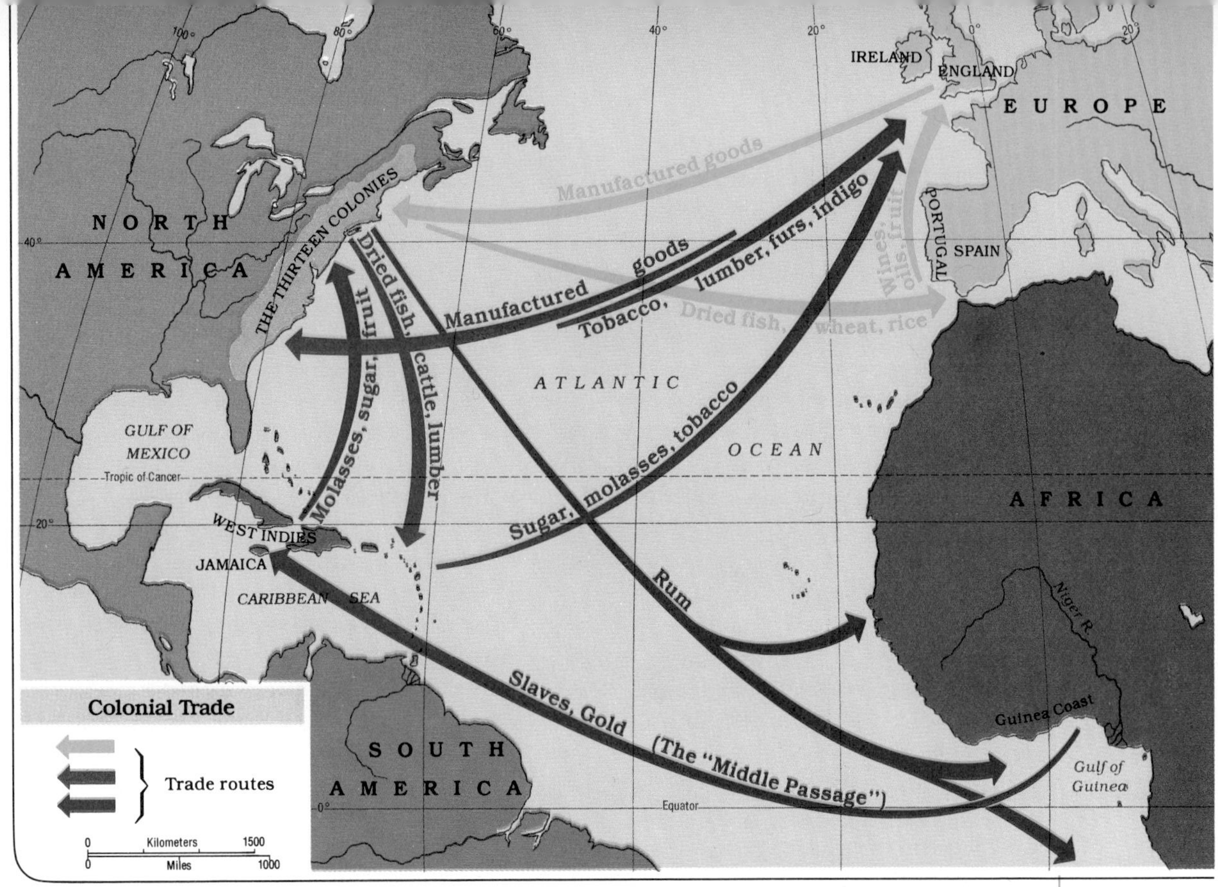

Foreign trade during America's colonial period consisted largely of the export of raw materials and the import of manufactured goods. Much of this trade was carried on with England. However, in order to make the best use of their sailing ships, owners worked out a pattern of triangular trade routes. How many examples of triangular routes can you trace out on the map above?

England and America. And in the backcountry of all the colonies, fur trapping and trading with Indians became an important business.

Finally, small manufacturing industries developed in several colonies. The making of rum from molasses was centered in a number of New England port cities, especially in Rhode Island. In several of the middle colonies, iron and iron products, such as kettles, nails, and stoves, were manufactured in dozens of small foundries.

A shortage of women. One of the important facts of life in America was the shortage of women in many of the colonies. When a shipload of 90 young women seeking mates arrived in Jamestown in 1619, it was a major event. As late as the mid-1600s, men outnumbered women in Virginia by six to one. Of the 10,000 indentured servants who left for America from one English port between about 1650 and 1680, males outnumbered females by more than three to one. Single women were generally reluctant to leave England for the American wilderness. Even in New England, where typically whole families migrated from England, males were in a three to two majority.

Promoters made special efforts, therefore, to attract women to the colonies. The tasks they performed were essential to the survival of the new settlements. The proprietors of Carolina included the following paragraph in their advertising pamphlet.

> If any maids or single women desire to go over to Carolina, they will think themselves in the Golden Age, when men paid dowries for their wives, for if they are only civil and under fifty years of age, some honest man or other will purchase them for their wives.

Women in colonial America not only were skilled in making clothing and in doing other kinds of work in their homes but also performed ably in other jobs vital to the colonial economy.

The writer's aim was to attract women to America. Without realizing it, he is also telling us a great deal about the position of women in England in the seventeenth century. See how much you can learn about women's status there from that paragraph.

Women's rights. Gradually the ratio of women to men improved. By the time of the Revolution, women made up nearly half the population. Partly because of the shortage of women in the colonies, their position was better than in England. Not that they had equal rights with men. Women could not vote. A wife had few legal rights over her children. The law gave husbands almost absolute power over their wives. And once women married, any property they owned passed to their husbands. For example, a wealthy Virginian named Daniel Custis died, leaving a large fortune to his widow Martha, and another large sum to their daughter "Patsy." When Martha married a young man named George Washington some years later, control of Martha's fortune passed to him. He also gained custody of the money left to Martha's daughter when the latter died shortly after Martha married George. Thus George Washington, already comfortable, was on his way to becoming one of the wealthiest men in America.

Still, women's property rights were better protected in America than in England. It became the custom that a husband could not sell or give away his wife's property without her consent. Single women and widows could own property of all kinds, could sue or be sued in colonial courts, and could run their own businesses.

Husbands had a higher status, but wives were by no means considered to be servants. One husband, who told his wife that "she was none of his wife, she was but his servant," was reported by his neighbors and fined forty shillings. Such an event was not an everyday occurrence, and by today's standards it seems a minor advance for women. At the time, however, it was an important step forward.

Women and the economy. A number of women owned and ran their own farms and business. Newspaper ads of the time show that there were women silversmiths, blacksmiths, gunsmiths, shoemakers, shipbuilders, printers, eyeglass makers and even undertakers. Many women sold goods that they sewed, ran taverns, and owned shops in which everything from hardware to foods and wines were sold. Many were widows who took over their husband's businesses or women who never married. A great many other women whose identities are lost to history worked in such trades alongside their husbands. Several large planters in the South were women, and women often helped manage their fathers' and husbands' plantations.

In colonial America almost all women married, and at an early age. Large families were the rule, for children were considered to be an advantage, helping with farm work. Thus the population

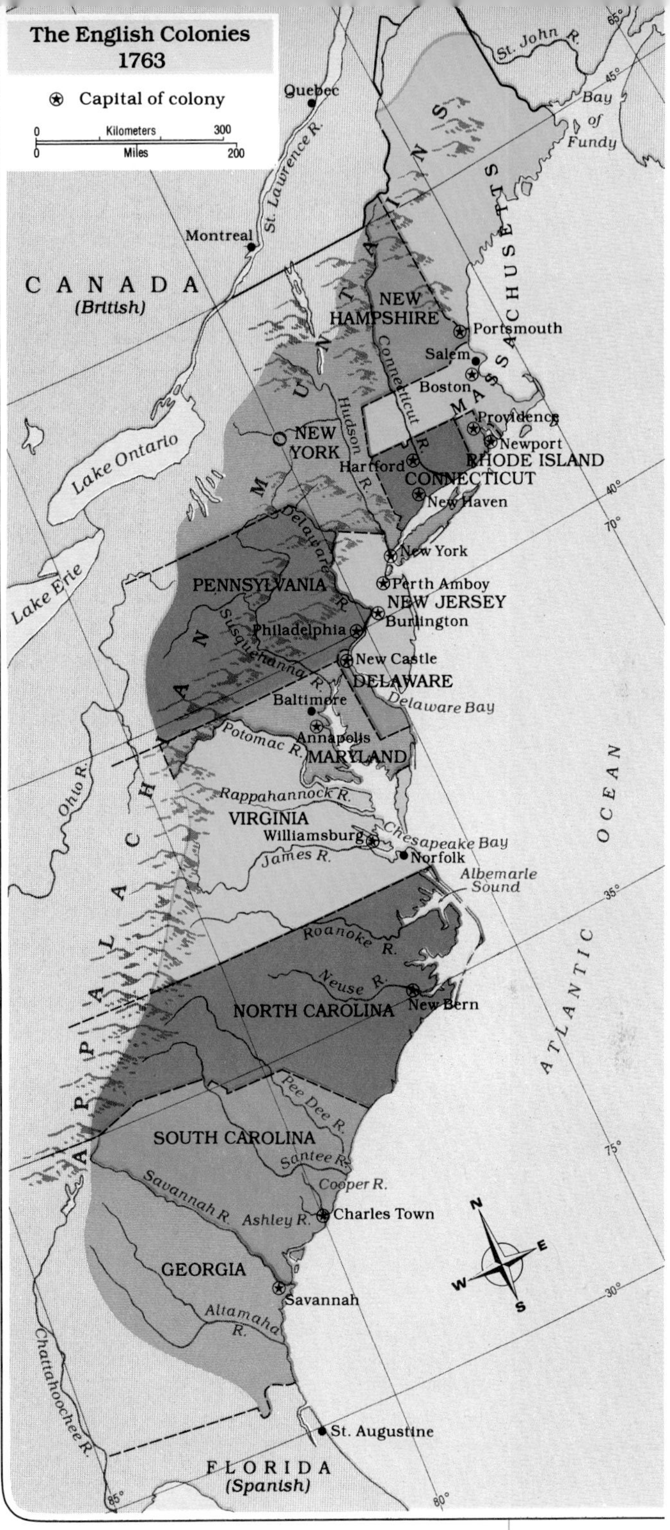

By the mid-1700s, about 1,300,000 people lived in the thirteen English colonies. To the south was Spanish Florida, and to the north lay Canada, under French control until 1763. Note that several of the colonies had more than one capital.

5. RESEARCH/ORAL REPORTS In the colonial period, women made great contributions as community builders and as apprentices in trades and professions. They often worked side by side with men in that society, in which every skilled hand was needed for survival, regardless of whether it was male or female. Some say that women were never so free as they were in colonial times.

Ask some of your students to read about Anne Hutchinson, Elizabeth Poole, and Anne Bradstreet and then to report their findings to the class. Ask others to find out more about the role of women in the colonies. There is an excellent article about the courage and durability of colonial women—though about the Revolutionary period—entitled "Patriots in Petticoats" in the October 1975 issue of *National Geographic*.

Perhaps some of your talented students would like to present their research findings in the form of a painting or drawing, poetry, music, or other appropriate creative expression.

doubled every generation. However, childbearing took its toll, and many women died young.

By far most women were members of farm families. The farm family was an economic unit, with defined jobs for each member. For women, these included the usual household tasks of cooking, spinning, weaving cloth, and a number of farming chores as well. Most women, however—always excepting slaves—did not work in the fields except at harvest time. These tasks were absolutely essential for the survival and well-being of the colonial family. Colonial males understood that, but few acknowledged it in the way one gentleman did in his diary of 1778.

> My wife's conduct verifies that old saying that "women's work is never done." [Among the tasks she performs are] getting prepared in the kitchen, baking our bread and pies, meat, etc. . . . cutting and drying apples . . . making of cider without tools . . . seeing all our washing done, and her fine clothes and my shirts, which are all smoothed by her . . . her making of twenty large cheeses, and that from one cow, and daily using milk and cream, besides her sewing, knitting, etc.

The closer to the frontier, the more blurred was the line between male and female roles. Women there had to know how to handle a plow and a rifle as well as a spinning wheel.

By no stretch of the imagination, however, can it be said that American conditions changed traditional male-female roles or greatly changed male-dominated institutions in the colonial era. This song of the American frontier suggests a woman's view of how much, or little, change had taken place:

> The heart is the fortune of all womankind,
> They're always controlled, they're always confined.
> Controlled by their families until they are wives,
> Then slaves to their husbands the rest of their lives.

The best "poor man's country." Despite America's abundance, colonial society had its poor in both countryside and city. Among them were farmers who had been unlucky enough to have bought poor land. And while some farm workers earned as much as the one the farmer complained about on page 47, others had to scrape for a living.

The poor were more noticeable in cities and towns than on farms. When trade and business declined, many of the unskilled went without work. Others fared poorly also. The fact that colonial cities and towns raised taxes for "poor relief" and built almshouses—homes for the poor—tells us that the penniless existed.

In the late 1750s, Boston, a city of 16,000, reported that "the poor supported either wholly or in part by the town . . . will amount to the number of about 1,000." In 1775 the city of Philadelphia was providing poor relief to 700 of its 35,000 people. These numbers do not include others who received help from churches or private groups. In at least one city there was an official whose job it was to discourage the poor from settling there.

Once again, however, our standard of comparison must be the England of that day. One third of England's population lived in poverty. Its cities were filled with beggars, who roamed the streets and found shelter in cellars and back alleys.

Continued on page 54

The Zenger Case

The case of John Peter Zenger, a printer, is a landmark in the struggle for freedom of the press. Born in Germany, Zenger came to America as a youth and was apprenticed at the age of fourteen to a printer. After learning the printing trade, he set up his own shop. In time he became the publisher of a newspaper, *The New-York Weekly Journal.*

In 1735 Zenger was brought to trial, charged with printing newspaper articles criticizing William Cosby, the royal governor of New York. Zenger was accused of criminal libel. (Libel is the publishing of material that damages someone's reputation.) Under English law, all that had to be proved to establish guilt was that Zenger's newspaper had printed the material damaging to Governor Cosby.

In the trial, Andrew Hamilton, Zenger's lawyer, frankly admitted that Zenger had printed the material that damaged the governor's reputation. But then Hamilton introduced a new idea. He declared that the statements printed in Zenger's newspaper were true. Because they were true, said Hamilton, and because men should be free "to complain when they are hurt," this was *not* a crime. The jury agreed with Hamilton's argument and found Zenger not guilty.

The verdict did not change the law. However, it did encourage newspaper writers to criticize those in authority—when the criticism was true. The Zenger case gave a great boost to the idea of freedom of the press.

This hand press was used in the shop where Benjamin Franklin learned the printing trade.

Answers To Review Questions

1. Many people sincerely believed in religious freedom. The promise of religious freedom increased the chances of attracting needed workers.
2. English people were used to the idea that laws should be made by an elected legislature. Furthermore, Parliament in London could not understand the problems of a wilderness settlement 3,000 miles away.
3. Members were usually appointed by the governor with the king's approval. In most colonies, the council was made up of the wealthiest and most important people.
4. Voters had to be white, male, twenty-one or over, and had to own a certain amount of property. Blacks, Indians, and most women were excluded from voting. A very large number of white male colonists did have the right to vote because land was so cheap that most could meet the property requirements.
5. Conflict developed because the assembly spoke for the interests of the colonists, while the governor and council represented the interests of the king and Parliament. The chief weapon possessed by the assembly was control over the spending of tax money. In many colonies, the assembly also paid the governor's salary.
6. Squatters simply moved out to the edge of settlement, or the frontier, cleared a piece of land, and farmed it without buying or getting a legal claim to it.

Nowhere in white colonial America did such conditions exist.

Touring England and Scotland in 1772, Benjamin Franklin noted the great wealth of a few and the poverty of the many.

> . . . the bulk of the people [are] tenants, extremely poor, living in the most sordid wretchedness, in dirty hovels of mud and straw, and clothed only in rags.

Franklin went on to compare that scene to America.

> I thought often of the happiness of New England where every man . . . had a vote in public affairs, lives in a tidy warm house, has plenty of good food and fuel, with whole clothes from head to feet, [made perhaps by] his own family.

Joseph Trumbull of Connecticut made a similar observation while traveling in England in 1764.

> We in New England knew nothing of poverty and want, we have no idea of the thing, how much better do our poor people live than seven eighths of the people of this much-famed island.

Indeed, the standard of living for ordinary people in the American colonies was probably higher than in any other country in the world. Because of the opportunities for so many, America came to be known throughout Europe as "the best poor man's country."

Although America opened up great opportunities, they were not unlimited. And they were not equally open to all. Indeed, opportunities for many often came at the expense of others who did not share them. This helped to create inequalities within America. In the next chapter, you will read about both the limits of opportunity and the growth of inequalities.

CHECKUP

1. How did most people in colonial America make a living? How was geographical mobility connected to opportunity?
2. In what ways did farming differ in the North and in the South?
3. Describe the trade patterns that developed in colonial America.
4. How was the status of women different from that of men in colonial times?

Key Facts from Chapter 3

1. There was increasing religious freedom in colonial America, and despite some serious restrictions, religious toleration was greater than in most European countries.
2. By 1700 each of the English colonies had its own legislature, usually composed of an upper house whose members were appointed by the governor and a lower house whose members were elected by the colonists.
3. The right to vote in colonial America was held, with few exceptions, by adult white males who owned property.
4. Though women played an important role in the development of the colonies, they were subject to many restrictions as compared to men.

★ REVIEWING THE CHAPTER ★

People, Places, and Events

The Great Awakening *P. 41*
Council *P. 41*
Assembly *P. 41*
Proprietary colony *P. 42*
Royal colony *P. 42*
Corporate colony *P. 42*
Geographic mobility *P. 45*
John Peter Zenger *P. 53*

Review Questions

1. Why did religious toleration gradually increase in America? *P. 39* Les. 1
2. Why did legislatures develop in the English colonies? *P. 41* Les. 1
3. How were members of the governor's council selected? *P. 41* Les. 1
4. What were the qualifications for voting in the colonies? Could many people satisfy those requirements? Explain your answer. *P. 43* Les. 1
5. Why did conflict develop between the colonial assembly and the governor? What power did the assembly use as a weapon in a conflict? *P. 44* Les. 1
6. How were squatters different from other landowners? *P. 44* Les. 2
7. How did farming differ from one part of the country to another? *Pp. 45–47* Les. 2
8. With whom did the colonial merchants trade? What goods and products were traded? *Pp. 47–48* Les. 2
9. Look at the map on page 49. Molasses and sugar were one side of a triangular trade route. Starting with the exportation of those products, trace the triangular trade. Les. 2
10. Describe the role women played in the colonial economy. *Pp. 51–52* Les. 2

Chapter Test

*On a separate piece of paper, write **T** if the statement is true and **F** if the statement is false.*

1. All people, regardless of their faith, were guaranteed religious freedom in colonial America. F
2. Most colonial governors, councils, and assemblies were elected by the colonists in the same manner in which we elect the President and members of Congress today. F
3. The power to control taxation gave the colonial assembly a strong hold over the governor. T
4. All male colonists over the age of 21 could vote. F
5. Squatters had no legal claim to their land. T
6. Southern farmers grew pay crops of rice, tobacco, and indigo. T
7. The middle colonies were called the bread colonies because they learned to make corn bread from the Indians. F
8. Free labor in the colonies was supplemented with indentured servants and slaves. T
9. Merchants carried on an active trade with southern Europe, England, the West Indies, and Africa. T
10. Women were an important part of the colonial economy, but they did not have equal rights with men. T
11. The chief difference in the three types of colonial government—proprietary, royal, and corporate—lay in the method of selecting a governor. T
12. The case of John Peter Zenger is considered a landmark in the struggle for freedom of religion. F

7. The South was a region mainly of large plantations and small farms. Plantations specialized in raising pay crops and depended on white indentured servants and, later, slaves for labor.

In New England and the middle colonies the lands were usually owned and worked by small farmers. New England's farmers raised corn as the main crop. Their soil was rocky and the growing season short. The middle colonies enjoyed soil and climate ideal for farming. Farmers raised wheat and corn on large farms that were worked with the help of many indentured servants.

8. Merchants did much trading among the thirteen colonies. Products and goods traded included fish and meat from New England, flour and iron goods from the middle colonies, and rice and tobacco from the South. Merchants also traded with the West Indies, southern Europe, England, and Africa.

9. Sugar was grown in the West Indies, where it was converted into molasses. The molasses, in turn, was taken to New England, where it was used to produce rum. Then the rum was transported to Africa and traded for slaves. To complete the cycle, slaves were sold for work on the West Indian plantations.

10. In addition to running the colonial household and working on the farm, women owned and operated a variety of businesses and shops.

Background Information

1. PICTURE This painting, entitled "Trustees of Georgia," was done by William Verelst in 1734 or 1735. It shows James Oglethorpe and the Indians whom he took home to London for a visit in 1734 with the trustees of Georgia. Oglethorpe had returned to England to revive the trustees' interest in the colony. The welcome by the press and the stir created by his Indian companions helped the Georgia governor to accomplish his purpose. "Trustees of Georgia" is at the Henry Francis duPont Winterthur Museum in Winterthur, Delaware.

THE LIMITS OF OPPORTUNITY

LESSON 1

TO EUROPEANS the discovery of the New World meant opportunity. To the native peoples who had lived there for thousands of years it meant catastrophe. The coming of the Europeans brought death to millions of Indians and destroyed entire tribes.

The first recorded contact between Europeans and the native peoples of the Americas came when Columbus's men set foot in the New World in 1492. In his first report Columbus described the people he met as gentle and loving. But he also made this ominous observation:

> These people are very unskilled in arms . . . with fifty men they could all be subjected and made to do all that one wished.

Columbus, of course, was describing only one Indian tribe. There were many others, some of them not so gentle and peaceful. But belligerent and peaceful alike, the Indians fell victim to European invaders over the next 400 years.

You have already read of the Spanish conquest of the native peoples of Central and South America. Forced by the Spaniards to work in the gold and silver mines under terrible conditions, the Indians died by the thousands. The Spaniards also used Indian slaves on sugar and tobacco plantations and on ranches. What the Spaniards did in most of Central and South America, the Portuguese did in Brazil.

The tragic results of the Indian encounter with Europeans in the sixteenth and seventeenth centuries in South and Central America can be put this way: Thousands fell to European guns. Hundreds of thousands died from overwork and mistreatment. Millions—perhaps many millions—died from such European diseases as smallpox, measles, and diphtheria, to which they had never before been exposed.

Indians and Colonists

The story of the encounter between the original native peoples of North America and the English and other European settlers does not read much better. There were some 600 different groups native to North America, speaking as many as 2,000 languages and dialects. Some were farming people, some fishing people, and some hunters. Among many of them there was fierce rivalry leading to frequent warfare. In fact, one of the reasons why Europeans were eventually able to conquer the continent was that the separate Indian tribes failed to unite against white settlers.

Estimates of the number of Indians in North America in 1492 range from 1 million to 10 million. The largest number lived in the western part of present-day United States. Far fewer lived in the Southeast. Fewer still were in the Northeast, where the English first settled.

Changing feelings. The pattern of English-Indian relations was pretty much the same wherever the two peoples met. Often the Indians were friendly at first and helped the Europeans adjust to the strange, new environment, teaching them to grow corn and other crops.

LESSON 1 *(2 days)*

Performance Objectives

1. To explain, either in writing or orally, the changes in the relationship between the Indians and the colonists in Virginia and New England. **2.** To name at least three reasons given by the English to justify taking land from the Indians, using source material in this lesson.

Famous People

Pocahantas, Powhatan, King Philip

Vocabulary

Smallpox, measles, diphtheria, Pequot War, King Philip's War

Activities

1. FILMS *The First Americans, Part I* (20 minutes, color) and *Part II* (32 minutes, color; both NBC) are available from the Audio-Visual Center of Indiana University.

Also recommended are the four sound filmstrips (79–88 frames), entitled *The Roots of the American Character,* that make up Set 1 of *The Social History of the United States.* These are available from Social Studies School Service, 10000 Culver Blvd., P.O. Box 802, Culver City, Calif. 90230. This service firm offers a variety of AV materials in all areas of social studies. It may be well worth writing for their catalog.

The map above shows the names and home regions of only a few of the hundreds of native-American tribes that lived, at the time of European exploration, in what is now the United States. Population estimates vary greatly, ranging from about 850,000 to several times that number.

This first period of good feelings soon gave way to mistrust and hostility. English greed was often the cause. Not satisfied with the lands the Indians offered or sold them, white settlers took more by force. Indian resistance and bloody warfare followed.

Warfare in Virginia. In Jamestown, the English foolishly angered the Indians, thus adding to the danger and misery of the first years of settlement. Peaceful relations were restored after an Indian princess, Pocahontas, saved the life of Captain John Smith, who had been captured in 1607. Her father, who was called Powhatan from the name of his tribe, became even more friendly with the English when his daughter married a Virginia planter, John Rolfe.

The period of peace ended after Powhatan's death in 1618. The Indians had come to realize that more English settlements would push them out of their lands. In 1622 the Powhatans launched an attack to drive the English from the area. The warfare was fierce. Despite the loss of a third of the settlers, the Jamestown settlement survived. The white settlers quickly struck back. "Now we have just cause to destroy them by all means possible," said one white leader. From that time on, warfare between Indians and whites in Virginia was continuous. Of the estimated 30,000 Indians who had lived in the area when the English first arrived, there were but 2,000 some 60 years later.

Warfare in New England. Indian resistance in New England flared up from time to time in the 1600s. Most Puritans thought the Indians were agents of the devil. The settlers angered the Indians not only by taking their land but by trying to force them to accept English ways and Puritan beliefs. Indians were punished if they hunted and fished on Sundays, and they were put to death if they used God's name in vain.

The Pequot War was the same kind of turning point in Indian-white relations in Massachusetts as the war in 1622 had been in Virginia. In 1637, without warning whites attacked a Pequot Indian village near the Mystic River in Connecticut. They set fire to the village, burning 600 men, women, and children alive.

Indian resentment erupted in 1675 in King Philip's War. By that time there were 90 white settlements in New England. Under the lead of King Philip, chief of the Wampanoags, a number of tribes were secretly united. The Indians then attacked more than half of the settlements, destroying twelve and killing hundreds of whites. One tenth of the grown white males in Massachusetts were either killed or captured.

The colonists responded with a vengeance. They destroyed Indian villages, beheaded chiefs (including King Philip), and sold hundreds of Indians as slaves to the West Indies. With the death of King Philip, Indian resistance in New England was crushed.

In every colony at one time or another, white settlers attempted to make Indian captives slaves. It rarely worked. For one thing, Indians did not do well in captivity, often falling victim to European diseases. For another, escape was easy, as the Indians could melt into the familiar forests and find their way back to their people.

Taking the Indians' land. How did Europeans, many of whom were religious people, justify the taking of Indian land?

This portrait of Pocahontas, a Powhatan princess, was painted in England where she went with her husband, John Rolfe, a Virginia planter. A year later, Pocahontas died of smallpox.

2. RESEARCH/ORAL REPORT King Philip was a son of Massasoit, the Wampanoag chief who had befriended the Pilgrims. Though Philip had been baptized and had been educated in colonial schools, as chief he saw no alternative for his people but to drive the English out of the land. (He called the English "Yinglees," hence the term *Yankee.*) Other tribes involved were the Narragansets and the Mohicans.

Have some of your students research these tribes and present their findings to the class. What were the tribes like? How did they dress? What were their customs? Are there any descendants of those people today? Where do they live?

3. LISTENING FOR INFORMATION After the students have read the lesson, present to them "King Philip's War," pages 107–111, in *The Oxford History of the American People* by Samuel Eliot Morison (New York: Oxford University, 1965). This gives a somewhat different account of the problem than is found in this text. Ask students to compare the two accounts.

Another interesting reading is Chapter IV, "The Wigwam People," in *A Pictorial History of the American Indian* by Oliver La Farge (New York: Crown Publishers, 1956). You may wish to have several students present the readings to the class.

4. WHAT IF? Discuss this possibility with your students: What if the conscience of the colonists had been such that they decided the land truly belonged to the Indians and they returned to England. What do you think America would be like today? On what do you base your opinion?

5. DEBATE Resolved, That the European colonists were justified in taking the Indians' land.

Have the students base their arguments on information given in the lesson text, but encourage them to engage in additional research if they so desire.

Solomon Stoddard, a Massachusetts minister, dealt with this question in a pamphlet he wrote in 1722.

> *Question VII.* Did we do any wrong to the Indians in buying their land at a small price?
> *Answer 1.* There was some part of the land that was not purchased, neither was there need that it should; it was vacant . . . and so might be possessed by virtue of God's grant to mankind. . . . The Indians made no use of it but for hunting. . . .
> *Answer 2.* The Indians were well contented that we should sit down by them. . . .
> *Answer 3.* Though we gave them but a small price for what we bought, we gave them . . . their price. And, indeed, it was worth but little; and had it continued in their hands, it would have been of little value. It is our dwelling on it, our improvements, that have made it to be of worth.

How does Stoddard justify the taking of some of the land without paying anything for it? How does he justify paying so little for the land that the English settlers did buy from the region's native Americans?

Less than human? Beneath such justifications was an attitude that many white settlers held about Indians. It was expressed by Henry Brackenridge of Pittsburgh, who went on a military expedition against the Indians in 1782.

Natives of the eastern woodlands go about their daily activities. The woman in the foreground is grinding corn in the top of a hollowed log. What else does the picture tell about these people?

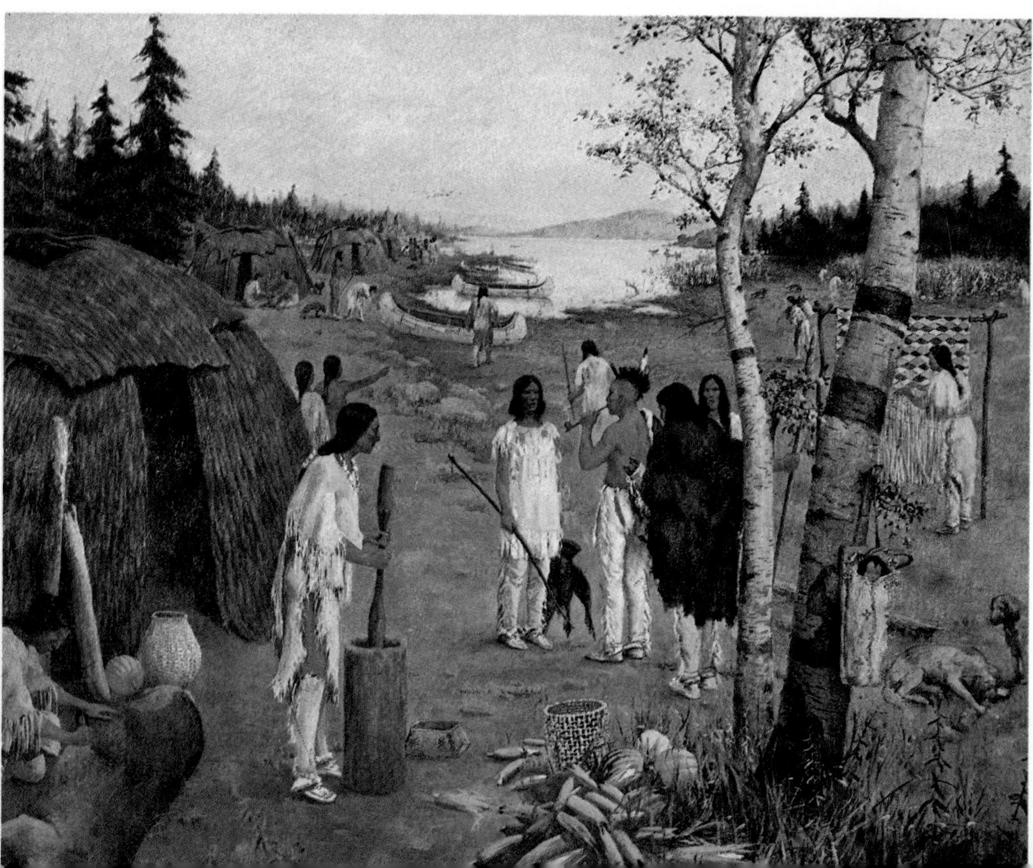

> [I offer] some observations with regard to the animals called Indians. . . What use do these ring-streaked, spotted and speckled cattle make of the soil? Do they till it? Revelations [a part of the Bible] said to man "thou shalt till the ground." This alone is human life. It is favorable to population, to science, to the information of a human mind in the worship of God . . . before you can make an Indian a Christian you must teach him agriculture and reduce him to a civilized life. To live by tilling is more [human], by hunting more [beastlike].

Can you see how making the Indians appear to be less than human would help Europeans justify to themselves taking over the Indians' land? Of what importance was the fact that the Indians were not Christians?

A circle of prejudice. Of course, the Indians bitterly resented the English view that they were less than human. They responded with hostility. Their hostility was proof to the whites that Indians were "savage" and should be treated as less than human. The circle of prejudice was complete. Using justifications like these, Europeans took more and more land, pushing the Indians steadily westward. From time to time, organized warfare would flare up. More usually there were simply isolated killings on both sides in the silence of the forest. Hate was answered with hate, and blood with blood.

Not all colonists believed it should be this way. Benjamin Franklin noted the source of the white prejudice against the Indians: "Savages we call them, [simply] because their manners differ from ours." Franklin also pointed out the illogic of warring on and mistreating all Indians just because of the actions of some.

> If an Indian injures me, does it follow that I may revenge that injury on all Indians? . . . if the French, who are white people, would injure the Dutch, are [the Dutch] to revenge it on the English because they are white people? The only crime [of the Indians] seems [to be] that they had a reddish-brown skin and black hair; and some people of that sort, it seems, had murdered some of our relations. If . . . any man, with a freckled face and red hair [should kill my wife], would it be right for me to revenge it by killing all the freckled red-haired men, women, and children . . . I met with?

Franklin's question answered itself, but few Americans were interested in either the question or the answer.

CHECKUP

1. How did the pattern of English-Indian relations change during the earliest years of colonization?
2. Where and why was King Philip's War fought? What was the outcome?
3. What views were put forth by those English who justified taking land from the Indians?

LESSON 2

Blacks and Whites

For millions of black Africans, as for the Indians, the opening up of the New World meant not opportunity but disaster. Torn from their villages and packed onto ships like so many cattle, they—and their descendants—became slaves in distant lands.

Slavery in early times. Slavery had existed for centuries in the western world. The ancient Greeks and Romans

LESSON 2 *(1 to 2 days)*

Performance Objectives

1. To describe in writing the horrors of the African slave trade. **2.** To explain orally how the concept of automatic inferiority was used to support the existence of slavery.

Vocabulary

Slave trade, middle passage, prejudice, Negroes, slave codes, free blacks, automatic inferiority

Activities

1. THOUGHT PROVOKER In an address to an Indian army regiment on March 17, 1865—less than a month before his death—Abraham Lincoln said, "I have always thought that all men should be free; but if any should be slaves, it should be first those who desire it for themselves, and secondly, those who desire it for others. Whenever I hear any one arguing for slavery, I feel a strong impulse to see it tried on him personally."

Ask your students to discuss what type of person would want to be a slave. In a modern age, how can people guarantee themselves a form of slavery?

An African raiding party marches its captives to the coast, where they are to be sold into slavery. The slaves will then be transported across the Atlantic to become laborers in New World lands.

enslaved the peoples they conquered. Moslems and Christians in the Middle Ages did the same. But that type of slavery differed from the African slavery of modern times in two important ways. First, it was not based chiefly upon race. And second, the children of slaves did not always automatically become slaves themselves.

A slave trade existed in Africa from early times, too. For centuries Africans had captured other Africans and sold them into a slavery, first to the Roman Empire in Europe and later to the Arabs and Moors in the Middle East. By the 1300s, however, this trade was quite small. Even when the Portuguese began to take Africans to Spain and Portugal in the mid-1400s, the slave trade remained small.

The changing slave trade. The European discovery of the New World changed the African slave trade dramatically. As their Indian slaves in the mines and plantations died off in the 1500s, Spanish and Portuguese colonists turned to Africa for laborers.

The Portuguese continued to be the main slave traders, but before long all the great trading nations of Europe—Holland, France, Sweden, and England—entered this profitable business. England, a latecomer, entered the trade in a big way in the last half of the seventeenth century. By the 1790s English ship captains dominated the business.

There is no exact record of how many Africans were brought to the Americas. The best estimate seems to be between 9 and 10 million. Of this number, 60 percent went to the Spanish and Portuguese colonies in South and Central America, and another 35 percent worked on the plantations of the West Indies islands. About 5 percent, or 500,000, went to the area that later became the United States.

It is hard for us today even to imagine the cruelty of the slave trade. It began with the capture of Africans by other Africans, as prisoners of war. As the demand for slaves increased, African tribes along the coast, working with the slave traders, sent bands into the interior to kidnap people. The captors chained their prisoners one to another and marched them single file to the slave-trading ports. There, ship captains and slave-trading companies purchased them, giving in payment iron bars, copper pans, cotton cloth, rum, guns, gunpowder, and the like. The captives were branded with a red-hot iron carrying the mark of their buyer.

The middle passage. The slaves were then herded onto ships for the voyage across the Atlantic. The trip from Africa to the West Indies was called the *middle passage*. It was the middle part of a triangular route that a slave ship usually followed. (See the map on page 49.)

The picture on this page explains better than words how tightly slaves were packed aboard these ships. Ships like this usually had several decks. Slaves were kept below decks for fear of mutiny,

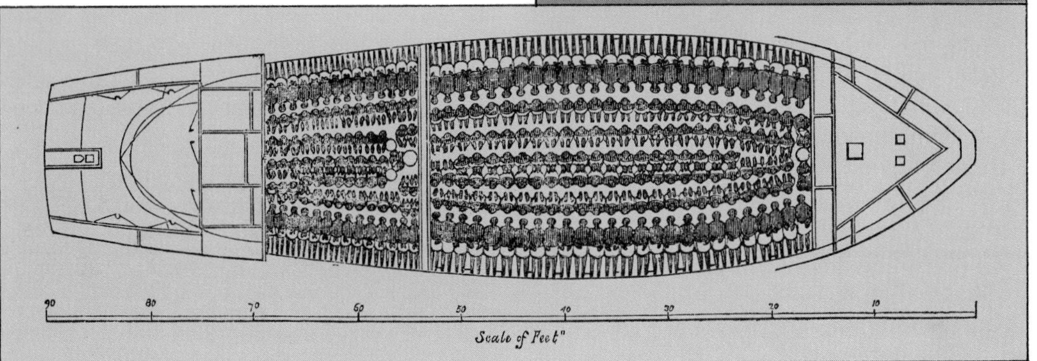

These diagrams of a slave ship show how the maximum number of Africans were loaded for the passage to the Americas. The slaves were usually chained, hands and feet, and permitted only enough exercise to provide for their survival. Even so, many of them died en route to the New World, the victims of disease.

2. CREATIVE WRITING After the students have read the lesson, ask them to describe the horrors of the African slave trade by writing editorials that might have appeared in an abolitionist newspaper. Before the students begin this activity, be sure they understand the personal and persuasive nature of an editorial. Most editorials are intended to influence opinion, although sometimes they are written to inform or merely entertain. Perhaps you would want to bring in examples of good editorial writing and discuss with students those qualities that each editorial possesses.

Depending upon your individual school situation, you may want to do this activity in conjunction with the English teacher.

3. LISTENING FOR INFORMATION To provide your students with insight into early conditions facing blacks, read to them the section "Black Men in a White Men's Country" in *Out of Our Past: The Forces that Shaped Modern America* by Carl N. Degler (New York: Harper & Row, 1970).

4. DISCUSSION Some historians have said that prejudice emanated from slavery. Others say that slavery emanated from prejudice. In this lesson, your students will read that free blacks, "even though free, . . . were subject to the same racial prejudice as slaves, which held that *black* automatically meant 'inferior.' " In *Democracy in America,* Alexis de Tocqueville said that "among the moderns the abstract and transient fact of slavery is fatally united with the physical and permanent fact of color. Slavery recedes but the prejudice to which it has given birth is immovable."

Ask your students to discuss the question of racial prejudice in America. What were and are its causes? Ask them to think about any negative attitudes they may have. Are these attitudes dislikes, or are they prejudices?

and were allowed on deck only for feeding and exercise. One officer of a slave ship has left us this description of their treatment:

> Some commanders . . . are [forever] beating and curbing them, even without the least offense . . . which [makes] those poor wretches desperate, and besides their falling into [sickness] through melancholy often is the occasion of destroying themselves.

We will never know how many slaves died in the middle passage. Estimates are that anywhere from 15 percent to 25 percent failed to make it to America alive. If that is correct, and if 9 to 10 million did reach the New World, then somewhere between 1.5 million and 3 million Africans died aboard these slave ships. That fact alone is powerful evidence of the horrors of the slave trade.

The meaning of *black*. The tragic relationship between African blacks and English whites in British North America may have been set even before they met. For centuries the word *black* carried a negative meaning in the English and other European cultures. One writer has noted:

> Black was the color of death, . . . of the devil; it was the color of bad magic and melancholy, of poison, of mourning, forsaken love, and the lowest pit of hell. There were black arts and black humors, blackmail and blacklists, blackguard and black knights, the Black Death . . . and there were countless legends of men turning black from sin and of black races sprung from hell.

One could add to the list from other English expressions: a black day, a black mood, a black sheep in the family, a black mark against one's name. Always, black meant "foul, wicked, sinful." *White,* on the other hand, stood for purity and good. Angels were clothed in white. Brides wore white. The dove of peace was white.

Thus when the English finally met black Africans, they already had a *prejudice* about them—that is, they had prejudged the Africans on the basis of their skin color. And the fact that the Africans were not Christian certainly reinforced the belief that they were sinful and connected with the devil.

White Europeans quickly noted other differences in appearance too, and placed a meaning on them.

> . . . the Europeans do not only differ from the . . . Africans in color . . . but also in their hair . . . in the shape of their noses, lips, and cheek bones, as also in the very outline of their faces and the mold of their skulls. They differ also in their natural manners, and in the internal qualities of their minds.

Different. Different in appearance, in religion, in customs, in language, in "the internal qualities of their minds." And different meant inferior.

It was not inevitable that the English would enslave such people. But when belief in the blacks' inferiority was combined with a severe shortage of labor, and with the example of the Spanish and Portuguese in Central and South America, slavery was not an illogical outcome.

Slavery in the English colonies. The first Africans to arrive in English North America landed in Jamestown in 1619. The Dutch ship that carried them had been bound for an island in the Caribbean Sea, but was blown off course. With workers in short supply, Jamestown settlers were glad to buy the services of these twenty black Africans, just as they bought the services of white indentured servants from England. The English called the Africans "Negroes," a term borrowed from the Portuguese and the Spanish word meaning "black."

More Africans came to Virginia and to Maryland during the next few decades, but they did not form a large part of the population. As late as 1650, only 300 of Virginia's 16,000 people were blacks.

Because of the sketchy records of that time, we know very little about these earliest Afro-Americans. It appears that at least some were treated as indentured servants and were freed after their terms of service. But it is also clear that even these blacks were treated differently than were white servants. For one thing, their terms of service were longer. For another, they were given more severe punishments. Also, black women were made to work in the fields—something that white women were not generally expected to do.

We know also that within twenty years of the first arrival of blacks in Jamestown, some were made slaves for life. A Maryland law of 1639 refers to "slaves." Records of the Virginia House of Burgesses indicate there were slaves in that colony in 1644. Virginia court records of the 1640s and 1650s also refer to slaves. But bits and pieces of evidence like these are all we have. We do not know who and how many blacks were slaves. And we know almost nothing about their lives.

It is clear, however, that by 1660 slavery was fairly widespread in Virginia and Maryland. In that decade, both colonies established slavery by law. In 1662 a Virginia law provided that

> . . . all children born in this country shall be held [slave] or free only according to the condition of the mother.

With those words, slavery became an inherited condition for all children born to a slave mother. Maryland passed a similar law a few years later. During the next half century, slavery was made legal in all the English colonies.

The first blacks arrive at Jamestown in 1619. The Dutch ship carrying them to the West Indies had been blown off course by a storm.

Indentured servants—or slaves? At first there was no great increase in the number of slaves in the North American colonies. Most landowners preferred indentured servants from England. They

5. **READING FOR INFORMATION/ORAL REPORT** Ask one or several of your students to read and to report to the class on "That Peculiar Institution," Chapter 13 in John Hope Franklin's *From Slavery to Freedom* (New York: Alfred A. Knopf, 1968).

You might assign a good reader to report on pages 52–80 in *Slavery: A Problem in American Institutional and Intellectual Life* (Chicago: University of Chicago Press, 1976). This selection compares slavery in the United States with that in Latin America. After the material is presented, encourage class discussion.

6. **FILMS** *Heritage of Slavery*, Black America series (56 minutes, 2 reels, color; BFA Educational Media). *The Black Rabbits and the White Rabbits* (8 minutes, color; Schloat House, Inc.). The latter film, an allegory, tells how two groups of rabbits enslave each other. Each group assumes that the other is inferior. Both films are available for rental from film depositories.

were of the same culture, spoke English, and were familiar with English ways of farming. Also, the initial cost of a slave was much higher. The price of an indentured servant's passage was only one fifth as much as the cost of an African slave. For the small planter without capital, that was a great difference.

In the latter part of the 1600s, the labor situation in the southern colonies changed sharply. With the formation in 1672 of the Royal African Company, a slave-trading company, British ships began to bring large numbers of slaves to the Americas. The price of slaves dropped. At just about the same time, white indentured servants began to be attracted to newer colonies—Pennsylvania, for example—where opportunities for their future seemed brighter.

The spread of slavery. Large tobacco planters now turned to black slaves for their work force. So did rice growers in South Carolina, who found it hard to get white men to do the backbreaking, unhealthy work in rice fields. The number of slaves increased rapidly. Maryland offers a good example of the change from white to black workers. In the 1670s, white indentured servants in that colony outnumbered black slaves by at least three to one. Thirty years later, black slaves outnumbered white indentured servants, 4,600 to 3,000.

By 1750, blacks made up 20 percent of the total population of England's North American colonies. By far most of the blacks were in the southern colonies, where they made up more than 40 percent of the population. Most slaves were located in the two main tobacco colonies, Virginia and Maryland.

The Number of Slaves in the Colonies 1650–1770

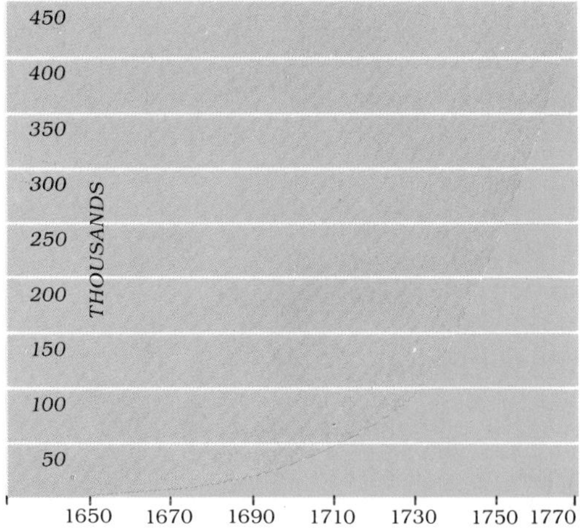

Slavery did not gain as great a hold in the colonies north of Maryland. The chief reason lay in the shorter growing season, which was not suited to plantation crops like tobacco and rice. Slaves in the North worked mainly as household servants, coach drivers, and porters. They were distributed unevenly. Slaves made up 14 percent of New York's population and about 10 percent of Pennsylvania's and New Jersey's. Rhode Island's population was also about 10 percent slave, but in the rest of New England, slaves made up only 2 percent of the population.

Slave codes. By the early 1700s almost all the American colonies had adopted special laws called slave codes. Under these laws slaves were treated differently from all others, including indentured servants. Servants had rights under their indentures—which were contracts—and they could use the courts to enforce those rights. And of course, once their service was ended they had the same rights as all other free persons.

Not so the slaves. Except in New England, slaves were not allowed to own property or to engage in any business. They could not testify in court, except in rare cases. Slaves were prohibited from gathering together in public places for fear they might plot a revolt. For the same reason, they were not allowed to have guns. In certain colonies they were forbidden to learn to read, lest they pick up dangerous ideas about freedom.

Many of the laws were aimed at keeping slaves from running away. Slaves were forbidden to leave their plantations without written permission. A South Carolina law required overseers to whip any slave on their plantations who did not have proper identification. Anyone —even a white person—who helped a slave to escape was subject to harsh punishments.

Slaves codes changed the status of blacks from human to a form of property. Slaves had almost no legal rights. Their marriages were not recognized in law, except in New England. Wives could be sold from their husbands, and children from their parents. Punishments set by law were severe, but that was only the half of it. The cruel treatment handed out by some owners was limited only by the master's imagination.

Nor could slaves look to the courts for protection. In Virginia and the Carolinas, if a master killed a slave while punishing him or her, the master was not subject to any penalties. Even for the outright murder of a slave by a master, there was usually only a light fine or other form of penalty.

The quarters for slaves were usually at a distance from, but within sight of, the plantation house. Cabins were small and poorly furnished and often lacked wooden floors.

LESSON 3 *(1 to 2 days)*

Performance Objectives

1. To compare the social structure of colonial America with that of seventeenth–century England. **2.** To compare the ways in which wealth was accumulated in the colonial South with the ways it was accumulated in the colonial North. **3.** To demonstrate an understanding of the concept of social mobility by comparing the social mobility of today with that of the colonial period.

Famous People

John Adams, Robert "King" Carter

Vocabulary

Equality, "proper station" in life, deference, political opportunity, periwig, standard of wealth, aristocracy, social mobility

Activities

1. FILMS *Tocqueville's America* (60 minutes, 2 reels, b & w; Indiana University Audio-Visual Center). This film, using many of the social concepts introduced in this lesson, lays a foundation for the eventual study of contemporary American social and political problems. Now is a good time to introduce the students to that foundation. *Equality and the Democratic Process* (29 minutes, b & w; Indiana University Audio-Visual Center).

Restraints on free blacks. With the status of slave passing from mother to child, the system was absolutely closed. A slave's only chance for freedom was to run away, or to be freed by a master. Both those things did happen, and there were indeed several thousand free blacks in the colonies, north and south. But for most of them life was little different than it was for slaves. They held low-paying jobs as house servants, dock workers, and sailors. If they wandered far from home, they could expect to have to prove they were not runaway slaves. At times, failure to prove this could result in their being made slaves again. They often could not join the colonial militia, could not vote, and often could not testify in court against whites. Even though free, they were subject to the same racial prejudice as slaves, which held that *black* meant "inferior."

To Americans of African descent—even free blacks—the call of opportunity that many Europeans heard from across the ocean was but a cry of despair.

CHECKUP

1. Describe the process by which slaves were brought to America.
2. How did the status of indentured servants and slaves differ?
3. Why did slavery gain a greater hold in the South than in the North?

LESSON 3

Opportunity Is Not Equality

The picture of colonial America as a land of opportunity was, except for Indians and blacks, fairly accurate. It is important, though, not to confuse the idea of opportunity with the idea of equality.

English writers of the seventeenth century pictured America as a land where all could find opportunity. But you would search their writings in vain for a promise that all persons in America would be equal. The reason is simple. The idea of equality did not figure much in the thinking of seventeenth century England.

English society. Society in England was made up of a number of ranks, or classes. It might help to think of them as a series of layers. In the top layer were the nobility. Great landowners, they held titles like duke, earl, and baron, which passed from father to son. In the next layer were the gentry, or landed middle class, including great merchants and professional men, like lawyers. Below them were the artisans, or skilled workers, as well as the small independent farmers called yeomen. The yeomen made up the largest class in England. In the bottom layer were the poor—farmers without land and workers without skills.

Although some persons managed to move up from one layer to another, most people lived out their lives in the layer into which they were born. Everyone, from top to bottom, was expected to be content to remain in his or her "proper station" in life. Those in the upper layers were the rulers; those in the lower were the ruled. People at the bottom were expected to "defer" to their "betters"—that is, to accept the views and the leadership of the upper classes in all matters. Members of the upper ranks did not mingle much with those of the lower. Laws even required that the people in the lower ranks dress differently.

The system of ranks by which the upper classes received the deference of the lower classes was accepted as right and necessary by all levels of English society. One might curse one's luck for having been born into a lower class, but few argued that the system should be changed. In seventeenth-century England, inequality, not equality, was the cement that held society together.

American society. Not all the layers of English society were carried over to America. Very few people in the top layer—the nobility—came. For those who had it so good, there was little reason to leave. Also, for reasons that are not known, few in the very lowest layer of English society came. These were the vagrants, the outcasts, the most wretched of the poor. The majority who came were from the middle and lower layers—yeoman farmers, skilled workers, and the farm and city laborers who came as indentured servants.

It was natural that the English who came would carry with them their ideas about rank and deference. John Winthrop, the Puritan leader of the Massachusetts Bay Colony, gave a little speech to his people in 1645 about how society should be run.

> God Almighty in his most holy and wise providence has so disposed the condition of mankind, as in all time some must be rich, some poor, some high and eminent in power and dignity; others mean and [controlled by their superiors].

Winthrop was making clear to his listeners that a system of ranks was in the natural order of things. The "gentlemen" who were among the first arrivals in Jamestown never doubted that others should defer to them. When a lowly tailor in that colony tried to enter his horse in a race in 1674, a judge fined him 100 pounds (45 kg) of tobacco. The reason the judge gave was that it was "contrary to law for a laborer to make a race, it being a sport only for gentlemen."

As in England, clothing was a sign of rank. The son of a poor carpenter gave us a good picture of Virginia society in the mid-eighteenth century when he wrote this paragraph in his memoirs:

> We were accustomed to look upon, what were called gentle folks as being of a superior order. For my part, I was quite shy of them, and kept off at a humble distance. A periwig [a white wig] in those

In colonial times, only the upper classes took part in this kind of musical activity.

2. DISCUSSION Have the students read this lesson and then discuss the similarities and differences between the social structure of colonial America and that of seventeenth-century England. Direct the students' attention to the source material on pages 69–70 and ask them to answer the questions about the paragraph on page 70.

Then ask students for their ideas about social structure in twentieth-century America. How does American society today compare with that in colonial America? Do the ideas of rank and deference still exist? If so, in what ways? Is there such a thing as an upper class in America today? a lower class? Of what importance is the idea of equality in society today? Throughout this discussion, encourage students to support their opinions and to raise questions for others to consider.

days, was a distinguished badge of gentle folks—and when I saw a man riding the road, near our house, with a wig on, it would so alarm my fears, and give me such a disagreeable feeling, that I would run off, as for my life. Such ideas of the difference between the gentle and simple, were, I believe, universal among all of my rank and age.

Why did this carpenter's son run away when the man with the periwig appeared? How would you describe his attitude? Does this help you understand the ideas of rank and deference?

Deference and politics. Did the idea of deference carry over into political life in America? That is, did Americans of the colonial era accept the idea of a ruling class? One place to look for an answer is in the makeup of colonial legislatures or assemblies.

In Chapter 3 you read how and why the legislatures developed. You read also that in most colonies the majority of white adult males had the right to vote. Since most voters in each colony were farmers, you might expect that they would send farmers like themselves to the legislature.

Is that what happened? John Adams, a Massachusetts colonial leader and later President of the United States, gives us the answer for the New England colonies.

> Go into every village in New England and you will find that the office of justice of the peace, and even the place of representative, which has ever depended on the freest election of the people, have generally descended from generation to generation, in three or four families at most.

What Adams saw in New England was equally true elsewhere. Candidates for office were almost always from "the better sort," or upper classes. It was understood that "the meaner sort," or common citizens, would choose between such gentlemen. In Virginia, for example, small farmers were in the great majority. But three fourths of all the men they elected to the House of Burgesses in the 1700s owned more than 10,000 acres (4,000 ha) of land each.

This does not mean that there were no farmers at all in the legislatures. There were. And as time went on, farmers from the western parts of many colonies demanded more seats for their sections. But for the most part, the idea of deference remained strong. Only rarely did a small farmer run against a gentleman. All in all, one would have to agree with the historian who wrote: "The governing class consisted of the wellborn who had wealth, prestige, and power. They monopolized the dominant offices of government."

The standard of wealth. By the early 1700s an upper class had developed in each colony. America's upper class, however, was not like England's. One big difference was that membership in the upper class in America was based mainly on wealth, not on birth. And in America, there were great opportunities for wealth. Some members of the upper class had gained their wealth through gifts of land or other special privileges from the King of England or from the proprietor or governor of a colony. The largest land gifts of all were made by the governor of New York. Several ran to

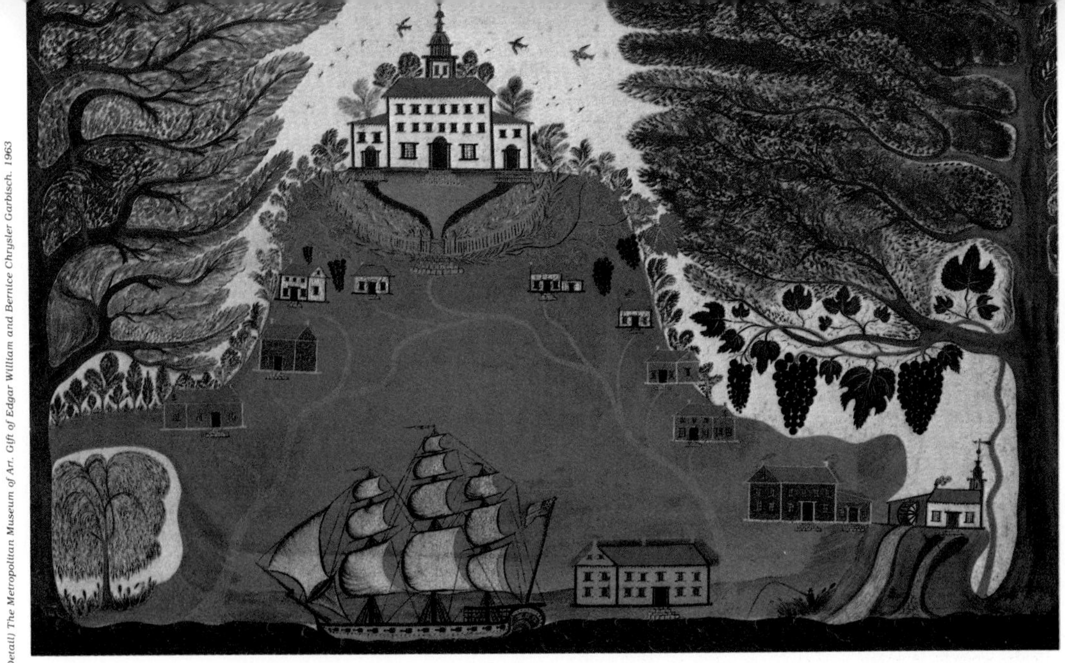

(Detail) The Metropolitan Museum of Art. Gift of Edgar William and Bernice Chrysler Garbisch, 1963

Wealthy Southern planters in colonial times often lived in elegant homes like the one shown above.

hundreds of thousands of acres. Three amounted to more than a million acres each. Needless to say, those who received them became instant members of America's wealthiest class.

But not all entered the upper class in this way. A good many families made their fortunes on their own. What they had in common was energy, ambition, some money, and an eye for the right opportunity. Family fortunes were often based on land inherited from parents and grandparents. Some families sold off part of this land as its value rose. They then used the money to buy still more unsettled lands that would later become valuable. Others used their large landholdings to raise pay crops. Many did both.

Prospering in the South. In the South, where slaves provided more and more of the labor, owning slaves was as important to success as owning land. Those who had saved or inherited enough money to buy slaves had an advantage over those who had not. With their profits, the owners then bought more slaves in order to raise more tobacco and rice, and their advantage widened.

By the early 1700s a powerful planter aristocracy had formed in Virginia, Maryland, and South Carolina, and to a lesser extent in North Carolina and Georgia. Robert "King" Carter was one of the wealthiest of these planters. Robert's father had settled in Virginia in 1649. With money he had brought from England, he bought land. He married five times, acquiring more land with each marriage. He also bought slaves to farm the land. His son Robert built on that solid base. When "King" Carter died, in 1732, he owned 600 slaves, at least 60,000 acres (24,000 ha), and 10,000 pounds in cash.

3. CREATIVE WRITING Divide the class into two groups. Ask one group to assume the role of Southern colonists; ask the other group to assume the role of Northern colonists. Tell each of them they have 1,000 pounds in cash. Ask the students to create identities for themselves and then to describe how they would seek to increase their wealth. Encourage them to use the factual information provided in this lesson and to "document" their accounts with actual people, places, and events of the colonial period.

4. DISCUSSION Ask your students to explain why colonial America was considered a highly mobile society. What opportunities awaited a newly arrived immigrant in colonial days? What opportunities are available today? What degree of social mobility is there in the United States today? Ask your students if there are examples of social mobility in their family histories.

5. WHAT IF? What if everyone were not only created equal (as Thomas Jefferson said) but also achieved equally, were rewarded equally, and ended equally? Ask your students to discuss the consequences of such conditions.

A few southern planters made it to the top in a single generation. Abraham Wood worked as an indentured servant for a planter who also traded with the Indians. When he became a free man, Wood did the same, only better. He collected thousands of acres, became a planter, traded with Indians, and speculated in western land. He became one of Virginia's most prominent men.

Not many made it as Wood did. The Carter family's path to wealth was more typical, though few families rose as high.

Prospering in the North. In the North it was the merchants who were able to take advantage of opportunity and who formed a new aristocracy of wealth. The northern merchants were not jacks-of-all-trades, but they were jacks-of-many. They sent ships with colonial products to the far corners of the world and then sold the goods the ships brought back. They loaned money, sold land, made rum, and bought and sold ships. When British trade laws stood in the way of profit, they were not above smuggling.

Here, too, inheriting money from an earlier generation was an advantage. But New England history is also filled with tales of poor Yankee lads who became rich merchants. John Hull and Thomas Hancock were but two examples. John Hull came from England in the 1630s with his father, a blacksmith. John himself became a silversmith. After a number of years, he branched out. He bought his own trading ships that went to the West Indies, Spain, and England and he sold goods in Boston. When he died, Hull was one of the wealthiest men in Boston.

Thomas Hancock arrived at the same point by a different path. The son of a Congregational minister, Hancock had the advantage of coming from a family of fairly high status, though not wealth. He was apprenticed to a bookseller at fourteen, and after learning the business, Hancock set up his own store. His marriage to the daughter of one of Boston's richest bookdealers added to his advantages. Hancock used her money and business connections to buy a fleet of ships, and was soon trading in many lands.

Elias Hasket Derby of Salem, Massachusetts, was typical of the merchants who made fortunes through foreign trade. His sailing ships took American products to Russia, China, and many other lands and brought back the goods of those countries for sale in American markets.

The growth of a wealthy upper class of merchants in Boston can be seen in the table below.

Distribution of Wealth in Boston

Percentage of Taxpayers	*Percentage of Wealth Held* 1687	1771
Bottom 30%	2	0.1
Low—mid 30%	11	9
Upper—mid 30%	40	27
Top 10%	47	63
(Top 1%	10	26)

Were the bottom 30 percent in Boston better off in 1687, or in 1771? How had the top 10 percent fared in that time? What does the table tell you about the top 1 percent of Bostonians?

Social mobility. Despite the development of social classes, America's society was very different from England's. First, the distance between the bottom layer of colonial society and the top was, except for the slaves, far less. The wealthy in America, in other words, were not nearly as rich as the rich in England. And as you read earlier, the poor were far, far better off than were the poor in England. In every colony, the great majority of white families, including those in the bottom layer, owned land. Even the few who did not had reason to hope that they or their children some day would own land. At the opposite end of the social scale, few of the wealthy in America could live like the idle rich in England. Nearly all of them—even the great planters—had to continue working to take care of their properties and their fortunes.

Second, Americans were not so fixed in their social rank. That was so because rank in America did not depend so much on birth as on wealth. And in America the opportunities to improve one's economic position, and with it one's rank, were far greater than in Europe.

Indentured servants offer the best example of this fact. Earlier you read that between 60 percent and 75 percent of the European immigrants during the colonial period were indentured servants. Their life was hard. They received no wages. They could own no property, except what their masters allowed, and they could not marry without their masters' permission. They were sometimes cruelly punished, especially for running away. A great many died before the end of their terms of service. Many of those who finished their terms became farm workers or laborers in towns and cities. It is estimated that eight out of ten never became landowners or rose into the middle class.

Now there are two ways of interpreting that fact. One is to emphasize the 80 percent of indentured servants who did not rise above the lowest layer. The other is to emphasize the 20 percent who did. Of the 20 percent, half became farm owners, and half became skilled workers who made a good living. For an age when most people in most countries remained fixed in their rank, this is an astonishing fact. Further, of the 80 percent who did not rise above the lowest class, the children and grandchildren of many did. Benjamin Franklin, whose grandparents were indentured servants,

6. THOUGHT PROVOKER In *Politics,* Book IV, Aristotle wrote, "Inferiors revolt in order to be equal, and equals that they may be superior. Such is the state of mind which creates revolution." Ask the students to reflect on the inequality that existed in England and the rest of Europe in the seventeenth century, the inequality that existed in colonial America, and the inequality that exists in America today. Have we made progress? What more must be done? How much equality can a society take?

7. LISTENING FOR INFORMATION Read to your class the section "A Poor Man's Country" in Carl N. Degler's *Out of Our Past: The Forces That Shaped Modern America* (New York: Harper & Row, 1970).

In America, even the poorest families might own land and could hope to rise in wealth and rank.

is the best known of these, but there were thousands of others.

The movement from one layer of society to another is called *social mobility*. In colonial America there was more social mobility than anywhere on earth. For example, the same carpenter's son who fled at the sight of a periwig (see page 70) rose to become an Anglican minister and one of Virginia's most important religious leaders.

In this highly mobile society, movement could go both upward and downward. Able and ambitious people could and did rise in wealth and rank. But a poor crop, a bad investment in land, or the loss of a ship at sea could wipe out a person's wealth, and with it one's high social status.

Opportunity—does it exist today? At the start of this unit, you read that America became identified with the idea of opportunity at the beginning of its history. Did the United States remain a land of opportunity between colonial times and the present? Does it remain a land of opportunity today? You noted earlier that the very opportunities in colonial America helped to make for inequalities in wealth. These inequalities grew during the next hundred years as fortunes were made in fur trading, commerce, industry, railroads, and real estate. Wealth was distributed more unevenly in 1820 than in 1775, and still more unevenly in 1850 than in 1820. In fact, in 1850 the top 1 percent of wealth holders owned 26 percent of the wealth of the United States; the top 2 percent owned 37 percent of the wealth. Although the distribution has become less uneven since 1850, it has continued to be a matter of concern.

Unquestionably there have been greater opportunities for people at the top than for those at lower levels. Yet there is evidence that opportunity has continued to exist for the great majority of Americans. A powerful proof of this fact is that from colonial times to the present day, millions of immigrants have continued to come to America. Had they not had the opportunity to better themselves, they surely would have stopped coming. (You will read more about this in Unit 6.) Other evidence can be found in studies of wealth in America in more recent times. These show that while wealth is still distributed very unevenly, the average person has made real gains in wealth during his or her life.

In judging the extent to which opportunity exists in America today, one must keep in mind, too, that opportunity is not measured by wealth alone. Opportunity has come to be measured today less by the chance to own land than by the chance to gain skills and education, to be free to enter a profession or other field of work, and to find a job where there is a chance to grow.

One of America's great challenges today is to open and keep open the door of opportunity, particularly to those groups to whom it has been shut. That is one of the nation's unfinished tasks. How well it is performed will determine whether America will be able to fulfill its promise to all as a land of opportunity.

CHECKUP

1. Explain how English society in the seventeenth century could be described as "a series of layers."
2. To what extent was society in the American colonies like society in England? How was it different?
3. Compare the ways of becoming wealthy in colonial times in the North and in the South.

Key Facts from Chapter 4

1. The coming of European settlers to America brought on the decline of the native peoples (Indians) whose lands were occupied by the colonists.
2. The first blacks in the colonies landed in 1619 in Jamestown, coming possibly as indentured servants. Within a short time, however, blacks were treated as slaves.
3. Colonial society was made up of a number of layers, ranging from the wealthy upper class to the lower class of farm and city workers who came as indentured servants. Below white indentured servants were black slaves and Indians.
4. It was easier in America than anywhere else in the world to rise in rank. The movement from one level to another is called social mobility.

Answers To Review Questions

1. The settlers took Indian lands and tried to force the Indians to accept English ways and religious beliefs.
2. The English justified their seizure of Indian lands by saying that the Indians did not use the land for anything except hunting, whereas the settlers improved the land and made it productive. Another English justification was the emotional argument that Indians were less than human.
3. The journey began with the capture of Africans by other Africans, who took them to slave-trading ports. There the slaves were exchanged for iron bars, copper pans, rum, or the like. The captives were branded with the mark of their buyer and herded onto ships for the voyage across the Atlantic. Many slaves never lived to reach America; they died of starvation, illness, and mistreatment aboard crowded, unsanitary ships.
4. For centuries the word *black* had carried a negative meaning in the English culture. It was the color of death, the devil, bad magic, poison, and forsaken love, to name but a few negative meanings. Black meant foul, wicked, evil, or sinful.
5. The price of slaves dropped at about the same time that white indentured servants began to be attracted to newer colonies where opportunities for their future seemed brighter.

6. Society in England was made up of the nobility, the gentry, the artisans and small farmers, and finally, the poor. Not all the layers of English society were carried over to America. For the most part, very few people in the nobility class or in the poor class came to America. The majority who did come were from the middle and lower layers—small farmers, skilled workers, and the farm and city laborers who came as indentured servants.
7. Membership in America's upper class was based mainly on wealth, rather than on birth. A person's wealth could be inherited or earned by taking advantage of the opportunities available in America. Membership in England's upper class was based largely on birth, although wealth was certainly important, too.
8. In the South the upper, or wealthy, class was represented by the large plantation owner. In the North it was the merchant who was able to take advantage of opportunity and who formed a new aristocracy of wealth.
9. The distance between the top and the bottom layers of colonial society, except for slaves, was far less than it was in England. Those on the top had to work to maintain their wealth, while even the poorest on the bottom usually owned land and had hope that they or their children might improve their economic position in life. In America the opportunities to improve one's economic position, and with it one's rank, were far greater than in Europe.

Answers for Chapter Test
1. d **2.** b **3.** h **4.** e **5.** j
6. a **7.** i **8.** f **9.** c **10.** g

★ REVIEWING THE CHAPTER ★

People, Places, and Events

Pocahontas *P. 58*
Powhatan *P. 58*
Pequot War *P. 59*
King Philip's War *P. 59*
Middle passage *P. 63*
"Negroes" *P. 65*
Indentured servants *P. 65*
Royal African Company *P. 66*
Slave codes *P. 66*
Free blacks *P. 68*
"Proper station" *P. 68*
Social mobility *P. 73*

Review Questions

1. What caused the conflict that developed between the Indians and the colonists? *Pp. 57–58* Les. 1
2. How did the English justify seizing Indian lands? *Pp. 59–61* Les. 1
3. Describe the journey of the Africans from their home in Africa to slavery in the New World. *Pp. 63–64* Les. 2
4. How did the English feel about the word L.2 *black*? Why did they feel that way? *P. 64*
5. Why did many plantation owners decide to use slaves instead of indentured servants? *P. 66* Les. 2
6. Compare the classes, or layers, of society in seventeenth-century England with society in America. *Pp. 68–69* Les. 3
7. How did America's upper class differ from L.3 England's upper class? *Pp. 70–71*
8. Who represented colonial America's wealthy class in the South? in the North? *Pp. 71–72* Les. 3
9. Why was there greater social mobility in L.3 colonial America than in England? *P. 73*

Chapter Test

In the first section below is a list of people and terms found in the chapter. In the second section is a list of descriptions. Match each person or term with the appropriate description. Write your answers on a separate sheet of paper.

1. Social mobility
2. King Philip's War
3. Slave code
4. Royal African Company
5. "Negroes"
6. Powhatan
7. Prejudice
8. Middle passage
9. Merchants
10. "Proper station"

a. Leader of the Indians of Virginia who helped the settlers
b. New England conflict between settlers and Indians
c. Members of the wealthy upper class in the northern colonies
d. Movement from one level of society to another
e. Slave-trading business
f. Trip from Africa to the West Indies
g. An idea popular in seventeenth-century England that one should stay in the layer of society to which one was born
h. Special laws to control the blacks in colonial America
i. An opinion formed without taking time or care to judge fairly
j. A term borrowed by the English from the Portuguese and the Spanish, meaning "black"

★ REVIEWING THE UNIT ★

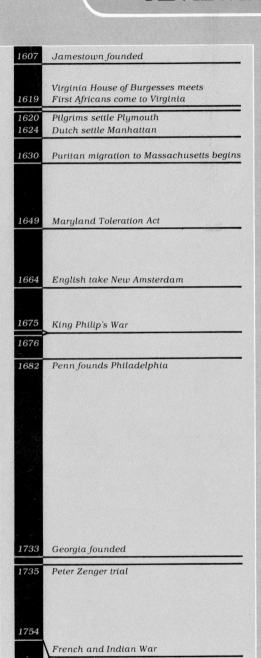

1607	Jamestown founded
1619	Virginia House of Burgesses meets First Africans come to Virginia
1620	Pilgrims settle Plymouth
1624	Dutch settle Manhattan
1630	Puritan migration to Massachusetts begins
1649	Maryland Toleration Act
1664	English take New Amsterdam
1675–1676	King Philip's War
1682	Penn founds Philadelphia
1733	Georgia founded
1735	Peter Zenger trial
1754–1763	French and Indian War

The first discoverers of America were the people Columbus called Indians. However, not until after Columbus's voyage in 1492 was there lasting contact between America and other lands. During the next century, explorers from Spain, Portugal, France, Holland, and England laid claim to vast territories in the New World.

The English were the most active colonizers. To them America meant opportunity—a place where settlers could own land, where they could worship God as they pleased, and where traders could make profits. Between 1607 and 1733, the English established permanent colonies along the Atlantic Coast, all the way from northern New England to Georgia. By 1700 every colony had its own legislature. Farming was the principal occupation, but trade and commerce were also important.

America's opportunities were not equally available to all. Voting was largely restricted to white, landowning males. Women were subject to many restrictions. Indians were forced from their lands by the colonists and were reduced in numbers by warfare and disease. Though the first Africans may have come as indentured servants, blacks were soon treated as slaves.

American society had various layers. The upper, or ruling, class was based largely on wealth. Yet there was opportunity for many in the lower classes to rise. In America there was more social mobility—movement from one layer of society to another—than anywhere else on earth.

 REVIEWING THE UNIT 

Skills Development: Creating a Time Line

Thinking clearly about time sequences is important in studying history. A good way to study sequences is through the use of a time line. A time line is a kind of schematic drawing that shows when an event happened and the time relationship of that event to other events.

Each time line is drawn to a certain scale. The scale depends on what you want to show. Let's compare the scales used for time lines in this unit. Look at the time line on page 77. Measure the distance for the years from 1607–1630. What does 1 inch (2.5 cm) represent? Now compare that scale with the one used in the time line on page 3. What is the scale for this time line? Approximately how many inches (centimeters) represent 100 years in the time line on page 77? on page 3? On which time line would there be more space to record the events of a century?

The important point to remember about scale is that it must be consistent within the particular time line. If, for example, 1 inch (2.5 cm) stands for 50 years, then that scale must be maintained throughout the time line. So before you draw a time line, you need to decide on the scale to be used in recording the events.

Drawing a Time Line

Now that you understand the importance of scale, try your hand at drawing a time line. The necessary information is provided in the right-hand column: a chronological listing of some famous explorers and their achievements. Before you begin to draw your time line, plan the scale carefully. You might wish to use different colors to show the countries for which each explorer sailed. Title your time line.

c. **1000** Leif Ericson believed to be the first European to reach the North American coast (Iceland)

1488 Dias first European to round Cape of Good Hope (Port.)

1492 Columbus visited West Indies (Sp.)

1497 Cabot reached Canada (Eng.)

1498 Da Gama first European to reach India by sea (Port.)

1499 Vespucci sailed to West Indies and South America (Sp.)

1500 Cabral claimed Brazil for Portugal

1513 Balboa crossed Isthmus of Panama and sighted Pacific Ocean (Sp.)

1513 de León explored Florida (Sp.)

1519 Cortes conquered Mexico (Sp.)

1520 Magellan commanded first voyage around the world (Sp.)

1524 Verrazano first European to see Hudson River (Fr.)

1525 Pizarro explored Peru (Sp.)

1535 Cartier sailed up St. Lawrence River (Fr.)

1540 Coronado explored Southwest and sighted Grand Canyon (Sp.)

1541 De Soto crossed the Mississippi (Sp.)

1565 St. Augustine founded by the Spanish

1572 Drake sailed around the world (Eng.)

1576 Frobisher searched for northwest passage to India (Eng.)

1584 Raleigh visited Virginia (Eng.)

1585 English settlers left on Roanoke Island

1603 Champlain sailed up St. Lawrence River (Fr.)

1607 Settlement of Jamestown (Eng.)

1609 Hudson explored Hudson River (Hol.)

Unit 2

Americans and Revolution

THE STRUGGLE FOR INDEPENDENCE

Background Information

1. PICTURE Painted by Johannes Oertal, this picture shows enthusiastic patriots attacking the statue of George III with crowbars and cables. The event occurred in New York City on July 9, 1776. That day the Declaration of Independence had been read publicly in New York for the first time, arousing the people to action. The lead statue was converted into musket balls—prompting one Patriot to observe that the king's troops "will probably have melted majesty fired at them." Shortly afterward, New York City fell into the hands of the British who occupied it for the duration of the war.

CHAPTER 5

DOWN THE ROAD TO REVOLUTION

LESSON 1

BENJAMIN FRANKLIN spent much of the 1760s in London as the agent in Parliament for the American colonies. During one of his appearances there, the following exchange took place.

> *Question:* What was the temper of America toward Britain before the year 1763?
> *Answer:* The best in the world. They submitted willingly to the government of the Crown, and paid in all their courts obedience to the acts of Parliament. . . . They had not only respect, but affection for Great Britain; for its laws, its customs, and manners, and even a fondness for its fashions, that greatly increased commerce.

The American Colonies in 1763

Franklin's statement was no doubt accurate. American colonists in 1763 were, for the most part, quite content to be British subjects. For one thing, more than half of them were of English origin. Many still had relatives in England. They were also tied to England by language and culture. English authors were their authors, and English artists their artists. Even though few of them had ever been to England, most spoke of it as "home." Among those colonists from other lands, most were speaking English by then and were becoming used to English ways.

The basic rights. When colonists boasted that they had the "rights of Englishmen," this was not a hollow term. It meant they enjoyed rights and liberties such as no other people on the earth enjoyed in that age. Among these were

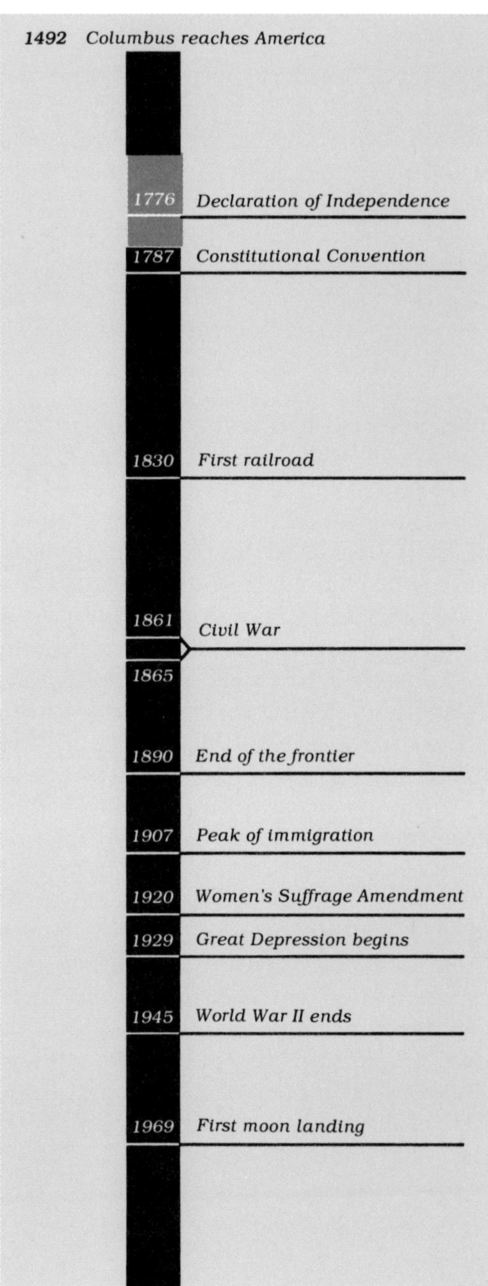

LESSON 1 *(2 to 3 days)*

Performance Objectives

1. To give written evidence in support of the fact that prior to 1763 most colonists were well satisfied with life within the British Empire. **2.** To explain orally the theory of historic inevitability and to relate the theory to the American Revolution.

Famous Person

Benjamin Franklin

Vocabulary

"Rights of Englishmen," monopoly, taxation without representation, Navigation Acts, inevitability, royal governor, proprietary colonies.

For this unit of study, you may wish to use **The American Revolution Picture Packet,** which contains twenty-four 19″ × 23″ display cards depicting major events of the American Revolution. The **Picture Packet** is published by Silver Burdett Company.

Activities

1. INTRODUCING THE UNIT Ask for, or provide, a definition of the term *revolution.* Then develop a discussion around the students' conception of a revolution. Encourage them to respond to questions such as the following. **(a)** What do you think it would be like to be in the middle of a revolution? **(b)** Where and when do we usually hear about revolutions? **(c)** How do Americans generally feel about revolutions? **(d)** Would you become involved in a revolution? Why or why not? **(e)** What do you think might possibly start a revolution in America today?

At some point, ease back into the colonial period with a question such as, Do you think people in the 1700s were more or less likely to start or join a revolution than people today? Try to establish the idea that it was somewhat difficult to interest people in revolution.

2. READING FOR INFORMATION/CREATIVE WRITING After students have read textbook pages 81–84, have them write letters to a relative living in England in 1763. The purpose of the letters is to deny the rumor that American colonists want to separate from England. Students should cite specific evidence from the textbook that colonists were, for the most part, quite content to be British subjects. Encourage students to be creative in their letter writing but at the same time to stick to the historical facts. Perhaps students would like to share their letters with classmates.

3. USING A MAP On outline maps of the United States have the students do the following:
a. Sketch the American colonies in 1763.
b. Label the major geographical areas that were important in the French and Indian War and the Revolution (Hudson River, St. Lawrence River, Appalachian Mountains, the Mohawk Valley, etc.).
c. Label the cities that were important (Philadelphia, Charleston, New York, Boston, etc.).

As events are described in the text, have students locate and label on their maps the sites of the events. Do not presuppose the students' knowledge of American geography.

private property, trial by jury, the right to meet together peaceably, and the right to petition their government.

Because of these "rights of Englishmen," Americans could not be taxed unless their representatives approved; in other words, "no taxation without representation." Their rights were guaranteed not only by the British constitution but also by the charter of each colony. Religious toleration in the colonies was not complete. Yet there was more of it there than anywhere else in the world.

The powers of government. The colonies also enjoyed a great deal of self-government. If a colonist were white, male, and the owner of a certain amount of property—and most white males were—he had the right to vote for his own representatives. Each colony had its own legislature and made most of its own laws. Only rarely did the British Parliament or king overrule these laws.

By the year 1763, Britain and the American colonies had worked out a compromise on dividing the powers of government. The king and Parliament were to control foreign affairs, war and peace, and overseas trade. The colonies, in most other matters, were to make their own laws. By 1763, colonial governments had won the right to levy their own taxes, appoint most of their own officials, and control their own militia. They had far more self-government than did the Spanish and French colonies in the New World.

Furthermore, most American colonists were rarely bothered by British officials. These officials were few in number and tended to be stationed in the larger seaport towns. Ninety percent of the colonists were farmers who lived in the countryside. They seldom saw a British official.

Economic advantages. American colonists also enjoyed certain trading advantages as members of the greatest empire in the western world. For one thing, the British government gave the colonists a monopoly on the sale in England of certain American products. Tobacco was one. English and Irish farmers were not allowed to raise it. And Britain placed a heavy tax on tobacco from any place except America.

Also, over a period of time, Parliament passed a number of laws to put in order the trade of the empire. They were called the Navigation Acts. They aimed to make the British empire both well-to-do and self-sufficient.Under these laws, the colonies were expected to produce raw materials for the empire and to buy manufactured goods from England. One act required that goods traded within the empire be carried only in ships made in England or America. As a result, the colonial shipbuilding industry boomed.

Britain also paid the colonists to produce certain products. Among them were indigo, used by British textile manufacturers, and tar and turpentine, needed for the British navy. That navy itself was one of the great advantages of being part of the British empire. It provided protection for American trading ships against pirates and foreign navies.

Some restrictions. It is true that the Navigation Acts restricted the colonists in some ways. They were not allowed to sell certain items, such as tobacco, rice,

Shipbuilding was a thriving industry along the Delaware River in Philadelphia. In colonial America—with its plentiful supplies of oak and pine—ships could be built more cheaply than in Britain.

indigo, and furs, to any countries outside the empire. Moreover, any goods they wished to buy from another European nation had to pass through England first. There, a special tax was placed on many of them. But all in all, the laws usually worked in the interests of the colonists as well as of the English. When they didn't, the colonists simply got around them by smuggling. That was not hard to do, because Britain had only a small number of officials in the colonies to enforce its laws.

Even British laws that discouraged or prohibited the making of certain goods in the colonies did not work much hardship—except, of course, for the few people engaged in such manufacturing. Generally, Americans were content to buy their manufactured goods from England. England was the most advanced industrial country in the world. It could make most products more cheaply than any other nation.

A few disagreements. There were, of course, some disagreements between Britain and the American colonists. A number of them involved the colonial governments. Colonists chose their representatives to the lower house of their colonial legislatures. But most governors were appointed to office—by the king in royal colonies and by the proprietor in proprietary colonies. Because of this, the legislative and executive branches battled constantly over which had the right to do what.

4. RESEARCH/ORAL REPORT Though not specifically mentioned in the text, the economic theory of mercantilism played a significant role in the coming of the American Revolution. Ask some of your more capable students to use encyclopedias and other appropriate reference books to do the following:

a. Define mercantilism as the British applied it to the American colonies.

b. Report informally to the class about how mercantilism could have been a major cause of the American Revolution.

5. THOUGHT PROVOKER Historical philosopher Isaiah Berlin believes that historical inevitability is not only a fallacy but also a danger in that it "saps the sense of individual responsibility. It engenders acquiescence and passive subjection to the mysterious and uncontrollable forces which are conjured up by the awed public as the masters of their destiny." Ask your students whether they agree with Isaiah Berlin, and encourage them to discuss their opinions.

6. DEBATE Resolved, That the American Revolution was inevitable. For more information on this interesting theory, have students read "Historical Inevitability" (Chapter 13) in *Debates with Historians* by Pieter Geyl (New York: New American Library).

LESSON 2 *(2 days)*

Performance Objectives

1. To list the events that indicate there was a growing distrust of British colonial policies by the American colonists. **2.** To define and give examples of the existence of the conspiracy theory in the minds of colonial leaders and intellectuals.

Famous Person

John Adams

Vocabulary

Seven Years' War, French and Indian War, writs of assistance, Stamp Act, conspiracy theory

Governors insisted that their instructions from London should be carried out to the letter. The colonists, on the other hand, wanted to be consulted. They felt that they should have a chance to modify the instructions to the governor. Americans also objected to the fact that they could not choose their own judges. Judges were appointed by the king and could be removed only by him.

A stunning turnabout. But by and large the colonists were well satisfied with life within the British empire in 1763. There was little talk of disloyalty to the king. Thinking back to that time, Benjamin Franklin later recalled, "I never heard in any conversation from any person, drunk or sober, the least expression for separation from England."

Thirteen years later the American colonies declared their independence.

Why? One historian has this to say:

> New soil had produced new wants, new desires, new points of view, and the colonists were demanding the right to live their own lives in their own way. As we see it today the situation was a dramatic one. On one side was the [unchanging and rigid] system of the mother country, based on precedent and tradition and designed to keep things comfortably as they were; on the other, a vital dynamic organism, containing the seed of a great nation, its forces untried, still to be proved. It is inconceivable that a connection should have continued long between [the] two. . . .

What shapes the course of events? That explanation contains an important idea about human affairs. It is the idea of *inevitability*. In this view, the course of events is not decided through acts and decisions of individuals nor by circumstances nor by chance. It is decided by great underlying forces and factors. Thus, the argument that the American colonies would have remained under English rule "if the colonists hadn't sent their troops to Lexington" or "if rabble-rousers like Sam Adams hadn't stirred up trouble" has no real importance. Things didn't happen differently, because they *couldn't* have happened differently. It was inevitable that the American colonies would seek their independence from Great Britain.

There is a problem with that view. We can never "do" history over again. We cannot bring back the exact circumstances of a time and place. Therefore, we cannot try out other approaches to see if the results would have been different. All we can ever know is what in fact *did* happen. And there is the problem. For the theory of inevitability tempts one to say that whatever did happen was bound to happen.

***Was* it bound to happen?** Was the American Revolution as inevitable as the historian suggests above? We cannot know. What we do know is that in 1763 there was little or no talk of separating from England. Ten years later there was a great deal of talk. And in 1776 the colonies declared their independence.

Even if it were true that separation was inevitable, it was the events of those years that determined when separation would come, and why. It was those years that decided what kind of a revolution the American Revolution would be, and over what issues it would be fought. And that experience, in turn, had much to do with shaping America's attitudes about revolution for years to come.

CHECKUP

1. How did most American colonists in 1763 feel about being British subjects?
2. When colonists talked of having the "rights of Englishmen," what rights were they referring to?
3. What economic benefits did Americans have from their association with Britain? What restrictions were placed on them?

LESSON 2

A Growing Distrust

The stage for the events of 1763–1776 was set in the previous ten-year period. In 1754, for the fourth time within three quarters of a century, Britain and France went to war. The stakes were high: control of nearly all the North American continent. In 1756 the European allies of each side entered the war. For the next seven years the battle raged on four continents—North and South America, Europe, and Asia.

The French and Indian War. Nowhere was the fighting more fierce than in North America, where the war first broke out. Known in Europe as the Seven Years' War, the conflict, in America, was called the French and Indian War. It was so named because of the number of Indian tribes that fought on the side of France.

The upper map on this page shows the areas of North America controlled by the big powers in 1700. The lower shows the area each controlled in 1763. American colonists had often expressed the

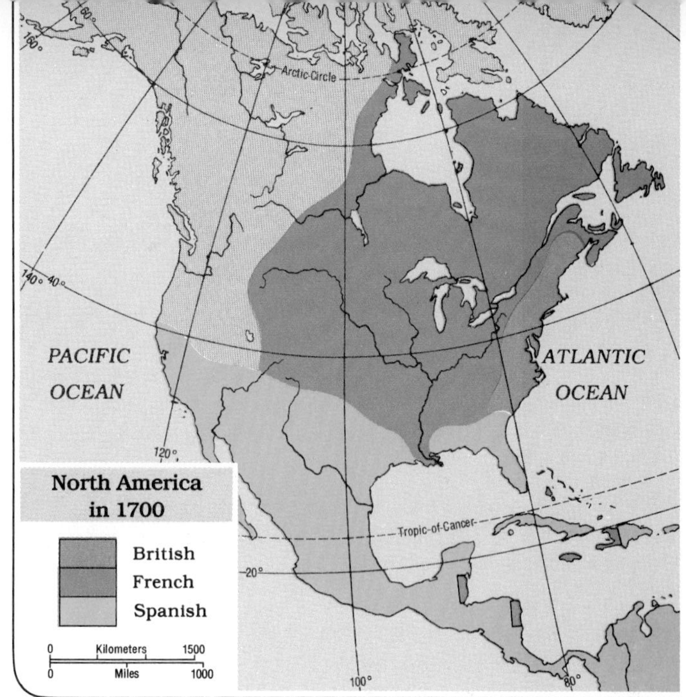

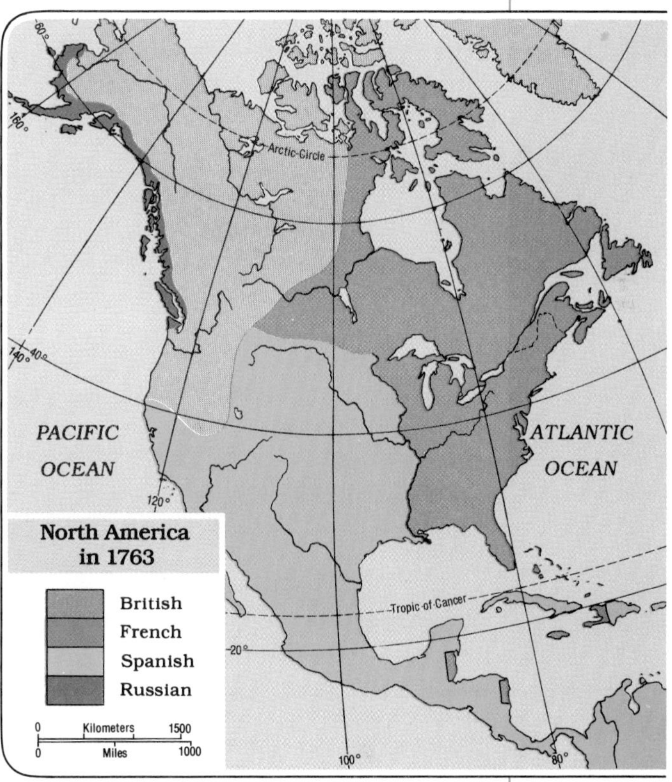

After the French and Indian War, which nation gained the most territory by the peace treaty? What other country made significant gains?

Activities

1. READING FOR INFORMATION The late Crane Brinton, an American historian, evaluated the English, French, Russian, and American revolutions. He concluded that there were similar preliminary signs or symptoms in all the revolutions. These symptoms were **(a)** an expressed discontent on the part of the middle class; **(b)** a growing inefficiency on the part of the central government; **(c)** an impending financial crisis in the government; **(d)** a dislike for certain classes of people; and **(e)** the beginning of vocal discontent on the part of the intellectuals, such as artists, authors, musicians, professors, ministers.

Ask your students to read this lesson carefully and to look for evidence that would confirm Brinton's conclusions. From the evidence, have students make a list of those events that showed the American colonists' growing distrust of British colonial policies.

2. WHAT IF? After students have studied the maps on page 85, ask them how the geography of America might have been different if the French had won the French and Indian War. How might the history of America have been different?

fear that they were being encircled by the French. Can you see why?

Even though Britain's American colonies had a large stake in the outcome, they contributed few soldiers and little money to the fight. It was British troops and British money that won the war. In the peace treaty of 1763, France gave up all its territory on the North American continent. Britain and Spain now shared control of the continent except for a thin strip claimed by Russia along the Pacific coast.

Paying the bills. The victory over France had been achieved at a great cost. During the war, Britain had run up a huge debt that now must be paid. Further, the cost of defending and running the British empire was five times what it had been before the war. To help pay these expenses, Britain looked to its American colonies.

It was the colonies who had benefited most by the removal of the French from America. It seemed only right that the colonies should now pay their fair share to defend the newly expanded empire. The money would come from two sources. One was new taxes. The other was better collection of the old taxes the colonists had been evading. This would come through stricter enforcement of the Navigation Acts and a general tightening up of Britain's control over its empire.

Threats to liberty? These moves came at just the wrong time for the colonies. As long as the French threat existed, the colonies depended on British military power to protect them. They were in no position to argue with their protector about taxes. But with the French threat gone, the colonies' attitude was quite different. They quickly objected to paying more taxes.

By this time a deep distrust had begun to develop between the American colonists and the British. In Britain's eyes, the new import taxes and tighter law enforcement were only fair and right. To the colonists, however, they were anything but fair. These actions, Americans believed, aimed at robbing them of their money and their property. American colonists believed there was a close connection between their property and their liberty. In their minds, therefore, these threats to their property were threats to their liberty, too.

They also objected to the *writs of assistance,* used by the British in enforcing the Navigation Acts. A writ of assistance was a kind of search warrant, often used in looking for smuggled goods. In the past, before searching for such goods, officials had been required to obtain a search warrant in court. Before they could get a warrant, they had to offer proof that there were indeed smuggled goods in the building or on the property they intended to search. Now, they no longer needed to offer such proof. Armed with a writ of assistance, British officials could search for smuggled goods anywhere they wished and at any time. They could even enter private homes. Was not that, thought a good many Americans, another threat to their liberty?

The Stamp Act. You can sense the growing distrust in the words of John Adams, Massachusetts lawyer and political leader, after Parliament passed the

Metropolitan Museum of Art, bequest of Charles Allen Munn, 1924

The required use of special tax stamps—like the one at left—aroused bitter opposition throughout the colonies. At right, New Hampshire citizens cheer the hanging in effigy of a tax collector.

Stamp Act of 1765. This law required the colonists to purchase special tax stamps for use on all newspapers, pamphlets, and legal documents. (We use similar tax stamps today on cigarette packages, packs of playing cards, and liquor bottles.) Special tax collectors sold the stamps. The money raised from the stamps was to be sent to England to help pay for the British troops stationed in America.

John Adams was no hothead. He was a thoughtful man, not given to exaggerated charges and fears. Yet here is how Adams interpreted the British motive behind the Stamp Act.

> There seems to be a direct and formal plan under way to enslave all America . . . to strip us in large measure of the means of knowledge . . . and to [take] from the poorer . . . people all of their little income and [confer] it on a set of stamp officers, distributors, and their deputies.

More than a tax? "Enslave." "Take from the poorer . . . people." "Strip us . . . of the means of knowledge." Those are strong words about a simple tax measure. But John Adams and other colonists were beginning to see in such actions something more than a tax.

Parliament had never before placed a direct tax on the colonies. Was this the first of more to come? English subjects were not supposed to be taxed without the consent of their representatives. That might happen to conquered peoples, but not to free English subjects. Yet here was a tax imposed on them by a Parliament in which they were not represented. Was this the start of an attempt to take away the "rights of Englishmen"? Further, those who broke the law were to be tried in a special kind of court in which there was no jury. Was not this another violation of the "rights of Englishmen"?

Background Information

DIRECT TAX One reason why the colonists were so angry about the Stamp Act was because it was a new kind of tax—a direct tax. It was the first time they had to pay money directly to the English government.

The old taxes were different. They were taxes on goods. When a ship sailed into Boston, Philadelphia, or some other American seaport, only the merchants had to pay a tax on the goods. After the merchants paid the tax, they raised the price of the goods. Later, when the colonists purchased something, they had to pay a little extra. Although they were really paying the tax for the merchants, they didn't feel it so much because the tax was hidden in the price. However, the new tax wasn't hidden at all. It was right out in the open. Every time the colonists bought a stamp, they had to pay for it out of their own pockets.

3. LISTENING FOR INFORMATION You might wish to read to the class "The Great War for the Empire" by Lawrence H. Gibson in *The American Story* edited by E. S. Miers (Great Neck, N.Y.: Channel Press, 1956). For additional information, see Gipson's *The Coming of the Revolution, 1763–1775* (New York: Harper & Brothers, 1954).

If some students are particularly adept readers, perhaps they could read selections to their classmates. Or you may wish to tape the reading of a selection and present the material in this fashion.

4. FILMS The following are recommended: *The French and Indian War: Seven Years' War in America,* (16 minutes, color; Encyclopaedia Britannica Films). *The American Revolution, Part 1: The Cause of Liberty,* (25 minutes, color; Robert Saudek Associates, Inc.). Indiana University Audio-Visual Center has these films available for reasonable rental.

5. ROLE-PLAYING Have the class dramatize a New England town meeting to protest the Stamp Act. Let your students act out the parts of common citizens affected by the direct tax. Use the tone of John Adams's arguments against the act as a guide. See also the "Resolutions of the Stamp Act Congress" (document number 38) in Henry Steele Commager's *Documents of American History* (New York: Appleton-Century-Crofts).

The conspiracy theory. The Americans were beginning to suspect that there was a plot, or conspiracy, to rob them of their liberty. Their suspicion is evident in the pamphlets and newspapers published in America between 1773 and 1776. In those, the British rulers are pictured as bent upon a conspiracy. Its aim was to deprive the Americans of their property and their rights as free people and to turn them into slaves.

At the center of this scheme—so the conspiracy theory went—were the king's ministers. These power-hungry men wished to destroy liberty both in Britain and in America. One way they planned to do this was to increase the number of British officials in America. Thus, the colonists, instead of governing themselves in most matters, would increasingly be governed by British officials. The salaries of these officials would be paid by taxing the colonists more. Slowly the Americans would have their property taken away, and they would be enslaved.

According to those who believed there was a conspiracy, the king's ministers would also undermine American liberties by working through American officials sympathetic to them. Promises of pensions, money, and titles of nobility would be used to bribe these colonial officials to do the bidding of the British.

Thomas Hutchinson, Lieutenant Governor and later Governor of the Massachusetts colony, was considered by many to be such an official. In truth, he was not. Yet in his private letters that American newspapers got hold of, Hutchinson had suggested the colonists' "rights of Englishmen" might have to be reduced if the British empire were to be preserved. A sellout of American liberties, claimed the accusers of Hutchinson.

Were British troops needed? The conspiracy theory also had an explanation for the presence of British troops in America. Britain kept more soldiers in America after the French and Indian War than ever before. British ministers claimed they were needed to protect the colonists against the Indians on the frontier. But the colonists wondered. The war with France was over and won. There was a need not for more troops but for fewer—unless, of course, the king's ministers had other plans for them.

After a few incidents between troops and civilians occurred, a writer in a Boston newspaper in 1768 reported:

> The inhabitants of this town have been of late greatly insulted and abused by some of the officers and soldiers. Several have been assaulted [for trifling reasons] and put under guard without any lawful warrant for so doing. A physician of the town walking the streets the other evening was jostled by an officer, when a scuffle ensued. He was afterward met by the same officer in company with another, both as yet unknown, who repeated his blows and (as is supposed) gave him a stroke with a pistol and so wounded him as to endanger his life. . . . *Here, Americans, you may behold some of the first fruits springing up from that root of bitterness, a standing army. Troops are quartered upon us in a time of peace, on pretense of preserving order in a town that was as orderly before their arrival as any one large town in the whole extent of his majesty's dominions; and a little time will discover whether we are to be governed by the martial [military] or the common law of the land.*

British troops disembark from Royal Navy ships in Boston Harbor in 1768. Their role was "to keep order," but their presence in the city led to clashes that heightened already tense feelings.

Do you think the writer held to the conspiracy theory? Was he justified in fearing the presence of a standing army?

Was there really a plot? New Englanders had their own special version of the conspiracy theory. Many of the original Puritan settlers, you will recall, had come to America to escape the persecution of the Anglican church. Now a fear spread through New England that Anglican bishops might be sent to make that church the official, established church in all the American colonies.

Looking back on the events of the 1760s, we know now that there was no British conspiracy to enslave the Americans. It is, however, not things as they are but as people imagine them to be that often determine the course of events. And once people begin to see the world through the lens of a conspiracy, there is no end to what they can imagine.

As you read of the events that followed, ask yourself how the colonists might in each case have applied their conspiracy theory.

CHECKUP

1. What effect did the French and Indian War have on the control of North America?
2. Why did Britain place new taxes on the colonies? What was the reaction of the colonists?
3. What was the conspiracy theory, in which some Americans believed?

LESSON 3

British Measures and American Reactions

The Stamp Act was met by violence and by political and economic protests. A new group, the Sons of Liberty, came into being to fight the act. They threatened and bullied tax collectors, and sometimes tarred and feathered them.

6. DISCUSSION Imagined evils, unfounded fears, and supposed conspiracies have caused humans, individually and collectively, to do some tragic things. In the text on page 89 it says, "Looking back on the events of the 1760s, we know now that there was no British conspiracy to enslave the Americans." In light of this knowledge, ask your students how they would justify the American Revolution. What other incidents in history were caused by imagined conspiracies?

7. THOUGHT PROVOKER In regard to the Stamp Act, Winston Churchill wrote in *The Age of Revolution,* Vol. 3 of *A History of the English-Speaking Peoples* (New York: Dodd, Mead, 1957): "With two exceptions it imposed no heavy burden . . . . it brought in £300,000 a year and its extension to America added another £50,000. But the Act included a tax on newspapers, many of whose journalists were vehement partisans of the extremist party in America, and the colonial merchants were dismayed because the duty had to be paid in bullion already needed for meeting the adverse trade balance with England. The dispute exposed and fortified the more violent elements in America, and gave them a chance to experiment in organized resistance." How does Churchill's description coincide with Crane Brinton's conclusions cited in Activity 1?

LESSON 3 *(2 to 3 days)*

Performance Objective

To define each of the following Parliamentary acts and explain what part each played in the coming of the American Revolution: Declaratory Act, Quartering Act, Townshend Acts, Tea Act of 1773, Intolerable Acts.

Famous Person

Samuel Adams

Vocabulary

Sons of Liberty, Stamp Act Congress, Declaratory Act, Quartering Act, Townshend Acts, Boston Massacre, Daughters of Liberty, Committees of Correspondence, Tea Act of 1773, Whig, Boston Tea Party, Intolerable Acts, Quebec Act of 1774, First Continental Congress, dominion theory of empire

Background Information

1. MOURNING CLOTHES In colonial times when a person died, the family usually observed a period of mourning. During this time, mourners wore distinctive articles of clothing. For example, a woman would wear a mourning bonnet. It was this custom of dress to which Franklin referred when he said, "The people have already struck off, by general agreement, the use of all goods fashionable in mourning."

Massachusetts asked that the colonies send delegates to meet in New York in 1765 to consider a common course of action, and nine colonies did. It was the first time this many colonies had met to discuss their common problems. The Stamp Act Congress, as it was called, asked Parliament to repeal the act. Meanwhile, many merchants refused to buy English goods, and colonists balked at buying the tax stamps. As a result, hardly a penny was raised.

Franklin on the Stamp Act. In the face of this opposition, Parliament took up the matter again. Among the things they considered was the testimony of Benjamin Franklin, who served as the colonial agent in England:

Question: If the act is not repealed, what do you think will be the consequences?
Answer: A total loss of the respect and affection that the people of America bear to this country, and all the commerce that depends on that respect and affection.
Question: How can the commerce be affected?
Answer: You will find that, if the act is not repealed, they will take very little of your manufactures in a short time.
Question: Is it in their power to do without them?
Answer: I think they may very well do without them.
Question: Is it in their interest not to take them?
Answer: The goods they take from Britain are either necessaries, mere conveniences, or [unnecessary luxuries]. The first, as cloth etc. with a little [effort] they can make at home; the second they can do without till they are able to [make] them . . . themselves; and the last . . . they will strike off immediately. They are mere articles of fashion. . . . The people have already struck off, by general agreement, the use of all goods fashionable in mourning.

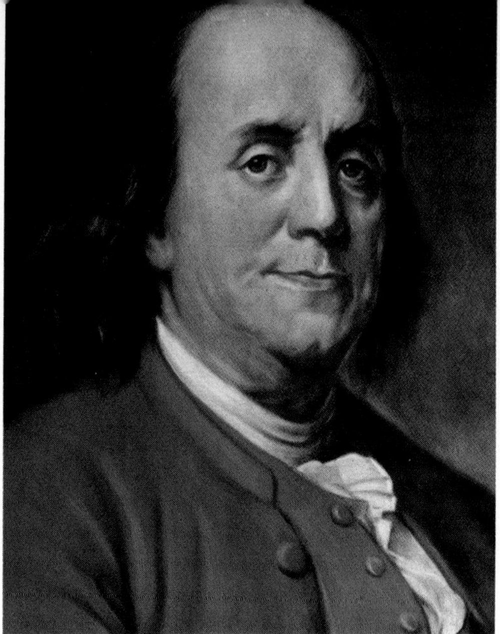

Benjamin Franklin—scientist, inventor, and diplomat—was the best-known man in colonial America. Although he had only two years of school, he never stopped educating himself.

Franklin rested his argument on the American refusal to buy English goods. In doing so, he hoped to worry British merchants so that they would ask Parliament to repeal the law. Read again Franklin's explanation of how the colonists could get along without "necessaries" from England. Do you see why English cloth manufacturers might also be worried?

In 1766 Parliament bowed to American pressure and repealed the Stamp Act. Just so there would be no question as to who was boss, however, the British passed the Declaratory Act on the same day. This act stated that Parliament had full authority over the American colonies "in all cases whatsoever."

The Quartering Act. Another British measure that angered colonists had to do with the support of the 10,000 troops the British planned to keep in North America. It seemed entirely reasonable to the British that the colonies should bear some of the costs for their own defense. Supplies and shelter would be needed for the troops. The most direct way to provide them, and the least costly way to the British government, was to require the Americans to furnish them.

This Parliament did in the Quartering Act of 1765. Some time later the British passed another act, permitting these troops to be quartered in inns, alehouses, and unoccupied buildings. When the New York legislature refused to furnish funds to supply the British troops, Parliament ordered the legislature shut down until it did as told. In this case, the order was never carried out. However, it is not hard to imagine how the colonists viewed an order to their representatives to knuckle under to Parliament.

The Townshend Acts. Still, taxes had to be raised, and so in 1767 the British tried again with the Townshend Acts. This time taxes were placed on certain imported goods such as tea, paper, paint, and lead. The money raised was to be used to pay the salaries of colonial governors and other royal officials. One of the acts set up in Boston a board of customs officials to crack down on colonists who were escaping the law. The British also set up more courts. There, violators would be tried—once again without the right of trial by jury.

The Townshend Acts fitted nicely into the conspiracy theory. Until now, the governor's salary in some colonies had been paid by the colonial legislature. The colonists believed control over a governor's salary gave them a powerful weapon. They could sometimes influence the governor by threatening to hold up his salary. What would happen when the governor no longer depended on the legislature for his salary?

Furthermore, Boston had been the spearhead of the anti-Stamp Act movement. Was it coincidence that the tough new customs officials were being sent to Boston? When the Massachusetts legislature sent a letter to the other colonies opposing the Townshend Acts, the British ministry reacted strongly. The royal governor was ordered to dissolve the legislature, and soldiers were sent into Boston. Was there any longer a doubt, the colonists asked, why the British were stationing so many soldiers in North America?

"All confidence is ended. . . ." Writing to an English friend, a Boston minister named Andrew Eliot expressed the feelings of many Bostonians in 1768.

> To have a standing army! Good God! What can be worse to a people who have tasted the sweets of liberty! . . . There will never be harmony between Great Britain and her colonies that there has been. All confidence is ended, and the moment any blood is shed, all affection will cease. . . .
>
> Tamely to give up our rights and allow ourselves to be taxed at the will of people so far away, and to be under military government is to consent to be slaves.

Do you see any evidence of the conspiracy theory in the Reverend Andrew Eliot's statement?

Activities

1. **FILMS** *The Boston Massacre* and *The Boston Tea Party,* You Are There series (each 26 minutes, b&w; CBS). Both films are available for rental from Indiana University Audio-Visual Center, Bloomington, Ind. 47401.

2. **USING A CHART** Have your students create a wall chart listing the main provisions of the acts named in the Performance Objective and the reasons why each act led a step closer to the Revolution. Encourage students to read the acts in Commager's *Documents of American History*.

3. **RESEARCH/ORAL REPORT** Impress upon your students the fact that the American colonists did have some friends in Parliament. Assign several students to read about and report on William Pitt the Elder and his eloquent speech to Parliament calling for the repeal of the Stamp Act. Ask others to report on Edmund Burke's speech calling for conciliation with America (March 22, 1775).

4. **RESEARCH/ORAL REPORT** If you did not have the opportunity to do Activity 4 in Lesson 1, you might wish to consider that activity now.

Then assign some students to research Adam Smith's theory of laissez-faire and contrast this economic philosophy with mercantilism.

5. DISCUSSION After reviewing the extent that mercantilism held sway over the minds of British leaders, ask your students for their opinions: Were the British deliberately trying to wrong the Americans, or were they the victims of an erroneous economic theory? Encourage students to support their opinions with facts.

6. RESEARCH/CREATIVE WRITING A key event that helped bring on the Revolution was the incident in Boston on March 5, 1770. The British called it a riot; the Americans called it a massacre. Have a group of students research the details of this incident and then write a one-act play or skit portraying the events of that day.

Ask other students to write newspaper accounts of the incident, first as it might have appeared in a Boston newspaper and then as it might have appeared in a London paper. Discuss the relationship of perspective, and impress on students the difficulties involved in historical objectivity.

7. RESEARCH/ORAL REPORT Following the Boston Massacre, there was a trial of the British soldiers involved in the incident. Their defense lawyer was John Adams, who, although a Patriot, felt bound to defend the soldiers in the name of justice. Ask several students to investigate this trial and present the information in the form of an oral report. Or, if the students want to try a creative presentation, encourage them to act out a courtroom scene with John Adams, the British soldiers, and other characters who might have been present at the trial.

Rising opposition. The Townshend Acts stirred greater opposition in the colonies than ever before. Once again American merchants agreed not to import British goods. England's trade with New York dropped by seven eighths, and with Pennsylvania and New England by one half.

To produce some of the goods they needed, American women began to manufacture clothing at home. A record of what happened has been left us by Peter Oliver, a Bostonian who sided with the British.

> [The clergy] were also set to Work, to preach up Manufactures instead of the Gospel. They preached about it and about it; until the Women and Children, both within Doors and without, set their Spinning Wheels a whirling in defiance of *Great Britain*. The female Spinners kept on spinning for 6 days of the Week . . . they generally clothed the Parson and his Family with the Produce of their Labor. This was a new Species of Enthusiasm and might be justly termed the Enthusiasm of the Spinning Wheel.

Why would New England ministers have taken the side of protestors? Does that account by an American who supported the British give us an indication of how widespread and deep the protest was?

The Boston Massacre ". . . the moment any blood is shed, all affection will cease." Two years after the Reverend Andrew Eliot wrote those words, the tension between the Americans and the British soldiers resulted in bloodshed.

As might be expected, Boston was the scene. Brawls between the redcoats and civilians had been going on there and elsewhere for some time. On the night of March 5, 1770, an angry, shouting crowd began throwing snowballs at British sentries. When the crowd would not stop, the soldiers called for help. In the noise and confusion, the soldiers, acting in fear and without orders from

In 1772, the burning of the British customs ship *Gaspee* increased tension between Britain and the colonies. While chasing a smuggler, the ship ran aground in Narragansett Bay. A group of Americans boarded the stranded *Gaspee*, removed the crew, and burned the ship to the waterline.

their commander, opened fire. Five Americans were killed. Among them was Crispus Attucks, the first black man to die in the Revolution. The colonists' leaders were quick to call the episode—for propaganda purposes—the Boston Massacre. To many Americans, the Boston Massacre was further proof of the conspiracy they believed in.

The Daughters of Liberty. Tensions between Britain and America relaxed temporarily after that incident. Britain once again retreated from its tough policy. In 1770 Parliament repealed all the Townshend duties except the one on tea. The colonists, responding measure for measure, ended their boycott of all goods except tea.

Groups of women calling themselves the Daughters of Liberty were especially active in seeing to it that the tea boycott was observed. They operated in a number of the larger colonial cities. In Boston, this public notice appeared.

> The following Agreement has lately been come into by upwards of 300 Mistresses of Families in this Town; in which Number the Ladies of the highest Rank and Influence. . . .
>
> Boston, January 31, 1770
>
> . . . we join with the very respectable Body of Merchants and other Inhabitants of this Town . . . in their Resolutions, *totally* to abstain from the Use of TEA: And as the greatest Part of the Revenue arising [from the latest acts from England] is produced from the duty paid on Tea . . . We the Subscribers do strictly [agree] that we will totally abstain from the Use of [Tea] (Sickness excepted) not only in our respective Families; but that we will absolutely refuse it, if it should be offered to us upon any occasion whatsoever.

What do you suppose was the aim of publishing this agreement in the newspaper? Why was it important to note that the group included "Ladies of the highest Rank and Influence"? To answer that question, you might want to think back to what you read about "deference" in Unit 1.

Samuel Adams's role. With the repeal of the Townshend duties, and except for the boycott on tea, business returned to normal. From mid-1770 to 1773 things remained quiet. Many colonists thought the crisis had passed. But not Samuel Adams. A distant cousin of John Adams, Samuel Adams was a leader of the Sons of Liberty. He had played a major part in anti-British activities.

During the lull in the tensions with Britain, Adams wrote a series of newspaper articles to alert Americans to the dangers they still faced. This one appeared in the *Boston Gazette* in 1771.

> I believe that no people ever yet groaned under the heavy yoke of slavery except when they deserved it. . . . The truth is that all might be free if they valued freedom and defended it as they ought. . . .
>
> The liberties of our country, the freedom of our civil constitution, are worth defending at all risks. . . . It will bring an everlasting mark of disgrace on the present generation . . . if we should allow them to be wrested from us by violence without a struggle, or be cheated out of them by the tricks of false and designing men. At present we are in most danger of the latter. . . . Instead of sitting down satisfied with the efforts we have already made, *which is the wish of our enemies*, the necessity of the times, more than ever, calls for our utmost carefulness, deliberation, fortitude, and perseverance.

Background Information

2. BOYCOTT The term *boycott* comes from the name of Captain Charles Cunningham Boycott (1832–1897), an English land agent for the estates of Lord Erne in County Mayo, Ireland. Boycott evicted many of his employer's Irish tenants. Such harsh treatment aroused the hostility of the people living in the district. They refused to have anything to do with Boycott or his family and organized a conspiracy to prevent the family from making any purchases, even the necessities of life.

Background Information

3. THOMAS HUTCHINSON (1711–1780) The son of a prominent Boston family, Hutchinson entered Harvard College at the age of twelve, graduated in 1727, and received a master's degree three years later. Upon graduation he worked in his father's counting house, but in 1737 he entered public life as a member of the Boston board of selectmen and shortly was elected to the Massachusetts Bay General Court, or legislature.

In 1760, after George III became king, he was appointed chief justice of the Massachusetts colony. By 1763, Hutchinson was the most influential person in Massachusetts politics. He was opposed to both the Sugar Act and the Stamp Act on the grounds that they would injure both British and colonial trade, but he did not deny the right of Parliament to govern and tax the colonies as it saw fit. This attitude on his part so aroused the colonists that in 1765 a mob sacked and destroyed his Boston mansion. Hutchinson barely escaped with his life. The experience convinced him that a more strenuous policy rather than a more lenient policy was necessary to make the colonists recognize their subjection to Parliament. In 1773 his refusal to allow the tea ships to leave Boston Harbor until the tea was landed resulted in the now-famous Boston Tea Party. That was his last important executive act. In 1774 he was permitted to go to England. Although he was well received, Hutchinson remained homesick for New England until his death in 1780. He was buried in England.

Adams worked hard to keep anti-British sentiment alive. To do so, he hit upon a clever scheme. In each Massachusetts town, a committee was formed to keep other towns in the colony informed whenever the British violated American liberties. These committees were called Committees of Correspondence. Later the idea was extended so that the several colonies could keep in touch with one another in the same way. These "engines of revolution," as they were called, became the machinery for organizing revolution throughout the land.

The dispute over tea. When the British blundered with the Tea Act of 1773, the Committees of Correspondence were ready to do their work. The British tax on tea, you will remember, was the only one of the Townshend duties not repealed. Britain kept that duty to show that Parliament had the right to tax the Americans. Just as stubbornly, the colonists refused to buy British tea—to show that Britain did *not* have the right of taxation. They bought their tea from the Dutch instead and smuggled it into the colonies.

This tug of wills might have gone on for years had not a new situation come up. The British East India Company was an important trading company. It controlled all trade in tea between India and the rest of the British empire. The company was being hurt by the American boycott. Finding itself with tons of unsold tea on hand, the company appealed to the British government for help. Parliament responded with an act that gave the company a monopoly on the sale of tea in America.

Since the colonists were not buying tea from the British, that act would not in itself do much good. But Parliament also lowered the price of British tea. The new price, even after the hated tea tax was added, would be cheaper than that of the Dutch tea the colonists were smuggling. By offering bargain prices, the British hoped to get Americans to buy their tea—and, at the same time, pay the tax. The Tea Act also named certain pro-British merchants in America, like the sons of Governor Thomas Hutchinson, as the only ones who could handle the sale of the tea. That shut out the Whig merchants. (An American who objected to British control and supported colonial interests was often referred to as a Whig. Many Whigs belonged to the Sons of Liberty.)

Opposing the tea tax. The colonists would have no part of the offer. They were *not* going to pay that tea tax, no matter what. When British tea ships began arriving in America, the Committees of Correspondence alerted the local Sons of Liberty to prevent the ships from unloading. In Charleston, South Carolina, the tea was unloaded but was then placed under guard so that it could not be sold. At Portsmouth, New Hampshire, and at Philadelphia, Americans forced the tea ships to turn back.

How this was done can be seen in this letter. It is addressed to Captain Ayres of the ship *Polly*, bound from London to Philadelphia.

> Sir: We are informed that you have [unwisely] taken charge of a quantity of tea which has been sent out by the [East] India Company, under the auspices of the Ministry, as a trial of American virtue and [will].

Now, as your cargo, on your arrival here, will most assuredly bring you into hot water, and as you are perhaps a stranger to these parts, we have concluded to advise you of the present situation of affairs in Philadelphia, that . . . you may stop short in your dangerous errand, [protect] your ship against the rafts of combustible matter which may be set on fire and turned loose against [it]; and more than all this, that you may preserve your own person from the pitch and feathers that are prepared for you.

In the first place, we must tell you that the Pennsylvanians are, to a man, passionately fond of freedom, the birthright of Americans, and at all events are determined to enjoy it.

That they sincerely believe no power on the face of the earth has a right to tax them without their consent.

That, in their opinion, the tea in your custody is designed by the Ministry to enforce such a tax, which they will undoubtedly oppose, and in so doing, give you every possible obstruction.

The Sons of Liberty made their point. Captain Ayres decided not to land.

The Boston Tea Party. In Boston, Samuel Adams and the Sons of Liberty were determined to have a show of force over the tea tax. The result was the Boston Tea Party in December 1773. During a town meeting, citizens demanded that two tea ships that had entered the harbor be sent back to England. When Governor Hutchinson refused this demand, Bostonians disguised themselves as Mohawk Indians, boarded the vessels, and threw the trunks of tea into the harbor.

A few years earlier, an act like this might have shocked many colonists. But by 1773, attitudes had hardened. John

The Boston Tea Party is pictured on this block of four postage stamps, issued on its 200th anniversary in 1973. Outraged Patriots throw cases of the hated tea into the harbor.

Adams recorded his feelings in his diary the day after the event.

This is the most magnificent move of all. There is a dignity, a majesty . . . in this last effort of the patriots that I greatly admire. The people should never rise without doing something to be remembered, something notable and striking. This destruction of the tea is so bold, so daring, so firm, intrepid, and inflexible, and it must have such important and lasting consequences that I can't help considering it a turning point in history.

Adams then went on to justify this act. As you read his words, again look for evidence of the conspiracy theory. Note also how Adams presents the choices available. Were there any other choices possible?

The question is whether the destruction of this tea was necessary? I think it was, absolutely and indispensably. They could not send it back. The Governor, Admiral, and Comptroller would not permit it. . . . Then there was no alternative except to destroy it. To let it be landed would be giving

Background Information

4. MOHAWK INDIANS The Mohawks were a tribe of North American Indians and a member tribe of the League of the Iroquois. The Mohawks held dominion over the land from Lake Champlain to the headwaters of the Susquehanna and the Delaware. They were renowned above all the Indian nations for their skill as warriors and were feared wherever they went. The name *Mohawk* came from an Algonquian term meaning "man-eaters." During the French and Indian War, the Mohawks supported the British side. In 1779, General John Sullivan, under George Wasington's orders, took revenge on them by destroying their villages. Most of the Mohawks moved to reservations in Canada.

> up the principle of taxation by Parliamentary authority against which the Continent has struggled for 10 years . . . and subjecting ourselves and our posterity forever . . . to desolation and oppression, to poverty and servitude.

As Adams predicted, the Boston Tea Party did become a "turning point in history." Relations between Britain and America grew worse. In America, the Whigs hoped this act of defiance would cause Britain to soften its policy. Resistance had done so in the past. In Britain, however, public opinion went against the colonists. The king himself was furious. "The die is now cast," wrote George III. "The colonies must either submit or triumph."

The Intolerable Acts. To punish the Americans, Parliament in 1774 passed a number of new acts. They were called the Intolerable Acts by the Whigs. One was the Boston Port Act, which shut down the port until Bostonians paid for the tea they had destroyed. Another was the Massachusetts Government Act. This act took away many of that colony's rights of self-government. It also made a British military man, General Thomas Gage, the new governor of the colony of Massachusetts.

Two other acts, passed at about the same time, further angered the colonists. One was a new Quartering Act, which allowed royal governors to board troops in occupied buildings. Under that act, colonists could even be required to put up soldiers in their own homes. The second was the Quebec Act of 1774. This law turned over the area north of the Ohio River to the newly formed British province of Quebec. The law deprived several colonies of their land claims in the West.

To colonists all over America, these acts came as a shock. They were regarded as further proof that a conspiracy against the colonists' liberties did exist. Two of the acts seemed to place the colonies under military rule. And all of them punished the entire colony of Massachusetts for the acts of a small number of people.

Were not these measures, Americans asked, acts of tyranny? Did they not deprive citizens of Massachusetts of their "rights as Englishmen"?

The First Continental Congress. The colonists' answer to the Intolerable Acts was to call on delegates from all the colonies to meet in Philadelphia in September 1774. This meeting was the First Continental Congress.

Most of the delegates were men who had been resisting Britain for some time. From Massachusetts came the two Adamses, Samuel and John; from Pennsylvania, Joseph Galloway and John Dickinson. Virginia sent George Washington, Patrick Henry, and Richard Henry Lee. New York's James Duane and South Carolina's Christopher Gadsden were also there. If the Continental Congress had done nothing else, it was important for bringing together for the first time many of the men who, within their own colonies, had long been opposing Britain.

But the Congress did more. Like the Committees of Correspondence, it became another part of the machinery of revolution. Members voted for another boycott of British goods, called the Continental Association. They also called for

Virginia lawyer and orator Patrick Henry, shown here arguing a case in court, was a fiery leader of the Patriot cause. In 1775 he urged resistance to Britain in these now famous words: "I know not what course others may take; but as for me, give me liberty, or give me death!"

repeal of the hated Intolerable Acts. They spoke out strongly against taxation without representation. Finally, they asked that the colonial militias be strengthened. (The militia was the group upon which each colony depended for its defense. It was made up of the colony's able-bodied men, who served as part-time soldiers.) The militias were urged to get new members and to arm and train them. This last measure was just short of war.

Theories of empire. But few Americans were yet ready to break cleanly away from England. Indeed, what they said over and over was that they wanted only to enjoy the "rights of Englishmen." What they sought was a way to protect those rights against the attacks of the king's ministers. To do so, they proposed various theories of empire.

During the meeting of the Continental Congress, Joseph Galloway, who would side with England when the revolution began, proposed to create an American government within the colonies. There would be a president chosen by the king, and a grand council, or congress, chosen by the colonial assemblies. Each colony would still run its own affairs. The president and grand council would manage affairs among the colonies. Most important, Parliament could not

8. LISTENING FOR INFORMATION Even before the battle of Lexington, there were people in America who firmly believed the only way to remain free was to break away from the British empire. One of the most fiery of these Americans was Patrick Henry (see photograph), a lawyer from Virginia who had often spoken out in the Virginia House of Burgesses against what he termed "British tyranny." On March 23, 1775, he made his most famous speech. It was made in response to the British punishment of Massachusetts for the Boston Tea Party.

Melvyn Douglas gives a fine rendering of Patrick Henry's "Liberty or Death" speech. It is in the album "Great American Speeches" from Caedmon Records, Inc. (505 Eighth Ave., New York, N.Y. 10018). If this recording is not available to you, perhaps one of your students might enjoy reading Henry's speech aloud.

Answers to Review Questions

1. The American colonies shared language and cultural ties with England. The colonists enjoyed considerable self-government, the "rights of Englishmen," and trade advantages.

2. "Rights of Englishmen" included free speech, trial by jury, right to assembly peacefully, and the right to petition the government. Because of these "rights of Englishmen," Americans could not be taxed unless their representatives approved.

3. Trade advantages: The British government gave the colonists a monopoly on the sale in England of certain products, such as tobacco, and placed a heavy tax on those products from any place except America. Britain also paid the colonists to produce certain products, such as indigo, tar, and turpentine. Colonial shipping was protected by the British Navy against pirates and foreign navies.

Trade restrictions: Colonists were not allowed to sell certain items, such as tobacco, rice, indigo, and furs, to any country outside the British Empire. Goods purchased from another European nation had to pass through England first and were taxed. British law discouraged or prohibited the colonies from manufacturing certain goods.

4. Great Britain received Canada and most French possessions east of the Mississippi River. The Spanish territory of Florida also went to Great Britain. Spain received all French land west of the Mississippi.

5. Britain looked to the American colonies to help pay the huge war debt and the increased cost of defending and running the empire. America

make laws affecting the American colonies unless the grand council had approved of them. The plan was voted on by the Continental Congress, but it lost out by a single vote.

Shortly after the congress adjourned, John Adams put forward another theory of empire. The colonies, he said, were not really part of the British Kingdom. Therefore they were not subject to Parliament. In Adams's plan, each colony would be considered entirely independent and would make its own laws. Each would be tied to the empire, however, by allegiance to the King of England.

This later became known as the *dominion theory of empire.* During the nineteenth and twentieth centuries this theory became the basis for the British Commonwealth of Nations. Adams was proposing the exact relationship that Canada and Australia have to Great Britain today. But in the 1770s, the British were not willing to consider the idea.

By the beginning of 1775 it was plain that Britain and its American colonies could not agree on measures that would keep the empire intact. The scene was now set for the final break between the two. In the next chapter we shall see how that break came about.

CHECKUP

1. What did each of the following provide for: the Stamp Act? the Quartering Act? the Townshend Acts? the Intolerable Acts?
2. In what ways did the colonists react to these measures?
3. Describe two events in Boston that contributed to rising tensions.

Key Facts from Chapter 5

1. Before 1763, American colonists were content, for the most part, to be British subjects. The Americans enjoyed many rights and liberties as well as economic advantages.
2. After 1763, when Britain won control of Canada and the French-held territories to the Mississippi, the attitude of many Americans toward Britain gradually changed.
3. Britain believed the American colonies should pay a larger share for the expenses of the French and Indian War, and took various steps to accomplish this goal.
4. The American colonists regarded the British actions as attempts to rob them of their money, their property, and even their liberties.
5. The Boston Massacre in 1770 and the Boston Tea Party in 1773 inflamed the feelings of both the Americans and the British toward each other.
6. By the beginning of 1775 it was plain that Britain and the American colonies could not agree on measures to keep the empire intact.

★ REVIEWING THE CHAPTER ★

People, Places, and Events

Navigation Acts *P. 82*
French and Indian War *P. 85*
Stamp Act *P. 87*
Conspiracy theory *P. 88*
Stamp Act Congress *P. 90*
Declaratory Act *P. 90*
Quartering Act *P. 91*
Townshend Acts *P. 91*
Boston Massacre *P. 92*
Boston Tea Party *P. 95*
Intolerable Acts *P. 96*
First Continental Congress *P. 96*

Review Questions

1. Why were the American colonies generally content to be British subjects before 1763? *P. 81* Les. 1

2. Explain what is meant by the phrase "rights of Englishmen." *Pp. 81–82* Les. 1

3. As British subjects, what trade advantages did the colonists enjoy? What trade restrictions did the British impose on the colonists? *Pp. 82–83* Les. 1

4. Look at the maps on page 85 and describe how the peace treaty changed the face of North America. Les. 2

5. How did British policy change toward the colonies after the French and Indian War? Why? *P. 86* Les. 2

6. Why did Americans object so strongly to the Stamp Act? Why did the British repeal the act? *Pp. 86–87, 89–90* Les. 2

7. What was the role of Samuel Adams? P. 93 Les. 3

8. Describe the accomplishments of the First Continental Congress. *Pp. 96–97* Les. 3

9. Suppose you were a Patriot and your best friend were a Loyalist. (A Loyalist was one who sided with the British.) What arguments might you use to win him or her away from the Loyalist cause?

Chapter Test

*On a separate piece of paper, write **T** if the statement is true and **F** if the statement is false.*

1. Before 1763, there was little or no talk of the American colonies separating from England. T

2. Under the Navigation Acts, the colonies were expected to produce manufactured goods for the empire and to buy raw materials from England. F

3. After the French and Indian War, Great Britain gained the most territory by the peace treaty. T

4. The colonists thought that, by taxing them without their consent, Parliament was trying to take away their political rights. T

5. During the Boston Massacre, the French killed many inhabitants of that city. F

6. Samuel Adams warned the colonists not to revolt against British laws. F

7. Under the Intolerable Acts, British troops could be quartered in colonial homes. T

8. The First Continental Congress brought together many of the people who would, in time, lead the Revolution. T

9. By the time the Revolutionary War began, all American colonists were united in their opposition to British rule. F

10. Life in the New World had produced new desires and new points of views that led the colonists to demand the right to live their own lives in their own way. T

had contributed few soldiers and little money to the war effort, so Britain believed it only right that the colonies should pay their fair share to defend the newly expanded empire in North America.

6. Americans objected strongly to the Stamp Act because never before had Parliament placed a direct tax on the colonies. The colonists saw this tax as an attempt to take away their "rights as Englishmen."

The British repealed the Stamp Act because it was met by violence and by political and economic protests.

7. Samuel Adams, a leader of the Sons of Liberty, wrote a number of newspaper articles to alert the colonists to the British threat. He also was responsible for organizing the Committees of Correspondence.

8. The First Continental Congress brought together those people who would lead the Revolution. It supported the boycott of British goods, demanded the repeal of the Intolerable Acts, and suggested the strengthening of the colonial militias.

9. Some suggested arguments include: Our "rights as Englishmen are being violated by such things as the writs of assistance and taxation without representation; the increase in the number of British officials and troops in the colonies threatens our right to self-government; the new custom laws and higher duties imposed by the British interfere with our right to operate our businesses as we see fit.

Background Information

1. PICTURE Shown here is a detail of the Battle of Bunker Hill, painted by an unknown artist. The picture is owned by the National Gallery of Art in Washington, D.C.

The famous command, "Don't fire till you see the white of their eyes," is alleged to have been issued at this battle. Gunpowder was scarce, so Col. Prescott ordered the patriots to reserve fire and aim low. It is said that Israel Putnam passed on the command in these words: "Men, you are all marksmen—don't one of you fire until you see the white of their eyes."

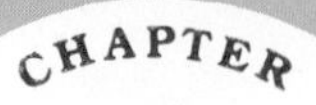

6

MOVING TOWARD INDEPENDENCE

LESSON 1

KING GEORGE III had his own theory of empire. He expressed it this way in 1774: "The New England governments are in a state of rebellion. . . . blows must decide whether they are to be subjects of this country or independent." For King George, there was no middle ground.

The Outbreak of War

Blows did indeed decide the fate of the empire. The first one came on April 19, 1775, when British soldiers and American militiamen faced each other for the first time. British General Thomas Gage learned that the Americans were secretly storing up guns and bullets in Concord, Massachusetts. On the night of April 18, he sent out soldiers from Boston to take them.

But even as the British marched through the darkness, American militiamen were arming to meet them. These Minutemen—so-called because they were to be ready at a minute's notice—had been warned by Paul Revere and others. Revere was a member of the Sons of Liberty. He and two companions had ridden along the country roads, awakening sleeping Patriots. (The Patriots were those Americans who resisted British control of the colonies.)

Shortly after dawn the British troops reached Lexington, on the road to Concord. There they found fifty Minutemen lined up across the village green. For a moment, the two groups—one large, uniformed, and well armed; the other small, in rough dress, and with fewer weapons—stood facing each other.

Two views of Lexington. Today we know that what happened next marked the beginning of the American War of Independence. Just what did take place? We have two conflicting accounts. For what we know about the exact details, we must rely upon them. One account was in a Massachusetts newspaper.

> At Lexington . . . a company of militia . . . mustered near the meeting house. The [British] troops came in sight of them just before sunrise; and running within a few rods of them, the Commanding Officer [Major Pitcairn] accosted the militia in words to this effect: "Disperse, you rebels—damn you, throw down your arms

After the Lexington encounter, a clash occurred at Concord. Why, do you think, did the poet Emerson describe the battle at North Bridge as "the shot heard round the world"?

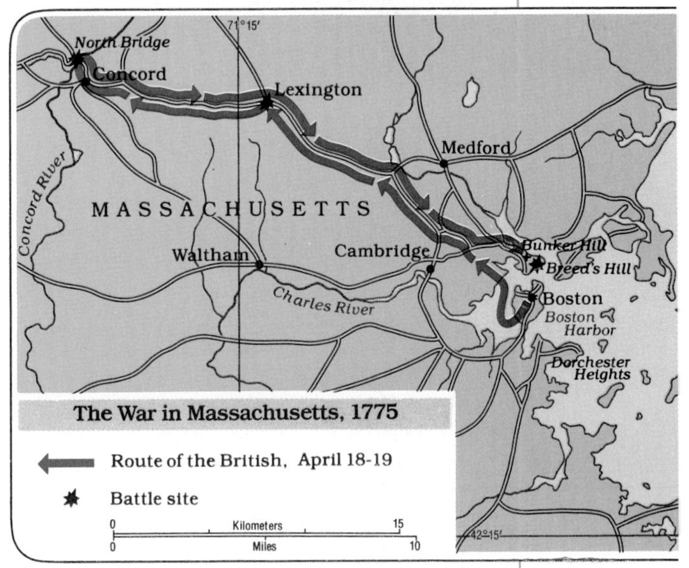

The War in Massachusetts, 1775

LESSON 1 *(2 days)*

Performance Objectives

1. To explain why newspaper accounts or eyewitness accounts of an historical event must be carefully analyzed before accepting them as facts.
2. To analyze, in writing or orally, the impact of propaganda writing, using Paine's *Common Sense*.

Famous People

Paul Revere, George Washington, Thomas Paine

Vocabulary

Lexington, Concord, Minutemen, Second Continental Congress, Fort Ticonderoga, Bunker Hill, *Common Sense*

Activities

1. ROLE-PLAYING Arrange for some of your students to create an attention-getting incident in the hall, the auditorium, etc. Then ask those who witnessed the incident to describe what happened. Have them analyze each other's eyewitness version to search for differences. Then ask them to account for those differences.

2. ANALYZING SOURCE MATERIAL The text mentions the fact that the ideas put forth by Thomas Paine were not unique unto him. Ask your students to read the excerpts from *Common Sense* and then to write in their own words the main ideas in those two passages. Does everyone agree on what Paine has actually said? If not, why not?

Next, have the students identify the words and phrases that especially attract their attention. Why did they pick out those particular words? Help them to recognize the emotion and drama conjured up by certain word combinations. Why did Paine use the words he did? Did he accomplish his purpose? Would he have been as successful if he had written in a more straight-forward, less colorful style?

Be sure students understand that propaganda writing is intended to influence people to believe certain ideas or take certain courses of action.

> and disperse"; upon which the troops huzzaed, and immediately one or two officers discharged their pistols, which were instanteously followed by the firing of four or five of the soldiers, and then there seemed to be a general discharge from the whole body. Eight of our men were killed and nine wounded. . . .
>
> In Lexington [the British] . . . also set fire to several other houses. . . . They pillaged almost every house they passed. . . . But the savage Barbarity exercised upon the bodies of our unfortunate brethren who fell is almost incredible. Not contented with shooting down the unarmed, aged, and infirm, they disregarded the cries of the wounded, killing them without mercy, and mangling their bodies in the most shocking manner.

The second account was printed in a British newspaper in London.

> Six companies of [British] light infantry . . . at Lexington found a body of the country people under arms, on a green close to the road. And upon the King's troops marching up to them, in order to inquire the reason for their being so assembled, they went off in great confusion. And several guns were fired upon the King's troops from behind a stone wall, and also from the meeting-house and other houses, by which one man was wounded, and Major Pitcairn's horse shot in two places. In consequence of this attack by the rebels, the troops returned the fire and killed several of them. . . .
>
> On the return of the troops from Concord, they [the rebels] . . . began to fire upon them from behind stone walls and houses, and kept up in that manner a scattering fire during the whole of their march of fifteen miles, by which means several were killed and wounded. And such was the cruelty and barbarity of the rebels that they scalped and cut off the ears of some of the wounded men who fell into their hands.

Newspaper accounts must often be used by the historian to discover what actually happened in any historic event. But their usefulness is limited. Do these two stories tell why? Do you suppose it at all likely that the first would have been written by a British soldier, and the second by an American?

Enter George Washington. The Second Continental Congress met in May 1775, fresh on the heels of this clash. It adopted as its own army the ill-organized force of New England militiamen that had now penned the British troops inside Boston. One of its main decisions was to choose George Washington as commander in chief of the army.

Washington was well equipped to handle the task because of his background, training, and personal qualities. The son of a well-to-do Virginia planter, he entered military service at the age of nineteen. He fought in the French and Indian War for five years, returning as Virginia's most celebrated hero. Following the war, he settled on his estate at Mount Vernon. There he gained valuable experience running a huge plantation. As a member of the Virginia legislature he took part in anti-British protests and helped train the Virginia militia.

Washington's abilities as a leader qualified him to become commander in chief. He had a cool head in an emergency and never lost his sense of dignity and bearing. His devotion to duty enabled him to carry on even during the darkest and most discouraging times of the war. And his strong will and

Continued on page 104

Fort Ticonderoga

At the time of the American Revolution, Fort Ticonderoga, in northern New York State, was regarded as the gateway to Canada. Lying at the foot of Lake Champlain, the fort was on the north-south military route that made use of Lake Champlain, Lake George, and the Hudson River. Built by the French in 1755, Fort Ticonderoga had been the scene of fighting during the French and Indian War.

At the outbreak of the Revolutionary War, a British force was occupying the fort. Soon after the events at Lexington and Concord, Americans made plans to take Ticonderoga. Two capable officers led the expedition. One was Benedict Arnold, who headed a force of Massachusetts militia. The other was Ethan Allen, leader of a rough-and-tumble group of Vermont men known as the Green Mountain Boys.

On the evening of May 9, 1775, the expedition reached Lake Champlain, across from Fort Ticonderoga. There were only a few boats available and only about eighty men were able to cross the lake during the night. But Arnold and Allen, determined to surprise the British, attacked at sunrise without waiting for the rest of their force. Although the main gate was locked, a small one was open. The Green Mountain Boys overpowered the sentries, and took the fort without the loss of a man.

Henry Knox, the commander of the Continental Army's artillery, had the idea of using the big guns from Fort Ticonderoga to drive the British army out of Boston. In December 1775, 43 cannon and 16 mortars were placed on sledges drawn by oxen and dragged for 300 miles (470 km) across Massachusetts. Once the Americans seized Dorchester Heights, most of Boston and its harbor would have been within range of Knox's artillery. The British, faced with this possibility, decided to get out of Boston and sailed with their army to Halifax, Nova Scotia.

Ethan Allen, waving his sword aloft, demands the instant surrender of Fort Ticonderoga from its surprised British commander.

3. ANALYZING A NEWSPAPER ARTICLE Have each student bring in a newspaper article that describes a recent happening, especially one that is controversial. Then ask each student to analyze the article for any indication of bias or subjectivity in reporting the details. What conclusions, if any, can be made about the author of each article? Request volunteers from the class to give a brief oral analysis of their articles and encourage other students to question or disagree if they have another opinion.

4. ANALYZING A PICTURE After students have read the caption, ask them to observe the picture and answer the following questions. **(a)** What characteristics did the artist attribute to Washington? **(b)** If you did not know anything about Washington as a leader, what impression of his leadership ability do you receive from this picture? **(c)** What techniques did the artist use to create that impression? (Washington is positioned in the center and riding a white horse; faces of the soldiers, flags lead one's eye toward Washington and emphasize his prominence; etc.)

5. LISTENING FOR INFORMATION Perhaps the best way to teach about revolutionary propaganda is to bring some examples into the classroom and have them read aloud. The following books are recommended: *Pamphlets of the American Revolution, 1750–1776* by Bernard Bailyn (Cambridge, Mass.: Harvard University Press, 1968); *The World Turned Upside Down: Prose and Poetry of the American Revolution,* edited by James H. Pickering (Port Washington, N.Y.: Kennikat Press, 1975); and *Trumpets Sounding: Propaganda Plays of the American Revolution,* edited by Norman Philbrick (New York: Benjamin Blom, 1972).

In analyzing any piece of propaganda, raise such questions as these: To whom was the propaganda directed? What explicit information did it give and how accurate was it? What implicit messages did it convey? What emotions was it likely to have aroused in a given audience at a given time?

Washington's taking command of the army was hardly as impressive as the artist has pictured it. It would be many months before the troops were as well trained and disciplined as shown here.

determination held the army together when others lost hope.

Bunker Hill. Before Washington took over his new command, however, an important battle had been fought. General Gage's troops in Boston were surprised when the Americans seized Breed's Hill in Charlestown. This hill, one of the many overlooking Boston, was located just below Bunker Hill, across the river from the city.

The British were determined to drive the untrained Americans from the commanding heights. On June 17, in what has become known as the battle of Bunker Hill, British troops charged the high ground three times before taking it. The Americans were finally forced to fall back after running out of gunpowder. The cost of this victory to the British was frightful. One eighth of all the British officers killed in the Revolutionary War died that day.

The battle had an electrifying effect on both sides. The Americans gained confidence in their fighting ability after they inflicted such heavy losses upon Britain's best soldiers. In England the great shedding of blood caused the government to become more determined to defeat and punish the colonists.

A reluctance to break away. In view of the fighting that had occurred by the end of 1775, you might find it surprising that most Americans still were not talking about breaking away from the British empire. They insisted, to be sure, that the old rules of empire were over. They maintained that there would have to be a new system, one that would protect their rights.

Yet at the same time most Americans hoped to find a way to remain within the empire. And they remained loyal to their king. It was not, they assured each other, George III who was responsible for Britain's harsh policies, but his evil ministers. Many still spoke of their affection for the king, and of their acceptance of the idea of monarchy.

Thomas Paine's pamphlet. Thomas Paine, a recent immigrant from England, destroyed whatever regard Americans still had for the king and monarchy. Early in 1776 he published a pamphlet called *Common Sense.* In harsh words he laid the blame for all that had happened directly at the door of the "royal brute of Britain," George III.

Paine urged Americans to stop fooling themselves that monarchy would ever bring a just government. Monarchy, said Paine, was an absurd form of government. One honest man, he wrote, was worth "all the crowned ruffians that ever lived." It was monarchy that was reducing the world to blood and ashes. Americans should abandon it forever and create a republican form of government. This meant throwing off completely all connection with Britain. Besides, added Paine, it was ridiculous that a continent—North America—should be ruled by an island—Britain. To those who still wanted to keep ties with Britain, Paine wrote:

> Men of passive tempers look somewhat lightly over the offenses of Great Britain, and still hoping for the best, are apt to call out, "Come, come, we shall be friends again in spite of this." But examine the passions and feelings of mankind . . . and then tell me whether you can hereafter love, honor and faithfully serve the power that has carried fire and sword into your land?

Paine followed this argument with a ringing defense of freedom.

> O, ye that love mankind! Ye that dare oppose not only the tyranny but the tyrant, stand forth! Every spot on the Old World is overrun with oppression. Freedom hath been hunted round the globe. Asia and Africa have long expelled her. Europe regards her like a stranger, and England has given her warning to depart. . . .
>
> But in America we have it in our power to begin the world over again. A situation similar to the present has not happened from the days of Noah until now. The birthday of a new world is at hand, and a race of men, perhaps as numerous as all Europe contains, are to receive their portion of freedom from the outcome of a few months.

Remember that Paine was writing to encourage reluctant Americans to break

6. CREATIVE WRITING Now that your students are familiar with propaganda writing, assign a topic, or allow them to choose their own, and request that they try their hands at writing propaganda pieces. The writing might take the form of an essay, short play, letter, poem, poster, or song.

7. RESEARCH/ROLE-PLAYING Assign your students to find out as much as possible about Thomas Paine and George III. Then give them time to create and act out an imaginary conversation between Paine and George III, capturing the personalities and beliefs of each.

8. LISTENING FOR INFORMATION You might wish to read to the class "Young Mackenzie Sees the World" from *The Way Our People Lived: An Intimate American History* by William E. Woodward (New York: Washington Square Press, 1968). This story, and the others in this remarkable paperback, push aside the great events of American history and give students an inside look at how the common, ordinary people lived at the times of those great events.

9. RESEARCH/ORAL REPORTS You may wish to have students report in more detail about the battles of Lexington, Concord, and Bunker Hill. For a readable and accurate account of those battles and all the other military engagements of the War of Independence, see *The War of the Revolution* by Christopher Ward (New York: Macmillan Company, 1952).

10. **RESEARCH/ORAL REPORT** As some of your students may know, Paul Revere was not the only messenger of alarm. William Dawes also set out to warn the countryside. When Revere and Dawes were both stopped by the British, Samuel Prescott was able to ride on and continue to spread the warning. Assign a student to find out more about these men and report back to the class. Perhaps you would want another student to introduce the report by reading Longfellow's poem, "Paul Revere's Ride."

with Britain and to set up a republic. Does this help you understand why he wrote that freedom will be "the outcome of a few months"?

The impact of *Common Sense.* In our day, when we are bombarded with arguments and information from a dozen different directions by television, radio, newspapers, movies, and magazines, it is hard to grasp the impact that this one little pamphlet had. In all, some 300,000 copies were sold. That would be comparable to 24 million today.

For every copy sold, there were probably several readers. In fact, a biographer of Paine estimated that one in every two Americans read it. Thomas Jefferson, John Adams, Samuel Adams, and several other colonial leaders had recently been putting forward the same ideas that Paine expressed. But none presented them with such force and passion as Paine. People talked about *Common Sense* on street corners and in taverns and inns. Paine may well have doubled the number of Americans who favored independence.

In *Common Sense,* Thomas Paine urged independence for the colonies. In the *Crisis* papers, he called upon all Americans to support wholeheartedly the Revolutionary cause.

National Portrait Gallery, London

CHECKUP

1. Where did the first clash between American and British troops take place? Why?
2. How did American and British newspaper accounts of the encounter differ?
3. What views did Thomas Paine put forth in *Common Sense?* What effect did this pamphlet have?

LESSON 2

Independence Is Declared

By the spring of 1776, the Second Continental Congress was moving boldly toward independence. In March, it gave *privateers* permission to attack British shipping. Privateers were privately owned vessels that were authorized by the government to be used as naval ships and to capture ships of other nations. Privateering was a form of legalized piracy. That meant that Congress was now authorizing acts of war against Britain at sea as well as on land. In May, Congress sent word to the assembly of each colony that it should write a new *state* constitution and set up a state government. In other words, each of the colonies was urged to be a colony no more.

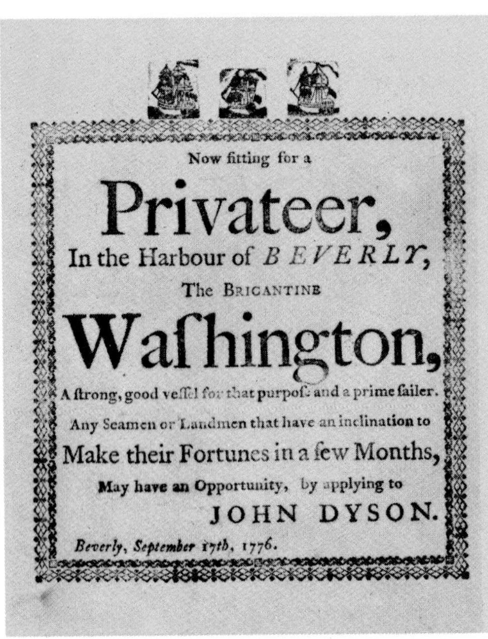

As a result of this broadside, the *Washington* quickly signed a crew. Half the proceeds from the sale of captured ships and cargoes usually went to the privateer's owner. The other half was shared by the ship's officers and crew.

By this time the colonies as a whole had practically made their break with Britain. All that remained was to declare it before the rest of the world. A small committee was appointed by the Second Continental Congress to write a declaration of independence. The committee turned over the task to one of its members, a quiet thirty-three-year-old Virginia lawyer and planter named Thomas Jefferson.

Explaining the Revolution. The rebellion of colonies was an extraordinary act, one that had not occurred before in modern times. Therefore, one of Jefferson's main purposes was to explain and justify the act in the eyes of the world.

He did this in two ways. One was to present a theory of government and society that explained when revolution is justified. Jefferson spelled out the theory in the first part of the declaration. There he made these five points:

- All men are created equal.
- People have a right to life, liberty, and the pursuit of happiness.
- The reason government was created in the first place was to protect people in the enjoyment of those rights.
- Government has to be based on the consent of the governed.
- When a government no longer follows the wishes of its people and becomes tyrannical, the people have a right to get rid of it and to set up a new one.

These ideas were not new when Jefferson set them down. Indeed, Jefferson calls them "truths" that are "self-evident"—that is, so obvious that they need no proof. People had long talked about these ideas. Political theorists and philosophers had written books about them for nearly a hundred years. But nowhere in the world had anyone dared actually to put them into practice. No people had fought a revolution on these principles or created a new government based on them.

The second means by which Jefferson explained and justified the American Revolution was to list the many ways the colonists believed the British had wronged them. Following Tom Paine's lead, Jefferson blamed all the wrongs on King George III rather than on his ministers or on Parliament. That list of wrongs takes up most of the Declaration of Independence, as you can see on the following pages.

LESSON 2 *(2 to 3 days)*

Performance Objectives

1. To list the four sections of the Declaration and identify the purpose of each. **2.** To list ten specific complaints that the colonists had against the King of England. **3.** To analyze the Declaration in terms of language and style to see how they were used to support the content and purposes of the document. **4.** To recognize the importance of the Declaration both as a justification for the American Revolution and as a model for other revolutionary movements.

Vocabulary

Written by one of the most literate people of the eighteenth century, the Declaration presents rather severe language problems for today's students. You may wish to make copies of a list of words (with their meanings) that you think your students will have trouble understanding. Or the students could do this as one of their first activities.

You may wish to emphasize the following terms: political bands, laws of nature, unalienable rights, tyranny, petitioned for redress

Background Information

1. THE DECLARATION OF INDEPENDENCE Richard Henry Lee, the leader of the Virginia delegation, would have been the natural choice of the Continental Congress to write the Declaration. But Lee wanted to go home early, so Jefferson was selected. Though Lee was a better orator, Jefferson was a better writer. Some say that if Benjamin Franklin had written the Declaration it would have contained many puns and jokes. Jefferson wrote the Declaration in a boarding house, where he had a second-floor room, at the southwest corner of Market and Seventh Streets in Philadelphia. The original draft, which contains numerous misspellings and scratch-outs, still exists.

2. "ALL MEN ARE CREATED EQUAL" In 1776, that phrase sounded much more inclusive than it was. It did mean men, but only those who were white, the efforts of Crispus Attucks, Salem Poor, and Peter Salem notwithstanding. Women were not even considered, as Abigail Adams wrote to her husband, John, then in the Continental Congress: "I cannot say, that I think you are very generous to the ladies; for, whilst you are proclaiming peace and good-will to men, emancipating all nations, you insist upon retaining an absolute power over wives."

IN CONGRESS, JULY 4, 1776

The Declaration of Independence

☆ ☆ ☆ ☆ ☆ ☆ ☆ ☆ ☆ ☆ ☆ ☆ ☆

When, in the course of human events, it becomes necessary for one people to dissolve the political bands which have connected them with another, and to assume, among the powers of the earth, the separate and equal station to which the laws of nature and nature's God entitle them, a decent respect to the opinions of mankind requires that they should declare the causes which impel them to the separation.

We hold these truths to be self-evident; that all men are created equal, that they are endowed by their Creator with certain unalienable rights, that among these are life, liberty, and the pursuit of happiness. That to secure these rights, governments are instituted among men, deriving their just powers from the consent of the governed; that whenever any form of government becomes destructive of these ends, it is the right of the people to alter or to abolish it, and to institute new government, laying its foundation on such principles, and organizing its powers in such form, as to them shall seem most likely to effect their safety and happiness. Prudence, indeed, will dictate that governments long established should not be changed for light and transient causes; and accordingly all experience hath shown that mankind are more disposed to suffer while evils are sufferable, than to right themselves by abolishing the forms to which they are accustomed. But when a long train of abuses and usurpations, pursuing invariably the same object, evinces a design to reduce them under absolute despotism, it is their right, it is their duty, to throw off such government, and to provide new guards for their future security.

Such has been the patient sufferance of these colonies; and such is now the necessity which constrains them to alter their former systems of government. The history of the present king of Great Britain is a history of repeated injuries and usurpations, all having in direct object the establishment of an absolute tyranny over these states. To prove this, let facts be submitted to a candid world.

He has refused his assent to laws the most wholesome and necessary for the public good.

He has forbidden his governors to pass laws of immediate and pressing importance, unless suspended in their operation till his assent should be obtained; and when so suspended, he has utterly neglected to attend to them.

He has refused to pass other laws for the accommodation of large districts of people, unless those people would relinquish the right of representation in the legislature, a right inestimable to them, and formidable to tyrants only.

He has called together legislative bodies at places unusual, uncomfortable, and distant from the depository of their

Activities

1. ANALYZING SOURCE MATERIAL Divide the class into four groups, and assign each group one of the following sections of the Declaration to work on. **(a)** Page 108 to top of page 109, from "When in the course" to "for their future security." **(b)** Middle of page 109 to middle of page 111, from "Such has been" to "of all ages, sexes, and conditions." **(c)** Middle of page 111 to top of page 112, from "In every stage" to "in peace, friends." **(d)** Page 112, from "We, therefore, the" to "our sacred honor." Have each group read the assigned section carefully and decide on a title that tells what the section is about. List the titles on the chalkboard for the class to copy. The titles should be similar to these: **(a)** Rationale for Declaration, and the purposes of government; **(b)** Complaints against the king; **(c)** Review of attempts to settle problems; **(d)** Declaration of freedom and independence.

2. ANALYZING LANGUAGE This activity may be done in the groupings used for Activity 1 or by the class as a whole. Have each group or student look at the second section, concerning complaints against the king, and make up a list of the ten most serious charges. Have students notice that the more serious charges were listed at the end. Ask: Why would the charges be arranged in this kind of order?

Then have students analyze the first four "He" statements, on Page 109, and compare the language with that used in the last four "He" statements, on page 111. In the latter passages, have students pick out the words that give the tone of the passages—words such as "death, desolation, and tyranny," "cruelty and perfidy," "executioners," and "savages." In the first passages, the key words are much less inflamatory—words such as "refused," "forbidden," "unusual, uncomfortable," and "fatiguing." You might mention that, at that time, the document would be listened to as much as, or more than, it would be read silently, so public speakers could present this section almost like a musical piece, building from a calm, quiet, presentation of grievances to a resounding crescendo of accusations. Students might like to try reading parts of this section as if they were reading it to Washington's army or another partisan group.

Then have the class study the other sections of the document to determine their tone. Point out the length of the sentences and their complexity. Have students try to read some of the long sentences in the same dramatic manner used for the complaints. Students should soon see that these sentences are wordy for a purpose: they make radical, risky ideas sound logical, rational, and almost ordinary.

Have students rewrite the first section ("When in the course" to "for their future security") in brief, concise, and blunt language; for example, "When you're going to revolt, you ought to tell people why." Ask: Do the different styles change people's reactions to the material? Why?

public records, for the sole purpose of fatiguing them into compliance with his measures.

He has dissolved representative houses repeatedly, for opposing, with manly firmness, his invasions on the rights of the people.

He has refused, for a long time after such dissolutions, to cause others to be elected; whereby the legislative powers, incapable of annihilation, have returned to the people at large for their exercise; the state remaining, in the meantime, exposed to all the dangers of invasion from without and convulsions within.

He has endeavored to prevent the population of these states; for that purpose obstructing the laws for the naturalization of foreigners, refusing to pass others to encourage their migrations hither, and raising the conditions of new appropriations of lands.

He has obstructed the administration of justice, by refusing his assent to laws for establishing judiciary powers.

He has made judges dependent on his will alone for the tenure of their offices, and the amount and payment of their salaries.

He has erected a multitude of new offices, and sent hither swarms of officers to harass our people and eat out their substance.

He has kept among us, in times of peace, standing armies, without the consent of our legislatures.

He has affected to render the military independent of, and superior to, the civil power.

He has combined with others to subject us to a jurisdiction foreign to our constitution and unacknowledged by our laws, giving his assent to their acts of pretended legislation:

For quartering large bodies of armed troops among us;

For protecting them, by a mock trial, from punishment for any murders which they should commit on the inhabitants of these states;

For cutting off our trade with all parts of the world;

For imposing taxes on us without our consent;

For depriving us, in many cases, of the benefits of trial by jury;

For transporting us beyond seas, to be tried for pretended offenses;

For abolishing the free system of English laws in a neighboring province, establishing therein an arbitrary government, and enlarging its boundaries, so as to render it at once an example and fit instrument for introducing the same absolute rule into these colonies;

For taking away our charters, abolishing our most valuable laws, and altering fundamentally the forms of our governments;

For suspending our own legislatures, and declaring themselves invested with power to legislate for us in all cases whatsoever.

He has abdicated government here, by declaring us out of his protection and waging war against us.

He has plundered our seas, ravaged our coasts, burned our towns, and destroyed the lives of our people.

He is at this time transporting large armies of foreign mercenaries to complete the works of death, desolation, and tyranny already begun with circumstances of cruelty and perfidy scarcely paralleled in the most barbarous ages, and totally unworthy the head of a civilized nation.

He has constrained our fellow-citizens, taken captive on the high seas, to bear arms against their country, to become the executioners of their friends and brethren, or to fall themselves by their hands.

He has excited domestic insurrection among us, and has endeavored to bring on the inhabitants of our frontiers, the merciless Indian savages, whose known rule of warfare is an undistinguished destruction of all ages, sexes, and conditions.

In every stage of these oppressions we have petitioned for redress in the most humble terms; our repeated petitions have been answered only by repeated injury. A prince whose character is thus marked by every act which may define a tyrant is unfit to be the ruler of a free people.

Nor have we been wanting in attentions to our British brethren. We have warned them, from time to time, of attempts by their legislature to extend an unwarrantable jurisdiction over us. We have reminded them of the circumstances of our emigration and settlement here. We have appealed to their native justice and magnanimity; and we have conjured them, by the ties of our common kindred, to disavow these usurpations, which would inevitably interrupt our connections and correspondence. They, too, have been

Here are some other points that you might mention to your students concerning the language of the Declaration. The word *revolution* is not used at all, probably because it implies breaking away from a legally established government. The word *insurrection* is used, but it is used to describe the king's actions, not the colonists' actions. Also, note that the colonies do not declare war. In fact, they claim that the *king* is waging war against *them.*

3. DISCUSSION Ask the class to identify various groups of people who would hear or read the Declaration. Have them try to decide what parts of the document the groups would like or dislike. The groups should include colonists (those who already favored the war, those opposed, and those in the very important undecided group), British citizens and government officials, and people and governments of other foreign countries. The discussion should touch on the fact that the writers were trying to win support at home and in foreign countries. (Colonists hoped that the Declaration would generate enough popular pressure in England to cause Parliament to abandon the war.) The colonists also wanted to rally their supporters, so they had to seem fearless and resolved, but not radical and unstable.

4. RESEARCH/ORAL OR WRITTEN REPORT The Declaration of Independence has served as a model for many varying movements. Have several students investigate the revolutions in South America as inspired by the writings of Antonio de Narino and Francisco Miranda; the writings of the Marquis de Mirabeau in the French Revolution; and the Seneca Falls Women's Rights Convention, which wrote a paraphrased version demanding women's rights.

5. RESEARCH/ORAL OR WRITTEN REPORT The ideas put forth in the Declaration of Independence did not occur in a vacuum. They had been suggested by political philosophers for many years. Have some students read and report on the writings of John Locke *(Two Treatises on Government)* and Jean-Jacques Rousseau *(The Social Contract)*. The famous phrase, "life, liberty and pursuit . . ." can be found almost word for word in Locke's work. It is interesting and thought provoking to note that Rousseau's ideas were also used as a basis for socialist and communist philosophies.

deaf to the voice of justice and consanguinity. We must, therefore, acquiesce in the necessity which denounces our separation, and hold them, as we hold the rest of mankind, enemies in war; in peace, friends.

We, therefore, the representatives of the United States of America, in General Congress assembled, appealing to the Supreme Judge of the world for the rectitude of our intentions, do, in the name and by the authority of the good people of these colonies, solemnly publish and declare that these United Colonies are, and of right ought to be, free and independent states; that they are absolved from all allegiance to the British crown, and that all political connection between them and the state of Great Britain is, and ought to be, totally dissolved; and that, as free and independent states, they have full power to levy war, conclude peace, contract alliances, establish commerce, and do all other acts and things which independent states may of right do. And, for the support of this declaration, with a firm reliance on the protection of Divine Providence, we mutually pledge to each other our lives, our fortunes, and our sacred honor.

John Hancock, President
(MASSACHUSETTS)

NEW HAMPSHIRE
Josiah Bartlett
William Whipple
Matthew Thornton

MASSACHUSETTS
John Adams
Samuel Adams
Robert Treat Paine
Elbridge Gerry

NEW YORK
William Floyd
Philip Livingston
Francis Lewis
Lewis Morris

RHODE ISLAND
Stephen Hopkins
William Ellery

NEW JERSEY
Richard Stockton
John Witherspoon
Francis Hopkinson
John Hart
Abraham Clark

PENNSYLVANIA
Robert Morris
Benjamin Rush
Benjamin Franklin
John Morton
George Clymer
James Smith
George Taylor
James Wilson
George Ross

DELAWARE
Caesar Rodney
George Read
Thomas McKean

MARYLAND
Samuel Chase
William Paca
Thomas Stone
Charles Carroll of Carrollton

VIRGINIA
George Wythe
Richard Henry Lee
Thomas Jefferson
Benjamin Harrison
Thomas Nelson, Jr.
Francis Lightfoot Lee
Carter Braxton

NORTH CAROLINA
William Hooper
Joseph Hewes
John Penn

SOUTH CAROLINA
Edward Rutledge
Thomas Heyward, Jr.
Thomas Lynch, Jr.
Arthur Middleton

CONNECTICUT
Roger Sherman
Samuel Huntington
William Williams
Oliver Wolcott

GEORGIA
Button Gwinnett
Lyman Hall
George Walton

A nation is born. Once Jefferson's task was completed, Congress prepared to act. On July 2, Congress voted in favor of independence. On July 4, it adopted Jefferson's Declaration of Independence.

The deed was done. At the end of the declaration, Jefferson wrote that, to the cause of American independence, "we mutually pledge to each other our lives, our fortunes, and our sacred honor." Those were not empty words to the fifty-six men who signed the document. Each well knew what would happen if the rebellion did not succeed. None summed up the need for unity better than Benjamin Franklin. "Gentlemen," he remarked, "we must all hang together, else we shall all hang separately."

CHECKUP

1. Who wrote the text of the Declaration of Independence?
2. According to the Declaration of Independence, when is revolution justified?
3. When was the Declaration of Independence adopted?

LESSON 3

The Opposing Sides

In the chapter before this you considered whether some events and outcomes are bound to happen. Was it inevitable that American colonists would want to become independent of Great Britain? You noted then the difficulties in answering such questions for sure.

We can say for certain, however, that it was *not* inevitable that the Americans would win the war after independence had been declared. This is what General Washington wrote at the end of the war.

> It will not be believed that such a force as Great Britain has employed for eight years in this country could be baffled . . . by numbers infinitely less, composed of men oftentimes half starved; always in rags, without pay and experiencing at times, every species of distress which human nature is capable of undergoing.

What were the disadvantages of the American side, according to Washington? Do Washington's remarks help you understand why many people at the start of the war thought the American rebels could not win it?

Comparing the armed forces. You need only look at the military picture at the start of the war to understand Washington's statement. In the fall of 1775, Britain's plans called for enlarging its army to 55,000 soldiers. More were added as the war went on. At the same time, Britain added 12,000 more sailors to its already large navy.

The British army also included *mercenaries*—that is, hired soldiers from other countries. The use of such soldiers was a common practice in those days. Over the course of the war, Britain hired 30,000 German troops. Most of them were from the German province of Hesse and were called Hessians. Some 50,000 Loyalists—Americans who remained loyal to King George III—took up arms for Britain. Most of the strong Indian tribes could also be counted upon to support the British. Furthermore, the British army was well trained and highly disciplined.

America's military power at the start of the war was, by comparison, pitiful. There was no army in existence. Washington had to build one from scratch. Even after an army was recruited, it was outnumbered by the

LESSON 3 (*2 Days*)

Performance Objectives

1. To list at least three advantages and five disadvantages that the Americans had in fighting for their independence. **2.** To describe orally or in writing the role of women in the War of Independence.

Vocabulary

Mercenaries, militia, Continental Army

Activities

1. MUSIC You may wish to use one of the following records with your class. "The Fifes and Drums Band of Music" from Colonial Williamsburg (Box C, Williamsburg, Va. 23185); "Music of the American Revolution" recorded by the Nathan Hale Ancient Fifes and Drums (Box 1776, Coventry, Conn. 06238); "Ballads of the American Revolution," a 2-record album from Folkways Records and Service Corp. (165 W. 46th St., New York, N.Y. 10036); "Oscar Brand's Songs of '76: A Folk Singer's History of the Revolution," a 4-record album from Miller-Brody Productions, Inc. (342 Madison Ave., New York, N.Y. 10017). The latter album is especially interesting because many of the songs reflect little-known episodes of the Revolution as well as the more important events. In addition, the songs present both the Tory and the Patriot point of view.

2. FILM PROJECT Fifth-grade students created a prize-winning super-8mm film about the American Revolution. Perhaps your students might enjoy doing a similar project.
Suggestion: Film an interview with George Washington as if it were a pregame analysis of the strengths and weaknesses of his army and of the British force.

3. THOUGHT PROVOKER You may wish to use the following quotation as a means of reviewing with your students what they know and understand about the American Revolution. Ask them whether they agree or disagree with the quotation. Be sure they support their opinions with facts they have learned.

Crane Brinton, in *Anatomy of Revolution,* writes: "The school of circumstances regards revolutions as a wild and natural growth, its seeds sown among tyranny and corruption, its development wholly determined by forces outside itself or at any rate outside human planning; the school of plot regards revolutions as a forced and artificial growth, its seeds carefully planted in soil worked over and fertilized by the gardener-revolutionists, mysteriously brought to maturity by these same gardeners against the forces of nature. Actually, we must reject both extremes, for they are nonsense, and hold that revolutions do grow from seeds sown by men who want change, and that these men do a lot of skillful gardening; but that the gardeners are not working against Nature, but rather in soil and in a climate propitious to their work; and that the final fruits represent a collaboration between men and Nature."

British, five to one. It was made up not of professional soldiers but of farmers, artisans, and merchants—men who were military amateurs.

On the high seas, the British navy was the finest in the world. British naval ships outnumbered American ships by a hundred to one. American naval vessels were often forced to sail shorthanded or with untrained crews.

Other British advantages. Great Britain's population was far greater than America's. There were about 9 million people living in Britain in 1775 compared with about 2.7 million Americans in the rebelling colonies. The latter included about 500,000 black slaves and a half-million Loyalists who would not or could not fight for the American cause. As a strong military power, Britain also had large amounts of war goods on hand. Britain was also far wealthier than the colonies. That meant its army could be well equipped. By comparison, the American army lacked gunpowder, food, and uniforms.

There was another reason for the difference in the equipment of the two armies. The British government had long since established its right to tax its people. During the war, then, it could raise the money it needed. But the Americans had started this rebellion largely over the issue of taxes. They were not ready to give the American Congress the same power to tax that they had denied to the British Parliament.

Without the power to tax, Congress had to ask the states to put up money and supplies. The state governments did so, but not in large enough amounts. Congress had to pay for supplies by borrowing money from the public, and by seeking loans and gifts from foreign countries. It also printed paper money. That led to other problems, as you will read in the next chapter.

What all this meant for America's war effort is summed up in this letter from General Washington to Congress early in the conflict.

> . . . my situation is inexpressibly distressing, to see the winter fast approaching upon a naked army, the time of their services within a few weeks of expiring, and not provision yet made for such important events. Added to this, the military chest is totally exhausted; the paymaster has not a single dollar in hand; the commissary-general [the officer in charge of food and daily supplies] assures me he has strained his credit to the utmost for the subsistence of the army. The quarter-master general [the officer in charge of quarters, clothing, and transportation] is precisely in the same situation; and the greater part of the army are in a state not far from mutiny (because they have not received what they were promised) . . . if the evil is not immediately remedied . . . the army must absolutely break up.

All through the war years, General Washington wrote letters like that to Congress.

The geographical factor. Against those British advantages, Americans had only a few. The greatest American advantage was geography. The supply line of the British army stretched 3,000 miles across the Atlantic. In many campaigns, troop movements were delayed because supplies were slow in arriving. Also, it took nearly six months to replace a British soldier who was killed or wounded in action. That was likely to

Continued on page 116

Paul Revere, Craftsman

To most Americans today, Paul Revere is known best as the rider on horseback who roused the countryside around Lexington with the cry, "The British are coming." But in his own time, he was better known as a craftsman. A genius at working with metals, Revere was a skilled silversmith, engraver, inventor, and even a maker of dental plates.

Revere fashioned many silver pieces for use in homes. The wide range of his household articles was astonishing. He made teapots, sugar bowls, salt shakers, trays, plates, and candlesticks.

In his shop in Boston, Revere used the tools of his trade to produce things of great beauty that, at the same time, expressed his political ideas. When ninety-two Patriots defied the Massachusetts governor before the Revolution, Revere made a handsome silver punch bowl honoring "the Immortal 92." After the Boston Massacre, Revere engraved a drawing showing British soldiers firing into a group of unarmed Boston citizens. He designed the first official seal used by the united American colonies as they waged their struggle for independence.

Revere's career mirrored that of the rising new nation. During the Revolutionary War, Revere used his skill to cast cannon for the Continental Army. After peace came, he turned to casting church bells. When the United States started building a navy to protect its trading vessels in the 1790s, Revere began rolling copper sheets to cover the bottom of warships. Later he began manufacturing copper boilers for the steamboats that Robert Fulton was sailing up the Hudson River. Revere also produced the sheet copper to cover the dome of the State House in Boston.

Revere typified the colonial craftworker of his day. Most Americans wanted to become farmers, and few entered the crafts and trades. The shortage of skilled artisans meant there could be little specialization. Anyone working with metal, like Revere, was called on to do many different things. Yet Revere's pride in anything he made was such that, no matter what he turned his hand to, it became a work of art.

This portrait of Paul Revere was painted in 1769 by the artist John Singleton Copley.

Museum of Fine Arts, Boston

4. DISCUSSION William Pitt, when looking at a battle map of the colonies, remarked, "You cannot conquer a map." Edmund Burke, in a statement about the conflict in the colonies, said, "Between the issuance of an order and its execution—months pass and seas roll." Both were alluding to the geographical hardships faced by the British in America. Ask your students to list and discuss the geographical advantages possessed by the Americans. In your discussion, have a wall map or other large map available and refer to it often.

5. RESEARCH/ORAL REPORT To give students a deeper understanding of the participation of colonial women in the protest movements leading up to the war and in the war itself, have a group of students present reports on the varied contributions of women. The following books offer a wealth of information on the role of women in American society: *Woman in America* by Edith Altbach (New York: D. C. Heath, 1974); *Herstory: A Woman's View of American History* by June Sochen (New York: Alfred Publications, 1974); and *Weathering the Storm: Women of the American Revolution* by Elizabeth Evans (New York: Scribner, 1975).

6. RESEARCH/ORAL OR WRITTEN REPORT In *The American Revolution Considered as a Social Movement* (Princeton, N.J.: Princeton University Press, 1940), J. Franklin Jameson wrote: "Let us not forget that a large part of the [Americans] heroism had to be expended in overcoming difficulties which need not have existed but for the slackness and indifference of their fellows."

Alistair Cooke, an English journalist, said of the Americans: "They were a frightened and divided body of men—divided between genuine revolutionaries and sunshine patriots, between dedicated colonial statesmen and secret Loyalists and a collection of money grubbers selling arms or commissions."

Have some of your more able students investigate the extent of participation in the war effort by Americans. Be sure to include women in this investigation. Ask students to pay particular attention to the various attitudes held by the colonists.

make a British general think twice before committing his troops to battle.

The vast expanse of the American continent gave the Americans endless space into which they could retreat. Thomas Paine likened the strategy that this space allowed to a game of checkers. "We can move out of *one* square to let you come in," he taunted a British general, "in order that we may afterwards take two or three for one; and as we can always keep a double corner for ourselves, we can always prevent a total defeat."

Fighting on familiar ground, with the feeling that they were protecting their families and homes, was also an advantage to the Americans. And most Americans were used to handling firearms.

Adding up the advantages and disadvantages of each side, the balance in 1776 seemed much in Britain's favor. Wars, however, are won not on the balance sheet but on the field of battle. That is where the great testing of American will and skill was to take place.

The militia. The American colonies had long opposed having standing armies in their midst in peacetime. Instead they relied on the local militia for their defense. The militia was made up of civilians who served as part-time soldiers.

During the Revolutionary War, the states continued to depend on the militia to fight many of the battles in their own areas. A total of about 165,000 militiamen saw service during the war.

The record of the militia members as fighters was mixed. In some situations, they proved to be useful. They could be called together quickly to meet a sudden attack nearby. Even if the British did take over an area, the militia made it hard for them to hold it. Once the British army moved on, it could control the territory only by leaving behind a large number of soldiers to guard against the local militia.

But the militia had serious weaknesses as a strong fighting force. Most militia members were short-term soldiers. They signed up for only three, six, or nine months under their state laws. And they didn't always stay that long. Once the British moved on to other states and the homes of the militia members were safe, the militia usually disbanded.

Washington himself had little faith in the militia. In the fall of 1776 he wrote to the President of Congress:

> To place any dependence upon militia is assuredly resting upon a broken staff. Men just dragged from the tender scenes of domestic life [are] unaccustomed to the din of arms, totally unacquainted with every kind of military skill, which . . . makes them timid and ready to fly from their own shadows.

The Continental Army. The backbone of the American military effort was the Continental Army. This was the national force raised by Congress. Altogether, 230,000 served in it as soldiers during the war, but there were never more than about 20,000 under arms at any one time. Continentals signed up for longer periods of service than militia members, usually from one to three years. They also served farther away from home. For these reasons, recruiting was difficult.

Among the soldiers who served in the Continental Army were 5,000 blacks. Some were free black men from the

North, but others were slaves. The latter were usually given their freedom after their military service. More probably would have served, except that Congress and several states worried about putting guns in the hands of blacks. For a time, enlistment by blacks was discouraged. Only when the British army began recruiting slaves with the promise of freedom did the American policy on recruiting blacks change.

Washington's leadership. Despite all these problems, Washington managed to shape the Continental Army into an effective fighting machine. He succeeded by the sheer force of his personality. He looked the part of a military commander. One of his acquaintances had described him earlier in life as follows:

> Measuring six feet two inches in his stockings and weighing 175 pounds . . . his frame is padded with well-developed muscles, indicating great strength. . . . His head is well-shaped, though not large, but is gracefully poised on a superb neck. . . . His movements and gestures are graceful, his walk majestic, and he is a splendid horseman.

One of the secrets of Washington's success as commander in chief was his ability to get along with Congress. He remained patient when he had good reason to be annoyed with that body. At all times he subordinated his needs as a military man to the civil authority of Congress. Members of Congress respected him for his high qualifications as a military commander.

Women and the war. Another important factor in the American military effort was the support accorded the Patriot cause by American women. This support took many forms.

In celebration of the Declaration of Independence, joyful citizens raise a liberty pole, a flagstaff with a variety of decorations.

Some women joined their husbands in the army camps. They did not have military duties, although there are records of a few who actually served in combat. For example, Deborah Sampson Gannett dressed herself like a man, enlisted in a Massachusetts regiment, and served in the Continental Army. But women played important roles in other ways. They cooked, washed, and kept conditions in the camps as clean and as sanitary as possible. The importance of these activities can best be explained by the fact that in those years fifteen or twenty times as many soldiers died from sickness as from battlefield wounds. Many women served also as nurses, tending the wounded in hastily built hospitals.

7. FILM *The American Revolution, Part 2: The Impossible War,* American Heritage Film series (25 minutes, color; Robert Saudek Associates, Inc.).

Answers To Review Questions

1. Washington possessed military experience from the French and Indian War. He operated his huge plantation successfully and gained valuable managerial experience in the process. As a member of the Virginia legislature, he took part in anti–British protests and helped train the Virginia militia. In addition, Washington was highly respected and possessed outstanding leadership qualifications.

2. Paine said that monarchy was an absurd form of government that would never bring a just government. True men and women could not honor and support a government that had used force against them. He called for Americans to rise to the defense of freedom, for it had disappeared from other parts of the world. Everywhere people talked about *Common Sense,* and its impact was such that it may have doubled the number of Americans who favored independence.

3. Jefferson's theory of government and society included: **(a)** all men are created equal; **(b)** people had the right to life, liberty, and the pursuit of happiness; **(c)** government was created to protect the people's rights; **(d)** government was based on the consent of the governed; **(e)** when a government no longer followed the wishes of its people, the people had the right to get rid of it and set up a new one.

4. Because it did not have the power to tax, Congress asked the states to provide money and supplies. It also borrowed money from the public, sought loans and gifts from foreign nations, and printed paper money.

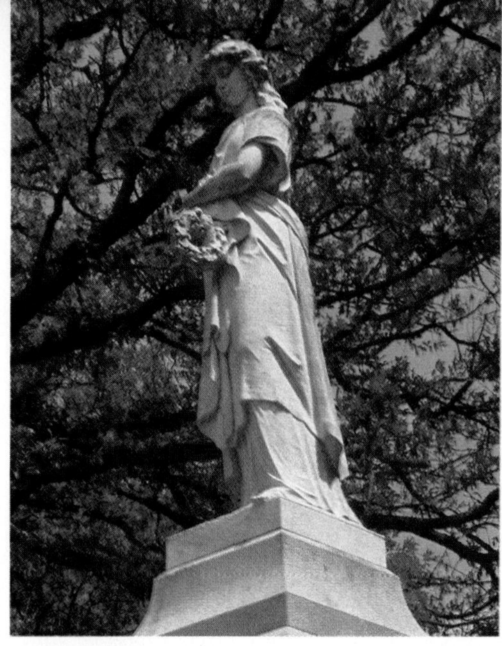

The heroic services of women during the Revolution are recalled by this monument at Moores Creek Bridge, North Carolina. It overlooks the grave of one of those women, Polly Slocumb. On this spot in February 1776, the Patriots defeated a Loyalist force in a battle often called "the Lexington of the South."

Women also made most of the uniforms and other clothing for soldiers. They helped make gunpowder by producing some of the ingredients within their homes.

Perhaps most important of all, women helped to keep the colonial economy going. Many a woman was left to run the family farm while her husband was off serving in the army or militia. The planting, cultivating, and harvesting that formerly had been done by husband and wife now had to be done by the woman alone. A remarkable fact of the period is that despite the loss of men to the army, farm production remained high.

In the next chapter we shall see how Americans were tested to the utmost on both the military and home fronts in waging the War of Independence.

CHECKUP

1. As the war got under way, what advantages did the British have? What advantages did the Americans have?
2. Distinguish between the militia and the Continental Army. Which was more effective as a fighting force?
3. In what ways did women make major contributions to the Patriot cause?

Key Facts from Chapter 6

1. The American War of Independence began on April 19, 1775, when British soldiers clashed with American militiamen at Lexington and Concord in Massachusetts.
2. Many Americans read and were influenced by Thomas Paine's pamphlet *Common Sense,* urging independence for the colonies.
3. The Declaration of Independence, written by Thomas Jefferson, was adopted on July 4, 1776.
4. The balance of strength between Britain and the American colonies in 1776, as measured by population, wealth, and the size of the armed forces, was much in Britain's favor.
5. The leadership of George Washington was a major factor in shaping the Continental Army into an effective fighting force.

★ REVIEWING THE CHAPTER ★

People, Places, and Events

Lexington and Concord *P. 101*
Minutemen *Pp. 101*
Paul Revere *Pp. 101, 115*
Second Continental Congress *P. 102*
George Washington *P. 102*
Bunker Hill *P. 104*
Thomas Paine *P. 105*
Privateers *P. 106*
Thomas Jefferson *P. 107*
July 4, 1776 *P. 113*
Mercenaries *P. 113*
Hessians *P. 113*
Militia *P. 116*
Continental Army *P. 116*

Review Questions

1. Why did the Second Continental Congress choose George Washington as commander-in-chief? *P. 102* Les. 1
2. Review the arguments given by Thomas Paine in favor of independence from Great Britain. What was the impact of *Common Sense*? *Pp. 105–106* Les. 1
3. Describe the theory of government and society that Thomas Jefferson included in the Declaration of Independence. *P. 107* Les. 2
4. How did Congress finance the war? *P. 114* Les. 3
5. At the start of the war, why did many people think that the American rebels could not win? *Pp. 113–114* Les. 3
6. What advantages did the Americans have in the war? *Pp. 114, 116* Les. 3
7. Suppose you were an American military officer and you were to lead a campaign against the British. Your superior officer gives you a choice of either **(a)** 500 regular troops and 100 militiamen, or **(b)** 500 militiamen and 100 regular troops. Which combination would you pick and why? *P. 116* Les. 3
8. Explain the roles women played in the war effort. *Pp. 117–118* Les. 3

Chapter Test

In the first section below is a list of descriptions. In the second section is a list of people and terms found in the chapter. Match each description with the person or term associated with it. Write your answers on a separate piece of paper.

1. Silversmith, engraver, and inventor
2. Writer of Declaration of Independence
3. Body representing all the colonies
4. British leader in Boston
5. Legal piracy
6. Hired soldiers
7. First armed conflict
8. Author of *Common Sense*
9. National military force
10. Part-time soldiers

a. Hessians
b. Lexington and Concord
c. Militia
d. Thomas Paine
e. Paul Revere
f. George Washington
g. Second Continental Congress
h. Thomas Jefferson
i. General Thomas Gage
j. Privateers
k. Continental Army
l. Parliament
m. Benjamin Franklin

5. Great Britain had a large, well-trained, and highly disciplined army and powerful navy. By comparison, America had no army, so one had to be built from scratch. American naval vessels were outnumbered a hundred to one by British ships. America had a much smaller population from which to draw soldiers, a serious shortage of war supplies, and very little money with which to finance the war effort.
6. The Atlantic Ocean hindered British communications and delayed the arrival of needed supplies and recruits. Americans were fighting on familiar ground, with the feeling that they were protecting homes and families. And most Americans were used to handling firearms in their civilian lives.
7. The better choice would be 500 regular troops and 100 militiamen. The militia was composed of civilians who served as short-term soldiers. They were not a strong fighting force, and often in combat they broke and ran before the enemy.
8. American women supported the Patriot cause by serving as nurses, by cooking, washing, and keeping the army camps clean, and even serving in combat on occasion. On the home front women produced clothing and uniforms for the soldiers, helped make the ingredients for gunpowder, and ran the family farm successfully.

Answers For Chapter Test
1. e **2.** h **3.** g **4.** i **5.** j
6. a **7.** b **8.** d **9.** k **10.** c

Background Information

1. PICTURE This is a detail from an engraving of the Battle of King's Mountain on October 7, 1780. The engraving is in the Anne S. J. Brown Military Collection at Brown University.

At King's Mountain, South Carolina, several bands of American frontiersmen defeated British-led Loyalist troops, compelling a British retreat. The significance of the battle was best described by Sir Henry Clinton, the British commander in chief, who wrote that this battle "proved the first Link of a Chain of Evils that followed each other in regular Succession until they at last ended in the total Loss of America."

CHAPTER 7

WINNING THE WAR OF INDEPENDENCE

LESSON 1

WASHINGTON REALIZED that the Continental Army was the symbol of the American cause. As long as it remained in the field, independence was possible. If it collapsed or was crushed, the cause of independence was lost. Washington, therefore, with great good sense fought a defensive war much of the time. He did not risk his troops in all-out battles. Not until the final campaign did he change his strategy.

The British opened the war with a different strategy. To win, they had to defeat the American army and take control of territory. That meant that the British must attack. In carrying out such a plan, their navy played a big part. With the navy, the British could easily move their troops. They could land along the coast, take key points, and march inland to pursue the American army.

In the British view, large cities on the coast were major goals. Holding them would provide ports for landing supplies. It would also, they thought, weaken the spirit of the Americans—particularly if they took control of the capital, Philadelphia.

Years of Strife

In the first two years of the war, the main military campaigns took place in the North. During those years, the British occupied America's three largest cities—Boston in 1775, New York in 1776, and Philadelphia in 1777. They gave up Boston and Philadelphia after less than a year, but they controlled New York up to the end of the war.

Early setbacks. The battle for New York in 1776 could have been the war's most important battle. The action began when a large British force under General William Howe landed on Long Island in late August. Had Howe acted decisively, he might have trapped Washington's army and ended the war then and there. However, he allowed the American troops to escape, under cover of darkness and fog, from Long Island into New York City. The British chased the American troops northward, skirmishing at Harlem Heights and fighting an inconclusive battle at White Plains. Washington's army then fled across the Hudson River to New Jersey.

The British pursued Washington's army, but never caught up for a clear-cut battle. In late autumn, the Americans withdrew farther, crossing the Delaware River into Pennsylvania. With winter coming on, Howe abandoned the campaign. He took most of his troops back to New York City for the winter, leaving some outposts in New Jersey.

Trenton and Princeton. Realizing that the enemy detachments in New Jersey were exposed, Washington struck a daring blow. On Christmas night in 1776, his small army recrossed the ice-choked Delaware River. The Americans surprised the British-paid Hessian troops at Trenton and took 900 prisoners.

Washington followed up this battle ten days later with an equally successful attack on the British troops at Princeton, New Jersey. Neither of those two victories, brilliant as they were, was a

LESSON 1 *(3 days)*

Performance Objectives

To show on an outline map of the eastern United States **(a)** the location of Revolutionary War battle sites, and **(b)** the general military movements of the American and British armies during the period 1776–1781.

Famous People

General William Howe, General John Burgoyne, Colonel Barry St. Leger, General Nicholas Herkimer, Marquis de Lafayette, Thaddeus Kosciusko, Johann Kalb, Friedrich von Steuben, Casimir Pulaski, George Rogers Clark, Francis Marion, General Nathanael Greene, Lord Cornwallis, Admiral de Grasse, John Paul Jones

Vocabulary

Trenton, Princeton, Hessians three-pronged attack, Oriskany, Saratoga, French-American alliance, Brandywine Creek, Germantown, *The Crisis,* Swamp Fox, Yorktown

Background Information

1. HESSIAN SOLDIERS When the British government realized it could not obtain sufficient troops in Britain to conquer the American colonies, it sought to purchase troops elsewhere. After being turned down by The Netherlands and Catherine the Great, the British ministers found a sympathetic hearing among the rulers of six German states. Greedy for British cash, these small monarchies were willing, and in some cases eager, to sell soldiers. One by one they entered into agreements by which they received large sums of cash and other concessions in return for a specified number of troops. Eventually, these German states provided almost 30,000 soldiers to the British army. The Landgrave of Hesse-Kassel personally sold 17,000, thereby giving the name Hessian to describe all German soldiers. Britain spent millions of pounds for the services of these mercenaries. Although the Germans were indispensable to the numerical strength of the British forces in the colonies, their regiments were not nearly as dependable as those of the redcoats.

In America, the use of foreign mercenaries was bitterly resented and greatly increased colonial enmity against the British government.

major step toward winning the war. But they were the first American victories after a long string of defeats. As such, the battles at Trenton and Princeton were an important boost to the morale of the Patriots.

A three-pronged attack. In 1777 the British came up with a grand plan to end the war. They would launch a three-pronged attack centered on the Hudson River valley. One army, under General John Burgoyne, was to march south from Canada by way of Lake Champlain toward Albany. A second force under Colonel Barry St. Leger, was to hurry east from Lake Ontario through the Mohawk Valley toward the Hudson. There it would link up with Burgoyne. General Howe, stationed in New York City, would go up the Hudson River and meet the other two. In this way, the British would drive a wedge between the southern states and New England, and control the state of New York. This was the area they considered to be the heart of the rebellion.

How many times did Washington's army meet the British in battle during 1776 and early 1777? In which battles were the Americans the victors?

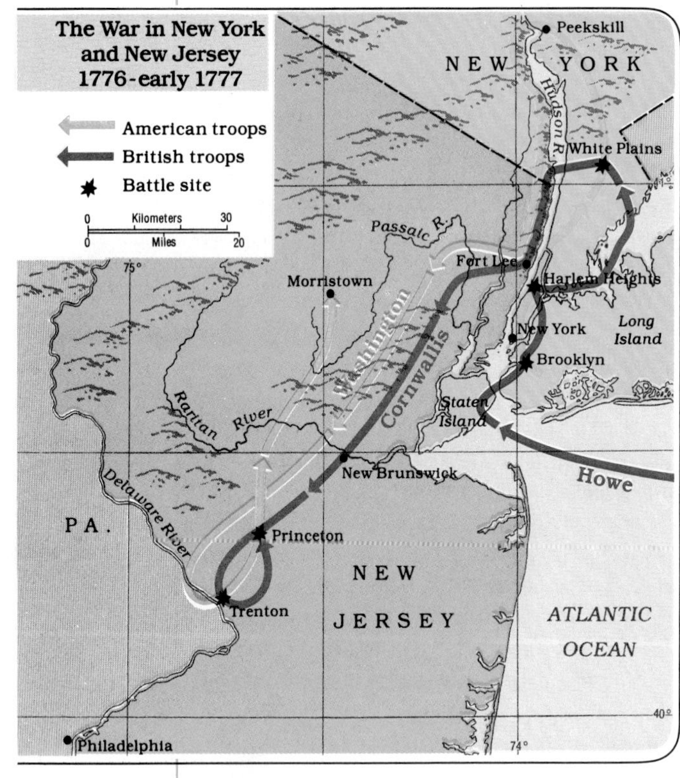

The plan made sense, but the British bungled it. A large part of the fault was General Howe's. Instead of going up the Hudson to trap the American army that lay between him and Burgoyne, he decided first to capture Philadelphia. There would still be time, he thought, to turn north and aid Burgoyne. But there wasn't time. The Philadelphia campaign occupied Howe until late September. By then Burgoyne's army had gotten as far south as Saratoga, New York. He was more than a hundred miles from his Canadian base, out of food, and harried by the Americans. Burgoyne had to surrender his entire army of 5,700. In the meantime, St. Leger's advance had been halted at Oriskany by General Nicholas Herkimer's militiamen.

The turning point. The surrender of Burgoyne's army on October 17, 1777, was the turning point of the war. Britain's old enemy, France, had been watching the American rebellion with more than passing interest. From the beginning of the war, the French had been secretly providing money and

General John Stark and his men prepare to meet a largely Hessian force near Bennington, Vermont. The force, sent by General Burgoyne to seize an American supply depot, was nearly wiped out.

supplies to the colonists. More than anything else, France wished to see Britain humbled. However, the French would not openly join the war until they were convinced that the colonies had a reasonable chance to win. Saratoga convinced them. For the first time, the Americans had defeated and captured a large British army.

The next year, in 1778, the French made an alliance with the United States and entered the war. That changed the entire character of the conflict. The United States had been at a great disadvantage because of the power of the British navy. Now the French fleet could help offset America's lack of seapower.

America's European allies. From the moment that France entered the conflict, the Revolutionary War became a world war. In 1779 Spain joined the United States and France in fighting Britain. The combined fleets of France and Spain outnumbered the British by far. Thus the navy that had controlled the seas from the beginning of the war found the tables turned. Britain was forced to defend itself against invasion at home, as well as to protect its colonies in America, Africa, and Asia.

In 1780, Holland followed France in recognizing America's independence and declared war on Britain. By this time, the British were on bad terms with practically every important European country trading on the Atlantic. The Royal Navy had abused the ships of many countries when Britain ruled the waves. Now, faced with many enemies, Britain was no longer able to commit its full resources against the Americans.

Activities

1. **USING A PICTURE** Ask students to observe the picture on page 123 and then ask, What problems of fighting a battle does this picture suggest? (Terrain; communication; scouting; organization; etc.) Encourage students to keep these problems in mind as they show the military movement of each side on their maps.

2. **MAP READING** At the beginning of this chapter, give students an outline map of the eastern United States. Using the maps in the text as a guide, have students indicate the location and general military movements of the actions described in the lesson.

In addition, ask students to answer the questions that accompany the maps in the lesson. If you find they are having difficulty reading the maps, perhaps you would want to take this opportunity to review basic map skills. Using the maps provided, devise questions about direction, latitude and longitude, boundaries, and distance measurement in miles and kilometers.

3. READING FOR INFORMATION/ESSAY After the students have read the text for this lesson, have them complete the following sentence and write several supporting paragraphs: British strategy in the American Revolution should have been ______.

4. DISCUSSION Suppose, for the purpose of discussion, that Country A ruled and dominated Country B, and that Country B wished to be free and independent. Suppose the United States was in a position to give Country B the necessary help to achieve independence. Ask students these questions: Should the United States help Country B? What information might you want to have before answering that question? What moral obligation, if any, does a nation have to help another free itself from domination? When should a nation mind its own business and refrain from becoming involved? What situations have arisen in America's history where the question of becoming involved or remaining neutral has been an issue?

5. LISTENING FOR INFORMATION You might wish to read to the class excerpts from *The War of the Revolution* by Christopher Ward (New York: Macmillan Company, 1952). This book is a classic and is available in most libraries. The battle of Saratoga (pages 532–542) is exceptionally well done.

FOREIGN HEROES OF THE REVOLUTION

Marquis de Lafayette, a French nobleman, became a major general in the Continental Army at the age of twenty. Wounded at Germantown, he later led troops at Yorktown. Washington regarded Lafayette almost as a son.

Thaddeus Kosciusko of Poland, an army engineer, built the defenses at Saratoga and West Point. A true champion of freedom, he bought slaves in order to free them. He later fought for the independence of Poland.

Johann Kalb, a native of Germany, came to America with Lafayette. He served with Washington at Brandywine, Germantown, Valley Forge, and Monmouth. He died from wounds suffered in battle at Camden, South Carolina.

Friedrich von Steuben, a Prussian army veteran, gained fame as a drill-master during the winter at Valley Forge. As a major general, he led troops at Monmouth and Yorktown. Later he became a United States citizen.

Casimir Pulaski, a Polish patriot who joined the Continental Army, headed a cavalry-infantry unit called Pulaski's Legion. Wounded while leading a cavalry charge at the siege of Savannah, he died two days later.

A change in British strategy. Under these new circumstances, the British changed their strategy. During the first two years of the war, they had launched a number of operations in the North from their base in New York City.

Their one notable success had been in taking Philadelphia. In the late summer of 1777 General Howe's army had moved by ship to the head of Chesapeake Bay and marched on Philadelphia. In a battle at Brandywine Creek, Washington's army failed to block Howe, whose troops advanced into Philadelphia. Three weeks later the Americans tried to retake the city, but were turned back at Germantown.

Despite this success, the British saw that their strategy of capturing large cities was failing. Tom Paine had pointed out the weakness of that strategy. Paine published a number of pamphlets called *The Crisis*. In one, he included this open letter to Howe.

> By what means, may I ask, do you expect to conquer America? . . .
>
> In all the wars which you have formerly been concerned in you had only armies to contend with; in former wars, the countries followed the fate of their capitals; Canada fell with Quebec, and Minorca [a Mediterranean island seized by Britain in 1708] with Port Mahon or St. Phillips; by subduing these, the conquerors opened a way into, and became masters of the country; here it is otherwise; if you get possession of a city here, you are obliged to shut yourself up in it, and can make no use of it, than to spend your country's money in [it] . . . This is all the advantage you have drawn from New York; and you would draw less from Philadelphia, because it requires more force to keep it, and is much farther from the sea.

Continued on page 127

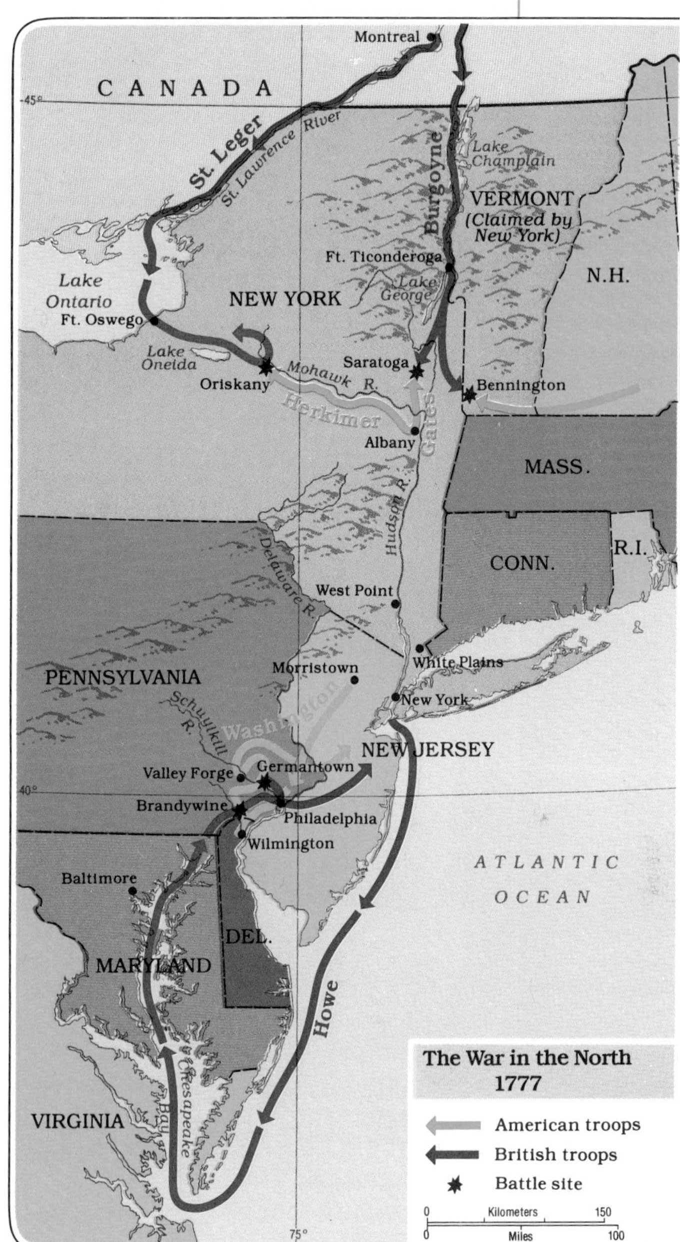

Armies have long made use of waterways as invasion routes. What waterways did Burgoyne's army use? How would the map be different if Howe had done what he was supposed to do?

George Rogers Clark's Northwest Campaign

When war broke out, the territory west of the Appalachian Mountains was mostly unsettled. During the war, however, the region became a battleground because British frontier posts were located in the Illinois country. From forts at Kaskaskia, Cahokia, Vincennes, and Detroit, the British and their Indian allies launched bloody raids upon American settlements. The goal of the British was to win complete control of the wilderness region.

George Rogers Clark, a Virginian who had explored and settled beyond the mountains in the Kentucky region, got approval to strike back. In the summer of 1778 he led an expedition through the wilderness and captured the British forts at Kaskaskia, Cahokia, and Vincennes. Colonel Henry Hamilton, the British commander at Detroit, resolved to win back the forts. He and his Indian allies retook Vincennes in December 1778. Planning to recapture the other forts in the spring, they settled down there for the winter. They were confident that control of the Illinois country was now within their grasp.

Clark's winter camp was at Kaskaskia, 180 miles away. He was working on a plan to attack Detroit in the spring when he heard of Hamilton's capture of the fort at Vincennes. Even though it was the middle of winter, Clark decided to strike at once. Gathering a band of about 180 men, he set out on one of the most amazing marches in American military history. A mid-winter thaw had caused the Wabash River to flood, turning much of the route into a huge lake. Nevertheless, Clark led his men in the dead of winter through icy floodwaters, sometimes shoulder high. Wet to the skin, exhausted, and hungry, the men survived the march. They surprised the British in February 1779, and Hamilton was forced to surrender the fort.

Clark's victory helped win this territory for the United States. When the peace treaty was signed in 1783, Britain gave up its claims to the region.

This postage stamp, issued in 1929, shows George Rogers Clark and his band of frontiersmen receiving the surrender of the British commander, Colonel Henry Hamilton, at Vincennes. To reach the British-held fort, Clark marched his men in the dead of winter through the icy floodwaters of the Wabash Valley. This amazing feat of endurance helped win the Northwest for the United States.

The new British strategy called for moving the fighting out of the North and into the South. There were, the British felt, a large number of Loyalists in that region. They hoped that those Loyalists would rise up to support a "friendly" invasion of British troops. At the same time, the British could depend more on their sea power to supply their troops in the South and to transport them from place to place. Finally, Britain decided that the war in America would have to take second place to the struggle in other parts of the world against its long-time enemy, France.

The southern campaign. The British southern campaign got off to a good start. In 1778 the British captured Savannah, Georgia. The next year they turned back a joint force of American soldiers and the French fleet, who tried to retake the city. The British then overran most of the state of Georgia.

Much of the state of South Carolina also came under British control after Charleston fell in 1780. In Charleston the Americans met with their worst defeat of the war when an army of 5,500 had to surrender. With almost no Continental Army force left in the area, Britain's southern strategy seemed to be working.

But Britain had not counted on the military ingenuity of the Americans. They now fought back with guerrilla warfare. Bands of militiamen swarmed over British outposts in a series of hit-and-run raids. When pursued, the Americans fled into nearby swamps and forests, where they could not be followed. Led by officers like Francis Marion of South Carolina, who earned the name Swamp Fox, these roaming bands kept the British off balance with their attacks.

Greene's strategy. To take charge of the new Continental Army formed in the South, Washington appointed Nathanael Greene, a Rhode Islander. Next to Washington, Greene was the most gifted general in the army. On taking command in North Carolina, Greene outlined his strategy.

> I am determined to carry the war immediately into South Carolina. The enemy will be obliged to follow us, or give up their posts in that state. If the former takes place, it will draw the war out of this state and give it an opportunity to [recruit men for the army]. If [the British] leave their posts to fall, they must lose more there than they can gain here.

The strategy was to fight and retreat, fight and retreat, always drawing the British farther away from their base. After one of Greene's generals dealt a British force a smashing defeat in 1781 at the battle of Cowpens in South Carolina, the British commander, Lord Cornwallis, determined to run down Greene's army. Although Cornwallis gave chase, he was never able to catch the American general.

Victory at Yorktown. Since it appeared that Greene was getting many of his men and much of his supplies from Virginia, Cornwallis moved north to invade that state. He marched to Yorktown, where he took up a position on the peninsula between the York and James Rivers. There he could count on being supplied from Chesapeake Bay by the British navy and, if necessary, rescued

6. RESEARCH/ORAL REPORT Have some students do a thorough study of guerrilla warfare and report to the class. How did this kind of warfare help the Americans in the War of Independence? Where has guerrilla warfare been used most successfully? What is the best strategy to use against guerrilla warfare?

7. ORAL REPORTS You may wish to assign students to report on each person listed under Famous People at the beginning of the lesson. If time does not permit a report on all of the people, perhaps you would want to concentrate attention on George Rogers Clark and John Paul Jones.

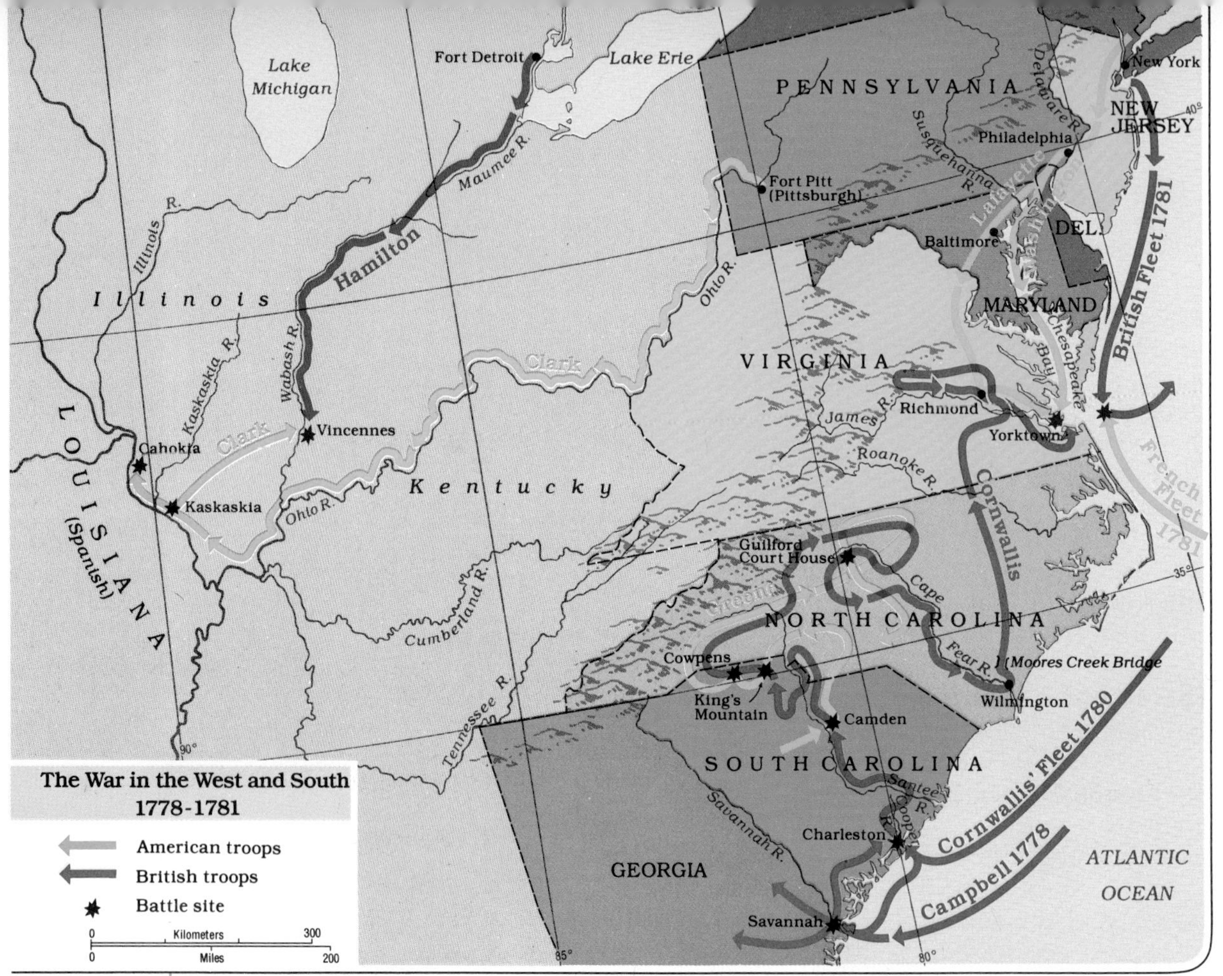

The location of Yorktown was a vital factor in bringing the War for Independence to a close. What opportunity did Cornwallis see that made him decide to take a stand there with his army? What opportunity did Washington see in that situation? Which general realized his opportunity?

by it. At least this was what he planned.

Washington decided it was now time to use French seapower and the French army to trap Cornwallis. The army France had sent moved south from its base in Newport, Rhode Island. Racing his own army south from New York, Washington joined up with the French and cut off Cornwallis by land. Admiral de Grasse, the French naval commander, bottled up Chesapeake Bay. Thus there was no chance for Cornwallis to escape by sea. A British fleet tried to rescue Cornwallis, but De Grasse fought it off. Confronted by more than 16,000 troops and 36 French warships, Cornwallis surrendered his army of 7,000.

British power in America was by no means ended by this defeat at Yorktown. The British still controlled much territory and held such major cities as New York, Charleston, and Savannah. But after years of fighting and the loss of two armies, the British were no closer to

Continued on page 130

John Paul Jones and the War at Sea

When the Revolutionary War broke out, there was no American navy. Slowly Congress began to build one. In the fall of 1775, four merchant vessels were purchased and armed. In December of that year, thirteen frigates were ordered built. The Continental Navy eventually put out to sea some fifty or sixty ships, although not all at one time.

Besides the Continental Navy, several states built their own navies. The navies in all totaled about forty ships. Together with the ships of the Continental Navy, these vessels sank or captured nearly 200 British craft. They were facing a British navy that numbered about 270 ships in 1775, and more than 460 in 1783.

The Continental Navy, although outnumbered, showed great seamanship and fighting qualities. Its most brilliant exploits were carried out by John Paul Jones. Born in Scotland with the full name of John Paul, Jones added his last name when he came to America. He probably did so to hide his true identity because he had been accused of murder in the death of a sailor. Appointed a lieutenant in 1775, Jones was soon given command of his own ship. He was later promoted to captain, and commanded a small squadron.

Jones boldly hunted enemy ships off the British coast, and even went ashore with raiding parties. In 1779 his vessel, the *Bonhomme Richard*, clashed with a bigger British warship, the *Serapis*, in the North Sea. When the *Bonhomme Richard* was almost sinking, Jones had it lashed with lines alongside the *Serapis* and continued the fight. After three hours of combat, the British commander called on Jones to surrender. Jones is said to have replied, "I have not yet begun to fight." The British ship finally surrendered, but the *Bonhomme Richard* was so badly damaged that it sank two days later.

Jones's efforts and those of the continental and state fleets were aided by another American naval force—the privateers (see page 106). More than 2,000 American craft became privateers. By the close of the war, these armed ships had sunk or captured more than 600 British vessels.

John Paul Jones raised this flag over the *Serapis*.

Background Information

2. PICTURE On the day of the surrender, Cornwallis pleaded illness and sent his deputy, General Charles O'Hara, to represent him. When O'Hara tried to surrender his sword to Washington, the American commander told O'Hara to offer his sword to General Benjamin Lincoln.

The reason for Washington's action was this: The previous year, General Lincoln had been forced to surrender his army under humiliating circumstances following the seige of Charleston. Military etiquette of the times decreed that an army that had fought bravely in defense of a fortified position but had been defeated should be permitted to march out with flags flying and with its band playing a tune of the victor nation. These concessions were called the honors of war. When Lincoln's army surrendered after putting up a stubborn fight at Charleston, the British had refused to grant them the honors of war. Thus, the Americans had been forced to march out with flags furled and with the band playing a Turkish tune. Now, in retaliation, Washington refused to grant the British the honors of war at Yorktown, and moreover, chose General Lincoln to receive the British surrender. As the defeated troops stacked their arms, the military band played a British march called "The World Turned Upside Down."

Yale University Art Gallery

The surrender of the British at Yorktown is shown in this painting by John Trumbull. General Benjamin Lincoln prepares to receive the surrender from General O'Hara, second-in-command to Cornwallis.

breaking the rebellion. British citizens were weary of the war. With other foes to face in Europe, Britain was now ready to seek peace. A peace treaty did not come until 1783. Yet in 1781, six years after the first shots rang out on the Lexington green, the War of Independence was, for all practical purposes, won.

Some battlefield "ifs." As we noted at the start of the previous chapter, there was nothing inevitable about the outcome of the Revolutionary War. If General Howe had moved quickly against Washington in New York City in 1776, the rebellion might have been crushed before the ink had dried on the Declaration of Independence. Several times during the war Howe had a chance to smash Washington's army, but he always let the Americans slip away.

Had the British succeeded in their plan to split New England from the southern states, there would have been no American victory at Saratoga—and probably no French-American alliance. Without French help, it is doubtful that the United States could have won. At the battle of Yorktown, for example, there were more French soldiers and sailors surrounding the British than there were Americans. One could build a long list of battlefield "ifs." After the war the British generals no doubt did.

CHECKUP

1. Why were the battles at Trenton and Princeton so important to the Patriot cause?
2. What grand plan did the British formulate in 1777 to end the war? What success did it have?
3. How did British strategy change in the later years of the war? Why did this strategy fail?

LESSON 2

Obstacles Overcome

Battles aside, there were times when the Continental Army could easily have collapsed. Always short of supplies, and with few victories to encourage them, the soldiers at times lost heart.

The plight of Washington's army was never worse than at its winter camp in Valley Forge, Pennsylvania, in 1777–1778. There, a shortage of food led to near starvation. For want of shoes, soldiers walked barefoot in the snow. Others, lacking clothing to protect them from the weather, remained penned up in miserably crowded cabins.

The money problem. There were also problems on the home front that might have lost the War of Independence. One was inflation. We have already noted that Congress printed paper money to pay for the war. This money was issued as Continental paper dollars.

At that time, the money that people trusted most was gold and silver. People did not like to accept paper money unless they felt sure they could exchange it for gold or silver. If the war was won and a new, strong government that could raise money was set up, there was a fair chance that people would be able to exchange their paper money for gold or silver. But if the rebellion failed—and for much of the war it looked that way—the paper money of Congress would be worth nothing.

Accepting paper money was, therefore, a gamble. People wouldn't take it for payment unless they were offered a lot more of it than of gold. And the more paper money Congress printed, the lower it fell in value. This table shows the amount of paper money Congress issued each year. It also shows the number of paper dollars it took each year to buy as much as a dollar in gold would buy.

Year	*Paper Money Issued*	*Value of Paper Money to Gold*
1776	$19 million	1 to 1
1777	$13 million	3 to 1
1778	$63 million	7 to 1
1779	$90 million	42 to 1

By the end of 1780, it took nearly 100 Continental paper dollars to buy as much as a dollar in gold would buy. Four months later, it took nearly 150. Since Congress was buying military supplies with Continental dollars, prices skyrocketed. Washington once commented that if one had a rat in the shape of a horse, one could probably sell it for 200 pounds. Some soldiers who were paid with these nearly worthless Continental dollars deserted; others mutinied.

State rivalries. Still another problem that might have led to an American defeat was *localism*—that is, the placing

LESSON 2 (*2 to 3 days*)

Performance Objectives

1. To demonstrate an understanding of inflation by giving examples of its symptoms and its effects. **2.** To demonstrate an understanding of the Loyalist position in the American Revolution by composing a statement of principles a Loyalist might have written to defend his or her position.

Famous People

Nathan Hale, Benedict Arnold

Vocabulary

Inflation, Continental dollars, civil war, Loyalists, Patriots, Tories, constitutions, ratified

Background Information

"NOT WORTH A CONTINENTAL" Continental dollars quickly lost value because the government printed so many of them. Consequently, Americans began to describe any worthless thing as "not worth a continental."

Activities

1. FILM *Anatomy of an Inflation* (22 minutes, color; McGraw-Hill). It is available for rental from Indiana University Audio-Visual Center, Bloomington, Ind. 47401.

2. DISCUSSION Have your students look for and bring to class copies of old newspapers (10–20 years ago). Have them compare the food and clothing prices as advertised then with prices advertised in newspapers today. Ask students to imagine that they were retired with a fixed income twenty years ago. How would you live today? What particular problems would you encounter in inflationary times? What effects might inflation have on the morale and character of a nation? What beliefs might a very principled person lose first?

3. CREATIVE WRITING Ask your students to think about how inflation might affect the soldiers of the Continental Army. Then have them compose letters from a wife with several children to her soldier husband serving in the army. What might her special concerns be? Encourage students to be creative but at the same time to pay attention to historical accuracy.

of a state's interests ahead of the national interest. You will remember that each state raised its own army, in the form of militia. Each state had its own navy and raised money for its own defense. With such division of effort, it was hard to get states to pull together in a single national effort. Each state was convinced that it was doing more than its share while others were doing less.

There were also boundary disputes between several of the states. Both New York and New Hampshire claimed what is now the state of Vermont. Virginia and Maryland argued over the former's claims to land west of the Alleghenies. Sometimes it seemed the states were busier quarreling with each other than fighting with the British.

A civil war. As soon as the Declaration of Independence was signed, the conflict between Great Britain and the Americans became—at least to the Patriots—a war between two countries. At the same time, however, another kind of war was going on at home. That was the civil war between the Loyalists and the Patriots.

Not all Americans, you will remember, favored independence. A large number remained true to the king and the British empire. Perhaps as many as 500,000, about one fifth of the white population, were Loyalists—or Tories, as they were scornfully called by the Patriots.

Loyalists came from all walks of life. A group of Loyalists arrested in New York City on suspicion of plotting to assassinate George Washington included the following: the city's mayor, a number of farmers, some tavernkeepers, two doctors, two tanners, two gunsmiths, a

Continued on page 134

Hero . . . and Traitor

Every war produces heroes and traitors. The Revolutionary War was no exception. In the careers of Nathan Hale and Benedict Arnold, one can see a clear example of this pattern.

Nathan Hale was born in Connecticut and attended Yale College. He was teaching school when war broke out, but entered military service in July 1775. Promoted to captain six months later, he went on duty near New York City. When General Washington called for a volunteer to spy on the British, Hale offered his services. Disguised as a Dutch schoolmaster, he visited enemy camps on Long Island and in New York City and drew sketches of fortifications.

This statue of Nathan Hale stands in New Haven, Connecticut, where Hale attended Yale College.

On the night of September 21, 1776, Hale was captured by British soldiers. His drawings were found hidden in his shoes, and he was sentenced to die. The next morning, as he faced death by hanging, he was allowed to speak. Tradition has it that Hale, with the rope around his neck, uttered these stirring words: "I regret that I have but one life to lose for my country."

The devotion of Nathan Hale to the American cause was not shared by Benedict Arnold, another native of Connecticut. Before the war, Arnold was involved in trade and managed a book- and drugstore. Once the war began, he quickly became an exceptional military leader. In the fall of 1775 he led a march of about 1,000 men through the Maine wilderness into Canada. In a swirling snowstorm in late December he and his men attacked the walled city of Quebec. Although the attack failed, Arnold's courage and daring were recognized, and he was promoted to brigadier general. He added to his reputation as a fiery leader in the campaign around Lake Champlain and in the battle of Saratoga. Although he was badly wounded at Saratoga, Congress recognized his worth and promoted him to major general.

But Arnold felt he had not been given the credit due him for the victory at Saratoga. Stories spread that he leaned toward the Loyalists, in part because he had married the daughter of one. Pennsylvania officials also accused him of overstepping his authority. Brooding over these matters, Arnold decided to cast his lot with the British. While in command of West Point in 1780, he worked out a plan to surrender that important fort to the enemy. When the plot was exposed, Arnold fled to the British.

After being made a British brigadier general, Arnold led the forces that burned Richmond, Virginia, and New London, Connecticut. Once the war was over, he went to England, where he became a merchant in the West Indies trade. He died in London in 1801, burdened by business debts and scorned by Americans as a traitor.

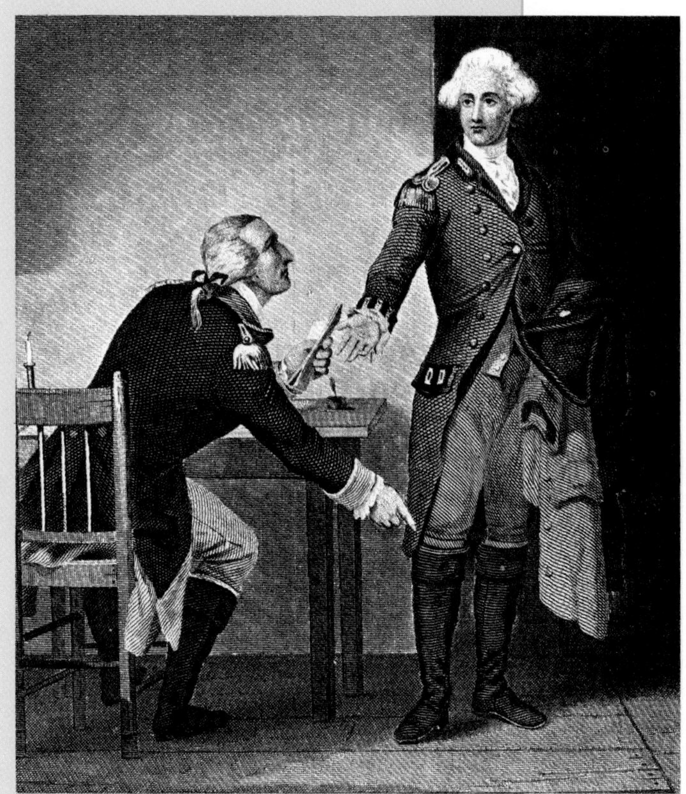

Benedict Arnold suggests to British spy John André that the defense plans for West Point be concealed in André's boot. Arnold's treachery was revealed when American soldiers stopped André, searched him, and found the papers.

4. ROLE-PLAYING Set up this imaginary situation: A Loyalist has been invited to appear as a guest on a news show, similar to *Meet the Press* or *Face the Nation,* in Philadelphia in 1780. Ask half of the students to prepare a list of questions they would want the Loyalist to answer. Ask the other students to compose a list of reasons defending the Loyalist's position and beliefs. Select different students to act as Loyalist and questioner.

Then reverse the situation and have the show take place in London with a Patriot as the guest. Follow the same procedure.

If your school has videotaping facilities, you might want to make this into a TV show to present to classes next year.

As background material for this activity, you may want to make available the following books: *The American Revolution Through British Eyes* edited by Martin Kallisch and Andrew McLeish (New York: Harper & Row, 1962); *Peter Oliver's Origin and Progress of the American Rebellion: A Tory View* edited by Douglas Adair and John A. Schutz (Stanford, Calif.: Stanford University Press, 1961); *The Good Americans: The Loyalists in the American Revolution* by Wallace Brown (New York: Peter Smith, 1969); and *The American Tory* by William H. Nelson (Boston: Beacon Press, 1961).

5. RESEARCH/DISCUSSION Have your students look up the Petition of Right (1628) and the Declaration of Rights (1689) and compare them with the guarantees asked for by the several states in their constitutions. Later, when you study the American Bill of Rights, you might want to refer back to these two British documents. In some cases, the American Bill of Rights is a word for word replication.

6. ROLE-PLAYING Consult Helen Miller's *The Case for Liberty* (Chapel Hill: University of North Carolina Press, 1965) for a readable account of important colonial court cases involving such civil-rights issues as freedom of religion, search and seizure, right to a jury trial, and freedom of the press. Have your students reenact the trials, taking the parts of defendants and prosecutors and developing the case for each side.

former schoolteacher, and a man described as "a damned rascal." Most Loyalists, like most Americans in general, appear to have been small farmers. A good many prosperous merchants and large landholders were also Loyalists. So were nearly all members of the Anglican clergy.

There were Loyalists in every colony, but there were more in certain areas than in others. A great many lived in the West, along the frontier. There were also large numbers in the coastal areas, especially in the middle colonies of New York, New Jersey, and Pennsylvania. The cities of New York and Philadelphia were Loyalist strongholds. The South also had a large number of Loyalists, especially in and around Charleston.

Loyalists proved to be a serious military threat to the Patriot cause. It is estimated that as many as 50,000 served with the British army. They took part in many of the war's major campaigns. There were Loyalists with Burgoyne's army at Saratoga. Loyalist soldiers fought in Savannah and aided in the capture of Charleston. They took part in the sacking of Connecticut towns, and in raids in Virginia.

Enemies within. Yet most Loyalists did not take part in the fighting. They tried to live as normally as possible during the war. Nevertheless, they were regarded by the Patriots as enemies within. The reason for this becomes apparent in this 1779 newspaper article. The article also gives you some idea of how high feelings ran.

> Who were the occasion of this war? The Tories! Who persuaded the tyrants of Britain to prosecute it in a manner before unknown to civilized nations, and shocking even to barbarians? The Tories! Who prevailed on the savages of the wilderness to join the standard of the enemy? The Tories! Who have assisted the Indians in taking the scalp from the aged matron, the blooming fair one, the helpless infant, and the dying hero? The Tories!

The same article went on to describe other practices in which the Loyalists supposedly participated.

> Who hold treasonous correspondence with the enemy? The Tories! Who send them daily intelligence? The Tories! Who take oaths of allegiance to the States one day, and break them the next? The Tories! Who prevent your battalions from being filled? The Tories! Who persuade those who have enlisted to desert? The Tories!

There was no wrong under heaven, apparently, for which the Loyalists were not to blame.

The treatment of Loyalists. With feelings like those, it is hardly surprising that people siding with the British were handled roughly. Their homes were sometimes looted or destroyed. Their moves were carefully watched. They were often kept from moving around freely. Those suspected of political or military acts were jailed, kept in their homes, or removed to faraway places. If one was caught returning home for a secret visit, the whole family might be sent into exile.

Those who served in the British army or gave aid to the enemy in other ways during the war were tried for treason. When convicted, they were sentenced to death. Such sentences were rarely carried out, and few Loyalists were actually executed. One reason for this was that General Washington urged that they not be. He feared that if Patriots executed Loyalists, the British would execute British-born American soldiers they had captured.

In the course of the war, the property of some wealthy Loyalists was seized. States passed laws confiscating the estates of certain offending Loyalists. Millions of acres were taken in this way. Usually the states sold the land at auction and used the funds to pay for the costs of the war. Some Loyalists were compensated by the British government for their losses, but many were not.

During the war, between 80,000 and 100,000 Loyalists left the United States so they could continue to live within the British empire. Some went "home"—that is, to England. Most, however, stayed in the Western Hemisphere, moving to Canada or to the West Indies.

It is clear the Loyalists suffered considerably. Yet, except for those who served with the British army, few lost their lives. Considering the bitterness of feelings in this civil war, that is a remarkable fact.

New governments. Once independence was declared, the former British colonies lost no time in writing state constitutions and setting up state governments. In 1776 alone, eight of them wrote new constitutions and two changed older ones. The remaining states followed within the next few years.

The experience of the recent arguments with Great Britain was stamped all over these constitutions. Colonists had gone to war to preserve the "rights of Englishmen." Now they wrote these rights securely into their constitutions. The following rights were guaranteed in most state constitutions.

- Trial by jury
- Bail
- A free trial in open court
- Writs of habeas corpus. These documents would protect citizens from being kept in prison without cause by requiring the authorities to explain to a judge why they were being held.
- Freedom of the press
- Freedom of religion
- The right to meet together peaceably and to petition the government

All constitutions, in addition, accepted the principle that government must be based on the consent of the governed. There were, however, limits to that idea. A person had to own a certain amount of property or pay a tax in order to qualify for voting. And in all but one state, the right to vote belonged only to adult white males.

The first restriction was not as great as might first appear. Most white male citizens were able to meet the property or tax requirement. In Massachusetts, for example, more than 80 percent owned enough property to give them the right to vote.

Restricting the vote to white males was far more limiting. Blacks, Indians, and women were all left out. The only exception was in New Jersey. There the constitution did not say "male," and for a time women could and did vote. In 1807, however, the constitution was changed and women could no longer vote. In spite of all those limitations, however, it remained true that nowhere in the entire world was representative

7. GUEST SPEAKER A representative of a local organization, such as the American Civil Liberties Union, or a lawyer or other knowledgeable person with an active interest in civil rights issues might be invited to speak to the class. Ask the speaker to present material that will help students compare the civil-rights issues of the past with those of today.

8. RESEARCH/USING A MAP At the peace negotiations in Paris in 1782, England, wanting to cultivate American trade and friendship and wishing to break America's close ties with France, was very generous in the peace terms. Assign a group of students to work together on a map that shows the boundaries of the United States in 1783, at the end of the Revolution, according to the Treaty of Paris.

Answers to Review Questions

1. Washington realized that the Continental Army was vital to the American cause. He therefore fought a defensive war by never risking his troops in an all-out battle. The British, on the other hand, had to defeat the American army and control territory in order to win. They planned to use their navy to move troops and supplies. A major goal was to take large coastal cities and hold them as bases for operations.
2. The purpose was to capture the Hudson River Valley, thereby driving a wedge between the southern states and New England and gaining control of New York State.
3. The battle at Saratoga was considered the turning point of the war. Not only were the British decisively defeated, but Britain's old enemy, France, openly decided to support the American war effort after that battle.
4. The defeat of Cornwallis at Yorktown did not mean the total defeat of British forces. The British still controlled large areas, but their will to fight was broken and they were ready to seek peace.
5. Congress lacked the power to tax and could only request funds from the states. To meet its financial obligations, Congress printed paper money called Continental dollars. These Continentals did not have backing in gold or silver, so accepting the paper money was a gamble. Because people were uncertain about the outcome of the war, they would not take the Continental dollars for payment unless they were offered a lot more of dollars than of gold. The more money Congress printed, the lower it fell in value. Eventually, the money was practically worthless.

government as advanced as in the United States.

At the same time, a constitution was drawn up for the nation. It was called the Articles of Confederation. You will study more about the Articles in the next unit. Here we need note only that the Articles were completed in 1777, but they could not go into effect until all thirteen states *ratified*, or approved, the document. That did not occur until 1781. By that time the war was almost over. Thus, throughout most of the war the Continental Congress operated as the national government.

The Peace of Paris. In September 1783, almost two years after Yorktown, Great Britain and the United States signed the Peace of Paris. Britain acknowledged that the United States was now an independent nation. The treaty set boundaries that were very favorable to the new nation. To the north, the Great Lakes; to the south, the border of Spanish Florida, at roughly 31° north latitude; and most important, to the west, the Mississippi River. This gave the United States the whole area between the Allegheny Mountains and the great river. Other terms had to do with American fishing rights off British-owned Newfoundland and the question of American treatment of Loyalists after the war was over.

The Peace of Paris brought forth something new in the world: the first modern nation born in revolution. That fact would forever affect the history of Americans and of the world. In the next chapter you will see several important ways in which this was so.

CHECKUP

1. How did inflation threaten to undo the struggle for independence? How did localism threaten it?
2. Who were the Loyalists? What role did they play in the war?
3. When new state constitutions were drawn up, what rights were generally guaranteed in them?

Key Facts from Chapter 7

1. During much of the War of Independence the British were on the offensive and the Americans on the defensive.
2. American victories at Trenton and Princeton were important in boosting the Patriots' morale.
3. The American victory at Saratoga was the turning point of the war. It induced France to come openly to America's aid.
4. The victory of the Americans and their French allies at Yorktown in 1781 was the last major battle of the war and assured American independence.
5. New state constitutions, written after independence was declared, guaranteed such basic rights as trial by jury, freedom of the press, and freedom of religion.

★ REVIEWING THE CHAPTER ★

People, Places, and Events

Gen. William Howe *P. 121*
Trenton *P. 121*
Princeton *P. 121*
Gen. John Burgoyne *P. 122*
Col. Barry St. Leger *P. 122*
Saratoga *P. 122*
Gen. Nicholas Herkimer *P. 122*
Brandywine *P. 125*
Germantown *P. 125*
The Crisis *P. 125*
George Rogers Clark *P. 126*
Savannah *P. 127*
Charleston *P. 127*
Francis Marion *P. 127*
Gen. Nathanael Greene *P. 127*
Cowpens *P. 127*
Lord Cornwallis *P. 127*
Yorktown *P. 127*
Admiral de Grasse *P. 128*
John Paul Jones *P. 129*
Valley Forge *P. 131*
Nathan Hale *P. 132*
Benedict Arnold *P. 133*
Peace of Paris *P. 136*

Review Questions

1. Compare Washington's war strategy with the British strategy. *P. 121* Les. 1
2. Define the purpose of the British three-pronged attack. *P. 122* Les. 1
3. What was the significance of the British defeat at Saratoga? *Pp. 122–123* Les. 1
4. Did the American victory at Yorktown end British power in America? Explain your answer. *P. 128* Les. 1
5. Describe America's money problem during the war years. *P. 131* Les. 2
6. How did rivalries between various states affect the war effort? *Pp. 131–132* Les. 2
7. How did the Patriots feel toward the Loyalists? How were the Loyalists treated? *Pp. 132, 134* Les. 2
8. List the individual rights included in the new state constitutions. *P. 135* Les. 2

Chapter Test

Complete each sentence. Write the answers on a separate piece of paper.

1. The strategic battles at Trenton and Princeton in New Jersey were the first American victories after a long string of defeats.
2. The surrender of Burgoyne's army at Saratoga convinced the French to join openly the Americans in their war for independence.
3. The British southern campaign got off to a good start with the capture of Savannah, Georgia.
4. Francis Marion, nicknamed the "Swamp Fox," and his band darted out of the marshes to attack the British and then disappeared before the redcoats could strike back.
5. John Paul Jones, an American naval hero, commanded the *Bonhomme Richard* in a successful attack on the British warship *Serapis*.
6. Washington appointed Nathanael Greene, one of the most gifted generals, to take charge of the new Continental Army formed in the South.
7. The surrender of Cornwallis at Yorktown forced the British to seek peace with America, although occasional fighting between the two sides continued for a time.
8. Those Americans who remained true to the King and the British empire were called Loyalists.
9. America financed the war by printing paper dollars called Continentals.
10. Great Britain acknowledged that the United States was an independent nation with the signing of the Peace of Paris, or peace treaty.

6. It was difficult to persuade the states to pool their troops and supplies in a single national effort. There were also boundary and land disputes that distracted from the war.
7. Patriots felt that Loyalists were a serious military threat. Loyalists were charged with acting as spies and encouraging the Indians to support the British and attack innocent settlers. Loyalists were accused also of trying to persuade American soldiers to desert the Continental Army.

As penalty for their British sympathies, Loyalists were carefully watched, their freedom of movement was curtailed, and sometimes their homes were looted or destroyed. Those suspected of political or military acts were jailed, kept in their homes, or sent to a faraway place. Loyalists who served in the British army or who gave aid to the enemy in some way were tried for treason. The property of some wealthy Loyalists was confiscated.
8. Most state constitutions guaranteed trial by jury; bail; free trial in open court; writs of habeas corpus; freedom of press, religion, and assembly; and petition of government.

THE ENDURING REVOLUTION

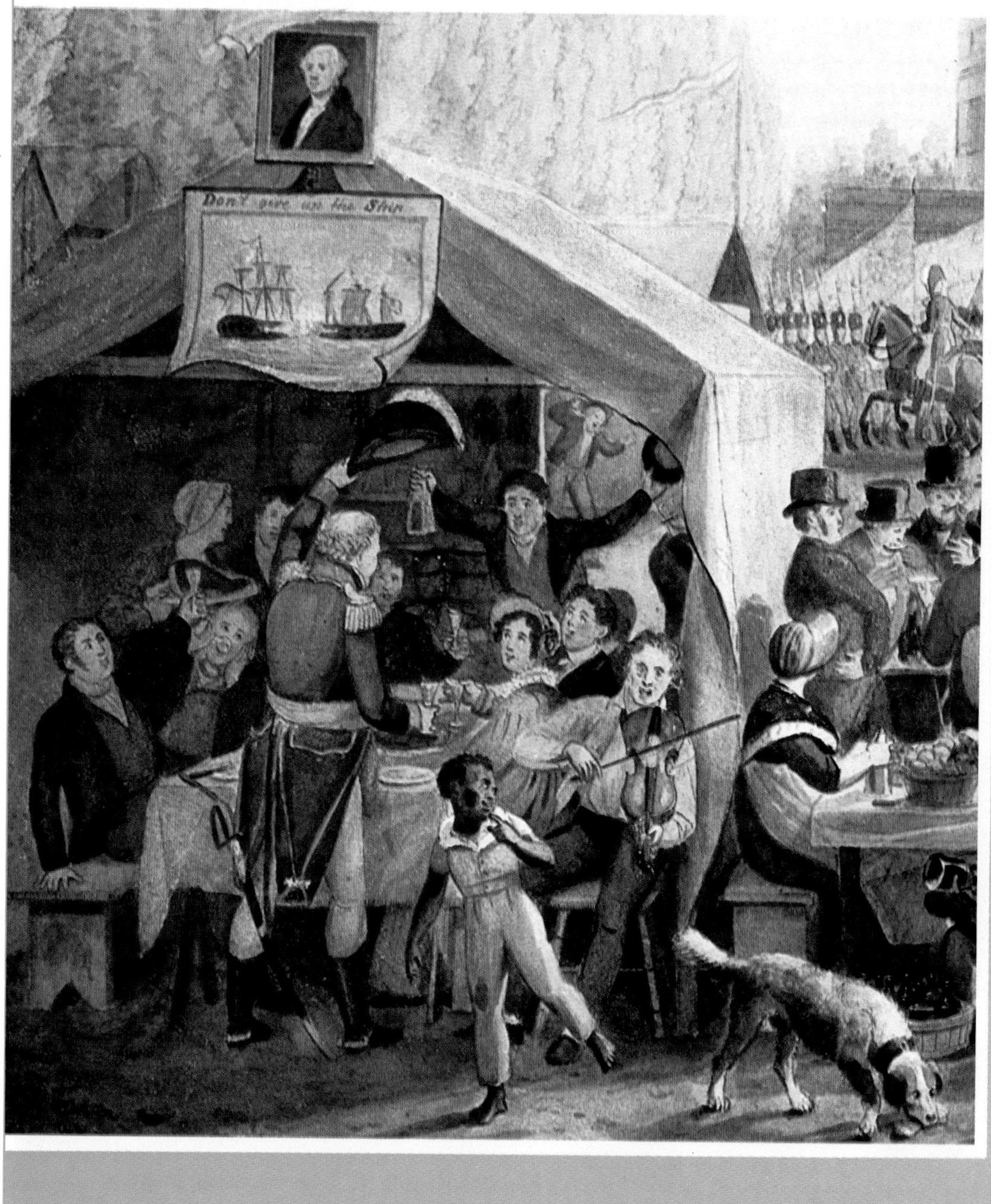

Background Information

1. PICTURE This is a detail from a painting by J. L. Krimmel in 1819. It shows the celebration of the Fourth of July in Philadelphia, the nation's birthplace. Most of the city's 130,000 people turned out to enjoy the festivities that included the usual banquets, fireworks, and patriotic speeches. At the time of this celebration, in 1819, almost a half century had passed since the signing of the Declaration of Independence. Only a handful of people were left who could recall the actual event, but the observance of the occasion had become a national tradition.

LESSON 1

THE AMERICAN REVOLUTION is the single most important event in the history of the United States. Without it, there would have been no United States. The American Revolution has also had a great effect on the way people in the United States have thought about themselves and about other countries. It has become the standard by which Americans judge all other revolutions.

What, then, was the meaning of the American Revolution? What kind of revolution was it? Perhaps as important, what kind of revolution *wasn't* it? Now that you have studied the course of events between 1763 and 1783, you will be able to find answers to those questions.

The Nature of the American Revolution

There are a number of ways to get at the true nature of a revolution. One is to study its leaders—to find out about their backgrounds, their social and economic positions, their occupations, and so on. Suppose we were to discover that the leaders of a revolution were all small farmers. That would suggest that farm problems were an important cause of the revolution. Suppose we found that a very large number of the leaders came from one part of the country—say, the South. That might be a clue that matters of special interest to that section had something to do with the revolution. If a great many of the leaders were from the poorer classes, what kind of clue might that give us?

Leaders of the American Revolution. What kind of people were the leaders of the American Revolution? Since we can't possibly consider all of them here, we have selected a sample. Our sample is drawn from the fifty-six signers of the Declaration of Independence—surely among the leaders of the Revolution. Here are short descriptions of twenty-eight—or one half—of the signers.

John Adams Graduate of Harvard College. Well-to-do lawyer; member of Massachusetts legislature.

Samuel Adams Graduate of Harvard College. Son of a wealthy brewer; most powerful leader in the legislature of Massachusetts.

Josiah Bartlett Doctor: colonel in the militia; member of the New Hampshire Provincial Congress.

Charles Carroll Attended colleges in France. Important landholder and political leader in Maryland; religious leader among American Catholics.

Samuel Chase Leading lawyer in the colony of Maryland; member of Maryland legislature.

George Clymer Prominent Philadelphia merchant and a leading Pennsylvania politician.

Benjamin Franklin Pennsylvania publisher; internationally known scientist.

Elbridge Gerry Graduate of Harvard College. Wealthy Massachusetts merchant and political leader.

Lyman Hall Graduate of Yale College. Doctor; minister; planter in Georgia.

John Hancock Graduate of Harvard College. Merchant; one of the richest men in Massachusetts.

LESSON 1 (*1-2 days*)

Performance Objective

To summarize the American Revolution by listing changes that occurred as a result of the conflict.

Vocabulary

Generalization, republicanism

Activities

1. **REFERENCE MATERIAL** *The Story of the Declaration of Independence* by Dumas Malone (New York: Oxford University Press, 1954) contains background information on the Declaration, with pictures and biographical sketches of each of the signers. This book is a standard reference on the subject and is available in most libraries.

2. **RESEARCH/ORAL REPORT** There were fifty-six signers of the Declaration. Some are famous and remembered by all Americans (John Hancock, Samuel and John Adams, Thomas Jefferson, Benjamin Franklin), but most of the other names are not "household words." Assign each student one of the lesser-known signers of the Declaration and ask the student to find out as much as possible about the signer's life, especially what happened to him as a result of the decision to sign the document. Franklin's remark about either hanging together or hanging separately was a grim forecast. Did the signers actually suffer hardships or were there no consequences to their act?

Background Information

PICTURE "Congress Approves the Declaration of Independence." The picture shows more than half of the fifty-six members of the Continental Congress who eventually signed the historic document. Standing in the group at the center are (left to right) John Adams of Massachusetts, Roger Sherman of Connecticut, James Wilson of Pennsylvania, and Thomas Jefferson of Virginia. Seated at the desk facing Jefferson is John Hancock of Massachusetts. This painting was begun by Robert E. Pine in 1785. When he died, Edward Savage finished the painting.

KEY 1. Richard Stockton, N.J.; 2 Josiah Bartlett, N.H.; 3. Thomas Nelson, Jr., Va.; 4. George Clymer, Pa.; 5. Francis Lightfoot Lee, Va.; 6. John Penn, N.C.; 7. Abraham Clark, N.J.; 8. John Morton, Pa.; 9. George Ross, Pa.; 10. James Smith, Pa.; 11. Samuel Adams, Mass.; 12. Robert Treat Paine, Mass.; 13. Button Gwinnett, Ga.; 14. Robert Morris, Pa.; 15. Benjamin Harrison, Va.; 16. Carter Braxton, Va.; 17. John Hart, N.J.; 18. John Adams, Mass.; 19. Roger Sherman, Conn.; 20. James Wilson, Pa.; 21. Thomas Jefferson, Va.; 22. Charles Thompson, (Secretary); 23. John Hancock, Mass.; 24. Francis Hopkinson, N.J.; 25. William Ellery, R.I.; 26. Edward Rutledge, S.C.; 27. Benjamin Franklin, Pa.; 28. Charles Carroll, Md.; 29. Richard Henry Lee, Va.; 30. George Read, Del.; 31. George Taylor, Pa.; 32. Stephen Hopkins, R.I.

Members of the Continental Congress met in Philadelphia to approve the Declaration of Independence. The serious expressions on their faces show how gravely they viewed a break with Great Britain.

Joseph Hewes A well-to-do North Carolina shipowner and merchant; a member of the North Carolina assembly.

William Hooper Graduate of Harvard College. A wealthy lawyer in North Carolina; member of North Carolina legislature.

Stephen Hopkins Wealthy merchant; chief justice of Rhode Island; chancellor of Rhode Island College.

Thomas Jefferson Graduate of William and Mary College. Owner of large plantation in Virginia; member of Virginia legislature.

Richard H. Lee Educated in England. Owner of large plantation in Virginia; member of Virginia legislature.

Philip Livingston Graduate of Yale College. Member of wealthy New York family that owned large amounts of land and had powerful ties with political leaders.

Arthur Middleton Educated in England. Son of one of the richest families in South Carolina; member of the South Carolina legislature.

Robert Morris Philadelphia merchant; partner in one of the largest firms in America doing business in Britain; member of Pennsylvania Assembly.

Thomas Nelson, Jr. Educated in England. Merchant and planter; member of Virginia Council; colonel in militia.

William Paca Graduate of College of Philadelphia (now University of Pennsylvania). Owner of a large plantation in Maryland; lawyer and politician.

Robert T. Paine Graduate of Harvard College. A well-known Massachusetts lawyer.

Caesar Rodney Well-to-do Delaware landowner. Member of provincial legislature; general in Delaware militia.

Benjamin Rush Graduate of College of New Jersey (now Princeton University) and University of Edinburgh (medical degree) in Scotland. Philadelphia physician; professor of chemistry.

Edward Rutledge Studied law in England. Owner of large plantation; member of one of the richest and most powerful families in South Carolina.

Roger Sherman At first a shoemaker; later a lawyer, judge, and legislator in Connecticut.

William Whipple Well-to-do merchant in New Hampshire; active in New Hampshire politics.

John Witherspoon Graduate of University of Edinburgh. President of College of New Jersey; prominent church leader.

Oliver Wolcott Graduate of Yale College. Lawyer and judge; colonel in Connecticut militia.

Let's say that these twenty-eight are a fair representation of those who led the American Revolution. What generalizations can you make about them? What could you say about their social position—that is, were they in the upper class or the lower? their economic position—were they well-off or not well-off? their educational backgrounds? In answering that last question, you will want to keep in mind that less than one percent of the total population of the American colonies attended college. College was usually for the upper classes only. Would you say that such people would be likely to make a revolution to change the economic system? Would they be likely to seek ways to redistribute wealth and property from those who had it to those who did not?

Power—before and after the Revolution. A second way to get at the true nature of a revolution is to see whether it brought a new group of people to power. Suppose, before a revolution, people of one religious group, or one social class, or one economic group were in power. Then, after the revolution, we found they were no longer in power. Might not that lead us to certain conclusions?

3. DISCUSSION In his book *The True Believer* (New York: Harper & Row, 1966), Eric Hoffer stated that revolutions are planned by men and women of words, carried out by fanatics, and tamed by people of action. Ask your students to determine if this is true by reviewing those people who played a significant part in the Revolutionary War era. Identify, as best you can, those who were people of words and those who were fanatics. Request that students wait until they have studied the making of the Constitution before identifying those who were practical people of action.

4. DISCUSSION In the major revolutions that have taken place (English, American, French, and Russian), most of the leaders have been young. Ask your students to characterize the ideal revolutionist and to explain why the young seem to be best suited for the role.

Or suppose those with certain values or beliefs—say, the value of republicanism, perhaps, or of rule by religious leaders—were in power before a revolution. Then, after it, we found people with very different values were in power. Might not that also lead us to certain conclusions? On the other hand, if the same persons, or type of persons, were in power both before and after a revolution, that would give an important clue about the meaning of the revolution.

You know, of course, that the chief aim of the American Revolution was to

Rhode Island

Office	*Officeholder Before Revolution*	*Officeholder During and/or After Revolution*
Governor	Joseph Wanton	Nicholas Cooke
Lt. Governor	Darius Sessions	William Bradford
Secretary	Henry Ward	Henry Ward
Treasurer	Joseph Clark	Joseph Clark
Attorney General	Henry Marchant	Henry Marchant
Chief Justice	Stephen Hopkins	Metcalf Bowler
Associate Justices	Job Bennett, Jr.	Shearjashub Bourne
	Metcalf Bowler	Jabez Bowen
	William Greene	William Greene
	Joseph Russell	Thomas Wells, Jr.
Assistants	John Almy	James Arnold, Jr.
	Peleg Barker	Thomas Church
	John Collins	John Collins
	John Congdon	John Jepson
	David Harris	Ambrose Page
	William Potter	William Potter
	Jonathan Randall	Jonathan Randall
	William Richmond	Peter Phillips
	John Sayles, Jr.	John Sayles, Jr.
	Thomas Wickes	Simeon Potter

end the power of the English king and Parliament over the colonies. It did that quite successfully. But within America itself, did power shift from one group to another? To answer that question, let us look at some Americans who held power before and after the Revolution.

Once again, we cannot examine here all the political leaders in each colony and state. We have selected leaders from two states, Rhode Island and Connecticut. For this example, a political leader is one who held high office in the colony or state at some time.

Connecticut *(Note that several people held more than one position.)*

Office	*Officeholder Before Revolution*	*Officeholder During and/or After Revolution*
Governor	Jonathan Trumbull	Jonathan Trumbull
Lt. Governor	Matthew Griswold	Matthew Griswold
Secretary	George Wylls	George Wylls
Treasurer	John Lawrence	John Lawrence
Attorney General	None	None
Chief Justice	Matthew Griswold	Matthew Griswold
Associate Justices	Eliphalet Dyer Samuel Huntington William Pitkin Roger Sherman	Eliphalet Dyer Samuel Huntington William Pitkin Roger Sherman
Assistants	Shubael Conant Abraham Davenport Eliphalet Dyer Jabez Hamlin James A. Hillhouse Jabez Huntington William Samuel Johnson William Pitkin Elisha Sheldon Roger Sherman Joseph Spencer Oliver Wolcott	Samuel Huntington Abraham Davenport Eliphalet Dyer Jabez Hamlin Richard Law Jabez Huntington William Williams William Pitkin Elisha Sheldon Roger Sherman Joseph Spencer Oliver Wolcott

5. RESEARCH/ORAL OR WRITTEN REPORT Nietsche said, "There are no facts, only interpretations." In the history of the American Revolution, several interpretations have emerged. Perhaps some of your students would be interested in delving into one of the following sources regarding these theories:
Empire theory—*The Coming of the Revolution, 1763–1775* by Lawrence H. Gipson (New York: Harper & Brothers, 1954)
Economic theory—*The Colonial Merchants of the American Revolution, 1763–1776* by Arthur M. Schlesinger (New York: Atheneum, 1968)
Social theory—*The American Revolution Considered as a Social Movement* by J. Franklin Jameson (Princeton, N.J.: Princeton University Press, 1940)
Conservative theory—*Out of Our Past: The Forces That Shaped Modern America* by Carl Degler (New York: Harper & Row, 1970)
Whig theory—*The American Revolution* by George O. Trevelyan (New York: McKay, 1964)
Neo-Whig theory—*Seedtime of the Republic* by Clinton Rossiter (New York: Harcourt Brace Jovanovich, 1953).

Yale University Art Gallery

Jonathan Trumbull was governor of Connecticut before, during, and after the Revolution. This portrait was painted by his son John, one of the outstanding artists of the period.

Not all the states would show results quite like those for Rhode Island and Connecticut. Judging by the record in those two states, however, would you say that there was, or was not, a major change of leaders during and after the Revolution? Keep in mind that death and retirement would account for the disappearance of at least some who held office before the Revolution.

The degree of change. There is a third way to get at the real meaning of a revolution. That is to see whether really great changes did take place in government and society during and after the revolution. Suppose an entirely new kind of government came into being. That would tell us a great deal about the revolution. If property were taken from one group and given to another, that would also tell us something important. If a social class that was formerly at the bottom of the heap was raised up, and one that was formerly at the top was pulled down, that would surely tell us something about the meaning of the revolution. If such changes did *not* take place, that, too, would be important to know.

Clearly, one change brought about by the American Revolution was the end of monarchy in America. Were there other important changes in government? Look back at page 135 where we talk about the new state governments, and decide.

Seizure of property. As for seizing the property of one group, you will recall that there was some of that. Estates of many wealthy Loyalists were seized by a number of state governments. That might suggest that a sweeping change in property ownership took place.

But two things must be noted. The first is that not all Loyalists lost their lands. In fact, most did not. The second is that when states did take land from wealthy Loyalists, they did not give it to those with little or no property. Generally, the lands were sold. Often wealthy people and speculators bought them.

Condition of the slaves. The condition of the lowest class in American society, the slaves, was not much changed by the Revolution. A small number gained their freedom by serving in the Continental

Army. And a number of northern states, including Rhode Island, Pennsylvania, Massachusetts, and Connecticut, took steps to abolish, or end, slavery. But in those states there were few slaves anyway.

In the parts of the country where most slaves lived, slavery remained. The most important change affecting slavery during the Revolution took place in Delaware, Virginia, Maryland, and South Carolina. These states agreed not to bring in any more slaves from Africa.

The colonists' rights. There is still another way to learn about the real meaning of a revolution. That is to see what those who made it *said* it was about.

Think back to events between 1763 and 1775. What were the colonists' grievances against England? What did they mean when they spoke of the "rights of Englishmen"? What did they believe was happening to those rights? What part did this play in their decision to rebel?

CHECKUP

1. What generalizations can you make about the backgrounds of the leaders of the American Revolution?
2. To what extent did the Revolution bring a new group of people to power?
3. What changes were brought about by the Revolution?

LESSON 2

The Significance of the American Revolution

From what you have learned so far, it is clear that the American Revolution, compared with many modern-day revolutions, did not bring great social or economic change. Yet Americans thought their revolution was an event of great significance. They saw it as such not only for themselves but for the rest of the world. And they were right. The American Revolution has been one of the three or four most important revolutions in the past two hundred years.

A surge of pride. For one thing, the Revolution had a great effect on the way Americans thought about themselves. Before that time, Americans had felt themselves inferior in many ways to Europeans. It was to Europe, and especially to England, that the colonists had looked for leadership on almost all things. If America lacked what Europe had, Americans had regarded this as a sign of America's weakness, not Europe's. Thus, when the English said that the absence of an aristocratic class, of an established church, and of a polished high society were marks of America's backwardness, many Americans had agreed. Some had tried to imitate England. The term Yankee, which the English used for the colonists, was one of ridicule, meaning something like "hick" or "hayseed."

All that changed with the Revolution. The Americans lost their inferiority complex. "It was," says one writer, "as if the colonists blinked and suddenly saw their society in a new light." Those characteristics that stemmed from their century and a half as colonists were no longer viewed as weaknesses. They were now seen as strengths. The American differences from the Europeans became pluses instead of minuses.

It was true that there was no American aristocracy—the better to form a

LESSON 2 (*2 days*)

Performance Objective

To demonstrate in writing an understanding of the significance of the American Revolution two hundred years later.

Famous Person

Louis Kossuth

Vocabulary

Yankee, aristocracy

Activities

1. READING FOR INFORMATION/CREATIVE WRITING After your students have read the text for this lesson, ask them to write about the significance of the Revolution two hundred years later. Students should be encouraged to express themselves in whatever creative writing style they choose. Perhaps different students would like to share their thoughts with others after they have completed the assignment.

new society. It was true that they had no national church—the better to develop religious freedom. The absence of that sign of national power and pride, a standing army, meant that there would be civilian and not military rule in America. As for the simple American life, it was well suited to a true republican form of government. Within such a government, liberty and equality for all citizens could be achieved.

The term Yankee now became one of pride, and Americans made "Yankee Doodle" one of their favorite patriotic songs. There was a swelling of national pride. Americans, boasted Alexander Hamilton, were a "young people" whose greatness lay ahead of them. England, he said, had already seen its best days.

A model for the world. Just as the Revolution affected the way Americans thought about themselves, it affected the way they were to think about revolutions in other countries. Americans believed their republic, dedicated to popular rule and liberty, would serve as a model for the rest of the world. Many expected that Europeans would soon overthrow kings and set up republican governments of their own. Thus, America would lead the world into a new golden age of freedom.

One historian has commented on the boldness of this view.

> The audacity [boldness] of the revolutionaries of 1776 in claiming that their little colonial rebellion possessed universal significance is astounding. After

During the French Revolution, armed Parisians prepare to storm the Bastille, a prison that held many political prisoners. Most Americans approved the revolutionists' goals, if not their methods.

all, those thirteen colonies made up a tiny part of the Western world, containing perhaps two-and-a-half million people huddled along a narrow strip of the Atlantic coast, living on the fringes of Christendom. To think that anything they did would matter to the rest of the world was the height of arrogance.

Yet the fact is that other peoples *did* look upon the American Revolution as Americans did. They watched the American experiment with much interest. And they were greatly influenced by it.

Support for revolutions. For many years, Americans looked with favor upon revolutions that appeared to be modeled on their own. They voiced approval in 1789 as the French removed their king and set up a republic. The public executions that followed shocked many Americans. Still more became disillusioned when the French republic ended in the dictatorship of Napoleon. But Americans were not discouraged by what happened in France. To them, it was simply a case of a promising revolution gone wrong.

Americans likewise saw the uprisings of Spain's colonies in South and Central America in the early 1800s as carbon copies of their own revolution. And the United States experience was in fact a powerful example for the new South American republics. Venezuela, the first of the Spanish colonies to become independent, even modeled its constitution after the Constitution of the United States.

In nineteenth-century Europe, too, Americans were sure they could see the inevitable march of republicanism. In 1821 they greeted with wild enthusiasm the outbreak of the Greek rebellion against Turkish rule. Long before the outcome was certain, South Carolina asked Congress to recognize Greece's independence. One leading American even asked that the United States lend a fleet to aid the Greeks in their fight for liberty. In his message to Congress in 1822, President James Monroe went out of his way to praise the Greek struggle for independence. Americans greeted the revolutions that broke out in a number of European states in 1848 with the same enthusiasm.

Americans were favorably disposed toward the revolutions led by Simon Bolivar in South America. They compared those struggles against Spain with their own struggle against Britain.

2. DISCUSSION It has been said that two main ideas from the American Revolution reverberated around the world: **(a)** that all people are created equal, that they are endowed by their Creator with certain unalienable rights, that among these are life, liberty, and the pursuit of happiness; and **(b)** that to secure these rights, governments are instituted among people, deriving their just powers from the consent of the governed. Ask your students to evaluate their community and school in terms of these two concepts. Would Thomas Jefferson be proud to live in your town and go to your school? If not, why?

Continued on page 149

3. FILMS To provide a background for your students, you might want to show one of the following films. All are available for rental from Indiana University Audio-Visual Center, Bloomington, Ind. 47401. *The French Revolution: The Terror,* Western Civilization: Majesty and Madness series (19 minutes, color; Learning Corporation of America). *The French Revolution* (17 minutes, color; Coronet Films). *Russia: Czar to Lenin* (25 minutes, b & w; McGraw-Hill Text Film Division).

4. RESEARCH/ORAL REPORT Assign a student to find out and report to the class about Simon Bolivar, a South American revolutionist mentioned briefly in the picture caption.

5. DISCUSSION Karl Marx, the founder of modern communism, called revolutions the locomotives of history. Ask your students what they think Marx meant by that expression. How might this expression apply to the American Revolution?

The Visit of Louis Kossuth

The feelings of Americans about revolution in the mid-nineteenth century can be seen in their reaction to Louis Kossuth. In 1848 Kossuth, a Hungarian patriot, led an uprising in the Austro-Hungarian Empire. He wanted to separate Hungary from Austria and to free his homeland from the rule of the Hapsburg monarchs. The revolution failed, but a sympathetic United States government sent a naval vessel to bring Kossuth from Turkey, where he had fled, to the United States for a visit.

Arriving in New York in 1851, Kossuth received a hero's welcome. Whenever he appeared in public, huge crowds—recalling their own country's struggle for independence 75 years earlier—turned out to cheer him. Countless banquets and parades were held in Kossuth's honor. Americans eagerly copied his clothes and hair style. Stores sold Kossuth hats and Kossuth overcoats, and men grew Kossuth beards. Hungarian music and dances became all the rage. It would be many years before Hungary would become independent, yet to Americans Louis Kossuth embodied the dreams they had had since 1776 of leading the peoples of other lands away from the rule of kings and queens.

A million Americans turned out to catch a glimpse of—and to cheer—Louis Kossuth when the Hungarian revolutionist was given a parade in New York City soon after his arrival in the United States. In the scene below Kossuth waves his plumed hat to admirers gathered outside New York's City Hall.

A changing attitude. The twentieth century has witnessed more revolutions than any previous age. But in this century, the attitude of Americans toward the idea of revolution has become more mixed. Some revolutions, like the anticolonial movements in Asia in the 1940s, were applauded by Americans. To others, they have given only lukewarm support. To still others, like the Russian Revolution of 1917–1918 and the revolution that brought the Chinese Communists to power in the 1940s, Americans were opposed.

Why? The answer is complex. Some believe it is because American feelings toward revolution have changed. More likely, it is because revolutions themselves have changed. The goals that were so important to Americans in their Revolution play little part today in many revolutions around the world.

Few modern revolutions aim to bring about representative government and real elections. Few have anything to do with the "rights of Englishmen"—free speech and free press, trial by jury, protection against illegal searches and arbitrary jailing, and other civil rights. Most modern revolutions have brought about sweeping changes. They have often been aimed against those classes that controlled the government and owned property. And they have often been accompanied by bloody executions.

How are Americans likely to feel about a particular revolution in our time? Again, there are many factors that will determine that. But one of them is the way Americans view that revolution in the light of their own. The more similarities they see to the goals of the Revolution that gave birth to their republic, the more sympathetic they are likely to be.

That fact alone attests to the vitality of the American Revolution today, and to its continued hold on the American mind.

CHECKUP

1. How did the Revolution affect the way Americans thought about themselves?
2. How has the American Revolution affected the way Americans think about revolutions in other countries?

Key Facts from Chapter 8

1. The American Revolution is the single most important event in the history of the United States.
2. Most of the leaders of the American Revolution were well educated and well-to-do and were regarded as leaders in their colonies.
3. The Revolution brought about the end of monarchy in America.
4. The Revolution did not result in widespread economic and social change.
5. The Revolution gave Americans a feeling of great national pride.
6. Americans have generally judged revolutions in other countries by how similar their goals were to the goals of the American Revolution.

6. USING A MAP On an outline map of the world, have your students color in blue the areas where the concepts mentioned in Activity 2 are being tried. Color in red the areas where such concepts are being repressed.

This activity provides an opportunity to review place geography. You might want to expand on the suggested map activity by devising additional map-drill exercises for the class.

7. RESEARCH/ORAL REPORTS For a better understanding of the cultural impact of the war, you might wish to have some students report on selections from the following books: *The Literary History of the American Revolution, 1763–1783* by Moses Coit Tyler (New York: Ungar, 1957) and *The Pursuit of Science in Revolutionary America* by Brooke Hindle (Chapel Hill: University of North Carolina Press, 1956).

For more information on the latest directions taken by historians engaged in research on the Revolutionary era, see *The American Revolution Reconsidered* by Richard B. Morris (New York: Harper & Row, 1967, and *Essays on the American Revolution* by Stephen G. Kurtz and James H. Hutson (Chapel Hill: University of North Carolina Press, 1973).

Answers To Review Questions

1. Revolutions may be evaluated by studying their political leaders, by determining where the ruling power rests before and after the revolution, and by observing the degree of change resulting from the revolution.
2. The signers of the Declaration of Independence were **(a)** upper class, **(b)** wealthy, and **(c)** well educated. Usually persons of this background would not start a revolution because they enjoy all the good things the society offers—education, wealth, power, and social position.
3. The group in power did not change to any significant degree as a result of the Revolution.
4. Although the condition of slaves did not change dramatically as a result of the Revolution, some improvement did occur. A small number gained their freedom by serving in the Continental Army. Some northern states took steps to abolish slavery. And several southern and middle states agreed not to bring any more slaves from Africa.
5. Louis Kossuth was a Hungarian patriot who led an uprising to separate Hungary from Austria and to free his homeland from the rule of Austrian monarchs. Although the revolution failed, Americans were sympathetic with Kossuth's dream of independence. In the nineteenth century, Americans enthsiastically supported revolutions in South and Central America and Europe that appeared to be modeled after their own Revolution.
6. Most revolutions of the twentieth century did not have the same goals as the American Revolution.

★ REVIEWING THE CHAPTER ★

People, Places, and Events

John Adams *P. 139*
Samuel Adams *P. 139*
Charles Carroll *P. 139*
Benjamin Franklin *P. 139*
Elbridge Gerry *P. 139*
John Hancock *P. 139*
Richard H. Lee *P. 141*
Robert Morris *P. 141*
Benjamin Rush *P. 141*

Review Questions

1. What are three ways to evaluate the true nature of a revolution? *Pp. 139, 141, 144* Les. 1
2. As you studied the information about the signers of the Declaration of Independence, what conclusions did you reach about **(a)** their social position, **(b)** their economic position, **(c)** their educational background? Would these people usually be the ones to start a revolution? Why, or why not? *Pp. 139–141* Les. 1
3. Look at the list of political leaders for Rhode Island and Connecticut on pages 142–143. Compare office holders before the Revolution with those during and/or after the Revolution. What conclusion can you reach about the group in power before and after? Les. 1
4. What effect did the Revolution have on the condition of slaves? *Pp. 144–145* L.1
5. Why did Americans give Louis Kossuth a hero's welcome? What does the reaction of the American people to Kossuth tell you about their attitude toward revolutions in the nineteenth century? *P. 148* L.2
6. Why did Americans tend to change their attitude toward revolutions in the twentieth century? *P. 149* Les. 2

Chapter Test

On a separate piece of paper, write ***T*** *if the statement is true and* ***F*** *if the statement is false.*

1. The chief aim of the American Revolution was to end the power of the English King and Parliament over the American colonies. T
2. When compared to many modern revolutions, the American Revolution did not bring great social or economic changes. T
3. The leaders of the American Revolution were mostly farmers without much formal education. F
4. The Revolution brought a new group of political leaders into power in the American colonies. F
5. As a result of the Revolution, many poor people were given land that had been taken away from the Loyalists. F
6. As a result of the Revolution some northern states took steps to end slavery, but, in general, the condition of slaves in America did not change much. T
7. The Revolution gave Americans a real sense of national pride that they had never had before. T
8. In the eighteenth and nineteenth centuries, Americans looked with favor upon revolutions that appeared to be modeled after their own. T
9. Americans were opposed to the Russian Revolution of 1917–1918, because the goals that were so important to them in the American Revolution played little part in the Russian Revolution. T
10. Few modern revolutions aim to bring about representative government and real elections. T

★ REVIEWING THE UNIT ★

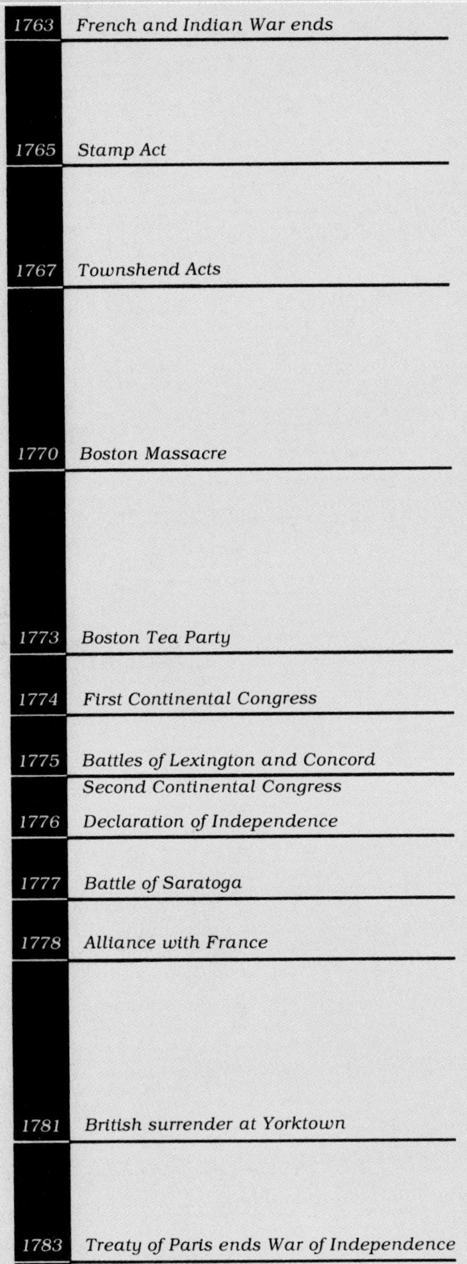

1763 French and Indian War ends
1765 Stamp Act
1767 Townshend Acts
1770 Boston Massacre
1773 Boston Tea Party
1774 First Continental Congress
1775 Battles of Lexington and Concord
Second Continental Congress
1776 Declaration of Independence
1777 Battle of Saratoga
1778 Alliance with France
1781 British surrender at Yorktown
1783 Treaty of Paris ends War of Independence

The 1760s saw rising tension between Britain and its American colonies. Britain put new taxes on the colonies. Most Americans regarded those taxes and other British measures as threats to their well-being and their liberty. The Boston Massacre in 1770 and the Boston Tea Party in 1773 inflamed the feelings of both British and Americans.

War began in 1775 when British soldiers clashed with American militiamen at Lexington and Concord. Soon afterwards George Washington of Virginia was made the leader of the American troops. Independence soon became the goal of the Patriots. On July 4, 1776, the Declaration of Independence—written by Thomas Jefferson—was adopted.

At first, Americans fought a defensive war. They won few victories but avoided a crushing defeat. A victory at Trenton in December 1776 and another at Princeton a week later boosted Patriot morale. The turning point of the war was the American victory at Saratoga in 1777. After that battle, France openly supported the American cause. In the later years of the war, fighting shifted to the South. The victory of the Americans and their French allies at Yorktown assured American independence.

The Revolution is the single most important event in United States history. It brought about the end of monarchy in America, but it did not cause great social or economic change. In later years, Americans have usually judged revolutions in other countries by how similar their goals were to the goals of the American Revolution.

Answers to Unit Questions

1. Philadelphia and New York were the largest cities in 1783. Boston, Charleston, and Baltimore had a population between 10,000 and 30,000.
2. Philadelphia
3. Georgia was both the westernmost and southernmost state in 1783.
4. Spain owned land south and west of the United States and Britain owned land north of the United States.
5. Eleven colonies. Only Delaware and Rhode Island are untouched by the Appalachian Mountains.
6. Baltimore to Charleston: approximately 500 miles (800 kilometers). Newport to Richmond: approximately 420 miles (400 kilometers)
7. Mississippi River
8. The Old Northwest included the present-day states of Ohio, Indiana, Illinois, Michigan, Wisconsin, and part of Minnesota. The Old Southwest included the present-day states of Kentucky, Tennessee, Alabama, and Mississippi.

★ REVIEWING THE UNIT 

Skills Development: Reading a Map

The Treaty of Paris, signed in 1783, recognized the independence of the United States and established its new boundaries. Study the map and then answer the following questions.

1. What were the two largest cities in 1783? Which cities had a population between 10,000 and 30,000?
2. Which city is located near the intersection of 75°N 40°W?
3. In 1783, which was the westernmost state? the southernmost state?
4. In 1783, which European nations owned land bordering on the United States?
5. The Appalachian Mountains extend through how many of the thirteen original American colonies?
6. Using the scale of miles, measure the distance from Baltimore to Charleston; Newport to Richmond.
7. What geographical feature formed the westernmost boundary of the United States in 1783?
8. Name the states eventually carved out of The Old Northwest and The Old Southwest. If you need help, refer to the map on pages 764–765.

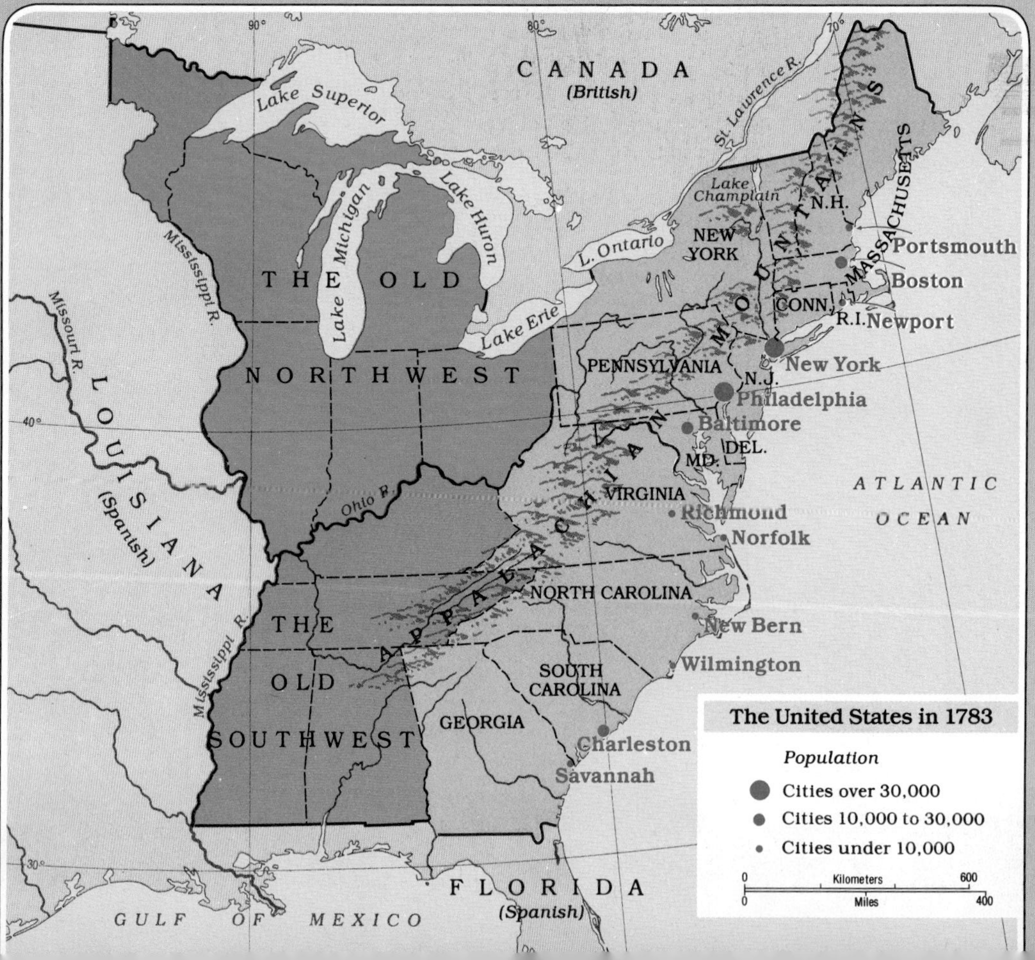

Americans and Limited Government

THE MAKING OF A NATION

CREATING A STRONG UNION

Background Information

SIGNING OF THE CONSTITUTION This picture of the last session of the Constitutional Convention on Sptember 17, 1787, was painted by Thomas Rossiter, a historical and portrait painter of the nineteenth century.

The last session began with a reading of the Constitution, although most delegates probably knew it by heart by this time. Then eighty-one-year-old Benjamin Franklin rose to make the speech that was intended to set the stage for the approval of the Constitution. However, since he was unable to stand for a long period because of poor health, Franklin asked James Wilson, another Pennsylvania delegate, to read the speech.

Before a vote on the Constitution could be taken, a motion was made to increase the number of members of the House of Representatives. Washington, president of the Convention, then surprised everyone by making a speech appealing for the passage of the motion. This was his second speech of the Convention.

After adopting the motion and approving the Constitution, the delegates began to come forward to sign the Constitution as shown in Rossiter's painting.

Ben Franklin did manage to get in the last word—according to James Madison's extensive *Notes* taken during the Convention. Watching the delegates as they signed the Constitution, Franklin remarked that during the Convention he had often looked at the rising-sun design on the back of Washington's chair and wondered if the sun was rising or setting. Madison

LESSON 1

ON APRIL 21, 1967, a group of military men overthrew the democratic government of Greece. The new government leaders quickly limited the freedom of the Greek people. One of their first steps was to abolish elections. They then moved to silence opposition. They censored newspapers, drove unfriendly editors from the country, and jailed political opponents. They even regulated personal conduct, forbade certain clothing, and dictated hair styles.

Very likely you reacted strongly to what you just read. Have you thought about why? Really, it is a matter of values or beliefs. A government had taken unlimited power over its citizens. In doing so, it had taken from them their liberty. And if you are like most Americans, that runs counter to your idea of what a government has a right to do.

No one has ever put the case against government power more strongly than Thomas Paine, the author of *Common Sense.* "Government," wrote Paine, "even in its best state, is but a necessary evil; in its worst, an intolerable one." Thomas Jefferson, author of the Declaration of Independence and third President of the United States, expressed his distrust of government only a little less strongly. "That government governs best," said Jefferson, "which governs least."

Government power—how much? In the two hundred years since Paine wrote, the world has changed in many ways. Most of us understand that government performs many important

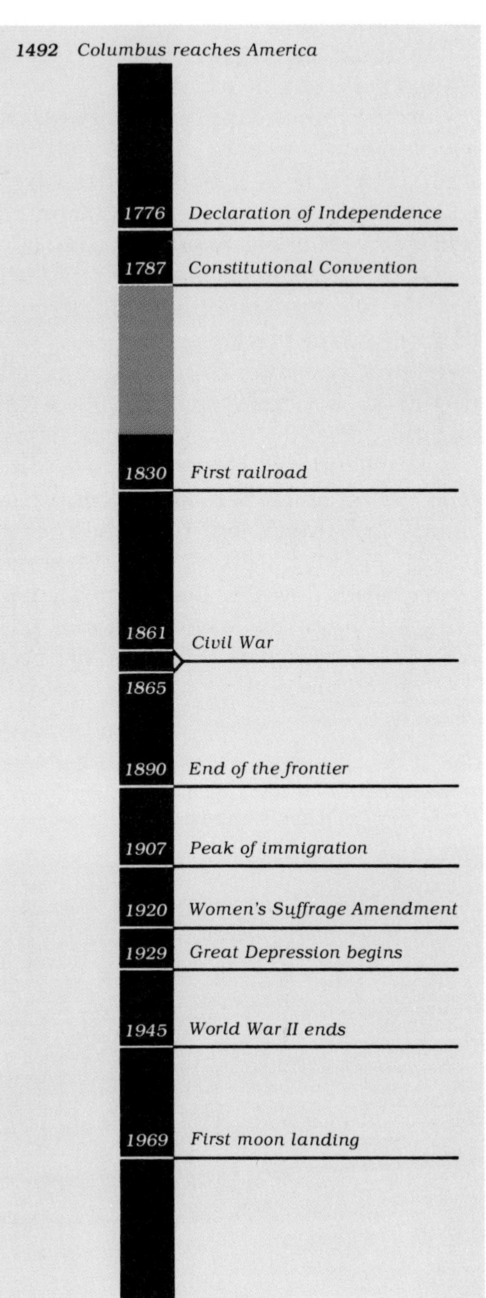

noted that Franklin concluded that it was definitely a rising sun. Note that Rossiter incorrectly interpreted Franklin's statement and painted a sunburst design on a tapestry instead of on Washington's chair.

Both this painting and Washington's chair with the rising-sun design are on display at Independence National Historical Park in Philadelphia, Pennsylvania.

LESSON 1 *(2 days)*

Performance Objectives

1. Given a list of actions involving the current federal government, to determine whether the government under the Articles of Confederation would have had the power to perform each action. **2.** To write an essay explaining the need for and the details of the legislation dealing with the Northwest Territory. **3.** To describe orally or in writing three events or situations that convinced a growing number of Americans of the need to strengthen the Articles of Confederation.

Vocabulary

Confederation, federal system, sovereignty, Northwest Territory, Land Ordinance of 1785, Northwest Ordinance of 1787, depression, Shays's Rebellion

Activities

1. INTRODUCING THE UNIT The central theme of this unit is the development of the federal government. Begin a discussion of the powers of the federal government today. Ask students to name some of the things the government can do that affect the lives of its citizens. (Draft; tax; arrest; etc.) Then draw up a list of those things the government cannot do. Here students may demonstrate their knowledge of the Bill of Rights. The following questions may aid your discussion. **(a)** What is the purpose of the actions the government can take that affect citizens? (Protect the nation; provide for general welfare; etc.) **(b)** What is the purpose of prohibiting the government from taking certain actions? (Protect individual rights; property; life; etc.) **(c)** Which is the more important, protecting the nation or protecting the individual's rights? Here students must be prepared to explain their answer.

This discussion can then lead to the new government that Americans attempted to establish after the Revolution. What particular fears would be uppermost in people's minds? (Too powerful a central government; too much power in one person's hands; etc.) What might happen if the government was too limited?

As you progress through this unit, there will be opportunities to refer back to this initial discussion when you study the Articles of Confederation, the Constitutional Convention, the Bill of Rights, the Virginia Resolutions, and the Hartford Convention.

tasks in a modern society. Even those who believe that government has too much power and does too many things today would agree that there are certain things government must do.

But few Americans would want the government to have power without limit. The title of a book written by a college president in America's bicentennial year probably expresses the concerns of many: *An Overgoverned Society.* Plainly there is a lingering distrust of government power.

In few if any other countries do people debate so seriously and so often the question whether their government has too much power. Newspaper accounts often tell of some person or group that claims the government has exceeded its power. Monday, the day the Supreme Court hands down its decisions, usually brings rulings on whether some government agency or official—or even Congress itself—has the power to do certain things.

Few things stir up Americans more than the belief that government officials have abused their power. When the Watergate scandal of 1973–1974 revealed that President Richard Nixon had engaged in doubtful and probably illegal activity, public opinion turned against him. Faced with impeachment by Congress, Nixon resigned on August 9, 1974, less than two years after he had been reelected by a huge majority.

A United States senator phrased the concern of Americans this way in a speech at one of the national party conventions in 1976:

> The issue this year, quite simply, is this: How much government is too much government? How many laws are too many laws? How much taxation is too much taxation? How much coercion [force] is too much coercion?

One of the landmarks of self-government by European colonists in America was the agreement by 41 adult males on the Pilgrim ship *Mayflower* to work for "just and equal" laws. The signing of the Mayflower Compact, as shown here, is as an artist imagined it many years later.

A deeply rooted belief. Our belief that limits should be placed on the power to govern carries over into almost every organization we form, from school groups to fan clubs. Nearly all of them quickly draw up rules which limit the powers of the officers.

The belief in limited government is rooted deeply in the American past. When colonists spoke of the "rights of Englishmen," they meant personal rights that no government could take away. At the bottom of the American Revolution was the question of government power. And the idea of limited government is at the very heart of the Declaration of Independence. You have already read that when Americans created their new state governments, they carefully set down which powers the governments had—and which they did not have. They did the same in writing the Articles of Confederation, the constitution of the new national government.

The Articles of Confederation

Those who wrote the Articles had to deal with another question. It was agreed that certain powers were to be denied to all governments, state as well as national. But of the powers that *would* be granted, which should be given to the national government, and which should be kept by the states?

A system in which powers are divided between a central government and local governments is called a *federal system*. The chief problem in federalism is deciding which powers should be given to each level of government. That may look easy, but it is really quite difficult. England and the North American colonies wrestled for a dozen years over the question of which powers should belong to the government in London, and which should be left to the colonial governments. When an answer could not be found, Britain lost much of its American empire.

Limiting the central government. In striking a balance in the Articles of Confederation, its writers came down on the side of local government. By no means, however, was the central government left without power. Congress could maintain an army and navy and thus could make war and peace. It could make treaties and alliances with other countries. It could regulate coinage, borrow money, establish a post office, and manage affairs with the Indians.

However, it is the powers *denied* to Congress that show the effect of America's unhappy experience with Britain's strong central government. Those who wrote the Articles, remembering how Britain had used the power to regulate trade with America, denied that power to their own central government. Recalling their quarrels over the Parliament's claim to levy taxes, they denied that right to the new Congress. Believing that the Parliament's control of the money supply had made for hard times, they gave the states the right to issue their own money. And with their grievances against George III fresh in mind, they decided the new government of the United States should have no chief executive, or president.

The Articles gave each state, no matter how large or small, one vote in Congress. For any important decision, nine states had to agree. The consent of all thirteen

2. DISCUSSION After students have read this lesson, have them reread the introduction to this unit on pages 155–157. Discuss ways in which, and reasons why, our lives are subject to government control. Bring out the point that government control need not be thought of in negative terms only. Is there a need today for more, or less, government involvement in areas such as education, television, sports, and transportation?

3. READING FOR INFORMATION/DISCUSSION Obtain a current-year copy of the *The Information Please Almanac,* published by Dan Golenpaul Associates in New York. Other current almanacs will also suffice for this activity. Turn to the section concerned with the news events for the preceding year. From that section, select events that concern actions by the federal government. Then ask your students to decide if the government under the Articles of Confederation had the power to perform the actions.

For example, the notation in the 1977 *Almanac* for April 10, 1976, is "U.S. and Soviet agree on treaty for limiting size of underground nuclear tests for peaceful purposes." The government under the Articles of Confederation had the power to make treaties and alliances with other countries, thus the government could have performed this action. Another example is the notation for December 19, 1975, that begins "Congress passes tax-cut extension bill. . . ." Under the Articles of Confederation the government did not have the power to levy taxes, so it could not have performed this action.

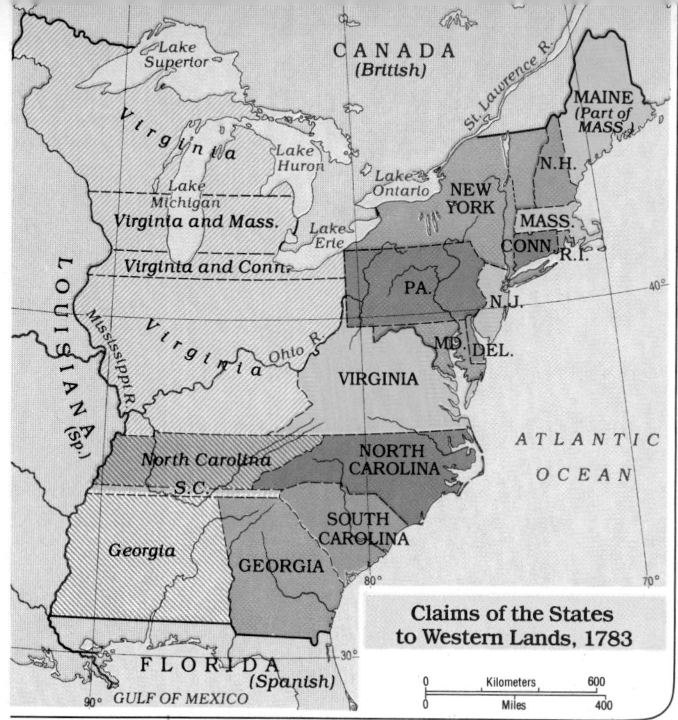

Claims of the States to Western Lands, 1783

In 1783, several of the original states still claimed land—as shown on the map above—between the Appalachian Mountains and the Mississippi River. But by 1787—as shown below—part of this region, known as the Northwest Territory, had been ceded to the federal government. By 1802, other claims were ceded.

The Northwest Territory 1787

was needed to *amend*, or change, the Articles. Thus no needed power could be given to the central government if even one state objected. That gave meaning to the statement in the Articles that "each state retains its sovereignty [supreme power], freedom, and independence."

The Articles' weaknesses. Two attempts were made to amend the Articles so that Congress could raise money through a 5 percent tax on imports. Each time, however, one state refused to go along, and the amendment failed. Without the power to regulate trade among the states, Congress looked on helplessly as some states taxed goods coming from other states.

These and other limits on the power of the central government were crippling. One of the weaknesses of the Articles was that, without the power to tax, Congress could only *ask* the states to give their share of money to pay the expenses of government. Since the states could not or would not do so, the central government was always without money. To make either the citizens or the states obey its laws, it had to depend on state courts, because the Articles did not set up federal courts. The states, in fact, often paid no attention to the wishes of Congress, and Congress could do nothing about it.

Despite these weaknesses, the government under the Articles of Confederation did win the war and gain a favorable peace. That was no small feat.

The Northwest Territory. The government also dealt wisely with the problem of western lands. Before the Articles went into effect, seven states had made claims—based on their colonial charters—to land west of the Allegheny Mountains. Some of these claims overlapped, and most of them were vague. Maryland refused to ratify the Articles until those states agreed to turn over their land claims to the new national government.

Congress passed two important laws dealing with the western region known as the Northwest Territory—that is, the lands west of Pennsylvania and Virginia and north of the Ohio River. The Land Ordinance of 1785 set up the policy for the sale of this land. It was divided into townships 6 miles (9.6 km) square—that is, each township was 36 square miles (93.6 square km). Each township was further divided into "sections" of 640 acres (256 ha), or 1 square mile (2.6 square km). The land was to be sold at auction in 640-acre units for a minimum of one dollar an acre. Congress required that one section of each township be set aside to maintain public schools. The law was more favorable to land companies than to small farmers, who found it hard to scrape up $640 at one time. But it did open the way for an orderly settlement of the region. The sale of land also provided much-needed revenue for the new government.

The Northwest Ordinance. The second and more important land law was the Northwest Ordinance of 1787. This law set up the system for governing the Northwest Territory. Under the law, Congress would appoint the governor and other officials until such time as there were 5,000 adult males in the territory. At that point, the settlers could choose their own legislature and send a

Land Survey in the Northwest Territory

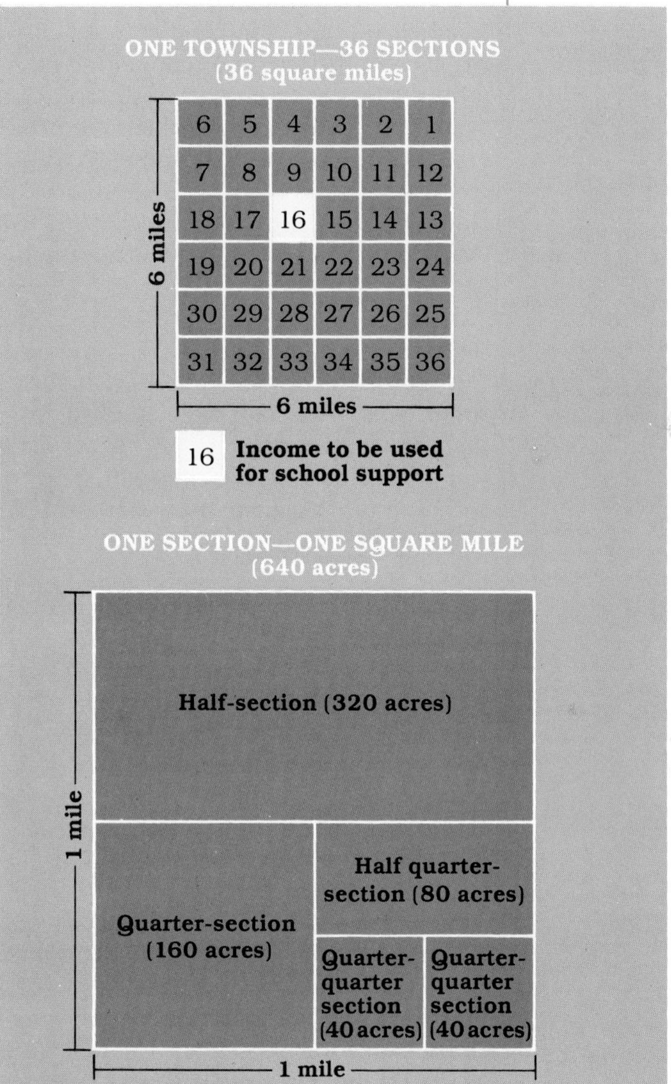

The rectangular system of survey devised for the Northwest Territory is used in most states west of the Appalachians. The system makes it possible to identify precisely any given piece of land. Roads sometimes follow section lines. The surveyed townships, six miles square, do not always conform with political townships.

4. **FILMS** *Debt to the Past: Government and Law* (16 minutes, color; Moody Institute of Science). This film summarizes the contributions of past civilizations to the development of American government and law. *Constitution of the United States* (22 minutes, b&w; Encyclopaedia Britannica Films, Inc.) portrays the historical background of the Constitution and includes explanations of the weaknesses of the Articles of Confederation and the significance of Shays's Rebellion.

5. **LISTENING FOR INFORMATION** You might wish to read to the class "Origins of the Convention" (pages 3–15) in *Miracle at Philadelphia* by Catherine Drinker Bowen (Boston: Atlantic Monthly Press, 1966). For additional information read "Editor's Introduction, 'Genesis of the American Constitution—The Confederation' " (pages lxx–lxxxvii) in editor Winton A. Solberg's *The Federal Convention and the Formation of the Union of the American States* (New York: Liberal Arts Press, 1958).

non-voting delegate to Congress. When the number of people in the territory reached 60,000, the people could draw up a constitution and ask Congress to admit their region to the Union as a state, on equal terms with all other states. Not less than three nor more than five states were to be created from this territory. Equally important, the law prohibited slavery in the Northwest Territory.

A weak government? The Confederation government satisfied a great many Americans. Ever suspicious of strong, distant, central government, a majority were satisfied to leave the main powers to the state governments, which were closer to home.

Yet, a growing number of Americans were beginning to wonder if the central government was not ineffective. In 1784, many blamed the government's weakness for the beginning of a *depression*—a time when business is poor and many people cannot find jobs. That was not entirely fair, since the government had nothing to do with crop failures that occurred in several parts of the country. On the other hand, lack of any power to regulate foreign trade probably did contribute to the economic troubles. While Britain sold all it wished in American markets, American merchants were blocked from freely selling in the British empire. This was because the American minister to England, unable to speak for all the states, could not win from Britain a favorable trade treaty. One Englishman mockingly asked why the United States did not send 13 ministers to represent them in London instead of just one.

The weakness of the United States did not go unnoticed elsewhere. Most European governments did not expect the United States to last. Several cast hungry eyes on its territory. Spain, which already held Florida and the land west of the Mississippi, hoped to slice off the region between the Appalachians and the Mississippi, south of the Ohio River. And England was not about to pull out of its profitable trading and military posts in the Northwest Territory, no matter what the Treaty of Paris said.

Many Americans found this situation humiliating. An increasing number were thinking of themselves less as Virginians or Pennsylvanians and more as Americans. They wanted a government that would express this growing national feeling. They wanted a government strong enough to command the respect of its own citizens as well as that of other nations.

Shays's Rebellion. An event in western Massachusetts in the fall of 1786 added to the growing belief that the central government could not govern. Falling crop prices that year hit small farmers there very hard. Many of the farmers had borrowed money to buy their land. After paying high taxes on their land, many of them did not have enough left to make mortgage payments. When those who held the mortgages took the farmers to court, judges ordered that the farmers' land be sold to pay off their debts. Some farmers were sent to debtor's prison. The Massachusetts legislature, meanwhile, turned a deaf ear to the farmers' requests for tax relief and for the printing of paper money that would help raise the price of their crops.

Several thousand desperate farmers, led by a Revolutionary War veteran named Daniel Shays, took matters into their own hands. In several small towns they kept the courts from opening, so that judges could not order the sale of any more of their lands. The troubles kept on for several months. In December 1786, Shays and his followers tried to seize arms from a government arsenal in Springfield. The state militia, however, beat them back. That broke the back of the uprising. Some farmers surrendered, and others, including Shays, fled the state. Yet many Americans took little comfort that the rebellion had been put down. They were troubled that the central government, with no army of its own, had had to ask the state militia to put down a small band of armed farmers.

Rising fears. The concerns of two important Americans may be seen in the two letters printed below. The first is from Abigail Adams to Thomas Jefferson. On hearing news of the events in Massachusetts, Jefferson had written his friends the Adamses for more information about the uprising. Abigail Adams replied:

> Ignorant, restless desperadoes, without conscience or principles, had led a deluded multitude to follow their standard. . . . Some of them were crying out for paper currency, some for an equal distribution of property. Some were for [wiping out] all debts. . . . you will see . . . the necessity of . . . vigorous measures to [put down this rebellion]. . . . these [rebels] are for undercutting the foundations of the government and destroying the whole fabric at once. . . .

The second letter is from George Washington to John Jay, a New York political leader.

> I do not believe that we can exist long as a nation without lodging, somewhere, a power which pervades the whole union. . . .To be fearful of giving Congress . . . ample authority for national purposes appears to me . . . madness. What then is to be done? Things cannot go on in the same train forever. It is much to be feared, as you observe, that the better kind of people, being disgusted in these circumstances, will have their minds prepared for any revolution whatever. . . .

The widespread discontent that brought on Shays's Rebellion in 1786 sometimes pitted neighbor against neighbor in violent disagreement over taxes, courts, and property rights.

6. ORAL REPORTS Have several of your students study and report to the class on Alexander Hamilton's famous letter of September 3, 1780, to his friend James Duane. Written by Hamilton when he was only twenty-three years old, this letter is considered a masterpiece in justifying the need for a constitution. A copy of the letter may be found in *The Basic Ideas of Alexander Hamilton* edited by Richard B. Morris (New York: Pocket Books, Inc., 1957).

7. THOUGHT PROVOKER In 1776, John Adams wrote to Richard Lee: "You and I, my friend, have been sent into life at a time when the greatest lawgivers of antiquity would have wished to live. How few of the human race have ever enjoyed an opportunity of making an election of government for themselves or their children." Ask: Does the opportunity that Adams wrote about still exist in the United States? Based on your knowledge of current events, are you able to cite any areas in the world today where people might have "an opportunity of making an election of government for themselves or their children?"

During the eighteenth century, Wall Street in New York City became a center of commerce. The merchants who traded there wanted a government strong enough to guarantee their property rights.

> . . . I am told that even respectable characters speak of a monarchical form of government without horror. From thinking proceeds speaking, thence to acting is often but a single step. . . .

Phrases like "ignorant, restless desperadoes" and "the better kind of people" tell us a good deal about the writers' attitudes and fears. George Washington was one of the largest landowners in America and a member of Virginia's upper class. The Adamses, while not rich, were among the more important families in Massachusetts because of John Adams's work as a lawyer and political leader. As leaders in the Revolution, Washington and the Adamses shared the fear of a too-strong government. But as members of an upper class, they also wanted a government strong enough to keep order and to protect their property.

That is why such people shuddered on hearing of the uprising against courts and property rights in Massachusetts. What happened in that state could happen elsewhere. Indeed, under pressure from farmers, more than half the state legislatures had already passed laws to help debtors at the expense of their creditors. The rights of property, and the right of "the better kind of people" to govern, was being challenged. "We are fast moving toward anarchy [absence of government] and confusion," wrote an alarmed Washington.

CHECKUP

1. What were the weaknesses of the Articles of Confederation?
2. How did Congress deal with the sale of land in, and the government of, the Northwest Territory?
3. In what way did Shays's Rebellion contribute to rising fears over the central government?

LESSON 2

The Constitutional Convention

In September 1786, even as Shays's Rebellion was under way, delegates from five states met at Annapolis, Maryland, to discuss problems of commerce under the Articles of Confederation. Concluding that this problem was only one of many, the delegates recommended that Congress call a general convention to revise and strengthen the Articles. Congress agreed. On May 25, 1787, what became known as the Constitutional Convention began its meetings in Philadelphia, Pennsylvania. Four months later, the new Constitution of the United States of America had been drafted, discussed, and approved by the delegates.

The Constitutional Convention was the greatest political gathering ever held in America. Chosen by their state legislatures, the fifty-five delegates were among the ablest and most experienced men in America. Many had served their country since the Revolution. George Washington, Alexander Hamilton of New York, and Charles Cotesworth Pinckney of South Carolina had been army officers. Former members of the Continental Congress included Benjamin Franklin, James Wilson, and Robert Morris of Pennsylvania, George Wythe and George Mason of Virginia, Elbridge Gerry of Massachusetts, William Livingston of New Jersey, and Roger Sherman of Connecticut.

One striking fact about these delegates was their youth. Five delegates were in their mid-twenties, and five more were in their early or mid-thirties. Franklin was the grand old man of the convention at eighty-one, but the average age was forty-two.

Also striking was their prominence and wealth. Included among them were planters, merchants, and lawyers. Their views were naturally colored by the fact that they were well-to-do.

This remarkable group was well aware of the high stakes in what its members were doing. Alexander Hamilton noted that what they did would "decide forever the fate of republican government." That is, if they could not solve the problem of federalism and failed to create a government that would work, it was unlikely that other peoples would soon experiment with republican government.

A search for balances. The story of the Philadelphia convention is the story of a search for two new balances. One was the balance between the central government and local governments. The other was the balance between liberty and order. The problem was to create a government strong enough to govern and maintain order, yet not so strong as to threaten the liberty of its citizens. Very early, the convention decided that in order to achieve these balances it would be necessary to write an entirely new constitution rather than to amend the Articles.

Nearly all the delegates agreed that the balances had to shift in the direction of centralism and order. The government

LESSON 2 *(2 to 3 days)*

Performance Objectives

1. To list at least three generalizations that describe the delegates to the Constitutional Convention. 2. To demonstrate an understanding of the concept of "checks and balances" by making a chart illustrating two ways in which the power of each federal branch is checked by another branch. 3. To describe, orally or in writing, three ways in which the Constitution protects the rights of citizens. 4. To demonstrate an understanding of three issues that caused disagreement at the Constitutional Convention by writing an essay explaining **(a)** three such issues, **(b)** the opposing viewpoints, and **(c)** the eventual compromises.

Vocabulary

Annapolis Convention, centralism, "supremacy clause," separation of powers, executive, legislative, judicial, bicameral, ratify

Activities

1. FILMS To introduce this lesson, you might wish to show one of the following films. *Our Federal Constitution* (21 minutes, b&w; Republic Steel Corporation) is part of the Building Political Leadership series. This film presents a comparison of unitary and federal systems and a discussion of the development of the Presidency and the system of checks and balances. *Constitution: One Nation,* Part 1 (30 minutes, b&w; Ford Foundation TV Workshop) dramatizes the Constitutional Convention by presenting many of the arguments for and against a constitution.

2. BULLETIN-BOARD DISPLAY After your students have read the lesson, have them review the system of checks and balances between the branches of the federal government as shown on page 165. Ask students to make charts illustrating two ways in which the Constitution protects the rights of citizens. This lesson offers a good opportunity to incorporate a review of current events. Ask your students to cite recent examples of the workings of the system of checks and balances.

Several of your students might create a bulletin-board display depicting the system of checks and balances. They may use newspaper or magazine headlines (and their dates), current news pictures, and political cartoons to help explain the various checks and balances mentioned in the display.

had to have the power to tax so that it would no longer need to beg the states for money. It must regulate trade among the states to prevent quarrels among them. It had to control trade with other countries so that it could negotiate trade treaties for all states. It needed to be able to raise its own army, without having to depend on the states to give men and money for defense. And it must be able to make citizens and the states obey its laws by having its own courts.

A group of Indian visitors stand before Independence Hall in Philadelphia. In this building in the summer of 1787, the nation's founders drafted the Constitution of the United States.

So clear was the need to give these powers to the central government that they were added almost without debate. Most important was the agreement that the new Constitution, and all the treaties and laws made under it, was to be the supreme law of the land. It was to be superior to state laws. This is stated in what is known as the "supremacy clause" of the Constitution (see pages 184–185).

Protecting liberty. Even as the delegates tipped the balance toward centralism and order, they built into the Constitution three ways to protect citizens from a too-powerful government. One was the idea of federalism itself. By dividing up the power of government between local and central levels, no one level was to have too much power. A second was by using the written Constitution to spell out certain things the central government could *not* do. It could not, for example, put a person in jail without a hearing. It could not take anyone's property without paying a fair price for it. It could not tax exported goods.

A third way of protecting liberty was the device of *separation of powers.* The Constitution created three independent branches of government—the *executive, legislative,* and *judicial*—and divided the powers of the central government among them. Congress, the legislative branch, was to make the laws. The President, as head of the executive branch, was to carry them out and enforce them. And the federal courts, the judicial branch, were to judge and interpret the laws.

To protect against the exercise of unlimited power by any one branch, the

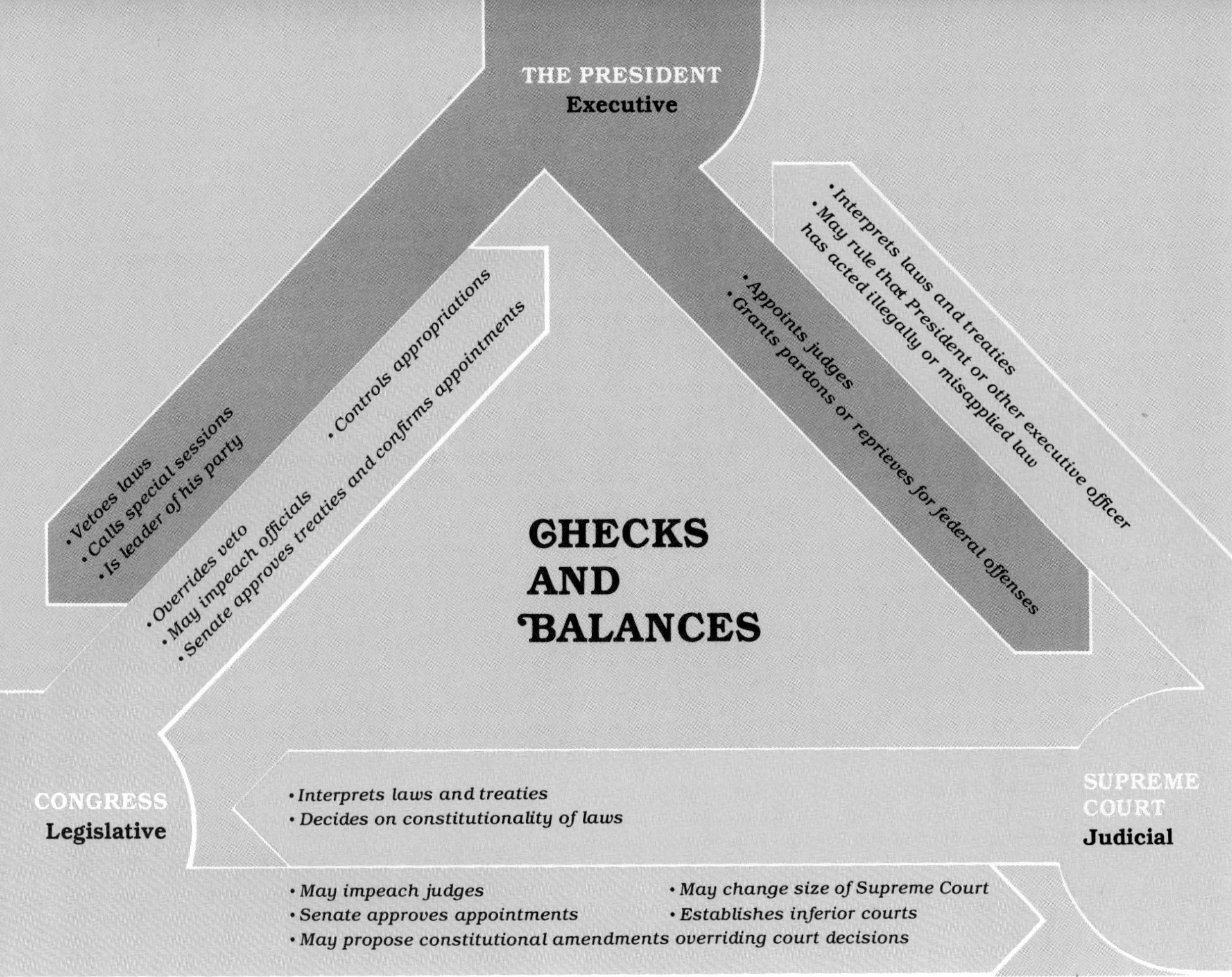
THE PRESIDENT
Executive
CONGRESS
Legislative
SUPREME COURT
Judicial
CHECKS AND BALANCES
• Vetoes laws
• Calls special sessions
• Is leader of his party
• Controls appropriations
• Overrides veto
• May impeach officials
• Senate approves treaties and confirms appointments
• Interprets laws and treaties
• May rule that President or other executive officer has acted illegally or misapplied law
• Appoints judges
• Grants pardons or reprieves for federal offenses
• Interprets laws and treaties
• Decides on constitutionality of laws
• May impeach judges
• Senate approves appointments
• May change size of Supreme Court
• Establishes inferior courts
• May propose constitutional amendments overriding court decisions

Constitution provides ways by which each branch may check and balance the others. The chart above shows the separation of powers. Can you see how the President may be checked? How may the Congress be checked? What means are there for checking and balancing the courts? Do you think there may be disadvantages as well as advantages in a system of checks and balances such as this?

None of these ideas—federalism, a written constitution, and the separation of powers—was new. In combining the three as they did, however, the delegates to the convention made their unique contribution. In doing so, they invented a new government.

The Great Compromise. Not all was harmony at the convention. On several subjects there was bitter disagreement. Delegates threatened at times to walk out of the convention, and it appeared the whole effort might fail. But in the end, compromises saved the day.

One major disagreement had to do with representation in Congress. Two ideas were put forth. The Virginia, or large state, plan would base representation in Congress on population. A state with twice as many people as another,

3. LISTENING FOR IFORMATION You might wish to read to the class "Establishing a Government (pages 93–98) by Irving Brant in editor E. S. Miers's *The American Story: The Age of Exploration to the Age of the Atom* (New York: Channel Press, 1956).

4. ESSAY After students have read the lesson, ask them to write essays explaining **(a)** three issues that caused disagreement at the Constitutional Convention, **(b)** the opposing viewpoints, and **(c)** the eventual compromises.

5. ROLE-PLAYING Have three students assume the roles of Edmund Randolph, William Paterson, and Roger Sherman as members of the Constitutional Convention. Each student should study the life of the delegate and the plan for organizing the legislative branch that the delegate presented to the convention—the Virginia Plan (Randolph), the New Jersey Plan (Paterson), and the Connecticut Compromise (Sherman). Another student might assume the role of a newspaper reporter to conduct a *Meet the Press* type of session with the delegates. After the reporter introduces each person, have the delegates present their plans. Point out to the class that this type of discussion for the press was not possible, because the convention had a secrecy rule.

6. WHAT IF? What if John Adams were right in his letter to John Taylor in which he said: "Remember, democracy never lasts long. It soon wastes, exhausts, and murders itself. There never was a democracy yet that did not commit suicide." Ask your students for their reactions to this statement. Do they believe that democracy is still alive in the United States? Encourage them to give examples to substantiate their points of view.

would have twice as many seats. On the other hand, the New Jersey, or small state, plan said that each state would have an equal voice in Congress, just as under the Articles. Thus, Rhode Island, with its population of less than 70,000, would have as many representatives as the largest state, Virginia, with more than 10 times as many people.

This issue nearly wrecked the convention. But finally Roger Sherman of Connecticut came forward with a plan that was adopted. Under the so-called Great Compromise, there would be two houses of Congress. In the upper, or Senate, each state would have equal representation. In the lower, or House of Representatives, representation would be based upon population. Such a lawmaking body made up of two houses is known as a *bicameral* legislature.

Roger Sherman of Connecticut was one of two men who signed all three of these great documents: the Declaration of Independence, the Articles of Confederation, and the Constitution. The other was Robert Morris of Pennsylvania.

The slavery problem. Two disagreements involved slavery. One was whether to count slaves as part of the population when determining the number of members each state should have in the House of Representatives. Clearly, to do so would give additional seats to Southern states. Northern delegates argued that since slaves had no political rights, they should not be counted. It was finally proposed that for purposes of assigning seats in the House of Representatives, every five slaves would count as three persons. To count a slave as three fifths of a person plainly did not make sense. Yet to reach agreement on a new constitution, delegates accepted this three-fifths compromise.

The second disagreement on slavery was whether or not the importing of slaves into America should continue. The compromise in this case was to prohibit Congress from passing a law on that subject for twenty years. After that, Congress would be free to stop the trade if it chose.

Executive power. Another compromise had to do with the Presidency. Some delegates felt that one executive would be little different from a king—especially if the term of office was a long one. They wanted an executive branch made up of several people. Some favored leaving the choice of the executive to Congress on the grounds that the people were not qualified to make such a choice. Other delegates said that for Congress to choose the executive would destroy the idea of the separation of powers.

In the compromise it was agreed there would be one executive known as the President. The President would be chosen for a four-year term by an indirect method—an electoral college—rather than directly by the people. Finally, it was agreed that the Constitution could be amended by a vote of two-thirds of each house of Congress and three-fourths of all the states.

Its work completed, the convention sent the Constitution to the Congress. Congress forwarded the document to a specially elected convention in each state. The delegates to these conventions were asked to *ratify*, or approve, the Constitution. It would go into effect after nine states ratified it.

CHECKUP

1. What generalizations can you make about the delegates to the Constitutional Convention?
2. In what three ways did the delegates act to protect citizens from a too-powerful government?
3. What were some of the compromises made in drawing up the Constitution?

LESSON 3

The Struggle Over Ratification

Those who favored the Constitution were called *Federalists*. They knew that ratification would not be easy, for most Americans still felt more loyal to their states than to the central government. Many Americans viewed the proposed new government as merely the old British tyranny in a new form.

A heated exchange. Debates in the state ratifying conventions often became heated. This exchange in the Massachusetts convention was typical of those that took place everywhere. Amos Singletary voiced the fears of the *Anti-Federalists*, as those who opposed the Constitution were called.

> We [fought against] Great Britain—some said for a three-penny duty on tea; but it was not that. It was because they claimed a right to tax us and bind us in all cases whatever. And does not this Constitution do the same? Does it not take away all we have—all our property? Does it not lay *all* taxes? . . .
>
> These lawyers, and men of learning, and moneyed men, that talk so finely and gloss over matters so smoothly, to make us poor illiterate people swallow down the pill, expect to get into Congress themselves. They expect to be the managers of this Constitution, and get all the power and all the money into their own hands. And then they will swallow up all us little folk . . . just as the whale swallowed up Jonah. . . .

Jonathan Smith, a Federalist, took a different point of view.

> I have lived in a part of the country where I have known the worth of good government by the [lack] of it. There was a black cloud [Shays's Rebellion] that rose in the east last winter, and spread over the west. . . . It brought on a state of anarchy. . . . People that used to live peaceably, and were before good neighbors . . . took up arms against the government. . . . They would rob you of your property, threaten to burn your houses; oblige you to be on your guard night and day. Alarms spread from town to town; families were broken up; the . . . mother would cry, O my son is among them!

LESSON 3 *(1 to 2 days)*

Performance Objective

To demonstrate an understanding of the arguments for and against the ratification of the Constitution by holding a debate in which the following points are covered: **(a)** two arguments used by the Federalists in support of the new Constitution, **(b)** two arguments used by the Anti-Federalists against the Constitution, and **(c)** the appeal of each argument to its respective group.

Vocabulary

Ratification, Federalists, Anti-Federalists, a workable federal balance

Activities

1. POSTERS After your students have read this lesson, have them make posters—some urging Americans to ratify the new Constitution and others urging Americans to retain the Articles of Confederation. Display the posters on the bulletin board.

2. DEBATE Resolved, That the citizens of the State of (your state) should ratify the Constitution created by the Constitutional Convention in Philadelphia in 1787. To sharpen opposing points of view, provide each student with a socioeconomic status—family background, occupation, residence, and property holdings.

3. FILM *Constitution: One Nation,* Part 2 (30 minutes, b&w; Ford Foundation TV Workshop) dramatizes many of the arguments for and against the Constitution.

4. RESEARCH/ORAL REPORTS William E. Gladstone served four terms as British prime minister during the second half of the nineteenth century. In 1887 he wrote a letter to the committee in charge of the Centennial Anniversary of the American Constitution in which he said: "I have always regarded that Constitution as the most remarkable work known to me in modern times to have been produced by the human intellect, at a single stroke (so to speak), in its application to political affairs."

Ask some of your more able students to study the constitution of Great Britain. In a report to the class, have them emphasize **(a)** the written and unwritten aspects of the British constitution and **(b)** the differences between the federal governments of the United States and Great Britain. Ask the class to speculate why Gladstone used the phrase "at a single stroke (so to speak)" in the above quotation.

Now . . . when I saw this Constitution, I found that it was a cure for these disorders. It was just such a thing as we wanted. . . . I got a copy of it and read it over and over. I had been a member of the convention to form our state constitution, and had learned something of the checks and balances of power; and I found them all here. . . .

I don't think the worse of the Constitution because lawyers, and men of learning, and moneyed men are fond of it. I don't suspect that they want to get into Congress and abuse their power. . . .

These lawyers, these moneyed men, these men of learning, are all embarked in the same cause with us, and we must all sink or swim together. And shall we throw the Constitution overboard because it does not please us [all] alike?

How does Smith's view of American society differ from Singletary's?

For and against ratification. The Anti-Federalists made three points. One was that the convention in Philadelphia had gone beyond its powers in writing an entirely new constitution. A second was that the Constitution did not have a bill of rights setting forth the basic liberties of the people—for example, freedom of speech and religion. The third was that the Constitution made the central government too strong and the state governments too weak. Among the Anti-Federalists were some of the leading Revolutionary figures—among them, Samuel Adams of Massachusetts and Patrick Henry and Richard Henry Lee of Virginia. Anti-Federalist arguments had the greatest appeal to small farmers, western frontier people, and debtors.

Federalists claimed that only a strong central government could prevent unrest at home and win respect for America abroad. Their strongest support came from merchants, businessmen, lawyers, land speculators, and southern planters. Generally speaking, the wealthier and more educated people favored ratification. The Federalists numbered in their ranks such well known men as Washington, Alexander Hamilton, James Madison, and John Jay.

The Federalists carry the day. Although the Anti-Federalists probably outnumbered the Federalists, the Constitution

Continued on page 170

This cartoon compares the ratification of the Constitution to the building of a dome held up by pillars. It was drawn at the time that eleven states had approved the document and two had not.

Father of the Constitution

James Madison was five feet four inches in height and weighed about one hundred pounds. Yet among those who founded the federal government, he was a giant. He deserves the title "Father of the Constitution" on several counts—as a debater and a recorder of events at the Constitutional Convention and as a leader in winning ratification of the Constitution.

Madison was well grounded for the vital role he played at the Constitutional Convention. Ten years earlier he had helped draft a new constitution for Virginia. Serving in both the Virginia legislature and the Continental Congress, he was regarded in each body as one of its ablest members.

Madison was thirty-six when he arrived in Philadelphia in 1787 as a Virginia delegate to the Constitutional Convention. During the debates he was a vigorous spokesman for a strong central government and for the separation of powers. The Virginia, or large state, plan was mostly his work. A number of its ideas were included in the new United States Constitution.

The debates were kept secret from the public, but Madison took notes at each session. Every evening he wrote out a full account of the day's happenings. His record, made public after his death in 1836, proved to be far more complete than the official record. Madison's account is the best we have of the Constitutional Convention.

Returning home from Philadelphia, Madison went to work to see that the new Constitution was approved by the people. He, Alexander Hamilton, and John Jay wrote *The Federalist*, a brilliant set of essays urging adoption of the Constitution. Many of the essays appeared in New York newspapers. They were then collected and published in book form. Thomas Jefferson called *The Federalist* "the best commentary on the principles of government which has ever been written."

This medallion shows James Madison as President. For his vital role in the creation and ratification of the Constitution, Madison was already assured a lasting place in American history.

5. THOUGHT PROVOKER "The power to tax is the power to destroy." This statement was made by John Marshall in the famous *McCulloch v. Maryland* case of 1819. The decision in the case stated that no state could tax an agency or institution of the federal government. How might Amos Singletary have used the same argument in his fight against the ratification of the Constitution? (See page 167 for Singletary's fears about the Constitution.)

6. WHAT IF? What if the Constitutional Convention proceedings had been public rather than secret? Note Singletary's comment on page 167. Thomas Jefferson, then in Paris, called the secrecy rule abominable. James Madison, forty-three years later, felt that the rule was correct because it allowed those who attended the convention with the original purpose of amending the Articles of Confederation to change their minds without "losing face." Would the ratification of the Constitution have been easier if the convention proceedings had been public? Would we have the same Constitution?

If the Constitutional Convention were being held today, what effects might the secrecy rule have on TV and newspaper reporters? How would the American people feel about being kept "in the dark" in this age of instant communication? Would the recent problems with Watergate, the CIA, the FBI, etc., make a secret constitutional convention impossible? Would secrecy be desirable today?

Answers To Review Questions

1. The central government under the Articles of Confederation could maintain an army and navy, make war and peace, regulate coinage, borrow money, establish a post office, manage affairs with the Indians, and make treaties and alliances with other countries. However, the central government was denied the power of taxation or the right to regulate trade. In addition, the central government did not have an executive or a judicial system.
2. England refused to send a minister to the United States, sign a trade treaty, or pull out its military and trading posts in the Northwest Territory. Spain was eager to seize the territory south of the Ohio River between The Appalachians and the Mississippi.
3. The convention decided that it would be necessary to write an entirely new constitution in order to achieve the desired balances between the central government and the local governments and between liberty and order.
4. The central government was given the power to tax, to regulate trade, to raise its own army so it would not have to depend on the states to give citizens and money for defense, and to have its own courts to enforce its laws.
5. The Constitution protects citizens from a too-powerful government by **(a)** dividing the power of government between local and central levels; **(b)** using a written constitution to spell out certain things that central government cannot do; and **(c)** creating three independent branches of government to ensure the separation of powers.

was ratified. How was this possible? For one thing, many of the Anti-Federalists simply did not take the trouble to vote for delegates to the state ratifying conventions. Only one-sixth of the adult white males voted in those elections. The Anti-Federalists also failed to organize their supporters. They were widely scattered throughout the country, and never found a single issue around which they could rally.

The Federalists, on the other hand, showed a genius for organization. They held the key political positions in many states, and they made the most of them. Many Federalists were leaders in their local communities. They had a large influence in the ratification debates. In many states they were able to quiet doubts by promising to add a bill of rights to the Constitution.

Delaware ratified the Constitution in December 1787. It was the first state to do so. Within eight months, ten more states did the same, and the new Constitution became the law of the land. North Carolina ratified it in 1789, and Rhode Island followed in 1790.

We know today that the founders of our government were amazingly successful in striking a workable federal balance. They provided a flexible constitution. Today it is the oldest written constitution in the world. In 1788, however, that was all in the untold future. Setting up the new government, breathing life into the words of the Constitution was the task of the moment. It was to that job that the victorious Federalists now turned. In the chapter that follows, you will see how that urgent undertaking was carried out.

CHECKUP

1. What arguments were put forth in favor of ratification of the Constitution?
2. What arguments were put forth in opposition to ratification?
3. Why were the Federalists able to bring about ratification of the Constitution?

Key Facts from Chapter 9

1. A system in which powers are divided between a central government and local governments is called a federal government.
2. The Articles of Confederation, which was the first constitution of the United States, gave the main powers to the state governments and severely limited the powers of the central government.
3. To strengthen the central government, delegates chosen by state legislatures met in Philadelphia in 1787 and drew up a new constitution.
4. Under the Constitution, the balance of power moved in the direction of the central government.
5. Under the Constitution, the powers of the central government were divided among the executive, legislative, and judicial branches.
6. The Constitution became the law of the land in 1788, after nine states had ratified it.

★ REVIEWING THE CHAPTER ★

People, Places, and Events

Articles of Confederation *P. 157*
Northwest Territory *P. 158*
Land Ordinance of 1785 *P. 159*
Northwest Ordinance *P. 159*
Shays's Rebellion *P. 160*
Constitutional Convention *P. 163*
Great Compromise *P. 165*
Virginia Plan *P. 165*
New Jersey Plan *P. 166*
Three-fifths compromise *P. 166*
James Madison *P. 169*

Review Questions

1. What powers were given to the central government under the Articles of Confederation? What important powers were denied? *P. 157* Les. 1
2. How did the weaknesses of the central government under the Articles affect American relations with foreign nations? *P. 160* Les. 1
3. Why did the delegates to the Philadelphia convention write an entirely new constitution rather than amend the Articles? *P. 163* Les. 2
4. Under the Constitution, what new powers were given to the central government? *P. 164* Les. 2
5. In what three ways did the Constitution protect citizens from a too-powerful government? *P. 164* Les. 2
6. How did the issue of slavery create disagreement at the convention? What compromises were made? *P. 166* Les. 2
7. Compare the viewpoints of the Federalists and the Anti-Federalists on the subject of the ratification of the Constitution. *P. 168* Les. 3

Chapter Test

In the first section below is a list of names and terms found in the chapter. In the second section is a list of descriptions. Match each name or term with the appropriate description. Write your answers on a separate piece of paper.

1. Virginia Plan
2. Bicameral legislature
3. Articles of Confederation
4. Anti-Federalists
5. Executive, legislative, judicial
6. New Jersey Plan
7. Federal system
8. Supremacy clause
9. Bill of Rights
10. Northwest Ordinance

a. Those who opposed ratification of the Constitution
b. Representation in Congress based on equal voice for each state
c. A system for governing western lands
d. Powers divided between a central government and local governments
e. Those who favored ratification of the Constitution
f. Protects basic liberties of the people
g. Representation in Congress based on population
h. Lawmaking body made up of two houses
i. Gave power to the state governments and limited the powers of the central government
j. Constitution was to be superior to state laws
k. Three independent branches of the government

6. The South wished to count slaves as population when determining representation in the House. The North did not. It was finally proposed that for purposes of assigning seats in the House of Representatives, every five slaves would count as three persons. This three-fifths compromise was accepted by the delegates in order to reach agreement on a new constitution. Another disagreement on slavery was whether or not the importing of slaves into America should continue. The compromise in this case was to prohibit Congress from passing a law on that subject for twenty years.
7. The Federalists favored ratification of the Constitution, because they believed that only a strong central government could prevent unrest at home and win respect for America abroad. The Anti-Federalists were opposed to ratification and cited the following points: **(a)** Constitutional Convention went beyond its powers when it wrote a new constitution; **(b)** the Constitution did not provide a bill of rights; and **(c)** the Constitution made the central government too strong and the state governments too weak.

Answers For Chapter Test
1. g **2.** h **3.** i **4.** a **5.** k
6. b **7.** d **8.** j **9.** f **10.** c

STUDYING THE CONSTITUTION *(3 to 4 days)*

You will notice that the Constitution is accompanied by annotations. These annotations include simplified explanations, definitions, questions on content, discussion questions, and suggested research topics. You will have to decide how much of this material your students can cover comfortably in the amount of time you allot to its study.

Performance Objectives

1. To identify, orally or in writing, the purposes and procedures of the articles of and amendments to the Constitution. **2.** To demonstrate, orally or in writing, an understanding of the effects of the principles, procedures, and interpretations of the Constitution on daily life in the United States.

We the people of the United States, in order to form a more perfect union, establish justice, insure domestic tranquility, provide for the common defense, promote the general welfare, and secure the blessings of liberty to ourselves and our posterity, do ordain and establish this Constitution for the United States of America.

Preamble. This very important part of the Constitution names whom as the final authority? How does Art. VII reinforce this? Who authorized the Articles of Confederation?

ARTICLE I

LEGISLATIVE BRANCH

SECTION 1.

All legislative powers herein granted shall be vested in a Congress of the United States, which shall consist of a Senate and House of Representatives.

CONGRESS

Two houses. If Congress has all legislative power, how can such agencies as the Internal Revenue Service make rules?

SECTION 2.

The House of Representatives shall be composed of members chosen every second year by the people of the several States, and the electors in each State shall have the qualifications requisite for electors of the most numerous branch of the State legislature.

HOUSE OF REPRESENTATIVES

Membership; term; election. Electors = voters. How has this been affected by Amend. 15, 19, 24, and 26? Is two years long enough? too long?

No person shall be a representative who shall not have attained to the age of twenty-five years, and been seven years a citizen of the United States, and who shall not, when elected, be an inhabitant of that State in which he shall be chosen.

*Representatives and direct taxes shall be apportioned among the several States which may be included within this Union, according to their respective numbers, which shall be determined by adding to the whole number of free persons, including those bound to service for a term of years, and excluding Indians not taxed, three fifths of all other persons.** The actual enumeration shall be made within three years after the first meeting of the Congress of the United States, and within every subsequent term of ten years, in such manner as they shall by law direct. The number of representatives shall not exceed one for every thirty thousand, but each State shall have at least one representative; and until such enumeration shall be made, the State of New Hampshire shall be entitled to choose three, Massachusetts eight, Rhode Island and Providence Plantations one, Connecticut five, New York six, New Jersey four, Pennsylvania eight, Delaware one, Maryland six, Virginia ten, North Carolina five, South Carolina five, and Georgia three.*

When vacancies happen in the representation from any State, the executive authority thereof shall issue writs of election to fill such vacancies.

The House of Representatives shall choose their speaker and other officers, and shall have the sole power of impeachment.

SECTION 3.

The Senate of the United States shall be composed of two senators from each State, chosen by the legislature thereof,† for six years; and each senator shall have one vote.

Immediately after they shall be assembled in consequence of the first election, they shall be divided as equally as may be into three classes. The seats of the senators of the first class shall be vacated at the expiration of the second year, of the second class at the expiration of the fourth year, and of the third class at the expiration of the sixth year, so that one third may be chosen every second year; and if vacancies happen by resignation, or otherwise, during the recess of the legislature of any State, the executive thereof may make temporary appointments until the next meeting of the legislature, which shall then fill such vacancies.†

No person shall be a senator who shall not have attained to the age of thirty years, and been nine years a citizen of the United States, and who shall not, when elected, be an inhabitant of that State for which he shall be chosen.

Qualifications. Must a candidate live in the district he wants to represent? What chance of election would he probably have if he did not live there?

Apportionment. "Those bound to service" were indentured. Who were the "three fifths of all others"? Did they pay taxes? Should they have been represented? On what basis? How did Amend. 13 change this?

What is the "enumeration" called today? When was the most recent one taken?

No amendment has changed "one for every thirty thousand," but Congress limits the House to 435. Without that limit, how many members would there be? Each representative represents an average of how many people?

Vacancies. Why may a governor appoint a Senator but not a representative?

Officers; impeachment. Impeach = accuse of wrongdoing. Who may be impeached (Art. II–4)?

THE SENATE

Membership; term. Under Amend. 17, who chooses the senators? Since when?

Expiration of term; vacancies. Only one third of the Senate is replaced or re-elected at each election, but each Congress is "new." What are some benefits or drawbacks of not having a totally new Congress each time? A governor may fill a vacancy until his legislature directs a new election. See Amend. 17.

Qualifications. How do the qualifications for senator and representative differ? Why are they different?

NOTE: Items that have been changed or replaced are underlined.

* Changed by the Fourteenth Amendment

† Changed by the Seventeenth Amendment

2. CROSSWORD PUZZLE
Have some students make up a crossword puzzle, using the terms from the Constitution. The words in the annotations in boldface type would be a good place to start. After you check the definitions that the students write, give the puzzle to the rest of the class as a way of reviewing the vocabulary.

A word-search grid would also do the same thing, but be sure the students make up clues for the words and not just list the words to find. Some students do better on these if the number of letters in the word is also given.

The Vice President of the United States shall be president of the Senate, but shall have no vote, unless they be equally divided.

The Senate shall choose their other officers, and also a president pro tempore, in the absence of the Vice President, or when he shall exercise the office of President of the United States.

Officers. As the Vice President may not be there, the president *pro tempore* acts as Senate president. Senators take daily turns presiding. Only the Vice President may break tie votes.

The Senate shall have the sole power to try all impeachments. When sitting for that purpose, they shall be on oath or affirmation. When the President of the United States is tried, the Chief Justice shall preside: and no person shall be convicted without the concurrence of two thirds of the members present.

Impeachment. Note that the Senate acts as a court in impeachment; House appointees prosecute the case.

Judgment in cases of impeachment shall not extend further than to removal from office, and disqualification to hold any office of honor, trust or profit under the United States: but the party convicted shall nevertheless be liable and subject to indictment, trial, judgment and punishment, according to law.

Punishment. What is the only punishment the Senate can give in impeachments? What might the U.S. Attorney General do after a conviction in the Senate?

SECTION 4.

The times, places, and manner of holding elections for senators and representatives shall be prescribed in each State by the legislature thereof; but the Congress may at any time by law make or alter such regulations, except as to the places of choosing senators.

ELECTIONS

Regulating elections. Remarkably, the first of many election laws was not passed until 1842. It set up election districts.

The Congress shall assemble at least once in every year, and such meeting shall be on the first Monday in December, unless they shall by law appoint a different day.*

Assembly. This contrasted with the king's calling and dissolving Parliament at will.

* Changed by the Twentieth Amendment

SECTION 5.

Each house shall be the judge of the elections, returns and qualifications of its own members, and a majority of each shall constitute a quorum to do business; but a smaller number may adjourn from day to day, and may be authorized to compel the attendance of absent members, in such manner, and under such penalties as each house may provide.

Each house may determine the rules of its proceedings, punish its members for disorderly behavior, and, with the concurrence of two thirds, expel a member.

Each house shall keep a journal of its proceedings, and from time to time publish the same, excepting such parts as may in their judgment require secrecy; and the yeas and nays of the members of either house on any question shall, at the desire of one fifth of those present, be entered on the journal.

Neither house, during the session of Congress, shall, without the consent of the other, adjourn for more than three days, nor to any other place than that in which the two houses shall be sitting.

SECTION 6.

The senators and representatives shall receive a compensation for their services, to be ascertained by law, and paid out of the Treasury of the United States. They shall in all cases, except treason, felony and breach of the peace, be privileged from arrest during their attendance at the session of their respective houses, and in going to and returning from the same; and for any speech or debate in either house, they shall not be questioned in any other place.

No senator or representative shall, during the time for which he was elected, be appointed to any civil office under the authority of the United States, which shall have been created, or the emoluments thereof shall have been increased during such time; and no person holding any office under the United States shall be a member of either house during his continuance in office.

SECTION 7.

All bills for raising revenue shall originate in the House of Representatives; but the Senate may propose or concur with amendments as on other bills.

Every bill which shall have passed the House of Representatives and the Senate, shall, before it become a law, be presented to the President of the United States; if he approve he shall sign it, but if not he shall return it, with his objections to that house in which it shall have originated, who shall enter the objections at large on their journal, and proceed to reconsider it. If after such reconsideration two

RULES AND PROCEDURES

Admitting members; quorum. The election winner must be accepted by the house he is elected to. Research: Sen. Hiram Revels, an interesting case of challenge. Since the power to punish is judicial, it cannot extend outside Congress. Explain.

Journals. The daily *Congressional Record* is the published journal. But since members can and do add to, change, or omit their remarks, no "reliable, accurate journal" exists.

Adjournments. This prevents one house from holding up the work of the other, as in Parliament under Charles II.

PAY, PRIVILEGES, AND LIMITS

Pay; privileges. In 1969, Congress raised top-level salaries, including its own, by 42% to 100%. Research these in an almanac. Safeguarding members from arrest is based on English experience. How does this affect the people?

Limitations. In parliamentary republics, one person can run two or more executive departments. What must an American official do if he wishes to change jobs or get a raise?

LEGISLATION

Bills for raising money. In which house must tax bills originate? Why?

Bills into laws. Describe the ways in which the President may veto a bill. When Congress overrides a veto, how large a majority must there be in the House? in the Senate? Which part of this clause is best

3. ANALYZING SOURCE MATERIAL Provide students with a list of the complaints that the colonists had against the king prior to the Revolution. These are stated in the Declaration of Independence (see pages 109–111). Have students find the article and section of the Constitution that deals with each complaint and explain how the Constitution expected to solve or avoid it.

4. BULLETIN BOARD Have your students make a display depicting the basic ideas of the Constitution (federalism, checks and balances, and civil rights).

thirds of that house shall agree to pass the bill, it shall be sent, together with the objections, to the other house, by which it shall likewise be reconsidered, and if approved by two thirds of that house, it shall become a law. But in all such cases the votes of both houses shall be determined by yeas and nays, and the names of the persons voting for and against the bill shall be entered on the journal of each house respectively. If any bill shall not be returned by the President within ten days (Sundays excepted) after it shall have been presented to him, the same shall be a law, in like manner as if he had signed it, unless the Congress by their adjournment prevent its return, in which case it shall not be a law.

described as a "pocket veto."

Of what value is the taking and recording of a roll-call vote when Congress overrides a veto?

Every order, resolution, or vote to which the concurrence of the Senate and House of Representatives may be necessary (except on a question of adjournment) shall be presented to the President of the United States; and before the same shall take effect, shall be approved by him, or being disapproved by him, shall be repassed by two thirds of the Senate and House of Representatives, according to the rules and limitations prescribed in the case of a bill.

Veto power. This stops Congress from bypassing a possible veto under the pretense of passing a resolution. Why is a constitutional amendment the only legislation the President need not see?

SECTION 8.

The Congress shall have power to lay and collect taxes, duties, imposts and excises, to pay the debts and provide for the common defense and general welfare of the United States; but all duties, imposts and excises shall be uniform throughout the United States;

To borrow money on the credit of the United States;

To regulate commerce with foreign nations, and among the several States, and with the Indian tribes;

To establish a uniform rule of naturalization, and uniform laws on the subject of bankruptcies through the United States;

To coin money, regulate the value thereof, and of foreign coin, and fix the standard of weights and measures;

To provide for the punishment of counterfeiting the securities and current coin of the United States;

To establish post offices and post roads;

To promote the progress of science and useful arts by securing for limited times to authors and inventors the exclusive right to their respective writings and discoveries;

To constitute tribunals inferior to the Supreme Court;

To define and punish piracies and felonies committed on the high seas, and offenses against the law of nations;

To declare war, grant letters of marque and reprisal, and make rules concerning captures on land and water;

To raise and support armies, but no appropriation of money to that use shall be for a longer term than two years;

To provide and maintain a navy;

POWERS OF CONGRESS

Taxes; defense; welfare. Research: "pork barrel." **Borrowing.** Jefferson called bonds "taxation without representation." Explain. **Commerce.** The tribes are likened to foreign nations. What is their situation now?

Naturalization; bankruptcy. If states say who may vote, why not who may be a citizen?

Money; standards. How is the guarantee that your money is real a kind of freedom? There are no official U.S. standards of weights and measures.

Copyrights; patents. How do these promote progress? Are they fair? Explain.

Courts; law. Highjacking = piracy. What laws do you recommend to control it?

War; armed forces. The President can send troops into foreign action without a declaration of war by Congress. How can Congress' "power of the

To make rules for the government and regulations of the land and naval forces;

To provide for calling forth the militia to execute the laws of the Union, suppress insurrections and repel invasions;

To provide for organizing, arming, and disciplining the militia, and for governing such part of them as may be employed in the service of the United States, reserving to the States respectively the appointment of the officers, and the authority of training the militia according to the discipline prescribed by Congress;

To exercise exclusive legislation in all cases whatsoever, over such district (not exceeding ten miles square) as may, by cession of particular States and the acceptance of Congress, become the seat of the government of the United States, and to exercise like authority over all places purchased by the consent of the legislature of the State in which the same shall be, for the erection of forts, magazines, arsenals, dockyards, and other needful buildings; and

To make all laws which shall be necessary and proper for carrying into execution the foregoing powers, and all other powers vested by this Constitution in the government of the United States, or in any department or officer thereof.

purse" curb such actions? **Navy.** Congress authorized a navy only when war with France was likely in 1798. **Militia** = National Guard, under command of governors until the President nationalizes them. **Captures.** In 1849 the Supreme Court ruled that the U.S. may not gain territory or property by right of conquest.

National capital. Maryland and Virginia both gave land for a national capital. Virginia took back its part in 1846.

Elastic clause. This is the famous battleground for contenders over how strong the central government shall be.

SECTION 9.

The migration or importation of such persons as any of the States now existing shall think proper to admit, shall not be prohibited by the Congress prior to the year one thousand eight hundred and eight, but a tax or duty may be imposed on such importation, not exceeding ten dollars for each person.

The privilege of the writ of habeas corpus *shall not be suspended, unless when in cases of rebellion or invasion the public safety may require it.*

No bill of attainder or ex post facto law shall be passed.

No capitation, or other direct, tax shall be laid, unless in proportion to the census or enumeration herein before directed to be taken.*

No tax or duty shall be laid on articles exported from any State.

No preference shall be given by any regulation of commerce or revenue to the ports of one State over those of another; nor shall vessels bound to, or from, one State be obliged to enter, clear, or pay duties in another.

No money shall be drawn from the Treasury, but in consequence of appropriations made by law; and a regular statement and account of the receipts and expenditures of all public money shall be published from time to time.

No title of nobility shall be granted by the United States: and no person holding any office of profit or trust under them, shall, without the consent of the Congress, accept of any present, emolument, office, or title of any kind whatever, from any king, prince, or foreign State.

SECTION 10.

No State shall enter into any treaty, alliance, or confederation; grant letters of marque and reprisal; coin money; emit bills of credit; make anything but gold and silver coin and tender in payment of debts, pass any bill of attainder, ex post facto law, or law impairing the obligation of contracts, or grant any title of nobility.

No State shall, without the consent of the Congress, lay any imposts or duties on imports or exports, except what may be absolutely necessary for executing its inspection laws: and the net produce of all duties and imposts laid by any State on imports or exports, shall be for the use of the Treasury of the United States; and all such laws shall be subject to the revision and control of the Congress.

No State shall, without the consent of Congress, lay any duty of tonnage, keep troops, or ships of war in time of peace, enter into any agreement or compact with another State, or with a foreign power, or engage in war, unless actually invaded, or in such imminent danger as will not admit of delay.

* Changed by the Sixteenth Amendment

FORBIDDEN POWERS

This was new! Kings were often curbed, but never a legislature. **Slavery.** In 1794 exports were banned; imports continued to 1865, despite the law of 1808.

Habeas corpus = you have the person; writ = written order. The writ's addressee must bring the prisoner promptly before the judge who issued the writ and who will decide if detention is legal. With right to counsel (Amend. 6), this clause ensures due process. Who can suspend this right? When? Why is it the most basic of civil rights? What others can be exercised without it? *Ex post facto* laws, passed after the act, make an innocent act a crime, make a lesser crime worse, increase the penalty, change rules of evidence to ensure conviction, and/or take away legal protections the accused would otherwise have had. Research: "due process of law."

POWERS FORBIDDEN STATES

With Secs. 8 and 9, this aims to help the States operate effectively without conflict among themselves or with the federal government. Study these sections to understand which powers are granted to or withheld from Congress, the States, or both. **Prohibited actions.** The outstanding part of this clause is "impairing the obligation of contracts." Research: contract. In hard times, Confederation legislatures often postponed payments of any debts. How would this affect interstate commerce? How else might State action affect interstate commerce?

ARTICLE II

SECTION 1.

The executive power shall be vested in a President of the United States of America. He shall hold his office during the term of four years, and, together with the Vice President chosen for the same term, be elected as follows:

Each State shall appoint, in such manner as the legislature thereof may direct, a number of electors, equal to the whole number of senators and representatives to which the State may be entitled in the Congress: but no senator or representative, or person holding an office of trust or profit under the United States, shall be appointed an elector.

The electors shall meet in their respective States, and vote by ballot for two persons, of whom one at least shall not be an inhabitant of the same State with themselves. And they shall make a list of all the persons voted for, and of the number of votes for each; which they shall sign and certify, and transmit sealed to the seat of the government of the United States, directed to the president of the Senate. The president of the Senate shall, in the presence of the Senate and House of Representatives, open all the certificates, and the votes shall then be counted. The person having the greatest number of votes shall be the President, if such number be a majority of the whole number of electors appointed; and if there be more than one who have such

THE EXECUTIVE BRANCH

PRESIDENT, VICE PRESIDENT

Terms. There was no executive under the old Articles of Confederation. Should the President's term be longer? Explain.

Presidential electors. Candidates for electors are chosen in various ways from State to State. All States determine electors by popular vote.

Electing executives. This entire paragraph was superseded by Amend. 12, ratified in 1804, which required electors to vote separately for President and Vice President. The amendment was seen to be necessary in 1800, when Thomas Jefferson and Aaron Burr were tied for first place, thus throwing the election into the House of Representatives. Only on the 36th ballot did Jefferson win. How-

*majority, and have an equal number of votes, then the House of Representatives shall immediately choose by ballot one of them for President; and if no person have a majority, then from the five highest on the list the said house shall in like manner choose the President. But in choosing the President, the votes shall be taken by States, the representation from each State having one vote; a quorum for this purpose shall consist of a member or members from two thirds of the States, and a majority of all the States shall be necessary to a choice. In every case, after the choice of the President, the person having the greatest number of votes of the electors shall be the Vice President. But if there should remain two or more who have equal votes, the Senate shall choose from them by ballot the Vice President.***

The Congress may determine the time of choosing the electors, and the day on which they shall give their votes; which day shall be the same throughout the United States.

No person except a natural-born citizen, or a citizen of the United States, at the time of the adoption of this Constitution, shall be eligible to the office of President; neither shall any person be eligible to that office who shall not have attained to the age of thirty-five years, and been fourteen years a resident within the United States.

In case of the removal of the President from office, or of his death, resignation, or inability to discharge the powers and duties of the said office, the same shall devolve on the Vice President, and the Congress may by law provide for the case of removal, death, resignation, or inability, both of the President and Vice President, declaring what officer shall then act as President, and such offer shall act accordingly, until the disability be removed, or a President shall be elected.

The President shall, at stated times, receive for his services a compensation, which shall neither be increased nor diminished during the period for which he shall have been elected, and he shall not receive within that period any other emolument from the United States, or any of them.

Before he enter on the execution of his office, he shall take the following oath or affirmation:—"I do solemnly swear (or affirm) that I will faithfully execute the office of President of the United States, and will to the best of my ability, preserve, protect and defend the Constitution of the United States."

SECTION 2.

The President shall be commander in chief of the army and navy of the United States, and of the militia of the several States, when called into the actual service of the

* Changed by the Twelfth Amendment

ever, Amend. 12 does not alter the fact that the people of the U.S. do not elect the President and Vice President but are required to elect others to do it for them.

Election day. By law, the election is held on the Tuesday after the first Monday in November every fourth year from 1788. The day on which the electors (Electoral College) meet to vote is the Monday after the second Wednesday in December.

Presidential qualifications. Except for the first (why?), the President must be a native. Washington was a native, but many well-qualified men of his era were not. Research: which signers of the Constitution were not natives? **Disability.** Amend. 25, ratified in 1967, enlarges upon this clause.

Salary. The intent is to avoid his catering to Congress or to the state governments for a raise or gifts.

Oath of office. "Or affirm respects Moses' commandment and Jesus' words in Matthew: "Swear not at all [say only] Yea . . . Nay . . . more than these come of the evil one."

PRESIDENTIAL POWERS

Military powers; reprieves, pardons. Executive departments accounted for 95% of the 3 mil-

United States; he may require the opinion, in writing, of the principal officer in each of the executive departments, upon any subject relating to the duties of their respective offices, and he shall have power to grant reprieves and pardons for offenses against the United States, except in cases of impeachment.

He shall have power, by and with the advice and consent of the Senate, to make treaties, provided two thirds of the senators present concur; and he shall nominate, and by and with the advice and consent of the Senate, shall appoint ambassadors, other public ministers and consuls, judges of the Supreme Court, and all other officers of the United States, whose appointments are not herein otherwise provided for, and which shall be established by law: but the Congress may by law vest the appointment of such inferior officers, as they think proper, in the President alone, in the courts of law, or in the heads of departments.

The President shall have power to fill up all vacancies that may happen during the recess of the Senate, by granting commissions which shall expire at the end of their next session.

SECTION 3.

He shall from time to time give to the Congress information of the state of the Union, and recommend to their consideration such measures as he shall judge necessary and expedient; he may, on extraordinary occasions, convene both houses, or either of them, and in case of disagreement between them with respect to the time of adjournment, he may adjourn them to such time as he shall think proper; he shall receive ambassadors and other public ministers; he shall take care that the laws be faithfully executed, and shall commission all the officers of the United States.

lion federal civilian employees in the early 1970's. How is the restriction on pardons part of checks and balances? How can Congress control the commander in chief?

Treaties; appointments. Who are some appointed officers not named in the Constitution? Research: some instances when the Senate refused its consent. How are checks and balances built into this clause?

Filling vacancies; interim appointments. How does this clause exemplify checks and balances?

PRESIDENT AND CONGRESS

Other duties. The President makes one or more reports to Congress soon after it meets each year. Usually he gives a State of the Union message to a meeting of both houses.

5. SCRAPBOOK PROJECT It is important for students to realize that the Constitution is a living document, not just a relic from the past. Have them compile a scrapbook of newspaper and magazine articles that pertain to the basic ideas of the Constitution or to specific activities concerning the Constitution. Articles might include decisions of the Supreme Court, a law being declared unconstitutional, a discussion about controlling the sale of hand guns, taxing church property, saluting the flag in school, censorship—the list is literally endless. You will probably have to discuss some of the possibilities before making the assignment.

SECTION 4.

The President, Vice President, and all civil officers of the United States, shall be removed from office on impeachment for, and conviction of, treason, bribery, or other high crimes and misdemeanors.

IMPEACHMENT

Removal of officers. Which elected officers may not be impeached? Why? Which appointed officers?

ARTICLE III

JUDICIAL BRANCH

SECTION 1.

The judicial power of the United States shall be vested in one Supreme Court, and in such inferior courts as the Congress may from time to time ordain and establish. The judges, both of the Supreme and inferior courts, shall hold their offices during good behavior, and shall, at stated times, receive for their services, a compensation which shall not be diminished during their continuance in office.

FEDERAL COURTS

Judicial power; federal judges. These judges are the only U.S. officers to hold lifetime jobs; their salaries cannot be reduced. How do these two facts help the parties in a lawsuit?

SECTION 2.

The judicial power shall extend to all cases, in law and equity, arising under this Constitution, the laws of the United States, and treaties made, or which shall be made, under their authority;—to all cases affecting ambassadors, other public ministers and consuls;—to all cases of admiralty and maritime jurisdiction;—to controversies to which the United States shall be a party;—to controversies between two or more States;—between a State and citizens of another State;—between citizens of different States,—between

FEDERAL JURISDICTION

Federal cases. How do federal court cases differ from State court cases? In 1798, Amend. 11 stopped anyone from suing a State in federal court. Equity, a judicial method of seeing that justice is done when a law causes specific injustice or hardship, is found only where

citizens of the same State claiming lands under grants of different States, and between a State, or the citizens thereof, and foreign States, citizens or subjects.

In all cases affecting ambassadors, other public ministers and consuls, and those in which a State shall be party, the Supreme Court shall have original jurisdiction. In all the other cases before mentioned, the Supreme Court shall have appellate jurisdiction, both as to law and fact, with such exceptions, and under such regulations as the Congress shall make.

The trial of all crimes, except in cases of impeachment, shall be by jury; and such trial shall be held in the State where the said crimes shall have been committed; but when not committed within any State, the trial shall be at such place or places as the Congress may by law have directed.

Anglo-American law prevails—Americans traveling or residing in other countries, beware!

Supreme Court jurisdiction. If a defendant objects to a court verdict, he may appeal to the next higher court. The Supreme Court is the highest U.S. court of appeals.

Jury trials. Amend. 5, 6, and 7 add further detail to the right of trial by jury in the State where the crime occurred.

SECTION 3.

Treason against the United States shall consist only in levying war against them, or in adhering to their enemies, giving them aid and comfort. No person shall be convicted of treason unless on the testimony of two witnesses to the same overt act, or on confession in open court.

The Congress shall have power to declare the punishment of treason, but no attainder of treason shall work corruption of blood, or forfeiture except during the life of the person attainted.

TREASON

Definition. A professor said he hoped the Communists would win the Vietnam war. Was he a traitor? What about war protesters? spies?

Punishment. Treason penalties include fines, prison, and death. In old times, the State took a traitor's property.

ARTICLE IV

THE STATES

SECTION 1.

Full faith and credit shall be given in each State to the public acts, records, and judicial proceedings of every other State. And the Congress may by general laws prescribe the manner in which such acts, records, and proceedings shall be proved, and the effect thereof.

RELATIONS OF THE STATES

Full faith and credit. Will an Iowa marriage be legal in Utah? If Idaho acquits a man of a specific crime, can Oregon try him for it?

SECTION 2.

The citizens of each State shall be entitled to all privileges and immunities of citizens in the several States.

A person charged in any State with treason, felony, or other crime, who shall flee from justice, and be found in another State, shall on demand of the executive authority of the State from which he fled, be delivered up to be removed to the State having jurisdiction of the crime.

*No person held to service or labor in the State, under the laws thereof, escaping into another, shall, in consequence of any law or regulation therein, be discharged from such service or labor, but shall be delivered up on claim of the party to whom such service or labor may be due.**

DUTIES OF STATE TO STATE

Citizens' privileges. A State may not discriminate unreasonably against nonresidents. **Fugitives.** Returning fugitives is extradition. Why might a governor refuse extradition?

Persons held to service. This provision refers to runaway slaves. How does this clause show that strong disagreements already existed over slavery?

* Changed by the Thirteenth Amendment

Background Information

3. NEW STATES Maine, until it became a separate state in 1819, was a part of Massachusetts. West Virginia became a state in 1863. Originally, the area made up the fifty western counties of Virginia, but the people there refused to recognize the secession of Virginia from the Union.

6. DISCUSSION The Constitution is the "supreme law of the land." Yet civil disobedience has always been a factor in American history; some people have felt that it is almost a social responsibility. Martin Luther King, Jr., made the following statement. Discuss it with your students.

"One may well ask: 'How can you advocate breaking some laws and obeying others?' The answer lies in the fact that there are two types of laws, just and unjust. One has not only a legal but a moral responsibility to obey just laws. One has a moral responsibility to disobey unjust laws. Any law that uplifts human personality is just, any law that degrades human personality is unjust. An unjust law is a code that a numerical or power majority group compels a minority group to obey but does not make binding on itself. This is difference made legal."

Ask: Is there a difference between civil disobedience and simply breaking a law that you do not like? Do people who engage in civil disobedience expect to be punished? How can that punishment help their cause? Are there any laws that you would consider attacking in this manner? What considerations would you have to make?

SECTION 3.

New States may be admitted by the Congress into this Union; but no new State shall be formed or erected within the jurisdiction of any other State; nor any State be formed by the junction of two or more States, or parts of States, without the consent of the legislatures of the States concerned as well as of the Congress.

The Congress shall have power to dispose of and make all needful rules and regulations respecting the territory or other property belonging to the United States; and nothing in this Constitution shall be so construed as to prejudice any claims of the United States, or of any particular State.

ADMISSION OF NEW STATES

Formation; admission. Can New York City become a new State, as many wish? How? Which States were formed from others?

Territories; federal property. Congress can either govern a territory directly or authorize it to set up a legislature and a court system.

SECTION 4.

The United States shall guarantee to every State in this Union a republican form of government, and shall protect each of them against invasion; and on application of the legislature, or of the executive (when the legislature cannot be convened) against domestic violence.

PROTECTION OF THE STATES

Guarantees. What does "republic" tell about how representatives are chosen or whom they represent? Explain the phrase *democratic republic.*

ARTICLE V

The Congress, whenever two thirds of both houses shall deem it necessary, shall propose amendments to this Constitution, or, on the application of the legislatures of two thirds of the several States, shall call a convention for proposing amendments, which, in either case, shall be valid to all intents and purposes, as part of this Constitution, when ratified by the legislatures of three fourths of the several States, or by conventions in three fourths thereof, as the one or the other mode of ratification may be proposed by the Congress; provided [that no amendment which may be made prior to the year one thousand eight hundred and eight shall in any manner affect the first and fourth clauses in the ninth section of the first article, and] that no State, without its consent, shall be deprived of its equal suffrage in the Senate.

AMENDMENTS

Amending the Constitution. In another world's first, a government set up ways in which it could be changed without violence. Describe two ways in which the Constitution may be amended. (*Note:* The Supreme Court says that "two thirds of both houses" means only members present, not entire membership.) What parts could not be changed before 1808? When were these parts changed? How?

ARTICLE VI

All debts contracted and engagements entered into, before the adoption of this Constitution, shall be as valid against the United States under this Constitution, as under the Confederation.

This Constitution, and the laws of the United States which shall be made in pursuance thereof; and all treaties made, or which shall be made, under the authority of the United States, shall be the supreme law of the land; and the

GENERAL PROVISIONS

Confederation debts. The Constitution guarantees payment of all debts contracted under the Articles of Confederation.

Supreme law. Why are treaties part of the supreme law of the land? How has the U.S. kept its treaties with the Indians? Re-

judges in every State shall be bound thereby, anything in the Constitution or laws of any State to the contrary notwithstanding.

The senators and representatives before mentioned, and the members of the several State legislatures, and all executive and judicial officers, both of the United States, and of the several States, shall be bound by oath or affirmation to support this Constitution; but no religious test shall ever be required as a qualification to any office or public trust under the United States.

ARTICLE VII

The ratification of the conventions of nine States shall be sufficient for the establishment of this Constitution between the States so ratifying the same.

Done in Convention by the unanimous consent of the States present the seventeenth day of September in the year of our Lord one thousand seven hundred and eighty-seven, and of the independence of the United States of America the twelfth. In witness whereof we have hereunto subscribed our names.

George Washington, President
(VIRGINIA)

MASSACHUSETTS
Nathaniel Gorham
Rufus King

NEW YORK
Alexander Hamilton

GEORGIA
William Few
Abraham Baldwin

DELAWARE
George Read
Gunning Bedford
John Dickinson
Richard Bassett
Jacob Broom

VIRGINIA
John Blair
James Madison

PENNSYLVANIA
Benjamin Franklin
Thomas Mifflin
Robert Morris
George Clymer
Thomas FitzSimons
Jared Ingersoll
James Wilson
Gouvernor Morris

NEW HAMPSHIRE
John Langdon
Nicholas Gilman

NEW JERSEY
William Livingston
David Brearley
William Paterson
Jonathan Dayton

CONNECTICUT
William Samuel Johnson
Roger Sherman

NORTH CAROLINA
William Blount
Richard Dobbs Spaight
Hugh Williamson

SOUTH CAROLINA
John Rutledge
Charles Cotesworth Pinckney
Charles Pinckney
Pierce Butler

MARYLAND
James McHenry
Daniel of St. Thomas Jenifer
Daniel Carroll

search: what those treaties promised the Indians.

Oath; religious test. How does State officials' support of the Constitution protect everyone? Banning religious tests was a first in world law. Was that a good idea? Why were religious tests banned?

RATIFICATION

Conventions, 1787–1790

Del.	7 Dec 87	Unanimous
Pa.	12 Dec 87	46–23
N.J.	18 Dec 87	Unanimous
Ga.	2 Jan 88	Unanimous
Conn.	9 Jan 88	128–40
Mass.	6 Feb 88	187–168 *
Md.	28 Apr 88	63–11
S.C.	27 May 88	149–73
N.H.	21 Jun 88	57–46 *
Va.	25 Jun 88	87–76 *
N.Y.	26 Jul 88	30–27 *
N.C.	21 Nov 89	187–77
R.I.	29 May 90	34–22

* Strongly urged Bill of Rights

Background Information

4. BILL OF RIGHTS Massachusetts, Virginia, New York, and several other states ratified the Constitution with the recommendation that a Bill of Rights be added to specifically safeguard individual rights. This was done by the First Congress in the form of twelve proposed amendments, ten of which were declared ratified by the necessary number of states on December 15, 1791.

The first eight amendments to the Constitution contain the fundamental rights and freedoms of every United States citizen. Amendments nine and ten forbid Congress to adopt laws that would violate these rights. But the Supreme Court of the United States has held that these rights have some limits. For example, freedom of speech does not protect a person who shouts "Fire!" in a crowded theater when there is no fire. Yet the government must respect these freedoms in all but extreme circumstances. The Supreme Court has held that freedom of speech may be limited only when its exercise creates a "clear and present danger" to society.

FIRST AMENDMENT—1791

Congress shall make no law respecting an establishment of religion, or prohibiting the free exercise thereof; or abridging the freedom of speech, or of the press; or the right of the people peaceably to assemble, and to petition the government for a redress of grievances.

Religion; speech; assembly. Some other democracies tax everyone to support religion. Why doesn't the U.S.? Discuss: "There can be no freedom of speech, press [etc.] for the foes of socialism."—Soviet official A. Vishinski, *The Law of the Soviet State.* Compare that with this Supreme Court comment: "Freedom... protect[s] criticism and agitation for [change], but it does not [protect him] who counsels... the violation of the law...."

SECOND AMENDMENT—1791

A well-regulated militia, being necessary to the security of a free State, the right of the people to keep and bear arms, shall not be infringed.

Right to bear arms. Are handguns or rifles of greater value to a militia? If you were a dictator, what would you do about privately owned firearms? Why?

THIRD AMENDMENT—1791

No soldier shall, in time of peace, be quartered in any house, without the consent of the owner, nor in time of war, but in a manner to be prescribed by law.

Housing troops. Explain how quartering soldiers in private homes could be a method of controlling the nation's civilian population.

FOURTH AMENDMENT—1791

The right of the people to be secure in their persons, houses, papers, and effects, against unreasonable searches and seizures, shall not be violated, and no warrants shall issue, but upon probable cause, supported by oath or affirmation, and particularly describing the place to be searched, and the persons or things to be seized.

Unlawful search. Do you think that the use of electronic "snooping" devices, including wiretapping, by the police violates a person's right to be "secure... against unreasonable searches"? Explain your answer.

FIFTH AMENDMENT—1791

No person shall be held to answer for a capital or otherwise infamous crime, unless on a presentment or indictment of a grand jury, except in cases arising in the land or naval forces, or in the militia, when in actual service in time of war or public danger; nor shall any person be subject for the same offense to be twice put in jeopardy of life or limb; nor shall be compelled in any criminal case to be a witness against himself, nor be deprived of life, liberty, or property, without due process of law; nor shall private property be taken for public use without just compensation.

Rights of accused. Jeopardy begins as a jury is sworn, and ends on acquittal; if jury can't agree, if a mistrial occurs, or if conviction is reversed on appeal, **due process** (= legal fair play) begins anew. Only Anglo-American law assumes accused is not guilty until so proved and stops anyone's being forced to witness against oneself. Each step of proof must protect accused's rights.

SIXTH AMENDMENT—1791

In all criminal prosecutions, the accused shall enjoy the right to a speedy and public trial, by an impartial jury of the State and district wherein the crime shall have been committed, which district shall have been previously ascertained by law, and to be informed of the nature and cause of the accusation; to be confronted with the witnesses against him; to have compulsory process for obtaining witnesses in his favor, and to have the assistance of counsel for his defense.

Criminal procedure. There are so many cases that years may elapse between indictment and trial. Should there be a cut-off time when, if there has been no trial, the indictment is dismissed and the accused is free? Why should the accused have the aid of counsel? Explain the proverb: He who is his own lawyer has a fool for a client.

SEVENTH AMENDMENT—1791

In suits at common law, where the value in controversy shall exceed twenty dollars, the right of trial by jury shall be preserved, and no fact tried by a jury shall be otherwise reexamined in any court of the United States, than according to the rules of the common law.

Civil suits. Many parties to civil suits prefer to let a judge decide. But no judge or appeals court can set aside a civil jury's decision. Jury trials are costly—should the lower limit of $20 be changed? Why? How much?

7. ORAL/WRITTEN REPORT There have been many major Supreme Court decisions affecting the Constitution. Assign one case to each of your more able students to research. Have each student report on the circumstances and significance of the case.

8. USING A CHART Have some students make a chart showing how their representatives and senators voted on major issues and how the total vote compared with the individual votes. The students might need to use the *Congressional Record* or the *Congressional Quarterly* to find some of the information, although most newspapers summarize voting records from time to time. Other students might write to their representatives and senators to make suggestions on how the legislators should vote on upcoming issues.

EIGHTH AMENDMENT—1791

Excessive bail shall not be required, nor excessive fines imposed, nor cruel and unusual punishments inflicted.

Bail, penalties. England forbade bails and fines so high as to deprive one of one's home or means of livelihood. Is death a "cruel punishment"?

NINTH AMENDMENT—1791

The enumeration in the Constitution of certain rights shall not be construed to deny or disparage others retained by the people.

People's rights retained. This amendment answers those who were against aiding a bill of rights. What must their arguments have been? Which of these do we still hear?

TENTH AMENDMENT—1791

The powers not delegated to the United States by the Constitution, nor prohibited by it to the States are reserved to the States respectively, or to the people.

Reserved powers. This guarantees the pre-Constitutional sovereignty of the States. Why was this important to the early Republicans?

ELEVENTH AMENDMENT—1795

The judicial power of the United States shall not be construed to extend to any suit in law or equity, commenced or prosecuted against one of the United States, by citizens of another State, or by citizens or subjects of any foreign State.

Suing States. This amends Art. III–2. Any nonresident must sue a State in that State's own courts, not in federal or other out-of-state courts.

TWELFTH AMENDMENT—1804

The electors shall meet in their respective States, and vote by ballot for President and Vice President, one of whom, at least, shall not be an inhabitant of the same State with themselves; they shall name in their ballots the person voted for as Vice President, and they shall make distinct lists of all persons voted for as President and of all persons voted for as Vice President, and of the number of votes for each, which lists they shall sign and certify, and transmit sealed to the seat of government of the United States, directed to the president of the Senate;—The president of the Senate shall, in the presence of the Senate and House of Representatives, open all the certificates and the votes shall then be counted;—The person having the greatest number of votes for President shall be the President, if such number be a majority of the whole number of electors appointed; and if no person have such majority, then from the persons having the highest numbers not exceeding three on the list of those voted for as President, the House of Representatives shall choose immediately, by ballot, the President. But in choosing the President, the votes shall be taken by States, the representation from each State having one vote; a

Separate election of President and Vice President. Must an elector vote for the candidates who win the popular election in his district? This amends Art. II–1–c. Amend. 20 changes March 4 to January 20, and tells what to do if neither a President nor a Vice President has been chosen by inauguration day.

quorum for this purpose shall consist of a member or members from two thirds of the States, and a majority of all the States shall be necessary to a choice. And if the House of Representatives shall not choose a President whenever the right of choice shall devolve upon them, before the fourth day of March next following, then the Vice President shall act as President, as in the case of the death or other constitutional disability of the President. The person having the greatest number of votes as Vice President shall be the Vice President, if such number be a majority of the whole number of electors appointed, and if the person have a majority, then from the two highest numbers on the list, the Senate shall choose the Vice President; a quorum for the purpose shall consist of two thirds of the whole number of senators and a majority of the whole number shall be necessary to a choice. But no person constitutionally ineligible to the office of President shall be eligible to that of Vice President of the United States.*

THIRTEENTH AMENDMENT—1865

SECTION 1.

Neither slavery nor involuntary servitude, except as a punishment for crime whereof the party shall have been duly convicted, shall exist within the United States, or any place subject to their jurisdiction.

SECTION 2.

Congress shall have power to enforce this article by appropriate legislation.

Slavery prohibited. Some laws passed to enforce this amendment deal with peonage, under which a person in debt to another must work without pay until the debt is "worked out." Isn't this an old-fashioned idea that no longer applies to anyone? If you don't think so, explain.

* Changed by the Twentieth Amendment

FOURTEENTH AMENDMENT—1868

SECTION 1.

All persons born or naturalized in the United States, and subject to the jurisdiction thereof, are citizens of the United States and of the State wherein they reside. No State shall make or enforce any law which shall abridge the privileges or immunities of citizens of the United States; nor shall any State deprive any person of life, liberty, or property, without due process of law; nor deny to any person within its jurisdiction the equal protection of the laws.

Citizens and the States. This, with the Preamble and Art. VII, reinforces the idea that the foremost political relationship is between the people and the federal government, which the people authorize. Before the Civil War, all States, not just southern ones, restricted citizenship to whites. How would States' Righters feel about this amendment?

SECTION 2.

Representatives shall be apportioned among the several States according to their respective numbers, counting the whole number of persons in each State, excluding Indians not taxed. But when the right to vote at any election for the choice of electors for President and Vice President of the United States, representatives in Congress, the executive and judicial officers of a State, or the members of the legislature thereof, is denied to any of the male inhabitants of such State, being twenty-one years of age, and citizens of the United States, or in any way abridged, except for participation in rebellion, or other crime, the basis of representation therein shall be reduced in the proportion which the number of such male citizens shall bear to the whole number of male citizens twenty-one years of age in such State.

Apportionment. This amendment adds to Art. I–2–c by saying that if a State denies the vote to any group, that State's delegation in Congress shall be reduced. If such reduction never took place in a State that denied blacks the vote for a hundred years, were the senators and representatives of that State legally present in Congress? (*Note:* Courts refuse to make decisions on this "political" question. Congress has never challenged a member for being elected under discriminatory laws or situations.)

SECTION 3.

No person shall be a senator or representative in Congress, or elector of President and Vice President, or hold any office, civil or military, under the United States, or under any State, who, having previously taken an oath, as a member of Congress, or as an officer of the United States, or as a member of any State legislature, or as an executive or judicial officer of any State, to support the Constitution of the United States, shall have engaged in

Dealing with rebels. This section denies the privilege of serving in any public office to any former officeholder who took part in the rebellion of the 1860's (See Art. VII.) Congress removed the disability in 1898 so that former Confederate officers could serve in the Spanish-American War.

insurrection or rebellion against the same, or given aid or comfort to the enemies thereof. But Congress may by a vote of two thirds of each house, remove such disability.

SECTION 4.

The validity of the public debt of the United States, authorized by law, including debts incurred for payment of pensions and bounties for services in suppressing insurrection or rebellion, shall not be questioned. But neither the United States nor any State shall assume or pay any debt or obligation incurred in aid of insurrection or rebellion against the United States, or any claim for the loss or emancipation of any slave; but all such debts, obligations and claims shall be held illegal and void.

Civil War debt. The Confederate states sold bonds and issued paper money. Can any of those former Confederate states pay off those bonds or redeem that money today? Explain your answer. (*Note:* In this section is the only use of the word *slave* in the Constitution.)

SECTION 5.

The Congress shall have power to enforce, by appropriate legislation, the provisions of this article.

FIFTEENTH AMENDMENT—1870

Right to vote. This third and last Reconstruction amendment was meant to guard the people against the misuse of State power. Look up "Jim Crow laws" and "Grandfather clause" to see how some States tried to evade this amendment.

SECTION 1.

The right of citizens of the United States to vote shall not be denied or abridged by the United States or by any State on account of race, color, or previous condition of servitude.

SECTION 2.

The Congress shall have power to enforce this article by appropriate legislation.

SIXTEENTH AMENDMENT—1913

Income taxes. This amendment gets around Art. I and its requirement for equal apportionment of taxes.

The Congress shall have power to lay and collect taxes on incomes, from whatever source derived, without apportionment among the several States, and without regard to any census or enumeration.

SEVENTEENTH AMENDMENT—1913

The Senate of the United States shall be composed of two senators from each State, elected by the people thereof, for six years; and each senator shall have one vote. The electors in each State shall have the qualifications requisite for electors of the most numerous branch of the State legislatures.

When vacancies happen in the representation of any State in the Senate, the executive authority of such State shall issue writs of election to fill such vacancies: Provided, that the legislature of any State may empower the executive thereof to make temporary appointments until the people fill the vacancies by election as the legislature may direct.

Direct election of senators. Corruption in state legislatures and deadlocked votes often allowed seats to remain vacant for long periods. How was this harmful to the people of the State?

EIGHTEENTH AMENDMENT *—1919

SECTION 1.

After one year from the ratification of this article the manufacture, sale, or transportation of intoxicating liquors within, the importation thereof into, or the exportation thereof from the United States and all territory subject to the jurisdiction thereof for beverage purposes is hereby prohibited.

SECTION 2.

The Congress and the several States shall have concurrent power to enforce this article by appropriate legislation.

SECTION 3.

This article shall be inoperative unless it shall have been ratified as an amendment to the Constitution by the legislatures of the several States, as provided in the Constitution, within seven years from the date of the submission hereof to the States by the Congress.

Prohibition. Forbidding the sale of intoxicating liquors was first proposed in the mid-nineteenth century. The Prohibition party was organized in 1869. By 1906, 18 states had at one time or another adopted prohibition, though only a few still retained it. The amendment resulted from the efforts of temperance organizations such as the Woman's Christian Temperance Union and the Anti-Saloon League.

This was the first amendment to include a time limit for ratification. Up to this time, about 1,500 proposed amendments had been sent to the States. How many had been approved?

* Repealed by the Twenty-first Amendment

NINETEENTH AMENDMENT—1920

SECTION 1.

The right of citizens of the United States to vote shall not be denied or abridged by the United States or by any State on account of sex.

SECTION 2.

Congress shall have power, by appropriate legislation, to enforce the provisions of this article.

Women's suffrage. Suffrage = right to vote. Women's votes were not new in the U.S. Women had voted in Wyoming since 1869; Colorado, 1893; Utah and Idaho, 1896; Washington, 1910. Montana sent Jeannette Rankin to the House in 1916, four years before this amendment went into effect.

TWENTIETH AMENDMENT—1933

SECTION 1.

The terms of the President and Vice President shall end at noon on the 20th day of January, and the terms of senators and representatives at noon on the 3d day of January, of the years in which such terms would have ended if this article had not been ratified; and the terms of their successors shall then begin.

SECTION 2.

The Congress shall assemble at least once in every year, and such meeting shall begin at noon on the 3d day in January, unless they shall by law appoint a different day.

SECTION 3.

If, at the time fixed for the beginning of the term of the President, the President-elect shall have died, the Vice

Terms of President, Congress. One big change made by this amendment was that Congress was already in session when the President took office. Thus, the outgoing President would no longer have to call a special session for the Senate to confirm new Cabinet appointments. The time between election and the beginning of terms was shortened by about one fourth of a year. What developments had made this possible as well as desirable?

This amends Amend. 12 by providing for the failure of both the President-elect and the Vice President-elect to

President-elect shall become President. If a President shall not have been chosen before the time fixed for the beginning of his term, or if the President-elect shall have failed to qualify, then the Vice President-elect shall act as President until a President shall have qualified; and the Congress may by law provide for the case wherein neither a President-elect nor a Vice President-elect shall have qualified, declaring who shall then act as President, or the manner in which one who is to act shall be selected, and such persons shall act accordingly until a President or Vice President shall have qualified.

qualify and for the possibility of deaths among candidates when the Electoral College has failed to elect a President and Vice President.

SECTION 4.

The Congress may by law provide for the case of the death of any of the persons from whom the House of Representatives may choose a President whenever the right of choice shall have devolved upon them, and for the case of the death of any of the persons from whom the Senate may choose a Vice President whenever the right of choice shall have devolved upon them.

SECTION 5.

Sections 1 and 2 shall take effect on the 15th day of October following the ratification of this article.

SECTION 6.

This article shall be inoperative unless it shall have been ratified as an amendment to the Constitution by the legislatures of three fourths of the several States within seven years from the date of its submission.

TWENTY-FIRST AMENDMENT—1933

SECTION 1.

The eighteenth article of amendment to the Constitution of the United States is hereby repealed.

SECTION 2.

The transportation or importation into any State, territory, or possession of the United States for delivery or use therein of intoxicating liquors, in violation of the laws thereof, is hereby prohibited.

SECTION 3.

This article shall be inoperative unless it shall have been ratified as an amendment to the Constitution by conventions in the several States, as provided in the Constitution, within seven years from the date of submission hereof to the States by the Congress.

Prohibition repealed; local option guaranteed. The Prohibition Amendment, passed 13 years earlier, had been widely violated. It had resulted in bootlegging—the illegal manufacture and sale of intoxicating beverages. Organized gangs had taken over the business of supplying illegal liquor, with a great rise in crime. The amendment repealing prohibition was swiftly ratified. But states and communities still have the option to prohibit the sale of alcoholic beverages within their boundaries.

TWENTY-SECOND AMENDMENT—1951

No person shall be elected to the office of the President more than twice, and no person who has held the office of President, or acted as President, for more than two years of a term to which some other person was elected President shall be elected to the office of the President more than once.

But this Article shall not apply to any person holding the office of President when this Article was proposed by the Congress, and shall not prevent any person who may be holding the office of President, or acting as President, during the term within which this Article becomes operative from holding the office of President or acting as President during the remainder of such term.

Two-term limit for Presidents. No President sought a third term until Franklin D. Roosevelt did so in 1940. Amend. 22 came about largely because Roosevelt broke this unwritten tradition. Roosevelt, a Democrat, was elected not only to a third term but to a fourth. When the Republicans gained control of Congress a few years later, they introduced this amendment. Note that it was worded so as not to apply to Harry S. Truman, the President at the time that it was proposed and adopted.

TWENTY-THIRD AMENDMENT—1961

SECTION 1.

The District constituting the seat of government of the United States shall appoint in such manner as the Congress may direct:

A number of electors of President and Vice President equal to the whole number of senators and representatives in Congress to which the District would be entitled if it were a State, but in no event more than the least populous State; they shall be in addition to those appointed by the States, but they shall be considered, for the purposes of the election of President and Vice President, to be electors appointed by a State; and they shall meet in the District and perform such duties as provided by the twelfth article of amendment.

SECTION 2.

The Congress shall have power to enforce this article by appropriate legislation.

Presidential vote for D.C. When the Constitution was drawn up, there was no District of Columbia. The right to choose electors for President and Vice President was granted only to the states. Amend. 23 finally gave the citizens of the District of Columbia the same rights in presidential elections that the citizens of the states had always possessed.

TWENTY-FOURTH AMENDMENT—1964

SECTION 1.

The right of citizens of the United States to vote in any primary or other election for President or Vice President, for electors for President or Vice President, or for senator or representative in Congress, shall not be denied or abridged by the United States or any state by reason of failure to pay any poll tax or other tax.

SECTION 2.

The Congress shall have power to enforce this article by appropriate legislation.

Poll tax. *Poll* is an old German word for head. A poll tax is one an individual pays just for existing.

TWENTY-FIFTH AMENDMENT—1967

SECTION 1.

In case of the removal of the President from office or his death or resignation, the Vice President shall become President.

SECTION 2.

Whenever there is a vacancy in the office of the Vice President, the President shall nominate a Vice President who shall take the office upon confirmation by a majority vote of both houses of Congress.

SECTION 3.

Whenever the President transmits to the president pro tempore of the Senate and the speaker of the House of Representatives his written declaration that he is unable to discharge the powers and duties of his office, and until he transmits to them a written declaration to the contrary, such powers and duties shall be discharged by the Vice President as Acting President.

SECTION 4.

Whenever the Vice President and a majority of either the principal officers of the executive departments or of such other body as Congress may by law provide, transmit to the president pro tempore of the Senate and the speaker of the House of Representatives their written declaration that the President is unable to discharge the powers and duties of his office, the Vice President shall immediately assume the powers and duties of the office as Acting President.

Thereafter, when the President transmits to the president pro tempore of the Senate and the speaker of the House of Representatives his written declaration that no

Presidential succession. When the Vice President should take over the President's duties in case of disability had never been defined. Some Presidents have had private agreements; others have not. But the numerous illnesses of Dwight Eisenhower in the 1950's and the tragic death of J. F. Kennedy in 1963 were behind the movement that resulted in this amendment.

inability exists, he shall resume the powers and duties of his office unless the Vice President and a majority of either the principal officers of the executive department or of such other body as Congress may by law provide, transmit within four days to the president pro tempore of the Senate and the speaker of the House of Representatives their written declaration that the President is unable to discharge the powers and duties of his office. Thereupon Congress shall decide the issue, assembling within 48 hours for that purpose if not in session. If the Congress, within 21 days after receipt of the latter written declaration, or, if Congress is not in session, within 21 days after Congress is required to assemble, determines by two-thirds vote of both houses that the President is unable to discharge the powers and duties of his office, the Vice President shall continue to discharge the same as Acting President; otherwise, the President shall resume the powers and duties of his office.

TWENTY-SIXTH AMENDMENT—1971

SECTION 1.

The right of citizens of the United States, who are eighteen years of age or older, to vote shall not be denied or abridged by the United States or by any State on account of age.

SECTION 2.

The Congress shall have power to enforce this article by appropriate legislation.

Eighteen made voting age. For the past 30 years the nation had been drafting young men below the age of twenty-one and sending them to war. Rarely were they allowed to vote. That, in addition to the fact that modern communications have resulted in a more knowledgeable and better educated group of under-21's, brought strong support for Amend. 26.

9. RESEARCH: EIGHTEEN-YEAR-OLDS AND THE VOTE Have students investigate the issue of voting by eighteen-year-olds since the inclusion of this right in the Constitution in 1971. How many have voted? How do they vote? Is the eighteen to twenty-one group a voting bloc on certain issues, or does the group split along geographic, party, or other lines?

10. RESEARCH: THE EQUAL RIGHTS AMENDMENT At the time of this writing, the amendment had not yet passed and was being contested in several states. Have some students investigate the history of the ERA, the problems encountered in its passage, and the current status of the amendment. Are there any other amendments that people wish to see passed?

CHAPTER 10

THE FEDERALISTS TAKE CHARGE

Background Information

WASHINGTON AT ASSUNPINK CREEK Washington was greeted by enthusiastic crowds all along his route from Mount Vernon to New York to be sworn in as President in 1789. The celebration in his honor at Assunpink Creek in Trenton, New Jersey, pictured here, was one of the highlights of his trip. As he approached the bridge, Washington recalled the time, a dozen years earlier, when his ragged band of men experienced their brief triumph followed by a near diaster at the hands of the Redcoats in Trenton. This time the bridge wore a triumphal arch of evergreens and flowers. Young girls dressed in white greeted Washington by singing songs and throwing flowers in his path.

J. Califano, a primitive artist, painted this picture a century after the event. He used descriptions of the scene provided by descendants of people who witnessed the celebration. Today the painting is in a private collection in Trenton.

LESSON 1

THE UNITED STATES OF AMERICA during the decade of the 1780s was not really a nation. States that had joined together in a common war for independence were soon putting *tariffs* —or import taxes—on each other's goods. New York and New Hampshire fought over Vermont lands, even while Vermonters themselves wanted to become a separate state. John Adams spoke of the United States as a house with thirteen clocks that had to be set to strike at the same time.

Washington's leadership. One reason the thirteen clocks began striking at the same time under the new Constitution was the leadership of George Washington. More than any other person in America, Washington had the trust of the people. In war, his character and conduct won him their loyalty. In peace, time and again he put his country ahead of his own self-interest. One reason why the delegates in Philadelphia were willing to give large powers to the office of the President was that they counted on Washington to take the job. Once the Constitution went into effect, Washington was the choice of every elector for President. His reelection in 1792 would be equally one-sided.

Filling In the Constitution

As Congress and the new President assembled in New York, the nation's temporary capital, in the spring of 1789, everyone realized that much must be done to fill in the new Constitution. All those in the government were very much aware that every one of their actions might set a *precedent,* or pattern that would be followed in the future.

Mr. President. Members of Congress agonized, for example, over how to address the President. Vice President John Adams suggested that he be called "His Highness, the President of the United States of America and Protector of Their Liberties." Others thought "His Excellency" was just about right.

The diary of Senator William Maclay of Pennsylvania gives us a glimpse into the feelings on this issue. We have changed a few of Maclay's words in order to make the meaning clearer.

> *May 1.* The minutes of yesterday's session were being read. When we came to the report of Washington's speech it was worded, "His most gracious speech." The secretary was going on. I interrupted him. "The words prefixed to the President's speech are the same that are usually placed before the speech of His Britannic Majesty. I consider them as improper. I therefore move that they be struck out."
>
> If such a thing appeared in our minutes, the enemies of the Constitution would not fail to represent it as the first step to royalty.

In the end it was agreed to address Washington simply as "Mr. President." Today this matter seems more amusing than important. But it was taken very seriously in 1789.

Setting precedents. Among the precedents that were to have a lasting effect on the American government was the

LESSON 1 *(2 days)*

Performance Objectives

1. Given a hypothetical civil liberties case, to make a decision based on knowledge of the freedoms guaranteed in the Bill of Rights. **2.** To demonstrate an understanding, either orally or in writing, of the American judicial organization as delineated in the Judiciary Act of 1789.

Vocabulary

Precedent, cabinet, two-term tradition, Bill of Rights, Judiciary Act of 1789

Activities

1. DISCUSSION After the students read the lesson and study the Bill of Rights, ask them how they feel about the following issues: **(a)** Should a person be required to salute the flag? **(b)** Should parochial school children be given public transportation to school? **(c)** Should a person be required to take a test before being registered to vote? **(d)** Should a person be required to serve in the armed forces? **(e)** Should a person who has publicly stated that the government of the United States should be overthrown be given the protection of the Constitution? Encourage your students to support their feelings with facts whenever possible.

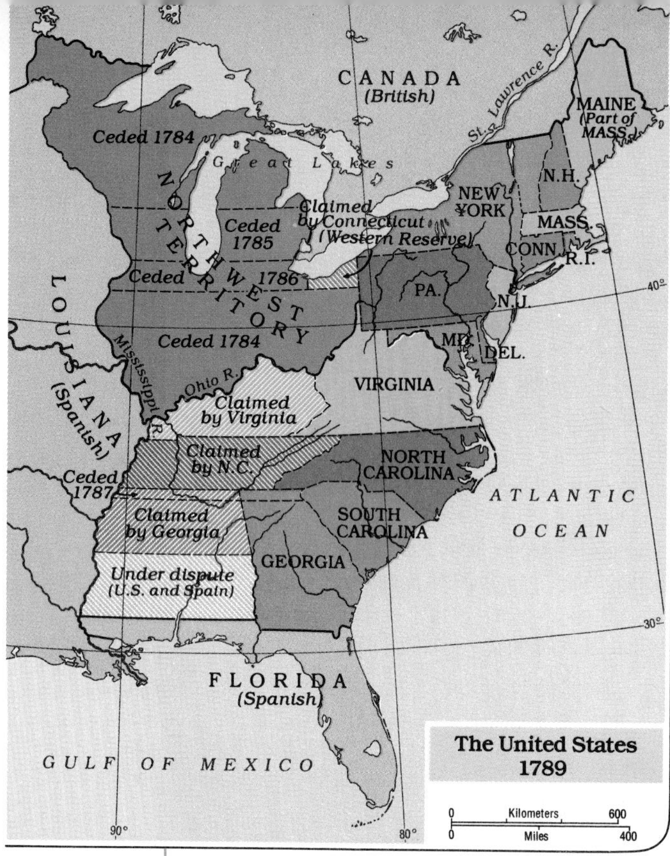

When Washington became President in 1789, the boundaries of the thirteen original states, though often poorly defined, were—except for Virginia—much as they are today. West Virginia was separated from Virginia in 1863.

2. USING A MAP Ask your students to study the map of the United States in 1789 on page 200. At the beginning of the Revolution, seven states claimed land extending to the Mississippi River. How many states still claimed land in 1789? Have students compare this map with a map of present-day United States.

In 1789 the area east of the Mississippi had thirteen states. What additional states are located east of the Mississippi today? What if the states refused to give up their land claims? What problems might have arisen if the states incorporated the area of the land claim within their state?

creation of a *cabinet.* The Constitution says that the President may seek advice from his department heads. As early as 1791, Washington began calling his department heads together to talk with them about a whole range of matters. They came to be known as the cabinet. American Presidents ever since have turned to their cabinets for advice.

Washington established another precedent some years later when he decided not to seek a third term as President. The two-term tradition he started lasted for nearly 150 years. It lasted until Franklin D. Roosevelt served a third term and part of a fourth. In 1951 the Twenty-second Amendment was added to the Constitution, limiting all future Presidents to two terms.

The Bill of Rights. In the Congress, James Madison of Virginia was the leader in taking steps to give the Constitution life. One step was the addition of a bill of rights. During the debates on ratification, delegates in several states had agreed to ratify the Constitution only because of a promise that such a bill would be added. Madison now proposed several amendments upholding the rights of individuals against actions by the federal government.

Ten of those amendments were ratified in 1791. Together, they are known as the Bill of Rights (see pages 186–188). Among the rights protected by these amendments are freedom of speech, freedom of religion and freedom of the press. The Bill of Rights also protects the rights of citizens to assemble peaceably, to petition the government, to bear arms, to be tried by a jury, and to have certain safeguards when accused of a crime.

The Judiciary Act of 1789. One of Congress's first acts was to use its taxing power to place a 5 percent tax on imported goods. Next, it set up federal courts under the Judiciary Act of 1789. There would be thirteen district courts—one for each state. There would be three circuit courts, and a Supreme Court with six judges. The number of district and circuit courts has been changed over the years. So has the number of judges on the Supreme Court. However, the framework of the court system has remained pretty much the same. The law set forth the kinds of cases that could be appealed from the district courts to the circuit and Supreme courts. Most important, it gave the Supreme Court of the United States the power to review the decisions of state courts. It could then declare unconstitutional those state laws that it felt violated the Constitution, acts of Congress, or United States treaties. This law, in other words, put teeth in the Constitution's "supremacy clause," which makes the document the supreme law of the land.

The Judiciary Act, however, did not deal with an important question. That was whether the Supreme Court had the power to review and declare unconstitutional acts of Congress, a co-equal branch of the government. But in 1803, in the case of *Marbury* v. *Madison* (which you will read about in the next chapter), Chief Justice John Marshall ruled that the Supreme Court did have this power.

CHECKUP

1. What were some of the precedents that were set in government while Washington was President?
2. Why was the Bill of Rights passed? What did it guarantee?
3. Describe the framework of the court system under the Judiciary Act of 1789.

LESSON 2

Hamilton and Jefferson

The Constitution, while referring to department heads, left to Congress the job of deciding what kind of and how many departments there would be. Under Madison's leadership, Congress in 1789 set up the departments of Treasury, State, and War, and made them parts of the executive branch of government. It created the posts of Attorney General and Postmaster General as well.

To head two of the new executive departments, Washington chose two of the most able people in America. Alexander Hamilton of New York, his former military aide, became Secretary of the Treasury. Thomas Jefferson of Virginia was named Secretary of State. These two men disagreed on almost every important policy, and became bitter foes. They, and their points of view, became the rallying points for two groups that later became political parties.

A nation of factories—or farms? To begin with, Hamilton and Jefferson saw America's future differently. In a 1791 report favoring a protective tariff, Hamilton spelled out to Congress his hopes for the United States.

> . . . the labor employed in agriculture is, in a great measure, periodical and occasional, depending on the seasons, and liable to various and long intermissions; while that occupied in many manufactures is constant and regular, extending through the year, employing, in some instances, night and day.
>
> . . . machinery forms an item of great importance. . . . It is an artifical force brought in aid of the natural force of man; and . . . is an increase of hands. . . . in general, women and children are rendered more useful, and the latter more early useful, by manufacturing establishment, than they would otherwise be. . . . Workers would probably flock from Europe to the United States, to pursue their trades and professions. . . .

If possible, obtain a copy of *The American Heritage Pictorial Atlas of United States History* (New York: American Heritage Publishing Co., Inc., 1966). Show your students Thomas Jefferson's 1784 plan for dividing the federal land (page 120).

3. BULLETIN-BOARD DISPLAY Have your students design a display for the bulletin board showing the judicial system of the United States as created by the Judiciary Act of 1789. For important excerpts from the Act, see Commager's *Documents of American History.*

LESSON 2 *(2 days)*

Performance Objectives

1. To draw a political cartoon that contrasts Hamilton's and Jefferson's views on one of the following issues: **(a)** the economy, **(b)** the extent of government power, **(c)** the interpretation of the Constitution, and **(d)** the basis for qualification of government leaders. **2.** To list, describe, and evaluate in discussion at least two financial plans initiated by Hamilton.

Vocabulary

Political party, protective tariff, funding program, speculators, assumption program, national bank, elastic clause, implied power, loose interpretation, strict interpretation

Activities

1. POLITICAL CARTOONS After your students have read the lesson, have them each choose a viewpoint expressed by either Hamilton or Jefferson and sketch a political cartoon that satirizes the viewpoint. Ask each student to write on a separate piece of paper a sentence or two explaining his or her cartoon. Then collect all the cartoons and explanations and ask the class to match each cartoon with the appropriate explanation.

2. FILMS *Alexander Hamilton* (18 minutes, b&w; Encyclopaedia Britannica Educational Corp.), presents the highlights of Hamilton's life. *Thomas Jefferson* (34 minutes, color; Handel Film Corp.) is part of the Americana series. The film presents Jefferson's opinion of his most noteworthy contributions to America.

3. THOUGHT PROVOKER In 1857, British historian Lord Macaulay wrote to an American friend: "Your Constitution is all sail and no anchor." What did Macaulay mean by this statement? Ask your students to discuss Macaulay's statement in relation to arguments over **(a)** strict and loose interpretation of the Constitution, **(b)** the funding program, **(c)** the concept of implied powers, and **(d)** the formation of the National Bank.

Contrast that view with Jefferson's version of the good society. We have changed a few of Jefferson's words in order to make his meaning clearer.

> Those who labor in the earth are the chosen people of God, if ever He had a chosen people. . . . Corruption of morals in the mass of farmers is something of which no age nor nation has furnished an example. . . . While we have land to labor, then, let us never wish to see our citizens occupied at a workbench. . . . Let our workshops remain in Europe.
>
> . . . .
>
> I think our governments will remain honest for many centuries; as long as they are chiefly agricultural. . . . When people pile upon one another in large cities, as in Europe, they shall become corrupt, as in Europe.

Which of the two wanted the United States to become a nation of cities and factories? What does he see as the advantages of manufacturing? Based on these writings, which one would you think wanted America to become a great trading nation?

How much power? The two men differed also on how much power the central government should have.

In Jefferson's view, the country was too big to be run by a single government. Public officials far away from the people would be tempted to be dishonest. He wanted the central government to be small and simple. Most governing power, he thought, should be left with the states.

Hamilton, on the other hand, favored a strong central government. He feared that strong, jealous states would keep the central government from acting effectively and would pull the union apart.

Paying the nation's debts. Hamilton's management of the new nation's financial affairs was brilliant. His first goal was to restore the government's credit, which was very low. During the Revolutionary War, Congress had borrowed heavily both from other countries and from American citizens. It raised money by selling certificates of indebtedness. These were a kind of bond, or IOU, promising to pay the money back at a later date. However, the Confederation government was never able to do so. So, the new government still owed $12 million to France, Spain, and Holland. It owed another $42 million to its own people. Many doubted the debts would, or could, be paid, at least in full.

Yet Hamilton proposed exactly that—full payment of the debts. Certificates of indebtedness were to be turned in for new interest-bearing United States bonds. Those bonds were to pay the original value of the certificates plus all unpaid interest. Money to pay off the new bonds was to be raised by new taxes. Hamilton's plan was known as the *funding program.*

The funding proposal touched off heated debate. It was not about whether the debts should be paid. Rather it was about to whom payments should be made. Many of the original lenders to the government, hard pressed for cash and discouraged about their chances of being paid back, had sold their certificates. They had done so for a small part of the original cost. James Madison, among others, felt that those who had originally lent the money to the government should get payment in full—rather than the speculators, who had bought the certificates from them at low prices. But Hamilton's plan was approved by Congress. The new bonds went to speculators and others who were holding the certificates.

Suspicions and objections. The credit of the United States government was soon restored among the nations of the world. But in the United States, the funding program left hard feelings and suspicions. The speculators, informed of the plan by Hamilton before it was made public, had hurried into the backcountry to buy certificates from unsuspecting farmers. Some of the speculators were the very Congressmen who later voted for the plan. Farmers who sold their certificates to those people at low prices rightly felt cheated.

Hamilton also proposed that the national government *assume*, or take over, responsibility for state debts left over from the war. The debts had been incurred for a national cause, he reasoned. Now they should be paid by the nation. The *assumption program*, as it was called, was also passed, but not without objection. Several states had already paid most of their debts. Virginia had paid all of its debt. Such states objected to being taxed by the federal government to pay off the debts of other states. In the end, enough votes were won to pass the bill by a compromise. Southern states, including Virginia, voted for assumption in exchange for northern votes to locate the permanent capital of the United States on the Potomac River.

Alexander Hamilton, the first Secretary of the Treasury, devised programs that placed the new nation on a solid financial foundation.

A national bank. The split between Hamilton and Jefferson widened when Congress accepted Hamilton's plan to charter a national bank. The bank, to be called the Bank of the United States, would have a charter to operate for twenty years. This bank was to have the power to issue bank notes that would circulate as money. It would also lend funds to the government when necessary, and serve as a place to deposit the government's money. Since the bank would help the nation's businesspeople, it was an important part of Hamilton's vision of the United States as an industrial and commercial nation.

4. DISCUSSION The essential conflict between Jefferson and Hamilton lay in the principles each held regarding the nature of human beings and government. Jefferson believed in **(a)** a democratic, agricultural society based on the free and individual landowner; **(b)** a broad distribution of wealth among the citizens; **(c)** freedom from the blights of city life, factories and industrial problems, and organized finance (banks); **(d)** sympathy for those in debt; **(e)** decentralized government; **(f)** the worth and perfectability of the individual human being; and **(g)** the ability of the people to govern themselves.

Hamilton believed in **(a)** a balanced and diversified system of business and finance; **(b)** the governmental encouragement of business of all kinds; **(c)** a strong central government; **(d)** the need for and value of a moneyed class (creditors); **(e)** the inherent weakness of human beings to govern themselves and to make the required decisions necessary to a good life; and **(f)** a government by the upper class.

Imagine that our early government was an airplane and that Hamilton's policies made up one wing, Jefferson's made up the other, and George Washington was the pilot. What would have happened to America if Washington had not maintained a balance between the views of these two antagonists? What would America be like today if all of Hamilton's views of government had dominated? if all of Jefferson's views of government had dominated?

The creation of a national bank was part of the program drawn up by Alexander Hamilton. The main office, shown above, was located in Philadelphia.

Did Congress have the right, under the Constitution, to charter a bank? President Washington had his doubts; the Constitution did not include this power among those given to Congress. Before signing the bill, Washington asked Hamilton and Jefferson for their opinions. In their statements, both referred to the so-called *elastic clause*—the last paragraph of Article I, section 8 of the Constitution. (You will find it on page 177.) This paragraph gives Congress the power "to make all laws . . . necessary and proper for carrying into execution the . . . powers" listed in the previous paragraphs of section 8. The key words in that clause are "necessary" and "proper."

Hamilton held that the Constitution *implied* that Congress had the power to set up a national bank, even if it did not state the power in so many words. Congress was expected to carry out the duties assigned by the Constitution. It was free to choose the means to do that as long as it didn't choose a means that the Constitution prohibited. In this case, setting up a national bank was a "necessary" and "proper" means to help collect taxes, regulate trade, and provide for defense—all of which were jobs of Congress.

Jefferson's view, however, was this:

> I consider the foundation of the Constitution as laid on this ground—that *all powers not delegated to the United States by*

the Constitution, nor prohibited by it to the states, are reserved to the states or to the people. . . .

The incorporation of a bank, and the powers assumed by this bill, have not, in my opinion been delegated to the United States by the Constitution.

The second general phrase is "to make all laws *necessary* and proper for carrying into execution the enumerated powers." But they can all be carried into execution without a bank. A bank therefore is not *necessary,* and consequently not authorized by this phrase.

Hamilton's belief that Congress has certain "implied powers" that are not stated by the Constitution has come to be known as the *loose interpretation* of the Constitution. Jefferson's position is known as the *strict interpretation.* Which of these two views is closer to the idea of limited government? In this case, Washington sided with Hamilton and signed the bill creating the Bank of the United States.

Who should govern? Hamilton's program was related to his ideas about which people could best run the government. On this subject, he and Jefferson were once again worlds apart. Here are Hamilton's ideas on popular rule:

> All communities divide themselves into the few and the many. The first are the rich and wellborn; the other, the mass of the people. The voice of the people has been said to be the voice of God. But that . . . is not true. The people are turbulent and changing; they seldom judge correctly. . . .

Hamilton believed that the new government could succeed only if it won the support and participation of the wise, the rich, and the wellborn. His way of winning them over was to offer them positions in government, and to make participation in government pay for them. By helping the government, they would be helping themselves.

Think back to Hamilton's plan. What class of people would hold most of the bonds under the funding program? Would they have reason to help the new government succeed? When the federal government assumed the state debts, which level of government did those same people want to see strengthened —state or federal? Which groups in society were most likely to benefit if the national bank and the new government succeeded? Describing Hamilton's position, one historian has said that Hamilton "proposed to use the federal government to enrich a class, in order that this class might strengthen the federal government."

Jefferson also believed that the ablest people should hold government office. But he did not believe they could be found only among the rich and the wellborn. And he had confidence that the people would have the good judgment to choose able leaders.

> I have such reliance on the good sense of the body of the people and honesty of their leaders that I am not afraid of their letting things go wrong to any length in any cause.
>
> . . . .
>
> Whenever the people are well-informed, they can be trusted with their own government; whenever things get so far wrong as to attract their notice, they may be relied on to set them to rights.

With Jefferson holding this view, it is not surprising that he differed with

Background Information

POSTAL SERVICE In 1789, Samuel Osgood was appointed the first Postmaster General under the United States Constitution. He took control of the existing postal system set up by the Continental Congress in 1782. Ben Franklin had played a large role in developing the postal system.

In 1790 the postal system had 75 post offices and about 2,000 miles of post roads. The main post road ran from Wiscasset, Maine, to Savannah, Georgia, and passed through Boston, Springfield, Hartford, New York, Philadelphia, Baltimore, Alexandria, Wilmington, and Charleston. Although some roads branched off from the main road, many towns had no direct link to the system. In 1790, stagecoaches carried most of the mail; post-riders handled the rest.

The amount of postage depended upon the distance a letter was to be carried. The milestone system devised by Franklin for the post roads helped a postmaster to determine the postage. Since adhesive postage stamps were not introduced until 1847, the postmaster simply wrote *Paid* on the envelope to indicate the postage had been paid. In 1792, uniform rates were put into effect. Distance still determined the amount of postage (e.g., up to 30 miles the cost was 6¢; over 450 miles it was 25¢). The postage was usually collected at the place of delivery. Letters and newspapers comprised most of the mail. Until 1816, every printer could send one newspaper free to every other printer of newspapers in the country.

Hamilton about who should run the government. Said Jefferson:

> Every government degenerates when trusted to the rulers . . . alone. The people themselves are its only safe depositories.
>
> . . . .
>
> I am not among those who fear the people. They and not the rich are our dependence for continued freedom.

Which of these two men, Hamilton or Jefferson, was more in favor of limiting government? Which do you think was more democratic-minded?

CHECKUP

1. What differing views did Hamilton and Jefferson have on the kind of country the United States should be?
2. How did Hamilton restore the credit of the federal government?
3. How did Hamilton and Jefferson justify their views on the right of Congress to charter a national bank?

LESSON 3

The Rise of Political Parties

Differences over the program of Washington and Hamilton, the question of government power and the future of the country led to the rise of two political groups. One was called the Federalists. While they took the same name as those who had supported ratification of the Constitution, they were a different group of people. By and large they shared Hamilton's views on popular rule, industry and commerce, and government power. Those sharing Jefferson's views on these matters formed the second group. They were called the Democratic-Republicans.

Members of these two groups did not divide neatly along occupational, class, or sectional lines, any more than today's political parties do. There were Federalist farmers as well as Democratic-Republican farmers. Nevertheless, it is safe to say that most of the strength of the Federalists came from New England and the coastal parts of the Northeast, and they were supported heavily by merchants, businessmen, and lawyers. The Democratic-Republicans drew most of their support from the small farmers, plantation owners, and frontier people of the South and West.

The French Revolution. Political divisions were further sharpened by foreign affairs. No event of the time had a greater impact upon Americans than the French Revolution. In 1789 the French overthrew their king and proclaimed the principles of liberty, equality, and brotherhood. They then set up a republican form of government. News of the event was received joyously by most Americans. They believed their own Revolution had served as an example for the French.

But in 1793 the French Revolution took a violent turn. First the King of France was executed. Then in the space of a few months, 17,000 others, including some of the revolution's own leaders who had fallen out of favor, were put to death. In that same year, France declared war on Great Britain. Except for a few short truces, their struggle lasted for the next twenty-two years. The Anglo-French conflict had a great effect on America's domestic and foreign politics.

The American reactions. Federalists were disgusted by what they felt were the disorder, mob rule, and godlessness

In Paris during the French Revolution, persons suspected of being disloyal to the government are arrested and taken to jail. Americans were divided in their reactions to events in France.

of the French Revolution. Some Americans were proud of the example the United States had given to France. However, the Federalists worried about the example the French might be setting for Americans. In the eyes of the Federalists, Britain remained the ideal society. It was ruled by the upper classes and was stable. It respected tradition and property. So, when the Anglo-French war broke out, the Federalists favored Britain.

Hamilton in particular disliked the French Revolution. He believed that America's prosperity depended upon good relations with England. Most of America's trade was still with Britain. The tariff collected from British imports was the main source of income for the United States. If it were cut off, Hamilton's entire funding program would be wrecked—and with it the credit of the United States.

Thomas Jefferson and the Democratic-Republicans, on the other hand, were pro-French. Before the French Revolution, Jefferson had visited France and had seen the terrible conditions there. Although he opposed the violence, he felt the revolution was justified because it replaced a monarchy with a republican government. "The liberty of the whole earth," said Jefferson, "was depending on the outcome of the contest, and was ever such a prize won with so little innocent blood?"

The Neutrality Proclamation. Most of the American people were pro-French. Some wanted to wage war on Britain.

LESSON 3 *(2 to 3 days)*

Performance Objectives

1. To demonstrate in writing an understanding of the issues that led to the development of political parties. 2. To demonstrate an understanding of the implications of the Alien and Sedition Acts by giving examples of ways in which the rights of citizens could be limited today if such acts were still in effect.

Famous People

Edmond Genêt, John Jay, James Madison, John Adams, Talleyrand

Vocabulary

Federalists, Democratic-Republicans, French Revolution, neutrality, Jay's Treaty, XYZ Affair, undeclared war, Alien and Sedition Acts, Kentucky and Virginia Resolutions, states' rights

Activities

1. RESEARCH/CREATIVE WRITING After your students have read this lesson, ask them to research the lives of the people mentioned in the lesson. Have them write a short biography that might serve to introduce the person before he made a speech at an imaginary fund-raising dinner in 1800. Encourage students to include the name of an appropriate organization to benefit from the funds raised, a brief biographical sketch, and a summary of the person's accomplishments.

2. ORAL REPORTS Commager's *Documents of American History* contains the text of many documents written during the time period covered in this lesson. Included are Washington's "Proclamation of Neutrality," Washington's "Proclamation on the Whiskey Rebellion," "The Alien and Sedition Acts," and "The Kentucky and Virginia Resolutions of 1798." Ask some of your better students to read the documents and to make reports to the class.

But other American citizens wanted the United States to side with Britain. Emotions were aroused further when a very enthusiastic minister from the French Republic, Edmond Genêt, arrived in America to ask for aid. Genêt was greeted by such huge crowds that he soon believed that he, rather than Washington, spoke for the American people. He even tried to recruit men and ships for the French cause without asking permission. President Washington finally had to ask the government of France to recall Genêt.

Washington, believing that America must have peace, steered a middle course. In 1793 he announced that the United States would remain neutral. The Neutrality Proclamation was unpopular, but history has shown that it was the wisest course to follow.

Britain, in the meantime, had begun to violate America's neutral rights on the seas. British captains stopped American ships and searched them. They seized those with cargoes for France. Americans on the western frontier had their own grievances against Britain. The British still held the forts they had promised to give up in the Treaty of Paris. Frontier settlers believed, with some justification, that the British were inciting the Indians against them.

Jay's Treaty. Once again, there was talk of war. And once again, Washington turned a deaf ear to it. In 1794 he sent John Jay, Chief Justice of the United States, to England to try to settle the differences between the two countries. Jay came back with a treaty some months later and almost immediately became the most unpopular man in America.

In truth, Jay's Treaty did not settle many issues. The British again agreed to leave the military posts on American territory in the Northwest. They allowed a few American ships to trade in the rich British West Indies market. But they added so many conditions to this trade that they greatly limited it. The treaty also referred several troublesome matters, such as the pre-Revolutionary War debt claims and boundary disputes, to boards of arbitration. The great accomplishment of the Jay Treaty, however, was not to be found in its words but in the fact that it prevented war.

Jay's Treaty outraged the pro-French Democratic-Republicans. They attacked it as the "death warrant of American liberty." The treaty also turned many people against Washington. One member of Congress even said the President should be impeached for signing it.

The first political party. The anger over Jay's Treaty caused the Democratic-Republicans to form a full-scale political party. They founded newspapers, formed local political clubs, and held rallies to influence voters. Those seeking local, state, and national offices agreed to help each other by running as members of the same party.

The chief builder of the new party was James Madison. With Jefferson, he had organized the opposition to Hamilton's program in 1791. Madison remained in Congress through both of Washington's terms and led the opposition to Federalist policies there. He also stayed in close touch with Jefferson after the latter retired as Secretary of State in 1793 and returned home to Monticello, Virginia.

(Detail) Metropolitan Museum of Art

Continued on page 210

The Whiskey Rebellion

An early test of the strength of the federal government under the new Constitution came in 1794 when the Whiskey Rebellion broke out in western Pennsylvania. Three years earlier Secretary of the Treasury Alexander Hamilton had gotten Congress to place a tax on a number of goods to help pay for his funding program. Among the taxed products was whiskey. The tax fell heavily on western farmers who distilled their grain into whiskey before shipping it to the East. They did this because of the difficulty of transportation. A pack horse could carry only 4 bushels (35 liters) of rye or corn in the form of grain, but 24 bushels (211 liters) in the form of whiskey.

To the frontier farmers, this tax on the product of their labor was unfair. In Pennsylvania, west of the Allegheny Mountains, they rose in rebellion. Mass meetings were held, and riots broke out. When the governor of Pennsylvania refused to send the state militia to restore order, President Washington, urged on by Hamilton, called upon 15,000 militia troops from neighboring states to do so. The rebellion was quickly put down. Two ring leaders, charged with treason, were pardoned by Washington.

In crushing the uprising, the federal government showed not only that it was strong enough to deal with an armed rebellion but also that it had the will to do it. The government's action in Pennsylvania was far different from the feeble way it had dealt with Shays's Rebellion.

The Whiskey Rebellion had another result that was not so pleasing to the Federalists. It made nearly all the western farmers angry with Hamilton and his Federalist supporters. Therefore, in the elections of 1796 and 1800, the western frontier people backed Jefferson and the Democratic-Republican party. After Jefferson became President in 1801, the whiskey tax was repealed.

3. CREATIVE WRITING
Washington's Farewell Address was never delivered by Washington. He arranged to have it published in a Philadephia newspaper on September 19, 1796. In the address, he explained his reasons for refusing a third term of office and warned against political parties and foreign entanglements. He stated that although political parties "may now and then answer popular ends, they are likely, in the course of time . . . to become potent engines by which cunning, ambitious, and unprincipled men will be enabled to subvert the power of the people and to usurp for themselves the reins of government."

After reading this quotation to your class, ask them to write a letter to President Washington explaining the developments that led to the rise of political parties. You might wish to have several students read their letters to the class.

In Maryland, Washington reviews the troops gathered to put down the Whiskey Rebellion.

Background Information

1. LOGAN ACT While President Adams was trying to bring about a peace with France in 1799, another American, a Quaker named George Logan, also made an attempt. A believer in the democratic ideas of the French Revolution and a follower of Jefferson, Logan traveled to France at his own expense. There he was warmly received by Talleyrand, who assured him that the French wanted peace. However, Washington and President Adams were not impressed by Logan's initiative. Federalist criticism of his actions led to Congressional passage of the Logan Act, which is still in effect in a modified form today. The act made it illegal for a private citizen to become involved in a controversy between the United States and a foreign country.

It is ironic that the first American political party was led by these two men. Jefferson had once said that if forming a party was the only way to get to heaven, he would rather not get there. Madison had often written that parties were undesirable. As one of the main authors of the Constitution, he had hoped that that document would discourage the growth of political parties.

Jefferson and Madison's views about political parties were shared by most leaders of their generation. They knew that disagreements among interest groups and among sections were bound to arise. They hoped, however, that the disagreements would never lead groups to form permanent political parties. Their main goal was national unity. To them, nothing threatened unity more than political parties.

Yet by 1796 they and others had decided that only by forming a party could they hope to block policies they opposed and promote policies they favored. And only through belonging to a political party could they expect to win election to office to seek those goals.

Adams succeeds Washington. In September 1796, Washington announced his plan to retire, and gave his farewell address. Among other things, he warned against the bad influence of party spirit. He was already too late, for the Democratic-Republicans were gearing up for the 1796 campaign. They nominated Jefferson for President. The Federalists were not yet organized enough to be called a party. Federalist members of Congress, however, chose Vice President John Adams as their candidate. In a close contest, Adams received 71 electoral votes and became President. Under the electoral system in use at that time, Jefferson, with 68 votes, became Vice President.

A dispute with France. John Adams proved to be a courageous President. His four-year term was one of the stormiest in American history. It was marked by an angry dispute between France and the United States. The French felt that the treaty of alliance they had made with the United States during the American Revolution meant that the United States must help France in its war against Britain. The French had become bitter when, in 1793, Washington had proclaimed neutrality. They were further angered when the Senate approved Jay's Treaty with their enemy, England.

Soon afterward, the French began to attack American shipping. Tension between the two countries mounted. President Adams sent three commissioners to Paris to try to settle matters peaceably. Talleyrand, the French foreign minister, refused to talk with the Americans. Instead, he appointed three agents to do so. These three, who became known as X, Y, and Z, demanded a large bribe as part of any deal. The Americans refused and broke off talks with the French.

An undeclared war. When Adams reported the XYZ affair to Congress in April 1798, Americans, angry and insulted over the bribery demand, prepared for war. Washington came out of retirement to head the army. Hamilton called for war and dreamed of leading an army against the French. American privateers received permission to attack

Continued on page 212

Charles Willson Peale

Patriot, portrait painter, naturalist, museum founder—these were some of the roles played by the remarkable Charles Willson Peale during the early years of the United States.

A native of Maryland, Peale was apprenticed to a saddle maker for seven years as a youth. However, he became interested in art, and showed much talent in painting portraits. In 1767 he went to London and studied under Benjamin West, one of the best known artists of the time. Upon returning to America, Peale kept busy doing portraits, and he also plunged into patriotic, political activities. He joined the militia and during the Revolution fought at Trenton, Princeton, and Germantown. While in the army, he did portraits from life of most of America's top military and naval officers. He is known particularly for his many portraits of George Washington, executed over a 23-year period. The versatile Peale also fashioned Washington's dental plates!

An ardent nationalist, Peale wanted Americans to be well educated. He promoted an interest in natural science as well as art. When he learned of the discovery of a mastodon skeleton in New York, he organized a scientific expedition to dig up the bones and put them on display. The museum that Peale opened in Philadelphia was one of the first of its kind in America. There he exhibited specimens of birds and animals, which he had stuffed and mounted, as well as many of his portraits.

To encourage American art, Peale helped to establish the Pennsylvania Academy of Fine Arts, one of the country's first public art galleries. He firmly believed that anyone could be taught to paint. Among those he instructed were members of his own family. Four of his sons, like their father, were both painters and naturalists. His niece, Sarah Miriam Peale, was very likely the first professional woman portrait painter in America.

In this self-portrait, Charles Willson Peale presents his Philadelphia museum.

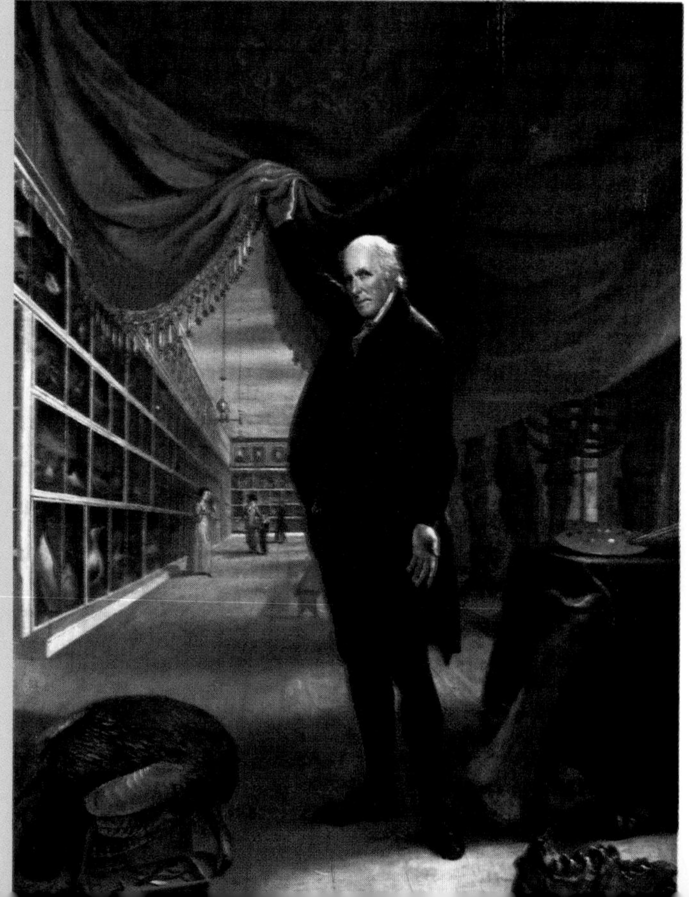

Background Information

2. MATHEW LYON One of those arrested and jailed under the Sedition Act was Matthew Lyon, a congressman from Vermont. Lyon published a periodical in which he often criticized the Federalists. One of his editorials urged Americans to resist the Federalist attempt to establish "a state of abject slavery and degrading subjection to a set of assuming High Mightinesses in our own country." He also published a letter that urged that the President be sent "to a mad house."

At his trial, Lyon tried in vain to prove the Sedition Act was unconstitutional and that his allegations were true. He was convicted on three counts of libel, sentenced to four months in jail, and fined $1,000.

Just before his trial, Lyon's term of office had expired. An election to fill the vacancy resulted in no majority for any candidate, as the Federalists had nominated several candidates to flood the field. Another election was held in December of 1798 and Lyon, considered a hero by this time, won easily. Released from prison in February of 1799, he immediately made his way to Washington. Enthusiastic crowds greeted him along his route in Vermont.

★**1**★

George Washington

1732–1799

Born in VIRGINIA
In Office 1789–1797
Party NONE

Elected and reelected by unanimous electoral vote. Helped erect government departments, agencies, and courts. Advised the United States to stay clear of permanent foreign alliances.

★ ★ ★ ★ ★ ★ ★ ★

French ships because of France's seizure of American ships. For the next two years, an undeclared war was fought on the high seas. President Adams told Congress: "I will never send another minister to France without assurance that he will be received, respected and honored as the representative of a great, free, powerful, independent nation."

Still, Adams, like Washington before him, knew that war would be a disaster for the struggling young nation. So while others shouted for war, Adams quietly looked for peace. Word came to him that Talleyrand would now properly receive an American minister. Without consulting his cabinet, Adams chose a minister to go to France. The move made him very unpopular among the other Federalists. They divided into two groups—one supporting him and the other favoring Hamilton.

Adams's second try at bringing about peace with France was successful. In the Convention of 1800, France and America agreed to end the alliance of 1778. Nothing further was said about the damage that the French had done to American shipping, but it was understood that the naval war would now end. As with Jay's Treaty, the most important achievement of this agreement was that it kept the young United States out of war. Adams himself said that this was his most important act as President.

The Alien and Sedition Acts. Affairs at home were as stormy as those abroad. Taking advantage of the war hysteria in 1798, Federalists in Congress passed a series of laws aimed at the Democratic-Republicans. Together, these laws are known as the Alien and Sedition Acts. One of them—the Naturalization Act—increased from five years to fourteen the time a foreigner had to live in the United States before becoming a citizen. Many new citizens had been siding with Jefferson and his party, and this would keep them from adding more voters to their ranks. The Alien Act gave the President the power to deport any foreigner whom he thought "dangerous to the peace and safety of the United States." The Sedition Act made it a crime for anyone to criticize the United States government, the President, or the Congress. Its aim was to silence Democratic-Republican newspaper editors.

Adams never deported any aliens, but the Sedition Act was used against newspaper editors. Twenty-five were tried. Ten were convicted and sent to jail by Federalist judges.

The Kentucky and Virginia Resolutions. The Alien and Sedition Acts raised a wave of disapproval among most people. Democratic-Republicans charged that the laws violated the guarantees of free speech and free press in the Bill of Rights. Jefferson and Madison wrote resolutions and had them passed by supporters in the Kentucky and Virginia legislatures. The Kentucky and Virginia Resolutions declared that the Alien and Sedition Acts were unconstitutional and would not be obeyed in those states. They also invited other states to pass such resolutions.

The resolutions were really intended more as political propaganda than anything else. But in claiming that a state had the right, by itself, to decide which federal laws would be obeyed within its borders, these resolutions put forth an idea—*states' rights*—that was filled with danger for the Union. You will read more about that idea in Unit 5.

The election of 1800. In the election of 1800, the Federalists were divided. John Adams failed to win a second term. Unexpectedly, however, Thomas Jefferson, the Democratic-Republicans' presidential candidate, and Aaron Burr of New York, the vice-presidential candidate, each got 73 electoral votes.

At that time, electors voted for two candidates, without distinguishing between President and Vice President. It had been expected that at least one of the Democratic-Republican electors would vote for Jefferson and not for Burr, avoiding a tie. But none did.

Under the Constitution, when no candidate has a majority, the final choice is made in the House of Representatives. At such times, each state has one vote. It took thirty-five ballots before Jefferson received the necessary majority. To prevent such an occurrence in the future, the Twelfth Amendment was added to the Constitution in 1804.

★2★

John Adams

1735–1826

Born in MASSACHUSETTS
In Office 1797–1801
Party FEDERALIST

Avoided a war with France, but was harshly criticized. To curb criticism, he helped pass unpopular Alien and Sedition Acts. Failed to win second term. First president to live in the White House.

★ ★ ★ ★ ★ ★ ★ ★

4. THOUGHT PROVOKER In Jefferson's *Autobiography* he tells of witnessing the demolition of the Bastille and of his delight in watching it. The mob violence and the decapitation of the Bastille guards did not appear to upset him. Earlier, in defense of Shays's Rebellion, he wrote a friend: "What country before ever existed a century and a half without a rebellion? And what country can preserve its liberties if their rulers are not warned from time to time that their people preserve the spirit of resistance? Let them take arms. The remedy is to set them right as to facts, pardon and pacify them. What signify a few lives lost in a century or two? The tree of liberty must be refreshed from time to time with the blood of patriots and tyrants. It is its natural manure."

Read Jefferson's statement to your class, and ask them to comment on his views. Ask how they react to his statement with regard to events in our recent history, such as Vietnam and Watergate. Point out that by justifying the excesses of the French Revolution, Jefferson argued, in effect, that the end justifies the means—the same argument that many totalitarian leaders and countries use today. Ask: How do you feel about Jefferson's arguments? Does the end always justify the means? Do ethics exist only for individuals—not for nations?

5. WHAT IF? What if the Alien and Sedition Acts were still in force? What aspects of American life would be affected? Is there any way these acts could be justified today? How were they justified in the 1790s?

Answers to Review Questions

1. The two precedents established were the creation of a cabinet and the two-term tradition.
2. The Bill of Rights guarantees freedom of speech, freedom of religion, and freedom of the press. It protects the rights of citizens to bear arms, to assemble peacefully, to petition the government, to be tried by jury, and to have certain safeguards when accused of a crime.
3. Hamilton's financial plan consisted of **(a)** the funding program; **(b)** the assumption program; and **(c)** the creation of a national bank.
4. **(a)** Hamilton envisioned America as a nation of cities and factories; Jefferson wanted the nation to remain chiefly agricultural; **(b)** Hamilton favored a strong central government, while Jefferson thought the central government should remain small and simple with most governing power left with the states. **(c)** Hamilton believed the new government should be governed by the wise, the rich, and the well-born, whereas Jefferson believed that the ablest people to hold government office could be found among the average citizens.
5. Hamilton believed in a loose interpretation of the Constitution by which the powers of the national government could be expanded through the use of the elastic clause of the Constitution. Jefferson, on the other hand, believed in a strict interpretation of the Constitution by which the national government could have only those powers specifically enumerated in the Constitution.

As the first woman to live in the White House, the well-informed, witty Abigail Adams enjoyed the give-and-take of the political scene.

It provided for electors to vote separately for President and Vice President.

The election of 1800 marked the end of Federalist rule. From 1789 to 1800, the Federalists had made impressive achievements. They had organized the new government. They had maintained peace in the face of serious threats from Britain and France. They had built a strong financial foundation for the new nation. It remained to be seen whether their opponents, the Democratic-Republicans and Thomas Jefferson could provide similar leadership.

CHECKUP

1. What were the first two American political groups called? How did they differ on foreign affairs?
2. What steps did Washington and Adams take to keep the nation out of war?
3. Why did the Alien and Sedition Acts arouse so much controversy? What were the reactions in Kentucky and Virginia?

Key Facts From Chapter 10

1. George Washington was the unanimous choice of the electors as the first President of the United States.
2. The first ten amendments to the Constitution are known as the Bill of Rights.
3. The Bill of Rights, ratified in 1791, guarantees to the people—against the power of government—certain basic liberties, including freedom of speech, religion, and the press and the right of assembly.
4. The differing ideas of Secretary of State Thomas Jefferson and Secretary of the Treasury Alexander Hamilton led to the formation of two political groups: the Federalists, who shared Hamilton's views, and the Democratic-Republicans, who shared Jefferson's views.
5. The Democratic-Republicans developed into the first political party in the United States.

★ REVIEWING THE CHAPTER ★

People, Places, and Events

Bill of Rights *P. 200*
Judiciary Act of 1789 *P. 200*
Alexander Hamilton *P. 201*
Funding program *P. 202*
Assumption program *P. 203*
Bank of the United States *P. 203*
Democratic-Republicans *P. 206*
The French Revolution *P. 206*
Neutrality Proclamation *P. 207*
Edmond Genêt *P. 208*
Jay's Treaty *P. 208*
Alien and Sedition Acts *P. 212*

Review Questions

1. What two precedents were established by George Washington during his presidency? *Pp. 199–200* Les. 1
2. List the rights of the people that are protected by the Bill of Rights. *P. 200* Les. 1
3. What were the three main points in Alexander Hamilton's financial plan? *Pp. 202–203* Les. 2
4. Contrast Hamilton's and Jefferson's views on **(a)** the future of America; **(b)** the amount of power the central government should have; and **(c)** who should run the government. *Pp. 201–202, 205* Les. 2
5. How did Hamilton and Jefferson differ in their interpretation of the power granted to the Congress under the Constitution? *Pp. 204–205* Les. 2
6. What was the XYZ Affair and how was it settled? *Pp. 210, 212* Les. 2
7. What was the significance of the Kentucky and Virginia Resolutions? *P. 213* Les. 3
8. Why was the Twelfth Amendment added to the Constitution? *P. 213* Les. 3

Chapter Test

*Write **H** if the phrase refers to Alexander Hamilton and **J** if the phrase refers to Thomas Jefferson. Use a separate piece of paper for your answers.*

1. Secretary of the Treasury H
2. Favored a small central government with most power left to the states J
3. Supported the idea of a national bank H
4. Wanted the United States to become a nation of cities and factories H
5. People with his political views were called the Democratic-Republicans. J
6. Believed in a strict interpretation of the Constitution J
7. Proposed the funding program to pay the nation's war debts H
8. People with his political views were called the Federalists. H
9. Belived that "those who own the country should govern it" H
10. Secretary of State J
11. Opposed the creation of a national bank J
12. Favored a strong central government H
13. Believed the average citizen was capable of holding government office J
14. Wanted the United States to remain a nation of farmers J
15. Supported the French Revolution J
16. Proposed the assumption program to pay the state debts left over from the Revolutionary War H
17. Opposed the French Revolution H
18. Believed in a loose interpretation of the Constitution H
19. Became the third President of the United States J
20. Wrote the Declaration of Independence J

6. When President John Adams sent three commissioners to Paris to try to restore good relations with France, the French foreign minister, Talleyrand, refused to talk with the Americans. Instead, Talleyrand appointed three agents, known as X, Y, and Z, to meet with Adams' commissioners. X, Y, and Z demanded a large bribe as part of any deal, so the Americans refused to pay and broke off talks with the French. When Adams reported the XYZ affair to Congress, it became angry and insulted over the bribery demand. A state of undeclared war existed between the two nations until the Convention of 1800 brought about an agreement to end the alliance of 1778. This agreement kept the United States out of war.

7. The significance of the Kentucky and Virginia Resolutions was the establishment of the idea of *states' rights*.

8. In the election of 1800, there was an electoral vote tie between Thomas Jefferson and Aaron Burr. It took thirty-five ballots before Jefferson received a majority of votes in the House of Representatives. To prevent such an occurrence in the future, the Twelfth Amendment was passed. It provided for electors to vote separately for President and Vice-President.

THE PERIOD OF REPUBLICAN RULE

Background Information

1. THE TRANSFER OF LOUISIANA This picture of the ceremonies attending the transfer of Louisiana from France to the United States was painted by Thure de Thulstrup. Born in Sweden in 1848, de Thulstrup studied art in Paris and eventually settled in Boston, Massachusetts.

The official transfer of Louisiana took place in New Orleans on December 20, 1803, in a large room on the second floor of the Cabildo, the building in the background of the painting. One report states that during the ceremony that took place in the Place d'Armes depicted here, only a handful of Americans were present to cheer the exchange of flags.

The Cabildo was built in 1795 and served as the seat of Spanish rule until the French took over briefly in 1803. At that time the building was one of the best examples of Spanish/Moorish architecture. The Spanish influence could be seen in the wide arches on both levels and the original flat tile roof. In 1847 a mansard roof was added, which altered the appearance.

Today the Cabildo houses the Louisiana State Museum. The museum's art collection includes de Thulstrup's painting.

LESSON 1

WHEN THOMAS JEFFERSON took office in 1801, he opened a long era of Republican control of the government. (The party name *Democratic-Republican* had by this time generally been shortened to simply *Republican*.) The Federalists would never again win the Presidency. Their belief in rule by an upper class made up mostly of merchants and large landowners was out of tune with the growing democratic spirit in the country. By 1816 the Federalists would fade from the scene completely.

The Republicans, who appealed more to small farmers, skilled workers, and plantation owners, were in command for the next twenty-four years. After eight years in office, Jefferson was succeeded by his friend James Madison. Madison also served two terms and was followed by James Monroe for another two. Because all three came from Virginia, their presidencies came to be called the Virginia Dynasty.

Jefferson's Program

Jefferson called his election "the Revolution of 1800." That was an exaggeration, of course. But it did point up a number of changes that Jefferson and the Republicans brought about. Hamilton had called the national debt "a national blessing." He meant that it would bind the wealthy, to whom it was owed, to the success of the government. Jefferson and Secretary of the Treasury Albert Gallatin believed the debt to be a burden rather than a blessing. They made plans to pay it off in sixteen years. Since they also favored lowering taxes, one of the chief ways to reduce the debt was to cut government costs. Jefferson reduced the number of government workers, cut the size of the Army and the Navy, and did away with a number of judgeships. Despite the unexpected cost of buying the Louisiana territory, Jefferson still was able to reduce the debt by nearly a third in his eight years in the White House.

Soon after Jefferson became President, the Republicans in Congress repealed the hated whiskey tax (see opposite page). They allowed the Alien and Sedition Acts to expire in 1801. They changed the waiting period for immigrants to become citizens from fourteen years back to five. And they repealed the Judiciary Act of 1801, passed in the final days of the Adams administration. You will read more about the repeal of the act later in this chapter.

Despite these changes, Jefferson left most of Hamilton's program untouched. The funding program and the assumption of state debts still stood. The Bank of the United States, or the B.U.S. as it was generally called, was allowed to run to the end of its twenty-year charter in 1811. And in spite of what Jefferson had written in the Kentucky Resolution in 1798, he made no move, as President, to shift the balance of federalism from the central government to the states.

A call for simplicity. Jefferson was the first President to begin his term in the nation's new capital city, Washington, D.C. In 1800 the capital had been moved

LESSON 1 *(2 to 3 days)*

Performance Objectives

1. Given a list of Jefferson's presidential actions from 1800 to 1804, to categorize the actions as consistent with Democratic-Republican ideals or reminiscent of Federalist policies. **2.** To demonstrate an understanding of the constitutional problems involved in the Louisiana Purchase and the case of *Marbury* v. *Madison* by writing an explanatory essay.

Famous People

Albert Gallatin, Pinckney, Napoleon Bonaparte, Toussaint L'Ouverture, Aaron Burr, John Marshall

Vocabulary

Republicans, Virginia Dynasty, Barbary pirates, Louisiana Purchase, Northern Confederacy, "midnight judges," *writ of mandamus, Marbury* v. *Madison,* judicial review, impeach

Activities

1. FILMS You might wish to show one of the following films to introduce this lesson. *Louisiana Purchase: Key to a Continent* (16 minutes, b&w; Encyclopaedia Britannica Films) presents the events that led to the purchase of the Louisiana Territory. *John Marshall* (18 minutes, b&w; Encyclopaedia Britannica Films) presents a biography of Marshall, which includes Supreme Court decisions important in establishing the authority of the Supreme Court.

Background Information

2. WASHINGTON, D.C., IN 1800 A visitor to the Federal City of the United States in 1800 might have been surprised to find only a village, albeit one with grandiose plans. When the government moved there in November of 1800, the new city had a population of more than 2,500. It boasted more than 400 private homes, but there was a noticeable lack of boardinghouses and hotels.

L'Enfant's design for the city was based on a gridiron superimposed with radiating broad avenues. The main features of the plan were the Executive Mansion and the Capitol. But neither of these buildings were completed by the end of 1800. Both houses of Congress as well as the Supreme Court met in the only completed section of the Capitol, the north wing. L'Enfant's "agreeable and convenient" central avenue, Pennsylvania Avenue, connected the Executive Mansion and the Capitol. But in 1800 it was almost impassable with its tangle of elder bushes, swamp grasses, and tree stumps.

Abigail Adams, wife of President John Adams, also came to the city in November of 1800. She was dismayed to find the Executive Mansion had no heat, water, or bathrooms. In a letter to her daughter she mentioned that she used the large-audience room (today the East Room) to hang up the family wash. Despite the inconveniences, she noted that Washington was "a beautiful spot, capable of every improvement, and the more I view it the more I am delighted with it."

there from Philadelphia. An unfinished city with a handful of buildings scattered along the Potomac River, this setting was fitting for an administration that called for simple, democratic ways. Jefferson dropped the practice of elegant weekly presidential receptions. He put into effect at the White House, the rule of first come, first served—regardless of one's social standing. He thought nothing of receiving foreign and American officials in the faded, threadbare coat and carpet slippers he often wore.

Jefferson set the tone of his administration with these words from his inaugural address:

> We have called by different names brethren of the same principle. We are all Republicans, we are all Federalists. Let us, then, with courage and confidence pursue our own Federal and Republican principles, our attachment to union and representative government. . . .
>
> Still one thing more, fellow-citizens—[we need] a wise and [thrifty] Government which shall restrain men from injuring one another . . . [and] shall leave them otherwise free to regulate their own pursuits. . . .

The election of 1800 had been a bitter political battle, but it was plain that Jefferson now wanted unity and harmony.

The Barbary pirates. Jefferson was a man of peace and a champion of the farmer. Yet one of his first acts as President was to use armed force to defend America's commerce.

For many years pirates from the Barbary States—Morocco, Algeria, Tunis, and Tripoli—had seized ships in the Mediterranean Sea off the coast of North

In 1804, during the Barbary War, Lieutenant Stephen Decatur led a daring raid into the harbor at Tripoli. He burned the captured American ship *Philadelphia*, which the pirates were refitting for use.

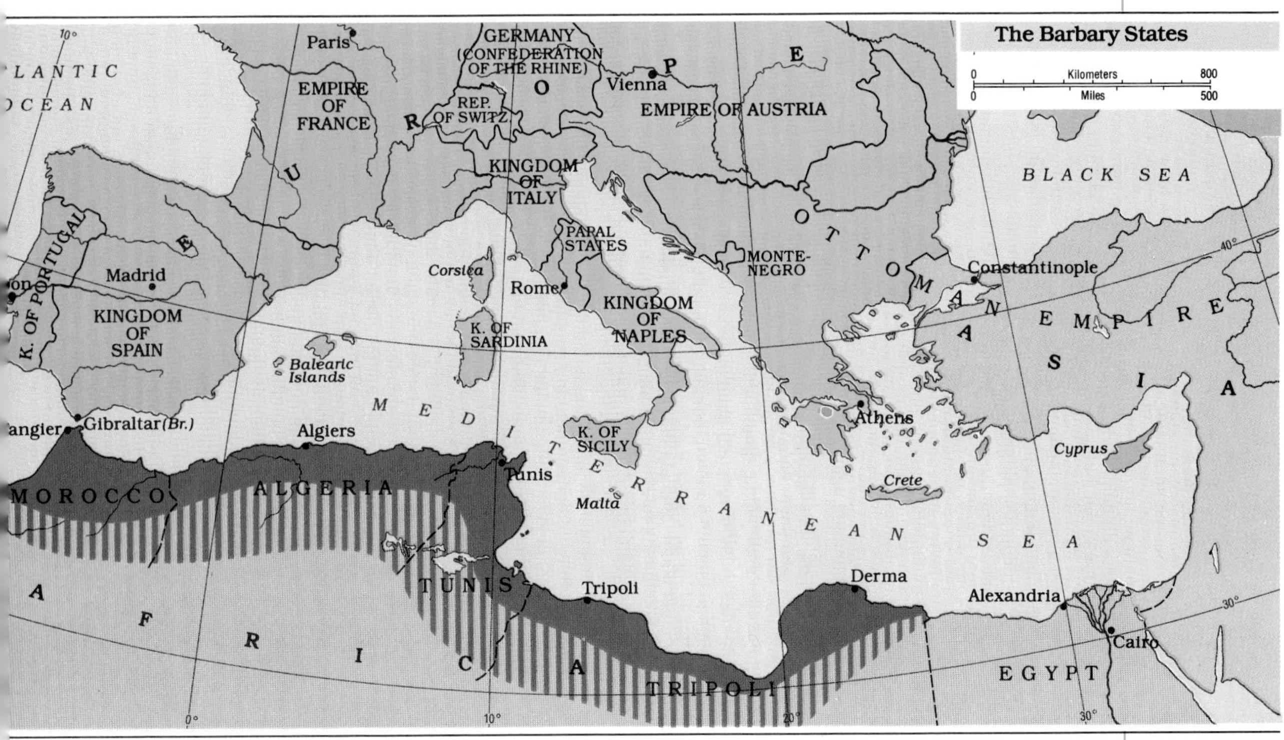

The pirates of Morocco, Algiers, Tunis, and Tripoli were a constant threat to American trading ships in the Mediterranean. After a temporary truce in 1804, pirate attacks continued off and on until 1815 when a United States fleet forced an end to pirate activity.

Africa. European nations found it easier to pay the pirates to leave the ships alone than to fight them. Under Washington and Adams, the United States had done the same.

Jefferson was opposed to paying such bribes. When Tripoli tried to raise the price for "protection" in 1801, the President put his foot down. Tripoli declared war, and Jefferson sent several naval ships to the Mediterranean Sea. The Barbary War lasted several years. The Navy failed to crush the pirates, as Jefferson had hoped. But America's show of force won new respect, and led to the end of some bribes. Tripoli made peace in 1805. Payments to the other Barbary States ended ten years later.

The Louisiana Purchase. The most important achievement of Jefferson's first administration was the purchase of the Louisiana territory. This was the vast region lying, for the most part, between the Mississippi River and the Rocky Mountains. The purchase was the result of a happy accident. Since 1763 Spain had controlled this area and also the

2. READING FOR INFORMATION After students have read this lesson, you might wish to have them study some of the topics in the lesson in more detail. Ask your students to read in Commager's *Documents of American History* some of the documents applicable to the time period of this lesson. Appropriate readings include 106, "Jefferson's First Inaugural Address"; 107, "Jefferson on the importance of New Orleans"; 108, "The Cession of Louisiana," and Chief Justice Marshall's opinion in 109, *"Marbury v. Madison."*

3. DISCUSSION After students have read the lesson, list on the chalkboard Jefferson's presidential actions from 1800 to 1804. Then ask students to discuss each action and categorize it as consistent with Democratic-Republican ideals or reminiscent of Federalist policies. Be sure students have a clear understanding of the political position of each party.

4. ESSAY Assign students to write explanatory essays identifying the constitutional problems involved in the Louisiana Purchase and the case of *Marbury* v. *Madison.* Ask students to imagine that the purpose of their essays is to explain the issues of each case to the average citizen of Jefferson's day. After they have finished the assignment, have volunteers read their essays. Ask the rest of the class to decide whether the average citizen would understand the constitutional problems after hearing the explanation. How might the essay be improved?

5. ORAL REPORTS The June 1975 issue of *American Heritage* has an article entitled "Cathcart's Travels" by Liva Baker; it could serve as the basis for an interesting oral report on life in the Barbary State of Algiers. James Cathcart, an American sailor, was captured by pirates of Algiers in 1785. The article traces Cathcart's career from slave to the position of consul general to the dey of Algiers. As consul general he acted as an intermediary between the dey and ambassadors from Christian countries. Freed after ten years, Cathcart was instrumental in negotiating the peace treaties for the United States with Tunis and Tripoli.

Mississippi River. The river was the western farmers' main route for getting crops to market. The crops were carried downriver on flatboats to New Orleans and were then shipped by ocean-going vessels to Atlantic ports and foreign countries.

In the Pinckney Treaty of 1795, Spain had given Americans the right to use the Mississippi. Spain also gave them the important "right of deposit" at New Orleans. This was the right to unload and store crops, without paying tariff duties, until they could be loaded onto larger ships for the ocean voyage. With about one third of its commerce going through New Orleans, the United States would have liked full control of the river and the port itself. But as long as Spain—a weak country—owned New Orleans and gave Americans permission to use the river, the United States was content with the situation.

Then, in 1802, Americans were shocked to learn that two years earlier Spain had secretly agreed to give Louisiana to France, and that the transfer would soon take place. Napoleon Bonaparte, the French dictator, wanted Louisiana to be a part of a new French empire on the North American continent. It would supply food for the sugar-rich French islands in the West Indies, especially the colony of Santo Domingo. The threat of a powerful and perhaps unfriendly nation—led by Napoleon—in control of New Orleans was cause for alarm.

Jefferson, greatly concerned, sent his friend James Monroe to Paris to join Robert Livingston, the American Minister to France. They were to try to buy New Orleans for $10 million. If they failed, Jefferson was willing to form an alliance with England to prevent the French from keeping New Orleans.

It was then that the United States had a stroke of good luck. It stemmed from a setback suffered by the French in the West Indies. On Santo Domingo, around the turn of the century, the slaves, led by Toussaint L'Ouverture, had rebelled. In 1801, Napoleon sent an army to put down the uprising; but disease and the rebelling slaves destroyed it. France lost control of the island.

Without Santo Domingo, Louisiana was of little value to Napoleon. Also, after a two-year truce, Napoleon was getting ready to make war again against England. He did not expect to be able to hold Louisiana against British attack. He therefore decided to get what he could for it. The startled American ministers, who were ready to offer $10 million for New Orleans, were told they could buy all of Louisiana for a little more money. Monroe and Livingston quickly agreed on a treaty. For $15 million, or less than three cents an acre, they doubled America's size. It was the biggest bargain in American history.

A constitutional problem. This windfall left President Jefferson with a problem. His vision of America was one of a nation of small farmers. By adding this territory, he believed that such a nation would be assured. However, Jefferson was also the champion of "strict interpretation" of the Constitution. In 1791 he had written to President Washington:

> I consider the foundation of the Constitution as laid on this ground—that all powers not delegated to the United States by

the Constitution, nor prohibited by it to the states, are reserved to the states, or to the people.

Yet nowhere did the Constitution say that the government had the right to acquire foreign territory.

For a while Jefferson considered a constitutional amendment that would allow the United States to buy Louisiana. He soon realized that by the time such an amendment could be ratified, Napoleon might have changed his mind. He therefore urged the Senate to approve the treaty and to worry about the constitutional problem later. The Senate did approve, and in December 1803 the United States took possession of the Louisiana Territory. It was not the last time in American history that the belief in limited government came into conflict with an opportunity or a national need. And it was not the last time that limited government came out the loser.

6. RESEARCH/DISCUSSION Presidents Lyndon Johnson and Gerald Ford had problems similar to Jefferson's problem with the Barbary pirates. Ask some of your students to research and describe to their classmates the *Pueblo* incident of 1968 and the *Mayaguez* incident of 1975. Have students compare these incidents with the Barbary pirate problem as to causes, actions, and results.

Among the first to explore the Louisiana territory were Meriwether Lewis and William Clark (see page 224) and Zebulon Pike. Pike explored the upper Mississippi region and, later, the Rocky Mountains. He sighted but did not climb the mountain now called Pike's Peak.

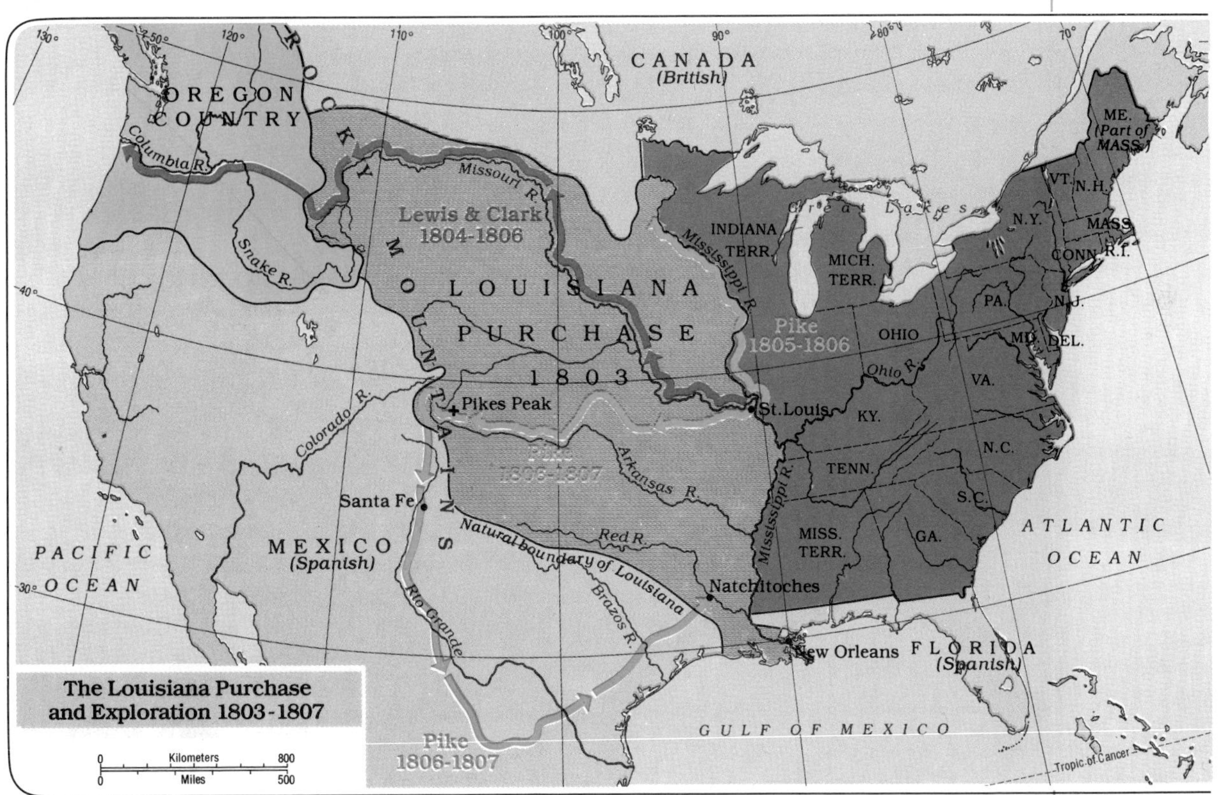

The Louisiana Purchase and Exploration 1803-1807

7. ORAL REPORTS One of the great heroes in American history was not an American but a black general from Saint Domingue, Toussaint L'Ouverture, a clever master of guerrilla warfare. By crushing the French forces invading his home island, he helped to save the Louisiana Territory from eventual French occupation, which made possible the American purchase of the territory. Have several of your students report on this amazing man.

8. LISTENING FOR INFORMATION You might wish to read to the class "History's Greatest Real Estate Bargain" (pages 107–111) by John Bakeless in editor E. S. Miers's *The American Story: The Age of Exploration to the Age of the Atom* (New York: Channel Press, 1956).

A minority view. Certain New England Federalists were dismayed by the purchase of Louisiana. The American West was filling up rapidly, and several new states—Kentucky, Tennessee, and Ohio—had already entered the Union. The Louisiana Purchase meant that still more western states would soon be created. The New England states, already in the minority, would then be so greatly outnumbered that they would have little influence in making national policy.

Led by Timothy Pickering of Massachusetts, these Federalists planned to lead the New England states out of the Union to form a "Northern Confederacy." When Hamilton and other leading Federalists rejected the idea, the planners turned to the ambitious Vice President, Aaron Burr. Burr wanted to run for governor of New York. The New England group approached Burr, hoping he would take his state into the proposed confederacy if he won. But Burr lost the election, with Hamilton leading the campaign against him. Nothing ever came of the confederacy scheme. But some months later, Burr had his revenge when he fatally wounded Hamilton in a duel.

In 1792 Kentucky became the first state in the lands west of the Appalachians. Soon afterwards the building shown below was built to serve as the state house at Frankfort, Kentucky's capital.

Unseating the "midnight judges." With a Republican majority in Congress and a Republican in the White House, the Federalists' last stronghold was in the federal courts. That was because federal judges hold office for life. Most of the judges were Federalists who had been appointed by Presidents Washington and Adams. And as Jefferson noted, "Few die, and none resign."

In the final weeks of the Adams administration, Congress had created still more judgeships, by the Judiciary Act of 1801, and Adams filled them with Federalists. Because he was still signing their commissions, or appointment papers, the night before he left office, they came to be called the "midnight judges."

Jefferson and the Republicans were furious. The new Congress repealed the Judiciary Act of 1801, leaving all of Adams's judges without salaries or jobs. The Federalists claimed this action was unconstitutional. They said that the judges had been appointed for life, and Congress could not change the situation by eliminating their positions.

When Jefferson learned that the commissions had not yet been delivered to several of Adams's appointees, he ordered Secretary of State James Madison to hold them back. One of those appointees, William Marbury, claimed that the commission was rightfully his. He asked the Supreme Court to order Madison to deliver it. The legal name for such an order is *writ of mandamus*, and the federal Judiciary Act of 1789 had given the Supreme Court the power to issue such a writ.

Marshall in *Marbury* v. *Madison*. In the case of *Marbury* v. *Madison* (1803), Chief Justice John Marshall ruled that Marbury ought to have his commission. He also said, however, that the Supreme Court could not order Madison to give it to him. The reason, said Marshall, was that the section of the Judiciary Act of 1789 giving that power to the Court was unconstitutional. Since the Constitution itself had not given this power to the Court, the Congress could not do so simply by passing a law.

Marshall's opinion was shrewd. In denying the Supreme Court a small power, Marshall had seized for it a much bigger one: the power to review acts of Congress and to declare them unconstitutional. From that time on, the Supreme Court has claimed this power. It is the power that raised the stature of the judiciary branch to the level of the other two branches of government—the executive and the legislative.

Striking at Federalist judges. Jefferson was angered by Marshall's claim of judicial power. More determined than ever to strike at Federalist judges, the President urged supporters in Congress to *impeach* a number of judges. Impeachment is the first step in removal from

John Marshall served as Chief Justice of the United States for 34 years. During that time, several decisions by the Supreme Court upheld the powers of the federal government.

office. The first target was John Pickering, a federal judge in New Hampshire. Pickering was both alcoholic and insane, but neither condition was constitutional ground for impeachment. Nonetheless, the House of Representatives impeached Pickering, the Senate convicted him, and he was removed from office.

The Jeffersonians' next target was Samuel Chase, a justice on the Supreme Court. Chase had offended the Republicans by his unfair treatment of several of them when they were tried under the Sedition Act. He had also attacked the Jefferson administration from the

Continued on page 225

9. THOUGHT PROVOKER
Jefferson's arrangement for the purchase of Louisiana was unconstitutional. In justification of his actions he wrote: "This treaty must of course be laid before both Houses. . . . They, I presume, will see their duty to their country in ratifying and paying for it . . . the Executive, in seizing the fugitive occurrence which so much advances the good of the country, have done an act beyond the Constitution. . . . It is the case of the guardian investing the money of his ward in purchasing an important adjacent territory, and saying to him when of age, I did this for your good!"

Some feel that Jefferson got away with this action for a good American reason—it worked. Discuss with your students the constitutional, political, and ethical problems involved in a do-it-now, ask-questions-later presidential outlook.

10. **ROLE-PLAYING** Sacagawea, when only a teenager, helped guide the Lewis and Clark expedition in 1805 and thus helped to open the West. She supposedly lived into her nineties. Facts about her death are unclear, but some believe she died in 1884 on the Wind River Reservation in Wyoming. Ask one of your better students to study Sacagawea's life and then to portray her in a *Today* show type of interview. The interviewers might represent different magazines. For example, a reporter from a women's magazine might question Sacagawea about her leadership role during the expedition; a travel magazine reporter might ask questions about the natural beauty of the area explored; and a financial reporter might inquire about the investment possibilities in the land west of the Mississippi.

The Lewis and Clark Expedition

President Thomas Jefferson began planning for exploration of the Louisiana territory even before the United States bought it. He was interested in promoting trade with the Indians in the lands west of the Mississippi. With the purchase of the territory from France in May 1803, the plans for exploration were quickly completed.

To lead the expedition, Jefferson selected Meriwether Lewis, his private secretary. Lewis chose William Clark, the younger brother of George Rogers Clark, to share the leadership with him. Both Lewis and Clark were Virginians and army officers and were used to dealing with the Indians.

The forty-five members of the expedition set out by riverboats from St. Louis in May 1804. After making their way slowly up the Missouri River, they stopped for the winter in the Mandan Indian country in what is now North Dakota. The next spring, they followed the Missouri River to its source. Then they traveled by foot, with pack horses, through the Rocky Mountains. They were helped through this wild, uncharted country by a remarkable Indian woman named Sacagawea. She and her husband, a French-Canadian trapper, served as guides and interpreters with the expedition. A member of the Shoshoni tribe. Sacagawea smoothed the way between her people and the explorers. During the trip the expedition met many different tribes of Indians, all of whom were friendly.

Lewis and Clark followed the Snake and Columbia Rivers until, in November 1805, they sighted the Pacific Ocean. Lewis wrote in his journal: "An Indian called me . . . and gave me . . . a piece of fresh salmon roasted . . . this was the first salmon I had seen and perfectly convinced me that we were on the waters of the Pacific Ocean."

The following spring the party started back. It reached St. Louis in September 1806. In the round trip the expedition had traveled 8,000 miles (12,800 km). It brought back much information regarding the geography, Indians, plant and animal life, and natural resources of the region. The trip also led to the growth of the fur trade. In later years the exploration became a basis for the United States' claim to the Oregon country.

The Lewis and Clark expedition meet a Chinook Indian party in 1805. Sacagawea, standing by Lewis, addresses the Indians in sign language.

bench, and had complained that allowing everyone to vote would cause the republic to "sink into a mobocracy." The House of Representatives impeached Chase, but the Senate did not convict him. With the failure to remove Chase, the Republicans gave up on their efforts to remove Federalist judges.

Despite the failure to root the Federalists out of the judiciary, Jefferson could look back on his first term with satisfaction. Most Americans felt the same way. In 1804 they reelected him by a wide margin over his Federalist opponent. Jefferson carried every state but Connecticut and Delaware.

CHECKUP

1. What changes in government did Jefferson bring about?
2. What did the United States achieve in the Barbary War?
3. What constitutional problem was involved in (a) the Louisiana Purchase? (b) the case of *Marbury* v. *Madison*?

LESSON 2

Neutrality, Embargo, and War

"Peace is our passion," Jefferson once wrote. But the world was not at peace when he began his second term. France and Britain had renewed their struggle in 1803, after a two-year truce. Within a few years, Napoleon's army was the master of Europe. Britain, with its great navy, was supreme on the seas. The war then settled into a long struggle, much like a fight between a tiger and a shark, each the master in its own element.

At first the European war brought great prosperity to the United States. As the major neutral nation, it doubled its sale of goods to France and England between 1803 and 1805. Shipbuilding boomed, and America's merchant fleet grew enormously.

Soon, however, the situation changed. Since the two foes could not strike directly at each other, they tried to weaken each other by upsetting their enemy's trade. Each seized neutral ships trading with their foe. The United States was caught in the middle. Between 1803 and 1807, Britain seized 1,000 American ships, and France seized 500 more.

The impressment of seamen. Even worse than the taking of ships was the British practice of *impressment*—the seizure of sailors for service on British ships. Horrible conditions in the Royal Navy had led thousands of sailors to desert to America. Many of them went to sea again on American ships, carrying fake naturalization papers. To get their sailors back, British captains stopped American ships and took off those seamen they believed were British. Often they were not too careful about whom they took. They simply wanted manpower for their own ships. As one British naval officer explained, "It is my duty to keep my ship manned, and I will do so wherever I find men that speak the same language with me." In the ten years after the British renewed war with France in 1803, they took between 5,000 and 10,000 sailors off American ships. Probably three fourths were American citizens.

In June 1807 an incident with the British enraged Americans. The British frigate *Leopard* stopped the American naval ship *Chesapeake* within sight of the Virginia coast and demanded to search its crew for deserters. When the American captain refused, the *Leopard*

LESSON 2 *(3 days)*

Performance Objectives

1. Given the events and legislative acts that led to the War of 1812, to create a time line from 1803 to 1812. **2.** Given an outline map of the United States, to plot the major military engagements of the War of 1812. **3.** To demonstrate an understanding of the causes of the War of 1812 by offering oral or written evidence to support the following statement: The War of 1812 was a "needless war."

Famous People

James Madison, Tecumseh, William Henry Harrison, Henry Clay, Oliver Perry, Thomas Macdonough, Andrew Jackson

Vocabulary

Neutrality, embargo, impressment, naturalization papers, *Leopard-Chesapeake Affair,* Embargo Act, Force Act of 1809, Non-Intercourse Act, Macon's Bill No. 2, Tippecanoe, "War Hawks," "Old Ironsides," battle of Lake Erie, battle of New Orleans, Treaty of Ghent, Hartford Convention, secede

A British boarding party seizes a sailor on an American ship. Such boarding parties claimed the men they took were deserters from the Royal Navy, but the seized men were often Americans.

fired, killing three seamen and wounding eighteen. The British then boarded the crippled ship and removed four sailors, only one of whom was British.

The Embargo Act. To Americans, this insult to their flag was the last straw. Many demanded war. Jefferson knew that would be unwise. With almost no Navy to fight back, he decided on economic pressure. On his urging, Congress—in 1807—approved the Embargo Act. This law forbade all exports, whether in American or foreign ships. Also, no American ship was permitted to leave for a foreign port, even without cargo.

Jefferson reasoned that if there were no American ships on the high seas, Britain and France could not seize them and the British could not impress American sailors. More important, by denying American goods to the warring countries, Jefferson hoped to force them to change their policies. Boycotts had worked against Britain in the years before the Revolution. Jefferson hoped that such economic pressure would work again.

However, the Embargo Act hurt the United States far more than it hurt France or Britain. Ships lay idle, goods rotted on docks, and crops remained unsold. Exports fell to one fifth of what they had been. Sailors and others whose jobs depended on trade were thrown out of work. Merchants lost trade that, even with the seizure of some of their ships, had been profitable. Western farmers also felt the embargo's effect as the loss of European markets caused prices of their crops to drop.

Resistance to the embargo. No measure in America since the days of British rule was resisted as much as the Embargo Act. Federalists declared that the Constitution gave Congress the power to regulate trade, not to stop it. In their eyes, the embargo was unconstitutional. When ship owners and captains tried to get around the law, Jefferson used harsh measures to enforce it. He sent the militia to prevent the smuggling of goods across the Canadian border. The government hired officials to police the ports. Under the Force Act of 1809, federal officers could seize, without a court order, any goods they suspected were going to be shipped in violation of the embargo. Jefferson, the champion of limited government, was now using strong powers to back up his embargo policy.

Jefferson finally gave up. In the last days of his administration, Congress repealed the Embargo Act. It was replaced by the Non-Intercourse Act. This law prohibited trade with Britain and France, but it allowed trade with all other countries. Trade with either or both of the warring nations could begin again only after the violation of American rights ended.

Madison and American rights. The embargo helped revive the Federalist opposition to the Republicans in the election of 1808, but the Republicans still won handily. James Madison, the new President, was no more successful in ending the violation of our rights than Jefferson had been. When it was clear after a year that the Non-Intercourse Act was not working, Madison and the Congress tried another measure. This was Macon's Bill No. 2, passed in 1810. Under it, the United States allowed trade again with both Britain and France, even though they were still violating our rights. The law added, however, that if either country agreed to end the violations, the United States would stop trading with the other.

In 1802, only one wing of the Capitol had been completed. Both the Senate and the House of Representatives met in this modest building, and the Supreme Court convened in the basement.

Activities

1. LISTENING FOR INFORMATION To introduce this lesson, you might wish to read to your students "Mr. Madison's War" by George Dangerfield (pages 116–121) in editor E. S. Miers's *The American Story: The Age of Exploration to the Age of the Atom* (New York: Channel Press, 1956).

2. CREATING A TIME LINE After students have read the lesson, ask them to draw a time line showing the events and legislative acts that led to the War of 1812. The understanding that students gain from this activity will be helpful to them in Activity 5.

3. USING A MAP After your students have read this lesson, assign this map activity. Have your students use the map on page 231 as a guide to locate and label the major engagements of the War of 1812 on an outline map of the United States. Ask them to summarize the American strategy and to offer alternative strategic plans that they think might have been more successful.

For a while it seemed that this law might work. A few months after its passage, Napoleon announced that France would honor America's neutral rights. But Napoleon meant only to trick Madison. France went right on seizing American ships. Meanwhile, taking the French at their word, Madison told the British that under the terms of Macon's Bill No. 2, the United States would end its trade with Britain in early 1811. The British pointed out that the French actually had not stopped seizing American ships. This was true, but America paid no attention. Tensions between the two countries grew worse as the British continued to seize our ships and impress seamen. In the United States, the clamor for war became louder.

Western grievances. Although Britain's actions hit the ports in the East most directly, the demand for war was stronger in the West. Westerners had several grievances. They blamed British interference with American trade for falling farm prices. And they believed that the British were encouraging Indians in the Northwest to attack American settlers there.

Actually it was the settlers' greed for Indian land in the West that caused the Indians to resist. Between 1800 and 1810, through force or through trickery, Indians had been driven off 100 million acres (40 million ha) in the Ohio Valley alone. In an attempt to halt the white settlers' advance into their lands, a Shawnee chief named Tecumseh or-

Mounted troops under General William Henry Harrison attack Britain's Indian allies at the Battle of the Thames in Canada. One of the casualties was the Shawnee chief, Tecumseh.

ganized Indian tribes from the Canadian border to the Gulf Coast. This Indian confederacy was effective for a time. But resistance crumbled after army troops under General William Henry Harrison fought Indians to a standstill at the battle of Tippecanoe in the Indiana Territory in 1811. That battle was only the beginning of a long, bloody period of frontier warfare.

Land hunger. Another reason why westerners wanted war against Britain was their hunger for even more land. Although over a million square miles (400,000 square ha) in the West had no permanent settlements, Americans along the frontier were casting hungry eyes on Canada. The belief that the British were stirring up the Indians from their base in Canada only added to the desire to take over the land. Settlers in the Southeast also saw war as a possible opportunity to seize Florida from Spain, Britain's weak ally. The United States had already seized a part of the Spanish territory in 1810.

A final factor in the West's demand for war was the desire to defend national honor. The issues of ship seizures and impressment did not affect the West as directly as they affected the East. However, westerners felt that America's honor should be defended against such British insults. In Congress these western views were expressed by a group called the War Hawks. They were led by the young Speaker of the House of Representatives, Henry Clay of Kentucky.

War is declared. Madison, like Jefferson, had hoped to avoid war. The growing demand for war was, however, too much for him to resist. On June 1, 1812, the President asked Congress to declare war on Great Britain. Seventeen days later, Congress did so. Most of the votes for war came from the South and the West. The majority of Congress members from the Northeast voted against war. Although that region had been hurt most by impressment and the seizure of American ships, its people feared that war would ruin their commerce completely.

The War of 1812 has been called a "needless war." Two days before Congress declared war, Britain had changed its policy of seizing American ships. But it took six weeks for that news to reach America. By that time, the two countries were already fighting.

Almost a disaster. The War of 1812 was almost a disaster for the young nation. Despite the demand for war, the country was ill-prepared. The army was tiny, and there were few volunteers. Leadership was poor. On the seas, Britain's navy greatly outnumbered America's. The country itself was badly divided, with New England bitterly opposing the war and withholding both money and men.

The American plans for war called for a three-way invasion of Canada. One force was to march from Detroit, a second along the Niagara River, and a third from the foot of Lake Champlain. All three invasions failed, and Americans soon were trying to keep the Canadians off American soil. Later, however, the United States won some victories in the West. American forces also defeated the Indians at the battle of the Thames in Canada in 1813 and at Horseshoe Bend in the Mississippi Territory in 1814.

4. READING FOR INFORMATION Assign students to read, in Commager's *Documents of American History*, some of the documents applicable to the time period of this lesson. Appropriate readings include 112, "Embargo Act," "Non-Intercourse Act," "Macon's Bill, No. 2"; 114, "Madison's War Message"; and 115, "Report and Resolutions of the Hartford Convention."

5. CREATIVE WRITING The War of 1812 might not have occurred if there had been a "hot line" between the leaders of the United States and Great Britain. Ask your students to create dialogue between President Madison and British Prime Minister Spencer Perceval that would have averted war. Encourage them to include the British acts that Madison later mentioned in his war message of June 1, 1812 (impressment of sailors, violations of American territorial waters, and the Orders in Council against neutral trade).

6. FILMS *War of 1812* (14 minutes, color and b&w; Coronet Films) presents the causes, major strategies, and effects of the war. *The War of 1812* (20 minutes, color; American Film Services) is part of the U.S. Navy series. The film concentrates on the events of the war through animated drawings and maps.

7. WHAT IF? What if the amendments to the Constitution proposed by the Hartford Convention had been ratified by the necessary number of states? How would the amendments have benefited the New England Federalists?

Matters went badly on the sea. At first, American privateers were active, capturing 1,300 British trading ships. But the privateers were soon swept from the seas by Britain's fleet. The same happened to the small American Navy. The American frigate *Constitution,* called "Old Ironsides," won some stirring sea battles. But soon it and other naval ships were blockaded in American ports by Britain's powerful navy.

America's military fortunes reached a low point in 1814. A British force entered Chesapeake Bay, marched to Washington, and burned most of the government buildings, including the White House. James and Dolley Madison had to flee for their lives, with Mrs. Madison carrying her parrot, a picture of Washington, and some official papers.

A few bright spots. Only on the Great Lakes did American forces prosper. Control of the lakes was important because they lay along the invasion routes between the United States and Canada. In the battle of Lake Erie in 1813, Captain Oliver Perry secured command of the lakes. The next year, Captain Thomas Macdonough, with his victory at the battle of Plattsburg on Lake Champlain, prevented an invasion from Canada.

Perry's and Macdonough's victories were important in bringing the war to an end. In 1814 the British defeated Napoleon and were free to use their huge army and navy against the United States. But when the Duke of Wellington, the leading British general, advised that little could be achieved without control of the Great Lakes and the invasion routes from Canada, a war-weary Britain decided on peace.

Despite earlier military disasters, America ended the war on a note of triumph. In January 1815, General Andrew Jackson's troops won a brilliant victory at New Orleans. But the battle

When the British bombarded Fort McHenry in Baltimore Harbor in 1814, Francis Scott Key, an American who watched the attack, feared the fort would fall. When he saw the American flag waving the next morning, he excitedly composed the words of "The Star Spangled Banner."

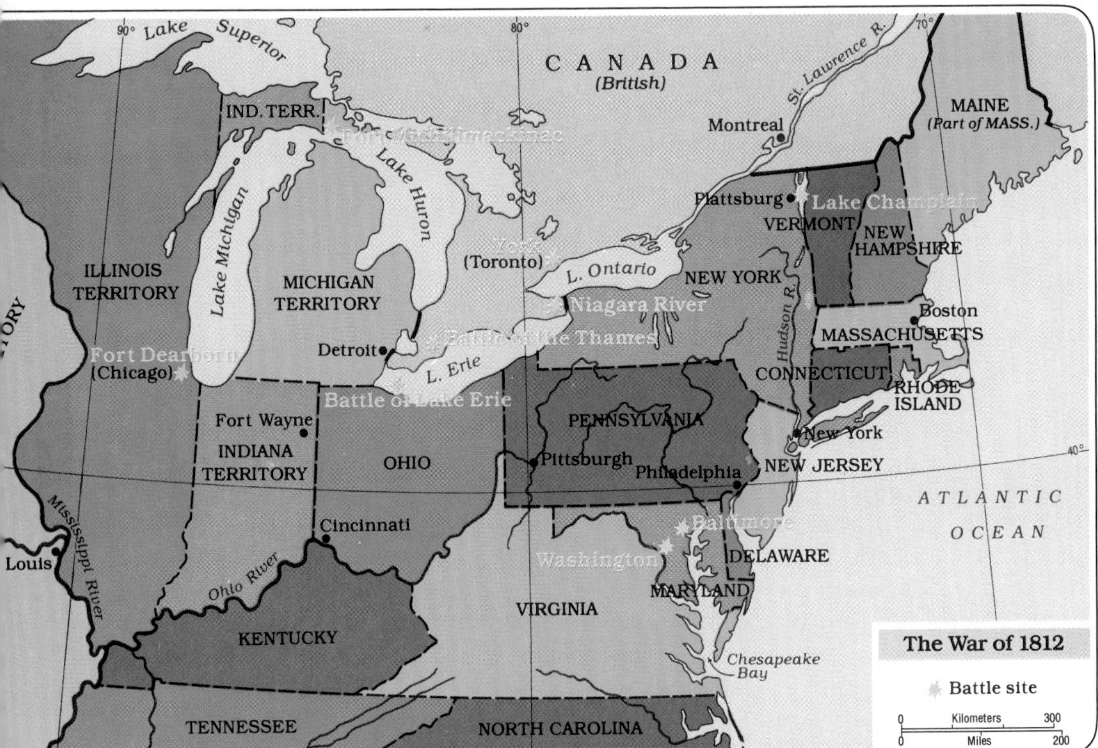

Though freedom of the seas was the big issue in the War of 1812, the major battles took place near the boundary between the United States and Canada. However, the only major land victory of the American forces occurred at New Orleans, far to the south of the area shown on the map.

was fought two weeks after the peace had been signed in Europe. The slow sailing ships that carried messages across the Atlantic played as important a role at the close of the war as they had played in the beginning.

The Treaty of Ghent. The peace treaty failed to settle a single question over which America and Britain had fought. By the Treaty of Ghent (1814), boundaries were to remain where they had been before the war, and all conquered territories were returned. There was no mention at all of America's neutral trade, impressment, or blockades. But America emerged from the war with a greater sense of independence. First, Americans had won the last battle of the war. The victory at New Orleans helped them forget earlier defeats. Second, Britain showed a greater respect to the United States during the treaty negotiations and afterward. For this reason, the conflict has sometimes been called "America's second war of independence."

Background Information

1. PEACE NEGOTIATIONS
In 1812, Czar Alexander I of Russia proposed to mediate the quarrel between the United States and Great Britain. He wanted Britain free to concentrate on the defeat of Napoleon and the United States free to end restrictions on trade, as Russia needed American raw materials. In response to the Czar's suggestion, President Madison sent Albert Gallatin and James Bayard to St. Petersburg (now Leningrad) to join the U.S. minister to Russia, John Quincy Adams, in the negotiations. Great Britain refused to participate.

However, to prevent the conflict in America from affecting the overall European settlement, the British Foreign Office proposed direct negotiations with the United States in 1813. The Flemish city of Ghent, about 30 miles northwest of Brussels, was chosen as the meeting place. President Madison named Henry Clay and Jonathan Russell as well as Adams, Gallatin, and Bayard as peace commissioners. The Americans met in Ghent in July of 1814, but the British kept them waiting until August.

In October of 1814 the news of the British burning of Washington reached Ghent. The British then demanded that peace be made on the basis of *uti possidetis,* or the idea that each country should retain existing holdings.

The news of American Captain Macdonough's decisive victory on Lake Champlain which frustrated the planned British invasion of New York reached Ghent in late October. The Americans then rejected the possibility of *uti possidetis* and insisted that all territory be restored to prewar ownership.

Other stumbling blocks were also encountered, but on December 24, 1814, the Treaty of Ghent was signed. The most significant achievement of the treaty was the restoration of peace between the two countries.

2. EMBARGO LEAKS Many attempts were made to break through Jefferson's embargo. Goods were smuggled over the Canadian border, over the Great Lakes and through Spanish Florida.

One man devised a way through the embargo that had Jefferson's unwitting approval. Jefferson ordered the necessary papers for "The Honorable Punqua Wingchong, a Chinese mandarin," to sail a 472-ton ship with $45,000 worth of merchandise and specie from New York to China to attend to some family matters. Wingchong was even permitted to return to New York with a full cargo from China. Jefferson thought this action might strengthen U.S. relations with China.

In reality, the ship was called the *Beaver* and was owned by John Jacob Astor, the noted fur trader and real estate investor. When the mandarin, who was one of Astor's clerks, returned to New York, Astor made a huge profit on the Chinese merchandise, as the embargo was still in effect.

The Hartford Convention. Earlier you read of the Northeast's opposition to the war. The people in New England called it "Mr. Madison's War." In December 1814, New England Federalists met in Hartford, Connecticut, to protest the war and to propose a convention to revise the Constitution. Some of the organizers wanted New England to *secede* from—that is, to pull out of—the Union. They were in the minority, however.

The Hartford Convention proposed a number of amendments to make it more difficult for the national government to exercise certain powers. The delegates proposed requiring in each house of Congress a two-thirds majority to declare war, to admit new states, or to limit trade under such laws as the Embargo Act and the Non-Intercourse Act. They called also for limiting the President to one term, and for prohibiting successive Presidents from the same state. The latter was a slap at the Virginia Dynasty. Taken together, these proposals aimed to change the federal balance by shifting power from the national government to the states.

The delegates also adopted a statement declaring that when an act of the federal government violated the Constitution, each state was to have the right to ignore or disobey the act. The state was to be the judge of when that violation occurred. This resolution by the Federalists was little different from the Virginia and Kentucky Resolutions supported by the Jeffersonian Republicans sixteen years before.

Nothing came of the Hartford Convention except ill for the Federalists. Since they had met in secret session while the war was going on, their actions raised many suspicions. Republicans claimed the convention was really a plot to break away from the Union. Actually, the Federalists had done nothing disloyal—no more than Republicans had done during the Adams years. But the Federalists were never able to recover from the charge. When news arrived that peace had been agreed upon, they were still protesting the war and predicting a British victory. Thus they were further discredited.

The idea of limited government. The position of the Federalists in Hartford on the powers the national government should have was far different from what it had been two decades earlier. At that time, the Federalists controlled both the Presidency and the Congress. They then favored a "loose interpretation" of the Constitution and more power for the central government. At the same time, the Republicans, led by Jefferson and Madison, opposed that view.

After the Jeffersonians won the Presidency and the Congress, those positions appear to have been reversed. Then it was the Jeffersonians who stretched the Constitution to purchase the Louisiana Territory and to pass and enforce the Embargo Act. And it was the Federalists who argued for a stricter interpretation of the Constitution. The Hartford Convention climaxed their opposition.

All of this raises an important question: Just how deeply did Americans of that time believe in limited government? At first glance, it may appear that what a group believed depended on whether or not it was in power. Certainly that was true in part. It is also true, however, that a major aim of the "outs"—those who

Continued on page 234

Webster's American Language

The burst of nationalism that America experienced after the War of 1812 expressed itself in many different forms. One way was through changes in language suggested by Noah Webster, a native of Connecticut. Soon after the Revolutionary War, Webster, a graduate of Yale College, had written, "America must be as independent in *literature* as she is in *politics* . . ." He wanted to form a national "American" language that would be distinct from English. He was convinced the first step toward achieving America's literary independence would be to establish a uniform language throughout the United States. To do so, he published an American dictionary. It simplified the British spelling of many words,—for example, *honour* became *honor.* The first version of his dictionary was published in 1806, but the full work, *An American Dictionary of the English Language,* was not finished until 1825. It was published three years later.

In addition, Webster was concerned about the spoken language. If the dialects spoken in various parts of the country were allowed to become more and more different from one another, sectionalism would win out over nationalism. Realizing the binding power of a common language, Webster in his dictionary suggested a single way for pronouncing words.

Webster first became interested in words and language during the Revolutionary War when he taught school to earn money to pay for his law studies. While teaching in Goshen, New York, he noticed that most of the textbooks he used were written by English authors. An ardent patriot, he decided to remedy the situation. In 1783 he published a spelling book that standardized the spelling of many words. At the time of his death in 1843, *The American Spelling Book* had sold 15 million copies. Today the famous "blue-backed speller" is the only American book to have sold 100 million copies.

Noah Webster's dictionary carried the definitions of 70,000 words. Revised many times, it is still published and still bears Webster's name.

LESSON 3 *(1 to 2 days)*

Performance Objective

To cite orally or in writing three Congressional actions in support of the idea that the period of Monroe's Presidency was an "Era of Good Feelings."

Famous People

James Monroe, Rufus King, Andrew Jackson, John Quincy Adams

Vocabulary

"Era of Good Feelings," Second Bank of the United States, protective tariff, "dumping" of goods, internal improvements, the National Road, acquisition of Florida

are out of office—is to become "ins." The fact that the "outs" believed they could win support by raising the cry of a too-strong government is an indication of the appeal that the idea of limited government had for most Americans.

CHECKUP

1. Why did Jefferson urge Congress to pass the Embargo Act?
2. Why did the Embargo Act encounter so much resistance?
3. What was accomplished by the War of 1812?

LESSON 3

The Era of Good Feelings

The years immediately following the war saw a great burst of national pride and feeling. Americans felt they had won the war, and the way seemed open to a secure and prosperous future. Americans busied themselves with building their nation and advancing their fortunes. The absence of party fights led people then, and some historians since, to label the times "the Era of Good Feelings."

The decline of the Federalists left the Republicans in complete control of the national government. James Monroe was elected President in 1816 by 183 electoral votes to just 34 for the Federalist Rufus King. Four years later there was not even an organized opposition to Monroe's reelection, and only one elector voted against him. Jefferson's comment of 1801 that "we are all Republicans, we are all Federalists," had been only a figure of speech. By 1817 it was very nearly a political fact.

Approving a national bank. The good feelings of the times were reflected in Congress. The two parties agreed on issues that had divided them for twenty-five years. One such issue was a national bank. In 1791, Jeffersonians had fought bitterly against creating the Bank of the United States. When the bank's twenty-year charter came up for renewal in 1811, however, many leading Republicans had changed their minds. A bill to renew the charter barely failed.

The difficulties of the government in financing the war led many to see how useful it might be to have a national bank that could lend money to the government in times of crisis. In 1816, the Republican Congress—with hardly a murmer—gave a twenty-year charter to the Second Bank of the United States.

Protecting American manufacturers. The Republican view on tariffs had also changed. In 1791, Hamilton had argued for a high tariff on imported goods in order to encourage the growth of manufacturing in the United States. The tariff would raise the price of foreign (mostly English) manufactured goods. This, reasoned Hamilton, would protect America's "infant industries" against foreign competition until they could grow stronger and more efficient.

Jeffersonians, who did not want an industrial America, blocked Hamilton's plan. Ironically, the Jeffersonian policies later gave American manufacturers more protection than could have been given by any Hamiltonian tariff. Embargo, nonintercourse, and finally war almost shut out English goods from 1808 to 1815. With such protection, American manufacturing grew.

With the war over, there was fear that British manufacturers might "dump" their goods in America—that is, sell

★3★
Thomas Jefferson
1743–1826

Born in VIRGINIA
In Office 1801–1809
Party DEM.-REPUBLICAN

Agreed to Louisiana Purchase, thereby doubling size of United States. Sent Lewis and Clark to explore the Northwest. To keep out of European war, supported embargo on foreign trade.

★ ★ ★ ★ ★ ★ ★ ★

★4★
James Madison
1751–1836

Born in VIRGINIA
In Office 1809–1817
Party DEM.-REPUBLICAN

Supported tariff to protect industry and urged national system of roads and canals. During War of 1812, had to flee from Washington when British burned the White House.

★ ★ ★ ★ ★ ★ ★ ★

★5★
James Monroe
1758–1831

Born in VIRGINIA
In Office 1817–1825
Party DEM.-REPUBLICAN

Obtained Florida from Spain. Warned European powers against colonizing in the Americas. Monroe's two terms were called by some the "Era of Good Feelings."

★ ★ ★ ★ ★ ★ ★ ★

below cost in order to drive American manufacturers out of business and recapture the American market for themselves. Republicans in Congress therefore voted a 20 percent duty on a number of imported goods. This was the first protective tariff in American history. Hamilton would have smiled.

Building roads and canals. A third subject on which Congress acted was "internal improvements"—the building of roads, canals, and the like. Such improvements would allow goods to move to and from markets, and would help tie together an expanding nation.

In 1811 work had begun on building the National Road from Cumberland, Maryland, across the Alleghenies to Wheeling, West Virginia. In 1816 Congress voted more money to extend the road to Vandalia, Illinois. Congress also passed a bill to set up a permanent fund to build internal improvements. President Madison, however, believed that this pushed the Constitution too far in the direction of government power. He vetoed the bill.

Activities

1. DISCUSSION A discussion about nationalism might serve as an effective motivation for this lesson. The "Era of Good Feelings" following the War of 1812 marked an upsurge in American nationalism—a time when Americans worked together to improve and strengthen their nation. Ask your students to define *nationalism.* Encourage them to conclude that nationalism refers to a national consciousness, a feeling of a sense of belonging together as a nation.

It has been said that nationalism can be good and evil. Many times nationalism is associated with a desire for national independence. What examples of this type of nationalism can your students offer? Discuss the emergence of new nations in Asia and Africa after World War II. What part has nationalism played in the history and development of these nations? Ask your students to give examples of leaders who have called for extreme forms of nationalism and demanded fierce loyalty to their national groups. Perhaps your students will mention Adolf Hitler of Germany and Benito Mussolini of Italy.

2. LISTENING FOR INFORMATION After your students have read this lesson, they may enjoy listening as you or a classmate read these two short selections: "Clinton's Ditch" (pages 126–131) by Carl Carmer in editor E. S. Miers's *The American Story: The Age of Exploration to The Age of the Atom* (New York: Channel Press, 1956) and "A Georgia Town in 1807" (pages 146–181) in William E. Woodward's *The Way Our People Lived: An Intimate History* (New York: Washington Square Press, 1970).

3. DISCUSSION Based on their reading of the lesson, ask students to cite three Congressional actions in support of the idea that the period of Monroe's Presidency was an "Era of Good Feelings." Would students characterize today's political climate as an "Era of Good Feelings?" Why or why not?

Acquiring Florida. The feelings of nationalism after the War of 1812 can be seen in the way that Florida was acquired from Spain. In 1810 and 1813, the United States had seized two small parts of West Florida, where Americans had settled. However, the rest of West Florida and all of East Florida remained in Spanish hands. This presented problems for the United States. Slaves from the southern states sometimes escaped into Spanish Florida. And Indians living there raided United States territory and then fled back to safety.

In 1818 President Monroe sent General Andrew Jackson into Florida to put a stop to these raids. Jackson defeated the Indians and also captured two Spanish forts. Spain, faced with revolts in its South American colonies, could do little to defend Florida.

Jackson's invasion strengthened the hand of John Quincy Adams, the Secretary of State. He had told the Spanish they should either control the Indians in Florida or else sell the territory to the United States. Fearing that the rest of Florida might be seized, the Spanish decided to sell. In 1819, the United States purchased Florida for $5 million. In the Transcontinental Treaty, Spain agreed also to give up its claims to territory in the Pacific Northwest.

The United States's southeastern boundary was established by the addition of East Florida.

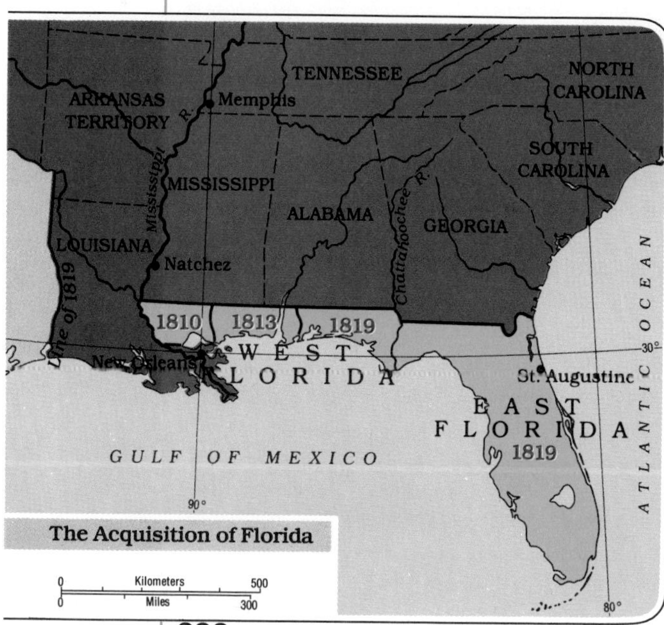

Curbing government power. On July 4, 1826, John Adams and Thomas Jefferson died within hours of each other. They were among the last giants of the Revolutionary era to pass from the scene. Their generation gave the United States independence and guided the young nation through difficult years.

It was the generation of Adams and Jefferson that also burned into the American mind the idea of limited government. No short document ever put the case for that idea better than the Declaration of Independence. No group ever translated that idea into a workable government better than the federal Constitutional Convention.

The Revolutionary generation was not unanimous, as you have seen, on exactly what powers government should have. There were even times when circumstances led some American leaders to approve of the exercise of government powers beyond those they approved in theory. The Alien and Sedition Acts that John Adams signed almost surely violated the Bill of Rights. Jefferson's purchase of Louisiana stretched the

Constitution to its limits. His embargo, and his strong enforcement of it, caused many to feel the hand of government.

Yet while there was disagreement about where to draw the line on government power, there was no disagreement at all that a line should be drawn. A useful way to gauge where Americans drew that line is to compare the United States government with others of the time. Nowhere else in the world did the power of government touch its citizens more lightly than in the United States.

That remained the case throughout the nineteenth century—except for the Civil War and the Reconstruction period—and well into the twentieth. Indeed, if Adams or Jefferson were to have returned to the United States of the 1880s, they would have found much that was familiar and comfortable in the practices of government at that time.

"How much government?" In time, industrialism, the rise of cities, and war—in short, modern society—would create the need for more positive roles for government. In our day, some of the ideas held by Jefferson and the Revolutionary generation on limited government seem almost quaint. Yet Americans are still fearful about unlimited government power. Even as government has taken on a larger role, a wary public continues to raise questions about it. Courts continue to protect the rights of individuals against abuses of governmental power. A watchful press continues to speak out when government overreaches itself.

"How much government is too much government?" asked the United States senator who was quoted at the start of this unit. It is a question that Americans have wrestled with from the very beginning. Every time it is asked, Americans approve once more the legacy of the nation's early years.

CHECKUP

1. How did the attitude of the Republicans change on (a) a national bank? (b) tariffs?
2. What action did Congress take during the Republican era regarding internal improvements?
3. How have Americans felt over the years about giving power to their government?

Key Facts From Chapter 11

1. The purchase of the Louisiana Territory from France in 1803 for $15 million doubled the size of the United States.
2. The United States went to war with Great Britain in 1812. A major reason was British interference with American shipping.
3. The War of 1812 ended without a clearcut victory for either side. It failed to settle a single issue over which the United States and Great Britain had fought.
4. A growth of national pride and an absence of party strife following the War of 1812 caused the period to be called by some "the Era of Good Feelings."

Answers To Review Questions

1. Jefferson made a number of changes in policy. He favored paying off the national debt, lowering taxes, repealing the whiskey tax, allowing the Alien and Sedition Acts to expire, changing the waiting period for immigrants to become citizens from fourteen years back to five years, and repealing the Judiciary Act of 1801.

2. The startled American ministers, who had been authorized to offer $10 million for New Orleans alone, were permitted by the French to purchase all of Louisana for $15 million, or less than three cents an acre. This land purchase doubled the size of America.

3. It established the precedence that the Supreme Court had the power to review acts of Congress and to declare them unconstitutional.

4. British seizure of American ships; British impressment of American sailors; falling farm prices due to British interference with American trade; a belief that the British were encouraging Indians to attack American settlers; American desire to take over Canada and Florida; and the desire to defend America's national honor.

5. The United States was poorly prepared. The army was tiny, with few volunteers and little leadership. The country itself was badly divided. American plans for the three-way invasion of Canada failed; Britain's powerful navy blockaded American ports and kept American naval ships bottled up; a British military force marched on Washington and burned most of the government buildings.

6. The Treaty of Ghent ended the war, but it failed to settle a single question over which America and Britain had fought. However, America did emerge from the war with a greater sense of independence and a greater degree of respect from Great Britain.
7. The significance of the Kentucky and Virginia Resolususpicion, in part because they had met in secret during the war and in part because some Federalists had wanted New England to secede from the Union. As a result of the convention, the Federalists were discredited, never to recover as a political party.
8. In the years immediately following the War of 1812, there was little party strife and a great burst of national pride and optimism. This period in history has been called "the Era of Good Feelings."
9. Florida, owned by Spain, was a haven for runaway slaves, marauding Indians, and lawless whites. President Monroe sent General Andrew Jackson to Florida to curtail the Indian raids. Jackson's successful invasion caused the Spanish to fear that the rest of Florida might be seized, so the Spanish decided to sell the land for $5 million.

★ REVIEWING THE CHAPTER ★

People, Places, and Events

Barbary states *P. 218*
Napoleon Bonaparte *P. 220*
Robert Livingston *P. 220*
Samuel Chase *P. 223*
Embargo Act *P. 226*
Tecumseh *P. 228*
War Hawks *P. 229*
Oliver Perry *P. 230*
Andrew Jackson *P. 230*
Treaty of Ghent *P. 231*
Noah Webster *P. 233*
Second Bank of the United States *P. 234*

Review Questions

1. How was Jefferson justified in referring to his election as "the Revolution of 1800"? *P. 217* Les. 1
2. Why was the Louisiana Purchase called the biggest bargain in American history? *P. 220* Les. 1
3. What was the real significance of the L.1 *Marbury* v. *Madison* case? *P. 223*
4. List the grievances that caused the United States to go to war with Great Britain. *Pp. 225, 228–229* Les. 2
5. Why was the War of 1812 almost a disas- L.2 ter for the United States? *Pp. 229–230*
6. What were the results of the War of 1812? *P. 231* Les. 2
7. How did the Hartford Convention contribute to the decline of the Federalist Party? *P. 232* Les. 2
8. Explain what is meant by the "Era of Good Feelings" and when did it occur? *P. 234* Les. 3
9. How did the United States acquire Florida? *P. 236* Les. 3

Chapter Test

Select the correct answer for each statement. Write your answers on a separate piece of paper.

1. The most important achievement of Jefferson's first administration was the purchase of the (Barbary states, Louisiana Territory, Florida).
2. The case of *Marbury* v. *Madison* was concerned with the issue of ("midnight judges," impeachment, impressment)
3. Jefferson tried to keep the United States out of the European war by urging Congress to pass the (Alien and Sedition Acts, Judiciary Act of 1801, Embargo Act).
4. The Federalists lost all popular support as a result of the (Barbary pirates, Hartford Convention, "Era of Good Feeling").
5. The War of 1812 was fought between the United States and (Great Britain, France, Spain).
6. A naval hero of the War of 1812 was (Oliver Perry, Andrew Jackson, William Henry Harrison).
7. The War of 1812 was ended by the (Treaty of Paris, Pinckney Treaty, Treaty of Ghent).
8. The growth of national pride encouraged Congress to give a twenty-year charter to the (War Hawks, Second Bank of the United States, Virginia Dynasty).
9. In 1819, the United States paid $5 million to Spain for the territory of (Oregon, Florida, Louisiana).
10. The main theme of this unit has been Americans' concern about (limited government, opportunity, revolution).

★ REVIEWING THE UNIT ★

1787	Constitutional Convention
	Northwest Ordinance
1789	New government goes into effect
1791	Bill of Rights adopted
1795	Jay's Treaty
1800	Washington becomes capital
1803	Louisiana Purchase
1805	Lewis and Clark reach the Pacific
1807	Embargo Act
1812–1814	War of 1812
1815	Battle of New Orleans
1819	Acquisition of Florida completed

Under the Articles of Confederation, which went into effect in 1781, the United States government was weak and ineffective. In 1787 a group of state delegates met in Philadelphia to revise the Articles. Instead, those at the meeting, now known as the Constitutional Convention, wrote a new constitution. It became the law of the land in 1788. The Bill of Rights was added in 1791.

George Washington, as the first President, oversaw organization of the federal government. Secretary of State Thomas Jefferson and Secretary of the Treasury Alexander Hamilton differed on many issues. Out of their differences there developed, in time, the first political parties. Washington and his successor, John Adams, kept the United States neutral during troubles in Europe. Adams had a stormy term of office, and failed to win reelection.

Thomas Jefferson's election in 1800 ushered in twenty-four years of Republican rule. In 1803 the purchase of the Louisiana Territory from France doubled the size of the United States. Freedom of the seas became a crucial issue when war between Britain and France threatened American shipping. Measures taken by Jefferson and his successor, James Madison, to meet the situation were unpopular. The issue of freedom of the seas brought on the War of 1812 with Britain. Though neither side could claim victory, the United States emerged with an upsurge of national pride. James Monroe's administrations (1817—1825) were called by some "the Era of Good Feelings."

Answers to Unit Questions

1. a. Jefferson thought that relations with the Indians should be as friendly as possible. He encouraged trade, if appropriate.
b. Knowledge of the new land's physical geography was important and should include information about soil, terrain, animals, minerals and climate.
c. Records are very valuable and should be protected against accidental loss. They should be written accurately and clearly enough for others to read and understand.
d. The explorers safety was more important than the complete success of the expedition.
e. American commerce should be expanded, especially by more direct water routes to the West coast.
2. Answers will vary.

 REVIEWING THE UNIT 

Skills Development: Analyzing Source Material

The following primary source material presents excerpts from President Jefferson's letter of instructions to Meriwether Lewis. Lewis, along with William Clark, led an expedition that explored the vast Louisiana Purchase. Read the source material and then answer the questions.

The object of your mission is to explore the Missouri River, and such principal stream of it, as, by its course and communication with the water of the Pacific Ocean may offer the most direct and practicable water communication across this continent, for the purposes of commerce.

Your observations are to be taken with great pains and accuracy, to be entered distinctly and intelligibly for others as well as yourself to comprehend all the elements necessary. . . . Several copies of these [observations] . . . should be made at leisure times and put into the care of the most trustworthy of your attendants. . . . A further guard [against accidental loss] would be that one of these copies be written on the paper of the birch, as less liable to injury from damp than common paper.

The commerce which may be carried on with the [Indians] renders a knowledge of these people important. You will therefore endeavor to make yourself acquainted . . . with the names of the nations and their numbers; . . . their language, traditions, monuments; their ordinary occupations in agriculture, fishing, hunting, war, arts, and the implements for these; their food, clothing, and domestic accommodations; the diseases prevalent among them . . . and articles of commerce they may need or furnish and to what extent.

Other objects worthy of notice will be: the soil and face of the country, . . . the animals of the country generally, and especially those not known in the U.S.; . . . the mineral production; . . . volcanic appearances; climate. . . .

. . . treat [the Indians] in the most friendly and conciliatory manner which their own conduct will admit; . . . make them acquainted with . . . our wish to be neighborly, friendly, and useful to them. . . .

As it is impossible for us to foresee in what manner you will be received by those people, whether with hospitality or hostility, so is it impossible to prescribe the exact degree of perseverance with which you are to pursue your journey. . . . To your own discretion, therefore, must be left the degree of danger you may risk, and the point at which you should decline, only saying we wish you to err on the side of safety, and to bring back your party safe, even if it be with less information.

1. Based on the evidence in the source material, tell how you think Jefferson felt about the following things.
   a. Relations with the Indians
   b. Knowledge of the new land's physical geography
   c. The value of keeping records
   d. The expedition's success compared with the explorers' safety
   e. Opening up trade routes and expanding American commerce

2. Write a paragraph describing the kind of person Jefferson must have been, as revealed by these instructions.

Unit 4

Americans: A People on the Move

EXPANSION AND DEMOCRACY

Background Information

PICTURE This picture from the New-York Historical Society shows the Erie Canal near Little Falls, New York. For a hundred years before the Erie Canal was built, people had talked about a canal to join the Great Lakes and the Atlantic Ocean. But even so farsighted a man as Thomas Jefferson declared that "talk of making a canal of three hundred and fifty miles through the wilderness—it is little short of madness." Much of the country between Albany and Buffalo, through which the canal was to be dug, was rugged and sparsely settled. Nevertheless, the canal's supporters persevered. The job took eight years and cost over $7 million paid for entirely by the state of New York. It soon earned its price many times over.

The original canal, completed in 1825, was 364 miles (582.4 km) long and had 82 locks. In addition to carrying freight, the canal provided two types of passenger service: slow boats (2 mph, or 3.2 km/hr) charged one and a half cents a mile and the faster "packets" (4 mph, or 6.4 km/hr) charged five cents. By 1862, the canal had been enlarged several times.

CHAPTER

12

WESTWARD THE FRONTIER

LESSON 1

STRETCHING FROM THE CAROLINAS on the East Coast to southern California on the West Coast is an arc of warm land called the Sunbelt. This area occupies about a third of the United States. It is the fastest-growing part of the country today. In the 1960s the population of the states in the Sunbelt grew one and a half times as fast as that of the other states.

Increases during the 1970s were even greater. By 1975 the population had gone up by the following percentages: Arizona, 25.3; Texas, 9.3; Florida, 23; South Carolina, 8.8; New Mexico, 12.7. During this same time, northern states such as Pennsylvania, Illinois, Indiana, New Jersey, Ohio, and Iowa were barely holding their own, and New York was losing ground.

This shifting of population is part of a much larger pattern. Today one of every three Americans lives in a state other than the one in which he or she was born. Of the remaining two out of three, a good many have moved from one place to another within the same state. Every year one in five Americans changes residence. One writer has suggested, perhaps not entirely in jest, that the national symbol is not the eagle but the moving van.

Our very language is the language of a people on the move. One widely used book on American slang uses thirteen columns of the index just to list all the slang expressions with the word *go* in them.

One writer has summed up this American characteristic in this way:

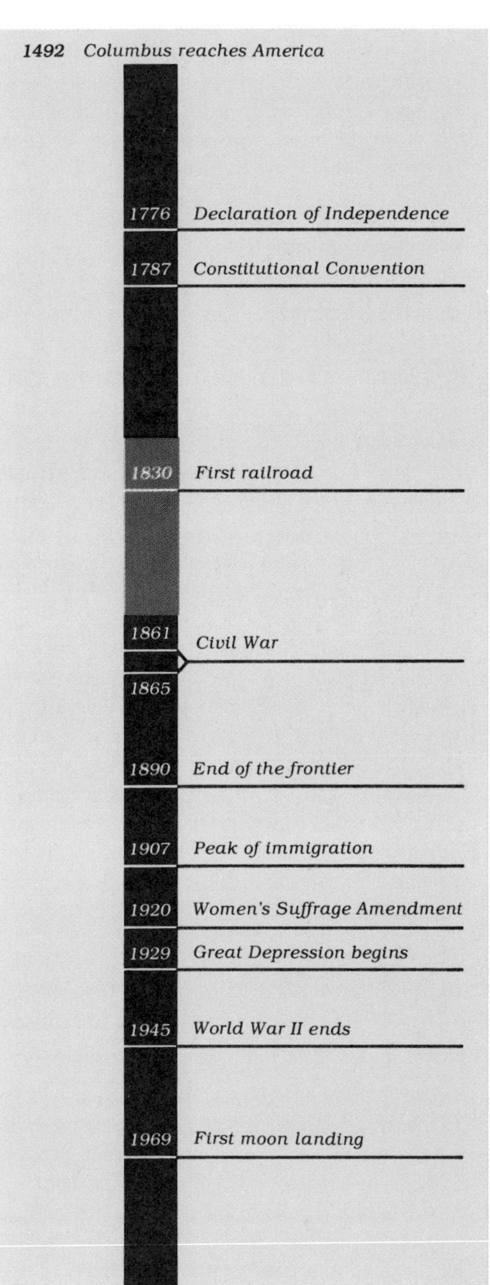

LESSON 1 *(1 to 2 days)*

Performance Objectives

1. To explain orally or in writing the reasons why Americans in general are such a restless people. **2.** To describe the typical pattern of settlement of western lands by writing an essay. **3.** To list at least five reasons why people were willing to leave settled areas and endure the hardships associated with moving to the frontier.

Famous People

Alexis de Tocqueville, Daniel Boone

Vocabulary

Sunbelt, Appalachian Mountains, Proclamation of 1763, squatters, permanent settlers

Activities

1. INTRODUCING THE UNIT The central theme of this unit is the westward migration of the American people that resulted in the expansion of the nation's boundaries from the Atlantic to the Pacific. As an introduction to the main ideas of this unit, discuss with students their thoughts and feelings about moving.

In his introduction to Chapter 1 in *A Nation of Strangers* (New York: PBI Books, 1974), Vance Packard quotes two Michigan women: "Many people prefer moving to staying around and saying goodby to everyone else." Ask students for their reactions to this statement. Then ask the following questions. **(a)** Have you ever moved? If so, what were your thoughts at that time? Did you enjoy the experience? **(b)** If you have never moved, have you ever wanted to? Why? **(c)** What are some of the advantages of moving? the disadvantages? **(d)** Do you think you will want to move away when you graduate from high school? For what possible reasons? **(e)** If you were to move, where would you choose to go? Why are you attracted to that particular place?

At this point in the discussion, present the information about the growing popularity of the Sunbelt. Have students locate the Sunbelt on a map of the United States and name the states that make up that area of the country. Ask students for possible reasons why the Sunbelt is experiencing such an increase in population. What are people seeking when they move to the Sunbelt? Are they seeking the same things their ancestors sought as they migrated westward in the 1700s and 1800s?

> . . . Americans have moved and have kept moving from farm to farm, from state to state, from town to town, back and forth, from job to job, around and around. There is a fever in our blood. We have itching feet. Here today and gone tomorrow. Let's go. 'Scuse our dust. Fill 'er up. Freewheeling. Howdy, stranger.

In short, Americans are the most mobile people on the face of the earth.

A restless people. The restlessness of Americans is nothing new. Travelers to our country have made note of it for 150 years. A South American visitor in the 1840s commented that "if God were suddenly to call the world to judgment He would surprise two thirds of the American population on the road like ants." A visitor from France had observed ten years earlier:

> [The American man is] not only a worker, he is a migratory worker. He has no root in the soil; he is a stranger to the worship of one's birthplace and family home; he is always in the mood to move on, always ready to start in the first steamer that comes along from the place where he had just now landed. He is devoured with a passion for movement; he cannot stay in one place; he must go and come. . . .

The most famous of all traveler accounts is *Democracy in America,* written in 1835 by a young Frenchman, Alexis de Tocqueville. In it, he said:

> In the United States a man builds a house in which to spend his old age, and he sells it before the roof is on; he plants a garden and [rents] it just as the trees are coming into bearing; he brings a field into tillage and leaves other men to gather the crops; he embraces a profession and gives it up; he settles in a place, which he soon afterwards leaves to carry his changeable longings elsewhere.

How can one account for the restlessness of Americans? One explanation may lie in the fact that America was populated by people from other lands. They had broken away from the village or piece of land to which their ancestors were tied for hundreds of years. Thus they were rootless. With no ties to any one place, they were always on the move.

Perhaps the restlessness comes from being part of a culture that stresses opportunity and rising in the world. Newspapers, political leaders, Fourth of July orators—all speak glowingly of America's opportunities. In such a society, the reasoning goes, one must be ready to seize the opportunity that arises, whether that be moving to lands in the West or to the growing cities. Perhaps that is what Tocqueville had in mind when he wrote:

> The American has no time to tie himself to anything. He grows accustomed only to change, and ends by regarding it as the natural state of man. He feels the need of it, more, he loves it; for the instability, instead of meaning disaster to him, seems to give birth only to miracles all about him.

Across the Mountains

Whatever may be the cause of the restlessness of Americans, much of their history is tied directly to this quality. More than anything else, it is the restlessness of the people that gave America its present-day boundaries. It affected our relations with other nations. It contributed to the tragic history of the native peoples of North America. It leveled forests, raised up cities, and settled a continent in an incredibly short time.

Continued on page 246

Daniel Boone

One of the first pioneers to venture into the wilderness across the Appalachian Mountains was Daniel Boone. As a youth on the North Carolina frontier, he first heard of a land called Kentucky. In 1769 he and his brother set out along an Indian trail. It led them through the mountains by way of a natural pass called Cumberland Gap. The country they came to was all that Boone had dreamed of. The soil was rich. Buffalo grazed on the bluegrass. Deer and panther roamed the forests. Great flocks of passenger pigeons darkened the skies.

Six years later, Boone guided the first permanent settlers to Kentucky. They founded a settlement called Boonesborough. The paths over which the group had traveled became the Wilderness Road, by which many later settlers made their way west.

Boone spent an adventurous life along the frontier, ranging as far west as the Yellowstone River. He became the most famous pioneer of his day. No one has caught the spirit of this legendary frontiersman and his times better than the poet Stephen Vincent Benét, who wrote:

When Daniel Boone goes by, at night,
The phantom deer arise
And all lost, wild America
Is burning in their eyes.

Daniel Boone was a fine shot with his favorite Kentucky rifle that he called *Tick-Licker*.

2. DISCUSSION After students have read the lesson, ask for reasons why Americans are such a restless people. Emphasize the source material on page 244. Then ask students for examples from today's culture that reinforce the idea of Americans as a restless people. (Slang expressions; lyrics of popular music; movie and television themes; increasing number of recreational vehicles; etc.)

3. ORAL REPORT Assign one of the students to read and report on Chapter XIII, "Why the Americans Are So Restless in the Midst of Their Prosperity" from Alexis de Tocqueville's *Democracy in America.* Editions of this book are available in most school and public libraries.

4. ESSAY Assign students to write essays **(a)** describing the typical pattern of settlement of western lands, including information about (1) hunters and trappers, (2) frontier men and women, and (3) permanent settlers and **(b)** giving at least five reasons why people were willing to leave settled areas and endure the hardships associated with moving to the frontier.

After students have completed this assignment, have them exchange essays with partners and critique their classmates' compositions.

5. DISCUSSION After students have read the special-interest material on Daniel Boone (page 245), ask them to discuss the meaning of the following statement: "If it was the ideas of such as Jefferson that invented a new nation, it was the hardihood of such as Boone that shaped and secured it."

The Applachian barrier. After the colonists had gained a foothold on the continent, they began to push the line of settlement steadily westward. By the time of the American Revolution, the frontier reached the Appalachian Mountains, about 300 miles inland from the Atlantic seaboard. A few pioneers had crossed the mountains in Pennsylvania and Virginia. Altogether, perhaps a few thousand made it to the western side of the mountains in the 1760s and 1770s. But for most, the Appalachians were a major barrier.

For a time, the westward movement slowed. Clearly, though, Americans regarded the mountains as a place to pause, not to stop. They had made that clear after the French and Indian War when King George III issued the Proclamation of 1763, forbidding settlement west of the Alleghenies. The colonists' anger over this act had added to the growing split with Great Britain.

An avalanche of people. Over the next twenty years Americans fought a war for independence and set up a government. During the first decade of independence, the government was engaged in clearing away the influence of the British and Spanish from its western lands, and in making treaties with Indian tribes. Those things accomplished, an avalanche of people began to roll down the western side of the mountains. From Virginia and North Carolina, they crossed through passes into Kentucky and Tennessee. To the north, settlers trekked from Massachusetts and Connecticut across New York to Ohio. From there, they soon pushed on to the Mississippi River, the nation's western boundary. To the south, planters moved westward into Alabama and Mississippi.

The table below reveals the speed of western settlement between 1790 and 1819. Of the new states listed there, only Vermont lay east of the Appalachians.

New States Formed from the Original Territory of the United States, 1791–1819

State	*Population in 1790*	*1800*	*1810*	*1820*
Vermont (1791)*	85,000	154,000	218,000	236,000
Kentucky (1792)	74,000	221,000	407,000	564,000
Tennessee (1796)	36,000	106,000	262,000	423,000
Ohio (1803)	—	45,000	231,000	581,000
Indiana (1816)	—	6,000	25,000	147,000
Mississippi (1817)	—	8,000	31,000	75,000
Illinois (1818)	—	—	12,000	55,000
Alabama (1819)	—	1,000	9,000	128,000

**The year in which each state entered the union is in parentheses. Under the terms of the Northwest Ordinance of 1787, sixty thousand people were required before a territory could become a state. (In the case of Illinois, the population requirement was not enforced.)*

In his inaugural message in 1801, President Thomas Jefferson had written that the United States had "room enough for our descendants to the thousandth and thousandth generation." So rapidly was the frontier being pushed back, however, that many people doubted there was room enough for the second and third generations. With good prices being paid for wheat, corn, and cotton, there was money to be made. Northern farmers and southern planters bought up western land as fast as the government put it up for sale. By 1819, states had been created in all the original territory of the United States, except for the area in the northwest that later became Michigan, Wisconsin, and Minnesota.

By the time Ohio became a state, however, Jefferson had completed the deal for the Louisiana Purchase. Sixteen years later, Florida was acquired from Spain. With these two additions, the territory of the United States was increased by more than 150 percent. Soon new states were being carved out of the newly acquired lands: Louisiana in 1812, Missouri in 1821.

The pattern of settlement. Western settlement followed a pattern. Typically, hunters and trappers were the first whites to enter an area and mark out trails. After the supply of furs ran out they departed, leaving no permanent settlement behind. Following them came the men and women pioneers. Often they were squatters. They moved to the edge of the frontier, threw up shelters, cleared patches of land, planted crops, and grazed their hogs in the nearby forest. To add to their food supply, the pioneers hunted animals. After a number of years, they moved on for a variety of reasons. Perhaps others were moving too close for their liking. Perhaps they could get a good price for the land they had improved. Or perhaps they had heard of still better lands beyond.

These men and women of the frontier might make half a dozen such moves in their lifetime. Thomas Lincoln was fairly typical. Born in western Virginia, he grew up in the central part of Kentucky. He had no schooling, but he knew something about farming and carpentering. In 1806 Thomas Lincoln married Nancy Hanks, an illiterate daughter of a farming family. He and Nancy settled on a farm in the western part of Kentucky. In 1809 their son Abraham was born. In 1816 the Lincolns moved to the southern part of Indiana. After "squatting" for a year, they bought land and built a log cabin without windows and with a roof made of mud and dry grass. Nancy Lincoln died, and Thomas remarried. In 1830 the Lincolns moved again, this time to Illinois. By then, Abraham was old enough to strike out on his own.

The permanent settlers. After the frontier people came the permanent settlers. These were the people who had enough money to buy the land and the tools they would need for farming. They finished the clearing, dug out the tree stumps, built fences, put up frame houses. As their harvests increased, they often bought extra land to sell at a profit at a later date. There was a bit of the speculator in most American farmers. Normally, these farm families expected to stay; but they were always prepared to

6. RESEARCH/ORAL REPORTS "We live too thick" is mentioned on page 248 as a reason why a Connecticut farmer would consider moving to the frontier. People today often move for the same reason. Have some of the students survey the population growth of their town. Has the population changed significantly? If so, when did the change occur? Why? What effect has the population change had on the community?

7. LISTENING FOR INFORMATION If you are able to locate a copy of *The American Story: The Age of Exploration to the Age of the Atom* (New York: Channel Press, 1956) read or play a tape you have prerecorded of the section titled "The Frontier Disappears." In this selection, Professor Ray Billington of Northwestern University describes patterns of American settlement and remarks that Americans are a wasteful people, unaccustomed to thrift or saving. He blames the frontier people for establishing this pattern. The students might enjoy discussing this idea and some of the other interesting judgments presented in this selection.

8. USING A GRAPH Ask some of the students to work in a group and make a bar graph showing the population growth in the new states formed from the original territory of the United States, 1791–1819. They will find the information they need in the table on page 246. Display the graph on the bulletin board.

LESSON 2 *(2 days)*

Performance Objectives

1. To explain orally or in writing the effect that the invention of the cotton gin had on western development. **2.** To identify and describe four developments in transportation that speeded western settlement. **3.** To explain orally or in writing how the federal government's land policies affected western settlement.

Famous People

Eli Whitney, Robert Fulton

Vocabulary

Cotton gin, National Road, Transportation Revolution, Erie Canal, speculators, "land-office business"

Activities

1. DISCUSSION Few inventions have altered history more than did Eli Whitney's cotton gin. After students have read the lesson, ask them to explain the impact of Whitney's invention on the westward movement. How did the cotton gin help to shape the course of events? Then ask students to compile a list of other inventions that have greatly affected history. What inventions may appear in the future that will have significant impact on history? Encourage several students to present a brief report about the laser and its proven and potential importance.

The Brooklyn Museum

The pioneers' first task was to clear the land for planting crops. They often killed the trees by cutting grooves around the trunks.

move if the fertility of their soil gave out or if they got a very good price for their land.

Whether one was a rootless pioneer or a permanent settler, it was a hard life. Why, wondered an Englishman, would anyone want to put up with all the hardships of the frontier?

> The rugged road, the dirty hovels, the fire in the woods to sleep by, the pathless ways through the wilderness, the dangerous crossing of the rivers. . . .

And for what?

> To boil their pot in gipsy-fashion, to have a mere board to eat on, to drink whiskey or pure water, to sit and sleep under a shed far inferior to English cowpens, to have a mill at twenty miles' distance, . . . and a doctor nowhere.

There were a number of answers to the Englishman's question, not all of them the same for each person who went to the frontier. Some of the answers you will find in the following items.

By a Connecticut farmer in the eighteenth century:

> Our lands being thus worn out, I suppose to be one reason why so many are inclined to Remove to new Places that they may raise Wheat: As also that they may have more Room, thinking that we live too thick.

By a New England traveler to the West, eighteenth century:

> Those who are first inclined to emigrate are usually such as have met with difficulties at home. These are commonly joined by persons who, having large families and small farms, are induced, for the sake of settling their children comfortably, to seek for new and cheaper lands. To both are always added the discontented, the enterprising, the ambitious, and the [greedy]. . . . Others, still, are [attracted] by the prospect of gain, presented in every new country to the [wise], from the purchase and sale of new lands: while not a small number are influenced by the brilliant stories, which everywhere are told concerning most [lands] during the early progress of their settlement.

One historian has written that the lure of the West made for a kind of "gold-rush mentality." Do these two accounts help you to see why?

CHECKUP

1. What were the major obstacles to western settlement in the early years of the United States?
2. Who were usually the first people to move to the frontier? What groups then followed?
3. Why did so many Americans leave settled areas and move to the frontier?

LESSON 2

Speeding Western Settlement

During the first 150 years after Jamestown was settled, the frontier had been pushed westward at a rate of 2 miles (3.2 km) a year. After 1790, it moved westward at a rate of 17 miles (27.2 km) a year. Three things contributed to this amazing increase: an important invention, developments in transportation, and changes in government land policy. Underlying all was the continuing land hunger of a people on the move.

The cotton gin. One development that speeded western settlement was the invention of the cotton gin in 1793 (see page 250). It made cotton raising highly profitable, and the production of cotton rose rapidly to meet the demand from English factories. From less than 4,000 bales in 1790, production climbed to 260,000 bales in 1816. Because cotton farming used up the fertility in the soil in just a few years, planters in South Carolina and Georgia were soon moving onto the rich coastal plains of Alabama, Mississippi, and Louisiana. Some large plantations were carved out of this land, but a good many smaller farms were located there, too. By 1820, half of America's cotton was grown in these newly opened lands.

Roads to the West. A second development that speeded western settlement was improved transportation. Beginning in the 1790s, a number of roads

Continued on page 251

Most early roads were dirt trails wide enough for a wagon. They were often muddy and developed deep ruts. The best of the major highways was the National Road. For most of its route, it was paved with stone and covered with gravel.

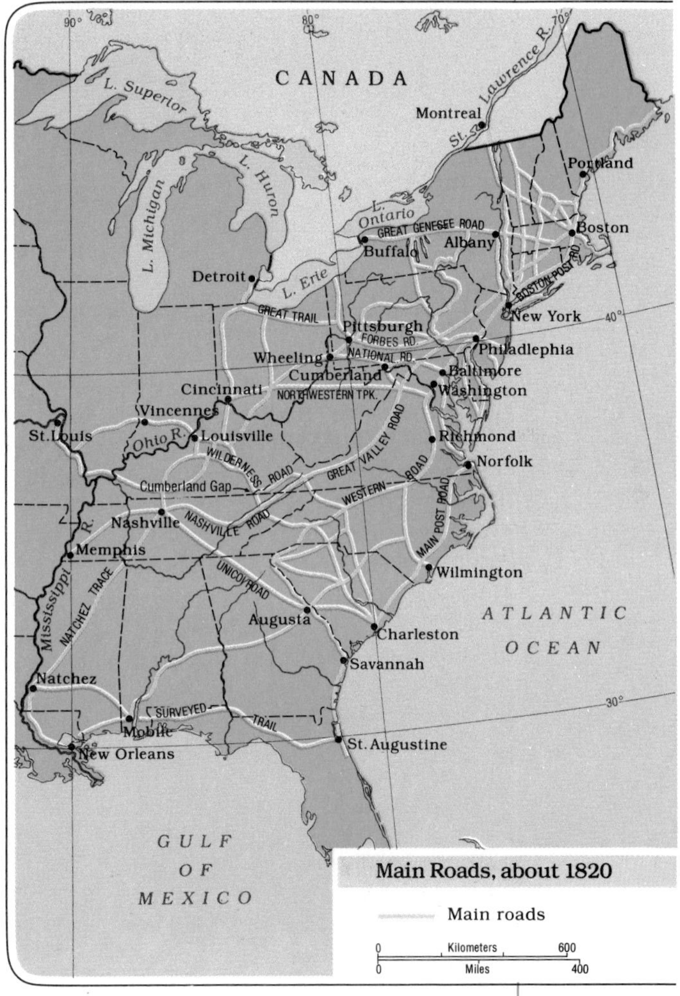

Main Roads, about 1820

2. RESEARCH / ORAL REPORT Whitney could not keep his invention a secret. The result was that others stole his idea for the cotton "engine," or 'gin. Ask a student to research and report on the protection offered inventors by today's patent laws.

Background Information

1. ELI WHITNEY (1765–1825) In 1793, Whitney applied for a patent for his cotton gin. While awaiting his patent, he and a partner began production of the gin. But the factory, in New Haven, Connecticut, burned down; and it took over a year for his patent to be granted. Other people began to manufacture the gin. Whitney sued. Many years were spent in litigation, but he was finally granted a renewal.

Eli Whitney also can be called the father of mass production. He started a second factory—this one for the manufacture of muskets for the government. Whitney invented tools and machines that turned out uniform musket parts. It was possible for unskilled workers to make the parts and assemble them into muskets in far less time than it took a skilled gunsmith to make one weapon. This, not the cotton gin, made Eli Whitney a rich person. It has also been said that while the cotton gin made the Civil War inevitable, mass production ensured a Union victory.

The Cotton Gin

Before the 1790s, not much cotton had been grown in America because processing it was difficult. Before cotton can be made into thread, the tiny seeds must be removed from the fluffy, white fibers. With "long-staple," or "Sea Island," cotton, the black, slippery seeds can be separated from the fiber by running the cotton between rollers much like those of an old-fashioned clothes wringer. However, this kind of cotton grew well only in small areas along the South Carolina and Georgia coasts. "Short-staple" cotton would grow well almost anywhere in the South, but its fuzzy seeds were so sticky that they had to be picked out by hand. Even a good worker could clean only a few pounds of cotton a day.

In 1793 Eli Whitney, a young Northerner, born in Massachusetts and educated at Yale College, went south to be a tutor on a plantation. While in Georgia, he became aware of the difficulty of removing seeds from short-staple cotton. Whitney had a mechanical bent, and within two weeks he had designed a hand-operated machine to do the job. The wire teeth of Whitney's engine—or as it came to be called, "gin"—tugged the cotton fibers through narrow slots. The seeds, however, were too large to pass through. A revolving brush then removed the fibers from the teeth. With Whitney's cotton gin, one person could clean as much as fifty pounds of cotton in a day.

The invention had electrifying effects. Cotton now became a profitable crop, and the South's faltering economy came to life. Planters, seeking fresh soil for cotton cultivation, moved westward. Mill towns grew up in the North to spin and weave the cotton. And the increased need for labor fastened the slavery system on the South. You will learn more in Unit 5 about the consequences of this last effect of Eli Whitney's invention of the cotton gin.

The cotton gin was a simple machine that any blacksmith could duplicate. Though Whitney held a patent on the machine, it was widely copied. He received little of the wealth that his invention brought for others.

were built to connect east and west. Usually they were built by private interests who charged a toll. State and local governments often helped pay the costs of road building. The federal government itself built one important highway—the National Road. Its first section was from Cumberland, Maryland, to Wheeling, on the Ohio River.

Paved with stone and gravel, these roads were a great improvement over the trails that early settlers had followed through the wilderness. Even so, they were crude affairs. In rainy seasons, they turned to mud. Some farmers in northern climates held their crops until winter, when they could ship them by sleigh over the snow-covered roads. It was also very expensive to ship goods over these roads. In fact, it was cheaper to send goods 3,000 miles (4,800 km) across the ocean than 30 miles (48 km) overland!

The steamboat. After 1800, improvements in transportation occurred that are important enough to justify the term *Transportation Revolution.* One was the invention of the steamboat. Rivers had long offered obvious avenues for transporting goods. However, because of the river current, traffic only went one way. In 1807, for example, 1,800 boats and rafts went downstream on the Mississippi River; only 11 went up. That same year, Robert Fulton, a Pennsylvania-born engineer, built the first practical steamboat. That invention turned rivers into two-way highways of commerce. Within twenty years, steamboats were plying the waters of nearly every large river in the country and giving western farm goods outlets to world markets.

Metropolitan Museum of Art, Gift of Mrs. John Sylvester, 1936.

This toll road ran between Baltimore and Reisterstown in Maryland. Coaches, wagons carrying freight, horses with riders, and even travelers on foot streamed through the busy tollgate.

Canal building. Another development in transportation that aided western growth was the digging of several thousand miles of canals. This created water highways where there were no rivers. The greatest canal was the Erie, running across New York State and connecting Buffalo to Albany. Building the Erie Canal was an enormous task. Every foot of its 364 miles (582.4 km) had to be dug by hand. With its opening in 1825, goods were transported to Buffalo from villages all along the shores of Lake Erie. From Buffalo, the goods went by canalboat to Albany and then down the Hudson River to New York City. In this manner, goods could travel by an all-water route from the Old Northwest to the nation's largest seaport and trading center.

Before the Erie Canal, the cost of shipping a bushel (35.2 l) of wheat overland from Buffalo to New York City was three times the value of the wheat itself. The canal reduced the cost to a few pennies, thus cutting the cost of shipping by 90 percent. In this way, canals encouraged settlement in the regions

3. ESSAY Have the students write essays in which they describe four important developments in transportation that speeded western settlement. Ask them to complete the following sentence at the conclusion of their essays and to substantiate their opinions: The most significant development in the Transportation Revolution was ____.

Background Information

2. TURNPIKE Toll roads, such as the one shown in the picture on this page, were called *turnpikes* because in the early days travelers stopped at tollgates, or turnpikes, to pay their fee before going further. The first recorded tolls were collected on a Persian military road between Babylon and Syria about 2000 B.C. The first turnpike in the United States was built in Virginia about 1785. The greatest activity in road construction occurred between 1795 and 1810. Roads were generally built with private capital and operated by corporations for profit under state regulation. By 1825, turnpike stocks were nearly worthless because the tolls seldom paid for more than the cost of keeping up the roads.

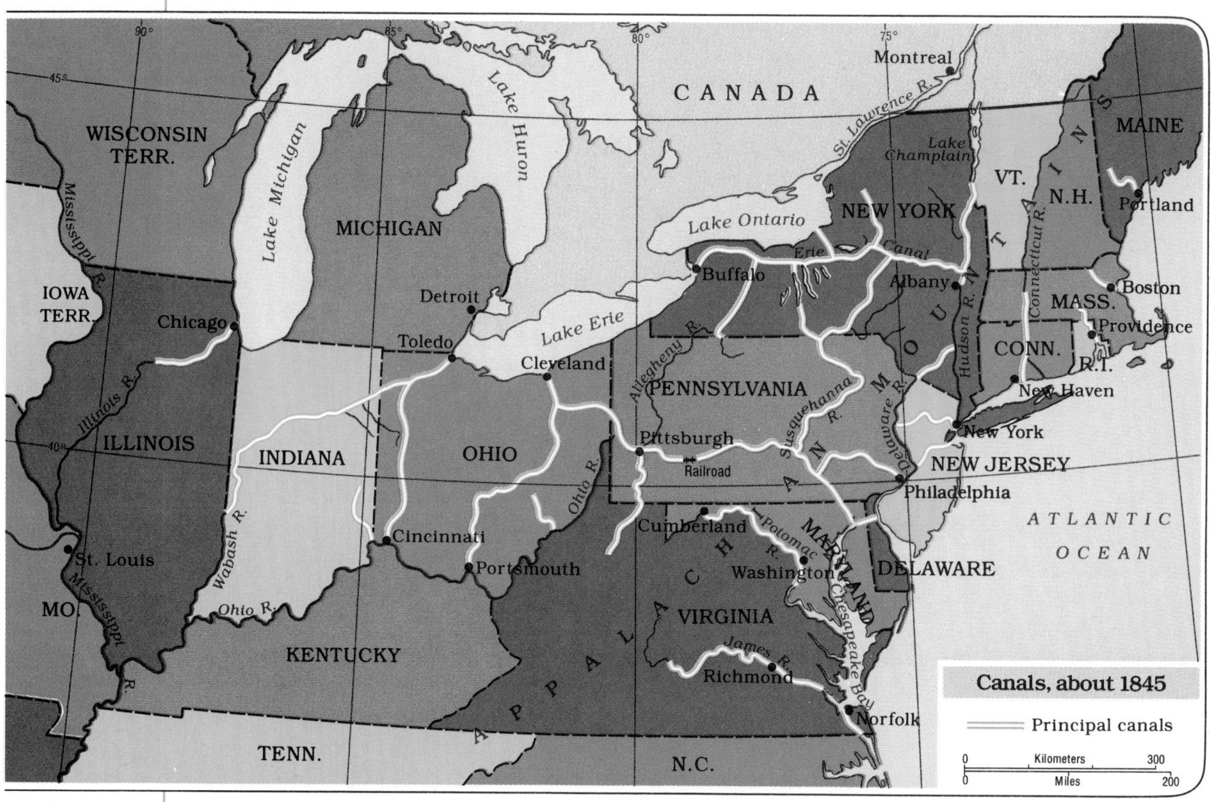

The success of the Erie Canal in New York State induced many other states to undertake canal building. Few of those canals proved to be profitable, but they contributed greatly to the development of the nation. Note that many canals followed the routes of rivers.

4. USING A MAP On outline maps of the eastern half of the United States, have students **(a)** locate the cities mentioned in this lesson; **(b)** draw the routes of the National Road, the Genessee Road, Great Valley Road, and the Natchez Trace; and **(c)** draw the principal canals. Refer students to the maps on pages 249 and 252 in their text.

around the Great Lakes, for farmers now knew they could ship their products to market cheaply.

The railroad. The transportation development that was the most important of all in opening up the West was the railroad. The first American railroad line was built in Baltimore in 1830 and was all of 13 miles (20.8 km) long. By 1840, 2,200 miles (3,520 km) of track had been laid. The railroad was now beginning to be a serious rival to the canal and the steamboat. During the next ten years, more than 6,000 miles (9,600 km) of track were added. By 1860, the United States had more than 31,000 miles (49,600 km) of track.

At first, railroad lines went from cities to the nearby countryside, much like spokes in a wheel, with each wheel separate from the other. Later, lines began to connect the hubs of these wheels—that is, the cities. By 1860, all the major cities of the North were tied to each other by rail.

Building railroads was expensive. Private investors from both the United States and England put up a good deal of the money. States and cities, believing that railroads would add to their prosperity, also bought stock in railroad corporations or loaned them money. Of the billion dollars spent in railroad building by 1860, perhaps one fourth came from public funds. In 1850 the federal government also began to support railroad building with grants of land to the companies.

Railroads opened up areas that were far from rivers and canals by providing cheap transportation for farm goods. One three-county area of rich farmland in Illinois, for example, had a population of only 8,500 in 1840. Farmers there raised 750,000 bushels (26,400 kl) of wheat and corn. Shortly after, a railroad line was built nearby. By 1860, there were 38,000 people living in these three counties. Farmers now raised more than 6,200,000 bushels (218,240 kl) of wheat and corn. Many eastern farmers found they were no longer able to compete with western farmers, who could now ship their crops cheaply. Therefore, those eastern farmers often pulled up stakes and moved west themselves.

Together, the steamboat, canal, and railroad lowered transportation costs dramatically. Before 1820, it had cost about twenty cents to ship a ton (.9 t) of goods one mile (1.6 km). By 1860, the cost had dropped to a penny, and the goods arrived five to ten times sooner. At the same time, passengers could be carried west for about one cent a mile and could go as far in six days as they used to go in three weeks.

5. RESEARCH / ORAL REPORTS Assign interested students to research and report on the following topics: Robert Fulton and "Fulton's Folly," the National Road, the Erie Canal, and the use of canals today. A valuable reference book, in addition to encyclopedias, is the *Concise Dictionary of American History* (New York: Charles Scribner's Sons, 1962).

6. LISTENING FOR INFORMATION Students may enjoy hearing Samuel Clemens's lively description of the effect the railroad had on the steamboat. This description is found in Chapter 58 of Mark Twain's *Life on the Mississippi*.

The first steam locomotive to operate on a commercial rail line was the *Tom Thumb* of the Baltimore and Ohio Railroad. In 1830 the *Tom Thumb*, designed by the New York inventor Peter Cooper, raced a horse. The horse won the race when the steam locomotive broke down.

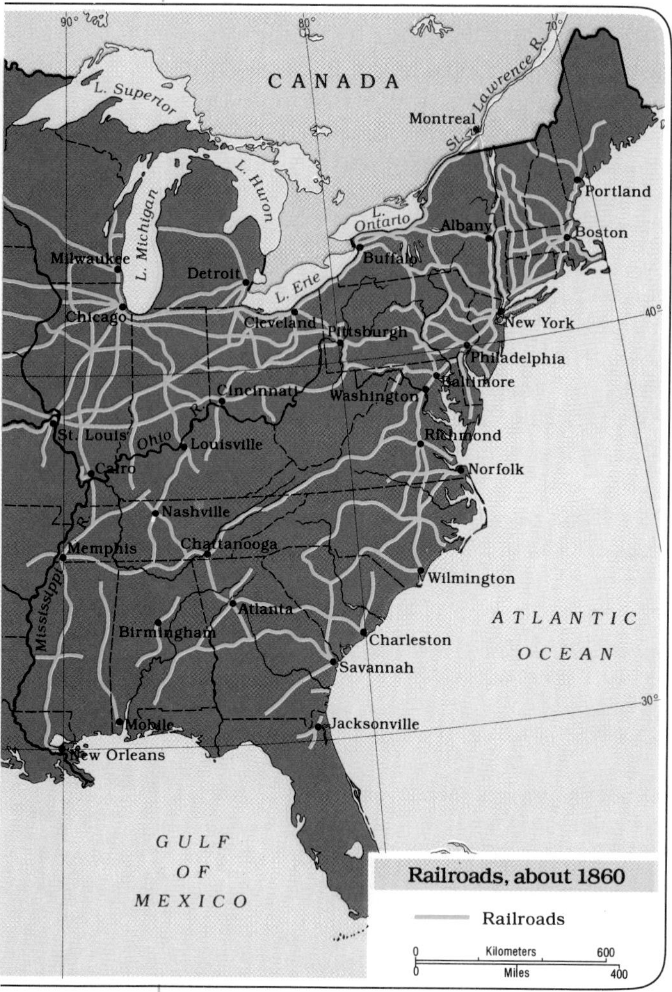

By 1860, America's railroads connected practically all the major cities east of the Mississippi River, and were pushing westward.

Government land policy. Another important development that speeded western settlement was government land policy. Following the Revolutionary War, the federal government controlled vast lands in the West. In Chapter 9 you learned how Congress, in 1785, set up a system for surveying and selling the land of the Northwest Territory to private individuals. The land was marked off into squares measuring a mile (1.6 km) on each side. Each square contained 640 acres (256 ha) and was called a section. Under the 1785 law, one had to buy an entire section at $1 an acre (.4 ha). That was more land than most settlers needed, and $640 was more money than they could afford. Most of the land was bought by *speculators.* These were people who bought the land not for their own use but in the hope it would rise in value so that they could sell at a profit.

Individuals and private land companies also owned huge tracts of land that they had acquired during colonial times or had bought from the states shortly afterward at bargain prices. Massachusetts, for instance, sold six million acres (2.4 million ha) to one buyer at about three cents an acre. A group called the Ohio Company arranged to buy 750,000 acres (300,000 ha). Not all such investors did well. Some bought unwisely and lost money. One of the investors, Robert Morris of Pennsylvania, spent several years in a debtor's jail after he went broke on land schemes. But many landowners made out quite well. They usually sold the land to settlers in quarter sections—160 acres (64 ha)—at a good price, and provided credit terms.

Most of the land by far, however, remained in the control of the federal government. Over the years, westerners pressured the federal government to sell land in smaller lots and at lower prices. How successful they were can be seen in the table at the top of page 255.

Requirements for Purchase of Land from the United States Government

Year of Law	*Minimum Number of Acres to Be Bought*	*Minimum Price per Acre*	*Terms*
1785	640	$1.00	Cash only
1796	640	$2.00	One half in cash, balance in one year
1800	320	$2.00	One fourth in cash, one fourth per year
1804	160	$2.00	One fourth in cash, one fourth per year
1820	80	$1.25	Cash only
1832	40	$1.25	Cash only

How much money did a settler need to buy land from the government in 1804? in 1820? in 1832? You can see how these changes in the law might have aided western settlement. Of course, settlers needed money for other things, too—tools, fencing, and so on. But by the early 1800s, farmland was within the reach of thousands, not only to raise crops on but to buy and sell for profit. The federal government set up land offices in various places where settlers could buy their land. During boom years, when land was in great demand, buyers lined up to purchase their land, giving us the phrase that we use today to describe a very good business—"a land-office business." In a two-year period during the land boom of the 1830s, the United States government sold 40 million acres (16 million ha) of land to settlers.

The growth of towns and cities. As settlers occupied the farmlands of the West, towns developed to provide goods and services to farmers. Some towns—like St. Louis, Cincinnati, and Pittsburgh—started as trading or military posts along rivers and at key road crossings. In some areas, towns were started even before the arrival of many farmers. Speculators bought land at places they thought would make good town sites and then advertised heavily, assuring buyers that the sites were certain to become great cities. Some places did. Most did not. Those people who guessed right became wealthy. The others moved on again to try their luck at other places.

The Erie Canal contributed greatly to the growth of towns and cities along its path. Buffalo, on Lake Erie, boomed. It was at the western end of the canal. Only a small village in 1780, Buffalo grew to a town of 12,000 by 1832. Rochester, New York, also owed much of its early growth to its location near the canal. By increasing traffic on the Great Lakes, the canal was responsible for the growth of a number of cities on the lakes. Cleveland, Ohio, hardly a village before the canal

7. DISCUSSION / USING A TABLE Ask students why it was necessary that the federal government change its requirements for purchase of land in the early 1800s. Have students answer the questions at the beginning of the first column on page 255, using the table above. After discussing the information presented in the table, ask students what effects they think the changes in requirements would have on the American frontier.

Background Information

3. THE FIRST STEAMBOAT In 1787 on the Delaware River, John Fitch built and launched the first mechanically successful steamboat. This was twenty years before Robert Fulton's *Clermont* made its famous trip. Fitch's boat had twelve long paddles, six on each side. It moved on the same principle as a canoe, but the paddles were powered by steam. In 1788, Fitch started the first regular passenger service between Philadelphia and Burlington, New Jersey. This and another, later attempt failed financially because of lack of interest. Steamboats built by Fulton and other inventors were successful business operations because people were ready for them by that time and the need was clearly established.

LESSON 3 *(2 days)*

Performance Objectives

1. To describe orally or in writing the injustices suffered by American Indians as the frontier moved westward.
2. To identify the attitude of white Americans toward the Indians in the nineteenth century.

Famous People

Andrew Jackson, William H. Harrison

Vocabulary

Native Americans, Battle of Fallen Timbers, Treaty of Greenville, Battle of Tippecanoe, "permanent Indian frontier," Indian Territory, Trail of Tears, Seminole, racism

Activities

1. FILM *Westward Expansion,* American History series (25 minutes, color; McGraw-Hill) traces the westward growth of the United States from the first colonial rumbles of discontent to the laying of the transcontinental railroad and the eventual disappearance of the "Old West." The film also contains an excellent section on the displacement of the American Indian.

2. CREATIVE EXPRESSION After the students have read the lesson, ask them to describe the injustices suffered by the Indians as the nation's frontier was pushed steadily westward. The description may take the form of any creative written or artistic endeavor that suits each student's talent and interest. Arrange to display the work.

At Lockport, New York, on the Erie Canal, a boat carrying passengers approaches the locks to be "lifted" upward. The steep incline there required locks at five levels.

opened, was a thriving city by 1840. Detroit and Milwaukee had a similar growth.

CHECKUP

1. How did the invention of the cotton gin affect western settlement?
2. What is meant by the term *Transportation Revolution?* In what ways did this development aid western growth?
3. How did the federal government's land policies affect western settlement?

LESSON 3

Pushing the Indians Westward

Americans were fond of talking about the "empty" continent that lay to the west. Thomas Jefferson wrote cheerfully in 1801 about settling "the extensive country still remaining vacant within our limits." Of course, as Jefferson and every frontier family knew, the continent was not empty at all. Indians inhabited much of it. Western settlement could advance only as the native Americans were moved out of the way.

Jefferson had written earlier that "it may be taken for a certainty that not a foot of land will ever be taken from the Indians without their own consent." That was an odd statement even then, since so much had already been taken without the consent of the Indians. In any case, American behavior made a mockery of Jefferson's statement. Time after time, white settlers pushed into Indian land and then cried "treachery" when the Indians resisted. Thousands on both sides paid with their lives in warfare that has few rivals for cruelty.

To satisfy the settlers' hunger for more land, the United States government pushed the Indians farther and farther to the West. The history of western advance can be told as a romantic story of a people on the move, clearing land, enduring hardships, and conquering a continent. It can also be told as an endless succession of broken treaties with Indians. Both stories are true.

Treaties—made and broken. After the American Revolution, the United States government had made a number of treaties with Indian tribes living within the boundaries it had won at the Peace of Paris. In each case, white settlers were forbidden to cross the treaty lines. They soon did, however, and fighting broke out. For a while the Indians held their own, and in 1791 and 1792 they defeated United States forces in a series of battles in the Ohio Territory. But in 1794 they were defeated at the battle of Fallen Timbers by General "Mad Anthony" Wayne. A year later, twelve tribes in the Northwest Territory signed the Treaty of Greenville with the United States by which they gave up most of the region. This treaty set a boundary between the Indian lands and the lands open for settlement. It was only then that settlers poured into the Ohio Territory in large numbers.

The years from 1800 to the 1830s were a disaster for the Indians. In the first decade, a dozen tribes were defeated in battles with the United States Army. In 1803, tribes in Indiana Territory were forced to sign a treaty giving up some of the lands granted to them only eight years earlier in the Treaty of Greenville.

For a brief time it appeared that the Indians might successfully draw a line. But the battle of Tippecanoe in 1811, followed by the death of Tecumseh in 1813 (see page 228), ended that hope. At about the same time, General Andrew Jackson was crushing the Creek Indians in Alabama Territory and forcing them from their lands. Jackson and General William H. Harrison, the hero of Tippecanoe, would later become Presidents of the United States. They owed much of their popularity to their reputations as Indian fighters.

Indian Territory. In 1825 Congress adopted a new Indian policy. It set aside land west of the Mississippi River, in present-day Oklahoma, to which all Indian tribes east of the river were to move. This was to be the "permanent Indian frontier." The lands would be "secured and guaranteed to them," with no white settlers allowed.

Indian nations to the East were pressured to give up their homelands in exchange for land in the Indian Territory. If they chose not to move, it was made clear that they would have to abide by

3. RESEARCH / ROLE-PLAYING Using *The Annals of America* (Chicago: Encyclopaedia Britannica, 1968) and other reference books with good primary source material, have students research the attitudes of white Americans toward the Indians in the nineteenth century. After the students have collected data, assign them to role-play characters from this time in history to show the various attitudes. They might portray members of a frontier family traveling west in a covered-wagon caravan, government spokespersons and politicians, merchants in western towns, and army scouts. Encourage those students who participate in this activity to develop specific attitudes toward the Indians. Be sure that some people speak out against the mistreatment and injustices.

4. CROSSWORD PUZZLE Have students use the specific vocabulary from this *chapter* to build crossword puzzles. After they have finished their puzzles, let students exchange them with partners and have the fun of trying to solve each other's puzzles.

5. WHAT IF? On page 257 a reference is made to a statement by Thomas Jefferson: "It may be taken for a certainty that not a foot of land will ever be taken from the Indians without their own consent." Ask students to discuss what might have happened if Jefferson's promise had been kept by the government. How might the history of America be different today?

Background Information

SEQUOYA After students have read President Jackson's comments on page 259, tell them about the Cherokee Indian named Sequoya, who created the Cherokee alphabet. As an adult, Sequoya came in contact with many white people and wished to learn the secret of their superior power. He became convinced that their secret was written language, which allowed them to accumulate and transmit knowledge far better than by memory or word of mouth. About 1809, Sequoya began working systematically to develop a written language for the Cherokees, experimenting first with pictographs and later with symbols representing the syllables of the spoken language. Twelve years after setting himself this task, Sequoya had perfected 86 letters, representing all the syllables of the Cherokee language.

The simplicity of his written system meant that pupils could learn it rapidly, and soon Cherokees throughout the nation were teaching it to one another. The tribe set up schools to teach Sequoya's alphabet, and it published books and newspapers in the Cherokee language. In 1827, the Cherokees organized a government with a written constitution. This was too much for the state of Georgia, and it demanded the Cherokees' land and the removal of the Cherokees to Indian Territory. After a bitter legal fight, in which President Jackson sympathized with Georgia, a treaty of cession was made in 1835. Within the next three years, all the Cherokees, with the exception of a few in North Carolina, were removed to the Indian Territory.

the laws and the ways of the settlers. Desiring to keep their own culture, the Indians had little choice. In the eight years that Jackson was President, Indian tribes signed 94 treaties, all of which added up to a transfer of millions of acres from Indian nations to the United States government. Having signed, they set out for Indian Territory. Indians called it the Trail of Tears. About 25 percent of the Cherokees and the Creeks who set out on the sad journey died along the way.

To the north, the Sauk and Fox tribes suffered the same fate as the southern Indians. They were removed from their lands in the upper Mississippi Valley. By 1840, all Indian tribes except the Seminoles in Florida had been pushed to areas beyond the Mississippi. In a series of fierce battles between 1835 and 1842, the Seminoles, too, were crushed, and their land was opened to white settlers.

A few whites spoke out against this treatment of the native Americans. One of them was James Barbour, Secretary of War under President John Quincy Adams. He wrote bitterly that "our promises have been broken . . . the happiness of the Indian is a cheap sacrifice to the acquisition of new lands."

The Seminoles attack an Army fort in Florida about 1835. Most of them were later forced to move to the West. In 1970 the Seminoles were awarded $12 million for the lands taken from them.

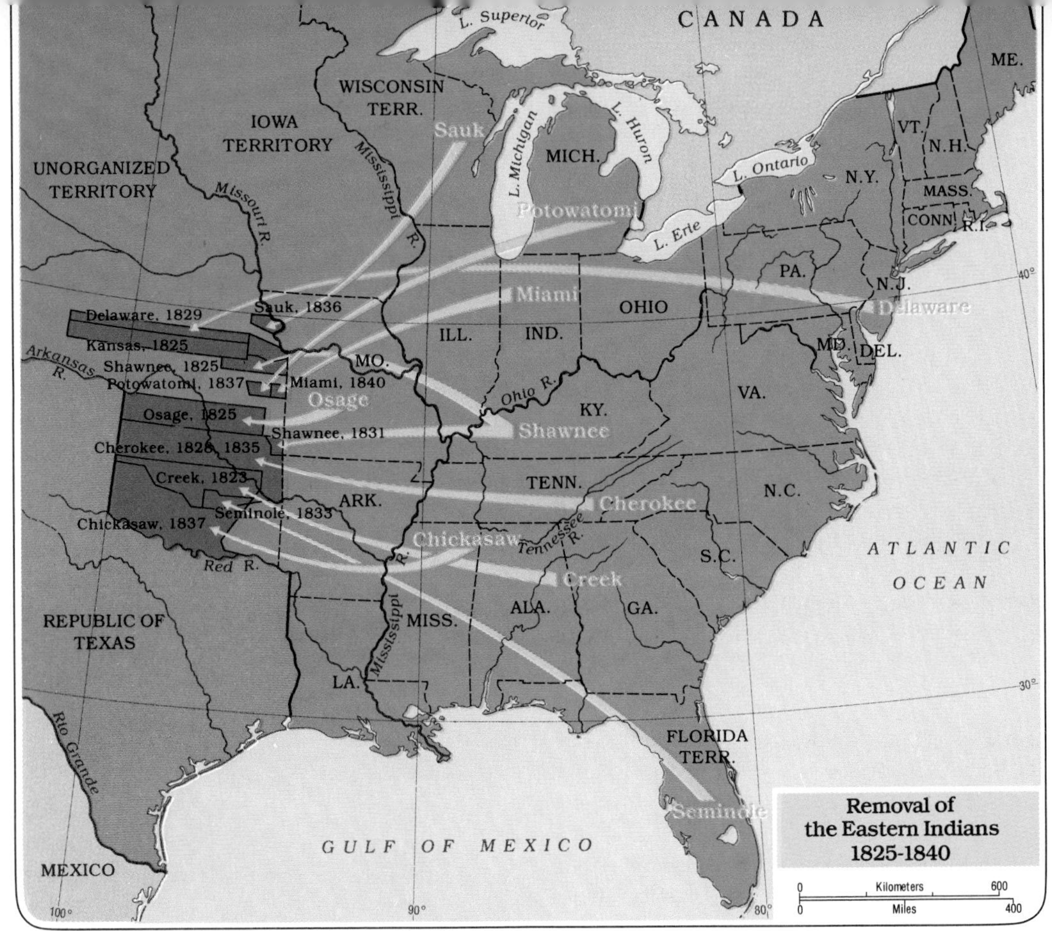

By 1840, most of the Indians east of the Mississippi had been forced to give up their lands and go to present-day Oklahoma. The Cherokees called their route to the West the Trail of Tears. The Seminoles resisted strongly, and a few hundred were allowed to stay in Florida.

But to most Americans, Indians were simply "wretched savages" who stood in the way of "civilization, of science, and of true religion."

The racism that infected white America's dealings with the Indians was never expressed more clearly than by President Jackson in 1833.

> They have neither the intelligence, the industry, the moral habits, nor the desire of improvement which are essential to any favorable change in their existence. Established in the midst of another and a superior race . . . they must necessarily yield.

And yield the Indians did. Within seven years of the removal of the Sauk and Fox tribes, there were 75,000 settlers in the Iowa and Wisconsin territories. Ten years later there were a half million. Iowa became a state in 1846; Wisconsin, in 1848. Minnesota, a part of the Wisconsin Territory, gained statehood in 1858.

Sequoya, as his tribe's representative in Washington, D.C., was instrumental in helping to settle bitter differences that arose among the Cherokees after they were forced from their lands. He worked toward the general advancement of Indians and also became an Indian historian.

The giant sequoia trees and Sequoia National Park in California are named in his honor. A statue of Sequoya represents Oklahoma (formerly Indian Territory) in Statuary Hall in the United States Capitol.

6. THOUGHT PROVOKER In *Alistair Cooke's America,* author Cooke writes: "They [the pioneers] were not philosophers or humanitarians. The schoolbooks tend to stress the twenty-four carat integrity of the families inspired by the prospect of free land. But apart from the old soldiers of two wars, and the mountain boys who had also known the Indian as the enemy, there was in any large company of pioneers a generous quota of prodigal sons, land jobbers, cattle thieves, criminals on the hop. They pulled up stakes for the usual wild variety of human motives, and, after an ambush or a scalping or two, they were inclined to think of the red man mostly as a fiend. Samuel Eliot Morison, with his usual sense of reality, has said it harshly and truly: 'These children of nature, white and red, could no more be made to respect a treaty than dogs can be kept from fighting by the friendship of their masters.' "

Ask the students to discuss Morison's statement in light of the fact that treaties were made in Washington but had to be carried out and lived on the frontier.

Answers To Review Questions

1. Americans are a people who have already broken ties with their ancestral homes. Thus, with no ties to any particular place, they are always on the move. Furthermore, American culture stresses the importance of seizing the opportunity that arises. This often means that people must move to another part of the country or a different city. Thus, Americans have grown accustomed to change as a natural part of life.

2. Hunters and trappers were the first whites to enter an area and mark trails. After the fur supply ran out, they departed, leaving no permanent settlement behind. Then came the men and women pioneers, who were often squatters. Although they erected shelters and cleared small patches of land on which to plant crops, eventually they moved on. Last came the permanent settlers, who bought their land and continued to improve their houses and fields.

3. (a) With Eli Whitney's cotton gin, one person could clean fifty pounds of cotton in a day. This revolutionary process made cotton raising profitable, and the production of cotton rose rapidly to meet the demand. Because cotton farming used up the fertility in the soil in just a few years, southern planters began to move westward in search of rich new lands. **(b)** The invention of the steamboat turned rivers into two-way avenues of commerce. With steamboats plying the waters of nearly every river in the country, Westerners had a way to ship farm goods to market. Thus more people began to move westward and farm for a living.

Osceola led the Seminoles in their resistance to moving west. When invited to discuss peace under a flag of truce, he was treacherously siezed and thrown into prison, where he died.

Farther south, planters quickly moved into the rich cotton lands after the departure of the Indians. Mississippi's population, 136,000 in 1830, increased by more than 200,000 in ten years. Arkansas, a territory of 30,000 in 1830, more than tripled its population in the next ten years and became a state in 1836. Florida, where the Seminoles had been crushed in 1842, became a state three years later.

The first American West was created, as you have seen, by the optimism, drive, and greed of a people on the move. In time, these people demanded a hand in shaping the policies of the federal government. The election of the first Westerner as President, Andrew Jackson, was a sign of that section's arrival in national politics. With that arrival, the old balance between northern and southern states was upset. You will read about these developments in the next chapter.

CHECKUP

1. In what respects were the 30 years or so after 1800 "a disaster for the Indians"?
2. What effect did the Indian policy adopted by Congress in 1825 have on native American tribes?
3. How did most Americans attempt to justify their treatment of the Indians?

Key Facts from Chapter 12

1. During colonial times, the Appalachian Mountains were the greatest obstacle to westward settlement by Americans.
2. After the American Revolution, hunters and trappers moved across the mountains, followed by restless pioneers, and finally by permanent settlers.
3. Among the developments that helped bring about movement into the West were the inventions of the cotton gin, the steamboat, and the railroad, and the building of canals.
4. The policy of the United States government in making western lands available at low cost led many Americans to move to the frontier.
5. As settlers moved into the West, the Indians were ruthlessly forced off their homelands and made to settle in other areas.

★ REVIEWING THE CHAPTER ★

People, Places, and Events

Sunbelt *P. 243*
Daniel Boone *P. 245*
Appalachian Mountains *P. 246*
Proclamation of 1763 *P. 246*
National Road *P. 251*
Robert Fulton *P. 251*
Erie Canal *P. 251*
Speculators *P. 254*
Fallen Timbers *P. 257*
Treaty of Greenville *P. 257*
Andrew Jackson *P. 257*
Trail of Tears *P. 258*

Review Questions

1. What explanations does the text offer for why Americans in general are such a restless people? *P. 244* Les. 1
2. Describe the typical pattern of settlement of western lands. *P. 247* Les. 1
3. Tell in what specific way each development encouraged western settlement of the United States: **(a)** invention of the cotton gin, **(b)** invention of the steamboat, **(c)** canal building, **(d)** railroad building. *Pp. 249—253* Les. 2
4. How did the Erie Canal contribute to New York City's development as an important trade center? *Pp. 251—252* Les. 2
5. How was railroad construction financed in the nineteenth century? *P. 253* Les. 2
6. Why was the federal government's land policy of 1785 unsatisfactory for the ordinary settler? *P. 254* Les. 2
7. What was the attitude of white Americans toward the Indians in the nineteenth century? How did this attitude affect government policy toward the Indians? *Pp. 257–259* Les. 3

Chapter Test

*On a separate piece of paper, write **T** if the statement is true and **F** if the statement is false.*

1. Many white people justified the removal of Indians from their lands on the grounds that they were ignorant savages unable to improve the land. T
2. Andrew Jackson and William Henry Harrison first gained national attention as Indian fighters. T
3. The Seminoles of Florida were the last tribe to resist the federal government's efforts to move them west of the Mississippi to Indian Territory. T
4. The National Road, built by the federal government to connect Washington, D.C., with Philadelphia, made it less expensive to ship goods between the two cities. F
5. Eli Whitney's cotton gin was largely responsible for improving the prosperity of the South. T
6. Fallen Timbers was an important lumbering company that helped western settlers clear their land for homesteading and farming. F
7. The Appalachian Mountains kept people from moving westward until the middle of the nineteenth century. F
8. The Erie Canal, built by engineer Robert Fulton and his crew, connected Buffalo and Albany. F
9. Between 1785 and the 1830s, the federal government eased the requirements for land purchase to enable more settlers to own land. T
10. The Sunbelt occupies about a third of the United States and is the fastest-growing part of the country today. T

(c) The building of canals gave farmers another way to ship their goods to market. In addition, canals reduced the cost of shipping by land by 90 percent. These factors encouraged people to settle farther west, secure in the knowledge that they could send their products to market cheaply. **(d)** Railroads opened up western areas that were far from rivers and canals by providing cheap transportation for products.
4. The Erie Canal connected the farmers and merchants of the Old Northwest with the markets in New York City.
5. Private investors from the United States and England put up most of the money. States, cities, and the federal government also provided funds.
6. In 1785 a settler had to buy a section (640 acres) at $1 per acre. That was frequently more land than a settler needed, and $640 was more than a person could afford. By 1832, the required number of acres to be bought had been reduced to 40, at $1.25 per acre. Most people could afford $50.
7. White Americans generally thought of the Indians as ignorant savages "who stood in the way of civilization, of science, and of true religion." With this attitude, most Americans agreed that the Indians must be pushed farther and farther to the West in order to make way for white settlers. Hence, government treaties were made and broken by the whites. Time after time, Indian tribes were forced to give up their ancestral lands and move to Indian Territory.

Background Information

PICTURE James Henry Beard painted this picture of North Carolina emigrants in 1845. This family was typical of the many restless Americans in the nineteenth century who were willing to move in search of a better life for themselves.

CHAPTER 13

THE AGE OF JACKSON

LESSON 1 *(1 to 2 days)*

Performance Objectives

1. To list and explain the major sectional issues confronting the nation in 1820.
2. To explain orally the issues present in the election of 1824.

Famous People

James Tallmadge, Henry Clay, John Quincy Adams, John C. Calhoun

Vocabulary

Sectionalism, electoral vote, tariffs, slavery, internal improvement, three-cornered rivalry, three-fifths clause, Missouri Compromise, American System, "corrupt bargain," National Republicans, tariff of 1828 (Tariff of Abominations), nullify, compact, states' rights, South Carolina Exposition and Protest, mudslinging

LESSON 1

FROM THE TIME of the Revolution, the West was a factor in national politics. The two major acts of Congress under the Articles of Confederation had to do with western lands. Getting the British out of the West and pushing back the Indians through war and treaty were important aims of the government under President Washington. It was the votes of the two western states of Kentucky and Tennessee that made Thomas Jefferson President. Later still, it was Westerners who led the cry for war against Great Britain in 1812. Even so, with few states and few seats in Congress, Westerners had little direct voice in politics at the national level.

The Growth of Sectionalism

The minor role of the West in national politics was sharply changed between 1810 and 1820 by the flood of restless Americans that rolled onto the lands between the Appalachians and the Mississippi River. During those years the population of the West went from one million to two million. Five new western states entered the Union. By 1820, there were three sections of the country with enough votes in Congress and enough electoral votes to have a voice in national politics. The North, the South, and the West each had developed differently. Each had its own special needs and desires. Each, therefore, now tried to use its say in national politics to advance its own interests and attain the goals that it felt were important.

Issues between North and South. The chief interest of the North was the growth of its industries. The North wanted Congress to place high import taxes, or tariffs, on goods brought in from other countries. These high tariffs would bring in money for the government. Their main purpose, however, would be to make the price of foreign goods so high that those goods could not compete with the products of northern industries.

The South, on the other hand, was bitterly opposed to high tariffs. As a planting rather than a manufacturing section, it bought its manufactured goods elsewhere, often from England. High tariffs pushed the prices of imported goods up to, or above, the prices of northern-made goods. Thus, whether southerners bought in the North or from England, they paid more because of the tariffs.

The South had another reason for opposing high tariffs. The South exported two thirds of its cotton to England. If Americans bought fewer goods from England because of high tariffs, England would be able to buy less cotton from the South.

A goal of even greater importance to the South was to protect slavery. The South wanted the federal government to do nothing that would interfere with slavery or with its spread into new territories. Northerners had no wish to interfere with slavery in the southern states. But they did oppose its spread into the territories, for they did not want more slave states to be created.

Activities

1. READING FOR INFORMATION / USING A CHART Assign students to read the lesson and to make charts showing the major sectional issues confronting the nation in 1820. Have students compare the attitudes of people in the three sections—North, South, and West—toward each of the following issues: **(a)** tariffs, **(b)** slavery, **(c)** internal improvements, and **(d)** land policy.

The West's interests. Slavery and the tariffs, burning issues in the two older sections, held little interest for Westerners. They were far more concerned with issues that bore on the development of their own section. In Chapter 12, you read of two of these. Westerners wanted internal improvements—roads and canals that would get their goods to eastern markets directly, quickly, and cheaply. Even more, they wanted the federal government to sell western lands cheaply, or even to give them away.

The North was generally in favor of internal improvements, for roads and canals would lead to more trade between the West and such states as New York and Pennsylvania. The South was more divided on this issue. Although some Southerners were in favor of internal improvements, others complained. They declared that the money paid by the federal government to build these improvements came from the tariff duties they, the Southerners, were paying. Still the issue of internal improvements was not as important to either of the older sections as it was to the West.

On land policy, neither North nor South agreed with the West. To both older sections, western land was part of the national treasure, to be sold at good prices. The North was especially opposed to a cheap land policy. Northerners felt it would encourage people to move west. That, they feared, would reduce the Northeast's population and thus its representation in Congress. Northern manufacturers felt, too, that such migration would make labor for their factories more scarce and costly.

Two other subjects of great importance to the West were banking and Indian policy. You have already read about the West's demand for Indian removal. Later in this chapter you will read about the West's position on banking and credit.

These were the issues at the bottom of the three-cornered rivalry that had been created by a people on the move. No one section was strong enough to control the federal government, but any two could outvote the third.

The explosive slavery issue. The strongest rivalry was between the North and the South. They became involved at this time in the first of the sectional issues to explode into national politics. This was the issue of the spread of slavery into the western territories.

In 1819 the territory of Missouri asked to enter the Union as a state under a constitution that allowed slavery. Congressman James Tallmadge of New York proposed an amendment to admit Missouri only if slavery were gradually abolished there. The House of Representatives approved Tallmadge's amendment, but the Senate blocked it. The debate—and the deadlock—went on for more than a year.

Tallmadge's amendment brought into focus differences between North and South on the issue of slavery. Missouri was part of the Louisiana Purchase, where slavery had existed under the French. Since the purchase, in 1803, Congress had made no law about slavery in the Louisiana Territory. Most people, however, thought of the Ohio River as the unofficial boundary between South and North—between slave states and free states. Missouri lay north of the latitude of the Ohio River. If Missouri came in as a slave state, argued Northerners, then other areas north of that latitude might become slave states, too. If so, the South would have greater power in Congress. Northerners complained that the South already had more seats in the House of Representatives than it was fairly entitled to. This was a result of the three-fifths clause in the Constitution (see page 166).

Southerners, on the other hand, were concerned that the population of the northern states was growing much more rapidly than that of the southern states. In the House of Representatives, members from the North outnumbered those from the South, 105 to 81, and that margin seemed sure to grow. With two senators from each state, the Senate was evenly divided, with eleven free states and eleven slave states. Slaveholders felt it was crucial that Northerners not get an advantage in the Senate, for then the North would control both bodies of Congress. It would then be able to pass laws harmful to the interests of the South.

The Missouri Compromise. Henry Clay of Kentucky, the Speaker of the House, finally arranged a compromise. Clay put the nation's interests, as he understood them, ahead of sectional interests. Maine, which had long been a part of Massachusetts, was also ready for statehood, so it was agreed to admit the two

In 1820 the Missouri Compromise seemed to solve the issue of the spread of slavery. But the solution was only temporary, and the issue would arise again after the Mexican War.

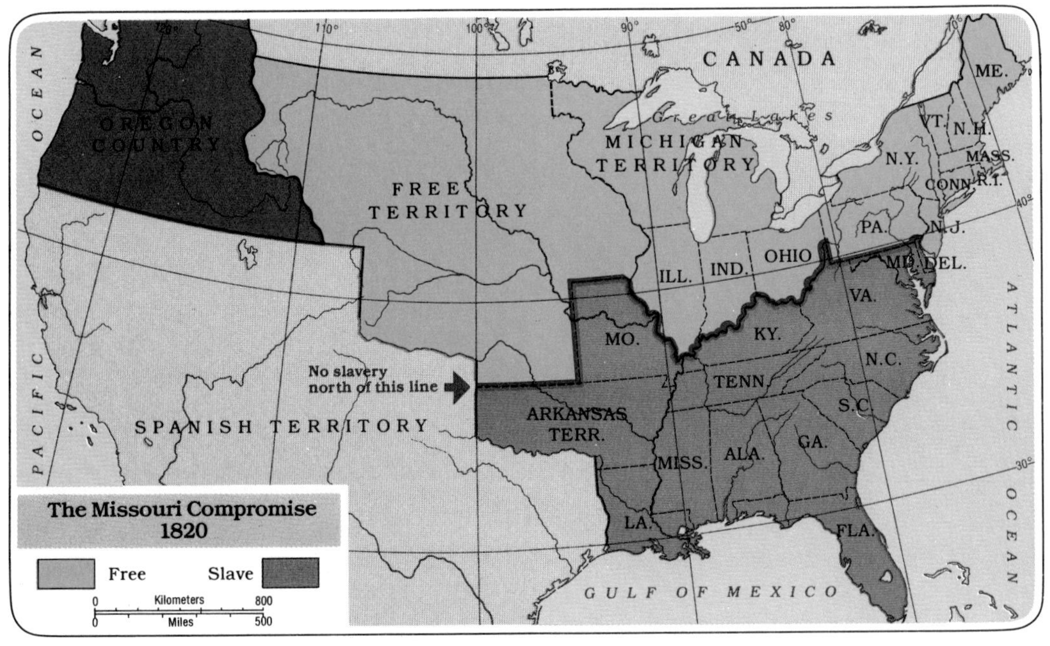

2. USING A MAP In 1820, of the original thirteen states, New Hampshire, Massachusetts, Rhode Island, Connecticut, New York, New Jersey, and Pennsylvania were free states (no slavery allowed). Delaware, Maryland, Virginia, North Carolina, South Carolina, and Georgia were slave states. Of the new states added to the Union after 1789, Vermont, Ohio, Indiana, and Illinois were free. Kentucky, Tennessee, Louisiana, Mississippi, and Alabama were slave states. That was the tally in 1820—eleven free and eleven slave.

On outline maps of the United States, have students use one color for the free states and another for the slave states in 1820. Have them use still another color for Missouri. Then ask the students to explain the controversy that developed when the territory of Missouri asked to enter the Union as a slave state and to tell what the resulting compromise was. After discussing the significance of the boundary established at latitude 36°30′, have students draw a dark line along that boundary (see the map on page 265).

You may wish to display the maps at the completion of this activity. Ask students to save their maps for comparison with the map of the Union just before the Civil War.

3. RESEARCH / ORAL REPORTS Ask several of the students to read from Commager's *Documents of American History* and report on the following subjects in Document 121: **(a)** the Tallmadge Amendment, **(b)** the Taylor Amendment, **(c)** the Thomas Amendment, **(d)** the Missouri Enabling Act, **(e)** selections from the Constitution of Missouri, and **(f)** Resolution for the Admission of Missouri. In addition to providing interesting background material on the Missouri Compromise, these documents increase student understanding of the legislative process.

4. LISTENING FOR INFORMATION When Thomas Jefferson (at age seventy-six) learned of the conflict over Missouri, he wrote to John Holmes: "But this momentous question, like a firebell in the night, awakened and filled me with terror. I considered it at once as the knell of the Union." Ask one of the better readers in the class to read this famous letter aloud. It is found on pages 603–604 in *The Annals of America*, Vol. 4, 1797–1820.

Ask students why Jefferson was so fearful. Why did he use the phrase "a firebell in the night?"

together, Missouri as a slave state and Maine as a free state. Thus the balance in the Senate would be kept. It was agreed, too, that slavery would not be allowed in the rest of the Louisiana Purchase north of latitude 36°30′, which served as Missouri's southern boundary.

The 1824 presidential candidates. The rivalry among the sections could be seen most clearly in the presidential contest of 1824. The Federalists were by then no longer a national party. Only the Republican party remained. Four Republicans, however, ran for the Presidency, each representing the outlook of a section. Northerners supported John Quincy Adams, Monroe's Secretary of State and son of the second President. William Crawford of Georgia, Secretary of the Treasury under both Madison and Monroe, spoke for the South. From the rising West came two men, Congressman Henry Clay of Kentucky and Senator Andrew Jackson of Tennessee.

Jackson was popular in the West not for his views—few knew what they were—but for what he was. Born in a cabin in the South Carolina backcountry in 1767, Jackson was a self-made man. By the age of twenty, he was practicing law, and soon afterward he was making money buying and selling land in western Tennessee. Jackson had led an army against the Creek Indians in 1814. He was also the hero of the battle of New Orleans (see page 230). Jackson believed in plain people. He judged people by their achievements, not by their family background. Westerners saw in him a man who shared their beliefs in individualism, equality, and democracy. Jackson's qualities brought him support in other sections of the country as well.

Clay's "American System." Of the four candidates, only Henry Clay had put together a program to appeal to more than one section. Clay called it the American System. It was based on a vision of a growing, self-sufficient America, with each section's interests tied to the well-being of the others. In his plan, a protective tariff would help manufacturing develop in the Northeast and make northern workers prosperous. Western farmers and southern planters would not need to depend on foreign markets, for the Northeast would become a dependable home market for western foodstuffs and southern cotton. Money raised by the tariff would pay for roads and canals that would bring farm goods to the East and manufactured goods to the West cheaply and quickly. A national bank would see that a sound currency and credit system helped the economy of all sections grow. There was less in this program for the South than for the East and West. Still it was the closest thing there was to a national program.

The election of 1824. The outcome of the election followed sectional lines. Adams took the New England states and New York. Crawford, who had suffered a stroke during the campaign, won Georgia and Virginia. Jackson won much of the West and a good part of the South. Clay, who was probably the second choice in most states, was the first choice of only three. The electoral vote stood 99 for Jackson, 84 for Adams, 41 for Crawford, and 37 for Clay.

Since no one had a majority, under the Constitution the House of Representatives had to choose from the top three candidates, with each state having one vote. Jackson's backers said that since he had won the most popular votes, the House should choose him. Clay, however, persuaded his supporters to vote for Adams, who shared many of Clay's ideas about the American System. Adams was thus elected. When Adams appointed Clay his Secretary of State—an office that had been the stepping stone to the Presidency for every President since 1808—Jackson's followers charged that the two had made a "corrupt bargain." There is no evidence that this was true, but the charge dogged Adams throughout his four years in office.

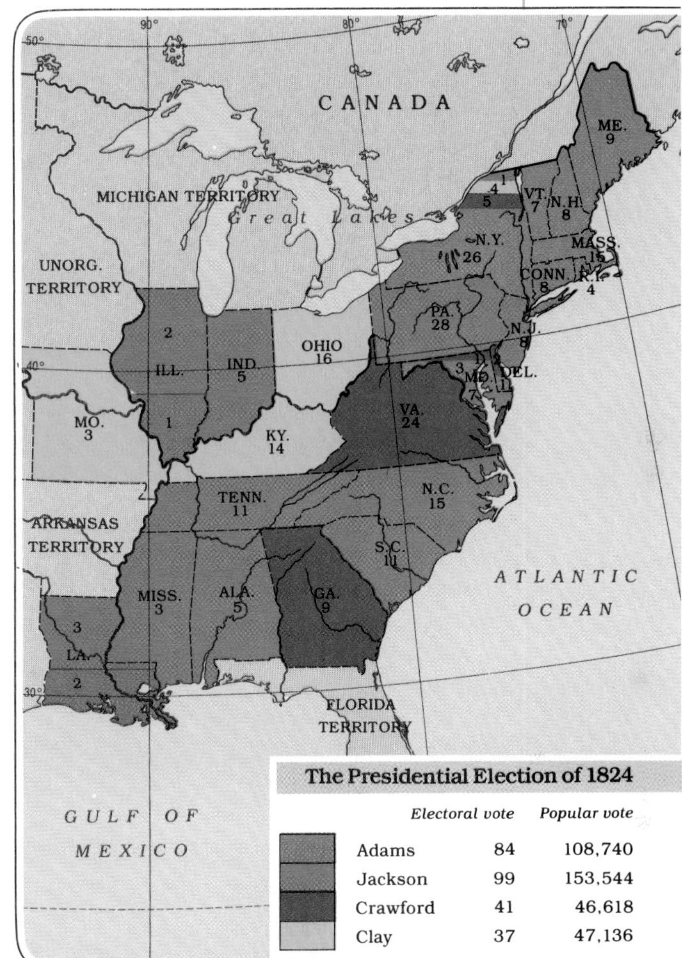

The totals in the key above show why Jackson's supporters were outraged over the outcome of the 1824 election. Jackson received almost 45,000 more popular votes and 15 more electoral votes than did John Quincy Adams.

Adams as Chief Executive. As President, John Quincy Adams showed little interest in gaining advantage for his own section of the country. He tried to be a truly national President. Adams favored internal improvements that would tie the country more closely together. In his belief that the federal government should give encouragement and financial aid to agriculture, science, and education, he was a century ahead of his time.

Except for internal improvements, which Congress supported, Adams made little headway. This was partly due to his own shortcomings as a political leader. Perhaps no President could have succeeded in bridging the sectional differences of the time. But Adams was especially unsuited to the task. A cold and uncompromising man, he lacked the political skills needed to build support for his nationalist views. Moreover, Jackson supporters in Congress had one main goal, and that was to elect their man in 1828. They spent the full four years of Adams's term blocking his

5. **ROLE-PLAYING** Divide the class into five groups and assign each group one of the following: John Quincy Adams, Andrew Jackson, William Crawford, Henry Clay, and members of the press. Each group that represents a presidential candidate in the 1824 election should establish that candidate's identity and be well informed on the issues of the election. The group that represents the press should prepare questions pertaining to the election and the issues involved. When all groups have established their respective roles, have the members of the press pose their questions for the presidental candidates to answer. Encourage the candidates to react to one another's statements.

6. **RESEARCH / ORAL REPORT** For in-depth information about the disputed election of 1824, ask a student to read and report on George Dangerfield's *The Era of Good Feelings* (New York: Harcourt Brace Jovanovich, 1963). This book won the Pulitzer Prize in History in 1953.

★6★

John Quincy Adams

1767–1848

Born in MASSACHUSETTS
In Office 1825–1829
Party NAT. REPUBLICAN

Elected by the House of Representatives after no candidate won a majority of electoral votes. His programs met opposition, and he was defeated in his bid for reelection.

★ ★ ★ ★ ★ ★ ★ ★

plans and trying to embarrass him. By the midpoint of Adams's term, Congress had divided into two groups. Supporters of Adams came to be known as National Republicans, while those backing Jackson took for themselves the old Jeffersonian name of Democratic-Republicans, or more simply, Democrats.

The tariff of 1828. The one important act of Congress in the Adams administration was the tariff bill passed in 1828. This act placed higher rates than ever before on imported manufactured goods. To win western support, it also protected western goods like raw wool and hemp (from which rope was made) from foreign competition. Southern opponents called the law the "Tariff of Abominations."

The most bitter foes of the protective tariff came from southern coastal states. These states were having economic problems and were losing population. The main reason for their troubles was that their cotton lands were wearing out. As a result, their cotton could not compete with cotton raised on the more fertile lands to the west—Alabama, Mississippi, Louisiana, and Missouri. Failing to understand this, however, the leaders of the Southeast fixed the blame for their problems on the tariff. They even argued that the tariff laws were an unconstitutional use of federal power.

Calhoun and states' rights. The Southerner who made the strongest argument against the tariff was John C. Calhoun of South Carolina. In a long statement written in 1828, Calhoun stated that a state had the right to *nullify,* or declare invalid, any federal law it believed to be unconstitutional. This was based on the claim that the Constitution was simply a *compact,* or an agreement, among sovereign states. In entering the Union, so the claim held, the states had not given up their rights. Most especially, they had kept the most important right of all—the right to secede.

This extreme statement of the *states' rights* position was not new in American history. The Virginia and Kentucky resolutions of 1798 had set forth similar views. Some New England Federalists during the War of 1812 had also talked of nullification and secession. Never before, however, had the idea been so fully developed and so carefully argued.

Calhoun's statement, which was called the South Carolina Exposition and Protest, was adopted by the South Carolina legislature in 1828. That body, however, did not try to act upon its theory. Also, Calhoun's authorship was kept secret. The reason was that Calhoun, who was then Adams's Vice President, was running for that office again in 1828, this time on the Democratic ticket with Andrew Jackson. Southerners hoped that he would be able to persuade General Jackson to adopt their point of view on the tariff. Jackson, at the age of sixty-two, was the oldest candidate ever to run for the Presidency. Moreover, he was in poor health: he carried lead in his body from a frontier duel. Many thought he would be a one-term President, at most, and that Calhoun would succeed him.

The election of 1828. The election of 1828 pitted Jackson, the Democrat, against Adams, who was seeking a second term as a National Republican. The campaign was a mudslinging affair that did little credit to either party or candidate. Each side made charges about the honesty, decency, and morality of the other. Jackson supporters painted their man as the champion of ordinary people and Adams as an aristocrat.

In the end, the popular Jackson won a big victory. He carried every part of the country except New England, New Jersey, and Delaware. Westerners had voted for him as a son of their own section. Southern planters felt he would understand their problems, since he, too, was a planter and slaveholder. Small business people looked to him as a self-made man who would encourage opportunity. City workers hoped for his support for certain laws that would improve their lot. Everywhere, Americans saw in Jackson a hero and a man of the people.

CHECKUP

1. What were the major sectional issues that confronted the nation by 1820?
2. Whose supporters made charges of a "corrupt bargain" following the election of 1824? Why?
3. What were the differing views put forth by North and South on the tariff of 1828?

This drawing, mocking John C. Calhoun for his strong stand on states' rights, pictures the South Carolina statesman as the biblical Joshua commanding the sun to stand still.

7. RESEARCH / ORAL REPORTS Following the election of 1824 and the charges of the "corrupt bargain," John Randolph remarked that it was "the combination unheard of till then, of the puritan with the black leg." A duel took place between Henry Clay and Randolph. The Harvard historian Samuel Eliot Morison remarked, "Both were bad shots." Ask several students to investigate this incident. Who was Randolph? If the puritan was John Quincy Adams, why did Randolph call Clay a blackleg?

8. DISCUSSION Today, American business people ask the federal government for protection against televisions, cars, textiles, cameras, etc., that are made abroad and sold in this country at cheaper prices than American-made products. After the students have studied about the Tariff of Abominations and the sectional rifts it caused, have them compare that tariff with a tariff of today. Ask: Who would benefit from a tariff? Who would be hurt? What responsibility does the federal government have to engage in trade with foreign countries? With whom should the United States trade? Why? Is there ever a time when the United States should not engage in foreign trade?

LESSON 2 *(1 to 2 days)*

Performance Objectives

1. To explain orally the meaning of the following statement: ". . . it was not Jackson's election that brought about the rise of the common man. It was, rather, the rise of the common man that made possible Jackson's election to the Presidency." **2.** To write an essay describing Andrew Jackson's Presidency.

Famous People

Robert Y. Hayne, Daniel Webster

Vocabulary

Jacksonian democracy, "rise of the common man," Old Hickory, caucus, nominating convention, spoils system, preemption, graduation, Foot Resolution, nullification, Webster-Hayne debates, secession, "legitimate sphere of State sovereignty," Maysville Road veto, Ordinance of Nullification, Force Bill

LESSON 2

Jacksonian Democracy

"I never saw anything like it before," said Massachusetts Senator Daniel Webster about the crowds that gathered in Washington for Jackson's inauguration on March 4, 1829. "They really seem to think the country is rescued from some dreadful danger." After the swearing-in at the Capitol, the cheering thousands followed the new President to the White House for a celebration. Jackson's supporters paraded across the carpeted floors in muddy boots, knocked over punch bowls, and stood on chairs to get a look at the President. A Washington woman who was present wrote this description of the scene.

> The President, after having been *literally* nearly pressed to death & almost suffocated & torn to pieces by the people in their eagerness to shake hands with Old Hickory. . . . escaped to his lodgings. . . . Cut glass and china to the amount of several thousand dollars had been broken in the struggle to get the refreshments. . . . Ladies fainted, men were seen with bloody noses & such a scene of confusion took place as is impossible to describe,—those who got in could not get out by the door again, but had to scramble out of windows.

"It was a proud day for the people," wrote a supporter of the new President. "General Jackson is *their own* President." But a conservative Supreme Court Justice saw it differently. The rule of "King Mob," he said, had now begun.

Rise of the common man. Jackson's Presidency has often been connected with the phrase "the rise of the common man." What that phrase meant is that in Jackson's time ordinary people came to have a greater say in government than ever before. The colonies and the new states, you will recall, limited voting to taxpayers and owners of property. As late as 1803, only Connecticut, Maryland, Vermont, and the new western state of Ohio allowed all adult white males to vote. In the years following the war of 1812, however, the growing democratic spirit led to broad changes. Between 1816 and 1821, six new western states entered the Union with no property qualifications on voting or holding office. At about the same time, older states dropped these requirements from their constitutions. By the late 1820s, all but a few states allowed all adult white males to vote. Most also dropped religious tests for holding office.

These changes appear far more limited today than they did at that time. The right to vote did not apply to women, who were half the population. It seldom included free blacks. In fact, in those very years, four states *took away* the vote from free blacks. By 1838, blacks could vote only in New England states. Yet in spite of these limits, in no country in the world was democracy more widespread at the time than in the United States. Visitors to America were struck more by this feature than any other. You may remember that the French author Alexis de Tocqueville called his book *Democracy in America.*

A broadening of democracy. Along with broader voting rights came a change in popular attitude that was just as important. In earlier times, you will recall, ordinary people were expected to vote for their "betters"—people of wealth and social position. Even the democratic

Collection of the Boatmen's National Bank of St. Louis

This George Caleb Bingham painting, showing the announcement of election results, catches the spirit of the time when "the common man" came to play a more active role in politics.

Thomas Jefferson expected that ordinary people would be wise enough to choose those with special ability and training as their leaders. By Jackson's time, however, Americans no longer deferred to their betters nor looked to people with special training. Why should they not choose leaders from among their own—people who were like them, who shared their experience, their values, their prejudices?

When people voted for Jackson, they were voting for such a man. He was the first President who did not have a background of social importance or family wealth. Jackson sprang from the plain people. They felt close enough to call him by a nickname—Old Hickory. It would never have occurred to anyone to do that to Washington, Adams, or any other earlier President.

Such changes in popular thinking broadened the meaning of democracy. Candidates for office now had to appeal to the desires, the pride, and the prejudices of ordinary people. After this time, it would be impossible to imagine someone like Alexander Hamilton—who had said, "Your people, sir, is a great beast"—long remaining in politics.

Changes in nominating and electing. The way in which Presidents were nominated and elected also became

Background Information

1. GEORGE CALEB BINGHAM (1811–1879) During the bustling decades of the mid-1800s, Bingham roamed the Missouri countryside with pencil and sketchbook, recording hundreds of local happenings and characters. From these sketches and notes, he later worked up oils, reproducing busy, bright-hued scenes like the one shown in this picture. His election scenes are remarkable studies of life in frontier towns. Bingham was an American regional artist who realistically and objectively depicted everything from drunks to flea-bitten dogs. His work reflects more than his own state and people.

In June 1978, a George Caleb Bingham painting of a Mississippi River scene ("The Jolly Flatboatmen, No. 2") set an auction record for American art when it was sold for $980,000. The previous high price ($320,220) had been paid in June 1976 for James Peale's "Washington and His Generals at Yorktown," painted in the eighteenth century. This price for Bingham's painting also set a new level for American artwork of the nineteenth century, well above the $275,000 paid for Winslow Homer's "The Angler" at an auction in May 1978.

2. "TO THE VICTOR BELONG THE SPOILS" This phrase was coined in 1832 by Senator William L. Marcy of New York, a state in which the spoils system was firmly established. Marcy made the following statement in the course of the debate on the nomination of Martin Van Buren as Minister to England: "It may be, sir, that the politicians of New York are not so fastidious as some gentlemen are, as to disclosing the principles on which they act. They boldly *preach* what they *practice.* When they are contending for *victory,* they avow their intention of enjoying the fruits of it. If they are defeated, they expect to retire from office. If they are successful, they claim, as a matter of right, the advantages of success. They see nothing wrong in the rule that to the VICTOR belong the spoils of the ENEMY."

more democratic. Since Jefferson's time, every candidate for President had been chosen in a *caucus,* or meeting of the party's congressmen. This method allowed a few insiders to keep control. The caucus system broke down in the 1820s and was soon replaced by the nominating convention. First used in 1831 by a minor party, the Anti-Masons, the nominating convention was adopted by both major parties the following year. The convention allowed much broader participation in the choice of candidates than had the caucus.

The manner of choosing presidential electors—those people who actually cast the ballots in the electoral college—also changed. By 1828, South Carolina was the only state in which electors were still chosen by the legislature. In all other states, they were elected by the people. These electors were publicly pledged to vote for one or another of the presidential candidates. This was very nearly the same as having the people vote for the President directly.

All these changes had happened, or were well underway, before the election of 1828. Thus it should be clear that it was not Jackson's election that brought about the rise of the common man. It was, rather, the rise of the common man that made possible Jackson's election to the Presidency.

There was an irony in this, for in many ways Jackson himself was anything but a common man. Despite his humble beginnings, he owned a large cotton plantation and slaves, and had long been a member of Tennessee's upper class. Many who knew Jackson commented on how he carried himself like an aristocrat.

The spoils system. Yet it is certainly true that Jackson glorified the common man and thought of himself as the champion of ordinary people. "Never for a moment believe," he said once, "that the great body of the citizens . . . can deliberately intend to do wrong." His faith in the ability of ordinary folks can be seen in his policy on federal officeholding. Shortly after taking office, Jackson replaced about 900 of the 10,000 federal jobholders, many of whom had opposed his election. He replaced them with his own supporters. Turning out officeholders and putting one's own supporters in was an old practice, and every previous President had done it. During his two terms, Jackson replaced 10 percent of the federal civil employees, about the same percentage that Thomas Jefferson had replaced. Jackson's political friends frankly justified the practice on the simple ground that "to the victor belong the spoils." From that phrase has come the term *spoils system.*

But Jackson explained the practice in democratic terms. No officeholder, he said, had a right to keep a government job as though it was private property. In fact, the public would gain from removing those who had stayed in office so long that they forgot they were supposed to serve the people. Most important, no class of people had a monopoly on the skills needed to work for the government. "The duties of all public officers are . . . so plain and simple," said Jackson, "that ordinary people of intelligence could perform them." Jackson further argued that it was desirable to "rotate" the offices among many people, so that more could have this "valuable training in citizenship." It is not a criticism of Jackson to note that many politicians then and later would use "rotation in office" not for "citizenship" but as a way of letting as many supporters as possible get on the federal payroll.

Jackson and the Presidency. Jackson brought to the Presidency a different view of that office than earlier Presidents had held. Congressmen might vote the interests of their districts, and senators of their states. But according to Jackson's view, only the President, elected by all the people, could look after the interests of all. To do that, the office of President must be one of strength and power. The President must make his own judgment of the meaning of the Constitution or of the wisdom of a bill. He must not simply accept the views of the other branches of government.

As a result, Jackson vetoed twelve bills—more than all the Presidents before him put together. He also tangled with the Supreme Court more than once. Because of these views, Jackson's foes called him King Andrew I.

Continued sectionalism. The election of Andrew Jackson, with support from nearly every part of the country, did not mean the end of the sectional struggle. Indeed, during Jackson's Presidency the struggle for sectional advantage heightened.

To their demands for lower land prices, Westerners had recently added two new proposals intended to speed settlement of their section. One proposal called *preemption*, was to allow frontier squatters first right to buy the land they were living on when the government put

This bitter Whig cartoon pictures Andrew Jackson on a pig growing fat on political spoils.

it up for sale. The second was to reduce the price of unsold land each year, with the government giving away any that was left over after four or five years. This plan was called *graduation*. Neither became law during Jackson's Presidency, but Congress did provide for preemption after 1841.

Northeastern interests, on the other hand, continued to oppose the rapid settlement of the West. In December 1829, Senator Samuel Foot of Connecticut proposed that the sale of western lands be stopped for the time being. Westerners in the Senate were enraged. Led by Senator Thomas Hart Benton of Missouri, they charged that the Foot Resolution was part of a manufacturer's plot to keep labor in the Northeast and prevent the growth of the West.

Activities

1. LISTENING FOR INFORMATION Read to the students or arrange for them to read "The Common Man's Hero" by Arthur Schlesinger, Jr., in *The American Story: The Age of Exploration to the Age of the Atom.*

2. DISCUSSION After students have read the lesson, ask them to discuss the statement on page 272 of the text: "Thus it should be clear that it was not Jackson's election that brought about the rise of the common man. It was, rather, the rise of the common man that made possible Jackson's election to the Presidency." Have students identify and explain the various changes that occurred in the 1820s that led to a broadening of democracy.

To extend this activity, discuss how a presidential candidate is selected. Begin with a comparison of today's process and that at the time of Washington's selection. Show the changes that took place in this process of selection from Washington to Jackson. Samuel Eliot Morison's *The Oxford History of the American People* (New York: Oxford University Press, 1965) will be of help for background information.

3. **ESSAY** Based on the information in this lesson, have students write essays describing Andrew Jackson's Presidency and character. Encourage students to be objective in their writing and to support their ideas with facts.

4. **RESEARCH / ORAL REPORTS** Select students to read and report on the following important documents, which may be found in Commager's *Documents of American History:* 138, "Jackson's Veto of Maysville Road Bill"; 143, "South Carolina Ordinance of Nullification"; 144, "Jackson's Proclamation to the People of South Carolina"; 145, "South Carolina's Reply to Jackson's Proclamation"; 146, "Nullification of the Force Bill."

Hayne versus Webster. Seeing a chance to split the North and West, the South entered the debate. The North's policies, argued Senator Robert Y. Hayne of South Carolina, were a threat to both the South and the West. Should not the two sections therefore make common cause? Let the West join in opposing high tariffs, and in exchange, the South would support a cheap land policy.

Hayne then went on to invite the West to support the idea of nullification—that is, that within its own borders a state could nullify a federal law. This brought Senator Daniel Webster of Massachusetts into the debate. Soon the Foot Resolution and the question of land policy were forgotten as the debate turned to the meaning of the Constitution and the nature of the Union. For nearly a week Hayne and Webster argued their views before a packed gallery in the Senate. Hayne, repeating Calhoun's arguments, insisted that the Union was made up of sovereign states. Each, he said, was free to nullify an act of Congress or even to pull out of the Union. Webster insisted the opposite—that the Union had been formed by the people, not by the states; that it was perpetual; and that nullification and secession were not possible.

Although the debate did not solve anything, it drew the issue squarely. Either the states were finally sovereign or the nation was. It remained to be seen if the West would accept the South's hand and Calhoun's view of the Constitution.

Jackson's stand. Many people now looked to President Jackson, the West's champion, for an answer. The South-

In Jackson's day, western roads were crude. In the picture above, note the stumps still standing in the road and, at right, the logs serving as a roadway over a marsh or stream.

Museum of Fine Arts, Boston

erners hoped that the President would side with them. In his inaugural address, Jackson had expressed himself in favor of a federal government of limited power. Warning against stretching the Constitution, he had spoken of the "legitimate sphere of State sovereignty."

But on the matter of preserving the Union and the supremacy of the federal government, Jackson was like a rock. At the Democratic party's Jefferson Day dinner in April 1830, Jackson gave his answer. Staring directly at Calhoun, the President proposed his toast: "Our Federal Union—it must be preserved!" Calhoun accepted the challenge. "The Union," he replied, "—next to our liberty, the most dear. May we all remember that it can only be preserved by respecting the rights of the states and distributing equally the benefits and burdens of the Union."

Relations between Jackson and Calhoun had been cool for some time. Their differences on this issue, plus several personal differences that arose later, left them enemies.

The Maysville Road veto. Westerners had reason to be satisfied with their President. He shared their outlook on most things. He agreed with their views on land policy. No one could ask for a stronger supporter of Indian removal. On the issue of internal improvements, however, the President disappointed the West. Jackson did favor roads and canals, but he thought that building them was mainly the job of the states rather than of the federal government.

In May 1830, Jackson's views became clear when he vetoed a bill to help pay for a 60-mile (96-km) road in Kentucky, between Maysville and Lexington. The road was expected to be a link in a future interstate highway. For the present, however, it lay entirely within one state. Thus, Jackson said, this road was "local," rather than "national," in character. For the federal government to pay for projects of this kind, he felt, would lead to waste, corruption, and a too-powerful central government. Jackson may also have had another reason for this veto. It allowed him to strike a blow at his main rival, Senator Henry Clay, whose home state was Kentucky.

Although Jackson lost some support in the West because of this veto, most Westerners remained loyal to him. Later, he approved bills for building roads in the territories and for extending the National Road. By the end of his two terms, he had approved more such spending than any President before him.

The nullification crisis. The opposition of Southerners to tariffs remained strong, and Calhoun and his fellow South Carolinians continued to nurse their grudge against Jackson. Actually, Jackson privately agreed that the tariff was too high. In late 1831 he urged Congress to reconsider it. Congress did pass a new tariff law in 1832, but it did little to lower rates.

South Carolina was now certain that the South could not hope for a low-tariff bill from Congress. Therefore, the state moved to put into practice the theories of the South Carolina Exposition. A specially elected convention met in November 1832 and passed the Ordinance of Nullification. It declared that the federal tariff laws of 1828 and 1832 were of no effect in South Carolina. It also forbade

5. WHAT IF? What if Jackson had allowed South Carolina's nullification of the Tariff of 1832 to go unchallenged? What might have been the short-term effects? the long-term effects?

6. DEBATE Ask students to imagine that Congress has passed a bill that threatens to seriously damage the economic conditions in your state. Conduct a debate: Resolved, That the state of ____ should nullify the ____ Act of Congress.

LESSON 3 *(1 to 2 days)*

Performance Objectives

1. To demonstrate an understanding of the controversy surrounding the Second Bank of the United States by **(a)** identifying the strengths and weaknesses of the Bank, and **(b)** describing the battle that ensued over the rechartering of the Bank. **2.** To create a ten-question recall test from the information contained in the lesson.

Famous People

Nicholas Biddle, Martin Van Buren, William Henry Harrison, John Tyler, James K. Polk

Vocabulary

Specie, hard money, bank notes, easy-credit practices, Panic of 1819, Bank of the United States, soft money, *McCulloch* v. *Maryland,* pet banks, wildcat banks, Specie Circular, Distribution Act, Panic of 1837, Whigs

the collection of tariffs in that state after February 1, 1833. If the federal government were to try to force South Carolina to obey the tariff laws, warned the convention, that would be grounds for withdrawing from the Union. Meanwhile, John Calhoun resigned the Vice Presidency, and South Carolina sent him back to Washington as its Senator.

There was never a question about what President Jackson's response would be. If the United States government were to allow this challenge to its authority to stand, the union of states would, he believed, be ended. Jackson warned South Carolina that nullification was not possible under the Constitution. Federal law, he said, would be enforced. Resistance to it was treason. The President sent a warship with reinforcements to the forts in Charleston Harbor, and said he stood ready to lead an army, if necessary. Privately, he threatened to hang Calhoun.

Seeking a compromise. In Congress, meanwhile, Henry Clay led an effort to find a compromise. In March 1833, Congress passed a bill to lower the tariff, over a ten-year period, to its 1816 levels. On the same day, the Force Bill was passed. This act allowed the President to use troops if necessary to enforce the law in South Carolina.

Although South Carolina had invited other southern states to follow its lead, none did. Standing alone against the United States government, South Carolina accepted the compromise. The convention met again and repealed its ordinance nullifying the tariff. But in a final act of defiance, it passed another ordinance nullifying the Force Bill.

Both sides claimed victory. Unionists declared that they had faced down the challenge. Southerners pointed out that they had won their objective, a lower tariff. Often it is desirable to have an outcome in which each side can feel it has won something. In this case, however, such an outcome may have done more harm than good. It left the key question of states' rights versus federal power unanswered. That question would rise again and again over the next quarter century. The answer would not finally come until the blood of hundreds of thousands had been shed.

CHECKUP

1. In what ways was Jackson's administration different from earlier ones?
2. Why did Jackson veto a bill to help pay for the Maysville Road?
3. How was the nullification crisis of 1831–1832 settled?

LESSON 3

Jackson and the Bank

One of the biggest struggles of the Jackson period concerned the Second Bank of the United States. To understand Jackson's war against the Bank, you will need to know something about money and banking in those days. The main money was gold and silver, also called *specie* and "hard money." Banks added to this money supply by printing paper money called bank notes. On the face of each note was stated the amount and the promise of the issuing bank to redeem, or convert, the note into dollars of gold or silver on demand. As long as people were confident that a bank could and would redeem its notes in hard money, few would bother to convert

Andrew Jackson spent his last years at the Hermitage, his home near Nashville, Tennessee.

them. The notes were just as good as hard money. A bank could safely issue several times as much in bank notes as it had gold and silver in reserve. It was unlikely that all of its noteholders would redeem their notes at one time.

The more notes a bank printed, the more money it had to lend. The more it lent, the more it could earn through interest charges. You can see the temptation, then, for a bank to print a lot of notes. On the other hand, if a bank issued too many notes, it ran the risk of not having enough gold or silver to redeem them when presented. If that happened, the bank would have to go out of business. A well-run bank, therefore, would not issue more than three or four times as much in notes as it had specie in its vault.

Easy-credit practices. Not all banks, however, were well run. In fact, not all people wanted them to be well run. Those who wanted easier credit were in favor of banks printing a great number of bank notes. The more paper money there was, the easier it would be to borrow.

That was the case in the West after the War of 1812. You will recall that high prices for cotton and farm products led to a great demand for land. Settlers bought more than they needed, planning to sell at a profit later. Speculators also bought up large pieces of choice land. Westerners, short on cash, financed these purchases by borrowing. This was easy to do, for state banks in the West—privately owned banks that operated under state charters—followed

Activities

1. GUEST SPEAKER Invite a local banker or economist to speak to the class about the history of money and banking in the United States. Before the speaker arrives, students should have carefully read the lesson and defined the important vocabulary terms.

2. DISCUSSION After students have read the lesson, list on the chalkboard the strengths and weaknesses of the Bank of the United States. Then ask students to explain how the question of rechartering the Bank arose some four years before the expiration of its charter. What was Jackson's view of the constitutionality of the Bank? Why was Jackson so opposed to the Bank? Why was his position on the Bank so appealing to the "common man"? How was the recharter issue resolved?

In the course of this discussion, have students pay particular attention to the cartoon on page 279 and relate its theme to the Bank controversy.

reckless practices. They printed and lent far more bank notes, and required far less security for the loans, than was wise. Since people could borrow easily to buy land, demand for land rose. And as demand rose, prices soared.

Second Bank of the United States. What did the Second Bank of the United States have to do with this? The Bank was chartered by Congress in 1816 for a twenty year period. It was like other banks in a number of ways. It took deposits, issued notes, and made loans.

But it was different in important ways. The Bank of the United States was the only bank chartered by the federal government, which also owned one fifth of the stock. With a capital of $35 million and deposits several times that much, the Bank of the United States was far larger than any other bank in the nation. It was the only bank that had branches—twenty-nine in all—in every part of the country. It held the deposits of the United States government, which could amount to several million dollars at any one time.

Most important, it had great power over other banks. This was because in the normal course of its large business the Bank of the United States received great numbers of the notes of other banks. At any time, the Bank would present notes for thousands of dollars to an issuing state bank and demand gold or silver in exchange. State banks all over the country therefore had to think twice before printing great amounts of paper money.

In the first few years of its life, the Bank did not use its power to redeem notes in gold or silver. In fact, between 1816 and 1818 its western branches overissued and overlent bank notes just as the state banks were doing. Thus the Bank helped to fuel the speculation and rising land prices in the West.

The Panic of 1819. Finally realizing that this was not sound banking, the Bank of the United States put the brakes on credit in 1818. It reduced its bank notes and cut down its loans. It also presented to the state banks large numbers of their notes for payment in gold and silver. This put the Bank in healthy condition again, but it forced out of business a number of state banks that didn't have enough hard money to redeem their notes. It also led the remaining state banks to cut down their note issues by half in less than two years. Fewer notes meant fewer loans; fewer loans meant fewer buyers of land; and less demand for land meant falling prices. Those who had counted on paying off bank loans by selling lands at high prices were caught in the squeeze. Thousands lost their lands and farms.

As word got out that the banks were in trouble, people hurried to convert bank notes into hard money. That only made more banks go under all the sooner. The Panic of 1819 was on. A depression followed that lasted in the West for two years.

The speculation probably would have led to a crash sooner or later, even had there been no Bank of the United States. But the Bank's action had clearly helped to bring it on. Westerners—farmers and bankers alike—were bitter about the Bank ever after. They agreed with the person who noted, "The Bank was saved and the people were ruined."

Differing views on the Bank. In 1823, Nicholas Biddle, a wealthy Philadelphian, became president of the Bank of the United States. Under his able leadership, the Bank became prosperous while performing important services to the American economy. It held one third of all the bank deposits in the United States, and it made one fifth of all the loans. These loans helped hundreds of small businesses to grow. The Bank's notes, as sound as gold or silver coin, added to the money supply. By helping to keep prices stable and the economy strong, the Bank won many supporters.

The Bank, however, also had many foes. State banks in all parts of the country were unhappy about having to compete for business against the branches of the Bank of the United States. Those who wanted to see more paper money and easier credit were against the Bank. Such "soft-money," or "cheap-money," people included not only farmers in the West and South but also rising business people in eastern cities. And hard-money supporters opposed the Bank because it allowed paper money to circulate at all. Many of those people were eastern workers.

There was also growing opposition on the grounds of privilege and power. The Bank of the United States was the only bank with a federal charter, and it had a monopoly on the government's deposits. This privilege brought great profits for its stockholders. Most of them were wealthy Northeasterners, and a good

Jackson attacks the Bank, shown as a many-headed serpent. The heads are those of Bank officials.

★7★

Andrew Jackson

1767—1845

Born in SOUTH CAROLINA
In Office 1829—1837
Party DEMOCRATIC

A symbol of the common man. Resisted South Carolina's nullification of federal tariffs. Killed the Bank of the United States. Used the spoils system in filling government jobs.

number were English investors. Further, although the directors of the Bank had great power over the whole American economy, they were not accountable to the public.

A rechartering proposal. President Jackson understood little about banking. A bad experience with paper money at the age of thirty had left him a hard-money man. "I do not dislike your Bank any more than all banks," he told Biddle. That, of course, was not much consolation for the Bank's president.

Early in his term, Jackson stated that he thought the Bank was not constitutional. In the Supreme Court case of *McCulloch* v. *Maryland* in 1819, Chief Justice John Marshall had ruled that it was. But Jackson believed the President had an equal right with the Court and Congress to decide on such questions for himself. Biddle worried about the Bank's future, tried to win support by granting loans to lawmakers and journalists on very favorable terms.

Biddle then made a fatal mistake. Henry Clay was planning to run as a National Republican against Jackson in 1832 and was looking for a winning issue. He believed the Bank would be one. Clay urged Biddle to ask Congress to recharter the Bank in 1832, four years before the old charter would expire. Clay knew that Congress would do so. Then, if Jackson signed the bill, the President would lose support in the West and South. If he vetoed it, he would lose support in the Northeast. Biddle agreed to ask for the recharter.

In July 1832 Congress passed the recharter bill. Jackson understood the strategy well. "The Bank, Mr. Van Buren, is trying to kill me," he said to his political ally and Secretary of State, "but I will kill it." Jackson vetoed the bill. Although his veto message was addressed to Congress, it was really aimed over Congress's head at the American people. The Bank, said Jackson, was unconstitutional because it was not really "necessary and proper." It was un-American, declared the President, because it had a large number of foreign stockholders. It was undemocratic because it put great "power in the hands of a few men irresponsible to the people."

Perhaps most important, Jackson argued, it was wrong for the government to give monopoly privileges to a few of its citizens—namely, the stockholders of the Bank.

> . . . when the laws [are used] . . . to make the rich richer, and the potent more powerful, the humble members of the society—the farmers, mechanics, and laborers—who have neither the time nor the means of securing like favors to themselves, have a right to complain of the injustice of their government.

Henry Clay had his issue. He could not have made a bigger mistake. Clay was able to rally Bank supporters to his side. But Jackson, by his veto message, once more appeared to be the champion of the common people and the foe of privilege. And in this new day of broader voting rights, there were many more common people than friends of the Bank. In the 1832 election, Jackson and his running mate, Martin Van Buren, overwhelmed Clay, 219 electoral votes to 49.

The "pet banks." The election of 1832 doomed the Bank of the United States to end when its charter ran out in 1836. Jackson, however, decided not to wait. On his orders, government deposits were withdrawn from the Bank and placed in certain state banks, which the opposition called "pet banks." Stripped of its business with the government, the Bank of the United States was little more than an empty shell by the time its charter ran out in 1836.

All together, 89 state banks received government deposits. They were supposed to have been chosen for political reasons, and a good number of the banks were less than sound. With the government's gold in their vaults, they could issue many more bank notes. Even those state banks that did not hold government deposits could do this, for the Bank of the United States was now without power to stop them. In the West, new "wildcat banks" sprang up—unreliable banks, issuing large numbers of notes with almost no specie to back them. Borrowing was easy. Between 1829 and 1836 the amount lent by state banks rose from $137 million to $475 million. These loans touched off wild speculation, especially in land. Government land sales doubled and then doubled again within a single year. Many buyers paid the United States Treasury with the cheap and nearly worthless paper money of the wildcat banks. And where was this money deposited? In the pet banks, which promptly lent it out again, adding to the speculation.

The Specie Circular. Hard-money men were aghast. They had cheered the death of the Bank because it issued paper money. Now they beheld the results of their victory—a country awash in cheap paper money. To stop this situation, President Jackson issued an order in July 1836 known as the Specie Circular. From that time on, said the order, the Treasury would accept only gold or silver as payment for public land.

The Specie Circular caused the sale of public lands to fall off sharply, for few people had gold or silver. Further, it led to a rush to convert bank notes into gold or silver. The weakest banks could not do this and quickly went under. At the very same time, Congress passed a law known as the Distribution Act. Receipts

3. RESEARCH / ORAL REPORTS Have several students read and report on the following books: Bray Hammond's *Banks and Politics in America from the Revolution to the Civil War* (Princeton, N.J.: Princeton University Press, 1957), concentrating on the section dealing with Jackson's war with the Bank; Arthur M. Schlesinger, Jr.'s *The Age of Jackson* (New York: Little, 1945), Chapters VII to X, dealing specifically with the bank war. *The Age of Jackson* was the 1946 winner of the Pulitzer Prize in History.

4. THOUGHT PROVOKER In his message vetoing the Bank Bill (July 10, 1832), Jackson wrote: "There are no necessary evils in government. Its evils exist only in its abuses. If it would confine itself to equal protection, and, as Heaven does its rains, shower its favors alike on the high and the low, the rich and the poor, it would be an unqualified blessing." Ask students for their reaction to this quotation. Are there any necessary evils in government today? What is meant by "equal protection"? What are some governmental abuses? Was Jackson's "spoils system" an abuse of government power?

5. DISCUSSION Several years ago, a number of prominent historians were asked to rank the Presidents of the United States according to ability and record. Andrew Jackson was ranked in the top five of every list. Ask students for their opinion of Jackson. Was he a good President? Some students, especially those who view the Presidency in idealistic terms, will see Jackson as a wheeling-and-dealing politician. Others will see him as a "people's President." Encourage some students to read more about the Jacksonian Period in the following books: Thomas A. Bailey's *Presidential Greatness: The Image and the Man from George Washington to the Present* (New York: Hawthorne, 1966) and Arthur B. Tourtellot's *The Presidents on the Presidency* (New York: Atheneum, 1970).

6. TESTING Have students each make up a ten-question recall test using material in this lesson. Then ask them to exchange tests and answer their partners' questions.

from land sales had paid off the national debt and left the United States government with a surplus, and this act provided that it be distributed to the states. This meant that the pet banks, among which the surplus was deposited, had to pay out a lot of money to the states at the very time they were feeling the effect of the Specie Circular.

The Panic of 1837. Soon panic spread, just as it had in 1819. The Panic of 1837 quickly turned into a depression. Struggling to survive, banks refused to renew old loans or to make new ones. Businesses failed. Thousands were thrown out of work. Unemployed workers in Philadelphia and New York rioted. Construction on roads and canals stopped, throwing thousands more out of work. Farm prices fell. Cotton, which had brought fifteen cents a pound in 1836, slid to six cents a pound by 1842.

In large part, the panic and depression were results of Jackson's policies. Killing the Bank of the United States removed an important check on the "cheap-money" tendencies of state banks. The speculation that followed would probably have led to a crash sooner or later, but it was Jackson's Specie Circular that made it sooner.

Van Buren as President. Fortunately for Jackson's popularity, he had left office by the time the panic and depression hit. The new President was Martin Van Buren, Vice President during Jackson's second term. Van Buren was called by some The Little Magician for his skills as a politician. A long-time political leader in New York State, he had been one of the first to understand the changes that the rise of the common man would bring to politics. He was one of Jackson's early supporters for the Presidency, and with Old Hickory's backing had easily won the Democratic party nomination in 1836.

The Democrats were opposed by the Whig party, a collection of groups and individuals that had little in common except opposition to Jackson. The Whigs took their name from the British party that had opposed George III, claiming that they, too, stood for liberty—against the authority of King Andrew I.

Knowing there was little chance of defeating Van Buren in a head-to-head race, the Whigs ran sectional favorites in different parts of the country. The hope was that together the candidates would win enough votes to keep Van Buren from getting a majority and thus throw the election into the House of Representatives. The plan failed. Only General William Henry Harrison, the Whig candidate in the West, ran well.

Van Buren was in office less than three months when the panic broke. In those days it was believed that a depression, like a common cold, had to run its course. It was felt there was nothing the government could do, or should do, to deal with it. Thus, during the next four years, Van Buren watched helplessly as the depression racked the country and wrecked his Presidency.

The election of 1840. The scent of victory was in the air as the Whigs gathered to choose their candidates for the 1840 election. To oppose Van Buren, they named General William Henry Harrison. The Indian fighter and hero of the battle of Tippecanoe had shown strength in

★8★

Martin Van Buren

1782—1862

Born in NEW YORK
In Office 1837—1841
Party DEMOCRATIC

First President who made a career of politics. Depression struck the nation soon after he took office, and it lasted throughout his term. He failed in his attempt to win reelection.

★ ★ ★ ★ ★ ★ ★ ★

★9★

William Henry Harrison

1773—1841

Born in VIRGINIA
In Office 1841
Party WHIG

Won fame fighting Indians at Tippecanoe and British in War of 1812. Served Ohio in Congress. At sixty-eight, the oldest man to be elected President. Served one month.

★ ★ ★ ★ ★ ★ ★ ★

★10★

John Tyler

1790—1862

Born in VIRGINIA
In Office 1841—1845
Party WHIG

First Vice President to become President on death of Chief Executive. A former Democrat, he clashed with Whigs after becoming President. Signed bill annexing Texas.

★ ★ ★ ★ ★ ★ ★ ★

the West in 1836. To carry the South, the Whigs chose for the Vice Presidency John Tyler, a states' rights Virginian. The party wrote no platform, for the varied elements in the party could not have agreed on one.

The campaign showed that the Whigs had learned well the strategy of politics in the new democratic age. Although Harrison was a country gentleman, living in a sixteen-room mansion in Ohio, the Whigs presented him as a simple man of the frontier, born in a log cabin. Meanwhile, Van Buren was pictured as a man with aristocratic tastes and no feeling for the common people who were suffering in the depression. It was a rerun of 1828, but with the sides reversed. The Whigs, with their slogan "Tippecanoe and Tyler too," claimed to be standing for the ordinary people against "Van, Van, the used up man."

Harrison won by a large majority of electoral votes, although the popular vote was somewhat closer. Shortly after taking office, however, Harrison died, and Tyler completed the term. Tyler's administration was marked by many

Answers To Review Questions

1. If Missouri came in as a slave state, then other areas north of the latitude of the Ohio River might become slave states too. If that occurred, the South would have greater power in the Senate.

2. Strengths: Tried to be a national President and heal the bitter sectional differences; favored internal improvements that would tie the nation together; believed the federal government should support agriculture, science, and education with encouragement and financial aid. **Weaknesses:** A cold personality and an uncompromising nature; lacking in political skills necessary to build support for his national views.

3. In Jackson's time, ordinary people came to have a greater say in government than ever before.

4. The caucus system was replaced by the nominating convention. And in all states except South Carolina, presidential electors were elected by the people instead of being selected by the state legislatures.

5. Jackson felt that since the President was elected by all the people, the office of the President was therefore one of strength and power. The President must make his own interpretation of the Constitution or judgment of a bill.

quarrels with the leaders of his own party. Four years later they refused to renominate him.

Though Tyler was not renominated, there occurred events of great importance to America's future during his administration and that of his successor, James K. Polk. The United States added more than a million square miles to its territory. This was the climax of the westward movement that you read about in Chapter 12. You will recall that in the early nineteenth century, Americans had steadily pushed toward their western boundary—first the Mississippi River, and then, following the Louisiana Purchase, the Rocky Mountains. Among most countries in the world, rivers and mountains have been thought to be logical and natural boundaries. For the first half century of this nation's history, Americans thought of them that way, too.

By the 1830s and 1840s, however, Americans were beginning to have a different vision. It was a vision of a great nation that extended from ocean to ocean. In the next chapter you will read how that vision became a reality.

CHECKUP

1. What were the strengths and the weaknesses of the Second Bank of the United States?
2. Why and how did Jackson "kill" the Bank? What was the effect of his action against the Bank in the 1832 election?
3. What part did Jackson's policies play in bringing on the Panic of 1837? How was Van Buren affected?

Key Facts from Chapter 13

1. As the nation's borders expanded during the early 1800s, three sections—the North, the South, and the West—developed differently with different interests.
2. Sectionalism—the attempt of each section to advance its own interests on the national scene—became a strong but divisive force in American politics and government.
3. Sectional issues included the tariff, slavery, government land policy, internal improvements, and banking policy.
4. The extension of the right to vote to almost all white adult males made possible the election of Andrew Jackson as President.
5. Jackson championed the cause of the "common man." During the Jacksonian era, ordinary people gained greater influence and participation in government.
6. Jackson's fight against the Bank of the United States was popular, but killing the Bank indirectly helped to bring on the Panic of 1837.
7. One issue that came to the fore during Jackson's administration was that of states' rights, especially the right of a state to nullify a federal law within its own borders.

★ REVIEWING THE CHAPTER ★

People, Places, and Events

Missouri Compromise *P. 265*
Henry Clay *Pp. 265, 266*
John Quincy Adams *Pp. 266–268*
"Tariff of Abominations" *P. 268*
John C. Calhoun *P. 268*
Maysville Road Bill *P. 274*
Panic of 1819 *P. 278*
Specie Circular *P. 281*
Martin Van Buren *Pp. 282, 283*

Review Questions

1. Why did Missouri's request for admission as a slave state cause so much controversy? *Pp. 264–265* Les. 1
2. What were John Quincy Adams's particular strengths and weaknesses as President? *Pp. 267–268* Les. 1
3. Why is Jacksonian democracy described as "the rise of the common man"? *P. 270* Les. 2
4. How did the procedures for nominating and electing a President change during the 1820s and 1830s? *Pp. 271–272* Les. 2
5. What were Jackson's views about the role of the President? *P. 273* Les. 2
6. Contrast the two points of view about the nature of the federal union as expressed by Hayne and Webster in their debate. *P. 274* Les. 2
7. Why were so many Americans opposed to the Second Bank of the United States? *Pp. 279–280* Les. 3
8. Why did Clay push for a rechartering of the Bank in 1832, when its charter did not expire until 1836? *P. 280* Les. 3
9. Why was the Whig party formed, and when was it successful? *Pp. 282–283* Les. 3

Chapter Test

For each sentence, write the letter of the correct ending. For some sentences, there may be more than one correct ending. Use a separate piece of paper.

1. The Specie Circular caused **(a)** the sale of public lands to fall off sharply, **(b)** a rush to convert bank notes into hard money, **(c)** the "Tariff of Abominations."
2. Robert Hayne and Daniel Webster argued their views on **(a)** slavery, **(b)** nullification, **(c)** specie.
3. President Jackson vetoed the **(a)** Distribution Act, **(b)** Maysville Road Bill, **(c)** Ordinance of Nullification.
4. The North and the West generally agreed on the following issues: **(a)** high tariffs, **(b)** internal improvements, **(c)** rapid western settlement.
5. The South objected to **(a)** high tariffs, **(b)** cheap land, **(c)** the spread of slavery.
6. The Missouri Compromise was arranged by **(a)** Andrew Jackson, **(b)** Daniel Webster, **(c)** Henry Clay.
7. John C. Calhoun's South Carolina Exposition and Protest upheld **(a)** the spoils system, **(b)** sectionalism, **(c)** states' rights.
8. Westerners opposed the strict money policies of **(a)** the Bank of the United States, **(b)** "pet banks," **(c)** "wildcat banks."
9. Jackson's Presidency has often been connected with **(a)** the rise of the common people, **(b)** the slavery issue in Missouri, **(c)** the spoils system.
10. Andrew Jackson was succeeded in office by **(a)** John Quincy Adams, **(b)** Martin Van Buren, **(c)** William Henry Harrison.

6. Hayne contended that the Union was composed of sovereign states that were free to nullify an act of Congress or even secede from the Union. Webster believed that the Union had been formed by the people, not the states, and that nullification and secession were not possible.
7. Farmers in the West and South and rising business people in eastern cities opposed the Bank's policies of limiting paper money and tightening up on credit. And hard-money people were against the Bank because it allowed paper money to circulate at all. In addition, there was opposition to the Bank because most of the stockholders were wealthy Northeasterns or foreign investors who enjoyed privilege and power.
8. Henry Clay was planning to run for President as a National Republican against Jackson in 1832, and he was looking for a winning issue. He pushed for a rechartering of the Bank because he knew that Congress would vote in favor of the action. Then, if Jackson signed the bill, the President would lose support in the West and South; if he vetoed it, he would lose support in the Northeast.
9. The Whig party was composed of those who had as a common goal oppostion to Jackson and his supporters. The Whigs were finally successful in electing their candidate, William Henry Harrison, in 1840.

Answers For Chapter Test
1. a, b **2.** b **3.** b **4.** a,b **5.** a, b **6.** c **7.** c **8.** a **9.** a, c **10.** b

Background Information

1. PICTURE With the Mexican Cession, the goal of the restless Americans to extend their national boundaries "from sea to shining sea" had been achieved. In 1783, after the peace treaty ending the Revolutionary War, the Mississippi River had been the nation's western boundary. In 1848, the western boundary became the Pacific Ocean, shown in this picture. By 1853, with the Gadsden Purchase, the United States had grown to its present North American limits, except for the state of Alaska.

2. PATAGONIA On page 287, the text mentions Patagonia, a region in the southern part of South America. In 1520 the Portuguese explorer Ferdinand Magellan became the first European to reach the region. Then Welsh settlers arrived in Patagonia in 1865. Prior to this time, however, the region was practically unexplored. In 1881, Chile and Argentina ratified a treaty that settled their dispute over Patagonia. The territory east of the Andes became part of Argentina, and the western coastal region became part of Chile. The region was named for the large feet *(patagones)* of the Indians who lived in Patagonia long before the white explorers arrived. The Indians were tall and wore large boots stuffed with grass.

FROM SEA TO SHINING SEA

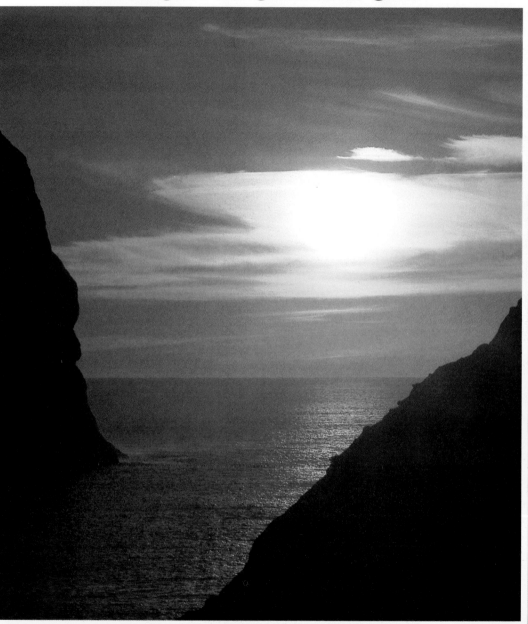

LESSON 1

MANY AMERICANS BELIEVED that their nation had a special mission to lead the rest of the world toward free institutions and a republican form of government. The nation's founders believed this mission would be fulfilled by example. A half century later their confident descendants declared that America should fulfill its mission not only by example but by "extending the area of freedom." With almost religious fervor, they proclaimed that more land should be brought under the American flag. To match such a grand vision, no boundary short of the Pacific Ocean itself seemed suitable.

The idea of the nation extending to the Pacific was not entirely new to Americans in the 1830s. When the United States was making the Transcontinental Treaty with Spain in 1819 (see page 236), Secretary of State John Quincy Adams told a cabinet meeting that it was a "law of nature" that all of North America should come under the American flag. Soon what Adams was saying privately was being said openly. There was nothing bashful about the way Americans stated their claims. Here, for example, is a speaker at a political convention in 1844.

> Make way, I say, for the young American Buffalo—he has not yet got land enough; he wants more land as his cool shelter in summer—he wants more land for his beautiful pasture grounds. I tell you, we will give him Oregon for his summer shade, and the region of Texas as his winter pasture. Like all of his race, he wants salt, too. Well, he shall have the use of two oceans—the mighty Pacific and the turbulent Atlantic shall be his. . . . He shall not stop until he slakes his thirst in the frozen ocean.

A member of Congress was just as open in a speech to the House of Representatives. Many of that body, he predicted, would live to hear the phrase from the Speaker's chair, "the gentleman from Texas." He wanted them also to hear "the gentleman from Oregon." He would even go further and have "the gentleman from Nova Scotia, the gentleman from Canada, the gentleman from Cuba, the gentleman from Mexico, aye, even the gentleman from Patagonia."

Manifest destiny. A Democratic journalist named John O'Sullivan summed up the urges of this restless people in 1845 when he wrote that it was America's "manifest [that is, self-evident] destiny to overspread the continent allotted by Providence for the free development of our yearly multiplying millions." The phrase *manifest destiny* was soon on the lips of editors, politicians, clergy, and ordinary Americans. It was a phrase with which many could agree, partly because it was so wonderfully vague. To some it meant expansion to the Pacific. To others it meant spreading over all of North America. To still others it meant controlling the Western Hemisphere.

Meanwhile, some people, both in government and out, were thinking of the more practical benefits that expansion would bring. Northern farmers were interested in the rich lands on the West Coast. Southern slaveholders saw Texas

LESSON 1 *(2 to 3 days)*

Performance Objectives

1. To list and explain the major events in Texas, from the first American settlement to statehood. **2.** To describe the circumstances under which the United States acquired full title to Oregon.

Famous People

Moses Austin, Stephen Austin, Santa Anna, Sam Houston, Jim Bowie, Davy Crockett, James K. Polk, John Jacob Astor, Kit Carson, Jim Bridger, Jim Beckwourth, Marcus and Narcissa Whitman, Joseph Smith, Brigham Young

Vocabulary

Manifest destiny, "Remember the Alamo!" Lone Star Republic, annexation, Oregon country, Columbia River, mountain men, Willamette Valley, Snake River, "Oregon fever," "Fifty-four Forty or Fight," 49° north latitude, Mormons

Activities

1. READING FOR INFORMATION / ORAL REPORT
Assign two students to report on *manifest destiny.* Have one read the section on it in S. F. Bemis's *Diplomatic History of the United States* (Gloucester, Mass.: Peter Smith, 1960). Have the other read about it in Thomas Bailey's *A Diplomatic History of the American People* (New York: Appleton, Century Crofts, 1969). The opinions of these two eminent historians differ. Have the students compare the opinions.

as a place where cotton culture and slavery could expand. The three great Pacific ports—at Puget Sound in the Oregon country and at San Francisco and San Diego in California—were seen by eastern merchants and government leaders as doorways to trade with the Far East. Most of all, the United States was aware that Great Britain was interested in acquiring the entire western area of North America. A strong European power was the last thing that Americans wanted along their country's western border.

George Caleb Bingham caught the spirit of manifest destiny in this painting of a determined band of pioneers, led by Daniel Boone, moving through Cumberland Gap on their way west.

Washington University Gallery of Art, St. Louis

Adding Texas and Oregon

What opened the way for the United States to "fulfill its destiny" was the crumbling of Spanish power in the Americas. Between 1808 and 1824, every Spanish colony in South, Central, and North America except Cuba rebelled and won its independence. The new Republic of Mexico inherited all of New Spain, which included the present-day American Southwest.

Settlers in Texas. One of the Mexican republic's early goals was to encourage settlement in Texas, the northern part of the state of Coahuila-Texas. A developed Texas could serve to buffer the rest of Mexico from Indian raids and from an aggressive United States. It would, moreover, strengthen Mexico's economy. The Mexican government therefore offered free land to groups of Americans who would settle there. In 1820, Moses Austin received the first land grant, but he died soon afterward. His son Stephen took over the grant and led the first groups of American emigrants into Texas. Learning that the land was good for cotton, others from nearby states in the South poured into Texas with their slaves. By 1830, there were 20,000 white Americans and 2,000 slaves in Texas. There were only a few thousand Mexicans.

The Mexican government soon realized it had made a mistake. The Americans were difficult to control and unwilling to live by Mexican law. That law forbade slavery, but American slaveholders found a way around it. The law required immigrants to be, or become, Catholic, but most of the Americans who came were Protestant, and

Courtesy San Antonio Museum Association, Witte Memorial Museum, San Antonio, Texas. Lent by Bexar County

San Antonio developed as a typical Mexican town, with a busy square lined by adobe buildings. This painting was made soon after Texas became a part of the United States.

they remained so. The Americans hardly bothered to learn more than a few words of Spanish. It was soon clear that they thought of themselves as Americans living in a place that, for the time being, belonged to Mexico.

In 1830 Mexico halted immigration from the United States and sent soldiers to Texas to tighten the rule. A few years later Mexico's president, General Antonio López de Santa Anna, dissolved the Mexican Congress, ended local government throughout Mexico—including Texas—and took on the powers of a dictator. Meanwhile, the Mexican government had been unable to enforce its law prohibiting Americans from entering Texas. By 1835, Americans there outnumbered Mexicans, 30,000 to 3,500. The Americans were in a rebellious mood over the loss of self-government. In that year there were a number of clashes between Mexican soldiers and the Texans. In 1836, Texas declared itself an independent republic.

The Alamo. Even as Texas proclaimed its independence an event was occurring that would give the Texans their battle cry. Determined to crush the rebellion, Santa Anna had led an army of some 4,000 soldiers against a Texas force of 187 men in San Antonio. The Texans took up a position in a deserted

2. LISTENING FOR INFORMATION Read to the students "Sam Houston, Statesman" by Marquis James from *The American Story.* Mr. James was twice the winner of the Pulitzer Prize in History.

3. CREATIVE WRITING After students have read the lesson, ask them to imagine they are settlers in Texas with relatives living back East. Have them write letters to relatives in which they explain the major events in Texas, from the first American settlement to statehood. Encourage students to base their imaginative accounts on facts from the text and outside readings. At the completion of this activity, ask for volunteers to read their letters aloud.

4. BOOK REPORT Have an interested student give an oral book report on Walter Lord's *A Time to Stand: The Story of the Alamo* (New York: Harper, 1960).

5. USING A MAP Direct the students' attention to the map on page 291. Ask: Why did the trails to the West start in Missouri? What effect do you think this had on the economy of St. Joseph and Independence? Why weren't there more trails to the West? What value was there in following where others had gone before?

6. DISCUSSION Discuss the development of the Oregon country from earliest American penetration to territorial status and statehood. In the discussion, refer to the map on page 294, and have students locate the important geographical features that are involved in the story of settlement.

7. DEBATE Resolved, That a "law of nature" commanded that all North America—from the Atlantic to the Pacific—should come under the American flag. To involve the entire class in this activity, before the debate begins have each student write down one reason for and one reason against extending the national boundary. Allow time for class discussion at the conclusion of the debate.

8. BOOK REPORTS A classic in American historiography is Francis Parkman's *The Oregon Trail.* This is available in many editions. Perhaps a student would be interested in reading the book and reporting on it to the rest of the class. Another book in this category is Bernard De Voto's *Year of Decision: 1846* (Boston: Houghton Mifflin, 1943).

mission known as the Alamo. Fierce fighting raged for ten days, and the Mexicans lost 1,544 men. But on March 6, the Mexicans overwhelmed the Texans. The six defenders who survived the Mexican attack were executed at Santa Anna's orders. Among those who died at the Alamo were Jim Bowie, inventor of the hunting knife that is named for him, and Davy Crockett, a former congressman from Tennessee. Thereafter, "Remember the Alamo!" became the slogan of Texas forces.

The Lone Star Republic. A short time later, Mexican troops wiped out another Texas force at Goliad, southeast of San Antonio. But in April 1836, General Sam Houston, leading an army of fewer than 800, struck at a Mexican force almost twice that size at the San Jacinto River. Houston's troops killed or captured the entire Mexican force. The Mexican army was soon driven out of Texas completely. Houston was made president of the Republic of Texas. Within a month the Lone Star Republic (named after its flag with a single star) asked the United States to annex it, or take it over.

The United States had long wanted Texas. Presidents Monroe, Adams, and Jackson had all offered to buy it from Mexico. American citizens had sent guns and supplies to the rebels. A good many Americans thought of annexation as simply bringing Americans in Texas back under the United States flag and Constitution.

By the 1830s, however, many in the Northeast were opposed to annexing Texas because they did not want to add more slave states to the Union. (You will read more about this opposition in Unit 5.) For nine years after Texas became independent, its annexation was blocked in Congress by these objections.

The annexation of Texas. Meanwhile, the young republic needed protection against a possible attempt at restoring Mexican control. Therefore, Texas developed close ties with England. England was interested in Texas as a source of raw cotton for its factories and as a market for its manufactured goods. It also saw an independent Texas as a barrier to American expansion farther west. When the United States Senate turned down a treaty of annexation in 1844, the Texans seriously thought about making an alliance with England.

Expansion became an issue in the American presidential election of 1844, however. The Democratic party and its candidate, James K. Polk of Tennessee, came out for the annexation of Texas. Henry Clay, running for the Presidency for the third time, was the Whig party candidate. Clay straddled the annexation question—that is, he did not come out clearly for or against it. When Polk won, it was generally felt that the American people had chosen him because of his stand on Texas. The retiring President, John Tyler, had long favored bringing Texas into the Union. Now, in the final days of his administration, Tyler persuaded Congress to pass a joint resolution annexing Texas. On December 29, 1845, Texas entered the Union as the twenty-eighth state.

The Oregon country. Farther to the north and west, the United States was gaining another large area. In the early nineteenth century, a number of coun-

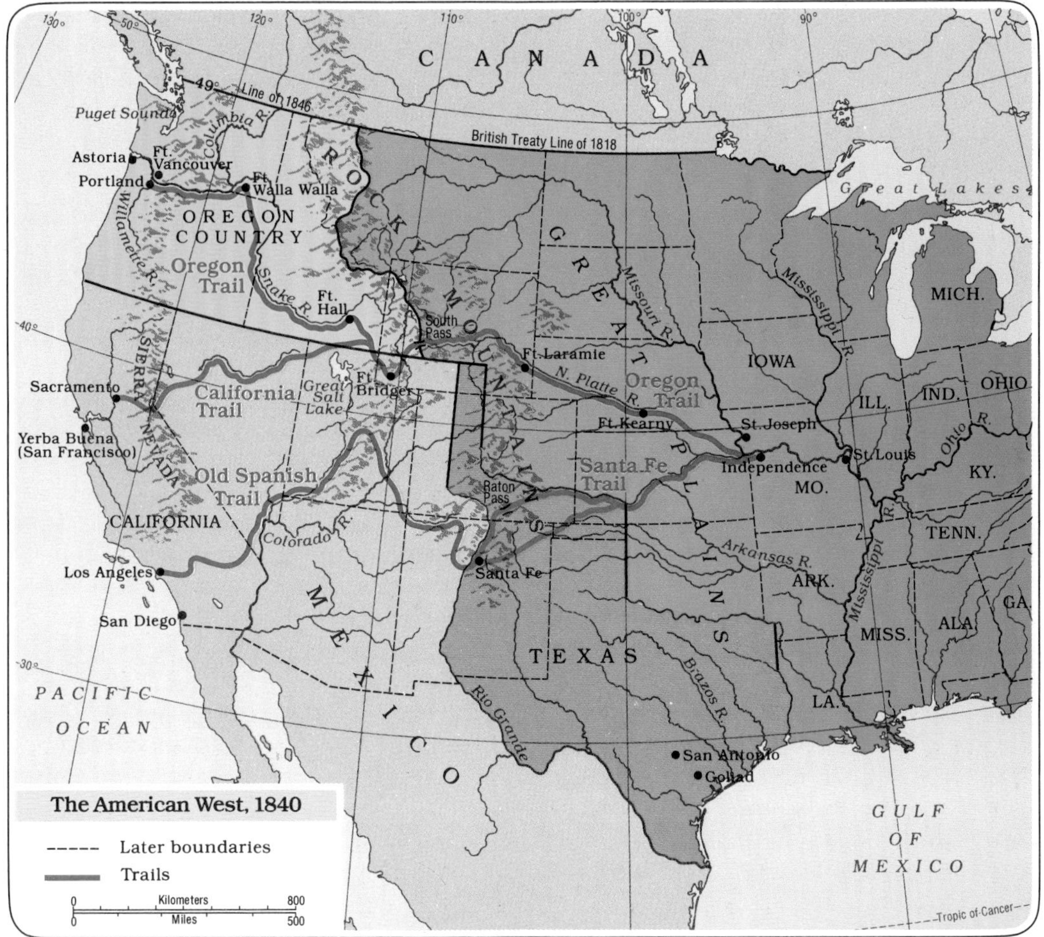

During the 1840s and 1850s, thousands of pioneers bound for Oregon and California made the grueling trip over the westward trails. As the wagon trains advanced, the trails were littered with articles cast aside to lighten the burden of the laboring horses and oxen. Alongside the rutted trails were markers over the shallow graves of those who had died along the way.

tries, including the United States and Great Britain, claimed the land called the Oregon country. It lay between the Rocky Mountains on the east and the Pacific Ocean on the west. From a southern boundary of 42° north latitude, it extended to 54°40′ north latitude, the southern boundary of Alaska. (At that time Alaska belonged to Russia.) The United States based its claim to the Oregon country mainly on the explorations of Lewis and Clark (see page 224). In 1810 an American merchant, John Jacob Astor, set up fur-

Continued on page 293

9. DISCUSSION Slogans have been important in rallying Americans to action. After the students have discussed "Fifty-four Forty or Fight," "Remember the Alamo!" and "manifest destiny," ask them how slogans influence the way people think. Present this quotation from James B. Conant: "Slogans are both exciting and comforting, but they are also powerful opiates for the conscience. . . . Some of mankind's most terrible misdeeds have been committed under the spell of certain magic words or phrases." This quotation may be used as a base for study not only of the slogans mentioned in this lesson but of slogans that will appear in other lessons and of slogans in use today.

10. COLLAGE Have students compile a list of popular slogans in use today. Then have them make a collage. American advertising is an especially rich source of slogans.

Background Information

3. JOHN JACOB ASTOR (1763–1848) Astor is the name of a prominent and wealthy American family, and John Jacob founded the family fortune. He was born in Waldorf, Germany, and came to New York City at the age of twenty. As a poor immigrant, Astor worked as a baker's boy and peddler, and ran a music store before he established his American Fur Company about 1787. He spent many years organizing the fur trade from the Great Lakes to the Pacific and from there to China and Japan, exchanging fur for tea at handsome profits. At one time, Astor had a virtual monopoly on the entire United States fur trade. The greater part of the family fortune, however, came from acquiring and developing real estate in New York City at a time when most of Manhattan Island was farmland. Astor was a leader in chartering the Second Bank of the United States. At his death, he left a fortune estimated at over $25 million.

The Mountain Men

In opening the way for settlement of the Far West, the "mountain men" played a key role. They were trappers and traders who, in the early 1800s, moved into the Rocky Mountain region in search of furs. As they pushed deep into this strange and hostile land, danger was ever present. Sometimes they fought the Indians, but on other occasions they lived with them and even adopted the Indian way of life. Many of the mountain men dressed in moccasins and buckskins, took shelter in winter in lodges of buffalo skins, and married Indian women.

The big event each year for the mountain men was the spring *rendezvous.* This was a meeting of trappers, Indians, and traders in a mountain valley in Wyoming or Utah. There the mountain men and the Indians exchanged their furs for the traders' guns, ammunition, knives, traps, and such luxuries as flour and coffee. For a week or so, a holiday air prevailed. Then the gathering broke up. The traders' pack trains, laden with furs, headed eastward for St. Louis and other cities. The Indians returned to their villages. And the mountain men made their way back into the wilderness for another lonely year.

During their search for furs, the mountain men traced the great western rivers to their sources. They named many of the peaks of the Rockies, and they found passes through the towering ranges. Kit Carson charted trails to Utah, Oregon, and California. Jim Bridger became the first white man to look upon Great Salt Lake. Jim Beckwourth, a free black from Missouri, discovered the pass in California that today bears his name.

By 1840, the beaver hat had gone out of style, and the fur trade declined. The mountain men became scouts and guides. Over the trails they had used so often as trappers, they now led wagon trains of settlers into California and the Oregon country.

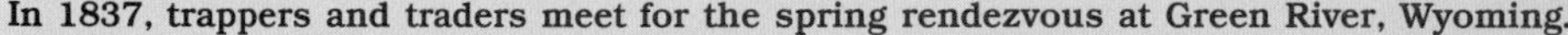

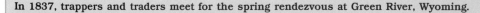

In 1837, trappers and traders meet for the spring rendezvous at Green River, Wyoming.

Pioneers going west listen intently as a trapper tells them of dangers that lie ahead.

trading posts along the Columbia River. Astor's Pacific Fur Company founded the settlement of Astoria. During the War of 1812, however, rival Canadian companies got their government to push Astor out with a show of force. After this, there was little American interest in the Oregon country for a quarter of a century.

Few people lived in the area. For that reason, the United States and Britain were willing to sign a treaty in 1818 to jointly occupy the Oregon country for ten years. In 1827 they renewed the treaty for an indefinite period, subject to cancellation on one year's notice.

In the 1830s a number of American missionaries and settlers went to Oregon. The first of them was Jason Lee, a Methodist missionary who arrived in 1833. Marcus and Narcissa Whitman were among the Presbyterians who arrived in 1836 to do work among the Indians. Four years later Father Pierre Jean De Smet arrived to represent the Catholics.

Many of the missionaries settled in the Willamette Valley and near the point where the Snake River enters the Columbia. They were soon sending word back east about the beauty of the Oregon country. Their descriptions of the

4. MARCUS AND NARCISSA WHITMAN In the 1830s, the Oregon Trail was traveled chiefly by fur traders and a growing number of Protestant and Catholic missionaries. One young missionary couple to journey west over the trail was the Whitmans. Married just before starting out for the Oregon country, Marcus and Narcissa Whitman spent their honeymoon making the difficult trek. In 1836 they opened a mission near Walla Walla. Whitman was a doctor, but he was unable to halt the terrible measles epidemic of 1847, which decimated the Indians in his area. Although the disease had been carried west by recent settlers from the East, the Indians felt that the Whitmans had poisoned them. Consequently, they attacked and burned the mission, killing Marcus and Narcissa Whitman and twelve other persons.

11. **PICTURE ANALYSIS** Ask students to study the pictures on pages 293 and 295 and to share their impressions of pioneer life as depicted in these scenes. Are the scenes generally realistic representations of pioneer life, or are they idealistic? Then ask the students each to choose one person in the pictures and tell how that person might have felt about moving west. If necessary, point out that despite the cheerfulness of the scenes, the journey was laborious and perilous. Have students describe the terrain, the dangerous encounters, the daily problems, the different animals seen, and so on.

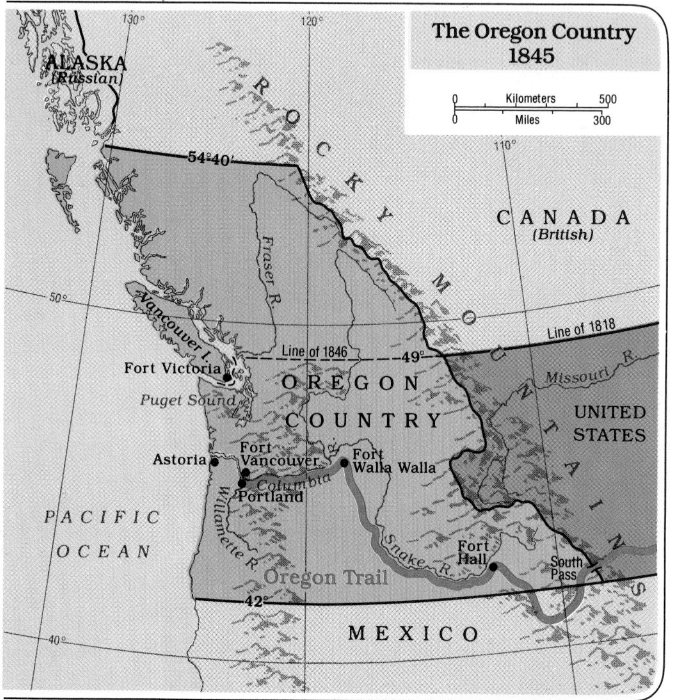

The territory originally claimed by the United States extended almost to the southern boundary of Alaska, then a Russian possession. However, the goal of most Oregon-bound pioneers was the fertile valley of the Willamette River.

mild climate and rich farmland aroused interest. Within a few years, Easterners had a case of "Oregon fever." In 1843 more than 1,000 people set out from Independence, Missouri, on the 2,000-mile (3,200-km) journey across plains, rivers, and mountains to the farmer's new paradise. Most of them traveled in groups for safety against Indian attacks as well as to help each other through the hardships of the five-month-long trip. By 1835, there were 5,000 Americans living in Oregon, with more on the way. They formed a provisional government and asked the United States to take them over.

Fifty-four Forty or Fight. Expansionists soon laid claim to the entire Oregon territory. Politicians and journalists raised the cry "Fifty-four Forty or Fight," though no American lived north of the 49° line and there were solutions other than fighting. The annexation of Oregon, as well as Texas, became an issue in the election of 1844. When Polk won, he spoke out in favor of taking the entire Oregon country. Privately, however, he let it be known to the British minister that the United States would be satisfied to divide the territory at 49° north latitude. That line was the boundary between Canada and the United States from Lake of the Woods westward to the Oregon country.

The British minister rejected the offer without even consulting his government. Polk then renewed his demand for all the land up to 54°40′. The United States gave England the necessary one-year notice to end their agreement of joint occupancy. For a time it looked as if there might be war. But neither side wanted to fight, and in 1846 cooler heads worked out an agreement to divide the Oregon country at the 49° north latitude line.

CHECKUP

1. What meaning in America's history does the term *manifest destiny* have?
2. How did the United States acquire Texas?
3. What is the significance of the slogan "Remember the Alamo"? "Fifty-four Forty or Fight"?

Continued on page 296

The Mormons

Most of the pioneers who moved westward across the dry region that was then called the Great American Desert were bound for Oregon or California. But one group of people stopped and settled on the arid lands. They were members of the Church of Jesus Christ of Latter-Day Saints, more commonly known as the Mormons.

The Mormon church had been founded by Joseph Smith in western New York State in 1830. Smith's teachings met with hostility among many people, and he and his followers moved westward. In time, they settled in Nauvoo, Illinois. But disputes broke out there between the Mormons and their neighbors, and Smith was killed by a mob.

The new leader of the Mormons was Brigham Young. He determined to take his people into the western wilderness, far from other folks. In 1847 he led an advance party westward. The site that Young chose for the new Mormon community was a spot near Great Salt Lake in what was then Mexican territory. During the following months, thousands of Mormons made the long journey across the Great Plains to settle in the region they called Deseret.

A people with less discipline and dedication would not have survived. But the Mormons stressed cooperation. They worked hard to irrigate the dry lands and raise wheat and corn. By 1850, there were more than 10,000 settlers. As a result of the Mexican Cession, the region was now within the United States. It became the Territory of Utah, with Brigham Young as its governor.

On their trek to Utah, Mormon pioneers, pulling handcarts loaded with their goods, prepare to stop for the night. Earlier arrivals are starting fires for cooking the evening meal.

LESSON 2 *(2 to 3 days)*

Performance Objectives

1. Given an outline map of Mexico and the southwestern United States, to locate **(a)** the Rio Grande, **(b)** the Nueces River, **(c)** Monterey, **(d)** Buena Vista, **(e)** Mexico City, **(f)** the area ceded to the United States as a result of the Treaty of Guadalupe Hidalgo, and **(g)** the Gadsden Purchase. **2.** To list and explain the issues that led to the Mexican War. **3.** To explain orally or in writing how the restlessness of the American people has affected American society.

Famous People

John C. Frémont, John Slidell, Zachary Taylor, Winfield Scott, Stephen Kearny, James Gadsden

Vocabulary

Rio Grande, Nueces River, "California fever," Buena Vista, Mexico City, Monterey, Treaty of Guadalupe Hidalgo, Gadsden Purchase, mobility

Activities

1. FILMS The following films are part of the United States Expansion series: *California* (15 minutes, color; Coronet Films) and *Texas and the Far Southwest* (14 minutes, color; Coronet Films).

2. DISCUSSION After students have read the lesson, list the causes of the war with Mexico on the chalkboard and discuss each one. Then consider the following questions: Was the war with Mexico inevitable? Could the Mexican War have been avoided if there had been instant communication between the White House and Mexico City? In the discussion, use such outside sources as Bemis's and Bailey's texts on American diplomatic history. See also the numerous articles that have appeared in *American Heritage* on the war.

3. ORAL REPORT / DISCUSSION Have one of your students deliver Polk's message on war with Mexico (see Commager's *Documents of American History).* Then ask the students for their reactions to Polk's message. Ask: Do you agree that Mexico started the war? What had Polk done that contributed to bringing on the war? How would you rate Polk as a President? Did he fulfill America's "manifest destiny"? What arguments can you give in favor of calling Polk our greatest imperialist President?

LESSON 2

The War with Mexico

One reason the United States was anxious to settle the Oregon dispute peacefully was that the country was rapidly moving toward war with Mexico. Angered by the annexation of Texas, Mexico broke off relations with the United States in 1845. Furthermore, the two countries disagreed over the location of Texas's southern border. Mexico claimed it was the Nueces River. The United States held that it was the Rio Grande, the mouth of which was more than 100 miles (160 km) farther south, on the Gulf of Mexico.

Had that been the only issue there would have been no reason for war. Few Americans or Mexicans lived in the disputed area, and there was plenty of time to work out a solution. At this moment, however, President Polk was determined to acquire another piece of territory owned by Mexico. That territory was California, lying on the Pacific Coast south of the Oregon country.

Americans in California. American interest in California had built slowly since the first contacts of New England whalers and merchants in the early nineteenth century. At that time California belonged to Spain. Spain had established a string of missions in order to teach the Indians agriculture and convert them to Christianity. Spanish ranchers traded hides and tallow for the goods brought by the American merchants. This trade continued after control of California passed to Mexico in 1822. The region was sparsely settled, with only a few thousand whites—mostly Mexicans—in addition to a larger Indian population.

A few Americans settled in California in the 1830s and urged others to join them. Many were encouraged to come by the appearance in 1844 of John C. Frémont's report of his explorations in California. Frémont, an army officer, was one of a number who were exploring the Far West in those years. He had led earlier exploring parties through much of the Rocky Mountain country, Oregon, and California. Frémont's report on California made special note of the great possibilities for farming and commerce, and led many to move there over the years. By 1845 there were about 700 Americans in California. There were ten times as many Mexicans and even more Indians, but it was clear that a "California fever" was building, among Americans. Further, there were already conflicts between the Americans and the Indian and Mexican inhabitants over land and cultural differences. Many of the 700 Americans were itching to "play the Texas game." That is, they wanted to become a majority and then rebel, declare their independence, and ask the United States to take them over.

War is declared. At this point, President Polk sent a representative, John Slidell, to Mexico. He was told to work out differences over the Mexican border and other matters. He was authorized to offer to buy California and New Mexico for up to $30 million.

When the Mexican government refused even to talk to Slidell, Polk decided on war. American troops under the command of General Zachary Taylor were already camped south of the Nueces. Polk ordered them to the Rio Grande, knowing that this would pro-

United States troops under General John Wool leave San Antonio, Texas, in 1846 on their way to Mexico. The drawing was made by one of the soldiers, sixteen-year-old Sam Chamberlain.

voke a clash. The President had already prepared his message asking Congress to declare war. When the report of a battle arrived, Polk added the news to his message, claiming that "American blood has been shed on American soil." Thereupon, Congress declared war.

Waging the war. Mexico's armies were soon overpowered by the better trained, better armed, and more numerous American troops. General Taylor carried the war into northern Mexico, crushing Mexican resistance at the battle of Buena Vista in February 1847. General Winfield Scott marched his troops into the heart of Mexico and conquered the capital, Mexico City, in September 1847.

Meanwhile, the New Mexico territory had also fallen into American hands. An American army led by Colonel Stephen Kearny had moved from the East into California. There it joined a naval squadron that had taken San Francisco

4. **WHAT IF?** Ask students what would have been the results, in their opinion, if the Mexicans had accepted the terms that John Slidell had offered. Is it possible that there would have been a war anyway? Why, or why not? Would Mexico have felt any differently toward the United States? Explain. After the Mexican War, how do you think most Mexicans felt toward the United States? How did the Mexican War affect the attitude of people in other Latin American countries toward the United States?

5. DEBATE Resolved, That the Mexican War was unjust; therefore, all territories taken from Mexico by the United States should be returned. In the course of this debate, students should discuss the idea of the feasibility of the suggested solution. At the conclusion of the debate, ask students: As you look back on this war, how do you feel about the role of the United States?

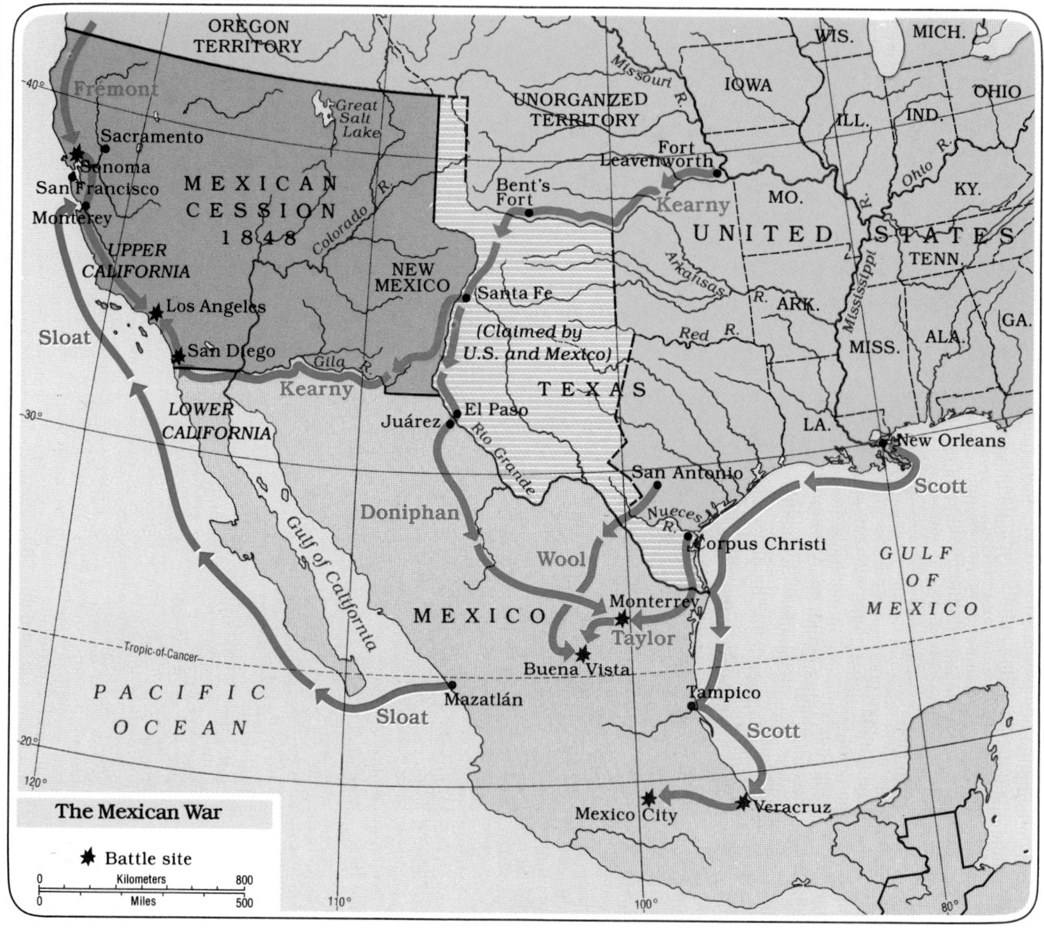

The Mexican War and the settlement that followed had unforeseen consequences for the United States. As you will see in Unit 5, the addition to the United States of the lands of the Mexican Cession revived old quarrels about slavery and thereby helped bring on the Civil War.

and Monterey. Even as the combined force was defeating the handful of Mexican troops, American settlers in California rebelled. Supported by soldier-explorer John Frémont, who was on another exploring trip to the region, they raised their bear flag (so called because it featured a picture of a grizzly bear) and declared California to be an independent republic.

The peace treaty. In February 1848, the United States and Mexico signed the Treaty of Guadalupe Hidalgo, which ended the war. The treaty included the following terms: (1) Mexico accepted the

Rio Grande as its boundary with Texas. (2) Mexico *ceded*, or gave up, New Mexico and Upper California to the United States. (3) The United States paid Mexico $15 million for the new territory. (4) The United States paid American citizens some $3 million that the Mexican government owed them.

With the transfer of these vast territories from Mexico came a hundred thousand Mexicans who were living there. The treaty further provided that these people were free to move to Mexico, but that those who chose to stay for one year would automatically be citizens of the United States. Most of the people stayed.

One further strip of territory south of the New Mexico territory was bought from Mexico in 1853. This was the Gadsden Purchase, so called because James Gadsden, the United States minister to Mexico, arranged it. The land was wanted for a southern rail route to the Pacific. The purchase gave the United States its present southwestern boundary.

In 1848 even the most extreme believers in manifest destiny could look back upon the previous three years with satisfaction. In that brief time, the United States had increased its territory by 1,200,000 square miles (3,120,000 square km), an incredible 66 percent. That, Americans agreed, was land enough even for a restless, land-hungry people.

★11★

James K. Polk

1795—1849

Born in NORTH CAROLINA
In Office 1845—1849
Party DEMOCRATIC

Followed an expansionist policy. Directed war with Mexico, by which U.S. got California and Southwest. Settled Oregon boundary dispute. First President not to seek reelection.

★ ★ ★ ★ ★ ★ ★ ★

At the beginning of this unit, we noted that much of America's history is tied to the restlessness of its people. You have read how that restlessness gave the country most of its present land before the middle of the nineteenth century. In a later chapter you will read how miners, cattle raisers, and farmers swept over plains, deserts, and mountains to fill in half the continent in little more than a generation.

This migration, incredible as it is, tells only a part of the story of this people on the move. Another part is to be found in the growth of American cities. For no movement of this endlessly mobile people has been more continuous or greater in size than the flow of people

Background Information

A TASTE OF THE FUTURE

The Mexican War brought together many of America's most promising and brilliant young officers: James Longstreet, George McClellan, George Pickett, Ulysses S. Grant, William T. Sherman, Thomas J. Jackson (later called "Stonewall"), Pierre Gustave Toutant Beauregard, Jefferson Davis, George Meade, Joseph Hooker, and Robert E. Lee. These men met as comrades in arms while fighting for one cause under one flag. They had no premonition of the tragedy that awaited them fifteen years hence, when, divided six to five between Confederacy and Union, they would clash on the bloodiest battlefields ever to divide a nation.

The Mexican War also brought Abraham Lincoln to the attention of the nation. As a member of the House of Representatives, he fought in Congress against the war. He insisted that the war had been unnecessarily and unconstitutionally commenced by President Polk. And he demanded that Polk tell him where the exact spot was that American blood had been shed and to say whether that exact spot was indeed American soil. When his constituents in Illinois censured him for his "base, dastardly, and treasonable assault upon President Polk," Lincoln knew he could not win reelection. He returned to Springfield at the age of forty, believing his political career had ended.

6. USING A MAP As a concluding activity for this study of the Mexican War, provide students with outline maps and have them locate the places specified in Performance Objective 1. Have students use different colors to show the areas added to the country by the Treaty of Guadalupe Hidalgo and the Gadsden Purchase. Refer students to maps on pages 298 and 300. In addition, you may wish to have them trace on the map the troop movements in the Mexican War. Remind students of the necessity for a map key.

7. CREATIVE WRITING Have students write brief editorials explaining how the restlessness of the American people has affected American society. Encourage them to express opinions, supported by facts from the text and their own life experiences. At the conclusion of this activity, poll the class to find out how many feel that mobility has had a good or positive effect on American society. How many feel that mobility has had a detrimental effect? Why?

8. USING A GRAPH The skills development activity on page 304 relates directly to the theme of mobility and makes a good concluding activity for this lesson and the entire unit.

from farm and village to town and city. That story, too, is for later chapters in this book. But one piece of information here will make the point clear. In 1790, the year of the nation's first census, only one in thirty Americans lived in a city of 8,000 or more. Today, nearly four out of five do.

Even this fact, however, does not give a complete picture of the moving Americans. It does not reveal the movement from one city to another. For example, the population of Boston, Massachusetts, grew from 383,000 to 448,000 between 1880 and 1890. That shows a gain of 65,000. But it does not show that nearly *fifteen times* that many—one and a quarter million—are estimated to have moved in and out of this one city during those same ten years! Studies of other cities of the time show much the same thing.

The effects of mobility. What have been the effects of this restlessness on the American people and their society? They have been many. As you have seen, there has been a clear connection between mobility and opportunity. The readiness to move about has made it possible for a

With the Gadsden Purchase of 1853, the United States great era of expansion on the continent of North America came to an end. The American people had spanned a continent. More than a century later, the state of Alaska and the offshore state of Hawaii would be added.

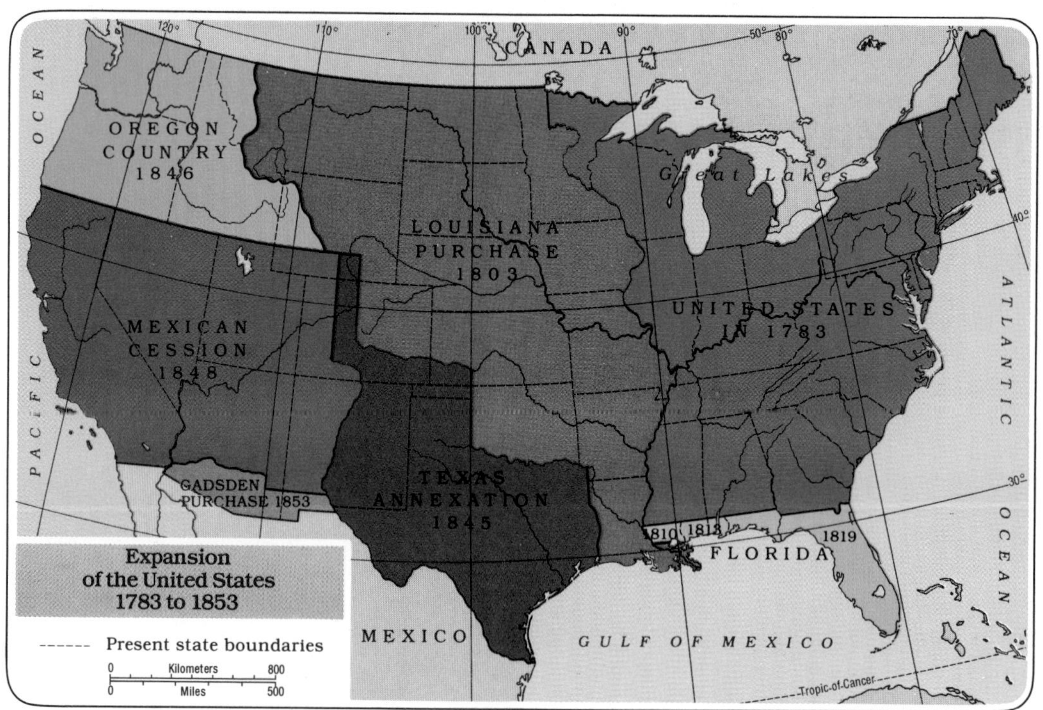

good many people to improve their positions and to rise in the world. It has also provided a safety valve for those who have not risen. Their luck, they say, will perhaps be better in the next town or in another part of the country.

Certainly all this mobility has had a great effect on the American family. We take for granted that young people will not be tied to the same place as their families. They will go wherever a job opportunity or their wish for adventure may take them. As a result, *family*, *home*, and *community* hardly mean the same in America as they do in a society where people are anchored to a place for generations.

Very probably this has something to do with the fact that Americans are a nation of joiners. The Elks and the Masons, churches and social clubs, may be substitutes for family, neighborhood, and village.

No doubt other possible effects of the rootlessness of Americans will occur to you. Knowing that friendships may be temporary, do Americans treat them differently? Americans are well known for their openness, their readiness to strike up new friendships, their first-name introductions to strangers. Are these traits connected to a need of an ever-moving people to form new relationships? Do Americans have less interest in local government, perhaps, or in preserving the quality of a town or neighborhood because tomorrow they may be someplace else? Does the practice of using things and then moving on affect their attitudes about conservation? These are some of the many questions that students of American society raise about the effects of mobility. Whatever may be the exact answer to any of them, it is clear that modern America has been shaped in important ways by the fact that its people, through all of their history, have been a people on the move.

CHECKUP

1. Why did the Mexican War take place?
2. How did the Mexican War alter the boundaries of the United States?
3. What territory was added to the United States by the Gadsden Purchase?
4. How has the restlessness of the American people affected American society?

Key Facts from Chapter 14

1. The term *manifest destiny* became popular during the 1840s as an expression of the expansionist goals of the United States.
2. Texas became independent of Mexico in 1836 and joined the United States in 1845.
3. A dispute between the United States and Great Britain over the Oregon country was settled in 1846 by dividing the region at 49° north latitude.
4. As a result of the war with Mexico, 1846–1848, the United States gained most of the lands that today make up the American Southwest.

Answers To Review Questions

1. National expansion could bring rich lands to the farmers, room for the spread of cotton culture and slavery, important ports on the Pacific Coast for trade with the Far East, and a way to block British expansion in North America.
2. At first, Mexico welcomed American settlers to Texas because that area was underpopulated and the settlers could serve as a buffer against Indian raids. However, the Texans, unwilling to learn local customs and language, did not obey Mexican laws against slavery or convert to Catholicism.
3. Many people in the Northeast did not want to add more slave states to the Union. The South, however, was eager for annexation in order to expand the cotton culture and slavery.
4. In spite of some opposition, most Americans favored the annexation of Texas. When expansionist candidate James K. Polk won election as President, the retiring President, John Tyler, persuaded Congress to pass a joint resolution annexing Texas in 1845.
5. On the explorations of Lewis and Clark; on the fur-trading posts established by John Jacob Astor; and on the activities of missionaries, such as Jason Lee, Marcus and Narcissa Whitman, and Father Pierre Jean De Smet.

6. Polk favored the annexation of Oregon as well as Texas.
7. (a) 1845–1848. (b) Disagreement over the location of Texas's southern border; American efforts to annex California; and the ordering of American troops to the Rio Grande—a deliberate action to provoke the Mexican army to attack. (c) Zachary Taylor, Winfield Scott, Stephen Kearny. (d) Treaty of Guadalupe Hidalgo. (e) Treaty terms: (1) Mexico accepted the Rio Grande as the boundary of Texas; (2) Mexico gave up New Mexico and Upper California (today's state of California) to the United States; (3) United States paid Mexico $15 million for the new territory; and (4) the United States paid American citizens some $3 million that the Mexican government owned them.
8. Americans exhibit a greater willingness to move in pursuit of a job opportunity or the spirit of adventure. They tend to be a nation of joiners of clubs and organizations. Because Americans are frequently on the move, they display an openness toward strangers and a readiness to strike up new friendships. Their mobility colors their attitudes toward local government and the conservation of resources.

Answers For Chapter Test
1. k 2. g 3. m 4. l 5. f 6. e 7. p 8. c 9. a 10. b 11. d 12. h 13. o 14. n 15. i 16. j

★ REVIEWING THE CHAPTER 

People, Places, and Events

Manifest destiny *P. 287*
Santa Anna *P. 289*
The Alamo *P. 289*
Sam Houston *P. 290*
James K. Polk *Pp. 290, 299*
John Jacob Astor *P. 291*
Marcus and Narcissa Whitman *P. 293*
Mormons *P. 295*
John C. Frémont *P. 296*
John Slidell *P. 296*
Gadsden Purchase *P. 299*

Review Questions

1. What practical benefits could national expansion bring? *Pp. 287–288* Les. 1
2. Why did the Mexican government encourage American settlement in Texas and then try to drive the settlers out? *P. 288* Les. 1
3. Why was public opinion divided about the annexation of Texas by the 1830s? *P. 290* Les 1
4. What finally persuaded the United States to annex Texas? *P. 290* Les. 1
5. On what evidence did the United States base its claim to the Oregon territory? *Pp. 291, 293* Les. 1
6. What was James K. Polk's position on the issue of expansion in the election of 1844? *P. 294* Les.1
7. Give the following information about the Mexican War: **(a)** dates, **(b)** three causes, **(c)** American military leaders, **(d)** name of treaty, **(e)** specific terms of the treaty. *Pp. 296–299* Les. 2
8. What have been some effects of mobility on the American people and their society? *Pp. 300–301* Les. 2

Chapter Test

Match the name in the first section with the correct description in the second section. Write your answers on a separate piece of paper.

1. Winfield Scott
2. James K. Polk
3. Zachary Taylor
4. John C. Frémont
5. Sam Houston
6. John Slidell
7. Brigham Young
8. Marcus Whitman
9. Santa Anna
10. Jim Beckwourth
11. Rio Grande
12. Moses Austin
13. James Gadsden
14. John J. Astor
15. Jim Bridger
16. Nueces River

a. Mexican leader at the Alamo
b. "Mountain man" in Nevada
c. American missionary in Oregon
d. Southern boundary of Texas, according to the United States
e. American diplomat sent to purchase California from Mexico
f. President of the Lone Star Republic
g. Expansionist President
h. Received a land grant from the Mexican government to settle in Texas
i. "Mountain man" and first white person to look upon Great Salt Lake
j. Southern boundary of Texas according to Mexico
k. American general who captured Mexico City
l. Soldier–explorer in the Far West
m. American general who first clashed with the Mexicans at the Rio Grande
n. Set up fur-trading posts in Oregon
o. Arranged a land purchase that gave the United States its present southwestern boundary
p. Mormon leader

★ REVIEWING THE UNIT ★

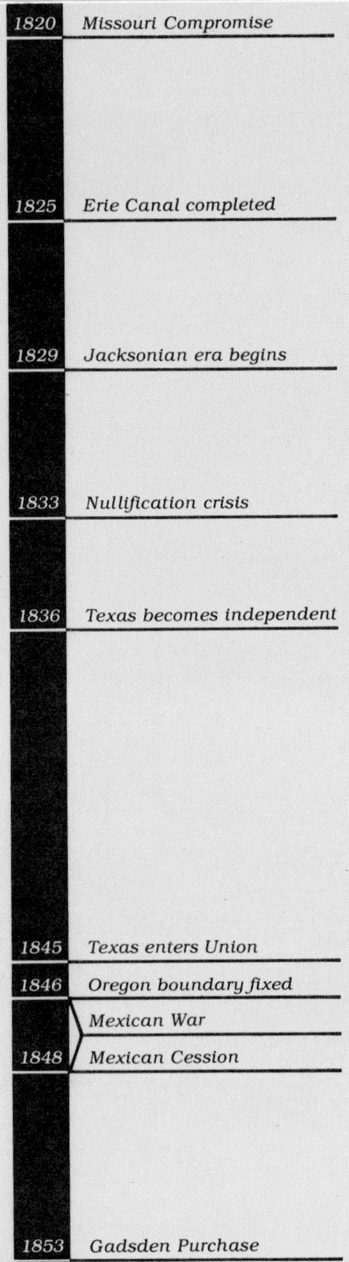

In the early 1800s, Americans started moving westward in large numbers. First to cross the Appalachians were hunters and trappers. Then came the pioneers and permanent settlers. The development of roads, canals, and railways hastened the westward movement. The federal government sold western lands at low prices. Tragic victims of westward expansion were the Indians, who were forced off their home lands.

As the nation grew, the North, the South, and the West developed differently, and sectional rivalries arose. With northern backing, John Quincy Adams was elected President in 1824. Andrew Jackson, with western support, won the 1828 election. Jackson's two terms saw ordinary people gain influence in government. In the tariff controversy, Jackson upheld the federal government's rights over states' rights. Jackson destroyed the Bank of the United States by stripping it of its business. The move, though popular, helped bring on a depression during Martin Van Buren's administration.

During the 1840s, a confident America continued its expansion. It gained the Oregon country up to 49° north latitude. Texas became independent from Mexico, and in 1845 it was annexed by the United States. Following the war with Mexico (1846–1848), California and most of what is today the American Southwest were added by the Treaty of Guadalupe Hidalgo. By 1848, Americans, ever on the move, had expanded the nation's boundaries from the Atlantic to the Pacific.

Answers to Unit Questions

1. Northeast, North Central, West, South
2. a. 3,900,000 or 3.9 million
   b. 2,400,000 or 2.4 million
   c. 5,000,000 or 5 million
3. Largest increase: Northeast, 1950–55; North Central, 1950–55; West, 1955–60; South, 1970–75. Smallest increase: Northeast, 1970–75; North Central, 1970–75; West, 1965–70; South, 1950–55
4. In 1970–75, the South experienced the greatest population growth and the Northeast experienced the smallest growth.

 REVIEWING THE UNIT 

Skills Development: Interpreting Graphs

One theme of this unit is the historical movement of the American people. As you study the graphs and answer the questions, think about how the information relates to the mobility theme.

1. What are the four regions named on the map?
2. Each bar on the graphs represents the increase in the region's population for a particular five-year period. The change is expressed in millions. For example, in the Northeast for the period 1950–55, the population increased by 2.7 million or 2,700,000.
   a. What is the increase in population for the West in the period 1960–65?
   b. For the North Central in 1965–70?
   c. For the South in 1955–60?
3. In which five-year period did each region experience the largest increase in population? the smallest increase?
4. In 1970–75, which region had the greatest population growth? Which region had the smallest growth?
5. In which region do you live? Describe the population trend in your region during the twenty-five year period.

Population Increase for 5-Year Periods by Region: 1950–1975
(Increase expressed in millions.)

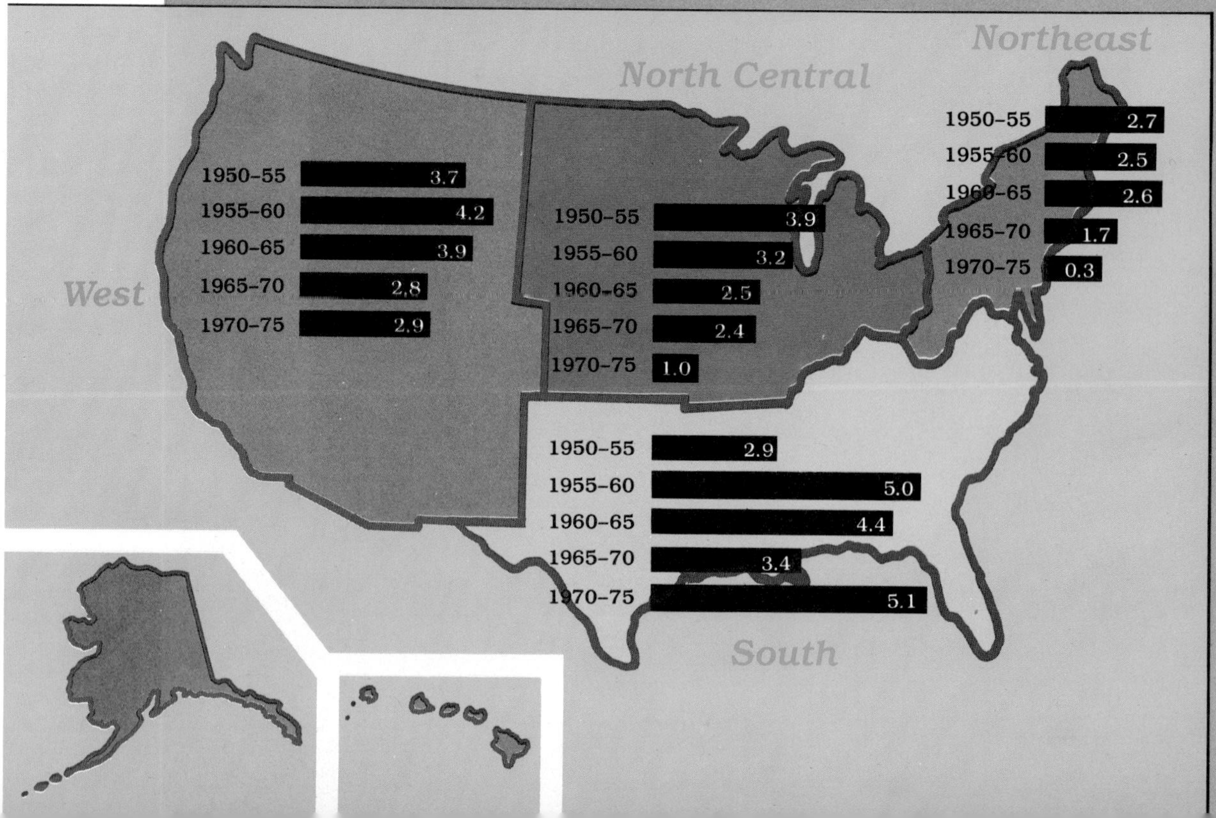

	West	North Central	Northeast	South
1950–55	3.7	3.9	2.7	2.9
1955–60	4.2	3.2	2.5	5.0
1960–65	3.9	2.5	2.6	4.4
1965–70	2.8	2.4	1.7	3.4
1970–75	2.9	1.0	0.3	5.1

Unit 5

Americans: Freedom and Equality

A NATION DIVIDED

Background Information

PICTURE "Upland Cotton" depicts black women harvesting cotton near Montgomery, Alabama. This is a detail from a painting by the famous American artist Winslow Homer (1836–1910).

THE WORLD THE SLAVEHOLDERS MADE

LESSON 1

"MY LIFE had its significance and its only deep significance because it was part of a Problem," wrote a famous American in his autobiography. "But that problem was, as I continue to think, the central problem of the greatest of the world's democracies and so the Problem of the future world." The writer of those lines was a noted American scholar and public figure. He had received a Ph. D. degree from Harvard and had taught at several American colleges. He was the author of dozens of books and articles. He was also one of the founders of the best-known civil rights organization in the United States, the National Association for the Advancement of Colored People (NAACP).

The writer was William Edward Burghardt Du Bois, a black American. The "central problem" of which he wrote was the problem of race. In a larger sense, it was the question of whether a multiracial society could make good on its claims of freedom and equality for all. For Du Bois as for many others, the extent to which it fulfilled those claims was the true measure of democracy. For that reason, the history of black people in America becomes a test case of American democracy.

Du Bois wrote his autobiography in 1940. In the years since then, and especially in the most recent twenty years or so, America has taken important steps in dealing with its "central problem." The evidence is not simply in laws passed or in court decisions handed down. It can be found, among other

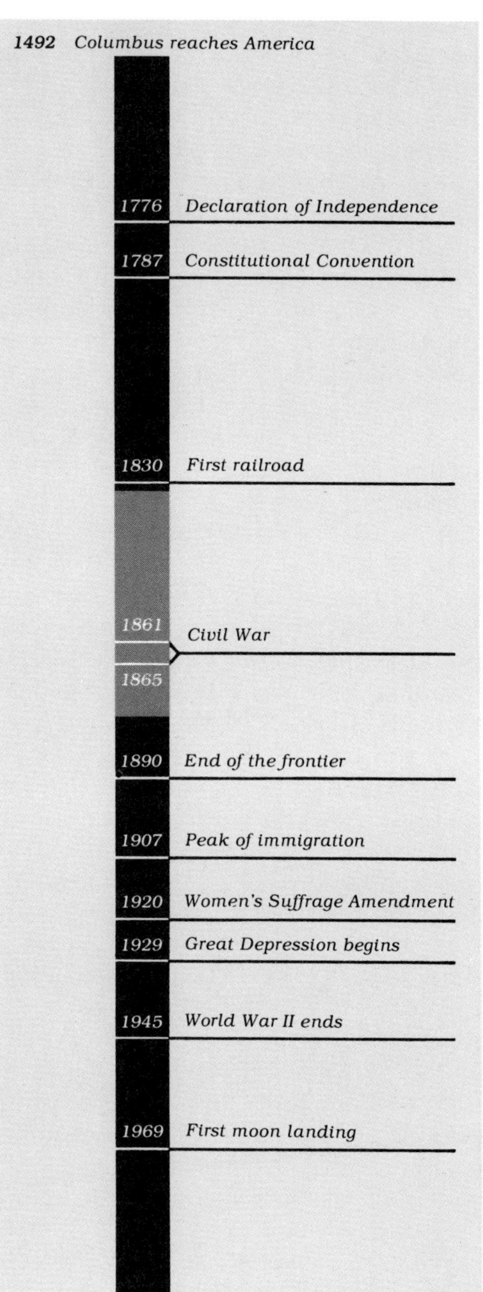

LESSON 1 *(1 to 2 days)*

Performance Objectives

1. To describe how black Americans were affected by the American Revolution. **2.** To cite evidence that supports and evidence that refutes the idea that slavery in America was dying out by the early 1800s. **3.** To describe the attempt at African colonization and to explain why it was unsuccessful.

Famous People

W. E. B. Du Bois, Benjamin Banneker

Vocabulary

National Association for the Advancement of Colored People (NAACP), multiracial society, Black Revolution, manumission, free blacks, prejudice, discrimination, three-fifths clause, cotton culture, Gabriel's rebellion, American Colonization Society, Liberia, Haiti

Activities

1. INTRODUCING THE UNIT The concepts of freedom and equality as major forces shaping America and Americans are the central themes of this unit. These themes are developed through a study of the experience of black people during the first hundred years of the nation's history. You may wish to begin the unit by discussing the status of various minority groups in the United States today. If possible, have students examine government statistics on unemployment, housing, poverty, and education and draw conclusions from this information about the position of minority people in American society. Ask: How successful have minority groups been in achieving their share of the American Dream? Why have black Americans, Hispanic Americans, American Indians, and other minorities had to work so hard to improve their social, political, and economic conditions? In answer to the last question, someone is bound to suggest the idea of racial prejudice and discrimination. At this time, introduce students to the ideas of W. E. B. Du Bois as presented in the text on pages 307 and 308. Point out that Du Bois wrote about the problem of race in 1940. Ask: In the years since 1940, what specific steps has the United States taken in dealing with the problem of race? Why, after all that has been done, does the problem still exist? As students mention the difficulty of changing people's attitudes, review those long-held ideas about race that were studied in Unit 1. Those ideas are important to an understanding of how and why slavery developed as a burning issue in the nineteenth century.

places, in the statistics on college graduates, entry into the professions, distribution of income, and the holding of positions in government. It can be seen in offices, on college campuses, and in the use of public facilities.

Many of these changes came as a result of the demands and organized efforts of blacks themselves. The movement for greater rights in the 1960s and 1970s, often called the *Black Revolution*, was an important force for improving the social, political, and economic conditions of black Americans. Hispanic Americans, American Indians, and other minorities have also pressed their claims for a share in the American Dream.

It is also true that these changes, so long in coming, have by no means achieved the goal of equality. That fact, too, can be found in statistics—those on unemployment and poverty, for example. And it can be seen in a drive through cities and rural regions.

At the root of the "Problem," as Du Bois suggested, are the long-held ideas of white Americans about race—ideas that are only now changing. You explored those ideas, their sources, and some of their tragic consequences in Unit 1. In this unit you will examine those ideas further. You will learn about the experience of black people in America during the first hundred years of the nation's history. You will learn how and why slavery came to be an important issue for an ever larger number of Americans. Unable any longer to square slavery with the value of freedom, they finally ended slavery.

Most Americans of the time were content to leave the matter at that. But for a minority even then, the freeing of slaves raised a host of new questions about the meaning of freedom. Does freedom mean merely the absence of slavery? Does it—must it—mean something more? Is equality—equal rights, equal opportunity—a necessary part of freedom? Or is it possible to have freedom with something less than equality? To the free blacks during the era of slavery, these were familiar questions. You will explore them in this unit.

Slave and Free

The American Revolution had an important effect upon the black Americans. For one thing, as you read in Unit 2, several thousand slaves gained their freedom in exchange for serving in the army. Even more important, the ideas of the Revolution caused many Americans to look at slavery in a different light. How could white Americans justify black slavery while complaining that Britain was trying to "enslave" them? As Abigail Adams wrote in 1774 to her husband, John, "It always appeared [wrong] to me to fight . . . for what we are daily robbing and plundering from [the slaves. They] have as good a right to freedom as we have."

There was surely a contradiction between slavery and the Declaration of Independence, which says that "all men are created equal." Thomas Jefferson, the author of the Declaration, understood that. In an early draft of the Declaration, he had condemned King George for violating "the sacred rights of life and liberty" of Africans by enslaving them. However, Southerners in the Continental Congress—especially those from

One slave who became free at the time of the American Revolution was Phillis Wheatley of Boston. Brought from Africa at the age of nine, she learned English quickly and showed a flair for writing verse. Her poetic talents were encouraged by her master's wife. Miss Wheatley's first book of poems, published in 1773, attracted much attention in both America and England.

South Carolina and Georgia, where the slave population was large—objected to this paragraph, and it was removed.

A spreading idea. Though the Continental Congress struck out Jefferson's words, it could not strike out the idea. In 1775 the first antislavery society in America was formed in Philadelphia, with Benjamin Franklin as its president. A year later the Society of Friends (Quakers) ruled that all of its members must free their slaves. Nearly all states, including those in the South, passed laws against the slave trade. During and right after the war, five northern states took steps to end slavery. To be sure, none had a large slave population. Furthermore, most did away with slavery gradually rather than at once, generally giving a slave freedom at the age of twenty-one. Still, those states were taking important steps toward freedom.

The effect of Revolutionary ideas about freedom was felt in the South, too. While Jefferson was governor of Virginia in the 1780s, he proposed that slavery be ended in that state, but the legislature did not accept the idea. Virginia and several other states did, however, pass laws making it easier for owners to set their slaves free. *Manumission* is the legal word for "setting slaves free." Many owners did this, most often in their wills. One North Carolina slave owner who freed his slaves at his death gave these reasons in his will:

> Reason the first: . . . every human being . . . his or her color what it may [be], is entitled to freedom. . . . Reason the second: My conscience . . . condemns me for keeping them in slavery. Reason the third: the golden rule directs us to do unto every human creature, as we would wish to be done unto. . . . Reason the fourth and last: I wish to die with a clear conscience that I may not be ashamed to appear before my master in a future world.

Free blacks. As a result of the spreading ideas about freedom, the number of free black people rose. By 1790, when the first federal census was taken, there were about 59,000 free blacks in the United States—about 8 percent of the black population. Most free blacks were in the southern states. By 1810, that number had tripled.

At the same time, it is important to understand that almost none of the

2. ORAL REPORTS Have some students read and report on Chapter XVIII, "The Present and Probable Future Condition of the Three Races That Inhabit the Territory of the United States" in Alexis de Tocqueville's *Democracy in America.* This is a remarkable chapter and closes with some quite accurate forecasts about the future of both the United States and Russia—especially amazing since the book was written in 1840.

3. DISCUSSION After students have read the lesson, list on the chalkboard the specific effects that the American Revolution had on black Americans. Ask: If so many people were sympathetic to the wrongs of slavery, why did so few people favor equality for black Americans? Help students to define *equality.* Ask: Is it possible to have freedom without equality? Does freedom refer only to the absence of slavery?

people who talked of the wrongs of slavery also favored equality for black Americans. Many states limited the number of free blacks or kept them from entering. Some even required that a freed slave must leave the state. Free blacks could not testify in court. Although they could vote in a number of states, they did not hold office. A few states limited the free blacks' chances to work in certain occupations. Even when laws did not limit job opportunities for them, prejudice did.

Making their way. To help themselves make their way in a society that discriminated against them, free blacks in northern cities formed their own organizations. They set up churches and schools and formed business and study groups and social clubs. Several of these organizations offered very practical help to their members—supplying insurance, making loans, and performing other services.

Through these groups, free blacks also tried to promote the cause of freedom for the slaves and equal rights for themselves. Because their numbers were small and their position was weak, the only way they had a chance of success was by persuading others to their views. One way of doing so was to set a high standard of personal conduct—

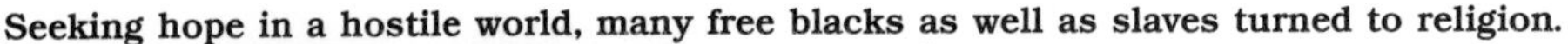

Seeking hope in a hostile world, many free blacks as well as slaves turned to religion.

hard work, a religious life, thrift, and so on. Such conduct would show that blacks were responsible citizens and deserved full rights. Another way of promoting their cause was to petition Congress and the state legislatures to end slavery and discrimination. At every opportunity, they reminded white Americans of the gap between the words of the Declaration of Independence and the condition of black people in America. One of the leaders in this effort was Benjamin Banneker, a mathematician who helped to plan the city of Washington.

Was slavery dying? At the Constitutional Convention, in 1787, a proposal by George Mason of Virginia to outlaw slavery had been defeated. In the debate, one northern delegate, also opposed to slavery, argued that Mason's plan was not necessary. "As population increases," he reasoned, "poor labor will be so plentiful as to [make] slaves useless. Slavery in time will not be a speck in our country." In the 1780s and 1790s, a good many Americans in both North and South agreed that slavery was on the way to its death.

There is some evidence to support this view. The number of slaves imported fell from an average of 6,500 a year in the 1760s to an average of fewer than 2,000 a year in the 1770s. In many parts of the South the profits of slavery shrank as overproduction of tobacco caused prices to drop and as the fertility of tobacco lands decreased. Many planters in Maryland and Virginia found themselves deep in debt. Further, as you have read, slavery was ending in the North, and the number of manumissions in the South was increasing.

Another view. On the other hand, there is strong evidence that slavery was *not* dying out. By the 1780s, southern states were having second thoughts about ending the importation of slaves. In that decade, the number of slaves brought into the United States climbed to an average of 5,000 a year. In the Constitutional Convention, southern states won a number of compromises that protected slavery. Among them were the three-fifths clause (see page 166) and the guarantee that runaway slaves would be returned.

Several of the reasons to believe that slavery would continue had little or nothing to do with profits. One of these was that slaveholders were unwilling to accept the changes in their way of living that would come with freeing slaves. Thus, even men like Thomas Jefferson and George Washington, who spoke out against slavery as a curse, did not give up their slaves until they died.

A second reason lay in the fact that most whites believed blacks to be inferior. They did not believe that a society in which blacks and whites lived side by side in equality could work. In other words, it was not just slavery that was the problem. It was that slavery and race had been tied together. Had the slaves been white, owners might well have worked out a way to free them and to live alongside them in the same society. They had done so with indentured servants. But few whites could bring themselves to do this with black people. African slavery, then, was not just a labor system. It was also a social system, with *African* having the meaning of "lower being" even when the African was not a slave.

4. LISTENING FOR INFORMATION Students may be interested in knowing more about the paragraph condemning slavery that was removed from the Declaration. Professor Carl Becker comments on this deleted paragraph in his classic *The Declaration of Independence* (New York: Harcourt, Brace and Company, 1922), pages 212–223. You may wish to read selections from Becker's book or have several good readers in the class present the information.

5. ESSAY Have students write essays in which they present evidence in one paragraph in support of the idea that slavery in America was on the way to its death by the early 1800s. In a second paragraph, students should cite evidence to refute that idea.

Effects of the cotton gin. As you read in Unit 4, Eli Whitney's invention of the cotton gin had far-reaching effects. The production of cotton rose rapidly. As planters opened up new cotton lands, slaves became more valuable. In the ten years after 1795, the price of slaves doubled, and the number of slaves imported rose sharply. Between 1790 and 1800 traders brought 80,000 slaves into the United States. By the time Congress ended the slave trade, in 1808, another 100,000 had entered. And even after it became illegal to import slaves, several thousand were smuggled in each year.

Touissaint L'Ouverture, a slave for almost fifty years, led the successful slave uprising in the 1790s against the French in Saint Domingue.

While the cotton culture was fastening slavery on the South, an event in the West Indies strengthened the South's belief that slavery was the only way to control black people. Slaves in the French colony of Saint Domingue rebelled against their masters. They took over the colony, fought off French and British armies, and eventually set up in Haiti the first black republic in the Western Hemisphere. All this took place between 1791 and 1804.

The idea that slaves could rise up and take over a society was terrifying to American slaveholders. They feared that ideas of freedom might infect their own slaves. Then in 1801 an uprising almost took place. A Virginia slave named Gabriel and his armed followers planned to seize a number of key points and hold them. Other slaves, Gabriel believed, would soon join them in a general uprising. At the last moment, the plot was discovered, and Gabriel and several dozen other slaves were executed.

As news of Gabriel's rebellion spread through the South, controls on slaves and even on free blacks were tightened. Blacks away from their home plantations had to produce either papers proving they were free or passes from their masters. Most southern states also now made it more difficult for a master to free slaves.

Still, there were people in the South who believed that slavery was wrong. They were also concerned about the effect that slavery had on white Americans. Thomas Jefferson, who knew firsthand what it meant to live in a slave society, explained this concern.

> There is an unhappy influence on our people produced by slavery among us.

> Every exchange between master and slave always includes the worst passions on the master's part, and degrading submission on the slaves' part. Our children see this, and learn to imitate it. The parent storms, the child watches . . . and puts on the same airs to smaller slaves, and thus learns tyranny. . . . When half the people trample the rights of the other half that way . . . it makes . . . tyrants of the masters and dangerous enemies of the slaves. . . . Also the masters will get used to having other people do their work, and no country can progress if half its people will not work.

Colonization in Africa. Although men and women of conscience were troubled by slavery, few were ready to liberate blacks and live alongside them in the same society. The best answer to the problem of slavery that white Americans could come up with was to plant a colony for blacks in Africa. In 1816 the American Colonization Society was formed with the support of such leading figures as Henry Clay, James Monroe, and John Marshall. The society planned to buy land in West Africa with contributions from Congress and from individuals. It hoped to transport to that colony 50,000 freed slaves a year.

The plan did not work out. To carry out its program, the society needed $1 million a year, but in its best year it raised less than $50,000. During the society's forty-year history, it settled only 8,000 Afro-Americans in Liberia, the nation it founded in West Africa.

The idea of "returning home" never had much appeal to American blacks. For one thing, by the time the American Colonization Society was founded, most blacks in America, both slave and free, had been born in the United States. To them, the United States, not Africa, was home. For another, some black leaders saw colonization as a means of strengthening, not ending, slavery. James Forten, a wealthy black sailmaker in Philadelphia, explained in 1818:

> Those slaves who feel they should be free and who thus may become dangerous to the quiet of their masters, will be sent to the colony; and the tame and submissive will be retained. . . . The bondage of a large portion of our brothers will thus become perpetual.

In 1830, Peter Williams, a New York minister, explained why free blacks opposed colonization.

> We are natives of this country; we ask only that we be treated as well as foreigners. Not a few of our fathers suffered and bled to purchase its independence; we ask only to be treated as well as those who fought against it.
>
> [The Colonization Society] professes to have no other object . . . than the colonizing of the free people of colour on the coast of Africa, with their *own consent;* but if our homes are made so uncomfortable that we cannot continue in them, or if . . . we are driven from them, and no other door is open to receive us but Africa, our removal there will be anything but voluntary.

Although free blacks had no wish to take part in a colonization scheme, some did favor leaving America for other lands. Between 1820 and 1825, several thousand free blacks moved to Haiti. However, Haitians thought of the new arrivals as foreigners. Moreover, the emigrants themselves found that they were more American in their ideas and customs than they had realized. After a few years, many returned to America.

6. DISCUSSION Many Americans insisted that slavery was immoral. Thomas Jefferson, a Virginian and himself a slave owner, declared: "I tremble for my country when I reflect that God is just; that his justice cannot sleep forever." Those who supported slavery in the South excused it as "a peculiar institution" that was necessary for the existence of the cotton plantations. Ask students how slavery might have been ended without causing economic ruin in the South. In the course of the discussion, have students describe the attempt at African colonization and explain why it was unsuccessful. Locate Liberia and Haiti on a world map.

7. FILM/FILMSTRIP The film *Black History: Lost, Stolen or Strayed* (53 minutes, color; CBS) compares the real history of the black American with the prejudiced and subverted history. *Black Odyssey,* a silent filmstrip in two parts, is produced by the Anti-Defamation League and available for purchase from Social Studies School Service (10,000 Culver Blvd., Culver City, Calif. 90230). Part 1 of this filmstrip deals with black Americans from the 1600s to the Civil War.

LESSON 2 *(2 to 3 days)*

Performance Objectives

1. To describe orally or in writing the life of plantation slaves, paying particular attention to the varieties of work performed and the social makeup of the slave groups. **2.** To explain how white masters were able to keep slaves under control. **3.** To describe the black resistance to slavery.

Famous Person

Frederick Douglass

Vocabulary

Overseer, driver, Gullah, Auntie, griot, sold "down the river," Nat Turner's rebellion

Activities

1. FILMS *The Angry Prophet: Frederick Douglass* (23 minutes, color; NBC Films). *In Search of a Past,* Of Black America series (53 minutes, color; CBS) tells of three teenage black Americans traveling in Ghana in search of their African heritage. *Heritage of Slavery,* Of Black America series (56 minutes, color; CBS). *Negro Slavery,* American History series (25 minutes, color; McGraw-Hill Films) shows the beginning and development of slavery as an institution in the United States and records the life of the slave.

CHECKUP

1. What effect did the American Revolution have on black Americans? How did free blacks promote the cause of freedom?
2. Why did some people in the 1780s and 1790s feel that slavery would die out? What were some of the reasons that it did not?
3. Why was African colonization unsuccessful as a solution to the slavery problem?

LESSON 2

Life Under Slavery

The world that the slaveholder made was filled with problems for white Americans. For black Americans, it was filled with danger and uncertainty. From the time that Africans were snatched from their homeland and packed into the cramped spaces below the decks of ships, there was never a moment's security for them.

The work routine. In the nineteenth century, about three fourths of all slaves worked the fields of the South. If they were on a small farm with fewer than five slaves, their owner often worked alongside them. Those on larger plantations worked under the eyes of an *overseer*—a manager. The overseer was often assisted by a black slave known as a *driver.* Slaves rose at daybreak, were in the fields at dawn, and usually stayed there until sunset. A break for breakfast, and two more for lunch and dinner offered a bit of relief and a chance to talk with other slaves. Such a workday was always at least ten hours long. Sometimes it was as long as sixteen hours.

As you read in Unit 1, a large plantation was much like a self-sufficient small town. Thus there was a need for many kinds of workers besides field hands. Slaves worked as shoemakers, carpenters, cooks, barbers, nurses, housekeepers, and at many other jobs requiring special skills. Sometimes they worked closely with their masters or overseers and often received special favors, such as gifts of cast-off clothing or home furnishings. Often the skilled slaves learned English better than the field hands, and a master might teach them to read and "figure." Attractive men and women slaves worked in the main house as cooks, maids, and butlers, or as caretakers for children of ill adults. At times, masters trusted talented slaves to treat the sick or to barter and trade for the household. These house slaves were at the top of the slave social order.

The slaves that were most often freed were the household servants and the slaves with special skills. Their master knew them as people. Moreover, they were the ones in the best position to make their way in a free society. By 1830 there were about 150,000 free blacks. They were centered in the cities of Baltimore, New Orleans, Charleston, and Washington.

Survival of African culture. For a long time it was thought that the slaves' African culture simply disappeared after they landed in America. However, as we have learned more about African society, we have come to realize that a considerable amount of African culture did survive. For example, in many African societies where farming was done in groups, one person sang to set a rhythm for the others to work by. This practice was carried over into the tobacco, rice, and cotton fields of the American South.

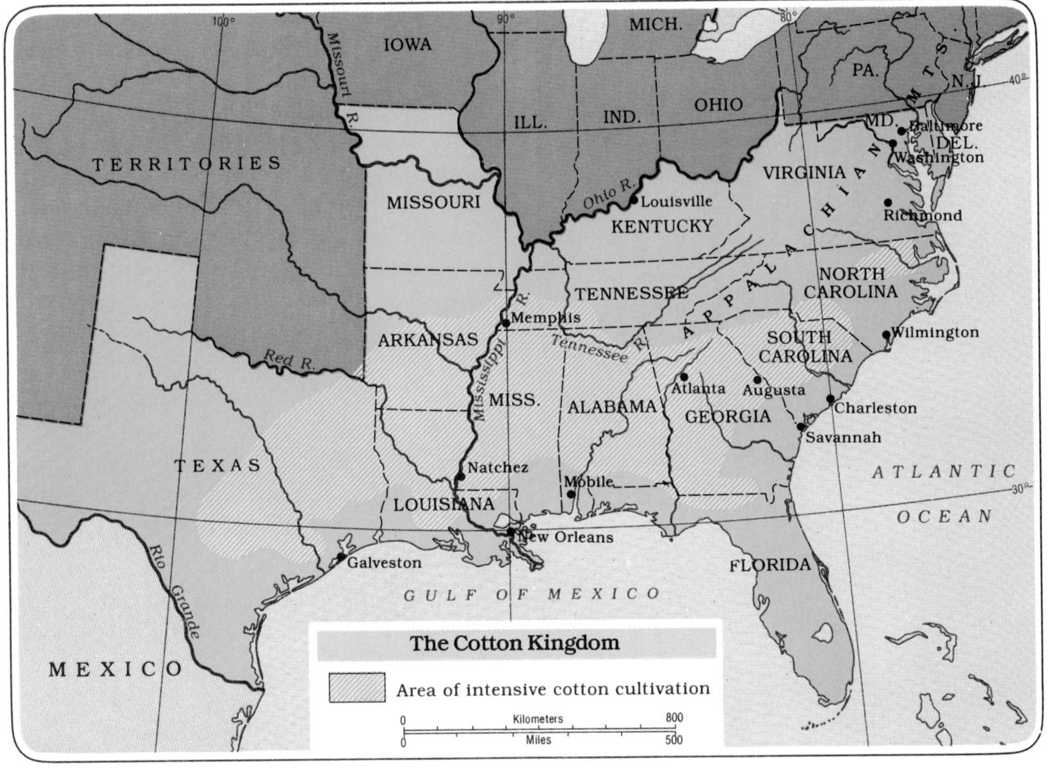

The slave population of the South was concentrated in the belt of intensive cotton cultivation.

On large plantations, slaves lived in small buildings not far from the main house. Floors were often of packed earth, and windows lacked glass. In the evenings, when the laborers came back to their quarters from the fields, there was singing and the telling of stories that had been passed on to the slaves by their parents and grandparents. The designs of the drums and stringed instruments that were used to make music were also African in origin.

Certain African religious beliefs and customs were brought to America too. When slaves were converted to Christianity, they often kept parts of their earlier religion.

African languages, too, survived for a time. Most slaves came from tribes along the western coast of Africa. Though tribal languages were different, they had some likenesses, as French and Spanish have, for example. Africans from different tribes, thrown together on large plantations, worked out new languages that combined their own languages and English. A number of African words made their way into the English language. These include *goober* (for peanut) and *yam* (for sweet potato).

2. ROLE-PLAYING After students have read the lesson, divide the class into three groups. Tell the first group that they are slave owners, the second group that they are slaves, and the third group that they are overseers. Explain to students that they are to act as they imagine those people would in the following hypothetical situations.

a. A slave requests permission of his or her master to marry another slave.

b. A runaway slave is returned to the overseer after being captured.

c. The master tells a slave family that he is going to sell two of the children to a neighboring slave owner.

d. The news of a slave rebellion in the next county is received by the master and the overseer; by the slaves.

Allow students time to meet in their groups and prepare their roles. Encourage different students to take part in each situation. At the conclusion of the role-playing, discuss with students their impressions of and reactions to each situation. Ask: How did you feel when you were involved in the actual role-playing? when you were watching? How true to life did the portrayal of each situation seem to be? Then explore with students the idea of how they each would have behaved if they had actually been the slave, overseer, or slave owner. Ask: To what degree can you really understand what slavery was like? What is the value today of attempting to understand slavery when it has been a dead institution for more than one hundred years?

Operation of the cotton gin on a Southern plantation was a job usually performed by slaves. At an early age, the slave children were assigned such tasks as carrying water to the older workers.

In time, English replaced the African languages. But in the low country of coastal South Carolina and Georgia, where the concentration of blacks was among the heaviest, a language called *Gullah* is still spoken. It was heavily influenced by African languages. Burial customs also show the African influence. One Afro-American cemetery in Georgia still has old grave markers that resemble West African carvings.

Role of the "Auntie." An important link in passing on parts of African culture from one generation to another was an older woman called the *Auntie*. She was often no longer able to do heavy field labor and so took care of the babies and small children of slave mothers who worked in the fields. The Auntie may have been a relative of the children she cared for. She entertained them with folktales that were frequently African in origin.

The Auntie also often served in the role that had been played in Africa by a man called the *griot*. It was the griot's job to memorize the history of births, family trees, wars, famines, and other local history. In Africa, this person was respected and protected and had no other work to do. As the griot grew old, he passed on his knowledge of local events to a successor.

The treatment of slaves. House servants were better treated than field hands. They played an important part in the family life of their owners and were in constant contact with them. Yet most owners treated field hands with some care too. The slave was a big investment. A master would indeed be very unwise not to take care of a field hand, who, by the 1850s, cost $1,700 to replace. Thus, recent studies of slave diets on large plantations show that the average slave probably got enough protein, vitamins, and calories to stay healthy. Though food was monotonous, the evidence is that slaves were not underfed.

Many masters encouraged slave marriages even though the marriages were not recognized by law. Masters did so partly because marriage conformed with their own ideas of a proper, moral life and partly because slaves with families made more stable workers. The threat to sell a member of the family also helped to discipline slaves.

Masters—kind and cruel. The most important factor in determining the treatment of the slave was the attitude of the master. Frederick Douglass, a Maryland slave who later escaped to the North, described one owner in this way:

> Instead of the cold, damp floor of my old master's kitchen, I was now on carpets. . . . I had a good straw bed, well-furnished with covers; instead of coarse meal in the morning, I had good bread and mush occasionally; instead of my old tow-linen shirt, I had good, clean clothes. I was really well off. . . . I was human, and she, dear lady, knew and felt me to be so.

But this lady was only one of several owners that Douglass had. Mr. Covey was very different.

> If at any one time of my life more than another, I was made to drink the bitterest dregs of slavery, that time was during the first six months of my stay with Mr. Covey. We were worked in all weathers. It was never too hot or too cold; it could never rain, blow, hail, or snow too hard for us to work in the field. Work, work, work was scarcely more the order of the day than of the night. The longest days were too short for him and the shortest nights too long for him. I was somewhat unmanageable when I first went there, but a few months of this discipline tamed me. Mr. Covey succeeded in breaking me.

Douglass's descriptions of these two owners are a reminder of the central truth of slavery: the power of one human, the master, over another, the slave, was total. The slave depended on the owner for food, clothing, and care. The master decided where, when, and at what task the slave should work. The master decided whether the slave might take a mate and whether and when they would be separated from each other and from their children. The slave's very life was in the hands of the master.

Physical punishment. Since there was no control of a master's use of force, it is not surprising that angry and brutal masters often did real harm to the helpless slaves. Whipping was routinely used, even by owners who thought of themselves as kind. Slaves who had not done enough work to please their owners were given a few lashes to make them pick up their pace. Slaves who broke rules or were disrespectful to their owners might be whipped in front of other slaves to set an example. The threat of physical beatings was one of the chief means of keeping slaves under control. As one Virginia planter said, "A great deal of whipping is not necessary; some *is*."

The breakup of families. One of the cruelest parts of the slave system was the breakup of families through the sale of slaves. This was done far more often for business reasons than for punishment. However, the reason hardly made a difference to the slave family that was separated. Between 1800 and 1860, about 100,000 slaves from the declining tobacco regions in Virginia and Maryland were sold "down the river" to cotton planters in the Deep South. Probably between 15 and 30 percent of the slave couples were separated by the sale of

3. DISCUSSION Sixty percent of the slaves in the United States in 1850 were employed in growing cotton. Ask students why slavery was considered to be an economic necessity by Southern plantation owners. Point out that by the 1850s, two thirds of the cotton crop was being exported to Great Britain and other European countries in return for the manufactured goods that the South needed. Ask students why it is dangerous for a region or a nation to ignore most of its natural resources and depend on a single crop, such as cotton. What if Eli Whitney had invented a synthetic fiber, such as nylon, instead of the cotton gin? What effect might this have had on American history?

4. DISCUSSION Henry F. Bedford in *The Union Divides: Politics and Slavery, 1850–1861* (New York: Macmillan, 1963) remarks: "James Madison thought he could abolish slavery in a way that would meet with almost universal approval if he had the miraculous ability to make the Negroes white." Ask students what Madison was really saying. Was he right? Bedford goes on to write, "Lacking such a power, Madison despaired of a solution." What does the word *despair* connote?

5. CREATIVE EXPRESSION From the variety of information given in the lesson, have students create a picture of life under slavery. What did it mean to be a slave? How did slaves live? What work did they do? Allow students to choose the methods or forms of creative expression that best suit their talents. Arrange to display their work at the completion of this activity.

Chicago Historical Society

Prospective buyers prepare to make bids at a slave auction in 1852. Such sales were held regularly in the cities of the slaveholding states. The auctions often separated the members of slave families.

one of the mates. More often it was the strong, young slaves who were sold, because they brought the best price.

Slave families knew that separation could occur at any time. Nevertheless, many slaves were able to make family life work. On many plantations, there were several generations of a slave family. Marriage into other slave families on the plantation made for a network of aunts, uncles, cousins, and other relations. Often, husband and wife were owned by separate masters on neighboring plantations. Then the husband was able to see his wife and children only one or two evenings a week, when he was allowed visiting rights by his owner. But slaves managed to keep their families intact whenever possible. Most slave marriages were broken only by death or by forced separation.

The response of the slaves. Some slaves accepted their lot. Others resisted. Between 2,000 and 3,000 slaves ran away each year. But escape was difficult. Masters sometimes hunted slaves with trained dogs. Nor could a runaway always count on other slaves to help, for they did not want to get into trouble themselves. Also, masters tempted their slaves with rewards for turning in runaways.

Even when runaways thought they had made good their escape, they could never feel sure they were safe. Professional slave catchers might retake them months or even years later. A captured runaway might then be branded or have a foot cut off to prevent another escape. The punishment was often performed in the presence of other slaves. The message was clear.

Resistance by rebellion. Before slavery was ended, there were more than 200 rebellions or plans for rebellion. Most of these were quite small, but some were major, such as the Stono rebellion in South Carolina and Gabriel's rebellion in Virginia. The largest was Nat Turner's rebellion in 1831 (see page 327).

Rebellion had even less hope for success than running away, for the whites had the guns. And even if a rebellion succeeded, where could the slaves go? The slaveholders were even more determined to track down rebels than to catch ordinary runaways. Rebellion, then, was an act of desperation. So were individual acts taken in rage, such as killing an overseer or clubbing a master. For the slave who committed such an act, execution was swift and certain.

Other kinds of resistance. There were forms of resistance, though, that were widespread though undramatic. Slaves would work very slowly. They would break tools or set fire to the toolshed or barn. They would either pretend to be ill or deliberately let themselves become ill. Some even went so far as to cut off a hand or foot so that they could not do field work. Masters were never sure whether the slaves had planned those things or whether they occurred by sheer accident. One Louisiana doctor actually thought this behavior was the result of a special slave disease. He gave it a Latin name, *dyaesthesia aethiopica,* and described it.

> Individuals affected with this complaint . . . do much mischief . . . owing to the stupidness of mind and insensibility of the nerves induced by the disease. Thus, they break, waste, and destroy everything they handle; abuse horses and cattle; tear, burn, or rend their own clothing. . . . When driven to labor the slave performs the task assigned him in a headlong, careless manner, treading down with his feet or cutting with the hoe the plants he is put to cultivate; breaking the tools he works with; and spoiling everything he touches that can be injured by careless handling.
>
> Hence the overseers call it "rascality," supposing that the mischief is intentionally done.

Many a slave would have laughed to know of the good doctor's findings.

Quite rare was the kind of resistance shown by Frederick Douglass against Mr. Covey. You read earlier that Covey had broken Douglass. But the time came when Douglass could strike back.

> Whence came the daring . . . to grapple with a man, who 48 hours before could . . . have made me tremble . . . I do not know. . . . The fighting madness had

Frederick Douglass, born into slavery in Maryland, fled to Massachusetts at the age of twenty-two. He later became an abolitionist leader.

Background Information

FREDERICK DOUGLASS (1817?–1895) Douglass was an abolitionist, an orator, and a journalist. Born a slave in Maryland, he was named Frederick Augustus Washington Bailey but assumed the name of Douglass after escaping from slavery and running away to Massachusetts in 1838. Although he was trained to work in a shipyard, Douglass had trouble finding work because other people refused to work with a black. Thus he was forced to take many menial jobs to stay alive. In 1841, Douglass successfully addressed a Massachusetts Anti-Slavery Society convention and was hired as a lecturer. In 1847 he published his autobiography, *Narrative of the Life of Frederick Douglass, an American Slave,* to answer those who doubted that a man of his abilities could ever have been a slave. When publication of his autobiography exposed his past, friends helped raise money to buy his freedom. After a period in England, Douglass moved to Rochester, New York, and started an antislavery newspaper, the *North Star.* He wrote almost as much about the prejudice and discrimination against the free black person in the North as he did about the horrors of slavery in the South. Seeking justice for his race, he successfully fought an attempt to segregate the schools in Rochester. His house was a station on the Underground Railroad. During the Civil War, his sons served in the Union army. Douglass himself conferred several times with President Lincoln about the problems of slavery. After the war, he held several positions with the federal government, including recorder of deeds in Washington, D.C., and minister to Haiti.

Answers To Review Questions

1. It was also a social system, with *African* having the meaning of "lower being." This was true even when the African was not a slave. Such an attitude on the part of whites meant that they could not envision a society in which blacks and whites lived side by side in equality. Even those whites who believed in the ideals expressed by the American Revolution could not free their slaves.
2. The production of cotton rose rapidly. Planters opened up new cotton lands and slaves became more valuable. The price of slaves doubled and the number imported rose dramatically.
3. Every exchange between master and slave always included the worst passions on the master's part and degrading submission on the slave's part. Slavery made tyrants of the masters and enemies of the slaves.
4. The field hand worked from dawn to sunset in the fields under the direction of the overseer and the driver. The skilled craftspeople and the house servants worked more closely with the master. They received better food, clothing, some education, and more of a chance to become free.

> come upon me, and I found my strong fingers firmly attached to his throat. . . . My resistance was entirely unexpected and Covey was taken all aback by it. . . . "Are you going to resist, you scoundrel," said he. To which I returned a polite "Yes, sir."

Douglass went on to describe a long fight between himself and this hated master, and the results of that fight.

> He had not, in all the scuffle, drawn a single drop of blood from me. I had . . . been victorious, because my aim had not been to injure him, but to prevent his injuring me. . . . He never again laid the weight of his finger on me. . . .
>
> I was no longer a servile coward. . . . This spirit had made me a free man in *fact* though I still remained a slave in *form.* When a slave cannot be flogged, he is more than half free. . . . From this time until my escape from slavery [more than four years later] I was never . . . whipped. . . . the easy manner in which I got off was always a surprise to me. . . . the probability is that Covey was ashamed to have it known that he had been mastered by a boy of sixteen.

The great majority of slaves, however, accepted their life. Because their masters' power over them was complete, they learned to walk, to talk, and to behave in ways that would please those masters, whatever the secret thoughts in their own hearts. And they turned to religion to find comfort in the hope of a better life in a world hereafter.

This was the world of the slave. Increasingly it became enmeshed with nearly every issue in American national politics—expansion, states' rights, and others. Finally, as we shall see in the next chapter, slavery overshadowed all other issues and eventually brought about America's most tragic conflict.

CHECKUP

1. How did the work of slaves vary on large plantations?
2. How were slaves kept under control by their masters?
3. In what ways did the slaves resist their lot?

Key Facts from Chapter 15

1. The Declaration of Independence, which says that "all men are created equal," caused many white Americans to question how slavery could be justified.
2. During the years immediately following the American Revolution, many whites came to favor freedom for slaves, and by 1810 there were close to 200,000 free blacks.
3. Among those whites who favored freedom for slaves, very few also favored equality for black Americans.
4. The invention of the cotton gin resulted in the increased planting of cotton and the need for more field labor, thus helping to fasten the slavery system on the South.
5. Many slaves accepted their lot, but many others resisted—by running away, by rebelling openly, or by doing their jobs poorly.

★ REVIEWING THE CHAPTER ★

People, Places, and Events

W. E. B. Du Bois *P. 307*
Black Revolution *P. 308*
Society of Friends *P. 309*
Manumission *P. 309*
Benjamin Banneker *P. 311*
Saint Domingue *P. 312*
Haiti *P. 312*
Gabriel *P. 312*
American Colonization Society *P. 313*
Overseer *P. 314*
Driver *P. 314*
Auntie *P. 316*
Frederick Douglass *P. 317*
Nat Turner *P. 319*

Review Questions

1. Why was African slavery more than just a labor system? *P. 311* Les. 1
2. What effects did the cotton gin have on cotton production and the issue of slavery? *P. 312* Les. 1
3. Why did Jefferson believe that slavery had a bad effect on the master as well as on the slave? *P. 313* Les. 1
4. Compare the lot of the field hand with that of the house slave on a plantation. *P. 314* Les. 2
5. Name four ways in which the African culture survived among the slaves in America. *Pp. 314–316* Les. 2
6. What was the special role played by the Auntie in the slave society? *P. 316* Les. 2
7. Besides physical punishment, what other hold did the slave owner have over his slaves? *P. 317* Les. 2
8. What methods could the slave use to "fight back" against the slave owner? *Pp. 318–319* Les. 2
9. Why did a slave rebellion offer little hope of success? *P. 319* Les. 2

Chapter Test

On a separate piece of paper, write **T** *if the statement is true and* **F** *if the statement is false.*

1. Freedom from slavery gave blacks equal rights and equal opportunity with whites. T
2. Leaders of the Revolution, such as Washington and Jefferson, favored abolition of slavery and freed their own slaves to set a good example. F
3. The plan to return blacks to Africa was enthusiastically supported by blacks, but colonization failed because of the lack of money. F
4. The African culture survived among the slaves, and in time even became part of the white culture. T
5. The Black Revolution refers to the slave uprising that took place in Louisiana during the 1830s. F
6. There were no free blacks in the South before the Civil War. F
7. A large plantation was much like a self-sufficient small town. T
8. In general, field slaves were better treated than house slaves because field hands cost a great deal of money to replace should something happen to them. F
9. A slave revolt in the French colony of Saint Domingue resulted in the eventual establishment of the first black republic in the Western Hemisphere. T
10. The attitude of the master was probably the most important factor in determining the treatment of slaves. T

5. The practice of one person singing to set a rhythm for the others to work by; the singing and telling of stories passed on to the slaves by their ancestors; certain religious beliefs and customs that influenced Christianity; African words made their way into the English language.
6. The Auntie memorized the history of births, family trees, wars, famines, and other local history. She passed on this knowledge to the other slaves.
7. The slave's greatest fear was that the master would sell one or more members of his or her family.
8. Some slaves ran away; some revolted; others worked very slowly, broke tools, set fires, pretended illness, or deliberately maimed themselves.
9. The whites had the guns and were determined to track down rebels. Furthermore, even if the rebellion succeeded, the slaves had nowhere to go.

Background Information

1. PICTURE This is a detail from a painting titled "Underground Railway" by the artist Webber. It depicts escaped slaves arriving safely at Levi Coffin's farm in Newport, Indiana, near the Ohio border. When Coffin learned that some runaways had been retaken because they had been clumsily hidden by well-meaning townspeople, he made his farm into a station on the Underground Railroad.

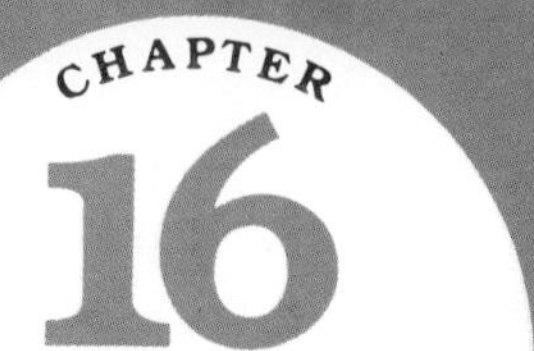

SECTIONALISM AND SLAVERY

THE ISSUE OF SLAVERY played no major part in national politics for the first thirty years after George Washington became President. Opinion was sharply divided between North and South, but most leaders were anxious to avoid an issue that might split the Union. Further, slavery was considered a local matter. Under the Constitution, each state decided for itself whether slavery would exist within its borders.

In 1819, however, slavery burst into national politics over the question of its spread into the territories. After a year of heated debate, Congress passed the Missouri Compromise. It set 36°30′ north latitude as the dividing line between slave and free territories (see page 266). Politicians breathed a sigh of relief. They believed they had now removed the dangerous issue of slavery from national politics.

The aging John Adams knew better. "I take it for granted," he wrote Thomas Jefferson, "that the present is a mere preamble—a title page to a great tragic volume." Whole chapters of that "volume" would soon follow. One of them was the nullification crisis of 1832–33 (see page 275). Although the apparent issue was the tariff, the question of slavery lay just beneath the surface. Southerners knew well that a federal government that could force a tariff on them could someday also interfere with slavery. "We are divided into slave-holding and nonslave-holding states," observed one South Carolinian at the time, "and this . . . must separate us at last."

The Antislavery Crusade

Most early opponents of slavery favored one of three approaches to the problem. They urged owners to treat their slaves more like human beings than like property. They tried to persuade owners to free slaves, at least in their wills. Or they supported colonization. By the 1820s, a small number of whites were working for *universal emancipation*—that is, the freeing of all slaves. But most of the whites proposed that this be done gradually, that slave owners be paid for their losses, and that the freed slaves be colonized. Such a person was Benjamin Lundy, a Quaker who published an antislavery newspaper.

Around 1830, however, there occurred an important change in the goals of the antislavery movement. Its leaders felt that they were making little progress and now began to demand that slavery be ended immediately.

The abolitionists. This demand that slavery be abolished right away gave antislavery reformers of the 1830s the name of *abolitionists.* Using the printing press, lecture platform, and pulpit, they spread their message on the cruelty of slavery. Many were deeply religious people for whom slavery was one of the worst of sins. Outstanding among these abolitionists was William Lloyd Garrison of Massachusetts. A former writer for Lundy's newspaper, Garrison began his own paper, *The Liberator,* in 1831. In the first issue, Garrison made clear that he no longer believed in a *gradual* freeing of slaves.

LESSON 1 *(1 to 2 days)*

Performance Objectives

1. To explain the methods that abolitionists used to achieve their goal. **2.** To describe the opposition white abolitionists received from **(a)** Northerners and **(b)** black abolitionists.

Famous People

William Lloyd Garrison, Theodore Dwight Weld, Angelina and Sarah Grimké, Harriet Tubman

Vocabulary

Compromise of 1820, universal emancipation, abolitionists, *The Liberator,* Underground Railroad, moral suasion

Background Information

2. UNDERGROUND RAILROAD Many fugitive slaves were helped by the Underground Railroad. One estimated figure is 50,000 escapees between 1830 and 1860. The Underground Railroad system included Southern blacks who were themselves unable to escape, free blacks in both the North and South, and white abolitionists. The railroad was most active in Ohio and Pennsylvania (see the map on page 392). Surprisingly, ads for the railroad appeared in the newspapers. One read: "The improved and splendid Locomotives . . . will run their regular trips during the present season between . . . the Patriarchal Dominion and Libertyville. . . . SEATS FREE, *irrespective of color.*"

3. HARRIET TUBMAN (1821–1913) Widely known as "the Moses of her people," Tubman was one of the most active "conductors" on the Underground Railroad. She was born a slave in Maryland and escaped in 1849, traveling north via the loosely organized network of abolitionists who made up what was called the Underground Railroad. Over a period of about ten years after her own escape, Tubman risked her life repeatedly by returning to Maryland nineteen times to guide others to freedom. Her aged parents were among the more than 300 slaves so aided. At one time, rewards offered for her totaled $40,000, but she always evaded capture. Harriet Tubman became a friend of leading abolitionists, and John Brown conferred with her about his plan to seize Harpers Ferry. During the Civil War, she served as a nurse, scout, and spy for the Union army in South Carolina. After the war, she lived in Auburn, New York, where she worked to raise money for black schools and to establish a home for elderly and needy blacks. In 1908 such a home was opened and later became known as the Harriet Tubman Home. In 1914 the city of Auburn honored her memory by placing a bronze tablet at the entrance to the Cayuga County Courthouse.

> I will be as harsh as truth, and as uncompromising as justice. On this subject, I do not wish to think, or speak, or write with moderation. No! No! Tell a man whose house is on fire to give a moderate alarm; . . . tell the mother to gradually extricate her babe from the fire into which it has fallen—but urge me not to use moderation in a cause like the present. I will not equivocate, I will not excuse—I will not retreat a single inch—AND I WILL BE HEARD.

Garrison helped organize the American Anti-Slavery Society in 1833. He published his newspaper until the end of the Civil War.

Another abolitionist leader, a New England minister named Theodore Dwight Weld, organized abolitionist groups in New York State and the Ohio Valley. Teams of his followers held public meetings in the spirit of religious revivals. With their message that slavery was cruel and sinful, and abolition was Christian, they organized nearly 2,000 antislavery societies by 1850. Most of the members, including many of the leaders, were women.

Two sisters from a South Carolina slaveholding family, Angelina and Sarah Grimké, wrote articles and made speeches. They were ridiculed and persecuted, not only for their ideas but for their boldness. The idea of women speaking before public groups was disapproved by most at the time.

The Underground Railroad. Some abolitionists did not wait for slaves to be freed voluntarily. They became involved in the *Underground Railroad*, a network of people who helped slaves escape from the South. In time, more than 3,000 people were involved in the railroad. Slaves would run away at a time arranged in advance and then be passed from house to house along the route to some safe place—often Canada.

Stories of spectacular escapes grew up around the railroad. A Maryland slave, Harriet Tubman, escaped and then risked her life by returning to the South nineteen times in order to guide other slaves to freedom.

At the height of its operation, the railroad probably helped about 500 slaves a year to escape. Actually, owners voluntarily freed more than that number each year. But the Underground Railroad was more threatening because it freed slaves without the owners' permission.

Northern opposition. Abolitionists were hardly the darlings of the North. Operators of mills that needed cheap cotton from the South were not anxious for slavery to end. Neither were those white workers who feared that free blacks would work for low pay and drive down wages. Even many whites who disliked slavery were irritated by the "troublemaking" of the abolitionists.

As a result, abolitionist leaders were often attacked and sometimes beaten. Garrison, arriving in Boston to speak to a women's antislavery group, was dragged through the streets by an angry mob. Weld was mobbed on numerous occasions. In New York and Philadelphia, abolitionist meetings were broken up. Philadelphia city officials stood by and watched a mob burn a building where abolitionists gathered. And in Alton, Illinois, in 1837, an angry mob of whites burned the printing press of Elijah Lovejoy, an abolitionist printer, and shot him to death.

A number of slave women flee with their children on what they hope will be the road to freedom. Runaway slaves usually hid in the woods or elsewhere by day and moved northward at night.

A political approach. Most abolitionists worked outside of politics. They expected to end slavery by *moral suasion*—that is, by convincing people to end it because it was morally wrong. "If we express frankly and freely our position," said one, "[slaveholders] will give up their slaves." By the end of the 1830s, however, some abolitionists were looking to achieve their ends through politics. They formed the Liberty party and chose James Birney, a former Kentucky slave owner, as their candidate for President in 1840. Their platform did not call for immediate abolition of slavery. Instead it focused on stopping the spread of slavery into the territories.

Birney polled only 7,000 votes in 1840. Running again in 1844, however, he received 62,000 votes. In New York State he drew enough votes away from Henry Clay, the Whig candidate, to cost Clay the state and thereby swing the election to James K. Polk of Tennessee, the Democratic candidate. Still, 62,000 was barely 2 percent of those who voted. More Americans than that felt slavery was wrong—antislavery societies had many more members—but most of them did not yet feel strongly enough about the issue to leave the Whig and Democratic parties.

No thought of equality. There was no more thought of equality for blacks in the North than there was in the South. Northern states that entered the Union after 1820 prohibited slavery, but many

Activities

1. **USING PICTURES** Call the students' attention to the pictures on pages 322 and 325. For each picture, have students reconstruct the feelings of the blacks at that particular moment. Ask: In what ways might the people's thoughts and feelings differ between the two pictures?

2. **LISTENING FOR INFORMATION** William Lloyd Garrison eventually came to be regarded as the leading abolitionist in the country. Students may enjoy reading aloud his manifesto from his first *Liberator;* this appears in Commager's *Documents of American History*, 149, "The Liberator, Vol. I., No. 1." An excerpt from this writing is shown on page 324 in the text.

3. RESEARCH/ORAL REPORT Have some of the students research and report to the class on William Lloyd Garrison, Angelina and Sarah Grimké, Harriet Tubman, and Frederick Douglass.

4. BOOK REPORT One or several of the students might be interested in reading and reporting to the class on John Hope Franklin's *From Slavery to Freedom* (New York: Alfred A. Knopf, 1956).

5. CREATIVE WRITING After students have read the lesson, ask them to imagine that they are members of the abolitionist movement. Assign each one to write a letter to a member of his or her family **(a)** explaining the methods used by abolitionists in order to achieve their goal and **(b)** describing the opposition that abolitionists encountered in their antislavery crusade. At the completion of this activity, encourage students to share their letters with the class.

6. DISCUSSION Alexis de Tocqueville, writing in the 1830s *(Democracy in America),* stated that "prejudice of the race appears to be stronger in the States which have abolished slavery than in those where it still exists." Have students analyze this statement in light of their knowledge of the treatment of free blacks in the United States prior to the Civil War. Ask: Do you think de Tocqueville was correct in his observation? If so, how do you account for this apparent paradox?

also discouraged free blacks from living within their borders. In the 1830s, several states took away the blacks' right to vote. By 1840, only 7 percent of the North's free blacks were allowed to vote. Only in Massachusetts could a black serve on a jury. By law or by custom, there was segregation in housing, public transportation, schools, theaters, and churches. It was plain that whites in the north as well as in the South felt that blacks should be kept "in their place."

Only some of the abolitionists favored equality for blacks. Garrison frequently had dinner with black friends and campaigned for integrated schools in Boston. Angelina Grimké went to social gatherings with her good friend, Sarah Mappes Douglas, a free black woman from Philadelphia. But many white abolitionists disapproved of such mixing with black people. Some antislavery groups would not let black people join. The American Anti-Slavery Society would not have a black minister speak to its meeting in 1836 because "the time has not come to mix with people of color in public." Most abolitionists were concerned with ending the moral wrong of slavery, not with fighting for equality for the Negro.

Black abolitionists. Free black Americans were deeply involved in the struggle to end slavery. In fact, a free black named David Walker published an abolitionist pamphlet in Boston in 1829, two years before Garrison's first issue of *The Liberator.* In his "Appeal . . . to the colored citizens of the world," Walker warned that if slaves were not freed immediately they might take their freedom by force. Indeed, until the mid-1830s, black people were the main source of support for the antislavery movement. Of the first 450 subscribers to Garrison's *Liberator,* 400 were black; of the 2,300 subscribers in 1834, 1,700 were black. Black abolitionists carried their message to other blacks and to whites through newspapers, books, and lectures. Autobiographies by former slaves, such as Frederick Douglass, were found to be especially effective.

Douglass's newspaper was named for the star by which escaping slaves made their way to freedom.

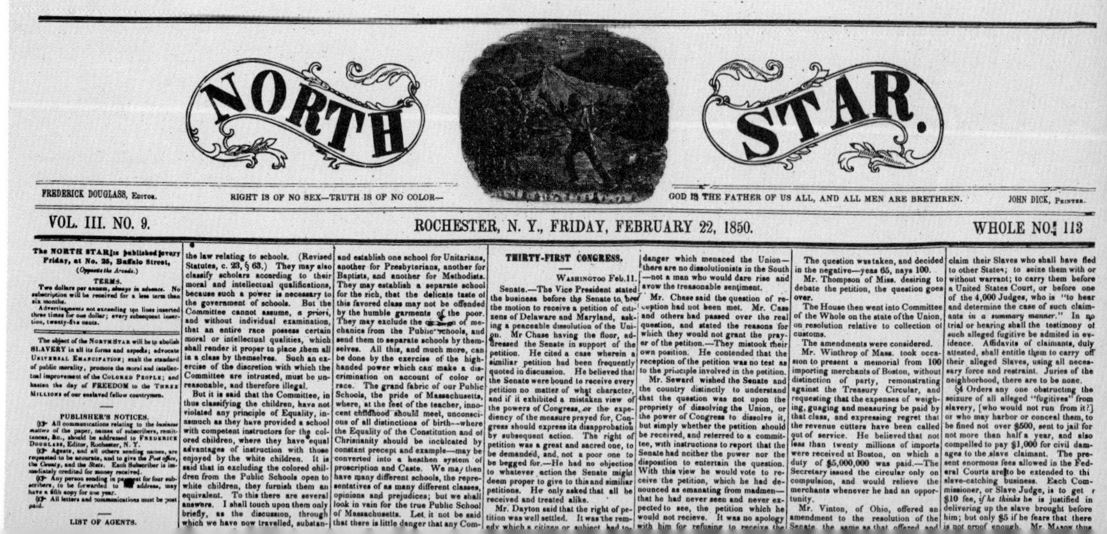

NORTH STAR.

FREDERICK DOUGLASS, Editor. RIGHT IS OF NO SEX—TRUTH IS OF NO COLOR— GOD IS THE FATHER OF US ALL, AND ALL MEN ARE BRETHREN. JOHN DICK, Printer.

VOL. III. NO. 9. ROCHESTER, N. Y., FRIDAY, FEBRUARY 22, 1850. WHOLE NO. 113

The NORTH STAR is published every Friday, at No. 25, Buffalo Street, (*Opposite the Arcade.*)

TERMS.

Two dollars per annum, *always in advance.* No subscription will be received for a less term than six months.

Advertisements not exceeding ten lines inserted three times for one dollar; every subsequent insertion, twenty-five cents.

The object of the NORTH STAR will be to abolish SLAVERY in all its forms and aspects; advocate UNIVERSAL EMANCIPATION; exalt the standard of public morality, promote the moral and intellectual improvement of the COLORED PEOPLE; and hasten the day of FREEDOM to the THREE MILLIONS of our enslaved fellow countrymen.

PUBLISHER'S NOTICES.

☞ All communications relating to the *business matters* of the paper, names of subscribers, remittances, &c., should be addressed to FREDERICK DOUGLASS, Editor, Rochester, N. Y.

☞ Agents, and all others sending names, are requested to be accurate, and to give the *Post office,* the *County,* and the *State.* Each Subscriber is immediately credited for money received.

☞ Any person sending in payment for four subscribers, to be forwarded to [illegible] address, may have a fifth copy for one year.

☞ All letters and communications must be post paid.

LIST OF AGENTS.

the law relating to schools. (Revised Statutes, c. 23, § 63.) They may also classify scholars according to their moral and intellectual qualifications, because such a power is necessary to the government of schools. But the Committee cannot assume, *a priori,* and without individual examination, that an entire race possess certain moral or intellectual qualities, which shall render it proper to place them all in a class by themselves. Such an exercise of the discretion with which the Committee are intrusted, must be unreasonable, and therefore illegal.

But it is said that the Committee, in thus classifying the children, have not violated any principle of Equality, inasmuch as they have provided a school with competent instructors for the colored children, where they have equal advantages of instruction with those enjoyed by the white children. It is said that in excluding the colored children from the Public Schools open to white children, they furnish them an equivalent. To this there are several answers. I shall touch upon them only briefly, as the discussion, through which we have now travelled, substan-

and establish one school for Unitarians, another for Presbyterians, another for Baptists, and another for Methodists. They may establish a separate school for the rich, that the delicate taste of this favored class may not be offended by the humble garments of the poor. They may exclude the [illegible] of mechanics from the Public schools, and send them to separate schools by themselves. All this, and much more, can be done by the exercise of the high-handed power which can make a discrimination on account of color or race. The grand fabric of our Public Schools, the pride of Massachusetts, where, at the feet of the teacher, innocent childhood should meet, unconscious of all distinctions of birth—where the Equality of the Constitution and of Christianity should be inculcated by constant precept and example—may be converted into a heathen system of proscription and Caste. We may then have many different schools, the representatives of as many different classes, opinions and prejudices; but we shall look in vain for the true Public School of Massachusetts. Let it not be said that there is little danger that any Com-

THIRTY-FIRST CONGRESS.

WASHINGTON Feb. 11.

Senate.—The Vice President stated the business before the Senate to be the motion to receive a petition of citizens of Delaware and Maryland, asking a peaceable dissolution of the Union. Mr Chase having the floor, addressed the Senate in support of the petition. He cited a case wherein a similiar petition had been frequently quoted in discussion. He believed that the Senate were bound to receive every petition no matter of what character, and if it exhibited a mistaken view of the powers of Congress, or the expediency of the measure prayed for, Congress should express its disapprobation by subsequent action. The right of petition was a great and sacred one, to be demanded, and, not a poor one to be begged for.—He had no objection to whatever action the Senate might deem proper to give to this and similiar petitions. He only asked that all be received and treated alike.

Mr. Dayton said that the right of petition was well settled. It was the rem-

danger which menaced the Union—there are no dissolutionists in the South—not a man who would dare rise and avow the treasonable sentiment.

Mr. Chase said the question of reception had not been met. Mr. Cass and others had passed over the real question, and stated the reasons for which they would not grant the prayer of the petition.—They mistook their own position. He contended that the reception of the petition was no test as to the principle involved in the petition.

Mr. Seward wished the Senate and the country distinctly to understand that the question was not upon the propriety of dissolving the Union, or the power of Congress to dissolve it, but simply whether the petition should be received, and referred to a committee, with instructions to report that the Senate had neither the power nor the disposition to entertain the question. With this view he would vote to receive the petition, which he had denounced as emanating from madmen—that he had never seen and never expected to see, the petition which he would not recieve. It was no apology

The question was taken, and decided in the negative—yeas 65, nays 100.

Mr. Thompson of Miss. desiring to debate the petition, the question goes over.

The House then went into Committee of the Whole on the state of the Union, on resolution relative to collection of customs.

The amendments were considered.

Mr. Winthrop of Mass. took occasion to present a memorial from 100 importing merchants of Boston, without distinction of party, remonstrating against the Treasury Circular, and requesting that the expenses of weighing, guaging and measuring be paid by that class, and expressing regret that the revenue cutters have been called out of service. He believed that not less than twenty millions of imports were received at Boston, on which a duty of $5,000,000 was paid.—The Secretary issued the circular only on compulsion, and would relieve the merchants whenever he had an opportunity.

Mr. Vinton, of Ohio, offered an amendment to the resolution of the

claim their Slaves who shall have fled to other States; to seize them with or without warrant; to carry them before a United States Court, or before one of the 4,000 Judges, who is "to hear and determine the case of such claimants *in a summary manner.*" In no trial or hearing shall the testimony of such alleged fugitive be admited in evidence. Affidavits of claimants, duly attested, shall entitle them to carry off their alleged Slaves, using all necessary force and restraint. Juries of the neighborhood, there are to be none.

§4 Orders any one obstructing the seizure of all alleged "fugitives" from slavery, [who would not run from it?] or who may harbor or conceal them, to be fined not over $500, sent to jail for not more than half a year, and also compelled to pay $1,000 for civil damages to the slave claimant. The present enormous fees allowed in the Federal Courts are to be extended to the slave-catching business. Each Commissioner, or Slave Judge, is to get $10 fee, *if he thinks he* is justified in delivering up the slave brought before him; but only $5 if he fears that there is not proof enough.

Black abolitionists were aware that for many of their white colleagues the fight was *against* slavery, not *for* equality for the black American. In his newspaper *North Star*, Douglass commented, "Until abolitionists [erase] prejudice from their own hearts, they can never receive the unwavering confidence of the people of color." Especially resented was the advice of some white abolitionists about how to behave. "Better have a little of the plantation speech," one white abolitionist told Frederick Douglass. "It is best that you seem not too learned." And Henry Highland Garnet, another abolitionist who had been a slave, sent this reply to a white abolitionist who disagreed with Garnet's views:

> I have dared to think and act contrary to you. . . . If . . . I must think and act as you do because you are an abolitionist, . . . then I say your abolitionism is abject slavery.

CHECKUP

1. How did the abolitionists try to attain the goal they were working for?
2. What groups in the North opposed abolitionism? Why?
3. On what matters did white and black abolitionists disagree?

LESSON 2

The South's Reaction

Hammered by attacks from the abolitionists, the South increasingly thought of itself as a nation apart. This feeling of isolation, of being a nation threatened, was heightened by the Turner rebellion in 1831. That event reminded the South of the grim dangers of slaveholding. Nat Turner, a Virginia slave, led a group of slaves in a three-day uprising against slave owners and their families in Southampton County. Before the rebelling slaves were caught, they had killed sixty people.

Silencing the critics. The South's response to these attacks from outside and inside was to tighten once more the controls on black people. It also tried to shut off criticism. Many Southern postmasters refused to deliver *The Liberator* and other antislavery writings. Several Southern states put a price on the head of Garrison and other abolitionists in the North. In Congress, Southerners in 1836 pushed through a *gag rule,* which prevented abolitionist petitions from being read or acted upon. The rule remained in effect for eight years, until former President John Quincy Adams, now a congressman from Massachusetts, led a successful fight to repeal it.

Southern critics were silenced too. The number of antislavery societies in the South shrank from 130 in 1827 to just 3 in 1832. Such citizens as James Birney and the Grimké sisters were pressured to leave the South. Others who held similar views fell silent. The South closed ranks in defense of its way of life. The generation of Jefferson, Washington, and Monroe had regarded slavery as a curse that must one day die out. John Calhoun, however, spoke for the new generation of Southerners.

> This agitation [against slavery] has produced one happy effect at least; it has compelled us in the South to look into the nature and character of this great institution and to correct many false impressions that even we had [about] it. Many in the South once believed that it was moral and

LESSON 2 *(1 to 2 days)*

Performance Objectives

1. To explain orally the justifications offered by Southerners in defense of slavery.
2. To describe in an essay how life in the South differed from that in the North.
3. To list the reasons why most Southern whites—slaveholders and nonslaveholders alike—supported the system of slavery.

Vocabulary

Gag rule, Southern hospitality, illiteracy, planter class, racial inferiority

Activities

1. **LISTENING FOR INFORMATION** For an accurate view of Southern life prior to the Civil War, arrange for students to hear "A Georgia Town in 1807," Chapter 6, in *The Way Our People Lived* by William E. Woodward (New York: Washington Square Press, 1970).

2. DISCUSSION The statements below present interesting justifications in defense of slavery. Divide the class into several groups and assign each group one or two statements to analyze. Ask students to give evidence **(a)** in support of the statement, and **(b)** in opposition to the statement. After the groups have had time to prepare this activity, have each group make a brief oral presentation to the class. The statements to consider are the following.

a. "A greater punishment could not be devised or inflicted upon the Southern slave at this day than to give him that liberty which God in His wisdom and mercy deprived [him] of. . . ." (Solon Robinson)

b. "There are great evils in a society where slavery exists, and the institution is liable to great abuse. But the whole of human life is a system of evils and compensations. The free laborer has few real guarantees from society, while security is one of the compensations of the slave's humble position." (William Harper)

c. "The right of property in a slave is distinctly and expressly affirmed in the Constitution." (Chief Justice Taney in Dred Scott case)

d. "The Africans brought to us had been slaves in their own countries and only underwent a change of masters." (William Harper)

e. "Free them from control, and how soon does poverty and wretchedness overtake them! . . . I boldly and truly assert that you may travel Europe over—yea, you may visit the boasted freemen of America—aye, you may search the world over—before you find a laboring peasantry who are [happier], more con-

Sarah Grimké, born in South Carolina, was one of two sisters who championed the causes of abolitionism and women's rights. She was an effective speaker on the lecture platform.

> political evil; . . . we see it now in its true light, and regard it as the most safe and stable basis for free institutions in the world.

The proslavery view. Southern minds and pens concentrated on creating a proslavery argument. They turned to the Bible, to the United States Constitution, to the ancient philosophers, and to the classical civilization of republican Greece (which had slavery) to find justification for their way of life.

Southerners contrasted also the treatment of their slaves with that of Northern workers. Every society, they pointed out, had a class of people who did the hardest and most unpleasant work. The people in this class in the South, the slaves, were cared for in sickness and in health, in old age as in youth. They had perfect security. But in the wage system of the "free" North, workers had no security at all. They received nothing in illness or in old age, and they could be thrown out of work during a depression.

In the South, wrote George Fitzhugh, a leading defender of slavery, all was harmony.

> A society of universal liberty and equality is absurd and impracticable. A state of slavery . . . is the only situation in which the war of competition ceases and peace and goodwill will arise. At the slaveholding South all is peace, quiet, plenty and contentment. We have no mobs, no trade unions, no strikes for higher wages.

The Southern way of life. As their differing ideas on slavery suggest, the South and the North had been growing apart for many years. By the middle of the nineteenth century, they stood as almost two different societies. In the North, although most people were still farmers, manufacturing and commerce were growing rapidly. Increasing numbers of people lived in cities. Immigrants, many of them from Ireland and Germany, added variety to the North's population.

The South, by contrast, was still almost wholly agricultural and rural. Less than 10 percent of its people lived in towns or cities of more than 2,500 people. There was a sameness to the white population. Few immigrants were willing to go to the South and compete for jobs with slaves. Thus the 1850 census showed that fewer than three Southerners in a hundred had been born outside the United States. Most white Southerners were descended from the English and Scotch-Irish who had settled in the South in the seventeenth and eighteenth centuries.

The pace of life in the South was slower than it was in the bustling, commercial North. Visitors often commented on this fact and on the warmth of the welcome they received in the homes of Southerners, rich and poor alike. *Southern hospitality* became a byword. At the same time, visitors noted the many ways in which the South seemed to lag behind the North. There were fewer newspapers and fewer schools, and illiteracy was high. Southern farms and villages often lacked the well-kept look of those in the more prosperous North.

Southern class structure. One's standing in the South was based mainly on ownership of land and slaves. The great planters, therefore, stood at the top of Southern society. They set the tone of Southern social life and held the main political offices—or chose those who did. A small, close-knit group, they were tied to each other by the bonds of blood and marriage.

The picture we often have of the wealthy plantation owner, living a life of ease in a mansion, was true for only a very few. Most owners worked hard. Usually they supervised the day-to-day operations of the plantations and kept the business records as well. While the homes of most were comfortable, they were hardly lavish. Profits were by no means certain, for the price that cotton would bring varied from year to year. In good times a planter might make large profits. At other times he might barely break even, or possibly lose money. Planters in the older parts of the South, where the soil was worn out, were often in debt.

This planter class was quite small. Only 8,000 slave owners owned as many as fifty slaves. Fewer than 40,000, or about 12 percent of all slave owners, owned as many as twenty slaves. This was probably the minimum number of slaves needed to run a good-sized plantation successfully.

Just below these great planters was the upper-middle class. This class included planters with between five and twenty slaves, as well as the successful merchants, bankers, doctors, and lawyers, who lived in towns.

The great majority of whites belonged to the middle class, made up mainly of independent small farmers. Most of these owned no slaves at all. The few who did usually owned but one or two and worked in the fields with them. At the bottom of the social scale were the poverty-stricken whites, who scratched out a bare living from the poor soil in the pinelands or the hill country.

More than three fourths of all the white families in the South owned no slaves at all. Why, then, were Southern whites so unified in their defense of slavery? The reasons varied. Many middle-class farmers favored slavery because they hoped to rise someday into the planter class and become slave owners themselves. Poor whites were assured that, however low they might be on the social scale, as long as there was slavery there would be others below

tented, as a class of people, or who are better clothed and fed and better provided for in sickness, infirmity, and old age, or who enjoy more of the essential comforts of life, than these so-called miserable, oppressed, abused, starved slaves. . . ." (Solon Robinson)

f. "But let me not be understood as admitting, even by implication, that the existing relations between the two races in the slaveholding States is an evil:—far otherwise: I hold it to be a good, as it has thus far proved itself to be to both and will continue to prove so if not disturbed by the fell spirit of abolition." (John C. Calhoun)

g. "Is it not palpably nearer the truth to say that no man was ever born free and that no two men were ever both equal, than to say that all men are born free and equal?" (William Harper)

h. "If all earthly power were given me, I should not know what to do as to the existing institution [slavery]. My first impulse would be to free all slaves and send them to Liberia—to their native land. But a moment's reflection would convince me that whatever of high hope (as I think there is) there may be in this in the long run, its sudden execution is impossible. If they all landed there in a day, they would all perish in the next ten days; and there are not surplus shipping and surplus money enough to carry them there in many times ten days. What then? Free them all and keep them among us as underlings: Is it quite certain that this betters their condition? I think I would not hold one in slavery at any rate; yet the point is not clear enough for me to denounce people upon. (Abraham Lincoln)

Out of the towns and cities, social life in the South centered about the great plantations.

3. ESSAY After students have read the lesson, assign essays based on Performance Objective 2. Ask them to describe the Southern way of life and to contrast it with life in the North by the middle of the nineteenth century.

4. DISCUSSION Ask students to identify the various groups that made up the white Southern class structure. List them on the chalkboard. Then ask students to name reasons why each group would favor slavery.

them. And whites of all classes were convinced that blacks were inferior people and not fit for freedom. Slavery fixed the relationship of blacks and whites. Southern whites were not able to imagine a society in which that relationship did not exist. Thus they were committed to the belief that slavery was necessary and desirable. Ending it, they believed, would threaten their very way of life.

CHECKUP

1. In what ways did the South respond to attacks on slavery?
2. How did the Southern way of life differ from the way of life in the North?
3. Why, with few exceptions, were Southern whites of all classes supporters of the slavery system?

LESSON 3

The Argument over the Spread of Slavery

The war with Mexico resulted, as you read in Unit 4, in the addition of millions of acres of land to the United States. At any other time, such an outcome would have been the cause of unmixed joy. But the slavery issue poisoned the well.

The Missouri Compromise had supposedly settled the question of where slavery could and could not extend. It had run a line through the United States. Below that line, slavery could exist; above it, slavery was outlawed. But the newly won Mexican lands were not covered by the Missouri Compromise. Whether slavery could be brought into that region became the subject of bitter argument.

The Wilmot Proviso. The argument started even before the war was ended, when Congressman David Wilmot of Pennsylvania offered an amendment to a money bill. His amendment provided that slavery would be prohibited in all lands acquired from Mexico. The view that slavery should not be allowed in any more territories was known as the *free-soil* position. The House of Representatives, with its Northern majority, passed the Wilmot Proviso twice. The Senate blocked it both times.

Southern leaders were enraged by the Wilmot Proviso. Calhoun saw it as the opening of a Northern campaign to destroy slavery in the South. He countered with his own resolutions in the Senate. Territories of the United States belonged to all the states, he said, and all states had equal rights in them. This meant that Congress could not prohibit citizens from taking their slaves or other property into the territories. Calhoun's resolutions did not pass, but no senator could fail to understand their meaning. In Calhoun's view, even the Missouri Compromise, which prohibited slavery above 36°30′ north latitude in the territory of the Louisiana Purchase, had been unconstitutional.

Search for a middle ground. Many looked for a middle ground between Wilmot and Calhoun. One proposal was simply to extend the 36°30′ line to the Pacific Coast. Another, known as *popular sovereignty*, was to let the people of each territory decide for themselves whether or not they wanted slavery. This view, supported mainly in the Midwest, was held by such Senate leaders as Lewis Cass of Michigan and Stephen A. Douglas of Illinois. It appealed to many because it appeared to be a democratic way to handle the problem. It also would take the dangerous question of slavery in the territories out of Congress, where it might divide the Union.

But supporters of popular sovereignty never made clear just *when* the people of a territory should vote on slavery. Should it be *before* slaveholders brought slaves in? Or *after* they did? The outcome of the vote would surely be different in the one case than in the other. More important, popular sovereignty ignored the fact that to more and more Northerners, slavery was a moral issue. If one person's owning another was morally wrong, a majority vote to allow it could not make it right.

The election of 1848. Both parties in the 1848 election avoided the issue of slavery expansion. The Democrats nominated Lewis Cass, an old party politician, and they wrote a platform that was silent on slavery. The Whigs, who had won with a general as their candidate in 1840, chose another war hero, General Zachary Taylor, and wrote no platform at all. Taylor, in fact, had never revealed his views on any of the important issues of the day.

In the North, a number of strongly antislavery Democrats left the party because of its stand—or rather its lack of a stand. They were called *Barnburners*, because it was said they were willing to burn down the barn (that is, destroy the party) to get rid of the rats (the proslavery Democrats). The Whigs likewise were split. One group, the *Conscience Whigs*, put the moral issue of slavery ahead of harmony with the South and the cotton

LESSON 3 *(2 to 3 days)*

Performance Objectives

1. To describe and explain the opposing view of David Wilmot and John C. Calhoun on the issue of slavery in the lands acquired by the United States through the Mexican Cession. **2.** To identify the views of Henry Clay, John C. Calhoun, and Daniel Webster in the debate preceding the Compromise of 1850. **3.** To explain how the Compromise of 1850 dealt with the slavery issue.

Famous People

Lewis Cass, Zachary Taylor, Martin Van Buren, Henry Clay, John C. Calhoun, Daniel Webster, Millard Filmore, Franklin Pierce

Vocabulary

Wilmot Proviso, free soil, popular sovereignty, election of 1848, Barnburners, Conscience Whigs, Cotton Whigs, Free-Soil party, nullification, Compromise of 1850, fugitive slave law

Activities

1. FILM The following film dramatically presents the struggles from 1790 to 1865 to keep the nation united: *Constitution: One Nation Indivisible, Part 1* (37 minutes, b&w) and *Part 2* (28 minutes, b&w; Ford Foundation Television Workshop). *Part 2* depicts the South's objections to high tariffs, presents the Dred Scott decision, Lincoln-Douglas debates, Lincoln's 1861 inaugural, the Emancipation Proclamation, and the secession of the South.

Background Information

HENRY CLAY (1777–1852)

For nearly forty years, Henry Clay was a prominent American political leader. He entered politics in 1801 as a member of the Kentucky constitutional convention and was elected to the Kentucky legislature in 1803. From there he went on to serve terms in the United States Senate and House of Representatives. During the War of 1812, Clay, as a "War Hawk," argued so strongly in favor of the war that some people called it "Mr. Clay's War." Then in 1814, as one of the five members of the United States peace commission, he played an active role in negotiating the Treaty of Ghent. In the postwar years, Clay proposed the American System—protective tariffs, a national bank, and internal improvements. He believed that such a nationalistic program would bring the United States "to that height to which God and nature had destined it." In 1820, Clay's brilliant handling of the Missouri Compromise earned him the title of the "Great Pacificator." The Compromise of 1850 again demonstrated his talent for arranging compromises. Clay is remembered for saying, "I'd rather be right than be President." Nevertheless, he nursed an ambition to become President that haunted him to his dying day. Three times he ran for the Presidency and lost. Despite personal disappointment, Clay remained a national patriot, devoted to public service. His home, Ashland, near Lexington, Kentucky, was a magnificent country estate. He imported pedigreed cattle and sheep to improve his own livestock. He also raised prizewinning horses. In fact, he helped to establish the area around Lexington as the famous horse-breeding area it is today.

trade. The other group, the *Cotton Whigs*, took a proslavery view. The Conscience Whigs left their party, and together with the Barnburners and members of the old Liberty party, they formed the Free-Soil party. Former President Martin Van Buren became their candidate. Taylor won the election. Yet the new Free-Soil party had taken more than 10 percent of the vote and had won nine seats in Congress.

The uproar about California. While Congress and the country argued about slavery in the territories, gold was discovered in 1848 in California. Within a year the population of California—still not an organized territory—reached 100,000. The area needed a government. President Taylor thought he saw a way to solve at a single stroke both California's problem and the question that was dividing the country. People could debate whether Congress had the power to block slavery in the territories. No one, however, could deny that a *state* could decide for itself whether it would have slavery. California had more than enough people to become a state. Why not, then, let California skip the territorial stage? Why not let it enter the Union directly as a state, with or without slavery, however it wished? That is what Taylor recommended.

Californians gladly took Taylor's advice. In December 1849, they asked to enter the Union with a constitution that prohibited slavery. (New Mexico prepared to do the same thing a short time later.) As Congress met that same month, Taylor declared that California's problem had been solved, and he urged Congress to admit it as a free state.

Far from solving the problem, the inexperienced Taylor set off an uproar that almost destroyed the Union. The South was furious. Taylor, a slaveholder himself, was seen as a traitor. With the more populous North already in control of the House of Representatives, the South's main stronghold in government was the Senate. There the slave and free states were evenly balanced in 1850. A free California would tip the balance to the North. Every Southerner who could read a map knew that the balance would be tipped sooner or later, for none of the remaining territories in the United States were fit for plantation slavery. One day soon, the House, the Senate, and the Presidency would all be in the hands of the North, where antislavery feeling was growing. The slave states would then be at the North's mercy. Many Southerners believed that before that day came, a bargain should be struck to protect slavery. Most felt that this was the time for such bargaining. If the North would not agree, then perhaps the South should leave the Union.

Clay's plan. Such talk alarmed Senator Henry Clay of Kentucky. Thirty years earlier, Clay had arranged the Missouri Compromise. Seventeen years earlier, he had worked out the compromise that ended the nullification crisis. Now, at seventy-two years of age, he set his talents one last time to the task of finding a middle way that both North and South could accept.

Clay hoped to settle differences not only on the territory question but on other important matters dividing the two. In January 1850, he presented his plan. It called for the following.

(1) California would be admitted to the Union as a free state.

(2) The rest of the Mexican Cession would be organized into two parts—the Utah and New Mexico territories—which would have no restrictions on slavery. Presumably, the people in each territory would eventually decide whether or not to permit slavery.

(3) Certain lands in dispute on the border between Texas and New Mexico would be given to New Mexico, but Texas would be awarded $10 million by the federal government.

(4) The trade in slaves would be forbidden in Washington, D.C., but slavery itself could continue there.

(5) A new fugitive slave law would make the recapture of runaways easier and provide for severe punishment of anyone who helped slaves escape.

(6) Congress would not interfere with the slave trade among the states.

In 1850 an aging Henry Clay of Kentucky urges the Senate to accept his compromise plan.

Hour after hour, Clay urged each side to back down. To Northerners who demanded the Wilmot Proviso, Clay pointed out that the deserts, plains, and mountains of the Southwest were not suited to plantation farming. Why insist on a statement forbidding something that would not happen anyway? "You have got what is worth more than a thousand Wilmot Provisos," Clay told them. "You have nature on your side." He warned the South that secession would lead to a bloody civil war.

Calhoun's and Webster's views. John C. Calhoun, the South's greatest spokesman, had no interest in compromise. Now dying of tuberculosis, he was carried on a stretcher on March 4, 1850 to the Senate floor. There a younger Southern senator read his speech. The Union could be saved, said Calhoun, only by "a full and final settlement" between North and South. The North must give the South equal rights in the new territories. It must return fugitive slaves. It must "cease the agitation of the slave question." If Northern senators could not agree to these conditions, said Calhoun,

> say so; and let the States we both represent agree to separate and part in peace. If you are unwilling we should part in peace, tell us so; and we shall know what to do, when you reduce the question to submission or resistance.

2. DRAMATIZATION The material in this lesson traces the important events leading up to the Compromise of 1850. You may wish to have the students write a television script, based on the lesson text, that re-creates the historic events of this period: the Wilmot Proviso; the counter-resolution offered by Calhoun; arguments put forth by supporters of popular sovereignty; the election of 1848; the uproar caused by California's request to enter the Union with a constitution that prohibited slavery; and the eloquent debate in Congress between Clay, Calhoun, and Webster that finally culminated in the Compromise of 1850.

Divide the class into small groups and assign each group one part of the story to recreate. Have students write imaginary dialogue, based on facts from their reading and any additional research they may have time to do. Then ask for volunteers from each group to act out that particular segment of the story as it occurs in the time sequence of the dramatization. At the beginning of the actual dramatization, encourage the more confident students to get the activity started.

3. DISCUSSION On the chalkboard, list the provision of the Compromise of 1850 and discuss the reactions of the North and the South to the five points. Ask students why these statutes did not magically calm the sectional storm.

It has been said that while the Compromise of 1850 was enacted because the issues seemed to be susceptible to compromise, it did not succeed because the issues compromised were not the basic causes of sectional differences. Ask students to analyze this statement. Why did the issues seem to be susceptible to compromise? If these were not the basic issues, what were?

In the discussion about compromise, you might wish to have students consider the following questions: Is compromise the best way to settle a dispute? Does it provide a permanent solution to the problem? Under what circumstances should a person refuse to compromise? Is it possible for one to be too uncompromising? Is the avoidance of a drastic solution a good reason for compromise? Was it right to compromise with slavery? In your opinion, what situations today cannot be compromised? Why?

Three days later Daniel Webster, the third of the Senate's aging giants, entered the debate. Like Clay, Webster was a Unionist above all. "I wish to speak today not as a Massachusetts man, nor as a Northern man," Webster told the Senate, "but as an American." Believing that only through this compromise could the Union be saved, Webster tried to make it acceptable to the North. He himself had supported the Wilmot Proviso, he said, but saving the Union was more important than insisting on an empty statement of principle. An opponent of slavery, he urged the North to accept the fugitive slave law.

Others had their say. Senator William H. Seward of New York argued against the fugitive slave law. Though the Constitution requires the return of runaways, there is a "higher law" than the Constitution, said Seward.

The Compromise of 1850. The debate in Congress lasted several months. Outside of Congress the debate went on as well. Southern extremists meeting in Nashville, Tennessee, in June 1850 talked openly of secession. Abolitionists in Webster's native New England condemned him for his support of the fugitive slave law. But moderates in both North and South generally supported a compromise. With President Taylor opposed, however, the chances of compromise were uncertain.

Taylor's sudden death in July opened the door to a solution. His successor, Millard Fillmore of New York, favored Clay's plan. In the autumn, with Douglas of Illinois taking up the work for an exhausted Clay, the Compromise of 1850 became law.

Reaction to the Compromise. Within each section, many opposed the Compromise. In the South, the "fire-eaters" predicted the North would not live up to its bargain. They favored immediate secession, before the North could become even stronger and better able to defeat the South. In the North, abolitionists and other opponents of the Compromise vowed they would not obey the fugitive slave law.

For the most part, however, there was a feeling of relief. Many political leaders regarded the slavery question as finally settled. Some said they would never bring up the matter again.

That seemed to be the meaning of the 1852 elections. For their candidate, the Democrats set aside such well-known leaders as Cass, Douglas, and James Buchanan in favor of a little-known former senator, Franklin Pierce of New Hampshire. Their platform stressed that the party accepted the Compromise. The Whigs also accepted the Compromise, but with little enthusiasm. Once again, they turned to a military hero, General Winfield Scott. This time it did them no good. Pierce won an overwhelming victory in the electoral college, 254 to 42, though the popular vote was much closer. The Free-Soil candidate received only half as many votes as in 1848.

CHECKUP

1. What were the opposing views of Wilmot and Calhoun on the issue of slavery in the lands acquired from Mexico?
2. Why did President Taylor's plan for admitting California to the Union set off an uproar?
3. How did the Compromise of 1850 deal with the slavery issue?

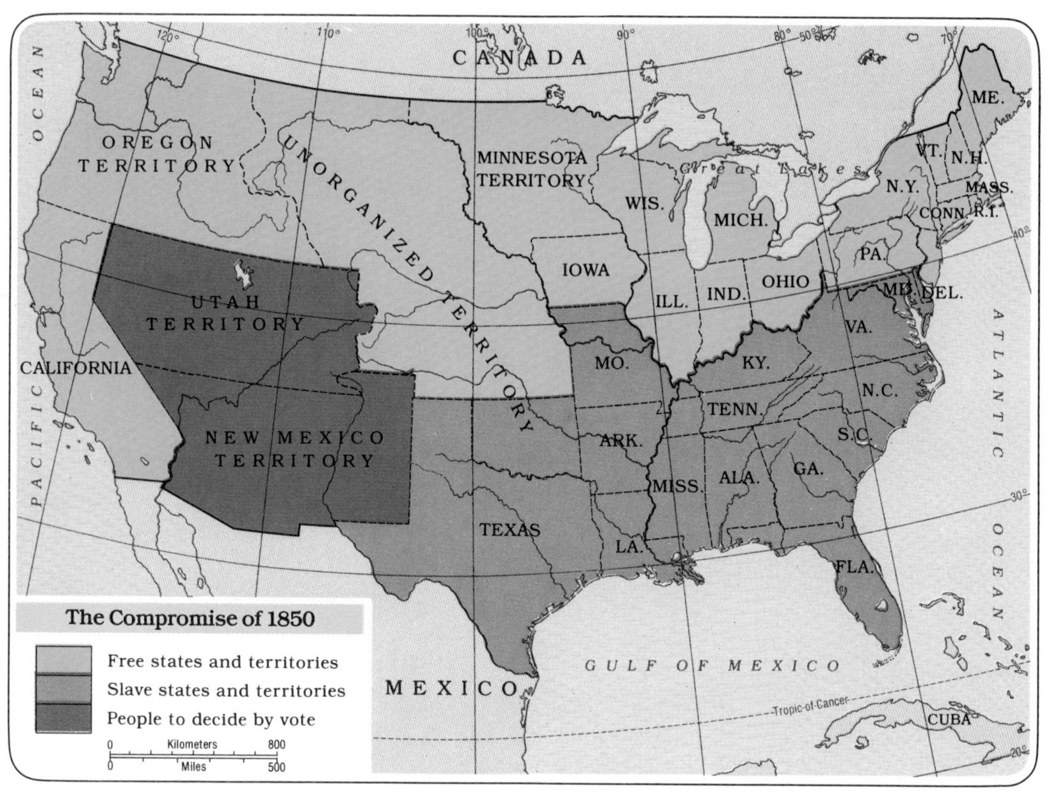

After the Compromise of 1850, the United States consisted of sixteen free states and fifteen slave states. The long-kept balance was slowly tipping toward the North. Events in the Western territories would eventually undermine the Compromise that Henry Clay had worked out.

LESSON 4

The Rising Storm

Despite a general acceptance of the Compromise of 1850, careful observers could see warning signals. By 1852, there were signs that the Whig party was splitting. In the North, Conscience Whigs refused to accept the Compromise, and in the South some Cotton Whigs moved over to the Democratic party. The death of both Henry Clay and Daniel Webster in 1852 took from the scene two powerful Unionists who had held the Whig party together. It was plain that the Whigs would not survive as a political party if the slavery question were opened again.

Though the Compromise of 1850 had included a strong fugitive slave law, Northerners tried, often successfully, to block the return of fugitive slaves. In 1852, Harriet Beecher Stowe's antislavery book, *Uncle Tom's Cabin,* created a sensation (see page 336). Far from being put out, the fire that threatened the Union still smoldered, ready to burst into flame at the next incident.

Continued on page 337

LESSON 4 *(2 to 3 days)*

Performance Objectives

1. To write an essay explaining the provisions of the Kansas-Nebraska Act and describing the consequences of the act's passage. **2.** To describe the change in American political parties during the 1850s. **3.** To explain orally or in writing the significance of the Dred Scott case in the slavery controversy. **4.** To identify Abraham Lincoln's views on slavery.

Famous People

Harriet Beecher Stowe, Stephen A. Douglas, John Brown, Charles Sumner, John Frémont, James Buchanan

Vocabulary

Uncle Tom's Cabin, Kansas-Nebraska Act, Know-Nothing party, "Bleeding Kansas," election of 1856, dough-face, Dred Scott case, Lecompton constitution, Lincoln-Douglas debates, Freeport Doctrine, Harpers Ferry

Uncle Tom's Cabin

No book published in America ever had a greater political effect than the novel *Uncle Tom's Cabin.* The author was Harriet Beecher Stowe. At the time she wrote the book, Mrs. Stowe was living in Brunswick, Maine, where her husband was a professor at Bowdoin College. Mrs. Stowe's aim was to show how terrible slavery was. The main character of her novel is Uncle Tom, a slave, one of whose masters is the brutal Simon Legree. Among the other characters are a young slave couple who flee to Canada.

Uncle Tom's Cabin appeared in 1852 at a time when there was great controversy over the fugitive slave law. Presses ran night and day to meet the demand for the book. Within 18 months, some 1,200,000 copies had been published. The story created great sympathy for the slaves. Senator William Seward of New York, an abolitionist, urged Southerners to read the book and learn the error of their ways. Southerners, on the other hand, charged that Harriet Beecher Stowe was a fanatic without firsthand knowledge of the conditions of slavery.

In a second book, *Key to Uncle Tom's Cabin,* Mrs. Stowe attempted to show that her novel was based on fact. Before moving to Maine, she had lived for some years in Cincinnati, Ohio, on the route of the Underground Railroad by which slaves fled northward. She had also visited a Kentucky plantation.

Because of its effect on public opinion, *Uncle Tom's Cabin* has been called the greatest of American propaganda novels. Senator Charles Sumner of Massachusetts declared that without this book Lincoln would not have been elected President. When Lincoln himself met Mrs. Stowe during the Civil War, he is said to have greeted her with these words: "So you're the little woman who made the book that made this great war."

Millions who never read the book *Uncle Tom's Cabin* saw the widely performed stage production. As the playbill shows, this company had given more than a thousand performances.

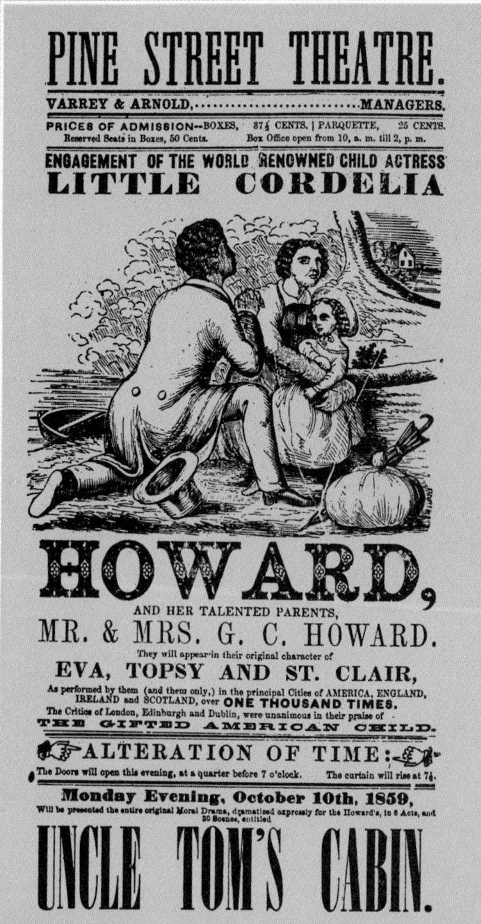

PINE STREET THEATRE.
VARREY & ARNOLD,..............................MANAGERS.
PRICES OF ADMISSION--BOXES, 37½ CENTS. | PARQUETTE, 25 CENTS.
Reserved Seats in Boxes, 50 Cents. Box Office open from 10, a. m. till 2, p. m.
ENGAGEMENT OF THE WORLD RENOWNED CHILD ACTRESS
LITTLE CORDELIA
HOWARD,
AND HER TALENTED PARENTS,
MR. & MRS. G. C. HOWARD.
They will appear in their original character of
EVA, TOPSY AND ST. CLAIR,
As performed by them (and them only,) in the principal Cities of AMERICA, ENGLAND, IRELAND and SCOTLAND, over ONE THOUSAND TIMES.
The Critics of London, Edinburgh and Dublin, were unanimous in their praise of
THE GIFTED AMERICAN CHILD.
ALTERATION OF TIME:
The Doors will open this evening, at a quarter before 7 o'clock. The curtain will rise at 7½.
Monday Evening, October 10th, 1859,
Will be presented the entire original Moral Drama, dramatized expressly for the Howard's, in 6 Acts, and 30 Scenes, entitled
UNCLE TOM'S CABIN.

The Kansas-Nebraska Act. Such an incident came in January 1854. At that time, Congress was considering several routes for a railroad to California. Senator Douglas of Illinois was anxious that the line run from Chicago in his home state to the Pacific. The route, however, would take the railroad through an unorganized territory inhabited by Indians and lacking a government. Douglas therefore introduced a bill to *organize* the Nebraska Territory—that is, open it to settlement and start it on its course to statehood. Nebraska lay north of 36°30′ north latitude in the Louisiana Purchase, however, and slavery was prohibited there. To win Southern votes for his bill, Douglas prepared to divide the land into two territories, Nebraska and Kansas. The bill specifically repealed the Missouri Compromise and provided for popular sovereignty instead. It was expected that the Northern territory of Nebraska would become a free state. With popular sovereignty, the South would have a chance to make Kansas a slave state. Supported by

Compare this map of the United States, after the Kansas-Nebraska Act, with the map on page 335, showing the nation four years earlier. Note the changes in the Western territories.

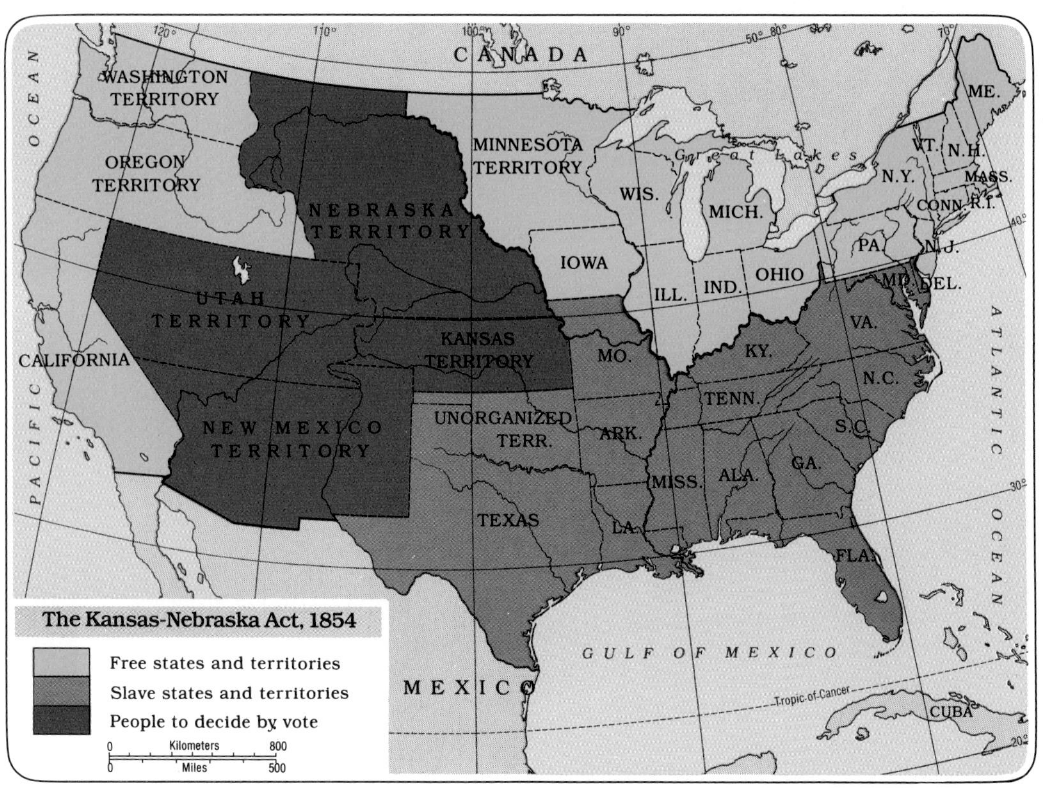

Activities

1. ORAL REPORTS Assign some of the more capable students to read and report on the following documents at the appropriate time in the lesson. From Commager's *Documents of American History:* 180, "The Kansas-Nebraska Act"; 183, "American Party Platform"; 185, "*Dred Scott* v. *Sandford*"; 186, "Lincoln's House Divided Speech"; and 189, "John Brown's Last Speech."

2. DISCUSSION / ESSAY After students have read the lesson, discuss the controversy over and consequences of the Kansas-Nebraska Act. You may wish to ask the following questions to stimulate discussion: How did the Kansas-Nebraska Act conbribute to national disunity? Did this Act threaten the balance-of-power concept between slave and free states? How did passage of the Act affect American political parties of the 1850s? Why did war break out in Kansas? Who were the opponents?

At the conclusion of the discussion, assign the essay suggested in Performance Objective 1.

3. USING A CHART The birth of the Republican party offers an opportunity to review the history of political parties in the United States. Have each student construct a chart or diagram showing the development of political parties from 1789 to 1860. Involve students at the beginning of the activity by asking for their suggestions about the kind of information to be included in the chart. List their ideas on the chalkboard and together decide upon the form that the chart should take. In the index in *Our American Heritage,* students will find references to the following political parties during the years 1789 to 1860: American party, Constitutional Union party, Democratic-Republicans (including Jacksonian Democrats and Jeffersonian Republicans), Federalists, Anti-Federalists, Free-Soil party, Liberty party, National Republicans, Republicans, and Whig party.

After students have completed their charts, review and tie together the story of political parties up to this time. Help students to eliminate confusion over party labels and to recognize that **(a)** the present Democratic party is an outgrowth of the first Republican party; **(b)** the Federalists, the National Republicans, and the Whigs shared a similarity of interests and viewpoints; and **(c)** the Republican party of the 1850s brought together the various shades of antislavery opinion in the North.

★**12**★

Zachary Taylor

1784–1850

Born in VIRGINIA
In Office 1849–1850
Party WHIG

An army officer, and a national hero after war with Mexico. Though once a slave owner, he sought the admission of California as a free state. Died after sixteen months in office.

★**13**★

Millard Fillmore

1800–1874

Born in NEW YORK
In Office 1850–1853
Party WHIG

Signed Compromise of 1850, which helped delay Civil War. But his enforcement of Fugitive Slave Law lost him Northern support, and Whigs did not make him their candidate in 1852.

★**14**★

Franklin Pierce

1804–1869

Born in NEW HAMPSHIRE
In Office 1853–1857
Party DEMOCRATIC

Served at time of great bitterness over slavery. Supported Kansas-Nebraska Act, angering Northerners. Approved Gadsden Purchase from Mexico. Protected rights of immigrants.

President Pierce and the Democratic party, Douglas pushed the Kansas-Nebraska Act through Congress.

In the North and West, the Kansas-Nebraska Act led to a storm of protest. To many people the repeal of the thirty-four-year-old Missouri Compromise to limit slavery was a betrayal. Protest meetings were held all over the North and West. Senator Douglas declared that he could have ridden across the country by the light of his burning effigies.

Antislavery Democrats and Whigs left their parties to form new local and statewide anti-Nebraska parties. Their main demand was an end to the spread of slavery into the territories. Soon these parties came together to form a new national party—the Republican party. The Whigs, meanwhile, collapsed. Many Southern Whigs now completed their shift into the Democratic party. Whigs in the North joined either the Republicans or another new party—the American, or Know-Nothing, party. The Know-Nothing party played down the slavery question and stressed its opposition to Catholics and immigrants.

"Bleeding Kansas." Since the question of slavery in Kansas was to be decided by the settlers themselves, both sides encouraged people to settle there. On the day set for the election of a territorial legislature, thousands of proslavery Missourians crossed into Kansas and voted illegally. They elected a proslavery territorial legislature and governor. This new body passed a slave code and set harsh punishments, including death, for anyone who interfered with slavery. Antislavery settlers, claiming fraud, held their own elections. They chose a free-state legislature and governor, and drew up an antislavery constitution. Thus, one year after the Kansas-Nebraska Act, the territory of Kansas had two legislatures and two governors.

In May 1856, the situation became violent. A proslavery band attacked the antislavery town of Lawrence, burning homes and newspaper offices. In revenge, a fiery, fanatical abolitionist named John Brown and six followers murdered five proslavery settlers at Pottawatomie Creek. This action touched off open warfare that claimed 200 lives and gave the territory the name of "Bleeding Kansas." Such was the first bitter fruit of popular sovereignty.

The violence in Kansas was soon matched in the halls of Congress. In a speech on "The Crime Against Kansas," Senator Charles Sumner of Massachusetts spoke out harshly against Senator Andrew Butler of South Carolina. Two days later, Butler's nephew, Representative Preston Brooks, walked over to Sumner at his Senate desk and beat him into unconsciousness with a cane. Sumner, seriously injured, did not return to the

4. ROLE-PLAYING Have students role-play the case of Dred Scott as it might have been argued before the Supreme Court. Be sure that participants bring out the three important issues involved in the case: **(a)** whether Scott was a citizen of Missouri and thus able to sue in a federal court; **(b)** whether his stay in free territory had made him legally a free person; and **(c)** the constitutionality of the Missouri Compromise.

In Kansas a band of antislavery settlers exchange fire with proslavery people. The upsurge of violence in this border state aroused feelings throughout the North and the South.

5. ORAL REPORTS The Supreme Court decision in *Dred Scott* v. *Sandford* caused great joy among white Southerners. Among Northerners, however, it aroused a storm of protest. Ask several students to read and report on the following protests found in *The Annals of America,* Vol. 8 (Chicago, Ill.: Encyclopaedia Britannica, Inc., 1968): "Negro Protest Over the Dred Scott Decision," pages 450–451; "Ohio Resolution on the Dred Scott Decision," pages 451–452; and "Abraham Lincoln: The Dred Scott Decision and the Declaration of Independence," pages 459–466.

6. LISTENING FOR INFORMATION Two books that infuriated Southerners were Harriet Beecher Stowe's *Uncle Tom's Cabin* and Hinton Rowan Helper's *Impending Crisis in the South.* You may wish to read to the class or have students read aloud selections from one or both books. Excerpts from both books appear in *The Annals of America,* Vol. 8. After students have heard or read the material, ask them for reasons why many Southerners considered these books dangerous.

Senate for three years. Many Southerners thought that the abolitionist Sumner had gotten only what he deserved, and a number of them sent Brooks canes to use against other Northerners. Meanwhile, in Northern eyes, Sumner's empty Senate seat became a symbol of the brutality of the slaveholding South.

The election of 1856. Against this background of violence, the election of 1856 took place. The new Republican party had been very successful in state elections in 1854 and 1855. Now its national convention nominated John Frémont, the soldier and Western explorer, for President. The party's chief position was to keep slavery from spreading into the territories. To enlarge its appeal in the North and West, however, it added planks favoring high tariffs for growing Northern industries, free homesteads, and a railroad to the Pacific.

The leading contender for the Democratic nomination was Stephen A. Douglas of Illinois. The Kansas-Nebraska Act, however, had made him too controversial. The Democratic party therefore turned to James Buchanan of Pennsylvania, a sixty-six-year-old party politician. As minister to England, he had had the good fortune to be out of the country during the Kansas-Nebraska uproar. Buchanan was generally favorable to the South. In nominating a *dough-face*—that is, a Northerner with Southern principles—the Democrats hoped to appeal to both sections. The American party nominated Millard Fillmore.

Buchanan won with 174 electoral votes to 114 for Frémont. Fillmore carried only Maryland. Frémont won most of the free states and only narrowly lost Pennsylvania and Illinois. Had he taken those two states, he would have won the Presidency. Thus the Republican party, a sectional party, had come very close to victory in its first national election.

The Dred Scott case. Two days after Buchanan took office in March 1857, the Supreme Court handed down an important decision on slavery. In the 1830s, Dred Scott, a Missouri slave, had been taken by his owner to Illinois, a free state, and later to the Wisconsin Territory, where slavery was prohibited under the Missouri Compromise. Some years later, he returned with his owner to Missouri. Claiming that his stay on free soil had made him a free man, Scott sued for freedom in the courts. In the 1850s the case reached the Supreme Court.

In *Dred Scott* v. *Sandford,* a majority of the justices, including Chief Justice Roger Taney, held that blacks—even free blacks—were not citizens under the Constitution. Therefore it was ruled that Scott could not sue in a federal court. Further, the Court stated that whatever Scott might have been while he was in Illinois and in Wisconsin Territory, he was a slave once he returned to Missouri.

This ruling was enough to decide the case, and the Court could have stopped there. But Chief Justice Taney, believing that a clear decision by the Court might settle the slavery issue once and for all, pushed further. The Fifth Amendment to the Constitution states that no person's property may be taken away "without due process of law." Slaves were property. It followed, then, according to Taney, that Congress had no power to deny a citizen the right to take property—slaves, cattle, furniture, or whatever—into a territory. That is exactly what the Missouri Compromise had done. That act of Congress, said the Court, had therefore been unconstitutional all along.

Far from quieting the slavery controversy, the Dred Scott decision created another uproar. Southerners rejoiced. The North was stunned and angry. Republicans were especially upset, for if there was no way in which Congress could keep slavery out of the territories, the party's very reason for being had been swept away. Republicans said that the Dred Scott decision was a bad ruling, and it would not last long. They pointed out that seven out of the nine judges on the Supreme Court were Democrats and that five of the seven were from the South. A Republican President would appoint different judges, they said, and the decision would be overturned.

★15★

James Buchanan

1791–1868

Born in PENNSYLVANIA
In Office 1857–1861
Party DEMOCRATIC

Caught up in storm over slavery. Tried to keep peace. Regarded Dred Scott decision as binding. Said states had no right to secede, but would not take action to keep them in the Union.

★ ★ ★ ★ ★ ★ ★ ★

The Lecompton constitution. Meanwhile, the proslavery forces in Kansas met in Lecompton. They drew up a proposed state constitution and sent it to the voters. Knowing that the majority of Kansans were antislavery, they rigged the vote. No matter how the people voted, they would be approving a constitution making Kansas a slave state. Antislavery Kansans refused to take part in the voting. As a result, the Lecompton constitution was adopted. Despite this trickery, President Buchanan recommended that Congress accept Kansas into the Union as a slave state. This was too much for Senator Douglas. Such action, he said, would make a joke of popular sovereignty and its idea of majority rule. Douglas split with Buchanan and the Southern Democrats, and Congress became deadlocked.

Antislavery Kansans now took matters into their own hands. They put the Lecompton constitution to a fair vote in another election, and it was voted down by a large margin. In yet another vote, ordered by Congress, the Lecompton constitution was rejected by a 6 to 1 margin. Kansas finally entered the Union as a free state in 1861.

7. ANALYZING SOURCE MATERIAL Arrange for students to read or hear portions of the 1858 Lincoln-Douglas debates at Freeport and Alton, Illinois. These debates may be found in a variety of sources, including Commager's *Documents of American History* and *The Annals of America,* Vol. 9. As students work with the debates, have them consider the following questions: What was Lincoln's attitude toward slavery? What was Douglas's position on slavery in the territories? Lincoln put this question to Douglas: "Can the people of a United States Territory, in any lawful way, against the wish of any citizen of the United States, exclude slavery from its limits prior to the formation of a state constitution?" How was the Dred Scott decision involved in that question? What was the political significance of the Lincoln-Douglas debates? Although these debates are not rated among the great oratorical contests of the past, why are they often called the most important debates in American history?

8. CROSSWORD PUZZLE A good way to review the many ideas presented in this chapter is to use the vocabulary terms and names of famous people in a crossword puzzle. Select those words and phrases that you particularly want the students to know and remember. Write the words on the chalkboard or make copies of the list. Have each student choose ten items from the list and make up his or her own puzzle using those words. Then have each student solve a partner's puzzle.

Background Information

STEPHEN A. DOUGLAS (1813–1861) Born on a farm near Brandon, Vermont, Douglas moved to Illinois at the age of twenty. In 1834 he was admitted to the bar and was elected prosecuting attorney for his district in 1835. Early in his career, he took an active interest in politics, and his rise was remarkably rapid. He affiliated with the Democratic party and was elected to the Illinois legislature in 1836, the United States House of Representatives in 1843, and the Senate in 1847. He was soon recognized as one of the ablest, most energetic of the Democratic leaders. His physical appearance—short stature with large head and broad shoulders—brought him the nickname of the "Little Giant." Douglas was an expansionist and an advocate of the doctrine of "popular sovereignty." He gained national prominence in the bitter controversy over slavery. Through his leadership, the Compromise of 1850 was adopted and the Kansas-Nebraska Act passed in 1854. When Douglas ran for reelection to the Senate in 1858, he engaged in a series of debates with his Republican opponent, Abraham Lincoln. These debates on the slavery issue attracted the attention of the entire nation. In 1860 Douglas was nominated for President by the northern Democrats, but those in the South refused to support him. He received only 12 electoral votes, against Lincoln's 180, although his popular vote was well over one million. When the Civil War broke out, Douglas denounced secession as criminal and offered his services to President Lincoln. At the President's request, he started on a tour of the border states to win support for the Union cause, but two months after the fall of Fort Sumter he died of typhoid fever.

"Cotton is King." Economic as well as political problems troubled the country. Overexpansion in railroads, land speculation, falling prices for grain, and problems in banking touched off a business panic and depression in 1857. It lasted for several years, and the North was hard hit. Because world demand for cotton remained high, however, the South was not as badly affected. Indeed, cotton accounted for nearly two thirds of the value of all United States exports.

The 1857 panic had important political results in both the North and the South. Northern manufacturers, more interested than ever in protective tariffs, moved to support the Republican party. Southern leaders became convinced that the real economic strength of the country rested in the cotton kingdom, with its system of slave labor. Thus they became more confident that the North would have to give in to their demands. As Senator Hammond of South Carolina said to his Northern colleagues in 1858, "You do not dare to make war on cotton. No power on earth dares to make war on it. Cotton is King." A Southerner named Hinton Rowan Helper wrote *The Impending Crisis of the South* in 1857. Because of this book, arguing that slavery actually made the South economically weaker, Helper was hounded out of the South.

Abraham Lincoln of Illinois. In the elections of 1858, Republicans made large gains in the North and West, and they won many seats in the House of Representatives. The most closely watched contest of that year was in Illinois, where Democrat Stephen Douglas was seeking reelection to the Senate. To oppose him, Republicans chose a young lawyer named Abraham Lincoln. He had served one term in the United States House of Representatives as a Whig during Polk's Presidency. With many other antislavery Whigs, Lincoln had shifted to the Republican party after the Kansas-Nebraska Act.

Lincoln was not an abolitionist. Nor, as he said during the campaign, had he "ever been in favor of bringing about in any way the social and political equality of the white and black races." But he did oppose slavery. "In the right to eat the bread . . . which his own hand earns," Lincoln would say, "he [the black man] is my equal, and the equal of Judge Douglas, and the equal of every living man." And while he did not believe that the federal government could interfere with slavery in the Southern states, he opposed its spread into a single foot of free territory. If slavery was thus limited, Lincoln believed, it would eventually die out.

The Freeport debate. The Lincoln-Douglas campaign featured a series of seven debates in Illinois towns. The most important one took place at Freeport. The Supreme Court had said in the Dred Scott case that Congress could not prohibit slavery in a territory. It followed that a territorial legislature, which was created by an act of Congress, could not do what Congress was prohibited from doing. Was there, then, asked Lincoln, any way in which an antislavery majority in a territory could keep slavery out? The question was a shrewd one. If Douglas said there was no way, he would be rejecting popular sovereignty, the idea on which he had built his career. If he said that slavery could still be kept out, he would be arguing against the Dred Scott decision. This would anger the South, whose support he hoped for in the next presidential election.

Douglas's reply was equally shrewd. Yes, he said, there was a way for a majority to keep out slavery, despite the Dred Scott decision. The territorial legislature could simply refuse to pass a slave code—those laws that protected slavery—for without it, slavery could not exist a single day.

Douglas's reply became known as the *Freeport Doctrine.* It satisfied enough Illinois voters for the Democrats to carry both houses of the state legislature narrowly, and it reelected Douglas to the United States Senate. But the Freeport Doctrine raised a storm among Southern Democrats, as Lincoln knew it would. No longer satisfied that slavery was *allowed* in the territories by the Dred Scott decision, they now demanded that Congress pass laws to *protect* it there. This would mean the end of popular sovereignty, and Northern and Western Democrats in Congress refused to go along. Meanwhile, despite the loss, Lincoln emerged from the election with a growing reputation.

Harpers Ferry. In the fall of 1859, John Brown—the same John Brown who had touched off the warfare in Kansas—led

Inside the arsenal at Harpers Ferry, John Brown and his men defend themselves against the militia and a company of marines. Only four out of nineteen were alive and unwounded upon Brown's surrender.

Answers To Review Questions

1. Owners should treat their slaves like human beings; owners should at least free slaves in their wills; freed slaves should be colonized.
2. There was no thought of equality for blacks in the North. In the 1830s, several states took away the free black's right to vote. By law or by custom, there was segregation in housing, public transportation, schools, theaters, and churches.
3. Harriet Tubman helped many slaves to escape using the Underground Railroad. David Walker and Frederick Douglass published articles and lectured in support of abolition. Many blacks purchased Garrison's *The Liberator.*
4. The South turned to the Bible, the Constitution, ancient philosophers, and to classical civilization of Greece to justify slavery. Southerners claimed that the slave had greater security than the northern wage earner.
5. Only a very small percentage of upper-and middle-class Southerners owned slaves. Three fourths of all white families in the South owned no slaves.
6. Popular sovereignty proposed that the people of each territory would decide for themselves whether or not they wanted slavery.

a small band of followers in an attack on a United States arsenal at Harpers Ferry in Virginia. With the guns stored there, Brown planned to arm Virginia slaves for an uprising. There was never any chance that this wild idea would succeed. Brown was quickly captured, tried for treason against the state of Virginia, found guilty, and hanged.

Most Northern citizens, political leaders, and newspapers condemned Brown's raid. Abolitionists, however, raised Brown to sainthood. He was an "angel of light," they said, whose execution would "make the gallows glorious like the cross." At their meetings, the abolitionists were soon singing:

> John Brown's body lies a-mouldering in the grave,
> His soul goes marching on.

It was the words of the abolitionists rather than those of Northern leaders and journals that frightened Southerners chose to hear. They were enraged to learn that some leading abolitionists had known of Brown's plan and had given him money to carry it out. That Northerners would help to bring about what Southerners most dreaded—a slave uprising—was to them further proof of the North's bad faith.

As the year 1860 opened, most of the ties that had held the Union together snapped. Every new episode, every new statement was taken by each side as proof of the aggressive designs of the other. By year's end, a sectional party would capture the Presidency, and secession of Southern states would begin. Soon after, the nation would be plunged into civil war. You will read of these events and their outcome in the next chapter.

CHECKUP

1. What were the results in Kansas of the passage of the Kansas-Nebraska Act?
2. How did the makeup of American political parties change during the 1850s?
3. In what ways did the Dred Scott case intensify the slavery controversy?
4. What were Abraham Lincoln's views on slavery?

Key Facts from Chapter 16

1. The antislavery movement was led by Northern abolitionists, both black and white. The abolitionists demanded that slaves be given their freedom.
2. As antislavery feeling became stronger, so did the defense of slavery by Southerners.
3. By the mid-1800s, the North and South were moving in different directions. The North was moving toward an industrial, urban society, while the South remained largely rural and agricultural.
4. Following the Mexican War, the overriding issue in national politics became the spread of slavery into the Western territories.
5. During the 1850s, the Republican party was formed. Its major goal was to keep slavery out of the territories.

★ REVIEWING THE CHAPTER ★

People, Places, and Events

Missouri Compromise *P. 323*
Abolitionists *P.323*
William Lloyd Garrison *P. 323*
Underground Railroad *P. 324*
Harriet Tubman *P. 324*
Wilmot Proviso *P. 331*
Compromise of 1850 *P. 334*
Kansas-Nebraska Act *P. 337*
Stephen Douglas *P. 337*
Republican Party *P. 338*
"Bleeding Kansas" *P. 339*
John Brown *P. 339*
Dred Scott case *P. 340*
Freeport Doctrine *P. 343*
Harpers Ferry *P. 343*

Review Questions

1. What three suggestions did early opponents of slavery offer to settle the problem? *P. 323* Les. 1

2. How were blacks treated in the North? *Pp. 325–326* Les. 1

3. In what ways did blacks contribute to the abolition movement? *P. 326–327* Les. 1

4. How did the South justify slavery? *P. 328* Les. 2

5. Did most Southerners own slaves? Explain. *P. 329* Les. 2

6. In what way did popular sovereignty propose to settle the argument over the spread of slavery? *P. 331* Les. 3

7. What were the views of John Calhoun and Daniel Webster in regard to the compromise offered by Henry Clay in 1850? *Pp. 333–334* Les. 3

8. Describe the impact of *Uncle Tom's Cabin*. *P. 336* Les. 4

9. How did the Panic of 1857 influence the political attitudes of Northerners and Southerns? *P. 342* Les. 4

Chapter Test

The statements below indicate events that occurred during the period 1820 to 1859. On a separate piece of paper, number 1 to 10. Beginning with number 1 for the earliest event, rearrange the events so that they are in the correct chronological order.

A. The Compromise of 1850 provided for the admission of California to the Union as a free state.

B. Open warfare between proslavery and antislavery forces claimed a number of lives in "Bleeding Kansas."

C. John Brown's raid at Harpers Ferry disturbed southern slave owners, who lived in constant fear of a massive slave revolt.

D. The Kansas-Nebraska Act specifically repealed the Missouri Compromise and provided for popular sovereignty as the method to settle slavery issue in the two newly created territories.

E. The Lincoln-Douglas debate at Freeport, Illinois argued the issues at stake in the Dred Scott decision.

F. The Missouri Compromise was the first great clash between North and South over the question of slavery.

G. Elijah Lovejoy, an abolitionist printer, was shot to death by an angry mob.

H. California sought to enter the Union as a free state.

I. As part of the decision in the Dred Scott case, the Supreme Court said that Congress could not bar slavery in any territories of the national government.

J. *Uncle Tom's Cabin* appeared at a time when there was great controversy over the Fugitive Slave Law.

7. Calhoun believed the North must give the South equal rights in the new territories, return fugitive slaves, and cease the agitation of the slave question. He had no interest in a compromise. On the other hand, Webster, a Unionist, believed that only through Clay's compromise could the Union be saved. Although he opposed slavery, he urged the North to accept the fugitive slave law and to quiet the opposition to slavery.
8. Among Northerners, the story created great sympathy for the slaves and generated much public opinion against slavery. On the other hand, Southerners charged that the book was pure fiction and painted an inaccurate picture of slave conditions. Whether the account was true or not, the book inflamed the nation.
9. The North was hard hit by the business depression resulting from overexpansion in railroads, land speculation, falling grain prices, and banking problems. So Northern manufacturers became more interested than ever in protective tariffs. And they consequently moved to support the Republican party. The South was not as badly affected because world demand for cotton remained high. Southern leaders became convinced that the real economic strength of the nation rested with cotton and the slave system. They grew confident that the North would have to give in to their demands.

Answers For Chapter Test
1. f **2.** g **3.** h **4.** a
5. j **6.** d **7.** b **8.** i
9. e **10.** c

Background Information

PICTURE This shows a typical scene in a northern city at the time of the Civil War. Troops march off to war, with friends and loved ones cheering.

SECESSION AND CIVIL WAR

LESSON 1

THE ELECTION OF 1860 took place against a background of rising sectional tension. Favored to win the Democratic party's nomination was Senator Stephen Douglas of Illinois. At the convention in South Carolina in April 1860, Southern delegates pressed their demand for a law to protect slavery in the territories. When Northern delegates refused to put this demand in the platform, Southerners walked out. The convention then adjourned without choosing a candidate. Six weeks later in Baltimore the Democrats tried again, but with the same result. This time the Northern delegates remained and nominated Douglas. Southern Democrats then met separately and chose John J. Breckinridge of Kentucky as their candidate. The Democratic party had now split into two sectional parties.

This split opened the door to a Republican victory. The new Republican party needed only to hold the support of those who had voted for it in 1856 and 1858. The strategy therefore called for choosing a candidate who would not frighten voters away. Mainly for that reason, party leaders at the Republican convention passed over the best known Republican, Senator William H. Seward of New York. Seward had once spoken of an "irreconcilable conflict" between North and South, and he was considered by some to be extreme. The Republicans named instead the more moderate Abraham Lincoln. The Republican platform, while promising not to interfere with slavery in the Southern states, opposed its spread into the territories.

A fourth party, the Constitutional Union party, also entered the field. Most of its leaders were former Whigs from the states of Maryland, Virginia, Kentucky, and Missouri. Those states lay between the North and the South. The leaders of the party desperately hoped to avoid war, knowing that if it came, their states would be the battleground. The Constitutional Union party nominated John Bell of Tennessee for President, and declared simply in favor of the Constitution and the Union.

Lincoln's election. Although Lincoln received less than 40 percent of the popular vote, he easily won the election. He received 180 electoral votes to 72 for Breckinridge and 39 for Bell. Douglas, who with 29 percent was second to Lincoln in popular votes, won only 12 electoral votes. The Democrats, however, kept control of Congress.

The presidential vote showed how deeply the country was split. Lincoln was not even on the ballot in ten Southern states. In the North, Breckinridge got a mere handful of votes. At the same time, the combined vote for these two clearly sectional candidates was far greater than that for the moderates, Bell and Douglas.

The South Leaves the Union

During the campaign, many Southern leaders warned that if Lincoln was elected the South would secede. They were true to their word. On December 20, 1860, South Carolina seceded from the Union. That state was followed in

LESSON 1 *(1 to 2 days)*

Performance Objectives

1. To explain orally or in writing how the election of 1860 reflected the national split over the slavery issue. **2.** To write in outline form the series of events that led to the outbreak of the Civil War at Fort Sumter.

Famous People

Stephen A. Douglas, John J. Breckinridge, John Bell, Abraham Lincoln, Jefferson Davis, Alexander Stephens

Vocabulary

Election of 1860, Constitutional Union party, secession, Confederate States of America, Fort Sumter, King Cotton

Activities

1. FILMS *Background of the Civil War* (20 minutes, color; Film Associates of California). *Abraham Lincoln, Part 2: The Illinois Years* (17 minutes, color; Francis R. Line). *Storm Over Sumter* (27 minutes, b&w; Westinghouse Broadcasting Company).

2. LISTENING FOR INFORMATION Read to your students "The Great Emotion" by David Donald and "Abraham Lincoln" by Benjamin P. Thomas from *The American Story: The Age of Exploration to the Age of the Atom* (New York: Channel Press, 1956). Or you may wish to have students tape-record the selections and play the tapes to the class.

3. RESEARCH / ORAL REPORTS Many articles have appeared in *American Heritage* on the coming of the Civil War. Assign some of these articles for students to read and report on to the class.

4. CREATIVE WRITING After students have read the lesson, ask them to write newspaper stories about the election of 1860. Be sure they understand that good newspaper English places a premium on accuracy and directness in telling a story, and is written to be read easily and quickly. The essential information—who, what, when, where, why—is usually given first, with details coming later. Have students write a headline for their election stories.

Before students begin to write their articles, you may want to conduct a class discussion about the election—the parties, candidates, issues, outcome, and significance of the outcome.

5. OUTLINING / DISCUSSION To help students gain a better understanding of the events that led to the outbreak of the Civil War at Fort Sumter, ask them to outline the main ideas of this lesson. This could be a homework assignment. When the students have completed this activity, have them discuss the information that they included in their outlines. List their ideas on the chalkboard and see if everyone can agree on the important points to include in the outline. Allow students to correct or modify their own outlines as the discussion proceeds.

the next six weeks by Mississippi, Florida, Alabama, Georgia, Louisiana, and Texas.

The Confederacy. On February 1, 1861, representatives of the seven seceding states of the Deep South met in Montgomery, Alabama, and formed the Confederate States of America. Four more Southern states—Virginia, North Carolina, Tennessee, and Arkansas—did not secede. However, they warned they would do so if force was used against the seven states that had withdrawn from the Union.

The Constitution of the Confederacy was much like that of the United States. The main differences were that the states in the Confederacy were sovereign, and slavery could never be abolished. Jefferson Davis of Mississippi, a former senator and cabinet member, became President. Alexander Stephens of Georgia, a former congressman, was made Vice President. Shortly after taking office, Stephens explained the reason why the Southern states formed the Confederate government.

> Our confederacy is founded upon the great truth that the Negro is not equal to the white man, that slavery is his natural and normal condition. This, our new government, is the first in the history of the world based upon this great physical and moral truth.

Meanwhile, the seceding states seized federal forts, post offices, and customs houses within their borders. Only Fort Sumter, in the harbor of Charleston, South Carolina, and Fort Pickens, off the Florida coast, remained under federal control. All these events took place while James Buchanan was still President. He did nothing to stop them. His position was that while secession was not possible under the Constitution, the federal government had no power under that document to stop it! Meanwhile, several compromise efforts in Congress failed.

Why the haste to secede? Why did the South hasten to secede at this time? Congress, after all, was still in the hands of the Democrats. On the Supreme Court, there was still a majority friendly to the Southern view. Even President-elect Lincoln had promised not to interfere with slavery in the Southern states. Despite the alarms of the fire-eaters, it is clear that there was no immediate threat to slavery in the South. Further, once it became a separate country, the South would have no claim at all to a share of the territories in the West. And getting back slaves who had run away to the North, now merely difficult, would then be impossible.

There are at least two reasons why the South seceded at this time. One is that its leaders were looking not to the present but to the future. Sooner or later, the rapidly growing, antislavery North would control all the branches of government. Better to leave now, said Southern leaders, than wait for that time when the North would be still stronger. A second reason is that after years of arguing with the North over tariffs, slavery, and states' rights, feelings had been built to a point where nothing but action would do. A South Carolina woman named Mary Chesnut later recalled her own feelings at that time.

My father was a South Carolina nullifier, Governor of the state at the time of the nullification row and then United States Senator; so I was of necessity a rebel born. . . . Come what would, I wanted them to fight and stop talking. South Carolinians had heated themselves into a fever that only bloodletting could ever cure. It was the inevitable remedy, so I was a seceder.

Would war follow? Not all Southerners shared Mary Chesnut's belief that secession would lead to war. Indeed, it was the belief that they could leave the Union without causing war that made many Southerners bold enough to take the step. In the North, many people agreed with the newspaper editor who wrote, "Let the erring sisters depart in peace." Many abolitionists were also pacifists. Further, Southerners believed that Northern manufacturers who needed cotton and Northern merchants who sold in Southern markets would never let the North go to war and ruin their businesses.

If war should come, the Southerners counted on King Cotton to give them victory. English and French textile manufacturers depended on Southern cotton. War would cut off their supply. Before England and France would allow their economies to be ruined, Southerners were sure that those nations would come into the war on the side of the South. Further, Southern slaveholders counted on the sympathetic support of the British upper class.

Lincoln's inauguration. On March 4, 1861, amid the nation's greatest crisis, Abraham Lincoln became the sixteenth President of the United States. In his inaugural address Lincoln tried to reassure the South. The President declared he would agree to a constitutional amendment that the government would never interfere with slavery in the South. At the same time, he said that secession was not possible under the Constitution. His oath of office required that he hold and protect government property, and he would do so. Whether this would lead to war was, the President said, a decision that lay in the hands of the South.

In February 1861, Jefferson Davis was sworn in as President of the Confederacy at Montgomery, Alabama. After Virginia seceded, the capital was moved from Montgomery to Richmond.

6. DISCUSSION Some historians have said that the Civil War might have been averted up to a certain point, but that after this point had been reached, war between the North and South was unavoidable. Ask: Could war have been avoided after the Kansas-Nebraska Act? after the Dred Scott decision? after John Brown's raid on Harpers Ferry? after the Democratic party nominated a Northern and a Southern candidate for President? after Lincoln's election as President? after the first seven states seceded from the Union? after the firing on Fort Sumter? Be sure students support their answers with logic.

7. **WHAT IF?** Suppose Abraham Lincoln had chosen to avoid war by recognizing the independence of the Confederate States. Ask: What effect might this recognition have had on the South? Would slavery have continued to exist until today? Would the economy of the South have remained largely agricultural? Encourage students to support their opinions with logic and reasoning.

8. **ORAL REPORTS** If students enjoy hearing excerpts from original documents that have shaped American history, arrange for several students to present the following documents to the class. From Commager's *Documents of American History:* 201, "The Constitution of the Confederate States of America" and 202, "Lincoln's First Inaugural Address."

The firing on Fort Sumter. Lincoln's determination was quickly put to the test. Major Robert Anderson, the army commander at Fort Sumter, reported that more arms, men, and supplies would be needed to hold the fort. Lincoln feared that sending men would cause Southern forces to open fire. Yet he was unwilling to allow the garrison to be starved into surrender. He therefore decided to send food only, and he notified authorities in South Carolina of this fact. But Confederate leaders were determined that the fort should fall. Their guns opened fire at 4:30 A.M. on April 12, before the supplies arrived. After thirty-four hours, Anderson and his men surrendered.

With the firing on Fort Sumter, Northern opinion, until now divided, rallied behind Lincoln. Two days later, the President called on the state militias for 75,000 volunteers to put down the rebellion. Virginia, North Carolina, Arkansas, and Tennessee promptly carried out their earlier threat to leave the Union. (The western part of Virginia, where Union sentiment was strong, broke away with the aid of Union troops. In 1863, it became the state of West Virginia.) Four other slave states—Maryland, Delaware, Kentucky, and Missouri—remained in the Union. Those states came to be called the *border states.* Keeping them in the Union became a chief objective of the Lincoln administration.

Within two weeks, Lincoln called for more troops and ordered a naval blockade of Southern ports. The Civil War had begun.

Confederate artillery pieces under the command of General P. G. T. Beauregard pound Fort Sumter in the harbor of Charleston, South Carolina. The barrage marked the beginning of the Civil War.

CHECKUP

1. In what ways did the election of 1860 reflect the split over the slavery issue?
2. Why did the South hasten to secede following Lincoln's election?
3. Under what circumstances were the first shots of the Civil War fired?

LESSON 2

Mounting the War Effort

How the war would be pursued by the two sides depended to a large degree on the resources available to each. A comparison at the start of the war shows that the Union and the Confederacy each had certain advantages.

Northern advantages. The twenty-three states remaining in the Union had a population of 22 million. In the eleven Confederate states there were only 9 million people, of whom 3.5 million were slaves. The North thus had a much larger population from which to draw soldiers.

With seven times as much manufacturing as the South, the North was able after 1862 to make all the war goods it needed, from guns to medical supplies. The South, on the other hand, had to buy many of its supplies from Europe. This was made difficult because of another of the North's advantages—its navy. Soon after the war started, the North set up a naval blockade that kept ships from entering or leaving Southern ports. Although far from airtight, the blockade became a powerful weapon.

Other Northern advantages included greater wealth to pay for a war and a better railway system. With twice as many miles of railroad lines as the South had, the North could move troops and supplies quickly. Moreover, as the war went on, Southern railroads fell into ever worse condition.

Southern advantages. A major advantage of the Confederacy was that, unlike the Union, it did not have to conquer any territory to attain its goal. To maintain independence, the Confederacy needed only to hold what it had. Thus its armies could fight a defensive war. That meant several things. One, the Confederacy's supply lines were short, while the enemy's were long. Also, the Southern soldiers fought on land they knew well. And finally, they felt that they were fighting to defend not only their way of life but their very homes, giving them a strong sense of purpose. Further, the South's strong military tradition gave it better military leadership at the start of the war. At the outbreak of the war, many officers in the United States Army were from the South. Most of those officers chose to resign and cast their lot with the Confederacy.

Raising an army: the North. Soon after the war began, it became clear to Northern leaders that they needed more than the three-month volunteers from the state militias. Lincoln therefore called for 42,000 volunteers for three-year terms in the regular army. Two months later, Congress increased the size of the army to 500,000. When enlistments slowed, Congress passed the nation's first draft law, in March 1863. There was a good deal of opposition to this law. *Peace Democrats*—Northern Democrats who opposed the war—were against it. So were many who believed that a draft violated their civil rights.

LESSON 2 *(2 days)*

Performance Objectives

1. To list and describe the advantages possessed by the North and the South in the Civil War. **2.** To identify the problems confronting Abraham Lincoln and Jefferson Davis as wartime leaders.

Vocabulary

Naval blockade, supply lines, defenders, state militia volunteer, draft law, Peace Democrats, substitute soldiers, "a rich man's war but a poor man's fight," desertion, National Banking Acts of 1863 and 1864, greenbacks, tax in kind, Copperheads, *habeas corpus*, *ex parte Milligan*, neutrality, Trent Affair

Activities

1. USING GRAPHS Before students read the lesson, present to them the following information about the resources of the Union and the Confederacy in 1860. Ask them to make a series of pie graphs based on the percentages given. Be sure students understand that the combined resources of the Union and the Confederacy represent 100 percent.

Population: Union, 71 percent; Confederacy, 29 percent.
Factories: Union, 85 percent; Confederacy, 15 percent.
Industrial Workers: Union, 92 percent; Confederacy, 8 percent.
Railroads: Union, 71 percent; Confederacy, 29 percent.
Value of Farmlands: Union, 72 percent; Confederacy, 28 percent.
Value of Livestock: Union, 65 percent; Confederacy, 35 percent.
Bank Deposits: Union, 81 percent; Confederacy, 19 percent.
Wealth Produced: Union, 91 percent; Confederacy, 9 percent.

After students have completed their pie graphs, ask them to compare the information and draw conclusions about the ability of each side to wage war. In the discussion of the graph statistics, point out that even though the material resources of the Union were greater than those of the Confederacy, it still took four years for the North to win the war. Ask: What factors that are not shown in the statistics might explain the Confederacy's ability to endure? As the students read the lesson text, have them look for answers to that question.

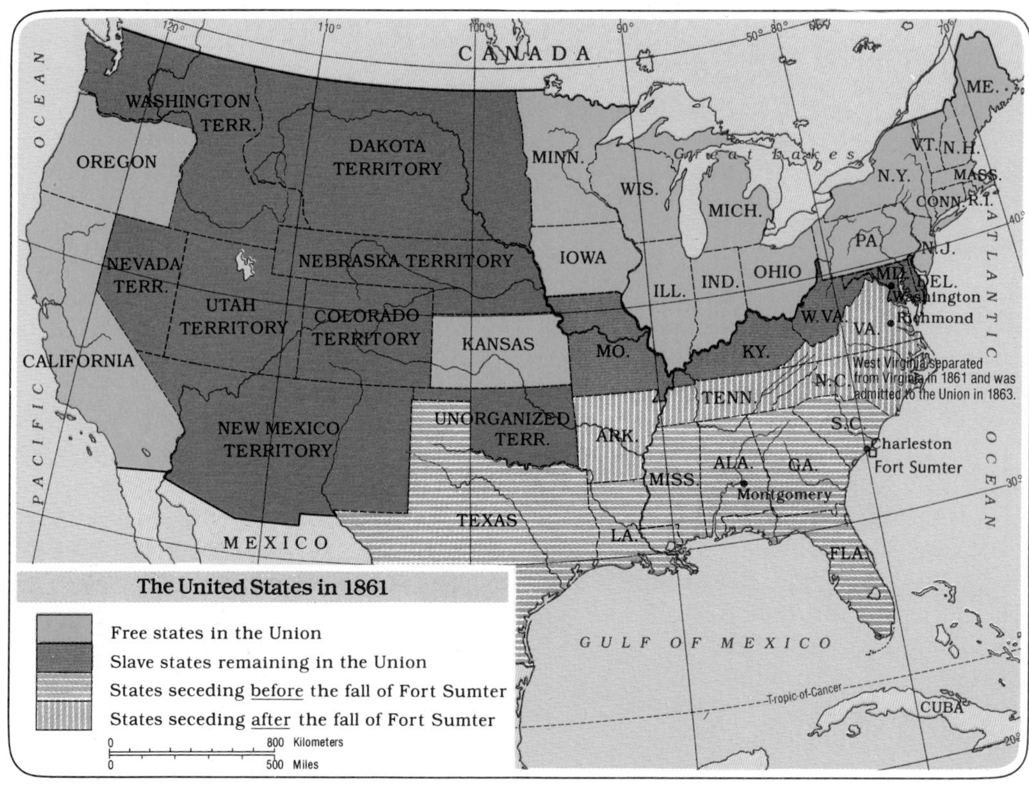

The Union consisted of twenty-three states following the admission of West Virginia in 1863. There were eleven states in the Confederacy. Most Western regions had territorial status.

Most opposition, though, centered on the fact that a draftee could keep from serving by paying the government $300 or by hiring a substitute to go in his place. This led some to complain that the war was "a rich man's war but a poor man's fight." In several cities there were draft riots. The worst was in New York City, where four days of rioting in July 1863 left several hundred dead. Union soldiers had to be sent to the city to restore order.

Black Americans were another source of troops for the army. At first, though, they were not allowed to enlist. When some blacks in Cincinnati tried to volunteer, they were told that "this"—a war that was about slavery—"is a white man's war!" After 1862, however, blacks were allowed to enlist. By the end of the war some 200,000, many of them former slaves, had served as members of the Union army.

Raising an army: the South. In the South, too, volunteers flocked to the colors at first. With a smaller population, however, the South had to turn to the draft nearly a year before the North did. Because the law allowed persons owning twenty or more slaves to be free from military service, it was bitterly opposed by many nonslaveholders. As casualties and desertions began to mount, the Confederacy raised the draft age to fifty. By early 1865, the Confederacy became so desperate that it passed a law to draft 300,000 slaves—into the very army that was fighting to preserve slavery! But the war ended before any slaves were drafted.

Paying for the war. The cost of fighting ran into billions of dollars for both sides. Both sides used three means to pay for the war: they taxed; they borrowed; and they printed paper money. The North, with far more of its wealth in money, was the more successful. Among its taxes was an income tax, the first in the country's history. It remained law until 1872. The federal government also raised a large amount of money by selling bonds to the public. In the National Banking Acts of 1863 and 1864, the government created a system of national banks, and it required these banks to buy United States government bonds. When these methods did not provide enough funds, Congress approved the issue of paper money. By the end of the war, $450 million in *greenbacks*, so

For both North and South, raising an army was an urgent task. This poster was used to recruit Union soldiers in Vermont. The photograph shows newly outfitted Confederate recruits.

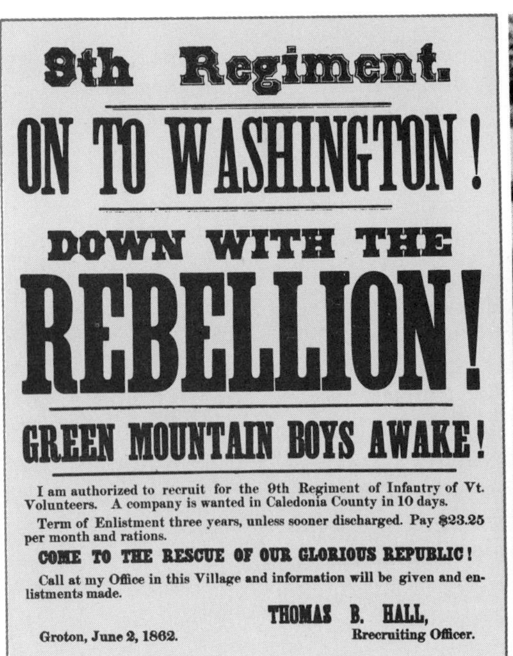

2. USING A MAP Have students study the map on this page and answer the following questions: If Lincoln had recognized the Confederacy, what states would have been lost to the United States? What special provisions would it have been necessary to make for the territories? What kind of relationship do you think the United States would have developed with the Confederacy?

3. USING A CHART After students have read the lesson, have them make charts comparing the North and the South with respect to **(a)** number of states, **(b)** population, **(c)** industrial development, **(d)** financial resources, **(e)** transportation facilities, and **(f)** military power. Tell students to evaluate each as a factor for strength in fighting the war.

4. ORAL REPORTS Assign several students to report on the role of blacks in the Civil War. Good sources are *Negroes in the Civil War* by Benjamin Quarles (Boston: Little, Brown & Company, 1969) and *Eyewitness: The Negro in American History* by William Katz (New York: Pitman, 1971).

5. ROLE-PLAYING Divide the class in half and assign one group to role-play Abraham Lincoln and the other group to role-play Jefferson Davis. Allow students to work together in small groups to develop the character of the person they will portray. If time permits, have them use reference books and primary source material to find more information about the two leaders. Tell students to concentrate on identifying the problems that confronted each man as he sought to provide leadership to his side in the Civil War. After students have prepared their treatment of Lincoln and Davis, ask for volunteers to participate in a *Meet the Press* style of question-and-answer session. The teacher may wish to serve as the press, directing questions alternately to each leader. Allow several different students to role-play each man. Then ask the rest of the class for their comments and/or observations about the role-playing situation. Did each student involved in the role-playing accurately portray his or her Lincoln or Davis? Did each person present accurate information about the events of the Civil War period?

called because of their color, had been issued. Greenbacks could not be redeemed for gold or silver. Therefore, their value at any time depended on how much faith people had in the government that issued them. When the war was going poorly for the North, greenbacks were worth as little as 30 cents. As Northern fortunes improved, so did the value of the greenbacks.

The South had a much harder time raising money. Most of its wealth was tied up in land and slaves, and the North's blockade kept the South from raising much money by selling cotton. Since few farmers had much money, the Confederacy passed a *tax in kind.* This required farmers to pay one tenth of their produce to the government. The Confederate government as well as individual Southern states sold bonds. The Confederacy turned to printing money earlier than the North did, and it printed more of it. By 1864, it had issued more than $1 billion in paper money. As the South's paper dollar fell in value, prices there skyrocketed. Flour came to cost $300 a barrel, and butter, $25 a pound. By the end of the war, the value of the Confederate dollar had dropped to less than a penny.

The home front. For the families of the millions who went off to war, normal life was disrupted. Women and children had to take on the work that had been done by the menfolk. Some Southern women had always run farms and plantations. Now, many more did. To their usual tasks they also added that of helping to manufacture war goods. A Georgia woman later recalled how every household "became a miniature factory" for making clothing after the North's blockade cut off supply lines from England and France.

A remarkable fact is that despite the absence of many men from Northern farms for long periods of time, farm production in that section actually increased during the war. That was partly due to the greater use of machinery. Much of the increased production, however, was the result of women picking up the farm work formerly done by men. A traveler to the Midwest in 1863 reported that "women were in the fields everywhere, driving the reapers, binding and shocking, and loading grain." One woman explained:

> Harvesting isn't any harder than cooking, washing, and ironing over a red-hot stove in July and August—only we have to do both now. My three brothers went into the army, all my cousins, most of the young men about here, and the men we used to hire. So there's no help to be got but women, and the crops must be got in all the same, you know.

Lincoln's leadership. One of the North's greatest strengths turned out to be the leadership of Abraham Lincoln. When he first entered the Presidency, many people thought of Lincoln as a small-town politician who was not big enough for the job. Several of his cabinet appointees, including Secretary of State William Seward, tried to dominate the President. Seward quickly learned, however, that Lincoln intended to run the government himself and had the ability to do it. From then on, Seward was the President's loyal supporter.

Throughout the war, Lincoln faced strong political opposition in and out of

Employees leave work at the Treasury Department building in Washington, D.C., during the Civil War. At that time, many women filled government jobs that had previously been held by men.

Congress. On the one side were those Northern Democrats who opposed the war. The *Copperheads,* as the Peace Democrats were called, wanted to invite the South back into the Union on the South's terms—a guarantee of states' rights. Some opponents of the war went so far as to form secret societies and plan acts of treason. On the other side were the Radical Republicans. They made up a growing wing of the party that wanted slavery abolished and the South punished. In Congress, the Radical Republicans created and controlled the Joint Committee on the Conduct of the War. Through this committee, they kept up a steady stream of criticism of Lincoln. With great patience and skill, the President steered between those two groups, moving always toward the main objective of saving the Union.

Stretching the Constitution. In his efforts to save the Union, Lincoln stretched the constitutional powers of the President to their very limits—and even beyond. Although the Constitution gives the power to raise an army only to Congress, Lincoln took it upon himself in May 1861 to call for three-year volunteers. Congress legalized that action when it returned to Washington two months later. Lincoln also acted without congressional authority in declaring the blockade.

To prevent interference with the war effort, especially in the border states, Lincoln suspended the writ of *habeas corpus* (see page 135). As a result, more than 13,000 civilians were arrested and held without trial in military jails—some for days, some for months, and a few for years. Those who were brought

Background Information

JEFFERSON DAVIS (1808–1889) Named for Thomas Jefferson, Jefferson Davis was born in Kentucky and moved with his family to Mississippi. There Jefferson and his brothers became plantation owners, with great wealth and prestige. Davis had graduated from West Point and, like many southern plantation owners, combined political and military activities with the management of his plantation. During the Mexican War, Davis commanded a regiment and was wounded at the battle of Buena Vista. Later he was a senator from Mississippi and secretary of war in Franklin Pierce's cabinet. During his term, Davis improved and enlarged the army. At the close of the Pierce administration, in 1857, he was reelected to the Senate from Mississippi and spoke out in defense of the rights of the South and slavery. After Lincoln's election in 1860, Mississippi seceded from the Union and Davis resigned from the Senate. It was his hope to be made head of the Army of the Confederate States, but he was asked to serve instead as president of the Confederacy.

Jefferson Davis had a difficult task as leader of the Confederacy. Although he was an eloquent orator and an able administrator, he tried to drive rather than lead public opinion in the Confederacy. He had problems with Congress and was condemned by bitter critics for his management of the war. Yet no one doubted his courage, sincerity, and integrity. Suffering acutely from neuralgia and other nervous disorders, he overworked himself with the details of government and military organization. Soon after Lee's surrender at Appomattox, Davis was captured in Georgia and imprisoned at Fort Monroe, Virginia. He was indicted for treason, held in prison for two years awaiting trial, and then released on bail; but he was never tried. Davis spent his last years traveling abroad writing, and studying at a friend's plantation near Biloxi, Mississippi. As a defense against his critics, he published *The Rise and Fall of the Confederate Government* in 1881.

to trial were tried in military courts. After the war, the Supreme Court ruled in *ex parte Milligan* (1866) that military trials of civilians were illegal where regular courts were still operating.

Lincoln justified his actions by saying that in order to preserve the Constitution, he had at times to disregard parts of it. Others might use the same justification for causes that were less good or when the danger to the nation and the Constitution was less clear.

Jefferson Davis's role. Jefferson Davis, the President of the Confederacy was less successful than Lincoln in directing the war effort. One reason was that Davis lacked Lincoln's skill in dealing with the trying problems of wartime leadership. Often Davis allowed himself to become bogged down with details. Further, his attempts to provide a unified leadership for the war effort were blocked by some states that insisted on states' rights. The doctrine of states' rights was, of course, one of the founding ideas of the Confederacy. At various times, some Southern states refused to take orders from the Confederate government. Once, South Carolina even threatened to secede from the Confederacy!

Wartime diplomacy. Both sides engaged in active diplomacy with European nations. The aim of the Confederacy was to bring England and France into the war on its side, or at least to get help from them. The North's aim was simply to keep those countries neutral.

The South, you will recall, had pinned most of its hopes on the need of Britain and France for cotton. However, when the war began, both countries had large supplies of cotton on hand. By the time they were used up, Britain and France had developed new sources of cotton in Egypt and India. Also, Britain's upper classes were sympathetic to the South, as the South had expected. But that sympathy was offset by the strong antislavery and pro-Northern feelings of the English working people.

Several crises arose between England and the United States. The first occurred when the commander of a United States warship stopped the British ship *Trent* and removed two Confederate diplomats who were traveling to Europe to seek aid for their cause. The British angrily protested this violation of freedom of the seas. This was the same right over which the United States had gone to war against England in 1812. The incident, which could have led to war, ended when President Lincoln ordered the release of the two Confederates.

Another dispute arose when English shipbuilders built two warships for the Confederacy and allowed them to put to sea in violation of international law. These warships, the *Alabama* and the *Florida*, destroyed a large number of Union merchant ships. Charles Francis Adams, the United States minister to England, had to threaten war to keep the British from delivering other warships built for the Confederacy.

CHECKUP

1. What advantages did each side have at the beginning of the Civil War?
2. How did the two sides secure troops and raise money for carrying on the war?
3. With what other problems did the two wartime leaders, Abraham Lincoln and Jefferson Davis, have to contend?

LESSON 3

The Agony of War

At the very beginning of the war, the North adopted a military plan with three parts. The first part was to blockade Southern ports. This would keep the South from sending its cotton to European nations and receiving supplies from them. The second part of the plan was to capture Richmond, Virginia. The capital of the Confederacy had been moved there from Montgomery, Alabama, after Virginia seceded. The third part of the plan was to control the Mississippi River. This would split the region lying west of the river—Texas, Arkansas, and most of Louisiana—from the rest of the Confederacy. It would deny the rebels a part of their manpower and supplies. Those Confederate states east of the Mississippi could then be squeezed between the blockade and armies moving in from west and north.

"Forward to Richmond!" Although the war began on April 12, 1861,with the firing on Fort Sumter, the first battle did not come until three months later. With the cry "Forward to Richmond!" a Union force marched out of Washington toward the Confederate capital. Civilians in a holiday mood trailed behind in their carriages, expecting to see the rebels turn and flee.

The two armies, neither of which was yet well trained, met on July 21 about 30 miles (48 km) from Washington, near a small creek called Bull Run. At first, Northern troops drove the Southern soldiers back. But one Confederate group led by General "Stonewall" Jackson held

LESSON 3 *(2 days)*

Performance Objectives

1. To mark on an outline map the major military actions of the Civil War described in the text. **2.** To describe the North's three-part military plan. **3.** To explain orally or in writing the timing and significance of the Emancipation Proclamation.

Famous People

"Stonewall" Jackson, George B. McClellan, Ulysses S. Grant, David G. Farragut, Robert E. Lee, George Meade, George Pickett, William T. Sherman

In this pencil sketch, an unknown onlooker caught the feeling of panic that swept through the Union troops fleeing back toward Washington from Bull Run after the first big battle of the war.

Vocabulary

Blockade, Richmond, Bull Run, Eastern theater of war, Western theater of war, Fort Henry, Fort Donelson, Shiloh, Seven Days' Battles, Antietam, Emancipation Proclamation, Gettysburg, Vicksburg, Chattanooga, the Wilderness, Sherman's march, Appomattox

Activities

1. LISTENING FOR INFORMATION The following selections from *The American Story* will be of interest to your students: "The Emancipation Proclamation" by Paul M. Angle; "Sherman and the Hard Hand of War" by Earl Schenck Miers; "Southern Yeoman in the Civil War" by Bell Irvin Wiley; and "Grant and Lee: A Study in Contrasts" by Bruce Catton. Arrange for some of the better students to read the selections to the class. If you prefer, have the students tape-record the selections and play the tapes in class.

2. USING A CHART Have students construct a chart of the Civil War. Have them list the strengths and weaknesses of both sides at the onset of war. Then have them list the battles separately and, under each, indicate the opposing generals, the battle casualties, and the results. After students have completed their charts, discuss the information in class.

its ground. With the arrival of reinforcements, Southern troops went on the attack. Northern troops retreated, and then broke in panic and ran. Soon the road to Washington was jammed with fleeing soldiers. The Southerners, however, were too inexperienced and disorganized to follow up their victory. After the battle of Bull Run, both sides settled in for a long war.

For the rest of 1861 the Eastern theater of war—the region between the Atlantic Ocean and the Appalachian Mountains—was quiet. It was plain that the Union soldiers needed training. To mold the volunteers into an effective army, Lincoln put General George B. McClellan in command.

The Western theater, 1862. In the region between the Appalachians and the Mississippi River, Union forces were more successful. Their aim there was to keep the border states of Missouri and Kentucky in the Union, while cutting the Confederacy off from the states west of the Mississippi. Early in 1862, General Ulysses S. Grant, then a little-known Union officer, moved a force into western Kentucky and Tennessee. In sharp fighting, Grant took Fort Henry on the Tennessee River and Fort Donelson on the Cumberland. Those losses forced Southern armies to withdraw into northern Mississippi. A Confederate counterattack just over the Tennessee border, near Shiloh, caught Grant by surprise and led to a bloody two-day battle. Grant's army was saved by reinforcements, however, and the Confederates had to withdraw.

Shortly afterward, a Union fleet under Captain David G. Farragut sailed up the Mississippi from the Gulf of Mexico, took New Orleans, and moved farther up river. By mid-1862, the Union controlled all the Mississippi except for the stretch between Vicksburg, Mississippi, and Port Hudson, Louisiana.

The Eastern theater, 1862. By the spring of 1862, the Confederacy was reeling. Northern victories in the West and a tightening blockade along the coast were squeezing the South. In Virginia, McClellan was preparing to move his well-trained army against Richmond. What followed, however, was a stunning reversal that revived the lagging fortunes of the Confederacy.

McClellan decided against attacking Richmond from the north. Instead, he had the navy move his troops to the York Peninsula, between the York and James rivers. From there he began a slow advance toward the Confederate capital. McClellan's caution gave Robert E. Lee, the brilliant Confederate general, time to make several bold moves. Lee sent Stonewall Jackson on raids into the Shenandoah Valley, making it appear that Washington would be attacked. The threat that Jackson posed tied up a large number of Union troops. Meanwhile, Jackson's troops, moving quickly, rejoined Lee's main forces, which now attacked McClellan's army. In the Seven Days' Battles—from June 25 to July 1, 1862—losses on both sides were severe, but Lee succeeded in halting the Union advance. A bolder commander than McClellan might have pressed on and taken Richmond. McClellan, however, withdrew. What is known as the Peninsula Campaign was thus a failure. Lincoln then removed McClellan from his

Continued on page 360

The Monitor *and the* Merrimac

One of the most significant naval battles in history was the engagement between the Union ship *Monitor* and the Confederate ship *Merrimac* at Hampton Roads, Virginia, in 1862. Until that time, almost all warships were made of wood. Such a vessel was the *Merrimac*, a United States naval ship at its berth in Norfolk, Virginia, when that state seceded in 1861. After the *Merrimac* was sunk by order of its commander, the Confederates raised it and covered its sides with iron plates, four inches thick. Armed with ten guns, the *Merrimac* (renamed the *Virginia* but usually called by its original name) steamed out of Norfolk harbor on March 8, 1862, to attack ships of the Union blockade. By nightfall, this strange-looking vessel with slanted sides had destroyed two Union ships and had caused another, the *Minnesota*, to run aground in shallow water.

On that very day, another ironclad was reaching Hampton Roads. This was the Union's *Monitor*, built in New York under the direction of John Ericcson, a Swedish-American inventor. The new *Monitor*, with its deck almost at water level and with a revolving gun turret, was variously described as "a cheesebox on a raft" and "a tin can on a shingle."

When the *Merrimac* moved out the next morning to attack the stranded *Minnesota*, the *Monitor* was waiting. For four hours the two ironclads blasted each other at close range. Shells clanged against the iron plates of each ship, but with little effect. Both ships finally withdrew. This first battle between ironclads made plain that the era of the wooden warship was over. To be effective, naval ships would henceforth have to be made of steel.

At point-blank range, the *Monitor* and the *Merrimac* pound each other. Nearby is the grounded *Minnesota*.

National Gallery of Art, Gift of Edgar William and Bernice Chrysler Garbisch

Background Information

WOMEN AS SPIES During the Civil War, women of both sides operated courageously as spies. The best-known Union spy was Pauline Cushman—"The Spy of the Cumberland." Cushman was born in New Orleans, but her sympathies were nevertheless with the Union cause. She was particularly skillful at obtaining Confederate military maps. Once when caught with a map, she was sentenced to be hanged but was rescued by Union forces.

Known as "The Cleopatra of the Confederacy," Belle Boyd became a spy at seventeen. She secretly gathered information from Union officers and relayed it to the Confederates. In 1862 and again the next year, Boyd was imprisoned for her spy activities but was released each time for lack of evidence. She published an account of her exploits, *Belle Boyd in Camp and Prison* (London, 1865), and lectured on her adventures.

3. ORAL REPORTS Assign students to read and report on the following documents from Commager's *Documents of American History:* 217, "McClellan Outlines a Policy for President Lincoln"; 218, "General Pope's Address to the Army of Virginia"; 222, "The Emancipation Proclamation"; 223, "Opposition to the Emancipation Proclamation—Resolutions of the Illinois State Legislature"; 224, "Appointment of General Hooker to the Command of the Army of the Potomac" (gives good insight into Lincoln, the commander in chief); and 228, "The Gettysburg Address." If time does not permit all the above to be presented, you may wish to have several students give dramatic readings of The Emancipation Proclamation and The Gettysburg Address.

post. McClellan's troops were placed under the command of John Pope, a more aggressive general. But when Pope attempted another invasion of Virginia from the north, Lee defeated him badly, at the second battle of Bull Run.

Antietam. The South was hoping for a victory that would both convince England to aid the Confederacy and encourage the border states to leave the Union. In pursuit of those goals, Lee moved into Maryland. Lee's battle plans, however, fell into the hands of McClellan, now in command of the Army of the Potomac. In September 1862, McClellan and Lee met at Antietam, Maryland, and after a bloody battle the Confederates withdrew. Had McClellan pursued the retreating Lee, he might have dealt Southern armies a crippling blow. Once again, however, McClellan's caution cost the chance for a major victory. And once again Lincoln removed McClellan from command.

Nurse Clara Barton writes a letter for a Union soldier in a field hospital. This great American devoted her life to helping others. In 1881 she founded the American Red Cross.

Museum of Fine Arts, Boston

The Emancipation Proclamation. Although Antietam ended in little more than a draw, it was nonetheless an important battle. From the beginning of the war, both Congress and President Lincoln had stated that their object was to preserve the Union, not to end slavery. One reason for their stand was that four slaveholding states—Maryland, Delaware, Kentucky, and Missouri—had remained in the Union. To declare that the government was fighting the war to free the slaves would have led those border states to secede. Their loss would have dealt a serious blow to the Union cause. Furthermore, Northern opinion had been more ready to support a war for the Union than for emancipation. Lincoln himself favored gradual emancipation, with payments made to owners, followed by colonization of the freed slaves.

When Horace Greeley, a New York newspaper owner and an abolitionist, demanded early in 1862 that Lincoln declare in favor of emancipation immediately, the President replied in a public letter.

> My paramount object in this struggle is to save the Union, and is *not* either to save or destroy slavery. If I could save the Union without freeing *any* slave I would do it; and if I could save it by freeing *all* the slaves, I would it; and if I could do it by freeing some and leaving others alone, I would also do that.

This, said Lincoln, was his view of his "official duty." However, he continued to hold the "*personal* wish that all men everywhere could be free."

But by mid-1862, opinion throughout the North was undergoing a change. More people were now in favor of making the end of slavery a war aim. By summer, Lincoln believed the time had come to announce that slaves would be freed. However, Union armies had suffered a string of defeats, and Secretary of State Seward advised Lincoln to hold off such a statement until a Union victory. Otherwise, the announcement might appear to be a desperate act.

Antietam was not the big victory Lincoln had hoped for, but it was enough. On September 22, 1862, the President announced that all slaves in areas still in rebellion against the United States as of January 1, 1863, "shall be then, thenceforward, and forever free." On the latter date, he issued the official *Emancipation Proclamation.*

The Emancipation Proclamation did not free a single slave immediately. There was no way of enforcing it within the areas still in rebellion. And it did not apply to the border states. Nor did it apply to parts of the Confederacy already under control of Union armies. This led critics of Lincoln to say that he would only free slaves where he could not, but would not free them where he could.

Nonetheless, the Emancipation Proclamation was of great importance. It committed the United States to ending slavery. By convincing the English masses that the war was being fought for human freedom, it also ended any chance that England might enter the war on the side of the South.

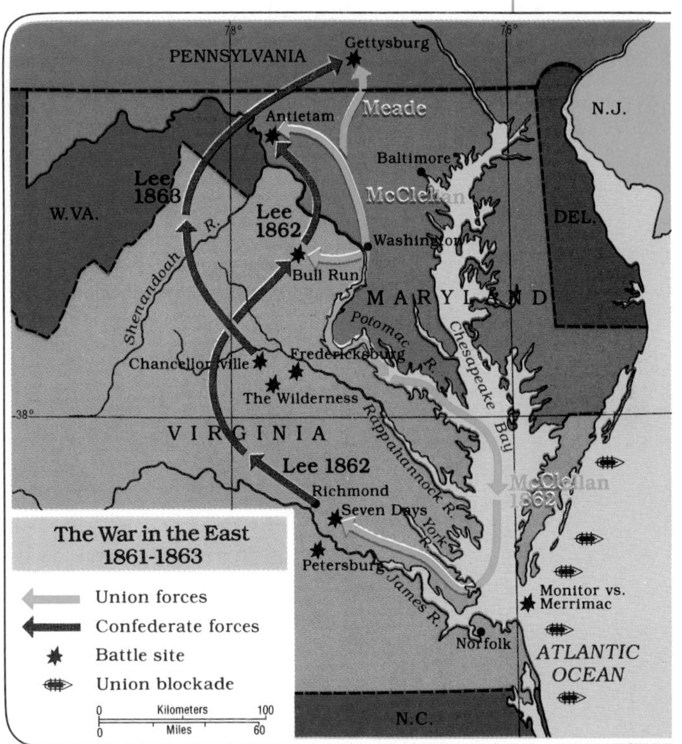

In the Eastern theater during 1862–1863, neither side had reason to be optimistic. The union forces failed to take Richmond, and the Confederates failed in their invasion of the North.

Gettysburg. Lee was well aware that time was on the side of the North. He decided therefore to try for a victory on Northern soil. Such a bold action would deal a blow to the North's morale and might lead it to quit the war. Thus, after brilliant victories in Virginia—at Fredericksburg in December 1862 and at Chancellorsville in May 1863—Lee pushed on into Pennsylvania. On July 1, 1863, his army met Union forces under General George Meade near the little town of Gettysburg.

4. USING MAPS As the students read the lesson text, have them pay careful attention to the maps showing military action in the Civil War. Then provide students with outline maps of the United States and have them trace the military actions described in the text. Be sure they understand the overall strategy of the war. Military historians state that the military tactics and strategy of both the Union and the Confederate generals were far advanced in comparison to other nations of that time.

5. ESSAY Have students write essays explaining the timing and significance of the Emancipation Proclamation.

6. ORAL REPORT Pickett's Charge is always of interest to students. Try to find several versions of this story, and then ask students to volunteer to present the material. An excellent account of the action was published in *American Heritage,* December 1957. This account was written by a Union officer, Frank A. Haskell, who was a member of the division that repulsed Pickett's troops.

For three days the battle lines flowed back and forth in the fields and over the ridges of southern Pennsylvania. The climax came on July 3, when 15,000 Confederates under General George Pickett charged up a slope toward Union positions. The attackers failed—barely—to take the ridge and had to fall back. The next day, Lee withdrew his army. He had lost so many men that he never again would have the strength to invade the North.

It was in the West, where Ulysses S. Grant first made his mark, that the tide turned in favor of the Union. The most important Union victories were at Vicksburg and Chattanooga.

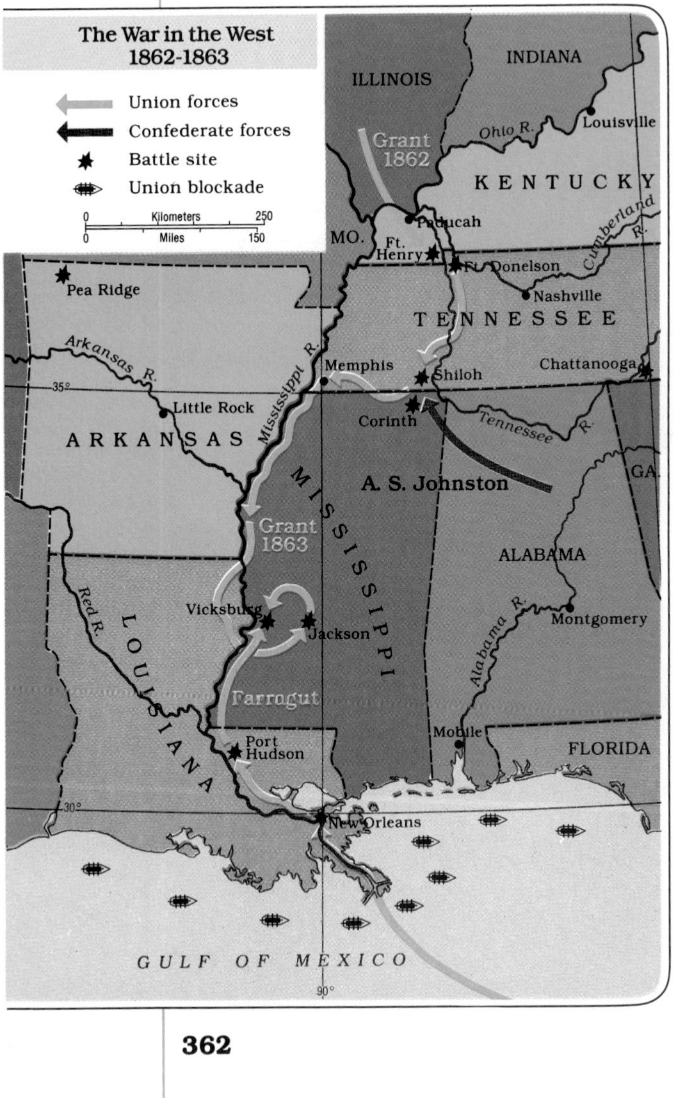

The War in the West 1862-1863

Union forces
Confederate forces
Battle site
Union blockade

Vicksburg and Chattanooga. Even while Northern armies were turning back Lee in the East, other Union forces were winning a major victory in the West. On July 4, 1863, after a siege that lasted for several months, Vicksburg on the Mississippi surrendered to General Grant. This put the entire river under Union control. Texas, Arkansas, and most of Louisiana were cut off from the rest of the Confederacy.

From the summer of 1863 on, Southern forces were mainly on the defensive. In the Western theater, Grant advanced on Chattanooga, Tennessee. This city was a key railway junction, and it stood in a gap in the Appalachian Mountains, commanding the route into Georgia. With victories at Lookout Mountain and Missionary Ridge, near Chattanooga, Grant drove the Confederate forces back. This opened the way for the Union invasion of Georgia, into the very heart of the Confederacy. After the Chattanooga operation, Grant was called to Washington and given top command of all Union armies.

Another move on Richmond. Grant now turned to the task at which so many other Union generals had failed—the capture of Richmond. Lee opposed him doggedly. In battles at the wooded region called the Wilderness, at Spotsylvania, and at Cold Harbor, the Union forces

Continued on page 364

Lee and Grant

The two men who rose to command of the opposing armies in the Civil War were men of vastly different backgrounds. Robert E. Lee was a member of one of Virginia's leading families. At West Point he made an outstanding record, and he fought brilliantly in the Mexican War. In the years that followed, his military reputation grew, and he was President Lincoln's choice to command the Union armies. Lee, torn between love of the Union and love of his native state, decided to stand by Virginia and fight with the Confederate forces.

By contrast, there was little in the career of Ulysses S. Grant before the Civil War to mark him as a coming leader. While at West Point, this son of an Ohio tanner did not distinguish himself. In the war with Mexico, he fought well but won no special recognition. Later, assigned to posts far from his family, Grant became lonely and took to drink. In 1854 he resigned from the army rather than face a court-martial. The start of the Civil War found him a clerk in a leather store in Galena, Illinois. Because the Union needed experienced officers, he was offered a troop command in Cairo, Illinois. After that, his great talents emerged.

In warfare, as in their early lives, Lee and Grant were a study in contrasts. Outnumbered in men and equipment, Lee used daring, surprise moves to keep the other side off balance. By comparison, Grant seemed a plodder. But unlike other Union generals, he understood that the key to victory was to put relentless pressure on the South. Thus the difference between these two great generals was as much the result of military circumstance as of personality.

Ulysses S. Grant *(left)* and Robert E. Lee *(right)* differed greatly in background and personality.

7. WRITTEN REPORTS A study of the Civil War offers a rich variety of topics suitable for written reports. The following are a few suggested topics: The Role of Women in the Civil War; The Effect of Technology in the Civil War; Foreign Relations During the Civil War; The Role of the Navy in the Civil War; The State of Medicine During the Civil War; Uniforms of the Civil War; The Role of Blacks in the Civil War; Life on the Homefront During the Civil War.

8. FILMS *Carl Sandburg at Gettysburg, Part 1: Facts About the Civil War* (28 minutes, b&w; CBS Films). *Carl Sandburg at Gettysburg, Part 2: The Gettysburg Address and Lincoln the Man* (24 minutes, b&w; CBS Films). *Carl Sandburg Discusses Lincoln* (12 minutes, b&w; Coronet Films). *Abraham Lincoln, Part 3: The War Years* (17 minutes, color; Francis R. Line Films). *The Civil War* (25 minutes, color; McGraw-Hill Films). *Gettysburg* (28 minutes, b&w; Westinghouse Broadcasting Company). *Grant and Lee at Appomattox,* You Are There series (26 minutes, b&w; CBS Films). *The Emancipation Proclamation,* You Are There series (26 minutes, b&w; CBS Films).

lost more than 50,000 men. But unlike the Union generals who had preceded him, Grant did not fall back. Though forced to alter his course, he kept within striking distance of Richmond.

Sherman's march. Meanwhile, farther south, the Union army that had taken Chattanooga was making rapid gains. That army, now led by General William T. Sherman, took Atlanta in September 1864 and then set off across Georgia for the coast. Abandoning its supply lines that extended back into Tennessee, Sherman's army lived off the countryside. As the Union forces advanced, they burned cotton gins, factories, and warehouses and destroyed railroads and bridges. After reaching Savannah, the army turned northward and advanced into South Carolina. Sherman's success lifted Union hopes for victory and contributed to Lincoln's reelection in 1864.

The spring of 1865 saw Sherman's army pushing northward toward Virginia. Its goal was to link up with Grant's forces. At this point, Lee's army, short of men and supplies, had to leave

Continued on page 366

The events of 1864–1865 in the East brought the Civil War to an end. With arrows and symbols, the map shows the three major factors in the Union victory: Grant's relentless drive on Richmond, Sherman's march across Georgia and then northward, and the Union blockade.

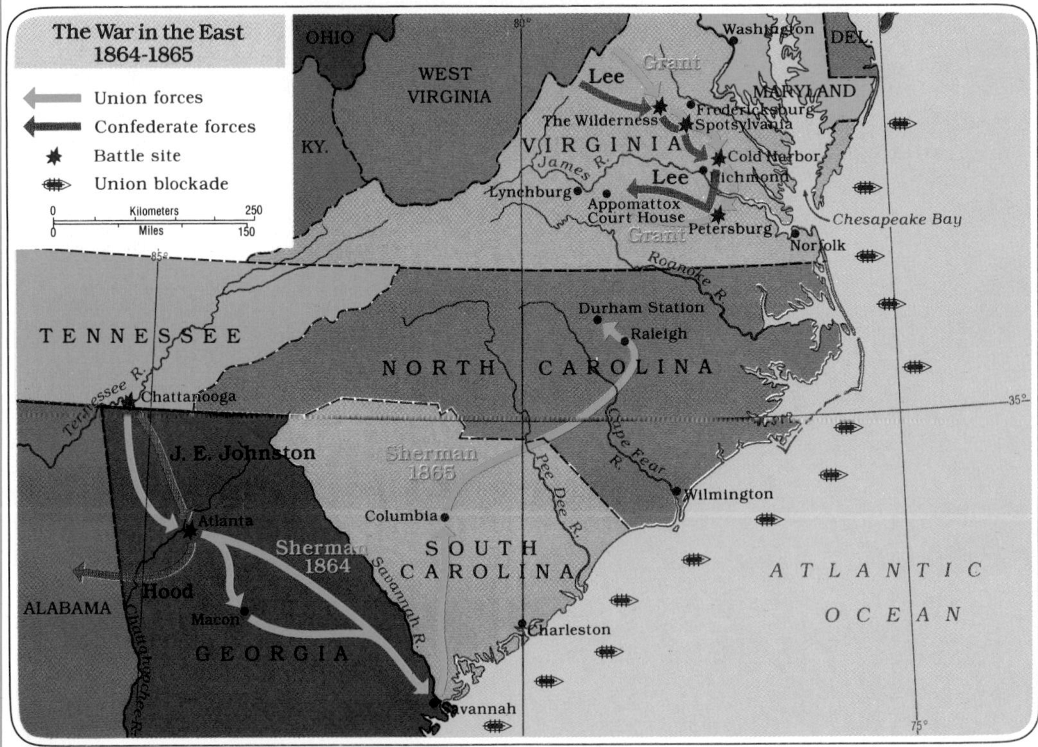

Matthew Brady, shown at lower right, is probably the best known American photographer of all time. Traveling with the Union army, he and his assistants took hundreds of photographs of soldiers, battlefields, and army camps. At upper right is the wagon that carried Brady's equipment. The other pictures are examples of Brady's work. At upper left is a black guard detail at a fort near Washington, D.C., and at lower left is a Union battery manned by troops from Connecticut.

Answers To Review Questions

1. Stephen Douglas, a Northern Democrat, ran on a no-slavery platform in the territories. John Breckinridge, a Southern Democrat, ran on a platform permitting slavery in the territories. Abraham Lincoln, a Republican, supported a no-slavery platform in the territories, but he would not interfere with slavery in the Southern states. John Bell, a Constitutional Unionist, simply declared in favor of the Constitution and the Union. The split in the Democratic party permitted the election of Lincoln, who received no Southern support.

2. South Carolina, Mississippi, Florida, Alabama, Georgia, Louisiana, and Texas immediately joined. Virginia, North Carolina, Tennessee, and Arkansas joined after Fort Sumter.

3. The main difference was that the states in the Confederacy were sovereign, and slavery could never be abolished.

4. Southerners believed that the Northern manufacturers needed cotton and the southern market for their goods. Furthermore, they anticipated that Britain and France would intervene in their behalf because cotton was needed in European textile mills.

Richmond. It was now plain that the South's position was hopeless. On April 9, Lee and Grant met in a private home at Appomattox Courthouse, Virginia. There Lee surrendered his army. As he left to join his defeated troops, the Union soldiers began a wild cheer. But Grant quickly silenced them. "The war is over," he said. "The rebels are our countrymen again."

The Civil War was the most tragic, destructive, and disruptive war in our history. About 2.5 million men served in the armies and navies at one time or another. More than 618,000 Americans were killed in battle or died of wounds. This compares with about 5,800 battle casualties among Americans in each of two previous conflicts—the War of 1812 and the Mexican War. The Civil War toll would have been even higher had it not been for the tireless work of doctors and nurses in the hospitals behind the lines and in the field.

Though the human costs had been staggering, the war had settled two main issues. The Union was preserved, and slavery was to be ended. But important questions remained. How would the seceding states be restored to the Union, and on what terms? What rights were the freed slaves to have? How would the races live together, and on what terms? Would freedom mean equality? These questions would be answered in the years immediately following. You will read about these answers in Chapter 18.

CHECKUP

1. What success did the North have in carrying out its three-part military plan?
2. Explain the importance of each of the following battles: Bull Run; Antietam; Gettysburg; Vicksburg.
3. To what extent did the Emancipation Proclamation change the status of slaves? In what other ways was this document important?

Key Facts from Chapter 17

1. The immediate cause of the Civil War was the South's determination to have its own government, the Confederate States of America, and the North's determination to keep the Union intact.
2. The Civil War started in 1861 with the firing on Fort Sumter in the harbor of Charleston, South Carolina. It ended in 1865 with the surrender of Confederate General Robert E. Lee to Union General Ulysses S. Grant at Appomattox Courthouse, Virginia.
3. The Emancipation Proclamation of January 1, 1863, put forth by President Abraham Lincoln, had no immediate effect in freeing the slaves but was important in that it committed the United States to ending slavery.
4. The Civil War was America's most tragic and disruptive war. There were more American casualties than in any other war in which Americans had fought.

★ REVIEWING THE CHAPTER ★

People, Places, and Events

Abraham Lincoln *P. 347*
Jefferson Davis *P. 348*
Fort Sumter *P. 350*
Richmond *P. 357*
Bull Run *P. 358*
Ulysses S. Grant *P. 358*
Robert E. Lee *P. 358*
Antietam *P. 360*
Emancipation Proclamation *P. 360*
Gettysburg *P. 361*
Vicksburg *P. 362*
William T. Sherman *P. 364*
Appomattox *P. 366*

Review Questions

1. Discuss the Presidential election of 1860 in terms of **(a)** the candidates, **(b)** the parties, **(c)** their platforms, and **(d)** the outcome of the voting. *P. 347* Les. 1
2. Which states immediately joined the Confederacy? Which states joined later? *Pp. 348, 350* Les. 1
3. How did the Confederate Constitution differ from that of the United States? *P. 348* Les. 1
4. Why were many Southerners convinced that there would be no war over secession? *P. 349* Les. 1
5. What effect did the course of the war have on the value of money in the North and South? *Pp. 353–354* Les. 2
6. Why was the South unsuccessful in gaining the support of Britain and France? *P. 356* Les. 2
7. List the North's strategy for winning the war and the reason for each part. *P. 357* Les. 3
8. Which issues were settled by the war? Which were not? *P. 366* Les. 3

Chapter Test

Match the names in the first section with the correct description from the second section. Write the letter of the description after the number of the name, using a separate piece of paper. Note: There may be more than one correct description for a name.

1. Robert E. Lee
2. George Meade
3. David Farragut
4. Antietam
5. Jefferson Davis
6. Abraham Lincoln
7. Bull Run
8. Ulysses S. Grant
9. William T. Sherman
10. George B. McClellan

a. Union victory that made it possible for the President to issue the Emancipation Proclamation
b. Top commander of the Confederate Army
c. Union general who captured Atlanta
d. Sixteenth President of the United States
e. Union general who failed to capture Richmond in the Peninsula Campaign
f. First battle of the war
g. Top commander of the Union forces
h. President of the Confederacy
i. Union naval leader who captured New Orleans
j. Defeated the Southern army at Gettysburg
k. Union general who took Vicksburg
l. Surrendered his army at Appomattox
m. Won the election of 1860 with less than 40 percent of the popular vote
n. Site of two important battles

5. When the war was going poorly for the North, greenbacks were worth as little as 30 cents. But as Northern forces began to win battles, the value of the paper money improved. In the South, the value of their printed money decreased with each Confederate defeat. Printing and issuing more money did not improve its value. As the South's paper dollar fell in value, prices soared. By the end of the war, the Confederate dollar was practically worthless.
6. Both European nations had large supplies of cotton on hand, so they were less dependent on the South. Among the English working people, there were strong antislavery and proNorthern sentiments. The United States minister to Britain threatened war to keep the British government from delivering warships built for the Confederacy.
7. The first part was to blockade Southern ports to prevent the South from exporting cotton and importing supplies. The second part was to capture the Confederate capital and demoralize the South. The third part was to gain control of the Mississippi and thereby split the Confederacy.
8. The Union was preserved and slavery was ended. Issues not settled were how the seceding states would be restored to the Union, what rights freed slaves would have, how the races would live together, and whether or not freedom would mean equality.

Answers For Chapter Test
1. h, l **2.** j **3.** b **4.** a **5.** i **6.** d, m **7.** f **8.** g, k **9.** c **10.** e

Background Information

1. PICTURE This is a photograph of Richmond, Virginia, at the end of the Civil War. In May 1861, a month after the outbreak of war, Richmond replaced Montgomery, Alabama, as the Confederate capital. The capture of Richmond became a prime goal of the Union forces, especially in the campaigns of 1862 and 1864. In April 1865, the Confederate government moved from Richmond to Danville, Virginia, which served as the capital for the last seven days of the war. The people of Richmond did not want the Union army to take the city undamaged, so they burned part of it. Immediately after the war, the task of rebuilding Richmond began.

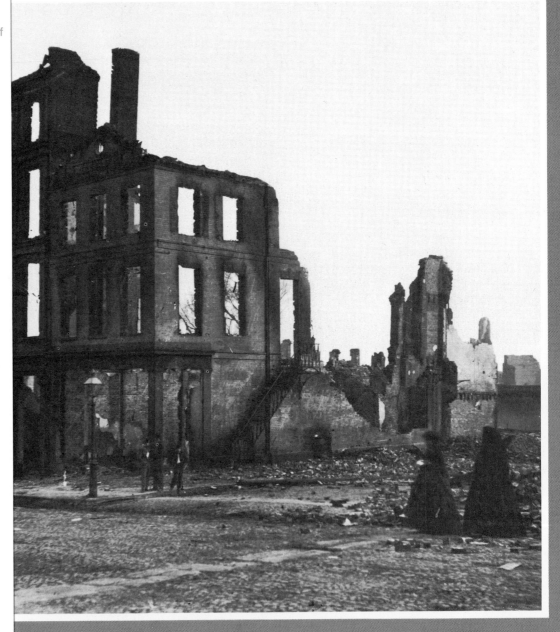

RECONSTRUCTION AND BEYOND

LESSON 1

ORGANIZED LIFE in the South had collapsed in the wake of the war. Travelers to that region were horrified by what they saw: blackened, burned ruins of towns and cities, uncultivated fields; torn-up railroad lines; and demolished cotton gins and factories. Describing Charleston, South Carolina, a Northern newspaperman reported:

> [It is] a city of ruins, a desolation, of vacant houses, of widowed women, of rotting wharves, of deserted warehouses, of weed-wild gardens, of miles of grass-grown streets. . . .

Capital, needed to bring the economy back to life, was not to be had. Emancipation wiped out the region's $2.5 billion investment in slaves, nearly two thirds of the South's wealth. The failure of Southern banks meant the loss of another billion dollars. Confederate currency was now worthless. With the credit system broken down, farmers were not able to buy the seed and tools they needed for planting.

Worst of all was the loss of the white South's young people. Nearly a quarter of a million men were killed, and many more were disabled for life. Of the white men in Mississippi old enough to fight, fully a third were either killed or maimed. One fifth of all the taxes taken in by that state in 1866 went to pay for artificial limbs.

The feeling of freedom. If the war devastated the Southern white society, it created both new opportunities and problems for the three million freed slaves. For many, the need to experience the feeling of freedom, to test it and be sure it was real, was overwhelming. "No, Miss," explained a former slave when asked to stay on at a South Carolina plantation, "I must go. If I stay here, I'll never know I am free." Large numbers of former slaves took to the road. For many, freedom meant the opportunity to rejoin wives, husbands, and children. To do this, most had to go no farther than to a neighboring plantation. But many hundreds set out on longer and more uncertain journeys to look for loved ones from whom they had been separated by sale.

Even so, many slaves stayed put. Of those who moved, most did not go far. The fact was that whether they moved or not, everyday life for most was not too different from what it had been before the war. They had been led by some Northerners to believe that freed slaves would receive "forty acres and a mule" to get started in their new life. That never happened. Without land of their own, therefore, the freed slaves worked for others, often their former masters, for wages or a share of the crop. And they shared in the general poverty and economic breakdown of the postwar South.

Restoring the Union

Even as the war was raging, government leaders were giving thought to how the Union should be restored. President Lincoln favored bringing the rebelling states back into the Union at the earliest

LESSON 1 *(3 days)*

Performance Objectives

1. To distinguish between the reconstruction plans of Lincoln and Johnson and those of the Radical Republicans by making a chart listing the components of each. **2.** To describe orally or in writing the efforts in the South to control the economic and social lives of the former slaves. **3.** To describe orally or in writing the events that led to the impeachment of Andrew Johnson and the outcome of the action.

Famous People

Thaddeus Stevens, Andrew Johnson, John Wilkes Booth, Edwin Stanton, Benjamin Wade

Vocabulary

Reconstruction, "forty acres and a mule," Radical Republicans, Wade Davis Bill, pocket veto, Thirteenth Amendment, black codes, Freedmen's Bureau, Civil Rights Act of 1867, Fourteenth Amendment, impeachment, Command of the Army Act, Tenure of Office Act, election of 1868, Fifteenth Amendment

★16★

Abraham Lincoln

1809–1865

Born in KENTUCKY
In Office 1861–1865
Party REPUBLICAN

Elected on antislavery platform. Was determined to preserve the Union. His leadership brought the nation through its great crisis—the Civil War. Killed by an assassin.

possible time. He proposed to do this by using the President's pardoning power. Under his plan, announced in December 1863, the President would pardon all—except a handful of top Confederate leaders and army officers—who took an oath of loyalty to the United States and agreed to an end to slavery. When 10 percent of the people who had voted in a state in 1860 had taken the oath, the state could draw up a new constitution, elect officials, and reenter the Union. Actually, Lincoln's view was that the states had never legally left the Union.

Lincoln's plan. The great strength of Lincoln's plan was that it would restore the Union quickly. But it had a great weakness. Although it ended slavery, it left the Southern states entirely free to decide how the freed slaves would be treated and what rights, if any, black people would have. Few could doubt that the South, left to its own wishes, would manage to control the former slaves.

The Lincoln plan was quickly put into effect in states controlled by the Union army. By the end of 1864, four states had met Lincoln's requirements and set up new governments. Lincoln's plan, however, had meanwhile brought a storm of protest from most Republicans in Congress. They insisted that Congress—not the President—should decide the terms for the return of the Southern states. Lincoln's plan for a quick and easy return, most of the Republican members of Congress felt, did not make the price of the rebellion high enough.

One group in the Republican party in Congress was known as the Radical Republican wing. These Republicans were radical in the sense that they wished to bring about a sweeping change in Southern society. Their goal was nothing less than to make good on the Declaration of Independence—to raise the freed slaves to equality with the whites. That meant that blacks should have the right to vote, enjoy full civil rights, and be free of discrimination.

Two of the main Radical Republicans were Representative Thaddeus Stevens of Pennsylvania and Senator Charles Sumner of Massachusetts. You will recall that Sumner was the abolitionist senator who was beaten at his Senate desk in 1856. Stevens had had a lifelong commitment to equality for blacks. He favored dividing public lands and large plantations in Southern states into forty-acre plots for the freed slaves. Only then, he believed, would they have a chance to be economically independent.

The Wade-Davis Bill. Radicals were able to get only a part of what they wanted into the Wade-Davis Bill. Passed in July 1864, it was Congress's plan for Reconstruction. For a state to be readmitted to the Union, said this bill, a majority of the white males in the state (not Lincoln's 10 percent of the voters) must take the oath of loyalty. The leaders could then meet to write a new state constitution. But no Confederate official, and no one who had willingly taken up arms against the United States could vote or hold office in the new government. Each new government must, of course, end slavery. It must also *repudiate* the state's war debts—that is, declare that they would not be paid.

Lincoln was able to keep the Wade-Davis bill from becoming law by means of a *pocket veto.* In a strong statement, however, Radical Republicans warned the President that making policy for Reconstruction was the business of Congress, not the President. Congress put teeth in what it said by refusing to seat representatives sent from the states that had followed Lincoln's plan. Congress could do this because the Constitution gives it the right to pass on its members' credentials. The stage was now set for a clash.

The election of 1864. So bitter were the Radical Republicans toward Lincoln that they tried to defeat him in the presidential election of 1864. Two years earlier, Lincoln had persuaded Republicans to join with those Democrats who supported the war in the National Union party. He himself was chosen in 1864 to head the National Union ticket. Andrew Johnson of Tennessee, a Southern Democrat who had remained loyal to the

The leaders of the Radical Republicans included (left to right) Representative Thaddeus Stevens of Pennsylvania, Senator Charles Sumner of Massachusetts, and Senator Benjamin Wade of Ohio.

Activities

1. FILMS *The Civil War and Reconstruction, 1861–1876,* History of the Negro in America series (19 minutes, b&w; McGraw-Hill Films). *Johnson and Reconstruction* (36 minutes, b&w; MGM). *The Years of Reconstruction, 1865–1877,* American History series (25 minutes, color; McGraw-Hill Films). *The Civil War: Postwar Period* (16 minutes, color; Coronet Films).

2. LISTENING FOR INFORMATION Read to the students "Johnson and the Radicals" by Howard K. Beale, from *The American Story.*

3. USING A CHART After students have read the lesson, have them construct charts identifying the policies that Lincoln and Johnson proposed for the reconstruction of the South. To the charts have them add a list of Republican policies. You may wish to assign the charts for homework. In class, discuss the information in the charts and make a master chart on the chalkboard. Have students compare the two plans. Discuss the merits of both plans, using Lincoln's "malice toward none" speech as a base.

Lincoln's funeral carriage, drawn by sixteen horses, proceeds through New York City.

Union, was the party's candidate for Vice President. He was chosen in order to attract the votes of Democrats. The Radical Republicans had already selected John C. Frémont, the Western explorer, as their presidential candidate. The Democrats nominated General George McClellan.

When the campaign began, Lincoln's chances were not bright. However, arguments over war aims weakened the Democrats, and the Radical Republican candidate, Frémont, decided to withdraw from the race. Union victories on Southern battlefields shortly before election day gave Lincoln's campaign a boost, and he won quite easily.

Johnson succeeds Lincoln. Less than a week after the end of the war, Lincoln was dead. He and his wife had gone to a play at Ford's Theater in Washington. During the performance, John Wilkes Booth, an actor and a Southern sympathizer, stole into the box occupied by the Lincolns and shot the President in the head. The President was taken to a house across the street and died there the next morning. Booth fled from the theater and was tracked to a barn in Virginia. There he died of gunshot wounds, possibly inflicted by himself.

A few hours after Lincoln's death, Vice President Andrew Johnson took the oath of office as the seventeenth President of the United States. Johnson had started life even poorer than Lincoln had. He rose to be a congressman from Tennessee and a two-term governor of that state, where he championed the interest of the small farmers against large planters. Radicals expected him to be one of them. "Johnson, we have faith in you," said Senator Wade of Ohio. "By the gods, there'll be no trouble now."

The Radicals had guessed wrong. They had mistaken Johnson's hatred of the planter class of the South for support of Radical goals. Although Johnson strongly supported the Union, he held Southern views on slavery.

Johnson's Reconstruction plan. In May 1865, Johnson announced a plan for Reconstruction very much like Lincoln's. To reenter the Union, Southern states needed only to wipe out their secession ordinances, state that they would not pay their war debts, and ratify the Thirteenth Amendment. This amendment provided for an end to slavery in the United States.

Radicals protested Johnson's plan, but they could do nothing to stop it because Congress was not in session. Johnson hoped that by the time it assembled again in December 1865, he could present Congress with an accomplished fact and the Radicals would have to accept it. By December, the Thirteenth Amendment had indeed been ratified. And all the states of the Confederacy except Texas had fulfilled most of the requirements of the Johnson plan.

Congress versus Johnson. The Republicans in Congress—Radicals and moderates alike—would have none of it. They resented Johnson's attempt to take Reconstruction out of their hands. They objected that the punishment for rebellion and war was so light. They demanded that the South repent. Proof that the Southerners had not had a change of heart was the fact that they had elected to Congress more than seventy leaders of the rebellion.

Further, Republicans deeply believed that the safety of the Union depended on their party's control of Congress. The return of Southern Democrats would threaten that control. Ironically, since an ex-slave would now be counted as a full person rather than three fifths of a person (see page 166), the South would now have fifteen *more* seats in the House than it had in 1860.

The black codes. Republicans were also angered by the *black codes* that Southern states were passing. These laws were meant to control the economic and social lives of the former slaves. The codes gave freedmen certain rights, such as to make contracts and to own property. Some of the codes also protected the freed slaves from dishonest merchants and employers. But one of the main aims of the codes was to guarantee that despite the end of slavery, there would still be a work force of blacks for Southern farms and plantations. Louisiana's code, for example, required blacks to sign contracts with employers during the first ten days of January. They then could not leave their jobs until the following January. South Carolina blacks were limited to farm jobs and housework. In a number of states a black who was considered to be a vagrant could be fined and then be required to work off the fine with months of labor. To many Northerners the black codes seemed proof that the South was still not willing to give the slaves freedom.

For all those reasons, Congress refused to accept Reconstruction as completed. It would not permit the members elected from the Southern states to take their seats. Instead, it set up the Joint Committee on Reconstruction, made up of members of both houses of Congress, to come up with a new program for Reconstruction. The state governments

4. ROLE-PLAYING Have the students imagine that they are freed slaves who have spent their lives on one cotton plantation. Now they have been turned out of the shacks that have been their only homes. They have no education and no money. Ask for student volunteers to role-play their feelings about their freedom and whether being free is what they expected it would be. Have students use the text material on pages 369 and 373–374 as a basis for their role-playing. Ask those students who watch the role-playing to react to their classmates' interpretations. At the conclusion of the role-playing, discuss how freed slaves should be treated and what rights they should have.

5. ANALYZING SOURCE MATERIAL Amendments to the Constitution often represent great changes in the thinking of the people of the United States. This was particularly true of the Thirteenth, Fourteenth, and Fifteenth amendments. Ask students to read the text of these amendments on pages 189–191. Have them make charts in their notebooks showing the major provisions of each amendment, the dates of ratification, and the general effect of each amendment. You may wish to conduct a class discussion, considering each amendment, section by section. Ask: What does the section mean? Is the provision actually in effect? (In the Fourteenth Amendment, Section 2, only the first sentence has been carried out. The rest has always been ignored. See the annotation to the right of that section.)

6. ORAL REPORTS As a basis for understanding the issues in the impeachment of President Johnson, have several students investigate and report on the Tenure of Office Act. Have one student state the terms of this law. Have another student explain why it is a law that no President could tolerate.

7. CREATIVE WRITING Ask students to imagine that they are newspaper reporters who have been following the events leading to the impeachment trial of President Johnson. Now the trial has ended and the verdict has been rendered. Have students write accounts of the whole affair for their newspapers. The purpose of the account should be to tell people who are unfamiliar with the details of the impeachment just what happened and why.

If time permits, present information about the part that Senator Edmund G. Ross of Kansas played in the famous impeachment trial. His "not guilty" vote made Johnson's acquittal possible. The story of the senator's great moral courage would add dramatic impact to the newspaper accounts. See the chapter on Senator Ross in John F. Kennedy's book *Profiles in Courage* (New York: Harper & Row, 1964).

that were set up under Johnson's plan stayed in office and continued to govern their states. However, they had no voice in national affairs. That situation would continue for the next fifteen months.

The Freedmen's Bureau. In the spring of 1866, Republicans in Congress passed two bills dealing with Reconstruction. The first was a bill to keep the Freedmen's Bureau alive. The Freedmen's Bureau had been set up in 1865 for one year, largely to help the freed slaves get started anew. This government agency saved thousands of freed slaves and white war refugees from starvation by providing food, clothing, and medical care. It also helped the freed slaves find jobs. It protected them against those white employers who might try to take advantage of them with unfair work contracts. Equally important, it started schools in which thousands of former slaves—parents as well as children—eagerly learned to read and write. The new bill added to the power of the Bureau by allowing it to fine or imprison, without a jury trial, persons whom it found guilty of depriving blacks of their civil rights.

President Johnson vetoed this bill as unconstitutional. Congress was not able to pass it over the President's veto. In July of 1866, however, Congress passed the bill again, and this time it easily overrode Johnson's veto. Since Congress was made of the same people both times, you can see that the Republican moderates were moving away from Johnson and toward the Radicals.

In setting up the Freedmen's Bureau, the United States government became involved for the first time in aiding large numbers of people at a time of catastrophe. The Bureau, for the most part, did good work. However, it also became caught up in politics. Some of its agents became more involved with promoting the interests of the Republican party in the South than with the proper work of the Bureau. Congress ended the Bureau in 1872.

The Civil Rights Act. The second bill passed by the Republicans that spring was the Civil Rights Act of 1866. This law stated that all persons born in the United States were citizens, regardless of race. All citizens were entitled to the same legal rights.

In passing this bill, Congress had in mind both the Dred Scott decision, which had said that blacks were not citizens, and the black codes of Southern states. This guarantee of equal rights for both races, the first in American history, could be enforced by federal troops.

The Fourteenth Amendment. Many congressmen feared that the Civil Rights Act might be held unconstitutional or would be repealed by a later Congress. To be sure that the act would always be in force, Congress put its provisions into a constitutional amendment, the Fourteenth. The Radicals had hoped to guarantee the vote to black people by this amendment. This would advance not only their goal of equality for blacks but also their aim to win Republican votes in the South and keep their party in power. They could not gain enough backing to guarantee black suffrage directly by their amendment. They did, however, put in a section that

Under the Freedmen's Bureau, schools for former slaves were set up throughout the South. The drawing above is of a primary school for freed slaves in the Mississippi city of Vicksburg.

was aimed to achieve that goal indirectly. This section provided that a Southern state that denied its adult male citizens the vote would lose seats in Congress in the same proportion.

The amendment also forbade former Confederates to hold federal or state office. They could be made eligible only by a two-thirds vote of Congress. Another section provided that the Confederate war debt would not be paid, and that no one could be paid for the loss of slaves.

Approval of the Fourteenth Amendment was, in effect, the price set by Congress for the former Confederate states' reentry into the Union. Tennessee ratified it and was promptly readmitted. Encouraged by President Johnson, however, the other ten states that had seceded turned it down.

The elections of 1866. That threw the question of Reconstruction policy into the congressional elections of 1866. In this contest, Democratic candidates were at a disadvantage. The Republican party presented itself as the party that saved the Union. It presented the opposition as the party of treason, which had brought four years of war. Stirring the emotions of war—a tactic known as *waving the bloody shirt*—Republicans urged veterans to "vote the way you shot." They pointed to recent race riots in New Orleans and Memphis as examples of how the South, if allowed to go its own way, would treat the freed slaves.

Johnson's support for Democratic candidates only made things worse for them. In an eighteen-day speaking tour of the North, he often lost his temper, took part in noisy arguments with people who jeered him, and behaved like anything but a President. In the election, Republicans gained enough seats to give them a two-thirds majority in Congress. It could now pass any bill it wished over Johnson's veto.

Background Information

2. ANDREW JOHNSON (1808–1875) What kind of person succeeded to the Presidency when Lincoln was assassinated? No one, not even Lincoln himself, ever reached the White House from humbler beginnings. Born to impoverished parents in North Carolina and orphaned at an early age, Andrew Johnson became a tailor's helper at ten. Though he did not attend school a day in his life, he taught himself to read. His wife, who was a teacher, later taught him to write and to do simple arithmetic. "Andy" Johnson moved to Tennessee when he was seventeen and entered politics as a Jacksonian Democrat. He favored small farmers rather than wealthy plantation owners, even though he eventually owned a few slaves himself. Johnson represented Tennessee in Congress and remained loyal to the Union when that state seceded. After Union armies regained control of Tennessee, Johnson served as the state's war governor with great success. The Union party nominated him as Lincoln's Vice President in 1864 to please War Democrats and voters in the border states. No one dreamed that an assassin's bullet would make him President from April 1865 to March 1869. One of his lawyers at the impeachment trial wrote, "He is a man of few ideas, but they are right and true, and he would suffer death sooner than yield up or violate one of them." After leaving the White House, Johnson ran unsuccessfully for Congress in 1869 and 1872. But he was elected to the Senate in 1874 and took his seat to a round of applause.

★17★

Andrew Johnson
1808–1875

Born in NORTH CAROLINA
In Office 1865–1869
Party DEMOCRATIC

Favored generous treatment for defeated South. Was opposed by Radical Republicans, who wanted to punish South. Bitter feelings led to impeachment, but he was not convicted.

★ ★ ★ ★ ★ ★ ★ ★

Triumph of the Radicals. Under the leadership of Stevens and Sumner, Radical Republicans now prepared a sweeping program of Reconstruction. The Reconstruction Act of March 2, 1867, made the Lincoln and Johnson state governments illegal (except for Tennessee, which was back in the Union), and placed the South under army rule. The region was divided into five districts, each under an army general, with troops to enforce federal law and keep order.

To come back into the Union, each state had to call a convention to draw up a new constitution. Blacks as well as whites (but not former Confederate officeholders) could vote for and serve as delegates. The new state constitutions must include negro suffrage and be approved by the voters. In addition, the state must ratify the Fourteenth Amendment. With this program, Radicals believed they were close to their goal of equality for the ex-slaves. Once Congress approved a state's constitution, the state could return, its congressmen would be seated, and federal troops would be withdrawn from within its borders.

By 1868, seven of the Southern states had met the terms of the Reconstruction Act and had been readmitted to the Union. In that year also, the Fourteenth Amendment was ratified and added to the Constitution. Three years later, the last state was reconstructed.

The impeachment of Johnson. Now firmly in control, Radicals in Congress were determined to have no interference from other branches of government. To protect against the chance that the Supreme Court might declare its program unconstitutional, they limited the Court's power to hear certain kinds of cases. To make sure that President Johnson could not get around their program with orders to the army generals in the South, Radicals passed the Command of the Army Act. It said that the President must put forth military orders only through the General of the Army, Ulysses S. Grant, who was working closely with the Radicals. Since the Constitution makes the President the Commander in Chief, this law was almost certainly unconstitutional. In the

Tenure of Office Act, Congress further limited the President by requiring the Senate's approval before he removed any official who had been appointed with the Senate's consent. Johnson believed this act was unconstitutional and decided to test it. He removed one of his cabinet officers, Secretary of War Edwin Stanton, who had been working hand in hand with the Radical Republicans.

For nearly a year, Radicals had been looking for an excuse to force Johnson out of office. His removal of Stanton now gave them that excuse. The Constitution says that a President may be removed from office for "treason, bribery, or other high crimes and misdemeanors." The House of Representatives put together a number of charges against Johnson. The charges centered on his alleged violation of the Tenure of Office Act. By making the charges, the House *impeached* the President—that is, formally accused him of "high crimes and misdemeanors." He then had to stand trial before the Senate.

Johnson went on trial in March 1868. The vote for conviction in the Senate was 35 to 19, just one short of the necessary two thirds. By that narrow margin, the Radicals failed to remove Johnson from office. Had they succeeded, the new President under the law at that time would have been Benjamin Wade, a Radical Republican who was president *pro tem* of the Senate.

The election of 1868. Even though the Radicals had failed to remove Johnson from office, they were still in control of Reconstruction policy. Now, in 1868, they hoped to win the Presidency as well. For their candidate, Republicans chose General Ulysses S. Grant, the war hero. Grant had cooperated with the Radical Republicans, and they felt that they could control him. The Democrats nominated Horatio Seymour, a former war governor of New York who was honest, wealthy, and colorless.

Grant won by a large margin in the electoral votes, but even with his party waving the bloody shirt, his popular majority was small—only 300,000. Without the votes of some 500,000 freedmen, giving Grant seven reconstructed states, Grant would not have had the majority of the popular vote.

The importance of the freedmen's votes was clear to the Republicans. To be sure that black men would not be kept from voting in the future the Republicans put forth the Fifteenth Amendment. No citizen could be kept from

Republican Senator James Grimes of Iowa breaks with his party by voting for acquittal in the impeachment trial of Andrew Johnson.

LESSON 2 *(1 to 2 days)*

Performance Objectives

1. To describe orally or in writing the role of blacks in governing Southern states during the Reconstruction period. **2.** To explain orally or in writing the response of Southern whites to Black Reconstruction. **3.** To identify and explain the bad points and the positive accomplishments of Reconstruction.

Famous People

Samuel J. Tilden, Rutherford B. Hayes

Vocabulary

Black Reconstruction, carpetbaggers, scalawags, Ku Klux Klan, Force Act of 1870, Ku Klux Klan Act, Amnesty Act, Civil Rights Act of 1875, Compromise of 1877, Hayes-Tilden election

voting "on account of race, color, or previous condition of servitude [slavery]." Congress required the three states still not back in the Union—Virginia, Texas, and Mississippi—to ratify this amendment as a condition of their return. In 1870 the Fifteenth Amendment was added to the Constitution.

CHECKUP

1. How did Lincoln's and Johnson's plans for restoring the Union differ from Congress's plan?
2. What steps did the Southern states take to control the economic and social lives of the former slaves?
3. How did the Radical Republicans try to assure that President Johnson could not interfere with their program? What success did they have?

LESSON 2

The Reconstructed South

Reconstruction brought about a sweeping change in the South. For the first time, black people had a political voice. Grateful to the party that brought them freedom, almost all of them voted Republican. Most whites voted Democratic, but with 150,000 whites barred from voting, black voters in the South outnumbered white voters, 700,000 to 625,000. Thus the Republican party, which in 1860 had not carried a single Southern state, was in control of all of them ten years later.

Black Reconstruction? Because blacks voted and held office, the decade from 1868 on came to be called *Black Reconstruction,* a phrase that seemed to say that blacks ruled the Southern states. That, however, was anything but the case. It was true that in every Southern state, blacks held many such local offices as sheriff and justice of the peace. State offices such as treasurer and superintendent of education were also sometimes held by blacks. Black men even served as lieutenant-governor in the states of Mississippi, Louisiana, and South Carolina.

Overall, however, the number of blacks who held office was quite modest, considering the number of black voters. During the whole Reconstruction period, blacks held a majority in a legislature in only one state—ironically, South Carolina, the leader of the secession—and that majority was in only one house and for only a few years. Of the more than one hundred Southerners elected to Congress during the Reconstruction period, only sixteen were black. There were never more than eight black congressmen at one time. Only two, Hiram Revels and Blanche K. Bruce, both of Mississippi, were sent to the United States Senate.

Carpetbaggers and scalawags. Whites held most positions of leadership in the Republican Reconstruction governments. A number of these were Northerners only recently arrived in the South. They were called *carpetbaggers* by Southerners because they were said to have carried their few belongings in suitcases made of carpeting. These men were a mixed lot. Some had come to the South looking for business opportunities. Others, such as teachers and clergy, had come to do educational, humanitarian, and religious work among the former slaves. Still other carpetbaggers were simply adventurers who meant to take advantage of the

Robert Elliott of South Carolina, one of seven blacks in Congress in 1874, delivers a speech.

upset conditions in the Southern states to advance their own interests by hook or by crook.

Most of the white leaders in the new state governments, however, were native Southerners. They, too, were a varied group. At one extreme were some who had opposed secession from the beginning. At the other were certain lower-class whites who had always envied the planters and now saw the chance to gain power over them. The great majority who joined the Republicans were, however, men of some standing—business people and some planters, for example. They believed that the best way to bring back prosperity was to cooperate with the ruling group. Southern Democrats regarded the Southern white Republicans as traitors and called them *scalawags,* a term applied to runty, worthless farm animals.

Among the blacks who served in Southern legislatures were a goodly number of uneducated ex-slaves.Some of them were easily used by others, and their inexperience gave Southern and Northern white critics of Reconstruction a field day. "Seven years ago these men [the black legislators] were raising corn and cotton under the whip of the overseer," sneered one white writer. "Today they are raising points of order and questions of privilege."

Activities

1. CREATIVE WRITING After students have read the lesson, have them imagine that they are Southerners writing letters describing the Reconstruction government. Students should be sure to mention the part played by blacks in government as well as the roles of carpetbaggers and scalawags. When students have finished their letters, make a list on the chalkboard of the words and phrases that accurately describe Southern governments during the Reconstruction period.

Such criticism took no notice of the fact that about half the blacks who held office during Reconstruction were not ex-slaves but free blacks. They included ministers and others who had already achieved some education. Two such men were George T. Ruby and Blanche K. Bruce. Ruby was an educated Northerner who had emigrated to Haiti. Returning to the United States when the Civil War began, he organized schools in Louisiana during the war. Later he served as a Freedmen's Bureau agent in Texas before being elected to the Texas state senate. Bruce, who had started life as a slave in Virginia, studied briefly at Oberlin College, Ohio, and taught school in Missouri before entering politics.

Black strategy. The criticism that black lawmakers simply did the bidding of white party leaders also missed the mark. Some of these men worked hard to advance the interest of all blacks. Knowing they could not hope to bring about all the changes black people needed, they concentrated on three areas. One was education. A second was preserving the right of blacks to vote—"our only means of protection," as one black man from Arkansas put it. A third area was the protection of black people against violence.

Because they were in the minority, black politicians knew they would need the support of at least some Southern whites to achieve their goals. The strategy they usually followed, therefore, was to ally themselves with the South's business people and members of the upper classes. The black politicians provided votes in the legislatures for laws that those groups wanted. They also urged black voters to support those whites at election time. In return it was hoped that those whites would support black leaders in their three major areas of concern. In the end this alliance did not do much for blacks. It was not because the idea was a poor one, but because the blacks' bargaining position was so weak. Still, the strategy did make possible some small gains for a while. And once the protection of the federal government was withdrawn, it was all the Southern blacks had to lean on.

Hiram Revels of Mississippi takes the oath of office as a United States senator during the Reconstruction period. He later served for many years as president of Alcorn University.

The Southern white response. Most of the white South resisted Black Reconstruction. What Northern Radicals saw as the beginning of biracial democratic government, most Southern whites saw as government by force and ignorance. Many whites were outraged at the sight of men who had been slaves but a few years earlier now voting and making laws. They resented being taxed to send black children to school, even though nearly all the schools were segregated. Basically, most white Southerners simply could not accept the idea of a society in which white and black were equal.

In 1866 the Ku Klux Klan was formed in Pulaski, Tennessee, and it spread quickly through the South. Its aim was to make the South once more a white person's country. Its weapons were the whip, the gun, the lynch rope, and fear. Wearing white robes and hoods, night-riding Klansmen struck terror among both blacks and those Southern whites who had befriended blacks. In addition to reminding blacks of their "proper place," the Klan aimed to keep them from voting. Other groups devoted to white supremacy also sprang up.

In 1870 Congress began to take action against these secret groups. The Force Act of 1870 and the Ku Klux Klan Act of 1871 gave the President the power to send troops to Southern counties that had fallen under Klan control. President Grant did so, and by the next year the Klan had very nearly disappeared.

Southern white control. By 1872, Radical Republicanism had passed its peak. The iron will by which the Radical wing had gained control of the Republican party was weakening. Thaddeus Stevens was dead, and Charles Sumner was an old man with little power left in the Senate. Much of the Northerners' interest in Reconstruction had been based on their desire to punish the South. As that desire faded, so did their interest.

The signs of change were clear. In 1872, Congress allowed the Freedmen's Bureau to expire. That same year, it passed a general Amnesty Act, granting a final pardon to all but a few hundred Confederates. The only new law to protect the rights of blacks was the Civil Rights Act of 1875. It said that all persons were to have the "full and equal enjoyment" of eating places, hotels, streetcars, and other public facilities.

Meanwhile, the Republican governments in the South were coming under heavy attack. Democrats charged them with being corrupt and inefficient. State debts and state taxes, it was pointed out, had shot upward under Republican rule. Most important, Southern white Democrats were determined to regain control of their states. To keep blacks from voting, they formed such groups as rifle clubs, the Red Shirts, and the White Leagues. Unlike the Klan, there was nothing secret about those groups. Through threats of violence and through economic pressure—such as firing or not hiring blacks who voted, and not allowing them to buy goods on credit—they kept down the black vote. By 1872, Democrats had already regained control of several Southern states. By 1876, only South Carolina, Louisiana, and Florida remained in Republican hands. That was only because federal troops remained in those three states. The following year the troops were removed, and white Democratic rule was restored.

2. DISCUSSION Ask students to cite reasons why most of the white South resisted Black Reconstruction. List the reasons on the chalkboard and discuss each one. Ask: Were white Southerners justified in their opposition to Reconstruction governments? Explain. Then ask students to discuss the following question: Was the Reconstruction period more difficult for defeated Confederates or for liberated slaves? Students should explain the reasons for their opinions.

3. RESEARCH / ORAL REPORTS You may wish to have students do research and report orally to the class on the following topics: Blanche Kelso Bruce, Hiram Revels, Rutherford B. Hayes, and the history of the Ku Klux Klan. This latter topic is usually of interest to students. If time permits, let them hear or read document 271, "The Ku Klux Klan—Organization and Principles," from Commager's *Documents of American History*.

★18★

Ulysses S. Grant
1822–1885

Born in OHIO
In Office 1869–1877
Party REPUBLICAN

Fame as military hero led to his election. Deferred to Congress in shaping national policy. His Presidency clouded by scandals brought on by some of his appointees.

★ ★ ★ ★ ★ ★ ★ ★

The Compromise of 1877. The withdrawal of the last federal troops from the South came as the result of the election of 1876. For the Presidency, the Democratic party chose Governor Samuel J. Tilden of New York. Tilden, who had made his reputation by exposing political corruption in New York City, made a strong candidate. Worried by the corruption issue, Republicans passed over the popular Senator James G. Blaine of Maine, who had been involved in a shady railroad deal. They chose instead Rutherford B. Hayes, governor of Ohio.

When the returns came in, Tilden appeared to be the winner. He had 250,000 more popular votes than Hayes, and he was one electoral vote short of a majority, with twenty votes in dispute. Nineteen of those votes were from Louisiana, South Carolina, and Florida, and the twentieth was from Oregon. Each of the four states sent two sets of returns to Washington—one making Hayes the winner, and the other Tilden. In January 1877, Congress set up a special body of five senators, five representatives, and five Supreme Court justices to decide which returns should be counted. Eight of the fifteen members of the Electoral Commission were Republicans. By a straight party vote of eight to seven, the Commission declared Hayes the winner. The decision, however, still had to be accepted in Congress, and outraged Democrats there threatened to block it. Working behind the scenes, Republican and business leaders won the support of Southern Democratic leaders for the Commission report. As their price, Southerners got a pledge of at least one cabinet seat for a Southerner in the Hayes administration, promises of support for internal improvements and federal aid for a railroad, and the withdrawal of remaining troops from the South. Thus in 1877, Reconstruction came to a close.

Reconstruction—success or failure? Radical Reconstruction lasted from about 1867 to about 1877. Ever since that time, it has been a subject of controversy. It has been described by one historian as "a clash between good and evil." And which of the two it was depended on one's viewpoint and biases.

However, most historians today agree that Reconstruction was a complex series of events, neither wholly good nor wholly bad but a mixture of both.

Those who have called Reconstruction bad point out that there was much corruption in the Southern state governments. It is true that public funds sometimes ended up in the pockets of corrupt politicians. Such corruption can never be excused, yet it must be judged in the framework of the times. The years following the Civil War saw a breakdown of moral standards all over the country. During this period, corruption was actually greater in certain Northern states and cities than it was in the South. As you will see in Unit 8, corruption even tainted the federal government during the 1870s.

A second charge often made is that the Reconstruction state governments spent money recklessly, causing the public debt—and taxes—to shoot upward. While there was some extravagance, it was a very minor cause of the spiralling costs of government and taxes. All Southern state governments were confronted with costs many times what they had borne before the war. Repairing the war damages was a very expensive undertaking. Moreover, the states were now called upon to supply services on a much larger scale than ever before. Those new responsibilities accounted to a very large degree for the mounting public debt and the higher taxes.

The Reconstruction period saw a number of positive achievements by the Southern state governments. The governments were reorganized along modern lines, and certain reforms were carried out. Many railway lines, factories, and other buildings destroyed during the war were rebuilt. One of the most impressive achievements was that of setting up schools in a region where public education had been almost nonexistent. In South Carolina, for example, the number of children in public schools climbed from 20,000 just before the Civil War to more than 120,000 in 1873.

It is clear that the Radical Republicans did not reach their goal of equality for black Americans. There were several

★19★

Rutherford B. Hayes

1822–1893

Born in OHIO
In Office 1877–1881
Party REPUBLICAN

Won disputed election by a single electoral vote. Withdrew last federal troops from South. Began civil service reform, by which appointments to federal jobs were based on merit.

★ ★ ★ ★ ★ ★ ★ ★

4. DISCUSSION In order to help students understand that Reconstruction was a complex series of events, neither wholly good nor wholly bad, make a list on the chalkboard of the negative aspects of the Reconstruction period. Then list the positive achievements of that period. Point out to students that for years historians have argued about Reconstruction. Some say it was a "tragic time" when there was a "blackout of honest government." Other historians contend that much good came from Reconstruction. After students have reviewed the evidence on the chalkboard, ask them which group of historians they think is right. Why?

5. WHAT IF? What if the South had won the Civil War? Have students compile a list of things that they think would be different today if such an event had happened.

LESSON 3 *(2 to 3 days)*

Performance Objectives

1. To describe orally or in writing the effects on the South of the sharecrop and crop-lien systems. **2.** To explain in an essay how blacks were deprived of rights granted them under the Fourteenth and Fifteenth amendments. **3.** To describe and compare the different approaches taken by Booker T. Washington and W.E.B. Du Bois to bettering the position of blacks.

Famous People

Booker T. Washington, W.E.B. Du Bois

Vocabulary

Sharecrop and crop-lien systems, *Plessy* v. *Ferguson,* Jim Crow laws, lynching, literacy test, grandfather clause, white primary, boycott, Atlanta Compromise, National Association for the Advancement of Colored People (NAACP)

reasons for this failure. Full equality would have required economic independence. In a farming society like the South's, that meant owning land. Radicals did propose that the government divide up large Southern farms into forty-acre pieces for the freed slaves, but there was never a chance that such a bill would pass. Ideas about the rights of private property and about limited government were simply too strong.

More important was that most Americans—Northerners as well as Southerners—never really accepted the Radical goal in the first place. In six of seven Northern states that voted on amendments to allow blacks to vote, the amendments were defeated. A Republican congressman who voted for all the Radical Reconstruction program probably spoke for the great majority when he admitted: "I never believed in Negro equality. I believe God made us, for his own wise purposes, a superior race."

Yet Reconstruction clearly started black Americans on the long tortuous road to equality. The Fourteenth and Fifteenth amendments gave blacks legal tools to use in chipping away at the discrimination that had so long blocked their progress. As blacks developed their own leaders and movements in the twentieth century, these tools made a crucial difference.

CHECKUP

1. What part did blacks take in ruling Southern states during the Reconstruction period?
2. How did Southern whites respond to Black Reconstruction?
3. What were some of the positive accomplishments of Reconstruction?

LESSON 3

The Aftermath of Reconstruction

In the years following Reconstruction, a number of Southerners began to talk of a New South. The South they envisioned was a prosperous region of cities, factories, and trade, supported by a diversified agriculture. Northern capital would be attracted by the hope of good returns. "The ambition of the South," said one of the boosters of the New South, "is to out-Yankee the Yankees." Many of the leaders in the new white governments of the South were business-minded men who hoped to make this New South a reality. In fact you will recall that in the Compromise of 1877 they won promises of capital for railroads and other improvements.

Some progress toward this goal was made in the 1880s and 1890s. New cities, such as Birmingham, Alabama, appeared, and older cities, such as Atlanta, Georgia, grew much larger. By 1900, mills in the South were making half of America's textiles and nearly all of its cigarettes. But the South of many factories and booming cities was still a hundred years away. Throughout the late nineteenth century, the South remained the most rural and agricultural region of the country.

The sharecrop and crop-lien systems. Nor did Southern agriculture become diversified. The lack of capital created special problems for Southern farming. Many small white farmers and nearly all freed slaves lacked the money to buy their own land or even to rent land on a cash basis. Many landowners, on the other hand, lacked the money to hire people to work their land. Out of these

As sharecroppers after the Civil War, many blacks found themselves cultivating the same fields that they had worked on as slaves. The people in this group are planting sweet potatoes.

situations there developed the *share-crop* and *crop-lien* systems. A landowner turned over a certain amount of land to a tenant. He also supplied the tenant with tools, seeds, and other supplies that had been purchased on credit from the local storekeeper. For all of this the tenant, or *sharecropper*, paid the landlord a share—usually a third to a half—of the crop he produced. To buy on credit, the landowner had to give the storekeeper a *lien* on his share of the crop. This was a pledge that whatever cash the landowner received from the sale of the crops would first go to pay off the storekeeper. To be sure of receiving payment, the storekeeper usually insisted that crops be raised that could be readily sold for cash. Such cash crops were almost always cotton and tobacco.

Because the sharecropper bought food, clothing, and other supplies on credit, he, too, gave a lien on his share of the crop. With prices and interest charges high—ranging from 40 to 100 percent—the harvest often did not bring in enough to pay off the debt completely. The sharecropper then had to pledge to work the same piece of land the next year or until the debt was paid.

The crop-lien system filled a real need in a society where credit was scarce. But it had three bad effects. It kept the South tied to a one-crop agriculture. It kept tenants from saving enough to buy their own land (70 percent of Southern farmers in 1900 were still tenants). And it caused many sharecroppers, usually blacks, to be bound to the land almost as if they were still slaves. The South's rural regions remained vast areas of poverty.

The blacks' loss of rights. The return of harmony between North and South came at the expense of black Americans. Southern whites were assured by President Hayes that the federal government would no longer "intrude" in their affairs. Soon they were exploring ways to get around the Fourteenth and Fifteeth amendments. Blacks were barred from restaurants, hotels, theaters, streetcars, and other public facilities, or they were made to sit in separate sections. Although these practices seemed clearly to

Activities

1. FILMS *Freedom Movement, 1877–Today* (21 minutes, b&w; McGraw-Hill Films). *Heritage of the Negro,* History of the Negro People series (30 minutes, b&w; National Educational Television). *The Negro and the American Promise* (59 minutes, 2 reels, b&w; National Educational Television).

2. DISCUSSION After students have read the lesson, have them define the sharecrop and crop-lien systems. Ask: Why were these agricultural relationships especially prevalent in the postwar South? How did the sharecropping and crop-lien systems restore cotton production? In what ways were these systems disastrous for the South? Can you think of a solution, other than sharecropping, through which the South could have restored agricultural production?

3. RESEARCH / ORAL OR WRITTEN REPORTS Have several of the students compare the Supreme Court decisions in the cases of *Plessy* v. *Ferguson* and *Brown* v. *Board of Education of Topeka, Kansas,* for similarities and differences.

4. DISCUSSION It has been said that *Plessy* v. *Ferguson* "represents the high-water mark of Jim Crow constitutional sanctions." Explore the meaning of this statement with the students. Ask: Do you agree with it? Why, or why not?

violate the Civil Rights Act of 1875, blacks found no protection in the courts. In the civil rights cases of 1883, the Supreme Court ruled that the law was unconstitutional, not the practices. The Fourteenth Amendment, said the Court, prohibited *states* from denying "full and equal enjoyment" of *public* accommodations, but it did not limit the acts of *private individuals.*

Soon the state governments, too, experimented with ways to get around the Fourteenth Amendment. They passed laws requiring segregation by race, arguing that this was not discrimination as long as equal facilities were provided to blacks. In *Plessy* v. *Ferguson* (1896), the Court agreed. It upheld a Louisiana law that required blacks and whites to ride in separate railroad cars. Three years later the Court applied the same "separate but equal" doctrine to state laws that set up segregated public schools. Such laws came to be known as *Jim Crow* laws (after a black song-and-dance man); the separate and almost always unequal facilities were called Jim Crow cars, Jim Crow lunchrooms, and so on. By the turn of the century, Jim Crow had extended to, among other things, theaters, ticket windows, waiting rooms, boardinghouses, hospitals, jails, toilets, and drinking fountains. Soon afterward, witnesses in courts were sworn in on Jim Crow Bibles.

In addition to these "legal" methods, the weapons of fear were used to "keep blacks in their place." The most brutal and ugly of these was lynching—killing carried out by a mob. In the 1880s an average of 150 lynchings a year took place in the United States. Most, but not all, were in the South. In the 1890s, the yearly average was 70.

Black citizens vote in an election soon after the Civil War. In later years, the right of black men to vote was drastically curtailed through such devices as the poll tax and literacy tests.

Keeping blacks from voting. The attack upon the Fifteenth Amendment, which assured blacks of the right to vote, did not come until the 1890s. Until then, many blacks in the South continued to vote. They generally supported the ruling white conservatives in return for small favors and a certain amount of protection from the worst kinds of oppression. In the 1890s, however, the reforming Populist party tried to win blacks as well as poor whites to its support. The prospect of different groups of whites bidding for black support alarmed many Southern whites. Most of the white South united during the next ten years to remove this threat to white supremacy by taking away the black man's right to vote. Several devices were used. The most popular were the *poll tax* and the *literacy test.* The poll tax was an annual tax that had to be paid before one could vote. The literacy test required the voter to demonstrate he could read and understand a passage—which could be made as easy or as hard as the examining official wished.

These devices would also prevent many poor whites from voting. In a number of states, however, exceptions were made that allowed whites to vote anyway. The favorite device was the *grandfather clause* (in the voting law.) Typical of this was the Louisiana law that allowed anyone to vote, even if he did not pay the poll tax or pass the reading test, as long as his father or grandfather had been a voter before March 1867. That was the date when black people were first allowed to vote in that state.

The *white primary* was still another device for keeping the vote of blacks from meaning anything. All Southern states were controlled by the Democratic party, a reaction against the Republican rule of Reconstruction days. The only election that meant anything, therefore, was the Democratic primary—the election in which the Democrats selected their candidates. By allowing only whites to vote in primaries, the blacks were effectively shut out from taking part in the democratic process.

The blacks' reaction. Here and there blacks resisted the taking away of their rights. During the first few years after 1900, blacks in twenty-five cities *boycotted* Jim Crow streetcars—that, is, they refused to use them. But these boycotts failed. Thus, most blacks—economically powerless, turned away by the courts, forgotten or ignored by the North, and faced with the opposition of Southern whites—believed that their best hope lay in an alliance with Southern white conservatives. To be sure, these conservatives upheld white supremacy, but they were often willing to give jobs to blacks and to give money to black schools. In return, they required that the blacks "stay in their place."

Many black Americans made their peace with this system. Some, like ex-slave Booker T. Washington, even saw this arrangement as an opportunity. In 1881 he began a school for blacks in Tuskegee, Alabama. His school stressed the teaching of job skills—carpentry, blacksmithing, sewing, and other forms of manual work. Washington's school was handsomely supported by whites, both Northern and Southern. They supported his effort because Washington was able to convince them that well-trained black workers would be responsible citizens.

The Atlanta Compromise. Washington's appeal for support in training blacks met with favor, especially in the South, for another reason. Washington made plain that blacks should not ask for social or political equality but should concentrate on advancing economically. In a famous speech at Atlanta, Georgia, in 1895, Washington held out a picture of white-black relations. Holding up his hand, he explained:

> In all things that are purely social black people and white can be as separate as the fingers, yet one as the hand in all things essential to mutual progress.

5. ESSAY Have students write essays that answer the following question: How was freedom for black Americans limited in the years following Reconstruction? After students have completed their essays, ask for volunteers to read their papers aloud.

6. WHAT IF? Ask students for their reactions to the following situations that existed in the United States not too many years ago. **(a)** What if you went to a water fountain for a drink of water and were told you couldn't drink from it because you were black? **(b)** What if you went to a lavatory and were told you couldn't use it because you were black? **(c)** What if you and a friend went to a restaurant but the waiter refused to serve your friend because he or she was black? **(d)** What if you and your friend boarded a bus but you were not allowed to sit together because you were black and your friend was not? While these situations do not exist today, what more must be done to ensure freedom and equality for every American?

7. ROLE-PLAYING Ask for volunteers to role-play Booker T. Washington and W.E.B. Du Bois speaking before an audience on the subject of bettering the position of black Americans at the beginning of the twentieth century. Perhaps first you would want to involve the whole class in this activity. Assign half the class to write speeches that Washington might have given and the other half to write speeches that Du Bois might have delivered. Have students use the source material in the text for information but rephrase the quotations in their own words.

8. CREATING A TIME LINE As a way to review the important events in this unit, have students create time lines covering the years 1860–1877. You may wish to provide the information to be included on the time lines or to allow students to select those events that they feel are important enough to be recorded. Arrange to display the time lines at the conclusion of the activity.

9. CONTEST For a review quiz, have students submit at least twenty objective questions based on the important items studied in this unit. After you or a committee of students have edited these questions, the class may enjoy using them in a contest situation. This review could precede a regular test on the unit.

Washington has been criticized for being willing to bargain away the rights of citizenship that had been so hard won by black Americans. Of late, however, historians have suggested that perhaps Washington was a smart politician who understood how to take the first step toward equality as preparation for the second. Often overlooked is the fact that Washington made clear that once blacks, as productive citizens, "proved themselves worthy," other steps toward equality must follow.

The approach of Du Bois. Booker T. Washington was widely looked upon as the top spokesman for black Americans in the years around the beginning of the twentieth century. But not all blacks accepted him as their leader. One who was highly critical of Washington's program of accommodation was William E. B. Du Bois. Blacks would never be able to gain self-respect, said Du Bois, while they willingly accepted the status of inferiors. They must seek full equality, not tomorrow but today. Du Bois and other militants met in Niagara, Canada, in 1905 to form the Niagara Movement. Du Bois issued a ringing declaration.

> We claim for ourselves every single right that belongs to a freeborn American, political, civil, and social; and until we get these rights we will never cease to protest and assail the ears of America.

Four years later, Du Bois and several other champions of equality—white as well as black—formed the National Association for the Advancement of Colored People (NAACP). The NAACP lobbied with legislatures and brought suit in courts to end discrimination. Its first major victory came in 1915, when the

Two leading spokesmen for black Americans in the early 1900s were Booker T. Washington *(top)* and William E. B. Du Bois. However, they had different approaches to white-black relations.

Supreme Court made the grandfather clause unconstitutional.

Until 1910 or so, most blacks favored Booker T. Washington's approach of accommodation. From then on, however, the Du Bois approach has dominated. Through appeals to conscience, through lobbying, politics, and court suits, black Americans and their white allies have worked to bring America face to face with the need to bring practice into line with idealism.

Equality can be defined differently by different people. Writing in 1903 Du Bois offered a vision of equality for the Afro-American that is startingly modern.

> One ever feels his two-ness—an American, a Negro. The history of the American Negro is the history of . . . a longing . . . to merge this double self into a better and truer self. . . . The Afro-American would not Africanize America, for America has too much to teach the world and Africa. He would not bleach his Negro soul in a flood of white Americanism, for he knows that Negro blood has a message for the world. He simply wishes to make it possible for a man to be both a Negro and an American, without being cursed and spit upon by his fellows, without having the doors of Opportunity closed roughly in his face.

What Du Bois wrote about the hopes of American blacks can be just as well applied to every other group living in America, as you will read in the next unit. It is the challenge by which, above all others, the success of America will have to be measured.

CHECKUP

1. What were the effects on the South of the sharecrop and crop-lien system?.
2. By what means were the rights given to blacks under the Fourteenth and Fifteenth amendments taken away from them?
3. What different approaches did Booker T. Washington and William E. B. Du Bois take to bettering the position of blacks in the late 1800s and early 1900s?

Key Facts from Chapter 18

1. The immediate task of the federal government at the end of the Civil War was to bring the rebelling Southern states back into the Union.
2. Presidents Lincoln and Johnson favored a plan that would restore the Union quickly and easily without punishing the South or causing sweeping changes in Southern society.
3. The Radical Republicans favored a plan for restoring the Union that would punish the South and raise the freed slaves to a position of equality in Southern society.
4. The Radical Republicans succeeded in putting their plan into operation, but they failed in their attempt to remove President Johnson from office. They also failed to raise the freed slaves to a position of equality with whites.
5. The Thirteenth, Fourteenth, and Fifteenth amendments prohibited slavery, made blacks citizens, and guaranteed that their rights, including the right to vote, were not to be denied by the states.
6. Despite these amendments, various methods were devised during and after Reconstruction to keep blacks from voting and to deny them social equality.

Answers To Review Questions

1. The great strength of Lincoln's plan was that it would quickly restore the Union. The great weakness, however, was that it left the Southern states entirely free to decide how the freed slaves would be treated and what rights, if any, black people would have. There was much doubt that the South was capable of according fair and equal treatment to the former slaves.

2. Congress limited the power of the Supreme Court to hear certain kinds of cases involving reconstruction. It limited the power of the President by requiring the President to issue military orders only through the General of the Army. When Andrew Johnson did not cooperate with Congress, the House impeached him for violation of the Tenure of Office Act. Impeachment failed by one vote, and Johnson remained in office.

3. The Thirteenth Amendment provided for an end to slavery in the United States. The Fourteenth Amendment made blacks citizens. The Fifteenth Amendment guaranteed each citizen the right to vote regardless of "race, color, or previous condition of servitude."

4. Since many white Southerners were barred from voting, Reconstruction governments were operated by blacks, carpetbaggers, and scalawags. Although they were accused of corruption and extravagance, Reconstruction governments were responsible for considerable rebuilding of the South, modernization of state governments, and expansion of public schools.

5. When the returns came in, the Democratic candidate Tilden appeared to be the winner. He was one electoral vote short of victory, with twenty votes in dispute. Nineteen of those votes were from four states that had each sent two sets of returns to Washington—one making the Republican Hayes the winner and the other Tilden. To resolve the matter, Congress set up an Electoral Commission. Eight of the fifteen Commission members were Republicans and they declared Hayes the winner. However, the decision had to be accepted by Congress where outraged Democrats threatened to block it. In order to get enough Southern Democratic votes, Republicans and business leaders worked out an agreement known as the Compromise of 1877. By this agreement, Southerners were given a pledge of at least one cabinet seat in the Hayes administration, promises of support for internal improvements and federal aid for a railroad, and the withdrawal of remaining troops from the South.
6. Jim Crow laws were Southern state laws enforcing segregation by applying the doctrine of "separate but equal" as sanctioned in *Plessy* v. *Ferguson.* The fact that the facilities were almost always unequal made such laws even more loathsome.
7. Both the poll tax and literacy test were devices used by the white South to take away the black's right to vote.

★ REVIEWING THE CHAPTER ★

People, Places, and Events

Wade-Davis Bill *P. 371*
Andrew Johnson *P. 372*
Freedmen's Bureau *P. 374*
Civil Rights Act of 1866 *P. 374*
Reconstruction Act *P. 376*
Tenure of Office Act *P. 377*
Black Reconstruction *P. 378*
Carpetbaggers *P. 378*
Scalawags *P. 379*
Ku Klux Klan *P. 381*
Amnesty Act *P. 381*
Compromise of 1877 *P. 382*
Rutherford B. Hayes *P. 382, 383*
Sharecropper *P. 385*
Plessy v. *Ferguson* P. 386
Booker T. Washington *P. 387*

Review Questions

1. What was the great strength of President Lincoln's plan to restore the Union? The great weakness? *Pp. 369–370* Les. 1
2. What action did Congress take in an effort to prevent any interference with their plans for southern reconstruction? *Po. 376–377* Les. 1
3. Distinguish between the following Constitutional amendments: Thirteenth, Fourteenth, and Fifteenth? *Pp. 373, 374, 377* Les. 1
4. Who operated reconstruction governments in the southern states and how effective was their leadership? *Pp. 378–380* Les. 2
5. What was the problem with the election returns in 1876? How was the matter settled? *P. 382* Les. 2
6. What was meant by the term *Jim Crow laws*? *P. 386* Les. 3
7. What was the purpose of the poll tax and the literacy test? *P. 387* Les. 3

Chapter Test

Complete each sentence using the vocabulary from this chapter. Write your answers on a separate piece of paper.

1. The House of Representatives impeached Andrew Johnson by charging that he violated the Tenure of Office Act.
2. The Wade-Davis Bill was Congress' plan for Reconstruction, but Lincoln was able to kill the legislation by using a veto or pocket veto.
3. The Electoral Commission declared Rutherford B. Hayes the winner of the disputed election of 1896.
4. Reconstruction came to an end when Democrats and Republicans accepted the Compromise of 1877.
5. The government agency established to give welfare to blacks and poor whites after the war was called the Freedmen's Bureau.
6. In *Plessy* v. *Ferguson*, the Supreme Court ruled in favor of the doctrine of "separate but equal" facilities for blacks.
7. Northerners who moved to the South for political reasons during Reconstruction were called carpetbaggers.
8. The Fifteenth Amendment provided that no citizen could be kept from voting "on account of race, color, or previous condition of servitude."
9. Segregation laws were referred to as Jim Crow laws.
10. Booker T. Washington advocated that blacks concentrate on advancing economically instead of asking for political or social equality.

★ REVIEWING THE UNIT ★

1831	*Nat Turner slave uprising*
1846	*Wilmot Proviso*
1850	*Compromise of 1850*
1852	*Uncle Tom's Cabin*
1854	*Kansas-Nebraska Act*
1857	*Dred Scott decision*
1858	*Lincoln-Douglas debates*
1859	*John Brown at Harpers Ferry*
1860	*Lincoln elected President*
1861	*Confederate States of America formed*
1863	*Civil War*
	Emancipation Proclamation
1865	*Lincoln assassinated*
	Thirteenth Amendment
1868	*Johnson impeachment trial*
	Fourteenth Amendment
1870	*Fifteenth Amendment*
1877	*Reconstruction ends*

The invention of the cotton gin brought about the expansion of cotton-growing lands and increased the demand for field laborers, thus fastening slavery on the South. Yet many people—both black and white—opposed slavery and sought to abolish it. The spread of slavery into the Western territories became a major issue in national politics. Compromises in 1820 and 1850 kept a shaky balance in Congress between free and slave states. Events during the 1850s brought the issue to a head. They included the publication of *Uncle Tom's Cabin,* the formation of the antislavery Republican party, the Kansas-Nebraska Act, the Dred Scott case, and John Brown's raid on Harpers Ferry.

Soon after Abraham Lincoln, a Republican, was elected President in 1860, the Confederate States of America was formed in the South. The Civil War started in 1861 as the North sought to restore the Union. After four years of destructive conflict, the war ended in 1865 with the North victorious. The slaves became free, gaining the rights and privileges of all other American citizens.

Following Lincoln's assassination, the Radical Republicans in Congress directed the Reconstruction of the South. They tried to remove President Andrew Johnson from office but failed. Reconstruction lasted from about 1867 to 1877. It restored the Southern states to the Union but failed to assure the freed slaves of a position of equality in American society. From the 1870s onward, many of the freed slaves' rights as citizens were taken from them.

Answers to Unit Questions

1. A principal station on the Underground Railroad
2. North, generally
3. Norfolk is the most southern station and Montreal is the most northern station.
4. Chicago
5. Atlantic Ocean; Lakes Michigan, Huron, Erie, and Champlain; St. Lawrence River, Hudson River and Ohio River
6. **(a)** From Norfolk: Atlantic Ocean to Boston, Fitchburg, Montpelier, and Montreal **(b)** From Davenport: Chicago, north on Lake Michigan and south on Lake Huron to Chatham
7. **(a)** Approximately 300 miles (480 kilometers) **(b)** Approximately 250 miles (400 kilometers)
8. The distance is approximately 640 kilometers. The trip would take about 34 days.
9. Beginning at the Ohio River, there were several stations on the Underground Railroad that would help a runaway to escape to the North and freedom.

 REVIEWING THE UNIT 

Skills Development: Reading a Map

Blacks and many white people who opposed slavery established a system of secret escape routes known as the Underground Railroad. People on the Underground Railroad used railroad language in the hope that they would not be found out. A "station" might be a house, a store, or a barn, where friendly people gave runaway slaves food and a place to rest. "Passengers" were the slaves themselves. They traveled mostly at night, going from station to station in secret, and led by a "conductor"—an abolitionist who knew the way. Canada was often the final destination for many escaping slaves.

As you study the map and answer the questions, try to imagine what it might have been like to be part of the Underground Railroad.

1. What does each dot on the map represent?
2. In what direction were runaway slaves traveling on the Underground Railroad?
3. As shown on this map, what is the most southern station? the most northern station?
4. Which station was located on the southwestern shore of Lake Michigan?
5. What bodies of water were routes on the Underground Railroad?
6. Trace the route an escaping slave would follow from: **(a)** Norfolk, Virginia to Montreal, Canada; **(b)** Davenport, Iowa to Chatham, Canada.
7. Using the scale of miles/kilometers, measure the distance from: **(a)** Chester, Illinois to Chicago, Illinois; **(b)** Fitchburg, Massachusetts to Montreal.
8. If the runaway slave could travel an average of 19 kilometers a day, approximately how many days would it take him or her to go from Philadelphia to Oswego, New York?
9. Why would a runaway slave be likely to head for the Ohio River?

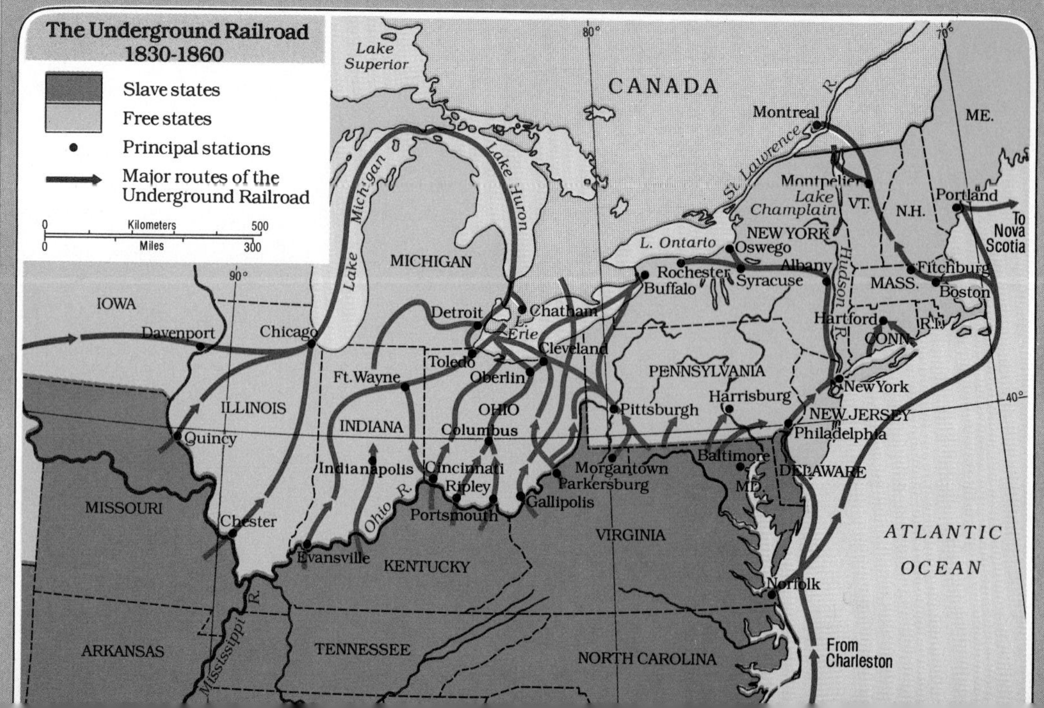

Unit 6

Americans: A Diverse People

IMMIGRATION

Background Information

1. IMMIGRANTS AND STEAMSHIPS In this 1903 photograph, immigrants crowd the deck of an Atlantic steamship as it approaches New York Harbor. The trip across the Atlantic probably took a little more than a week at that time. By sail during the 1830s this voyage usually took forty days, but in unfavorable weather it took as long as three months. The development of the ocean steamship greatly reduced the length of the voyage across the Atlantic.

LESSON 1 *(2 days)*

Performance Objectives

1. To demonstrate an understanding of Greeley's three observations about America and its ethnic groups by giving an oral explanation of each observation. **2.** To list five examples of areas of American society affected by ethnic diversity.

Vocabulary

Social scientist, ethnic group, nationality, ethnic diversity, immigrant, migration, survey, "balanced ticket," revival, ethnic pride

CHAPTER 19

A NATION OF NATIONS

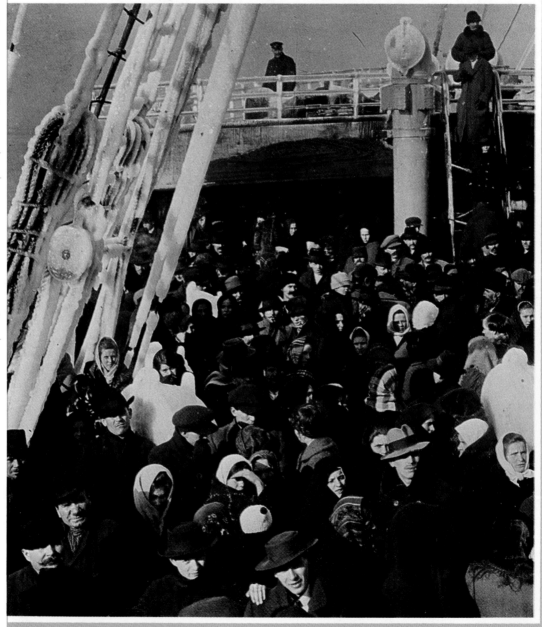

LESSON 1

THREE OR FOUR HUNDRED YEARS from now, when historians look back at our times, which developments will they find the most interesting and important? One development, believes Andrew Greeley, a leading social scientist, "will be the formation of a new nation on the North American continent made up of widely different nationality groups." Greeley explains why scholars three or four centuries hence will wonder at this development.

> [The historians] of the future will find it hard to believe it could have happened that English, Scotch, and Welsh, Irish, German, Italians and Poles, Africans, Indians—both Eastern and Western—Frenchmen, Spaniards, Finns, Swedes, Lebanese, Danes, Armenians, Croatians, Slovenians, Greeks and Luxembourgers, Chinese, Japanese, Filipinos and Puerto Ricans would come together to form a nation that not only would survive, but, all things considered, survive reasonably well.
>
> They will find it especially astonishing in light of the fact that ethnic differences, even in the second half of the twentieth century, proved far more important than differences in philosophy or economic system. Men who would not die for [a difference in economic systems] . . . would more or less cheerfully die for a difference rooted in ethnic origins. Chinese and Malay fight each other in Southeast Asia; Ibo and Hausa in Nigeria; Greek and Turk on Cyprus; Czech and Slovak in Czechoslovakia; Arab and Jew in the Middle East.

In fact, Greeley states, "What is fascinating about American society is that despite its incredible diversity there has been so little ethnic conflict."

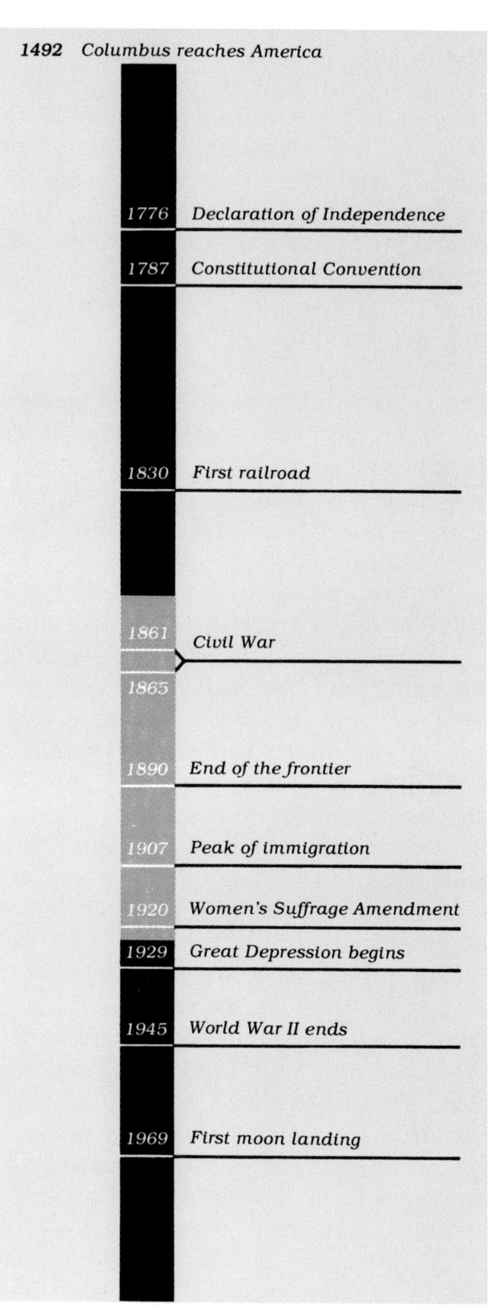

Activities

1. INTRODUCING THE UNIT The central theme of this unit is the reaction of various immigrant groups to America and America's reaction to them. Develop a discussion around the idea that Americans are almost all "immigrants or children of immigrants." You might begin by asking how many of the students think of themselves as immigrants or children of immigrants. Then ask how many consider themselves to be a member of an ethnic group. Discuss the significance of the distinction in the terms. Because these are opinion questions and involve feelings, there should be few "wrong" answers.

You might use the following questions in your discussion. **(a)** What are some of the ethnic groups that have come to America? **(b)** Why do you think they came? **(c)** What kinds of jobs were they able to do? What kinds of jobs did they actually find in America? **(d)** In what ways was their life in America different from that in their homeland? **(e)** What special problems did these people face in a new country? **(f)** What ethnic groups are a part of your community today? What evidence is there of their presence? (Holidays; churches; foods; etc.)

It might be useful to lead the discussion to a consideration of why America needed immigrants and how the nation continues to benefit from the achievement of immigrants (Henry Kissinger; Wernher von Braun). This discussion will tie into the first several activities below.

Conclude this discussion by introducing students to Greeley's three observations about America and its ethnic groups (pages 395–396).

2. DISCUSSION A possible motivation for this lesson, this activity will help make students aware of the ethnic backgrounds of famous Americans. Have each student compile a list of candidates for the five most famous living Americans. Undoubtedly these lists will contain names of movie stars, athletes, and politicians. Have the students try to guess each one's ethnic origin based on knowledge of the person named or from the last name. If time permits, ask several of your students to find out if the class speculations were accurate. The *Information Please Almanac,* published each year, has a list of famous people that might help, especially with the movie stars or singers who may have changed their names; e.g., John Denver's name was Henry John Deutschendorf, Jr.

America's Ethnic Variety

Greeley is writing about America's numerous *ethnic* groups. An ethnic group is one with a shared culture and a sense of identity based on common origin. Usually the common origin is nationality, but it can also be religion or race. American Indians and blacks, for example, are often regarded both as ethnic groups and as racial groups. As Greeley uses the term, however, he means mainly *nationality* groups. That is how we will use the term here.

The greatest migration. In the passage you have just read, Greeley makes three important observations about America and its ethnic groups. The first is that America is a nation of immigrants. More than 220,000,000 people live in the United States today. Except for the 800,000 or so American Indians, all of them are descendants of immigrants or are immigrants themselves. They came from all over the world—Asia, Africa, Central and South America—but mostly from Europe. They were part of the greatest migration in all human history. In the hundred years from 1830 to 1930, more than sixty million Europeans pulled up roots and left for other lands. Almost two thirds of them went to one country, the United States.

That in itself is a remarkable fact. What is equally remarkable is the great variety of nationality groups who came here. This is Greeley's second point. A few other countries—such as Australia, Argentina, and Canada—have also been the product of immigration. No other, however, has been settled by such a great variety of people. Of the immigrants to Australia, for example, four fifths came from the British Isles. Of those who went to Argentina, nearly four fifths were from Spain and Italy. Three fourths of all immigrants to Canada came from Britain and the United States.

How varied is America's ethnic makeup? A recent survey sent to all colleges in one eastern state listed the ethnic groups living in that state. The list began with Algerians and Armenians at one end of the alphabet. It ended with Welsh, West Indians, and Yugoslavs—and included seventy other ethnic groups in between!

Greeley's third point may be the most important. While some other countries have been torn apart by conflicts and even killings among their ethnic groups, America works.

This great ethnic variety is a fact of central importance to an understanding of America today. Every ethnic group could compile, and almost every group does, long lists of members who have contributed to American politics, religious life, art, business, music, science, and so on. There is scarcely a part of American society that is not influenced by our ethnic diversity.

The ethnic candidate. Consider politics, for example. A candidate for office might start the day with a tour of a Greek neighborhood. He or she might then lunch on pizza or sauerbraten, and take part in an afternoon parade honoring a Polish saint. After conferring with local Puerto Rican or black leaders at dinner, the candidate might then deliver a talk at the local synagogue. Those who run for office or who shape American foreign policy must be sensitive to the views and interests of ethnic voters. They must be concerned with the feelings of Jews for Israel, of Poles and Hungarians for the fate of those eastern European nations, and of Irish Catholics for the condition of their people in Northern Ireland. All this reflects what every political leader understands: in the voting booth, many Americans vote the interests and causes of their own ethnic group.

Given a choice, many ethnics simply vote for one of their own. Thus, in Buffalo, New York, a Polish name is a major asset for an office seeker. In Boston, an Irish name is indispensable. In Milwaukee, German is magic, while a Hispanic name is favored in many parts of the Southwest. In cities with several large ethnic groups, parties have long nominated "balanced tickets." That is, they reserve a place on the ticket for each of the largest ethnic groups. In New York City, that has traditionally meant that persons of Irish, Italian, and Jewish backgrounds would be nominated for the three major elective offices. The recent growth of that city's Puerto Rican and black populations will just as surely result in places on the ticket for them.

Senator Edward Muskie of Maine shows a Polish-American audience the true spelling of his name. The senator's father changed the family name after coming to America from Poland in 1903.

Ethnic pride. For many years it was unfashionable to talk about the ethnic backgrounds and differences among Americans. In recent times, stimulated by the movement of black Americans for recognition and a greater share of power, there has been a revival of ethnic awareness and pride. Many seem anxious to identify themselves as members of ethnic groups. A bumper sticker may proclaim "Italian Power" or "Kiss Me, I'm Polish." Or it may display the national or regional colors with which the car owner identifies: red, white, and green for Italy; blue and white for Israel; red, black, and green for Africa. Novels, movies, and television reflect this growing ethnic consciousness. Detectives and other "good guys" are now as likely to have Italian, Hispanic, or Greek names as English-sounding ones. In a word, in today's America, ethnic is "in."

3. BULLETIN-BOARD DISPLAY A bulletin-board display showing the ethnic backgrounds of your students could also be used to motivate the class. Tack a large map of the world on the bulletin board. Mark the spot where your school is located. Supply students with pieces of yarn. Have the students pin their yarn to the point on the map where your school is located and to the country or countries of their ancestors. Tag each piece of yarn with the students' name.

LESSON 2 *(1 day)*

Performance Objective

To explain orally the meaning of the statement "The history of America *is* immigration."

Activity

THOUGHT PROVOKER

This activity, concerned with the meanings popularly associated with the words *colonist* and *immigrant,* might serve as an effective motivation for this lesson. On the chalkboard, list the adjectives your students use to describe a colonist. In another column, write the adjectives they use to describe an immigrant. Do the adjectives in the lists overlap? Undoubtedly the lists will have some different adjectives. Then read the following thoughts of Marcus Lee Hansen from his book *The Immigrant in American History* (Cambridge, Mass.: Harvard University Press, 1940). "Popular usage recognizes a distinction between those settlers who reached America before 1776 and those who came later. The former are described as 'colonists,' the latter as 'immigrants.' . . . [But the] Puritan who landed in Massachusetts Bay with his blunderbuss and Bible was an immigrant. The peasant from Eastern Europe who [sixty] years ago passed through Ellis Island with a pack upon his back was a colonist. They were all colonists, all immigrants." Ask: Do you agree with Hansen's opinion? Would you still use the same adjectives to describe colonists and immigrants?

At the conclusion of this discussion, ask students to sum up the main points by explaining the meaning of the statement "The history of America *is* immigration."

How was it that America came to be the home of so many different peoples? How did immigrants fare in America? How has American society felt about this great variety of ethnic groups? How have these groups felt about America? What is the future of ethnic diversity in America? This unit will deal with those and other questions about American ethnicity.

CHECKUP

1. What is an ethnic group? Why does ethnicity have more meaning in the United States than in many other countries?
2. How does ethnicity make itself felt in the selection of candidates for office?
3. What are some of the ways in which ethnic pride is shown?

LESSON 2

The First Wave

"The history of America *is* immigration," one historian of the subject has written. That was not true for the first hundred years after Columbus, when few Europeans came to North America to settle, but it has been largely true ever since. When you read about the settlers of Jamestown, Plymouth, and Massachusetts Bay earlier in this book, you may not have thought of them as immigrants. But they were, as were the thousands of other colonists who settled in the thirteen colonies along the eastern coast of America.

The English—and others. Even among the earliest immigrants, the great ethnic variety that became an American characteristic was in evidence. Most of the colonists in New England were English, as were perhaps half or more of the people in the other colonies. But there were also Dutch in New Amsterdam (later New York City) and along the Hudson River, Swedes and Finns along the Delaware River, French in South Carolina and several other colonies, and a sprinkling of Jews in several seaport towns. William Penn's colony resembled a map of Europe, with one third English, with another third German, and with French, Dutch, Swiss, and Scotch-Irish making up the remainder.

Since we have already learned about the coming of black Americans in an earlier unit, we will not be studying them in this unit on ethnic diversity. However, one cannot write about the ethnic composition of the colonial South without noting that blacks made up a third of the population of that region, and in some parts of it more than half.

Germans and Scotch-Irish. The population in Britain's North American colonies grew slowly during the seventeenth century, but it increased rapidly in the eighteenth century. In the fifty years before the American Revolution, the population rose by 400 percent. A large part of that increase was due to immigration. People continued to come from many lands. The two largest groups, though, were the Germans and the Scotch-Irish. The latter were Scots who had been living in northern Ireland. Although the larger number of each group went to Pennsylvania, both the Germans and the Scotch-Irish quickly spread through all the colonies from New York to Georgia. Immigration reached 20,000 to 30,000 a year just before the beginning of the American Revolution, and about 10,000 each year were Scotch-Irish.

CHECKUP

1. Among the earliest immigrants, what was the largest ethnic group? What other ethnic groups were among the earliest settlers?
2. From what two countries did the largest immigrant groups come during the 1700s?

LESSON 3

A Rising Tide

For the first thirty years after independence, immigration dropped to an average of about 8,000 a year. There were two reasons for this drop. For more than twenty of those thirty years, European powers were at war on the sea as well as on land. A voyage of any kind was extremely dangerous. Also, European governments made it difficult for their citizens to leave. Some prohibited it altogether.

A period of peace that began in 1815 removed, however, the main danger of the Atlantic crossing. And in the 1820s many European governments ended their restrictions on emigration. The result was an increased flow of immigrants to America, as can be seen in the graph on the next page.

Note especially the number of people who came in the years 1845–1854. The entire population of the United States at the start of that ten-year period was only about 20 million. During those years, America's immigration was greater in proportion to its population than in any

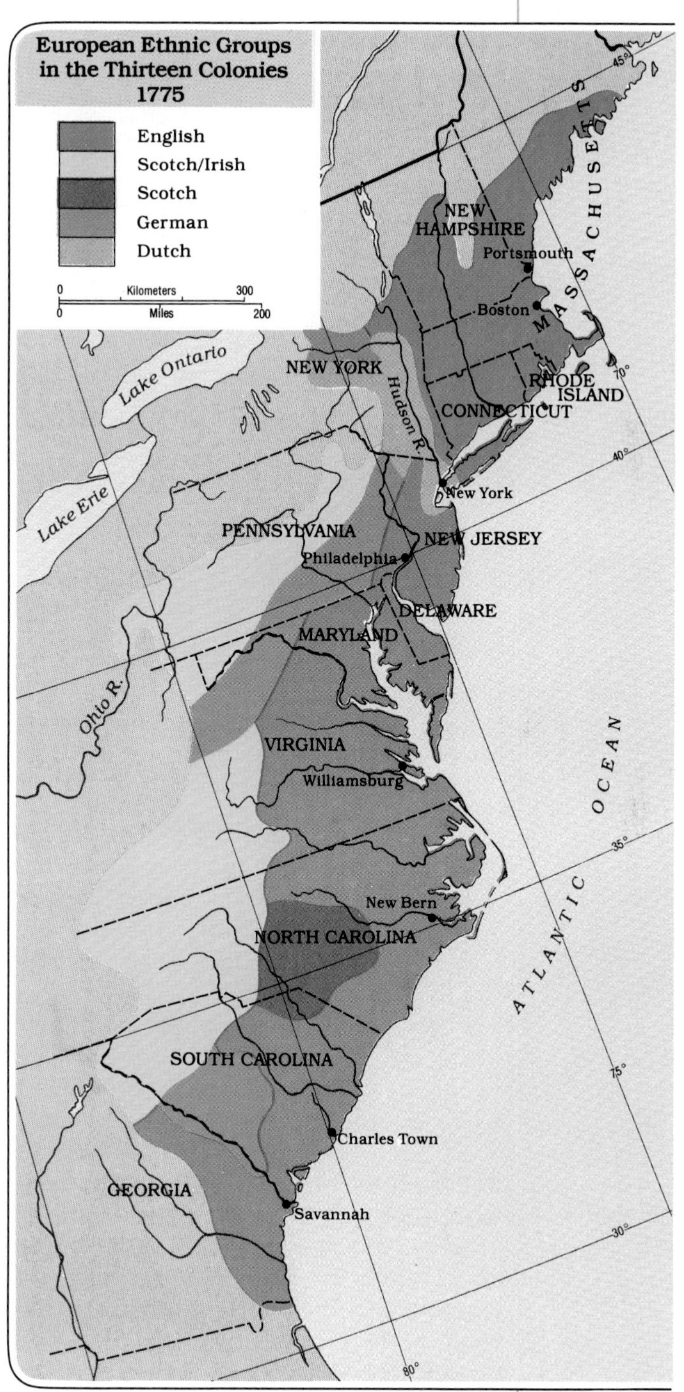

The map shows the regions where various European ethnic groups were living at the time of the American Revolution. In most regions there were also people with ethnic backgrounds different from that of the majority group.

LESSON 3 *(2 to 3 days)*

Performance Objectives

1. To demonstrate the ability to read a graph by formulating three questions based on the information given in the graph on page 400 entitled "Immigration, 1820–1970." **2.** To demonstrate an understanding of the term "the push of immigration" by compiling a list of at least five reasons why immigrants were forced to leave their homelands. **3.** To demonstrate an understanding of the term "the pull of immigration" by compiling a list of at least eight reasons why immigrants were attracted to America.

Vocabulary

Emigration, factory system, Irish land problem, peasant, absentee landlord, Irish potato famine, American Letters, American "fever," "push" factor, "pull" factor

Activities

1. RESEARCH Many of your students may have ancestors who came to America during the time period covered in this lesson. The personal nature of this activity may help to motivate your students. It is said that the attics of American homes are filled with history not yet known. Ask your students to look in their homes for any links to their immigrant past—letters, pictures, clothing, tools, etc. If response is great enough, you could display items in the school library or in your classroom.

Immigration 1820-1970

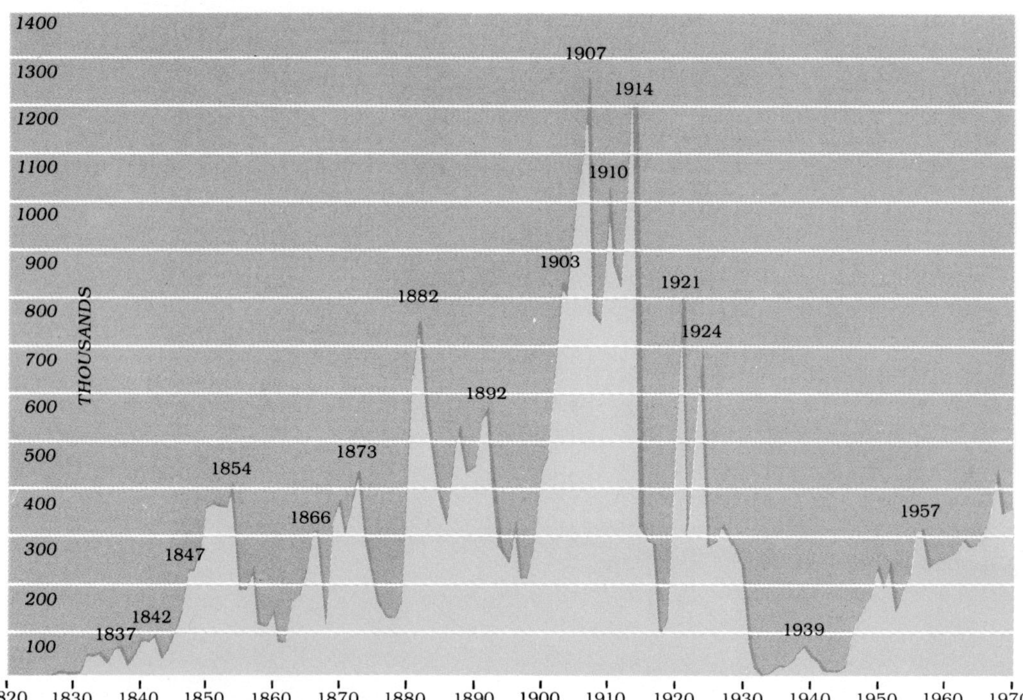

other period of its history except the colonial era. The greatest number of immigrants settled in Massachusetts, New York, Pennsylvania, Ohio, Illinois, and Wisconsin, giving those states a distinctly foreign flavor.

Where did the immigrants come from? By far, most came from countries in northern and western Europe. Over half were from the British Isles: two million from Ireland and three quarters of a million from England, Wales, and Scotland. Germans numbered a million and a half, and French, 200,000. Immigrants from Norway, Sweden, the Netherlands, and Switzerland accounted for most of the rest. One hundred thousand French Canadians came across the border, settling in several northern states. The West Coast received 40,000 from China.

Why the immigrants came. The question "Why did they come?" is really two questions: What caused them to leave their familiar surroundings, their hometowns, often their families, and always most of their friends? And why was it America that they chose to come to? The reasons were not the same for all. In general we can say, though, that there was a "push" and a "pull" in every decision to leave one's own country for the United States.

The "push" had to do with conditions in their own lands. The most important factor in that push was a huge increase in population. Between 1750 and 1850, Europe's population doubled. This was in large part because of a declining death rate—a result of better knowledge about medicine and sanitation and the absence of serious plagues. In a modern society, industries create jobs that soak up increases in population. But most European nations in the early and middle 1800s were still farming countries. For them, a sharp increase in population was a problem.

The case of Sweden. Sweden offers a good illustration. In the 1850s and 1860s Sweden was mostly rural. Only 10 percent of its population lived in towns and cities. As population increased, people had to be absorbed into farming. One way to do that was to bring new land under the plow. About a million more people were taken care of in this way between 1750 and 1850.

But there was a limit to the unused land that was suitable for farming. By 1850 the limit had been reached. After that, the only way to create more farms would be to cut up existing ones. Otherwise, an increasingly large part of the population would have to find work on farms owned by others. Either way, more people had to be supported by the same amount of land. In days before modern fertilizers and machinery, that would be difficult under the best conditions. A bad turn in the weather, a blight, or anything that would reduce the harvest could lead to disaster.

That is what happened. A crop failure in the years 1867—1868 brought ruin to thousands of people. The result can be seen in the table in the next column.

Emigration from Sweden

Years	*Number*
1841–1850	About 7,000
1851–1860	About 10,000
1867	9,000
1868	27,000
1869	39,000

Most of those people went to the United States.

The slide into poverty. German farmers had experienced the same slide into poverty thirty years earlier. They started to emigrate to America in the 1830s. Even some of the better-off farmers left, for they could read the handwriting on the wall. When crop failures struck in the 1840s, hundreds of thousands more departed for the New World.

In the case of the Germans and the English, another factor added to the flow of emigrants. Both were experiencing the beginnings of the factory system. In time, factories would mean more jobs, not fewer. But in the earlier stages of the factory system, machines threw skilled laborers out of work. Some took jobs in the new factories, but many others emigrated. More than half the English who came to America in the 1830s and 1840s had been skilled workers in their own land. The same was true of thousands of Germans.

The Irish land problem. But it remains true that a very large number of immigrants were peasants who had been forced off the land. Nowhere in Europe

2. DISCUSSION After students have read the lesson, list on the chalkboard, in random fashion, the various reasons why immigrants were **(a)** forced to leave their homelands, and **(b)** attracted to America. Using the terms "push" factor and "pull" factor, have students classify and discuss each reason.

3. USING A GRAPH Relate students' understanding of the "push" and "pull" factors to the graph on page 400. What events were occurring in Europe when immigration was at a particularly high level? Then ask students to write three questions based on the information *in the graph.* Help them to distinguish between factual information as presented by the graph and the application of knowledge after studying the text material. When students have finished writing their questions, have them exchange questions with another student and answer that set of questions.

4. USING A MAP While students are reading Lesson 3, have them notice the many different places mentioned. After they have read the lesson, supply them with an outline map of the world. Have them locate and label the following places on the map.

a. Countries: Ireland, England, Wales, Scotland, Germany, France, Norway, Sweden, Netherlands, Switzerland, China, and Canada

b. States: Massachusetts, New York, Pennsylvania, Ohio, Illinois, Wisconsin, New Hampshire, Kansas, Iowa, Minnesota, Nebraska, the Dakotas, Texas, and Missouri

c. European cities: Arnhem, Netherlands; Quebec, Canada; Le Havre, France; and Westport, Ireland

d. U.S. cities: Boston, New York, Philadelphia, Baltimore, New Orleans, Cincinnati, Milwaukee, St. Louis.

On another piece of paper, have the students write a sentence to explain the significance of each of these places in the history of immigration.

5. FAMILY HISTORY RESEARCH Except for your students who are American Indians, all others are either immigrants or descendants of immigrants. Have each one inquire in their families to find out **(a)** the countries their ancestors came from, **(b)** their journey across the Atlantic or Pacific, and **(c)** the "push" and "pull" reasons for coming to America. Students could present their findings in a written or oral report.

At this time you may wish to introduce the skills development activity on page 460. This activity could then be developed throughout this unit.

was the situation more desperate for such people than in Ireland. Ireland had the highest population density in Europe. Its people were poorer than those from almost any other place in Europe. Absentee English land owners held most of the land. They rented it in small parcels to the Irish. One landowner divided 240 acres (96 ha) among 39 families. From such tiny plots, each Irish family barely scratched out a living raising potatoes. Little wonder the average age at death in Ireland was nineteen, and only one in five reached forty.

When landowners converted their land from farming to pasture in the early 1800s, they combined the tiny rented farms into a few large ones. Fewer families were needed to work these larger farms. The landowner mentioned above, for example, combined the thirty-nine farms into five. Nine of the thirty-nine families were hired as farm workers. The others had to leave the land. As people all over Ireland were forced off the land, they turned to the United States. Between 1815 and 1845, 850,000 Irish came to America.

Thousands of Irish immigrants came to America in the late 1840s. They did so after their main food crop—potatoes—failed because of a plant disease. Many of the newcomers from Ireland during this period settled in New York, Boston, Philadelphia, and other eastern cities.

The potato crop failure. Beginning in 1846, Irish immigration swelled to new highs. In that year and for the next several years, the potato crop failed. What that meant in human terms was recorded by an eyewitness who visited Ireland in 1847.

> The town of Westport was in itself a strange and fearful sight, like what we read of in beleaguered cities; its streets crowded with gaunt wanderers, sauntering to and fro with hopeless air and hungerstruck look—a mob of starved, almost naked, women around the poorhouse clamouring for soup tickets—our inn, the headquarters of the road engineer and pay clerks, beset by a crowd of beggars for work. . . . As we went along, our wonder was not that the people died, but that they lived. . . . One poor woman whose cabin I had visited [earlier] said, "There will be nothing for us but to lie down and die." I had tried to give her hope of English aid, but, alas! her prophecy had been too true. Out of a population of 240 I found thirteen already dead from want. The survivors were like walking skeletons—the men gaunt and haggard, stamped with the livid mark of hunger—the children crying with pain—the women in some of the cabins too weak to stand. When there before I had seen cows at almost every cabin, and there were besides many sheep and pigs owned in the village. But now all the sheep were gone—all the cows—all the poultry killed—only one pig left—the very dogs which had barked at me before had disappeared—no potatoes—no oats.

The "pull" of America. Accounts of that kind help us understand the "push" of immigration. What of the "pull"? What attracted people to the United States? What ideas did people have about America, and where did they get them?

One important source of information was the newspaper. There was great curiosity in Europe about this newest of nations. Newspapers regularly carried stories about life in America. Books, especially those written by travelers to America, also provided information. In England alone, 200 books were written by travelers between 1825 and 1850. During those same years, guidebooks to America appeared in half a dozen languages. A hundred such books were printed in the German language alone.

This great flow of information made many Europeans familiar with America. Years later, one immigrant told how surprised his group had been on landing here to learn that "we knew far more about conditions both in Iowa and Illinois than did the native Americans with whom we conversed."

The American Letters. People were influenced most by letters from relatives and friends who had already moved to America. These letters have come to be called the American Letters. They were passed from one member of a family to another, and were often published in the local newspaper. As you read them, you can discover what immigrants themselves regarded as the "pull" of America. In comparing America with the European countries they left, the writers also give you further information about the "push" of immigration. You might try to draw up a list of the "push" and "pull" factors in these letters.

From an Englishman in New Hampshire, 1821:

We now have a comfortable dwelling and two acres of ground planted with potatoes, Indian corn, melons, etc. I have two hogs,

6. CREATIVE WRITING/ ROLE-PLAYING Divide your students into small groups and ask each student to assume the role of a member of an immigrant family. Using the varied experiences given in the text as examples, have each group, or "family," write a short dialogue in which the members of the family speak about their hopes, dreams, and fears as they spend their last night aboard ship before disembarking in America. Students in each group may either read their script to the class or tape-record their dialogue and use their imagination to enhance the script by adding sound effects.

Background Information

1. PATRICK KENNEDY One of the haggard, gaunt Irish wanderers of the 1840s, much like the one mentioned in the source material on page 403, was a bankrupt farmer named Patrick Kennedy, the great-grandfather of President John F. Kennedy. After losing his farm in County Wexford, he decided to try his luck in America. Kennedy landed in Boston, as did many other Irish, simply because Boston was the end of the steamship line. He was one of the 1.7 million Irish who emigrated to America in the 1840s and 1850s.

one ewe and a lamb: cows in the spring were as high as 33 dollars, but no doubt I shall have one in the fall.

From a Swede in Illinois, 1850:
This is a free country and nobody has a great deal of authority over another. . . . nobody needs to hold his hat in his hand for anyone else. Servants are not bound for a fixed time. This is not Sweden, where the higher classes and employers have the law on their side so that they can treat subordinates as though they were not human beings.

From a Dutch woman in Massachusetts, 1846:
Nearly all people eat three meals a day . . . Arnhem [a Dutch city] can't compare with it. One sees no poor here. . . . Schools are free . . . there are no taxes. . . . The finery is great, one cannot discern any difference between the cobbler's wife and the wife of a prominent gentleman . . . nobody steals here . . . no night watchman.

From a Welshman in Kansas, 1869:
I am amazed at the efforts made by the Welsh in Wales to get a farm. When one

In the latter years of the nineteenth century, a Swedish immigrant family poses before its farm home in Minnesota. The states of the upper Midwest welcomed many settlers from Sweden.

comes vacant there are hundreds trying to get it. But here you can be your own master without fear of being turned out and you can do what you like with your own land. . . . The land is very good here, the corn is four yards tall and a field of it is like a wood.

From a Norwegian in New York, 1835:
It would greatly please me to learn that all of you who are in need and have little chance of supporting yourselves and your families have decided to leave Norway and come to America: for even if many more come, there will still be room here for all. Those who are willing to work will not lack employment or business here. It is possible for all to live in comfort and without want.

From a Welshman in New York, 1817:
Dear wife, . . . If you will let the two eldest boys come over to me for a while it will be of great benefit to them. They will be taught for nothing until they are fourteen years old. Here are the best schools in the world at the cost of the state.

Letters like these were responsible for periodic outbreaks of "American fever." At such times the desire to move to America might sweep through an entire village and carry away many residents.

Unfavorable views. Not all letters home were so favorable to America. Here are some others.

From a Norwegian in New York, 1837:
I have looked around day after day to find jobs for my countrymen; but when they have been employed for a day or two, their employers send them back to me and say that they cannot use them because they do not speak the language.

From a Welshman in New York, 1818:
This country is not what we had heard about it in any way. The wages are not as high as we had heard . . . I do not think that the corn or the hay is half as good as the corn and hay in the Old Country. . . . Be Happy in your country and do not be surprised to find me back in Wales.

From a Norwegian in Wisconsin, 1844:
. . . almost all reports and letters received in Norway from America are good. But this is very wrong; only about a third part of these letters are true. People only write down accounts of the good, although they themselves have had no experience of it . . . I do not advise any of my relatives to come to America. If you could see the conditions of the Norwegians in America at present, you would certainly be frightened; illness and misery are so prevalent that many have died.

Compare the two letters from Norwegians in New York in the 1830s. Also compare the two letters from Welsh immigrants living in the same state in 1817 and 1818. How might one account for the claim that some letter writers had exaggerated about America? What problems do these letters suggest that immigrants to America might expect to have?

Tickets to America. Letters like the last three that you read might bring down the American fever for a short while. But then would come another letter with money saved by the immigrant. Here was proof of America's plenty. A single money order from a new American sometimes more than equaled the cash that many a European villager might see in years of hard work. Sometimes the money was a gift to help out relatives who had stayed behind. More often it was meant to be set aside to buy tickets to America. Often, the immigrant sent

7. ORAL REPORTS Many studies of immigration concentrate on data collected by the government, by newspapers, and by other nonfiction accounts. However, the use of fiction and autobiographies can provide valuable insight to your students. The May 1976 issue of *The History Teacher* (Vol. IX, No. 3) contains a bibliography of novels and autobiographies concerned with the immigrant experience in America. There are numerous books mentioned for 24 ethnic groups. The following are some of the classic books on American immigration. *My Name Is Aram* by William Saroyan (New York: Harcourt Brace and World, 1940) tells about an Armenian community in California. *My Antonia* by Willa S. Cather (Boston: Houghton Mifflin Co., 1954) describes a Hungarian immigrant family on the Dakota prairies. *Autobiography of Andrew Carnegie* tells the story of the self-made steel tycoon and philanthropist from Scotland. *Plow the Dew Under* by Helen C. Fernald (New York: Longmans, Green and Co., Inc., 1952) deals with Russian immigrants in Kansas. *A Daughter of the Samurai* by Etsu Inagaki Sugimato (Norwood, Pa.: Norwood Editions, 1934) tells the story of a young Japanese girl who came to America as a bride in the 1890s. *The Making of an American* by Dane Jacob Riis (New York: Macmillan Publishing Co., 1924) is the story of an immigrant whom Theodore Roosevelt called "America's most useful citizen." And of course, *Roots* by Alex Haley (New York: Doubleday & Co., 1976).

8. THOUGHT PROVOKER
After your students have read this lesson, encourage them to evaluate the role that ethnicity has played in American events and trends. Several statements by Nathan Glazer and Daniel Patrick Moynihan in their book *Beyond the Melting Pot: The Negroes, Puerto Ricans, Jews, Italians, and Irish of New York City* (Cambridge, Mass.: M.I.T. Press, 1970) might be used to stimulate a consideration of the role of ethnicity. Glazer and Moynihan make the three following statements. (1) "Ethnicity is more than an influence on events, it is commonly the source of events." Ask: Do you agree? What examples can you offer to substantiate or disprove this statement? (2) "Religion and race seem to define the major groups into which American society is evolving as the specifically national aspect of ethnicity declines." Ask: What religions and races were Glazer and Moynihan probably referring to? Do you feel this statement is true? Why, or why not? (3) "The American nationality is still forming: its processes are mysterious, and the final form is as yet unknown." Ask: What traits would you cite to describe the "average" American? Would a European cite the same traits? Could there ever be such a thing as a truly American ethnic group (besides the Indians)?

back prepaid tickets instead of money. Probably a third or more of all who emigrated in the 1830s went in this way.

One writer has observed that at the beginning of the 1800s the idea of moving from one country to another across the ocean "would have been unimaginable to any but the boldest," but that by the end of the 1800s millions were accustomed to the idea. Certainly one reason for this was the great amount of information that people had received. Another was the sharp drop in the cost of travel to America. In 1816 it cost a passenger twelve English pounds to go from England to the United States. Thirty years later the fare had dropped to just three pounds. To go from Ireland to Quebec, Canada, in the 1820s cost only one tenth as much as it had in 1810. The fare from Ireland to Boston fell almost as much.

The hardships of travel. The voyage to America was hardly a pleasure trip, even though it was not as risky as it had been in colonial times. The crossing on sailing ships lasted anywhere from one month to three months, depending on wind and weather. An average trip took forty-four days.

Ships were designed to carry freight, not passengers, a fact of which the passengers had daily reminders. Fifty bunks, all crowded into one huge, airless room belowdecks, had to do for 250 or more passengers. The immigrants often had to provide their own food and prepare it. Sometimes food could be obtained from the ship's captain, but at high prices.

Again we have letters of immigrants to describe conditions.

> First I want to warn all those of you who are planning to undertake the journey to America to make contracts with the shipper with whom you are emigrating. You must insist that you be given at least three quarts of water a day. We got no more than one pint and almost died of thirst. It was not very good water either, for it tasted and smelled so bad that we had to throw it up. . . .
>
> I and the people with me went by freighter and were underway for more than a month, and we suffered great misery. We neither had room to sit down nor stand up. We felt like so many pigs stowed together . . . . In the galley there was a large stove, but as there were always a lot of people who wanted to cook, the only law that prevailed here was club law. The strongest and most aggressive could always . . . get something cooked, while the weaker and more timid got nothing or had to content themselves with being the last in line. . . . Fights and quarrels were daily occurrences. . . . The crossing was terrible. Three days after we had left land, we had a frightful storm . . . Many of the berths on the lower deck collapsed.

A new life. Where did the newcomers settle? What kind of work did they do? What was their life like in America? Answers differ from one group to another, and even among members of the same group. Because they traveled on a freighter, immigrants had no choice but to go to the freighter's regular port.

Most freighters docked in the ports of New York, Philadelphia, Boston, and Baltimore, and those East Coast cities are where most immigrants landed. Norwegians and Swedes tended to move directly on. They looked for good farming country with a climate not too different from that of their homeland. Many settled in Wisconsin, Iowa, Minnesota, and Illinois. Later in the century they moved on to Kansas, Nebraska, and the Dakotas.

Some freighters did dock at other ports. Immigrants who left Europe from the French port of Le Havre, for example, probably landed in New Orleans. That is the route most Germans followed. From New Orleans they made their way up the Mississippi River and carved out farms or moved to the young cities in the Mississippi Valley. So more than half the Germans who came between 1815 and 1860 settled in the states of Ohio, Illinois, Wisconsin, and Missouri. Others scattered from New York to Texas.

Where immigrants settled was often determined by the occupation skills—or the lack of them—they brought from Europe. A Welsh miner would head for the coal mines of eastern Pennsylvania. A British textile worker would go whereever cottons, woolens, and carpeting were manufactured. And of course, like attracted like: immigrants tended to go where relatives, friends, and others from the old country were already living. Thus some counties in Illinois or Wisconsin came to have large clusters of Germans. Others had mainly Swedes or Norwegians.

The attraction of the cities. The great majority of immigrants remained in the cities. That may seem surprising, for to many of them the promise of America was plentiful land and a good life in farming. Of course, many hundreds of thousands did move on to the land throughout the North and Midwest. But there were several reasons why most

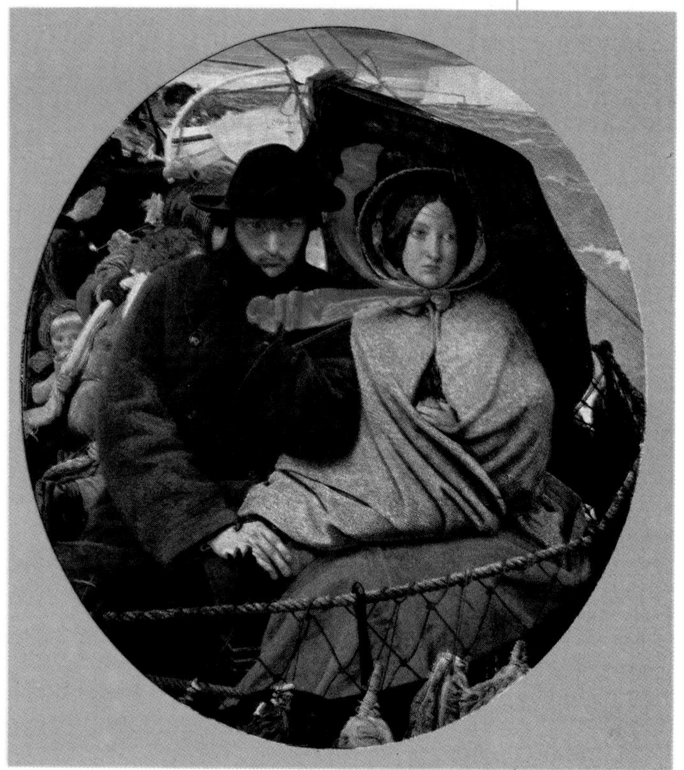

A young couple bound for a new life in America watch the coast of England disappear as their ship heads out into the Atlantic. They know that they may never again see the land of their birth.

immigrants became city dwellers. About 20 percent of those who came before the year 1860 were skilled workers—cabinetmakers, tailors, bookbinders, textile workers, and so on. Most of those people found the greatest demand for their services in the cities.

Of the unskilled immigrants, most were far too poor when they arrived to buy a farm. They had to find work quickly, and this they could do in the cities. With nothing to sell but their

9. WHAT IF? What if the recent revival of ethnic awareness intensifies? What consequences would this type of action have on America? What conditions could advance such a revival? What conditions would work against such a revival?

10. GUEST SPEAKER Perhaps you could arrange for the mayor or another official of your community to speak to the class about the effect, if any, of ethnicity upon local politics. In preparation for the talk, ask several students to visit the local library and ask the librarian for any available statistics detailing the ethnic background of your town or city. These findings could be organized in tabular or graph form and distributed to the class before the guest speaker's talk on local politics.

Background Information

2. PROFESSIONAL READING You might wish to obtain the following books for a classroom loan during this unit or for your own personal reading. All were written or edited by Oscar Handlin, an internationally known historian specializing in American history and immigration. Born of Russian immigrant parents in New York, Handlin studied at Brooklyn College and at Harvard University. Handlin's books applicable to this unit include *The Uprooted* (New York: Grosset & Dunlop Publishers, 1951); *Immigration as a Factor in American History* (Englewood Cliffs, N.J.: Prentice-Hall, Inc., 1959); and *A Pictorial History of Immigration* (New York: Crown Publishers, Inc., 1972). The bibliography in the last book mentioned lists a great number of other books suitable as background material for this unit.

muscles, they took whatever work they could get at whatever pay was offered.

They worked as street cleaners, porters, waiters, dock workers, stable cleaners, ditchdiggers. Their jobs required muscle power and wearying hours of labor. According to the New York State Census of 1855, there were 20,000 such jobs in New York City. More than 19,500 of them were held by immigrants. Domestic work—that of a maid or housecleaner—was another kind of job open to unskilled immigrants, especially women. Before long, most domestics were immigrants.

The poorest and least skilled of all were the Irish. In Boston in 1860, two of every three domestic workers, and more than one of every two common laborers, were Irish. Half of all New York City's Irish in 1855 were employed as domestics or unskilled laborers. In Boston the proportion was two thirds.

Irishmen who found it difficult to get even such jobs as those in the cities hired out to work on railroad, canal, and other construction projects in the South and West. In later years, Chinese, Mexicans, and Italians also provided the muscle power that built America's railroads, but before 1860 most of that work was performed by the Irish. Leaving families behind in the cities for months at a time, Irishmen worked and lived under harsh conditions in labor camps hundreds of miles away.

When the lines of the Central Pacific Railroad were built soon after the Civil War, Chinese laborers constructed the roadbed and laid the tracks through mountain passes and deserts.

European immigrants come ashore at Castle Garden. This island at the southern tip of New York City was an immigration station from 1855 to 1890. Landfill later tied the island to the city.

11. DISCUSSION America has received a larger number of immigrants than any other country in history. These immigrant groups were (and are) composed of people of different races, religions, cultures, languages, and creeds. Divide your class into groups of four or five students. Ask each group to list several reasons why there has been no widespread fighting between these groups in America. Compare the various lists after the small-group discussions.

It was not the Irish alone who filled America's cities. French Canadians moved into the mill towns of New England. Large numbers of Germans settled in New York, Cincinnati, Milwaukee, and St. Louis. In fact, the Germans were the largest single immigrant group in each of those cities. English were scattered among a number of cities. Only among the Swedish and Norwegian immigrants did less than half settle in cities.

City housing. What were living conditions like for immigrants in American cities? Investigators for the state of New York have given a description of the housing that Irish-born residents lived in in New York City. The house they describe here was at 16 Washington Street.

This is a three-story building . . . accessible through a narrow door and steep stairway, ascending over a stable wherein an express company's horses are kept. The dilapidation of this entire building is extreme; its rickety floors shook under the tread, and portions of the wall, black and mildewed, were continually breaking off. . . . A poor woman who occupied an apartment on the second floor complained, . . . "The ould ceiling . . . is ould as meself, and its full uv the *dhrop* it is," i.e., it was soaked with water that entered through the broken roof whenever it rained; . . . in wet weather the upper floors of this ruinous habitation were completely flooded, and the poor occupants were obliged to move their drenched beds from spot to spot. . . . In the rear of this building was another of the same height. . . . The number of tenants in both houses was reported as seventy, all Irish. . . . In one of the rooms of the front

Answers To Review Questions

1. America **(a)** is a nation of immigrants, **(b)** has a great variety of nationality groups, and **(c)** has witnessed few ethnic conflicts.
2. Americans vote for ethnic candidates, display bumper stickers, and identify with ethnic characters and situations in novels, in movies, and on television.
3. English, German, and Scotch-Irish settled in large numbers, but there were also smaller numbers of many other ethnic groups, including Dutch, French, Swiss, and Jewish.
4. Huge increase in population; shortage of farmland; famine; industrialization, which caused skilled workers to lose jobs; poverty.
5. Books and newspaper articles favorable to America; the American Letters; money sent by relatives in America.

house, an apartment six by ten feet in area, a widow lived with five children.

Compare the description of life in America, above, with the descriptions in the immigrants' letters you read earlier. How can one explain the differences? Is it possible that both views are accurate?

A vote for America. In view of the description above, one might think immigrants were unhappy with life in America. No doubt some were. But not all immigrants—not even all the immigrants in big cities—lived in these conditions. Those who came as skilled workers had few problems in adjusting to American life. This was especially true of those who came from Great Britain. Such immigrants, not troubled by language differences, were quickly made to feel at home. They were paid as well as the local American skilled workers. Most were far better off than they had been in the old country. Furthermore, as the American Letters show, thousands who took up farming found a very satisfying life in America. For such persons, America truly was a land of opportunity. It was mostly the unskilled, crowded into cities, who sometimes had to live in discouraging conditions.

Few immigrants, however, had reason for long to regret their move, as they compared their new life with the one they had left behind. In America there was hope for the future, especially for their children. That was why immigrants saved and scrimped to bring their families over to join them. Each immigrant who purchased a boat ticket to send to a relative in the old country was casting a vote for America.

In the next chapter we shall see how the stream of immigration increased and, as the 1800s came to an end, how that stream was fed by a new source.

CHECKUP

1. What were the "push" factors that led people to leave their own countries for the United States?
2. What were the "pull" factors?
3. How did life in America differ for various immigrant groups?

Key Facts from Chapter 19

1. An ethnic group is one with a shared culture and a sense of identity based on common origin.
2. The United States—except for its American Indians—is a nation of immigrants, representing many ethnic groups.
3. There is today in America a growing ethnic awareness and pride.
4. Poverty, famine, lack of land, and lack of opportunity are among the "push" factors that have led people to leave their homelands for America.
5. Land, jobs, and the opportunity to carve out a better life for themselves and their children are among the "pull" factors that have brought immigrants to America.

★ REVIEWING THE CHAPTER ★

People, Places, and Events

Ethnic group *P. 396*
Ethnic diversity *P. 396*
Nationality *P. 396*
"Balanced ticket" *P. 397*
Ethnic pride *P. 397*
"Push" factor *P. 400*
Irish land problem *P. 402*
Irish potato famine *P. 403*
"Pull" factor *P. 403*
American Letters *P. 403*
American "fever" *P. 405*

Review Questions

1. What three points does Andrew Greeley make about America and its ethnic groups? *P. 396* Les. 1
2. What are some of the ways in which Americans show their ethnic pride? *P. 397* Les. 1
3. What ethnic groups settled in the thirteen American colonies? Refer to the map on page 399. Les. 2
4. List some of the happenings in Europe that encouraged men and women to come to America in the eighteenth and nineteenth centuries. *P. 401–402* Les. 3
5. Discuss the "pull" factors that attracted people to America. *P. 403* Les. 3
6. Why did most immigrants settle in the cities? What kinds of work did they do? *Pp. 406–407* Les. 3
7. What were some of the problems that immigrants faced upon their arrival in America? *Pp. 407–410* Les. 3
8. Refer to the graph on page 400. Can you think of a reason why immigration declined in the years 1915–1919 and 1931–1945? Why did immigration begin to increase after 1945?

Chapter Test

*For each sentence, write the letter of the answer that is **not** true. Use a separate piece of paper.*

1. An ethnic group is one with a common **(a)** culture **(b)** nationality **(c)** occupation.
2. America is a nation of **(a)** immigrants **(b)** great ethnic variety **(c)** great ethnic conflict.
3. Americans show their ethnic pride by **(a)** voting for ethnic candidates **(b)** choosing a job **(c)** displaying bumper stickers.
4. During the colonial period, most immigrants were **(a)** Italian **(b)** English **(c)** German.
5. Some "push" factors that have caused people to leave their homelands for America include **(a)** shortage of land **(b)** loss of jobs **(c)** epidemics.
6. Some "pull" factors that have brought people to America include opportunities for **(a)** travel by freighter **(b)** farmland **(c)** employment.
7. American "fever" was caused by **(a)** mosquitoes **(b)** favorable newspaper articles **(c)** letters written by people in America.
8. Immigrants tended to settle where **(a)** they could find employment or best use their job skills **(b)** good housing was available **(c)** relatives and friends were living.
9. In America, most immigrants found **(a)** wealth and riches **(b)** hope for the future **(c)** a satisfying life.
10. The graph on page 400 shows immigration increasing during the following periods: **(a)** 1842–1854 **(b)** 1854–1862 **(c)** 1900–1907.

6. Freighters on which immigrants traveled to America usually docked in the ports of major cities (New York, Boston, Philadelphia, Baltimore, New Orleans). Although some immigrants moved on immediately in search of good farming country, most remained in the cities for a variety of reasons: not enough money to purchase farmland; desire to join relatives and friends already living in the cities; employment opportunities for both skilled and unskilled workers. Those with job skills worked as cabinetmakers, tailors, bookbinders, textile workers, and so on. Unskilled workers toiled as street cleaners, porters, dock workers, waiters, ditchdiggers, stable cleaners, maids or housecleaners.
7. Many immigrants arrived in poverty and were forced to settle in slum areas. Others were discriminated against because they didn't speak English and had different customs. The kinds of jobs available to the many unskilled immigrants were usually low-paying and physically demanding.
8. Immigration declined during those years because of World War I and, later, the rise of Hitler in Europe and World War II. Immigration began to increase after World War II ended, in 1945.

Answers for Chapter Test
1. c **2.** c **3.** b **4.** a **5.** c
6. a **7.** a **8.** b **9.** a **10.** b

Background Information

1. CLEARING PROCEDURE ON ELLIS ISLAND In this picture, taken around the turn of the century, a public nurse on Ellis Island is administering an intelligence test to a young immigrant couple. This was only one of the examinations that were administered to would-be immigrants before they were allowed entry into the United States.

Beginning in 1892, immigrants were assigned a number while they were still aboard the ship, before a barge or ferry carried them to Ellis Island. Inspectors called out numbers in German, Italian, Polish, Russian, Yiddish, and other languages. Once the immigrants were organized into small groups, the clearance procedure began. Doctors quickly evaluated the health of the immigrants. An "H" chalked on an immigrant's back referred to suspicion of heart disease; an "L" referred to a limp associated with rickets or other deficiency disease.

Two feared symbols were a circle with a cross in the middle, which referred to feeblemindedness, and an "E," which which referred to trachoma, a disease common among southern and eastern Europeans. Deportation was certain for any who wore these symbols.

The final ordeal was a series of questions from an immigration inspector. Those who survived the clearing process then changed their money into dollars at the currency booth. Those bound for places inland met a railroad agent or a ticket agent. Those planning to stay in New York might have met relatives, representatives from an immigrant aid society, or politicians looking for a vote.

CHAPTER 20

IMMIGRATION–OLD AND NEW

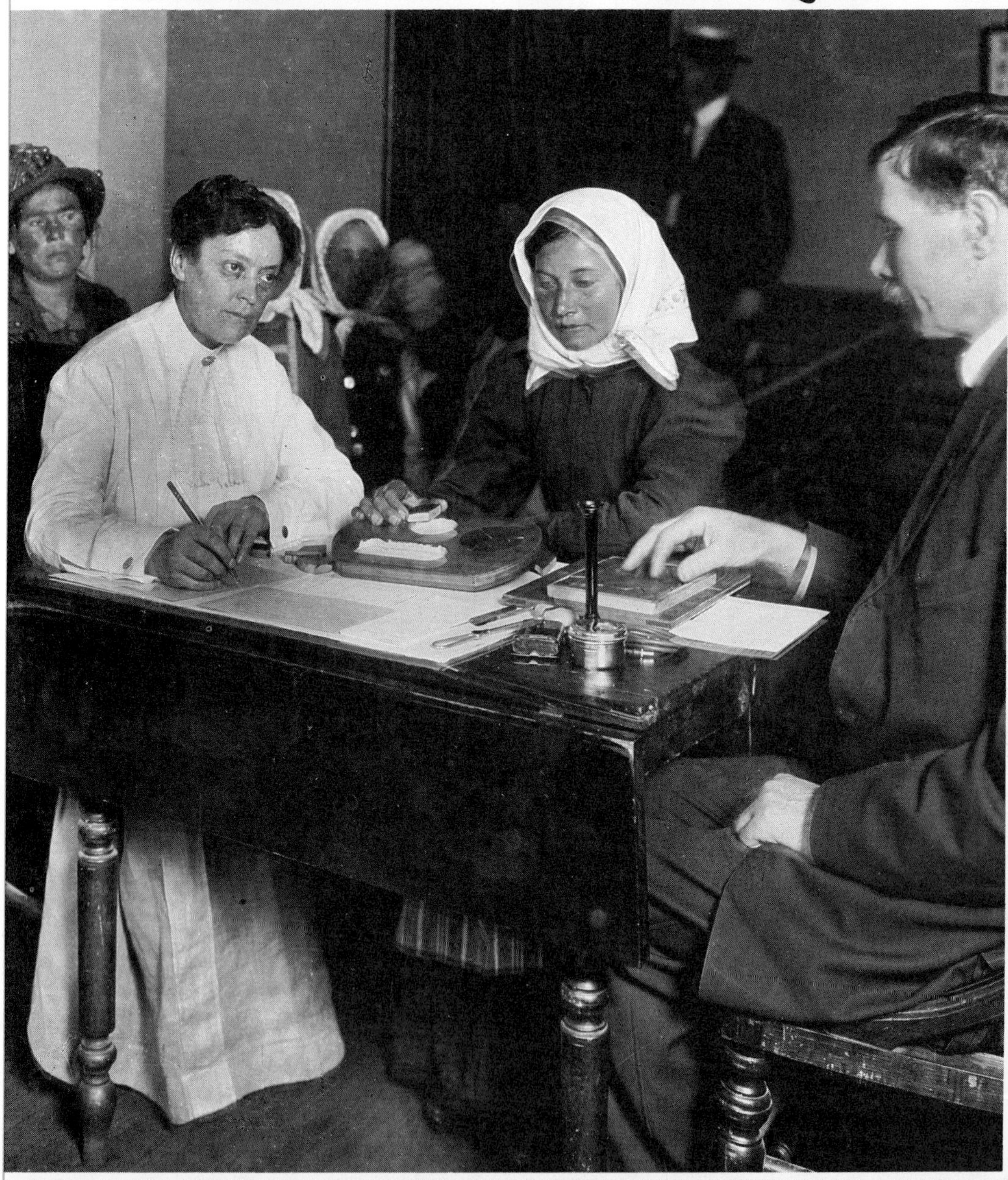

LESSON 1

LOOK AT THE GRAPH on page 400. What happened to the rate of immigration between the years 1855 and 1865? Can you account for this change? The time line on the first page of this unit will help you answer this question.

By the mid-1860s, immigration had picked up once again. Then it declined briefly when the United States went through a severe depression in the mid-1870s, but recovered along with the economy a few years later.

As the graph shows, immigration reached a peak in 1882. Most of the immigrants that year were from the same countries as before. The number from Britain and Ireland—179,000—was down somewhat from the desperate years of the potato famine. But the 105,000 who came from Sweden, Norway, and Denmark were more than had ever before or have ever since come from those countries in a single year. The same was true of the 250,000 who came from Germany.

The reasons these people came were much the same reasons that had influenced the immigrants from their countries thirty or forty years earlier. Hard times for farmers, especially in Germany, provided much of the push. Visions of a good life, derived from newspapers, books, and letters, provided most of the pull. From city dwellers came word of good wages. From farmers came stories of richer soil, bigger crops, creamier milk. Ordinary people could relate to letters like the one Johann Schmitz sent to his brother in 1890: ". . . this is a free land. No one can give orders to anybody here, one is as good as another, no one takes off his hat to another as you have to do in Germany."

Emigrants who returned to the old village, whether for a visit or to stay, were another source of information about the New World. One can imagine the impression made by these returning heroes. Sporting the signs of unmistakable prosperity, they reported on the land of plenty to gatherings of eager listeners—and maybe for effect embroidered on the truth a bit.

Railroads and steamships. There were two additional pull factors, both having to do with advertising. One was the effort of railroad companies to attract immigrants to the thinly settled areas of the Midwest and Far West, where they had built their lines. On page 414 is a poster typical of the thousands the railroads distributed in European towns and cities. Why is the railroad trying to attract settlers? What promises does the railroad make to attract them?

Such advertising paid off handsomely. Many thousands did settle along the lines of this railroad in Wisconsin, Minnesota, and Iowa.

The second new pull factor was the advertising carried out by western states in several European nations. Here is a section from an advertising pamphlet.

> Those who are restless in their old homes, or who seek to better their condition, will find greater advantages in Colorado than anywhere else in the West. Our mining resources offer inducements which no state

LESSON 1 *(2 to 3 days)*

Performance Objectives

1. To offer evidence to support the following statement: Technological advances and advertising techniques influenced the New Immigration. **2.** To formulate three generalizations based on the information presented in the tables entitled "Immigration from Southern and Eastern Europe" and "Immigration from Northern and Western Europe." **3.** To list the national groups included in the New Immigration and the reasons why they emigrated. **4.** To explain the interrelationship between immigration and urbanization during the late nineteenth century.

Vocabulary

Old Immigration, New Immigration, hectare, Austro-Hungarian Empire, Magyars, excise duty, czar, kopek, "pogrom"

Activities

1. GUEST SPEAKER To motivate your students perhaps you could arrange for a talk by a person in your community who emigrated from southern or eastern Europe. Points to include in such a talk might be **(a)** reasons for coming to America, **(b)** the journey across the Atlantic, and **(c)** problems involved with adjusting to American society.

2. FILM Another possible motivational activity is the viewing of the film *The Huddled Masses* (52 minutes, color; BBC-TV and Time-Life Films), which is Part 9 of the series America: A Personal History of the United States. The film, adapted from Alistair Cooke's book *America,* may be rented from Time-Life Films Multimedia Division, 100 Eisenhower Dr., Paramus, N.J. 07652. The film centers on the turn-of-the-century immigration, with views of Ellis Island, ships' holds, New York's Lower East Side, and garment factory sweatshops.

3. DISCUSSION/ADVERTISING BROCHURES After your students have read this lesson, ask them to cite evidence in support of the idea that technological advances and advertising techniques influenced the New Immigration. Then ask them to create advertising brochures aimed at attracting immigrants to your community today. Have them emphasize the positive aspects of your community. Photographs of scenery, industrial plants, schools, libraries, homes, town celebrations, etc., could enhance the brochures.

east of the mountains can present, and for stockmen and agriculturalists Colorado can make a better exhibit than any other region. The climate possesses peculiar charms and those in failing health, or invalids, can find here a sure panacea for nearly every human ill. The poor should come to Colorado, because here they can by industry and frugality better their condition. The rich should come here, because they can more advantageously invest their means than in any other region. The young should come here to get an early start on the road to wealth, and the old should come to get a new lease on life, and to enjoy their declining years in a country unequalled for its natural beauty and loveliness. In short, it is the Mecca for all classes and all conditions, and we confidently recommend it to the thoughtful examination of the public.

Posters like this one, distributed by railroads, induced many Europeans to come to America.

"To the West, to the West, to the Land of the Free."

EMIGRATION

TO

IOWA and NEBRASKA, U.S.

The next Colony will leave Rochdale for Lincoln Nebraska, on Wednesday, June 28th, 1871.

The Burlington and Missouri River Railroad Company will provide the Colony with Through Tickets from Liverpool to Lincoln, at the following Rates:

					£	s.	d.
Steerage on Steamer and 3rd class Railway				....	11	11	0
Ditto	Ditto	1st	Ditto	....	15	2	5
Intermediate	Ditto	1st	Ditto	....	18	5	5
Cabin	Ditto	1st	Ditto	....	24	11	5

A Guide will be furnished to accompany the Party from the Landing Port to their Destination, and every arrangement will be made for the care and comfort of the Colony, until they are finally settled in their New Home.

HOMES FOR ALL!

More Farms than Farmers! More Landlords than Tenants!

WORK FOR ALL WORKERS!

2,000,000 Acres of LAND for SALE

At from Four to Fifteen Dollars per Acre, on Ten Years' Credit, and only charged Six per Cent. Interest.

Those intending to join the Colony, should apply to the undersigned at once for full information and Copy of the Guide to Iowa and Nebraska.

ASHWORTH & PARKER,

2, River-Street, Rochdale; and 4, Corporation-Street, Manchester,

Agents to the Burlington & Missouri River Railroad Company.

JOHN TURNER, PRINTER, DRAKE-STREET, ROCHDALE.

At the same time, the development of the ocean steamship made the Atlantic crossing much faster. Because these steamships were designed to carry passengers, the trip was also more comfortable. Instead of an average voyage of forty-four days under sail, the steamer had by 1867 cut the trip to less than two weeks. Thirty years later the trip was down to five and a half days. Because of these advantages, steamships took over the passenger business from sailing ships. In 1856, 96 percent of all immigrants landing in New York came by sail. By 1873, the situation was reversed: 96 percent of the immigrants landing in New York arrived on steamers.

The New Immigration

Return once more to the graph, page 400. What does it tell you about the rate of immigration in the years 1880 to 1914? The chief reason for what you see is that beginning in the 1870s and increasing each year, the stream of immigration was fed by a new source. Immigrants began to come from countries in southern and eastern Europe. Barely a trickle before the 1870s, immigration from this region thickened to a steady stream in the 1880s and 1890s, and became a flood in the early 1900s. This came to be called the New Immigration. Those who had come earlier from northern and western Europe were referred to as the Old Immigration.

Immigration from Southern and Eastern Europe

Country	1861–1870	1871–1880	1881–1890	1891–1900	1901–1910
Italy	11,725	55,759	307,309	651,893	2,045,877
Greece	72	210	2,308	15,979	167,519
Russia	2,512	39,284	213,282	505,290	1,597,306
Romania	—	11	6,348	12,750	53,008
Austria-Hungary	7,800	72,969	353,719	592,707	2,145,266

Immigration from Northern and Western Europe

Country	1861–1870	1871–1880	1881–1890	1891–1900	1901–1910
France	35,986	72,206	50,464	30,770	73,379
Ireland	435,778	436,871	655,482	388,416	339,065
Germany	787,468	718,182	1,452,970	505,152	341,498
Norway	71,631	95,323	176,586	95,015	190,505
England	222,277	437,706	644,680	216,726	388,017

The tables on this page tell much of the story of those years. Compare the numbers of the New Immigration with the numbers who came from northern and western European countries during those same years.

What general statements about the sources of immigration can you make from these tables?

In addition to the Europeans, there were perhaps 100,000 people who came to the United States from Japan in these years. Most lived in the West, as did the 300,000 Chinese who had entered the United States by the 1880s. Thousands of other aliens moved across the borders from the neighboring countries of Mexico and Canada. Six times between 1900 and 1914, immigration topped one million a year. The average annual immigration during that stretch was almost 900,000.

From eastern and southern Europe. Many of the same push factors that affected northern and western Europe in the first half of the nineteenth century hit eastern and southern Europe in the second half. Population increased, but with no more land to go around, farms were divided into smaller plots. In one eastern European country just before the turn of the century, half the landholders had plots no larger than seven

4. USING TABLES The tables on page 415 tell much about the patterns of immigration between the years 1860–1910. Have students compare the information presented in the tables and formulate three general statements about the sources of immigration. Then list on the chalkboard those generalizations that are valid. In discussion, be sure students can distinguish between the Old Immigration and the New Immigration.

Background Information

2. POLISH IMMIGRATION The table entitled "Immigration from Southern and Eastern Europe" on page 415 does not list Poland as a source of U.S. immigrants, but large numbers of Polish immigrants came to America between 1899 and 1919. During that period, Poland was not an independent nation; it had been divided among the Austro-Hungarian Empire, Russia, and Prussia (later part of Germany). For that reason, it is difficult to estimate the number of Polish immigrants, since they were counted among the immigrants from Austria-Hungary, Russia, or Germany.

5. RESEARCH/ORAL REPORTS Have several of your students research German history to determine why the period between 1881 and 1890 was the greatest period for German immigration. Encourage students to include the rapid growth of industrialism and a working class, the rising belief in socialism among the German people, and the antisocialist and anti-Catholic policies of Chancellor Bismarck.

acres (2.8 ha). Such a farm plot was far smaller than was needed to produce a decent living. In Italy, Greece, Hungary, and other countries in the region, millions could no longer make a living on the land. Since many had to leave their homes anyway, they decided to try their luck in America.

In certain countries and for certain groups, special factors added to the push of emigration. Eastern Europe was a hodgepodge of nationalities. Czechs,

In 1907, the United States admitted the record number of 1,285,349 immigrants. About 93 percent of this total came from Europe. Economic conditions and persecution were among the reasons for immigration at that time. The country supplying the largest number of immigrants in 1907 was Austria-Hungary, with ten or more nationality groups. After Austria-Hungary came Italy and Russia.

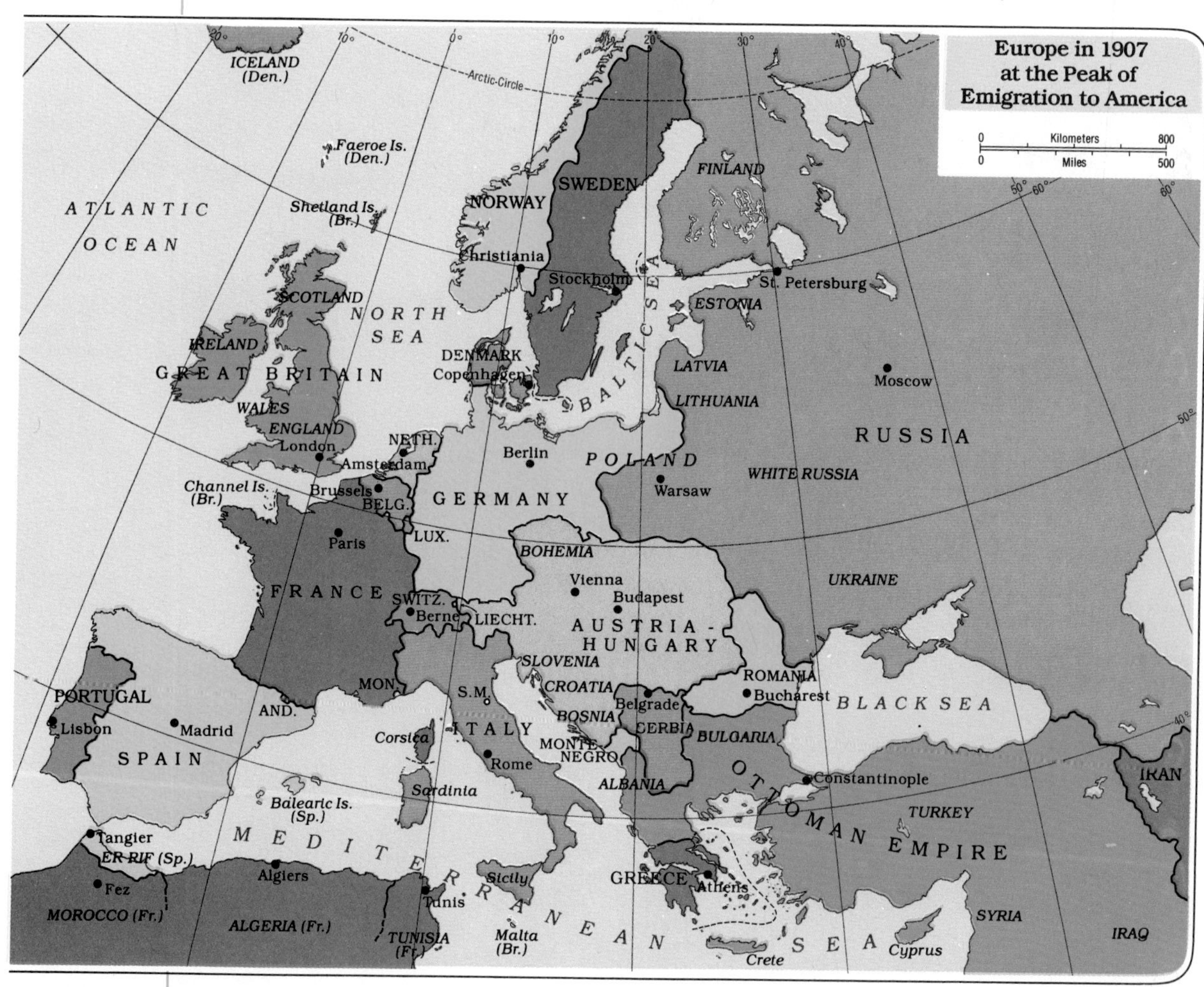

Slovaks, Croatians, Serbs, and a half-dozen others found themselves living under the rule of the Austro-Hungarian Empire. The dominant people of the eastern half of that empire were called Magyars. What this could mean to a member of another nationality group in that region was described by Emily Balch in 1910.

> Then came the unhappy decision to give a forced monopoly in pulpit, schools, courts of justice, and so far as possible in daily life, to the Magyar language. . . .
>
> In Hungary to take a Slovak newspaper, or if an educated man, to speak the Slovak tongue, is to brand oneself in Magyar eyes as a political traitor, and to insure every possible obstacle in one's path. The upper schools . . . , formerly conducted in Slovak and founded and supported by private contributions, have been closed.
>
> . . . the Slovak literary association has been dissolved and its building seized. It is almost impossible for a company of Slovak shareholders to receive the necessary permission to carry on business even, since the undertaking is considered a nationalistic enterprise.
>
> . . . Even to study for the priesthood a Slovak must pass through the Magyar seminary, and there any study of the language of the future flock is treated as ground for expulsion.

What does Emily Balch see as the main reasons why Slovaks might want to leave their country?

Life under the czars. Throughout eastern and southern Europe, people felt the heavy hand of government. Nowhere was it heavier than in Russia. Two passages from the autobiography of a Russian immigrant named Mary Antin tell us what it was like to live there.

> It was bewildering to hear how many kinds of duties and taxes we owed the Czar. We paid taxes on our houses, taxes on our business, taxes on our profits. I am not sure whether there were taxes on our losses. The town collected taxes, and the county, and the central government; and the chief of police we always had with us. There were taxes for public works, but rotten pavements went on rotting year after year; and when a bridge was to be built, special taxes were levied. . . .
>
> My uncle explained to me all about the excise duties on tobacco. Tobacco being a source of government revenue, there was a heavy tax on it. Cigarettes were taxed at every step of their process. The tobacco was taxed separately, and the paper, and the mouthpiece, and on the finished product an additional tax was put. There was no tax on the smoke. The Czar must have overlooked it.
>
> . . . .
>
> In your father's parlor hung a large colored portrait of Alexander III. The Czar was a cruel tyrant . . . and yet his portrait was seen in a place of honor in your father's house. You knew why. It looked well when police or government officers came on business.
>
> You went out to play one morning, and saw a little knot of people gathered around a lamp-post. There was a notice on it—a new order from the chief of police. You pushed into the crowd, and stared at the placard, but you could not read. A woman with a ragged shawl looked down upon you, and said, with a bitter kind of smile, "Rejoice, rejoice, little girl! The chief of police bids you rejoice. There shall be a pretty flag flying from every house-top today, because it is the Czar's birthday, and we must celebrate. Come and watch the poor people pawn their samovars [vessels used to boil water for tea] and candlesticks, to raise money for a pretty flag. It is a holiday, little girl. Rejoice."

6. PICTURE ANALYSIS Using pictures in this unit, ask students to describe the immigrant's lifestyle in his or her new homeland. What can one learn about the immigrant experience from picture sources? Then share with the class the information and pictures about immigrants and cities in the late nineteenth century in the following two books. You will find appropriate chapters in *This Fabulous Century, 1870–1900* (New York: Time-Life Books, 1970) and *The Nineties* by the editors of American Heritage (New York: American Heritage Publishing Co., Inc., 1967). In the Time-Life book, the chapter entitled "The City" (pages 218–245) presents many photographs of the major urban areas in the late nineteenth century. "Chicago" by Robert S. Gallagher in *The Nineties* (pages 12–29) describes the Windy City of the 1890s with text and photographs.

7. **THOUGHT PROVOKER** American humorist Robert Benchley (grandfather of the author of *Jaws*) once remarked, "We call England the Mother Country because most of us came from Poland or Italy." Ask: What did Benchley mean by this remark? Although the remark was made in jest, does it have any truth in it? What examples of characteristics of American society can students offer to prove or disprove Benchley's statement?

8. **WHAT IF?** What if the rate of unemployment became so high in the United States that many Americans had to consider emigrating to another country? Ask: What country would you choose? What are your reasons for your choice? What difficulties do you believe you would encounter in a new country?

9. **USING A GRAPH** Ask your students to study the pie graphs "Foreign-born in Four Cities in 1910" on page 419. Then ask: Which city had the highest percentage of immigrants in 1910? Why? What part did geography play in determining the total percentages of foreign-born in these four cities? Which city had the highest percentage of immigrants from eastern and southern Europe? Why? Why were a considerable number of Irish located in all cities except Minneapolis? What group of foreign-born is represented in all cities? Mention to your students that Germany was the largest single source of immigration to the United States between 1820 and 1972—6,933,000 Germans immigrated during that period.

You might like to have your students make a pie graph showing the ethnic backgrounds of the class members.

> You know the woman is mocking—you are familiar with the quality of that smile—but you accept the hint and go and watch the people buy their flags. . . . One customer puts down a few kopecks on the counter, saying, "Give me a piece of flag. This is all the money I have. Give me the red and the blue; I'll tear up my shirt for the white." You know it is no joke. The flag must show from every house, or the owner will be dragged to the police station, to pay a fine of twenty-five rubles.

Plight of the Russian Jews. Jews had a special reason to leave Russia. They were restricted to certain parts of the country by order of the government. They were also prohibited from working in industry, agriculture, and the professions. Only a small quota were allowed to enter the universities. And there was still another kind of persecution.

> [In] the Passover season, when we celebrated our deliverance from the land of Egypt, and felt so glad and thankful as if it had only just happened, was the time our Gentile [non-Jewish] neighbors chose to remind us that Russia was another Egypt. . . . Somebody would start up that lie about murdering Christian children, and the stupid peasants would get mad about it, and fill themselves with vodka, and set out to kill the Jews. They attacked them with knives and clubs and scythes and axes, killed them or tortured them, and burned their houses. This was called a "pogrom." Jews who escaped the pogroms came to Polotzk [the town in which the writer lived] with wounds on them, and horrible, horrible stories, of little babies torn limb from limb before their mother's eyes. Only to hear these things made one sob and sob and choke with pain. People who saw such things never smiled any more, no matter how long they lived; and sometimes their hair turned white in a day, and some people became insane on the spot.

In the face of such treatment, it is not hard to understand why, of the two million Jews who poured into America in the New Immigration, 70 percent were from Russia.

The promise of the cities. Like the people of the Old Immigration, these new Americans settled in every part of the country, though only a few went to the South. The greater part of them stayed in the Northeast—mostly in New York, Pennsylvania, New Jersey, and southern New England. Also, like those of the Old Immigration, most lived in cities and for much the same reasons. Without money or job skills, they needed work on arrival, and it was in the cities that jobs could be found.

Of those who entered America through the port of New York in the years 1908–1910, three fourths gave "joining relatives" as their reason for coming; and it was in the city that their relatives lived. About half of the new immigrants, in fact, had their passage to America paid by these American relatives. Finally, unlike earlier immigrants, most of the new immigrants never expected to be farmers in America. It was not the promise of land in the country but of jobs in the city that had drawn this new wave of immigrants to the Land of Opportunity.

As you have seen, most large cities already had a distinctively foreign flavor. The New Immigration added a babel of new languages, and new customs, dress, and tastes. The graphs on page 419 show the number and percentage

The Foreign-born in Four Cities 1910

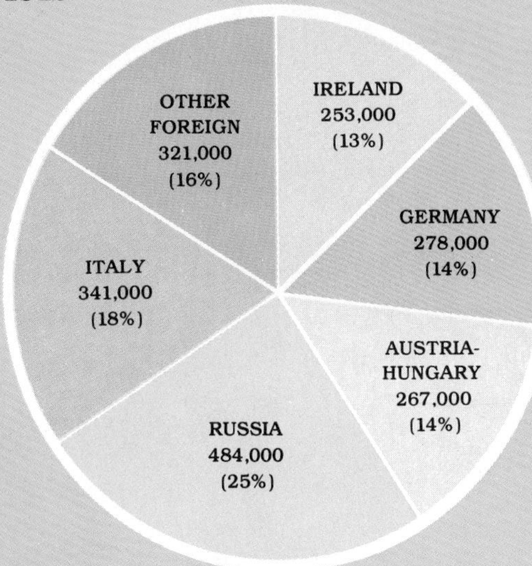

NEW YORK CITY
1,944,000 foreign-born,
(40% of 4,767,000)

IRELAND 66,000 (8%)
OTHER FOREIGN 189,000 (24%)
GERMANY 182,000 (23%)
RUSSIA 122,000 (16%)
SWEDEN 63,000 (8%)
AUSTRIA-HUNGARY 161,000 (21%)

CHICAGO
783,000 foreign-born,
(36% of 2,185,000)

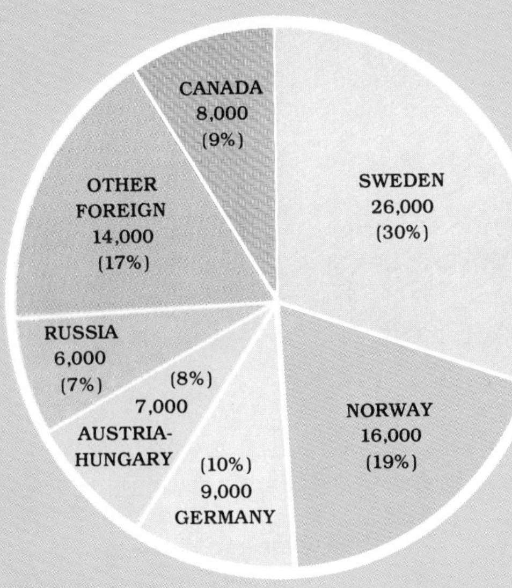

MINNEAPOLIS
86,000 foreign-born,
(29% of 301,000)

GERMANY 24,000 (17%)
OTHER FOREIGN 61,000 (43%)
ITALY 17,000 (12%)
IRELAND 23,000 (16%)
(5%) 7,000 CHINA
(7%) 10,000 ENGLAND

SAN FRANCISCO
142,000 foreign-born,
(34% of 417,000)

Charles R. Clark, Chicago Historical Society

Street markets, like this one in Chicago at about 1906, were common sights in the ethnic neighborhoods of big cities. At such markets, buyers could find everything from vegetables to clothing.

of the foreign-born in several cities in 1910. If one adds to them the second generation—that is, the children of the immigrants—one gets some startling figures. By 1910, immigrants and their children made up three fourths of the population of New York, Chicago, Detroit, Cleveland, and Boston. They made up more than half the population of another half-dozen large cities. In 1916, 72 percent of San Franciscans spoke a foreign language. It is, in fact, one of the great ironies of American life that the rapid urban growth of the late nineteenth century was mainly the product of European peasants.

CHECKUP

1. From what areas did most of the Old Immigration and most of the New Immigration come?
2. What were some of the conditions in their homelands that induced Slovaks and Russians to come to America?
3. In what geographical regions of the United States did most of the new immigrants settle? Did they settle more in rural areas or in the cities?

Background Information

3. SAN FRANCISCO POPULATION IN 1910 In 1910 more than a third of the population of San Francisco was foreign-born, as the pie graph on page 419 shows. The 61,000 people represented by "Other foreign" included people from the following countries: Austria-Hungary, 4,500; Canada, 6,000; Denmark, 3,000; Finland, 2,000; France, 6,000; Greece, 2,000; Norway, 4,000; Russia, 4,500; Scotland, 3,500; Sweden, 7,000; and Switzerland, 2,500. The remaining 16,000 were from many other groups.

Perhaps several of your students might create a pie graph of the total population of San Francisco in 1910 using these figures and those on the existing pie graph on page 419.

LESSON 2

Builders of Modern America

In his autobiography, Louis Adamic recalls talking with a man who had returned to live in his European village after a number of years in America. Pointing to a picture of New York, the man says:

> I—we helped to build these buildings—we Slovenians and Croatians and Slovaks and other people who went to America to work. We helped to build many other cities there, cities of which you have never heard, and railroads, and bridges, all made of steel which our people make in the mills. Our men from the Balkans are the best steelworkers in America. The framework of America is made of steel. And this smoke that you see here—it comes from coal that we have dug up; we from the Balkans and from Galicia and Bohemia. . . .

Then the man told of his last days in New York, as he walked the streets.

> I looked up, and can hardly describe my feelings. I realized that there was much of our work and strength, my own work and strength, frozen in the greatness of New York and in the greatness of America. I felt that, although I was going home to Blato [a village in Croatia, now a part of Yugoslavia] I was actually leaving myself in America.

Were feelings like these shared by other immigrants? Were this man's claims to a share in the building of modern America justified? You can test them by studying the chart on this page.

What does the chart tell us about the kinds of jobs the new immigrants held? and the kinds they did not hold? Can you make any generalizations about which kinds of jobs were open to most immigrants and which were not? Why, do you suppose, did immigrants hold few jobs in the categories near the top?

Percentage of Foreign-born Workers by Occupation, 1910

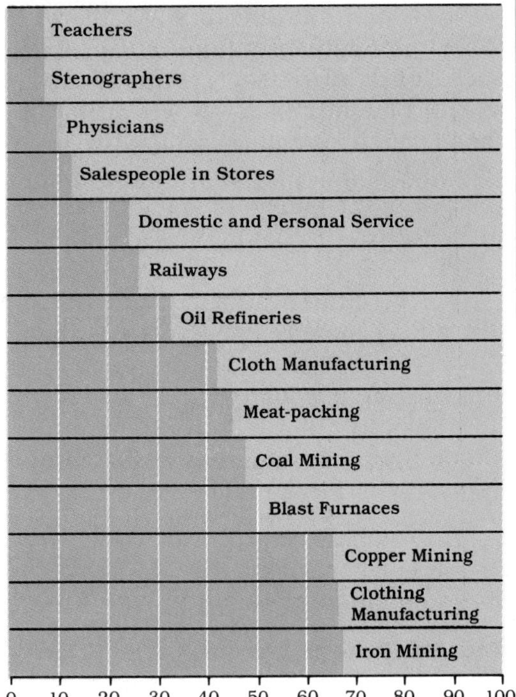

The hard jobs. It is clear that immigrants, and of course the descendants of black slaves, provided much of the physical labor that built modern America. One important reason why this was so is to be found in the age and sex distribution of immigrants. More than four fifths of all newcomers were between the ages of fourteen and forty-five, a person's most productive work years. Almost two thirds of them were male. Among some groups the percentage of males was higher: 78 percent of Italians, and 95 percent of Greeks, Chinese, and Japanese.

Why this high proportion of males? Many did not plan to stay in America.

LESSON 2 *(2 days)*

Performance Objectives

1. To demonstrate an ability to distinguish between fact and opinion by selecting three examples of facts and three examples of opinion from the primary source material in the lesson. **2.** To list at least three reasons why most immigrants were denied access to all but the lowest-paying jobs.

Vocabulary

Slovenian, Croatian, Slovak, Balkans, Galicia, Bohemia, Yugoslavia, "birds of passage," *padrone,* occupational ladder, "sweatshops"

Activities

1. ANALYZING SOURCE MATERIAL The ability to distinguish between fact and opinion is particularly useful to students when reading primary source materials. After your students have read the lesson, ask them to find three factual statements and three statements of opinion in the primary source material within the lesson.

2. RESEARCH/CREATIVE WRITING The low wages that accompanied employment in factories and mines and on railroad construction jobs in the late nineteenth century were further reduced by the competition among the oversupply of unskilled immigrant workers. The combination of low wages and the inevitable periodic layoffs made it impossible for most families to live on one salary. To make ends meet, many immigrant wives and children had to contribute to the family earnings.

Have your students gather information about the types of jobs that were available to immigrant women and children. Have each one choose an imaginary person and write a diary entry about one day's activities. The entry might include descriptions of **(a)** family members, **(b)** housing, **(c)** transportation to work (if not employed at home), **(d)** place of employment, and **(e)** employment activities.

3. RESEARCH/ORAL REPORTS Have several of your students report to the class on "The Padrone System," a report by the Industrial Commission on Immigration and Education that can be found on pages 403–409 in *The Annals of America,* Vol. 12 (Chicago: Encyclopaedia Britannica, Inc., 1968). The report describes the development of the padrone system and its status in 1901.

They came to work for a few years, save money, and return to the Old Country. About a third of the immigrants who came in the early twentieth century were such "birds of passage." Among those who did intend to stay, it was usual for the father and perhaps a son or two to go on ahead and earn enough to bring over the rest of the family. It sometimes took years to get the family under one roof again.

Wherever they worked, the new immigrants generally got the lowest-paid jobs. This newspaper advertisement for workers on a construction project in New York in 1895 tells you where one group of new immigrants stood in the job market as measured by wages per day.

Common labor, white, $1.30 to $1.50
Common labor, colored, $1.25 to $1.40
Common labor, Italian, $1.15 to $1.25

And the Italians got the hardest jobs, much as the Irish had a generation or two earlier. They worked in mines, in steel mills, and on track gangs laying railroad track in the West.

Laying track. One Italian immigrant has described work on a track gang. The man Fulvio in this account was a *padrone*. The padrone was the boss. In this case, he was a sort of labor contractor who secured workers for an employer, the railroad company. The padrone signed up immigrants, usually from his own country, to work and paid their wages from a sum of money given him by the employer. Whatever he didn't have to spend was his profit. It was to the benefit of the padrone to work his gang hard and pay the laborers little. In most cases, he did both.

On the morning of the first day our gang was divided in groups of ten and put under the supervision of a boss who was directly responsible to Fulvio and his associate contractors. The treatment for a week was tolerable, but as time wore away, Fulvio's henchman kept applying a pressure which increased almost in geometric ratio. From seven in the morning till seven in the evening you saw nothing, you heard nothing but picks and shovels, rising and falling in incessant monotone. Men sweated like sponges and melted like candles under the blazing sunheat and the ceaseless admonitions of the bosses to hurry up. Once a man stopped to fill his pipe and was severely reprimanded on the ground that he was wasting time.

One day we were laying some rails. Ordinarily six or eight men with tongs are employed to carry them. Fulvio insisted that four were sufficient. It was the most strenuous work and not without danger. As a huge rail was being moved, one man was borne down by the weight, and the rail fell on his partner, cutting his foot badly.

"Come, come, that is nothing," said the boss.

"Are we slaves, beasts, or men, sir?" inquired a man, his eyes flashing with anger.

"Whatever you like," replied Fulvio, brusquely. "If you don't like the job you may quit."

I saw a fearful struggle going on in the man's face. He quivered all over like a leaf. I heard him mutter, almost in an agony of prayer, "God, if I did not have a wife and children in Italy!" and with that he resumed his work with the patience and the resignation of a slave.

Grinding toil. Living conditions for new immigrants were as poor as they had been for the immigrants who had come a half-century earlier. Many immigrants lived in run-down, unhealthy surroundings in the cities.

Theodore Roosevelt, who would later become President of the United States, made a personal investigation of working and housing conditions among New York's new arrivals in the 1880s. The people he visited worked as cigar makers in their own homes. The impression of that visit was still clear in his mind when he wrote his autobiography thirty years later.

> I have always remembered one room in which two families were living. . . . There were several children, three men, and two women in this room. The tobacco was stowed about everywhere, alongside the foul bedding, and in a corner where there were scraps of food. The men, women, and children in this room worked by day and far on into the evening, and they slept and ate there. They were Bohemians, unable to speak English, except that one of the children knew enough to act as interpreter.

Up the ladder. Yet this harsh picture of city living, while accurate, is incomplete. For one thing, the employment of new immigrants in the hardest and lowest-paid jobs had an important effect on the old immigrants. Coal mining offers a good example. Where English, Welsh, Scotch, and Irish had dug the coal out of the mines of Pennsylvania, West Virginia, and Kentucky in the 1860s and 1870s, they were replaced

These Italian workers, photographed about 1905, are building one of the numerous tunnels that lie under New York City. Many Italian immigrants at that time found work on construction jobs.

4. DEBATE Resolved: The American economy profited from the New Immigrants. Ask several of your students to research this topic and present their facts and interpretations to the class in the form of a debate. Introduce your students to *Immigration as a Factor in American History* by Oscar Handlin (Englewood Cliffs, N.J.: Prentice-Hall, Inc., 1963). Chapter 3 of that book, entitled "The Economic Adjustment," has many articles that will familiarize your students with different points of view about the impact of immigration on the economy of the United States.

Background information

SOUTHERN ITALIAN IMMIGRANTS Daniel Moynihan and Nathan Glazer in *Beyond the Melting Pot* (Cambridge, Mass.: M.I.T. Press, 1970) report that 2,300,000 Italian immigrants came to the United States between 1899 and 1910. Almost 90 percent of those Italian immigrants were from southern Italy. Of those, less than one half of one percent were professionals and only 15 percent were skilled workers. Most of the remaining were farm workers or laborers with no saleable skill to an urban, industrial setting except their physical labor.

Answers To Review Questions

1. Advertisements distributed in European towns and cities by the railroads and western states attracted many thousands of immigrants to settle in thinly populated areas of the United States. Development of the ocean steamship made the Atlantic crossing much faster and more comfortable for passengers, thereby improving travel conditions which in turn attracted more immigrants.
2. Immigrants began to come from countries in southern and eastern Europe. Immigration from this region came to be called the New Immigration.
3. People of the New Immigration had many of the same reasons for leaving Europe as did those of the Old Immigration. In addition, many southern and eastern Europeans came to America because in their homelands they were members of minority groups who were being mistreated and often persecuted.
4. Jews were restricted to certain parts of Russia by government order, were prohibited from working in industry, agriculture, and the professions, were usually denied a university education, and were killed or tortured in the pogroms.
5. Because many immigrants lacked job skills, they often worked at hard manual labor in mines and steel mills, meat-packing plants, and clothing manufacturing.

by Poles, Slovaks, and Italians in the 1890s and 1900s. As that happened, the old immigrants moved up the ladder to better jobs in the industry. Thus, in coal mining and many other occupations, the continuing supply of new immigrants who took jobs at the bottom of the heap provided a push upward for the immigrants who had come before.

Furthermore, at least some of the immigrants managed to rise rapidly. It was true, for example, that almost all the employees in the clothing industry were immigrants. Pay was low, hours long, and working conditions so poor that these factories were called "sweatshops." But it was also true that many owners of these shops were also immigrants, often from the same group as their workers. A few immigrants did spectacularly well. Several of the nation's largest department stores in 1900 had been started by immigrants who began life in America as simple peddlers. A good many other immigrants could look back on a satisfying if less spectacular improvement during their lifetime in their new homeland.

Still more could see a better future for their children. And they were right. Thousands of sons and daughters of these immigrants became doctors, lawyers, teachers, business leaders, scientists, and government leaders (and authors of textbooks such as this).

Before a better future for the immigrants and their children could be realized, however, obstacles had to be overcome. One was the attitude of many who had come earlier to America toward those who followed them. Those are the attitudes that we will turn to in the next chapter.

CHECKUP

1. What kinds of jobs did immigrants generally get upon arrival in America?
2. What were living conditions like for newly arrived immigrants?
3. How did the arrival of new immigrants affect the occupational status of those who had come earlier?

Key Facts from Chapter 20

1. Until the late 1800s most immigrants to the United States came from northern and western Europe. This inflow is called the Old Immigration.
2. During the late 1800s increasing numbers of immigrants came from southern and eastern Europe. By the early 1900s those regions were the major source of immigration to the United States. This is called the New Immigration.
3. Many who came in the Old Immigration settled in rural areas.
4. Most who came in the New Immigration settled in cities.
5. Immigrants generally had the hardest and lowest-paid jobs, but they moved up the ladder to better jobs as later immigrants replaced them.

★ REVIEWING THE CHAPTER ★

People, Places, and Events

Old Immigration *P. 414*

New Immigration *P. 414*

Austro-Hungarian Empire *P. 417*

Czar *P. 417*

Pogrom *P. 418*

Padrone *P. 422*

Sweatshop *P. 424*

Review Questions

1. In what ways did advertising and the development of the ocean steamship in the late 1800s influence immigration to America? *Pp. 413–414* Les. 1
2. How did immigration change in the 1870s? *Pp. 414–415* Les. 1
3. Compare the reasons for the New Immigration with those for the Old Immigration. *Pp. 415–417* Les. 1
4. Explain why Jews had a special reason for leaving Russia. *P. 418* Les. 1
5. Why can we say that the rapid urban growth of the nineteenth century was mainly the product of European peasants? *Pp. 418, 420* Les. 1
6. Look at the chart on page 421. What kinds of jobs were open to the new immigrants? Why? *Pp. 421–422* Les. 2
7. Les. 2 Explain the fact that most immigrants were young and male. *Pp. 421–422*
8. How was the occupational position of old immigrants affected by the arrival of the new immigrants? *Pp. 423–424* Les. 2
9. Look at the graphs of city populations in 1910, on page 419. Why, do you think, are ethnic groups from Austria-Hungary and Russia not found in San Francisco? Account for the fact that Germans could be found in all cities.

Chapter Test

*On a separate piece of paper, write **T** if the statement is true and **F** if the statement is false.*

1. Railroads and western states used advertising to attract immigrants to settle in thinly populated areas. T
2. After the 1870s, more immigrants came from northern and western Europe than from southern and eastern Europe. F
3. During the 1800s, Europeans entered the United States on the East Coast as Chinese and Japanese were arriving on the West Coast. T
4. Southern Europeans had entirely different reasons from northern Europeans for coming to America. F
5. Many of the immigrants who came after 1880 were members of minority groups in their European countries. T
6. Russian Jews were eager to come to America in order to escape persecution by their government and their peasant neighbors. T
7. Most of the new immigrants never intended to be farmers in America but expected to join relatives in the cities. T
8. Much of the rapid urban growth of America in the late nineteenth century was due to the presence and the labor of the immigrants. T
9. Sweatshops were factories that were so cold the workers had to wear sweaters to keep warm. F
10. As more new immigrants entered the work force, members of the Old Immigration moved up the ladder to more skilled and better paying jobs. T

6. Most members of the New Immigration were from the peasant class, and they settled in urban areas. They provided much of the labor that built the cities and worked in industries that contributed to urban growth.
7. They came to America during their most productive work years in order to work, save money, and eventually earn enough to bring over the rest of the family. About a third of the immigrants returned to the Old Country after saving enough money in America.
8. The employment of new immigrants in the hardest and lowest-paid jobs provided opportunities for the old immigrants to move up the ladder to better jobs.
9. People from Austria-Hungary and Russia were the most recent arrivals. They had not had time to reach the West Coast. Germans had arrived as early as the colonial period, so they had had ample time to penetrate all parts of the country.

Background Information

1. CARTOON "Looking Backward" is the title of this cartoon, which first appeared in the January 11, 1893, issue of *Puck*. The subtitle is "They would close to the newcomer the bridge that carried them and their fathers over." The shadows behind the rich Americans reveal the poor immigrants they once were.

A satirical weekly magazine, *Puck* was founded by Joseph Keppler, who emigrated from Austria in 1867. The magazine was published from 1877 to 1918. During the early years, Keppler drew the three cartoons that appeared each week. He brought to America the German conception of cartooning, with its emphasis on caricature. Most of his cartoons were large and contained many people. Only a portion of the original cartoon is pictured on this page.

Although Keppler generally championed the cause of the Democratic party, he attacked any form of graft or injustice. Labor unions, woman's suffrage, monopolies, and Catholicism were also subjects of his ridicule.

CHAPTER 21

WHY CAN'T THEY BE LIKE US?

LESSON 1

FROM THE GARDEN OF EDEN ONWARD, observes one writer, "no age or society seems wholly free from unfavorable opinions of outsiders." Some believe it almost a law of human behavior to fear or dislike aliens. Certainly Americans have been no different from other people in dividing the world into "we" and "they." The firstcomer has almost always discriminated against the latecomer as an outsider, at times savagely. This opposition to foreigners is known as *nativism*. America has experienced periods when nativism was strong.

But there has been another side to America. Even as Americans held "unfavorable opinions of outsiders," they have often welcomed immigrants to their shores. Partly this was because immigrants were needed to live in and build the country. But partly it was because Americans were sure that in the New World, foreigners could not stay foreign very long.

Becoming an American

The process in which one is absorbed into another culture is called *assimilation*. For much of our history, Americans have been sure that the millions of immigrants would be assimilated within a generation. They would shed their separate cultures and enter the mainstream of American life.

A melting pot. The French immigrant Michel Guillaume Jean de Crèvecoeur, writing at just about the time of the nation's birth, expressed that confidence.

> What then is the American, this new man? He is . . . a strange mixture of blood, which you will find in no other country. I could point out to you a family whose grandfather was an Englishman, whose wife was Dutch, whose son married a French woman, and whose present four sons have now four wives of different nations. . . . Here individuals of all nations are melted into a new race . . . whose labors and posterity will one day cause great changes in the world.

One hundred twenty-five years later another immigrant expressed the same idea in a play dealing with immigration. His name was Israel Zangwill, and the play was called *The Melting Pot*. At one point, as though welcoming new arrivals to America, Zangwill has one of his characters say:

> America is God's crucible, the great Melting Pot where all the races of Europe are melting and re-forming. Here you stand good folk, think I, when I see you at Ellis Island, here you stand, in your fifty groups, with your fifty languages and histories, and your fifty blood hatreds and rivalries. But you won't be long like that, brothers, for these are the fires of God you come to—these are the fires of God. A fig for your feuds and vendettas! German and Frenchmen, Irishmen and Englishmen, Jews and Russians, into the Crucible with you all! God is making the American!

And in another line, he writes about America.

> There she lies, the great Melting Pot—listen! Can't you hear the roaring and the bubbling? . . . Ah, what a stirring and seething! Celt and Latin, Slav and Teuton, Greek and Syrian . . . East and West, and

LESSON 1 *(2 days)*

Performance Objectives

1. To demonstrate an understanding of the difference between the melting-pot view of assimilation and the dominant-culture view of assimilation by giving specific examples of how each type of assimilation should function. **2.** To offer evidence to support the following statement: A degree of nativism has existed since the beginning of American history.

Vocabulary

Nativism, assimilation, melting pot, dominant culture

Activities

1. ANALYZING SOURCE MATERIAL After the students have read the lesson, ask them to distinguish between the melting-pot theory and the dominant-culture theory using the source material on pages 427 and 428. What ideas did Crèvecoeur and Zangwill express? How do their ideas differ from the dominant-culture view of assimilation?

2. PICTURE ANALYSIS Ask students to observe the political cartoon on page 428. Ask: Does the cartoon reflect a melting-pot view of assimilation or a dominant-culture view? On what do you base your opinion?

Background Information

2. UNCLE SAM Uncle Sam originated as a nickname during the War of 1812. It is said that Samuel Wilson, an Army meat inspector, was the progenitor of America's nickname. When asked what the initials EA-US on barrels of meat represented, a worker at a Troy, N.Y., meat plant supposedly answered that the EA stood for Elbert Anderson, a meat contractor, and added in jest that the US stood for "Uncle Sam" Wilson. The nickname appeared in a Troy newspaper in 1813, and by the end of the War of 1812, its usage as a symbol for the United States was widespread. During the 1830s Uncle Sam began to appear in political cartoons dressed in stars and stripes. In 1961 Congress recognized Uncle Sam as a national symbol.

> North and South . . . how the great Alchemist melts and fuses them with his purging flames!

Crèvecoeur and Zangwill had similar notions about how the immigrant would be assimilated in America. Both saw America as a great melting pot. Whether by intermarriage or just by living side by side and mixing with one another, a new person would emerge. This new person would be different from any one part of the mixture. And, of course, better.

Accepting the dominant culture. There was a second notion of how assimilation would, or at least should, work.

> Everywhere these people [immigrants] tend to settle in groups or settlements, and to set up their national manners, customs, and observances. Our task is to break up these groups or settlements, to assimilate these people as a part of our American race, and to implant in their children, so far as can be done, the Anglo-Saxon conception of righteousness, law and order, and popular government, and to awaken in them a reverence for our democratic institutions and for those things in our national life which we as a people hold to be of abiding worth.

Under this idea of assimilation, newcomers give up their own cultures and accept the dominant English-American culture. How is this idea different from that of the melting pot?

Probably few Americans made a clear distinction, as we have, between assimilation by the melting pot and assimilation by full acceptance of the dominant culture. Their concern wasn't *how* aliens among them would be changed

In this cartoon drawn in the early years of the twentieth century, Uncle Sam perspires at his back-breaking job of turning immigrants into American citizens. Do you think the cartoonist saw assimilation more as a melting-pot process, or as full acceptance of the nation's dominant culture?

into Americans, but *whether* they would be. During much of our history, most Americans were sure that they would. As long as that confidence remained, immigrants were welcomed. When confidence evaporated, so did the welcome.

Two minds about immigration. From the beginning of its history, then, America has been of these two minds about immigration. Needing people to settle the land, work on it, and help defend the frontier, the colonies welcomed immigrants. To attract them, several colonies offered free land, free tools, and lower taxes.

But the welcome was not for all. In the seventeenth and eighteenth centuries, religious belief played an important part in the lives of most. Except in a few colonies, Protestants put out no welcome mat for Catholics. Also, no colony except Georgia liked England's practice of sending over prison convicts.

The mixed feeling about immigration is well illustrated in colonial Pennsylvania. In 1718 an official named James Logan warmly welcomed Scotch-Irish settlers to Pennsylvania. Eleven years later, watching the arrival of several thousand more, he wrote that there were "some grounds for the common apprehension [fear] of the people that if some speedy method [were] not taken," the Scotch-Irish would "soon make themselves Proprietors [owners] of the Province."

Likewise, William Penn and his successors had encouraged Germans to settle in his colony from its earliest days. By the mid-1700s at least a third of Pennsylvania's population was German. But many Germans chose to keep to themselves. They formed tightly knit communities. They continued to speak German, publish German-language newspapers, and maintain their German culture.

Benjamin Franklin, one of the most tolerant and broadminded people of the age, was irritated by this resistance to assimilation. On one occasion he exploded:

> Why should the Palatine Boors [Germans] be suffered to swarm into our Settlements, and by herding together, establish their Language and Manners, to the Exclusion of ours? Why should *Pennsylvania*, founded by the *English*, be a Colony of *Aliens*, who will shortly be so numerous as to Germanize us instead of our Anglifying them?

Did Franklin believe in the melting pot, or did he believe in the acceptance of the dominant Anglo-American culture in the colonies?

Continuing attitudes. The mixed feelings about immigrants continued to exist in the years following independence. At about the same period that Crèvecoeur boasted of a "new race of men," George Washington wrote, "The bosom of America is open to receive not only the Opulent [wealthy] and respectable Stranger, but the oppressed and persecuted of all Nations and Religions." And Thomas Jefferson, lover of liberty, welcomed the victims of European tyranny to our shores.

But each of the nation's founders had reservations. The immigrants should share "all our rights and privileges," said Washington, but they must "merit" them by "decency and propriety of conduct." And Jefferson, who regarded

3. THOUGHT PROVOKER Historian Carl Degler noted in *Out of Our Past: The Forces That Shaped Modern America* (New York: Harper & Row, 1962) that "the metaphor of the melting pot is unfortunate and misleading. A more accurate analogy would be a salad bowl, for, though the salad is an entity, the lettuce can still be distinguished from the chicory, the tomatoes from the cabbage." Ask your students to interpret Degler's statement. What evidence can they offer to support the idea that America is a melting pot? a salad bowl?

4. RESEARCH/ORAL REPORTS Ask several of your students to research the life of Crèvecoeur and report their findings to the class. Encourage them to discuss his collection of twelve essays entitled *Letters from an American Farmer,* published in 1782 under his American name, J. Hector St. John. These essays helped to persuade many Europeans to emigrate to America. If your students locate a copy of the essays, have them look for the passages that describe the adjustments of new immigrants.

5. LISTENING FOR INFORMATION Perhaps you might read to the class Chapter 1, "Patterns in the Making" (pages 3–11) in John Higham's *Strangers in the Land: Patterns of American Nativism* (New Brunswick, N.J.: Rutgers University Press, 1955). In this chapter, Higham discusses the major ideological background of American nativism. He cites anti-Catholic and anti-radical feelings and opposition to immigrants not of the "Anglo-Saxon race" as the main themes of nativism. If an opaque projector is available, you might wish to share with the class the political cartoons and photographs located between pages 210 and 211 in this book about nativism.

LESSON 2 *(1 to 2 days)*

Performance Objectives

1. To demonstrate an understanding of the rise and fall of nativist feelings from the 1830s to the 1890s by writing a newspaper article that explains the underlying issues that led to these feelings.
2. To distinguish between fact and opinion in the theory of race.

Vocabulary

Know-Nothing Party, naturalization papers, American Protective Association, race

Activities

1. **DISCUSSION** A discussion about the nature of prejudice might serve as an effective motivation for this lesson. Ask your students for their definitions of *prejudice*. One textbook defines prejudice as an emotional bias with no foundation of knowledge or experience. Prejudiced attitudes may be favorable or unfavorable, but current usage implies the negative connotation. Prejudicial opinions are learned, not inherited.

Prejudicial thinking is often reinforced by the use of common expressions in the forms of stereotypes, epithets, and clichés. Stereotypes refer to beliefs that assign uniform characteristics to certain groups of people. Ask your students to give examples of stereotypes that connote an inaccurate image of various ethnic groups. Ask: In what ways are these stereotypes perpetuated? What are some of the common epithets or unflattering names applied to ethnic groups that encourage stereotypical opinions?

Europe as corrupt and decaying, worried whether the very victims we would shelter might bring some of Europe's corrupting influences with them to their new country.

Some people noted with concern the tendency of immigrant groups to settle in separate regions. It was true that a good many immigrants hoped to keep their own ways by living apart. A few had an even bolder dream.

> What would Philadelphia be in forty years if the Germans there were to remain German, and retain their language and customs? It would . . . be a German city, just as York and Lancaster are German counties. What would be the result throughout Pennsylvania and Maryland? . . . An entirely German state where, as formerly in Germantown [a suburb of Philadelphia], the beautiful German language would be used in the legislative halls and the courts of justice.

Consider Benjamin Franklin's comment in the light of this statement.

But it was not possible to stay permanently isolated in America. The same rich soil or climate that made a region attractive to one group soon attracted others, foreign-born and native alike. There were no walls to keep them out. A pocket here and there, perhaps a whole county, might remain the special preserve of a small group, but not much more. Moreover, at least as typical as the German quoted above was the Norwegian who wrote home in 1835 after a short period in America, "Our son attends the English school and talks English as well as the native-born." And language, as one American political leader had observed years earlier, was one key to assimilation.

> . . . the triumph and adoption of the English language have been the principal means of melting us down into one people, and of extinguishing those stubborn prejudices and violent animosities [hatreds] which formed a partition [wall] between the inhabitants of the same land.

CHECKUP

1. Explain the meaning of the following words: *nativism, assimilation.*
2. How does the melting-pot theory of assimilation differ from the dominant-culture theory?

LESSON 2

The Rise of Nativism

Until the 1830s and 1840s, immigrants were far more welcome than not. But the influx of Irish and German immigrants in those years led to uneasiness of many, and alarm of some Americans. The immigrants, it was noted, clung to their languages and customs. Several million were Catholic. They tended to cluster in the cities. Two thirds of New York City's 100,000 Germans lived in one section of the city, which came to be called Kleindeutschland—little Germany. Nativists charged that immigrants were illiterates, paupers, criminals, and drunkards, a threat to American democracy, an indigestible lump in America's throat.

The Know-Nothing party. In the 1830s and 1840s there were several grave incidents in which immigrant Catholics were victims. Secret nativist societies sprang up and in 1850 joined in a single national group, the Order of the Star Spangled Banner. Many of its members in turn joined a political party called the American party. It came to be known as the Know-Nothing party because its members, sworn to secrecy, answered all questions with "I know nothing." The party wanted to hold down immigration. For those foreign-born already here, it would delay citizenship and the right to vote.

Know-Nothings elected a number of candidates to office in northeastern states in the mid-1850s. The party died down soon after, however, and achieved none of its goals. Even at its peak, nativism did not represent the feelings of most Americans. During the same years in which Know-Nothings were winning office in Massachusetts and Connecticut, western states and territories were advertising in Europe for more immigrants.

Anti-Chinese feelings. In one part of the country the current of nativism ran strong even after the Know-Nothings died out. That was in the Far West. There, nativists focused on the Chinese. The Chinese had begun to come to the United States in the 1850s. They worked the goldfields of California, ran small shops, and laid track on the western railroads.

Everywhere the Chinese were ridiculed and discriminated against. They were often the victims of robbery, beatings, and even murder. These crimes were rarely punished, partly because in California Chinese were not allowed to testify in court against white persons. On one horrible night in 1871, white residents of the small village of Los

In 1877, Chinese immigrants undergo inspection upon arrival in San Francisco. Note that there are only a few women in the group. Most Chinese immigrants were men whose families stayed in China.

2. RESEARCH After discussing prejudice as suggested in Activity 1, ask your students to search for examples of prejudice in magazines and books. The stereotypes, clichés, and epithets mentioned in the discussion about prejudice can often be found in advertisements in older issues of magazines, which may be borrowed from the library. Also have the students look for examples of prejudice in television shows and commercials.

3. RESEARCH/ORAL REPORTS Ask several of your students to investigate the reasons why the Chinese began coming to the United States in the 1850s. Encourage them to report on the isolation of China from the Western world until the mid-1850s. Factors important in the opening of China to the West include the Opium War (which began in 1839), the treaties of Nanking (1842) and Tientsin (1857), and the Tai-ping Rebellion against the Manchu Dynasty. The discovery of gold in California in 1848 was one of the "pull" factors of the United States.

One student might prepare a combination time line and bar graph that shows major events in Chinese history and numbers of Chinese immigrants to the United States from 1840 to 1882.

4. CREATIVE WRITING After reading the lesson, ask students to write a newspaper article about the rise and fall of nativist feelings from the 1830s to the 1890s. The article should make clear the changing moods in America during those years and the reasons for the change.

Background Information

NATURALIZATION The concept of naturalization of citizens developed during the 1800s. Until that time, people were considered to be a citizens of the lands of their birth no matter where they lived. One of the causes of the War of 1812 was the British refusal to acknowledge the naturalization of British subjects in the United States. Not until 1870 did Great Britian recognize the right of a British person to become a citizen of another country.

Congress approved the first naturalization law in the United States in 1790; it set up certain courts to naturalize citizens. Only "free white persons" could be naturalized. Other groups eventually became eligible; for example, blacks in 1870 and Chinese in 1943. The Immigration and Nationality Act of 1952 did away with all racial bars to naturalization in the United States.

Today the naturalization procedure involves three steps. To file a petition for naturalization, a person must be 18, must have been a United States resident for five years, and must be of good moral character. The second step involves an investigation by and interview with officers of the Immigration and Naturalization Service. The prospective citizen must be able to read, write, and speak some English, have some knowledge of United States history and government, and provide two citizens who offer assurance of the qualifications of the person. The final hearing—the third step—is held in a public court. If approved for citizenship, the new citizen must denounce allegiance to foreign countries and pledge to defend and support the Constitution of the United States.

Angeles shot or hanged twenty Chinese. During the next decade anti-Chinese sentiment grew. Congress finally passed a law in 1882 bringing to an end Chinese immigration.

Changing moods. Elsewhere in the United States, however, nativism died down for the moment. Immigration once again rose after the Civil War, but now the newcomers were welcomed. The United States Treasury Department estimated that through the work that immigrants would do, each would add $800 to the country's wealth. Others placed the value even higher. Confidence returned that all comers would quickly become Americans. "We are the Romans of the modern world, the great assimilating people," boasted the famous American writer Oliver Wendell Holmes. Most Americans agreed.

That confident feeling lasted for another two decades and several million more immigrants. Then the mood changed once more. The following editorial, which appeared in a Philadelphia newspaper in 1891, tells the story.

> Agents of the ocean lines report that the coming season will be the busiest ever known. Every vessel will come over loaded down with new recruits for America. More immigrants will be landed this year than ever before in history. What kind of people are these new citizens? Some are honest men seeking a home. They will go West, take up land and add to the resources of the Nation. This is the desirable class. Others will get no farther than New York where they will get on the police force, take out naturalization papers, sell themselves to Tammany and the corrupt politicans who feed upon their stealings from the city, and in time share in the plunder themselves. . . . Others will be fresh from jails and prisons, brigands, outlaws, murderers, midnight assassins, cowardly thugs, like the Mafia of New Orleans. Isn't there food for thought in the greatly increasing number of immigrants? No respectable person seeking to settle down and become a worthy citizen is unwelcome. He may not have an education. He may not even know how to read, but if he will work at some useful trade or turn his attention to the cultivation of the soil America will open her arms to him. But what shall we do with the assassins and criminals driven to this country in the expectations of finding a new field for their villainy? Where is this thing to end?

A congressman in 1897 put forth the following views.

> Immigrants work for wages upon which American workingmen cannot live. The evidence abundantly shows that they habitually live in shanties, that they eat the rudest food, that they do not have even the most common sanitary appliances, that they expose themselves to all the diseases that are generated by filth. The American workingman cannot support churches and decently clothe his children and send them to school and enjoy any of the comforts of civilization, so long as he must come into this degrading competition.

And a political leader in California demanded:

> We must keep out the restless, revolutionary hordes of foreigners who are now seeking our shores from every part of the world.

What are the main concerns expressed above about the immigrants? What differences do the writer and speakers believe there were between the New Immigration and the Old?

A different immigrant? How different *was* the new immigrant from the old? Certainly the new ones were culturally different. Immigrants from southern and eastern Europe had different customs, dress, and language. As you saw earlier, a smaller percentage of new immigrants became farmers, and a larger percentage worked in industrial jobs. (Of course by the time the new immigrants arrived, industry had grown greatly and there were many more jobs to be had.) On the whole the new immigrants were poorer, more unskilled, and less educated.

Still, in most important ways, new and old immigrants were not that different. Their reasons for coming to America were pretty much the same. Their wish to live near others from their own country was the same. Their clinging to old-country ways was the same. While a larger percentage of new immigrants were "birds of passage," the rest were no less desirious of becoming Americans than the earlier immigrants had been.

People were more aware of the new immigrants, however, because they were so highly visible. We have already seen that the new immigrants lived mostly in cities. There were more foreign-born living in Brooklyn, New York, in 1890 than in all the states on the Atlantic Coast from Virginia to Florida. Immigrants from Norway, speaking their native language and following their old customs on Minnesota farms in the 1840s might be hardly noticed. But how could one fail to note the foreign ways of the thousands of Slavs, Jews, and Italians who crowded together in the cities?

The children of an immigrant neighborhood, undisturbed by clotheslines and lack of open space, join in a game of baseball in a tenement alley. In the early 1900s, there were few playgrounds.

Nativists began to demand strict limits on immigration. In 1887 a powerful nativist organization named the American Protective Association was formed. Its aim was to resist foreign influence and what it called "the Catholic menace." This secret society reached its highest point in the mid-1890s. About a half million belonged to the society and it influenced a number of members of Congress. Soon after, however, it faded

5. ANALYZING SOURCE MATERIAL Have students carefully read the theory of race put forth in the source material on page 434. Ask students to identify three statements of fact and at least three statements of opinion. Discuss the influence of the theory of race on immigration.

LESSON 3 *(1 to 2 days)*

Performance Objective

To explain, orally or in writing, the purpose and provisions of the Immigration Act of 1924.

Vocabulary

Immigration act of 1917, Communist, "Red scare," "we-they" argument, Immigration Act of 1924, "national origins," quota, Ellis Island

Activities

1. USING A MAP The Immigration Act of 1924 discriminated against immigrants from certain areas of the world. A list of the quotas established for countries may be found in "The Immigration Act of 1924" in Commager's *Documents of American History.* Ask your students to use different colors or patterns to graphically show the quotas assigned to the various countries. You may wish to provide them with outline maps of the world with 1924 political boundaries.

First have the students create a legend using the quotas in the Immigration Act. One breakdown might be countries with quotas that fall into the following categories: **(a)** 100, **(b)** 100–500, **(c)** 500–1,000, **(d)** 1,000–5,000, **(e)** 5,000–10,000, **(f)** 10,000–52,000, and **(g)** no quota limitations.

After your students complete the map, have them write at least three generalizations about the Immigration Act of 1924 from the information provided by their maps.

about as quickly as the Know-Nothings had forty years before, and with not much more success.

The theory of race. Around the turn of the century a new word was introduced into the argument over immigration. The word was *race.* One of the founders of an organization that favored limiting immigration wrote the following.

> A few years ago practically all of our immigrants were from northern and western Europe, that is, they were more or less closely allied to us, racially, historically, socially, industrially, and politically. They were largely the same elements which had recently made up the English race. As experience has shown, they found little difficulty in assimilating with the American people, and what is more, they were as a whole eager to become assimilated. They intermarried among themselves and with the older American stock, which was akin to the English. Now, however, the majority of the newcomers are from southern and eastern Europe, and they are coming in rapidly increasing numbers from Asia. These people are alien to us, in race . . . in language, in social, political and industrial ideas and inheritance. . . . Among the families of our newest immigrants, children are born with reckless regularity. . . .
>
> The question before us is, therefore, a race question. Slav, Italian, Jew, not discouraged by the problem of maintaining high standards of living with many children, are replacing native Americans. . . .
>
> There can, then, be absolutely no doubt that the recent change in the races of our immigrants will profoundly affect the character of the future American race.

According to those who wrote about the different "races" of Europe, each race had certain distinct characteristics. Some of these differences were physical: hair, color, height, skin shade, size of head, and so on. But the races were supposedly different in other ways as well. In the following passage, you will see how far the racial theory was carried by one writer.

> Mental, spiritual and moral traits are closely associated with the physical distinctions among the different European races. The Alpine race is always and everywhere a race of peasants. . . . The Nordics are, all over the world, a race of soldiers, sailors, adventurers, and explorers, but above all, of rulers, organizers and aristocrats.

Nonsense? Of course. But the racial argument was seriously presented by writers like this one as though it were scientific fact. What is worse, many readers believed it.

CHECKUP

1. What forms did nativism take in America in the 1800s?
2. In what ways were the new immigrants different from the old immigrants? In what ways were the two similar?

LESSON 3

Restricting Immigration

As you can see on the graph on page 400, immigration reached its highest point ever in the early years of the twentieth century. During World War I, 1914–1918, immigration dropped off. But it started again when the war ended.

Under a 1917 law, every immigrant over sixteen had to be able to read in some language. That discriminated against those who had had little chance for schooling, and it did keep out some. Still, in 1920, 430,000 came. Over

Continued on page 436

The Island of Tears

From the early nineteenth century on, New York was the main point of entry for immigrants to the United States. For most of those years they were received at Castle Garden, a converted fort at the tip of Manhattan. In 1892, the United States opened a new receiving station, on Ellis Island in New York Harbor. This facility could handle up to 5,000 people a day, many more than Castle Garden. Within a few years, even this proved too small. The island's three acres (1.2 ha) grew to twenty-seven acres (10.8 ha) with landfill dumped into the harbor, and new buildings were added. By 1900 the enlarged facility handled as many as 15,000 immigrants a day. All told, 16 million people passed through Ellis Island upon their arrival in America.

One can only imagine how immigrants felt as they waited to be cleared for entry. Their biggest hurdle, they knew, would be the medical examination. Two out of ten were turned back because of disease. To travel so far and then be sent back to Europe—that was the greatest fear of all. After the medical examination came the immigration inspectors with their list of questions. Your name? Any relative in America? Why are you coming? Where will you live? Do you have a job waiting for you? Many an immigrant's name was changed by an inspector who gave his own spelling to what he heard, or thought he heard, the immigrant say. The three or four hours that most immigrants spent on Ellis Island were among their most anxious times in America. For good reason, Ellis Island came to be known as the Island of Tears.

After the immigration laws of the 1920s, Ellis Island was little used as an immigration center. In 1954, it was shut down. Ellis Island was once again opened to the public in 1976, as part of the nation's bicentennial celebration. Eventually the island is to be restored as a national historic site and a recreation center.

During the height of immigration, Ellis Island in New York Harbor was the first American soil on which millions of immigrants set foot. The stop there brought tears to some, but hope to many.

2. ANALYZING SOURCE MATERIAL Have your students carefully read the statements made by several congressmen in favor of the bill to limit immigration (see page 436). Then have them list the various arguments to limit immigration used by the congressmen. Ask: Which arguments were based on facts? Which arguments appealed to the emotions? What beliefs did these congressmen have in common with members of the Know-Nothing party? How were the two groups different?

3. THOUGHT PROVOKER
The "Red scare" of 1919–1920 against radicals was led by Woodrow Wilson's Attorney General A. Mitchell Palmer. He capitalized on the uneasy feelings of many Americans caused by the reports of Communist revolts sweeping across Europe. Historian John Higham believes the absolute loyalty demanded during World War I carried over into peacetime. He stated that "along with death and sacrifice the war had brought the warmth of a common purpose into millions of lives; . . . it had given them catharsis for a host of aggressive impulses. These were experiences to cherish deeply, and men who had discovered them in the heat of national conflict had little difficulty supposing that the war had not ended, that the adversary had merely assumed another guise and still presented a deadly challenge to loyalty and a summons to hatred."

Write Higham's statement on the chalkboard and have the students interpret it. Ask: Do you feel that the Immigration Act of 1924 would have been approved even if the Communist Revolution had not occurred? Do you feel, as Higham did, that World War I drew people together and the following peacetime created a vacuum that needed to be filled with another enemy (real or imaginary)?

800,000 more came in 1921. Amid wild stories that another 15 to 20 million would soon be coming, nativist hysteria rose once more.

This fear of a flood of foreigners was fed by another event. During World War I a Communist government had been set up in Russia. The Communists, or Reds as they were called, preached world revolution. Indeed a few revolutions did break out in several European countries right after the war, although they did not succeed for long. In America there were those who spread the fear that foreigners with radical ideas might try to start such revolutions here. This "Red scare" gripped many people in 1919 and 1920 and added to the demand that Congress do something immediately to limit immigration.

The debate in Congress. The following statements were made by congressmen in 1921 during the debate on a bill to limit immigration. What seem to be the main reasons why these speakers want to limit immigration? Which immigrants are most of these statements aimed at?

Congressman Parish (Texas):
It is time we act now, because within a few short years the damage will have been done. The endless tide of immigration will have filled our country with a foreign and unsympathetic element . . . and the true spirit of Americanism left us by our fathers will gradually become poisoned by this uncertain element.

The time once was when . . . the oppressed and downtrodden people . . . came to us . . . with the sincere purpose of making true and loyal American citizens. . . . But that time has passed now; new and strange conditions have arisen in countries over there; new and strange doctrines are being taught.

Congressman Heflin (Alabama):
I plead for the preservation of the institutions of my country. I plead for the great army of wage earners of America, to protect and defend them against the horde of unfit foreigners who want to come here to take their places in our industrial establishments. I plead for the honor and glory of my flag and for the preservation . . . of American institutions.

Congressman Raker (California):
No one . . . can object to our taking time to assimilate those who are here. . . . Instead of that we find communities in this country that are as foreign as to language and thought as any city in any foreign land today. That must be avoided, and now is the time to stop.

Congressman McClintic (Oklahoma):
Practically all of them [recent immigrants] were weak, small of stature, poorly clad, emaciated, and in a condition which showed that the environment surrounding them in their European homes was indeed very bad. It is for this reason that I say the class of immigrants coming to the shores of the United States at this time are not the kind of people we want as citizens of this country.

One congressman who did not favor limiting immigration noted the "we–they" nature of the arguments.

Just now we hear nothing but hatred, nothing but the ravings of the exaggerated I—"I am of the best stock, I do not want to be contaminated; I have produced the greatest literature; my intellect is the biggest; my heart is the noblest"—and this is repeated . . . in every country . . . by every fool all over the world.

But in the climate of the time, such statements made little impression.

This cartoon of the early twentieth century pictures Uncle Sam as Noah welcoming immigrants to the American "ark." The signs remind the new arrivals of the advantages of life in America.

The immigration act of 1924. In 1924 Congress passed a law that limited total immigration to the United States, except from the Western Hemisphere, to about 150,000 each year. A nation was given a quota based on the proportion of the white population in 1920 that traced its origin back to that country. For example, it was decided that about one sixth of the white population had its origin in Germany. Therefore the German quota was 25,814—about one sixth of 150,000.

The law was hard to understand, and very unscientific. How could one possibly find the "national origin" of an American whose grandparents had been Irish and German on the mother's side and Polish and American on the father's? But the law asked for that.

The table on the next page shows the number who came from several European nations between 1890 and 1920,

The cartoon below, drawn more than fifty years ago, takes a less favorable view of immigration than the cartoon above. On what grounds does the lower cartoon criticize the admission of immigrants to the United States? Are the differing views put forth in these two cartoons still put forth about immigration today? How has immigration changed in the last half century?

Copyright, 1921, by Chicago Tribune — McCutcheon in Chicago Tribune

4. ANALYZING CARTOONS The cartoons on page 437 present contrasting views of immigration in the early twentieth century. After students have observed the cartoon at the top of the page, ask them to discuss the kinds of people who were boarding the ark and their reasons for emigrating to the United States. Then ask students to observe the cartoon at the bottom of the page and answer the questions posed in the caption.

5. ROLE PLAYING Before voting on a bill, both the House of Representatives and the Senate hold separate hearings before standing committees or *ad hoc* committees to discuss the bill. Have your students conduct a mock hearing before an imaginary Senate committee that is meeting to discuss a proposed immigration policy in 1924. Encourage them to use the information they have read in their textbook about **(a)** the nature of the new immigrant, **(b)** the recent rapid increase of number of immigrants, **(c)** the influence of nativist feelings in the nineteenth century, and **(d)** the traditional view of America as a haven for the "huddled masses yearning to breathe free."

LESSON 4 *(2 to 3 days)*

Performance Objectives

1. To write three generalizations that characterize the nature of immigration to the United States in the last half century. **2.** To offer evidence, orally or in writing, that supports the following statement: The ultimate purpose of the immigration law of 1965 was different from that of the Immigration Act of 1924. **3.** To write an essay that explains the reasons why, and the ways in which, Japanese Americans were victims of discrimination in twentieth-century America.

Vocabulary

Refugee, immigration law of 1965, anti-Semitism, Nisei, "relocation center," "Go for Broke"

Activities

1. FILM A possible motivational activity for this lesson is the showing of the film *Guilty by Reason of Race,* (51 minutes, color; NBC), an NBC documentary that has attracted much attention. Beautiful photography and interviews help to tell the story of the internment of Japanese Americans during World War II. For information about the film, contact National Broadcasting Corporation, 30 Rockefeller Center, New York, N.Y. 10020.

Immigrants from Several European Nations, 1890–1920

Country or area	*Number* (rounded to nearer 10,000)	*Quota set by 1924 law*
Austria and Hungary *(combined)*	3,630,000	3,282
Germany	990,000	25,957
Great Britain and Northern Ireland	1,140,000	65,721
Greece	370,000	307
Irish Free State	870,000	17,853
Italy	3,810,000	5,802
Russia	3,020,000	2,712
Sweden	550,000	3,314

and the quota assigned to each by the 1924 law. Do you see any pattern as to which nations were favored by their quotas and which were discriminated against? Would you say that the arguments against the New Immigration had had an effect, or not?

The number of immigrants went down sharply following the 1924 quota law. During the 1930s, the average net immigration to the United States per year was only about 8,000. That is barely what it had been at the start of our nation's history 150 years earlier. At that time the population had been only one thirtieth the size it was in the decade of the 1930s. Clearly, an era had come to an end.

LESSON 4

CHECKUP

1. Why were restrictions placed on immigration during the 1920s?
2. In what ways did the immigration act of 1924 limit immigration?

New Patterns of Immigration

Though immigration to the United States fell off, it did not end. During the 1930s, several thousand refugees, many of them Jews, fled the persecution of Adolf Hitler in Germany. Among them was the famous scientist Albert Einstein. In the years after World War II, special laws and presidential orders allowed the entrance of more thousands—persons made homeless by war as well as refugees from Communist-controlled lands. Since the 1920s, however, the main source of immigration has shifted from Europe to the Western Hemisphere. You may recall that immigration from countries in this hemisphere was not limited by the 1924 law. Thus, while all European and Asian countries could send no more than 150,000 a year, nearly a million entered the United States from Canada alone during the 1920s. But the greatest source of immigrants since then has been south of the border. The last half-century has been the great era of Spanish-speaking immigration.

The Mexican Americans. Large numbers of Mexicans first became citizens of the United States in the 1840s. They did so simply by staying on the land the United States won from Mexico in war. This was most of the present-day Southwest.

During the next half-century many immigrants came from Mexico. They provided the back-breaking labor that built the railroads of the Southwest, just as the Irish, Chinese, and Italians had earlier done in other parts of the country. They also provided much of the farm labor in the states of Texas, Arizona, and California.

Between 1920 and 1940, possibly another million Mexicans came; since 1940, perhaps another two million. No one really knows for sure. Through most of our history it has been easy to cross the border from Mexico without meeting the legal requirements. Almost certainly several million have done so. The wages these newcomers earn in America have usually been very low. Yet Mexican laborers came because these wages were five times what they could earn at home. Some, like the European "birds of passage," came to work during the harvest season and then returned to Mexico. Others stayed.

Today there are probably between six and seven million people in the United States who trace their origin to Mexico. Some believe the number is closer to ten million. Next to blacks, Mexican Americans are the nation's largest minority. Eighty percent live in the Southwest, but there are large numbers in other areas also.

These two young women of Mexican-American ancestry operate a fast-food shop in a community in the Southwest. Their specialty, as the sign under the flag indicates, is Mexican food.

Because so many Mexican Americans have worked as farm laborers, they are often thought of as rural people. Most of them, however, are not. In fact, four of five live in cities. A million are in Los Angeles alone. Another 300,000 live in Chicago.

Other Hispanic groups. Other large Spanish-speaking ethnic groups are also recent arrivals. Because the island of Puerto Rico is part of the United States, its people were already citizens before

2. DISCUSSION After your students have read the lesson, encourage them to compare the immigrants to the United States during the New Immigration (1880–1920) with the immigrants who have arrived since 1920. Ask: What countries were the main sources of the two groups of immigrants? Can you account for the shift in source countries? What similar problems did both groups face? What different problems?

At this point tell your students the leading sources of newcomers to the United States in 1975: Mexico, 62,205; Philippines, 31,751; South Korea, 28,362; Cuba, 25,955; and Republic of China (Taiwan), 18,536. Ask: What problems do you think these immigrants are experiencing? Are the problems similar to, or different from, those of earlier groups? What could your community do to ease the adjustment of newcomers?

3. **ANALYZING MAGAZINE ARTICLES** Ask each of your students to read one recent magazine or journal article about Mexican Americans. If necessary, show them how to use the *Readers' Guide to Periodical Literature.* Have the students analyze the articles, organizing their reports into three parts: **(a)** bibliography entry, **(b)** short summary of the article, and **(c)** evaluation of the author. To evaluate the author, students should include any information provided about the author in the article and answer the following questions (if possible).

Does the author appear to have relevant expertise, based on education or experience, to write the article? Is there any evidence of bias held by the author that might have influenced his or her observations? Was the author an eyewitness to the items reported, or was the article written on the basis of someone else's observations?

4. **ANALYZING SOURCE MATERIAL** The text states that the Japanese Americans were the victims of the worst episode of discrimination in America since the end of slavery. Have students re-read the source material on page 441 and discuss the questions that are posed in the paragraph following General DeWitt's letter. Then ask students to react to the source material on page 442. Ask: Why, in your opinion, were Japanese Americans treated so differently from German and Italian Americans? Do you think that, given the time and circumstances, General DeWitt's reasons were valid?

they even set foot on the mainland. Today about two million persons of Puerto Rican background live in mainland United States. A majority live in New York City. Most of the remainder are in cities of the Northeast. Nearly all have arrived since 1945.

The Mexican and Puerto Rican experience has been very much like that of earlier immigrant groups. Puerto Ricans live in some of the cities' worst housing, and hold some of the lowest-paying jobs. In fact, many now have the same jobs that earlier immigrants once held. In the garment industry, for example, Puerto Ricans have largely replaced the Jews and Italians who used to make up the work force.

A second group of recent comers are the Cubans. Most have come since 1959 because they were against the Castro government that came to power that year in Cuba. Almost a million Cubans are now in the United States. More than half live in Florida, almost 400,000 in and around Miami. In the short time they have been here, Cubans have become a very important part of the society and economy in Florida.

The immigration law of 1965. In 1965 a new immigration law was passed. The discriminatory quota system based on national origin was ended. There was still a limit to total immigration: 170,000 from outside the Western Hemisphere, and 120,000 from within. The law gave preference to those who had relatives in the United States, to refugees, to those who had skills that were needed in the United States, and to certain unskilled workers as well.

Under this law, many thousands of doctors, engineers, and scientists came to the United States. So also did several thousand war refugees from Vietnam.

A Filipino medical student, backed by two witnesses, takes the oath of United States citizenship. In recent years, Filipinos have made up one of the largest groups of American immigrants.

5. CREATIVE WRITING
Divide your class into groups of five or six students. Ask each group to compose a present-day immigration bill to be presented to Congress for consideration. Tell the students they must decide to what degree (if any) they want to use restrictions or exclusions for any national groups. Personal characteristics and relationship to United States citizens are important parts of our current immigration policy. Ask your students to include a description of desirable and undesirable personal characteristics in each proposed bill.

Lingering discrimination. Discrimination against ethnic groups did not stop with the passage of immigration laws. In the 1930s there was a rise of anti-Semitism—discrimination against Jews. While most of that has subsided, more than a trace still remains. Both Mexican Americans and Puerto Ricans have found themselves the victims of "we—they" thinking.

The history of mistreatment of Japanese in America is a long one. This was especially true in the states on the West Coast, where not only people but laws discriminated against them. In 1913 California made it illegal for Japanese aliens to own land in that state. Under federal law, Japanese were the only immigrants who could not become citizens, although, of course, any of their children born in the United States were citizens. And in the immigration law of 1924, Japan was the only country to be denied even the minimum quota of 100 per year.

Anti-Japanese feeling. During World War II, Japanese Americans were the victims of the worst episode of discrimination in America since the end of slavery. On December 7, 1941, the armed forces of the Japanese Empire brought the United States into World War II with an attack upon the naval base at Pearl Harbor, Hawaii. That episode fueled the flames of anti-Japanese feeling in America. With no evidence at all, high American officials hinted that Japanese Americans were cooperating with the Japanese government against the United States.

In California, Washington, and Oregon there was talk of Japanese spying and sabotage. Otherwise sensible people demanded that Japanese Americans be forced to leave the West Coast. General Benjamin DeWitt, United States Army commander on the West Coast, urged the government to order their removal from that region. In this letter to the Secretary of War, DeWitt gives his reasons.

> Hostile naval and air raids will be assisted by enemy agents signaling from the coastline and the vicinity thereof; and by supplying and otherwise assisting enemy vessels and by sabotage. . . . The Japanese race is an enemy race and while many second- and third-generation Japanese born on United States soil, possessed of United States citizenship, have become "Americanized," the racial strains are undiluted. . . . It, therefore, follows that along the vital Pacific Coast over 112,000 potential enemies of Japanese extraction are at large today. There are indications that these are organized and ready for concerted action at a favorable opportunity. The very fact that no sabotage has taken place to date is a disturbing and confirming indication that such action will be taken.

What are DeWitt's reasons for wanting the Japanese removed? Read General DeWitt's last sentence again. With this kind of reasoning, was there any way for Japanese Americans to defend themselves against the charge of disloyalty?

A shameful episode. Pressed by the Army and a hysterical public, President Roosevelt reluctantly agreed to the removal of more than 110,000 persons of Japanese ancestry from the western states. Most of them were *Nisei*—sons and daughters of immigrant Japanese parents, themselves born in the United States and therefore American citizens.

A group of Japanese Americans are trucked to a relocation center in a western state soon after the United States entered World War II. Their internment was a tragic case of discrimination.

Some were even third-generation Americans. They were forced to leave their homes, businesses, and jobs on short notice.

Allowed to take only what they could carry, the Japanese Americans sold most of their possessions for whatever they could get. Often that wasn't much. This passage explains why.

> Many opportunists were waiting for the prices on Japanese-owned property to go very low before they bid on it. Henry Takemori and his wife owned a grocery store in Phoenix, Arizona, inside the prohibited zone. "When it came time to sell . . . potential buyers knew that the longer they held out, the less it would cost them. Finally, only two days before the Takemoris were scheduled to board the Greyhound buses leaving for Mayer assembly center with 242 bewildered passengers, they sold the $15,000 property for $800—about the price of a new meat case."

Behind barbed wire. It is estimated that Japanese Americans lost $400 million as a result of their forced removal. They were then shipped to ten "relocation centers" that were set up in isolated parts of California, Arizona, Wyoming, and several other western states. There, behind barbed-wire fences, they tried to establish some kind of normal existence for the duration of the war.

Those who were herded into these camps were understandably bitter. One, testifying before a United States Senate committee, put it this way.

> Our citizenship has even been attacked as an evil cloak under which we can expect immunity for the nefarious purpose of conspiring to destroy the American way of life. To us—who have been born, raised, and educated in American institutions and in our system of public schools, knowing and owing no other allegiance than to the United States—such a thought is manifestly unfair and ambiguous.
>
> . . . We cannot understand why General DeWitt can make exceptions for families of German and Italian soldiers in the armed forces of the United States while ignoring the civil rights of the Nisei Americans. Are we to be condemned merely on the basis of our racial origin? Is citizenship such a light and transient thing that that which is our inalienable right in normal times can be torn from us in times of war?

The questions in that last paragraph were not answered by the committee. It was, indeed, difficult to understand why Japanese Americans should be treated one way and German and Italian Americans, against whose ancestral land America was also at war, another way. The reasons most often given were those cited by General DeWitt above. Were they, do you think, valid reasons?

Continued on page 444

"Go for Broke"

Even as the Japanese Americans on the West Coast were being herded into camps, others were joining the United States Army. In Hawaii alone, 16,000 Americans of Japanese descent were drafted into the Army. More than three times that many eventually served in the United States armed forces in World War II. At first the Army did not accept Nisei (American-born offspring of Japanese immigrants). When it changed its policy, thousands—determined to prove their loyalty to the United States—signed up. Among them were over a thousand young men who were living in the relocation centers!

The most famous Nisei units during the war were the 100th Infantry Battalion and the 442nd Regimental Combat Team. These units fought in Europe, first in Italy and then in France. From September 1943 to early February 1944, the 100th was in action almost continuously. In June 1944 the 100th became a unit of the 442nd, which went into action at that time in Italy. The members of this combat team fought with a bravery and reckless heroism that was summed up in their battle cry, "Go for Broke." They took heavy casualties: more than 1,700 killed and nearly 5,000 wounded. They were also among the most decorated units in the United States Army. Commenting on the heroism of the Japanese Americans, General Joseph Stilwell, one of the outstanding generals of World War II, declared, "The Nisei bought an awfully big hunk of America with their blood."

In later years many who served in the 100th and 442nd held important positions in private and public life. Both Daniel Inouye and Spark Matsunaga, United States senators from Hawaii as these words are written, proudly count themselves as "graduates" of the 442nd.

In 1944, General Mark Clark and Navy Secretary James Forrestal review Nisei troops in Italy.

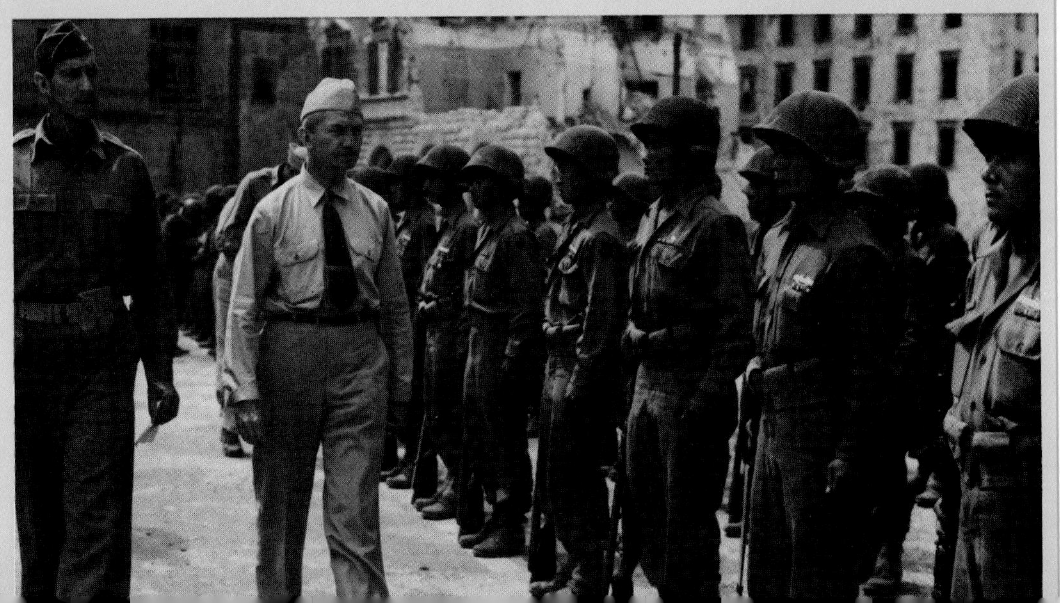

6. ORAL REPORTS Ask several of your students to present oral reports based on a book of photographs of the relocation of Japanese Americans during World War II. If possible, obtain a copy of *Executive Order 9066: The Internment of 115,000 Japanese-Americans* by Maisie and Richard Conrat (California Historical Society, 1972). This excellent book of photographs offers some commentary, but the pictures tell their own story.

7. CREATIVE EXPRESSION The "shameful episode" of the relocation of Japanese Americans has been called the most blatant form of discrimination in America since slavery. Encourage your students to consider how they might have felt if they were among the Nisei herded into a relocation center during World War II. Ask them to express their imagined feelings in creative ways. Possibilities for expression include poems, paintings, collages of pictures, skits, models of the type of housing provided for the Nisei, political cartoons, and musical compositions.

Answers To Review Questions

1. Melting-pot theory: all ethnic groups would blend together to form a new group known as Americans. Dominant-culture theory: the immigrant would abandon all his/her own culture and adopt the dominant Anglo-American culture.
2. At some times, immigrants have been welcomed in order to settle the land, provide labor, and defend the country. At other times, the mood has changed and Americans have opposed foreigners because they have a different religious belief or different language and culture, which they seek to preserve in America.
3. Nativists charged that immigrants were illiterates, paupers, criminals, and drunkards,—a threat to American democracy.
4. Some Americans feared that foreigners with radical ideas might try to start revolutions here. This "Red scare" caused many people to demand that Congress take steps to limit immigration.
5. The purpose of the immigration act of 1924 was to limit total immigration to the United States, except from the Western Hemisphere, to about 150,000 each year. A nation was given a quota based on the proportion of the white population in 1920 that traced its origins back to that country.

Perhaps there was also another reason that few mentioned. As a member of a nativist organization said, "This is our time to get things done that we have been trying to get done for a quarter of a century."

At the end of the war, the Japanese Americans were released. Most returned to their homes in West Coast states to pick up the pieces of their shattered lives, but some moved on. Prejudice against the Japanese remained high for several years, but as war memories faded, it died down.

Into the mainstream. There is encouraging evidence that discrimination and prejudice against ethnic groups have declined during the past generation. The decline is probably due, in large part, to education. Another factor in the decline is that most ethnic groups have now entered the mainstream of American life.

The answer to the question "Why can't they be like us?" is "More and more they are." That in turn raises two more questions. How did the immigrant groups enter the mainstream? And now that most of them have, what is the future of ethnicity in America? We shall explore those questions in the next chapter.

CHECKUP

1. What countries have been the main source of immigration to the United States since the 1920s?
2. How did the law enacted in 1965 change the immigration system?
3. In what way were Japanese Americans the object of discrimination during World War II?

Key Facts from Chapter 21

1. Assimilation is the process by which one is absorbed into another culture.
2. Under the melting-pot theory, assimilation would come about by immigrants blending their separate cultures into an entirely new culture.
3. Under the dominant-culture theory, assimilation would come about by immigrants giving up their own cultures and fully accepting the dominant Anglo-American culture.
4. There have been periods in American history when nativism—opposition to foreigners—was strong.
5. At the same time that nativism has existed, foreigners have been welcomed in order to settle the land, provide labor, and defend the country.
6. For many years immigration laws favored the admission of immigrants from northern and western Europe.
7. In recent years the main source of United States immigration has been the Western Hemisphere.

★ REVIEWING THE CHAPTER ★

People, Places and Events

Nativism *P. 427*
Assimilation *P. 427*
Melting-pot theory *P. 427*
Dominant-culture theory *P. 428*
Know-Nothing party *P. 430*
Immigration act of 1917 *P. 434*
Immigration act of 1924 *P. 437*
Quota *P. 437*
"National orgin" *P. 437*
Immigration law of 1965 *P. 440*

Review Questions

1. Compare the melting-pot and dominant-culture theories. *Pp. 427–429* Les. 1

2. Describe the mixed feelings about immigration that many Americans have held at different times in the country's history. *Pp. 429–430* Les. 1

3. In general, what reasons did the nativists give for their anti-immigrant attitude? *P. 430* Les. 2

4. How did the "Red scare" of 1919 and 1920 influence American attitudes toward immigration? *P. 436* Les. 3

5. Explain the purpose and provisions of the immigration act of 1924. P. 437 Les. 3

6. Who, after blacks, make up the nation's largest minority group today? Why have these people come to the United States? *P. 439* Les. 4

7. What other ethnic groups have been recent immigrants to the United States? *Pp. 439–440* Les. 4

8. In what ways did the immigration law of 1965 change the rules for immigration? *P. 440* Les. 4

9. What happened to many Japanese Americans following December 7, 1941? Why? *Pp. 441–442* Les. 4

Chapter Test

In the first section below is a list of names and terms found in the chapter. In the second section is a list of phrases. Match each name or term with the phrase associated with it. Write your answers on a separate piece of paper.

1. Melting-pot theory
2. Immigration act of 1924
3. "Red scare"
4. Immigration Law of 1965
5. Mexican Americans
6. "Relocation centers"
7. Assimilation
8. Know-Nothing party
9. Black Americans
10. Nativism
11. Immigration act of 1917
12. Japanese Americans

a. Largest minority group in the United States
b. Fear of revolution
c. Detention camps for Japanese Americans
d. Set quotas for immigration of the basis of national origins.
e. Process of being absorbed into another culture.
f. Immigrants over sixteen had to be able to read in some language.
g. Ended the quota system
h. Second-largest minority group in the United States
i. Opposition to foreigners
j. Victims of discrimination during World War II
k. A political organization that wanted to hold down immigration
l. "America is God's crucible"

6. Mexican Americans. They have come to the United States in search of economic opportunity.
7. Puerto Ricans, Cubans, and other Hispanic groups; Vietnamese; Filipinos.
8. The new immigration law ended the discriminatory quota system based on national origin, which had favored immigrants from northern and western Europe. Immigration was still limited: 170,000 from outside the Western Hemisphere, and 120,000 from within. The law gave preference to those who had relatives in the United States, to refugees, to those with skills needed in the United States, and to certain unskilled workers as well.
9. Following the Japanese attack on Pearl Harbor, Japanese Americans living in western states were forced into "relocation centers" and detained there for the duration of the war. The discrimination against and mistreatment of Japanese Americans resulted from Army charges of disloyalty and long smoldering prejudice.

Answers for Chapter Test
1. l **2.** d **3.** b **4.** g **5.** h **6.** c **7.** e **8.** k **9.** a **10.** i **11.** f **12.** j

Background Information

PULASKI DAY These girls are participants in a Pulaski Day parade in New York City. The parade is held every year on the first Sunday in October. Many Polish-American organizations participate. Red and white are the colors of the Polish flag.

Casimir Pulaski—Polish noble and patriot, and soldier in the American Revolution—is the man the Polish Americans honor on this day. He was born in 1748 in the Polish province of Podolia, which is now part of the Ukrainian Soviet Socialist Republic. In his twenties, Pulaski was arrested after leading an unsuccesful revolt against Poland's Russian rulers. He eventually reached France, where he heard about the American cause from Ben Franklin.

Arriving in America in July 1777, Pulaski joined George Washington's forces. Congress commissioned him to organize a cavalry corps, known as Pulaski's Legion. He was wounded during the siege of Savannah and died two days later, on October 11, 1779.

CHAPTER 22

THE IMMIGRANTS' RESPONSE

LESSON 1

UP TO THIS POINT you have looked at the ways America responded to the immigrants. But the meeting of the immigrants and America was a two-way street. What was the immigrants' response to America? How did they react to the pressure to assimilate? How did their descendants react? Has America really been a melting pot for those millions who came here?

Easing the Adjustment

Earlier, you noted that immigrant groups usually stayed together. Most large cities had a little Italy, a Kleindeutschland, an Irishtown, a little Warsaw. One reason for this you read in the last chapter: a large number of later immigrants came to join relatives already here.

A second reason was simply that immigrant families wanted to be with "their own kind"—people with whom they had something in common. Often they sought out people who came from the same village in the old country. Such people could be trusted. They could be depended on for help in making the adjustment to the new life. Thus, as social scientist Andrew Greeley has explained:

> . . . in the Italian neighborhoods of New York's lower east side in the early 1920's it was possible to trace, block by block, not only the region in Italy but also the very villages from which the inhabitants had come. Indeed, it is no exaggeration to say that some of these blocks were nothing more than foreign colonies of Sicilian villages.

An immigrant family that could not find others from its own village would look for people who were at least from the same country. Their reason was the same: these were the people who shared their language, their experiences, and their values. By banding together they could help each other in the strange new world they now lived in.

Even after settling into a neighborhood of familiar people, the immigrants found adjustment to American life anything but easy. The newcomers found themselves in an environment that was coldly neutral at best. They often encountered discrimination and were ridiculed as "greenhorns." It seemed to them that America was demanding that they adopt its ways immediately. One immigrant told why this was difficult.

> . . . the alien who comes here from Europe is not the raw material that Americans suppose him to be. He is not a blank sheet to be written on as you see fit. He has not sprung out of nowhere. Quite the contrary. He brings with him a deep-rooted tradition, a system of culture and tastes and habits—a point of view which is as ancient as his national experience. . . . And it is this thing—this entire Old World soul of his—that comes in conflict with America as soon as he has landed.

Were the native Americans' demands for conformity a kind of "we—they" thinking? Do you think the attitudes described are unique to Americans?

Their own churches. Newcomers eased their adjustment to the New World in several ways. First and most important,

LESSON 1 *(2 to 3 days)*

Performance Objective

To compile a list of at least six factors in immigrants' lives that helped to ease their adjustment to American life, and to explain the need fulfilled by each factor.

Famous Person

Jane Addams

Vocabulary

Mutual-aid society, Americanization program, assimilation through public schools

Activities

1. **GUEST SPEAKER** You might wish to invite a guest speaker to talk to the class as a motivating activity for this lesson. A community member who immigrated to America might be willing to discuss his or her adjustment to American life. Provide the speaker with the text of this lesson before the talk. The speaker might choose to discuss a personal reaction to the items mentioned in the text or to speak about other ways in which his or her adjustment to American life was facilitated.

2. **READING FOR INFORMATION/DISCUSSION** After students have read the lesson, ask them to make a list of at least six factors in immigrants' lives that helped to ease their adjustment to American life. List the factors on the chalkboard and discuss the need fulfilled by each factor. Then ask students to identify some of the problems and criticisms associated with the assimilation efforts.

3. **RESEARCH/CREATIVE WRITING** The social functions of the mutual-aid societies were often based on religious celebrations. Many ethnic organizations today sponsor enormously successful feasts and festivals. Ask your students to find out more about the traditions of such annual festivals and to write publicity releases for the next festivals. Library resources and local ethnic organizations are possible sources of information. Have students include the origins of the festivals and the festivities associated with them.

For example, some students might choose to write about the San Gennaro Festival, held in Little Italy in New York City each September. During this eleven-day festival, thousands of Italians and others join together to honor San Gennaro, the third-century saint who led the people out of Naples when Mount Vesuvius erupted. Festivities include hundreds of stands which feature both food and games of chance, a parade, band concerts, dances, and a mass to honor the saint. However, many would agree that the food—including baked ziti, homemade manicotti, sausage and peppers, and canolli—is the main attraction.

they tried to re-create the religious life they had known in the Old World. Every immigrant group since the Pilgrims and the Puritans had done this. From their small wages they scraped together money to build their own church. They did this even when there was a church of exactly the same religion nearby.

In their own church, members could speak the same language, share the same religious customs, celebrate the same holidays. Most Poles, Italians, and Portuguese were Catholic, for example. Yet they honored their own saints with festivals at different times of the year, and in different ways. Also, in their own church and church schools, parents could teach children the religious customs and values of their own people.

Mutual-aid societies. Immigrants also formed groups to help one another. Through these mutual-aid societies they could buy life and health insurance. Some societies loaned small sums of money in time of need. Such groups set up their own orphanages, hospitals, and old-age homes. They founded their own cemeteries, for it was important that they not be buried among strangers.

Their organizations also had a social purpose. At their picnics and dances, members could spend their leisure time together. There they could see that their sons and daughters would meet and marry their own kind.

The great social function was the parade. It was the parade, writes one historian of immigration, that "enabled the group to display before the whole world the evidence of its solidarity, which enabled the individual to demonstrate that he belonged. . . ."

Foreign-language newspapers. Another important part of immigrant life was the foreign-language newspaper. About 1900 there were more than 1,000 such newspapers, and in almost every language. Through them, immigrants kept up with news of the old village and country. They also read the news of marriages, births, deaths, and honors received in their own community. Such news was not likely to be carried in the local English-language newspaper.

Some Americans criticized foreign-language newspapers. These papers, they charged, slowed down assimilation. A well-known German American offered a different view.

> . . . that press does the country a necessary and very important service. In the first place, it fills a real and very urgent want. That want will exist so long as there is a large number of German-born citizens in this republic. There will always be many among them . . . who arrived on American soil without any knowledge of the English language, who may be able to acquire enough of it to serve them in their daily work, but not enough to enable them to understand newspaper articles on political or similar subjects. Such persons must receive the necessary information about current events . . . from journals published in the language they understand, or they will not have it at all.

The writer of this piece sees the foreign-language newspaper as a bridge to Americanization. Others saw it, the mutual-aid society, and immigrant clubs as obstacles to Americanization.

Who was right? Very likely both. Certainly there were those who wanted simply to re-create the old village in their corner of America. Ethnic institutions helped them do this. Many others wanted to become part of the America beyond their neighborhoods. Ethnic institutions gave them a secure home base from which they could go forth to meet America. Ethnic social groups, it is true, reminded members of the ways of the old country. But they also urged members to become American citizens, and prepared them for it by teaching the language and ways of America.

Americanization programs. Concerned about the large numbers of newcomers, some Americans around the turn of the century decided that America's assimilating powers needed a push. They launched Americanization programs. Patriotic societies printed millions of pamphlets to teach the immigrant about American government and society. Several business organizations did the same.

Volunteer groups, churches, and state and city governments ran evening schools and other programs where immigrants learned English. There were numerous special programs that drove the point home to the immigrants: they—the immigrants—were the problem, Americanization was the answer. A writer has described one such program that he witnessed.

Laotian immigrants learn English at a Christmas party in Boulder, Colorado. From the refreshments they learn the words for various foods. By playing Bingo, they are taught the words for numbers.

4. THOUGHT PROVOKER In 1852, Massachusetts enacted the first law that compelled children to attend public school. In a recent education journal, the following statement was made: "Compulsory education paid off magnificently. . . . Immigrant children, by the millions, were brought into the mainstream of American life. And a sense of national unity developed as children from different parts of the country, from different families, lived and worked through 10 to 12 years of schooling—sharing a heritage of knowledge, goals, and attitudes and often singing the same songs from sea to sea and border to border."

Have your students analyze this statement. Ask: Do you think the statement is realistic, or idealistic? Does the writer of this statement believe in the melting-pot theory, or the dominant-culture theory? Ask your students to reread the sections entitled "The ethnic candidate" and "Ethnic pride," on pages 396–398. Can a "sense of national unity" and ethnic pride be compatible? Ask your students to recall the school courses they had in grammar school. Ask: Which courses would have been particularly helpful to an immigrant child? If a large number of immigrant children were enrolled in this school district this year, what new courses might be helpful to them?

5. CREATIVE WRITING The Americanization programs often resulted in the establishment of settlement houses in the urban ghettos. One such house was Hull House, which is described on page 451. These settlement houses were places where Americans taught the ways of the new land to immigrants and their children. Ask your students to imagine that a large group of immigrants have recently settled in their community. Ask them to devise a curriculum for a settlement house that would teach the immigrant adults and children how to live in America.

6. LISTENING FOR INFORMATION This lesson discusses several organizations that were designed to ease the immigrants' adjustment to their new life. Many people have argued that these organizations hindered the immigrants rather than helped them. The controversial neighborhood politicians, who often served as lifelines between the immigrants and the new society, have been both cursed and praised for their influence with immigrants. Oscar Handlin's *Immigration as a Factor in American History* (Englewood Cliffs, N.J.: Prentice-Hall, Inc., 1959) presents both sides of the issue about the neighborhood politician. You might like to read excerpts from the chapter entitled "The Immigrant in American Politics" (pages 94–116). Opinions by Lincoln Steffens and about G. W. Plunkitt of Tammany Hall are found in that chapter.

For a festival sponsored by Henry Ford during the early 1920's a giant pot was built outside the gates of his factory. Into this pot danced groups of gaily dressed immigrants dancing and singing their native songs. From the other side of the pot emerged a single stream of Americans dressed alike in the contemporary standard dress and singing the national anthem. As the tarantellas and the polkas at last faded away only the rising strains of the national anthem could be heard as all the immigrants finally emerged.

Efforts to bring the newcomer into the mainstream of American life were mostly well intended. There was probably much good in them. But those who ran the programs were not always sensitive to the feelings of the people on the receiving end. The next piece that you read explains the feelings of one such person, who recalls the difficulty in becoming adjusted to life in America.

How unkind, how cruel are the methods sometimes used in connection with our so-called Americanization program. Think of our saying to these foreign peoples, some of whom have been in this country for perhaps a brief period: Forget your native land, forget your mother tongue, do away in a day with your inherited customs, put from you as a cloak all that inheritance and early environment made you and become in a day an American. . . .

This was precisely the talk I used to hear when I first came to this country. There was then as now, I regret to say, a spirit of compulsion in the air. "Either become an American citizen or get out," was in substance the attitude of certain people. But how was I to choose so suddenly? "Give me time for try," Thomas Daly makes an Italian say. I needed as every immigrant does, this "time for try," to see whether I could honestly become an American.

The public schools. Most of the Americanization effort of the early twentieth century focused on the children of the immigrants. The greatest aid in this work was the public school. There the children learned to speak and write English. American-born teachers taught about American history and American government.

"Go and see in our public schools the children of the German, Irish, Bohemian, and Italian parents, waving the Stars and Stripes on the Glorious Fourth," a political leader assured his listeners, "and you will fully appreciate . . . that education is solving the problem." And all the while, in school and out, these second-generation Americans were becoming accustomed to American ways, tastes, habits, dress, and values that touched every aspect of life.

CHECKUP

1. What were the main problems that confronted immigrants trying to adjust to life in America?
2. Describe some of the groups and programs that were intended to help immigrants adjust to American ways.

LESSON 2

Coming to Terms with America

As the children became Americans, differences arose with their immigrant parents. From the parents' point of view, their children were carelessly throwing off a valuable heritage. The parents wanted to keep what they had always learned about family life: the proper relationship of husband to wife, of child to parent, of young to old; the proper place of religion and of education. The children, speaking one language at home and another at school and on the

Continued on page 452

Jane Addams of Hull House

Among the institutions that helped immigrants adjust to America were the settlement houses. In these neighborhood centers, local residents could find social activities, libraries, and classes in English, music, drama, and a host of practical skills. Among the settlement houses, not any was better known than Chicago's Hull House, founded by the remarkable Jane Addams.

Born into a comfortable Illinois family in 1860, Jane Addams was among the first generation of American women to attend college. After graduating from Rockford Seminary in 1881, she looked for a career where she could be of service to others. She found it on a trip to England in 1883, when she visited an English settlement house called Toynbee Hall. On her return to America she and a college friend, Ellen Gates Starr, arranged for the purchase of the old Hull mansion, then in a poor neighborhood in Chicago. In 1889 Hull House opened its doors. Some 70 other settlement houses were to follow in American cities in the 1890s and early 1900s. Hull House remained, however, the most famous and the largest, growing to 13 buildings and a staff of 65 people.

Actually, settlement houses were meant to aid the poor generally and not just immigrants. But in many cities, it was mainly the immigrants who *were* the poor. The idea was, as one settlement leader explained, "to give the people of the neighborhood some of the advantages which unfortunately have been denied to them." Because settlement workers lived among the people they were serving, and didn't look down on the immigrants' customs and values, they were trusted. Social workers like Jane Addams performed services for the neighborhood—washing newborn babies, tending children, nursing the sick, and burying the dead. But the settlement houses were also intended to help residents work together on all kinds of community problems. These houses became one of the great sources of reform ideas in urban America.

Through her work in settlement houses, her writings, and her many reform activities, Jane Addams became known to millions. She shared the Nobel peace prize in 1931 for her work with women's peace organizations.

Jane Addams chats with some of the girls for whom Hull House offered opportunities for betterment at the start of the present century.

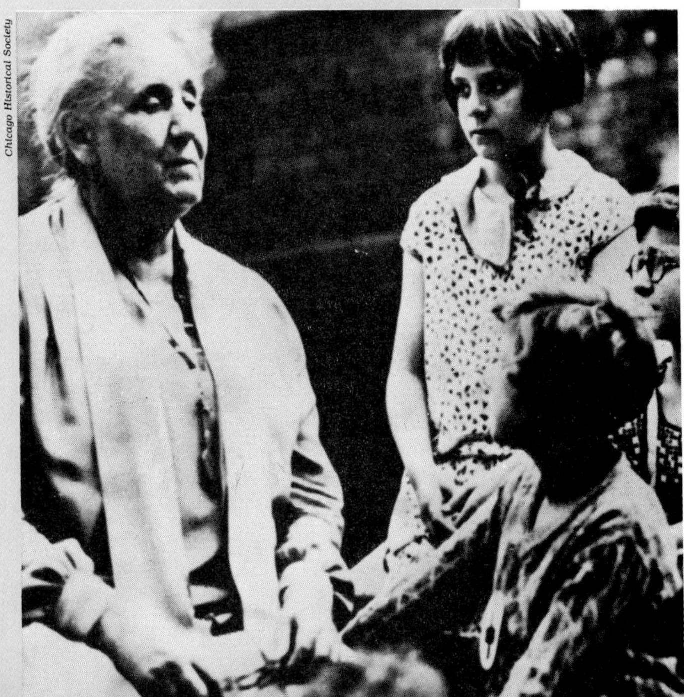
Chicago Historical Society

LESSON 2 *(2 days)*

Performance Objectives

1. To list at least five possible conflicts over values that might develop between generations as children of immigrants become assimilated into American culture. **2.** To demonstrate an understanding of the issues discussed in this unit by presenting at least three generalizations that support and three generalizations that refute the following statement: The melting pot is a desirable goal for America.

Vocabulary

Heritage, generation gap patriarchy, assimilation through marriage, intermarriage, assimilation through opportunity, cultural pluralism

Activities

1. ORAL REPORTS To supplement the information provided about Jane Addams on page 451, have several of your students report to the class on her educational philosophy. Many of her views on the education of immigrant children in the primary grades are included in a speech she made during the National Education Association's annual meeting in July 1897. In that speech she emphasized that education is based on experience. She criticized the public school system for relying on abstract thinking instead of relating to the children's real-life experiences. Excerpts from the speech may be found in *The Annals of America,* Vol. 12 (Chicago: Encyclopaedia Britannica, Inc., 1968) pages 130–135.

streets, found their old-fashioned parents a block to their being accepted as Americans. Never has there been a larger generation gap.

A conflict in values. The next three passages that you read deal with the conflict in values between generations. Try to define what values are at issue. Compare the differences between these generations and what you believe to be the difference between generations today.

> One Saturday Sammy came home rich with seventy-five cents jingling in his pockets. His father, struggling to maintain his last shred of authority, the patriarchy of his own home, demanded to know why he was not at cheder [religious school].
>
> "I hadda chance to make a dollar," Sammy said.
>
> "Sammy!" his father bellowed. "Touching money on the Sabbath! God should strike you dead."
>
> The old man snatched the money and flung it down the stairs.
>
> Sammy glared at his father. . . .
>
> "You big dope!" Sammy screamed at him, his voice shrill with rage. . . .
>
> The old man did not respond. His eyes were closed and his lips were moving. He looked as if he had had a stroke. He was praying.
>
> Sammy went down and searched for the money until he found it.
>
> His mother came down and sat on the stairs above him. She could never scold Sammy. She was sorry for Papa but she was sorry for Sammy too. She understood. Here in America life moves too fast for the Jews. There is not time enough to pray and survive. The old laws like not touching money or riding on the Sabbath—it was hard to make them work. Israel [Sammy's brother] might try to live by them but never Sammy. . . .

. . . .

> I am nervous when I bring friends to my house; the place looks so Italian. Here hangs a picture of Victor Emmanuel, and over there is one of the Cathedral of Milan, and next to it, one of St. Peter's, and on the buffet stands a wine-pitcher of medieval design; it's forever red and brilliant with wine. These things are heirlooms belonging to my father, and no matter who may come to our house, he likes to stand under them and brag.
>
> So I begin to shout to him. I tell him to . . . be an American once in a while.

. . . .

> My contemporaries had labeled me Italian. . . . I didn't want to be Italian. Or Swedish. Or Irish. Or anything "different." Like countless bewildered young people before me—and to come—I just wanted to be myself. "Why can't I just be Joe," I thought.

The role of women. Life in America not only added to the conflict between generations. It also upset old ideas about the role of women. Traditionally, women kept house, cooked, and raised the children and looked after their religious upbringing. Few, including women themselves, questioned that woman's place was in the home. In America, however, many younger immigrant women grew dissatisfied with that role.

Just as important, a good many found it necessary to take jobs outside of the home in order to help with the family income. Many found jobs in the "needle trades," as the clothing industry was called. Others found jobs as clerks in stores and as office workers. Once out of the home, a good many questioned the traditions that had kept them there. This led to many conflicts, sometimes between husbands and wives, but more often between parents and daughters.

The third generation. It was the third generation that made its peace with America. Few still spoke the language of the old country. No longer torn between two worlds, the third generation was comfortable in its Americanness.

Except for the newest arrivals, most descendants of immigrants have reached this stage. One sign has been the drop in foreign-language newspapers. In 1910 there were 142 such daily newspapers and more than 800 weekly papers. Fifty years later the daily newspapers had decreased by half, and the weekly ones by three fourths.

Most of the mutual-aid societies are gone. So are many of the social organizations. Of the older immigrant groups, only among the Poles and the Italians do the social clubs remain strong. Church is still important to many. No longer, though, need the church serve only one's own ethnic group. With better incomes, some second- and third-generation Americans began to drift out of the tight neighborhood community and into new city neighborhoods or suburbs. There, in the schools and on the block, they have met and mixed with people of different backgrounds and from other ethnic groups.

Assimilation through marriage. One of the important values of each immigrant group was the belief in "marrying your own kind." Has this value continued? Or has there been an increase in intermarriage among ethnic groups? Here are the data on intermarriage in one city over a period of eighty years.

What does this table indicate about intermarriage (marrying outside the group) the longer a group is inside America? To answer this question, first compare old immigrant groups with new immigrant groups. Then compare the figures for each group over the 80-year period.

Percentage Marrying Within Own Ethnic Group in New Haven, Connecticut, 1870—1950
(to nearer percent)

Ethnic Group	*1870*	*1900*	*1930*	*1940*	*1950*
Jewish	100	99	95	94	95
Italian	—	98	87	82	77
British	93	78	59	55	54
Irish	93	75	74	45	50
Polish	—	100	68	53	41
German	86	55	40	27	27
Scandinavian	40	83	33	18	22
All ethnic groups	92	75	66	63	61

2. CREATIVE WRITING/ ROLE-PLAYING The conflict of values between generations frequently resulted in family quarrels in immigrant homes. Parents often wanted their children to learn and keep the old ways; the children frequently wanted to adopt the new American ways. After your students have read this lesson, divide the class into groups of five or six. Have each group write and perform a short skit that shows the possible nature of one such argument. You might wish to have one group of students investigate and report to the class about the plot of *Flower Drum Song,* a musical that deals with conflicts between two generations in families of San Francisco's Chinatown.

3. DEBATE Resolved: The melting pot is a desirable goal for America. Divide the class into six groups; have three groups prepare arguments in support of the resolution and three groups prepare arguments that refute the resolution. Encourage students to seek additional information from sources other than the text. Have each group choose a person to represent them in the debate.

4. READING FOR INFORMATION Lerner Publications Company of Minneapolis publishes a series of books for young people about various ethnic groups in America. The series, entitled In America, includes books about the following groups: Chinese, Czechs and Slovaks, Dutch, East Indians and Pakistanis, English, French, Germans, Greeks, Hungarians, Irish, Italians, Japanese, Jews, Mexicans, Negroes, Norwegians, Poles, Puerto Ricans, Russians, Scots and Scotch-Irish, Swedes, Ukrainians, and American Indians. Each volume covers conditions in the country of origin, the immigrant experience, and the achievements of notable immigrants of the group. You might wish to have students choose one of these books to read as a concluding activity for this unit.

The view of the immigrant generation, and of some of the second generation, toward these developments is expressed by this middle-aged Czech woman in New Jersey.

> The old Czechs are dying and moving away. Our parents are the ones who were very active. The people of my age still had their parents around. They remember the customs, and that is something you can't forget. But you can't pass memories on to your children. The younger generation marry people who are not Czech and don't keep up the language with their children. I go to see a friend of mine who's 83, and I talk Czech with her. If I didn't I'd forget the language.

Assimilation through opportunity. One thing that has advanced assimilation in America has been opportunity. The streets of America were not lined with gold as stories in some European villages had it. But by and large the immigrants, or at least their children and grandchildren, have "made it" in America.

That does not mean that every member of every group is now well-off. Nor does it mean that all groups have achieved the same degree of success. But large numbers of every group have improved their position, and some have fared extremely well. There is no group that cannot point to some of its members who have become prominent as doctors, business leaders, professors, scientists, political leaders, lawyers, and so on.

Of those arriving most recently, Cubans are among the most well-off. Many of them were middle-class before they came here. They brought their skills and professions with them from Cuba.

Continued on page 456

The Motion-Picture Industry

The immigrant contribution to American cultural life has been enormous. American art, writing, theater, and music have all been enriched by this source of talent. In the 1930s, for example, the conductors of all America's major symphony orchestras had been born outside the United States. That is still true of the majority of symphony conductors today. Such writers of America's popular music as Irving Berlin ("Easter Parade," "God Bless America," "White Christmas") and George Gershwin (*Rhapsody in Blue, Porgy and Bess,* "Swanee") were immigrants or the children of immigrants.

In no area of cultural life, however, did immigrants have a greater impact than in the movies. To begin with, they made key contributions to the technology of the movies. The modern motion picture itself was invented by W.K.L. Dickson, Thomas Edison's English-born assistant. Sigmund Lubin, who came to the United States from Germany at age twenty-five, invented the motion-picture projector. Lubin also founded one of the earliest movie studios, and is sometimes called "the father of the moving picture industry."

Immigrants had a major part in developing that industry. Nearly every major movie company was created and run by them. Hungarian-born Adolph Zukor first had a job as a film sales-

James Wong Howe (right), born in China, won many awards for motion-picture camera artistry.

5. ORAL REPORTS Several of your students might enjoy reading *Life Goes to the Movies* (New York: Time Inc., 1975), a book full of photographs of the history of the movie industry. Thirty-six years of *Life* magazine's coverage plus photographs of early film history are included. Have the students select pictures of immigrant movie stars and directors to show to the class.

person and then became owner of a nickelodeon (a theater presenting entertainment for an admission price of five cents). He teamed up with a young glove manufacturer named Jesse Lasky, the son of Polish immigrant parents, to found Paramount Pictures. One of Lasky's glove salesmen, a Polish immigrant named Samuel Goldwyn, joined with a Russian-born junk dealer named Louis B. Mayer to form Metro-Goldwyn-Mayer—MGM. Carl Laemmle, born in Germany, started life in America as a clothing salesperson. Like Adolph Zukor, Laemmle entered the world of the movies as a nickelodeon owner. Eventually he founded Universal Pictures. William Fox, another immigrant from Hungary, followed almost the same path on his way to forming Twentieth Century-Fox. Finally, Warner Brothers was founded by the four sons of a Russian immigrant shoemaker.

Immigrants have also made a huge contribution to American films as producers, directors, photographers, and of course actors and actresses. Spiro Skouras (Greek), Greta Garbo (Swedish), Charlie Chaplin and Bob Hope (English)—these are some of the best known. James Wong Howe, born in China, won many awards for moving-picture photography.

It has been said that the most distinctively American art form is the motion picture. It seems especially appropriate that in this nation of nations, immigrants from many lands should have played such major roles in developing this art form.

6. LISTENING FOR INFORMATION You might wish to read to your students excerpts from Sam Levenson's *Everything but Money* (New York: Simon & Schuster, 1949). In this book, humorist Levenson tells of life in a crowded New York tenement where he lived with his Russian parents. Mr. Levenson offers a humorous account of the hardships of ghetto living and the benefits such a life provided him.

7. THOUGHT PROVOKER In *Beyond the Melting Pot,* Glazer and Moynihan state: "Ethnicity is more than an influence on events; it is commonly the source of events. Social and political institutions do not merely respond to ethnic interests; a great number of institutions exist for the specific purpose of serving ethnic interests. This in turn tends to perpetuate them. In many ways, the atmosphere of New York City is hospitable to ethnic groupings: it recognizes them, and rewards them, and to that extent encourages them." Ask your students to interpret this statement. Ask: What are some of the ways in which New York City appears to be hospitable to ethnic groups? Are other large cities in the United States also hospitable to ethnic groups? In what ways, if any, does your town or city recognize or reward ethnicity?

To retain their cultural heritage, these Cuban guitar students play the music of their homeland.

Puerto Ricans and Mexicans have not fared so well. When they arrived, they were often at least as poor as those who came earlier from Ireland, Italy, and Russia. They have come at a time when many of the opportunities for unskilled workers that earlier groups found in America no longer exist. They have also run into a good deal of prejudice. Even so, these groups too are beginning to start the upward climb. A growing number of their young people are attending college. They are finding better jobs on graduation.

Has America, then, been the melting pot that Crèvecoeur and Zangwill said it was? The authors of a book entitled *Beyond the Melting Pot* don't think so. "The point about the Melting Pot," they write, "is that it did not happen." Many others share this view. Nor do they believe immigrant groups have given up all their culture and adopted the dominant Anglo-American culture, as some demanded. They offer a different description of what has happened.

Immigrant groups, they believe, have become thoroughly American, and have adopted much of the dominant Anglo-American culture. At the same time, they have kept much that was distinctive about their own cultural heritage. This process of change has come to be called *cultural pluralism.* The American motto is "Out of Many, One." Some say that "Out of Many, Many" would be as accurate.

The future of ethnicity. What lies ahead for cultural pluralism in America? Many think ethnic differences will soon disappear. They point to the drop in foreign languages, the rise in ethnic intermarriage, the greater assimilation that has taken place with the upward social and economic movement of ethnic groups.

Certainly all the immigrant groups of colonial times, except for a few small ones, have lost their identities.

Is it, then, only a matter of time until later ethnic groups do the same? The writers of a recent book on ethnic Americans think so. "We believe," they say, "that we are on the threshold of the disappearance of the European ethnic minorities." And one of America's greatest sociologists wrote in 1945, "The future of American ethnic groups seems to be limited; it is likely that they will be quickly absorbed." The ethnic revival of the 1960s and 1970s is seen by these people as a passing thing, a sort of last gasp of ethnicity.

But Andrew Greeley, the social scientist who is quoted earlier, sees the present and the future differently. "Ethnic diversity seems to be alive and well," Greeley writes. He explains: "Ethnic diversity seems to be something that man grimly hangs onto, despite overwhelming evidence that he ought to give it up." And Richard Gambino, in a book on Italian Americans entitled *Blood of My Blood* (1974), writes, "Today it is no longer in doubt that ethnicity is a powerful force on the American scene and is likely to remain in the open rather than resubmerging." Still another writer sums up his views in the title of his book: *The Unmeltable Ethnics.*

We cannot know for sure the long-term future of ethnicity in America. What we can be reasonably sure of is that for at least some time to come, ethnic diversity will continue as one of the important facts of life in modern America.

CHECKUP

1. What kind of value conflicts arose between immigrant parents and their Americanized children?
2. What is meant by the phrase "assimilation through marriage"? Is there more—or less—intermarriage today among ethnic groups as compared with earlier years?
3. How has "assimilation through opportunity" advanced the status of ethnic groups in America?

Key Facts from Chapter 22

1. To ease the difficult adjustment in a new country, immigrants tended to settle in neighborhoods with others from their old country.
2. Other aids to the immigrants' adjustment included churches, mutual-aid societies, foreign-language newspapers, and Americanization programs.
3. The greatest aid in Americanizing the children of immigrants has been the public schools.
4. Conflicts in values often arose between the immigrants and their Americanized children.
5. Ethnic groups have adopted much of the dominant Anglo-American culture, while keeping much that was distinctive in their own cultures. This process of change is called cultural pluralism.

8. FILMSTRIPS Accent on Ethnic America is a series of six filmstrips with either records or cassettes available from Social Studies School Service, 10,000 Culver Blvd., Culver City, Calif. 90230. The filmstrips examine the cultural problems of six immigrant groups. Each filmstrip discusses common stereotypes of the ethnic group, the culture each group brought to the United States, and the effect of that culture on present-day members of the various groups. Titles are *The Polish Americans*, *The Mexican Americans*, *The Puerto Rican*, *the American Jew*, *The Italian American*, and *The Chinese Americans.*

Answers To Review Questions

1. To be with relatives and other people with whom they had something in common. By banding together, immigrants could help one another adjust to the new life.
2. Settled among members of their own ethnic group; established their own church in which they could re-create the religious life they were used to in the old country; formed mutual-aid societies and social organizations; held parades; founded foreign-language newspapers.
3. Mutual-aid societies made loans; helped the orphans, sick, and aged; founded cemeteries; and provided opportunities for social occasions, such as picnics, dances, and parades.
4. Foreign-language newspapers gave immigrants news of the old village and country; news of their own community; information about American politics, current events, and customs; and encouragement to become American citizens. Some people criticized these papers and charged that they slowed down assimilation by encouraging immigrants to re-create the old village in their corner of America.

5. Immigrants continued to hold many of the values and customs of their ethnic background, while their children were becoming accustomed to American ways, tastes, habits, dress, language, and values.
6. Traditionally, European women remained at home, caring for the house and children. In America it was necessary for many women to seek employment outside the home. This introduced them to different ideas about the rights and role of women and led them to question the traditions that had kept them in the home.
7. Decrease in foreign-language newspapers; disappearance of most mutual-aid societies and many social organizations; increase in ethnic intermarriages; decrease in importance of ethnic neighborhoods and churches.
8. Assimilation has advanced because of foreign-language newspapers, Americanization programs, public schools, intermarriage, and economic opportunity.
9. The later the date of arrival in America, the greater the chance of intermarriage.

★ REVIEWING THE CHAPTER ★

People, Places, and Events

Mutual-aid society *P. 448*
Americanization program *P. 449*
Assimilation through public schools *P. 450*
Jane Addams *P. 451*
Settlement house *P. 451*
Generation gap *P. 452*
Assimilation through intermarriage *P. 453*
Assimilation through opportunity *P. 454*
Cultural pluralism *P. 456*

Review Questions

1. Why did immigrant groups usually remain together in the United States? *P. 447* Les. 1
2. How did newcomers ease their adjustment to America? *Pp. 447–449* L. 1
3. In what ways did mutual-aid societies help the immigrant adjust to America? *P. 448* Les. 1
4. How did foreign-language newspapers help immigrants become assimilated? Why did some people criticize these newspapers? *Pp. 448–449* Les. 1
5. What caused a generation gap between L.2 immigrants and their children? *P. 450*
6. How did the role of women change in America as a result of immigration? *P. 452* Les. 2
7. What facts are given to show that most of the new immigrants have become Americanized by the third generation? *P. 453* Les. 2
8. Summarize the reasons why assimilation has advanced in the United States. L. 1, 2
9. Study the table on p. 453. What conclusions can you reach about the relationship of intermarriage and date of arrival in America? Les. 2

Chapter Test

Complete each sentence by writing the correct answer on a separate piece of paper.

1. Immigrants often settled in neighborhoods peopled by those of the (same) (different) ethnic background.
2. Immigrants eased their adjustment to America by establishing their own (churches) (states).
3. Orphanages and old-age homes were organized through (mutual-aid societies) (government agencies).
4. (Foreign-language newspapers) (The Know-Nothing Party) informed immigrants not only about their own communities but also about American culture and politics.
5. Patriotic societies encouraged (immigration) (assimilation) through Americanization programs.
6. The children of immigrants became Americanized largely through (volunteer groups (public schools).
7. The differences that developed between immigrants and their Americanized children may be called a (quota) (generation gap).
8. It took an immigrant family about (one) (three) generations to become Americanized.
9. In America, assimilation through opportunity means that (every member of every ethnic group is well off) (large numbers of every group have been able to improve their position).
10. A situation where the immigrant group has adopted the dominant Anglo-American culture while keeping much of its own cultural heritage is (cultural pluralism) (intermarriage).

★ REVIEWING THE UNIT 

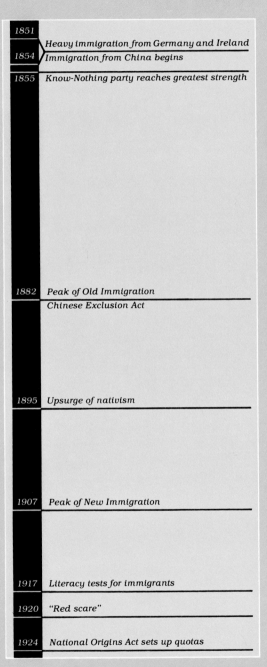

- 1851–1854 *Heavy immigration from Germany and Ireland*
- 1854 *Immigration from China begins*
- 1855 *Know-Nothing party reaches greatest strength*
- 1882 *Peak of Old Immigration*
  Chinese Exclusion Act
- 1895 *Upsurge of nativism*
- 1907 *Peak of New Immigration*
- 1917 *Literacy tests for immigrants*
- 1920 *"Red scare"*
- 1924 *National Origins Act sets up quotas*

Except for the American Indians, the people of the United States are all the descendants of immigrants or are immigrants themselves. Coming from all over the world, they represent many ethnic groups.

Most of the earliest colonists were English, but there were also Dutch, Swedish, French, Spanish, and others. In later colonial times, many Germans and Scotch-Irish came to America. The mid-1800s saw the coming of the Irish and more Germans. This inflow from northern and western Europe is known as the Old Immigration. From 1896 to 1918 most immigrants were from southern and eastern Europe. This is called the New Immigration.

Beginning in the late 1800s, Congress placed restrictions on immigration. The earliest laws were aimed at Asians. Later laws had the effect of favoring immigration from northern and western Europe. In 1965 the discriminatory quota system was ended.

Immigrants came to America in hope of a better life. The first years were difficult. The newcomers toiled at the hardest, lowest-paid jobs. Living conditions, especially in the cities, were often bad. Immigrants frequently met up with nativism—prejudice against foreigners.

Once the difficult adjustment period was over, however, immigrant groups have fared well in America. For most, life has been better than in the old country. They have adopted much of the Anglo-American culture but have retained much that was distinctive in their own cultures.

★ REVIEWING THE UNIT ★

Skills Development: Gathering Source Material

As you study this unit dealing with the American immigrant experience, you may have wondered about your family's national origins. Or perhaps you already know something about your origin and would like to fill in the missing pieces. One way to find out about your roots is through a study of your family history. Such study may help you to trace your ancestors. You probably will not find a really famous person in your family background. But you will discover that your ancestors were real people who may have been involved in some of the great events of history. And you may also discover that they were people with many of the same problems, hopes, and desires that you have.

The purpose of this activity is to aid you in gathering basic historical information that you will use to write or tell a history of your family. You must begin at home with your parents, grandparents, or close relatives. One of the best ways to go about collecting the data is to conduct an oral interview. That is, you prepare a set of questions to ask a family member and then listen carefully as he or she answers. Before interviewing anyone, however, explain why you are asking questions and be sure to respect the person's right to privacy.

At this point, you are ready to start the activity. Below is a list of sample questions for you to consider asking in your interview. Write each set of questions on a 3 x 5 card or a piece of paper.

1. Where were you born? What were the names of your parents?
2. What was your mother's maiden name? Where did her family come from?
3. What memories of your school years do you have? What has been the value of schooling to you?
4. Do you know where our immigrant ancestors came from? When did they emigrate to the United States? Why did they come?
5. Where did the first members of our family originally settle in this country? Why did they choose that particular place?
6. Have our ancestors moved from one place to another over the years? For what reasons?
7. Do you know if any of our ancestors have been directly connected with certain great events in history?
8. Does our family have any legends or stories about the family's past?
9. Does our family have any customs or values that have been passed on from one generation to another?

Those questions are a good starting point for your interview. Now write at least five questions of your own.

After preparing your questions, conduct at least one interview with an older member of your family. Be sure to listen carefully to the responses.

Based on the evidence gathered in your interview, write or tell a brief history of your family. If you have your family's permission, perhaps you would want to include photographs, old letters, or whatever other documents you might have discovered in your research.

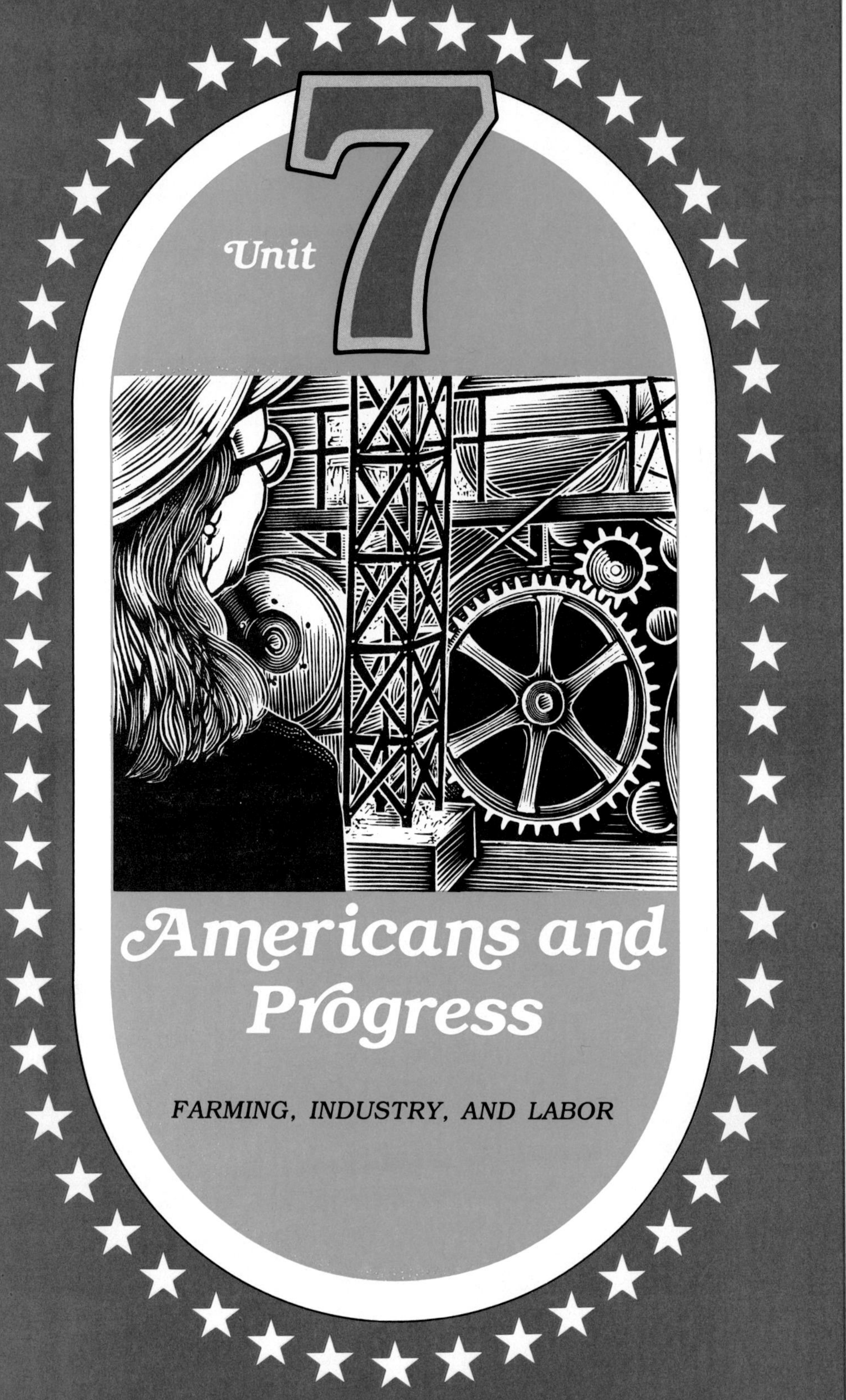
Unit 7
Americans and Progress
FARMING, INDUSTRY, AND LABOR

Background Information

"FORGING THE SHAFT" In a nineteenth-century foundry, an iron shaft is being withdrawn from the furnace before being hammered. This particular foundry, in Cold Spring-on-Hudson, N.Y., produced some 3,000 cannon for the Civil War. The John Ferguson Weir painting (1877) hangs in New York's Metropolitan Museum of Art.

CHAPTER 23

AMERICA'S INDUSTRIAL BEGINNINGS

LESSON 1

ONE of the most popular exhibits at both Disneyland and Walt Disney World is the Carrousel of Progress. Since it first opened at the New York World's Fair in 1964, the show has been seen by more than 70 million people. In this exhibit, the audience is taken by means of a moving platform past various scenes inside an American house in about 1900, in the 1920s, in the 1940s and in the present day. Each scene shows how inventions have made life easier and more pleasant than in the earlier years. An electric refrigerator and freezer replace the old ice box. The family is cooled by an air conditioner instead of by a fan blowing over a cake of ice. A washing machine and clothes dryer have taken over for the scrub board and clothesline. Television sets, stereos, and many other electrical items appear in the last scene. During the show, the sound track informs the audience that every tomorrow can be "The Best Time of Your Life."

One reason for the popularity of the show is that its main theme so well suits the temper of an optimistic, hardworking people. That is the theme of progress. With faith in the future and with hard work, the voice on the sound track tells us, we shall all have a better life.

The meaning of progress. Further, most Americans would agree with the way the Carrousel show defines that better life. Progress, the show seems to tell us, means an abundance of goods. To a people who glory in their country's ability to produce, that definition makes

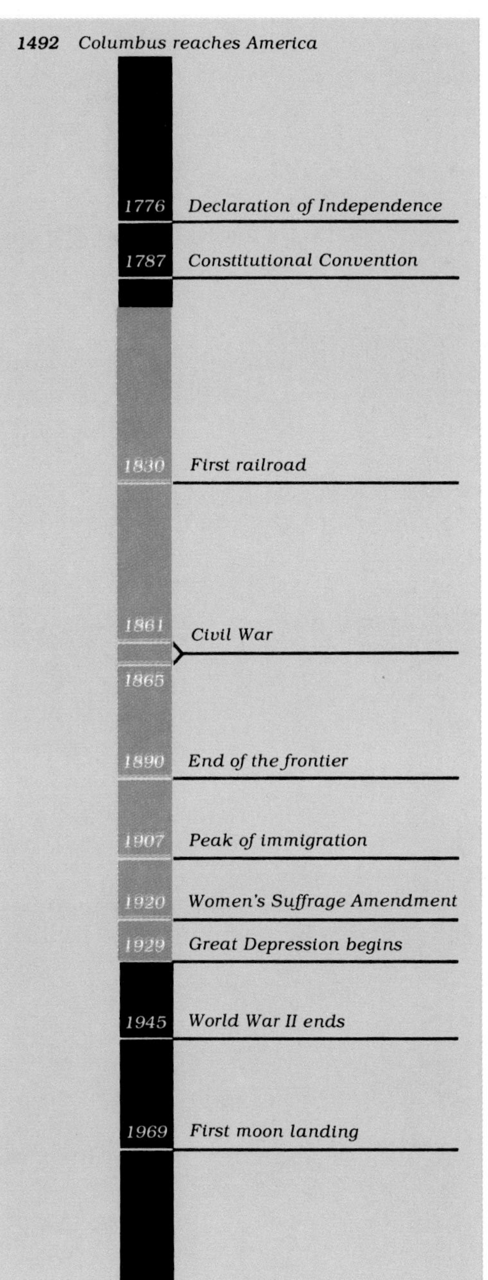

LESSON 1 *(2 days)*

Performance Objectives

1. To discuss orally and to distinguish between the following definitions of progress: **(a)** as prosperity, **(b)** as plenty, **(c)** as moral reform, and **(d)** as reform of institutions. **2.** To identify orally or in writing the factors that brought about the introduction and early expansion of industry in America.

Famous Person

Samuel Slater

Vocabulary

Progress, industrialism, spinning machine, Boston Manufacturing Company

Activities

1. INTRODUCING THE UNIT The central theme of this unit is that Americans have usually associated the idea of progress with increasing material prosperity. However, there have been costs involved, in terms of people excluded from the prosperity and exploitation of resources, both human and natural. The problems peaked with the Great Depression but have been present throughout industrialization. These problems have triggered various responses, including the formation of labor unions, the expansion of rights for women, and the resistance to new ideas and groups.

Develop a discussion concerning a definition of the term *progress*. This could be done before or after reading pages 463–465. Ask if all students favor progress; if there are different kinds of progress; if these different kinds sometimes conflict. Below are several quotations that your students could analyze as part of the discussion of the meaning of progress. It might be useful to make copies of the quotations so that the students may understand them more easily.

"Progress is our most important product." General Electric Company.

"Pity this busy monster, manunkind,/not. Progress is a comfortable disease." e. e. cummings in *One Times One,* 1944.

"The test of our progress is not whether we add more to the abundance of those who have much; it is whether we provide enough for those who have too little." F. D. Roosevelt in Second Inaugural Address, January 20, 1937.

"All progress is based upon a universal innate desire on the part of every organism to live beyond its income." Samuel Butler in *Notebooks.*

"There can be no progress (real, that is, moral) except in the individual and by the individual himself." Charles Baudelaire.

"'D'ye think th' colledges has much to do with th' progress iv th' wurruld?' asked Mr. Hennessy. 'D' ye think,' said Mr. Dooley, ''tis th' mill that makes th' wather run?' " Finley Peter Dunne in *Mr. Dooley's Opinions: on Wall Street.*

As you discuss these quotations with the students, try to establish the four definitions of progress listed in Performance Objective 1.

sense. Most Americans place a high value on material things. Indeed, a good many, believing that "more" is "better," measure their personal progress in life by the number of goods they own.

Progress also means, according to this show, advances in invention and technology. That, too, most Americans would agree with. No nation has been more identified with that kind of progress than the United States. No nation has contributed so much to industrial know-how in the world.

Associating America with the idea of progress is hardly new. In earlier times, some Europeans even dated the beginnings of modern progress from the discovery of America. They were not thinking, however, of goods or technology. They had in mind the unique opportunity America offered to people to begin anew: to build a society free from the traditions and injustices of the Old World. In this new setting, people would achieve moral growth and improvement of the mind. They would reach new heights of political and religious liberty.

Progress as plenty. As time went on, Americans began to think of progress more and more in terms of material plenty. America, of course, had been considered a land of plenty ever since the earliest promoters lured settlers to the New World. But to most of these people "plenty" had meant enough to meet a family's needs for food, clothing, and shelter, with possibly a little left over for a small luxury here and there.

By the 1820s, however, opportunities for real wealth were multiplying. The piling up of wealth now became a measure of progress for both the individual and the nation. "There are no bounds among us to the restless desire to be better off," observed one American in 1845, "and this is the ambition of all classes of society." Through such striving by individuals, it was believed, the whole society gained, and progress was achieved.

Certainly not all Americans shared this view. A good number continued to think of progress in nonmaterial terms. To them, progress meant the reform of individuals or institutions, or even the perfection of the human race.

But for the great majority, plenty was the yardstick of progress—that and the inventions and technology which made that plenty possible. Americans cheered each new machine that added to the flow of goods, each new invention that shortened distances. Walt Whitman, the American poet, exulted over the mountain of goods available to Americans.

> Think of the numberless . . . inventions for our comfort and luxury which the last half dozen years have brought forth—of our baths and ice houses and ice coolers—of our fly traps and mosquito nets—of house bells and marble mantels and sliding tables—of . . . serving machines and street-sweeping machines—in a word, give but a passing glance at the fat volumes of Patent Office Reports and bless your star that fate has cast your lot in the year of our Lord 1857.

By 1876—the end of the country's first century—progress, plenty, invention, and technology were firmly linked in the minds of most Americans. Nearly all would have agreed with the minister Henry Ward Beecher when in that year he declared, "He that invents a machine increases the power of a man and the well-being of mankind."

The First Factories

Today we can see that Jefferson's vision of America as a land of small farms was doomed from the beginning. Even as Jefferson was praising agriculture and deploring the appearance of factories, events were moving America toward industrialism. Indeed, the first factory in America had appeared in 1790, during Washington's first term as President.

Slater's cotton mill. In 1788, Samuel Slater was a textile worker in a cotton mill in England, where the Industrial Revolution had begun. At that time, the British were trying to keep their ideas secret about machines and manufacturing so that they would have no competition. Parliament passed laws prohibiting textile workers and textile machinery from leaving the country.

However, Slater was lured to America by the promise of a rich reward for anyone who knew Britain's industrial secrets. Disguised as a farm boy, the twenty-one-year-old Slater slipped out of England, taking with him in his head his knowledge of the latest machines. Arriving in America in 1789, he built a spinning machine completely from memory. He helped set up America's first cotton mill on the Blackstone River in Pawtucket, Rhode Island.

Effects of the War of 1812. The real beginning of America's industrial revolution came with the War of 1812. Before that time, the United States had been forced to rely upon Britain for most manufactured goods. American manufacturers lacked capital, for Americans with money were more likely to invest it

America's first factories, like this restored mill in Massachusetts, were powered by falling water.

2. READING FOR INFORMATION After the students have read the lesson, have them compile a list of the advantages that the Northeast had in developing industrialism. (See page 466.) After the list has been made, check those advantages that still exist. Ask: Which advantages have vanished? Why, do you think, did they disappear? Today there are different kinds of advantages for geographical regions. These may include availability of natural resources, cheap labor, or low tax rates.

As a follow-up activity, give students the following list of major industries: automobile, steel, oil, aircraft, lumber, computer, electronics, meat packing, food processing, textiles. Ask: Are these industries scattered, or located in one or a few locations? Why do some industries locate in specific areas? (Examples: steel in Pittsburgh and Birmingham; oil in Southwest; textiles from New England to South) Conclude with a discussion of your local area. Ask: Does this area offer anything special for a certain industry? Do certain industries locate here? Why do towns want industry?

3. DISCUSSION The text claims that the War of 1812 aided the growth of American industry. Using appropriate reference material, have the students make a list of products that Great Britain would certainly have attempted to keep America from importing during the war. After putting the list on the chalkboard, discuss with the class which American industries would have been stimulated by the war. Encourage students to use their imagination and reasoning as well as their textbooks and outside resources.

4. BULLETIN-BOARD DISPLAY If Americans generally accepted the definition of progress as plenty during this period, what kinds of things did they want plenty of? How do those consumer items compare with things Americans want today? Ask students to bring in the oldest newspapers, magazines, or mail-order catalogs they can find. Have them make a product-comparison display for the bulletin board, showing, for example, an early radio and a contemporary one, or obsolete items and their replacements.

5. FILMS *America Becomes an Industrial Nation,* American History series (25 minutes, color; McGraw-Hill Films). *The Industrial Revolution in England* (25 minutes, color; Encyclopaedia Britannica Films). *Beginnings and Growth of Industrial America* (10 minutes, b&w; Coronet Films). *The Industrial Revolution: Beginnings in the United States* (25 minutes, color; Encyclopaedia Britannica Films).

6. MODEL / DISPLAY Mechanically inclined students might enjoy making a model of a water-wheel or demonstrating how a steam engine works in a factory to power many machines. Although any pictures would show students what the machines looked like, the textbook *Adventures in American History* (Morristown, N.J.: Silver Burdett Co., 1976) has excellent drawings on pages 148–150.

in land speculation or trade. There was a shortage of labor, for most people preferred to become farmers rather than to work in factories. Also, manufacturers found it hard to get their goods to market.

The War of 1812 changed many of these conditions. The embargo, the Non-Intercourse Act, and the war itself shut off the supply of British goods from 1808 to 1815. With the scarcity of imported products, Americans were encouraged to go into manufacturing. In 1800 there were but 7 mills making cotton thread in the United States. But in the single year 1809—when the embargo was followed by the ban on trade with Britain and France—89 new mills were built. By the end of the war, there were 213 such mills. Other manufacturers were soon making cloth, nails, guns, and other products. This was the start of America's industrial revolution. From these small beginnings, the United States was to rise to the top of all industrial countries in less than a century.

Advantages of the Northeast. Most American manufacturing was located at first in the Northeast—the New England states and New York, New Jersey, and Pennsylvania. The region had abundant waterpower. Since most early machinery was driven by the power of falling water, the river valleys became centers of industry. Mills making cotton and woolen cloth were built on such New England rivers as the Connecticut, the Merrimack, and the Housatonic.

When the War of 1812 cut off trade and commerce, many well-to-do merchants in the Northeast turned to manufacturing, and supplied the capital that had been lacking earlier. In the words of one historian, they made the shift from "the wharf to waterfall," as they built their mills to run with waterpower. Most of the important banks and other financial institutions were also located in this part of the country.

The Northeast had numerous other advantages for starting manufacturing. In the 1820s, almost half of all Americans lived in that part of the country, and many began to look to the factories for work. The Northeast also had larger cities, bigger ports, and more roads and canals than other parts of the country. And in the states of New York, New Jersey, and Pennsylvania there were big deposits of coal and iron.

The Waltham factory. In 1814 a group of wealthy men known as the Boston Associates built a textile factory in Waltham, Massachusetts. It was the first factory to bring under one roof all the steps in manufacturing cloth, from spinning the raw cotton to dyeing the finished cloth. Most of the factory's machines were driven by waterpower. The Boston Manufacturing Company, as it was called, was a success from the start. In the late 1820s the Boston Associates built more factories at a Massachusetts site named Lowell after one of the Associates.

After the successes in Waltham and Lowell, textile-mill towns sprang up in New Hampshire and Rhode Island as well as in Massachusetts. When New Englanders moved westward into the Mohawk and Hudson river valleys of New York State, they took the system of textile manufacturing with them. By 1830, the United States had 800 cotton mills.

CHECKUP

1. In what ways have Americans measured progress?
2. Why did the War of 1812 help to bring on America's industrial revolution?
3. In what part of the country was most American manufacturing located at first? Why?

LESSON 2

The Expansion of Industry

At first, factories were pretty much confined to the Northeast. The South lacked capital, which was tied up in land and slaves. The lightly settled West lacked both capital and labor.

A westward move. In time, however, people moved westward. The states carved out of the Northwest Territory provided a larger market. They also provided a greater labor supply and a growing number of cities from which goods were distributed. Some of these cities began processing the farm goods grown in the region. This gave rise to such new industries as flour milling, lumber manufacturing, meat-packing, and the making of leather goods.

As population increased in the West, there developed a belt of manufacturing rivaling that of the Northeast. Stretching from Pittsburgh to St. Louis, the industrial buildup was especially strong along Lake Erie and in the Ohio River Valley. Besides meat, flour, and lumber products, the factories of the region manufactured farm machinery, whiskey, bagging, and other things. In most cases, these industries could manufacture products and sell them in the West more cheaply than they could be imported from the East.

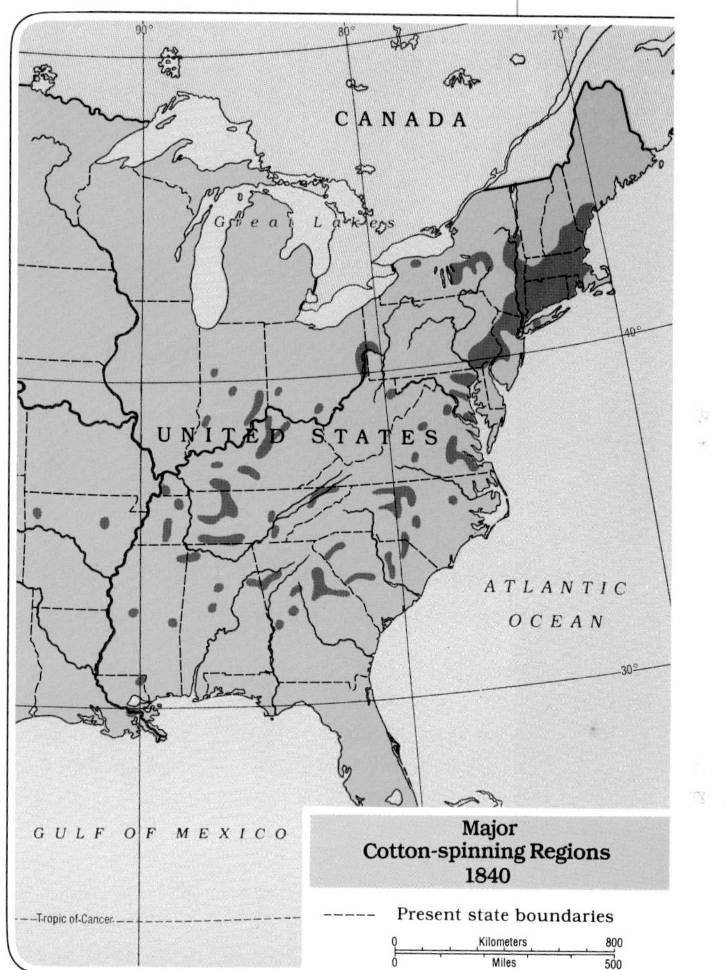

By 1840, cotton spinning was a major industry in the United States. Most spinning mills were in the river valleys of the Northeast.

The effect of inventions. A number of inventions spurred the rapid expansion of America's industry. As early as 1804, Oliver Evans, a mechanic and shopkeeper from Delaware, had revolutionized flour milling. His inventions included a conveyor-belt system, an elevator,

LESSON 2 *(2 days)*

Performance Objectives

1. To describe in writing or orally how American industry was affected by **(a)** inventions and technological improvements, **(b)** the American system, **(c)** the growth of railroads, and **(d)** the Civil War.
2. To list two reasons why corporations became increasingly popular in the mid-1800s.

Famous People

Oliver Evans, Charles Goodyear, Elias Howe, John Deere, Obed Hussey, Cyrus McCormick, Eli Whitney, Gail Borden, Gordon McKay

Vocabulary

Conveyor belt, automated factory, reaper, revolver, mechanization, division of labor, ingenuity, interchangeable parts, "American system," corporation

Activities

1. TIME LINE / RESEARCH Refer to the "Chart of Inventions Throughout History" in the *World Book Encyclopedia* (Vol. 10, pages 280–284) or a similar listing of inventions. Have some of the students construct a time line using the items. Ask other students to research different American inventions and/or inventors to add to the time line. (The "Invention/Study Aids" section in *World Book Encyclopedia* could be used as a basis for these other research assignments.) The activity can be expanded by using the bulletin board to display one large time line. It also combines well with Activities 2 and 4.

Industry developed rapidly in Pittsburgh where the Allegheny and Monongahela rivers join.

and a new grinding process. These operations were all automatic, and by combining them, Evans devised the first *automated* factory.

Between 1825 and 1850, there was a rash of new inventions and processes. In 1844, Charles Goodyear succeeded in making rubber that could withstand heat and cold. This made it possible to produce such articles as raincoats and rubber boots. In 1846, Elias Howe received a patent for his sewing machine, thereby providing the basis for a ready-made clothing industry. Hundreds of smaller inventions, including friction matches, lead pencils, the Colt pistol, and screw-making machines, served as the start for new industries.

In Europe, wage earners often feared such new inventions. They thought technological advances might cause them to lose their jobs. British visitors were therefore surprised to find that in America workers "hail with satisfaction all mechanical improvements." The reason, of course, was that like Walt Whitman, American working people saw inventions as the agents of progress and material well-being.

Machinery on the farms. Inventions also led to greater production on farms. In 1819, Jethro Wood, a farmer in central New York, patented a cast-iron plow that was an important advance over the centuries-old wooden plow. In 1847, John Deere built the first all-steel plow. At his factory in Moline, Illinois, he was soon making thousands of plows each year to meet the demand.

Another major development in agriculture was the invention of the reaper. This machine did the work in reaping grain that had hitherto been performed by men with scythes. In the 1830s, Obed Hussey of Ohio and Cyrus McCormick of Virginia patented reaping machines that were much alike. But by the 1850s, McCormick's reaper dominated. He established a manufacturing plant in Chicago, and by 1860, about 100,000 of his machines had been sold. During the Civil War, another 250,000 came into use. "The reaping machine," according to one report of that period, "is a saving of more than one third the labor when it cuts and rakes."

The American system. America's great progress in technology and industry was soon noticed throughout the world. In 1851, the British held a large industrial fair at the Crystal Palace in London. Among the American products shown there were the McCormick reaper, the Colt revolver, and some Goodyear rubber products. The British were amazed. A London newspaper wrote: "Their reaping machine has carried conviction to the heart of British farmers. Their revolvers threaten to revolutionize military tactics."

So impressed were the British that they sent a committee to the United States to investigate the reasons for America's economic progress. One main reason they discovered was that Americans applied the ideas of *mechanization* and *division of labor* to all processes of manufacturing. Wherever possible, Americans used machines rather than human hands to perform a task. Americans also tended to break down the process of production into separate steps. A machine performed a single operation on the raw material, which would then be moved on to the next step.

Americans also employed labor-saving devices in moving materials through the factory process. As the British committee observed:

> ". . . everything that could be done to reduce labor in the movement of materials from one point to another was adopted. This includes mechanical arrangements for lifting materials from one floor to another, carriages for conveying materials on the same floor, and the like."

America's system of manufacturing also included the idea of *interchangeable parts.* Eli Whitney (the same person who devised the first cotton gin) had used this idea in his Connecticut firearms factory as early as 1798. Before that time, a gun was manufactured by a gunsmith, who made each part separately. If any part of the gun was broken, a new part had to be made to fit that particular gun. To meet a contract deadline for supplying guns to the government, Whitney hit upon the idea of manufacturing identical parts. Each part would fit any gun of the type being made. This meant that the broken gun could be repaired very quickly simply by slipping in a new part. Moreover, with large numbers of identical parts on hand, unskilled workers could assemble the guns.

This approach to manufacturing, sometimes called the "American system," was soon applied to hundreds of machines. It paved the way for mass production in the factory system. The procedure proved to be one of the most important developments in America's industrial history.

2. RESEARCH / ORAL OR WRITTEN REPORTS Some of the students will enjoy finding the story behind certain inventions. Arrange to have those interested students report to the rest of the class. Reports might include the following: Goodyear's accidental discovery of the Vulcanization process; Edison's experiments on the electric light bulb; Bell's reasons for inventing the telephone. A good source for research is National Geographic Society's *Those Inventive Americans* (Washington, D.C.: National Geographic Society, 1971).

3. DISCUSSION After students have read pages 470–472, discuss the railroads as an industry upon which other industries depended for success. (Demand for iron, jobs, transportation) Help the students to conclude that the railroads therefore affected the entire economy. Ask what industries are in that position today and why. (Auto, steel, coal, etc.) What happens when one of these industries goes on an extended strike or drastically cuts production?

Background Information

COLT REVOLVER Patented by Samuel Colt (1814–1862) in 1835, the Colt revolver was made in Hartford, Connecticut. It had a cylinder of several chambers that could be fired without reloading. Although the first models used ball and powder, later versions used cartridges. Colt was an honorary colonel of the Connecticut militia, but he died before his company brought out the "Peacemaker," which became the famous army and gunfighter weapon. (See *The Gunfighters* in *The Old West* series by the Editors of Time-Life Books [New York: Time-Life Books], pages 40–51.)

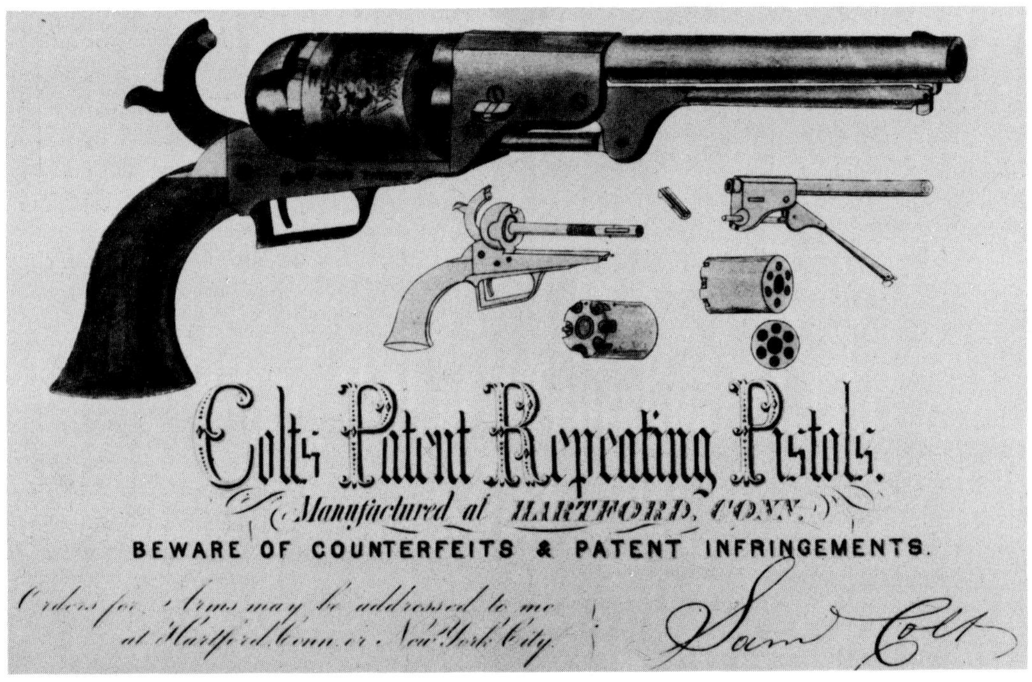

The revolver that Samuel Colt of Connecticut invented was assembled by a series of workers, each of whom did a single task. Thus the assembly line was added to the "American system."

Rise of corporations. Another development in the mid-1800s was the rise of the corporation as a form of business organization. Up to about 1850, the two most common types of business organization were the single ownership and the partnership. But now, for several reasons, the corporation became increasingly popular. First of all, a business could raise large amounts of money by selling stock, or certificates of ownership, in the corporation. Secondly, a corporation received a charter; this gave it lasting life, so that its business was not interrupted by the death of the owner or the death or withdrawal of a partner. Finally, a person who invested in a corporation had only a limited liability—that is, if the corporation failed, the stockholder would lose only the amount of money that he or she had invested. In a partnership, each of the partners was personally accountable for all the debts.

Because of all these advantages, the corporation came into wide use as a form of business organization. During the 1850s, the number of corporations in manufacturing doubled.

American railroads. One industry that boomed in the years before the Civil War was the railroads. During the 1850s, four railroad companies pushed their lines from the Atlantic Coast deep into the interior. In 1851 the Erie was the world's longest railroad, with 537 miles (859 km) of track. It linked the Hudson River north of New York City and Lake Erie. The following year, the Baltimore and Ohio connected Baltimore and Wheeling, West Virginia. In 1853, the New York Central was formed out of eight small lines, tying together Albany and Buffalo. And in 1858, the Pennsylvania Railroad ran its line across the Appalachian Mountains from Philadelphia to Pittsburgh.

By 1860, most of the nation's 31,000 miles (49,600 km) of track linked the Northeast to the Old Northwest. (This development had political as well as economic meaning, in that the two sections were tied together before the Civil War.) The rail network connected New York, Philadelphia, and Baltimore to such cities as Chicago and Cincinnati. About half of the lines were west of the Appalachian Mountains. Because of its strategic location. Chicago became the great railroad center of the Midwest.

Railroads had a great economic effect on the country. They made it possible to ship raw materials to factories over long distances. Manufacturers could also reach out to larger and more distant markets to sell their goods. Passengers could travel quickly and easily. In 1855 one could go by rail from the East Coast to Chicago or St. Louis in forty-eight hours. Thirty years before, such a trip would have required two or three weeks.

The railroads themselves were now big business. In many states they were the most important corporations with the largest amounts of capital. More than $1.2 billion was invested in railroad lines between 1830 and 1860, much of it coming from Europe. Public funds also went to the railroad industry. Local and state governments gave loans, or grants or purchased railroad stock. In 1850, Congress passed a bill providing for the first of many federal land grants. To help finance a railroad through Illinois, the federal government gave that

4. RESEARCH/ORAL REPORTS Many giants of American industry got their start during this period. Assign the following names to individuals or pairs of students. Have them find out the name of the company their person started, when it was started, and what products it made originally and what it makes today.

William Colgate (Colgate-Palmolive-Peet Co.); Ezra Cornell (Western Union Telegraph Co.); Éleuthère Irénée Du Pont (E.I. Du Pont de Nemours Co.); Pierre Lorillard (American Tobacco Co.); Matthias W. Baldwin (Baldwin Locomotive Works); Isaac Merrit Singer (Singer Sewing Machine Co.); Francis A. Pratt and Amos Whitney (Pratt & Whitney Co.); Linus Yale (Yale Lock Co.); William Procter and James Gamble (Procter & Gamble); Clement and Henry Studebaker (Studebaker-Packard Co.) Note that the present company names have been given here.

A train of the Michigan Central line is about to leave a sidetrack in the railroad yards in Chicago. The location of that Middle Western city made it a foremost railroad center.

5. DISCUSSION / DEBATE
On pages 472–473 the text states that the Civil War had a great impact on American industrialization. Historians have said the same thing about World War I, World War II, the Korean War, and the Vietnam War. Discuss how any war affects the economy and industry; then have the students answer this question: Is war necessary for industrial development? In the discussion, be sure students deal with the moral issue as well as the economic one. For example, assuming President Roosevelt believed joining World War II would get the United States out of the depression, would he have been justified in declaring war (or in pursuing a course that he knew would eventually lead to war)? Also try to handle the long- and short-term impact of war. For example, though Japan's industry was destroyed by World War II, rebuilding it allowed the Japanese to include the most modern technology and efficient designs. American industry, on the other hand, is still using some buildings from the 1800s and some machines that are almost as old. Insist that your students support their opinions with logical arguments, not just emotion. This could be presented as a formal debate topic: Resolved, That periodic wars are necessary to stimulate industrial growth.

state 3 square miles (7.8 square km) of federal land in alternate sections on both sides of the proposed line. This set an important precedent for future federal aid. By 1860, about 28 million acres (11.2 million ha) of federal lands had been given to the states to help them build railroads.

The iron and steel industries. The manufacture of locomotives, rails and other railway equipment, and machinery for America's factories required great amounts of iron. Iron had been produced in small quantities for many years, but the industry did not expand significantly until after the War of 1812. Then the introduction of machinery permitted manufacturing operations to be carried out on a larger scale. Also, new coal and iron deposits were discovered in western Pennsylvania and in the Ohio River Valley.

After the 1820s, the iron industry boomed. High tariffs kept out foreign iron imports. As the textile industry grew, so did the demand for textile machinery. Iron stoves came into common use, and by 1850, more than 300,000 were being made each year. The growing railroad industry had to have rails, locomotives, and other equipment made of iron. In 1860, railroads purchased about $15 million worth of iron in the form of locomotives, rails, and other equipment. This was nearly half the nation's iron output.

As the iron industry grew in size, it became more concentrated in location. Pennsylvania produced almost half of America's iron by 1860, with Ohio ranking second. Pittsburgh gained a permanent place as a leader in the iron and steel industries. But the output of steel was still small compared with that of iron. In 1860, steel output was only 12,000 (10,800 t) tons.

Industry at the takeoff point. American industry by 1860 was, despite its growth in the previous decade, still only in the early stages of development. Though some mills made steel and other "heavy industry" articles, most American manufacturing continued to be directed toward the simple processing of farm products. Factories were usually small, averaging about ten workers each. Moreover, America was still a large importer of foreign manufactured goods because it could not satisfy its own needs.

The 1860 census showed more than 140,000 manufacturing places and 1.5 million workers in industry. Nearly 60 percent of America's labor force was still involved in agriculture, but the picture was changing rapidly. The United States was on the verge of a great industrial breakthrough, which would change the country from a farming to a manufacturing nation.

Industry and the Civil War. The Civil War had a great impact on America's industrial development, though historians sometimes argue exactly what it was. Some evidence seems to show that industrial development might have gone farther if there had been peace instead of war. Certain industries, such as cotton textiles, were actually hurt by the war, and the war destroyed most of the South's factories. Many industries, however, boomed. The McCormick reaper plant could not keep up with the orders that poured in. The great meat-

The Civil War hastened America's industrial development. Soldiers like these in a Confederate camp in Mississippi became acquainted with new products that they would continue to use after the war.

packing plants in Chicago and Cincinnati, the flour mills in Minneapolis and St. Paul, and the iron and steel mills in Pittsburgh worked night and day to supply the Union army's needs.

The Civil War proved to be a technological turning point for the food industry. To get food to the soldiers in the field, large quantities had to be processed and shipped long distances. The meat-packing industry in the Midwest, the sardine canners in New England, and the vegetable and fruit canners in both regions all profited from the needs created by the war. Condensed milk, a product that Gail Borden had patented in 1856, came into wide use. Soldiers returned home with a taste for canned foods eaten in the army, and this created a new market for such products.

Another industry—the manufacture of shoes—was also greatly affected by the war. In 1862, Gordon McKay of Massachusetts made a machine that could sew the soles of shoes to the uppers. Factories rushed to manufacture shoes for soldiers, and the demand for ready-made shoes continued after the soldiers returned to civilian life.

CHECKUP

1. What were some of the inventions that led to the expansion of industry and the increase in farm production during the nation's first century?
2. What were some of the factory processes that brought worldwide attention to the American system of manufacturing?
3. How did the Civil War affect America's industrial development?

6. DISCUSSION Give the students, either orally or in writing, the following quotations concerning corporations. Have them decide which, if any, agrees with the opinion in the text. Afterward, ask which they agree with, and discuss with them the advantages and disadvantages of corporate ownership of industries.

"Business corporations attained prominence in this period (1830s–1850s) permitting through the separation of ownership and management, these side investments by businessmen whose major energies were occupied elsewhere." Thomas Cochran and William Miller in *The Age of Enterprise (New York: Harper & Row, Publishers, 1961).*

". . . (stockholders) seldom pretend to understand anything of the business of the company; and when the spirit of faction happens not to prevail among them, give themselves no trouble about it, but receive contentedly such half-yearly or yearly dividend, as the directors think proper to make to them." John Kenneth Galbraith in *The Age of Uncertainty* (Boston: Houghton Mifflin Co., 1977).

LESSON 3 *(2 days)*

Performance Objectives

1. To identify orally or in writing the criticisms of industrialization by people such as Thoreau, Emerson, and Melville. 2. In a short story or essay, to describe conditions in early factories such as the Lowell mills. 3. To describe orally or in writing the origin and early growth of American unionism.

Famous People

Henry David Thoreau, Herman Melville, Ralph Waldo Emerson

Vocabulary

Walden, Lowell girls, child labor, Workingmen's Party, National Trade Union, *Commonwealth* v. *Hunt*

LESSON 3

The Dark Side of Industrialism

Not all Americans agreed that tons of steel or yards of cloth were the proper measure of progress, either for the nation or for individuals. Surely, they believed, there were measures of greatness other than material goods—for example, things of the mind and of the spirit.

Thoreau's criticism. One of these critics was Henry David Thoreau, a native of Massachusetts. Thoreau believed that the scramble for wealth was changing American society and destroying both human and natural resources. The new emphasis on "getting ahead" was, according to Thoreau, a false value. He wrote:

> There is no more fatal blunderer than he who consumes the great part of his life getting a living . . . It is not enough to tell me that you worked hard to get your gold. So does the Devil work hard.

And at another time, Thoreau wrote:

> Most men are so occupied with the . . . cares and . . . hard labors of life that its finer fruits cannot be plucked by them.

All these bad effects were, to Thoreau, the evil products of industrialism. To him, the railroad, symbol of progress to so many Americans, was the symbol of a change that was making people the slaves of machines. "We do not ride on the railroad," he wrote. "It rides upon us."

In 1846, Thoreau built a hut in the woods at Walden Pond, near Concord, Massachusetts. There he lived alone for more than two years, free from machines, government, and the products of modern civilization. Thoreau later explained his purpose:

> I went to the woods because I wished to live deliberately, to front only the essential facts of life, and see if I could not learn what it had to teach, and not, when I came to die, discover that I had not lived.

Some years afterward he published *Walden*, a classic book about his ideas and experiences during that period.

Emerson and Melville. Another who expressed concern about the changing American values was Thoreau's friend, Ralph Waldo Emerson. Also a native of Massachusetts, and a writer and philosopher, Emerson was the most famous public lecturer of his day. Emerson did not dislike industrialism as did his friend Thoreau. But Emerson was much troubled by the growing emphasis in America upon material things. To him, the measure of progress lay in such things as the growth of democracy, of individualism, and of self-reliance. These were the true values that Americans should hold high.

Continued on page 476

Thoreau declared that Americans, intent on success, were basing their lives on false values.

The Lyceum Movement

Education has long been part of the American Dream, but it has not always taken place in the classroom. In the late 1820s the desire for more knowledge and culture led to the rise of groups known as lyceums. The lyceum movement was an effort to spread popular learning among adults who were interested in improving their minds.

The movement actually began in Great Britain and then spread to America. In the United States its father was Josiah Holbrook of Connecticut, a traveling lecturer and part-time schoolmaster. He founded the first American lyceum in 1826 in Millbury, Massachusetts. Within six years, there were more than three thousand lyceums in America.

In the lyceums, people could hear talks or debates on such public issues as capital punishment, school curriculum reform, and popular science. Ralph Waldo Emerson, Oliver Wendell Holmes, and other outstanding thinkers and writers gave lectures. Musical artists performed, and scientists gave demonstrations of their experiments. Holbrook often supplied lyceum groups with pamphlets on various subjects and with mathematical and scientific materials that he had made himself.

The lyceum movement thus became a powerful force for social and political reform. Lyceum groups conducted discussions, established libraries, and lobbied for better schools. In some instances, the lyceums were responsible for setting up educational institutions. The Lowell Institute of Boston and Cooper Union in New York both began as lyceums. The lyceum movement faded after the Civil War. In its day, however, it satisfied the thirst for knowledge and culture that many Americans deeply felt.

The famous writer and philosopher Ralph Waldo Emerson lectures at a Massachusetts lyceum.

Activities

1. ROLE-PLAYING It must have been exciting, scary, and difficult to start a new union when unions were illegal and severely opposed by factory owners. Divide the class into three groups and tell them to imagine they are workers talking about forming a union. Have one group of students represent workers who strongly favor forming the union, another group represent those who strongly oppose it, and the third group represent those who are undecided but asking questions. Be sure students discuss whether women and children should be included in the union. After the discussion, let the class vote on whether to attempt the effort of forming the union. Students should base their votes on the arguments presented by each side.

For added interest, let someone role-play the owner of the factory talking to the people who favor the union. Another situation to role-play would be a court room or legislative hearing concerning the formation of labor unions. Arguments could be presented as to why they should or should not be allowed.

2. CREATIVE WRITING/ RESEARCH After students have read the lesson, have them write essays or short stories concerning someone working in a factory in the 1830s or 1840s. The students should be encouraged to do research on working conditions, living conditions, and general life-styles.

3. THOUGHT PROVOKER In his essay "*Wealth,*" Emerson wrote: "Wealth begins in a tight roof that keeps the rain and wind out; in a good pump that yields you plenty of sweet water; in two suits of clothes, so to change your dress when you are wet; in dry sticks to burn, in a good double-wick lamp, and three meals; in a horse or a locomotive to cross the land, in a boat to cross the sea; in tools to work with, in books to read; and so in giving on all sides by tools and auxiliaries the greatest possible extension to our powers; as if it added feet and hands and eyes and blood, length to the day, and knowledge and good will."

After reading the quotation to the students, ask if they would define progress in the same way Emerson defined wealth. Where would they differ? How would Emerson's attitude, held by many, affect industrialization?

4. ORAL REPORT Criticism of industrialism has persisted throughout American history. Emerson and Thoreau have been joined in the twentieth century by Alvin Toffler. Assign three groups of sophisticated students to each read one of the following: Emerson's essay *"Wealth,"* Thoreau's *Walden,* and Toffler's *Future Shock.* After each group has reported on its reading, the views of the three authors should be compared concerning wealth, progress, and industrialism.

Herman Melville, one of America's greatest writers, was another who rejected the idea that material plenty necessarily meant progress for a society. In one of his essays, Melville described the lives and working conditions of young girls in a paper mill. His essay was a protest against the way humans were becoming secondary to machines.

As famous writers and lecturers, Thoreau, Emerson, and Melville could make their criticisms heard. But there were thousands of other people whose doubts that industrialism was bringing progress to America were never heard. These were the working poor who labored in America's factories and mines.

Factory workers. In 1800, nearly nine of every ten Americans were members of farm families. Although the remaining one in every ten included some skilled and unskilled workers in the cities, there was no large, ready pool of labor from which the rising new industries could draw. Workers in the early factories were therefore drawn from the poorer farm families nearby. Sometimes whole families were hired. More often it was just the women and children.

In Samuel Slater's first American factory, most of the workers were children. By 1820, about half of all the factory workers were children of nine or ten. Working from sunup to sundown six days a week, they received less than a dollar for their week's work. Yet at a time when children often worked full days on farms, few people thought it was bad for children to work in factories. The work was not considered hard, and the children's earnings, however small, added to their families' income.

The Lowell girls. The Boston Associates followed a different path in their factories, especially in the Lowell mills. Several of the Associates had visited England and had been horrified by the miserable working and living conditions of factory workers there. They hoped to avoid the development of such a permanent, depressed, wage-earning class in America. Therefore, they hired mostly young, unmarried women from New England farm families. During their employment, usually a year or two, the girls lived in company boarding houses. These lodgings were so well kept and supervised that parents were willing to allow their daughters to work and live in Lowell. Rules were strict: no drinking or card playing, everyone in bed by ten o'clock, and church attendance on Sundays. To improve their minds, the girls were encouraged to read books, to write letters, and to listen to lectures. Employees even published a magazine of their own poetry and other writings. Of their weekly wages of $2.50 to $3.00, about half went for room and board. The rest they saved, sent to their families, or spent.

For a time, Lowell was a showplace for foreign visitors. One visitor in 1842 was the famous English writer Charles Dickens. A short time before, Dickens had written a novel dealing with the desperate condition of the English working class. But after touring the mills in Lowell during his American tour, he wrote that he saw "no face that bore an unhappy and unhealthy look."

Yet other reports and events suggest that all was not what it seemed in the New England mills. A visitor to another cotton mill of the Boston Associates, in

Two "Lowell girls" operate looms in one of the textile mills that the Boston Associates built along the Merrimack River. The mills gave employment to hundreds of young women in New England.

Manchester, New Hampshire, wrote: "The atmosphere . . . is charged with cotton thread and dust, which, we are told, are very injurious to the lungs." And another visitor, writing about the Lowell girls shortly before Dickens did, reported that "the great mass wear out their health, spirit, and morals without becoming one whit better off than when they started."

In 1834, about one thousand Lowell girls walked off their jobs to protest a 15 percent wage cut. A few years later, several thousand were forced to leave the company boardinghouses after they formed an association to fight against worsening conditions in the mills. On another occasion, the Lowell girls tried without success to get the Massachusetts legislature to limit their workday to ten hours.

A changing industrial scene. Meanwhile, hundreds of other factories were rising elsewhere in America. They appeared not only in rural communities like Lowell and Manchester but, more and more, in such large cities as Boston, New York, and Philadelphia. In these places, bright, clean factories and comfortable boardinghouses were seldom, if ever, found. Instead, dark, dirty mills and slum housing were the rule. Moreover, during the 1840s and 1850s, the work force changed. Instead of farm girls who came to the factories for a year or two, there developed a wage-earning class made up mostly of immigrants. Soon the company boardinghouses of Lowell disappeared. It had now become clear that the experiment of the Boston Associates was not the pattern that American industry would follow.

5. THOUGHT PROVOKER Duplicate and distribute to the class the following excerpt from the diary of George T. Strong, an attorney from New York. It was written on January 11, 1860. After they have read the excerpt, have the students discuss this question: At what point must progress bend to the needs of humanity?

"News today of a fearful tragedy at Lawrence, Massachusetts, one of the wholesale murders commonly known in newspaper literature as accident or catastrophe. A huge factory, long notoriously insecure and ill-built, requiring to be patched and bandaged up with iron plates and braces to stand the introduction of its machinery, suddenly collapsed into a heap of ruins yesterday afternoon without the smallest provocation. Some five or six hundred operatives went down with it—young girls and women mostly. An hour or two later, while people were working frantically to dig out some two hundred still under the ruins, many of them alive and calling for help, some quite unhurt, fire caught in the great pile of debris, and these prisoners were roasted. It is too atrocious and horrible to think of.

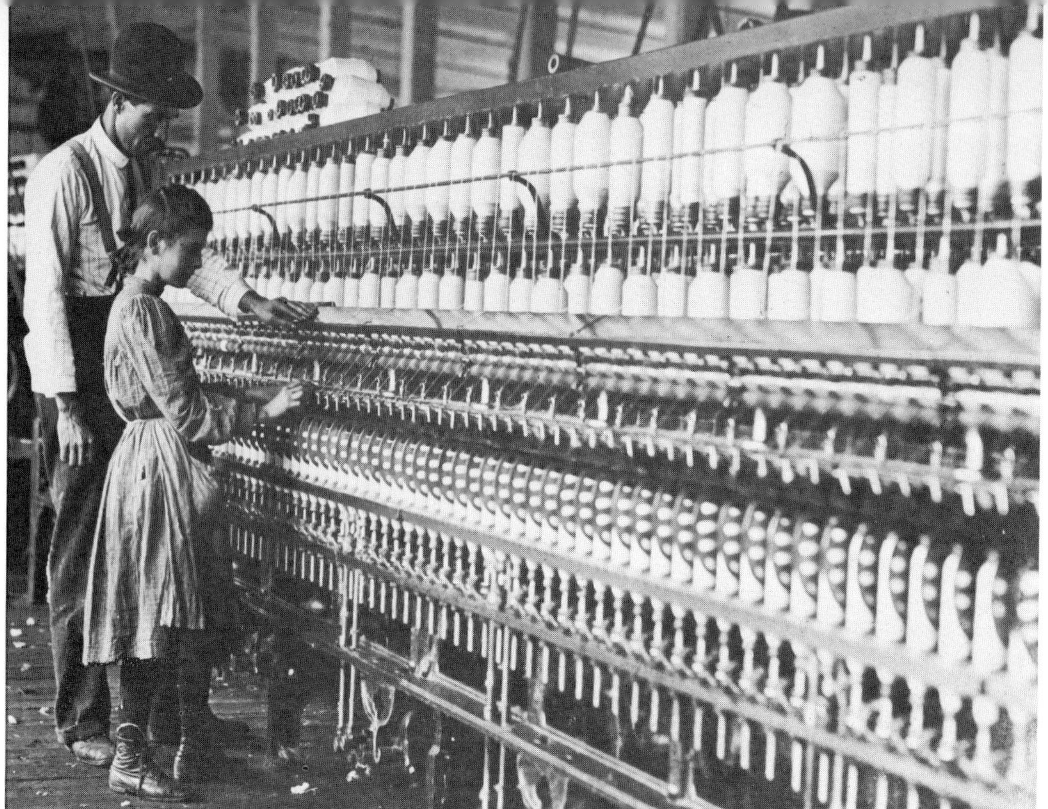

A supervisor instructs a child laborer in her duties at a textile mill. During the 1800s, children made up a significant part of the labor force in factories of this kind.

At the same time, the rise of factories dealt a blow to the artisan class. This group consisted of independent skilled workers who until then had made most of America's clothing, boots, furniture, and other goods in their homes and small shops. By the middle of the nineteenth century, artisans were finding it impossible to compete with goods made by machines run by low-paid workers. A few artisans were able to get enough capital to hire other workers and even to start factories of their own. Most, however, had to give up their independent businesses. They were pushed down into the wage-earning class, although at a higher level than that of the unskilled worker.

Women and children in the mills. In most factories of the 1800s, hours were long—in fact, a 70-hour workweek was normal! Wages were low, and working conditions were grim. Women made up probably 20 percent of the factory work force. They were most numerous in four industries: boots and shoes, ready-made clothing, cotton textiles, and woolens.

Children made up another large percentage of the workers. Beginning in the 1830s, child labor in the factories began to be a matter of deep concern. This was partly because factory conditions for child labor were growing worse. Seth Luther, a labor reformer, described what a visitor to a cotton mill in 1832 might expect to see.

He might see, in some instances, the child taken from his bed at four in the morning, and plunged into cold water to drive away his slumbers . . . After all this, he might see that child robbed, yes, robbed of a part of his time allowed for meals by moving the hands of the clocks backwards or forwards, as would best accomplish this purpose. . . .

The other part of the concern over child labor had to do with the growing awareness that education of the young was important. And as one person noted, "If thirteen hours actual labor is required each day, it is impossible to attend to education. . . ."

The birth of unions. Workers responded to the conditions of industrialism in the 1820s by forming "workingmen's organizations." These were the first American labor unions. Most of them were made up of skilled workers who were no longer independent but were employed by others. These workers organized to protest lower wages and also their loss in status. At first, the workers in a given trade—weaving or printing, for example—organized locally. They also took part in local politics. In 1828 a political party called the Workingmen's party was formed in Philadelphia. There were local labor parties in at least fifteen states.

Soon these local organizations were banding together to form national unions of printers, carpenters, and other skilled workers. And in 1834 these groups came together to form the National Trades Union. However, size was deceiving. This national union was, in fact, weak. A depression that began in 1837 (see page 282) dealt this national movement a blow from which it did not recover.

In 1842 the labor movement made an important gain. Before that time, the courts had held that workers' organizations were "conspiracies"—that is, criminal plots—and therefore unlawful. But in *Commonwealth* v. *Hunt*, a Massachusetts court ruled that it was legal for workers to form unions. This gain, however, was limited. First of all, it applied only in Massachusetts. Secondly, when unions tried to use the weapons of the strike and the boycott, the courts ruled against them.

The growth of unions during this period lagged. Hostile newspapers, unfavorable public opinion and court decisions, and the use of strikebreakers by employers—as well as court decisions—held down union growth. So also did the fact that many workers did not yet see themselves as a group with a common interest that could be advanced through common action. Therefore, up to the Civil War, the numbers who joined unions were small. Most who did join were skilled workers. The organization of unskilled factory workers would not come until many years later.

Two new groups. By the mid-1800s, no one could argue the fact that America, measured in material terms, had made great progress in half a century. With Walt Whitman, millions of Americans blessed their stars that they were living at such a time.

Accompanying these growing national riches was the appearance of two new groups: industrialists and factory workers. A disturbing aspect of this development was the uneven way in which the

"Of course, nobody will be hanged. Somebody has murdered about two hundred people, many of them with hideous torture, in order to save money, but society has no avenging gibbet [gallows] for the respectable millionaire and homicide. Of course not. He did not want to or mean to do this massacre; on the whole, he would have preferred to let these people live. His intent was not homicidal. He merely thought a great deal about making a large profit and very little about the security of human life. He did not compel these poor girls and children to enter his accursed mantrap. They could judge and decide for themselves whether they would be employed there. It was a matter of contract between capital and labor; they were to receive cash payment for their services.

"No doubt the legal representatives of those who have perished will be duly paid the fractional part of their week's wages up to the date when they became incapacitated by crushing or combustion, as the case may be, from rendering further service. Very probably the wealthy and liberal proprietor will add (in deserving cases) a gratuity to defray funeral charges. It becomes us to prate about the horrors of slavery! What southern capitalist trifles with the lives of his operatives as do our philanthropes of the North?" (Allan Nevins and M. H. Thomas, III, eds., *The Diary of George Templeton Strong* [New York: Macmillan, 1952].)

Answers To Review Questions

1. Progress usually means an abundance of material goods brought about through invention and technology.
2. The war cut off British manufactured goods to the United States. The scarcity of imported products encouraged Americans to go into manufacturing.
3. Oliver Evans—conveyor-belt system, elevator, new grinding process; Charles Goodyear—vulcanized rubber process; Elias Howe—sewing machine; John Deere—first all-steel plow; and Cyrus McCormick—reaper.
4. An approach to manufacturing that includes mechanization, division of labor, and interchangeable parts.
5. The corporation became a popular form of business organization for three main reasons: large amounts of money could be raised by selling stock in the corporation; the corporation received a charter that gave it unlimited life, not subject to interruptions due to the death of a corporate officer or stockholder; and, the stockholders had only limited liability in the event that the corporation should fail or experience financial difficulties.
6. With the expansion of American manufacturing as a result of the War of 1812, the demand for iron production increased. New coal and iron deposits were discovered in Pennsylvania and Ohio, and these states became the center of the industry. High tariffs kept out foreign iron imports, so the American industry boomed. The production of iron and steel meant

earnings of industry were divided. Parke Godwin, a newspaper writer, provided this picture of the growing gap between wealth and poverty in America in the 1840s.

> Walk through the streets of any of our crowded cities; see how within a stone's throw of each other stand the most marked and frightful contrasts. Here, look at this marble palace reared in a pure atmosphere and in the neighborhood of pleasing prospects. . . . Look you, again, to that not far distant alley, where some ten destitute and diseased families are nestled under the same rickety and tumbling roof; no fire is there to warm them; no clothes to cover their bodies. . . . the rain and keen hail fall on their almost defenceless heads. . . . Look you, at this, we say, and think that unless something better than what we now see is done, it will grow worse!

At the time Godwin was writing this, the wealth of America was spread more unevenly than ever before. By 1850, the top 1 percent of wealth holders owned 26 percent of the wealth in the United States. And the top 2 percent of wealth holders owned 37 percent of the nation's wealth.

In every country, industrialism has come at a high human price. As you have seen, America was no exception. At the same time, it is important to note that the human cost was lower in America than elsewhere. Workers in America, though by no means well-off, were far better-off than workers in other industrial countries. Proof of that fact lies not only in the statistics on wages but in the statistics on immigration of European workers to the United States.

While industrialism was changing the face of much of the eastern part of the nation, another drama was unfolding in the Far West. There, pursuing progress of a different kind, Americans were taming and filling half a continent. You will read about that in Chapter 24.

CHECKUP

1. How did Thoreau, Emerson, and Melville feel about the growth of industrialism?
2. In what ways did the lives of the workers differ in the first mills in Lowell and in later factories?
3. Why were the first American labor unions formed? Why was their growth slow in the years before the Civil War?

Key Facts from Chapter 23

1. The first American factories, powered by falling water, were located alongside the rivers of the Northeast.
2. By cutting off trade with other countries, the War of 1812 stimulated America's industrial development.
3. The "American system" of manufacturing stressed the use of machinery, the division of labor, and the interchangeability of parts. It paved the way for mass production.
4. The factory system brought material plenty to many Americans, but to many others it brought grim working and living conditions.
5. Workers reacted to the ills of industrialism by forming labor unions.

★ REVIEWING THE CHAPTER ★

People, Places, and Events

Samuel Slater *P. 465*
Boston Manufacturing Company *P. 466*
Charles Goodyear *P. 468*
Elias Howe *P. 468*
John Deere *P. 468*
Cyrus McCormick *P. 469*
Pittsburgh *P. 472*
Gail Borden *P. 473*
Gordon McKay *P. 473*
Lowell girls *P. 476*

Review Questions

1. What does the term progress usually mean to Americans? *Pp. 463–464* Les. 1
2. How did the War of 1812 stimulate America's industrial development? *Pp. 465–466* Les. 1
3. Name five important inventors and their inventions of the first half of the nineteenth century. *Pp. 467–469* Les. 2
4. Exactly what is meant by the "American system"? *P. 469* Les. 2
5. What form of business organization became popular in the mid–1800s? Why? *P. 470* Les. 2
6. Explain the role of the iron and steel industries in the economic development of the nation. *P. 472* Les. 2
7. What specific criticisms of industrialism did the following people make: **(a)** Henry David Thoreau **(b)** Ralph Waldo Emerson **(c)** Herman Melville? *Pp. 474, 476* Les. 3
8. What were working conditions like in the early factories? How did workers try to protect themselves against such conditions? *Pp. 478–479* Les. 3
9. What two new social groups emerged in America as a result of the industrial growth of the 1800s? *P. 479* Les. 3

Chapter Test

Copy the statements below and complete them by filling in the blanks. Use the vocabulary that has been introduced in this chapter.

1. In the 1820s, workers banded together to form "workingmen's organizations" and these became the first American labor unions ________.
2. The event that brought about the real beginning of America's industrial revolution was the War of 1812 ________.
3. Samuel Slater ________, an English textile worker, who brought to America his knowledge of the latest machines, helped set up America's first cotton mill ________ in Rhode Island.
4. Most American manufacturing was located in the Northeast ________ because this region had abundant waterpower ________.
5. The invention of the sewing machine by Elias Howe ________ provided the basis for a ready–made clothing industry.
6. One reason why the corporation ________ came into wide use as a form of business organization was the fact that it had unlimited life.
7. By 1860, the state of Pennsylvania ________ produced almost half of America's iron.
8. The growth of industrialism changed the United States from a farming ________ to a manufacturing ________ nation.
9. Two important inventions that led to greater agricultural production were John Deere's first all-steel plow ________ and Cyrus McCormick's reaper ________.
10. The three major characteristics of the "American system" were division of labor ________, mechanization, ________ and interchangeable parts ________.

employment for many people and contributed indirectly to increased employment in all other industries that were dependent upon iron and steel for their manufacturing processes.

7. (a) Thoreau believed that industrialism made people the slaves of machines. He also criticized Americans for placing too great an emphasis upon material goods and "getting ahead" at the sacrifice of human and natural resources. **(b)** Emerson did not dislike industrialism, but he was deeply troubled by the growing emphasis in America upon the acquisition of material things. **(c)** Melville, too, was concerned about the emphasis placed upon material plenty and about the way humans were becoming secondary to machines.

8. Work hours were very long and wages were poor. The atmosphere in many factories was injurious to health. Children, who made up a large percentage of the work force, were frequently exploited by being made to toil long hours in unsafe working conditions. In addition, they were denied any opportunity for education due to the rigorous demands of their workday. Workers responded to these unfavorable aspects of industrialism by forming labor unions to protest the grim working conditions. Many local unions were later merged into the National Trades Union.

9. The two new socioeconomic groups were the industrialists and the factory workers.

Background Information

1. "THE LONE PROSPECTOR" Heading off to the diggings, the prospector carries everything he needs. Strapped to his bedroll are a pick and shovel for loosening the soil and a pan for washing it (see page 484). The placer system was highly inefficient, probably washing away some $300 million in gold over the $550 million obtained. For protection in surroundings that were often both dangerous and lawless, the miner carries a rifle and a revolver.

The painting was done by Alburtis Browere around 1850 and presently hangs in the Knoedler Galleries in New York City. Browere made two trips to the mining country to research his pictures and habitually painted himself into them. The prospector here looks much like Browere the miner in some of his other paintings.

CHAPTER 24

THE LAST FRONTIER

LESSON 1

IN THE NINETEENTH CENTURY, the ideas of Americans about progress led them to change their thinking about the relationship of humans to nature. Up to then, they had believed that people were meant to live closely with nature. To be sure, God *did* intend for humans to "improve" the land—to clear it, till it, and make it fruitful. (Indeed, the claim that Indians were not doing this was the justification for taking land from them.) But—so earlier thinking went—people were to take from the land only *what was needed.* They would cut only enough trees for shelter and fuel. They would kill only enough game for food and clothing.

However, as progress came to be measured by the piling-up of wealth, the relationship of humans to nature changed. Nature was now seen as a storehouse of unclaimed wealth. The proper aim of humankind was no longer to live in harmony with nature but to tame it. The more nature could be bent to the human will—the more forests cut, the more mines opened, the more lands fenced and put to the plow—the greater the progress.

Such thinking was encouraged by the existence of the vast, untapped West, which lay before Americans at mid-century. Prospects for wealth were dizzying. Thus, in the last half of the nineteenth century, Americans devoured the West in great gulps. In the name of progress, they exploited the resources of half a continent without much care for the future. While doing this, they created one of the most colorful eras in American history. They also ruthlessly smashed the Indian civilizations that stood in their way.

The Mining Frontier

In January 1848, James Marshall was building a sawmill on the American River in California, about 40 miles (64 km) from Sutter's Fort. A glint of yellow metal in the stream bed caught Marshall's eye. A hundred times since Jamestown, newcomers to an area had become excited by such sights, only to be disappointed. But not this time—what Marshall had found was pure gold.

The California gold rush. As news of the discovery spread through California, people rushed off to stake out claims on likely land. San Francisco, a growing port city not far from the site of Marshall's find, was soon half deserted. Dozens of ships lay helplessly at anchor, their sailors having flocked to the gold fields.

By mid-1848, the news reached the eastern United States and Europe, and the great gold rush was on. Within months, thousands descended on California. In 1849, another 80,000 people arrived, and the following year California entered the Union as the thirty-first state.

Most of the migrants were from the settled parts of the United States, but the lure of gold drew people from Europe, Asia, and Australia as well. The migrants were mainly males who came without family. Only about 10 percent of

LESSON 1 *(1 day)*

Performance Objectives

1. Using a map of the United States, to locate three or four places where gold or silver was discovered between 1848 and 1878. **2.** To describe orally or in writing the life of people in the areas where the gold and silver strikes took place.

Famous Person

James Marshall

Vocabulary

Placer mining, "forty-niners," "Pikes Peak or Bust," Comstock Lode, Big Bonanza

Activities

1. FILM An excellent film describing life in the early western lands, especially mining towns, is *Eyeball Witnesses,* the Glory Trail series (30 minutes, b&w; National Educational Television). The film focuses on the descriptions of the land by Greeley, Clemens, and Bret Harte.

2. USING A MAP After making a list of locations of mining strikes named in the text, the students should locate the sites on an outline map of the United States (see map, page 492). Be sure to label the states they are in. Compare the locations with this recent list of leading gold- and silver-producing states. Gold: (1) South Dakota, (2) Nevada, (3) Utah. Silver: (1) Idaho, (2) Arizona, (3) Colorado, (4) Utah. Ask: Which states had strikes after 1878? Which states that had early strikes are continuing to produce gold or silver? (Remind the class that these places were not states when gold was discovered. It was the lure of the gold or silver that drew the needed population to the areas.)

3. DISCUSSION Have students compare the attitude of prospectors toward wealth, as described in this lesson, with the attitudes of Thoreau and Emerson described on page 474. Ask: Why would a prospector's attitude be so different?

4. LISTENING FOR INFORMATION Read to the class the following parts from Irving Stone's *Men to Match My Mountains,* Mainstream of America Series (New York: Doubleday, 1956): pages 100–106, the discovery of gold in California; pages 108–121, the gold rush; pages 207–213, the Comstock Lode. Have the class take notes as they listen and then collectively decide what is important to remember from the material.

the "forty-niners" who crossed the plains to California were women, and another 5 percent were children. Armed with little more than pick and shovel, the miners swarmed over the streams, gulleys, and canyons of the western slopes of the Sierra Nevada.

Mining was crude but effective. The prospector scooped the dirt and gravel with its flakes of gold, or "pay dirt," into a washing pan or a long open box set near running water. By swirling water in the pan or box, the miner separated the mud and gravel from the gold. This method, called *placer mining,* yielded more than $550 million in the first ten years of the California gold rush.

The fortune seekers. All sorts of people were thrown together in the mining camps—farmers and traders, poor workers and sons of wealthy families, southern whites and northern free blacks, natives, and immigrants. In one camp numbering 216 people, there were 73 white Americans, 18 black Americans, 37 Chinese, 35 people from Great Britain, 29 Mexicans, and 24 people from various countries in Western Europe. All were seeking their fortunes. Some did not care how they got it. One person described the camps in this way.

> Hordes of pickpockets, robbers, thieves, and swindlers mixed with men who had come with honest intentions. . . . Murders, thefts, and heavy robberies soon became the order of the day.

A few miners did make fortunes. Most did little better than make a living, for nearly everything they took out of the streams and ground went to pay for food and supplies, or was spent in a few hours in saloons and gambling houses. Those who went into the business of selling goods and services to the miners did better. A Boston woman who went west reported baking and selling $18,000 worth of pies in 1852, clearing a profit of $11,000. Many other women ran boardinghouses and hotels. Stores that sold mining supplies never lacked for customers. As one writer has put it, many more people became wealthy by mining miners than by mining gold.

A California gold miner pauses in his task of shoveling dirt into a wooden box. Running water washed away the dirt, while the heavier gold particles went to the bottom to be recovered.

In less than ten years, most of the surface gold had been taken. Rich deposits remained, but they were locked into hard quartz rock and lay deep beneath the surface. Machinery far beyond the means of the ordinary prospector was needed to get at this gold. By the late 1850s, most of the mining in California was being done by large companies. Some of the 200,000 people who were drawn to California by the lure of gold stayed to scratch out a living in a placer mine here and there. A good many settled down to farming or other work and raised families.

For many thousands of people, however, "prospectin' " became a way of life. For the next twenty years and more, they wandered the West, chasing after every new report of a strike, knowing that the next time for sure—in Nevada or Colorado, Idaho or Montana, Washington or South Dakota—they would strike it rich. Few ever did. But in their search for instant wealth they helped to settle the West. Each new gold rush brought men and women who ran the stores, farmed the land, and started schools, churches, and newspapers. When the mining boom passed, many of these people stayed on, raised families, and built up the country.

"Pikes Peak or Bust." Colorado Territory was the scene of the next gold rush. In the summer of 1858 the discovery of a small amount of gold near Denver touched off wild rumors. Within a year, 100,000 people flocked to Colorado Territory with the cry, "Pikes Peak or Bust."

For most who went, it turned out to be not one or the other, but both. There was little gold to be found, and within a year or two most moved on. As in California, however, some stayed on to farm or to raise cattle. Later discoveries of silver and gold in the 1870s brought other miners to Colorado, and in 1876 it became a state.

Other strikes. The same year that prospectors flocked to Pikes Peak brought the discovery of the Comstock Lode in western Nevada, which was at that time a part of the Utah Territory. This vein of gold and silver was the richest in western mining history. In less than twenty years, this one find yielded over $300 million. This discovery was followed by other strikes, the most notable of them being the Big Bonanza in 1873.

Meanwhile, gold had also been discovered in Washington, Idaho, and Montana in the 1860s. Although none of the strikes could compare with the Comstock Lode or the Big Bonanza, they were large enough to bring thousands of miners to this region.

The last of the great gold rushes on the mining frontier was in the Black Hills of South Dakota. This area was part of the Sioux Indian reservation. The United States government had agreed it was to be the Indians' land forever. But rumors of gold led to demands that the Army allow in prospectors. After a year, the Army gave in, and miners swarmed over the Black Hills.

By the 1880s, prospectors with pack horse, pick, and shovel could still be seen wandering the West, but their day had passed. Nearly all mining was in the hands of large companies. Gold and silver continued to be produced in great amounts. Even more important were

Background Information

2. "FORTY-NINERS" The trip to California was not easy for the "forty-niners." The easiest but most expensive route was by ship, around the tip of South America and north to San Francisco. The journey cost approximately $500 (now about $5,000) and took several months. There were alternatives. **(a)** One was by sea to Panama, then across the isthmus, and by sea again to San Francisco. This was most dangerous because of the threat of disease while crossing the isthmus. **(b)** Another route was to Mexico, across bandit-ridden deserts, and then by sea to San Francisco. **(c)** others were overland routes, by trails through the Southwest or from St. Joseph, Missouri, due west.

One of the most popular books of the time was *An Emigrant's Guide to California.* There were many different publications, each supposedly written by an experienced Indian scout. One of the most popular was written by a man from St. Louis who never left his state!

3. BIG BONANZA Located in Nevada near the Comstock Lode was the huge ore deposit called Big Bonanza. Its silver was discovered at the depth of 1,167 feet after many people had looked at shallower depths. The mine produced about $1.5 million in silver per month from 1873 through 1877, with a total of $135.8 million. Four men made huge profits ($10 to $25 million), some made by unethical if not illegal means.

Much of the money in silver and gold mining was made by knowing when to buy and sell shares of a mine. Shares that were worth $3.00 one year could be worth $1500 or more the next if there was a strike, or find. If the mine went dry, the shares were worthless. Obviously, this led to all kinds of cheating and spying. A seller might salt a mine—that is, place gold or silver where a prospective buyer would be sure to find it. Miners were sometimes bribed with shares or even locked up to keep them from talking about strikes.

This wealth was often spent as quickly as it was earned. Immense fortunes were made and lost in just a few years. One woman, Eilley Orrum Bowers, who owned a small claim in the Comstock Lode, had a showplace mansion built in 1861, only to be reduced to giving tours of it for a living by 1874. Scandal was rampant also. Colorado mining millionaire Horace Tabor divorced his wife in 1883 to marry a beautiful young divorcée named Baby Doe. President Chester A. Arthur was at the gala Washington wedding, that featured a $7,000 wedding dress. Huge political contributions by Tabor had led to his short senatorial career at the time, but by 1897 he was flat broke. After Tabor died, in 1899, Baby Doe Tabor lived in the tool shack of his last worthless mine until her death in 1935. (See *The Miners* and *The Forty-niners* in The Old West series by the Editors of Time-Life Books [New York: Time-Life Books] for more details.)

Forbestown, in the foothills of the Sierra Nevada, was a lively community in the days of the California gold rush. Like many other mining communities, it became a ghost town in later years.

copper and lead. By 1900, the value of copper mined each year topped that of gold and silver put together. The rowdy, roaring, get-rich-quick days of Deadwood, Silver City, Tombstone, and Last Chance Gulch were gone by then, as were such characters of the mining frontier as Wild Bill Hickock and Poker Alice, but the real business of mining the West's treasures had only begun.

CHECKUP

1. How did each new mining strike in the West affect the region in which the strike took place?
2. In what places were the major discoveries of gold and silver made?
3. In the process of extracting gold or silver from the earth, what changes took place over the years?

LESSON 2

The Last Stand of the Indians

With the mining frontier pushing eastward from California and filling in the region between the Pacific Ocean and the Rocky Mountains, there remained but one vast unsettled area in the United States. That was the region lying generally between the 100th meridian and the Rockies, and from Canada southward to Mexico. We know the region as the Great Plains. Until the 1860s, however, it was called the Great American Desert.

Settlement, which had raced westward more than 200 miles (320 km) every decade, had halted at the edge of of this region in the 1840s. The reason was that the 100th meridian is the dividing line between two sharply different climates. The line cuts almost in half the Dakotas, Nebraska, and Kansas and then runs across eastern Texas. To the east of the 100th meridian, rain is plentiful, and the weather is humid. To the west, rainfall drops below 20 inches (50 cm) a year, and in some places is less than 10 (25 cm). Wind sweeps over the flat lands, which are bitterly cold in winter and like a furnace in summer. With no trees for houses, fences, or fuel, the Great Plains were long thought to be unfit for settlement. This was a region to be passed through as quickly as possible on the way to green Oregon or golden California.

The Plains Indians. On these arid lands, shunned by white settlers, lived about 250,000 Indians. Although divided among a number of tribes, they were generally called the Plains Indians. A wandering people, they followed the herds of buffalo across the endless grasslands. For the Plains Indians, the buffalo was, as someone put it, "a galloping department store." The buffalo's flesh, hide, and bones provided food, clothing, tepees, blankets, and tools.

For centuries, the Plains Indians hunted the buffalo on foot. In the late 1700s, they started using horses, which had multiplied and spread northward since the Spanish brought them to Mexico. The horse made the Plains Indians more efficient hunters. It also made their skilled warriors more effective in battle, first against each other, later against the whites.

Broken promises. Until the 1840s, the policy of the United States government had been to regard the plains region as one big Indian reservation. That policy was changed as the miners, settlers, and traders who crossed the plains demanded protection against the Indians. First, the government built Army posts along the main western trails. Then, in 1851, it called a council of all Plains Indian chiefs at Fort Laramie. The government persuaded each chief to accept a smaller area for his tribe—"forever."

But the new policy did not last long. Many Indians refused to be bound by agreements that gave away their lands. More important, it was beginning to dawn on whites that the Great American Desert was really among the richest regions in the world. They were discovering that the mountains held great treasures of minerals, and that the land, if watered, would yield rich harvests of wheat. They were determined to have this land for themselves. Soon, white settlers were demanding that Indian lands in parts of Kansas, Nebraska, and the Dakotas be opened to settlement. Farther west, rumors of gold at Pikes Peak brought thousands of miners swarming over land that had been set aside for the Cheyenne and Arapaho Indians. Just ten years after solemnly promising these lands to the Indians forever, the government made the tribes give them up. Meanwhile, corrupt government officials cheated the Indians in trading, and tricked them out of some of their remaining reservation lands.

Warfare on the plains. In 1862, fighting broke out on the Minnesota frontier. Sioux Indians attacked white settlements and killed 450 people. The Indians were soon defeated by the Minnesota militia and as punishment were forced to give up all their lands in that state. Farther west, the Cheyenne and

LESSON 2 *(2 days)*

Performance Objectives

1. To describe in writing or orally the life-style of the Plains Indians and tell how and why their life-style changed during the nineteenth century. **2.** To identify the various official positions of the federal government toward the Plains Indians from the 1850s to the 1930s. **3.** To describe how the general public felt about Indians in the 1800s.

Famous People

Crazy Horse, George Custer, Sitting Bull, Geronomo, Col. J. M. Chivington

Vocabulary

Great American Desert, Plains Indians, buffalo, Cheyenne, Arapaho, Sioux, Nez Percé, reservation, Wounded Knee, Dawes Act, Indian Reorganization Act

Activities

1. FILMS *People of the Buffalo* (14 minutes, color; Encyclopaedia Britannica Films). *End of the Trail: The American Plains Indians* (52 minutes, b&w; NBC-TV), North American Indians: Part I, *Treaties Made, Treaties Broken* (17 minutes, color); Part II, *How the West Was Won* (25 minutes, color); Part III, *Lament of the Reservation* (23 minutes, color). Parts I–III in series by McGraw-Hill Films; narrated by Marlon Brando, with songs by Buffy St. Marie.

2. DISCUSSION Stereotypes are standardized mental pictures that members of a group have of other people. These are generally overly simplified and often quite distorted. They are often formed from prejudice and are used to justify discrimination. For example, the settlers did not like the Indians' ways, so they decided the Indians were savages; then, because the Indians were savages, the colonists felt justified in taking their land. The rationalization process is obvious. In the 1950s and 1960s, TV "westerns" gave a whole generation of Americans a specific stereotype of the Plains Indians. The movies had given earlier generations the same view, and at an even earlier time the "dime novels" were spreading the stereotype.

Red Horse, a Sioux chief, drew this picture of the battle of Little Bighorn from memory.

Arapaho had gone on the warpath the year before in an effort to hold onto their lands. Three years of bloody fighting followed. In 1864, the Colorado militia, led by Colonel J. M. Chivington, fell upon an Indian camp of 500. The soldiers ignored the Indians' efforts to surrender. In a few hours of savage killing, they wiped out nearly all of the Indians.

In the warfare between the Indians on one side and the white settlers and the Army on the other, the Plains Indians were, for a time, able to hold their own. They even managed to force the government to give up a plan to build a road across a favorite hunting ground. The Indians were skilled horsemen and fighters. While on horseback, they could fire 20 to 30 arrows in the time it took a soldier or settler to reload a rifle. Gradually, however, superior technology—especially the Colt repeating revolver—tipped the balance to the whites.

Another government plan. In seeking a solution to the problem of Indian-white relations, white Americans were generally divided into two groups. Both held racist views. One group, which included most Westerners and Army leaders, favored a policy of extermination, that is, killing the Indians. That view was

Continued on page 490

The Pony Express

The rapid settlement of California created an urgent need for mail service to and from the West Coast. In 1857, John Butterfield's Overland Mail Company was awarded a contract to carry the United States mails in the West. Butterfield's stagecoaches, traveling the southern route through New Mexico territory, made the trip from Missouri to California in a little more than three weeks.

William H. Russell, who headed a freight-carrying company, believed that a route across the central part of the country would be faster. He hoped to win a valuable mail contract for his firm. What was needed, it was decided, was a dramatic demonstration that the central route was better. Thus was born the pony express.

The pony express was like a great relay on horseback. Stations were set up 15 miles (24 km) apart between St. Joseph, Missouri, and Sacramento, California. At each station, the rider transferred his mailbags to fresh ponies—he was allowed two minutes to do this—and rode on. A rider generally went 75 miles (120 km) before a new one took over. The express was nonstop—night and day, winter and summer, through rain and snow. Service began on April 3, 1860. Ten days later a rider arrived at the final station, more than 2,000 miles (3,200 km) from the starting point. Later trips were made in eight or nine days, nearly two weeks faster than the Overland Mail.

The backers of the pony express proved their point, but it was all for nothing. Just eighteen months after the first trip, telegraph lines connected the East and West coasts. No longer was there need for the pony express, and the service stopped. William Russell's freight company never got the hoped-for mail contract, and the high costs of the pony-express experiment brought the company to financial ruin. The pony express, with its daring riders galloping over desert, plains, and mountain trails, quickly passed into the folklore of the Old West.

Posters like this were used to drum up business for the pony express as well as to recruit riders.

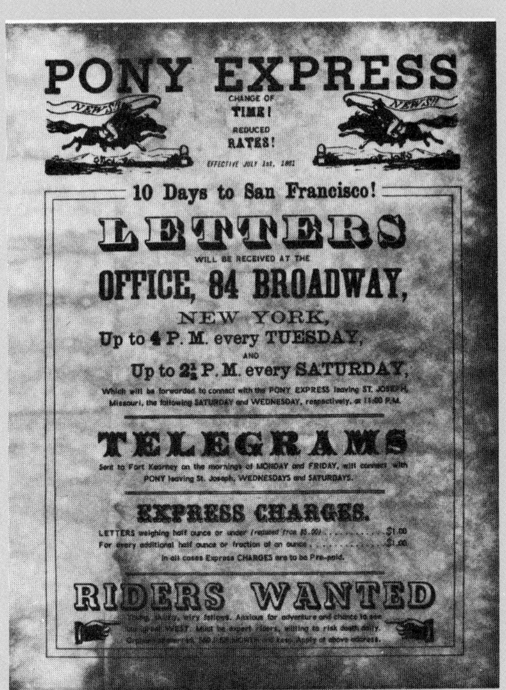

Discuss with the class this stereotype. This could be done by listing on the chalkboard terms that describe characteristics of the Indians as they were shown in movies and TV shows. From the text, determine the stereotype of the Indians that whites had in the nineteenth century. Compare and contrast the stereotypes, how they were formed, and the effects. Ask: How does having a stereotype of a historical group differ from having a stereotype of a present group? Which is harder to change? How did the nineteenth-century stereotype affect relations with the Indians? How do present stereotypes affect relations with present groups? How do historical stereotypes of Indians affect people's personal relationships with Indians today?

After this discussion, read to the class from Oliver La Farge's *A Pictorial History of the American Indian* (New York: Crown, Inc., 1974), Chapter VII, "The Great Open Spaces." The chapter describes the traditions and ways of life of the Sioux, Cheyenne, Blackfoot, and other groups. Have the class distinguish between the reality of Indian life and the stereotype. If La Farge's book is not available, use another source that describes accurately the life-style of the Plains Indians.

3. DEBATE Resolved, That the United States government was justified in taking the land away from the Indians. Have students research their positions carefully and try to anticipate and answer each other's arguments. An excellent source for this debate is *The Annals of America* (Encyclopaedia Britannica, Inc., 1968). Be sure students start with the essays in the Conspectus, Vol. I, pages 97–99, and Vol. II, pages 6–9. Specific articles are referenced on pages 28–30 in Vol. I and pages 110–111 in Vol. II. This series gives students a good chance to work with primary sources.

4. RESEARCH / ORAL OR WRITTEN REPORTS Have students select a topic related to this lesson for their reports. Suggestions might be the expeditions against the Indians at Sand Creek in 1864 or at Wounded Knee in 1890.

summed up in the saying, "The only good Indian is a dead Indian." The other group was against extermination but believed that the Indians' only hope of survival was to adopt the ways of the white Americans as quickly as possible. This approach, while surely more well-meaning than the other, was almost as destructive. It would bring about the end of Indian customs, religion, and society.

In the late 1860s, the United States government accepted the second view. It created a plan to put all the Plains Indians on two reservations. One was in the Black Hills of Dakota, the other in present-day Oklahoma. Government officials hoped that placing the Indians on reservations would force them to settle down on farms and give up their wanderings on the plains. In 1867 and 1868, worn down by war, the chiefs of the major tribes accepted the plan.

Many Indians moved onto the reservations, but a good many others refused to accept their chief's decision to give away millions of acres of land. For the next seven years, there was war along the frontier. In 1875, after more than 200 battles with the Army, the Indians were forced back to their reservations.

The last resistance. For a brief period there was quiet. Then the government yielded to the demands of miners that they be allowed to dig for gold on the Black Hills reservation. Once again a promise had been broken.

Fighting continued, off and on, for the next ten years. Now and then, the Indians won a big victory. For example, in June 1876, a large force of Sioux, led by Crazy Horse and Sitting Bull, ambushed and killed General George Custer and his 265 soldiers near the Little Bighorn River in Montana. The following year the Army captured most of Sitting Bull's people, and the chief himself fled to Canada. In the Far West, the Nez Percé Indians led the Army on a chase of 1,300 miles (2,080 km) for two months through Idaho and Montana. Weakened by starvation and disease, the Indians were finally taken and forced onto a reservation. Farther south, near the Mexican border, the capture of the Apache chief Geronimo marked the end of that tribe's resistance. The last "battle" of the Indian wars took place in 1890 at Wounded Knee, South Dakota. There soldiers slaughtered several hundred Indian men, women, and children.

End of the buffalo. The buffalo herd was the Indians' source of livelihood. The destruction of that huge herd ensured the end of Indian resistance. In 1860, there had been 12 or 13 million buffalo on the Great Plains. During the next ten years, workers laying railroad track across the plains killed many of these animals. Many more were killed for sport by hunters.

In 1871, the buffalo's doom was sealed with the discovery that buffalo hides could be sold at a profit. Over the next three years, 9 million buffalo were killed. By 1878, the great herd was almost wiped out. A few years later, there were less then 1,000 buffalo left in all North America.

The Dawes Act. As the fighting ended, the government moved to force the Indians to accept the ways of white Americans. The Dawes Act of 1887 aimed to

This hunting scene was painted by George Catlin, who spent six years with the western Indians.

break down the tribal organization of Indian life, and to make the Indian a farmer and landowner. In place of the traditional tribal ownership of land, each head of a family could claim 160 acres (64 ha) of reservation land to farm. Single persons would get smaller amounts. To protect the Indians from being cheated out of their land, the law said that the land could not be sold for 25 years. Those who accepted the offer of land would become citizens of the United States.

Some Indians made the adjustment to farming, but most of those who accepted the offer of land fared poorly. There was nothing in their tradition to prepare them for life as individual farmers. Nor did government schools do much to help them learn. Furthermore, the government sold much of the best reservation land to whites, leaving the poorest land to the Indians. In time, even those poor plots were divided by inheritance or sale.

Many Indians, including both those who had accepted farmland and those who had not, became dependent on the government. They accepted government aid, and in turn, the government used the threat of holding back aid to make the Indians give up tribal customs and loyalties. Under the Dawes Act, the lot of the Indians became ever more desperate. Population actually dropped because of poverty and disease. The fact that Congress in 1924 made all Indians citizens did not improve their lives.

In 1934, the Dawes Act was followed by the Indian Reorganization Act. It ended the breakup of the reservations, and gave back land and authority to the tribes. The government also taught the

5. MAKING A CHRONOLOGY Dee Brown's *Bury My Heart at Wounded Knee* (New York: Holt, Rinehart and Winston, 1971) contains the following memorable quote by an unknown Indian: "They [the white men] made us many promises, more than I can remember, but they never kept but one; they promised to take our land, and they took it." Have students make a chronology of government policies and treaties with the Indians. The chronology should indicate when the policies changed or treaties were broken. Students should start with information in the text and then research other treaties and laws. (See Activity 3 for sources.) Brown's book is also an excellent reference for this assignment. It is available in paperback (New York: Bantam Books, 1972) and also on tape cassettes. It, or a similiar study, should be read by anyone teaching or studying this material.

Indians better farming methods. For the first time, government policy left the Indians with some hope for the future. In the last unit of this book, you will read about the Indians in modern times.

CHECKUP

1. What was the traditional way of life of the Plains Indians?
2. How was the way of life of these Indians changed during the latter years of the nineteenth century?
3. What did the Dawes Act aim to do? Why was it unsuccessful?

LESSON 3

The Cattle Ranchers' Frontier

Even as the Indians were being pushed back, other Americans were sweeping over the Great Plains. Among the first to recognize the value of the region were the cattle ranchers. Cattle were brought to the Western Hemisphere by the Spanish in the early sixteenth century. Roaming freely in northern Mexico and Texas, they multiplied over the years, and by the middle of the nineteenth century numbered some five million in Texas alone. Some of the Americans who settled in Texas in the 1820s and 1830s be-

By 1880, the frontier was rapidly disappearing as miners, homesteaders, and ranchers moved into the American West. Between 1880 and 1900, seven new states would be carved out of that region.

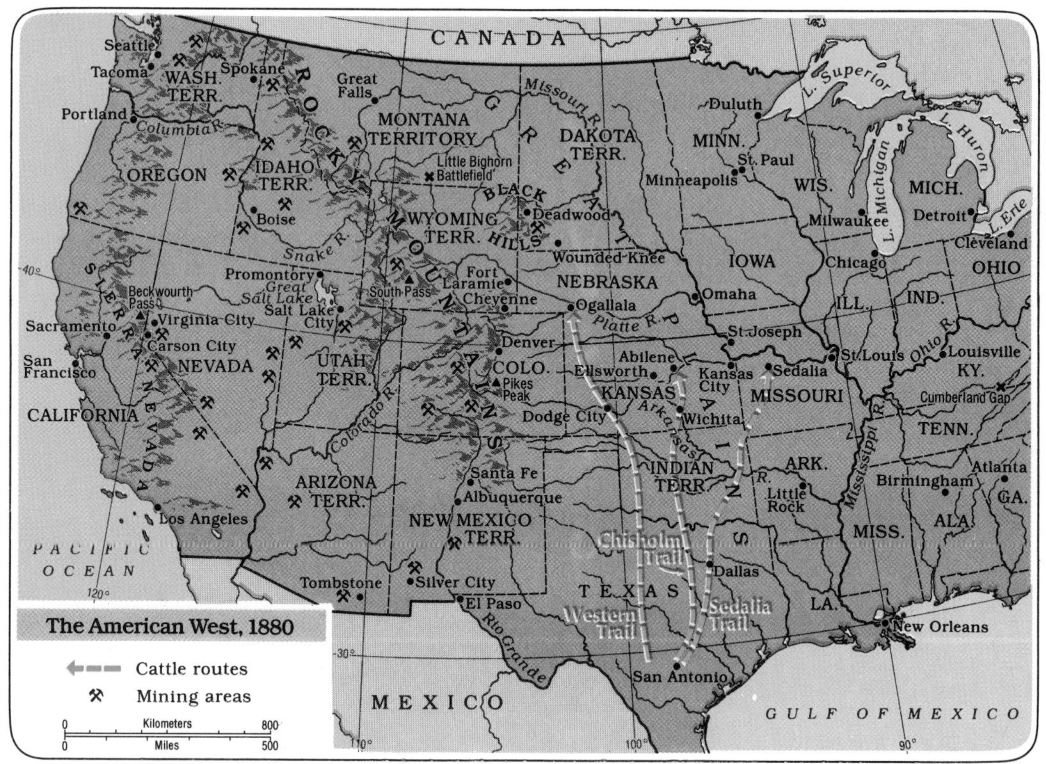

came large-scale ranchers overnight by rounding up and branding thousands of head of cattle.

The great market for beef, however, was in the cities of the East. A Texas longhorn that brought $3 or $4 in Texas could sell for $40 or more in the East, if it could be brought there. That became a possibility after the Civil War, when the railroad pushed westward into Missouri and then to Kansas. But the ranchers still had to get the cattle to the railroad lines.

The long drive. In 1866, Texas cattle raisers organized the first *long drive.* The plan was to drive the cattle northward the thousand or so miles (about 1,600 km) to the nearest railhead at Sedalia, Missouri, grazing them along the way. The route of the cattle drive, leading through wooded areas and across settled farmlands and Indian reservations, was not well chosen. Most of the 260,000 cattle that started the trip died or were lost or stolen. Still, those that reached Sedalia brought $35 a head. If the route was wrong, the idea was right.

The following year, a route farther west was chosen, leading across unsettled plains to Abilene, Kansas. Seventy-five thousand cattle were driven to Abilene in that first year and shipped to the East at large profits. In the next five years, about one and a half million cattle were driven to Abilene. As railroads pushed westward, other "cow towns" grew up in Kansas—Wichita, Ellsworth Falls, Dodge City. All in all, between 1866 and 1888, some six million cattle were driven north from Texas over several well-used trails across the plains.

The western cowboy. The long drive gave to American folklore, movies, and television one of its favorite figures, the western cowboy. In real life, cowboys were hardly the romantic characters of television, experiencing a new and exciting adventure weekly. On the long drive, a half dozen of these young men (most were age eighteen to twenty-five) would spend 18 hours a day in the saddle. They went on, day after day, in all kinds of weather, for two or three months. They were highly skilled, using the tools of the trade—the western saddle, the bit, the bridle, spurs, lariat, chaps, and the cowboy hat—developed long before by the Mexican *vaquero* (cowboy). In fact, many of the western cowboys were Mexican. About one in four was Mexican, Indian, or black.

The cowboy's greatest worry was the stampede. Thunder, lightning, anything that might give the cattle fright could set them off. It was then that the cowboy had to call on all his skills, for failure to head off a stampede could mean loss of the herd, or even serious injury or death to himself. For this largely dull but sometimes dangerous work, the cowboy received the use of a horse and about $30 a month.

Grazing on public lands. As cattle ranchers discovered that their animals could survive the winters on the northern plains, the cattle empire moved north. Nearly all that land was in the public domain, that is, owned by the government, so that young herds could be grazed for three or four years on public lands without a dollar's cost. By 1880, four and a half million head of cattle grazed on the open range.

LESSON 3 *(1 day)*

Performance Objective

To describe and explain orally or in writing the rise and decline of the cattle empire.

Vocabulary

Ranchers, long drive, cow towns, *vaquero,* water rights, rustlers, sheepherders, Hereford stock

Activities

1. **FILM** *Settling the Great Plains, 1850–1885,* American Adventure series (11 minutes, color; McGraw-Hill).

2. **USING A MAP** The cow towns are what most people think of in connection with the old West. Have the students use the map on page 492 to locate Abiline, Wichita, Ellsworth Falls, and Dodge City. Ask: Why did the cattle industry start where it did? What do you think would end the necessity for the long drives?

3. **LISTENING FOR INFORMATION** Read to your students or have them read aloud other information about the life of the American cowboy. Chapter 7 of *Alistair Cooke's America* by Alistair Cooke (New York: Alfred A. Knopf, Inc., 1977, paperback) would be useful. Compare the stereotype, from TV and movies, with the real cowboy.

4. **RESEARCH** Have students investigate the cattle industry today. Where is it? How do the ranchers avoid the problems of the 1880s? Where do they sell their cattle?

Background Information

COWBOY SUITS The fancy "western" clothes that entertainers have popularized are quite different from the early cowboy outfits, which cost about $135 each. Cowboys usually tried to buy the best hat, boots, and saddle they could find. Most of their other clothes and equipment came from the catalog houses, such as Montgomery Ward. The pices that follow are from a Montgomery Ward catalog of the 1880s: revolver—$12.20; cartridge belt with holster—$2.00; saddlebags—$5.00; spurs—$.70; leather boots—$20.00; chaps and pants—$8.00; bridle—$2.30; rain slicker—$2.75; cotton shirt—$1.25; leather vest—$3.00; Stetson hat—$10.00; kerchief—$.10; lasso (braided leather)—$7.75; rifle—$20.50; saddle—$40.00. Another necessity, a horse, usually cost around $35.00 but it was provided by the rancher.

These cowboys are "breaking" wild horses—that is, accustoming them to bridles, saddles, and riders.

By buying a few hundred acres near a river or a spring and taking advantage of loopholes in the law, the ranchers soon controlled large areas of the public lands. A few of these ranchers claimed areas of 5,000 square miles (13,000 square km). Sometimes they held the land by general agreement among ranchers, with each honoring the other's claim. At other times they held it by force against all comers. Cattle ranchers were continually fighting small wars in the range country—against other ranchers for water rights, or against rustlers, Indians, and sheepherders.

The 1870s and early 1880s were a time of great prosperity for the cattle empire. By this time, ranchers had bred the Texas longhorn with Hereford stock to produce a better quality of beef, and eastern and European markets were paying high prices for it. Stories of huge profits attracted more people into ranching. Fifty percent profit a year was common, and some people told of getting 800 and 1,000 percent return on their money in four years.

The end of the open range. Such prosperity was too much of a good thing. The ranges soon were overstocked and overgrazed. With a surplus of cattle, prices in the East and in Europe began to fall. Then a hard winter in 1885–86 followed by a hot, dry summer and another brutal winter in 1886–87 brought the cattle empire crashing down. Parched by the summer drought, and overcome by the winter blizzards, between 80 and 90 percent of the cattle on the range died. Millions of dollars of investment were lost, and many ranchers were ruined.

This disaster marked the end of open-range ranching. Thereafter, those who raised cattle followed more settled ways. They acquired land of their own, and turned to ranching with smaller herds. No longer able to depend on a sea of publicly owned grassland to fatten their cattle, they raised hay for feed, and sank wells for water. The cowboy, who had been the master of the open range, was reduced to the role of a farm laborer—just as he was being romanticized by writers of the western novel. By the end of the 1880s, the day of the cattle empire had passed. By then, the possessor of most of the plains was not the great rancher but the small farmer.

CHECKUP

1. What were some of the problems that ranchers faced in raising and marketing cattle?
2. How did the life of the cowboy of the 1870s differ from that of the cowboy usually portrayed on television?
3. In what ways did the cattle-raising business change during the 1880s?

LESSON 4

The Farmers' Frontier

Even as the cattle ranchers were starting to exploit the grasslands in the 1860s, some farmers began to move onto the Great Plains. The big rush of settlement came after 1870.

Why, after decades of shunning the Great American Desert, did farmers now flock to it? Part of the answer lies in the hold that the West had on the American mind as the place where opportunity was renewed. Part lies in the optimism of a confident and restless people that they could tame even a hostile nature. That optimism was encouraged by three things: eight years in a row of above average rainfall on the plains, which many took to be a permanent change in climate; a new government land policy; and the promoting activities of large landholders, especially railroads.

The Homestead Act. In 1862, Congress passed the Homestead Act. By this law any citizen or person who applied could get 160 acres (64 ha) of public land free, provided he or she lived on it and farmed it for five years. The law was meant to allow poor people to start family farms. Even with free land, however, poor Americans could still not afford the costs of moving a family, building a house and barn, sinking a well, and buying work horses, fencing, tools, and machinery. Most homesteaders on the plains were people who had been farmers in the East and had saved some money.

Between 1862 and 1900, the United States government gave away 80 million acres (32 million ha) under the Homestead Act. Much of this land fell into the hands of speculators. They hired people for $10 or $20 each to register for 160-acre homesteads, which were then signed over to the speculators. But during that same period, farmers bought from five to six times as much land from railroads, land companies, and state governments, all of whom had acquired large tracts of land before passage of the Homestead Act.

Railroads had a special interest in attracting people to settle in the West. Not only would it mean income from the sale of their lands, it would also provide customers who would ship their farm goods to market. Railroads, therefore, advertised heavily in the East and in Europe.

LESSON 4 *(1 day)*

Performance Objective

To identify orally or in writing **(a)** those events that led to the settlement of the Great Plains, **(b)** the problems the settlers faced, and **(c)** the various solutions to the problems.

Vocabulary

Homestead Act, sod house, dry farming, barbed wire, barn-raising bees.

Activities

1. **FILM** *The Real West,* Project 20 series (51 minutes, b & w; NBC and McGraw-Hill Films), narrated by Gary Cooper.

2. **CREATIVE WRITING** Ask students to read the lesson. Then have them write letters as though they were members of young farming families writing to their parents who are farmers in the East. They should include why they came, the kinds of problems they have faced, how their lives are different and what they like and dislike about it. (See page 496.) Beth Millstein and Jeanne Bodin's *We, the American Women* (Chicago: Science Research Associates, Inc., 1977) has letters and diaries that could be used for samples. Remind students that sometimes overcoming difficulties is part of the fun and certain people would seek such challenges.

3. RESEARCH Life on the prairies was exceptionally hard on women. Alistair Cooke, in *Alistair Cooke's America,* wrote, "Many otherwise healthy women went mad from the scrimping, the droughts, the burning summers, the polar winters, the loneliness. . . ." Perhaps the term *cabin fever* originated in this period. Have some students study the daily activities of these prairie women, finding answers to questions such as these: What jobs did the women do? What kind of social life did prairie families have, since they lived so far from neighbors? How were children educated? What games did they play? Have students present the information to the class by reports or by constructing a bulletin-board display.

4. POSTER Discuss the poster shown on page 496. Have students draw their own posters "advertising" the West but really indicating problems; for example, "See the millions of grasshoppers! Experience the droughts!"

This ad was used by a western railroad in 1873 to attract settlers to the Great Plains. Note the various inducements that were offered.

Life on the Great Plains. Farmers who settled on the plains found a climate and land different from anything they had known in the East or in Europe. Summer temperature reached 110°F (43°C), and water was scarce. The tough sod would not yield to the old-style eastern plow. There was no wood for buildings, fencing, and fuel.

A farm family's first house was usually made from blocks of sod. These were the matted roots of tough plains grasses, cut after rain or melted snow softened the hard soil. Piled one upon another, the blocks of sod made a surprisingly tight building. With their thick walls, sod houses were cool in summer and snug in winter. They were very small, however. A New England woman who had moved to the Kansas frontier wrote back, "We have but one room, in which we all eat, drink, and sleep, and that is not as large as your kitchen."

To deal with the lack of rain, some plains farmers sank wells 200 to 300 feet (60 to 90 m) deep, using windmills to pump the water. But that was too costly for most, and was not a widely used method until after 1900. Most farmers used a method known as "dry farming." This involved turning over the soil after each infrequent rain, moving the wet surface soil nearer to the roots. Doing this slowed down evaporation.

Inventions helped the plains farmers solve other problems. Barbed wire, invented in 1874, allowed them to fence off their land. Thus they could keep range cattle from trampling their crops and prevent their own animals from wandering off. New steel plows and other machinery helped break the tough sod, cultivate the land, and harvest the crops.

A harsh existence. Some of the difficulties of life on the plains, however, could not be relieved by inventions. For example, grasshoppers appeared every few years in such numbers as to darken the sky. A young settler described what happened to the family farm in a grasshopper plague that swept over a large part of the plains in 1873.

> So thick were the grasshoppers in the cornfield of which both of us had been so proud, that not a spot of green could be seen. And within two hours of the time that they had come not a leaf was left in all

that field. The stalks that still were left were merely ragged stumps, and where many a stalk had stood, a hole in the ground was all that remained—a hole where the grasshoppers had eaten the stalk off an inch or more below the ground.

Probably the hardest thing about life on the plains was the loneliness. Farms were far apart. For many years there were not even small villages nearby to break up the monotony and isolation. One relief for this loneliness was the *bee.* At a bee, frontier families came together to help each other with their work and also have a good time. There were barn-raising bees, sod-house-building bees, quilting bees, and many other kinds as well. A British woman traveling on the western frontier reported that the people "have a craze for giving and going to bees, and run to them with as much eagerness as a peasant runs to a race-course or a fair; plenty of strong drink and excitement making the chief attraction of the bee. . . ."

Despite the hardships, farmers moved onto the Great Plains in large numbers. For a number of years they were rivals of the cattle ranchers, and the two often fought, especially for control of water holes and streams. With the aid of barbed-wire fencing and sheer numbers, however, the farmers finally came out on top.

A family of homesteaders lounge by their wagons on their way to a new life in the West.

Answers To Review Questions

1. Prior to the nineteenth century, Americans believed that people were meant to live closely with nature. They were to take from the land only what was needed. However, in the nineteenth century, the ideas of Americans about progress led them to change their thinking. Nature was now seen as a storehouse of unclaimed wealth. And the proper aim of humankind was no longer to live in harmony with nature but to tame it.
2. Whereas very few miners made their fortunes moving from place to place in search of gold or silver, those who went into the business of selling goods and services to the miners did better financially.
3. The Great Plains had less rainfall than the settlers were used to; the temperatures ranged from very cold in winter to extremely hot in summer; winds swept over the flatlands; there were no trees for houses, fences, or fuel.
4. One group favored a policy of extermination. The other group believed that the Indians' only hope of survival was to adopt the ways of white Americans.
5. The Dawes Act sought to break down the tribal organization of Indian life by giving each head of a family 160 acres of reservation land to farm. This land policy would take the place of traditional tribal ownership of land. The purpose of the Dawes Act was to make Indians farmers and landowners, thereby forcing them to accept the ways of white Americans. The Indian Reorganization Act sought to end the breakup of the reservation and give back land and authority to the tribes.

Larger crops. As farm machinery came into use, more land came under cultivation. Without machines a wheat farmer in 1800 could harvest no more than eight acres (about 3 ha) a season. But by using farm machinery on the flat plains, a single farmer in 1900 could harvest 135 acres (54 ha). The economics of plains agriculture thus encouraged large farms. Farming corporations soon entered the picture, and "bonanza farms" of 5,000 to 10,000 acres (2,000 to 4,000 ha) were not unusual. There were a few huge farms of 100,000 acres (40,000 ha) in the Dakotas.

By the end of the nineteenth century, the Great Plains had become the nation's chief producer of grain. Of the five leading wheat-growing states in 1900, four were wholly or in part on the plains. With a growing population, North Dakota, South Dakota, and Montana entered the Union as states in 1889, along with Washington. Wyoming came in the following year.

The drama of the miners and the cowboys, of cattle ranchers and rustlers and sheriffs, was played out on the stage of the American West in the years between 1860 and 1890. It has fascinated Americans ever since. During those same years, other events of great significance were unfolding farther east. They had much to do with the making of modern America. You will read about those developments in the next chapter.

CHECKUP

1. What were some of the factors that led farmers to settle on the Great Plains?
2. What new problems on the Great Plains confronted settlers who had farmed in other regions?
3. How did they solve those problems?

Key Facts from Chapter 24

1. The discovery of gold in California in 1848 and later discoveries of gold and silver elsewhere in the West brought thousands of wealth seekers to those regions and helped open them for settlement.
2. As whites moved into the West, the Plains Indians were forced off lands that had been promised them forever in treaties with the United States government.
3. The destruction of the buffalo herd, government actions that broke down tribal authority, and confinement to reservations undermined the way of life of the Plains Indians, and put them into a long period of decline.
4. Cattle ranching on the Great Plains reached its peak during the 1870s and 1880s, and gave to American folklore one of its favorite characters, the western cowboy.
5. The Homestead Act of 1862 and the promotional activities of railroads were among the factors that induced farmers to settle on the Great Plains. By 1900, this was the chief grain-producing region in the United States.

★ REVIEWING THE CHAPTER ★

People, Places, and Events

"Forty-niners" *P. 484*
"Pike's Peak or Bust" *P. 485*
Comstock Lode *P. 485*
Great Plains *P. 486*
Plains Indians *P. 487*
Pony Express *P. 489*
Little Bighorn *P. 490*
Wounded Knee *P. 490*
Dawes Act *P. 490*
Indian Reorganization Act *P. 491*

Review Questions

1. In what way did Americans change their thinking about the relationship of humans to nature? *P. 483* Les. 1
2. Explain the statement, many more people became wealthy by mining miners than by mining gold. *P. 484* Les. 1
3. Why had the settlers of the 1840s avoided the Great Plains? *P. 487* Les. 2
4. Contrast the two views held by most Americans regarding a solution to the problem of Indian-white relations. *Pp. 488, 490* Les. 2
5. Compare the Dawes Act of 1887 with the Indian Reorganization Act of 1934. *Pp. 490–491* Les. 2
6. What factors contributed to the decline of the cattle empire during the 1880's? *Pp. 493–495* Les. 3
7. Briefly describe the hardships that confronted a farm family living on the Great Plains. *Pp. 496–497* Les. 4
8. The people who settled the West had different ideas about the land. Tell how each of the following groups might have answered the question, How shall the land be used? **(a)** miners, **(b)** Indians, **(c)** ranchers, **(d)** farmers.

Chapter Test

For each sentence, write the letter of the correct ending or endings.

1. "Pike's Peak or Bust" became the cry of miners flocking to **(a)** Montana, **(b)** Colorado, **(c)** California.
2. The region lying between the 100th meridian and the Rockies, and from Canada southward to Mexico, is called the **(a)** Great Plains, **(b)** Black Hills, **(c)** Great American Desert.
3. The last "battle" of the Indian wars took place at **(a)** Little Bighorn, **(b)** Ft. Laramie, **(c)** Wounded Knee.
4. The Dawes Act of 1887 aimed to **(a)** break down the tribal organization of Indian life, **(b)** protect dwindling buffalo herds, **(c)** make the Indian a farmer and landowner.
5. The Plains Indians were **(a)** victims of broken government promises, **(b)** skilled horsemen and fighters, **(c)** buffalo hunters.
6. Custer and his soldiers were killed in battle by the Sioux under the leadership of **(a)** Geronimo, **(b)** Sitting Bull, **(c)** Crazy Horse.
7. Land in the public domain may be owned by **(a)** the state, **(b)** cattle ranchers, **(c)** the federal government.
8. The purpose of the long drive was to move the cattle herd to the nearest **(a)** railhead, **(b)** grazing land, **(c)** watering hole.
9. Sod houses were popular with the **(a)** Plains Indians, **(b)** Great Plains farmers, **(c)** Mexican vaquero.
10. Land and authority were restored to the Indians by the **(a)** Indian Reorganization Act, **(b)** Homestead Act, **(c)** Dawes Act.

6. The open ranges were overstocked and overgrazed; a surplus of cattle caused prices to fall; adverse weather conditions caused between 80 and 90 percent of the cattle on the range to die; millions of dollars of investment were lost, and many ranchers were ruined.
7. In their answer, students should mention such hardships as adverse climate, scarcity of water and wood, grasshopper plagues, wandering range cattle, and loneliness.
8. Although this question calls for opinions, encourage students to support their beliefs with facts.

Suggested type of answer may be as follows: **(a)** Miners—The land should be used as a source of mineral wealth; **(b)** Indians—The land is the source of many good things in life and should be shared by all people; **(c)** Ranchers—The land should be kept as open range; **(d)** Farmers—The land should be divided into homesteads and improved in those ways necessary to ensure agricultural production.

Answers For Chapter Test
1. b **2.** a, c **3.** c **4.** a, c
5. a, b, c **6.** b, c **7.** a, c
8. a **9.** b **10.** a

THE INDUSTRIAL GIANT

Background Information

1. "THE BIG BLOW—THE BESSEMER PROCESS" was painted in 1948 by Aaron Bohrod and is presently owned by the National Steel Corporation. The Bessemer process was invented in 1856 in England by Henry Bessemer. It involves blowing air through molten pig iron, thus burning out much of the carbon. Too much carbon makes iron too brittle for major industrial use. This cheap, efficient way to make steel was introduced in America by Alexander Holley, who combined Bessemer's ideas with those of William Kelley. The Bessemer process was also the basis for Andrew Carnegie's steel empire. The Bessemer process was most important during the 1880s. By 1900 it had been surpassed by the open-hearth method as the major steel-producing method.

LESSON 1

At the time of its one hundredth birthday in 1876, the United States threw itself a six-month-long party—a world's fair. The fair took place in Philadelphia, the city of the nation's birth, and was called the Centennial Exposition. Some eight million people visited the 167 buildings that housed more than 30,000 exhibits from the United States and 50 other countries.

Of all the buildings, it was Machinery Hall to which most people flocked. There visitors were awed by the sight of 8,000 machines, powered by a single steam engine 40 feet (12m) high. Among the recent inventions were the sewing machine and the high-speed printing press, the typewriter and the telephone (". . . it *talks*!" exclaimed the visiting Emperor of Brazil). Models of the latest inventions from other countries stood beside those from the United States. To a people that fairly worshipped technology the comparison was deeply satisfying. One writer boasted:

> All that Great Britain has sent is insignificant in amount when compared with our own contributions. The superior elegance, aptness, and ingenuity of our machinery is observable at a glance. Yes, it is in these things of iron and steel that the national genius most freely speaks.

At the end of the country's first century, the machine was, beyond doubt, America's symbol of progress.

The two moods of America. The Centennial Exposition took place during a sharp depression. The downturn began in 1873 with the failure of a large banking house that had loaned too much money to railroads. The depression then spread through the rest of the economy. Industrial production fell. Railroad building in 1874 was but half what it had been the year before. Between one and three million people were thrown out of work.

In July 1877, the Baltimore and Ohio Railroad announced a wage cut, the fifth since 1874. Railroad workers, whose pay had now gone down by nearly 40 percent in three years, rose in protest. Firemen on the B & O walked off the job. The strike quickly spread to other lines across the country. In a number of places, violence broke out. Strikers in Martinsburg, West Virginia, set fire to the roundhouse.

In Pittsburgh other workers joined the strikers. Twenty-five hundred loaded railroad cars and 125 locomotives were destroyed. For several days, mobs roamed the streets, smashing windows, burning, and looting. Dozens of lives were lost. Millions of dollars' worth of property was ruined. Violence also broke out in nearly a dozen other cities. Order was restored only when President Rutherford B. Hayes called out federal troops.

The Centennial Exposition of 1876 and the violence of 1877 showed the two moods of America as it entered the industrial age. The one looked confidently toward a future of boundless plenty to be brought by the machine. The other raised deep doubts about the human costs of industrial progress.

LESSON 1 *(2 days)*

Performance Objectives

1. To contrast orally or in writing the two moods of America indicated by the Centennial Exposition and the railroad strikes of 1877. **2.** To list and explain orally or in writing the main factors contributing to American economic growth from 1875 to 1900. **3.** To explain orally or in writing the contributions made, and problems created, by Andrew Carnegie and John D. Rockefeller. **4.** To explain orally or in writing the consequences of a belief in social Darwinism in a culturally diversified nation.

Famous People

Cornelius Vanderbilt, Thomas Scott, Schuyler Colfax, Gustavus Swift, Andrew Carnegie, John D. Rockefeller, Horatio Alger

Vocabulary

Centennial Exposition, material progress, patents, exploitation, federal subsidies, Crédit Mobilier, vertical integration, Standard Oil Company, horizontal integration, rebates, consolidation, pool, trust, holding company, finance capitalism, *Origin of Species,* "survival of the fittest," natural selection, social Darwinism, Gospel of Wealth

Activities

1. FILMS This is a particularly good lesson for media, since the worker-owner differences can be shown so easily. Possible films include the following: *Toward the Gilded Age,* Exploring series (25 minutes, color; NBC). *Andrew Carnegie* (18 minutes, b & w; Encyclopaedia Britannica Films). *Darwin and the Theory of Natural Selection* (15 minutes, color; Coronet Films). *The Railroad Builders,* Western Movement series (14 minutes, color; Encyclopaedia Britannica Films). If the particular film or filmstrip you use includes the term *Gilded Age,* be sure to discuss what it means.

2. BULLETIN-BOARD DISPLAY After students have read page 501, have them look for news articles from recent magazines or newspapers that show the same conflicting moods in America today. Have students arrange the articles in two collages for the bulletin board.

3. READING FOR INFORMATION/NOTE-TAKING Have students take notes from pages 502–509 to find ten factors that aided industrialization. The factors should be listed using brief headings, such as Raw materials, Capital, Inventions, Population, Material progress, Government subsidies, Railroads, Leadership, Consolidation, Social Darwinism. This would be a good time to check students' understanding of the ideas of the lesson.

The Pursuit of Progress

In the fifteen years following the Centennial Exposition, the United States became a mighty industrial country. In that time, production of coal tripled. The output of iron ore increased four times, of lead nearly three times, and of copper more than eight times. Production of finished steel rose from little more than a half million tons (450,000 t) in 1877 to nearly five million tons (4.5 million t) in 1892. In 1890, for the first time, the value of manufactured goods exceeded the value of farm products. In 1894, the United States moved into first place among the manufacturing countries of the world.

Factors for growth. What were the reasons for this amazing industrial growth? There were several. America was rich in raw materials. It had half the world's known supply of iron ore, two thirds of its copper, and one third of its lead. It also had huge amounts of coal, oil, zinc, and other metals. Its capital was increasing, and what it lacked, European investors happily provided. A population that tripled in 50 years—31 million in 1860, 92 million in 1910—provided both workers for industry and buyers for its products. Hundreds of inventions each year increased output per worker and created wholly new industries. In 1850, 883 patents were issued for inventions; in the centennial year, 1876, 14,169; and in 1900, 24,644. And a growing railroad network moved goods cheaply and swiftly from Atlantic to Pacific, turning the entire 3,000-mile (4,800-km) span into one great market. In 1885, a ton of goods could be carried one mile (1.6 km) for less than seven tenths of a cent. That, marvelled an economist of the time, was less than the smallest coin one could "give a boy as a reward for carrying an ounce (28 g) package across a street."

Yet those factors do not fully explain America's rapid industrialization. Just as important was an idea central to American culture: *material* progress, both personal and national. Tocqueville had noted how America's boast of opportunity and its promise of a place for those with drive and ability created not only a desire among Americans to grow rich but an anxiety about it. And opportunities never seemed greater than in the last half of the nineteenth century.

A helpful government. Government policy also encouraged economic growth in a number of ways. A stable banking system and constitutional guarantees for property made a healthy climate for business. Patent laws encouraged invention by reserving the rewards for the inventor. Generous *subsidies*—that is, payments of government funds—to railroads, the largest business of the times, helped open the West for development. High tariffs gave many businesses an advantage in the American market by keeping out foreign goods.

Perhaps most important of all, the government opened up America's treasures to exploitation by private interests, large and small. An example was the Timber and Stone Act of 1878. For $2.50 an acre (0.4 ha), anyone could buy 160 acres (64 ha) of land in the Far West so long as it was "unfit for cultivation." This land included the thick forests of Washington, Oregon, and California, where there were hundreds of trees on

America's timber resources have often been ruthlessly exploited in the interests of "progress."

each acre. It has been pointed out that $2.50 was "about the price of one good log." Lumber companies used this law to gain thousands of acres. They hired people to put in claims at the land office. Then each person was paid a few dollars to sign over the deed.

Millions of acres of trees were soon cut without either plan or thought of renewing them. Yet this ruthless exploitation, too, could find some of its roots in the American belief about progress. For a part of that belief was, as you will recall, that nature was to be tamed, overcome, and bent to human will.

The railroad era. The railroad industry captured the imagination of people everywhere after the Civil War. Between 1860 and 1890, railroad mileage tripled. By 1900, the United States had 193,000 miles (308,800 km) of track—more than in all of Europe.

Most of this increased mileage was east of the Mississippi River. There, leaders like Cornelius Vanderbilt of the New York Central and Thomas Scott of the Pensylvania Railroad were bringing the many independent and competing lines into a few great systems. The drama, however, was in the West. Soon after the Civil War, two railroads combined to build the first line spanning the continent. Both the Union Pacific and the Central Pacific had received generous federal subsidies. The Union Pacific, with its gangs of Irish workers, started laying track westward from Omaha, Nebraska. The Central Pacific, with its work force of Chinese laborers, set out eastward from Sacramento, California. In May 1869 the two lines met in Utah, just north of Great Salt Lake. The nation cheered as a golden spike was driven into the last tie. As the spike received its final tap, the news was carried to the rest of the country by telegraph. During the next 24 years, four more transcontinental lines would be built, along both northern and southern routes.

Background Information

2. THE VANDERBILT FAMILY The Vanderbilts were fascinating if atypical examples of the leaders of the time. Several generations of the family have included business leaders, from "Commodore" Cornelius (1794–1877), owner of steamship and railroad lines, through grandsons William (1849–1920) and Cornelius (1843–1899) and down to the present Cornelius, Jr. (1898–). Extremely successful but coarse and uneducated, the Commodore was not accepted into New York society, but by his grandson's time, the Vanderbilts were social leaders also. The following will give an idea of the wealth this family controlled. When the Commodore turned over control of his railroad lines to his son, William Henry (1821–1885), William sold some 250,000 shares. He then reinvested the proceeds from his sales in U.S. government bonds and other stocks and bonds. William's income from these holdings was $10,350,000 a year! Based on an eight-hour day, and a five-day week, (2080 hours per year), the hourly wage for this amount would be $4,975.96—more than $80 per minute! Ironically, he and many of the others of his family were very hard workers, often arriving at their jobs before the office staff. They did find ways to spend their money, however. The Vanderbilts built seven mansions in New York City and two summer "cottages" at Newport, Rhode Island, which was the summer resort for the rich. The larger "cottage," named "The Breakers," cost $5 million unfurnished, while the smaller was furnished for $3 million. Of course, there were the necessary expenses, ranging from servants (no respectable house could have less than fifteen) to the cost of importing the cast and set of a Broadway play for an evening's entertainment. A housewarming ball could cost $250,000. Another $250,000 was needed for the *North Star,* a luxury yacht to transport them from Newport to New York City or even to Europe.

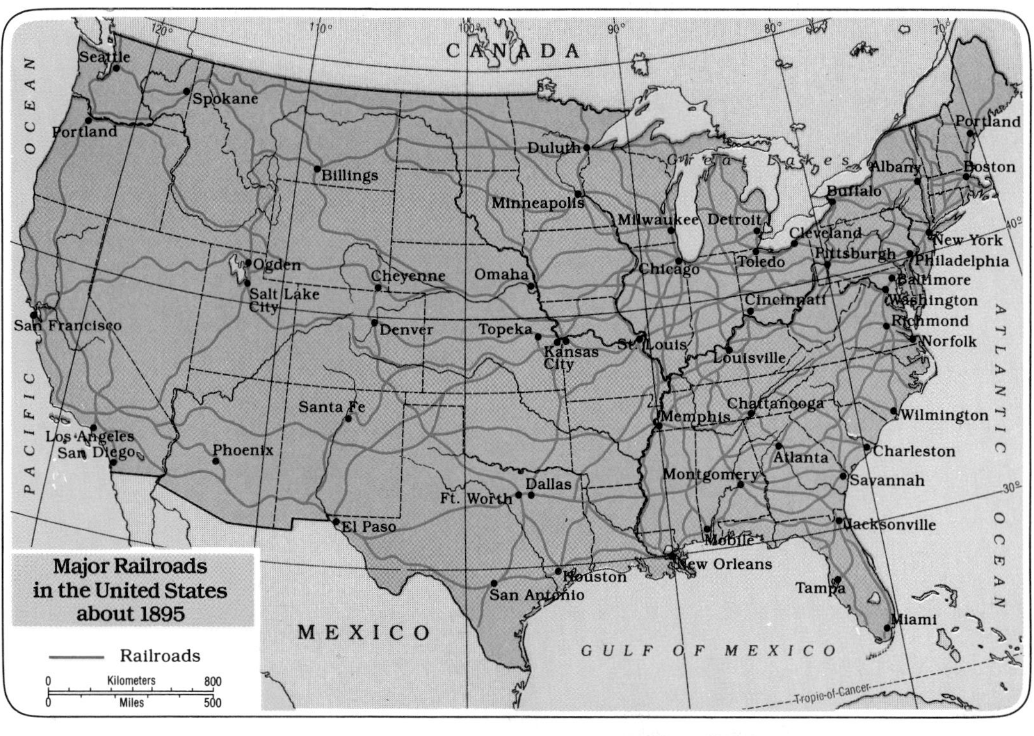

By 1895, America's railroad network was nearly complete. The years of greatest growth had been during the 1880s when some 70,000 miles (120,000 km) of new railroad lines were built.

Subsidies and scandals. These railroads were to be built through unsettled regions and could not look forward to profitable traffic for some time. Congress therefore offered subsidies in the form of loans and grants of land for each mile of track laid. All but the last of the transcontinentals, the Great Northern, received these grants. Between 1850 and 1871, the United States government gave away a total of 134 million acres (53.6 million ha) to the railroads. States added another 49 million (19.6 million ha). Estimates of the value of these gifts run from $130 million to $500 million—more than enough to cover the cost of building the roads.

The huge sums of money involved in building railroads led to a great deal of corruption. In one scandal, the officials of the Union Pacific awarded contracts to build their railroad at wildly inflated prices to the Crédit Mobilier, a construction company they secretly owned. Most of the money would in the end come from the loans of the federal government. To head off an investigation, the Crédit Mobilier bribed with company stock a number of members of Congress. Among them was Schuyler Colfax of New York, soon to be Vice President under Grant. None of those accepting bribes went to jail or received anything worse than a rebuke for his part in the deal. Meanwhile the Credit Mobilier made a profit of more than $23 million.

Industrial leadership. A number of remarkable business leaders contributed to America's industrial growth in the late nineteenth century. They were persons of great vision, with a genius for organization, an ambition to attain power and wealth, and—more often than not—a ruthlessness to match. Often they started their upward climb by being among the first to see how a change in technology could be used to build a new business.

Gustavus Swift, for example, very early saw that the refrigerated railroad car would make it possible to send fresh beef from Chicago to eastern cities. This fresh meat would replace the shipments of less tasty smoked, salted, or canned meat. In 1878, Swift made his first such shipment. Ten years later his company dominated the industry.

Andrew Carnegie. One of the most remarkable business leaders of the age was Andrew Carnegie. Carnegie came to America from Scotland at the age of twelve, and immediately went to work in a cotton mill for $1.20 a week. He became, in succession, a Western Union messenger, a telegraph clerk, and private secretary to Thomas Scott of the Pennsylvania Railroad. As Scott rose, so did Carnegie, becoming an executive of the railroad himself.

It was, however, the iron and steel business rather than the railroads in which Carnegie would make his mark. After building iron railroad bridges for a number of years, Carnegie turned to steel. Although Bessemer and Kelley had discovered a way to make steel cheaply in 1856, less than 20,000 tons (18,000 t) a year were being made in the United States a decade later. In 1872, Carnegie and a few others built a huge steel mill in western Pennsylvania. Carnegie shrewdly named the plant after the head of the Pennsylvania Railroad, J. Edgar Thompson. Needless to say, when the plant began to produce steel rails in 1875, the Pennsylvania Railroad bought them. So did most other railroads, not only because Carnegie was a good salesman and knew many of the railroaders firsthand, but also because steel rails lasted 20 times longer than iron rails. Carnegie prospered even during the depression of the 1870s, and was able to buy out a number of steel companies that were failing. By 1880, there were more than 1,000 iron and steel companies in the United States, but Carnegie's company was by far the largest of all.

Many of those companies fell by the wayside over the next ten years as Carnegie tightened his grip on the steel business. A brilliant organizer, Carnegie had a gift for choosing able associates. He also reinvested profits in the most up-to-date machinery and methods. To assure regular supplies of the raw materials needed in the manufacture of steel, Carnegie bought iron mines in Michigan and Minnesota, the richest iron ore district in the world. He purchased limestone quarries and coal mines in Pennsylvania and elsewhere. He also bought ore boats and railroads

4. RESEARCH / ORAL REPORTS Have some of the students read and report on John Kenneth Galbraith's *The Age of Uncertainty*, Chapter 2, "The Manners and Morals of High Capitalism." This chapter is a clear and witty explanation of social Darwinism. Richard Hofstadter's *Social Darwinism in American Thought, 1860–1915* (Philadelphia: University of Pennsylvania Press, 1945) goes even deeper into the subject.

to carry those materials to his plants in Pittsburgh. To assure a source of coke, used as fuel in the steel mills, he took in as a partner Henry Clay Frick, owner of a rich coke business in Pennsylvania. Bringing under single control all the steps in manufacturing from raw materials to finished product, is called *vertical integration.*

In vertically integrating the steel industry Carnegie was able to increase profits and effect great economies. He himself marvelled at it all.

> To make a ton of steel, one and a half tons of iron stone has to be mined, transported by rail a hundred miles to the Lakes, carried by boat hundreds of miles, transferred to cars, transported by rail one hundred and fifty miles to Pittsburgh; one and a half tons of coal must be mined and manufactured into coke and carried fifty-odd miles by rail; and one ton of limestone mined and carried one hundred and fifty miles to Pittsburgh. How then could steel be manufactured and sold without loss at three pounds for two cents? This, I confess, seemed to me incredible, and little less than miraculous, but it was so.

And it was true. When Carnegie began to make steel rails in 1875, the price was $160 a ton. In 1898, it was just $17 a ton. By that time Carnegie had long since become the greatest single force in the steel industry, and the United States the world's leading producer of steel.

John D. Rockefeller. What Carnegie was to steel, John D. Rockefeller was to oil. In 1859, Colonel Edwin Drake drilled the first successful oil well in Titusville, Pennsylvania. Soon a forest of oil rigs rose in western Pennsylvania, as hundreds rushed to mine the "black gold."

Andrew Carnegie, shown in the cartoon at top, gave away millions of dollars. The cartoon refers to the gifts he made to universities in his native Scotland. John D. Rockefeller, below, gave a large sum to the University of Chicago.

The result was waste, overproduction, and falling prices. At the time Colonel Drake struck oil, John D. Rockefeller was a successful young businessman in wholesale meats and grain in Cleveland. Rockefeller had many of the same qualities as Carnegie. He was highly intelligent, frugal, and hard-working. He had a genius for organizing and a passion for order and efficiency.

Rockefeller saw that there was money to be made in oil, not in the disorderly business of drilling for it but in refining it. The chief product of oil refining was kerosene, used for home lighting. Rockefeller entered the refining business in 1863, and set out to gain control of it, first in Cleveland, later in the entire United States. By controlling this one step in the manufacture of oil products, he could decide what price would be paid for crude oil, and what would be charged for the finished product. Bringing a single key step of production in an industry under one company is known as *horizontal integration.*

By 1870, Rockefeller had most of the refineries in Cleveland under his thumb. With 20 percent of the market. he was the leading oil refiner in the country. In that year he formed the Standard Oil Company and soon dominated the entire oil industry. By 1879, only nine years later, Standard Oil controlled more than 90 percent of refining. It would remain the major firm in the oil industry, not only in the United States but in the world.

The efficient use of modern business methods and machines had a good deal to do with Standard Oil's success. So too did a number of questionable business practices. As the largest shipper of oil, the company was able to demand and get secret rebates on freight charges by threatening to take its business to other railroads. Standard Oil, in fact, not only got back a part of what it paid but also a part of the freight charges its competitors paid. Standard Oil also gained control over the pipelines that were built later. The company was thus able to turn those advantages into both higher profits and lower prices—which drove out competitors. Rockefeller often made generous offers to buy out competitors. If they refused, however, he would use fair means or foul to drive them to the wall.

Big business. Steel and oil were only two of many businesses in which competing units were *consolidated,* or joined together, into a single company—or, more often, into a very few companies. No doubt the effort to do away with competition involved a desire for power and profits. But there were other reasons also. Some industries were just not suited to small-scale operation. Without large investments of capital in steel, refining, and dozens of other businesses, small firms simply could not compete for very long against large ones. Also, the economy in the late nineteenth century was changing rapidly. New industries, offering great opportunities for riches, attracted a great many people, much as the oil fields of Pennsylvania had. The result almost always was overproduction, price cutting, business failures, and broken dreams. To avoid such situations and to keep out of ruinous price wars, business people looked for ways to match production more closely to demand.

5. THOUGHT PROVOKER
Discuss with your students the following statement made by John D. Rockefeller, Jr. (son of the founder of the Standard Oil Co. and father of Nelson Rockefeller. former Vice President): "I believe that every right implies responsibility; every opportunity, an obligation; every possession, a duty." Ask: While it is very easy and popular to criticize the Rockefellers, Carnegies, and others of the time, would our nation have advanced as far as it had without the efforts of such people? What responsibilities did a person such as Carnegie have? What obligations? What duties? How does the comment by Rockefeller, Jr., compare with that by Rockefeller, Sr., quoted on page 509? What factors may have influenced Rockefeller, Jr.'s change in attitude and philosophy? Does it make sense that his son Nelson would go into politics (public service)?

As the trusts became powerful, they came under attack in political cartoons. Here the trusts are shown hitting the consumer with high tariffs in order to make their profits shoot upward.

One method was the *pool*. This was a secret agreement among rival companies to divide the market among them and keep prices up. Railroads covering the same territory often tried to form pools, as did some producers. Pools, however, were "gentlemen's agreements" that could not be enforced by law. Sooner or later, one or more members would reach out for a bigger share than agreed upon, touching off a price war among the rival companies.

More dependable than the pool was the *trust.* Stockholders in competing corporations turned over their stock to a single group of trustees. In exchange they received trust certificates entitling them to dividends but no power. The trustees now could set policies for all the firms in the trust and run them as a single company. Invented by a lawyer for Standard Oil in 1882, this device was soon used by dozens of industries. By the late 1880s, consumers had heard of the whiskey trust, the lead trust, the sugar trust, the cottonseed oil trust. Because of legal problems, the trust was discarded in the 1890s, but the word *trust* continued to be used by the general public to mean any big business combination. The trust was replaced by the *holding company.* It got the same results as the trust by owning a controlling share of stock in a number of corporations in the same business.

By the 1890s, banks were among the leading promoters of business consolidation. As suppliers of money for business expansion, they wanted to be sure that their investments were not threatened by price cutting. The surest way to do that was to end competition and bring industry under the control of bankers. Under this arrangement, known as *finance capitalism,* many businesses passed into the hands of a few financial giants, such as J. P. Morgan.

Social Darwinism. Captains of industry built up fortunes greater than many a prince or king. Between 1896 and 1900, Carnegie, who was worth hundreds of millions of dollars, received an average income of $10 million a year from his steel companies. This was about 20,000 times the income of the average wage earner of that day. Charles Schwab, president of the Carnegie Steel Company, built a four-story mansion occupying a city block in New York. It had a bowling alley, a gym, 90 bedrooms, and a laundry to meet the daily needs of 100 guests. Members of the Vanderbilt family, whose fortune was based on the New York Central Railroad, built seven houses within seven blocks on New York's Fifth Avenue. The cost: $11 million. Two Vanderbilts put as much money, if not more, into summer palaces at Newport, Rhode Island.

Some people justified such fortunes, and the growth of the big businesses and trusts that created them, through ideas based upon the work of the English scientist Charles Darwin. In the *Origin of Species* (1859) Darwin showed that in nature there was a constant struggle for survival, and that only the fittest survived. Soon people claimed that Darwin's findings about the world of animals and plants applied equally to human society. Social Darwinists argued that in the struggle for existence among individuals and among businesses, the fittest would survive. Some individuals would be hurt, of course, but in the grand plan of nature, that was the price of progress. John D. Rockefeller put it this way:

> The growth of a large business is merely the survival of the fittest . . . the working out of a law of nature and a law of god. . . . The American Beauty rose can be produced . . . only by sacrificing the early buds which grow up around it.

These ideas were spread by writers, lecturers, professors, and clergymen. One of the people who held this view was William Graham Sumner, a professor at Yale University, who wrote:

> The millionaires are a product of natural selection, acting on the whole body of men to pick out those who can meet the requirements of certain work to be done. . . . They get high wages and live in luxury, but the bargain is a good one for society.

A few, like Andrew Carnegie, while agreeing entirely with Sumner, also insisted that the rich were simply trustees of their millions, and were obliged to spend them wisely for the public good. This, wrote Carnegie, was the real Gospel of Wealth. True to his own word, Carnegie spent the last eighteen years of his life giving away his millions for libraries, scientific and educational research, and the cause of world peace.

John D. Rockefeller held much the same view. "The good Lord gave me my money," he said, "and how could I withhold it from the University of Chicago?" Thereupon he gave that worthy institution a founding gift of $34 million. It must be added, however, that while a few like Carnegie and Rockefeller were moved by the spirit of "earn and give," most of the wealthy of the age lived by a philosophy of "grab and hold."

CHECKUP

1. What were the main factors in America's economic growth during the 25 years after the Centennial Exposition?
2. How did such leaders as Andrew Carnegie and John D. Rockefeller contribute to America's industrial growth?
3. How did social Darwinism justify the growth of great fortunes?

Continued on page 511

6. ROLE-PLAYING Have several students serve as a Congressional subcommittee that is conducting investigative hearings into the activities of John D. Rockefeller and Andrew Carnegie. Have other students represent witnesses at the hearing. Some witnesses should be in favor of big business while others should be against it. For example, Ida Tarbell might be a witness (see page 586). Have two students role-play Rockefeller and Carnegie as they testify before the subcommittee about whether they have helped the United States or hurt it. Those on the subcommittee should represent the spectrum of views concerning these men. Instruct the subcommittee members to ask questions of the witnesses and allow witnesses to answer questions and make statements.

After all the witnesses, including Carnegie and Rockefeller, have testified, let the whole class act as the Congressional subcommittee and vote on whether there should be laws making the activities of Carnegie and Rockefeller illegal. If so, what kind of laws?

LESSON 2 *(2 days)*

Performance Objectives

1. To describe in writing the working conditions prevalent in most factories in the latter half of the nineteenth century.
2. To list and explain the major advances and setbacks enjoyed and suffered by organized labor from the 1850s to 1900.

Famous People

Terence V. Powderly, Samuel Gompers, Eugene V. Debs

Vocabulary

Laissez faire, Sherman Anti-Trust Act, *Progress and Poverty,* "needle trades," collective bargaining, National Labor Union (NLU), Knights of Labor, Haymarket Riot, anarchists, American Federation of Labor, yellow dog contract, blacklist, injunction, Homestead Strike, Pullman Strike

From Rags to Riches

The dream of success in terms of personal progress was a persistent theme in American novels during the period after the Civil War. An almost endless stream of books encouraged boys to feel that they could go from rags to riches. With a few variations, those books told the same tale: how a poor youth of noble character overcame setbacks to achieve worldly success.

One author who made a career of writing such books was Horatio Alger. The son of a Massachusetts clergyman, he became a minister himself because his father insisted on it. But in 1866 he left the pulpit, settled in New York, and began his writing career. His books—such as *Luck and Pluck* and *Tattered Tom*—dealt with penniless lads who rose to fame and fortune. Alger's novels made the moral that in America, success could come to anyone who worked hard, had courage, was of good character, and was blessed with good luck. Alger wrote 130 books all on this same theme, and more than 20 million copies were sold.

Girls were also provided with success stories, but such stories for girls focused on home and family rather than on the business world. Martha Finley was to girls what Horatio Alger was to boys. Thousands of girls followed the trials of Elise Dinsmore, the pure-in-heart heroine in a number of Martha Finley's novels.

About 1900, a new kind of popular literature—the dime novel—appeared. Printed on cheap paper in magazine form, the dime novel offered stories with such titles as "From Bootblack to Senator" and "Winning the Dollars."

For more than half a century, the success stories of Horatio Alger, Martha Finley, and others were read by countless boys and girls. Those novels shaped the views of a great many Americans about personal progress and success.

This dust cover from a book by Horatio Alger indicates the rags-to-riches theme of that writer's stories. The penniless newsboy will surely go on to win fame and fortune through perseverance, courage, and a bit of luck.

LESSON 2

The Cost of Progress

By no means did all Americans agree with the justifications of social Darwinism. They pointed out that most of those who talked of *laissez faire*, that is, no government interference, in fact sought and received government aid. Such aid included high tariffs and land grants from the federal government and tax breaks from local ones. Those who talked about the need for competition were often the same ones who did whatever they could to prevent it. Indeed, they often acted illegally to avoid it.

Critics of big business. Some Americans did not accept the idea that government should never interfere, nor that business consolidations were natural, necessary, and good. They demanded a law to outlaw trusts and other such combinations. In 1890, Congress responded with the Sherman Anti-Trust Act. This law declared that combinations that restrained trade in interstate commerce were illegal. Little came of the law for a number of years as court decisions sharply limited its use.

Many people also rejected the social Darwinist view that progress could only come through the elimination of the weak by the strong. In *Progress and Poverty* (1879) Henry George, a newspaper writer, reformer, and self-taught economist spoke for many when he wrote:

> So long as all the increased wealth which modern progress brings goes but to build up great fortunes to increase luxury and make sharper the contrast between the House of Have and the House of Want, progress is not real and cannot be permanent.

It was in the cities that the contrast between the House of Have and the House of Want was most striking. Just blocks from Charles Schwab's mansion was the shantytown in which the Irish immigrant poor lived in crude huts of wood and cardboard. Some blocks farther away were neighborhoods whose very names—Hell's Kitchen and Bandit's Roost—told of the desperate conditions of life there. It is doubtful that these people saw millionaires as the same "bargain" for society that William Graham Sumner did.

The workers' lot. The working conditions in America's mills, factories, and mines had hardly improved over what they had been before the Civil War. As late as 1900, the average workweek was 58 hours. In the steel industry, it was 72 hours. Women made up 20 percent of the work force in manufacturing. They generally received less pay than men, although they worked the same long hours. Women made up the largest part of the work force in the "needle trades," making dresses and other clothing.

Children made up another important part of the work force. In 1890, 600,000 boys and girls between ten and fourteen years of age were working 10 to 12 hours a day in factories and mines. Even younger children worked the 12-hour night shift in some southern cotton mills. A nineteenth-century reformer named Sarah Cleghorn captured the unfairness of child labor in these bitter lines.

> The golf links lie so near the mill
> That almost every day
> The laboring children can look out
> And see the men at play.

Activities

1. ESSAY After students hare read the lesson, have them write brief essays describing wages and working conditions in American industry during this period. They should try to show why people would consider joining unions.

2. USING A CHART Today's unions are much different from the first unions. The direction of change can be seen between the time of the NLU and the AF of L. Have students construct a chart showing similarities and differences between the NLU, the Knights of Labor, and the AF of L. The categories might include Leaders, Membership (who belonged), Goals, and Accomplishments. All the information can be found in or inferred from the text, except that William Sylvis was the leader of the NLU. For a more complex exercise, have students decide what categories to use.

Background Information

1. SHERMAN ANTI-TRUST ACT In its early years this act was used primarily in the opposition of labor unions and thus actually helped the businesses it was designed to limit. The courts ruled that labor unions were organizations that worked "in restraint of trade" and thus were prohibited by the law under the commerce section of the Constitution. The leaders of the unions were served injunctions by the court to stop striking or even to stop organizing the workers. If they refused, they could be sent to jail for contempt of court. The Norris-LaGuardia Anti-Injunction Act, the Wagner Act, and changing court opinions ended this practice by the 1940s.

3. RESEARCH/ORAL OR WRITTEN REPORTS Some sophisticated students could try to discover why there was so much resistance to unions. Aside from the fear of losing their jobs for joining, many American workers were opposed to unions. (See *Annals of America* Conspectus, Vol. II, Chapter 17.) Have the students present oral or written reports of their findings.

4. THOUGHT PROVOKER Havelock Ellis, an eminent British psychologist at the turn of the century, wrote: "The greatest task before civilization is to make machines what they ought to be, the slaves, instead of the masters of men." He also remarked that "all civilization has from time to time become a thin crust over a volcano of revolution." Ask your students to analyze the two statements and agree or disagree with them. Could the first statement be a cause of the second? The students might be interested in discussing current as well as historical applications of the statements.

Working conditions were often unsafe. On railroads alone in 1891, the first year for which there were records, more than 7,000 workers were killed and 33,000 injured. Mining was even more dangerous. In many factories, a split second of inattention near an unprotected gear or press could cost a life or leave a worker crippled. Each year, 20,000 or more workers were killed on the job, and more than ten times that number were injured. And those numbers do not include the many thousands whose lives were shortened by coal dust in the mines, fiercely high temperatures at the steel furnaces, and bad working conditions elsewhere.

Wages, averaging about $9 a week, hardly changed at all during the last half of the nineteenth century. It must be noted, however, that prices of goods dropped throughout these years. Thus, the real income of workers did increase. However, most workers earned barely enough to make ends meet. Unemployment was a constant fear.

Toiling garment workers ply their trade in a New York City shop in 1908. Working conditions in such shops were often unsafe and insanitary.

Many workers lived in company towns, where employers owned the homes and the stores. At times the employers even paid the workers in scrip (paper money issued by the company). It could be used as money only in the company towns. Prices there were often higher than elsewhere.

Many employers thought of workers simply as a cost of production, and one that could be lowered more easily than could the cost of machines. With an even hand, one New England manufacturer stated that he felt the same about his workers as he did about his machines. "So long as they can do my work for what I choose to pay them, I keep them, getting out of them all that I can." Individual workers had no power to bargain with employers. "I have always had one rule," said a factory owner. "If a workman sticks up his head, hit it."

The first unions. Unable to improve their conditions by bargaining with their employers individually, workers formed unions to bargain collectively. By the Civil War years, several hundred thousand workers had joined national unions organized along the lines of each skill: printers, cigar makers, iron molders, and so on. In 1866, a number of these unions of skilled workers joined in the National Labor Union (NLU). At one time, membership reached 600,000.

The NLU had little in common with modern unions. Its leaders did not believe in strikes. Instead, they talked grandly of abolishing the wage system and forming cooperatives, with workers owning the factories and mines and becoming their own employers. Except for the eight-hour day, the NLU leaders ignored the immediate needs of labor. Rather, they favored more general long-range social and humanitarian reforms. After a time, the NLU turned itself into a political party. It disappeared after being crushed in the election of 1872.

The Knights of Labor. More important than the NLU was the Knights of Labor. This organization appeared in 1869 under the leadership of Uriah S. Stephens. The Knights attempted to unite "all who toiled"—skilled and unskilled, of whatever race, color, or nationality—into one big union. The only people excluded were gamblers, liquor dealers, bankers, and lawyers. Like the NLU, the Knights of Labor opposed strikes. They also favored a number of social reforms having little to do with improving the immediate condition of workers. But at the same time, they sought an eight-hour day, equal pay for both sexes, and an end to child labor.

The Knights grew slowly, having fewer than 10,000 members as late as 1879. Until that date, the Knights were a secret organization, at least partly in order to protect members from being fired for joining. Soon afterwards, the Knights dropped their secrecy, and under a new president, Terence V. Powderly, entered a period of growth. Although Powderly, too, opposed strikes, local assemblies of the Knights of Labor called a series of successful strikes between 1884 and 1886. Those strikes attracted most of the new membership. Following a successful strike against a large railroad in the Southwest, membership climbed to 700,000.

The Haymarket Riot. In 1886, however, the Knights suffered several crippling blows. First was the loss of a number of strikes, especially a major one against the same railroad it had defeated the year before. Second was the Haymarket Riot. Police had killed four strikers at the McCormick Harvesting Machine Company plant in Chicago during a strike for an eight-hour day. Seeking to take advantage of the workers' anger, *anarchists* (radicals who did not believe in any form of government) called a protest rally at Haymarket Square. As police moved in near the end of the rally, someone threw a bomb that killed one policeman and injured seven others.

Though no one ever knew who threw the bomb, a hysterical public demanded scapegoats. Eight anarchists were tried and convicted, four were hanged, and a fifth took his own life. Although the Knights of Labor were also working for the eight-hour day, they had nothing to do with either the strike or the rally in Haymarket Square. Yet in the public mind they became connected with the violence. As a result of these setbacks, workers dropped out of the Knights of Labor in droves. The Knights were never an effective force after this.

The AF of L. The American Federation of Labor (AF of L), first formed in 1881 and reorganized in 1886, was based on ideas quite different from those of the Knights of Labor. While the Knights supported the solidarity of all working people, the AF of L organized only skilled workers. All Knights were members of a

5. DISCUSSION: THE HAYMARKET RIOT Some historians say the Haymarket Riot was an example of the overreaction of police authorities. Discuss with the class what constitutes an overreaction. Ask: What might an underreaction be? What is police brutality, and how does it compare with criminal brutality? Could overreaction be good? What makes it bad? What makes a particular reaction "over" or "under?" Is it possible to know ahead of time whether a reaction will be too great? What criteria should police follow in situations such as the Haymarket Riot, the incident at Kent State, and the 1968 Democratic Convention in Chicago? How are those situations different from a rowdy victory celebration after a college football game?

Background Information

2. SAMUEL GOMPERS (1850–1924) An English immigrant, Gompers was the first registered member of the Cigar-Maker's International Union when he joined at age fourteen. He made it into one of the most successful trade unions. As president of the AF of L, he tried to make member unions rely on bargaining with management rather than appealing for government help or combining with political parties.

At a union convention in Richmond, Virginia, delegate Frank Farrell *(left)* introduces Terence Powderly, head of the Knights of Labor.

single big union. In the AF of L, however, workers organized into national unions along craft lines. These nationals, though part of the AF of L, kept much of their independence.

Furthermore, the Knights had talked of ending the wage system, running cooperatives, and making "every man his own employer." The AF of L, on the other hand, accepted the idea that industrial capitalism was here to stay, and that most workers would remain workers all their lives. The union's job, therefore, was to improve the condition of those workers by concentrating on immediate "bread-and-butter" goals—wages, hours, and working conditions. Samuel Gompers, who headed the AF of L for all but one year from 1886 until his death in 1924, once said that his union's philosophy could be summed up in six words: "More, more, more; now, now, now." To gain those ends, the AF of L was willing to use the strike.

Fighting the unions. Acceptance of the unions did not come easily. Companies used many means to weaken or destroy them. One was the *yellow dog contract.* In order to be hired, workers had to sign this contract, promising that they would never join a union. Employers passed among each other *blacklists,* which were lists of names of union members who should not be hired.

To break strikes, employers hired other workers to take the place of those who had walked off the job. Often the newly hired people were blacks who were desperate for work. Employers also turned to courts for *injunctions* (court orders that forbade unions to strike or engage in various activities). And some employers hired small private armies, often from the Pinkerton Detective Agency, to fight the strikers.

A time of strikes. During the last twenty years of the nineteenth century, there were some 24,000 strikes. Most of them were for union recognition, or to prevent wage cuts, rather than to increase wages. Some of the strikes were marked by violence. Earlier you read of the railroad strike of 1877. In 1892, striking miners and company guards shot it out in the Coeur d'Alene mining district of Idaho. Federal troops moved in, broke the strike, and the strikers were fired. That same year, wage cuts at Carnegie's Homestead steel plant in Pennsylvania led to a strike by the iron and steel work-

Background Information

3. YELLOW DOG CONTRACT
This term was invented by labor leaders to describe mangement's practice of making workers promise to not join a union as a condition for getting their jobs. If the workers then tried to join a union, they were fired for breaking their contract. The union leaders claimed that a worker would feel "like a cowardly dog with its tail between its legs." The practice died out after the Norris-LaGuardia Anti-Injunction Act of 1932 made the contract unenforceable in the courts, and the National Labor Relations Act (also called the Wagner Act) of 1934 gave workers the right to join any union.

ers' union of the AF of L. The company brought in 300 Pinkertons, and a pitched battle led to the death of 10 strikers and 3 detectives. After several months, the strike was broken, and the union crushed. Homestead took back 10 percent of the strikers and blacklisted the rest.

Two years later came the Pullman strike, the largest upheaval in the 1890s. The strike began with factory workers in the company town owned by George Pullman, maker of the sleeping cars that carried his name. Pullman had cut wages five times in one year. In Chicago, the American Railway Union, to which the Pullman workers belonged, refused to handle trains that included Pullman cars. Because these trains also pulled mail cars, the Attorney General of the United States, on the urging of the railroads, got an injunction forbidding the union to interfere with the United States mails. When President Grover Cleveland sent 2,000 troops to Chicago on July 4 to make sure the injunction was obeyed, violence broke out. Looters, most of them not strikers, destroyed railroad cars, and other property was burned or stolen. Twelve people were killed, and dozens were injured. The strike was broken, and Eugene Debs, head of the union, was sent to jail for disobeying the court. While there, Debs became a socialist, and later would be the Socialist party's candidate for President in five elections.

Despite such setbacks, organized labor made steady gains. Between 1897 and 1904, total union membership rose from 440,000 to 2 million before leveling off. The AF of L accounted for better than three fourths of the membership.

CHECKUP

1. What were working conditions like in most factories in the latter years of the nineteenth century?
2. How did the National Labor Union, the Knights of Labor, and the AF of L compare in the ways they were organized and in their goals.?
3. What setbacks did organized labor suffer during the 1890s?

LESSON 3

The Outlook for Further Progress.

January 1, 1900, the beginning of a new century, was for many people a time to take stock. As Americans did so, they were, by and large, quite satisfied with what they saw. They looked forward confidently to still more progress. A *New York Times* editor spoke for most.

> The year 1899 was a year of wonders . . . in business and production . . . prosperity left scarcely any of our industries untouched, and touched nothing it did not enrich. It would be easy and natural to speak of the twelve months just past as the banner year were we not already confident that the distinction of the highest records must presently pass to the year 1900. . . . The outlook on the threshold of the new year is extremely bright.

The *Times* even ran a special supplement, telling "the story of the nation's material progress." Throughout ran the theme that progress for Americans meant material plenty. If arts and letters, science and learning were "the noble products of civilization," they nonetheless rested on a foundation of material prosperity.

Problems there were, a whole range of them, from poverty to child labor, from

LESSON 3 *(1 day)*

Performance Objectives

1. To explain orally or in writing why Americans were optimistic about the future at the beginning of the twentieth century. 2. To describe and explain the growth of the consumer society in America.

Famous Person

Thomas Alva Edison

Vocabulary

Infant mortality, Flatiron Building, Bakelite, capital goods, consumer society, mail-order houses, chain stores, mass consumption, mass production, "Pain Economy," "Pleasure Economy"

Activities

1. **RESEARCH/DISCUSSION** Optimism usually results in great achievement, but sometimes abysmal failures turn the optimism into a total lack of faith in anything. The period before World War I was an optimistic period that ended in an era of nihilism. This phenomenon occurred not only in America but in Europe as well. Ask your students to construct a list of the great achievements that occurred in this period. Ask them to consider those things that brought on the loss of faith.

2. RESEARCH Mass production would have been useless without mass consumption. Mass consumption in turn is dependent on advertising to encourage buyers. Have some students research the beginnings of the advertising industry and some of the interesting people and products involved. (See *Pioneers of American Industry* [Hammond, 1964], pages 68–75, and 148–155 for a start on the research.) Reports could be written, oral, or perhaps in some form of display.

Background Information

THOMAS A. EDISON (1847–1931) Though Edison had only three months of formal education and he was deaf for much of his adult life, he received 1093 patents on his inventions and on improvements of other people's inventions. Among his inventions were the electric light bulb, the phonograph, the mimeograph machine, the kinetoscope (peep-show movie), and the projecting kinetoscope (movie projector). His first commercial movie show was on April 23, 1896, and featured scenes from a prize fight, a dancer, and waves on a beach. He developed the first research laboratory complex, in Menlo Park, N.J., but most of the experiments concerned trial-and-error efforts to find practical inventions rather than work on the development of theoretical science. He had worked for 72 hours straight on his phonograph when this photograph was taken in 1888.

corrupt city government to poor working and living conditions. As America came out of the depression of the 1890s, however, there arose a reform movement to meet those problems. You will read about that movement, called *progressivism*, as you study American Reform in the next unit. Here, we need only note that a characteristic of that reform movement, as it got underway around 1900, was its optimism that it could solve those many problems.

An optimistic outlook. One reason for this optimistic outlook was the belief that science and technology, which had contributed to many of America's problems, would soon find solutions for them. Such confidence seemed justified by great gains in recent years. Education would help. The number of people attending schools and colleges was on the rise. Between 1890 and 1915 the number of high school graduates increased by nearly six times, and the number of college graduates tripled. By 1900, medical science had already found the causes of many diseases. By 1915, medical science would cut infant mortality to a third of what it had been in 1885. Between 1900 and 1930 it would add 10 years to the life expectancy of Americans.

At his laboratory in New Jersey, Thomas Edison listens to the phonograph that he has invented.

Further, recent gains in science and technology were already providing answers to many problems. Thomas Alva Edison, an inventing genius, had produced the electric light bulb and the arc lamp before 1880. In 1882, he built the first central power station to sell cheap electricity to nearby buildings in New York. By the turn of the century, downtown streets and buildings as well as a growing number of city homes were being lighted by electricity. By 1900, just 13 years after the first electric street railway was tried in Richmond, Virginia, electricity powered the street railways in nearly every American city. Developments in steelmaking and architecture made possible the modern skyscraper, which appeared first in Chicago in 1885. By 1902, New Yorkers were craning their necks to see the top of the new 22-story Flatiron Building, the tallest office building in the world. Science produced other marvels as well, from the long-distance phone to indoor plumbing. The creation in 1909 of Bakelite, the world's first plastic, opened up a whole new range of possibilities. The idea that humans could make to order materials not found in nature was exhilarating.

An emerging consumer society. During the first fifteen years of the new century, such optimism seemed confirmed. America's industrial output rose. Steel production, for example, tripled in those years. By 1915, the amount of capital invested in industry was 22 times what it had been in 1860. The United States accounted for one third of the industrial output of the whole world.

By 1915, moreover, an important shift in the American economy had begun to take place. A consumer society was beginning to appear. Most of the goods made by American industry in the latter years of the nineteenth century were *capital goods,* that is, goods used in the making of other goods. Capital goods included steel, coke, timber, and of course machinery. The main consumer goods included stoves, kerosene for lamps, and meat products. By 1910, however, average real income had increased nearly 70 percent over what it had been fifty years earlier. Thus, although life remained a struggle for millions of people, more and more people had income left over after paying for necessities. This surplus created a demand for consumer goods, and American business and industry adjusted to meet it.

The signs of the consumer society were everywhere. A century earlier, nearly all food and clothing were prepared in the home. By 1914, Americans spent millions for packaged cereals, canned vegetables, bakery-made bread, and ready-made clothes. In the dollar value of their products, the food and clothing industries ranked first and second. Mail-order houses and chain stores catering to the consumer grew rapidly.

When this ad appeared in 1910, the automobile was still not in general use, but it would soon change the living patterns of Americans. In 1916, for the first time the production of motor vehicles exceeded one million in a year.

Further, whole industries based on new inventions arose to make goods for consumers. Edison's phonograph and George Eastman's camera were but two. Two more inventions that would shortly change the way millions spent their free time were the automobile and the moving picture. By 1915 the movies had moved out of empty stores with folding seats and into "movie palaces" that seated several thousand.

3. COLLAGE Have some of the students make a collage of consumer goods that are available today. Have some other students make a display of capital goods. Be sure students understand the difference between them. (Capital goods are used to make other goods. Consumer goods are made to be used to satisfy human wants directly.) The consumer-goods collage could be easily made using ads from any of the popular magazines, while the capital-goods display might require some trade or speciality magazines for appropriate pictures. After the class has examined the collages, ask: Which goods are more important to society? Why? Who decides whether to produce capital or consumer goods?

Answers To Review Questions
1. The value of America's manufactured goods exceeded the value of its farm products.
2. Abundant raw materials; a rapid increase in population that provided workers and consumers; hundreds of inventions; emphasis on the idea of material progress, both personal and national; and, government policies that encouraged economic growth: a stable banking system, constitutional guarantees for property, patent laws, generous subsidies, high tariffs, and the opening up of America's treasures to exploitation by private interests.
3. Carnegie founded a business organization that was vertically integrated. Rockefeller, on the other hand, founded an organization that was horizontally integrated.
4. Elimination of competition that resulted in increased power and profits for those companies remaining in business; larger investments of capital than would be possible in small firms; greater control over production.
5. The pool was a secret agreement among rival companies to divide the market among them and keep prices up. There were no legal restrictions binding on the pool. A trust was a combination of firms or corporations formed by a legal agreement. Because of legal problems, the trust was discarded in the 1890s and was replaced by the holding company. It got the same results as the trust by owning a controlling share in a number of corporations in the same business.

The need for mass consumption. There was in fact a close and necessary connection between America's industrial advances and the beginnings of a consumer society. Mass production required mass consumption. Henry Ford recognized that fact when he astounded the country by paying the workers in his automobile plant the unheard-of wage of $5 a day. One of his reasons, Ford explained, was to make it possible for workers to buy the products industry was making—including, of course, Ford cars. At the same time, Ford's mass-production methods allowed him to lower prices. The cost of a Ford car dropped from $950 in 1909 to $360 eight years later. Thus Henry Ford put his cars within the reach of millions.

An economist of that time wrote that America was moving out of a "Pain Economy," that is, an economy of scarcity, and into a "Pleasure Economy," or one of surplus. A half century later an author writing about that era chose for his title *The Good Years.* So the years 1900 to 1920 seemed—to most Americans living through them—years of growing plenty and of material progress. They would make a fitting preface to the decade of the 1920s, when Americans more than ever before were convinced that they were on an endless upward escalator of progress and plenty. You will read about that decade, and about its shattering conclusion, in the next chapter.

CHECKUP

1. As the twentieth century began, what basis did Americans have for feeling optimistic about the future?
2. What important shift took place in the American economy during the early years of the twentieth century?
3. What effect did Henry Ford's mass-production methods in the automobile industry have on consumption?

Key Facts from Chapter 25

1. Among the factors leading to industrial growth were an ample supply of raw materials, a growing population, new inventions, government aid to industry, and the desire of Americans for material progress.
2. During this period of growth, industrial leaders built up great fortunes, sometimes by ruthless exploitation of both workers and natural resources.
3. The theory of social Darwinism held that in the struggle for existence among individuals and businesses, only the fittest would survive.
4. The last years of the nineteenth century saw many strikes by workers, usually for union recognition or for preventing wage cuts. The disputes between unions and companies were sometimes accompanied by violence.
5. The early years of the twentieth century saw a major shift in the economy away from the production of capital goods towards the production of consumer goods.

★ REVIEWING THE CHAPTER ★

People, Places, and Events

Crédit Mobilier *P. 504*
Andrew Carnegie *P. 505*
John D. Rockefeller *P. 506*
Social Darwinism *P. 508*
Horatio Alger *P. 510*
Sherman Anti-Trust Act *P. 511*
Knights of Labor *P. 513*
Haymarket Riot *P. 513*
American Federation of Labor *P. 513*
Samuel Gompers *P. 514*
Homestead strike *P. 514*
Pullman strike *P. 515*
Eugene Debs *P. 515*

Review Questions

1. What was the significance of the year 1890 to the American economy? *P. 502* Les. 1
2. What were the reasons for America's rapid industrial growth? *Pp. 502–503* Les. 1
3. How did the business organization founded by Andrew Carnegie differ from that founded by John D. Rockefeller? *Pp. 505–507* Les. 1
4. What were the advantages of business consolidation? *P. 507* Les. 1
5. What is the difference between a trust, a holding company, and a pool? *P. 508* Les. 1
6. What attempts were made to control the practices of big business in the United States? *P. 511* Les. 2
7. Describe the tactics used by big business to weaken or destroy the labor unions. *P. 514* Les. 2
8. What were the grounds for public optimism in 1900? *P. 516* Les. 3
9. Explain the significance of the rise of a consumer economy. *P. 517* Les. 3

Chapter Test

In each of the lists below, choose the word or phrase that is not related to the other terms. Write your answers on a separate piece of paper. In two lists, all of the terms are related, so write the word All beside those numbers.

1. John D. Rockefeller, William Graham Sumner, Cornelius Vanderbilt, Andrew Carnegie
2. Centennial Exposition, federal government subsidies, Union Pacific Railroad, Crédit Mobilier
3. Trust, holding company, labor union, pool
4. Consumer goods, ready-made clothes, chain stores, capital goods
5. Automobile, moving pictures, camera, phonograph
6. Haymarket Riot, anarchists, Sherman Anti-Trust Act, Knights of Labor
7. Samuel Gompers, Charles Darwin, Eugene Debs, Terence V. Powderly
8. Horizontal integration, Standard Oil Company, New York Central Railroad, John D. Rockefeller
9. Andrew Carnegie, Gospel of Wealth, Scotland, vertical integration
10. Yellow-dog contract, blacklists, injunction, strike
11. *Origin of Species*, "survival of the fittest," Sarah Cleghorn, Charles Darwin
12. Government subsidies, company towns, patent laws, high tariffs
13. *Luck and Pluck*, Horatio Alger, "rags to riches," Social Darwinists
14. Timber and Stone Act of 1878, Homestead Strike, AF of L, Pinkerton Detective Agency

6. Critics of big business demanded a law to outlaw trusts and the government responded with the Sherman Anti-Trust Act.
7. Big business used the yellow-dog contract, blacklists, and injunctions.
8. The belief that science and technology would find solutions to America's problems; the spread of education; medical science having found cures for diseases that once killed many people; new inventions that were made to order by humans rather than found in nature.
9. The increase in the average real income of many Americans meant that they had income left over after paying for necessities. This surplus created a demand for consumer goods and American industry responded by producing more of such goods. New products appeared and were readily accepted by the public. New businesses, such as mail-order houses and chain stores, began to cater to consumer needs. In addition, whole industries based on new inventions arose to make goods for consumers.

Background Information

1. THE AUTOMOBILE No single invention had a more revolutionary effect on American society than the automobile had. Between World Wars I and II, the car became a distinct part of the American way of life. In 1920 there were about 9 million cars registered, but by 1930 there were nearly 30 million. "Why do you need to study what's changing this country?" asked one observer. "I can tell you what's happening in just four letters: A-U-T-O!" The change affected some fundamental areas of American life. Skilled workers could now live miles away from their jobs and commute to work. Farmers could leave their isolated homes and travel into the city for pleasure or to sell produce. Women could drive to do their shopping and were no longer confined to their homes. Young people could go out on dates where they would not be under the eyes of their parents or could join the family for the ritual of the "Sunday drive." Cities were able to extend their boundaries, and suburbs enjoyed a building boom. As America became a "nation on wheels," growing numbers of Americans took to the road to see how the people in other parts of the country lived. As a result, some of the differences separating various regions tended to disappear.

THE NEW ERA

LESSON 1

THE 1920s seemed to many Americans a fulfillment of their faith in progress. The American economy came out of the great war of 1914—1918 as the strongest in the world. Following a sharp depression in 1921 and 1922, the economy took off on the longest period of rising prosperity in American history.

An Economic Boom

The prosperity of the 1920s was based on several factors. One was the growth of a number of industries. Several of those industries were fairly new.

The auto industry. The most important of the newer industries was automobile manufacturing. In 1910, the car was still something of a rich person's toy. But by the 1920s, the automobile had become the center of life for many American families. To some people, owning a car was more important than owning a bathtub. As one person explained, "You can't go to town in a bathtub." By 1930, the number of cars in the United States had grown to nearly 30 million, or almost one per family. That was an increase of 21 million cars for the decade.

The automobile industry had a great effect on the whole economy. It brought about a demand for other goods, such as steel, glass, paint, and rubber. The oil industry was already large enough in 1900 to make John D. Rockefeller America's richest person. Yet in the first thirty years of the century, the oil industry grew to be sixteen times as large, mostly because of the automobile. Gas stations and garages were built, as were tourist cabins and roadside stands. Ten billion dollars were poured into road building in the 1920s. Directly and indirectly, the automobile created about four million jobs.

Other vital industries. The construction industry was another mainstay of the economy in the 1920s. Construction of new homes, factories, and office buildings had slowed during World War I, but reached a record rate in the 1920s. Skyscrapers sprouted, giving new skylines to New York and several other cities.

A booming electrical industry added to America's growth. In the first thirty years of the century, the production of electricity increased nearly twenty times. As it did so, the cost came down sharply. By 1929, nearly all city homes and apartments had electricity. This, in turn, made possible many new household products, such as refrigerators, vacuum cleaners, irons, toasters, heaters, and radios.

Chemicals became a big industry in the 1920s. By 1929, chemical companies were making plastics and other products worth $3.7 billion a year. The industry was now strong enough to compete for foreign markets against companies from other countries.

Gains in productivity. The economic boom of the 1920s was based not only on those key industries, but on a great

LESSON 1 *(2 days)*

Performance Objectives

1. To list and explain those factors that helped cause the economic boom of the 1920s. 2. To identify orally or in writing the goals of big business and to explain how the federal government helped support those goals. 3. To explain orally or in writing why some American intellectuals were discontented with and criticized the national industrial system of the 1920s.

Famous People

Warren G. Harding, Calvin Coolidge, Andrew Mellon, Herbert Hoover

Vocabulary

Economic boom, productivity, scientific management, advertising, consumer credit, welfare capitalism, company unions, mergers, Fordney-McCumber Tariff, Teapot Dome, farm bloc, McNary-Haugen bill

Activities

1. FILMS *Chronicle of America's Jazz Age* (67 minutes, b&w; March of Time). *Productivity: Key to America's Economic Growth* (28 minutes, color; Sutherland Educational Films, Inc.). *A History of Economic Growth: The Market Economy* (20 minutes, color; Treiburg Films). *Economic Growth,* American Business series (29 minutes, b&w; National Educational Television).

2. CREATIVE WRITING Ask some students to imagine that they are working on a production line in a factory. Have them each write an imaginary conversation with another worker, including workers' complaints and the solutions they can see for their problems. Other students might enjoy a research project concerning the problems management is having today with workers on the production lines. They may use *The Reader's Guide* to find recent articles about solutions—for example, "flexitime."

improvement in productivity. In manufacturing, the same number of workers, putting in fewer hours a week, turned out 64 percent more goods in 1929 than in 1922. During the decade, output per working hour increased by 35 percent in the economy as a whole.

Such large gains in productivity during the 1920s were made possible by two things. One was improved technology. New inventions and greater use of machines meant that each worker could produce more. Horsepower per worker rose by 50 percent. The moving assembly line had first been used in the Ford factory in 1914. Now it was adopted by hundreds of companies. American industry, 30 percent electrified in 1914, was 70 percent electrified by the end of the 1920s.

Productivity gains were made also by applying efficient methods in the factories. Before the turn of the century, Frederick W. Taylor had developed *scientific management.* He divided production into a series of simple tasks, and organized them so as to get rid of wasted motion. He showed that by doing

A car moves down an early assembly line at the Ford plant in Highland Park, Michigan. The idea of bringing the unfinished product to a succession of workers helped to boost productivity.

this, a factory could increase production and lower costs. By the 1920s, most large manufacturers were applying Taylor's ideas.

The combination of more and newer machines and better ways of using them made possible the mass-production miracles of the 1920s. In 1913, it had taken 14 hours for workers to make a new Ford car. The next year, Ford put in a moving assembly line, and the time was cut to 93 minutes. During the following ten years, Ford built a bigger plant, brought in newer machinery, and adopted still more improved methods. By 1925, a shiny new car was coming off the assembly line in Ford's factories every 10 seconds.

Advertising and credit. Two "inventions" of earlier times also helped the economy grow. One was advertising, which used techniques that appealed to the desire for status and success. Advertising helped create a market for hundreds of goods from soup to cigarettes. The second "invention" was consumer credit, or installment buying. The idea is a very old one, but until 1920 few goods could be bought by installment payments. In the 1920s, however, older ideas about thrift gave way. Now sellers were happy to give credit to those who wanted goods at once, but could not fully pay for them. Some 60 percent of the cars sold in the 1920s were bought "on time."

Advertising made people want more material things, and credit allowed people to obtain them. Thus the consumer society, which had begun to develop soon after 1900, now emerged full-blown. The rise in real wages and the increase in the number of married women working outside the home gave more families a surplus to spend on wants rather than needs. By far the greatest part of the incredible flow of goods and gadgets in the 1920s was intended for the home. Where only one of America's twenty leading industries was in the consumer-goods area in 1920, nine out of twenty were in 1930. For people who gloried in acquiring material goods, the 1920s seemed a golden age. People soon called it the New Era.

Prosperity—but not for all. The prosperity of the 1920s by no means reached all Americans. Most of the increase in wages went to skilled workers. Wages of the unskilled, which included many blacks, Mexican-Americans, and recent immigrants, rose hardly at all. Coal mining, cloth manufacturing, and shipbuilding were sick industries with many workers laid off. The 1920s were also bad times for farmers, as you will read later in this chapter. It is a fact that in 1929, some 60 percent of American families received less than $2,000 a year. At that time, families needed an income of at least $2,000 in order to buy basic necessities. Even the New Era had not solved the riddle of progress and poverty posed by Henry George.

Yet prosperity is relative. While only a minority of Americans shared in the prosperity of the 1920s, that minority was a far larger part of the population than had ever before known prosperity in America. It was also a far larger part than had enjoyed prosperity in any other country. The fact was that Americans, on the whole, had the highest standard of living the world had ever known.

3. RESEARCH/ORAL REPORTS Consumer credit was a factor in the buying boom of the 1920s and the depression of the 1930s. A relatively recent aspect has been the "plastic fantastic," or credit-card boom. A couple of statistics give an idea of the extent of the boom. Bank credit expanded from $828 million in 1967 to $11 billion in 1976. Total personal debt expanded from $21.5 billion in 1950 to $217.8 billion in 1976. Have students research this area of the economy and decide if Americans are borrowing themselves into trouble.

4. RESEARCH/ORAL REPORTS The text mentions the management methods devised by Frederick W. Taylor in which production was divided into a series of simple tasks and then organized to eliminate wasted motion. Teaching has been subjected to the ideas presented by Taylor; he is the father of the Management by Objectives process. Have students investigate Taylor's ideas and then decide how they might organize their classroom activities in the way Taylor proposed that production lines be organized. They should also decide if there is anything about the teaching-learning process that defies a management system.

Background Information

2. HENRY FORD (1863–1947) As a machinist experimenting in a Detroit workshop, Ford completed his first automobile in 1896 and started the Ford Motor Co. in 1903. Up until then, cars had been playthings of the rich, but Ford "had a better idea"—a cheap "farmer's car" that almost everyone could afford. The car was the Model T, or "Tin Lizzie." The first Model T went on sale in 1908 for $850 (it later went down to about $600) and featured ease of driving and reliability rather than good looks. (The driver's door, for example, was only painted on. This meant that the driver had to enter from the passenger's side. And as for color, Ford said "You can have any color you want, as long as you want black.") By 1920, the ideas of mass production aided by the moving assembly line had speeded production of the "flivver" to one per minute. The Ford Motor Co. eventually owned iron mines, steel plants, lake barges and freighters, and many of the companies that made parts for Ford cars. Iron mined on Monday morning, it was said, could be transformed into a Ford automobile by Friday afternoon. Ford became the world leader in the use of mass-production techniques. Industrialists from around the world would come to inspect, admire, and copy Henry Ford's system.

Hail to big business! Many people were still living in poverty. Yet the proud boast of the New Era was that America was the first society in world history to solve the problem of scarcity. It was only a matter of time and a few adjustments, some declared, before plenty would be enjoyed by all. The greatest credit for this achievement went to business. If prosperity was nearly a national religion, then the businessman was its high priest. "The business of America is business," said President Calvin Coolidge. "The man who builds a factory builds a temple; the man who works there worships there." In a poll among a group of college students to choose the greatest figure in history, Henry Ford came in third, trailing only Christ and Napoleon. Even the journalist Lincoln Steffens, a critic of big business in the early 1900s, was now saying, "Big business is producing what the socialists held up as their goal: food, shelter, and clothing for all."

A quartet of New Era businessmen sings the praises of the President. Coolidge believed that wholehearted government support of big business would assure lasting prosperity.

Americans were not alone in hailing the business leaders of the New Era. Many countries sent engineers and managers to America to study the industrial methods that the Germans called "Fordismus." Even the leaders of Soviet Russia admired and studied Ford. As a British traveler noted, just as a visitor to Rome might go to the Vatican to try to see the pope, so a visitor to Detroit would go to the Ford Motor Company and try to see Henry Ford.

The decline of unions. Americans believed that the New Era had also solved the conflict of capital and labor. This "solution" took the name of *welfare capitalism*, a phrase used to describe an arrangement between employers and workers in some large industries. Those employers provided the workers with many benefits. Among them were paid vacations, group insurance, educational and recreational programs, health care, and profit sharing. The employers' motives were generally mixed. While they really wished to spread the benefits of capitalism to their employees, they hoped that by doing so, they would undercut the appeal of unions. In a further effort to keep the workers under their control, some employers started *company unions*. These unions, made up of only the workers in a single company, were under the influence of the firm's owners.

Welfare capitalism did help bring about the decline of organized labor in the 1920s. However, that decline owed more to other causes. The failure of strikes in steel, coal and several other large industries in 1919 hurt the unions. They also lost public backing as their opponents unfairly but successfully pinned the Communist label on them and their leaders. These setbacks, together with weak leadership in the AF of L, caused a drop in the number of union members. Many people wrongly took the unions' decline to mean that the big differences between capital and labor had now disappeared.

Big business gets bigger. During the 1920s, one striking feature of the economy was the increase in *mergers.* In a business merger, or consolidation, two or more companies combine under the same ownership. Through such mergers, thousands of firms in banking, manufacturing, and public utilities disappeared. Thus, giant companies controlled more and more of American business. By 1929, nearly half the business wealth of the country was owned by just 200 corporations. These, in turn, were controlled by about 2,000 persons. Although competition remained strong in some industries, it all but disappeared in many others. In the telephone industry and a few others, a single company dominated. In most industries, however, control rested with several firms. Thus, four meat packing companies controlled 70 percent of that business. Ford, General Motors, and Chrysler made 83 percent of the autos. General Electric and Westinghouse accounted for most of America's electrical equipment. Despite the many brand names of cigarettes, more than 90 percent of them were made by just four companies.

Most of the mergers occurred with the consent of the government, which sought few antitrust actions. The antimonopoly argument of the 1880s and 1890 seemed out of date in the prosperous twenties. Those few who raised it appeared meanspirited. Since business leadership was credited with progress and prosperity, many people believed that business should be left altogether free from government interference.

The Harding years. The all-powerful role of business in America in the 1920s was strongly supported by the men who sat in the White House. In 1920, Senator Warren Harding of Ohio was the choice of the Republicans for President. In his campaign he declared that "what this country needs is less government in business and more business in government." This statement summed up his view of the proper relationship between the two. In the election, Harding won an easy victory over the Democrats' choice, James Cox, also of Ohio. As President, Harding supported most of the goals of business. To protect American products from foreign competition, he favored a high tariff. In 1922 the Fordney-McCumber Tariff set the highest rates in history.

Harding was a friendly, likeable man with a weak will and a poor eye for talent. Although he chose persons of real ability for a few high posts, most of his appointees were cronies and politicians

5. DISCUSSION After reading this lesson, the students should make a list of the factors named in the text that contributed to the economic boom of the 1920s. Discuss how many of the factors are present today. Ask: Is America in a boom today? Why, or why not? After discussing these factors with the students, have them find out which groups of people were excluded from the boom of the 1920s. Ask: Do these groups seem to be doing better, or worse, today? What about the attitude of government toward business in the 1920s and today? (Would there have been environmental restrictions then, for example?)

6. DISCUSSION The ideal citizen in the 1920s was involved in business. Discuss why business people were accorded such high status in America in the 1920s. Ask: Do business people have the same status today? The class will probably have to decide what gives people status. (Is it money, fame, the envy of others?) What does today's ideal citizen do? Ask how many students want to become involved in business careers. Why, or why not?

7. LISTENING FOR INFORMATION From *The American Story,* read to your students "Back to Normalcy" by Quincy Howe. If that is unavailable, read excerpts of Frederick Lewis Allen's *Only Yesterday* (New York: Harper & Row, 1957). Encourage your students to read some of the novels, essays, and poems of authors who were critical of America of the 1920s, including Sinclair Lewis, Vachel Lindsay, Theodore Dreiser, H. L. Mencken, Sherwood Anderson, and F. Scott Fitzgerald.

looking for financial gains. His administration turned out to be one of the most corrupt in American history. His attorney general, Harry Daugherty, sold pardons and paroles, liquor permits, and immunity from prosecution. Only a jury that could not agree on a verdict saved Daugherty from jail. Charles Forbes, the man Harding made head of the Veterans Administration, was less lucky. Forbes was sent to prison for selling to private buyers Veterans Administration supplies worth $250 million in return for kickbacks. Others in the administration also went to jail.

The best known scandal of Harding's administration centered on Teapot Dome, Wyoming, and Elk Hills, California. These were government-owned oil lands held in reserve to meet the Navy's future oil needs. In return for large bribes, Secretary of the Interior Albert Fall secretly turned over the oil rights to privately owned oil companies. Eventually the government took back the oil lands, and Fall went to prison.

"UGH!"

The Republican party, nicknamed G.O.P. (for Grand Old Party), shudders at the effect of the Teapot Dome oil scandal of the 1920s.

Coolidge and business. Harding died in 1923, before most of the scandals became known. He was succeeded by Calvin Coolidge, who had been Governor of Massachusetts before becoming Vice President. Coolidge ran a far more honest administration than Harding did. He was, however, even more a supporter of the businesses they were supposed to ulating agencies, Coolidge appointed people who shared the point of view of the businesses they were supposed to regulate. Coolidge chose persons of similar outlook for other government jobs and for judgeships. Andrew Mellon, head of the aluminum monopoly and secretary of the treasury from 1921 to 1932, became Coolidge's chief adviser. Mellon favored lowering taxes on high incomes. He believed this would encourage investment and create jobs. Under Coolidge and Mellon, the federal tax on the highest income bracket was lowered from 65 percent in 1920 to 20 percent in 1928.

Coolidge favored an inactive government. He set the standard himself with afternoon naps in the White House and an average working day of four hours. To dwell on Coolidge's inactivity, however, overlooks the very great and active aid that the government gave to business during the years he was in office. Much of the help came from the Department of Commerce, headed by the talented Herbert Hoover. The department gave businesses information on foreign markets. To help companies be more efficient, Hoover's department put forth all kinds of facts and figures, as well as other forms of aid. Hoover believed that the old-fashioned kind of competition was wasteful and inefficient. The country would benefit more, he felt, if businesses cooperated with each other. Hoover encouraged firms in the same industry to form trade associations. Through these organizations they could exchange information, standardize methods and products, and better predict market needs. Thus they could avoid overproduction.

Labor and the farmers. While government looked warmly upon business in the 1920s, it was unsympathetic to organized labor. Harding's Secretary of Labor, James J. Davis, had little interest in labor's problems. Rulings in many federal and state courts went against unions. In 1922, Attorney General Daugherty got a court injunction to break a strike of 400,000 railway shop workers who were protesting a wage cut.

Farmers fared little better. Following a time of high prices during and after World War I, overproduction caused prices to fall sharply in 1921. Though prices partly recovered during the following years, they never came near earlier levels. Meanwhile, farmers' costs for taxes and mortgages remained high. Caught in this squeeze, most farmers never shared in the prosperity of the 1920s.

During this period, members of Congress from farm states joined together in a group known as the *farm bloc*. Under the leadership of the farm bloc, Congress passed a number of laws to help farmers. One law made it easier for farmers to get credit. The main effort to raise income was the McNary-Haugen bill. Under this bill, the government would sell surplus crops abroad for whatever they would bring. At the same time, crop prices inside the United States, protected by a tariff, would be kept at a higher level. The bill, twice passed by Congress, was vetoed each time by President Coolidge.

Critics of the New Era. The New Era was not without critics. Some were simply unhappy about the passing of familar ways. But others raised deeper questions about the direction in which America was headed. In the mid-nineteenth century, Thoreau, Emerson, and Melville had raised such questions. But after that, few writers criticized the great American producing machine.

By the early 1900s, however, authors were again expressing doubt that piling up material goods was the same as progress. By the 1920s, writers such as Sinclair Lewis, Sherwood Anderson, and T. S. Eliot were strongly attacking the values of a business civilization.

Many of those who were concerned over America's material values were worried even more by the effect of industrialism on the human spirit. The philosopher and educator John Dewey warned that the machine was being "harnessed to the dollar" rather than to the "liberation and enrichment of human life." And Edward Sapir, a noted anthropologist, sighed, "Part of the time we are [work] horses, the rest we are listless consumers of goods . . . Our

Background Information

3. ELMER RICE (1892–1967) One of the outstanding plays that made American drama famous in the 1920s was Rice's *Adding Machine,* an expressionistic satire using distorted settings and nonrealistic acting to show the tortured mind of the main character, Mr. Zero. After twenty-five years on the job, Mr. Zero is replaced by an adding machine. He responds by killing his boss. Executed, he is unsatisfied in heaven and is reincarnated to become the perfect, soulless industrial slave. Rice's other most famous play, *Street Scene* (1929), realistically depicted life in a crowded big-city apartment building.

Background Information

4. CHARLIE CHAPLIN (1889–1977) Chaplin was a motion-picture actor, writer, and director. From the days of silent pictures well into the time of the "talkies," his most famous character was the optimistic and indomitable, if unsuccessful, Tramp. The character made the transition to sound movies, but Chaplin seemed to become more serious in his films, focusing on the lack of fulfillment in human life. *Modern Times* was made in 1936 and showed humans overwhelmed by technology. One of his most famous satirical films was *The Great Dictator* (1940), which ridiculed Adolf Hitler. During the 1940s and 1950s, Chaplin was criticized as immoral and Communistic. Born in London, Chaplin had been in the United States since he was about twenty but had never become an American citizen. So in 1952, when he was out of the country, the government refused him reentry unless he submitted to an investigation. He refused, and chose to live in Switzerland. He returned to the United States in 1972 for several special awards, including an honorary Oscar. In 1975 he was knighted by Queen Elizabeth II of England. He died on Christmas Day, 1977 and was buried in Lausanne, Switzerland. In March 1978 his body was stolen from its grave and held for ransom for 76 days until the grave robbers were caught.

spiritual selves go hungry, for the most part, pretty much all of the time."

Mass production—at a cost. Mass production and the drive for efficiency came at a high cost to those who worked in the modern factories. Too often, work was dull and boring. "The aim of scientific management," stated one of Frederick Taylor's followers frankly, "[is] to induce men to act as nearly like machines as possible." Elmer Rice's play *The Adding Machine* (1923) was but one of several plays and books of the time that wondered aloud whether that aim was not rapidly being reached.

Modern advertising, drawing upon the findings of psychology and playing to secret desires, seemed, too, to be saying that humans were simply objects to be moved about like pieces on a chessboard. Some wondered whether democracy would any longer have meaning when office holders and candidates could slyly change public opinion with advertising techniques.

Those who put forth doubts and criticisms, however, were small in number, and few of them found an audience. It was plain that most Americans were content with the material gains being made.

CHECKUP

1. What factors helped bring on the economic boom of the 1920s?
2. How did the Harding and Coolidge administrations support the goals of big business?
3. On what grounds did some people criticize America's industrial system during the 1920s?

In the motion picture *Modern Times*, Charlie Chaplin caught the feeling of the New Era as expressed by critics. They complained that technology had made human beings secondary to machines.

LESSON 2

Social Change and Mounting Tensions

The 1920s were a time of great social change in the United States. Among the most important changes were those relating to the position of women and the place of the home and family. Those changes continued what had begun in the late nineteenth century. By 1870, 15 percent of American women held jobs outside their homes. In the years that followed, the great growth of cities opened still more opportunities for women. The opening of department stores meant thousands of sales jobs. The invention of the typewriter and of other business machines, plus the increase in office work, made more thousands of jobs. As the school population swelled, more women found work as teachers.

It is easy to exaggerate the job opportunities that cities made available to women. As late as 1910, nearly 80 percent still worked in factory jobs or in domestic service. For one and a half million women, in other words, a job outside the home meant working in textile or shoe factories or in the garment industry, where pay was low and working conditions often poor. For another million and a half, working outside their homes simply meant working in someone else's. Thousands of other women did piecework, such as making cigars or sewing clothes, in their own homes. Pay for women was generally poor. A survey in Boston for the years 1907 through 1909 showed that only women in professional fields were earning the $500 or more a year that was then required for decent living. Even so, however, the 10 percent who held jobs as clerks and secretaries found office work a clear step up

Having won the right to vote in 1920, women soon made their influence felt at the ballot box. Some, like Nellie Tayloe Ross of Wyoming, the first woman governor, ran successfully for public office. Here she turns the first spadeful of soil at an airport construction project.

LESSON 2 *(2 days)*

Performance Objectives

1. To describe orally or in writing the mood of the country in the 1920s and how it reflected the times. **2.** To identify and explain the major population trends of the 1920s. **3.** To list the major social tensions of the period and identify the causes of each. **4.** To describe the changing role of women in the 1920s.

Famous People

Marcus Garvey, Nicola Sacco, Bartolomeo Vanzetti, Clarence Darrow, Alfred E. Smith

Vocabulary

Flapper, population trend, migrants, boll weevil, "Red scare," Ku Klux Klan, Scopes Trial, fundamentalists, prohibition, bootleggers

Activities

1. MAKING A BIBLIOGRAPHY Have the class compile a bibliography on the social developments during the 1920s. The class could be divided into committees to work on separate sections, such as Women, Race, Ethnic Groups, Fads, Laws, Media, Literature and Drama, Jobs, Entertainment, Famous People, or other categories that students might list. They should be sure to decide which are primary sources and which are secondary.

Background Information

1. THE GOLDEN AGE OF RADIO The 1920s saw the rise of radio, and the late 1940s saw the rise of television. The years in between are known as the Golden Age of Radio. Many of the stars of vaudeville moved into the new medium and became favorites of the nation. George Burns and Gracie Allen, W. C. Fields, and Bob Hope were some. In an era of fast-talking comics, Jack Benny acquired instant fame by introducing himself and then saying there would be a pause while everyone said, "So what?" The long pause was one of his trademarks through his long career. The comedy show *Amos 'n' Andy* was so popular that movie houses stopped their features for 15 minutes every night so that people could listen. The show is now criticized, since it was done by two white comics and made fun of blacks. Adventure shows and dramas were also big on radio. Serial dramas, called "soap operas," because of the predominant kind of sponsors, were popular in the daytime, while *The Shadow, Superman, The Lone Ranger,* and *Gangbusters* were evening favorites.

from the factory workbench and the scrub board. Furthermore, the fact remained that earning money allowed women to become more independent.

Gains for women. During the next several decades those trends kept on. At the end of World War I, there were 8 million women workers. Many held jobs that women had never been able to get before. Though men got back most of those jobs at the end of the war, women held on to some of them. By 1930, women made up 22 percent of the work force. Nearly 2 million were doing secretarial or other office work, and 750,000 held sales jobs in stores. Nearly a million women held jobs in the various professions.

Women won the right to vote in 1920. (See Chapter 29.) Yet, in the long run, that victory was less important in freeing women than the new economic independence they were gaining. Holding a job made it less necessary for women to stay in an unsatisfactory marriage, a fact that could be seen in the changing divorce rate. Divorces had been on the rise since 1870, and by 1900 had reached the rate of one for every twelve marriages. In the 1920s, however, there was one divorce for every five marriages.

In many things and in many ways, women in the 1920s made clear that they wanted the same freedoms that men had. Women began to ignore old restraints upon their behavior. They began, for example, to smoke in public. They cast aside confining corsets. Skirts, ankle length in 1919, rose to the knee by 1927. The symbol of the New Era woman was the pleasure-seeking flapper—a young woman with bobbed hair and loose-fitting clothes, her face painted with lipstick and rouge.

Once again, one must put these changes in perspective lest they be exaggerated. Most women of the 1920s remained in the home. Their way of life was much like that of women in earlier times. Cooking and cleaning continued to be "women's work." The average city housewife spent 51 hours a week at her household tasks.

Even more to the point was the fact that in literature, in the movies, and in real life, women were seen not as whole persons in their own right but rather as beings that found their meaning only through their relationship with men and families. As long as that continued, wrote one feminist, "nothing new or strange or interesting is likely to happen" to women. Still, there is no question that a good many women in the 1920s enjoyed a position far different from that of women fifty years earlier.

Home and family. During the 1920s, the importance of the home and family changed rapidly. Both were losing many of their traditional roles.

Educating the young was more and more being done by the school. High school enrollment rose from 1.3 million in 1915 to 4.4 million in 1930. The canned food and ready-made clothing industries took over several of the chief tasks formerly performed by members of the family.

The sports stadium and the motion-picture theater took the place of the home as the center of family entertainment. Time spent watching Babe Ruth hit a home run, Jack Dempsey box, and college football teams battle it out on

Continued on page 532

The Coming of the Radio

From the day the first commercial station (KDKA in Pittsburgh) took to the air with the 1920 election returns, radio was an instant success. Within two years, five hundred stations were operating. Radio quickly became a major industry, not only through the manufacture of sets but also through the selling of air time to advertisers.

With two of every five American families owning sets by 1929 and four of every five owning sets by 1940, radio also became a major influence in American culture. By the 1930s, it was the main source of family entertainment. Programs ranged from music to soap operas, from adventure to comedy, from news to sports. Drama was played out on the stage of the listener's imagination. Play-by-play accounts of baseball and football games made the world of sports come alive for millions. Radio also encouraged popular interest in current events through news and public-affairs broadcasts, and it brought the voices of political leaders into the homes of the citizens. One of its most important effects was to relieve the isolation and monotony of rural life. But it was also important to millions of city dwellers.

The dramatic possibilities of radio were most clearly shown on Halloween Eve, 1938, when Orson Welles broadcast a radio script of H. G. Wells's science-fiction book of 1898, *The War of the Worlds.* Although the announcer stated that the show was fictional, when Welles broadcast the invasion of Martians in Grover's Mills, N.J. (a town Welles picked by sticking a pin in a map), panic spread, with many people fleeing their homes and several ending up in hospitals in shock. President Roosevelt used the radio to reassure Americans in his famous fireside chats during the depression. The real-life drama of World War II was also played out on the radio as thousands listened nightly for reports from the front made by daring reporters.

In the 1920s, listening to the radio was a popular evening pastime for all members of the family.

2. RESEARCH/ORAL OR WRITTEN REPORTS The period called the Roaring Twenties has provided a seemingly endless supply of colorful stories and characters. It was probably partly the times and the people themselves, but it was definitely the energetic reporting of the "tabloid" newspapers that prevented these stories from being lost to oblivion. Have students research some of the people of this era to get an idea of the type of story the papers sensationalized. These are some of the people they could start with: Aimee Semple McPherson, an evangelist whose lovers and mysterious kidnapping kept her in the news as much as her preaching; Leopold and Loeb, two young men who killed a boy as a "scientific experiment"; Charles Ponzi, whose financial empire turned out to be just a pyramid confidence game. The Time-Life series This Fabulous Century, Vol. III, *1920–1930* (New York: Time-Life Books, 1971) has information on the tabloids as well as on these and other characters. Have students summarize their research for the class.

Saturday afternoons was time not spent in the home. The number of moviegoers climbed from 40 million a week in 1920 to 100 million in 1930. Some people began to wonder if America was not becoming a country of spectators. In addition, the car, by making it easy to move about, did more than anything else to undercut the home as the center of family life.

These changes were in turn connected with the country's mood which stressed pleasure-seeking and the dropping of old restraints. It was this mood in the 1920s that caused old attitudes toward thrift to give way in favor of buying on credit. It was this mood also that helped form the consumer society. Although church membership rose, attendance declined, despite ministers' warnings that God could not be found on the golf course. Free-flowing jazz became the rage, and the Charleston replaced the waltz and the fox-trot. Attitudes about modesty in male-female relationships changed. Chaperones became a thing of the past. The movies caught the changing mood: shy, curly haired Mary Pickford, "America's Sweetheart," was set aside for Clara Bow, the "It" girl.

Population trends. The 1920s saw the continuation of four major population trends. The first was the growth of cities. In 1920, for the first time, more Americans lived in cities than in rural areas. Large cities became even larger. Those of 250,000 to 500,000 people nearly doubled in number between 1920 and 1930.

The second population trend was the rapid growth of the West. Not only Easterners but also migrants from neighboring Mexico helped swell the population of the western states. During the 1920s, the population of several western states rose by about 20 percent, while that of California rose by a huge 66 percent.

The automobile was mainly responsible for the third population trend: the growth of suburbs. As street railway lines moved outward from the city, new communities sprang up along them. In the 1920s there began a growth of suburbs that is still going on. The automobile made it possible not only for more people to move to the suburbs but also for new communities to be started ever farther away from the city.

The fourth important shift in population during this time involved the movement of black people from the South to the North. A small flow of black people to the North had started soon after the end of the Civil War. In the years following, the number of black migrants increased greatly. There were three reasons for this. One was the boll weevil, an insect that damaged the cotton crop in Louisiana, Mississippi, Alabama, Georgia, and Florida in 1915 and 1916. The damage threw many southern farmers, black and white, out of work. The second was the blacks' belief that they would find better treatment and more rights in the North than they had in the South. The third was the growth of job opportunities in northern factories as the result of World War I.

Racial tensions. In the North, racial prejudice flared in a number of communities as blacks competed with whites for jobs and entered their neighborhoods. In 1917, whites in East St. Louis, Illinois, attacked blacks, touching off a riot that took the lives of 39 people. Two years later a race riot broke out in Chicago. It started when a young black at a beach was killed after swimming into an area that whites reserved for themselves. In the next six days, 15 whites and 23 blacks were killed. More than 500 people were injured, and twice that many were left homeless as their houses burned. The Chicago riot was the most destructive of the twenty-five that broke out in cities across America during the tense summer of 1919.

Nonetheless, blacks kept on pouring northward. While the black population of the South increased by little more than 5 percent in the 1920s, in the North it rose by 64 percent. As blacks moved north, and also west, this traditionally rural people became urban. In 1930, 68 percent of the black population of the South still lived in rural areas, but 88 percent of northern blacks lived in cities. So, too, did 82 percent of the black people living in the West. In both New York and Chicago, the number of blacks more than doubled during the 1920s.

The rough treatment of blacks gave rise to black protest and resistance. One of the most widely followed black leaders of the early 1920s was Marcus Garvey, a West Indian immigrant who founded the Universal Negro Improvement Association. Garvey urged pride in race, and proclaimed that black people were not only the equal of whites but superior to them. His followers contributed money to buy ships for Garvey's back-to-Africa movement, but the ships that were bought turned out to be broken-down tubs. Garvey was convicted of mail fraud, jailed, and then deported to his native Jamaica. Black leaders like W. E. B. DuBois and A. Philip Randolph had no use for Garvey, regarding him as a false prophet. Yet Garvey gave hope to many blacks. One person observed that putting Garvey in prison was like "jailing a rainbow."

In the 1920s, Marian Anderson was beginning to attract attention as a singer. During the following years, she won worldwide fame.

Fear of foreign influences. To some Americans the many changes that were taking place were troubling and frightening. Mostly rural and small-town folks, these people distrusted the cities with which they identified most of the changes. They also felt that America needed to be purified of foreign influences. As a result, social tensions filled the 1920s.

Background Information

2. PHILIP RANDOLPH (1889–) Randolph gained his reputation as a labor leader and civil rights leader. He founded the Brotherhood of Sleeping Car Porters in 1925. Later he was vice-president of the AFL-CIO. During World War II, Randolph threatened to lead a march on Washington, D.C., to demand jobs in the defense industry for blacks. Roosevelt responded with a fair labor practices bill. Randolph later helped organize the 1963 civil rights march on Washington.

3. RESEARCH In much of the literature in the past, there has been blatant disregard, disrespect, or contempt for the role of women in American society. Ask students to find examples in older literature and watch for examples in current literature. If you have old editions of textbooks or reference books, give some out for students to examine for sexism. Have students check indexes for the number of references to individual women and individual men as well as for what subjects are "women's" topics. Examine the language used in describing women. Also have students look for topics under which women should be included but are not, such as the American Revolution.

Have some of the students compile a list of sexist terms—such as salesman, poetess, housewife, stewardess, mankind—and the words that should replace them. (Sales representative, poet, homemaker, flight attendent, humanity)

4. FILMS *Modern Women: The Uneasy Life* (60 minutes, b&w; National Educational Television). *Social Change and the American Woman* (52 minutes, b&w; National Educational Television). *Population Patterns in the United States* (11 minutes, color; Coronet Films).

Battles were fought out along a number of lines. One took place even before the decade began. The hatred whipped up by World War I did not end with the coming of peace, but was loosed against groups and beliefs that were looked at as un-American. When the Communist revolution in Russia in 1917 was followed by similar movements in other European countries in 1919, fear of Communists, or "Reds," swept the country. Although there were a few bombing incidents, these fears were greatly exaggerated.

Nonetheless, as a result of the "Red scare," Attorney General A. Mitchell Palmer began a series of illegal raids on private homes and labor organizations. His goal was to round up the so-called "Reds." Several thousand suspects were arrested and jailed. In the end, most were released.

The same fear of foreigners and radicals could be seen in the trial of Nicola Sacco and Bartolomeo Vanzetti. They were Italian immigrants accused of a murder at South Braintree, Massachusetts. Both were convicted and were sentenced to death. A good many Americans believed that Sacco and Vanzetti, both of whom were anarchists, had really been convicted for their radical ideas. For six years they tried to get a new trial. Their efforts drew international attention. All efforts failed, however, and in 1927 Sacco and Vanzetti were put to death.

A revived Ku Klux Klan. One of the more ugly expressions of this desire to "save" America was the Ku Klux Klan. The new Klan was still antiblack, as the original one had been. But it was even more anti-Catholic, anti-Semitic, and anti-immigrant. One of its recruiting pamphlets pulled no punches.

> Every criminal, every gambler, every thug, every libertine, every girl ruiner, every home wrecker, every wife beater, every dope peddler, every moonshiner, every white slaver, every Rome-controlled newspaper, every black spider—is fighting the Klan. Think it over, which side are you on?

By the mid-1920s, the Klan claimed more than 4 million members. While the actual count was surely less than that, the KKK was very strong in many midwestern states, and had considerable political influence. Only in the late 1920s, after its leader was involved in scandal, did its influence decline.

The Scopes trial. The fears felt by many people about changes in American life can be seen in an event that took place in Tennessee in 1925. That year the Tennessee legislature passed a law forbidding public schools to teach "any theory that denies the story of the divine creation of man as taught in the Bible." Schools were forbidden to "teach instead that man had descended from a lower order of animals." This law had been passed at the urging of *fundamentalists*—those who believe that the Bible is to be taken as a literal historical record and prophecy. John T. Scopes, a high-school biology teacher in Dayton, Tennessee, decided to test the law. In his classroom he presented the theory of evolution. He was then arrested and went on trial.

William Jennings Bryan, a fundamentalist, and three times the Democratic candidate for President, went to Ten-

Clarence Darrow *(left)* and William Jennings Bryan, the opposing lawyers at the Scopes trial, confer.

nessee to help the prosecution. Clarence Darrow, a famous criminal lawyer and a foe of fundamentalism, offered his services in defense of Scopes. A circus atmosphere enveloped Dayton as reporters and spectators by the hundreds crowded into town. All over the country newspapers carried daily accounts of the trial on their front pages. To no one's surprise Scopes was convicted—he had clearly violated the law—but his fine was later canceled. What had given the trial so much drama and such widespread attention, though, was the clash between the old beliefs and ways of life and the new ones.

Prohibition. One final arena of battle between the old and the new was prohibition. In 1920, the Eighteenth Amendment prohibited the manufacture and sale of liquor. Prohibition turned out to be a failure almost from the beginning. Instead of changing popular habits, it made lawbreakers of millions of Americans who either brewed liquor or bought it from sellers known as *bootleggers.* The government had 2,000 officers to enforce the law when a hundred times that many were needed. Supplying liquor for Americans brought organized crime an income of $2 billion a year. The prohibition issue divided Americans until it was ended by the Twenty-first Amendment in 1933.

The election of 1928. Many of the tensions between rural small-town America and urban America came to the surface in the 1928 Presidential election. When Coolidge decided not to seek another term, the Republican party made Herbert Hoover its choice for the country's highest office.

Hoover had grown up on an Iowa farm. Left without parents at the age of

Continued on page 537

Background Information

3. CLARENCE DARROW (1857–1938) Although primarily a criminal lawyer, Darrow was perhaps the first labor lawyer. In both areas, he was involved in some of the most controversial cases of his time. He defended the Socialist leader Eugene V. Debs in a labor strike case and John T. Scopes in the "Monkey Trial." In the Loeb-Leopold case, he defended two "thrill killers"—the wealthy, brilliant young men who committed cold-blooded, premeditated murder of a fourteen-year-old boy. In spite of the nation's revulsion, which was enflamed by sensationalist press coverage, Darrow succeeded in keeping them from execution.

5. DISCUSSION After students have read the lesson, discuss with them the colorful decade of the 1920s in the United States. Nicknamed the Roaring Twenties, the Jazz Age, and the Dollar Decade, this was a restless era that brought spectacular economic growth, generally rising prosperity, and far-reaching social change. Ask students to consider the following questions. What was the mood of the nation in the 1920s? How did it reflect the times? What were the major social tensions of the period and the causes of each? In the discussion, have students make up two lists of events, ideas, and people of the period. One list should show the light side of the 1920s (flappers, bathtub gin, the Charleston, etc.), while the other should show the dark side (KKK, Red scare, racism). Discuss with the class possible reasons for the dichotomy.

6. RESEARCH/ORAL REPORT Have one or several students read in Commager's *Documents in American History* Document 172, "Woman's Rights—The Seneca Falls Declaration of Sentiments and Resolutions—July 10, 1848." Ask the student(s) to report to the class on how the American woman of today stands in relation to those sentiments and resolutions.

The "Lone Eagle"

Charles Lindbergh captured the imagination of millions of people when he flew alone across the Atlantic from New York to Paris in 1927. In a spectacular display of courage, coolness, and endurance, he flew nonstop for more than thirty-three hours in his single-engine plane, *Spirit of St. Louis.* His performance won for him a prize of $25,000, offered to the first aviator to make a New York-to-Paris nonstop flight.

Upon his return, the "Lone Eagle," as newspapers called him, was welcomed by wildly enthusiastic crowds. Lindbergh's book *We* (the title referred to him and his plane) became a best-seller. An air tour took him to seventy-five cities in America. Everywhere, huge crowds turned out to cheer the courageous young aviator.

What secret spring had Lindbergh touched to trigger such a response? In an age when many people felt helpless before the impersonal forces of society, Lindbergh's daring act was a glorious fulfullment of the individual. People who yearned to take a bold step of their own identified with the "Lone Eagle." Because he embodied their secret desires, they made him the hero of the age.

Charles Lindbergh, the most famous flyer of his time, poses before his plane, *Spirit of St. Louis.*

ten, he worked his way through college. He then became a mining engineer, traveled all over the world, and was a millionaire at the age of forty. Thereafter, he devoted himself to public service. He won praise for his relief work in Europe during and after World War I. As Secretary of Commerce under Harding and Coolidge, Hoover showed leadership talents that were widely recognized.

To run against Hoover, the Democrats chose Alfred E. Smith, the progressive governor of New York. In the good times of the 1920s, when the majority of Americans voted Republican, probably no Democrat could have defeated Hoover. Smith, however, had special disadvantages. He had grown up in New York City and had begun his career in politics in the Tammany Hall organization. He was a Catholic, the first to run for President. On the liquor issue, he was a "wet," that is, he favored repeal of prohibition. In short, he was everything that many rural small-town Americans were against.

On election day, Hoover won 58 percent of the votes and carried forty states. Among them were five southern states that had voted for Democrats since Reconstruction days. Nonetheless, Smith, running well in the big cities, doubled the vote of John W. Davis, the Democrats' candidate in 1924.

CHECKUP

1. How did women's role both within and without the family change during the 1920s?
2. What were the major population trends of the 1920s?
3. In what ways did social tensions come to the surface during this period?

LESSON 3

The End of the Economic Boom

Herbert Hoover, Americans believed, was an ideal President to guide the country toward continued prosperity. He had shown himself to be a talented engineer, a strong administrator, and a skillful problem solver.

Prosperity forever? In accepting his party's nomination for President, Herbert Hoover had said:

> We in America are nearer to the final triumph over poverty than ever before in the history of any land. . . . given a chance to go forward with the policies of the last eight years, we shall soon with the help of God be in sight of the day when poverty shall be banished from this nation.

Republicans had campaigned on the slogan "A Chicken in Every Pot, Two Cars in Every Garage." Hoover himself took note of how far America's material progress had advanced. "The slogan of progress," he said, "is changing from the full dinner pail," the promise of the Republicans in William McKinley's day, "to the full garage."

The first months that Hoover was in office seemed to bear out this feeling. Business and government leaders talked about the United States as having arrived at a "permanent plateau of prosperity." John J. Raskob, chairman of the Democratic party and a millionaire industrialist, wrote a piece for the *Ladies' Home Journal* in August 1929 with the title, "Everybody Ought To Be Rich."

> If a man saves $15 a week, and invests in good common stocks, and allows the dividends and rights to accumulate, at the end of twenty years he will have at least

LESSON 3 *(2 days)*

Performance Objectives

1. To explain orally or in writing the immediate causes of the stock market crash of 1929. **2.** To identify and explain in an essay the underlying weaknesses in the American economy that were ultimately responsible for the depression. **3.** To describe orally or in writing the effects of the depression on the lives of Americans.

Famous Person

John Maynard Keynes

Vocabulary

Stock market crash, panic selling, wild speculation

Activities

1. ESSAY After students have read pages 538–539, they should write essays in which they explain the underlying causes of the depression and how it might have been prevented. Also have them explain why the stock market crash was so important if so few people were involved in speculation.

2. **INTERVIEW** If some students have relatives or acquaintances who lived through the depression, ask them to prepare a series of questions to investigate life during the depression. Be sure to check the questions before the students ask them, and discuss proper behavior and how to conduct the interview. Have the students report their findings to the class. It could be interesting to compare interviews of people living in America with those living in another country at the time, since the depression was worldwide. If tape recorders are available, have students record the interviews and make the tapes available to the class for further study. (Warning: Don't be surprised if some of the interviewees do not view the times as particularly bad; discuss with students the implications of this.)

3. **RESEARCH/ORAL REPORTS** The depression contributed certain rather colorful terms to the language and gave new meaning from the times to some other terms. Have some students look up and report on the origins, meanings, and implications of the following terms associated with the depression: dust bowl, Hooverville, riding the rails, flophouse, bread lines, soup kitchens, selling apples, Okies, Black Thursday, bank holiday, buying on margin.

4. **FILM** *Life in the Thirties,* Project 20 series, (53 minutes, b&w, National Broadcasting Company).

$80,000 and an income of around $400 a month. He will be rich. And because income can do that, I am firm in my belief that anyone not only can be rich, but ought to be rich.

The stock market crash. Two months after Raskob's article appeared, disaster struck. Since 1924, prices of shares in American corporations, sold on the New York Stock Exchange, had been rising. For a time, the rise was a fair reflection of the large profits that companies were making. Beginning in 1927, however, speculation took over. People bought stock not with regard to the real earnings of a company, but because they felt sure they could sell to other buyers later for a higher price. Actually, only a little more than one percent of Americans owned stock. Fewer than half of these people, along with some banks and companies, were engaged in wild speculation. But these were enough to send the prices of stocks skyrocketing.

All speculative crazes come to an end sooner or later. This one did in the fall of 1929. In late October, the prices of stocks broke. Panic selling followed, and prices tumbled in a dizzying spin. In just a few months, billions of dollars in stock values were wiped out. Many people had been speculating with borrowed money. Not only did they lose everything, but so did those bankers and brokers who had lent them money.

The headline and cartoon convey the shock of the stock market crash. The speculator is pictured as the victim of forces he cannot control.

STOCK PRICES SLUMP $14,000,000,000
IN NATION-WIDE STAMPEDE TO UNLOAD;
BANKERS TO SUPPORT MARKET TODAY

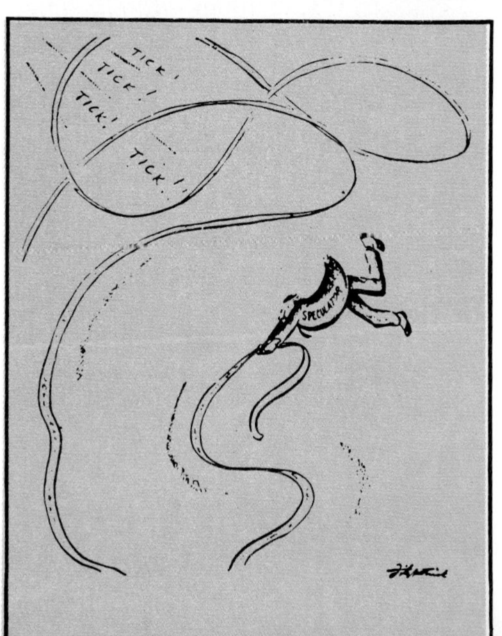

Beginning of the depression. The stock market crash of 1929 was followed by a depression that spread over the country like a cold fog. The real causes of the downturn lay, however, not in the stock market but in certain weaknesses of the American economy of the 1920s. By the end of the decade, American ability to produce goods had outrun the ability to buy them at current prices.

That might have been dealt with in two ways. One was to lower prices. The other was to increase the earnings of those who bought the goods. Neither of those things happened. New machines and better ways of manufacturing had lowered the costs of production. With less competition in many industries, however, businesses chose to keep prices up and increase their profits. While wages rose during the 1920s, they did not rise enough to let wage earners buy the many goods being made. Had labor unions been stronger, they might have won higher pay for their members, but, as you know, unions were weak during the 1920s. You will recall, too, that farmers, another important part of the consuming public, had low incomes during that time. Millions of others with low-paying jobs had not fully shared in the prosperity of the 1920s, and had little money for buying goods.

Thus, there was a great imbalance in the distribution of income in the United States. In 1929, the income of the top one tenth of one percent of the population equalled that of the bottom 42 percent. Plainly there was a limit to the number of refrigerators, vacuum cleaners, and radios that the rich would buy. And there was a limit to the number that poorer people *could* buy. A banker of the time later summed up sadly, "Capital kept too much, and labor did not have enough to buy its share of things."

Some of the large share of wealth kept by the rich was invested in more capital goods—machines and factories. That, of course, increased the flow of consumer goods. Some of the new wealth went for luxury items for the well-to-do. And some—surely too much—went into speculation in the stock market.

Hard times. Soon after the stock market crashed, business and government leaders made optimistic public statements. President Hoover assured the people that "the fundamental business of the country . . . is on a sound and prosperous basis." In December 1929, the head of the Bethlehem Steel Company said, "Never before has American business been as firmly entrenched for prosperity as it is today." As time went on, a few were more ready to admit that there was trouble. As one person put it, "You are going to have, once in so many years, difficulties in business." But these people seemed to feel that if an occasional downturn did happen, then recovery was bound to take place.

The economy, however, did not bounce back. Conditions grew steadily worse. As orders for goods fell, factories laid off workers. That cut buying power still more, and the downward spiral went on. Businesses failed. Banks, weakened by unpaid loans and by losses in stock speculation, went under. In 1931 alone, two thousand banks closed their doors, with the loss of millions of dollars to their depositors. Farm prices tumbled.

The human toll was terrible. Unemployment mounted: 4 million in 1920, 8 million in 1931, 12 million in 1932. Unable to keep up payments, hundreds of thousands lost their homes and farms. In the cities, breadlines and soup lines spread around whole blocks. William Green, president of the AF of L, reported that "the men are sitting in the parks all day long and all night long, hundreds and thousands of them, muttering to themselves, out of work, seeking work." On vacant lots, families with no place else to live threw up makeshift shelters. Hunger stalked the land.

In a country where success was often measured by income, to have no income at all meant that one was a failure. In some families, husbands who could no longer fulfill the role of breadwinner lost the respect of wives and children. Some men took to drink. Some abandoned their families. Some committed suicide.

Hundreds of thousands of Americans left their homes in search of jobs. Many were migrant workers from the Great Plains and the rural South. In 1932,

5. ROLE-PLAYING The effects of the depression varied greatly, depending on a person's occupation, financial situation, location, and perhaps luck. Divide the class into small groups to role-play improvisationally or with their own prepared scripts various people's reactions to the depression. Here are some possible groups and situations: a "Walton" type of family on its own place in the country; a "Dust Bowl" family that has lost its farm; a business leader and his or her advisers trying to deal with the situation; a politician and advisers considering their next campaign; a laid-off urban factory worker and his or her family; two police officers chasing homeless people out of a park at 3:00 A.M.; soup-kitchen workers and patrons; men or women "riding the rails"; two unemployed men in a flophouse; two unemployed and homeless women in the city. (The last two situations should show the great difference between the ways men and women in the cities, especially, dealt with the depression. More women, it seems, just quietly starved or froze to death rather than ask for help. Being less visible, needy women did not receive even the inadequate help made available to needy men.)

6. RESEARCH/ORAL REPORTS John M. Keynes is aptly described and analyzed in Robert Heilbroner's *The Worldly Philosophers* (New York: Simon and Schuster, Inc., 1972), Chapter 9, "The Sick World of John Maynard Keynes." Assign several students to read this analysis and report to the class.

7. ORAL REPORT One of the most gripping of all novels about the American scene is the classic *Grapes of Wrath,* written by John Steinbeck in 1939. In it, he dramatized the exodus of the unemployed, starving victims of the dust bowl of Oklahoma as they migrated to California. Some students might be interested in reading all or part of this book and reporting to the class the impressions the author gives of the depression.

Background Information

JOHN MAYNARD KEYNES (1883–1946) John M. Keynes (kānz) was a most interesting economist. He was certainly not a traditionalist. During the depression, Keynes saw that as the economy withered, income shrank and people's savings vanished. Many people, especially those of the middle class, were left destitute, causing despair and frustration to build upon one another. Keynes felt that it was the government's job in good times as well as in bad to stir up the economy. Business on its own was not sufficient. It took the power of the government to "prime the pump." Keynes's ideas were in direct contrast to those of economists who believed in laissez faire, under which the government stayed out of the marketplace. It is hard to say if Keynes was right or wrong. Depending upon one's politics, economic savvy, and current bent of mind, Keynes is either a devil or an angel. Some say that without him Western civilization as we know it would have disappeared long ago. Others say that Western civilization as we know it will disappear in the future because of Keynes.

Unemployed men line up in New York City to receive food from a charitable group during the depression. Such breadlines were common sights in all large American cities during that period.

some 2 million people were wandering around the country. About 200,000 of them were boys and girls. The Southern Railroad reported the removal from their trains of 680,000 people who were "riding the rails."

A shattering effect. The depression struck a mighty blow at Americans' belief in progress. That belief had always rested on the fact of material plenty. Yet it now seemed that this very plenty was causing misery. Grain elevators overflowed, yet people were going hungry. Cotton filled the warehouses, yet people were in need of clothing. Factories lay idle. As the British economist John Maynard Keynes said, the depression was "not a crisis of poverty but a crisis of abundance."

America's belief in progress had always included boasts about its rapidly swelling population. Now, marriage rates and birthrates dropped sharply, and the average age of the population began to rise. Immigration also dropped. In 1932, for every person who came to America, three left.

In place of the optimism of earlier years, there was now a widespread feeling of helplessness and hopelessness. Predictions of progress had a hollow ring. The promise of personal riches now brought only bitter laughter. Here and there, respected voices were raised against the American system. A conservative congressman warned, "If we don't give [security] under the existing system, the people will change the system. Make no mistake about that." The editors of a major magazine recommended, "Appoint a dictator." An Oklahoma rancher who had lost everything said, "We have got to have a revolution here like they had in Russia." Such opinions were held by only a small minority of Americans. But because of their conservative sources, those views were indeed disturbing.

In time the depression would end. You will read in Chapter 30 about efforts to deal with it. Since the depression, Americans have gone on to build a consumer society that far outdistances that of the 1920s. For many millions of Americans now, as then, possessing goods is an important goal. The statistics of production are still the chief measure of the nation's progress.

Yet time has brought differences. Americans today are more aware that we cannot go on exploiting and abusing nature without paying a heavy cost. We have come to understand that resources are not limitless. We know that the production and enjoyment of goods must be balanced by a concern for preserving a healthful environment. We no longer believe that the destruction of forests or the building of highways is certain evidence of progress.

Even as Americans are aware of these things, however, it is typical of them to trust to invention and technology to resolve new problems. That faith in progress through invention and technology is one of the many things that ties Americans of today to those of very different yesterdays.

CHECKUP

1. Why did the stock market crash of October 1929 take place?
2. What were the underlying weaknesses in the American economy that really brought on the depression?
3. How did the depression affect the lives of Americans? What effect did it have on Americans' belief in progress?

Key Facts from Chapter 26

1. Among the factors creating the economic boom of the 1920s were the growth of the automobile, chemical, and electrical industries; large gains in industrial productivity; and the widespread use of advertising and consumer credit.
2. During the 1920s, big business flourished. Many mergers took place, and business received favorable treatment from the federal government.
3. The 1920s saw women gain both political equality at the ballot box and greater economic opportunity.
4. The stock market crash of October 1929, brought on by reckless speculation, ushered in the worst depression in American history.
5. A major reason for the depression was that industry's ability to produce goods had outrun people's ability to buy them.

Answers To Review Questions

1. Scientific management refers to the application of efficient methods in the factories. Production is divided into a series of simple tasks and organized so as to get rid of wasted motion. By operating in this fashion, a factory could increase production and lower costs.
2. Unskilled workers, in general; workers in such industries as coal mining, cloth manufacturing, and shipbuilding; farmers.
3. Most Americans hailed big business as the producers of the highest standard of living the world had ever known. People believed that it was only a matter of time before plenty would be enjoyed by all. The greatest credit for the nation's prosperity went to business.
4. Welfare capitalism; the failure of strikes in steel, coal, and several other large industries; the popular belief that unions were tainted with Communism.
5. Women were employed in sales jobs in department stores; in business offices as secretaries, typists, and clerks; in the factories as unskilled or semiskilled laborers; in the home as pieceworkers or domestic workers; in the professions as teachers, nurses, or librarians.
6. The boll weevil so damaged the cotton crop that many southern farmers were thrown out of work; the blacks believed that they would find better treatment and more rights in the North; as a result of World War I, there were more job opportunities in Northern factories.

7. Fear of Communists caused a "red scare" that swept the nation and resulted in a series of illegal raids on private homes and labor organizations. The Sacco-Vanzetti case attracted worldwide interest as a number of notable Americans protested the conviction on the grounds that the two immigrants had really been convicted for their political beliefs. The Ku Klux Klan was revived as an anti-Catholic, anti-Semitic, and anti-immigrant group in addition to being antiblack. The Scopes trial evoked strong emotion among many Americans who felt that their way of life was threatened by the teaching of the theory of evolution in schools.
8. Wild speculation sent the prices of stocks skyrocketing. In late October, 1929, when the prices of stocks broke, panic selling followed and caused prices to tumble even more drastically.
9. Americans' belief in progress had always rested on the fact of material abundance. Through the depression years, there was a plentiful supply of goods, but few people had the income to buy them. America's belief in progress had included boasts about its rapidly growing population. During the depression years, however, marriage rates and birthrates dropped dramatically and immigration also declined.

★ REVIEWING THE CHAPTER ★

People, Places, and Events

Warren Harding *P. 525*
Teapot Dome scandal *P. 526*
Calvin Coolidge *P. 526*
McNary-Haugen Bill *P. 527*
Marcus Garvey *P. 533*
Nicola Sacco *P. 534*
Bartolomeo Vanzetti *P. 534*
John T. Scopes *P. 535*
Eighteenth Amendment *P. 535*
Twenty-First Amendment *P. 535*
Herbert Hoover *P. 535*
Alfred E. Smith *P. 537*
Depression *P. 538*

Review Questions

1. What is meant by the term *scientific management?* How did this method contribute to the economic boom of the 1920s? *P. 522–523* Les. 1
2. Who did not share in the overall prosperity of the times? *P. 523* Les. 1
3. What was the general attitude of most Americans toward big business in the decade of the '20s? *P. 524* Les. 1
4. What factors caused the decline of labor unions? *Pp. 524–525* Les. 1
5. What employment opportunities were available to women in the 1920s? *P. 530* L.2
6. Why did blacks continue to leave the South and migrate North? *P. 533* Les. 2
7. In what specific ways did Americans demonstrate their fear of foreign influences and changes in their traditional way of life? *Pp. 533–535* Les. 2
8. What brought about the stockmarket crash in October 1929? *P. 538* Les. 3
9. How did the depression affect Americans' belief in progress? *P. 540* Les. 3

Chapter Test

*On a separate piece of paper, write **T** if the statement is true and **F** if the statement is false.*

1. The great increase in the gross national product during the 1920s meant that all Americans shared in the prosperity. F
2. The development and growth of the automobile industry was important because it had a stimulating effect on the entire American economy. T
3. Scientific management, first developed by Frederick W. Taylor, refers to the use of chemicals to manufacture plastics and explosives. F
4. Both Presidents Harding and Coolidge supported the interests of big business during their administrations. T
5. The Sacco-Vanzetti case was a famous trial that attracted international attention in the 1920s. T
6. A major reason for the depression was that the American public demanded more goods than industry could produce at that time. F
7. Marcus Garvey, a West Indian immigrant, tried to persuade blacks to return to the South in order to lessen racial tensions in northern cities. F
8. Prohibition was soon recognized as a failure because so many Americans ignored, or broke, the law. T
9. In the 1928 Presidential election, Herbert Hoover defeated the Republican candidate Alfred E. Smith. F
10. As a result of the many economic and social changes of the 1920s, most women were employed outside the home and enjoyed the same freedoms that men had. F

★ REVIEWING THE UNIT 

1793	*Slater's cotton mill*
1814	*Waltham textile factory*
1834	*Reaper invented*
1848	*Gold discovered in California*
1862	*Homestead Act*
1869	*First transcontinental railroad*
1876	*Centennial Exposition*
	Custer's defeat at Little Big Horn
1881	*American Federation of Labor formed*
1894	*Pullman strike*
1920	*Prohibition amendment*
1929	*Great Depression begins*

In the 1790s and early 1800s, America's first factories were built along the rivers of the Northeast. After the War of 1812, inventions and advances in technology spurred industrial growth. The American factory system stressed the use of power-driven machinery, the division of labor, and the interchangeability of parts. Progress became a major goal of the American people. For most Americans—but not all—progress was measured by material gains and advances in technology. To achieve progress, Americans exploited such natural resources as timber, soil, and minerals. Moving westward, they settled on the Pacific Coast and on the Great Plains. As the settlers advanced, the Indians were forced onto reservations.

After the Civil War, the United States became a great industrial nation. Its growth was based on ample raw materials and capital, a plentiful labor supply, advances in technology, and a growing transportation network. The period saw the growth of big businesses and great personal fortunes, as well as much conflict between capital and labor.

In the early 1900s, a consumer society appeared, its growth hastened by advertising and consumer credit. In the 1920s, business thrived under favorable treatment by the federal government. The 1920s was a time of social change, and tensions were created as old ways of life clashed with new ones. The economic boom of the 1920s came to a halt in 1929 when the October stock market crash ushered in the worst depression in America's history.

Answers to Unit Questions

1. In 1840 most Americans lived in rural areas.
2. In 1860 the rural population was four times larger than the urban population.
3. In 1920 the urban population exceeded the rural for the first time.
4. In 1850: 1,174,668. In 1910: 20,302,138.
5. The 1920 urban population was nine times larger than it had been in 1860.
6. The 1920 rural population was about two times larger than it had been in 1860.
7. In 1850: 20 percent. In 1920: a little over 50 percent.
8. The decade between 1840 and 1850 showed the smallest increase, only 105 urban centers
9. Although the rural population was steadily growing during that period, it was not increasing as rapidly as the urban population.
10. Urban and rural populations will continue to grow, but the rural population will probably increase more slowly than the urban. Accept any other variation on this answer that the student can defend.

 REVIEWING THE UNIT 

Skills Development: Reading a Table

Urban and Rural Population 1840–1930

Year	*Rural*	*Urban*	*Total Number of Urban Centers**	*Total Population in Cities of 100,000 or more*
1840	15, 224, 398	1, 845, 055	131	517,216
1850	19, 648, 160	3, 543, 716	236	1,174,668
1860	25, 226, 803	6, 216, 518	392	2,638,781
1870	28, 656, 010	9, 902, 361	663	4,129,989
1880	36, 026, 048	14, 129, 735	936	6,210,909
1890	40, 841, 449	22, 106, 265	1,348	9,697,960
1900	45, 834, 654	30, 159, 921	1,737	14,208,347
1910	49, 973, 334	41, 998, 932	2,262	20,302,138
1920	51, 552, 647	54, 157, 973	2,722	27,429,326
1930	53, 820, 223	68, 954, 823	3,165	36,325,736

**Places over 2,500 people*

Study the table and then answer the following questions.

1. In 1840 did most Americans live in urban areas or rural areas?
2. In 1860 approximately how many times larger was the rural population than the urban population? (Hint: Begin by rounding off each population figure to the nearest million.)
3. In what year did the urban population first exceed the rural population?
4. How many Americans were living in cities of over 100,000 people in 1850? in 1910?
5. Compare the urban population of 1860 with that in 1920. How many times larger was the 1920 population?
6. Compare the rural population of 1860 with that in 1920. How many times larger was the 1920 population?
7. Approximately what percentage of the American people lived in urban areas in 1850? in 1920?
8. In which decade did the number of urban centers show the smallest increase?
9. Compare the urban and rural population figures for the years 1840-1930. What significant pattern do you see developing in that time period?
10. Based on the trends shown in the population figures in this table, what conclusion can you draw about urban and rural populations from 1930 to the present?

Unit 8

Americans and Reform

ECONOMIC, SOCIAL, AND POLITICAL CHANGE

Background Information

"NEW ENGLAND COUNTRY SCHOOL" This is a detail from a painting by Winslow Homer in the 1870s. The painting is displayed at the Addison Gallery of American Art, Phillips Academy, Andover, Massachusetts. Now recognized as one of the great American painters, Homer was considered rather too simplistic by many of his contemporaries. He consistently chose mundane aspects of everyday life over dramatic scenes. As he grew older, he "retired" to an isolated beach house where he not only painted but also fished, hunted, and enjoyed life. He wrote, "The Sun will not rise or set without my notice, and thanks." Many of his best paintings depict the sea and those involved with it.

CHAPTER 27

THE FIRST GREAT PERIOD OF REFORM

LESSON 1

SCRATCH AN AMERICAN, it has been said, and you will find a reformer. That is no doubt an exaggeration. Yet the desire to improve upon existing conditions has been a characteristic of the American people. "Americans," wrote a noted historian, "do not abide very quietly the evils of life. We are forever restlessly pitting ourselves against them, demanding changes, improvement, remedies. . . ." An optimistic people, Americans believe that tomorrow can be better than today and that they can make it so through their own actions.

Though Americans use the word *reform* approvingly, it often means different things. You would have no trouble finding a majority who favor reform of city government, education, the welfare program, or the tax laws. However, they would have quite different ideas about exactly what the changes should be. At times, *reform* has meant simply "to bring up to date," as in reforming an old system of bookkeeping. At other times, *reform* has meant "to make more efficient." Usually that is what we mean when we speak of reforming the civil service. In this unit you will find examples of both kinds of reform.

Most often, however, reform in America has had two goals. The first has been to make America's political life more democratic. The second has been to make for human betterment. While you will read about many kinds of reform in this unit, it is reform of this second kind that you will be examining most fully.

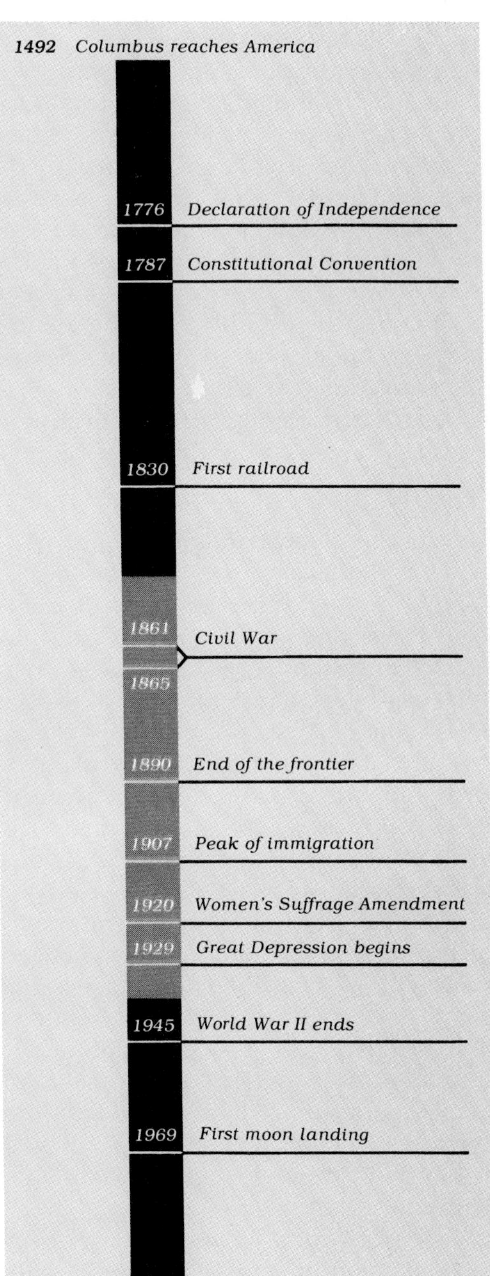

LESSON 1 *(2 days)*

Performance Objectives

1. To explain orally or in writing the nature of the reform spirit in America by describing the spirit's sources and limits.
2. To demonstrate an understanding of the American need for reform by listing several current reform movements.

Vocabulary

Reform, human betterment, character, radical change

Activities

1. INTRODUCING THE UNIT The central theme of this unit is reform as a major aspect of American history. A secondary theme of the unit is the ebb and flow of the reform spirit in American history. Although most people claim to favor it, reform is not always a high-priority item.

Discuss with your students the meaning of the word *reform*. Compile a list of problems in America today. If necessary, expand the discussion by asking what is wrong with America. Everyone likes to find fault! After you have a sufficient list, ask the class to decide which of the problems could be solved, assuming people were really interested in solving them. If the cynicism is so great that few students think problems will be solved, have them cite some problem situations that have at least been improved, such as air and water pollution, working conditions, and political corruption. After the students have discussed which problems might be solved, ask them who they would expect to solve each problem—individuals or the government. This question will point out the change in attitude about reform from the nineteenth to the twentieth century; reform is now considered part of the government's job. Have the students pick a particular problem and decide how they would go about getting that problem solved. What if there was much opposition? How would the class get priority for the problem when there are so many groups trying to get attention for other problems? Have the class examine some of the tactics that groups use to draw attention to their causes. These would run the gamut from ads in newspapers and door-to-door canvassing, to picketing and demonstrating, to rioting and bombing. Ask which technique they think is most effective. Why?

2. ESSAY Have the students write on the following essay topic, using the textbook as the resource: "Reform is as American as apple pie." In the first paragraph, have them *attack* the statement by showing the limits that Americans place on reform. In the second paragraph, have them *defend* the statement by citing the sources of reform in America. In the third paragraph, have them state their opinions of America's attitude toward reform and reformers, being sure to support their arguments with logic and evidence.

This activity not only will reinforce the students' reading of the material in the lesson but also will show their ability to find, sort, and use the material in the text. Some discussion about the techniques of essay writing should probably follow this activity so that the students can improve these skills.

The Nature of Reform

How can the lot of human beings be improved? During the course of American history, reformers have had two answers. One answer has been to change peoples' character. Changing a person's moral character would produce the reformed drinker, the reformed criminal, the reformed sinner. This kind of reform, as you will read later in this chapter, was very important before the Civil War. The second answer of reformers has been to change the conditions that are believed to create poverty, inequality, and injustice, and to help the disadvantaged. Much of the reform in the twentieth century, as you will read, has been of this kind.

Sources of reform. What are the sources of the reform spirit in America? No one knows for certain. Religion is said to be one source. By stirring our consciences, the argument goes, religion has led us to seek remedies for social ills. Some church groups have also inspired reform, it is said, through their message that humans can improve, and even reach perfection, by following the example of Christ. Further, religious leaders and deeply religious people have been at the front of many reform movements in America, such as antislavery, civil rights, peace, and efforts to help the poor. At the same time, it must be noted that religion has also often been the source of a conservative outlook. In turning attention to the world of the hereafter, religion may have weakened demands to improve conditions in this world.

A second source of American reform has been said to be the ideas and ideals of the Declaration of Independence. One writer has pointed out how reformers all through our history have used that great document as a measuring stick by which to judge their own times.

> If all men are created equal, demanded the abolitionists, why are black men being held in bondage? If all are created equal, cried the feminists in their time, why are women denied their rights? If human beings are equally entitled to life, liberty, and the pursuit of happiness, asked others in their turn, how justify the plight of the distressed farmers, underprivileged children, the hungry poor, the innocent victims of war?

Yet here, too, the evidence is mixed. Some of the most basic ideas of the Declaration, such as majority rule and consent of the governed, were never accepted by a good number of important reformers. Would William Lloyd Garrison, for example, have agreed to go along with slavery just because most whites were not in favor of abolishing it? Also, like religion, the Declaration has probably inspired as many conservatives as reformers in our history. "Thousands of Americans who have never supported a reform movement," one authority reminds us, "drew moral and intellectual nourishment from the supposed 'roots' of reform."

Limits of reform. If we cannot pick out the sources of reform in America, neither can we explain why, in a nation so favorable to change and improvement, reform is not always uppermost in people's minds. Why is reform not a continuing process? A number of reasons have been offered. As you study the eras of reform described in this unit, you may see how one or more of these have placed limits on reform.

One reason is the strong feeling of Americans for the idea of limited government. In modern times, reform often calls for action by the federal government. Many Americans have been slow to agree to this approach. Another reason has to do with the strong feelings that Americans have about the right of private property. When the law limits owners in their right to use their property as they wish—for example, refusing to sell or rent to certain groups, or selling unsafe goods—reform takes second place to property rights.

A third reason why reform is limited involves the nature of our political parties. These parties are groups of people with many points of view. To hold them together, compromise is often necessary. Thus, clear-cut reform goals are sometimes put aside for the sake of party harmony.

A fourth reason why reform is limited, some believe, lies in the reformers themselves. As one reformer of the 1830s sadly noted, there is a "tendency of every reform to surround itself with a fringe of the unreasonable and half-cracked." That puts the matter too strongly, but there is some truth in it. Even the most generous, kind, and pleasant reformers upset some people. After all, as one person has put it, reformers are "disturbers of peace." When they include in their numbers people who are self-righteous, unbending scolds, as they often do, reformers "turn off" some of the very people they seek to win over.

Clearly, there are a good many Americans who not only are not reformers themselves but who strongly oppose re-

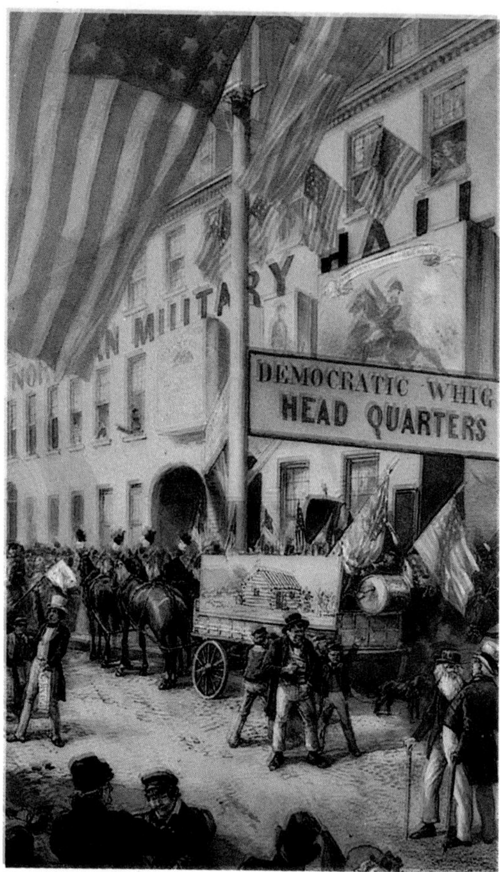

The spirited campaign of 1840 reflected political reforms that had brought about greater democracy. However, political parties were often indifferent to other types of reform.

form efforts. Some do so because they are better off under existing conditions. Others see in every change the first step toward revolution. Still others believe there is little that people can do to change the wrongs in life. Those Americans cling to such mottoes as: "Leave well enough alone"; "The cure may be worse than the disease"; and "The more

3. DISCUSSION After the students have read page 547, ask if they are optimistic that tomorrow will be better. The cynics might not be, but they should see that most Americans act under the assumption that things can and should get better. (An important, it off-the-point, discussion would be to consider what happens when people no longer think things will get better. Rioting, suicide, alcoholism become more likely occurrences.) From the second paragraph, point out the possibility of conflict among reformers and different meanings of the word *reform.* To some, for example, tax reform may mean a new system for determining taxes, while to others it may simply mean that the tax burden should be shifted from them to other people. For some, reform in education means giving the schools more money to improve education, while to others it means cutting the budget to eliminate waste and frills.

Discuss the phrase *human betterment.* Ask: Do you think that people can be changed by reformers? Give examples. Can the conditions of human life be changed? Is this easier, or harder? Do laws affect only the behavior of people, or do they also influence feelings and attitudes indirectly?

4. RESEARCH Ask your students as a class to compile a list of the most important reformers in history. Among them might be Jesus Christ, Mohammed, Martin Luther, Thomas Jefferson, Saint Thomas Aquinas, Saint Augustine, Saint Francis of Assisi, Abraham Lincoln, Woodrow Wilson, Mohandas Gandhi, Martin Luther King, Jr. Have some students give brief summaries of their reformers' lives and reforms.

5. **USING A CHART** Have your students individually compile a list of current reformers at the national, state, and local levels. Have them arrange the names in a chart to show the name of the reformer or group and what is being reformed. Examples of current reformers and reforms include Ralph Nader, Billy Graham, and zero population growth.

6. **THOUGHT PROVOKER** Ask your students to discuss the following quotation: "To know how to say what other people only think is what makes men poets or sages; to dare to say what others only dare to think makes men martyrs or reformers." Why do reformers sometimes become martyrs?

7. **ANALYZING SOURCE MATERIAL** Finley Peter Dunne's Irish anti-intellectual characters, Mr. Dooley and Hinnissy, made fun of the reform movement of the early twentieth century. Read the following Dooleyisms to your class for their reaction: "A man that's expict to thrain lobsters to fly in a year is called a loonytic; but a man that thinks men can be tu-rrned into angels be an iliction is called a rayformer an' remains at large." Later Dooley said, "A rayformer thinks he was ilicted because no wan knew him. Ye can always ilict a man in this counthry on that platform. If I was runnin' f'r office, I'd change me name an' have printed on me cards: 'Give him a chanst; he can't be worse.' "

things change, the more they stay the same."

Some people oppose reform not because it seeks to change too much but because it does not seek to change enough. For them, reform merely nibbles at the edge of a problem, leaving its real cause untouched. For such people, only sweeping, radical change will do.

Political reform. One of the reforms that had the broadest support was the movement in the early nineteenth century to make America's political life more democratic. In Chapter 13, you read how the vote was extended to all adult white males. You learned, too, how the process of choosing a President was made more democratic. These changes brought about the beginning of modern American politics. To win the new voters' loyalties and to get people to vote on election day, strong party organizations had to be set up. Those seeking office tried to present themselves in ways with which the common man and woman could identify. Back in 1800, no one cared the least bit that candidate Thomas Jefferson owned the fine estate of Monticello. But by 1840, it was to the advantage of candidates to link themselves with ordinary folk. Though William Henry Harrison also owned a large estate with a sixteen-room house, his backers thought it important to claim that Harrison had been born in a simple log cabin.

As a result of all these changes, ordinary people began to take a greater part in national politics. In 1824, only 27 percent of the white males in America voted in the presidential election. In 1840, about 78 percent voted.

CHECKUP

1. What two approaches have reformers in America used in bettering the lot of human beings?
2. From what sources is the reform spirit in America said to have sprung?
3. What factors have tended to limit reform?

LESSON 2

Ideas of Social Reform, 1830–1860

The period of democratic change in politics was followed by one of the great eras of social reform in American history. During the 1830s and 1840s, a small army of reformers examined American society inside and out. Through dozens of reform societies with thousands of branches, they reached out to help the unfortunate and to heal the sick. They championed everything from the abolition of slavery to changes in diet as the keys to further development toward human perfection.

The reform movements drew on several sources. One was the idea of progress, about which you read in Unit 7. To a people who had built a nation from a handful of small settlements, progress was more than an idea—it was a proven fact. A second source was concern over the new problems caused by the coming of industrialism to America. A third source was religion. Between the 1820s and the 1840s, religious revivals swept across much of the North. Americans were moved by the desire to save their own souls and those of others and to move the country closer to the goal of perfection. Thousands of men and women joined reform movements. Most of these movements were aimed at the moral reform of individuals.

The temperance movement. One major reform action was the temperance movement. Between 1790 and 1830, the average consumption of whiskey and hard cider was 17 gallons per male American each year. Temperance reformers believed that too much drinking was the main cause of poverty, crime, insanity, broken homes, and other social ills. Supported by many Protestant ministers, the American Society for the Promotion of Temperance was formed in 1826. Within eight years it had 5,000 local chapters. Through songs, plays, and pamphlets, temperance people carried their message to Americans with the skill of today's advertisers. They called their method *moral suasion*—that is, persuading drinkers to cut down or stop their drinking. About a million people "took the pledge" to do so, though no one knows how many kept it.

Members of the temperance movement occasionally used more than moral suasion to achieve their goals. Here, at a saloon in the Midwest, temperance reformers are smashing barrels of rum and emptying bottles of whiskey.

In the late 1830s the emphasis in the temperance movement shifted toward *abstinence*—no drinking at all. Public meetings now featured parades through city streets and confessions of reformed drinkers. In addition to moral suasion, temperance reformers began to press state legislatures to prohibit the sale of liquor. Maine did so in 1851, and a dozen other states followed over the next ten years.

After the Civil War, many of those states changed their minds and repealed those laws. The temperance movement itself, however, did not die out. It remained an important force in local and state politics. In 1920, *prohibitionists* succeeded in obtaining a constitutional amendment, barring the sale of liquor. It was repealed thirteen years later.

Education as a cure-all. Another group of reformers saw education as the cure for all social ills. What existed in education in the 1820s could hardly be called a school system. Only in New England, where laws required that schools be maintained with taxes, were there public schools. Even there, they existed mainly in a few larger cities. Elsewhere, children of parents who could afford it went to private schools or studied with tutors. Many children went to no school at all. It is surprising that as many learned the three Rs as did.

Lesson 2 *(2 days)*

Performance Objectives

1. To identify orally or in writing the six major reform movements between 1830 and 1860. **2.** To identify and explain orally or in writing the issues concerning women's rights during this period and what reforms were accomplished. **3.** To explain orally or in writing the history and significance of utopian communities in America.

Famous People

Horace Mann, Dorthea Dix, William Ladd, Elizabeth Blackwell, Lucretia Mott, Elizabeth Cady Stanton, Susan B. Anthony, Robert Owen

Vocabulary

Religious revivals, temperance movement, moral suasion, abstinence, prohibitionists, curricula, paupers, rehabilitation, pacifists, Seneca Falls convention, utopian communities, socialist, New Harmony, phrenology

Activities

1. OUTLINING Have students outline this lesson using the boldface titles as main topics. If necessary, review outlining techniques as described in Unit 1, Chapter 1, Activity 2. Emphasize the need to pick only the essential facts for the outline and to keep entries to brief phrases, clauses, or single words.

2. FILMSTRIP AND SIMULATION *Feminism as a Radical Movement* (Multimedia Productions) presents the history of the feminist movement from the nineteenth century to the present in two color filmstrips with record or cassette. *Women's Work: America, 1620–1920* (Warren Schloat Productions, Inc.) traces the history of women's rights from colonial America through the 1920s in four color filmstrips with records or cassettes. Also available is a simulation exercise of the Seneca Falls convention. You can involve the entire class in the activities of that convention. The simulation exercise is available from Social Studies School Services, 10,000 Culver Blvd., Culver City, Calif. 90230.

3. LISTENING FOR INFORMATION Read to the class from Margaret Truman's *Women of Courage* (New York: Bantam Books, Inc., 1977). In this paperback are twelve stories of American women who had the courage to stand up for their rights and say what had to be said. Included are Susan B. Anthony and Elizabeth Blackwell from this lesson. Your students will enjoy hearing or reading every story.

4. DISCUSSION Many reasons have been given for the failure of the utopian communities in America. The most frequently cited was faults in the character of the inhabitants of these communities. What character traits would be necessary to make a utopian society work? Do you think you could join such a society?

Beginning in the 1830s, educational reformers led by Horace Mann in Massachusetts and Henry Barnard in Connecticut and Rhode Island worked to open free, tax-supported primary schools. Mann spoke for all reformers when he said, "I have faith in the improvability of the [human] race." This would be brought about, he believed, through education. Mann played not only upon faith but upon fear. The growing gap between rich and poor in industrial America was a danger to society, he warned, and only education could close it. Mann believed that working people, through education, would improve their position. They would then acquire property. "For," said Mann, "such a thing never did happen, and never can happen, as that an intelligent and practical body of men should be permanently poor."

Support for public schools came from many quarters. Businesspeople needing workers who could read, write, and "figure" favored free public schools. So did members of workers' groups, who saw schooling as the key to their own advancement and that of their children. Perhaps the most telling argument was that with white male suffrage, it was important for voters to be educated.

Opposition was strong and often bitter. "Giving away" education would cause the children of the poor to grow up lazy, claimed some. Others, raising the fear of a powerful government, objected that public schools would interfere in the parent-child relationship. A good many saw no reason why they should pay taxes that would be used to educate other people's children.

By the 1850s, however, all states outside the South were committed to tax-supported education in elementary schools. Most states also passed attendance laws, lengthened the school year, and updated curricula and teaching methods. Mann and Barnard also got several states to set up schools for the training of teachers.

Reformers did not have total success, however. Many of the attendance laws were quite loose. As late as 1860, only one white child in every six actually went to school. (Hardly any blacks received schooling.) Further, these reforms touched only elementary schools. In 1860 there were barely 300 public high schools in the country, and nearly 100 of those were in Mann's state of Massachusetts. In that same year there were some 6,000 private "academies," or high schools. The great majority of young people did not go to high school, and of those who did go, nearly all paid for it themselves.

Treatment of the unfortunate. A number of humanitarian reformers worked to improve treatment of the unfortunate. Dorothea Dix of Boston spent forty-five years of her life improving the lot of the insane. Samuel Gridley Howe, a Boston doctor, trained the deaf and blind. Such reformers believed that the lives of all men and women, no matter what their present condition, could be made better.

Other reformers, moved by the same feeling, focused on the treatment of criminals. Prisons and jails before the Civil War were primitive. One prison in Connecticut was actually an old mine shaft. Hardened criminals, first offenders, debtors, paupers, and the mentally ill were all thrown together. Treatment

Continued on page 554

Dorothea Dix

What makes a person become a reformer? Sometimes it is a chance happening. That is how Dorothea Dix (1802–1887) became a crusader for the humane treatment of the insane.

Dorothea Dix had taught school for twenty-five years when a friend asked her to teach a Sunday-school class for women inmates in the East Cambridge jail near Boston. Her visit to that jail on a March morning in 1841 changed her life. Miss Dix was horrified by the conditions. Among the people held in the filthy, unheated jail were a number of insane. In an age when insanity was thought to be incurable, most communities wanted only to keep these unfortunates where they could do no harm. Generally that meant in jails and poorhouses, where they were either neglected or cruelly treated.

Dorothea Dix made the humane treatment of the insane her life's cause. During the next three years, this woman of frail health traveled 10,000 miles, visiting every one of the 800 penitentiaries, county jails, and poorhouses in Massachusetts. One entry in her notebooks tells of people held "in *cages, closets, cellars, stalls, pens! Chained naked, beaten with rods,* and *lashed* into obedience!" In 1843, Dorothea Dix's findings were presented to the Massachusetts legislature. Her evidence was so overwhelming and shocking that the legislature was moved to vote money for mental hospitals.

From Massachusetts, Miss Dix carried her work to other states, ranging as far west as Illinois and as far south as Alabama. Everywhere her method was the same: study the conditions thoroughly, and then present the findings to the public and the legislature in such detail that the situation could not be ignored or denied. In the years from 1843 to 1880, the number of mental hospitals in the United States increased from 13 to 123. Most of the credit belongs to this remarkable reformer who happened to visit the East Cambridge jail in 1841.

Dorothea Dix did much to change the attitude of Americans toward the treatment of the insane. During the Civil War, she also served as Superintendent of Woman Nurses for the Union.

5. RESEARCH / ORAL OR WRITTEN REPORT The communes of the 1960s were the spiritual descendants of the utopian communities of the 1800s. Have some of the students research the commune life-style, its history and current status in America and compare it with the utopian communities described in the text.

6. BULLETIN-BOARD DISPLAY Many fads have come and gone in America. Have your students research and describe some of these fads (marathon dances, swallowing goldfish, flagpole sitting, filling telephone booths or cars with people, bobby-sox, fan clubs, panty raids, hoola hoops, yo-yos, and so on). They could make a bulletin-board display showing fads that indicate that "old-timers" did strange things too.

7. ANALYZING SOURCE MATERIAL From page 555, read to the class the quotation from Abbey Kelley and have the students discuss the "many" chains binding women of the period. To bring the discussion up to date, read the following quotation by Shirley Chisholm, the first black woman to be elected to the House of Representatives: "I have pointed out time and time again that the harshest discrimination that I have encountered in the political arena is antifeminism both from males and brainwashed, Uncle Tom females. When I first announced that I was running for the United States Congress, both males and females advised me, as they had when I ran for the New York State Legislature, to go back to teaching—a woman's vocation—and leave the politics to the men." (From Beth Millstein and Jeanne Bodin's *We, the American Women* [Chicago: Science Research Associates, 1977, page 285])

Background Information

1. WOMEN'S CHRISTIAN TEMPERANCE UNION (WCTU) Founded in 1874, the WCTU was for years the most powerful and influential women's organization in America. Dedicated to ending drinking, the WCTU employed tactics that ranged from invading the all-male saloons for the purpose of Bible reading and hymn singing to smashing the saloons with hatchets. The most famous of the crusaders was Carry Nation (1846–1911), and she was as comfortable with the hatchet as with the Bible. She had been drawn into the struggle by her marriage to an alcoholic. It should be emphasized that families had no protection against fathers who were alcoholic or abusive for any other reason. As legal head of the family, a husband could use not only his money but also any property or wealth his wife might have brought with her to the marriage or earned since. Although Carry Nation generated much publicity by her actions, she was totally atypical of the reformers and rather an embarrassment to the WCTU. The undue emphasis placed on such eccentrics by the contemporary opponents of the women's movement and by later historians has tended to make the whole movement seem ridiculous. Although students should be allowed to enjoy these colorful characters, teachers should be careful not to generate fallacious stereotypes. A much more typical leader was Frances Willard (1839–1898), who was president of the WCTU. Under her outstanding leadership, the WCTU was involved in many causes, including suffrage.

was cruel and inhumane. Reformers argued that the goal of imprisonment should be the rehabilitation of the prisoner. They proposed new penal methods and designed new prisons. Some of their ideas seem strange today. One "reform" was to keep prisoners isolated and in silence, in the belief that they would then meditate on their evil behavior. This, reformers said, was the first step in rehabilitation. A number of prisons incorporating reform ideas were built. The prison that was built at Auburn, New York, was regarded as a model for its time.

The peace movement. Still another reform movement was begun by *pacifists*, people who were against war as a means of settling disputes between nations. This movement drew its inspiration from the biblical prophecy of a time

The women's rights movement of the 1800s brought about limited gains in educational opportunity for girls. However, the courses of study in girls' schools sometimes differed from those in boys' schools. In the classroom shown here, needlework and penmanship were emphasized.

when nations "shall beat their swords into plowshares and their spears into pruning hooks." In 1828 a Maine man named William Ladd drew together several dozen peace groups to form the American Peace Society. Much of the pacificism of Ladd and his followers came from Quaker thinking. Their American Peace Society strongly opposed the war with Mexico. One of its members, the writer and philosopher Henry David Thoreau, went to jail rather than pay taxes that would support the war.

Ladd devised a plan for an international court to settle all disputes. Public opinion, rather than armed force, would see that the decisions were carried out. However, on the question of whether a nation had the moral right to fight if attacked, pacifists split. An even more difficult question faced them with the coming of the Civil War. Most members of peace societies were also abolitionists. They found themselves with the choice of peace and slavery or war and an end to slavery. Most supported the latter as the greater need of the time.

Women's rights. The same era of reform also saw the birth of the movement for women's rights. The position of women had improved but little since colonial times. Husbands still had control of the property of their wives. In a divorce, a husband usually kept the children. Women still could not sue in court or serve on juries. Schooling was not thought important for girls. Their proper path in life was felt to be marriage and homemaking. Colleges were closed to them, as were professions like law, medicine, and the ministry. A woman might become a teacher, but her pay would be lower than a man's. Only among Quakers were women allowed to speak in public before mixed groups.

Here and there, a few determined women broke through these barriers. In 1821 Emma Willard founded the Troy Female Seminary in Troy, New York, to improve women's education. It was the first higher-level school for women in America. Angelina and Sarah Grimké, the South Carolina abolitionists, were the first women to speak in public to mixed audiences. Lucy Stone became the first American woman to lecture on women's rights. She was a graduate of Oberlin College in Ohio, the first school to award college degrees to women. Elizabeth Blackwell won her struggle to be admitted to medical school, and she received an M.D. degree in 1849. But these women were exceptions.

Women were very active in all the great reform movements of the day. About half the members of abolitionist groups were women, and hundreds of women were conductors on the underground railroad. Through their work in the abolitionist movement, some women began to see parallels between their own condition and that of slaves. Abby Kelley, a Massachusetts abolitionist, said:

> We have good cause to be grateful to the slave for the benefits we have received to *ourselves*, in working for *him*. In striving to strike his irons off, we found most surely, that *we* were manacled *ourselves*: not by *one* chain only, but by many.

The point was driven home in 1840 at a world antislavery meeting in London. A number of women abolitionists were told they could watch from the balcony

Background Information

2. EDUCATION FOR WOMEN In the early 1800s, education for men was stressed to ensure more responsible voters. Since women did not vote, it was felt they did not have to be educated beyond basic homemaking skills. Emma Willard (1787–1870) established her school to produce teachers as well as better-educated homemakers. The courses offered were those of a typical high school program. The Willard School taught gymnastics and physiology, although visitors' disapproval of women studying the human body forced the school to cover parts of the textbook pictures. As for colleges, in 1837 Oberlin College in Ohio became the first coeducational institution. Later that same year, Mary Lyon opened the first college exclusively for women—Mount Holyoke Seminary in South Hadley, Massachusetts.

3. SENECA FALLS CONVENTION The convention was attended by over 300 people, 40 of whom were men. It was chaired by Lucretia Mott's husband, James, since none of the women had had any such experience. For the Declaration of Sentiments, Elizabeth Cady Stanton suggested the resolution for the right to vote. It was considered to be a controversial item but not the most important. More important were the right to control their property and earnings, the guardianship of children, educational and job opportunities, and their legal status.

Background Information

4. BROOK FARM Another type of experimental socialistic community was established in Massachusetts in 1841. The transcendentalists started Brook Farm to implement their philosophy of the union between intellectual growth and manual labor. All residents worked the same hours, received the same pay, and paid the same expenses. The farm school featured some ideas that foreshadowed later progressive educational methods. The community folded in 1847 due to increasing debts.

but could not have seats on the convention floor and take part.

Several of the women reformers decided to work for women's rights. Among the leading feminists were Lucretia Mott, Elizabeth Cady Stanton, and Susan B. Anthony. In 1848, Mott and Stanton organized the Woman's Rights Convention at Seneca Falls, New York. The Declaration of Sentiments and Rights adopted by the convention was modeled on the Declaration of Independence. It began by proclaiming that "all men *and women* are created equal." It listed many of women's grievances.

The women reformers wanted women to be able to control their own property and earnings after marriage. They demanded equal rights with men before the law. They also wanted to be able to enter schools and the professions. Gaining the right to vote was at this time one of their lesser goals. The resolution favoring woman suffrage was the only one that received less than a unanimous vote at the Seneca Falls convention.

In the following years, some of the convention's aims were won. Several states passed laws giving married women control over their own property. During the 1850s, however, it was the antislavery movement that occupied most reformers. Most women agreed that abolitionism should be put ahead of all other reform movements. At that time, little further progress for women's rights was made.

Women could vote in New Jersey until that right was taken from them in 1807. For many years afterward, women concentrated on other issues.

Utopian communities. A number of reformers decided to build entire communities based on their own ideas of reform. Some were religious communities, some socialist, some a mixture of both. Nearly all were based on cooperation of the members and the sharing of property. Altogether there were about a hundred utopian communities. Each one believed that it held the key to the perfect society. At first it might seem odd that people who aimed to reform society should withdraw from it. But the idea of starting an entirely separate community was explained by one of these reformers.

The community of New Harmony, Indiana, was based on theories of socialism and human betterment.

> Now if we can . . . build one house rightly . . . we can, by taking it for a model and building others like it, make a perfect and beautiful city; in the same manner, if we can, with a knowledge of true social principles, organize one township rightly, we can, by organizing others like it, and by spreading and rendering them universal, establish a true Social and Political Order.

Today we would call such an undertaking a "pilot project." The idea, though, was thoroughly American. It was little different from the Puritans' goal of building "a City upon a Hill" that would serve as a shining model to the rest of the world.

The best known of those communities was at New Harmony, Indiana. It was started in 1825 by Robert Dale Owen, a wealthy English manufacturer turned socialist. Neither New Harmony nor the other utopian communities lasted very long. The lives of few Americans were changed by these efforts to form a utopian society.

Other roads to betterment. In an age so ready to seek improvement, some of the ideas on how humans might best realize their potential were strange indeed. Some people believed that the road to perfection lay in diet. Eating only vegetables and avoiding tobacco and coffee were some of the more popular ideas. The graham cracker was named for a Doctor Sylvester Graham, who preached that eating breads made of coarse whole wheat would lead not only to good health but to the good society.

One of the most popular fads of the era was the "science" of phrenology. This fad held that one's personality and character could be learned by studying bumps on his or her head. Through such knowledge, it was claimed, humankind could be renewed. One of the reasons for the popularity of this notion was that the democratic age was sweeping away ideas of the need for special training. It was comforting to many people to think that almost anyone

Background Information

5. ROBERT OWEN (1771–1858) As part owner of a cotton mill in Scotland, Owen had set up a model community in which the children were in schools instead of working and the working conditions of the mill were carefully supervised. His success there encouraged him to start cooperative communities where farming and industry could be combined with ideas of equality for all. In 1825 he started this type of community in New Harmony, Indiana. By 1827, his antireligious views and the lack of cooperation by some of the residents caused the town to fail. Owen returned to England, where he was involved in attempting to organize industrial workers into cooperatives. This effort failed due to government and management opposition, but Owen's ideas have continued to influence cooperative movements.

6. PHRENOLOGY Founded by Franz J. Gall in the early 1800s, phrenology claimed that differences in people were due to the physical shape of the brain. This shape was reflected in bumps on the head or the shape of the skull. A phrenological chart (see *World Book Encyclopedia*, Vol. 15, page 382) shows supposed locations for such characteristics as hope, imitation, and combativeness as well as the locations for the perception of time, language, size, and so on. Although scientists today do associate different parts of the brain with different functions, the shape of the skull has no relationship to the functioning of the brain. Scientists do not yet fully understand the brain's role in causing differences in people.

Answers To Review Questions

1. For some Americans, reform meant "to bring up to date." For others, it meant "to make more efficient." For most Americans, however, reform implied two fundamental goals: to bring about more political democracy and to improve the conditions of people's lives.

2. Government's role in reform has been limited by the concept of restricted powers of government and the right of the individual to use property as he or she wishes. Political parties must maintain a middle-of-the-road position in order to gain widespread support. Many reform movements or ideas have attracted zealots whose excesses repelled the average citizen.

3. People oppose reform for a variety of reasons: they like things the way they are; they fear reform will lead to revolution; they believe there is little that can be done to right the wrongs in life; they think reform would not change enough.

4. The temperance movement sought to reform America's drinking habits through a method called moral suasion. Later on, reformers advocated abstinence and began to lobby for legislation to prohibit liquor sales.

5. For educational reform: people needed an education to work in the business world; through education people would have a chance to improve their lives; voters should be better educated. Against educational reform: "giving away" education would cause poor children to grow up lazy; public schools would interfere with parent-child relationships; people should not have to pay taxes to educate other people's children.

could become an instant scientist and psychologist.

"Reforms" and fads of this sort make it easy to see many of the reformers of the period from 1830 to 1860 as crackpots. Even many of the reforms that came closer to the mainstream were led by people who were impractical and self-righteous. Their single-minded devotion to their causes often made them hard to get along with. Yet it should be remembered, as the historian David B. Davis reminds us, that

> the main issues raised by the reformers are still very much alive. We have by no means solved the problems of racial and sexual discrimination. . . . We are still perplexed by the discrepancy between our penal institutions and our ideal of reforming and rehabilitating criminals. We argue endlessly over the most effective methods for redeeming . . . what we now term "the culturally deprived." If we are usually more cynical than the antebellum reformers, we have not abandoned their dream of a world without war.

As you have read, most of the reforms of this period were based on the hope of changing the individual. Except for the prohibitionists, these early reformers did not come into conflict with American ideas of limited government, for their reforms did not require the use of government. The belief that government had no role in reform would change in the last half of the nineteenth century. Why it changed, and what the results of this change were, you will read in the next chapter.

CHECKUP

1. What were the major reform movements between 1830 and 1860? With what degree of success did each meet?
2. How was the cause of women's rights advanced by reformers?
3. How did utopian communities attempt to bring about reform?

Key Facts from Chapter 27

1. The two broad goals of reformers in America have been to bring about more political democracy and to improve people's lives.
2. One approach to the goal of human betterment has been to change a person's character. Most reform movements before the Civil War took this approach.
3. A second approach has been to change the social and economic conditions that have created poverty, inequality, and injustice.
4. Among the limits to reform in America have been the idea of limited government, the attachment to private property, the diverse interests of each major political party, and the nature of the reformers themselves.
5. The goals of reform movements before the Civil War included the abolition of slavery, temperance, free education, humane treatment for the unfortunate, the abolition of war, and equal rights for women.

People, Places, and Events

Horace Mann *P. 552*
Henry Barnard *P. 552*
Dorothea Dix *P. 552*
Samuel Gridley Howe *P. 552*
William Ladd *P. 555*
American Peace Society *P. 555*
Emma Willard *P. 555*
Angelina and Sarah Grimké *P. 555*
Lucy Stone *P. 555*
Elizabeth Blackwell *P. 555*
Lucretia Mott *P. 556*
Elizabeth Cady Stanton *P. 556*
Susan B. Anthony *P. 556*
Seneca Falls convention *P. 556*
New Harmony, Indiana *P. 557*

Review Questions

1. What different meanings might people give to the term *reform*? *P. 547* Les. 1
2. Why have the efforts of reformers had only limited success? *P. 549* Les. 1
3. Why are a number of Americans opposed to reform efforts? *Pp. 550—551* Les. 1
4. How did the temperance movement seek to reform American society in the first half of the nineteenth century? *P. 551* Les. 2
5. What arguments were advanced in favor of educational reform? against educational reform? *P. 552* Les. 2
6. How successful was the educational reform movement? *P. 552* Les. 2
7. Which groups of people especially benefitted from the efforts of humanitarian reformers? *P. 552* Les. 2
8. Define the term *pacifist*. *P. 554* Les. 2
9. What specific rights were women reformers advocating for all women? *P. 556* Les. 2

Chapter Test

For each sentence, write the letter of the correct ending or endings.

1. Temperance reformers sought to influence Americans' drinking habits by using a method called **(a)** pacificism, **(b)** prohibition, **(c)** moral suasion.
2. The Woman's Rights Convention was organized by **(a)** Elizabeth Cady Stanton, **(b)** Lucretia Mott, **(c)** Lucy Stone.
3. The reform spirit in America is said to have sprung from **(a)** religion, **(b)** the Declaration of Independence, **(c)** the American Peace Society.
4. Support for public schools came from **(a)** Horace Mann, **(b)** businesspeople, **(c)** members of workers' groups.
5. Dorothea Dix and Samuel Gridley Howe were involved with **(a)** educational reform, **(b)** humanitarian reform, **(c)** the women's rights movement.
6. Most members of the peace movement were also **(a)** members of a political party, **(b)** abolitionists, **(c)** Social Darwinists.
7. A well-known utopian community was **(a)** Seneca Falls, **(b)** Haddonfield, **(c)** New Harmony.
8. Women reformers of the nineteenth century wanted women to have the right to **(a)** control their own earnings and property after marriage, **(b)** equal employment opportunities, **(c)** equal pay with men for performing the same work.
9. As a result of the educational reform movement, most states **(a)** passed attendance laws, **(b)** established tax-supported high schools, **(c)** offered schooling to blacks.
10. Most reforms were based on the hope of changing **(a)** the individual, **(b)** society, **(c)** the spoils system.

6. Moderately successful. Attendance laws were passed, but not always enforced, and curricula and teaching methods were updated. Although most states were committed to tax-supported elementary schools, they did not endorse high-school education for the masses.
7. The insane, the physically disabled, such as the deaf and blind, and criminals in prisons.
8. Pacifists are people against war as a means of settling disputes between nations.
9. Women reformers wanted the following rights for all women: control of their own property and earnings after marriage; equality with men before the law; entrance to schools and the professions. Gaining the right to vote was at this time one of their lesser goals.

Answers For Chapter Test
1. c **2.** a, b **3.** a, b
4. a, b, c **5.** b **6.** b
7. c **8.** a **9.** a **10.** a

Background Information

1. THE GRANGER. The old Grange poster from which this was taken is now in the Library of Congress. This part depicts the type of yeoman farmer that the Grange, and later Populism, was trying to help. The rest of the poster shows Grange activities and family life on a farm as well as the slogan "I pay for all," reflecting farmers' grievances.

Oliver Kelley, the founder of the organization, wisely provided that farm women as well as men were eligible to join the Grange. So, too, were young people of both sexes. In order to attract young members, Kelley said of the Grange: "In its proceedings a love for rural life will be encouraged, the desire for excitement and amusement, so prevalent in youth, will be gratified." For old and young, the goals of the Grange were, in Kelley's words, "to advance education, to elevate and dignify the occupation of farmers, and to protect its members against the numerous combinations by which their interests are injuriously affected."

CHAPTER 28

THE POPULIST REVOLT

LESSON 1

THE REFORM MOVEMENTS of the pre-Civil War era had lost most of their momentum by the 1860s. As a result of the Civil War, the abolitionists reached the goal they had worked for. However, other reform movements were overwhelmed by the happenings of the war years. What passed for humanitarian reform after the war was but a faint echo of the earlier effort to reform prisons, train the deaf and blind, and find the path to world peace. Except in the South, school reform fell behind. Between 1850 and 1890, the percentage of children going to elementary schools did not increase at all. Although free public high schools began to spread in the 1870s, attendance was not compulsory, so few young people went. Of the early reform movements, only temperance was still strong.

Feminists were among the many reformers who found at the war's end that their moment had passed. In the 1850s they had put aside their own goals in favor of the fight to free the slaves. Now they expected that women as well as the freed slaves would gain the right to vote. However, male abolitionists told them they must wait because "this is the Negro's hour." It was plain that many of the women's male allies in the abolitionist movement had little interest in women's rights. The Fourteenth Amendment, adopted in 1868, said that the right to vote belonged only to males. And the Fifteenth Amendment, which forbade denying the right to vote because of race, said nothing about denying it on the grounds of sex.

New Patterns of Reform

This did not mean that Americans no longer thought of reform in the late 1800s. Those who looked for change, however, turned to quite different kinds of problems than those that had occupied reformers in the years before the Civil War.

The corrupt Tweed Ring. To a number of Americans of the 1870s and 1880s, the greatest problem in American life was corruption in government. One currupt politician was William "Boss" Tweed of New York City. He and his gang ran the Tammany Hall organization. This was a political club that controlled the local Democratic party, which in turn governed New York City. Through kickbacks, bribery, the padding of bills, and every other kind of shady deal, the Tweed Ring looted the city treasury. It stole at least $50 million and perhaps as much as $200 million before it was brought down in 1871. Typical of the bill-padding was the charge to the city of $11 million for a courthouse that cost $3 million to build.

Many state legislatures were known to be open to bribery. The going price for a lawmaker's vote on important bills in the New York State legislature was said to be $20,000. During one struggle between two large railroads for the lawmakers' favors, representatives from each railroad actually appeared on the floor of the legislature with suitcases full of money. One writer in 1881 said that Standard Oil did everything to the Pennsylvania legislature but refine it.

LESSON 1 *(1 day)*

Performance Objectives

1. To explain orally or in writing the changes in the reform movement after the Civil War. **2.** To describe and explain orally or in writing examples of corruption, why it was such a serious problem in the 1870s and 1880s, and what reformers did about it. **3.** To explain orally or in writing the plans for dealing with poverty that were suggested by Henry George, Edward Bellamy, and the Social Gospelers.

Famous People

Henry George, Edward Bellamy

Vocabulary

Fourteenth Amendment, Fifteenth Amendment, Tweed Ring, kickbacks, patronage, Pendleton Act, Civil Service Commission, merit system, nationalized, Social Gospel

Background Information

2. THOMAS NAST (1840–1902) Beginning his career as a cartoonist in the 1860s, Nast popularized the political symbols of the Democratic donkey, the Republican elephant, and the Tammany Tiger. His caricatures of Boss Tweed were instrumental in breaking up the Tweed Ring, but not until after Nast was bribed, bullied, and threatened by Tweed's gang. In seeming contradiction to his political cartoons, Nast also created the modern-day version of Santa Claus in some of his early cartoons in *Harper's Weekly*.

Activities

1. DISCUSSION After students have read page 561, discuss the following questions: Why, do you think, were women excluded from the Fourteenth and Fifteenth Amendments when they were so important in the abolitionist movement? What other reform movements were weaker after the Civil War? Why?

2. READING FOR INFORMATION Have students carefully read the section in the text concerning the reform ideas of Henry George, Edward Bellamy, and the Social Gospelers. In their notes, students should compare those reforms with the current programs and ideas about how to end poverty.

3. ORAL OR WRITTEN REPORTS Have some students investigate and report on some examples of corruption during this time period. Have others report on the civil service system and how it was designed to prevent corruption. Still other students could report on other means of fighting corruption, such as Thomas Nast's cartoons and other newspaper crusades.

This cartoon pictures President Ulysses S. Grant as a circus strong man, using his strength to support his associates. The six figures below Grant were all charged with corruption during their service with the government.

Corruption in Washington. On the national level, the administration of President Grant was one of the most corrupt in America's history. The Secretary of War accepted a bribe in exchange for profitable trading rights on an Indian reservation. A special agent in the Treasury Department kept for himself and for the Republican party one half of the $427,000 in taxes he collected. President Grant's own private secretary was involved with some whiskey distillers in a scheme to cheat the government out of millions in taxes. Dozens of members of Congress took payoffs from a construction company that was building railroads with government subsidies. The company then overcharged the government by millions of dollars.

Such corruption was seen by some people as a threat to the very existence of democracy. Many who led the movement to reform these conditions were members of older, upper-class families. These people now felt themselves pushed from their old positions of leadership by a new class of industrialists and by professional politicians. To these "genteel reformers," reform meant bringing back honesty and economy to government. That in turn could be done simply by putting good people like themselves in office. They believed in limited government and *laissez-faire,* and they had no wish to change the social and economic system.

Civil service reform. You will recall that under the spoils system, people were given government jobs as rewards for service to the party. The reformers now proposed to replace the spoils system by choosing civil service employees through written examinations. Merit would decide which persons received the government jobs.

Through the 1870s, reformers worked to end the system of *patronage*—that is, the naming of people to government jobs for reasons other than merit alone. In 1881 a tragic event aided the reformers' cause. President James Garfield was killed by a disappointed office seeker. Garfield's death shocked the public and won support for reform. In 1883, Congress passed the Pendleton Act, marking the beginning of the merit system in the federal civil service. The Pendleton Act set up a Civil Service Commission. This group would draw up examinations and give them to those people seeking certain offices in the federal government. Appointments to offices would go to those who proved best fitted to fill them. The act forbade making officeholders kick back part of their salary for political purposes. Although only 10 percent of federal jobs were covered by this first law, the merit system has been extended over the years. Today it applies to nearly 90 percent of such jobs.

★20★

James A. Garfield

1831–1881

Born in OHIO
In Office 1881
Party REPUBLICAN

Last President to be born in a log cabin, and second to be assassinated. Shot by disappointed job seeker, he died after six months in office. His death helped end spoils system.

★ ★ ★ ★ ★ ★ ★ ★

The plight of the poor. Reform of the federal civil service was a step forward, yet it by no means ended corruption. Industrialists, and politicians working with them, still bent government to their own purposes. Political machines continued to enrich their members at public expense. In addition, civil service reform did not touch the problems faced by the great mass of people in industrial America, especially the poor. The genteel reformers looked upon these people as "the dangerous classes."

Two reformers who turned their attention to the troubles of the poor were the writers Henry George and Edward Bellamy. In *Progress and Poverty* (1879), George offered an answer to this riddle of modern society: Why is progress always accompanied by poverty? It is, he felt, because people are allowed to keep the value that is added to their land, when such value is gained not by their own efforts but by society—as, for example, when the value of land increases because a city grows up around it. George proposed that this unearned value be returned to society through a tax. This Single Tax, as it was called would raise money for all the government's needs and would end poverty.

In *Looking Backward* (1887), Edward Bellamy proposed a utopian society in which all business and industry would be *nationalized*, or owned and operated by the government. All strife between capital and labor would then be ended, and there would be plenty and happiness for all. Unlike reformers of the early nineteenth century, George and Bellamy did not seek to save society through reforming millions of people but rather through one grand change.

Another important group of reformers of the late nineteenth century was

4. FILM *The Tiger's Tail: Thomas Nast vs. Boss Tweed* (20 minutes, b&w; Teaching Films Custodian). This is an old film (1953) but well done dramatically.

5. READING FOR INFORMATION Some of your students might enjoy reading some of the anecdotes in Eric Goldman's *Rendezvous with Destiny* (New York: Random House, 1956). It is available in paperback and could also be read to the whole class. There are several references to this book in later chapters.

6. DISCUSSION Have students discuss and defend opinions on the following question: Can poverty be eliminated by giving money to the poor?

LESSON 2 *(2 days)*

Performance Objectives

1. To explain orally or in writing why farmers' incomes were declining in the post–Civil War years when farm production was increasing. **2.** To explain orally or in writing the differences between inflation and deflation. **3.** To explain orally or in writing how the Grange and the Farmers' Alliances helped the farmers and why the Grange declined.

Famous Person

Oliver H. Kelley

Vocabulary

Specialization, cash crop, worldwide market, grain elevators, tax assessor, crop-lien system, inflation, deflation, world overproduction, Grange, middlemen, cooperatives, interest-group reform, Farmers' Alliances

Activities

1. DISCUSSION After students have read this lesson, discuss the answers to the Checkup questions on page 569.

2. READING FOR INFORMATION / REPORT There are fourteen terms in the vocabulary section above. Assign each term to one or two students. Individuals or partners should become experts on their own terms and be responsible for the other students clearly understanding those terms also.

★21★

Chester A. Arthur

1830–1886

Born in VERMONT
In Office 1881–1885
Party REPUBLICAN

Though a veteran of New York machine politics, he proved to be an efficient and honest President. Supported civil service reform and worked for economy in federal government.

★ ★ ★ ★ ★ ★ ★ ★

made up of certain Protestant ministers who preached the "Social Gospel." Before that time, ministers had held that the cause of poverty lay in sin. The Social Gospel held that for millions in an urban industrial society, it was the other way around—the cause of sin lay in poverty. To end sin, the working and living conditions of ordinary people must be improved. Social Gospelers were willing to use the powers of government to reach that goal.

None of those reformers—George, Bellamy, or the Social Gospelers—were able to form a movement to carry out their proposed changes. Their role instead was to stir consciences. The actual fashioning of the first major reform movement to respond to the effects of industrialism fell to the farmers.

CHECKUP

1. Why was corruption in government considered by some to be the greatest problem in American life in the 1870s and 1880s?
2. How did reformers attempt to make government more honest and efficient?
3. What different ways of dealing with poverty were put forth by Henry George and Edward Bellamy?

LESSON 2

The Problems of the Farmers

By the late nineteenth century, the independent farm family that grew everything it needed was disappearing. A great many American farmers were now really business people who specialized in one or two cash crops. Specialization increased the farmers' chances for large incomes. However, it also made those incomes dependent on factors over which they had no control.

A worldwide market. One of those factors was the worldwide market for farm crops. Trains and steamships now carried crops swiftly and cheaply from one part of the world to another. Grain grown on the Great Plains competed with grain grown in Russia, Canada, South America, and Australia. The price of each crop was thus determined by world supply and world demand.

Most farmers in the late nineteenth century never understood the full meaning of this fact. They had always lived by the simple idea that the harder they worked and the more crops they grew, the more money they would earn. And so they increased their production. In about a twenty-year period following the Civil War, the wheat and corn crops more than tripled. Between 1860 and 1890, cotton production rose by 126 percent.

Farmers and the railroads. Farmers were highly dependent on the railroads. People in rural towns believed that a railroad meant prosperity for them. They soon found, however, that their prosperity depended on men who sat in distant cities and set the railroads' freight rates. Railroads lowered rates on routes where there was competition and raised them on routes where there was none. For example, at one time the rate for carrying a ton of goods one mile was 95 cents on the heavily traveled route east of Chicago, but it was $1.52 from Chicago to the Missouri River, and $4.80 west of the Missouri. Farmers often paid more to ship a crop a short distance than a long one. It cost more, for example, to ship wheat from points in the Dakotas to Minneapolis, in neighboring Minnesota, than to send it from Chicago to Liverpool, England. At times, half the market price of crops was eaten up by railroad charges.

Moreover, farmers paid high charges for storing their crops in grain elevators and warehouses, many of which were owned by railroads. Farmers would have liked to hold their crops until they could get a good price. Unable to afford the storage rates, however, they often had to sell when prices were low.

3. FILM Inflation and deflation are difficult concepts to teach. Perhaps if you show your students the film *Economic Stability: The Goal of Full Employment Without Inflation* (30 minutes, b&w) before you attempt to explain the concepts, they might have a firmer base for learning. This film is part of the Economics for Concerned Citizens series and was produced in 1970 by the University of Nebraska. It is available for rental from the Audio-Visual Center at Indiana University.

4. ORAL OR WRITTEN REPORT Money has intrigued humans for a long time. For a better understanding of this important item, have some of your students read and report on John Kenneth Galbraith's *Money: Whence It Came and Where It Went* (Boston: Houghton Mifflin Company, 1975).

This reaper, bearing the name of its inventor, was known as McCormick's "Old Reliable." The use of new types of farm machines helped to increase crop production after the Civil War.

5. USING A CHART For the following activity you will need a chart of corn production from 1866 to 1970. The most common source of such information is *Historical Statistics of the United States, Colonial Times to the Present,* which is put out by the U.S. Department of Commerce, Bureau of the Census. The particular chart is on pages 510–512; it is also referred to as Series K 502–516. (*Note:* If the chart must be manually reproduced, just do the figures for every five years: 1870, 1875, 1880, etc., but include 1866 and 1919.) After you have distributed and explained the chart, have the students answer the following questions.

a. Identify the overall trend in each of the following areas from 1866 to 1910: (1) amount of land used for corn, (2) total corn crop harvested, and (3) prices.

b. If you were an average farmer on an average farm in the years 1866 to 1910, would you think you were improving your position, or losing ground?

c. What happened between 1890 and 1895 to acreage, production, and prices? How can you explain what happened to prices?

d. What would have happened if a farmer borrowed money in 1890 that he had to pay back in 1895? Would it be easier, or harder, to pay it back in 1895 dollars compared with 1890 dollars?

e. Does the law of supply and demand explain why prices dropped from 1925 to 1930?

f. How would you explain the drop in crop production from 1920 to 1925? (Answer: Bad weather, disease, etc.) How would you explain the rise in prices during the same years?

Taxes and credit. Farmers also complained of unfair taxation. This taxation took two forms. One kind of tax was imposed by the tariff laws passed by Congress. Tariff duties added from 33 percent to 60 percent to the cost of more than a hundred articles that farm families bought, from machines to clothes. The second kind of tax was the personal property tax. In earlier times, the wealth of most farmers had been in land, buildings, and animals. All of those things were property that a tax assessor could quickly see. Those who owned more property paid more taxes. In the late nineteenth century, the assessor could still see the farmers' property. However, the wealth of a good many rich people was in the form of stocks and bonds that were easily hidden. Thus the farmers bore the burden of taxation.

Farmers were also hurt by the high cost of credit. Many of them were accustomed to borrowing money in order to expand in good times and to stay in business in bad times. Banks, insurance companies, and private lenders often charged western farmers interest ranging from 17 percent to 25 percent a year. There were sometimes good reasons for such high rates. Loans to Plains farmers were often risky, and more than a few lenders lost their money. However, to farmers whose profits were eaten up by those rates, such explanations had little meaning. In the South, where farmers borrowed from storekeepers under the crop-lien system (see page 385), rates ran from 40 percent to 100 percent.

The money supply. Farmers also claimed that an inadequate supply of money in circulation was a major cause of low crop prices. This issue needs some explanation. The price of goods at any time depends partly on the amount of money in circulation. If the amount of money for each person increases greatly, prices will rise, and the dollar will buy less. This condition is called *inflation.* If, on the other hand, the amount of money in circulation per person decreases greatly, prices will go down, and the dollar will buy more. That is known as *deflation.*

In the thirty years following the Civil War, the amount of money in circulation per person in the United States decreased by 27 percent. Partly as a result of this situation, the prices of all goods, including crops and other farm products, declined during the last part of the nineteenth century.

At first, that might not seem to be a special problem for farmers. After all, while they were receiving less for their goods, were they not also paying less for the goods they bought? The answer to this question is not as simple as one might think. There were two special factors that affected the farmers. One was world overproduction of crops, which caused the prices of farm goods to drop a lot faster and further than the prices of other goods. The other factor was that farmers were almost always in debt. As income dropped, it became harder to pay off debts. Take, for example, a farmer who borrowed $1,000 in the 1860s. If he were paying off the loan the same year, he could do it with the money received for 1,200 bushels (42,240 kl) of grain. But if he were paying off the same loan twenty years later, when grain prices were lower, it would take 2,300 bushels (80,960 kl)—nearly twice as

In 1873, members of the Grange hold a mass meeting near Winchester, Illinois. They wanted to unite farmers against the practices of corporations that owned the railroads and elevators.

many—to pay off the loan. Farmers were correct, therefore, when they said they were paying back dollars worth far more than the ones they had borrowed.

A final grievance of farmers was harder to pinpoint but just as important. It was the feeling that they were not sharing in the progress of the nation. They were isolated from the exciting material and cultural advances of the cities. They felt left behind. Once they had been the ideal citizens, the backbone of the republic. "God's chosen people, if ever He had a chosen people," Jefferson had called them. Now they felt that city folks looked down on them as hicks and hayseeds.

The Grange. In the latter part of the nineteenth century, farmers organized to deal with their problems. In 1867 they set up the Patrons of Husbandry, more commonly known as the Grange. This organization was started by Oliver H. Kelley, a clerk in the United States Department of Agriculture. At first, the purpose of the Grange was to help farm families fight the loneliness and isolation of farm life by bringing them together for social and educational gatherings. When hard times hit in the early 1870s, however, farmers turned the Grange into a group for protest and action. By 1875, the Grange had over 1.5 million members.

g. What accounts for the extremely good prices for the years 1916 to 1919? (War years) Why the sudden drop afterward? (European farms back in production, world trade back to normal)

h. Which decade was the best one for farmers? (1940–1950) Which was the worst? (1950–1960) Why do prices vary so suddenly for farmers?

6. REFERENCE MATERIAL
The most important element in this lesson is the emphasis on economics. The Joint Council on Economic Education (1212 Avenue of the Americas, New York, New York 10036) has produced a 101-page booklet entitled *Teaching Economics in American History* (price $4). This will give you many excellent ideas for class discussion and classroom activities. There is also an entire kit available for $30.

The Grange undertook both political and economic actions. In politics, it sometimes backed minor-party candidates. More usually it supported friendly candidates in the two major parties. In the early 1870s, Grangers won control of several legislatures in the Midwest. Between 1871 and 1874, the Illinois, Iowa, and Wisconsin legislatures passed laws to regulate rates charged by railroads, grain elevators, and warehouses, and to prohibit certain discriminatory practices of the railroads.

At the same time, Grangers joined together to eliminate the *middlemen*—the agents or dealers between the producers and the consumers. They believed that the middlemen were underpaying the farmers for what they produced and overcharging them for what they bought. Pooling their efforts and their money, the Grangers set up *cooperatives*—organizations owned and operated by those using their services. Among these cooperatives were grain elevators and warehouses, stores and insurance companies, and even factories that made farm machinery and other products. In time, nearly all these cooperatives failed, mostly because of poor management and lack of capital.

The failure of many cooperatives and the return of better crop prices in the late 1870s led to a huge loss of membership in the Grange. By 1880, there were barely 100,000 members left. The Grange was no longer a force in politics. Furthermore, the railroads won back the right to fix freight rates in most cases. The Supreme Court held that when railroad traffic passed through more than one state, as most of it did, states could no longer regulate the rates.

Interest-group reform. Although the Grange was strong for only a few years, it is important for several reasons. Much of modern American reform has grown out of economic grievances. The Grange was the first important movement to concern itself with economic problems. It was also important as the first major reform movement to seek to use the government to limit the power of private interests.

Another reason for the Grange's importance is that it represented a kind of reform different from reforms you read about earlier. Those reforms could be classified as *humanitarian reforms*—changes championed by some people to better the condition of other people. In the Grange movement, reform was promoted by the *same* group that would receive the benefits. The name given to this kind of reform is *interest-group reform*. This variety of reform has been an important part of modern reform in America.

Good times and bad. From the late 1870s to the mid-1880s, the growers of major crops generally did well. Increased rainfall in Kansas, Nebraska, and the Dakotas brought large crops at the very time that production in foreign countries was low. Through much of the West, there were two sure signs of good times: freshly painted barns, and new bank loans with which to buy more land and machinery.

Good times ended soon. In 1886 a fierce blizzard followed by summer drought spelled the end for many Kansas farmers. By the last months of that year, a stream of wagons was heading eastward. Some carried signs, such as

"In God we trusted, in Kansas we busted." Crop failures took their toll. Beginning in 1887, farm prices slid downward for the next ten years. As prices dropped, farmers did the only thing they could think of to keep up their income: they raised more crops. This, of course, added to the overproduction, and prices fell even lower. No longer able to pay mortgages, many farmers lost their land.

In the South, most poor farmers had no land to lose. They were tenants and sharecroppers. This was especially true of black farmers. In 1880 in Georgia, for example, barely 1 percent of the black farmers owned their own land. By 1900, nearly half of all southern farms were being run by tenants. Many of those who did own their land, you will recall, were prisoners of the crop-lien system. To pay their debts, farmers grew more cotton, making prices fall further. In 1894, cotton farmers received less income from 23 million acres (9,200,000 ha) than they had received in 1873 from 9 million acres (3,600,000 ha).

Cowboys drive cattle to a feeding station during the harsh winter of 1886–1887. The weather reduced the herds and brought financial ruin to many cattle raisers on the Great Plains.

The Farmers' Alliances. Once again, farmers responded by organizing. Local groups combined, forming regional Farmers' Alliances. Members totaled more than 2.5 million. Like the Grange, the Farmers' Alliances had both social and educational goals. Almost from the beginning, however, the Alliances emphasized politics. Through politics they tried to raise farm prices, lower transportation costs, and reform the country's financial system.

In 1890 the Alliances ran candidates for local and state offices and for Congress on a number of party labels. Candidates supported by the Alliances won the governorships of five states, controlled ten state legislatures, and took over nearly fifty Congressional seats.

CHECKUP

1. Why, in spite of increased crop production, did farmers' incomes go down in the latter years of the nineteenth century?
2. Why was the amount of money in circulation a matter of concern to farmers?
3. What steps did the Grange and the Farmers' Alliances take to help their members?

LESSON 3 *(2 days)*

Performance Objectives

1. To list the goals and objectives of the Populist party as stated in the Omaha platform. **2.** To describe and explain orally or in writing the various aspects of the issue of inflationary or deflationary currency. **3.** To describe the extent of Populist support by indicating on a chart how Populist candidates fared in the elections of 1892 and 1896.

Famous People

James B. Weaver, Grover Cleveland, Mary Lease, Jacob Coxey, William Jennings Bryan, William McKinley

Vocabulary

Populists, Omaha platform, graduated income tax, postal savings banks, initiative, referendum, subtreasury plan, legal tender, legal ratio, Sherman Silver Purchase Act, silver certificate, Panic of 1893, Coxey's Army, high protective tariff, "cross of gold," front-porch campaign

★**22**★

Grover Cleveland

1837–1908

Born in NEW JERSEY
In Office 1885–1889
Party DEMOCRATIC

First Democrat to become President after Civil War. His honesty, following a time of graft and corruption, appealed to the voters. He sought lower tariffs and fought the trusts.

LESSON 3

The Populist Party

Alliance leaders, encouraged by their political success, decided to form a third party. The People's party, or Populist party, held its first national convention in Omaha, Nebraska, in July 1892. Most of the Populists were farmers. In their ranks, too, were small-town merchants, cattle ranchers, and miners. Many of their leaders were lawyers, editors, and professional politicians. Populists thought of their party as one in which farmers and industrial workers—the true producers of the nation's wealth—would join to remove the evils from American society.

A call for justice. What the Populists believed those evils to be, they described in the preamble to the party platform.

> We meet in the midst of a nation brought to the verge of moral, political and material ruin. Corruption dominates the ballot box, the Legislatures, the Congress, and touches even . . . the Bench. The people are demoralized; most of the States have been compelled to isolate the voters at the polling places to prevent universal intimidation or bribery. The newspapers are largely subsidized or muzzled, public opinion silenced, business prostrated, our homes covered with mortgages, labor impoverished, and the land concentrating in the hands of the capitalists. The urban workmen are denied the right of organization for self-protection; imported pauperized labor beats down their wages; a hireling standing army, unrecognized by our laws, is established to shoot them down, and they are rapidly degenerating into European conditions. The fruits of the toil of millions are boldly stolen to build up colossal fortunes for a few and the possessors of these in turn despise the Republic and endanger liberty. From the same source of governmental injustice we breed the two great classes—tramps and millionaires.

Here is pictured American society in the 1890s as the Populists saw it—great wealth and monopoly in league with the politicians to oppress the ordinary people. It was a struggle, as one Populist put it, "between the robbers and the robbed."

"In the interests of the people." The Omaha platform has become one of the landmark documents in the history of American reform. Populists demanded that the federal government own the railroad, telephone, and telegraph companies, and run them "in the interests of the people." They also demanded a graduated income tax and postal savings banks. Under the latter proposal, people could turn over their savings to United States post offices instead of putting them in the hated banks.

To return the government to the hands of ordinary people, Populists demanded the secret ballot and the direct election of senators, who were at that time chosen by the state legislatures. They also asked for two devices to allow the people to take part more directly in lawmaking. One device was the *initiative*, by which a certain number of voters could propose a law by petition and submit it to the people or to the state legislature for approval. Through the other device, the *referendum*, a certain number of voters could require that the people have the opportunity to vote whether to keep or revoke a law passed by the legislature.

The People's, or Populist, party was met with ridicule by the old political order. This cartoon pictures the party, following a regional meeting in Cincinnati, as a leaky balloon patched together by several small political groups.

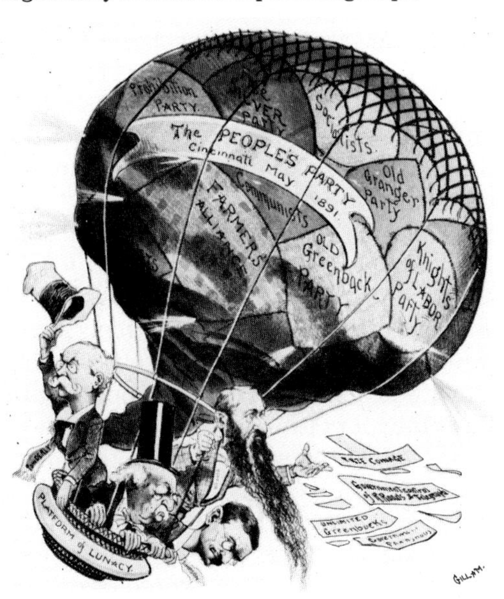

The subtreasury plan. One plank in the Omaha platform dealt directly with crop surpluses. It called for the United States government to set up a subtreasury office and warehouse in every large agricultural county. When prices were low, farmers could hold their nonperishable crops, such as cotton and grains, off the market by storing them in those warehouses. They could then borrow up to 80 percent of the crops' value at 2 percent interest. When prices rose, the farmers would sell the crops and repay the loans.

Paper money and silver coins. Another plank dealt with the demand for increasing the money supply. Populists believed there were two ways to do this. One was for the government simply to print paper money and declare it *legal tender*—that is, money that must be accepted in payment of debts. During the Civil War, the United States had more than doubled the money supply by issuing $415 million in paper money called *greenbacks*. Now, in 1892, Populists picked up the demand for the government to print paper money.

A second way to increase the money supply was to coin silver into dollars. In 1792,[1] Congress had provided for the coinage of both gold and silver. Since gold was worth far more than the same

Background Information

1. GOLD AND SILVER TODAY The history of gold and silver as coins and as backing for paper money in the United states is long and confusing. The two most recent periods of change and adjustment were the 1930s, due to the depression, and the 1970s, due to significant changes in the international monetary structure. In 1933 and 1934, America stopped minting gold coins and made it illegal for citizens to buy or trade gold. It was still used for international exchange and was traded for U.S. dollars held by other countries. This practice was stopped in 1971, but since 1974, Americans have been able to buy and sell gold at market prices. Prior to that time, all gold was exchanged by the government at $35 per troy ounce.

As for silver, in 1934 the government agreed to issue silver certificates (bills) for silver brought to them. This plan was stopped in 1963, and all silver certificates were taken out of circulation. Since 1970, no coins except special-issue silver dollars have contained silver.

Activities

1. READING FOR INFORMATION Using their textbooks and/or copies of the Omaha platform (see Commager's *Documents of American History,* 325), students should make a list of the Populists' demands and goals. After compiling the list, students should decide what group each plank was designed to appeal to. The students should also check off those demands that have been accepted, wholly or in part, into the American political system today. Which still have not been accepted? This last part of the activity will show the real value of the Populists as forerunners of and ground breakers for the reform movement.

amount of silver, that fact had to be shown in the weight of the coins. The *legal ratio* was set in 1834 at 16 to 1. That meant there were to be sixteen times as many grains of silver in the silver dollar as there were grains of gold in the gold dollar. No sooner was this ratio set, however, than people stopped taking silver to the mint to be turned into coins. For the same amount of silver used in coining a dollar, they could get more than a dollar from a silversmith or other buyer in the open market. Not only were no new silver coins being minted, but people melted down their old coins to sell the metal. Thus silver stopped circulating.

Bricks of silver await shipment at a mine in the West about 1880. During the previous ten years, many new mines had been opened. Because of the quantity of silver produced, prices dropped.

In 1873, Congress voted to end the coinage of silver dollars. Since none were being coined anyway, no one paid much attention to Congress's action. Then silver began to pour out of new western mines. As the supply rose, the price of silver fell. By 1877, the number of grains of silver in a dollar brought only ninety cents when sold commercially. Now mine owners turned to the mint again, only to find that silver was no longer being coined. Farmers, meanwhile, anxious to raise farm prices, saw the coinage of silver, like the printing of paper money, as a way to inflate the currency. They and the silver-mine owners joined forces to demand that Congress restore the free and unlimited coinage of silver at the ratio of 16 to 1. They denounced the law that had ended coinage as "the crime of 1873." They declared it had been a scheme of bankers and creditors to deflate the currency and to squeeze farmers.

The Sherman Silver Purchase Act. In 1878, Congress enacted a law requiring the United States to buy a certain amount of silver each month. However, that law fell far short of the free and unlimited coinage of silver. So did the Sherman Silver Purchase Act of 1890. That act required the government to buy 4.5 million ounces (126 million g) of silver at the market price each month. It would be paid for with paper notes called *silver certificates.* These notes could be redeemed for either gold or silver.

Few were long satisfied with the Sherman Silver Purchase Act. "Sound money" people saw it as a threat to the value of the dollar. Mine owners wanted free coinage at 16 to 1. That would pay them a dollar for the same amount of silver that, by 1892, was bringing less than seventy cents on the commercial market. Western and southern farmers looked to free coinage as a way of creating millions of new dollars that would cause farm prices to rise. Thus the Omaha platform came out for the "free and unlimited coinage of silver at a ratio of 16 to 1."

The election of 1892. As its candidate for the Presidency in 1892, the People's party chose James B. Weaver of Iowa. Weaver, a Civil War general, had run for President in 1880 on the Greenback-Labor ticket, and was a veteran of third-party politics. President Benjamin Harrison sought reelection as a Republican. Grover Cleveland was the choice of the Democrats. Cleveland had already served one term as President but in 1888 had lost his bid for reelection. At that time, he received 90,000 more popular votes than the winner Harrison but trailed in electoral votes, 168 to 233.

Populists entered the race with high hopes. Their rallies had the spirited air of camp meetings. Populist leaders were a colorful lot, as suggested by their nicknames: Governor Davis "Bloody Bridles" Waite of Colorado; James "Cyclone" Davis of Texas; "Sockless Jerry" Simpson of Kansas; and from Minnesota, Ignatius Donnelly, "the Sage of Nininger." They were also fiery speakers. None expressed the bitterness and frustration of the western farmer better than Mary Elizabeth Lease, a Kansas Populist and a fiery orator.

> We were told two years ago to go to work and raise a big crop, that was all we needed. We went to work and plowed and planted; the rains fell, the sun shone, nature smiled, and we raised the big crop they told us to; and what came of it? Eight-cent corn, ten-cent oats, two-cent beef, and no price at all for butter and eggs—that's what came of it. Then the politicians said that we suffered from overproduction.

Mary Lease's advice to the farmers was to "raise less corn and more hell."

Many eastern politicians looked upon Populists as ignorant yokels. Some politicians poked fun at the Populist programs, especially the subtreasury plan. If the idea was a good one, they asked, why stop at storing wheat and cotton? Why not also set up a warehouse for poetry? Then poets could borrow on their work, holding it off the market "until poetry goes up." Other eastern politicans, however, found little that was funny in ideas that they thought dangerously radical.

Grover Cleveland won the election of 1892 by a wide margin. Yet the Populists were encouraged by their showing. Weaver got more than a million popular votes and 22 electoral votes. A dozen Populists were elected to Congress, as were many Alliance candidates, who ran as Democrats in the South.

Panic and depression. Almost as soon as Cleveland took office, the country was hit by the Panic of 1893. It marked the beginning of the worst depression in American history up to that time. By the end of that year, 500 banks, 15,000 businesses, and 156 railroads—including some of the country's largest—had failed. Twenty percent of the workers were unemployed. Farm prices, skidding since the late 1880s, plunged sharply.

2. DISCUSSION Discuss with the class the issue of money and the farmers. Take the time to define the economic terms used, since people generally have trouble with this topic. Why did the farmers want soft, or inflationary, money? What was the Populist position? What were the positions of the Democratic and Republican parties? How was the decline of the Populists related to developments in the area of money? The discussion can be brought up to the present by examining who is hurt by and who benefits from inflationary and deflationary times today.

3. USING A CHART Have students make up charts of the 1892 and 1896 elections, showing candidates, parties, platforms, and results. Use these charts as bases for discussion of these elections.

4. ANALYZING SOURCE MATERIAL Have the students read the quotations from Bryan's "cross of gold" speech on pages 575 and 576. What was the gold standard? Who did Bryan think was the more important citizen—the farmer or the city dweller? Where did Bryan get the idea of the "crown of thorns" and the "cross"? Why would these terms appeal to the farmers in that time? (Religious metaphors would appeal to the farm population because it was basically fundamentalist.)

5. ORAL OR WRITTEN REPORTS Have some of your students read and report on the issues of this period as presented in the following primary source materials from Commager's *Documents of American History:* 319, "The Judicial Review of Railroad Rates"; 321, "The Sherman Silver Purchase Act"; 322, "Cleveland's Silver Letter"; 323, "Tillmanism in South Carolina"; 325, "Populist Party Platform" (July 4, 1892); 327, "Cleveland's Message on the Repeal of the Sherman Silver Purchase Act" (August 8, 1893); 328, "Repeal of the Sherman Silver Purchase Act" (November 1, 1893); 332, "Coxey's Program" (1894).

6. LISTENING FOR INFORMATION Read to your class from *The American Story,* "The Farmers Protest: Populism" by J. D. Hicks. This story describes the background to the 1892 Populist party convention.

The depression had many causes. To Grover Cleveland, however, there was one simple explanation: the loss of business confidence. That was caused, in Cleveland's opinion, by the drain of gold out of the Treasury. The drain created fear that the Treasury would no longer be able to redeem all of its notes in gold, as the Sherman Silver Purchase Act of 1890 permitted. By 1893, the value of a silver dollar had slipped to sixty cents. Naturally, people exchanged their certificates for gold. Soon the Treasury's gold reserve fell almost to $100 million, the lowest level then considered safe.

To restore confidence and end the depression, Cleveland insisted that the Silver Purchase Act must be repealed. He called Congress into special session. The debate was bitter and heated as western and southern Democrats opposed the President. Finally, however, Cleveland got enough support from other members of Congress, both Republicans and Democrats, to repeal the act.

No government action. Despite the repeal of the Sherman Silver Purchase Act, the depression deepened. Misery was widespread. Cleveland, like many Americans, held to the old belief that there was nothing the government could do to end a depression. Nor, in his view, was it proper for the federal government to relieve suffering. That was the job of private charities and local governments.

Not everyone agreed, however. Private charities and local governments were running out of money. Voices were raised calling for the federal government to act. Jacob Coxey, a successful Ohio businessman and also a Populist, proposed that the government print $500 million in paper money to pay for a road-building program. This would provide jobs and at the same time inflate the currency. Coxey and several hundred supporters marched from Ohio to Washington to present their demands, only to be arrested for walking on the lawn of the Capitol. The demands of "Coxey's Army" for government action were ignored.

Growing tension. Meanwhile, hard times led to growing tension. Workers were haunted by unemployment. Farmers blamed low prices and the loss of their farms on a conspiracy of eastern bankers. On the other hand, conservatives thought they heard in every Populist speech the beginnings of revolution. The year 1894 saw hundreds of strikes, many of them the result of wage cuts. Some were accompanied by violence. The largest was the Pullman strike, which President Cleveland broke by sending in troops (see page 515).

The depression, Cleveland's support of gold, and his antilabor policies cost the Democratic party dearly in the congressional elections of 1894. Republicans swept the Democrats out of the House and barely missed gaining control of the Senate. Populist candidates did well, receiving 42 percent more votes than they had two years earlier.

Many Democrats in the South and West were now in open revolt against President Cleveland. "Pitchfork Ben" Tillman, a Democratic congressman from South Carolina, campaigned with the promise of "going to Washington with a pitchfork and prod[ding] him in his fat old ribs." The rebelling Democrats were determined to win control of the party from the eastern "gold wing" that Cleveland represented.

As 1896 approached, the money question dominated American politics. Each side came to see the struggle between gold and silver as a struggle between good and evil, even between God and the devil. Each believed that the very future of civilization rested on the outcome. Both major parties were divided into gold and silver wings, though most Republicans favored gold.

The conventions of 1896. In 1896 the Republican party chose as its presidential candidate William McKinley, then governor of Ohio and a former congressman. McKinley was best known as the champion of a high protective tariff. The convention voted to oppose the free coinage of silver and to support gold as the basis of the nation's currency. Western silver delegates walked out.

The Democratic convention was controlled by silver forces from the West and South. They wrote a platform that rejected almost all of Grover Cleveland's policies. The Democrats came out in favor of the free coinage of silver at 16 to 1. The debate over the money issue also gave the Democrats their candidate for President, William Jennings Bryan, a thirty-six-year-old lawyer from Lincoln, Nebraska. Bryan had served two terms in Congress. Although unknown to most eastern delegates, he was well known to the silver forces. No one, however, would have said that Bryan was a strong contender for the nomination—that is, until he rose to speak in the debate over the money plank in the party platform.

Coxey's Army makes its way through a Pennsylvania town. Bound for Washington, the marchers sought economic and social reforms.

Bryan's speech was the most electrifying in convention history. Bryan declared that he was speaking for the small farmers of the nation who "are fighting in the defense of our homes, our families, and prosperity."

> You come to us and tell us that the great cities are in favor of the gold standard; we reply that the great cities rest upon our broad and fertile prairies. Burn down your cities and leave our farms, and your cities will spring up again as if by magic; but destroy our farms and the grass will grow in the streets of every city in the country.

At the end of his speech, Bryan threw down the challenge to the opponents of silver.

> We will answer their demand for a gold standard by saying to them: You shall not press down upon the brow of labor this crown of thorns, you shall not crucify mankind upon a cross of gold.

With that, the convention erupted. The silver plank was adopted. On the fifth ballot, William Jennings Bryan was named the Democratic party's candidate for President.

In this cartoon, William Jennings Bryan is ridiculed for his "cross of gold" speech, which electrified the Democratic convention in 1896.

A problem for the Populists. The Democrats' choice of Bryan on a silver platform created a grave problem for the Populists. If they ran their own ticket, it was certain to split the silver vote. That would give the election to the Republicans. On the other hand, to agree to join the Democrats and support Bryan would mean the end of the Populist party. As Populist Tom Watson of Georgia put it, Populists would be playing Jonah to the Democratic whale. Further, many Populists were disturbed that the silver issue was overshadowing the many other reforms they were seeking.

In the end, most Populists felt they had no choice. Their convention voted to support Bryan. However, they would not accept the Democratic nominee for Vice President, Arthur Sewall, a Maine shipbuilder and banker. Instead, they nominated Tom Watson for that post.

The election of 1896. The campaign of 1896 was dramatic, mainly because of the emotions that were poured into it by each side. The two candidates differed greatly in style. The young and energetic Bryan traveled 18,000 miles and gave 600 speeches to 5 million listeners. McKinley ran a front-porch campaign at his home in Canton, Ohio, delivering speeches to visiting groups. However, the Republican campaign was heavily financed with a fund much larger than that of the Democrats.

McKinley won the election by more than 600,000 votes. He received 271 electoral votes to 176 for Bryan. Bryan

★23★
Benjamin Harrison
1833–1901

Born in OHIO
In Office 1889–1893
Party REPUBLICAN

Trailed Cleveland by more than 90,000 popular votes but won 1888 election with more electoral votes. Supported higher tariffs, Sherman Anti-Trust Act, and pensions for veterans.

★ ★ ★ ★ ★ ★ ★ ★

★24★
Grover Cleveland
1837–1908

Born in NEW JERSEY
In Office 1893–1897
Party DEMOCRATIC

Only President who served two terms that did not run successively. Used army to end Pullman strike. Was against annexing Hawaii. Insisted on maintaining the gold standard.

★ ★ ★ ★ ★ ★ ★ ★

★25★
William McKinley
1843–1901

Born in OHIO
In Office 1897–1901
Party REPUBLICAN

Saw United States become power in Caribbean and the Pacific following war with Spain. Reelected on prosperity platform, promising "the full dinner pail." Killed by an assassin.

★ ★ ★ ★ ★ ★ ★ ★

won most of the South and the West, but his failure to gain the support of workers and the middle class in the cities of the East and Midwest cost him the election. These people were fearful that free silver would bring higher prices. They were also attracted by McKinely's argument that a high tariff would mean jobs.

The decline of the Populists. Soon after the election of McKinley, business improved. Farm prices rose as crops in Europe failed. In one year, American wheat farmers doubled their sales to other countries. The finding of gold in Alaska, Australia, and South Africa, together with a new process for removing the metal from the ore, greatly enlarged the gold supply. This brought the increase in the currency, and the inflation, that Populists had demanded through silver. In the first ten years of the new century, the prices of crops and other farm products and the value of farmland doubled.

The 1896 election marked both the high point and the beginning of the end for the Populist party. By giving up their

Background Information

2. WILLIAM JENNINGS BRYAN (1860–1925) Bryan was born in Salem, Illinois. He practice law in Lincoln, Nebraska, until 1891, when he began the first of two terms in the House of Representatives. He ran for the Senate in 1894 but did not make it and so became a newspaper editor in Omaha. In 1901, after two unsuccessful attempts to gain the Presidency, he founded a newspaper of his own. *The Commoner* came out weekly, and in the editorials Bryan expressed his views on the control of government by big business, the coinage of money, and other matters. Bryan stayed active in the Democratic party. He ran again for the Presidency in 1908 and helped Woodrow Wilson get the nomination in 1912. Wilson appointed Bryan his secretary of state. Bryan favored arbitration as the means of settling international disagreements. Bryan negotiated thirty treaties; the Senate ratified twenty-eight of them. He resigned in 1915 because he was afraid that Wilson would involve the United States in the war as a result of the sinking of the *Lusitania.* Bryan urged United States neutrality until we were actually committed in 1917, at which point he gave his support to the President. Bryan spent his last years traveling across the country lecturing. He continued to support Populist ideals, strict interpretation of the Bible, and temperance. Shortly before he died, he assisted the prosecution in the Scopes "Monkey Trial."

Answers To Review Questions

1. City: Tweed Ring in New York looted city treasury. State: Members of New York legislature accepted bribes from railroad interests. National: Secretary of War sold trading rights with the Indians; Grant's private secretary schemed with whiskey distillers to cheat the government out of millions in taxes.
2. Under the merit system, job appointments would go to those who proved best fitted to fill the positions. Under the system of patronage, people were named to government jobs for reasons other than merit.
3. Social Gospel, preached by Protestant ministers, said that poverty caused sin. The Gospel of Wealth held that the rich were obliged to spend a portion of their earnings for the public good.
4. Railroads and grain elevator operators charged farmers high rates. Farmers were hurt by unfair taxation and the high cost of credit, deflation, and the feeling that they were not sharing in the progress of the nation.
5. World overproduction caused the price of farm goods to drop a lot faster and further than the prices of other goods. As income dropped, it became harder for farmers to pay off their debts. And it was a fact of life that farmers were almost always in debt. So farmers ended up paying back dollars worth far more than those they had borrowed.

own principles to join the Democrats, the Populists had destroyed their own party. The return of prosperity quieted the protests of most farmers. After a last, feeble effort in 1900, the Populist party disappeared.

The Populists' lasting influence. In looking back on the Populists, one can see that some of their fears were exaggerated. In many ways, they were backward looking. They rejected much that was modern in American life. They longed for that earlier, "golden age" when, they believed, farmers and honest toilers ruled the country and had high standing.

However, the Populist party was the first important American party to favor the use of government to deal with social and economic ills. "We believe," said the Populists, "that the power of government—in other words, of the people—should be expanded . . . to the end that oppression, injustice, and poverty shall eventually cease in the land." In proclaiming this, they broke through longstanding fear of government as well as the ideas of social Darwinism and of *laissez-faire*.

Conservatives at the time thought the Populists' ideas were "wild" and "radical." Yet within a decade those ideas were part of the mainstream of American reform. Many of the ideas would in time become law. However, they were carried out as part of a reform movement which was much different from that of the Populists. You will read about that new era of reform in the next chapter.

CHECKUP

1. What were the goals set forth in the Omaha platform of the Populist party?
2. In what two ways did the Populists want to increase the money supply?
3. How did the Populists fare in the elections of 1892 and 1896? Why did the Populist party disappear?

Key Facts from Chapter 28

1. Corruption in government became a major target of reformers in the 1870s and 1880s.
2. The Pendleton Act (1883) marked the beginning of the merit system, in place of the spoils system, in the federal civil service.
3. The first major reform movement to respond to the effects of industrialism was organized by farmers, mostly in the Midwest.
4. The Grange, a farm organization, was the first important reform group to concern itself with economic problems. It was also the first to represent interest-group reform.
5. The Grange and, later, the Farmers' Alliances undertook political as well as economic action. Alliance leaders founded the People's, or Populist, party.
6. The Populist party was the first important political party to favor the use of government to deal with social and economic ills.

★ REVIEWING THE CHAPTER ★

People, Places, and Events

Tweed Ring *P. 561*
Pendleton Act *P. 561*
Civil Service Commission *P. 561*
Grange *P. 567*
Populists *P. 570*
Omaha platform *P. 570*
"Crime of 1873" *P. 572*
Sherman Silver Purchase Act *P. 572*
Grover Cleveland *P. 573*
William McKinley *P. 575*

Review Questions

1. Cite examples of corruption found on the city, state, and national levels of government following the Civil War. *Pp. 561–562* Les. 1
2. How did the merit system differ from the system of patronage? *P. 562* Les. 1
3. Compare the Social Gospel with the Gospel of Wealth. *Pp. 563–564* Les. 1
4. Identify at least four major problems confronting the farmers in the late nineteenth century. *Pp. 564–567* Les. 2
5. Why was the farmer especially hurt by the continuing deflation? *P. 566* Les. 2
6. What was the original purpose of the Grange? What political and economic actions did the Grange undertake in the 1870s? *Pp. 567–568* Les. 2
7. What was the origin of the Populist party? What did Populists hope to accomplish? *P. 570* Les. 3
8. What steps did Grover Cleveland take to deal with the panic and depression of the 1890s? *P. 574* Les. 3
9. How was the gold-silver struggle finally resolved? *Pp. 575–577* Les. 3
10. What was the lasting influence of the Populist party? *P. 578* Les. 3

Chapter Test

Complete the sentences below by writing the correct answers on a separate piece of paper. Use the vocabulary that has been introduced in this chapter.

1. Two writers who wanted to reform society by eliminating poverty were Henry George and Edward Bellamy.
2. In the election of 1896, the Republican candidate, William McKinley, supported gold as the basis of the nation's economy while the Democratic candidate, William Jennings Bryan, endorsed silver.
3. The corrupt political machine that operated in New York City was called the Tweed Ring.
4. Deflation is a condition in which the amount of money in circulation per person decreases greatly, causing prices to go down and making the dollar worth more.
5. The goals of the Populist party were set forth in the Omaha platform.
6. In order to restore confidence and end the depression of the 1890s, Cleveland urged the repeal of the Sherman Silver Purchase Act.
7. Money that must be accepted in payment of debts is called legal tender.
8. Originally, the Grange was formed as a social and educational organization, but later it became involved in protests of a political and economic nature.
9. The Pendleton Act established a Civil Service Commission to draw up and administer examinations to federal government office seekers.
10. The high cost of credit hurt farmers because they were often in debt.

6. Originally, the Grange was organized to bring together farm families for social and educational gatherings. When hard times hit in the 1870s, however, the Grange used the votes of its members to support political candidates and promote laws to improve their economic position.
7. The Populist party emerged from the Farmers' Alliances, the successors of the Grange. Populists hoped to unite the industrial worker with the farmer for their common benefit and to work against corruption in government and the cominance of big business.
8. Cleveland called the Congress into special session and insisted that the members vote to repeal the Sherman Silver Purchase Act of 1890. The President believed that to repeal the act would stop the drain of gold out of the Treasury. This, in turn, would restore people's faith and confidence in the government's ability to redeem all of its notes in gold.
9. In the election of 1896, the Republicans and their candidate, William McKinley, were committed to the gold standard while the Democrats and their candidate, William Jennings Bryan, were in favor of the free coinage of silver. The victory of McKinley, coupled with new gold strikes and a new smelting process that enlarged the gold supply, settled the money debate in favor of gold.
10. It was the first important American party to favor the use of government to deal with social and economic ills. Within a decade many Populist ideas were part of the mainstream of American reform.

Background Information

1. "CLIFF DWELLERS"
Painted by George Wesley Bellows (1882–1925), "Cliff Dwellers" (1913) shows life in the immigrant-packed Lower East Side of New York. Taught by Robert Henri, the founder of the Ashcan school of painting, Bellows used that genre in this depiction of city life. Inner cities in those days were not so much melting pots as minature maps of Europe, with each section reflecting a particular ethnic nature. Bellows himself was an excellent athlete and supported his early career by playing semi-pro baseball and basketball. His first great picture, "Stag at Sharkey's" (1907), was of a boxing match. Sports and urban life became his principal themes. A truly great career was cut short by his sudden death at age forty-two.

CHAPTER 29

THE PROGRESSIVE ERA

LESSON 1

BY THE START of the twentieth century, three forces—industrialism, urbanization, and immigration—brought shattering changes to America. To deal with the problems these forces created, a new reform movement arose. This was the movement known as *progressivism*. Some of the reform activities began before 1900, and some continued beyond America's entry into World War I in 1917. However, those dates mark the period of the progressive movement's greatest energies and accomplishments in the area of reform.

Urban Growth and Problems

Much of the progressive movement was concerned with conditions in America's cities. The last half of the nineteenth century had seen an explosion in urban growth. Cities doubled, tripled, even quadrupled their size in a decade. Between 1880 and 1890, the greatest decade of growth, Omaha's population rose from 30,500 to 140,000; Kansas City's, from 60,000 to 132,000; Minneapolis's, from 47,000 to 164,000; and Portland, Oregon's, from 17,000 to 46,000. In that same decade, many small towns became cities. The population of Birmingham, Alabama, went from 3,000 to 26,000; Wichita, Kansas, from 5,000 to 23,000; Duluth, Minnesota, from 3,300 to 33,000; Seattle, Washington, from 3,500 to 42,000.

Especially notable was the growth of very large cities. In the fifty years between 1860 and 1910, Chicago's population zoomed from 109,000 to more than 2 million; Philadelphia's tripled, to 1.5 million; and New York's grew fourfold, to nearly 5 million. In 1860, 8 percent of the population lived in cities of 100,000 or more; by 1900, 18 percent lived in such cities.

Why cities grew so fast. Why did cities grow with such breathtaking speed? Of prime importance was the railroad. Horses and boats could carry enough food to feed a small city, but not one of a million or more souls. The refrigerator car was an especially important invention. As railroads moved across the country, new cities grew up at key junctions, old cities became larger. Kansas City, Missouri, for example, got its start as a city when a railroad company decided to run its line through that town rather than through nearby Fort Leavenworth. And Chicago, already a growing city, increased greatly in size as it became the chief railroad center of the nation.

Many a city owed a good deal of its growth to a single large industry. In Pittsburgh and Birmingham it was steel; in Cleveland, oil refining. Milwaukee had beer; Omaha, meatpacking and grain selling; Minneapolis and St. Paul, wheat milling. After the turn of the century, Detroit had automobiles. Very large cities combined many functions. They were centers for railroads, industries, banking, finance, commerce, and government.

Among the advances in technology that were important to the growth of cities, four stand out: the electric street

LESSON 1 *(2 days)*

Performance Objectives

1. To explain orally or in writing the phenomenal growth of cities in the last half of the nineteenth century. **2.** To describe orally or in writing the living conditions in the cities during this period. **3.** To list several reasons for the inefficiency of city government. **4.** To explain orally or in writing America's concern with the growth of trusts and banking.

Vocabulary

Progressivism, urbanization, migration, "dumbbell" tenement, political machine, "honest graft"

Activities

1. DISCUSSION After the students have read this lesson, have them answer the Checkup questions on page 586 orally as a way to check basic understanding of the objectives. The questions could also be used as a "pop" quiz prior to discussing the material.

2. SIMULATION The simulation kit entitled *Urban America* by John A. Kappel may be used to involve 20 to 36 students in the problems and crises of cities and in the decisions that must be made to save the cities. This kit is available from Social Studies School Service, 10,000 Culver Blvd., P.O. Box 802, Culver City, California 90230.

Background Information

2. SKYSCRAPERS The first skyscrapers in the United States were built in Chicago and New York City. William Le Baron Jenney designed the first skyscraper in 1884. It was for the Home Insurance Company in Chicago. It was torn down in 1931. One of New York City's early skyscrapers was the Flatiron Building, which was twenty-one stories high and was erected in 1902. It is still standing. Iron girders provided the strong skeletons of the early buildings. Skyscrapers today have skeletons made of steel and concrete. Completed in 1931, the tallest skyscraper for many years was the Empire State Building in New York (1,250 feet; 381 meters). During the 1970s, two taller buildings were completed—the Sears Tower in Chicago (1,454 feet; 443 meters) and the World Trade Center in New York City (1,350 feet; 411 meters).

car, the elevator, steel construction of buildings, and the telephone. The first allowed cities to grow out, the second and third allowed them to grow up. Telephones made communication possible between distant points.

Where city folks came from. Where did the enormous increase in city population come from? As you read in Unit 6, one important source was immigration. A second was America's own countryside. Forty percent of the townships in the United States saw their population decline during the late 1800s. Most of the decline resulted from the movement of people to the cities. For every city dweller who moved to a farm, twenty left the farm for the city.

Alexander Graham Bell, inventor of the telephone, presides at the opening of a long-distance line. His invention was one of several developments that contributed to the growth of cities.

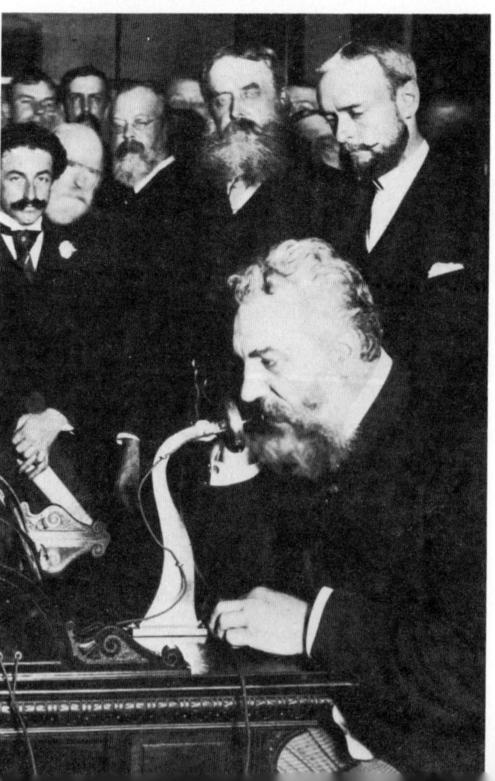

A small but growing part of this movement from farm to city was made up of black people leaving the rural South. At first, black farm families moved into southern cities, where there had been sizeable numbers of free blacks before the Civil War. In the late nineteenth century, however, there began the migration of blacks from the South to northern and western cities. Between 1870 and 1910, more than 280,000 black people left the South.

Why people left the farm. Why did so many people leave the farm for the city? The answer in part lies in the conditions of farm life. A woman named Kate Sanborn explained what life was like on many eastern farms in 1891.

> It's all work, with no play and no proper pay, . . . and how can the children consent to stay on, starving body and soul? *That* explains the 3,318 abandoned farms in Maine at present. And the farmers' wives! What monotonous, treadmill lives! Constant toil, with no wages, no allowance, no pocket money, no vacations, no pleasure trips to the city nearest them. . . . Someone says that their only chance for social life is in going to some insane asylum! There have been four cases of suicide in farmers' families near me within eighteen months.

For many people, and especially for the young, the city represented variety, social life, excitement, and bright lights. (As late as the 1930s, only 10 percent of America's farms had electricity.)

Another reason why people went to the city was economic opportunity. While a few no doubt hoped for fame and fortune, most hoped simply for a little better life than they had on the farm.

Living conditions. As thousands of newcomers poured into the cities month after month, problem piled upon problem. Street paving came nowhere near keeping up with city growth. Not one of Minneapolis's 200 miles of street was paved in 1890, and only 100 of New Orleans's 500 miles were paved. Roads were dusty in dry weather and muddy in wet. City water supplies were often inadequate and almost always impure. Factory wastes and raw sewage were poured into the same rivers from which cities drew their drinking water.

The greatest single failure of the American city was in providing housing. The problem was especially bad in the large cities, where the population was dense. On the lower East Side of New York, 330,000 people lived in one square mile (2.6 square km). One section of Manhattan averaged 986 people per *acre* (0.4 ha)! At that density, the entire population of the United States today would fit into three of New York City's five boroughs. An inspection in New York just before 1900 disclosed that in one part of the city only 300 out of 250,000 people had the use of toilets in their buildings. Under such conditions, disease spread quickly.

With the development of a new kind of building, named the "dumbbell" tenement because of its shape, crowded housing conditions went from bad to worse. Since the dumbbell tenement made possible a large number of apartments on a small plot of land, it was popular with builders. On one block, 39 dumbbell tenements were squeezed in, with 2,800 people living in them. More people were crowded into less space, as the floor plan at right indicates.

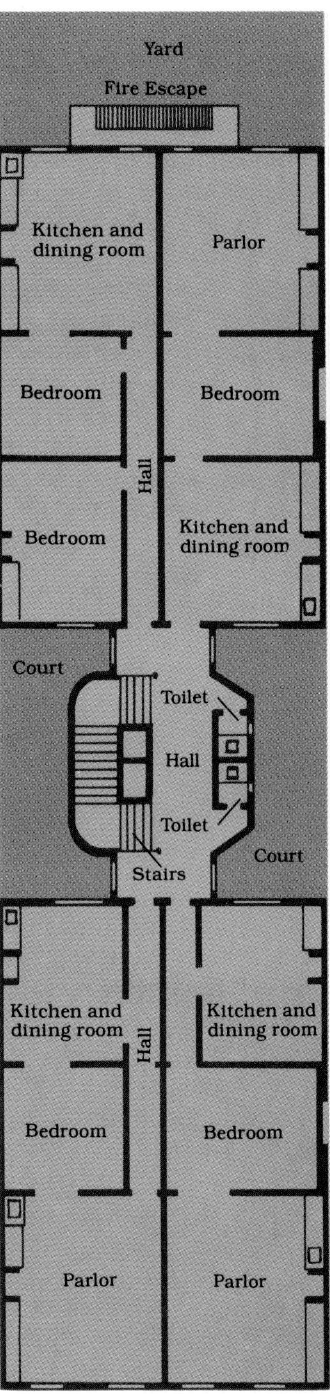

3. DISCUSSION When Boss Tweed was confronted with a list of illegalities, he is said to have asked his detractors, "What are you going to do about it?" Discuss with your students the checks and balances needed to prevent people like Tweed from getting to a position where they dare to say such a thing. How much power is too much for a city mayor? When can a leader be too weakened by restrictions on his or her power?

4. USING A CHART Have some students use the U.S. Department of Commerce's *Historical Statistics* or a similar resource to make a chart showing the growth of population in urban areas versus that in rural areas for the years between the Civil War and the present. Population information could also be charted for specific states, sections, groups, or races. Have the students make up questions for the other students to answer using the chart. Let the first students grade and return the answers.

5. ORAL REPORTS Have one or more students research the career and pictures of Jacob Riis and report to the class about him and the effects of his pictures. Jacob Riis was one of the first photojournalists to use pictures to make a point rather than to simply record an event. Encourage the students to circulate and analyze some of Riis's pictures if possible. (See Life Library of Photography, *Documentary Photography* [New York: Time-Life Books, 1972], pages 48–55.)

6. ORAL OR WRITTEN REPORTS Have students research and report on the technological improvements that were so important to the growth of cities: the refrigerator car, the electric street car, the elevator, steel construction of buildings (skyscrapers), and the telephone system. Have them give the background of the inventor and the invention and show the importance of the invention to city life.

7. FILMS *The City* (44 minutes, b&w, American Documentary Films, Inc.). Though old (1939), *The City* is an excellent presentation of the transformation of the United States from a country of small towns to an urban society. *A City Is to Live In,* The Cities series (54 minutes, color; CBS Films). *Trusts and Trust Busters,* American History series (25 minutes, color; McGraw-Hill Films).

City governments. One well-traveled college president of the time called America's city governments "the worst in Christendom—the most expensive, the most inefficient, and the most corrupt." The governments of older cities had been designed at a time when the population of each city was perhaps no more than 50,000. Now these governments had to deal with problems of cities that had grown to ten or twenty times that size. The mayor was often weak. Power lay with a few dozen city councilmen, each of whom was more interested in the neighborhood that elected him than in the needs of the city as a whole. The political machine and the boss provided what little unity there was to city government. The boss decided who would get the contracts for paving roads and sidewalks, for building sewage systems, for constructing public buildings, and for providing such public utilities as water, gas, electricity, and street railways. He exacted a high price. Those who received the contracts paid handsomely, as did the criminal rings that wanted protection against arrest.

There were still a few instances of the kind of open thievery that the Tweed Ring had performed. But most machine politicians now enriched themselves through more subtle means. One such politician, a Tammany lieutenant named George Washington Plunkitt, explained a favorite method, which he called "honest graft."

> My party's in power in the city, and it's goin' to undertake a lot of public improvements. Well, I'm tipped off, say, that they're going to lay out a new park at a certain place. I see my opportunity and I take it. I go to that place and I buy up all the land I can in the neighborhood. Then the board of this or that makes its plan public, and there is a rush to get my land, which nobody cared particular for before. Ain't it perfectly honest to charge a good price and make a profit on my investment and foresight? Of course, it is. Well, that's honest graft. . . . Wouldn't you? It's just like lookin' ahead in Wall Street or in the coffee or cotton market. It's honest graft, and I'm lookin' for it every day in the year.

The main supporters of the machine were the immigrant masses in the city. The machine befriended the immigrants. It speeded along their naturalization papers, tided them over with food and coal in hard times, and helped their children who had brushes with the law. And it got them jobs. In return, immigrants gave their grateful support on election day. The arrangement was scorned by one foreign visitor as government "of the alien, by the alien, for the alien," but it helped thousands in their struggle for survival.

The power of big business. Another problem that troubled Americans deeply at the turn of the century was the growth of bigness in business. You read about the growth in Unit 7. The size of some businesses dwarfed state governments. In 1888, for example, Massachusetts employed 6,000 people and collected taxes of $7 million. In that same year, a single railroad company with offices in Boston employed 18,000 people and had receipts of $40 million.

Of special concern was the sudden increase of business consolidations around the turn of the century. An example was the United States Steel Corporation, a holding company. With the stroke of a pen, 213 manufacturing plants and transportation companies, 78 blast furnaces, 41 mines, more than a hundred ore boats and a thousand miles of railroad, and coal and iron deposits of millions of tons were swallowed up in the nation's first billion-dollar corporation. U.S. Steel thus controlled 60 percent of America's steel production. By 1904, such basic industries as copper, oil, and steel, and such consumer industries as sugar and tobacco, had been consolidated. In 1902 or 1903, it must have seemed that all of American business would soon be controlled by a handful of giants.

The influence of banks. While the trusts were gaining greater control of industry, banks were gaining greater control over the trusts. During the depression of the 1890s, banks took over bankrupt railroads and consolidated them. By 1904, two thirds of the railroad mileage in the country was controlled by four groups of financiers. Only the banker J. P. Morgan could have afforded to buy Andrew Carnegie's steel companies. He bought them for $447 million and put together U.S. Steel. A committee of Congress in 1912 showed how far bank influence in American business had gone. According to its study, Morgan and Rockefeller banking interests controlled 341 directorships in 112 corporations—railroads, insurance companies, public utilities, manufacturing firms, and so on—worth $22 billion. That was more than a tenth of the estimated national wealth.

Such developments troubled people for a number of reasons. For one thing, monopolies were free to set their own

This giant figure of William H. Vanderbilt symbolizes the degree of control that he and his associates held over the railroads.

prices. Consumers were especially aware of this because the cost of living was rising sharply in those years. Also, people feared that those business combinations would become so powerful that they would control all of American life—politics, the marketplace, the job market, and everything else.

LESSON 2 *(1 to 2 days)*

Performance Objectives

1. To list several important muckrakers and explain each one's accomplishments. 2. To name and explain reforms made in city and state governments during the progressive era. 3. To explain orally or in writing the political and social status of American women during this period and describe the reforms accomplished.

Famous People

Ida Tarbell, Lincoln Steffens, Tom Johnson, Robert La Follette, Carrie Chapman Catt, Dr. Anna Howard Shaw, Alice Paul

Vocabulary

Muckrakers, commission form of government, city-manager system, direct primary, Triangle Shirtwaist Company fire, woman suffrage, Nineteenth Amendment

Activities

1. **FILMS** *The Progressives,* American History series (25 minutes, color; McGraw-Hill Films). *Susan B. Anthony* (19 minutes, b&w; Encyclopaedia Britannica Films).

CHECKUP

1. Why did cities grow so fast during the last half of the nineteenth century?
2. What were living conditions like in the cities? Why were many city governments inefficient?
3. Why was the growth of trusts and banks a matter of great concern to large numbers of Americans?

LESSON 2

Progressive Reform

A group of journalists known as the *muckrakers* did much to show the need for reform. Reaching millions through the new mass-circulation magazines, they exposed corruption in government and unethical methods in business.

Among the earliest and ablest of the muckrakers were Ida Tarbell and Lincoln Steffens. Tarbell wrote on Standard Oil's method of driving competition out of business. Steffens exposed the corruption of many city governments. The muckrakers aimed to stir the conscience of people and move them to action.

The nature of progressivism. It is no simple thing to describe progressivism. The movement was made up of different kinds of people seeking different reforms. Generally, progressives concentrated on problems that they had studied or worked with firsthand. Some spent their energies on reforming city government. Others turned to the areas of housing or health. Still others worked to end child labor or improve working conditions for women. Even progressives who worked in the same reform cause often had different goals. Some urban reformers, for example, wanted to make city government more democratic. Others cared far less about making government democratic than about making it efficient.

Similarly, the motives of reformers were often different. Clearly, many agreed that certain social injustices must be ended. Certain of the reformers wished to do this for humanitarian reasons. Others, however, acted out of a fear that desperate people, if not helped, might turn to radical or revolutionary ideas. And still others supported reforms because they could advance the interests of their own group. What held the reform groups together, though, was the belief that government power could and should be used to deal with America's ills.

Most progressive leaders came from the middle class of the cities. Especially important were the university-trained experts in such fields as social work, public health, conservation, and education. Like others, they saw the need to improve the conditions of urban industrial life. But they also understood that only people with training and skill like themselves would be able to do this. No ward politician had the medical knowledge to run a department of public health and prevent epidemics. Loyal party work did not qualify one to manage a school system for a city of a million, plan housing and parks, or draw up programs to conserve the forests. Because society needed their talents, these experts rose to positions of power and status.

These new reformers provided much of the drive and optimism of the progressive movement. Some reformers, like Jane Addams (see page 451) and Lillian Wald, founded settlement houses. Others, like Florence Kelley, started

Continued on page 588

The Birth of Muckraking

Reviewing plans for the January 1903 issue of *McClure's Magazine*, owner Samuel McClure discovered that this issue was to carry three articles dealing with corruption in American life. *McClure's Magazine* had exposed corruption before. Lincoln Steffens's piece titled "Tweed Days in St. Louis" had run in the October 1902 issue, and Ida Tarbell had started her series on Standard Oil the following month. But three exposés in the same issue—that seemed significant. McClure quickly penned an editorial, commenting on this theme.

> The leading article, "The Shame of Minneapolis," might have been called "The American Contempt of Law." That title could well have served for the current chapter of Miss Tarbell's *History of Standard Oil*. And it would have fitted perfectly Mr. Baker's "The Right to Work." All together, these articles come pretty near showing how universal is this dangerous trait of ours. . . .
>
> Capitalists, workingmen, politicians, citizens—all breaking the law, or letting it be broken. Who is left to uphold it? The lawyers? Some of the best lawyers in this country are hired, not to go into court to defend cases, but to advise corporations and business firms how they can get around the law. . . . The judges? . . . for some "error" or quibble they restore to office and liberty men convicted on evidence overwhelmingly convincing to common sense. The churches? We know of one . . . which had to be compelled . . . to put its tenements in sanitary condition. The colleges? They do not understand.
>
> There is no one left; none but all of us. . . . We all are doing our worst and making the public pay. The public is the people. We forget that we all are the people; that while each of us in his group can shove off on the rest the bill of today, the debt is only postponed; the rest are passing it on back to us. We have to pay in the end, every one of us. And in the end the sum total of the debt will be our liberty.

From that issue on, exposés became the hallmark of *McClure's Magazine*. As circulation soared, other magazines picked up the same theme. Thus, Samuel McClure's editorial marked the birth of the muckraking movement.

Lincoln Steffens was one of several muckrakers whose writings appeared in *McClure's Magazine*.

2. ORAL REPORT/CHART Have each student make a chart to show the muckrakers and their accomplishments. The items on the charts should include the name, the issue, the publication (the name of the magazine or novel), and result of the campaign. Not all the following muckrakers are dealt with in this lesson, but all were active at this time. Assign several students to investigate each muckraker and report to the class so that other students can complete their charts. **Journalists:** Ida Tarbell (the Standard Oil Monopoly), Lincoln Steffens (corruption in government), Burton Hendrick (insurance company abuses), Ray Stannard Baker (railroads), David Graham Phillips (corruption in the Senate). **Novelists:** Upton Sinclair *(The Jungle)*, Frank Norris *(The Octopus)*. **Painters:** (The Ashcan school of painting shows real-life slums in a naturalistic style.) John Sloan, William Glackus, Robert Henri, George Luks. Some other students might be assigned to get similar information on more recent muckrakers, such as Rachel Carson *(Silent Spring)* and Ralph Nader.

Background Information

1. MUCKRAKING The muckrakers played an important part in the reforms of the progressive era. The term itself was first used by Teddy Roosevelt, who got it from John Bunyon's *Pilgrim's Progress*, in which the "man with the muckrake" never looked up at the beautiful things but only looked down at the mud and filth. Although it was intended as a pejorative label, the term was soon proudly embraced by *McClure's* and other magazines for authors of the new exposés.

3. GUEST SPEAKER Invite someone from the local government to address the class concerning their local government. Be sure to have the class research the history of their government before inviting the speaker. It might be a good idea to make up a series of questions to ask the speaker. These might include the following: What checks and balances exist in the system? What office holds the power in the local government structure? What role does the average citizen play? If your questions need specific answers, it would probably be polite to send questions to the speaker ahead of time.

such organizations as the the National Consumers League and the National Child Labor Committee. The latter group gathered statistics on child labor and lobbied with legislatures to end the practice. A reform group led by housing experts wrote New York City's housing reform act of 1901 and got it passed. The law outlawed the dumbbell tenement and required better fire escapes, indoor plumbing in each apartment, and open spaces outside the buildings.

Rescue workers hunt for victims in the wreckage at Galveston, Texas, after a hurricane and tidal wave in 1900. The disaster brought into existence the commission form of city government.

Reform of city government. In a number of cities, reform forces won control of the government. In each case, they were led by a strong mayor. One such person was Tom Johnson, mayor of Cleveland from 1901 to 1909. After making a fortune in street railways, Johnson was converted to reform by reading Henry George's *Progress and Poverty*. Believing that citizens should become involved in public issues, Johnson held public meetings in a circus tent. There, citizens and city officials discussed ideas about dealing with Cleveland's problems. Johnson also attracted able people to take important city jobs and brought honesty and efficiency to Cleveland's government. Other reform mayors included Hazen Pingree of Detroit and Samuel "Golden Rule" Jones of Toledo, Ohio.

Progressives also brought about two important forms of city government. The first, the commission form of government, came about by accident. In 1900, Galveston, Texas, was hit by a hurricane and tidal wave from the Gulf of Mexico. One third of the city was destroyed. When the outdated and corrupt city government was not able to deal with the emergency, the state appointed a commission of five experts to run the city departments. The people of Galveston were so pleased with the results that they changed the form of their city government permanently. Other cities, mostly of small or medium size, followed. By 1914, some 400 cities had adopted commission government.

The second form of government begun by progressives was the city-manager form. In this system, elected commissioners appoint a nonpartisan expert to run the city with modern business methods. First used in Staunton, Virginia, in 1908, the city-manager system really caught on after it was adopted in 1913 by Dayton, Ohio.

Reform of state government. At the beginning of this unit you read that the two main goals of reform in America have been to increase democracy and to make for human betterment. Much of progressive reform on the state level fitted into these two goals. To bring about lasting reform in state government, progressives believed they must destroy the alliance between the machine and the special interests. Government could then be returned to the people.

Progressives tried to do this through a number of devices meant to allow the voice of the ordinary voter to be heard. Many states adopted the initiative and the referendum (see page 571). These, you will recall, allowed citizens to get around a corrupt legislature and get rid of poor elected officials. Another device was the *direct primary* by which voters, rather than a convention controlled by special interests, would choose party candidates. By 1916, all but three states had a form of direct primary for at least some of their state and national offices. Through the Seventeenth Amendment (1913), United States senators were chosen by direct vote of the people rather than by the state legislatures.

For human betterment. Progressives sought to achieve their second broad goal—making for human betterment—by using the power of the state. Many of their laws aimed, as one writer has put it, to "heal the casualties" of industrial society. By 1914, every state but one prohibited the employment of children under a certain age, usually fourteen in northern states, twelve in southern states. At the same time, states required children to attend school until they reached legal working age. Other laws limited the number of hours children under sixteen could work, usually ten hours a day, and prohibited their working in certain dangerous jobs.

Several states set maximum hours of work for women in the early 1900s. Several states also passed laws setting minimum wages for women. States also tried to limit hours of work for men, but the Supreme Court upheld only those that dealt with dangerous jobs. Otherwise, the court said, the state could not interfere with the "liberty" of a man to work any number of hours he wished.

States also improved their laws requiring safety inspections of factories. Many of these improvements came after a fire in the Triangle Shirtwaist Company in New York in 1911. This fire took the lives of 145 women, trapped in the factory by locked doors leading to the fire escapes. To "help heal the casualties of industrialism," twenty states by 1915 were giving aid to widows with dependent children, and to families in which the husband was physically unable to work. The aim of these laws, called mothers' assistance acts, was to help children in their own homes instead of moving them into institutions for the poor. By 1920, all but five states provided compensation for workers injured on the job.

At the same time, many states started conservation programs. They also expanded public education, and set up

4. ORAL OR WRITTEN REPORTS Throughout the history of the United States, women have been among the leading reformers. Although some of these are identified in other places in this textbook, it might be effective to have the class realize the extent of women's contributions to reform by dealing with these women as a group. In teaching "women's history," the danger of treating the topic as a "special item" must be weighed against the myth that "there aren't any important women anyway." You must handle the topic in the way that will be most beneficial to your class. The following is a list of women and the areas of reform in which they were active from the 1890s to the 1920s. The list is not complete but includes names that students should be able to find in women's history books without much trouble. Have the students investigate the reformers' lives, accomplishments, and the obstacles they had to overcome to make their contributions. This activity could also be done in conjunction with Activity 2 on the muckrakers. **Reformers:** Florence Kelley (social reform), Frances Willard (temperance), Carry Nation (temperance), Jane Croly (women's clubs), Mary Church Terrell (civil rights), Jane Addams (social reform), Grace Dodge (vocational training), Sara Josephine Baker (child hygiene), Albion Fellows Bacon (housing conditions), Margaret Dreier Robins (Women's Trade Union League), Emma Goldman (labor radicalism), Mary Harris "Mother" Jones (labor agitator), Charlotte Perkins Gilman (economic rights of women), Elizabeth "Nellie Bly" Cochrane (reporter), Carrie Chapman Catt (suffrage),

Susan B. Anthony (suffrage), Elizabeth Cady Stanton (suffrage), Lucy Stone (suffrage), Harriet Blatch (suffrage), Alice Paul (suffrage), Lucy Burns (suffrage), Anna Howard Shaw (suffrage). If you think it is appropriate for your class, you could add Victoria Woodhull and/or Margaret Sanger.

5. READING FOR INFORMATION Have several students read Eric Goldman's *Rendezvous with Destiny* (New York: Vintage Books, 1956), pages 128–133, for an interesting description of Tom Johnson and Robert La Follette.

Background Information

2. WOMAN SUFFRAGE In colonial times some of the colonies did allow women to vote if the women owned property, but after the Revolution, suffrage was denied in all states except New Jersey (which took away the vote in 1808). The fight for woman suffrage symbolically started with the Seneca Falls convention in 1848. Some progress was made when Wyoming became a state in 1890 and gave women the right to vote. By 1917, twelve states had followed Wyoming's lead. In January 1918, President Wilson reluctantly gave his support to a constitutional amendment granting women the right to vote. He had opposed it for political and personal reasons (the Southern Democrats were strongly opposed, and he felt the states should control suffrage). In 1919, the amendment made it through both houses of Congress and went to the states for ratification. Wisconsin was the first to ratify it, and Tennessee completed the necessary thirty-six (three fourths of the states). The Nineteenth Amendment was officially added to the Constitution on August 26, 1920.

This lad is working as a helper on the night shift in a glass factory in Virginia about 1900.

commissions to regulate the rates of railroads and public utilities. Under Governor Robert M. La Follette, the state of Wisconsin became a laboratory for these and other progressive reforms. Iowa and Oregon were not far behind.

Woman suffrage. One final democratic reform of the progressive era was woman suffrage. After women failed to win the vote in the Fourteenth Amendment, the women's movement split into two groups in 1869. One group concentrated on winning the vote. The second group sought not only the vote but other rights as well. This split divided the energies of the movement until the two groups joined forces once more in 1890. At that time, they formed the National American Woman Suffrage Association. By 1900, women had won the vote in eleven states. All but one of them were west of the Mississippi River.

But winning the vote one state at a time was a long, slow process. In many states, opposition was strong. It came not only from persons with traditional attitudes about the role of women, but from interest groups who feared women's influence in politics. The liquor interests, for example, feared that women might vote for prohibition. That was because women were members of, and leaders in, the main prohibitionist groups. Some industry leaders worried that women would be "softhearted" and vote for reforms in child-labor laws and other laws affecting working conditions.

With a new generation of leaders, including Carrie Chapman Catt, Dr.

Anna Howard Shaw, and Alice Paul, women launched a major effort to win the vote through a Constitutional amendment. Their techniques ranged from petitions, education, and gentle persuasion to parades, picketing, and hunger strikes. To dramatize their demands, a few women even chained themselves to the White House fence.

The position of women was made stronger by their growing role in all areas of American life. During the progressive era, women were active in many reform movements. By 1910, about 80 percent of public-school teachers were women. It was hard to argue that persons trusted to educate the young could not be trusted with the vote. During World War I, many women held jobs in factories making war goods. Even President Wilson, who had not at first favored woman suffrage, came around to supporting it. In 1920, the Nineteenth Amendment, giving women the right to vote, was added to the Constitution.

With this victory, the old split in the women's movement returned. Some women felt they should now fight for other feminist goals. But most women felt they had achieved what they had set out to win, and were satisfied. A drive led by Alice Paul in the 1920s for an equal-rights amendment to the Constitution made little headway. Some of its chief opponents were women who believed that if the amendment should be adopted, they would lose the special protection that women had under many laws.

CHECKUP

1. What part did the muckrakers play in promoting reform?
2. What reforms did progressives accomplish in city and state governments?
3. What reforms pertaining to women did the progressives bring about?

In 1917, women demonstrate near the White House for voting rights, a goal they achieved in 1920.

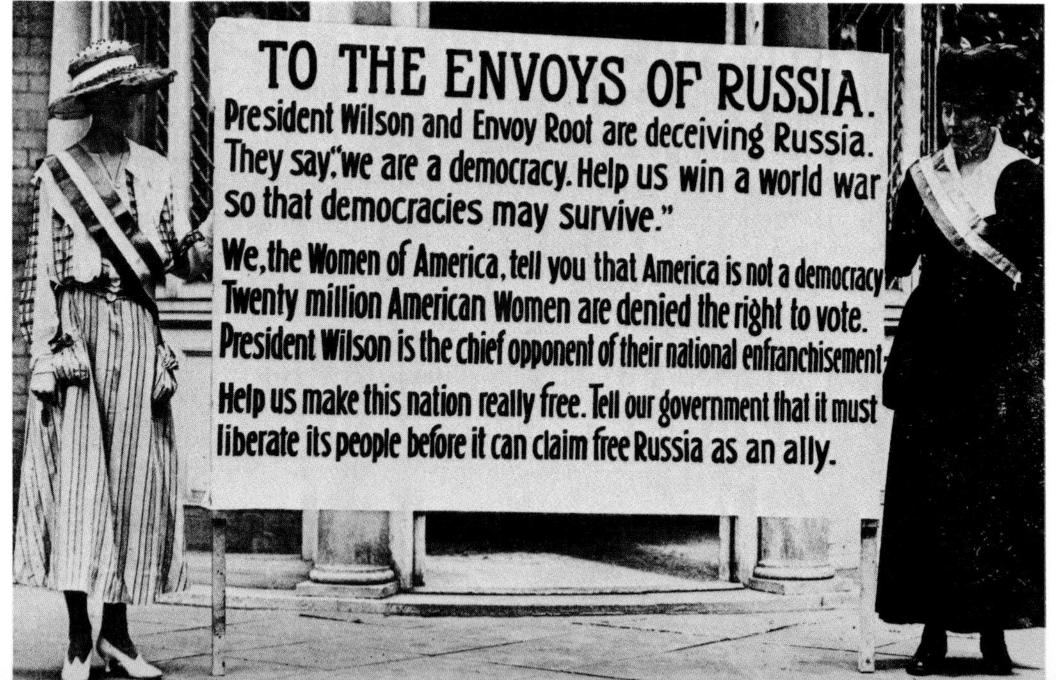

TO THE ENVOYS OF RUSSIA.
President Wilson and Envoy Root are deceiving Russia.
They say:"we are a democracy. Help us win a world war
so that democracies may survive."
We, the Women of America, tell you that America is not a democracy
Twenty million American Women are denied the right to vote.
President Wilson is the chief opponent of their national enfranchisement
Help us make this nation really free. Tell our government that it must
liberate its people before it can claim free Russia as an ally.

6. DISCUSSION After the class has read pages 588–589 and reviewed pages 561–562, discuss why reform was needed in city and state governments. What suggestions did reformers have for correcting the problems? How did each reform try to prevent a particular problem?

7. DISCUSSION In 1920 the Nineteenth Amendment, giving women the right to vote, was finally passed. It had been introduced in Congress as early as 1878 and had become known as the Susan B. Anthony amendment as it was reintroduced each session. Ask the class why it might have taken so long to be passed by Congress. Who might have opposed it? Why? Why did it not die out completely? Why was it finally approved?

Background Information

3. PICTURE In June 1917, President Wilson met with leaders of Russia's provisional government, which had taken over after the fall of the Czar in March. Wilson was trying to keep Russia in the war to maintain an eastern front against Germany. Although it tried to continue the war, the government collapsed and was overthrown in November 1917. The Bolsheviks made peace with the Germans and withdrew from the war. "Free Russia" referred to the institution of woman suffrage in Russia by the provisional government. Wilson ended his lack of support for woman suffrage in 1918.

LESSON 3 *(2 days)*

Performance Objectives

1. To compile a list of the major reforms accomplished during the progressive era. **2.** To explain orally or in writing why Theodore Roosevelt has been called "the first modern President." **3.** To compare and contrast in an essay the progressivism of Teddy Roosevelt with that of Wilson. **4.** To compare and contrast orally Populism and progressivism.

Famous People

Theodore Roosevelt, Upton Sinclair, William Howard Taft, Woodrow Wilson

Vocabulary

Trusts, Northern Securities Company, combination in commerce, trust regulation, anthracite coal strike, arbitration, Square Deal, Hepburn Act, Elkins Act, Interstate Commerce Commission, *The Jungle,* Pure Food and Drug Act, Payne-Aldrich Bill, Mann-Elkins Act, Progressive party, New Nationalism, New Freedom, Underwood-Simmons tariff, income tax, Federal Reserve Act, Clayton Anti-Trust Act of 1914, Federal Trade Commission

Background Information

1. "T.R." AND CARTOONISTS Theodore Roosevelt was a favorite of political cartoonists throughout his career. His rimless glasses, bushy moustache, and energetic personality were easy to capture in caricature. One cartoon, showing T.R. with a bear cub, prompted a new toy—the "Teddy Bear."

LESSON 3

Progressivism's High Tide

Progressivism on the national level began with the Presidency of Theodore Roosevelt of New York. The son of well-to-do parents, Roosevelt set out at an early age to be "a member of the governing class." He entered Republican politics in New York and served in the state legislature. Then, in succession, he became a United States civil service commissioner, New York police commissioner, and assistant secretary of the navy. Returning from the Spanish-American War as a hero in 1898, he was elected governor of New York.

Roosevelt proved to be an effective reform governor. In 1900 the boss of New York's Republican party, anxious to get rid of this reformer, arranged to have him nominated for Vice President on the Republican ticket headed by President McKinley. Senator Mark Hanna, a close friend of McKinley and the head of the Republican National Committee, was upset. "Don't you realize," he warned, "that there's only one life between this madman and the White House?"

Only a few months after McKinley began his second term, he was shot by a crazed man and died soon afterward. At the age of forty-two, Roosevelt became President, the youngest man up to that time to occupy the office. T.R., as the newspapers called him, proved to be anything but a madman. Roosevelt was careful to stay on good terms with Republican leaders in both houses of Congress. He had the upcoming presidential election in mind. Four Vice Presidents had moved up when Presidents died, but none had been elected President in his own right—or even nominated by his party.

T.R. and the trusts. Though Roosevelt moved cautiously, two actions in 1902 showed that he had ideas different from those of most earlier Presidents about the proper roles of the federal government and the Chief Executive. In one action, he ordered the attorney general to bring suit under the Sherman Anti-Trust Act of 1890 to break up the Northern Securities Company. This company had recently been formed by two great railroads and two banking houses, one of which was J. P. Morgan's. The purpose of the merger was to gain control over the railroads of the Northwest.

Roosevelt's move startled many, for the Sherman Act had been almost a dead letter since its passage. In *E. C. Knight* v. *U.S.* (1895), the Supreme Court had ruled that the law did not apply to the sugar trusts, which controlled 98 percent of the sugar refining in the country. The Court's reasoning was that the Sherman Act applied only to combinations in commerce, not those in manufacturing.

In 1904, the Supreme Court ordered that the Northern Securities Company be dissolved. However, the ruling had less than the intended effect. The bankers and railroaders in that company found other ways to achieve consolidation. But the case was important for reviving the Sherman Act and for making clear to business leaders that they were accountable before the law. During his administration, Roosevelt brought suit against forty-four trusts.

These actions earned Roosevelt the nickname "the Trustbuster." That was ironic, for while Roosevelt believed that illegal acts of trusts should be prosecuted, he did not believe that trusts should be "busted" if they conducted their affairs properly. Bigness, Roosevelt felt, was a natural and desirable development in modern business. The efficiencies of mass production could benefit consumers and help the country compete with other nations for world markets. The proper course, believed Roosevelt, was for the federal government to *regulate* the trusts rather than to break them up.

Settling the coal strike. Another action by Roosevelt in 1902 involved the anthracite coal strike in Pennsylvania. Mining was probably the most dangerous occupation in America. Hours were long, and the work was backbreaking. For this work, miners averaged about $600 a year. Most of the Pennsylvania mines, as well as the company towns, were owned by the Reading Railroad. In turn, the railroad was dominated by J. P. Morgan.

In the spring of 1902, the miners struck for a 20 percent wage increase, an eight-hour day, and union recognition. The strike dragged on for five months, with the mine operators not budging. But as winter neared, Roosevelt decided to step in. He got the mine operators to agree to *arbitrate*—that is, to submit the dispute to the judgment of an impartial person or group. The strike then ended. The union won a 10 percent wage increase and a nine-hour day, but no union recognition. The most important thing, however, was that a President had intervened in a major labor dispute in the public interest. Unlike Presidents Hayes and Cleveland, who had used troops to break strikes, Roosevelt had used federal power to insist on a fair settlement.

Theodore Roosevelt brings the trusts under control with the approval of a smiling Uncle Sam.

The idea of an impartial but active government, prepared to step in to see that everyone was treated fairly in an industrial society, was what Roosevelt meant by the phrase "the square deal." In 1904, Roosevelt was nominated for the Presidency. Campaigning on the theme of the Square Deal, he was elected by a large margin over a conservative Democratic candidate, Alton B. Parker of New York. Now President in his own right, Roosevelt set about winning enactment of his program.

The Hepburn Act. One of the most important measures sought by Roosevelt was a strengthening of the regulation of

2. FOOTBALL One of the minor reforms made by Theodore Roosevelt was in the "brutal" sport of football. The first college football game was played by Rutgers and the College of New Jersey (now Princeton) in New Brunswick, New Jersey, on November 6, 1869. Rutgers won, 6 goals to 4. The sport, a derivative of English rugby, became extremely violent. In 1905, eighteen players were killed in football games and 159 were severely injured. President Roosevelt, keenly interested in sports, authorized an investigation of the sport and drastic reforms resulted. Still, the changes did not eliminate injuries from the game. One player who suffered a serious knee injury a few years later was a young West Point cadet named Dwight David Eisenhower.

Background Information

3. THEODORE ROOSEVELT A sickly youth, Roosevelt exercised in a private gymnasium that his father had built for him until he overcame all his physical weaknesses except nearsightedness. An equally dedicated student, Roosevelt got good grades at Harvard, from which he graduated in 1880. In the same year, he married Alice Lee and soon entered politics. In 1884 the double tragedy of his wife's and mother's death led Roosevelt to give up politics and buy a ranch in the Dakota Territory. He became a regular cowpuncher, often riding for sixteen hours a day, and once even aiding law officers in catching a band of outlaws. Roosevelt's frontier days led him to become a staunch conservationist and protector of public lands. He even went camping in the national parks when he was President.

The severe winter of 1885–1886 ended Roosevelt's cattle days, so he returned to New York City, where he failed to win the mayoral office but did win the hand of Edith Carow, whom he married in 1886. They had five children of their own plus Alice Roosevelt, the daughter who had been born two days before Alice Lee Roosevelt died.

the railroads. The Interstate Commerce Act of 1887 had never been effective. The act forbade railroads to give rebates to favored shippers, to charge more for short hauls than for long ones, and to enter pools to keep rates high. A commission had been set up to see that railroad rates were "reasonable." But the law did not say what "reasonable" was. The law also allowed railroads to delay putting new, lower rates into effect while they appealed to the courts. Such appeals often took years.

In 1903 the Elkins Act had made it illegal once again for railroads to give rebates, this time making both the railroads and the shippers liable to prosecution. This law, a reform of sorts, was actually drafted by an attorney for the Pennsylvania Railroad. The railroads themselves were the main supporters of the law, because without it they had been unable to resist the demands of large shippers for rebates. Meanwhile, farmers, small shippers, and the public at large continued to complain about rates. Moreover, rebating continued.

That was the situation when Roosevelt asked for a law that would give the Interstate Commerce Commission real power. The result was the Hepburn Act. It gave the Interstate Commerce Commission the power to investigate complaints and to set new rates. Railroads might still appeal to the courts, but in the meantime, the new rates were to be in effect. Further, the burden of proof in court was not to be on the railroad. The Interstate Commerce Commission's power was also extended over interstate pipelines and sleeping cars.

How was this reform brought about? In large part, it was achieved because it had the support of a President who believed in using federal power to regulate industry. He dramatized the reform and made compromises when necessary. Then he persuaded the lawmakers to support it. The law passed also because there was a broad public feeling that tighter regulation of the railroads was long overdue. Finally, it passed because those who depended on the railroads—farmers, small shippers, and businesses such as the new mail-order houses of Sears, Roebuck and Montgomery Ward—lobbied with Congress for fair, stable rates and better regulation.

Protecting the consumers. An important part of progressive reform was its concern for the protection of consumers. Around the turn of the century, a number of experts had shown that the food industry was using several harmful

This ad appeared in a catalog of one of the mail-order houses that sought railroad reforms.

preservatives and additives. They urged a law that would regulate the food and drug industries.

In 1905, President Roosevelt proposed such a law, but Congress took no action. Then in 1906, Upton Sinclair's book *The Jungle* appeared. Its descriptions of filthy conditions in the meat-packing plants created an uproar. Roosevelt ordered an investigation, which proved Sinclair's account to be true. The President then threatened to make public the entire report unless opposing members of Congress promptly agreed to a law. They did, and in June 1906, Congress passed the Meat Inspection Act and the Pure Food and Drug Act.

Conserving natural resources. Roosevelt also took important steps in the field of conservation. Forests were being cut at a shocking rate. The guiding rule in mining minerals appeared to be today's profits rather than tomorrow's needs. No one proposed that natural resources not be used; the challenge was to make the wisest use of them. This meant replanting forests and protecting watersheds as trees were harvested.

Understanding the need for trained experts in these fields, Roosevelt appointed such people to government jobs. Gifford Pinchot, an expert in forest management, was put in charge of the national forests. Roosevelt also increased the amount of national forestland by about 400 percent. In addition, he withdrew from public sale millions of mineral-rich acres as well as thousands of water-power sites. In 1908, a White House conference of governors and conservation experts focused national attention on the need for conservation.

The first modern President. Theodore Roosevelt has been called "the first modern President." Claiming that the President was the "steward of the people," he expanded the role of the President. With Theodore Roosevelt began the tradition of an active federal government led by a strong Chief Executive. Without those changes, little reform could have occurred then or since on the federal level.

Much of Roosevelt's support of progressive reform grew from his sense of right and justice. It also derived partly from his fear that if nothing were done, the victims of industrialism might turn to socialism. Thus he viewed the Hepburn Act as heading off a demand for government ownership of the railroads. He saw his role in the anthracite coal strike as standing "between them [the mine owners] and socialist action."

The Taft administration. In 1908, William Howard Taft of Ohio was handpicked by Roosevelt to be the Republican nominee for President. For the third time, William Jennings Bryan was the Democratic choice. Taft defeated Bryan and succeeded Roosevelt as President. Roosevelt expected that Taft would continue the Roosevelt policies. There is no doubt that Taft honestly intended to do so. However, Taft lacked Roosevelt's political skills and was more conservative by nature. Therefore, he soon alienated progressives. Although Taft called for a reduction in the tariff, he signed the Payne-Aldrich bill, a law that raised duties. He became involved in a fight over conservation policies between Secretary of the Interior Richard Ballinger and Chief Forester Gifford Pinchot. When he fired Pinchot, President Taft

As a reform police commissioner in New York, Roosevelt even went out into the streets at night to find evidence of corruption and end it. He received the job of assistant secretary of the navy as a grudging reward for his campaigning for William McKinley in 1896. After service in Cuba in the Spanish-American War, the Rough Rider returned to New York and was elected governor, even though the party machine feared his independence. In 1900 the Vice Presidency looked like a good place to use his popularity and keep him out of the way, so the Republicans nominated him to run with McKinley. After McKinley's death, Roosevelt promised to maintain McKinley's policies but soon set his own ideas in motion. When he ran for election on his own in 1904, his $2\frac{1}{2}$-million-vote plurality was the greatest margin of victory in an election to that time.

With an active President, six children, and innumerable pets and friends in the White House, life was never dull there. Ponies and snakes were invited inside, tennis was regularly played on the lawn, and winter hikes often included swimming across the Potomac River through chunks of ice. Roosevelt lost the use of his left eye while boxing with a military aide in the White House, but he did not reveal the fact for fifteen years. The marriage of his daughter, "Princess Alice," to Nicholas Longworth was a historic Washington social event. Many of Alice's pithy comments on people and events since then have also been historic.

Background Information

4. WILLIAM HOWARD TAFT Taft never wanted to be President; his ambition was to be a justice of the Supreme Court. He was a lifelong Republican from a prominent Ohio family active in politics. His career was largely a series of appointments to increasingly important positions. He entered public life as an assistant prosecuting attorney. Later he was appointed a collector of internal revenue in Ohio. Several years later he sat as a judge on the superior court of Ohio. This position and the Presidency were the only public offices he held by popular election. Next he was an extremely successful solicitor general. He won fifteen of the eighteen government cases he argued in his first year. Taft then spent eight years as a federal circuit court judge. In 1900, President McKinley appointed Taft the first civil governor of the Philippines. Taft was a brilliant colonial administrator who made many improvements, including creating a limited form of self-government for the colony. He became Theodore Roosevelt's secretary of war in 1904. He supervised the construction of the Panama Canal and set up the government of the Canal Zone. As President, along with the accomplishments mentioned in the text, Taft saw a law passed that mandated the public disclosure of campaign expenses in federal elections. After leaving office in 1913, he taught constitutional law at Yale. When Warren Harding appointed Taft as Chief Justice on the Supreme Court in 1921, Taft felt that he had finally achieved his life's ambition. He retired in 1930 because of ill health.

appeared, incorrectly, to be an enemy of conservation.

During Taft's administration, Congress passed the Mann-Elkins Act, further strengthening the Interstate Commerce Commission. It established postal savings banks, an idea dating back to the Populist reformers. It approved and sent to the states one proposed constitutional amendment allowing an income tax and another for the direct election of senators. Taft approved of these changes. Yet progressives in Congress felt that Taft's support for their goals in these and other matters was less than complete. Even the fact that Taft started twice as many antitrust suits in four years as Roosevelt had in seven earned him few points with progressives.

The election of 1912. Roosevelt, who returned to the country in 1910 after a year abroad, was disappointed with Taft's performance. Roosevelt soon became openly critical of his old friend, and in 1911 the two split. Early the next year, Roosevelt announced that he would fight Taft for the Republican nomination for President. Although Roosevelt won most of the delegates in states that had primary elections, Taft forces controlled the party machinery at the convention, and Taft became the Republican candidate. Roosevelt's supporters walked out of the convention. Some weeks later they started the Progressive party, with Roosevelt as its candidate for President.

The platform of the Progressive party was a remarkable expression of the two main goals of American reform. It aimed to make political life more democratic by the initiative, referendum, direct primary, woman suffrage, and a law to end certain corrupt election practices. To improve the lot of people in industrial society, the platform favored all the advanced reforms of the day. The platform promised the eight-hour day, minimum wages for women, and an end to child labor. It would regulate industries to prevent "accidents, occupational disease, overwork, and involuntary unemployment." And it favored workmen's compensation laws, unemployment insurance, and old-age pensions.

The split in the Republican ranks assured the Democrats of victory. They

By 1912, Theodore Roosevelt and President William H. Taft, once completely in accord, found themselves headed in opposite directions on the political path.

nominated Woodrow Wilson, the progressive governor of New Jersey and a former president of Princeton University. The campaign was lively, with most attention focusing on Wilson and Roosevelt. Roosevelt called his program the New Nationalism, and Wilson called his the New Freedom. One of the main issues on which they differed was the trusts. Roosevelt restated his well-known position that size itself was not bad and that the trusts should be regulated rather than broken up. Wilson, on the other hand, believed that trusts were illegal and should be broken up.

Wilson, with but 42 percent of the vote, still had 2 million more votes than Roosevelt and won easily. Taft trailed badly. Eugene Debs, who had been sent to prison for his part in the Pullman strike, ran as the Socialist candidate and received nearly 900,000 votes, about 6 percent of the total. The combined votes for Wilson, Roosevelt, and Debs showed how deep the progressive tide was running in America.

Tariff and banking reforms. Wilson proved to be an able President. Using remarkable political skills, he got Congress to pass two important measures in short order. The first was the Underwood-Simmons tariff, placing duties at the lowest level in two generations. The law included an income tax, the first under the new Sixteenth Amendment.

The second major law was the Federal Reserve Act, which reformed the banking system of the country. Banking remained a private business, but it was placed under federal supervision. The law created twelve regional banks rather than one central bank. Each of the regional banks was owned by the member banks in the system. Over the whole system stood the Federal Reserve Board, whose members were appointed by the President. The law corrected a number of the problems of the banking system, though not all. Most important, the Federal Reserve Board, a government agency, could decide when and whether to expand the money supply and also could regulate interest rates.

Progressivism under Wilson. In dealing with the trusts, Wilson at first sought a measure that followed his campaign position but soon switched course. The result was two laws. One was the Clayton Anti-Trust Act of 1914. Intending to maintain competition and prevent trusts, it listed and prohibited certain unfair business practices. But the

Wilson signs the first federal child-labor act. It was, however, declared unconstitutional.

Background Information

5. THE BULL MOOSE PARTY
In the election campaign of 1912, the Progressive party came to be known also as the Bull Moose party. The name came from Roosevelt's answer to a newspaper reporter's query concerning how he felt—"I feel as strong as a bull moose."

Activities

1. READING FOR INFORMATION After the students have read this lesson, have them make a list of the laws identified in this lesson, including a short explanation of what each law was designed to do and under whose administration it was passed.

2. ESSAY Using the notes taken in Activity 1 and the information in their textbooks, the students should write essays comparing and contrasting the progressivism and personalities of Roosevelt and Wilson.

3. DISCUSSION After students have read page 599, have them compare and contrast progressivism and Populism. Good documents to use for this discussion are the Omaha platform of 1892 and the Progressive party platform of 1912. (See Commager's *Documents of American History,* 325 and 384.)

4. RESEARCH/ORAL OR WRITTEN REPORT In almost every article or book that purports to rate American Presidents, Theodore Roosevelt gets high grades. Have some students research several of these evaluations to report on why he is so highly rated and why he has been called "the first modern President." Someone else might try to determine why he is the only "modern" President to be immortalized on Mount Rushmore.

5. LISTENING FOR INFORMATION Read excerpts of *The Jungle* by Upton Sinclair. You may wish to give the book to a student to read and locate interesting sections for the class to hear.

★26★

Theodore Roosevelt

1858–1919

Born in NEW YORK
In Office 1901–1909
Party REPUBLICAN

Youngest man (42) ever to become President. Favored regulating "big business." Started Panama Canal. Had Pure Food and Drug laws enacted. Worked to conserve natural resources.

★27★

William H. Taft

1857–1930

Born in OHIO
In Office 1909–1913
Party REPUBLICAN

Recommended by Roosevelt as his successor. Acted against the trusts. Set up Department of Labor. His conservatism caused split in Republican party, and he was not reelected.

★28★

Woodrow Wilson

1856–1924

Born in VIRGINIA
In Office 1913–1921
Party DEMOCRATIC

Undertook many reforms. During World War I, became strong leader of Allied cause. His program became basis of peace, but his health broke down while seeking support for League of Nations.

★ ★ ★ ★ ★ ★ ★ ★

law made these practices illegal only when they tended to reduce competition. This last phrase made the law almost useless, for it was always a matter of judgment whether in any given case the practice was responsible for reducing competition.

The second law dealing with trusts was the Federal Trade Commission Act, also passed in 1914. With this act, Wilson adopted Roosevelt's views of the need to regulate big business. The law set up a five-person commission with power to investigate business behavior and to order firms to stop practices and procedures that the commission found to be illegal.

Wilson's progressivism was more limited than that of many others. With the enactment of the tariff, banking, and antitrust laws, he considered his program complete. Progressives in Congress, however, went on to enact other laws in the next two years, and Wilson accepted them. One new law reformed the dreadful working conditions aboard American ships. Another made it easier for farmers to get low-cost credit.

The first Wilson administration marked the high tide of progressivism. In 1916, Wilson could rightly claim that the Democrats had not only carried out their own campaign promises but a good part of the Progressive party platform as well. In that year, Wilson successfully sought a second term, defeating Charles Evans Hughes, the Republican candidate, in a very close election. But with the beginning of Wilson's second term, the conduct of foreign affairs took most of his time. Although reform continued for some years. America's entry into World War I in 1917 marked the end of the progressive period.

Populism and progressivism. Was there a connection between Populism and progressivism? As you have seen, progressives adopted as their own a number of the Populists' demands, such as the initiative and the referendum, the income tax, and direct election of senators. The two reform movements also shared the belief that government should be an active force in the lives of people. One writer of the time said that progressive leaders had "caught the Populists in swimming and stole all of their clothing except the frayed underdrawers of free silver."

Yet the differences between these two reform movements may have been greater. Populism was mainly a rural protest movement of the farmers of the South and West. Progressivism was urban in its concerns, its leadership, and its support. Whereas Populists looked backward to a "golden" age, progressives accepted the challenge of dealing with the new age of industrialism and urbanism. While Populism glorified the average person, progressivism looked to the experts to deal with modern problems.

Progressivism differed from other varieties of nineteenth-century reform in another important way. Many earlier reform movements had been based on the belief that there was a single cure for all of society's ills: reform the civil service; stop the sale of liquor; tax away the unearned value of land; coin silver at 16 to 1. Progressives saw the world as much too complex for single answers. Nor did they expect to come up with final solutions. Their aim, instead, was to find a way to manage the many problems of an ever-changing world.

The limits of progressivism. The democratic reforms of the progressive period have had, as one writer has said, "only a marginal effect on the conduct of American government." Political organizations found ways to get their own candidates chosen through the direct primary. Senators elected directly seemed to be neither much better nor much worse than senators chosen by state legislatures. Old-line politicians soon learned how to manipulate the referendum and the initiative to confuse the voters and get what they wanted. City machines and bosses did not disappear. The reason they survived was simply stated by the political boss of Boston: "There's got to be in every ward somebody that any bloke can come to—no matter what he's done—and get help. Help, you understand; none of your law and justice but help."

Further, some people were dismayed at how limited were the many progressive reforms. The socialist Upton Sinclair, author of *The Jungle*, spoke for many of these. Sinclair had hoped to

6. ORAL OR WRITTEN REPORT In 1957 a United States Senate special committe, headed by the junior senator from Massachusetts, John F. Kennedy, was instructed to select the five most outstanding senators in American history. The five selected were Henry Clay, Daniel Webster, John C. Calhoun, Robert A. Taft, and Robert M. La Follette. La Follette's ideas are under study in this lesson and were also studied in the previous one. Have one or several of your students research Senator La Follette and his career to determine what caused him to be selected for such an elite group.

7. READING FOR INFORMATION For a primary-source look at the progressive era, have your students read the following documents in Commager's *Documents of American History:* 363, "*Northern Securities Company v. United States*"; 369, "The Conservation of Natural Resources" (Roosevelt's Seventh Annual Message to Congress); 370, "Declaration of the Conservation Congress"; 374, "Taft's Defence of the Payne-Aldrich Tariff"; 379, "Roosevelt's Candidacy in 1912"; 380, "Roosevelt and the New Nationalism"; 384, "The Progressive Party Platform"; 402, "The Federal Trade Commission Act"; 403, "The Clayton Anti-Trust Act."

8. FILMS *Theodore Roosevelt—American* (20 minutes, b&w; U.S. Department of Defense). *Theodore Roosevelt* (26 minutes, b&w; McGraw-Hill Films).

Answers To Review Questions

1. Immigrants, farm families, and blacks from the rural South were especially attracted to life in cities. To them, the city represented economic opportunity, variety, social life, and such technological innovations as electricity.
2. Unpaved streets, pollution, inadequate water supplies, poor housing, corrupt city governments.
3. The political machine helped immigrants obtain naturalization papers, gave them food and fuel in hard times, aided their children who had brushes with the law, and most importantly helped immigrants find jobs.
4. (a) City government: Brought about two forms of government: commission and city-manager. **(b)** State government: Brought about widespread use of the direct primary, initiative, and referendum. **(c)** Worked for the passage of a variety of legislation to aid and protect workers, the disadvantaged, and children.
5. Brought suit against the Northern Securities Company and broke that trust; intervened to settle coal strike of 1902; passed the Hepburn Act to strengthen the ICC; passed the Meat Inspection Act and the Pure Food and Drug Act; made the public aware of the need for conservation measures.
6. Roosevelt believed that government should be prepared to step in and insure justice and fair treatment for everyone. The President should provide strong leadership for the federal government.

arouse Americans to the horrible conditions in which men, women, and children found themselves working in the meat-packing industry.

> I had not been nearly so interested in the condemned meat as in something else, the inferno of exploitation. I realized with bitterness that I had been made a celebrity, not because the public cared anything about the workers, but simply because the public did not want to eat tubercular beef.

He had aimed at the hearts of Americans, Sinclair observed sadly, and had hit them in their stomachs.

Nor did state and federal efforts to end the trend toward business consolidation succeed, as you read in Chapter 25. Indeed, in the interest of getting full production from American factories in World War I, President Wilson dropped his opposition to the growth of large business combinations.

Despite these limitations, progressivism was an important reform movement. It showed the way toward more systematic government of our cities and the use of experts to solve all manner of problems. It shattered the old idea that there was no public responsibility to deal with large social problems. If its humanitarian laws were not always well enforced and well funded, they were nonetheless important breakthroughs. Once on the law books, they could always be improved later, and they often were. And if progressives did not succeed in fully regulating business, they at least established the principle that business must be accountable. Finally, progressives committed the federal government to an active role in social reform and in all other affairs. Many of these achievements would serve as important precedents in the next major era of American reform, the New Deal. You will be reading about that in the next chapter.

CHECKUP

1. Why has Theodore Roosevelt been called "the first modern President"? In what ways did he support progressive reform?
2. How did the progressivism of Woodrow Wilson compare with that of Theodore Roosevelt?
3. How were the reform movements of progressivism and populism alike? How were they different?

Key Facts from Chapter 29

1. The progressive reform movement dealt mainly with the problems created by the growth of industry and cities.
2. Progressivism looked to experts to solve the problems brought about by industrialism and urbanism.
3. Progressivism committed the federal government to an active role in carrying out reforms.
4. Progressivism established the principle that business must be held accountable for its actions.
5. Theodore Roosevelt began the tradition of an active federal government with a strong Chief Executive.

★ REVIEWING THE CHAPTER ★

People, Places, and Events

Seventeenth Amendment *P. 589*
Nineteenth Amendment *P. 591*
Theodore Roosevelt *P. 592*
Hepburn Act *P. 593*
William Taft *P. 595*
Mann-Elkins Act *P. 596*
Woodrow Wilson *P. 597*
Underwood-Simmons Act *P. 597*
Clayton Anti-Trust Act *P. 597*
Federal Trade Commission *P. 598*

Review Questions

1. Which people were espcially attracted by life in cities? Why? *P. 582* Les. 1
2. What were the drawbacks associated with urban living? *P. 583* Les. 1
3. Why did immigrants generally support the city political machine? *P. 584* Les. 1
4. List the reform accomplishments of the progressives in each of the following areas: **(a)** city government, **(b)** state government, **(c)** human betterment. *Pp. 588–590* Les. 2
5. Briefly identify the important actions taken by the government at Theodore Roosevelt's direction. *Pp. 592–595* Les. 3
6. What were Roosevelt's ideas about the proper roles of the federal government and the President? *P. 595* Les. 3
7. Why was there doubt as to whether or not Taft was a progressive? *P. 595* Les. 3
8. Under the banner of the New Freedom, what legislation did Woodrow Wilson support? *Pp. 597–599* Les. 3
9. What were the provisions of the Federal Reserve Act? *P. 597* Les. 3
10. How might you evaluate the success of progressivism? *Pp. 599–600* Les. 3

Chapter Test

Match the description in the first section with the individual associated with it from the second section. Write the letter of the individual after the number of the description, using a separate piece of paper. Note: Individuals may be used more than once or not at all.

1. Founded a settlement house
2. Active in woman-suffrage movement
3. Signed the Payne-Aldrich Tariff
4. Wrote *The Jungle*
5. Nicknamed "the Trustbuster"
6. Led progressive reforms in Wisconsin
7. Reform governor of New York
8. Wrote exposé on Standard Oil
9. Campaigned on slogan of "square deal"
10. Called *muckrakers*
11. Progressive governor of New Jersey
12. Encouraged government intervention in the coal strike of 1902
13. Progressive Party candidate in 1912
14. Succeeded Roosevelt as President
15. Supported the Hepburn Act
16. President shot to death
17. Forester fired from office
18. Urged Congress to pass the Federal Reserve Act
19. President during World War I
20. Reform mayor of Cleveland

a. Jane Addams
b. Carrie Catt
c. Tom Johnson
d. Florence Kelley
e. R. La Follette
f. William McKinley
g. Gifford Pinchot
h. Hazen Pingree
i. T. Roosevelt
j. Upton Sinclair
k. Lincoln Steffens
l. William Taft
m. Ida Tarbell
n. Woodrow Wilson

7. Although Taft supported many progressive measures, he also signed the Payne-Aldrich Tariff calling for higher rates and became involved in a fight over conservation policies. Both situations put him in the position of appearing to be against such popular progressive ideas as tariff reform and conservation.
8. Wilson supported the Underwood-Simmons tariff, the Federal Reserve Act, the Clayton Anti-Trust Act, and the Federal Trade Commission Act.
9. Banking remained a private business under federal supervision. Twelve regional banks were created and placed under control of the Federal Reserve Board whose members were appointed by the President. The Federal Reserve Board had the responsibility of regulating the amount of money in circulation and fixing interest rates.
10. Political reforms enjoyed only limited success because politicians soon found ways to circumvent the laws. Little success was achieved in controlling business combinations, either. However, progressivism shattered the old idea that government had no public responsibility to deal with social problems. Some beginnings were made in humanitarian and business reforms and the foundations were laid for New Deal reform legislation.

Answers For Chapter Test
1. a **2.** b **3.** l **4.** j
5. i **6.** e **7.** i **8.** m
9. i **10.** j, k, m **11.** n
12. i **13.** i **14.** l **15.** i
16. f **17.** g **18.** n **19.** n
20. c

Background Information

1. VANITY FAIR COVER
This cartoon was painted for the cover of the October 1934 issue of *Vanity Fair.* Started in 1914, *Vanity Fair* was one of several important literary publications in the early twentieth century. Posters of old covers of some of these magazines, such as *Vogue* and *Vanity Fair,* have recently been in style as works of art. This particular cartoon is making fun of the many New Deal agencies, all of which were known by their initials. These initials are being tattooed on a less than enthusiastic "Uncle Sam." The tattoo artist, "Dr. Braintrust," represents Roosevelt's advisers from the academic world.

CHAPTER 30

THE NEW DEAL

LESSON 1

THE ERA OF REFORM that has left the greatest mark upon America came in the 1930s. It occurred in the Presidency of Franklin D. Roosevelt and came to be known as the New Deal. The New Deal drew on the achievements and goals of earlier reform eras, but it also charted new directions for American reform.

The Great Depression

Much of the New Deal was a response to the Great Depression, about which you read in Chapter 26. That depression, you will remember, began with the stock-market crash of 1929. Herbert Hoover had become President only a half year before the depression began. Americans had always believed that in hard times the role of the government was to cut expenses to the bone and wait until a depression ran its course. This had been the approach of President Rutherford B. Hayes in the depression of the 1870s and President Grover Cleveland in the depression of the 1890s.

Hoover's approach. President Hoover refused to accept this view. He believed that certain things could be done to end business downturns, or at least to keep them from becoming worse. Very soon after the stock-market crash, he called on businesses to keep people employed and not cut wages. He urged businesses, states, and cities to go ahead with their plans for new construction and even to hasten them. He also asked Congress to increase its own spending for public works—roads, post offices, and the like. At the same time, the Federal Farm Board, an agency created by a new farming law, entered the market and bought up large amounts of wheat, cotton, and other crops. This was intended to reduce supplies and thus keep crop prices up. Hoover's aim in all that he undertook was to keep up purchasing power.

To reach this goal the President counted on the voluntary cooperation of thousands of businesses. For Hoover, the voluntary approach was basic to the American way. He believed that the government could and should deal with the depression by pointing out what needed to be done and encouraging private groups to do it. But he felt the government should not become too directly involved in the economy. How well Hoover's program worked, therefore, depended on how willing and able the businesses of the country were to cooperate voluntarily.

A further decline. For nearly a year, many businesses did keep employment and spending up. When conditions did not improve quickly, however, employers were faced with losses as business fell off. They felt they now had no choice but to cut spending and production and to lay off workers if their companies were to survive. Also, despite the purchases of the Federal Farm Board, farm prices continued to slide, cutting the farmers' incomes. As purchasing power of workers, farmers, and business people declined, the depression became worse.

LESSON 1 *(2 days)*

Performance Objectives

1. To compare and contrast in an essay Herbert Hoover's and Franklin Roosevelt's philosophies concerning government involvement in the economy. **2.** To list and identify actions taken by Roosevelt to deal with banking, farming, and industrial recovery and to aid the victims of the depression.

Famous People

Herbert Hoover, Franklin D. Roosevelt, Henry Wallace

Vocabulary

New Deal, Great Depression, voluntary approach, Hawley-Smoot Tariff, Reconstruction Finance Corporation, Federal Home Loan Bank Act, polio, first hundred days, bank holiday, fireside chats, "brain trust," Securities and Exchange Commission (SEC), Federal Emergency Relief Act (FERA), Civilian Works Administration (CWA), Civilian Conservation Corps (CCC), Home Owners Loan Corporation (HOLC), Tennessee Valley Authority (TVA), Agriculture Adjustment Act (AAA), National Industrial Recovery Act (NIRA), National Recovery Administration (NRA)

Activities

1. USING A CHART Have the class make a chart of the New Deal legislation enacted during the first hundred days. Items for the chart should include the name of the act, its "alphabet" designation, a brief explanation of what it did, and what problem it was designed to solve. This chart should be continued in the next lesson. Since there are so many "alphabet agencies," you may want to note those that you think your students should remember. After students have completed the chart, it can be used as a basis for discussing the magnitude of the New Deal and evaluating its successes and failures.

2. FILMS *The New Deal,* American History series, (25 minutes, color; McGraw-Hill Films). *Election of 1932,* Making of the President Voter Education series (20 minutes, b&w; Films, Inc.). *Franklin D. Roosevelt, Part I: The New Deal* (26 minutes, b&w; McGraw-Hill Films). *Life in the Thirties,* Project 20 series, (53 minutes, b&w; NBC).

★29★

Warren G. Harding

1865–1923

Born in OHIO
In Office 1921–1923
Party REPUBLICAN

Campaigned on slogan "Back to Normalcy." Deferred to Congress, which raised tariffs and put quotas on immigration. His unwise appointments brought on scandals. Died in office.

★ ★ ★ ★ ★ ★ ★ ★

★30★

Calvin Coolidge

1872–1933

Born in VERMONT
In Office 1923–1929
Party REPUBLICAN

Became President upon Harding's death. Supported business. Favored economy and reduced national debt. Served during time of prosperity, but farmers did not share in it.

★ ★ ★ ★ ★ ★ ★ ★

★31★

Herbert C. Hoover

1874–1964

Born in IOWA
In Office 1929–1933
Party REPUBLICAN

Supported aid for farmers, but depression struck and economic conditions became worse. Steps to reduce unemployment were not effective. Defeated in attempt for second term.

★ ★ ★ ★ ★ ★ ★ ★

Meanwhile, Congress responded to the demands of manufacturers and workers to protect American industry from foreign competition. It passed the Hawley-Smoot Tariff in 1930, the highest tariff in our history. Other countries responded by throwing up tariff walls of their own, thus shrinking the market for American goods. Congress also increased its spending for public works, but not by a large amount. Hoover and most members of Congress believed that too much spending would unbalance the budget.

Some limited successes. The Hoover administration did help certain large businesses, such as banks and insurance companies. If such companies went under, millions of depositors and policyholders would suffer losses. The whole economy might be brought down. In 1931, Congress carried out Hoover's plan to set up the Reconstruction Finance Corporation (RFC). This agency was given the power to lend $2 billion to help financial institutions, railroads (the largest employers of the time), and other such businesses.

By another act, Congress indirectly aided homeowners who could not keep up their mortgage payments. It did so by helping the lending institutions that held mortgages. The Federal Home Loan Bank Act allowed the government to lend $125 million to savings and loan associations, savings banks, and insurance companies. Thus those groups would not be forced to foreclose on mortgages—that is, to take the property of those unable to make payments.

Who should provide relief? One of the greatest problems in the depression was providing help for the millions who were unemployed. President Hoover had long worked in humanitarian causes, and he was deeply concerned about those families in need. He strongly believed, however, that providing relief was the job of private charities and local and state governments—not the federal government. If the federal government gave money directly to the needy, Hoover believed it would sap their initiative, their self-reliance, and their self-respect.

Hoover may have been correct in this belief. But what else was there to do to help the millions who were without jobs? The problem was so massive that it overwhelmed the charities and local governments. In many cities, funds ran out and people had to go without the food and clothing they needed.

During the first year or two of the depression, most Americans probably agreed with Hoover's approach. They shared his feelings about self-reliance, voluntary cooperation, a limited role for government, and the balanced budget. By 1931, however, dissatisfaction was growing. Eight million people were out of work, and there was no end of the depression in sight. Many people felt that the government must do more than it had done in past depressions. Further, many found it hard to follow Hoover's reasoning about relief. Why, they wondered, would receiving money from the federal government lead to a loss of self-respect, while receiving money from a charity or local government would not?

It was without much optimism, then, that the Republican party in 1932 nominated Herbert Hoover for a second term as President. Franklin D. Roosevelt was the Democratic candidate.

Franklin D. Roosevelt. Like his distant cousin Theodore, Franklin D. Roosevelt was a member of a wealthy New York family. Unlike Theodore, however, Franklin D. Roosevelt was a Democrat. He had served in the New York legislature and was assistant secretary of the navy for seven years under President Wilson. In 1920 the Democrats gave him their vice-presidential nomination. But the ticket of Cox and Roosevelt was swamped, and Warren G. Harding became President.

The following year, Roosevelt was stricken with polio. He lost the use of both legs, yet he remained active in politics. In 1928 he was elected governor of New York, and in 1930 he was reelected by a large margin. It was during his second term as governor that Roosevelt became the Democratic nominee for President. In accepting the nomination, he promised a "new deal for the American people."

Roosevelt's approach. In his campaign, Roosevelt gave little indication of the program that was to come. Walter

3. DISCUSSION In the year that Roosevelt came to office, 273,000 American families had been evicted from their homes for nonpayment of rent or mortgage. Twenty-five percent of the American work force was unemployed. What kind of a person does it take to begin to find solutions to such problems? What kind of people would a President have to find to help him? Where does a President begin? Ask your students to discuss this problem, which is faced by many new Presidents. For an indication of the character and style of the new President, read to the class the following quotation by John Gunther after observing a Roosevelt press conference. "In twenty minutes Mr. Roosevelt's features had expressed amazement, curiosity, mock alarm, genuine interest, worry, rhetorical playing for suspense, decision, playfulness, dignity, and surpassing charm. Yet he *said* almost nothing. Questions were deflected, diverted, diluted. Answers—when they did come—were concise and clear." (*Roosevelt in Retrospect* [New York: Harper & Row, 1950])

4. **DISCUSSION** With so many unemployed and under-skilled young people in America today, should there be a new organization like the Civilian Conservation Corps? Have your students find out what the CCC was like. Ask: Do you know anyone who served in it? Would you join something like it today?

5. **BOOK REPORT** Have some of your students read John Kenneth Galbraith's *The Great Crash, 1929* (Boston: Houghton Mifflin Company, 1955) and report their findings to the class.

6. **LISTENING FOR INFORMATION** Read to your students from Eric Goldman's *Rendezvous with Destiny*, pages 255–268, for an excellent description of the first hundred days of the FDR administration.

Lippmann, one of the country's leading newspaper writers, dismissed Roosevelt as "a pleasant man who, without any important qualifications for the office, would very much like to be President." Yet in two important speeches, Roosevelt revealed a great deal about his approach. In Georgia he said:

> The country needs bold, persistent experimentation. It is common sense to take a method and try it. If it fails, admit it frankly and try another. But above all, try something.

And in San Francisco:

> Every man has a right to life, and this means that he has also a right to make a comfortable living. . . . Our government . . . owes to everyone an avenue to possess himself of a portion of [America's abundance] sufficient for his needs, through his own work.

In the November election, Franklin D. Roosevelt won by a large majority over Herbert Hoover. There were also big Democratic majorities in both houses of Congress. Hoover and the Republican party were victims of the depression.

In the months between the election and Roosevelt's inauguration on March 4, 1933, government drifted, and the depression grew worse. Farm prices fell further, and thousands lost their farms. Unemployment climbed to between 13 and 15 million, fully 30 percent of the work force. Since 1930 more than 5,500 banks had shut down. At those banks still open, long lines of worried people waited to take out their savings. To stop the panic, many states ordered a temporary closing of the banks. As Roosevelt took the oath of office on March 4, banks were closed in forty states.

The First Hundred Days

In his inaugural address, Roosevelt expressed his faith that the nation would revive and prosper. He told his listeners that "the only thing we have to fear is fear itself." And he promised that he would ask Congress to act speedily. But if it did not, said Roosevelt:

> I shall not evade the clear course of duty that will then confront me. I shall ask the Congress for the one remaining instrument to meet the crisis—broad Executive power to wage a war against the emergency, as great as the power that would be given to me if we were in fact invaded by a foreign foe.

The President had struck the right note. People were looking for confidence and leadership. Roosevelt offered both. Nearly a half million letters poured into the White House after the speech.

The banking crisis. The *first hundred days* of the Roosevelt administration produced some of the most far-reaching laws in American history. The President turned first to the banking crisis. He proclaimed a "bank holiday," during which all the banks in the country would be closed. He then called Congress into special session and gave it a draft of an emergency banking bill. The bill prohibited the hoarding of gold and gave the Treasury Department the power to examine banks before they could reopen. In less than eight hours the bill passed both houses of Congress and was signed into law by the President. As an example of how government could act in a crisis, the action was electrifying. It was also a bit frightening. There had not been enough time to print copies of the bill for each member of

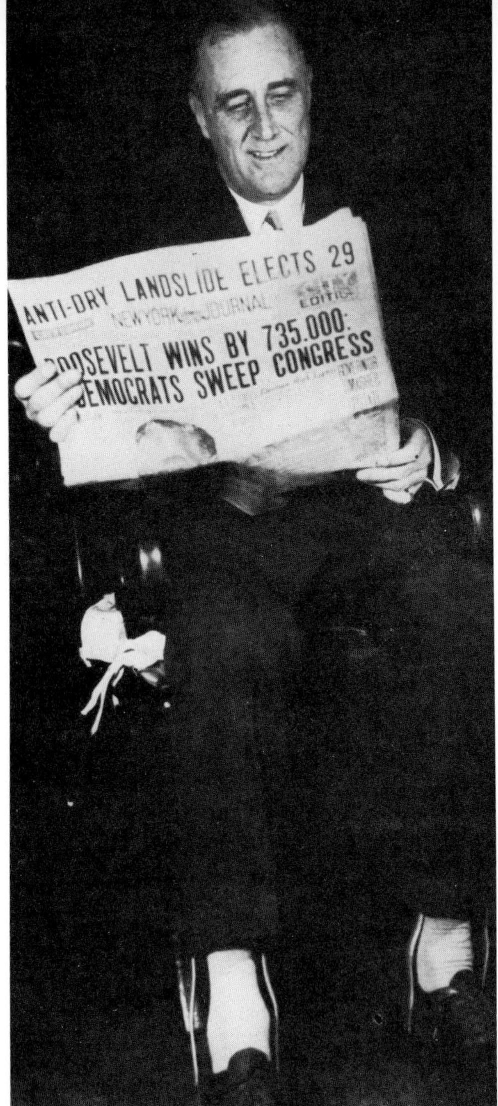

Franklin D. Roosevelt reads about his reelection as governor of New York in 1930. Two years later, in the midst of the Great Depression, he would win his first term as President.

Congress, and most of them voted without having read it.

On Sunday evening, March 12, the President made the first of many radio "fireside chats" to an audience of 60 million people. He assured them that any bank that was allowed to open again would be safe. During the next three days, three fourths of the banks in the Federal Reserve System opened. There were no runs on banks, and people once more deposited their savings. The banking crisis had passed.

Banking reforms. Roosevelt sent Congress a flood of plans for dealing with the depression and for reform. Many of them were the work of what came to be called the Brain Trust, a group of advisers drawn from universities.

Several of the proposals were aimed at reforming banking and the securities business. So that banks could not again speculate in stocks with depositors' money, they were required to separate investment activities from their regular commercial banking. The Securities Act required that full information be given the public on any new issue of stock that corporations offered for sale. Later, another law created the Securities and Exchange Commission (SEC), an agency to regulate the business of buying and selling stocks. Congress also created the Federal Deposit Insurance Corporation (FDIC) to insure small depositors against loss.

Helping the needy. Another group of acts were aimed at relieving human suffering. Most important of those were laws to help those without jobs. For example, the Federal Emergency Relief Act (FERA) gave half a billion dollars to the states for relief payments to the unemployed. One of the aims of the act was also to increase purchasing power. Over the next three years, $3 billion would be spent on this program.

Background Information

2. MARY MCLEOD BETHUNE (1875–1955) In 1904 Mary Bethune opened a school for black girls in Daytona Beach, Florida. In 1923 the school merged with a boys' school to form a college now called Bethune-Cookman College. Mary Bethune remained its president until 1942. She served three Presidents in government posts; for example, she was Roosevelt's Special Adviser on Minority Affairs. She was also the founder of the National Council of Negro Women.

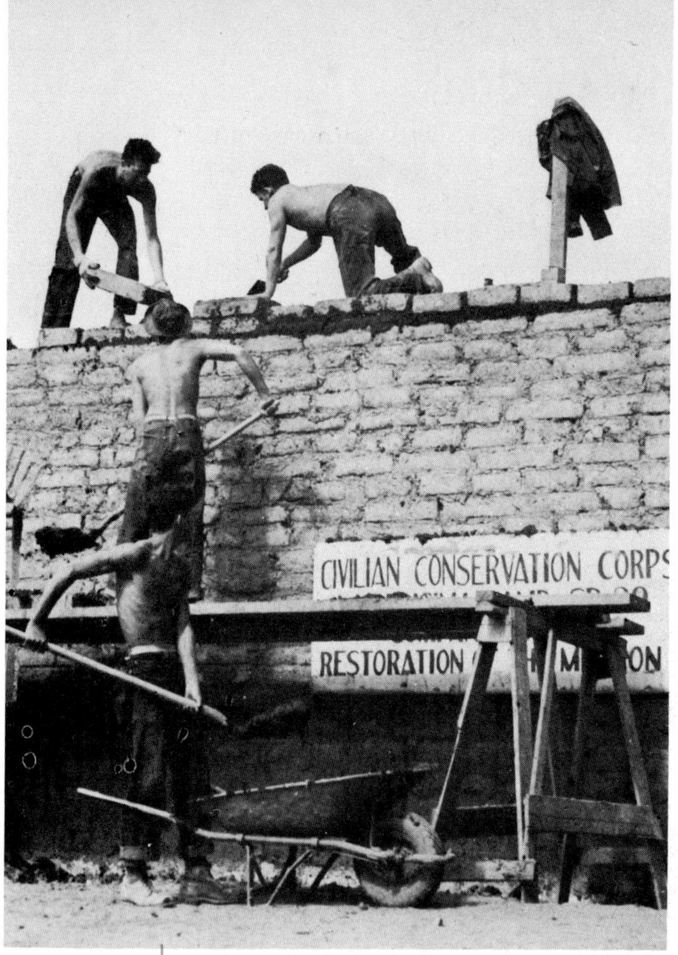

These young men of the Civilian Conservation Corps are putting up a barracks wall at their camp near Santa Barbara, California.

While Roosevelt knew how important it was to get money into the hands of the poor, he also knew that people wanted jobs, not handouts. The Civil Works Administration (CWA) was set up to create temporary jobs for people. During the winter of 1933–1934, CWA workers built or repaired a half million miles of road, 40,000 schools, and several thousand playgrounds. The program was criticized for its high cost and the way it was run, and in 1934 Roosevelt ended the program. But CWA had been a remarkable experiment. For the first time, the federal government had hired the unemployed directly. For the 4 million workers and their families who were helped through the winter, the program came as a godsend.

The CCC and the HOLC. Still another creation of the first hundred days was the Civilian Conservation Corps (CCC), combining unemployment relief and conservation. From needy families, the CCC hired 250,000 young men, ages eighteen to twenty-five, to work on conservation projects in rural areas. During the ten-year life of the CCC, more than 2.5 million young men worked in it. They stocked streams with a billion fish, built 30,000 wildlife shelters, thinned millions of acres of trees, and planted more than 2 billion seedlings. More than half of all the forest planting in all American history was done by the CCC.

Homeowners were among those to feel the depression most painfully. Unable to meet payments on mortgages, 250,000 families had lost their homes in 1932. Congress therefore created the Home Owners Loan Corporation (HOLC). It allowed homeowners to lower their mortgage payments and spread them out over a longer time, at a low interest rate. In three years, HOLC refinanced the mortgages of more than a million Americans who might otherwise have lost their homes.

The Tennessee Valley Authority. The most sweeping reform measure of the hundred days was the creation of the Tennessee Valley Authority (TVA). During World War I, the government had begun a dam and had built two plants for making nitrates (used in explosives) on the Tennessee River at Muscle Shoals, Alabama. At the end of the war some government officials, including President Harding, favored selling the plants and the dam to private business. That plan, however, was blocked by Senator George W. Norris of Nebraska and other progressives in Congress. They wanted the government to keep the dam and to provide cheap electric power for people in the area. Twice Congress passed bills to do this, but Presidents Coolidge and Hoover vetoed them.

The Tennessee Valley Authority of the New Deal used Muscle Shoals as its base, but it went beyond even Senator Norris's dreams. Roosevelt proposed a great effort in regional planning in the seven-state area of the Southeast through which the Tennessee River flowed. This region was one of the poorest sections of the country. Through a network of dams and canals, TVA would control flooding, conserve soil and forests, aid navigation, produce and sell cheap electric power and fertilizer, and help industry and business to grow throughout the region. Over the years,

The Tennessee Valley Authority developed industrial and recreational sites in seven states.

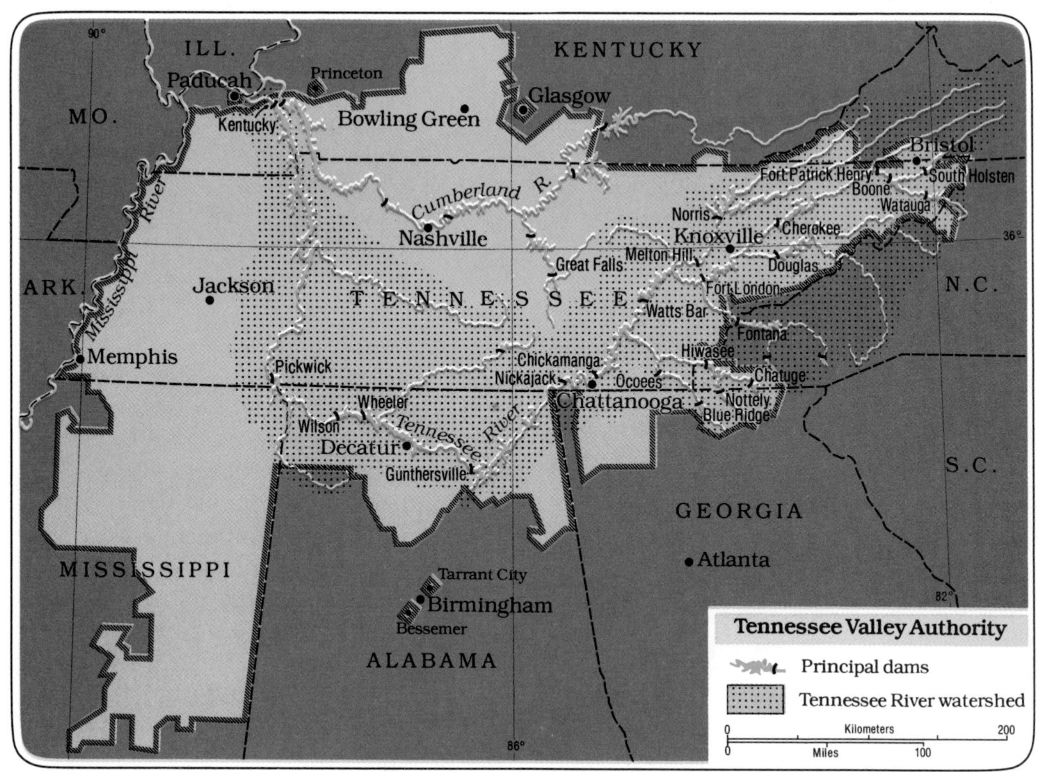

7. ESSAY After the students have read and discussed this lesson, assign an essay question designed to compare Hoover's and Roosevelt's plans for ending the depression and their philosophies concerning government involvement in the economy. If desired, the essay question could ask for opinions concerning the long-range (thirty or forty years) effects of the philosophies. (For example, Has the New Deal encouragement of dependence on the federal government to solve personal problems contributed to the weakening of the family structure in America?)

8. DISCUSSION Some critics of FDR's social reforms claim that it was World War II, not the New Deal, that brought America out of the depression. Ask your students what they think. What are the implications if the criticism is true?

9. DISCUSSION Ask: Which is more dangerous—a depression or uncontrolled inflation? Have students let their imagination flow, but occasionally bring them back to economic reality. In the discussion, encourage them to read and study the classics of economics.

Background Information

3. PICTURE In the 1930s the Farm Security Administration appointed an economist from Columbia University, to publicize the need for the program to relocate farmers who had lost their land. Roy Stryker, the economist, decided to use photography as his main weapon. He brought together a group of photographers and sent them around the country to get pictures that would make people understand the need for massive help for these displaced farmers. The result was a collection of 150,000 pictures that captured the feeling of a time as well as any pictures ever taken. Several of the photographers became famous for their techniques. Walker Evans's pictures established the pattern of sharp detail and harsh reality that is characteristic of the collection. Ben Shahn was already a well-known painter when he took three months off to try photography. His were among the most persuasive pictures taken. Dorothea Lange's photographs best expressed the humanity of the people suffering through the depression; they were credited with responsibility for getting migrant camps set up in 1935. Russell Lee succeeded in making the life and suffering of rural America understandable to a largely urban population. For pictures and more information, see these volumes in the Life Library of Photography: *Photojournalism* (New York: Time-Life Books, 1971), pages 118–134, and *Documentary Photography* (1972), pages 66–84.

TVA has accomplished many of those goals. In doing so, it has raised the standard of living for millions of people.

The Agricultural Adjustment Act. To bring about farm recovery, the Agricultural Adjustment Act (AAA) was passed. It brought together a variety of ideas for ways to raise farm income. The main method was to raise prices by limiting production. This was to be accomplished by offering a benefit payment to raisers of staples who agreed to cut down their acreage or, in the case of those who marketed hogs or dairy products, their production. The program was voluntary. Before any crop program could start, a majority of the growers of that crop had to vote for it. The program was to be paid for by a tax passed on to the consumer in higher prices.

At the time the act was passed (May 1933), a new crop was already in the ground and millions of pigs had been born. If the crops and animals were allowed to grow to maturity, they would simply add to the surpluses that were pushing down prices. The AAA therefore paid farmers to plow under a quarter of their crops and to kill more than six million pigs. A severe drought on the Great Plains made it unnecessary to reduce the planting of wheat.

At a time when millions were hungry and poorly clothed, many people were shocked by the destruction of pigs and crops. As criticism of the AAA mounted, Secretary of Agriculture Henry Wallace lashed out:

> I suppose it is a marvelous tribute to the humanitarian instincts of the American people that they sympathize more with little pigs which are killed than with full-grown hogs. Some people may object to killing pigs at any age. Perhaps they think that farmers should run a sort of old-folks home for hogs and keep them around indefinitely as barnyard pets.

In fact, however, Wallace too was troubled by having to take these actions to bring about scarcity. Millions of Americans would ever after associate the AAA with crop destruction, even though this was the only time it was carried out.

The AAA was reasonably successful in raising farm income. Prices improved in 1933 and 1934, though the decline in production owed more to the drought in the Midwest than to AAA programs. Rural debts declined sharply, and cash income increased by 50 percent between 1932 and 1936, though it still was well below the 1929 level.

The NIRA and NRA. The measure meant to bring about industrial recovery was the National Industrial Recovery Act (NIRA). Business had long held that recovery was being slowed by too much competition. The act therefore allowed industries to limit competition by the use of codes of fair practice. Through these codes, industries could prohibit price-cutting, divide markets, and plan production—thereby avoiding overproduction. Because such acts violated the antitrust laws, those laws would be suspended for companies that entered into codes. Once companies were sure that they could make a profit, it was hoped they would again hire workers, make goods, and set out on the road to recovery. To balance the advantages to business, the NIRA required that each code set minimum wages and maximum hours for workers in that industry. It also guaranteed workers the right of collective bargaining.

The drawing up of the codes and their operation would be supervised by the National Recovery Administration (NRA). To head the NRA, Roosevelt chose General Hugh Johnson, who had helped direct the production effort during World War I. Johnson held parades and rallies to whip up public support for NRA and to get businesses to enter into codes quickly. Businesses that did so were allowed to display the NRA symbol, a blue eagle with the words "We Do Our Part." The public was urged to deal only with those firms. Within four months, more than 700 industries had agreed to join in self-regulation. In all, 2.5 million firms and 22 million workers were eventually brought under NRA codes.

To prime the pump—that is, get money into the hands of people who would buy goods and services as the industries started up again—the second part of the National Industrial Recovery Act created the Public Works Administration (PWA). It was authorized to spend $3.3 billion on roads, buildings, dams, and the like. Because the money was actually spent very slowly, the PWA never fulfilled the role expected of it.

Before long, NRA was in trouble. After a brief spurt, industrial production fell again. The promised recovery did not take place, and the cooperative spirit of the first few months began to come apart. Prices rose, making consumers unhappy. Employment rose but slightly. Business dragged its feet on recognizing the rights of workers to form unions. Organized labor soon was calling the NRA the "National Run Around." Small businesses complained that they could not survive under codes tailored to the big firms.

During the 1930s, dust storms worsened the plight of farmers on the western Great Plains. In the region known as the Dust Bowl, croplands were oftened buried under wind-driven dust.

NRA added to the troubles by spreading itself too thin. Instead of concentrating on putting the large industries under codes and making them work, it spent its energy on drawing up codes for such groups as the gravediggers, pinsetters, and the dog-food industry. It became involved with trying to enforce all those codes, with almost no power to police them. By 1934, it was clear the NRA was not working. Little was lost

LESSON 2 *(2 days)*

Performance Objectives

1. To list the major New Deal accomplishments of the second hundred days. **2.** To explain orally or in writing the purpose and effects of Roosevelt's attempt to alter the composition of the Supreme Court. **3.** To describe orally or in writing the relationship between the American labor movement and the New Deal.

Famous People

Huey Long, the Reverend Charles Coughlin, Dr. Francis Townsend, Alfred M. Landon, John L. Lewis

Vocabulary

Works Progress Administration (WPA), National Youth Administration (NYA), Social Security Act, unemployment insurance, National Labor Relations Act (Wagner Act), collective bargaining, Rural Electrification Administration (REA), "pack the court," CIO, sit-down strike, "Roosevelt Recession," Fair Labor Standards Act

Background Information

1. HUEY LONG (1893–1935) Born a poor Louisiana farm boy, Long passed the bar examination with little formal education and went into politics. He was elected governor of Louisiana in 1928 on a program of social reform for poor farmers and workers. Long was known as "Kingfish," and his slogan was "Every Man a King." Surviving an impeachment attempt by the state legislature for alleged misuse of funds, Long

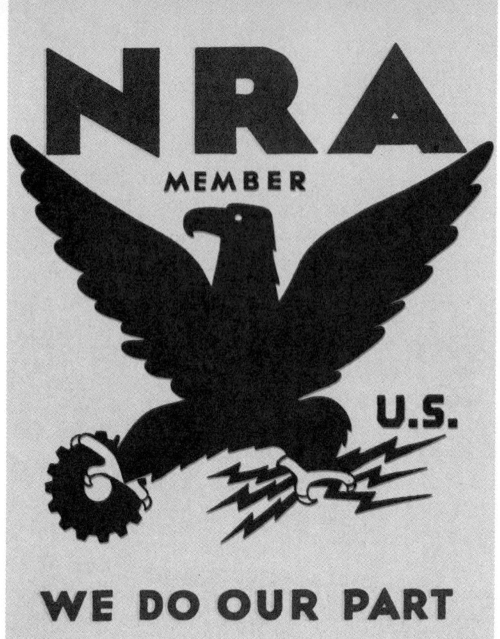

During the New Deal era, many businesses displayed the blue eagle, emblem of the NRA.

when, in 1935, the Supreme Court declared the act of Congress that created NRA unconstitutional.

The NRA nonetheless had some important results. For the first time, it brought about federal regulation of wages and hours. In many industries, the codes abolished child labor, a goal of reformers for half a century. And though it did not succeed in finally bringing about recovery, NRA did help for a while to give jobs to some 2 million workers.

CHECKUP

1. How did Franklin D. Roosevelt deal with the banking crisis?
2. In the early days of the New Deal, what steps were taken by the government to relieve human suffering?
3. What New Deal laws promoted farm and industrial recovery? What did the laws provide for? How successful were they?

LESSON 2

Achievements and Setbacks

For much of 1933, President Roosevelt enjoyed the support of nearly all groups. Sooner or later, however, this coalition was bound to come apart. To some people, the New Deal reforms seemed like wild radicalism. Others grumbled that the New Deal reforms were not going far enough. By any standard, however, the New Deal had not ended the depression. Business activity by the fall of 1934 was well below 1929 levels. National income, while higher than when FDR took office, was only half what it had been before the depression. Unemployment was down by 4 million, but 9 million were still without jobs.

The situation was made to order for the rise of people with simple answers. By 1934, three such people led growing movements. One was Senator Huey Long of Louisiana. Under his "Share Our Wealth" plan, wealth would be taken from the very rich. It would then be redistributed so that each person would have a homestead worth $5,000 and a yearly income of about $2,500. The Reverend Charles Coughlin, a Roman Catholic priest who spoke to some 30 million in his weekly radio talk, wanted to nationalize the banks and inflate the currency by coining silver. As time went on, he sought out scapegoats for America's problems, and his weekly talks became anti-Semitic in tone. Dr. Francis Townsend, a retired physician, proposed that the government pay a pension of $200 a month to all people sixty-five years of age and older. The one requirement was that they spend it all each month, thus helping the economy.

Long, Coughlin, and Townsend each claimed to have millions of followers.

The ideas that the three put forth were not economically sound, but they had an appeal to desperate people.

A new burst of reform. Despite a growing number of critics, Roosevelt enjoyed the support of a large majority. In the congressional elections of 1934, Democrats made large gains. One Republican editor wrote about Roosevelt, "He has been all but crowned by the people."

With a heavily Democratic Congress, the President undertook a new burst of reform in 1935. This period has been called the *second hundred days*. First, Roosevelt proposed an emergency program of public employment to give jobs to 3.5 million people. The initial cost of the program, called the Works Progress Administration (WPA), was $4.8 billion. This was the largest single appropriation in the history of Congress and about half what the government would spend for that year.

Under the direction of Harry Hopkins, WPA built or improved nearly 6,000 school buildings, 13,000 playgrounds, and over 2,500 hospitals. It employed writers to write, actors to act, musicians to entertain, and artists to paint. In four years, the Federal Theater played to audiences of some 30 million people. More people learned about art and music through lessons given at this time by WPA workers than in all the rest of our history.

Another agency created in 1935 was the National Youth Administration (NYA). It gave part-time jobs to at least 600,000 college students and 1.5 million high school students to allow them to stay in school. It also gave jobs to 2.6 million young people not in school.

Social security, labor, and REA. Some months later, the Social Security Act brought about one of the New Deal's most far-reaching reforms. This law set up a system of old-age pensions paid for by a tax on workers' wages and employers' payrolls. It also set up a federal-state system of unemployment insurance. The act was far more limited than many reformers would have wished. Some who were most in need of such protection—like farm workers, domestics, laundry workers, and people who were out of work—were not covered by the act. Still it was an important first step. Over the years, Congress has brought many other groups under the act.

Another important law dealt with organized labor. When the Supreme Court

Working under a grant from the WPA, these artists paint a mural for a government building. The WPA gave jobs to many kinds of workers.

was elected to the United States Senate in 1930, keeping his governorship until 1932. In the Senate, he originally supported Roosevelt but broke with him when FDR would not become more radical. In 1934, Long announced his Share-the-Wealth plan for homestead allowances and a guaranteed minimum annual income. In 1935, boosted by the support for this plan, Long became a candidate for President. On September 8, 1935, he was shot by Carl A. Weiss, whose father's judgeship was threatened by Long. Long's bodyguards riddled Weiss's body with a total of sixty-one bullets. Two days later Long died, ending what some people thought was a serious challenge to Roosevelt's leadership of the Democratic party. The new Union party tried to absorb Long's supporters but with little success. Long's widow, Rose, completed his Senate term. His brothers, George and Earl, and his son, Russell, have also been important Louisiana political figures.

Background Information

2. CHARLES E. COUGHLIN 1891–) A priest at the Shrine of the Little Flower at Royal Oak, Michigan, Coughlin became popular through his Sunday radio show, which featured his brand of economic panacea and also his angry tirades against Communists, Jews, New Dealers, internationalists, labor unions, industrial capitalists, and others. When he started his own political party in 1934, five million listeners signed up in the first two months. In June 1936, Coughlin tried to unite his party with the followers of Dr. Townsend and the remains of Huey Long's supporters. The result was the ill-fated Union party. The coalition did not last, because Coughlin tried to take control and antagonized former supporters with his statements, such as one comparing the choice between FDR and Landon to that between carbolic acid and rat poison. Attacked on all sides, Coughlin was even publicly chastised by the Vatican for calling Roosevelt a liar. In time, radio stations stopped broadcasting his show, and he faded from the political scene.

3. THE TOWNSEND PLAN The money for the plan was to come from a 2 percent sales tax. (A modified version of the plan was actually introduced in the House of Representatives in 1939 but was defeated.) Dr. Francis Townsend was a political force himself, however. In the mid-1930s it was said that he had the power to control politics in several western states. But by the end of World War II, Townsend's movement had faded from popularity, as had most of the other radical movements, including the pro-Nazi bund and communism.

ruled the National Industrial Recovery Act unconstitutional, Senator Robert Wagner of New York sought to replace the section of that law dealing with labor. The result was the National Labor Relations Act. This law, also known as the Wagner Act, threw the support of government behind the right of collective bargaining. Employers were not allowed to interfere with efforts of workers to form unions. They were also required to "bargain in good faith" and were prohibited from using a number of practices long used to keep out unions.

Among several other laws enacted in 1935 was one creating the Rural Electrification Administration (REA). This act changed the lives of millions by providing electricity in rural areas. In 1935, only 1 farm family in 10 had electricity. In 1941, 4 in 10 had it, and by 1950, 9 in 10.

A powerful coalition. As the presidential election of 1936 approached, Roosevelt and the Democrats could point to very real gains in the struggle for recovery. Although 8 million remained unemployed, that was 6 million fewer than when FDR took office. National income was 50 percent higher than in 1933. Industrial production had almost doubled, and corporate profits were up. Farm net income, while still below that in 1929, had greatly improved.

The measures of 1935 had brought bitter opposition from big business and the wealthy. However, those same measures had helped Roosevelt put together a winning coalition: farmers, organized labor, ethnic groups and blacks in the large cities, and many others who were helped in one way or another by the New Deal. The shift in voting loyalties of blacks is especially worth noting. Over the years, blacks had supported the Republicans, remembering Lincoln and the Emancipation Proclamation. The New Deal brought no major gains in civil rights. In fact, one New Deal program—the AAA—probably hurt blacks by forcing many sharecroppers off the land. But the New Deal did provide relief and jobs for many black people. It also broke some patterns of discrimination. Especially influential in bringing the plight of blacks and other minorities to the attention of the President was his wife Eleanor (opposite page). Mrs. Roosevelt was in large measure responsible for the appointment of a number of blacks to federal offices. In 1936, most blacks voted the Democratic ticket. Since that time, they have continued to do so.

The election of 1936. The Republicans nominated Kansas Governor Alfred M. Landon to run against Roosevelt. A third party, the Union party, chose Congressman William Lemke of North Dakota as its presidential candidate. In the election, Roosevelt swept forty-six states. Landon carried the other two—Vermont and Maine. Lemke managed to get barely 800,000 votes.

Roosevelt began his second term with greater popular support than any other President since the earliest years of the republic. He could count upon a Congress controlled by large Democratic majorities. His statement in his inaugural address, "I see one-third of a nation ill-housed, ill-clad, ill-nourished," held out the promise of action to deal with those conditions. Three things,

Continued on page 616

Eleanor Roosevelt

Of all the First Ladies of America, Eleanor Roosevelt was the best known and the most influential. Few who knew her as a young girl would have predicted this. Although born into the wealthy and prominent Roosevelt family (she was a niece of President Theodore Roosevelt), Eleanor was shy, awkward, and insecure. The deaths of her mother and alcoholic father whom she adored left her an orphan at the age of ten. Possibly it was her own personal tragedy that helped develop in Eleanor a life-long sensitivity to and compassion for the less privileged. By the age of nineteen, she was working in a settlement house. She also was making a study of working conditions for women.

In 1905, Eleanor married Franklin Roosevelt, a distant cousin. During their forty years of marriage, Eleanor did a great deal to advance her husband's political career, even as she pursued her own interests. This was especially the case after an attack of polio in 1921 robbed Franklin of the use of his legs. From then on, writes a biographer of F.D.R., Eleanor "served as his eyes and ears." She became active in New York State Democratic politics, attending meetings for Franklin and helping to keep his name before the public. Roosevelt was elected governor of New York in 1928, and four years later he became President.

The new First Lady served not only as her husband's eyes and ears but as his conscience. She constantly kept before him the need to remedy injustices to women, to racial and religious minorities, and to the poor. These concerns, her travels across the country, and her daily newspaper column, "My Day," made her name a household word.

After the President's death in 1945, Eleanor Roosevelt thought her public life was over. She was wrong. President Truman appointed her to the American delegation to the General Assembly of the United Nations, where she served for six years. She headed the UN's Commission on Human Rights.

In later years, Eleanor Roosevelt remained active, traveling, writing, lecturing at universities, and taking part in Democratic politics until the time of her death in 1962.

Four Japanese-Americans in Tacoma, Washington, confer with Mrs. Roosevelt. Throughout her life, Mrs. Roosevelt strongly supported minority groups in their quest for civil rights.

Activities

1. **USING A CHART** Have the students add the laws of the second hundred days to the chart of New Deal legislation that they started in Lesson 1.

2. **DISCUSSION** Examine the political cartoon on page 616 concerning FDR and the "court packing" plan. What opinion does the cartoonist have of the plan? What are the advantages and disadvantages of this method of expressing opinions compared with the normal editorial? Perhaps some students could bring in examples of political cartoons to compare with editorials concerning the same subjects.

3. **CREATIVE EXPRESSION** Following Activity 2, have students volunteer to draw political cartoons on issues of concern to them. Have other students write editorials on those subjects. Arrange both for display in the classroom and/or submit some to the school paper for publication.

4. **ROLE-PLAYING** Roosevelt was either the greatest hero or the worst villian of his time, depending on who was talking about him. Have several students research opinions of Roosevelt held by his contemporaries and then present a role-playing situation in which labor union members and leaders are discussing Roosevelt with factory owners and managers.

5. **DISCUSSION** It has been said that a reformer faces two serious problems: **(a)** not reforming enough and **(b)** reforming too much. Ask your students their views of the New Deal. Was it too little? Was it too much? Or was it just right?

however, soon brought the New Deal to a grinding halt. They were Roosevelt's plan to change the Supreme Court, aggressive union tactics, and a new economic downturn.

The Supreme Court proposal. Roosevelt saw the conservative majority on the Supreme Court as an obstacle to New Deal reform. By the end of 1936, nine cases involving New Deal laws had come before the Court. In seven of the cases, the Court had ruled against the New Deal. Among the laws ruled unconstitutional were the two major New Deal recovery laws: the National Industrial Recovery Act (by 9 to 0) and the Agricultural Adjustment Act (by 6 to 3). Though these two decisions had not crippled the New Deal, Roosevelt's worry was that the conservative majority on the Court would make it impossible for him to carry out the rest of his reform program. The Court might even strike down such measures as the Wagner Act and the Social Security Act.

Roosevelt therefore sent a Court reorganization plan to Congress. Claiming that the aging judges of the Supreme Court were not able to keep up with their work, he proposed a voluntary retirement age of seventy. For each judge who chose not to retire, the President could appoint an additional judge so long as the total number of judges on the Court did not exceed fifteen. Since six judges were already past seventy years of age, this plan would give Roosevelt six new appointments.

The proposal raised a storm of opposition. The claim that the Court could not keep up with its workload was quickly shown not to square with the facts. Even when Roosevelt did state the problem frankly, he appeared to be attacking an institution almost sacred to Americans. Roosevelt's liberal supporters as well as his conservative opponents joined to oppose this effort to "pack the Court." While the battle raged in Congress, the Court took the wind out of Roosevelt's sails by upholding both the National Labor Relations Act and the Social Security Act by 5-to-4 decisions. Further, the resignation of one of the conservative justices gave Roosevelt an appointment. However, the President insisted on continuing the fight for his plan. In the summer of 1937, Congress defeated the President's proposal. The fight cost Roosevelt dearly, for it helped to revive conservative opposition to the rest of his program.

President Roosevelt's Supreme Court plan inspired this cartoon, showing a reorganized Court with six new justices, all in Roosevelt's image.

S. J. Ray in Kansas City Star

Rise of the CIO. The New Deal was set back also by public reaction to developments in the labor movement. The National Industrial Recovery Act had encouraged the organization of labor unions. John L. Lewis, head of the AFL's United Mine Workers, added 300,000 members to his union in less than six months. But Lewis and several other union leaders were becoming dissatisfied with the AFL's policy of organizing mainly skilled workers. In 1935, Lewis and his supporters left the AFL and formed what later became the Congress of Industrial Organizations (CIO). The CIO quickly planned drives to organize the semiskilled and unskilled workers in such mass-production industries as steel, rubber, autos, and textiles.

In December 1936, workers at several General Motors plants sought company recognition of their union, the United Auto Workers. To gain their goal, they began a *sit-down strike.* That is, instead of walking off the job, they sat down at their machines, took over the factories, and held them against court orders and police efforts. The federal and state governments refused to use force to break the strike. After several weeks, General Motors agreed to bargain. The illegal sit-down tactic quickly spread across the country.

The CIO had remarkable success. By the end of 1937, most of the biggest firms in the steel, auto, rubber, textile, and electrical industries were unionized. Although there had been some violence, it was surprising how little bloodshed attended this great change. By 1940, union membership was 8.5 million, more than twice what it had been five years before. But this rapid growth, and especially the illegal sit-down strikes, led to public hostility toward the union movement. Since the New Deal had supported the unions, this hostility rubbed off on it. Opposition increased inside and outside of Congress to other New Deal measures.

Last days of the New Deal. By 1937, Roosevelt believed that recovery was well on the way. Fearing that continued high spending would bring on harmful inflation, FDR sharply cut back on government spending. Private business, however, was not yet ready or willing to take up the slack in government spending by buying new plants and machines. Thus, the drop in government spending brought a sharp economic downturn in the fall of 1937. In nine months, payrolls fell by 35 percent, and production of some goods fell by 50 percent. Unemployment climbed once more to 10 million. The administration's enemies called the downturn the "Roosevelt Recession." In 1938, Roosevelt and his advisers finally decided on new spending programs that helped to reverse the decline. But the recession cost the New Deal greatly. If the New Deal claimed credit for the recovery before 1937, then it had to accept blame for the decline after it.

The final important New Deal reform law was enacted in 1938. That was the Fair Labor Standards Act. It set minimum wages and maximum hours in industry, and it abolished child labor. But after 1938, the Republicans and the conservative Southern Democrats became strong enough to block further New Deal laws. By 1939, the Roosevelt administration seemed to have run out

6. DISCUSSION In 1935, President Roosevelt created the National Youth Administration by executive order. Lyndon Johnson, then a young congressional aide, was appointed to direct the NYA in Texas. His work there became a model for the other states. In 1936, Eleanor Roosevelt visited Texas and asked to see "this brilliant young man about whom I have heard so much." How do you think Johnson's future career and programs were affected by the fact that he started out in New Deal programs?

7. ORAL OR WRITTEN REPORTS John Kenneth Galbraith says that John Maynard Keynes's book *The General Theory of Employment, Interest and Money* became the basis for the New Deal economics. Have some students make reports on Mr. Keynes. Refer them to Galbraith's book *The Age of Uncertainty* (New York: Houghton Mifflin Company, 1977) and Robert L. Heilbroner's *The Worldly Philosophers* (New York: Simon & Schuster, Inc., 1972).

8. SIMULATION The New Deal is a simulation game in which your students can play the roles of President, cabinet members, and congressional leaders as they attempt to find solutions to the problems caused by the depression. The game is available for purchase from Social Studies School Service (10,000 Culver Blvd., Culver City, Calif. 90230).

LESSON 3 *(1 day)*

Performance Objectives

1. To compare and contrast orally the progressive reforms and the New Deal reforms. **2.** To explain in an essay the successes and the failures of the New Deal. **3.** To explain orally or in writing how the relationship between the federal government and the people changed during the New Deal.

Vocabulary

Great American bonanza, Council of Economic Advisers, Maximum Employment Act, welfare state, Big Labor, limited government, Gallup poll

Activities

1. DISCUSSION Using whatever notes and charts they may have from previous lessons in addition to the information in this lesson, the students should compare and contrast the two reform movements known as progressivism and the New Deal. What were their motivations? Who were involved? What areas did they reform? What areas did they ignore?

2. ESSAY Have the class answer an essay question evaluating the successes and failures of the New Deal. Let the students use whatever notes they may have as well as the text. This essay could be a good review for a chapter test.

President Roosevelt signs the Social Security bill in 1936. Standing directly behind him is Frances Perkins, the secretary of labor.

of energy and ideas. Moreover, it was increasingly occupied with the threat of war in Europe. The New Deal was over.

CHECKUP

1. What were the major New Deal accomplishments of the second hundred days?
2. How did President Roosevelt try to alter the Supreme Court? What success did he have?
3. How did developments in the labor movement in 1936 and 1937 increase opposition to the New Deal?

LESSON 3

The Place of the New Deal

What is the place of the New Deal in the history of American reform? Certainly we can find many similarities to the progressive era that preceded it. In common with the progressives, New Dealers sought humanitarian reforms and a greater measure of social justice. In both the progressive era and the New Deal period reformers were willing to use government to bring about those goals. Neither movement offered a single grand answer to all of America's ills, as so much of nineteenth-century reform did. Instead, each movement proposed concrete answers to specific problems. Progressives had begun the shift away from earlier efforts to reform the character and behavior of individuals and toward reforming social conditions in America. The New Dealers of the 1930s completed that shift.

A different kind of reform. There were important differences, however, between progressivism and the New Deal. Progressive reform took place during a time of economic growth. When progressives turned to the use of government, therefore, it was mainly to do only two things. One was to break up monopolies, or at least to regulate them in the public interest. The second progressive goal was "to broaden the number of those who could benefit from the great American bonanza."

The New Deal, on the other hand, took place when America's economic life seemed to be grinding to a halt. Its major effort was to make sure that there would be a bonanza. It continued and expanded the regulation of business, begun by the progressives. But now the general welfare required a more active and positive government than the progressives had thought of. Progressives never pictured the government paying farmers not to grow crops; lending billions of dollars to businesses, homeowners, and tenant farmers; providing for electricity in rural areas; and hiring millions of people to plant trees, build roads, paint pictures, and write books. Indeed, as the New Dealers undertook these activities, many old progressives turned against it.

A further difference can be seen in the way the New Dealers felt about the two issues that were most important to the progressives. One was the problem, as the progressives put it, of "restoring the government to the people" by getting rid of the bosses and the machines. The New Dealers showed almost no interest in this issue. In fact, Franklin D. Roosevelt drew a great deal of support from big-city political groups. The second issue was the problem of monopoly and bigness in business. At times, New Dealers renewed the old progressive debate over whether the trusts should be broken up or regulated. The New Deal was far less interested in that problem than in the larger one of how to get the economy moving again. In fact, you will recall that the NIRA actually *suspended* the antitrust laws for businesses that were under codes.

The permanent New Deal. Critics of the New Deal have correctly pointed to some of its shortcomings. The New Deal did not end the depression; World War II did. As late as 1940—the end of Roosevelt's second term—there were still 8 million people out of work. Nor did the New Deal solve the farm problem. Though farm income improved under the AAA, it did not even reach the 1929 level until 1941, and surpluses held by the government mounted at record rates. Many people were left out of such New Deal programs as social security. And no civil rights laws came out of the New Deal.

But to focus on its limits is to miss the importance of the New Deal in the history of American reform and its long-term impact upon the country. Much of this impact can be seen in the changed role of the federal government. To most Americans of an earlier day, "the government" meant local or state government. When we use that phrase today, there is no question that we mean the federal government. The federal government touches our lives in countless ways. One way to measure this change is to think of the things that government does which we take for granted and then to note how many were started or greatly expanded in the New Deal.

Before the New Deal, few believed that the federal government had a responsibility for the economy. Today nearly everyone does. We expect government to act to prevent economic breakdown. The President has a Council of Economic Advisers to keep a close watch on the economy and recommend action to avoid recession. Indeed, many of the New Deal's humane reforms—such as social security, minimum wages, and unemployment insurance—have the effect of softening any downturn by keeping up consumer buying power. Further, some of the measures used by the government to aid the economy today go back to the New Deal. The

3. BULLETIN-BOARD DISPLAY In doing either of the above activities, the students should have become aware of how the relationship of the government to the people of the United States has changed as a result of the New Deal. To emphasize this point, have the students find and bring in pictures, articles, pamphlets, and so on, that show how the government is involved in people's lives today. Display these items in the classroom on the bulletin board.

4. THOUGHT PROVOKER
The New Deal is synonymous with Franklin D. Roosevelt. Read to your students this description of Roosevelt by one of his most vehement detractors, journalist Westbrook Pegler.

"As a social and political liver-shaker he has had no equal in our time in this country, Ornery, tricky, stubborn, wayward and strong as a bull. . . . He looked nice and dressy back there in 1932 . . . there was nothing in his past record to indicate what a cantankerous hide he would turn out to be. . . . Anyone who gentles Mr. Roosevelt is simply imposing a handicap on himself, for he won't gentle you back. . . . But never in our time have people been so conscious of the meanness which a complacent upper class will practice on the help, and of the government's duty to do something real and personal for the assistance of those who are so far down that they can't help themselves. He needs to be fought all the time, for he has an enormous appreciation of himself and of any idea which he happens to approve, but if the country doesn't go absolutely broke in his time, it will be a more intelligent and a better country after him."

Ask the class to analyze that opinion of Roosevelt. What did the journalist mean by "more intelligent" and "better"? Ask the students if they think it is a more intelligent and better country now.

★32★

Franklin D. Roosevelt

1882–1945

Born in NEW YORK
In Office 1933–1945
Party DEMOCRATIC

Proclaimed New Deal to fight depression. Gave support to labor. During World War II, a leader of Allies. First President to serve more than two terms. Died during his fourth term.

★ ★ ★ ★ ★ ★ ★ ★

AAA's plan for raising farm income by combining lower production with subsidies is still used today.

If times are generally good but one region is suffering, we expect government to lend a helping hand. Americans in the 1930s were not sure whether TVA, which aimed to develop a poor area in the Southeastern states, was a proper project for government. But few Americans in the 1960s thought it wrong for President John F. Kennedy to propose a program to help develop a poor region known as Appalachia.

The government is also responsible for seeing to it that those who want to work can find jobs. Congress took on that responsibility in 1946 when it passed the Maximum Employment Act.

If a downturn should occur, it is unthinkable that the federal government would stand by and "let it run its course." It is expected that government will do whatever is necessary—heavy spending, work programs, tax incentives, or other measures—to bring about recovery. And in the meantime, it is taken for granted that the unemployed will look to the federal government for relief—not as a matter of charity, but as a matter of right.

The welfare state. The New Deal created the welfare state in the United States. This was a logical outgrowth of the reform tradition, which, as one writer has put it, "sought to make the industrial system more humane and to protect workers and their families from exploitation." The outlines of the welfare state in America had begun to emerge in the social legislation of the progressives and in the ideas of Theodore Roosevelt's Progressive party of 1912. But it was such New Deal measures as old-age pensions, unemployment insurance, wages-and-hours laws, relief payments and jobs for the unemployed, and help for the small homeowner and the small farmer that actually created the welfare state. It is unlikely that any of this shall be undone, no matter what party is in power. Indeed, with the addition of health insurance and similar programs, the welfare state has grown.

Two other results of the New Deal have been the increase in the power of the

Presidency and the rise of "Big Labor." Both would almost certainly have taken place sooner or later, for they were long-term trends. But the New Deal hastened both.

Not everyone cheers all the long-term results of the New Deal. Nor would all agree that everything it did was really reform. Much of what the New Deal did runs counter to the American tradition of limited government. The enlargement of the power of the Presidency has not always had happy results. It is also clear that in trying to solve some problems, the New Deal may well have brought on others. But whatever the judgment, there can be no doubt that this era of reform left a permanent mark upon America.

In this unit you have examined some of the achievements of the reform tradition in America and some of the failures. Will the reform tradition continue? A Gallup poll taken in 1945, right after the end of World War II, showed that only 39 percent of Americans wanted "to see many changes or reforms made in the United States," while 52 percent preferred to have things stay the same. Polls taken in the 1950s revealed much the same mood. Yet in the 1960s the mood reversed once more. In Unit 10 you will read about the burst of reform laws and activities during the Presidency of Lyndon B. Johnson.

It seems safe to say that the reform tradition will continue in America. The historic goals of reform, which have included human betterment and the extending of political participation to more and more people, are deeply embedded in America. As long as American society is less than perfect, the reform tradition will continue.

CHECKUP

1. How were the New Deal reforms similar to the reforms of the progressive era? How were they different?
2. In what respects did the New Deal succeed? In what respects did it fail?
3. How did the New Deal alter the role of the federal government in time of economic crisis?

Key Facts from Chapter 30

1. The goals of the New Deal under President Franklin D. Roosevelt were to restore the health of the economy and to relieve suffering during the depression of the 1930s.
2. The New Deal was partially successful in attaining its goals, but it failed to end the depression.
3. Through such measures as old-age pensions, unemployment insurance, wage-and-hour laws, relief payments, and jobs for the unemployed, the New Deal established the idea that the federal government has a major responsibility for the welfare of its citizens.
4. The New Deal enlarged the power of the Presidency.
5. The New Deal years saw a tremendous growth in the power of labor unions.

Answers To Review Questions

1. Hoover called on businesses to keep people employed and not reduce wages, authorized increased spending for public works, and supported the Federal Farm Board's purchase of surplus farm goods. Economic conditions, however, did not improve enough and the market for American goods abroad shrank after Congress passed the highest tariff bill in the nation's history. The success of the Reconstruction Finance Corporation and the Federal Home Loan Bank Act were not enough to reverse the steady decline of the economy.

2. Hoover believed that providing relief was the job of private charities and state and local governments. Federal government handouts would only ruin people's self-reliance. FDR, on the other hand, thought that government owed everyone the opportunity to work in order to satisfy needs. To accomplish this end, Roosevelt was willing to experiment until he found a method that would produce results.

3. Senator Huey Long proposed a "Share Our Wealth" plan whereby money would be taken from the rich and redistributed. Charles Coughlin wanted to nationalize banks and inflate the currency by coining silver. Dr. Francis Townsend proposed that the government pay a pension of $200 per month to those 65 or older with the proviso that all the money must be spent to aid the economy.

4. Farmers, organized labor, ethnic groups, urban blacks, and many others who were helped by New Deal programs.
5. The Social Security Act and the National Labor Relations Act.
6. The rejection of FDR's plan to alter the Supreme Court; the aggressive tactics used by unions that had received encouragement from the government; and the cutbacks in government spending that led to a recession.
7. FDR wanted to change the conservative Supreme Court because he viewed it as an obstacle to New Deal reform.
8. Both movements were alike in that they sponsored humanitarian reforms and sought social justice. They expected the government to bring about these goals. They were different in that progressivism occurred during a period of economic growth while New Deal reforms took place during the depression. While progressivism sought to curtail "big" government, the New Deal saw a mushrooming of government bureaucracy.
9. Increased involvement of the federal government in the lives of American citizens; creation of the welfare state; increase in the power of the Presidency; rise of powerful labor unions.

Answers For Chapter Test
1. Recovery, b **2.** Relief, a
3. Reform, k **4.** Reform, f
5. Relief, d **6.** Relief, g
7. Recovery, c **8.** Reform, i
9. Reform, e **10.** Reform, j
11. Reform, h **12.** Relief, l

★ REVIEWING THE CHAPTER ★

People, Places, and Events

Franklin D. Roosevelt *P. 605*
Securities Act *P. 607*
Federal Deposit Insurance Corp. *P. 607*
Federal Emergency Relief Act *P. 607*
Civilian Conservation Corps *P. 608*
Home Owners Loan Corporation *P. 608*
Tennessee Valley Authority *P. 608*
Agricultural Adjustment Act *P. 610*
National Industrial Recovery Act *P. 610*
National Recovery Administration *P. 611*
Social Security Act *P. 613*
National Labor Relations Act *P. 614*

Review Questions

1. How did President Hoover propose to deal with the depression? Why didn't his plans work? *P. 603* Les. 1
2. Compare the philosophies of Hoover and Franklin Roosevelt as to the role of government in a time of financial crisis. *Pp. 605–606* Les. 1
3. Name three people who offered alternatives to the New Deal. What did they propose? *P. 612* Les. 2
4. What were the two most important laws passed during the second hundred days? *Pp. 613–614* Les. 2
5. Which groups of people tended to support Roosevelt's New Deal? *P. 614* Les. 2
6. What three factors caused the New Deal to lose its momentum during FDR's second term? *P. 616* Les. 2
7. Explain FDR's reason for trying to change the Supreme Court. *P. 616* Les. 2
8. Compare progressivism to the New Deal. *Pp. 618–619* Les. 3
9. What were the lasting effects of the New Deal? *Pp. 620–621* Les. 3

Chapter Test

Below is a list of New Deal legislation and phrases that describe each law. Classify the legislation by using one of three labels: Reform, Relief, or Recovery. Write the correct label after the number of the law. Then write the letter of the phrase that describes the law.

1. Agricultural Adjustment Act
2. Civilian Conservation Corps
3. Fair Labor Standards Act
4. Federal Deposit Insurance Corp.
5. Federal Emergency Relief Act
6. Home Owners Loan Corporation
7. National Industrial Recovery Act
8. National Labor Relations Act
9. Securities Act
10. Social Security Act
11. Tennessee Valley Authority
12. Works Progress Administration

a. Hired young men to work on rural conservation projects
b. Sought to raise farm income
c. Established codes of fair practice
d. Gave the states money for relief payments to the unemployed
e. Public must be given full information about new issues of stock for sale
f. Insured small depositors against loss
g. Offered refinancing for mortgages
h. Provided cheap electric power
i. Gave workers the right to collective bargaining
j. Set up system of old-age pensions
k. Set minimum wages and maximum hours
l. Emergency program of public employment directed by Harry Hopkins

★ REVIEWING THE UNIT 

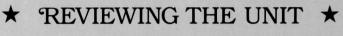

1848	*Women's Rights Convention*
1867	*The Grange founded*
1871	*Tweed ring exposed*
1883	*Pendleton Act*
1892	*Omaha platform of Populist party*
1900	*Progressive Era begins*
1903	*Elkins Act*
1906	*Pure Food & Drug Act*
	Hepburn Act
1914	*Clayton Antitrust Act*
1920	*Woman suffrage amendment*
1933	*New Deal begins*
1935	*Social Security Act*
	Wagner Act
1938	*Fair Labor Standards Act*

The broad goals of reform in America have been to make political life more democratic and to achieve human betterment. Most early reform movements aimed to change individual character. They included the abolition of slavery, free education, temperance, humane treatment for the unfortunate, the abolition of war, and equal rights for women. The first reform movement that aimed to remedy the effects of industrialism was started by midwestern farmers. Both the Grange and the Farmers' Alliances undertook economic reform and political action. The Populist party urged the government to deal with social and economic ills. After its candidate for President failed to win the election of 1896, the Populist party died out.

The reform movement called progressivism flourished from about 1900 to about 1917. It focused on problems created by the growth of industry and cities. It called for action by the federal government, and it used experts to tackle the problems of reform of city and state governments. Theodore Roosevelt and Woodrow Wilson supported the federal government's role in reform.

During the 1930s, President Franklin D. Roosevelt's New Deal came as a response to the Great Depression. Sweeping reforms were carried out. Among other things, they dealt with banking, farm and industrial recovery, and the relief of human suffering. The New Deal enlarged the power of the Presidency, and it established the idea that the federal government has a responsibility for the welfare of its citizens.

Answers to Unit Questions

1. The signers of the Declaration of Independence continued to vote because their names were among those used fraudulently.
2. The letters were returned because there was no such person; the address was used for a fraudulent voter.
3. People could vote at poll after poll because the election officers and the police were controlled by the party machine.
4. Answers will vary.
5. Answers will vary.

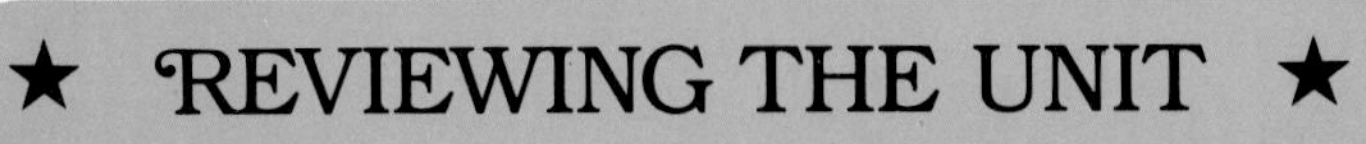

★ REVIEWING THE UNIT ★

Skills Development: Analyzing Source Material

Lincoln Steffens wrote a famous series of muckraking articles called The Shame of the Cities, *published in 1904. One of the cities that Steffens visited was Philadelphia. In his article, he explained how a political machine, or ring, headed by the political bosses ruled the city. Read the following source material and then answer the questions.*

The machine controls the whole process of voting, and practices fraud at every stage. The assessor's list is the voting list. [The assessor is the city official who values property for the purpose of determining the tax to be paid on it] . . . and the assessor is the machine's man . . . . The assessor pads the list with the names of dead dogs, children, and nonexistent persons. One newspaper printed the picture of a dog, another that of a little four-year-old negro boy, down on such a list.

A ring orator in a speech resenting sneers at his ward [voting district] as "low down" reminded his hearers that that was the ward of Independence Hall, and naming over signers of the Declaration of Independence, he closed . . . with the statement that "these men, the fathers of American liberty, voted down here once. And," he added with a catching grin, "they vote here yet."

Rudolph Blankenburg, a persistent fighter for the right and the use of the right to vote . . . sent out just before one election a registered letter to each voter on the rolls of a certain selected division. Sixty-three percent were returned marked "not at," "removed," "deceased," etc. . . .

The repeating [voting more than once by the same person] is done boldly, for the machine controls the election officers, often choosing them from among the fraudulent names . . . . The police are forbidden by law to stand within thirty feet of the polls, but they are at the [ballot] box and they are there to see that the machine's orders are obeyed and that repeaters . . . are permitted to vote . . . on the names they, the police, have supplied. . . . The repeaters go from one polling place to another, voting on slips, and on their return rounds change coats, hats, etc. The business proceeds with very few hitches. . . .

1. What did the machine orator mean when he said that the signers of the Declaration of Independence "vote here yet?"
2. Why were 63 percent of the letters, sent to the voters on the rolls of one district, returned to the sender?
3. How were people able to go from one polling place to another and repeat their votes without getting caught?
4. Who, in your opinion, was to blame for such widespread voting fraud as Lincoln Steffins described? Explain your answer.
5. If you were running for mayor of Philadelphia on a reform platform, what specific recommendations might you propose after reading this excerpt?
6. You have learned that reformers try to turn what *is* into what *should be*. Make a list of at least three existing conditions in your school, your community, and the United States. For each existing condition describe what *should be* and why you think it should be that way.

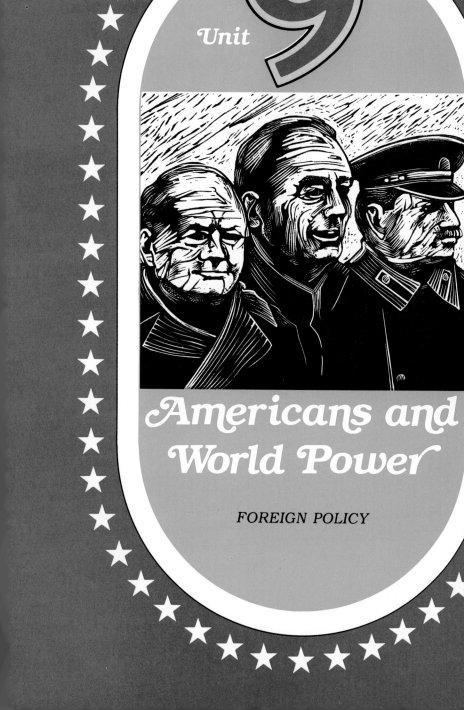

Americans and World Power

FOREIGN POLICY

FROM ISOLATIONISM TO IMPERIALISM

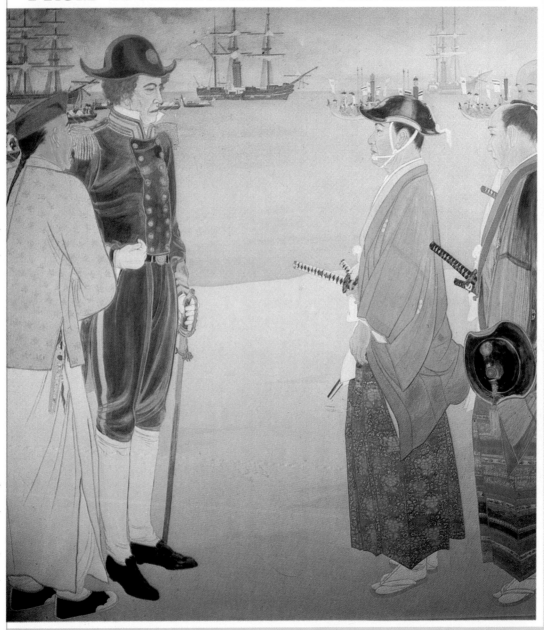

Background Information

1. COMMODORE MATTHEW PERRY (1794–1858) Brother of Oliver Perry, the famed naval hero of the War of 1812, Matthew Perry sailed the first United States Navy ships into Tokyo Bay in 1853. By a show of force and bold diplomacy, Perry succeeded in obtaining the first trading rights granted by that isolationist country. The opening of Japan changed the course of history, because it inspired the Japanese to imitate the West in industrial and military development. By 1900, Japan was a major modern power that would soon dominate Asian affairs. The painting shown here was done by an anonymous Japanese artist.

LESSON 1 *(2 days)*

Performance Objectives

1. To describe the foreign policies of the first three Presidents of the United States and explain why those policies were followed. **2.** To explain orally or in writing the purposes of the Monroe Doctrine and how the policy expressed American isolationism. **3.** To explain orally or in writing the arguments of those who thought that the United States should take a more active role in foreign affairs in the latter half of the nineteenth century.

Famous People

Josiah Strong, John W. Burgess, Alfred Mahan

Vocabulary

Neutrality, Farewell Address, alliances, isolationism, Monroe Doctrine, imperialists

LESSON 1

WHAT ROLE should our country play in world affairs? Few people in modern times have been as free as Americans to ask themselves that question. For most countries, the need for security has determined what their role must be in their relations with other nations. Many are separated from strong neighbors by only a river, as France is along part of its border with Germany, and as Uruguay is from Argentina. Between other countries there is only an imaginary line running across an open plain, as between Poland and Russia, or across flat desert sands, as between Egypt and Libya. For such countries, security has required them to be alert to every shift in the attitudes and power of their neighbors. It has meant becoming involved with other countries and often making alliances with them.

The fortunate geographic position of the United States has relieved Americans of such concerns through most of the country's history. To the north lies Canada, a friendly country with a small population. To the south lies Mexico, a nation that also has posed no military threat to America's borders. And to the east and west lie thousands of miles of ocean. An envious French ambassador once described the United States as having "weak neighbors to the north and south, and to the east and west, fish." Thus the security that other nations have paid for with standing armies, big navies, and continuous involvement in foreign affairs was given to America by nature.

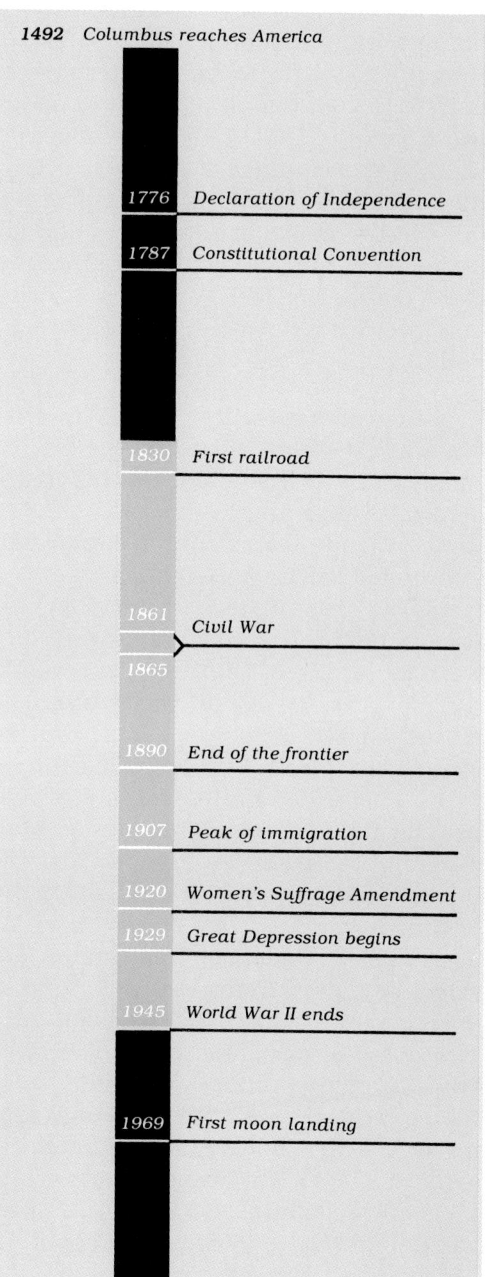

Activities

1. INTRODUCING THE UNIT The central theme of this unit is the shifting attitudes of Americans toward involvement in world affairs. As a motivational activity, poll the students concerning their opinions and attitudes about current United States foreign policy. Below is a list of basic questions that could be included in your survey. In addition, you could include questions about United States relations with specific countries that are in the news currently.

For each statement, students should respond by writing a number from 1 to 5—1 indicating that they strongly disagree with the statement; 2, that they mildly disagree; 3, that they are undecided; 4, that they mildly agree; and 5, that they strongly agree. You can make copies of the statements or read them to the class, making sure students do not respond aloud. **(a)** The U.S. spends too much money helping foreign countries. **(b)** The U.S. should have armies around the world in order to be prepared for any attack. **(c)** The U.S. should keep NATO (its alliance with Western European countries) strong to prevent the Soviet Union from dominanting Europe. **(d)** If Communist countries send advisers to aid revolutionary guerrillas in an African country, the U.S. should send advisers to help the government there. **(e)** The U.S. should have secret agents in countries that might be attempting to hurt the U.S. **(f)** The U.S. government should seek trade agreements with other countries in order to help American businesses. **(g)** The U.S. should have high tariffs to keep foreign goods from competing with American-made products. **(h)** The U.S. should attempt to prevent Communists or socialists from taking over in a major foreign country even if they do it through elections. **(i)** If someone like Fidel Castro were to take over in another Latin American country, the U.S. should send in an armed force to drive him out of the country. **(j)** The United Nations has been a failure. **(k)** The President should try to get treaties limiting nuclear arms signed by all major countries. **(l)** The U.S. should follow a foreign policy that emphasizes its own needs. **(m)** The U.S. should defend "human rights" around the world. **(n)** The U.S. should lead by example, not by being involved in every situation. **(o)** A "paper agreement," such as a strategic arms limitation treaty is a waste of time, since the other side will break it if they want to. **(p)** International terrorism is the most serious new foreign policy problem in the past ten years. **(q)** The U.S. should oppose the spread of communism in the world.

Once the students have completed the survey, discuss their answers and the ramifications. As a rough guide, those students who strongly agreed with statements **a, g, l, n,** and **o** are probably rather isolationist, while those who agreed with **c, d, h, i, k, m,** and **q** are more internationalistic in their opinions. These breakdowns could vary, though, because no distinction is made here between liberal and conservative viewpoints. As you go over the statements, encourage discussion. Point out contradictions and inconsistencies in the students' opinions when you see them.

Setting America's Course in World Affairs

Only during the first years after America became independent was the safety of the country a chief factor in determining its role in world affairs. You read about those years in Unit 3. At that time, you will recall, a number of nations, believing that the weak young country would not survive, hoped to take pieces of it for themselves. England kept its foothold in the forts in the Old Northwest. Spain schemed to seize most of the present Southeast.

A policy of neutrality. It was in that situation in the 1790s that the United States faced its first major test in foreign affairs. Britain and France had gone to war. Among Americans, feelings ran strong for and against each country. President Washington feared that the nation might find itself plunged into war. He realized that nothing would threaten the success of the young government more than war. Therefore, he issued the Neutrality Proclamation of 1793. The United States, he said, would be "friendly and impartial" toward both warring countries. In other words, the United States would not take sides and be drawn into war. Three years later, as he left the Presidency, Washington advised the nation in his Farewell Address that it was America's "true policy to steer clear of permanent alliances with any portion of the foreign world."

Succeeding Presidents followed Washington's advice. John Adams stubbornly resisted war with France in the late 1790s, even though Congress was prepared for fighting. Thomas Jefferson, in his inaugural address, expressed the same sentiments as Washington. Jefferson called for "friendly relations with all nations [but] entangling alliances with none." Even President Madison, while stumbling into the War of 1812 over neutral rights, made certain that the United States did not enter into an alliance with other countries that were also fighting Britain.

Isolationism. These events during the country's early years set a powerful tradition in American history. It was the policy of staying out of the affairs of other countries (mainly European) and having them stay out of America's affairs. Such a policy, it was believed, best promoted the nation's security. That policy came to be called *isolationism.*

Of course, *complete* separation from other nations was neither possible nor desirable. There were many reasons why the United States had to deal with other countries. One was that, as a trading nation, it had a strong interest in making favorable trade treaties. Another was that countries like England, Spain, France, and even Russia had claims to land that bordered the United States. But for the most part, the United States managed to follow the policy of noninvolvement and nonintervention in the affairs and quarrels of other countries.

America's economic interests reinforced this policy. As a neutral in a time of war, the United States sold goods to countries on both sides. Thus during a three-year period of war between Britain and France in the early 1800s, America's trade doubled.

The tradition of isolationism was also strengthened by America's sense of mission. As you read in Unit 4, Americans felt they had a special mission to bring democracy, liberty, and free institutions to the rest of the world. During the 1840s they believed this should be done by acquiring neighboring territories, thereby "extending the area of freedom." But throughout almost all of America's first hundred years, most of its people thought that their country could best fulfill its mission by steering clear of foreign involvements and providing a democratic model for other countries to follow.

The Monroe Doctrine. Thus security, economics, and mission all combined to support the tradition of isolationism in the nineteenth century. One expression of this was the Monroe Doctrine in 1823. Spain's colonies in Central and South America had rebelled and set up independent governments. There was concern, however, that some European nations might try to take control of them. Therefore, President Monroe said to the European powers, in effect, hands off the New World.

> In the wars of European powers in matters relating to themselves, we have never taken part, nor does it [fit] with our policy to do so. . . . The political system of the allied powers in Europe is essentially different . . . from that of America. . . . We owe it, therefore, . . . to declare that we should consider any attempt on their part to extend their system [of government] to any portion of this hemisphere as dangerous to our peace and safety.

At the time, Monroe's statement had little effect. In fact, the Monroe Doctrine was practically forgotten for years. But in later years, as you shall see, it became very important.

Looking inward. Through most of the nineteenth century, the attention of Americans was focused on their own affairs. The slavery struggle, the Civil War, and the settling of the continent took most of the nation's energies. While European countries were busy gaining overseas empires in the 1870s and 1880s, America showed little interest in such matters. The United States, it is true, acquired Alaska from Russia in 1867. But the territory was purchased rather than conquered, and it was, after all, on the North American continent.

As late as 1885, President Grover Cleveland summed up American policy

President Andrew Johnson and Secretary of State William Seward were much ridiculed for the purchase of Alaska, widely regarded as a frozen, worthless land. Here they greet Alaska's "senators"—an Eskimo and a penguin.

Background Information

2. CARTOON: SEWARD'S FOLLY In 1867, Secretary of State William Seward bought Alaska for $7,200,000—less than two cents an acre (0.4 ha). It was termed "Seward's Icebox" and "Walrussia" by opponents. No government was even set up. No one knew what Seward had purchased. This cartoonist, for example, did not even know that penguins live only in the Southern Hemisphere. This all changed in 1880, when Joe Juneau discovered gold and the rush started. Later, the Klondike gold rush provided real foolishness, as the prospectors in 1898 not only risked their lives in the cold but spent $60 million on food, transportation, and equipment to mine about $10 million in gold. Other resources, such as timber and oil, have proved the purchase of Alaska to be one of the greatest "bargains" of all time.

Background Information

3. WASHINGTON'S FAREWELL ADDRESS The following longer quotation from the address gives a better view of the rationale for Washington's isolationism. This could be read to the class instead of or in conjunction with Activity 5.

"Europe has a set of primary interests which to us have none, or a very remote, relation. Hence she must be engaged in frequent controversies, the causes of which are essentially foreign to our concerns. . . .

"Why forego the advantages of so peculiar a situation? Why quit our own to stand upon foreign ground? Why, by interweaving our destiny with that of any part of Europe, entangle our peace and prosperity in the toils of European ambition, rivalship, interest, humor, or caprice?"

2. ESSAY After students have read the entire lesson and discussed the terms and ideas, assign an essay topic that requires them to identify and explain those aspects of United States history that contributed to the isolationist tradition and those aspects that, by the 1890s, had begun to change this attitude.

3. BOOK REPORT Assign several students to read Admiral Mahan's book *The Influence of Sea Power upon History.* Have them pay particular attention to the introduction of the book. Ask them to report to the class on Mahan's thesis and to decide whether they think the thesis is obsolete or still important in this age. Critics of American foreign policy maintain that the Soviet Union is following Mahan's thesis and that the United States has lost power to them.

toward the rest of the world in these words: "It is the policy of neutrality, rejecting any share in foreign [disputes] and ambitions upon other continents and repelling their intrusion here." In fact, some Americans wanted the country to play so small a role on the world stage that a New York newspaper actually recommended that the United States call all its foreign ministers home and abolish its entire diplomatic corps!

Looking outward. Even as these sentiments were being expressed, however, certain forces were at work undermining America's traditional attitude and role in world affairs. Several small but important groups of Americans showed an awakened interest in the rest of the world.

One group, composed of a number of business people and political leaders, urged that the United States seek new markets for its surplus goods. "Today," said one, "we are raising more than we can consume. Today we are making more than we can use. Therefore we must find new markets for our produce, new occupations for our capital, new work for our labor." The export of American manufactured goods, valued at $21 million in 1870, would reach $805 million by 1900. With goods pouring from American factories in ever greater amounts, failure to keep pace with new markets abroad could lead to depression.

A second group wanted America to enter the race for empire. This group, called *imperialists,* consisted of certain clergymen, professors, and writers, as well as military and government leaders. These imperialists drew on the ideas of Charles Darwin (see page 509). The struggle for existence, they said, goes on among nations as among biological species. And America, as a strong nation, was destined by the very laws of nature to gain control over the weaker nations. There was a strong racial overtone in the thinking of this group. In his widely read book *Our Country* (1885), the minister Josiah Strong wrote that the Anglo-Saxon race, and especially its American branch, had a "genius for colonization. God . . . is training the Anglo-Saxon race for . . . *the final competition of races.*" Strong predicted that the United States would soon push its institutions upon the lesser people of Latin America, Africa, and Asia. "Can anyone doubt that the result of this . . . will be the 'survival of the fittest'?" The American people, wrote Professor John W. Burgess, had a duty to "uplift less fortunate people, even to force superior institutions upon them if necessary." In this talk of an "American mission," one can hear echoes of the Manifest Destiny of the 1840s.

Some of those in the first group—those concerned mostly with the need for markets—agreed with some in the second group on the need for colonies. Competing for markets with other countries was all well and good, they pointed out. But if America had colonies, the markets the colonies offered would be "ours alone." Further, with other great trading countries already seizing colonies around the world, the United States dare not be left behind.

Mahan's argument. One of the most important speakers for imperialism was Admiral Alfred Thayer Mahan. In the

Foreign flags wave over the international trading area in the port of Canton, China. During the 1890s the United States sought increased trade with China and with other Asian lands.

1890s in several widely read books, Mahan made the point that all the great nations in history had been sea powers. To be truly great, he went on, the United States, too, must develop its sea power. To Mahan, this meant merchant shipping, a navy to defend that shipping, and colonies. The colonies would serve both as bases for the navy and markets for the nation's surplus products. Mahan urged that the United States build a canal across Central America to allow its ships a shorter route between the Atlantic and the Pacific; acquire bases to defend the canal; and take colonies in the distant Pacific. "Whether they will or no," he wrote, "Americans must now begin to look outward."

By the time Mahan had written his books, the United States had begun to "look outward." Trade with China had brought American ships into contact with the Samoa Islands in the South Pacific. In 1878 the United States gained the right to build a naval station at the Samoan harbor of Pago Pago. Britain and Germany also had an interest in the islands, and for a time, control of Samoa was shared by all three. After 1899, however, these South Pacific islands were divided between the United States and Germany.

CHECKUP

1. During the administrations of the first three United States Presidents, what policy did the nation follow in world affairs?
2. How did the Monroe Doctrine relate to this policy?
3. What arguments were put forth later in favor of a more active role for the United States in world affairs?

4. THOUGHT PROVOKER In 1898 an American magazine, *The Overland Monthly* observed: "The subjugation of a continent was sufficient to keep the American people busy at home for a century. . . . But now that the continent is subdued, we are looking for fresh worlds to conquer." Ask: Is this statement true? Did the closing of the American frontier have anything to do with the increased activity in American foreign policy?

5. ANALYZING SOURCE MATERIAL In Commager's *Documents of American History* or a similiar source, locate a copy of Washington's Farewell Address and the Monroe Doctrine (part of Monroe's Seventh Annual Message to Congress). Assign several students to read the policies and report on them. They should try to decide which ideas seem to still apply and which were only important at the time. If the ideas do not apply any more, the students should explain why not.

6. ANALYZING SOURCE MATERIAL In this activity several students will interpret the results of the survey taken in Activity 1. After they have tabulated the results, have the students look at them from the point of view of a potential politician. Ask: In order to be elected by your class, what positions would the politician take on foreign policy? What areas might the candidate try to avoid because any position would antagonize many people? Is it easier to campaign on foreign policy issues, or on domestic issues? Why? Have the students write their answers and advice to the politician in the form of a position paper from a campaign staff member.

LESSON 2 *(2 days)*

Performance Objectives

1. To list in writing the reasons why the United States entered the war with Spain. **2.** To explain orally or in writing how the treaty of peace with Spain changed America's traditional isolationist policy of world affairs. **3.** To describe and explain the contrasting views regarding American policy in the Philippines.

Famous People

General Valeriano "Butcher" Weyler, Dupuy de Lôme, Commodore George Dewey, Emilio Aguinaldo

Vocabulary

Spanish-American War, yellow journalism, "Remember the *Maine!*" De Lôme letter, Teller Amendment, Rough Riders, Philippines, Puerto Rico, Guam, white man's burden, guerrilla warfare, Jones Act of 1916

Background Information

1. YELLOW JOURNALISM The term originated in the battle between the *World* and the *Journal* over the first newspaper cartoon strip, *Hogan's Alley,* which was started in 1895 by Richard Outcault. Its hero was a young boy known as the "Yellow Kid." Originally published in the *World,* the *Hogan's Alley* strip moved to the rival *Journal* when Outcault was offered a huge salary by publisher William Randolph Hearst. The *World* continued to publish its strip—now called *The Yellow Kid* and drawn by a new artist—and the battle was

LESSON 2

The Spanish-American War

The event that led the American people to debate the question of what role their nation should play in world affairs was the Spanish-American War, in 1898. The war broke out over events on the Caribbean island of Cuba. This island, together with Puerto Rico, some 500 miles (800 km) east of Cuba, were all that remained of Spain's once great empire in the New World.

Rebellion in Cuba. A ten-year rebellion by Cubans against Spanish rule had ended in 1878 with promises of better conditions. But over the next two decades, Spain kept few of those promises. In 1895, rebellion broke out again. Hard times in Cuba were one factor in touching off the uprising. Throughout several areas in Cuba, desperate rebels burned and destroyed property.

Spain used harsh measures against the rebels. To deprive them of support, Spanish General Valeriano Weyler herded about 400,000 civilians into concentration camps. Tens of thousands died from disease and lack of food, earning for Weyler the nickname "Butcher." Spanish troops also destroyed crops and buildings.

Yellow journalism. These events received wide coverage in American newspapers. The *New York Journal* and the *New York World* were then involved in their own war for circulation. To stir emotions and sell more newspapers, each published sensational and not always truthful accounts. Such reporting came to be called *yellow journalism.* Similar accounts were carried in other newspapers around the country.

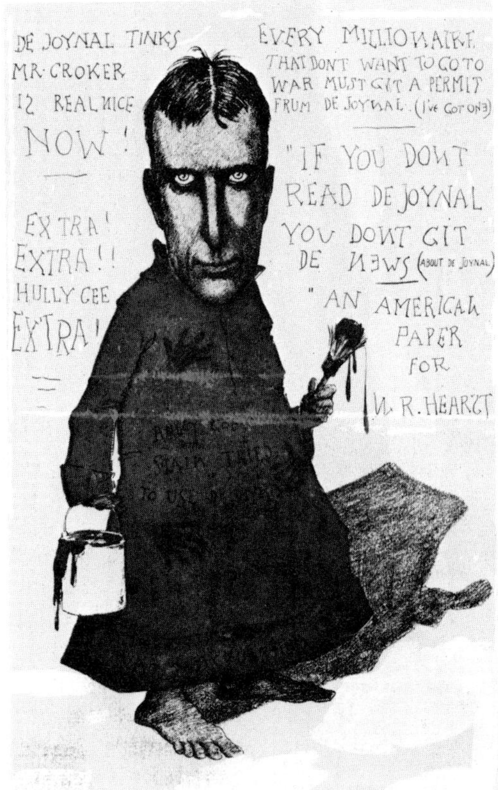

The cartoon shows William Randolph Hearst, publisher of the *New York Journal*, inciting war with Spain. Hearst is pictured as the "Yellow Kid," a popular cartoon character of the day.

Stories of the brutal events in Cuba stirred American consciences. Talk arose of America's "moral responsibility" to stop the killing of Cubans and to free Cuba from Spain. Both in and out of Congress, there was open sympathy for the rebels. However, outgoing President Grover Cleveland held to a neutral course. William McKinley, who became President in 1897, also opposed war. But others in his party—for example,

Assistant Secretary of the Navy Theodore Roosevelt—urged that the United States join the fight. His aim was not only to help Cuba but to gain colonies. Meanwhile, McKinley protested to Spain about Weyler's "uncivilized and inhuman" conduct. When Spain recalled the general in 1897 and spoke of Cuban self-rule, it appeared that war might be avoided.

"Remember the *Maine!*" Two events in February 1898, however, pushed the United States closer to war. The first was the publication of a private letter written by Dupuy de Lôme, the Spanish minister to the United States. In it, De Lôme called McKinley "weak and a bidder for the admiration of the crowd." After the letter was made public, the embarrassed minister quickly resigned, but the incident outraged McKinley and angered most other Americans.

The second and more important event occurred a week later. It involved the American battleship *Maine*, which had been sent to Cuba to protect Americans there. While lying at anchor in Havana harbor on February 15, the *Maine* was blown up and sunk, with the loss of 260 lives. The explosion was probably caused by a mine, but it has never been possible to determine who was responsible. Influenced by headlines in the yellow press, however, most Americans blamed the Spaniards. Soon the slogan "Remember the *Maine!*" was on everyone's lips.

War is declared. The demand for war now became irresistible. Clergymen, newspapers, and others talked of humanitarian responsibilities in Cuba. Expansionists pressed the President. Republican leaders warned McKinley that to go against the public now could cost him and his party victory in the election of 1900.

McKinley yielded. Even though Spain gave in to his demands for an armistice and an end to the concentration camps, the President on April 11 sent a war message to Congress. A week later, the United States was at war. As though to show the world that America's interest in acquiring Cuba for itself had nothing to do with the action, Congress passed the Teller Amendment. This measure stated that the United States would not seek to annex Cuba.

Action in the Philippines. The first blow in the war to free Cuba was struck half a world away in the Philippine Islands, another Spanish possession. Expansionists had cast their eyes on those Pacific islands for some time as a likely prize in a war with Spain. In fact, some weeks earlier, Commodore George Dewey, commanding the United States fleet in the Pacific, had been told that if war came, he was to engage the Spanish ships guarding the Philippines. On May 1, 1898, the American fleet entered the harbor of Manila, the main city of the Phillipines. Dewey's ships, part of America's new, all-steel navy, destroyed every vessel in Spain's old, wooden fleet. American troops, arriving in the middle of August, worked with Filipino forces under Emilio Aguinaldo to take the city of Manila.

Action in Cuba. In Cuba, an ill-trained and poorly equipped American army landed in late June. The Spanish army

joined. Nicknamed "the Yellow Kid journals" by the other newspapers, the *World* and the *Journal* used senationalism as their main, but not only, weapon in the circulation wars. It should be pointed out that along with encouraging the war spirit leading to the Spanish-American War, these journals crusaded against bossism, big business, and corruption.

2. JOSEPH PULITZER (1847–1911) A Hungarian who was recruited to fight in the Union Army after European armies had rejected him for poor health, Pulitzer served until 1865. He then settled in St. Louis, Missouri, where he rose to managing editor of a German-language newspaper and served in the state House of Representatives. In 1883 in New York City, he bought the *World*, which was nearly bankrupt. By turning it into a innovative, crusading newspaper, he won for it the highest circulation in the country. By 1887, he was almost totally blind and extremely sensitive to noise, so he ran his paper from seaside resorts or his yacht. In his will he left $2 million to establish a graduate school of journalism at Columbia University and to finance the awards that bear his name today. Approximately twenty-four awards are given annually to individuals or newspapers in areas ranging from cartoons and reporting to drama and music. A prize of $1000 goes with each award, although the honor and recognition are worth much more.

Background Information

3. WILLIAM RANDOLPH HEARST (1863–1951)
Hearst's father was a California mining magnate and United States senator. In 1885, Hearst was thrown out of Harvard for pulling a practical joke. His father then gave him the *San Francisco Examiner* to run. A success at that, Hearst bought the *New York Journal* in 1895. The ensuing circulation battle with Joseph Pulitzer's *World* led to increasing sensationalism. When told by artist Frederic Remington, whom Hearst had sent to Cuba, that there would be no war, Hearst replied, "You furnish the pictures, I'll furnish the war." After the *Maine* exploded, Hearst redoubled his efforts toward obtaining a declaration of war. When the war came, he referred to it as "Our War" in proud recognition of the *Journal's* efforts to create it. After this success, he continued buying newspapers and magazines, eventually owning twenty-five large newspapers and several highly successful magazines, such as *Good Housekeeping* and *Harper's Bazaar.* His estate at San Simeon, California, rivaled the homes of the robber barons his newspapers attacked. It included some 50 miles (80 km) of ocean coastline, some 240,000 acres (97,100 ha) of land, and four separate castles. In 1958 the main castle and some of the land was given to the state for a park. In 1974, the kidnapping of Hearst's granddaughter Patricia by a group known as the Symbionese Liberation Army was given substantial coverage in the news.

in Cuba, however, was even less prepared. In two brief battles in July—at El Caney and San Juan Hill—the Spanish troops were routed. Theodore Roosevelt had resigned from the Navy Department to lead a group of volunteers nicknamed the "Rough Riders." At San Juan he led his men in a charge that won him instant fame.

The Spanish fleet was cornered in the harbor of Santiago. With American guns controlling the hills overlooking the harbor, the Spanish ships were forced to make a dash for the open sea. Waiting United States vessels, however, swiftly destroyed every Spanish ship. Two weeks later, Spanish troops in Santiago surrendered. Soon afterward, an American army took Puerto Rico with almost no resistance. By this time, Spain had decided to seek peace.

Acquiring an empire. The war had been the least costly in American history. Of the 5,200 who died, only 369 were killed in battle; the remaining fatalities were victims of disease. After just three months, the American flag flew over

The *Maine* is blown up in Havana harbor. Two explosions occurred. The more powerful one was probably caused by the ship's ammunition. But the cause of the first explosion is still unknown.

Chicago Historical Society

Cuba, Puerto Rico, the Philippines, and the small Pacific island of Guam. Small wonder one of the American expansionists called it a "splendid little war."

The peace treaty marked a sharp shift from America's traditional policy. Cuba was to be free and independent, as promised in the Teller Amendment. However, the United States received Puerto Rico, Guam, and the Philippine Islands from Spain in exchange for $20 million. President McKinley had at first been undecided about keeping the Philippines. But expansionists urged that the United States keep what it had won and become a colonial power. The general public, elated with the victory and enjoying a new feeling of mastery, agreed. McKinley therefore instructed his negotiators to hold out for those Pacific islands. Their transfer to the United States was included in the treaty signed in December 1898. Two months later, the treaty was approved by the Senate.

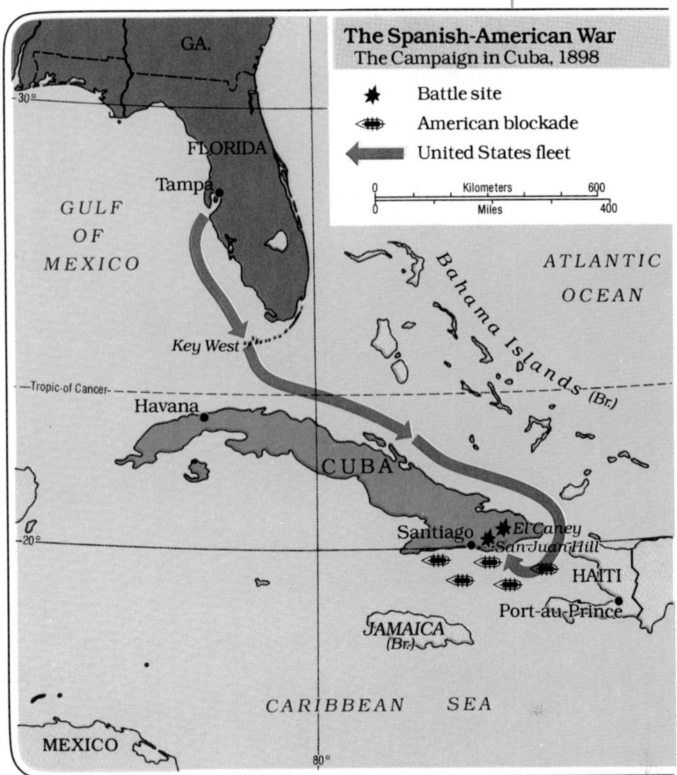

The most decisive action in the Cuban campaign was the destruction of the Spanish fleet near Santiago. Without the support of their fleet, Spanish ground troops had to surrender.

Debate over the Philippines. Americans well understood that keeping the Philippines marked a departure from the historic role that their country had played in world affairs for a century. During much of 1898 and 1899, they debated the wisdom of this change that the war with Spain had brought about.

Imperialists argued that America had a God-given responsibility to carry its superior civilization and democratic institutions to "backward" people. "We cannot retreat from any soil where Providence has unfurled our banner," said Senator Albert Beveridge of Indiana. "It is ours to save that soil for Liberty and Civilization." They also asserted that control of the Philippines gave America a foot in the door of Far Eastern trade. And it would also provide a naval base in the far Pacific. Some, like the President himself, even spoke of the obligation to Christianize the Filipinos, unaware that most Filipinos had been Roman Catholics for centuries.

Anti-imperialists, on the other hand, raised some serious questions. How, asked one, could a country whose birth certificate had been the Declaration of

Activities

1. FILMS *Admiral Dewey's Victory at Manila,* You Are There series (27 minutes, b&w; CBS Films). *Naval Decline, the New Navy, and the War with Spain, 1865–1898,* History of the U.S. Navy series (21 minutes, color; Creative Arts Studio).

2. USING A MAP Have the students use a world map to locate the colonies that the United States obtained as a result of the Spanish-American War. Ask: Why would expansionists want each of them? How would the additional land force a change in United States foreign policy?

3. RESEARCH/WRITTEN REPORT Some historians claim that McKinley showed himself to be a weak executive when he gave in to congressional and public demands for war. Have some students do research papers agreeing or disagreeing with this statement. These should be graded on the basis of the evidence the students present for their arguments. Refer them to Julius W. Pratt's *Expansionists of 1898,* Walter Millis's *The Martial Spirit,* Margaret Leech's *In the Days of McKinley,* and Frank Freidel's *The Splendid Little War.*

4. BULLETIN-BOARD DISPLAY Have several students research yellow journalism as it appeared in New York's *World* and *Journal.* Have them draw copies of the pictures and summarize some of the kinds of sensationalistic articles the papers featured. Have other students find headlines, stories, and pictures in today's newspapers and magazines that feature sensationalism. Put the items on side-by-side bulletin boards for comparison.

5. ORAL OR WRITTEN REPORT Have one or several students trace the origin of the phrase *white man's burden.* After they have discovered that it came from a poem written in 1899 by Rudyard Kipling, have them analyze the poem for its racial and class prejudices. Then let them try to find out if Kipling's ideas were typical of British colonial thinking at the time. (Since he was considered the unofficial historian and defender of the empire, he probably was typical.) Since Kipling wrote several famous books for children, the students could examine them to see if they subtly encouraged racism.

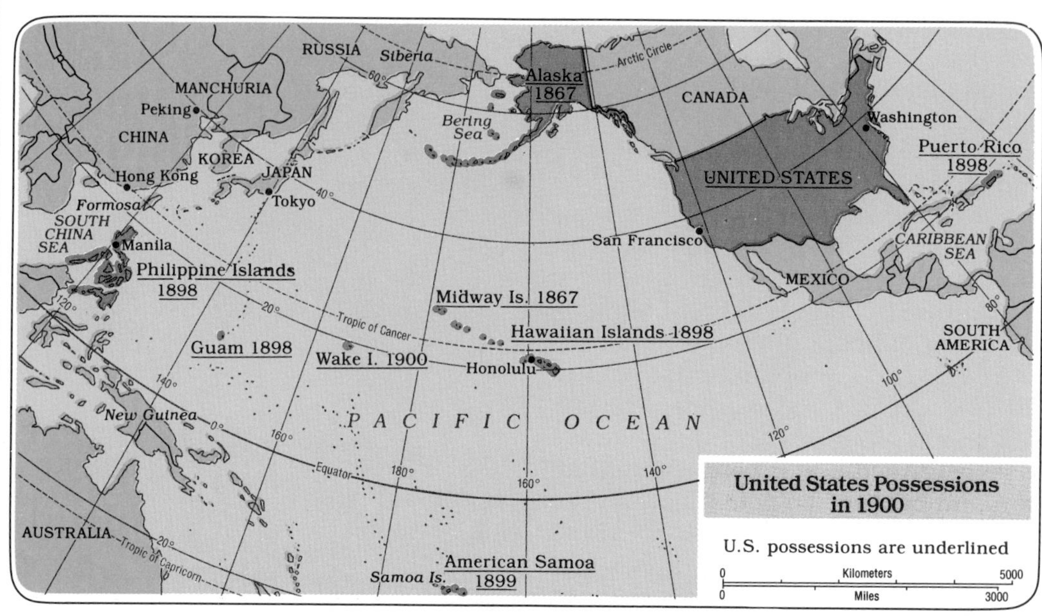

During the 1890s the United States acquired a colonial empire stretching from Puerto Rico to the Philippine Islands. More than 8 million people were brought under United States rule.

Independence rule a land without the consent of the governed? What effect would ruling an alien people thousands of miles away have on republican institutions at home? One anti-imperialist warned that in forsaking George Washington's advice, America would become just like "the nations of the Old World, groaning under militarism and its burdens."

Imperialists were not the only ones to bring up race in their arguments. Senator Tillman of South Carolina was opposed to "incorporating any more colored people" into the United States. And labor leader Samuel Gompers stressed the threat to American workers of cheap labor coming to the country from annexed territories.

It remained for Professor William G. Sumner of Yale University to offer the most prophetic statement about imperialism. Those who talked of the "white man's burden" to carry civilization to "lesser" peoples did not understand the true situation at all, warned Sumner.

> We assume that what we like and practice, and what we think better, must come as a welcome blessing to Spanish-Americans and Filipinos. This is grossly and obviously untrue. They hate our ways. They are hostile to our ideas. Our religion, language, institutions, and manners offend them. They like their own ways. . . . The most important thing which we shall inherit from the Spanish will be the task of suppressing rebellions.

Guerrilla warfare. The United States quickly enough discovered the truth of Sumner's statement. While fighting in the Philippines, Americans had had the help of Filipino revolutionaries led by Emilio Aguinaldo. Those revolutionaries expected not only the overthrow of the hated Spanish rulers but independence for the Philippines. When it became clear that the islands would not be given their independence, Aguinaldo turned his fight against the occupying American armies. A savage guerrilla war followed, which took 120,000 American soldiers three years to end. In the fighting, the American army used some of the same methods—such as the use of concentration camps—that the Spanish had used in Cuba. "You seem to have about finished your work of civilizing the Filipinos," the anti-imperialist Andrew Carnegie wrote bitterly to an imperialist. "About 8,000 of them have been completely civilized and sent to Heaven. I hope you like it."

In 1902 the Filipino guerrillas ended their struggle for independence. Self-rule was promised, however, under the Jones Act of 1916. Thirty years later, on July 4, 1946, the Philippines were granted complete independence.

CHECKUP

1. How did yellow journalism help to bring on the Spanish-American War?
2. How did the peace treaty alter America's traditional policy in world affairs?
3. Following the war, what opposing views were put forth by Americans regarding the United States role in the Philippines?

6. READING FOR INFORMATION Have the students use their textbooks to **(a)** list the reasons why the United States got involved in the Spanish-American War and **(b)** identify the arguments for and against keeping control of the Philippine Islands after the war with Spain.

Emilio Aguinaldo, leader of the Philippine revolutionaries, defies Uncle Sam. What Americans have called the Philippine Insurrection is known to many Filipinos as their war for independence.

LESSON 3 *(1 day)*

Performance Objectives

1. To explain orally the purposes and procedures of the Open Door policy in China. **2.** To explain orally how Theodore Roosevelt attempted to maintain the balance of power in Asia. **3.** To define and explain orally the term *dollar diplomacy* and its effects on United States relations in Asia. **4.** To describe and explain orally the attitude of Americans toward Asia and Asians during this period.

Famous Person

John Hay

Vocabulary

Open Door policy, spheres of influence, Boxer Rebellion, balance of power, Russo-Japanese War, "yellow peril," Gentlemen's Agreement, dollar diplomacy.

Activities

1. DISCUSSION Very often the interpretation of an event by contemporaries and historians is more important than the event itself, especially for future history classes. Different schools of thought may see different motives and goals behind the same action. To help your students become aware of this problem, discuss with them two opposing viewpoints of the actions taken by these people: Hay concerning the Open Door, Roosevelt with the Russo-Japanese War, and Taft with dollar diplomacy. First use the assumption, still seen in some books, that these people were completely noble and straightforward in their intentions to help the people of these areas. (e.g.,

LESSON 3

The United States and the Far East

With the expansion of American interests in the Pacific, American merchants looked to open the door to further trade with China. However, events in that Far Eastern country were threatening to close the door.

The Open Door in China. Great Britain, France, Russia, and Japan were carving the weak Chinese empire into *spheres of influence.* A sphere of influence is an area of one country in which another country has been granted special trading rights and other privileges for itself alone. The United States feared that the division of China into spheres of influence would keep Americans from expanding their trade there. Yet the United States was not strong enough to force European powers and Japan to give up their special interests inside China.

Hoping to achieve with pen and ink what could not be won through force of arms, Secretary of State John Hay sent notes to the imperial countries in 1899. Hay asked each to agree that within its sphere, it would follow an Open Door policy, under which it would allow other nations equal opportunity for trade. Although the answers were vague at best, Hay boldly announced in 1900 that the countries had agreed to America's Open Door policy.

That same year a group of Chinese patriots known as *Boxers* tried to drive the foreigners out of China. The Boxer uprising in Peking, the capital of China, was put down by an international army. Fearing that the major powers might use the Boxer Rebellion as an excuse to take over still more of China, Hay sent a second note to each of them. In it, he stated that the policy of the United States was to "preserve Chinese territorial and administrative entity"—that is, China should be controlled by the Chinese. Moreover, all nations should have equal trading opportunities.

Preserving a balance of power. Americans applauded Hay's bold diplomacy. They credited him with keeping trade open with China and with keeping China from being further carved up. However, Hay and Theodore Roosevelt, who became President in 1901, both understood that it was not the Open Door notes that did this. The Open Door, Roosevelt wrote later, was "an excellent thing." But it "completely disappears as soon as a powerful nation determines to disregard it, and is willing to run the risk of war." And the reason no nation had risked war was that there was a *balance of power* in the Far East. A balance of power exists in an area when no one nation, or group of nations acting together, is strong enough to dominate others in that area.

Accordingly, Roosevelt's aim was to preserve a balance of power in the Far East. Since America did not have enough military force to keep the balance, Theodore Roosevelt did the best he could through diplomacy. Roosevelt believed that the greatest threat in the Far East was Russia, which was trying to expand. In 1904, Japan went to war against Russia in a dispute over Korea and Manchuria. Roosevelt was privately pleased by Japan's early naval victories because he believed that "Japan is playing our game." However, he was concerned lest either power emerge from the

Uncle Sam informs the European colonial powers, who are busy cutting China into spheres of influence, that he intends to trade freely with China in accordance with the Open Door policy.

war too dominant. When Japan, victorious but nearing exhaustion, asked the United States to help arrange a peace conference, Roosevelt gladly agreed. The peace conference was held at Portsmouth, New Hampshire, in 1905, with Roosevelt acting as mediator. For his role in bringing about the end of the Russo-Japanese War, Roosevelt was awarded the Nobel peace prize in 1906.

Strained relations. Roosevelt hoped that by building a good relationship with Japan, the United States might increase its influence in Asia. However, strains between the two countries soon appeared. At Portsmouth, Japan had demanded a large cash payment from Russia. Roosevelt persuaded the Japanese that Russia would never agree to this, and the demand was dropped. Later, many Japanese held Roosevelt responsible for the fact that they did not get all they wanted in the peace treaty.

Worse, in the face of a sharp increase in Japanese immigration to the West Coast of the United States, the American press began to run racist stories about the threat of the "yellow peril." In 1906 the San Francisco Board of Education ordered that the ninety-three Japanese children in that city must go to a separate school. This segregation order was an insult to Japanese racial pride, and stirred a storm of protest in Japan. Roosevelt was angered by the school board's action, but because school boards are under local and state laws, there was not much he could do. The President finally persuaded the school board to drop its order in return for a promise that he would get Japan to curb the heavy immigration. This was done through what was called the *Gentlemen's Agreement* with Japan in 1907. Thus the crisis passed.

the Open Door to keep China free; the conference at Portsmouth to end the killing; American investment to help Latin America develop). Then examine the same actions using the assumption seen in some recent works, that these people were selfishly exploiting opportunities to advance American imperialism (e.g., the Open Door so that American goods could be sold everywhere; treaty to maintain balance of power so that the United States could not be forced out; American investment for profit only). After the students compare the two interpretations, have them try to determine the textbook's point of view of these actions.

2. DISCUSSION The textbook asserts that Roosevelt was primarily interested in maintaining the balance of power in Asia when he agreed to mediate a peace treaty for the Russo-Japanese War. Since he had his own interests, was he a good candidate for mediator? Should he have been awarded the Nobel peace prize for his efforts? (Does the motivation for an action matter as much as the result?) In 1973, Henry Kissinger and the North Vietnamese negotiator shared the Nobel peace prize for their efforts in negotiating a cease-fire in the Vietnam War. By the same logic, should they have received the award?

3. THOUGHT PROVOKER Isolationists said that America had no business interfering in the affairs of China or any other country. Read to the class this statement from the platform of the American Anti-Imperialist League (October 8, 1899): "We hold, with Abraham Lincoln, that 'no man is good enough to govern another man without that man's consent. When the white man governs himself, that is self-government, but when he governs himself and also governs another man, that is more than self-government—that is despotism.' Our reliance is in the love of liberty which God has planted in us. Our defense is in the spirit which prizes liberty as the heritage of all men in all lands. Those who deny freedom to others deserve it not for themselves, and under a just God cannot long retain it."

Ask your students if they would have joined the Anti-Imperialist League at that time. Some historians say that if the United States had not taken the Philippines, Germany would have. Would this information change the minds of any who would have joined the League? Have some students examine the entire platform in light of today's post-Vietnam anti-imperialism. (See Commager's *Documents of American History*, 351.) Do the ideas in the platform still apply? Are there still problems with the ideas?

4. READING FOR INFORMATION Have several students read Commager's *Documents of American History*, 367, "Japanese Immigration—The Gentlemen's Agreement." Ask: Who was actually excluded? Why not everyone? Why these?

Roosevelt was concerned lest the Japanese think he was negotiating from fear or weakness. He therefore took a dramatic step. He ordered the entire American battleship fleet to sail around the world. Though the fleet was to make friendly calls in the ports of many nations, including Japan, its clear purpose was to make a show of American naval might. Some were concerned about what Japan's reception would be. When the fleet reached that country in 1908, however, it was warmly received. For a time, Japanese-American relations improved, and the two countries agreed to respect each other's possessions in the Far East and to honor the Open Door policy.

Dollar diplomacy. President Taft, who took office in 1909, believed that the Open Door should apply to investments as well as to trade. His policy of promoting American investment abroad came to be known as *dollar diplomacy*. Taft believed that American foreign policy could be made to serve the purpose of American investors, and vice versa. In theory this idea seemed to make good sense. The chief result of Taft's efforts to create investment opportunities in China and Manchuria, however, was to raise the suspicions of Japan and Russia and drive those two old rivals together. American bankers, moreover, were hesitant to invest large sums in a part of the world where the American government's power to safeguard them was so small. When Woodrow Wilson, who became President in March 1913, said that his administration would not support such investments in China, American bankers withdrew them.

Thus, a decade and a half after imperialists trumpeted the arrival of the United States as an Asian power, American trade with and investment in China remained small. Further, the United States still had not found a way to exercise real influence in the Far East for any long period of time.

CHECKUP

1. What steps did John Hay take to promote America's trading rights with China?
2. How did Theodore Roosevelt influence relations between the United States and Japan?
3. What is meant by *dollar diplomacy?* What success did this policy have in the Far East?

LESSON 4

The United States in Latin America

The Caribbean was a far more promising region than the Far East for American influence and domination. For one thing, it was close to the United States. The area was also one in which the United States had long asserted an interest through the Monroe Doctrine. And American military and naval power could easily make its presence felt there.

Growing American influence. Another reason why the United States was interested in the Caribbean area was its desire to build a canal to connect the Atlantic and Pacific oceans. The logical place for such a canal was the isthmus, or narrow strip of land, connecting North and South America. The Spanish-American War had dramatized the need for moving the navy quickly from one ocean to another. A canal would shorten the travel time im-

LESSON 4 *(2 days)*

Performance Objectives

1. To explain the Platt Amendment and tell how it strengthened the influence of the United States in Latin America. **2.** To describe and explain how the United States obtained the right to build a canal in Panama. **3.** To explain how the policies of Theodore Roosevelt, Taft, and Wilson were received by the Latin American countries.

Famous Person

Philippe Bunau-Varilla

Vocabulary

Platt Amendment, protectorate, Hay-Herran treaty, Republic of Panama, Hay–Bunau-Varilla Treaty, Roosevelt Corollary to the Monroe Doctrine, Dominican Republic

mensely, and it would also promote the growth of America's foreign trade.

Once a canal was built, the approaches to it would have to be guarded. This could be done by controlling the islands and small Central American countries that form the rim of land around the Caribbean Sea. It would not be necessary to take them over as colonies. Having a dominant influence in their affairs would be enough.

Already the United States had expanded into the region economically. American investors eagerly poured money into mining operations and sugar, tobacco, and banana plantations. In a number of the Caribbean lands, American companies and banks became the most important economic and political forces. This growing American influence was, in effect, turning the Caribbean Sea into an "American lake."

The Platt Amendment. The pattern of influence that the United States was to follow in the Caribbean area had been marked out in Cuba. In entering the Spanish-American War, Congress had promised not to annex the island. However, before withdrawing, the American army required that Cuba accept certain limitations on its independence. Together, these limitations were known as the *Platt Amendment.* Under the Platt Amendment, Cuba's sovereignty was limited. The United States kept the right to send troops back to the island under certain conditions. Cuba thus became an American *protectorate*—that is, it was placed under United States protection. But the United States would decide when Cuba needed protection.

Acquiring a canal site. In choosing a site for a canal, the United States considered two locations. One was in Nicaragua. The other was in Panama, then a province of the South American country of Colombia. In 1902, Congress voted in favor of the Panama route. Some twenty years earlier, Colombia had given a French company the exclusive right to build a canal across Panama. The company had failed, and its

On its world cruise from 1907 to 1909, the American fleet visited ports on four continents.

Activities

1. ESSAY After the students have read this lesson, have them write essays showing the change in American foreign policy as indicated by the progression from the Monroe Doctrine (page 629) through the Platt Amendment and to the Roosevelt Corollary to the Monroe Doctrine. The essays should reflect the idea that America was assuming more and more responsibility and privilege in Latin America.

2. ORAL REPORT Have a student read Chapter 13 of David McCullough's *The Path Between the Seas* (New York: Simon & Schuster, 1977), which describes the formation of the Republic of Panama. Ask the student to report to the class, supplementing the information in the textbook.

3. USING A MAP On an outline map of Latin America, have students draw in the locations of American intervention during the administrations of Roosevelt, Taft, and Wilson. Have them indicate the countries and the dates of occupation and elsewhere indicate the reason for each intervention.

successor, the New Panama Company, gladly sold its rights to the United States for $40 million.

In 1903, Secretary of State John Hay worked out a treaty with a representative of Colombia. Under the Hay-Herran Treaty, the United States was to pay Colombia $10 million plus an annual rental of $250,000 for a ninety-nine-year lease on a strip of land 6 miles (9.6 km) wide. The New Panama Company was also to get its $40 million. The United States Senate quickly ratified this treaty, but the Colombian Senate refused. It demanded $20 million and a clearer statement guaranteeing Colombia's sovereignty over the zone.

Revolt in Panama. Roosevelt, furious over the delay, accused Colombia of bad faith. The Colombians were "contemptible little creatures," said Roosevelt. The United States would be right to take what it wanted "without any further parley with Colombia."

A man named Philippe Bunau-Varilla was also upset. He was the chief engineer of the New Panama Company and one of its largest stockholders. Should the United States turn to the Nicaragua route, he and his fellow stockholders stood to lose $40 million. Bunau-Varilla promptly helped a number of Panamanians to organize a revolution against Colombia. Although Roosevelt did not incite this revolution or give it aid, he did know about it in advance. The revolt broke out in October 1903. It was nearly bloodless and lasted little more than a day. The presence of an American cruiser off Panama prevented Colombian troops from landing to put down the uprising.

Three days later, the United States recognized the new Republic of Panama. Nine days after that, with Bunau-Varilla acting for Panama, the Hay–Bunau-Varilla Treaty was signed. The sums of money were the same as in the earlier treaty, but the Canal Zone was widened to 10 miles (16 km), and the lease was to be "in perpetuity"—that is, forever. Construction started soon after on what became one of the world's greatest engineering feats. In 1914 the first ship moved through the canal.

The whole episode left a bad taste in the mouths of Latin Americans. In 1913, President Wilson urged Congress to apologize and make a cash payment to Colombia, but Congress refused. In 1921, however, although refusing to offer an apology, Congress voted a payment of $25 million to Colombia. In 1978, Congress approved a treaty turning the Canal Zone back to Panama in the year 2000.

The Roosevelt Corollary. With the site of a canal secured, the United States intended to keep other nations from gaining a foothold in any of the countries around the Caribbean. The finances of a number of those countries were shaky. Large sums were owed to European investors. The United States feared that failure to pay the debts might lead to intervention by the creditor nations.

Roosevelt wanted to avoid this, and he argued that the Monroe Doctrine forbade such intervention. Yet he also believed that the Doctrine must not be used as a shield against paying one's debts. The President therefore announced a policy in 1904 that came to be called the *Roosevelt Corollary* to the

Continued on page 644

Digging the "Big Ditch"

The building of the Panama Canal was one of the great engineering feats of all time. The route chosen for the "Big Ditch" ran for about 40 miles (64 km) across the Isthmus of Panama, through jungles, hills, and swamps. Before the canal was put into operation, many questions and problems developed.

One question was whether the canal should be built at sea level or should employ locks. After much debate, it was decided to build the canal with locks to raise and lower ships from one level to another. Perhaps the biggest problem of all was assembling a huge labor force and keeping the workers healthy in the tropical, disease-ridden climate of Panama. When the French had tried unsuccessfully to build a canal in Panama some twenty years earlier, many workers had died of yellow fever. Later, however, Walter Reed, an American army doctor in Cuba, had proved that yellow fever was carried by mosquitoes. Thus, Colonel William C. Gorgas, chief sanitary officer for the canal, made the destruction of the mosquitoes' breeding grounds a first objective. Through his efforts, yellow fever was almost eliminated, and malaria—also carried by mosquitoes—was greatly reduced.

In 1907, Colonel George Goethals, a brilliant army engineer, took charge of the huge construction project. Thousands of laborers were brought in from the West Indies. By hand labor, dredges, and steam shovels, millions of cubic yards of earth were moved. The Chagres River was dammed to form a lake 24 miles (38 km) long; it serves as one section of the canal. Three sets of gigantic locks were built; at one point, ships are lifted 85 feet (25.5 m) above sea level. The soil was soft, and there were frequent landslides, one of which delayed work for ten months.

The Panama Canal was the largest and most expensive undertaking (except for war) that the world had seen up to that time. After ten years of work, construction was completed in 1914. On August 15, the first ship passed through the "Big Ditch" from the Atlantic to the Pacific.

Construction proceeds at Culebra (now Gaillard) Cut. Landslides caused great delays in this area.

Detroit Institute of Arts

4. DISCUSSION After students have completed Activities 1–3 or have otherwise become familiar with the lesson, discuss what the reactions of Latin Americans would be to such actions. What impression would they have of Americans? How could the interventions backfire by causing the Latin Americans to seek outside aid in defending themselves from American "help"? Has the distrust of America that developed in this period fully disappeared even today? Is it justified today?

5. THOUGHT PROVOKER
On March 23, 1911, Theodore Roosevelt, in a speech at the University of California in Berkeley, said, "The Panama Canal I naturally take special interest in because I started it. There are plenty of other things I started merely because the time had come that whoever was in power would have started them. But the Panama Canal would not have been started if I had not taken hold of it, because if I had followed the traditional or conservative method I should have submitted an admirable state paper occupying a couple of hundred pages detailing all of the facts to Congress and asking Congress' consideration of it. In that case there would have been a number of excellent speeches made on the subject in Congress; the debate would be proceeding at this moment with great spirit and the beginning of work on the canal would be fifty years in the future. Fortunately the crisis came at a period when I could act unhampered. Accordingly I took the Isthmus, started the canal and then left Congress not to debate the canal, but to debate me."

Read the above speech to your students and ask them for their reaction to Roosevelt. Was he a superb leader, or a brash braggart? Was Roosevelt boasting, or telling history? Secretary of State Hay said of the remark about taking the isthmus, "it was a concise impropriety." What did Hay mean? Does America need more Presidents like Theodore Roosevelt? Why, or why not?

Monroe Doctrine. The United States, he said, would exercise "an international police power" in this hemisphere to see that Latin American republics observed their international obligations.

Applying the Roosevelt Corollary. The Roosevelt Corollary was first applied in 1905 in the Dominican Republic. At that time, Roosevelt pressured the government of that country to invite the United States to handle its finances. The United States got creditors to agree to scale down their claims. American banks then lent the Dominican government money to pay off the creditors. With money no longer owed to Europeans, the threat of European intervention was removed. United States officials then proceeded to collect and distribute the taxes and run the customs houses of the Dominican Republic.

This method of removing the danger of European intervention by substituting American lenders for European creditors was used by the Taft administration in Honduras, Haiti, and Nicaragua. Taft also sent United States marines into Nicaragua in 1912 to put down a revolution against its government, which the United States considered to be friendly. A few American soldiers stayed on in Nicaragua until 1925. Taft likewise followed his dollar diplomacy in the Caribbean. As a result, Americans invested heavily in Central America and in the Caribbean island republics during his administration.

For many years the United States exerted strong control over the lands of the Caribbean area. It exercised this control for the most part through application of the Roosevelt Corollary.

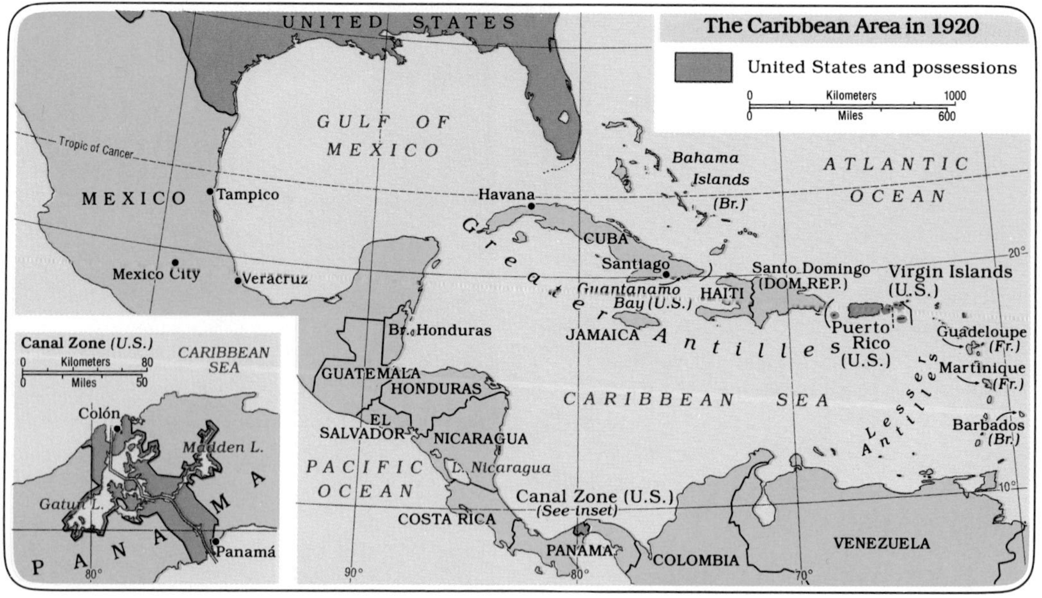

6. RESEARCH/ORAL OR WRITTEN REPORT
Have students research the controversy surrounding the 1978 decision to turn control of the Canal Zone back to Panama in 2000. Ask: What arguments were presented on both sides? Do you feel the decison was just? Was the United States forced into it? Did it hurt, or help, the international position of the United States?

When President Wilson came into office, he assured the countries of this hemisphere that the United States did not want any of their land. His statement seemed to signal a reversal of American policy. But in practice, Wilson's policy differed little from that of Roosevelt or Taft. The security of the canal remained the central goal. Wilson also felt a missionary call to promote democracy. "I am going to teach these South American republics to elect good men," he once said. When disorders broke out in Haiti and the Dominican Republic, Wilson sent in United States military forces and turned each country into an American protectorate. He also approved of a treaty that did the same in Nicaragua.

Relations with Mexico. Wilson likewise intervened in Mexican affairs for a number of years—though with far less success. In 1911 a revolution led by Francisco Madero ended forty years of dictatorship in Mexico. Madero's victory brought the hope of social reform, which Mexico badly needed. Foreign investors, great landholders, and the military owned most of Mexico's wealth, while the masses lived in dreadful poverty. But after two years, Madero was overthrown by General Victoriano Huerta, who then had Madero murdered.

President Wilson was horrified and refused to recognize this "government of butchers." He also expressed support for democratic forces who were rebelling against Huerta. Wilson called his policy "watchful waiting," but in fact he did more than wait for Huerta to fall. He prohibited the sale of arms to Huerta but allowed it for the rebels. Seizing on a minor incident in the spring of 1914, the President ordered marines to occupy the Mexican port of Vera Cruz in order to keep a shipment of German arms from reaching Huerta. This action almost touched off war. Mexicans ranging from Huerta to Venustiano Carranza, the leader of the rebel democratic forces, objected to American troops on Mexican soil. Both sides accepted the offer of Argentina, Brazil, and Chile to mediate, however, and war was avoided.

Realizing he could not win, Huerta fled in the summer of 1914 and Carranza took over. The writing of a new constitution and the election of a democratic government followed. Carranza made clear, however, that Mexico would not welcome Wilson's further advice or involvement. Relations between the United States and Mexico remained strained. Shortly afterward, Pancho Villa, a rival of Carranza and really a bandit, led a new rebellion. Hoping to provoke American intervention, Villa crossed the border into New Mexico in 1916 and killed seventeen Americans. With Carranza's permission, Wilson sent General John J. Pershing into Mexico after Villa. But as Pershing's troops pushed into Mexico trying to catch Villa, Carranza insisted they withdraw. With a possible war with Germany looming, Wilson pulled American troops back, ending the affair.

America's foreign policy under Roosevelt, Taft, and Wilson created ill will toward the United States in much of Latin America. One Mexican diplomat, for example, declared that the effect of the Roosevelt Corollary upon Latin American public opinion had been utterly disastrous. He put forth these views:

ANSWERS TO REVIEW QUESTIONS

1. The United States has not had to worry about having its security threatened by countries that border on it. Canada has always been a friendly neighbor, and Mexico has never posed a military threat to America.
2. Through most of the first hundred years of the United States history, most Americans thought that their country could best fulfill its mission to bring democracy, liberty, and free institutions to the world by staying clear of foreign involvements and providing a democratic model for others to follow. Economic interests also reinforced the policy of neutrality by making it possible for the United States to sell goods to countries that were at war with each other.
3. American expansionists were pleased because—for a war that had been the least costly in American history—America had taken control of Cuba, Puerto Rico, the Philippines, and Guam when the war was over.
4. Americans who argued against annexing the Philippines advanced the following reasons: **(a)** The idea of annexing the Philippines without consent of the governed was against the intent of the Declaration of Independence. **(b)** America should avoid entangling relations in Asian affairs. **(c)** The United States should avoid incorporating any more "colored people." **(d)** The United States should prevent the threat to American workers that would be posed by cheap labor from annexed territories.

No document has proved more harmful to the prestige of the United States in the Western Hemisphere. No White House policy could be more distasteful to Latin Americans. . . . Monroe's doctrine . . . simply told Europe what it should not do. But the Roosevelt Corollary became aggressive, because, even without actual European attack, it urged United States "protection" of Latin America—and that was outright intervention. . . .

President Monroe had merely shaken his head, brandished his finger, and said to Europe, "Now, now, gentlemen, if you meddle with us, we will not love you any more," while Teddy Roosevelt, brandishing a big stick, had shouted, "Listen, you guys, don't muscle in—this territory is ours."

Thus, to the question "What role should our country play in world affairs?" Americans of the early twentieth century gave a different answer from that of the early Presidents. At the same time, they had not abandoned completely the advice of Washington's generation. They still believed that the country should stay aloof from European diplomacy and avoid entanglements with the Old World. Those beliefs were soon tested by events. Another generation of Americans would be faced anew with the question "What role should our country play in world affairs?" You will read about that generation's answer in the next chapter.

CHECKUP

1. How was United States influence in Latin America strengthened by the Platt Amendment? by the Roosevelt Corollary?
2. How did the United States acquire the right to build a canal in Panama?
3. What was the reaction in Latin America to the policies of Roosevelt, Taft, and Wilson in that part of the world?

Key Facts from Chapter 31

1. From the administration of George Washington onward for many years, the United States followed a policy of isolationism in its relations with the rest of the world.
2. The Monroe Doctrine (1823) warned European powers not to intervene or establish new colonies in the Western Hemisphere.
3. The Spanish-American War (1898) brought a sharp shift in America's policy of isolationism. As a result of the war, the United States acquired overseas possessions and became involved in Caribbean and Far Eastern affairs.
4. In the early years of the twentieth century, the United States exerted influence in Latin America through such means as trade, investments, the establishment of protectorates, and intervention with troops.
5. The Panama Canal, connecting the Atlantic and Pacific oceans, was built by the United States in the early 1900s. Safeguarding the canal was a major reason for United States involvement in the Caribbean area.

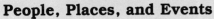

 REVIEWING THE CHAPTER 

People, Places, and Events

Admiral Alfred Mahan *P. 630*
The Spanish–American War of 1898 *P. 632*
General Valeriano Weyler *P. 632*
George Dewey *P. 633*
The *Maine* *P. 633*
William G. Sumner *P. 636*
Emilio Aguinaldo *P. 637*
John Hay *P. 638*
Open Door policy *P. 638*
Russo-Japanese War *P. 639*
Dollar diplomacy *P. 640*
Platt Amendment *P. 641*
Philippe Bunau-Varilla *P. 642*

Review Questions

1. How has the geographic position of the United States affected its foreign relations? *P. 627* Les. 1
2. How did economic interests and America's sense of mission help to reinforce the policy of neutrality in foreign affairs? *Pp. 628–629* Les. 1
3. Why did American expansionists call the Spanish–American War a "splendid little war?" *Pp. 634–635* Les. 2
4. What were American arguments against annexing the Philippine Islands? *Pp. 635–636* Les. 2
5. How did the Boxer Rebellion assert self-determination in China? *P. 638* Les. 3
6. What international events led to the decision by President Theodore Roosevelt to restrict immigrants from Japan? *P. 639* Les. 3
7. What are the similarities and differences between the Monroe Doctrine of 1823 and the Roosevelt Corollary of 1904? *Pp. 642, 644* Les. 4

Chapter Test

Complete each sentence using the vocabulary from this chapter. Write your answers on a separate piece of paper.

1. The foreign policy of the first three presidents of the United States was one of neutrality that came to be called isolationism.
2. Some American imperialists in the late 1800s wanted to seek new markets for manufactured goods to avoid depression.
3. Josiah Strong's book *Our Country* reflected the thinking of imperialists who drew on the ideas of the scientist Charles Darwin.
4. American press coverage of events in Cuba was called yellow journalism.
5. The first American naval victory in the Spanish-American War occurred when Commodore Dewey took the city of Manila in the Philippines.
6. Anti-imperialists argued that annexation of the Philippines was against American principles stated in the Declaration of Independence.
7. Due to a weak government in China, European powers carved this country into "spheres of influence" for the purpose of trade monopolies.
8. During the Taft Presidency, the policy of promoting American investment abroad was known as dollar diplomacy.
9. Americans supported the Panama Canal plan for trade and military benefits.
10. After disorders in Haiti and the Dominican Republic, President Wilson sent in United States military forces and turned each country into an American protectorate.

5. In 1900 the Boxers tried to drive from their homeland foreigners who were involved in trying to establish spheres of influence to promote trade opportunities and other privileges in China.
6. The United States persuaded Japan not to demand a large cash payment from Russia to settle the Russo-Japanese war, and many Japanese held Roosevelt responsible for the fact that they did not get all that they wanted. Further, there was a sharp increase in Japanese immigration to the West Coast of the United States, and the San Francisco Board of Education ordered that Japanese children attend a separate school. Roosevelt promised to restrict heavy immigration from Japan when the school board agreed to drop its order.
7. Both the Monroe Doctrine and the Roosevelt Corollary were conceived to give the United States an international justification for preventing its adversaries from gaining influence and power in Latin America and the Caribbean. The Monroe Doctrine prevented European creditors from intervening in countries around the Caribbean to collect their debts. However, Roosevelt announced his corollary in 1904 to state that the United States would exercise an international police power to see that Latin American republics observed their international obligations. Under the Roosevelt Corollary, the U.S. tried to support the objective of the Monroe Doctrine to prohibit European intervention in Latin America by trying to avoid the needs or reasons for intervention.

Background Information

1. PICTURE This painting of the Allies Day Parade along Fifth Avenue in New York City symbolizes the Allied unity that was expressed when the United States entered World War I. The painting is done in the style of the French impressionists by Childe Hassam (1859–1935) who introduced the technique to America. Although Hassam began painting scenes from Manhattan, he later used his soft-focus style to portray New England countrysides and small towns.

CHAPTER 32

WORLD WAR AND WORLD PEACE

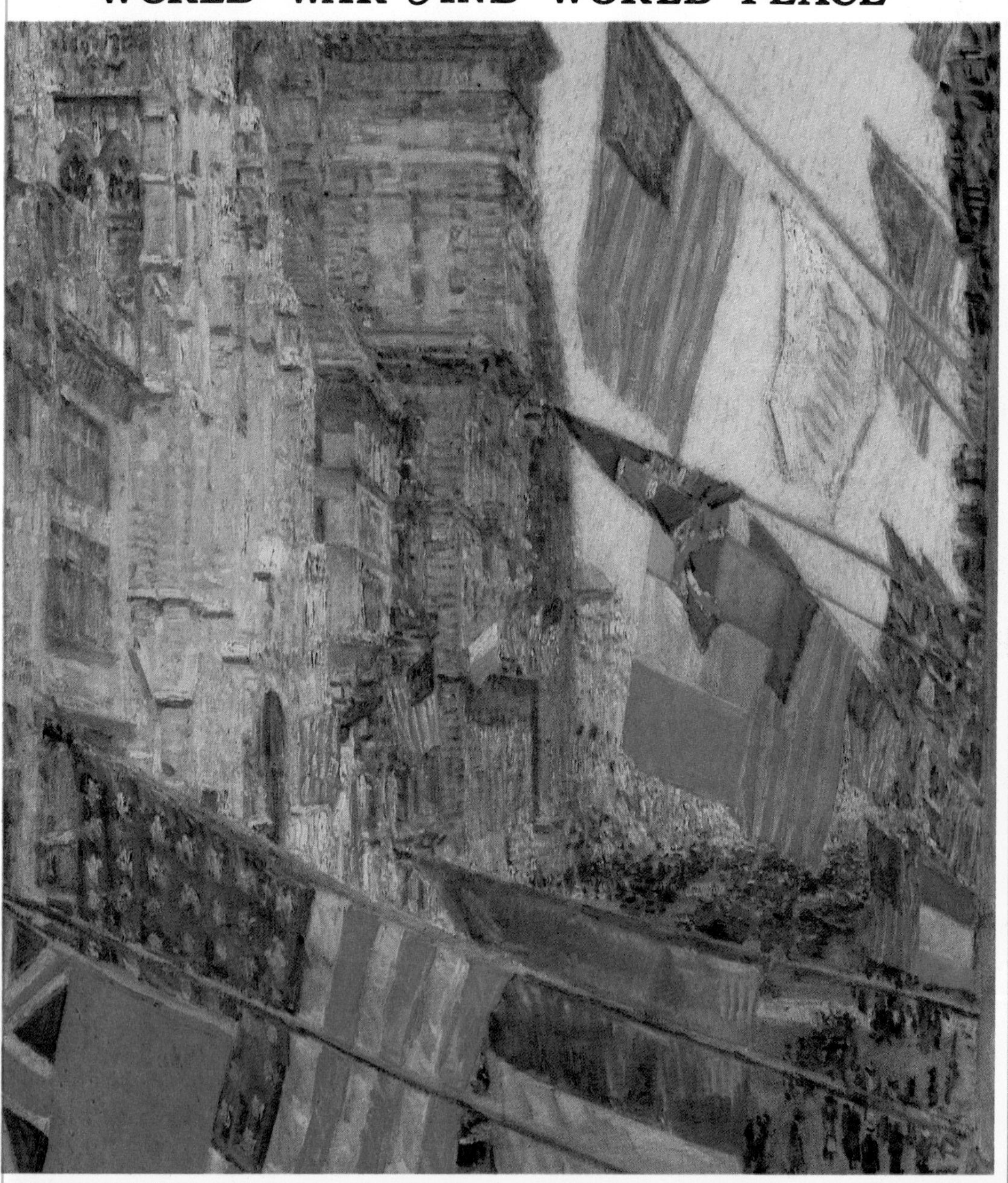

LESSON 1

ON JUNE 28, 1914, in the city of Sarajevo in the Austro-Hungarian Empire, a Serbian nationalist shot and killed Archduke Franz Ferdinand, heir to the throne of Austria-Hungary. That incident touched off a chain of events that led, one month later, to the outbreak of war in Europe. A system of alliances, fashioned over a period of years, quickly drew nearly every European power into the Great War, or as it was later called, World War I. On the one side stood the *Allied Powers*, the chief of which were Great Britain, France, and Russia. On the other side were the *Central Powers*—Germany, Austria-Hungary, and Turkey.

Americans were shocked when war broke out. Most, however, adopted the view expressed by one newspaper: "Luckily we have the Atlantic between us and Europe. It is their war, not ours." In proclaiming America's neutrality, President Wilson told his people that the war was one "with which we have nothing to do, whose causes cannot touch us." By remaining neutral the United States would be free "to do what is honest . . . and truly serviceable for the peace of the world." He urged Americans to be "impartial in thought as well as in action."

The Road to War

It was probably too much to expect Americans to be "impartial in thought." Nearly one in every three was of European birth or parentage and many had relatives living in some of the countries now at war. Observing the conflict in Europe, those Americans with European roots sympathized more often than not with the countries from which they or their ancestors had come.

America's ties with the Allies. Yet most Americans sympathized with the Allies. Americans spoke the English language and shared a literature as well as traditions of government, law, and liberty. For the previous two decades Britain, in sharp contrast to Germany, had cooperated with rather than competed with America in foreign affairs. French aid to the United States during the American Revolution had left a heritage of good will. Many high American officials, in fact, had strong pro-Allied feelings.

The United States also had strong economic ties with the Allies. From the nation's earliest days, Britain had been America's most important trading partner. In 1914, trade with the Allies was already $825 million, compared with $169 million with the Central Powers. Allied orders for goods kept machines humming and brought prosperity to the United States. American farmers and manufacturers were free to sell to the Central Powers too, but Britain's blockade cut off most of their ports. By 1916, America's trade with the Allies had reached $3.25 billion. Its trade with the Central Powers had fallen to barely more than $1 million.

The problem of loans. In August 1914, Secretary of State William Jennings Bryan told American bankers that the government did not approve of their

LESSON 1 *(1 to 2 days)*

Performance Objectives

1. To explain orally or in writing why American sympathies were largely with the Allies at the beginning of World War I. **2.** To describe orally how America's neutral rights were violated by both Great Britain and Germany. **3.** To list and explain the events that led America into World War I.

Famous People

Archduke Ferdinand, Kaiser Wilhelm II

Vocabulary

Sarajevo, Allied Powers, Central Powers, blockade, belligerents, contraband, visit and search, U-boat, neutral rights, *Lusitania*, *Arabic* Pledge, *Sussex* Pledge, peace without victory, Zimmerman note

Activities

1. READING FOR INFORMATION Have students outline in their notes the events that led America into World War I. When discussing this material in class, put steps on the chalkboard leading to the word *WAR.* Fill in the events that took the United States to that final step. If possible, leave these steps on the board for use with Activity 3.

2. DISCUSSION Ask the class why American sympathies were on the Allied side at the beginning of the war. Would this sympathy affect how violations of neutrality were viewed? Discuss some examples of violations and American reactions to them. If possible, find and show some of the political cartoons of the time. Have the class decide if the sympathies toward the Allies were reflected in those opinions.

3. WHAT IF? Winston Churchill wrote in his book about World War I *(The Crisis),* "The terrible Ifs accumulate." In this text, we have included from time to time a "What If?" section. There were many points prior to World War I when the war might have been avoided had different decisions been made. Ask your students to write "What If?" scenarios in which the war is avoided.

plan to buy Allied bonds—that is, to lend money to the Allies. This was a change from usual practice under international law, which allowed neutrals to lend to *belligerents,* or countries at war. Bryan's intention, of course, was to avoid having America help one side or the other. (Since Britain and France needed the loans and the Central Powers did not, some argued that Bryan's neutrality was, in effect, putting America on the side of the Central Powers.)

In 1915, President Wilson reversed this policy, and loans were again allowed. However, the reason had little to do with the rights of neutrals to lend. With Britain and France running low on money, a sharp drop in their orders might have led to a depression in America. Wilson's advisers persuaded him that loans must be permitted in the interest of the American economy. By 1916, Allied purchases were being paid for largely with funds lent by American bankers. By 1917, American bankers had lent more than $2 billion to the Allies but only $27 million to the Central Powers.

Neutral rights and England. From the start of the war, the United States found itself in controversies over the violation of its neutral rights on the seas. Most of those disputes were with Britain. To keep goods from reaching Germany, the British illegally planted mines in the North Sea in the fall of 1914. The British also enlarged the list of *contraband*—that is, war goods that they would not permit a neutral ship to carry to a belligerent. The United States insisted that contraband should be defined narrowly as guns, ammunition, and the like. But by 1915, the British insisted that metals, oil, cotton, and even food be included as contraband. In trying to keep such goods from getting to Germany, the British abused the right of *visit and search.* This is the right of a naval ship of a country at war to stop a neutral on the high seas and see if it is carrying contraband. Often the British navy would take American ships into British ports and hold them for weeks before releasing them. In 1916, Britain also forbade its citizens to trade with some eighty-five American firms because those firms also traded with Germany.

Such actions angered Wilson, and the United States protested them strongly. At times America's relations with Britain became very strained. The British, however, were careful never to go so far with their actions as to cause a break with America.

Neutral rights and Germany. British violations, however, were overshadowed by those of the Germans with their new weapon—the submarine, or *U-boat.* The submarine was Germany's chief weapon in the struggle for control of the seas. In the end, it was Germany's use of this weapon without regard for the rights of neutrals that brought America into the war.

Under international law, the commander of a warship had to give warning before sinking an enemy passenger or merchant ship. This was required in order to provide for the safety of passengers and crew, who were considered to be civilians. For this reason, it was supposed to be safe for citizens of neutral countries to travel on the ships of countries at war. Under international law,

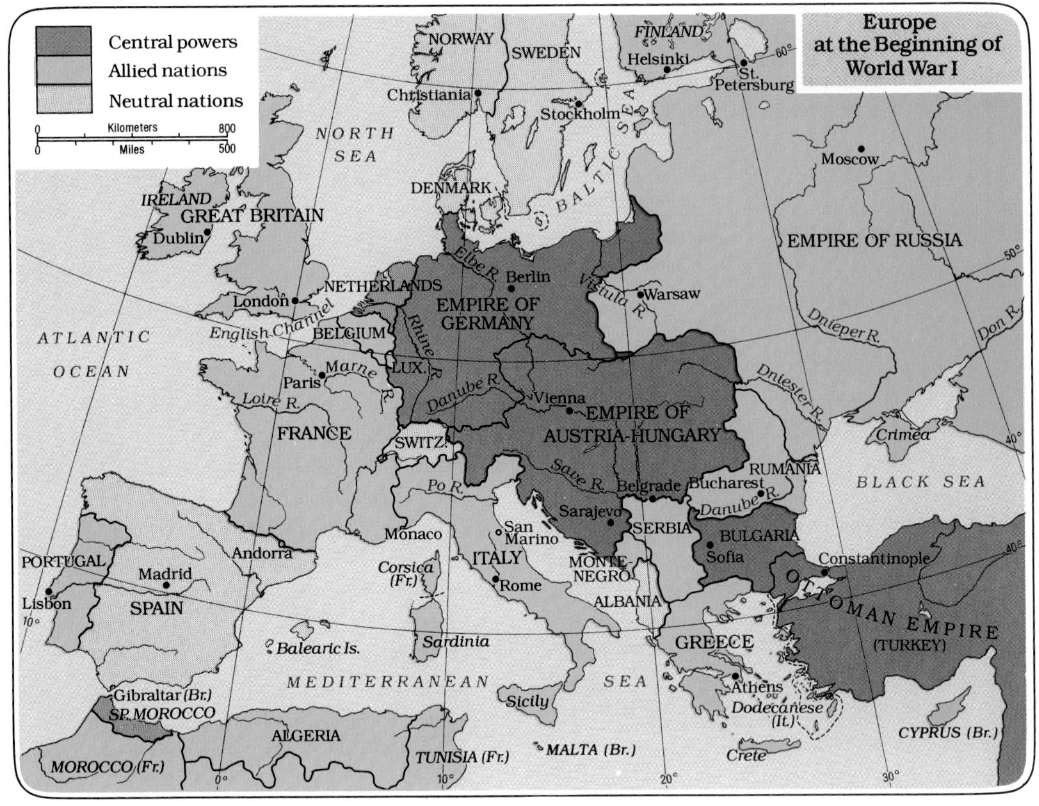

Europe, only slightly larger than the United States, was divided among some twenty nations.

those citizens had the right to do so. These rules were agreed upon in an age when such a warning could cost an armed and armored warship nothing but a little time. The submarine, however, was a frail ship. A U-boat that surfaced to give warning could easily be sunk by a light deck gun or by ramming. The submarine could be effective only by violating international law.

On February 4, 1915, the German government declared the waters around the British Isles to be a war zone. German submarines would sink, without warning, all enemy vessels in those waters, including passenger and merchant ships. Because the British sometimes disguised their ships by flying the flags of neutral nations, neutral ships were warned that they entered the zone at their own risk. "It may not always be possible," Germany further warned, "to save crews and passengers."

Six days later, President Wilson sent a sharp reply to Germany. America, he said, would continue to exercise its neutral rights. Were any American ships or lives lost as a result of this illegal use

4. RESEARCH REPORT For a thorough account of the assassination of the Archduke Ferdinand, have some students read *The Origins of the World War* by Sidney Bradshaw Fay (New York: Free Press) Vol. II, Chapters 2 and 3, "The Assassination Plot" and "The Responsibility for the Sarajevo Assassination." As in the Kennedy assassination, there has been much written about conspiracies and complications in the Ferdinand assassination. Have the students report these interesting details as well as the full story of the reasons for the assassination.

5. ANALYZING PRIMARY SOURCES Have some of your students read the following in Commager's *Documents of American History:* 405, "The First *Lusitania* Note"; 409, "The *Sussex* Affair"; 416, "Peace Without Victory" (Wilson's Address to the Senate Jan. 22, 1917); 417, "The Zimmermann Note." Ask them to show how each of these contributed to America's entrance into World War I. Can they find a progression in tone that indicated a hardening of position?

6. FILMS *Assassination in Sarajevo: Pretext for War* (16 minutes, b&w; Films, Inc.). *The Sinking of the* Lusitania, World War I series (17 minutes, b&w; CBS Films). *The Secret Message That Plunged America into World War I,* You Are There series (25 minutes, b&w; CBS Films).

7. BOOK REPORT There has always been much controversy concerning the sinking of the *Lusitania.* Have one or more students read Colin Simpson's *Lusitania* (Boston: Little, Brown & Company, 1973) for one of the more recent investigations. Mr. Simpson's evidence indicates that the Germans were correct in stating that the *Lusitania* was carrying munitions.

of the submarine, the United States would hold Germany to "strict accountability." To Wilson the submarine was an inhumane weapon of war.

The sinking of the *Lusitania.* On May 7, 1915, the British liner *Lusitania* was torpedoed off the Irish coast with a loss of 1,198 people, including 128 Americans. The sinking led to the first major crisis between the United States and Germany. A great wave of resentment against Germany swept over the country. Some Americans even called for war.

Wilson protested sharply to Germany. He demanded an apology, compensation to the families of the victims, and an end to German submarine warfare as it was then being conducted. Germany replied—correctly—that the *Lusitania* carried guns and ammunition in its hold. In a newspaper ad, Germany had warned Americans not to travel on this ship. Therefore, Germany could accept no responsibility for the deaths. Wilson's reply defended the right of neutrals to travel on the seas. The note was so strong that Secretary of State Bryan resigned. Bryan believed that the United States should warn its citizens against traveling on the ships of belligerents, so as to avoid incidents that might draw the nation into war.

Two other sinkings. While Germany and the United States wrangled over the *Lusitania,* another incident occurred. Despite secret German orders not to sink other passenger ships without warning, a U-boat sank the British liner *Arabic* in August, killing two Americans. Anxious to avoid a break with the United States, the German government quickly pledged that its subs would sink no more unarmed passenger ships without warning. The *Arabic* Pledge calmed relations between the two nations and was regarded as a victory for Wilson's patient but firm diplomacy.

Germany kept this pledge until March 1916, when a U-boat torpedoed the *Sussex,* an unarmed French passenger ship, injuring several American passengers. Furious, Wilson warned that unless the Germans abandoned their method of submarine warfare, the United States would break off diplomatic relations—a step that often preceded war. A month later Germany issued the *Sussex* Pledge. It declared that its subs would no longer sink either passenger or merchant ships without warning. At the same time, it insisted that Wilson must make the Allies also observe international law. Germany was referring to Britain's illegal blockade and its violations of other rights of neutrals. To Wilson, the two were separate matters. One violation involved only property rights. The other involved human lives. A Boston newspaper said of the two warring parties that one was a "gang of thieves" and the other a "gang of murderers." "On the whole," it said, "we prefer the thieves, but only as the lesser of two evils."

"He kept us out of war." With the *Sussex* Pledge, it appeared that Wilson had managed to avert war. At the same time, he had forced the Germans to use the submarine only within the limits of international law. Indeed, Wilson was reelected in 1916 largely because, as his followers chanted, "He kept us out of war." But Wilson knew that the longer the war lasted, the greater the chance the United States would be drawn into it.

The best way to avoid being drawn into the war was to get the parties to make peace. Wilson had earlier tried to do this several times without success. Following his reelection, he tried once more in December 1916. Neither side, however, was ready to settle for anything short of a clear victory, and the effort failed. Thereupon, Wilson went before the Senate on January 22, 1917, to give his own ideas on a peace settlement. There must be, he said, a "peace without victory," for any other kind would breed hatred and more wars. "Only a peace between equals can last," Wilson declared. The President spoke also of a need for an international organization to keep the peace.

A fateful decision. Wilson did not know that two weeks before his speech, a decision had been made that would draw the United States into the war. On January 9, Germany decided to resume unrestricted submarine warfare. This meant torpedoing, without warning, any ship that entered the waters around the British Isles, neutrals included.

The crew of a surfaced German U-boat watches the sinking of a British ship in the Atlantic.

Background Information

2. U-BOATS *Unterseebooten,* as they were called in German, were not the first submarines used in a war. (The *Turtle,* a one-person, hand-powered submarine, failed in an attempt to sink a British warship during the Revolutionary War.) However, U-boats established the importance of submarines in naval warfare. In 1914, for example, one German U-boat sank three British cruisers in less than one hour. U-boat activity reached its peak in 1917 when unrestricted submarine warfare was declared.

LESSON 2 *(1 to 2 days)*

Performance Objectives

1. To describe orally the special efforts made on the home front to win the war. **2.** To explain orally the part the United States Navy played in World War I. **3.** To explain orally how the A.E.F. contributed to the Allied victory.

Famous People

John J. Pershing, Field Marshall Hindenburg

Vocabulary

Selective Service Act, War Industries Board, Liberty Loan drives, Associated Powers, A.E.F., convoy system, Western Front, Caporetto, "race for France," Battle of the Marne, armistice

Activities

1. **FILMS** *Home Front, 1917–1919; War Transforms American Life* (17 minutes, b&w; CBS Films). *The Great War,* Project 20 series (52 minutes, b&w; NBC Films). *The Day the Guns Stopped Firing* (17 minutes, b&w; CBS Films).

2. **DISCUSSION** After students have read the lesson, ask them to list the sacrifices and contributions made by Americans at home during World War I. Ask: Why were people willing to do so much? Would people today respond in the same way? Under what circumstances might Americans today be willing to make personal sacrifices?

"I know full well," said one German official, "that by taking this step we run the danger of bringing about a break and possible war with the United States." But the Germans concluded that in light of the large loans and heavy trade in war goods with the Allies, the United States could hardly do more harm in the war than it was doing out of it. The German army and navy leaders believed that it would take a year before American forces could become a factor in the fighting. By then, with the submarine strangling Britain and with German armies advancing on the continent, the war would be over. On a draft of the submarine-warfare statement, Wilhelm II, the German emperor, or kaiser, penciled a note: "Now, once and for all, an *end* to negotiations with America. If Wilson wants war, let him make it, and let him then have it."

The United States goes to war. The German announcement of unrestricted submarine warfare came on January 31, 1917. As expected, Wilson broke off diplomatic relations three days later. The President still hoped that the Germans would not go through with their threat. But in March, five American ships were sunk. That same month, the contents of a secret note sent by Alfred Zimmerman, the German foreign secretary, to the German minister in Mexico were made public. The Zimmerman note, which had been intercepted, proposed an alliance with Mexico in the event that the United States entered the war. As a reward, Mexico would get back its "lost territories" of Texas, New Mexico, and Arizona. The note stunned and angered Americans.

On April 2, 1917, Wilson asked the Congress to declare war on Germany, saying that "the world must be made safe for democracy." Four days later Congress responded, and the United States was at war.

CHECKUP

1. When World War I broke out in Europe, why were America's sympathies largely with the Allies?
2. In what ways were the neutral rights of the United States violated by Great Britain? by Germany?
3. What specific events contributed to drawing the United States into the war?

LESSON 2

America in World War I

Once war was declared, America quickly mobilized. Congress passed the Selective Service Act in May 1917. It required men between twenty-one and thirty to register for the draft. A later law put the age limits at eighteen and forty-five. Before the end of the war, 24 million men had registered, of whom 2.8 million were drafted. Another 2 million men volunteered for service. Although there was some grumbling about the draft—one congressman said he saw "no difference between a conscript and a convict"—there were no draft riots such as occurred in the Civil War.

Home-front efforts. To increase America's industrial output, Congress granted Wilson wide powers. The President, in turn, created the War Industries Board, which had the power to act as a virtual economic dictator. The Board decided which manufacturers would have first call on scarce materials, what would be produced, what prices would be charged, and to whom the goods would be sold. Such regimentation was unknown in America, but it got the job done.

To increase food production and cut down on its consumption at home, Wilson appointed Herbert Hoover to head the Food Administration. Farmers were guaranteed high prices for wheat and other crops. Americans were asked to observe "wheatless Mondays" and "meatless Tuesdays," and when eating apples, to be "patriotic to the core." As a result of this "Hooverizing," America tripled its exports of meat, breadstuffs, and sugar in 1918.

Similar efforts were made to save fuel. Daylight saving time was introduced. There were "gasless Sundays" for motorists and "fuelless Mondays" for homeowners. Electric light displays were darkened, and some plants that made nonessential goods were shut down.

Winning public support. None of these efforts could have been successful without the full support of the American people. To win that support, the government engaged in a vast propaganda campaign. The Committee on Public Information distributed millions of leaflets describing America's war aims and urging patriotism. Well-known people were enlisted to give brief talks at public gatherings. Organizations of every kind joined the government's campaign "to sell the war to the American people."

This popular support was expressed in financial support as well. Through four Liberty Loan drives and one Victory Loan drive, nearly $22 billion was raised by selling government bonds to the public. This accounted for two thirds of the total cost of the war. The remaining third was raised through taxes on many items, plus higher taxes on private and corporate incomes.

During World War I, as increasing numbers of men entered the armed services, women were called upon to fill many jobs the men had held. Here, at the headquarters of a city streetcar company, conductors await their tour of duty.

3. ORAL REPORTS Have several students research the military aspects of World War I. Divide the assignments so that students report on different topics, such as the contributions of the United States Navy and the A.E.F., the new technology invented for the war, trench warfare, casualties (both civilian and military), and the heavy property losses that resulted from the war. One good source would be *The West Point Atlas of American War,* edited by Vincent J. Esposito (New York: Frederick A. Praeger, 1959). This book describes in detail the American participation on the Western Front.

4. **RESEARCH / ORAL AND WRITTEN REPORTS** Wartime propaganda reached new heights with World War I. This topic is discussed in Chapter Six of Phillip Knightley's *The First Casualty* (New York: Harcourt Brace Jovanovich, Inc., 1975). Some students may want to read this source. Have others look for examples of wartime propaganda in newspapers of the time or in other historical sources. The students should report to the class about the techniques and purposes of wartime propaganda as well as prepare a written report for your grading.

5. **BOOK REPORT** Ask an interested student to read *All Quiet on the Western Front* by Erich M. Remarque. This famous novel presents a realistic picture of war based on the author's own experiences. Have the student report to the class on the advantages and disadvantages of studying about this period in history through a work of historical fiction.

6. **USING A CHART** Have several students prepare a wall chart showing casualties of World War I (see *World Book Encyclopedia*, Vol. 21, page 377). In addition to the military casualties, at least 5 million civilians died, most from disease and starvation. After the class has looked at the chart, ask: What effect would these figures have on the kind of peace treaty demanded by the people of the victorious countries? Be sure to refer to these figures when you discuss the peace conference.

Aid for the Associated Powers. Although the United States entered the war on the side of the Allies, it made no treaty with them. Old prejudices against "entangling alliances" were too strong. Instead the United States referred to the Allies as the Associated Powers. Soon after the United States entered the war, representatives from the Associated Powers came to Washington to discuss their needs. They were short of food, munitions, and supplies, as well as ships to carry them. Help would also be needed from the American Navy to combat German submarines. President Wilson put General John J. Pershing in command of the American Expeditionary Force (A.E.F.) and, hoping to lift Allied morale, sent him to France in June 1917 with a small force.

The United States Navy was quickly involved in the fighting. With the renewal of unrestricted submarine warfare in the spring of 1917, Allied shipping suffered terrible losses. German submarines were sinking ships at twice their rate of replacement. Britain's naval leader reported that "it is impossible for us to go on, if losses like this continue. . . . The Germans . . . will win unless we stop these losses—and stop them soon."

The United States began to build ships that could be used on antisubmarine duty. More important, American strategists devised the *convoy system.*

During World War I, the Western Front created a swath of destruction across northeastern France.

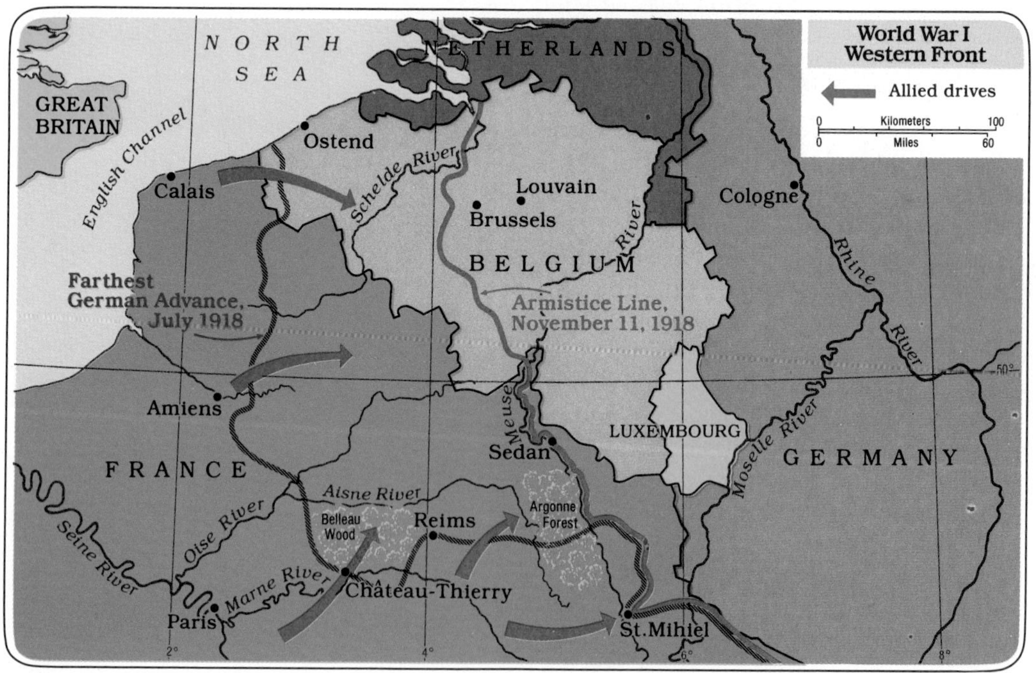

This drew together large fleets of freighters and troop carriers to cross the Atlantic under the protection of destroyer escorts. This system and other changes succeeded in reducing shipping losses from 881,000 tons in April 1917 to 289,000 tons in November. The antisubmarine campaign by the American and British navies proved so successful that not a single American troop ship was lost during the war.

A deadly stalemate. After the first German advance into France in 1914 was stopped, a deadly stalemate had developed. From then through the spring of 1917, both sides dug in along a line of trenches and forts extending from the North Sea across France to the border of Switzerland. Along this line, known as the *Western Front,* the French and German armies pounded away at each other. Hundreds of thousands of men died in battle, yet neither side made significant gains.

Italy had entered the war in 1915 on the Allied side. But in October 1917, Italian troops were mauled by the Austro-Hungarian army at Caporetto in northern Italy, with the staggering loss of 600,000 men. In Russia, Communists seized control of the government in November 1917 and soon took that country out of the war. By the spring of 1918, the Central Powers had shifted their armies from Russia to the Western Front.

The A.E.F. in France. The call now went out for American troops to help defend against the expected spring offensive of the Germans. What followed was called the "race for France." Field Marshall Hindenburg, commander of the German armies, later wrote: "Would [the United States] appear in time to snatch the victor's laurels from our brows? That and that only was the decisive question! I believed I could answer it in the negative." But the United States won the race for France. During the critical months—March to October 1918—1,750,000 American soldiers landed in France. "America," Hindenburg concluded, "thus became the decisive power in the war."

In the shattered courtyard of a farmhouse near St. Mihiel, France, American troops take a brief rest before launching another attack.

The Germans launched a new offensive in March 1918. For two months they drove the French and British armies back. On May 31, however, Allied troops reinforced by Americans halted

Continued on page 659

Background Information

WOMEN AND WORLD WAR I

The shortage of men caused by World War I gave women new opportunities, albeit limited and temporary, in many industries. More than one million women moved into jobs that men had left. Although their efforts were almost always outstanding, they were generally paid less, promoted less often, and let go when the war was over. Besides filling jobs, women were deeply involved in all aspects of the home-front effort. Dr. Anna Howard Shaw headed the Committee of Women's Defense, which coordinated efforts to conserve food and other resources, to raise money, and to fill job vacancies. Black women made the same kinds of efforts but were rewarded with even lower paying and less important jobs. Segregation even in government jobs was a common practice, as was discrimination. Women were also directly involved in the military aspects of the war; many served in the Red Cross, the Nurse Corps, and the Naval Reserve, where they filled many noncombat jobs.

The War in the Air

World War I saw the introduction of a new military weapon—the airplane. Its use in war came only eleven years after the first successful flight of an engine-driven, heavier-than-air machine. That flight took place in 1903 at Kitty Hawk, North Carolina, when the flimsy flying machine made by Orville and Wilbur Wright of Dayton, Ohio, lifted off the ground for twelve seconds. The value of such a machine in warfare was so obvious that in 1907 the United States Army Signal Corps set up a group to develop planes and balloons.

The first military planes were flimsy, slow, and difficult to fly. When World War I broke out, planes were used by France, England, and Germany for observing enemy forces and military bases. Soon, however, rival pilots were firing at each other from their open cockpits with rifles and pistols. Machine guns were then installed in the planes, and the pilots engaged in air battles known as *dogfights*.

At first, American pilots volunteered in the French Air Force. When America entered the war in 1917, most of the American pilots transferred to the United States Air Service, commanded by General Billy Mitchell. The best-known American pilot was Eddie Rickenbacker, who had driven racing cars before the war. Though he did not reach the front until 1918, he shot down twenty-two German planes and four observation balloons.

In the skies over France, the American airmen fought the "Flying Circus," the German fighter group headed by Baron Manfred von Richthofen. During the war, Richthofen in his red plane shot down eighty Allied planes. The "Red Baron" was himself finally shot down in 1918.

The airplane did not change the outcome of World War I, but its use set the pattern for future warfare.

Posters such as this one induced many adventurous young men to enlist in the Air Service. By the end of the war, more than 10,000 Americans had undergone training as flying cadets.

the German advance at the Marne River, only 40 miles (64 km) from Paris. In mid-July, French General Ferdinand Foch, commander in chief of the Allied forces, launched a counteroffensive. Wave after wave of American, British, and French troops forced the German armies to retreat. By August, with more fresh American troops ready to enter the conflict, the tide of battle had clearly turned.

Through the early autumn, Allied and American troops continued to push toward the German border. By late September it had become clear to the Germans that they could not hope to win. With resistance crumbling, Germany signed an armistice on November 11, 1918. World War I was over.

CHECKUP

1. What special efforts were made on the home front toward winning the war?
2. What part did the United States Navy play in the war?
3. How did the American Expeditionary Force contribute to the Allied victory?

LESSON 3

Making Peace

In a message to Congress in January 1918, President Wilson outlined the "only possible program for peace." It was contained in his Fourteen Points.

Wilson's Fourteen Points. The first five of these points dealt with broad principles as a basis for the peace settlement. They included open diplomacy (an end to secret agreements), freedom of the seas, reduction of arms, ending the barriers to free trade, and an adjustment of colonial claims that kept in mind the interests of the colonial populations. The next eight points dealt with the need for territorial adjustments in Europe. Such adjustments would be based on the principle of *self-determination*—that is, allowing each national group to live in a country of its own.

The fourteenth point—and to Wilson the most important one—proposed the creation of "a general association of nations" to afford "mutual guarantees of political independence and territorial integrity" of all countries. With these words, Wilson was offering to have the United States take a continuing role in an international organization to keep the peace. This move was a great departure from the American tradition of isolationism.

The Allies did not immediately agree to all of Wilson's points. Britain could not accept the second point, dealing with freedom of the seas. Some of the points were in conflict with secret treaties, in which the Allies had agreed upon the spoils each would get at the end of the war. By the time of Wilson's speech, those treaties had been made public by the Russians.

In the United States, too, there was not total agreement with Wilson's Fourteen Points. Supporters of a high tariff did not favor lowering the barriers to free trade. But for most Americans and most of the peoples of the world, Wilson's Fourteen Points held out the vision of a just and lasting peace.

By the fall of 1918, the Germans were faced with defeat. Regarding Wilson's plan as a program for peace without vengeance, the Germans asked for peace on the basis of the Fourteen Points. Wilson made clear that he would negotiate

LESSON 3 *(1 to 2 days)*

Performance Objectives

1. To describe and explain in an outline the opposition to Wilson's Fourteen Points. 2. To list and explain in an outline the major provisions of the Treaty of Versailles. 3. To explain in an essay why the United States did not join the League of Nations.

Famous People

Vittorio Orlando, Lloyd George, Georges Clemenceau, Henry Cabot Lodge

Vocabulary

Fourteen Points, self-determination, "general association of nations," peace without vengeance, Paris Peace Conference, Big Four, Treaty of Versailles, mandate system, League of Nations, League Covenant, Article X, irreconcilables, strong reservationists, mild reservationists, Senate Foreign Relations Committee

Activities

1. **FILMS** *Woodrow Wilson,* Biography series (26 minutes, b&w; McGraw-Hill Films). *Wilson's Fight for Peace,* Twentieth Century series (26 minutes, b&w; CBS Films). *World War I: Building the Peace* (11 minutes, b&w; Coronet Films).

2. LISTENING FOR INFORMATION Read to your students from *The American Story,* "Failure After Versailles" by John A. Garraty. Also, Chapter 12, "Isolationists in Peace," in Eric Goldman's *Rendezvous with Destiny.*

3. DISCUSSION In *Alistair Cooke's America* (New York: Alfred A. Knopf, 1973), Cooke says there were three things that elevated Woodrow Wilson to the status of a world savior: "his unwavering high moral tone, his self-intoxicating eloquence, and his true concern for the dispossessed." Cooke also says it was these three things that helped bring him down. Ask your students to provide evidence that supports Cooke's analysis. Then have them try to provide evidence that he was wrong.

only with representatives who could speak for the German people. Thereupon, Kaiser Wilhelm II was overthrown, and a new government was set up in Germany to make peace.

The peace conference. The victorious powers prepared to meet in Paris in January 1919 to work out the terms of a peace settlement. Wilson decided to head the United States delegation to the peace conference himself. He believed rightly that he was the only American with enough standing to win a peace based on his Fourteen Points. As the head of the only nation that asked for neither territory nor other spoils, the President felt he would have the moral standing to win a just peace, fair to both victors and losers. Wilson believed his hand was further strengthened by the cheers of thousands who greeted him as he toured the Allied capitals before the conference opened. Many looked upon Wilson as a savior.

The peace conference opened in Paris in January 1919. Representatives of more than thirty countries took part, but the "Big Four"—Great Britain, France, Italy, and the United States—shaped the terms of the treaty. Prime Minister Vittorio Orlando of Italy, Prime Minister Lloyd George of Great Britain, and Premier Georges Clemenceau of France represented their countries. Among those three there was no talk of a generous peace. Each led a country exhausted by war, fearful for its future security, and burning with revenge. Britain was determined to end the German naval challenge and to have Germany pay for the costs of the war. France, invaded twice by German troops in less than 50 years, wanted to cripple the war-making power of Germany by taking some of its land, resources, and industry. Italy wanted pieces of the crumbling Austro-Hungarian Empire.

With this background of ambition, fear, and hate, there was no possibility that Wilson's Fourteen Points would be translated into a peace treaty. Wilson had thought that the cheering crowds of Europe were cheering his vision of a just peace. Most, however, were only expressing their gratitude for victory. Their own leaders, not Wilson, spoke for their desires at Paris.

Leaders of the "Big Four" were *(left to right)* Lloyd George of Britain, Orlando of Italy, Clemenceau of France, and Wilson of the United States.

The Treaty of Versailles. The peace treaty was signed in June 1919 at the Palace of Versailles, near Paris. The Treaty of Versailles was not a peace without

The Treaty of Versailles profoundly changed the face of Europe, since new nations were created and old ones disappeared or were altered. Compare this map with the one shown on page 651.

victory. It was a victor's peace, dictated to the defeated. Germany was forced to accept guilt for the war and to pay a reparations bill that was finally set at $56 billion. France and Poland together took 10 percent of Germany's land area, and the French occupied some of Germany's most valuable mining regions as well. Germany was also stripped of all its colonies and its navy.

Still the treaty was less harsh than one the Allies would have written without Wilson. Indeed, it is remarkable that Wilson was able to save as much of his Fourteen Points as he did. Poland became independent, as did several of the subject peoples of the Austro-Hungarian Empire. Boundaries were generally adjusted on the basis of nationality, although in several places the principle of self-determination was violated. In the Far East, Wilson had to give in to the demand that Japan, for its help in the war, should take over Germany's sphere of influence on the Shantung Peninsula in China. And Italy acquired some land

4. READING FOR INFORMATION / DISCUSSION Have the students take notes from the text, comparing the Fourteen Points with the Treaty of Versailles. Have them include the specific issues dealt with in each document. Then compare and contrast the handling of each issue. Be sure that the students include reasons for the differences between the Fourteen Points and the final treaty. After they have completed their note-taking, have the students discuss the conflicting philosophies underlying the treaty. Wilson supported the idea that peace could only be maintained if every country was happy with its general situation. Britain and France believed that peace depended on their enemies being too weak to fight them. Ask the class to indicate which ideas of the treaty reflect each philosophy. Which philosophy does the class support—destroy your enemies so that they cannot attack you, or be nice to them to earn their friendship? Why?

5. ESSAY The text claims that the Treaty of Versailles, including the League of Nations, could have been approved had Wilson acted differently. Have the students write essays in which they explain how Wilson could have won Senate approval for the Treaty of Versailles and especially the League of Nations. Make sure they point out early mistakes, such as not having senators and important Republicans among the negotiators. The main part of the essays should identify the various opposition groups and how Wilson could have dealt more successfully with them. The essays should show the students' understanding of why the treaty was defeated and also the general concept of how changing certain factors in a given situation can dramatically change the outcome.

peopled mainly by Austrians. Yet never before had the ethnic populations of Europe and the boundaries of nation-states more closely matched.

Wilson was not able to force the Allies to give up Germany's former colonies, but he did prevent an old-style takeover. The treaty provided for a *mandate* system. The Allied nations would hold those colonies as trustees and would prepare them for self-government.

Most important, Wilson won agreement to his fourteenth point, a *League of Nations.* He believed that through the League, the imperfections of the peace treaty could be worked out later. The League *Covenant,* or constitution, was a part of the peace treaty.

The most important part of the Covenant—"the heart of the Covenant," Wilson would call it—was Article X. Members agreed "to respect and preserve against external aggression the territorial integrity and . . . political independence of all members of the League." The League could not outlaw war, but it would discourage it by the principle of *collective security.* This was the idea that all would act together against an invasion of another's country. Through this article, Wilson hoped to replace the old alliance system that had led to wars. In case of a threat of aggression, the League could ask—but not compel—members to use economic, financial, or military pressure.

American public opinion. Wilson returned to the United States in June 1919. The tide of public opinion seemed to be running strongly in favor of a League of Nations. A survey showed 1,196 newspaper editors in favor of the United States joining the League and only 181 opposed.

On the other hand there were many groups unhappy with one or another part of the peace treaty. Irish Americans were angered because Wilson had not pressed for Irish independence from Britain. Italian Americans were angry because Wilson insisted on self-determination and blocked Italy's claim to the port of Fiume on the Adriatic Sea. Many German Americans resented the harshness of the treaty. A number of those who had believed in Wilson's vision of a peace without victory were shocked by the terms of the treaty. Some Americans, disillusioned by the war, just wanted to forget Europe. "The whole continent is rotten," said one.

Traditionalists saw the Covenant of the League, and especially Article X, as an entangling alliance with the Old World. An advertisement for an anti-League meeting in Boston read in part:

> Shall We Bind Ourselves to the War-Breeding Covenant?
>
> It Impairs American Sovereignty!
>
> Surrenders the Monroe Doctrine!
>
> Flouts Washington's Warning!
>
> Entangles Us in European and Asiatic Intrigues!
>
> Sends Our Boys to Fight Throughout the World by Order of a League!

Rough seas ahead. Wilson, a Democrat, faced the task of winning a two-thirds majority for the treaty in a Senate controlled by the Republicans, 49 to 47. The task was made more difficult by the fact that the President had done nothing in advance to enlist support from the groups whose backing he now needed.

This cartoon is critical of the three senators who led opposition to the League of Nations.

Although Wilson could count on the votes of nearly all the Democratic senators, he would also need the votes of some Republicans. Yet in choosing the peace commissioners to accompany him to Paris, he had named no senators and only one inactive Republican.

As early as March 1919, Wilson had had a warning of rough seas ahead. He had left the peace conference briefly to return to America, where he explained the League Covenant to the senators. As the President prepared to return to Paris, thirty-nine senators signed a statement opposing acceptance of the kind of League that Wilson had outlined. Even though thirty-three were enough to block the treaty, Wilson was confident that in a final vote those senators opposing it would not dare reject it. And in voting for it, they would be accepting the League Covenant, which was part of it.

The Senate opposition. The most extreme opponents of the League of Nations in the Senate were some twelve to fifteen Republicans. They were called *irreconcilables,* because they opposed a League in any form. Their motives included traditional isolationism, partisan opposition to anything a Democratic President proposed, and racism. They refused to enter a League in which nations of black and brown people would have equal votes with the United States.

The rest of the Republican senators were willing to accept United States membership in a League, but only with *reservations,* which are similar to amendments. These senators were divided into a large group of *strong reservationists* and a smaller one of *mild reservationists.* The strong reservationists were led by Senator Henry Cabot Lodge of Massachusetts, who was chairman of the Senate Foreign Relations Committee. The key reservation insisted upon by Lodge's group was to Article X, the article on collective security. Under that article, member states were not required to send troops to fight aggression but only to consult with each other on how "their obligation shall be fulfilled." It was, as Wilson explained, a "moral not a legal obligation." Wishing to leave no room for misunderstanding, the strong reservationists insisted on a statement that the United States had no obligation, moral or otherwise, to send troops unless Congress approved in each and every case. Wilson insisted that such a reservation would cut the very heart out of collective security. Finding a middle ground was difficult because Lodge and Wilson hated each other personally.

6. DISCUSSION On October 2, 1919, a month after his doctor ordered his trip around the country cancelled, Woodrow Wilson fell to the floor of his White House bedroom unconscious, a victim of a cerebral thrombosis. He was bedridden for several months, paralyzed in his left side, and left with thickened speech. Wilson was emotionally upset. He was quick to anger, distrusted his friends, and was easily moved to tears. His wife assumed some of his duties, and many thought she was the "real" President. This period is described in the book *When the Cheering Stopped* by Gene Smith (New York: William Morrow Co., 1971). Wilson's illness was partly responsible for the Twenty-fifth Amendment (ratified in 1967), detailing what must be done in case of presidential disability. Ask: What kind of disability would be severe enough to warrant the President's removal? Is there the possibility of abuse under the new system?

Background Information

HENRY CABOT LODGE (1850–1924) From a wealthy Boston family, Lodge was an editor and an influential historian before entering politics. He served first in the House of Representatives and then, after 1883, in the Senate. A staunch Republican, Lodge was responsible for sponsoring such legislation as the civil service reform and the Pure Food and Drug Act. He opposed the League of Nations because he feared the United States was becoming too involved in European affairs. His grandson, Henry Cabot Lodge, Jr., also was a senator, as well as a diplomat in several administrations and Richard Nixon's vice presidential running mate in the unsuccessful 1960 campaign.

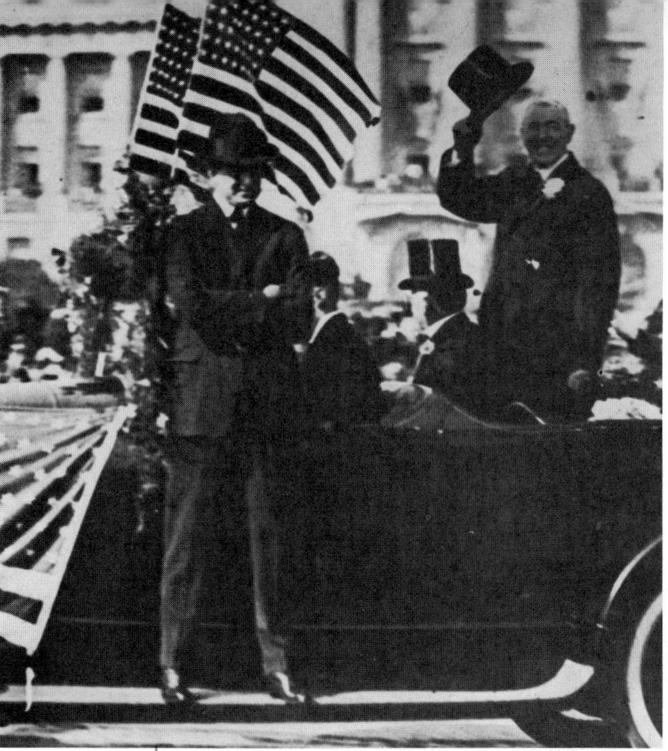

In San Francisco in 1919, President Wilson campaigns for approval of the Treaty of Versailles.

The strategy of the League opponents was to delay a vote while opposition to the treaty could be aroused. For two months, Lodge tied up the treaty in hearings before his Foreign Relations Committee.

Defeat of the treaty. Fearing that support for the League was slipping, and hoping to force the Senate to act, Wilson set out on a cross-country speaking tour in early September. For a time he seemed to make headway. Everywhere, he was greeted by large cheering crowds. But the strain was too much for a sixty-three-year-old man in frail health. After speaking in Pueblo, Colorado, on September 25, Wilson collapsed. He was hurried back to Washington where, early in October, he suffered a stroke that left him bedridden. The pro-League forces were now without a leader.

Shortly afterward, the Treaty of Versailles was brought to the floor of the Senate. There the irreconcilables and the reservationists combined forces to tack on fourteen reservations proposed by Lodge. Only a simple majority was needed to add a reservation. Included was the Lodge reservation on Article X. It was clear that only a compromise could save the treaty. President Wilson insisted from his sickbed that the reservations destroyed the League's effectiveness. He urged Democrats to vote against the treaty with reservations. With both Wilsonian Democrats and irreconcilables voting against it, the treaty was defeated, 35 to 55. The Senate also voted on the treaty without reservations. With Wilson Democrats the only ones in support, the treaty was defeated again, 30 to 53.

Between reservationists and Wilsonian Democrats, more than two thirds of the senators were willing to accept the League of Nations in some form. Moderates in and out of the Senate urged a compromise. In March 1920 the Senate once again voted on the League with the Lodge reservations. Wilson again urged Democrats not to support the League in this form, insisting that the 1920 presidential elections could instead be made a "solemn referendum" on this issue. This time twenty-one Democrats broke with the President, making the vote 49 to 35. But that was still seven short of the needed two thirds, and the treaty and League Covenant were defeated.

The election of 1920 did not prove to be a referendum on the League. Warren

G. Harding, the Republican candidate, had no deep convictions about the League and never took a clear stand in the campaign. Governor James Cox of Ohio, the Democratic candidate, strongly backed the idea of America's joining the League. Harding chose to interpret his landslide victory as a rejection of the League, and the issue was dead. In 1921, Congress passed a joint declaration—of just two sentences—formally ending the war with the Central Powers.

America and collective security. A later generation would view America's decision not to join the League as a tragedy. Had the United States joined, it has been argued, there need never have been a second World War. Those who hold this view cite Wilson's prophecy during his speaking tour for the League: "I tell you, my fellow citizens, I can predict with absolute certainty that within another generation, there will be another world war if the nations of the world do not concert the method by which to prevent it."

Yet the critical question was not whether the United States joined the League. Rather it was whether the United States and the other nations were prepared to accept the responsibilities of collective security. The history of the League in the 1930s shows that the other nations were not yet ready to do this. The Lodge reservations and the mood of America in the 1920s and 1930s show that the United States was not yet ready either. Such a change in the country's traditional role in world affairs was, as yet, too great for most Americans to accept.

CHECKUP

1. What opposition to his Fourteen Points did Wilson encounter from the Allies?
2. What were the major provisions of the Treaty of Versailles?
3. Why did the United States not join the League of Nations?

LESSON 4

Foreign Policy in the Postwar Years

The years 1918 and 1919 marked the high tide of American idealism and internationalism. Thereafter, the tide receded rapidly. Disillusionment set in as Americans learned about secret war aims of the Allies. In the 1920s and 1930s, a majority of Americans wanted their country to draw back from involvement in world affairs.

Leaders in the American government as well as some in private business understood, however, that it was not possible to return to the years before 1914. At the end of the World War, the United States was, by any measure, the greatest power in the world. Its exports, $2.4 billion in 1914, climbed to more than $7 billion in 1929. Americans' private investments in other countries rose from $3.5 billion to $17.2 billion in the same period. A nation whose well-being was so closely tied to the economy of other countries could not turn its back on the world. Leaders were therefore willing and anxious for the United States to enter into treaties and agreements with other nations in the interest of keeping a stable world order. At the same time, however, they were careful to draw the line at any agreement that would commit America to use force or limit its freedom of action.

LESSON 4 *(2 days)*

Performance Objectives

1. To describe orally or in writing how the Washington Conference of 1921 helped ease international tensions.
2. To explain orally the conflicting views concerning the repayment of war debts owed to the United States.
3. To describe on a chart the steps taken by the United States to ensure peace in the 1920s.

Famous People

Dwight Morrow, Frank Kellogg, Aristide Briand

Vocabulary

Disillusionment, Washington Conference, Five-Power Treaty, Nine-Power Treaty, Four-Power Treaty, World Court, war debts, Kellogg-Briand Pact

Activities

1. USING A CHART Have the students prepare charts on which they list the major peace-keeping efforts involving the United States during this period. Have them use four columns: one for the action involved (signing Five-Power Treaty, renegotiating war debts, joining World Court, etc.); another for listing the other countries involved in the action; a third for explaining the purpose of the action (to limit size of navy, to solve specific problem, etc.); a fourth for problems that the action itself could cause or aggravate. This last column will require the students to analyze the original action and purposes to see if any country would be unhappy with the result, or if there was any particular weakness in the idea that could cause it to fail. For example, look at the treaty limiting the size of the navies. As Japan continued to grow, it would be unhappy because it would not be entitled to equality with Britain and the United States. The Kellogg-Briand Pact had the obvious weakness of having no enforcement procedures. Since students' answers in this column may vary, be sure to discuss what you think are the most important problems. It might also be advisable for you to fill in the first column in class so that all students know exactly what actions they should be thinking about.

2. FILMS *An Essay on War* (22 minutes, color; Encyclopaedia Britannica Films). *The Twenties,* American History series (25 minutes, color; McGraw-Hill Films).

The Washington Conference. Both of these tendencies could be seen at work in the Washington Conference of 1921–1922. Japanese ambitions for territory on the mainland of Asia had caused tensions to rise in the postwar years. Some people expressed concern for the security of America's possessions in the Pacific. There were signs that the United States, Britain, and Japan might get caught up in a naval building race that all were anxious to avoid.

To deal with these problems, Charles Evans Hughes, Harding's secretary of state, called a conference of interested countries to meet in Washington in late 1921. Out of the Washington Conference came three treaties that succeeded for a time in easing tensions and keeping the international balance of power in the Far East.

The Five-Power Treaty provided for a reduction of naval armaments. It also set a ratio on the tonnage of battleships and heavy cruisers (over 10,000 tons). For every five tons for Britain and the United States, Japan would have three, and France and Italy would have 1.75 each. No new battleships would be built for ten years.

In the Nine-Power Treaty, all the nations with overseas empires agreed to respect China's independence and territorial integrity. This was the first time that nations had agreed to the Open Door in a treaty.

In the Four-Power Pact, the United States, Britain, Japan, and France agreed to respect each other's possessions in the Pacific. Should a dispute arise among them, or should another nation threaten the peace, they agreed to consult with each other before taking action. The United States Senate approved all three treaties. To be certain there could be no misunderstanding, however, the Senate added this reservation to the pact: "There is no commitment to armed forces, no alliance, no obligation to join in any defense."

A continuing isolationism. During the 1920s the United States government was careful to hold the League of Nations at arm's length. For a time, mail from the League was even returned unopened by the State Department. Gradually, however, the United States agreed to take part in a few minor committees of the League. Americans went only as observers, however, not as members, and they had no power to commit the United States to any action.

One international body for which there was support in the United States was the Permanent Court of International Justice. This body had been set up in the Netherlands to arbitrate international disputes. Both Presidents Harding and Coolidge recommended that the United States join this body, popularly known as the *World Court.* The Senate actually voted to join in 1926, but it so hedged its vote with reservations that the other members of the Court refused to accept the bid.

The war debts. One issue that nagged the United States relations with several European countries during the 1920s was the war debts. During and immediately after World War I, the United States government had lent billions of dollars to the Allies. Now the Allies said that the United States should regard those loans as its contribution to the joint war effort. Their contributions, they said, had been made in the blood of their armed forces and in the destroyed property within their borders. Therefore the United States should not demand payment of the loans. While willing to spread out the payments and cut down the interest, the United States insisted the debts should be paid. "They hired the money, didn't they?" asked President Coolidge. Further, it was pointed out, the Allies had received territory and reparations from Germany, while the United States received neither.

France and Britain then insisted that they could only pay their debts to the United States as they collected reparations from Germany. When Germany was unable to make payments on its debts—as was the case in 1923—the Allies felt they should not have to do so either. Officially, the United States refused to accept the argument that one had anything to do with the other. Unofficially, however, the United States recognized the connection. In 1924 and again in 1929, the United States took the lead in getting German reparations on a more manageable payment plan. But the worldwide depression of the 1930s, plus events in Germany, ended the payment of both the reparations and the Allies' war debts. Only Finland completed its payments to the United States.

The vast debts brought on during World War I were a matter of great concern during the post-war years. The debts were regarded everywhere as serious obstacles to economic recovery.

Relations with Latin America. In Latin America, the United States remained determined to dominate. American investments, less than $1 billion in 1914, rose to $5.4 billion in 1929, and the United States controlled the finances of ten Caribbean countries. The United States tried to install friendly governments in those lands, and on several occasions intervened with the use of troops.

Even in Latin America, however, American officials backed away from earlier policies that too readily committed the United States to action, especially the use of troops. Thus in 1928 the United States announced that it would no longer use the Roosevelt Corollary to justify intervening in the affairs of another country. In Mexico, when American oil interests complained that the lands they owned had been seized under Mexican laws, the United States reacted neither with threats nor with armed intervention. Instead, President Coolidge sent a skillful ambassador, Dwight Morrow, to straighten out matters. Morrow did succeed in getting some changes in the laws, and relations between the two neighbors improved.

3. DISCUSSION Have the class discuss the various arguments concerning the payment of war debts to the United States after World War. I. If your class did the wall chart of casualties (Lesson 2, Activity 6), refer to that when discussing the question of payment in blood versus payment in money. Have the students also consider possible consequences for the United States had it not lent the Allies the money. Explain and discuss the effect of the war debts and the reparations on the inflation and depression of the 1920s and 1930s.

4. ANALYZING SOURCE MATERIAL After discussing relations with Latin America during this period, read the following to the class from Commager's *Documents of American History:* 460, "American Intervention in Nicaragua" and 469, "The Stimson Doctrine." Ask why the United States intervened. Would the United States today intervene in similar circumstances? Should it? What advantages and disadvantages did Stimson's policy have? Was it similiar to, or different from, United States policy today?

5. DEBATE Divide the class for a debate on the following topic: Resolved, That a new peace pact signed by all the major world powers would ensure peace today.

6. CROSSWORD PUZZLE Have students, perhaps working in pairs, make up crossword puzzles using the terms, and names of people and events from this chapter. This will serve as a review device. You may wish to duplicate and distribute several of the best puzzles and/or keep them for use with another class.

ANSWERS TO REVIEW QUESTIONS

1. Many Americans or their parents were born in European countries and felt loyal to those countries. Many German Americans sympathized with Germany. Irish Americans hoped for defeat of hated England. Most Americans sympathized with England and France due to a shared heritage and/or tradition of cooperation and support. Economic ties also created close relations with the Allies.
2. On January 31, 1917, Germany announced its intention to resume unrestricted submarine warfare—torpedoing without warning any ship that entered waters around the British Isles. President Wilson broke off diplomatic relations with Germany. Five American ships were sunk in March. Wilson learned that month that Germany had proposed a secret alliance with Mexico in the event that the United States entered the war. Wilson asked Congress to declare war on Germany, which it did on April 6.
3. The United States accounted for two thirds of the total cost of the war by selling government bonds to the public. The remaining third was raised through taxes on many items, plus higher taxes on private and corporate incomes.
4. The United States Navy was needed to combat the German submarines and to supplement the badly decimated British fleet for transporting provisions and for military maneuvers. The United States began to build ships that could be used on antisubmarine duty. More important, the convoy system was devised to escort large fleets of freighters and troop carriers safely across the Atlantic under the protection of destroyers.

The Kellogg-Briand Pact. One final expression of the new direction in American foreign policy came in 1928 in a pact drawn up by Secretary of State Frank Kellogg and French Foreign Minister Aristide Briand. The sixty-three nations that eventually signed the Kellogg-Briand Pact agreed to "renounce war as an instrument of national policy." All agreed to settle their disputes by peaceful means only. But this pact to outlaw war did not commit any signer to do anything in the event the pact was violated. With this assurance, the United States Senate happily voted for the pact, 85 to 1.

Following its rejection of the League of Nations, the United States had moved cautiously during the 1920s toward putting together a structure that it hoped would keep the peace. Among the parts of the structure were the Washington Conference treaties, aimed at stabilizing the Far East, as well as a number of security treaties among European nations. The capstone of the structure was the Kellogg-Briand Pact. How these measures would stand up to a challenge remained to be seen. And what America's response would be to such a challenge was also unknown. In the next chapter, you will read about a challenge to peace and America's response to it.

CHECKUP

1. How did the Washington Conference of 1921 help ease international tensions?
2. What were the conflicting views during the 1920s on the war-debts issue?
3. What steps did the United States take in the late 1920s in the interest of peace?

Key Facts from Chapter 32

1. When World War I broke out in Europe in 1914, the United States was determined to remain neutral, even though its sympathies lay with the Allies.
2. The sinking of American ships by German submarines was a major factor in the decision of the United States to enter the war in 1917 on the side of the Allies.
3. Even before the war ended in 1918 with an Allied victory, President Woodrow Wilson proposed his Fourteen Points as the basis for a just and lasting peace.
4. The peace conference in Paris in 1919 produced the Treaty of Versailles. Although it included several of Wilson's Fourteen Points, it was a victor's peace. It forced Germany to accept guilt for the war, to pay large reparations, and to give up its colonies and part of its territory.
5. In the Treaty of Versailles, the Allies approved Wilson's plan for a League of Nations, but the United States Senate rejected American membership in the League.

★ REVIEWING THE CHAPTER ★

People, Places, and Events

Sussex Pledge *P. 652*
British blockade *P. 652*
Selective Service Act of 1917 *P. 654*
Liberty Loan and Victory Loan *P. 655*
General John J. Pershing *P. 656*
Convoy system *P. 656*
American Expeditionary Force *P. 656*
General von Hindenburg *P. 657*
General Ferdinand Foch *P. 658*
Mandate system *P. 662*
Henry Cabot Lodge *P. 663*
Permanent Court of World Justice *P. 666*
Kellog-Briand Peace Pact *P. 668*

Review Questions

1. What old-country ties and loyalties caused differing sentiments among Americans toward the nations at war in Europe in 1914-1915? *P. 649* Les. 1
2. What steps led to the United States entry into the war after Wilson's "peace without victory" speech? *Pp. 653–654* Les. 1.
3. How was World War I financed by the American government? *P. 655* Les. 2
4. Why was the United States Navy needed so desperately in 1917, and what solutions did it offer? *P. 656* Les. 2
5. What events led up to the "race for France?" *P. 656* Les. 2
6. Why did the Russians reveal the secret treaties about spoils among the Allies? *Pp. 657, 659* Les. 3.
7. What basically different attitudes toward a peace treaty existed between President Wilson and the Allied leaders? *P. 660* Les. 3
8. What were the main arguments against the League of Nations in the United States? *P. 662* Les. 3
9. How did the United States attempt to promote the cause of international peace after World War I? *P. 665* Les. 4

Chapter Test

On a separate piece of paper, write **T** *if the statement is true and* **F** *if it is false.*

1. Wilson's decision in 1915 to allow American loans to the Allies was primarily influenced by the threat of recession in the United States. T
2. President Wilson's war message to Congress argued that the world must be made safe for democracy. T
3. The War Industries Board had the power to allocate scarce materials and set prices for manufactured goods. T
4. As soon as the United States entered the war, the Associated Powers requested ground forces and defense against submarines. F
5. In his Fourteen Points, President Wilson proposed reinstating the Czar to power in Russia. F
6. The Treaty of Versailles forced Germany to pay reparation, to give up land and colonies, and to disband its navy. T
7. The League of Nations was designed to replace international alliances with a system of forced arbitration. F
8. War debts owed the United States by the Allies were renegotiated in the Nine–Power Treaty. F
9. Although cautious about military commitments in the 1920s, the United States tried to protect investments in the Caribbean. T
10. The Washington Conference treaties succeeded for a time in stabilizing the Far East. T

5. During March and April of 1918, the Germans drove French and British armies backward to the Marne River, within 40 miles of Paris. American troops reinforced the Allied forces and halted the German advance on May 31. A counteroffensive was begun in July by the French General Ferdinand Foch, commander-in-chief of the Allied forces, and drove the German armies back to the German border.
6. The Communist government in Russia wanted to reveal the secret treaties to show that the Great War was an imperalists' war.
7. The people and governments of England, France, and Italy were exhausted by the war, fearful for future security, and burning with revenge. Their representatives did not want a generous peace. President Wilson of the United States wanted neither territory nor other spoils from Germany.
8. First, traditionalists didn't want an entangling alliance that would require the United States to send troops to the defense of other countries. Second, racists refused to enter a League in which nations of black and brown people would have equal votes with the United States.
9. The United States was eager to enter into treaties and agreements with other nations in the interest of keeping a stable world order. These treaties came out of the Washington Conference in 1921: The Five-Power Treaty, the Nine-Power Treaty, and the Four-Power Pact.

Background Information

1. U.S.S. *HORNET* Artist Tom Lea saw this view of the U.S.S. *Hornet* from its deck shortly before a Japanese pilot made a suicide attack on the carrier in 1942. The plane hit the bridge and went through the deck before exploding. This attack, along with damage from other bombs and torpedoes, so disabled the carrier that the Navy was forced to sink it the next day. Lea, working for Time Inc., painted a series of pictures of the incident in which 111 people died. The other 895 of the crew were saved, as were all of the carrier's planes.

CHAPTER 33

GLOBAL POWER AND RESPONSIBILITIES

LESSON 1

EARLY IN THE 1930s, the structure of peace fashioned in the previous decade was challenged, and it collapsed. The first challenge came in the Far East. In 1931, Japan satisfied a long-held imperial ambition on the Asian mainland by seizing Manchuria, China's northern province. This attack violated both the Nine-Power Treaty and the Kellogg-Briand Pact. The United States, powerless to do anything else, announced that it would not recognize any territorial changes. After the League of Nations issued a report mildly critical of Japan's action, Japan withdrew from the League in 1933. The following year Japan announced that it would no longer be bound by the naval limits of the Five-Power Treaty.

The next challenge came in Europe. In Germany, the fanatical Adolf Hitler and his National Socialist (Nazi) party rose to power in 1933. They did so by playing on resentment over the Treaty of Versailles and by taking advantage of the disorganization and hard times brought on in Germany by the depression. Hitler soon took the powers of a dictator. Although Hitler promptly began to persecute the Jews in Germany, the world was still uncertain about how seriously to take his raving about a "master race" and "inferior peoples." In 1933, Germany withdrew from the League of Nations and proceeded to tear up the Treaty of Versailles. Two years later, Hitler sent troops into the Rhineland. This was German territory bordering on France. Under the Treaty of Versailles, no German troops were to be stationed there. The League of Nations protested, but it took no effective action.

Farther south, another dictator, Benito Mussolini of Italy, had gained power soon after World War I. He and his Fascist party turned attention away from Italy's economic problems with talk of restoring the glories of the Roman Empire. In 1935, Italian armies attacked and conquered helpless Ethiopia in eastern Africa. An attempt by the League of Nations to punish Italy failed, and in 1937, Italy also walked out of the world body. Meanwhile, Mussolini and Hitler were providing aid to General Francisco Franco of Spain in his revolution against the republican government of that country. By 1939, Franco had become Spain's dictator.

In all these countries, the dictators glorified the state and the use of force. All had a contempt for democracy. In 1936, Germany and Italy entered a military alliance. From that moment on, Mussolini bragged, the world would turn on the *axis* between the two capitals—Berlin and Rome. For this reason, Germany and Italy were called the *Axis powers*. Later that year the two signed a treaty of cooperation with Japan. Eventually those three countries would become military allies.

Isolation or Cooperation?

In responding to these challenges to international order and peace, the United States had two choices. It could work closely with other nations to discourage

LESSON 1 *(2 to 3 days)*

Performance Objectives

1. To describe orally or in writing the international situation that the United States faced in the 1930s. **2.** To identify in a chronology the actions taken by Congress in the 1930s to keep America out of war. **3.** To explain orally or in writing why and how the United States came to the aid of Great Britain in the late 1930s. **4.** To explain why the Japanese government chose to go to war against the United States.

Famous People

Adolf Hitler, Benito Mussolini, General Francisco Franco, Neville Chamberlain, Wendell Willkie, Prince Konoye, Hideki Tojo

Vocabulary

Manchuria, Nazi party, "master race," Rhineland, Ethiopia, Axis powers, Johnson Debt Default Act, neutrality acts, "quarantine," Ludlow Resolution, Good Neighbor policy, Sudetenland, Munich Pact, nonaggression pact, cash-and-carry, Maginot Line, *sitzkrieg, blitzkrieg,* Dunkirk, RAF, Fortress America, Committee to Defend America, destroyer deal, Lend-Lease, U.S.S. *Greer,* Japan's New Order, Dutch East Indies, oil embargo, Pearl Harbor

Activities

1. MAKING A CHRONOLOGY Have the students use their textbooks and possibly other resource materials to make a chronology of events leading up to Pearl Harbor. Identify the events in Europe and Asia that led to the war in those areas. For the United States, include both the efforts to avoid the war and the actions that involved the United States more deeply in the conflict.

After the students have completed the chronologies, use them while discussing the ideas in the performance objectives above. You will probably also want to discuss some of the classic questions of this era; for example, "Where could Hitler have been stopped if Britain and France had been willing and prepared?" Or "Did the isolationist movement in the United States mislead Japan and Germany into thinking that the United States would not enter or support the war?" Another favorite is "Did FDR know about the attack on Pearl Harbor beforehand but let it happen in order to assure America's entry into the war?" These questions could also stimulate additional research for some students.

aggression. Or it could try to separate itself from the problems abroad and from any war that might follow.

There was no doubt as to which course the United States intended to take. The mood of America in the early 1930s was one of withdrawal. Disillusionment with America's participation in World War I was still high. Journalists, writers of plays, and some historians developed the theme that America's entry into World War I had been a mistake. A Senate committee studying the roles of munitions makers and bankers during that conflict concluded, with little evidence, that these groups had been responsible for getting the United States into war. The failure of European countries to pay their war debts added to the feeling that America had been tricked into entering the war. In fact, Congress in 1934 passed the Johnson Debt Default Act, prohibiting American loans to any government that had not paid its war debts. A magazine in 1935 claimed, with only small exaggeration, that "ninety-nine out of one hundred would today regard as an imbecile anyone who would suggest that in event of a European war the United States should again participate in it."

The neutrality acts. Between 1935 and 1937, Congress passed a series of laws aimed at keeping the country out of war. This was to be done by prohibiting the kinds of actions that Congress believed had drawn the United States into the last war. Congress enacted laws that (1) prohibited loans to any nation at war, (2) forbade Americans to travel on belligerent ships, (3) forbade the sale of munitions to any nation at war, and (4) forbade American ships to carry war goods anywhere during wartime.

Not all Americans agreed with the laws. Some pointed out that the United States was giving up freedom of the seas, a principle it had fought for in the War of 1812. Others pointed out that by denying help equally to victims and aggressors, the laws would encourage aggression. But there is little question that the neutrality acts had the overwhelming support of Americans.

Two further episodes, in 1937 and 1938, served to confirm the mood of Americans. In the fall of 1937, Japan opened a full-scale attack upon China, beginning an undeclared war that would last for the next eight years. President Roosevelt suggested in a speech that "peace loving nations" should "quarantine" aggressors and make "positive endeavors to keep the peace." When isolationists protested, however, Roosevelt quickly backed off. He denied that he was proposing any active role for the United States. Then in January 1938, Congress only narrowly defeated the *Ludlow Resolution.* This was a proposal for a constitutional amendment to require a nationwide vote before Congress could declare war, except in case of an invasion. Polls showed that a majority of the public favored the Ludlow Resolution.

The Good Neighbor policy. As the United States was pulling back from Europe, it was drawing closer to the nations of the Western Hemisphere. President Roosevelt continued the policy, begun in the late 1920s, of improving relations with countries closer to home. His program for dealing with the nations to the south came to be called the *Good Neighbor policy.*

At a Pan-American conference at Montevideo, Uruguay, in 1933, the United States and the Latin American countries signed a pact declaring that "no state has the right to intervene in the internal or external affairs of another." As evidence of its acceptance of this policy, the United States in 1934 cancelled the Platt Amendment, which had allowed American intervention in Cuba (see page 641). The President also ordered the removal of American troops stationed in Haiti.

War in Europe. For some years Hitler had been demanding that all German-speaking peoples be brought together under the flag of Germany. In 1938 he began to act. In March he sent his troops into Austria and annexed that country without a fight. Next he demanded that the Czechs hand over the Sudetenland, a section of Czechoslovakia where a large number of German-speaking people lived. Czechoslovakia prepared to fight rather than yield, and for a time it appeared that war might result. If war did break out, it would draw in France and the Soviet Union, both of which were bound by treaties to come to the aid of Czechoslovakia. Britain would also probably be drawn into the conflict. Fearing a war for which they were unprepared, the leaders of France and Britain met with Hitler at Munich, Germany, in September 1938. They were assured by the German dictator that this was his last territorial demand, and they gave in to him. Without the support of France and Britain, Czechoslovakia had no choice but to yield. On his return to England from Munich, British Prime Minister Neville Chamberlain said that the settlement meant "peace in our time."

The Cleveland Plain Dealer

Under the Good Neighbor policy of the Roosevelt administration, Uncle Sam exchanges a hearty handshake with a Western Hemisphere friend.

The value of a promise from Hitler became clear in February 1939 when German troops seized the rest of Czechoslovakia. Britain and France now began to rearm. They promised also to defend Poland against attack, for Hitler had already turned his demands upon that country. They tried to get the Soviet Union, Hitler's sworn enemy, to join in their guarantee of Poland. Instead, Russia stunned the world in August 1939 by

2. FILMS *Adolf Hitler* (52 minutes, b&w; McGraw-Hill Films). *Benito Mussolini*, Biography series (26 minutes, b&w; CBS Films). *The Fascist Revolution*, Twentieth Century Revolutions in World Affairs series (29 minutes, b&w; NET). *The Nazi-Soviet War: Partisan* (25 minutes, b&w; CBS Films). *Parallels: The President and the Dictator*, Part I (23 minutes, b&w; Reaction Films).

If possible, show one movie that has newsfilm of the leaders making speeches. This would be helpful in Activity 4. Since this war also saw film being used much more effectively as a propaganda device, both for home and foreign consumption, much of the contemporary film can be studied for several purposes.

3. ANALYZING PRIMARY SOURCES Have several of your students examine Commager's *Documents of American History* for documents that apply to this lesson. Several different assignments might be made: **(a)** read and summarize several of the isolationist documents, **(b)** read and compare the isolationist and the interventionist documents, **(c)** read FDR's speeches for propaganda techniques.

joining with Germany in a *nonaggression pact*—an agreement that neither would make war on the other. The pact also contained secret clauses for dividing up Poland. With the way now cleared for action, German planes, tanks, and troops attacked Poland on September 1. Honoring their pledge to Poland, Britain and France declared war on Germany two days later. World War II had begun in Europe.

America's response. As soon as war broke out, President Roosevelt declared that the United States would remain neutral. "But," he added, "I cannot ask that every American remain neutral in thought as well." Indeed, Americans were not neutral in thought. A poll showed that 84 percent hoped that the Allies—Britain and France—would win. Only 2 percent favored Germany. A clear majority also favored giving aid to the two democracies. Yet that majority also wanted the United States to stay out of the war.

Soon after the war started, President Roosevelt called Congress into special session to repeal the arms embargo part of the neutrality laws. The repeal would allow the United States to sell arms to France and Britain. The President's proposal touched off a bitter debate. Isolationists warned that the sale of arms would be the first step on the path to war. On the other side, it was argued that Germany, which had long been preparing for aggression, was well armed, while the peaceful democracies, Britain and France, were not. Keeping the embargo would have the effect of helping the aggressors. In November, Congress did repeal the embargo. However, it was anxious to avoid an incident that could involve the United States. Therefore Congress placed sales on a *cash-and-carry* basis—that is, the goods had to be paid for in cash and carried away in the ships of the buyer. The law also authorized the President to define war zones—that is, areas into which American ships could not go.

The fall of France. Despite their guarantee to come to Poland's aid, Britain and France were not strong enough even to attempt it. About two weeks after German forces crossed Poland's borders, the Soviet Union invaded Poland from the east. In less than a month, Poland fell. For the remainder of the fall and winter of 1939–1940, the battlefronts were quiet. The French settled in behind the Maginot Line, their fortifications along the German border. The Germans made no effort to break through. Some reporters began to call this quiet time the "phony war," or the *sitzkrieg* (sitting war).

But in the spring of 1940, the *sitzkrieg* suddenly became the *blitzkrieg* (lightning war). In April, Hitler's troops invaded and conquered Norway and Denmark. In May, German bombers, tanks, and paratroopers attacked Holland, Belgium, and Luxembourg without warning. Within a few days, German armies had overrun those Low Countries. They wheeled into France through Belgium, bypassing the Maginot Line. As the Germans smashed forward, they trapped British and French troops along the coast of the North Sea. Only a miraculous effort by a makeshift fleet saved those British and French soldiers. In hundreds of boats of all kinds, the cornered troops were rescued and ferried from the French port of Dunkirk across the English Channel to Britain. Though the men escaped with their lives, they were forced to leave behind most of their military equipment.

France could do nothing to stave off defeat. Nazi tanks drove on toward Paris. With France's defenses crumbling in the north, Hitler's ally, Mussolini, declared war and invaded France from the south. Late in June, France was forced to surrender.

Britain now stood alone. During the summer and fall of 1940, German planes filled the skies over England. They tried to bomb Britain into surrender or to soften it up for an invasion. The heroic efforts of the Royal Air Force saved Britain during those months, and Hitler had to postpone his planned invasion of England.

Becoming prepared. Americans and the world were stunned at how quickly the war had changed. They now asked themselves what it meant to America that the Axis powers controlled the European continent, and that Britain stood at the edge of defeat. Walter Lippmann, a noted journalist, wrote:

> Our duty is to begin acting at once on the basic assumption that the Allies may lose the war this summer, and that before the

Background Information

2. THE MAGINOT LINE Designed to prevent invasion from Germany, the Maginot Line stretched along France's eastern border. The series of forts were built after World War I and consisted of tank barricades, barbed-wire entanglements, and artillery and machine-gun stations. Below ground level were several stories containing barracks, recreation areas, hospitals, and storage areas. There were tunnels and rail lines connecting the forts and there were even garages for tanks and hangars for airplanes. The Germans never really attacked the line. After they overran Belgium, they were able to capture the defense system from the rear. The Maginot Line was rebuilt in the 1950s to be used in case of nuclear attack.

A hastily assembled fleet rescues British and French troops from the burning port of Dunkirk.

Imperial War Museum, London

Messner in Rochester Times-Union

"A Huff and a Puff and I'll Blow Your House Down!"

NEUTRALITY

San Francisco Chronicle

snow flies again we may stand alone and isolated, the last great Democracy on earth.

The first response of the United States was to rearm. Congress had already begun to build up the Navy. In 1940, it voted to spend $18 billion on the Army, Navy, and Air Corps. In September 1940, Congress passed the first peacetime draft law in American history.

The United States also took steps to shore up its hemispheric defenses. In 1936 and 1938, the United States and twenty other countries in the Western Hemisphere had agreed to consult promptly to decide what action should be taken if the security of any one of them was threatened. This was an important step, involving all the countries of the New World in enforcing the "hands off" idea of the Monroe Doctrine. In 1940, Congress declared that it would not permit any transfer of territory in the Western Hemisphere. This was done to prevent Germany from taking any of the Caribbean islands belonging to the European nations it had defeated.

A great debate. On the question of aid to embattled Britain, a great debate now began in the United States. It would continue until December 7, 1941. On the one side were those who believed the United States should do nothing that might draw it into the war. Those people were divided into two groups. One group agreed that Hitler was a menace to the United States. But its members believed

The differing views of these two cartoonists on the wisdom of maintaining American neutrality reflect the great debate that began about 1940.

that a well-armed America, protected on both sides by oceans, could stand alone if necessary. This view, which was held by former President Hoover, came to be called *Fortress America*. The other group insisted that a German victory created no threat to America. "In the future," said Charles Lindbergh, the famous aviator, "we may have to deal with a Europe dominated by Germany. . . . An agreement between us can maintain peace and civilization throughout the world as far into the future as we can see." Lindbergh and others formed the America First Committee to lead the fight against aid to Britain and against possible American involvement.

On the other side of the issue were those who believed that the United States must give all necessary aid to Britain, even at the risk of war. They held that Britain was fighting America's fight as well as its own. A group called the Committee to Defend America by Aiding the Allies warned that those countries that had tried to remain neutral had been invaded by the Nazis. Hitler, it was held, was a madman who would destroy civilized values. A poll in September 1940 showed that 60 percent of the American people agreed with that position. American thinking had undergone a great change, for such a policy meant, as one writer has said, throwing "the old concepts of neutrality . . . out the window in favor of self-interest."

This was the position President Roosevelt took. "We will extend to the opponents of force the material resources of this nation," he said. In September 1940, Roosevelt made an executive agreement with Britain to exchange fifty overage American destroyers for ninety-nine-year leases on eight British naval and air bases in the Western Hemisphere. Britain desperately needed those destroyers for convoy duty. Winston Churchill, the British prime minister, later wrote that Roosevelt's act would have justified Germany in declaring war, had it wished to do so at that time.

That autumn, Roosevelt ran for a record-breaking third term as President. Wendell Willkie, the Republican nominee, shared Roosevelt's views on the need to help Britain. Therefore America's foreign policy was not a major issue in the campaign. Both Democrats and Republicans favored a strong national defense, aid to Britain, and keeping America out of the war. Roosevelt won by a large margin, although not so large as in his victory in 1936.

The Lend-Lease plan. Soon after the election, Roosevelt received an urgent message from Churchill that Britain would soon run out of cash to pay for war goods in the United States. Roosevelt knew how strongly Americans felt about creating new war debts. He therefore came up with a plan to "lend" goods to England, which would return or replace them at the end of the war. The President likened this plan to lending a garden hose to a neighbor whose house was on fire.

Of course, Roosevelt's Lend-Lease plan was far more than that. "Lending equipment is a good deal like lending chewing gum," grumbled one senator. "You don't want it back." Opponents claimed that the plan was certain to lead to war. Senator Burton K. Wheeler of Montana, referring to the New Deal's farm policy

4. LISTENING FOR INFORMATION If possible, obtain records or tape recordings of speeches by Roosevelt, Churchill, and perhaps Hitler. Have the students imagine they are various people of the time listening to the speeches. Ask them to determine how people would react to the speeches. (The emotionalism in Hitler's speeches is apparent even without translation.) Some students could be directed to *Bartlett's Familiar Quotations* (Boston: Little, Brown & Company) for additional quotations from the men. Churchill's quotations are particularly inspiring and interesting.

5. LISTENING FOR INFORMATION Read to your students from *The American Story*, "FDR and Global War" by Nathaniel Peffer. Also from Winston Churchill's *The Second World War: The Gathering Storm* (Boston: Houghton Mifflin Company, 1948), pages 405–421. Have the students note the feelings that accompany a declaration of war.

Background Information

3. PICTURE This picture of a crying, injured baby in the remains of a railway station became a classic of wartime photography. The baby's mother had been killed in the bombing of the Chinese city by the Japanese. In 1937 mass killing of innocent civilians was considered immoral and outrageous. In the years following, such scenes have unfortunately become more familiar and thus less shocking.

of 1933, called Lend-Lease "the New Deal's 'triple-A' foreign policy; it will plow under every fourth American boy." Both Congress and a majority of the public, however, favored the measure, and the Lend-Lease plan became law in March 1941.

Britain began to receive supplies immediately. For all practical purposes, the United States was now an ally of Britain, though not actually in the war. After Hitler tore up his treaty with Russia and attacked that country in June 1941, goods also went to the Soviet Union. In all, the United States gave $50 billion in Lend-Lease aid to its allies. This program was one of the most important acts of the war. It was also one of the most unneutral.

To make sure that supplies reached Britain, the United States Navy began to convoy British ships across the Atlantic in the summer of 1941. In September, a German submarine attacked the United States destroyer *Greer* on convoy duty. Roosevelt thereupon ordered the Navy to "shoot on sight." Following other sinkings in October, Congress repealed what was left of the neutrality laws. A deadly shooting war, though an undeclared one, had begun on the Atlantic.

Japan's "New Order." When outright war came, however, it would be not in the Atlantic but in the Pacific. There Japan was on the march. The United States had remained neutral following Japan's invasion of China. However, the unprovoked invasion of that country and Japan's bombing of civilians created much sympathy among Americans for the Chinese people. By 1938, Japan controlled most of China's main cities, but Chinese forces continued the fight in China's vast interior. Meanwhile, Japanese leaders made clear their intent to establish a "New Order" in which Japan would control or dominate China, the lands of Southeast Asia, and the islands of the Pacific.

The defeat of France and the Netherlands and the desperate position of Britain gave Japan new opportunities in mid-1940. All those European countries had colonies in southeast Asia. Several, like the Dutch East Indies, were rich in oil, rubber, tin, and other resources that Japan needed. In June 1940, Japan demanded that the French government give it the right to build airfields in

This picture, taken in 1937 just after a Japanese bomb struck the railway station in Shanghai, China, stirred up outrage in the United States and elsewhere over the bombing of civilians.

French Indochina. The French government, now under Germany's control, had no choice but to agree.

America's changing role in Asia. Just as the role of the United States was changing in Europe, so was it also in Asia. American leaders were now convinced they must act to halt Japan's expansion. To discourage further such actions by Japan, the United States tried economic pressure. It put an embargo on aviation gasoline to Japan, and limited the sale of certain other goods. The United States also made a large loan to China. Japan's response in September 1940 was to make a full-scale military alliance with Germany and Italy. Should the United States become involved in war with one, it would face a fight with all three.

By 1941, the aims of Japan and the United States in the Far East were hopelessly at odds. Japan was determined to defeat China and to replace European nations as the imperial power in Asia. The United States, with its long-held Open Door policies regarding China, insisted that Japan end its war and withdraw from the Asian mainland.

Japan's fateful decision. Japan's military and civilian leaders were divided on a course of action. The military believed that war was the only answer to America's interference with Japan's ambitions. Prince Konoye, the Japanese prime minister, looked for a more peaceful course while still holding to Japan's aims in Asia. But the position of the military grew stronger when Germany invaded the Soviet Union in June 1941. Now all possibility of the use of Soviet forces against Japan was removed. Japan had a freer hand to do what it wanted in the Far East.

In July 1941 Japan forced France to give it control of the rest of Indochina. From bases in Indochina, Japan could threaten British and Dutch colonies throughout Southeast Asia. Roosevelt promptly ordered the cut-off of nearly all goods to Japan—including oil, the item that Japan needed most. With little more than a year's supply of oil left, Japan now had to make a decision. It could yield to the United States, give up most of its ambitions in China and elsewhere, and have American trade restored. Or it could plunge forward and seize the oil-rich Dutch East Indies, a move that would probably result in war with the United States.

Japan decided on the latter course. On September 6, 1941, the Japanese War Council secretly voted for war if American aid to China did not stop within six weeks. During that time General Hideki Tojo, who had long favored war against the United States, replaced Prince Konoye as prime minister. Throughout the fall of 1941, American and Japanese negotiators met, but they did little more than restate their positions. Meanwhile, Japan prepared for war.

The attack on Pearl Harbor. By the end of November, United States leaders knew what was in store. Military decoding experts had broken Japan's secret codes and had intercepted messages that told them that war was coming. The only thing the United States did not know was *where* in the Pacific the blow would fall. It was believed that an attack

6. DISCUSSION In the June 5, 1978, issue of *Newsweek* magazine, Meg Greenfield's column entitled "The New Quagmire" refers to the "Post-Vietnam Syndrome." This means that because of fears of having another "quagmire" like Vietnam, many senators and representatives are afraid of making any commitment to African nations under attack from rebel forces. Critics of the past have often stated that if France, or Great Britain, or the United States had individually or collectively opposed Hitler and the Nazis when they first started their illegal conquests in the 1930s, World War II could have been prevented. What do your students think about that argument? If possible, show them Ms. Greenfield's column. Suppose she had said the same thing in 1937. Would she have been called a warmonger? Is she today?

7. ESSAY Have the students write essays in which they defend the Japanese attack on Pearl Harbor. This experience will force them to view the war from another aspect. The essays should identify the goals and assumptions behind the Japanese decision as well as the specific reasons for the decision. Some students might want to do additional research, such as reading biographies of Japanese leaders, before writing their essays.

Background Information

4. JEANNETTE RANKIN (1880–1973) The first woman ever to serve in Congress, Jeannette Rankin of Montana was in her first year when war was declared on Germany in 1917. Being a lifelong pacifist, Rankin voted against America's entry into the war. Her vote cost her her seat in Congress. She was not reelected until 1940. Then her lone vote against the declaration of war on Japan ended her political career. Still active in the 1960s, Rankin continued her pacifist work and campaigned against the war in Vietnam.

In this panoramic painting of the attack on Pearl Harbor, bombs splash beside the battleship *Nevada*.

might be made on the Dutch East Indies, or possibly on the Philippines. Instead, a Japanese force of thirty-three ships, including aircraft carriers, was already crossing the 3,000 miles (4,800 km) of ocean toward Pearl Harbor, Hawaii. There the United States Pacific fleet was based.

At 7:55 A.M. on Sunday, December 7, 1941, Japanese carrier planes approached Pearl Harbor. "Pearl Harbor was asleep in the morning mist," later wrote the Japanese officer who led the first formation. "Calm and serene inside the harbor . . . important ships of the Pacific Fleet [were] strung out and anchored, two ships side by side." Japanese bombs quickly knocked out practically the whole fleet, except for three aircraft carriers that were at sea.

The following day, President Roosevelt asked Congress for a declaration of war; Congress promptly voted it. Three days later, Germany and Italy, in keeping with their alliance with Japan, declared war on the United States. America was now in World War II.

CHECKUP

1. What steps did Congress take in the 1930s to keep America out of war?
2. Why and how in the late 1930s did the United States come to the aid of Great Britain?
3. What led the Japanese government to go to war against the United States?

LESSON 2

America in World War II

Two weeks after Pearl Harbor, British Prime Minister Winston Churchill and his advisers went to Washington to plan overall strategy. One of the important results of that meeting was the Declara-

Dense clouds of smoke from the fiercely burning battleship *Arizona* blot out the morning sun.

tion of the United Nations of January 1, 1942. Twenty-six nations signed this treaty of alliance, pledging to stay in the war against the Axis powers to the finish. One of those countries was the United States, which was departing from its long tradition against alliances. The public's approval of this treaty was an indication of a sharply changing view of the role that America must play in world affairs.

War in the Pacific, 1942. For the first six months after America entered the war, the outlook was grim for the Allies. In the Pacific, Japan topped one success with another. The Japanese forces seized the Malay Peninsula with the British naval base of Singapore, the British colony of Hong Kong, the Philippine Islands, the Dutch East Indies, and the American outposts of Guam and Wake Island. Japan also landed troops in the northern Solomon Islands, threatening Australia. In the battle of the Java Sea, the Japanese navy inflicted heavy losses on a joint fleet of the United States, Britain, Australia, and the Netherlands. By the end of April 1942, Japan controlled the entire western Pacific as well as the mainland of Southeast Asia up to the border of India.

No one realized it at the time, but the early spring of 1942 marked the high tide of Japan's fortunes in World War II. In May the Japanese navy received its first setback when carrier-based planes from a British-American naval force sank or damaged thirty warships in the battle of the Coral Sea. This battle halted the Japanese advance on Australia. A month later the Japanese suffered even heavier losses in a fierce battle with

LESSON 2 *(2 to 3 days)*

Performance Objectives

1. To indicate on a map the strategy and events that led to the Allied victory in Europe.
2. To indicate on a map the American strategy in the Pacific that led to the Allied victory over the Japanese.
3. To describe and explain orally or in writing the preparations made by the Allies for the postwar world.

Famous People

Winston Churchill, Admiral William Halsey, General Erwin Rommel, General Bernard Montgomery, General Douglas MacArthur, Harry S. Truman

Vocabulary

Declaration of the United Nations, Singapore, Wake Island, Coral Sea, Midway, Guadalcanal, *Afrika Korps,* Suez Canal, El Alamein, Sicily, Stalingrad, June 6, 1944, Normandy, battle of the Bulge, death camps, "final solution," island-hopping, Iwo Jima, Okinawa, atomic bomb, Hiroshima, price controls, rationing, "Rosie the Riveter," Atlantic Charter, Tehran Conference, Yalta Conference, United Nations Charter

American warships and planes at Midway Island. Those victories stemmed the Japanese tide in the Pacific. From that point on, Japan was on the defensive. In August 1942, American troops landed on Guadalcanal, one of the Solomon Islands. Fighting raged for four months before Americans took control. When the Japanese tried to retake the island, Admiral William Halsey and the American fleet delivered a crushing blow to the Japanese navy in a four-day battle.

War in Europe and Africa, 1942. In Europe, too, 1942 started out bleakly for the Allies. On the eastern front, German forces had taken the Ukraine, Russia's breadbasket. They had seized the oil

The United States armed forces faced a gigantic task in reducing the area of Japanese control.

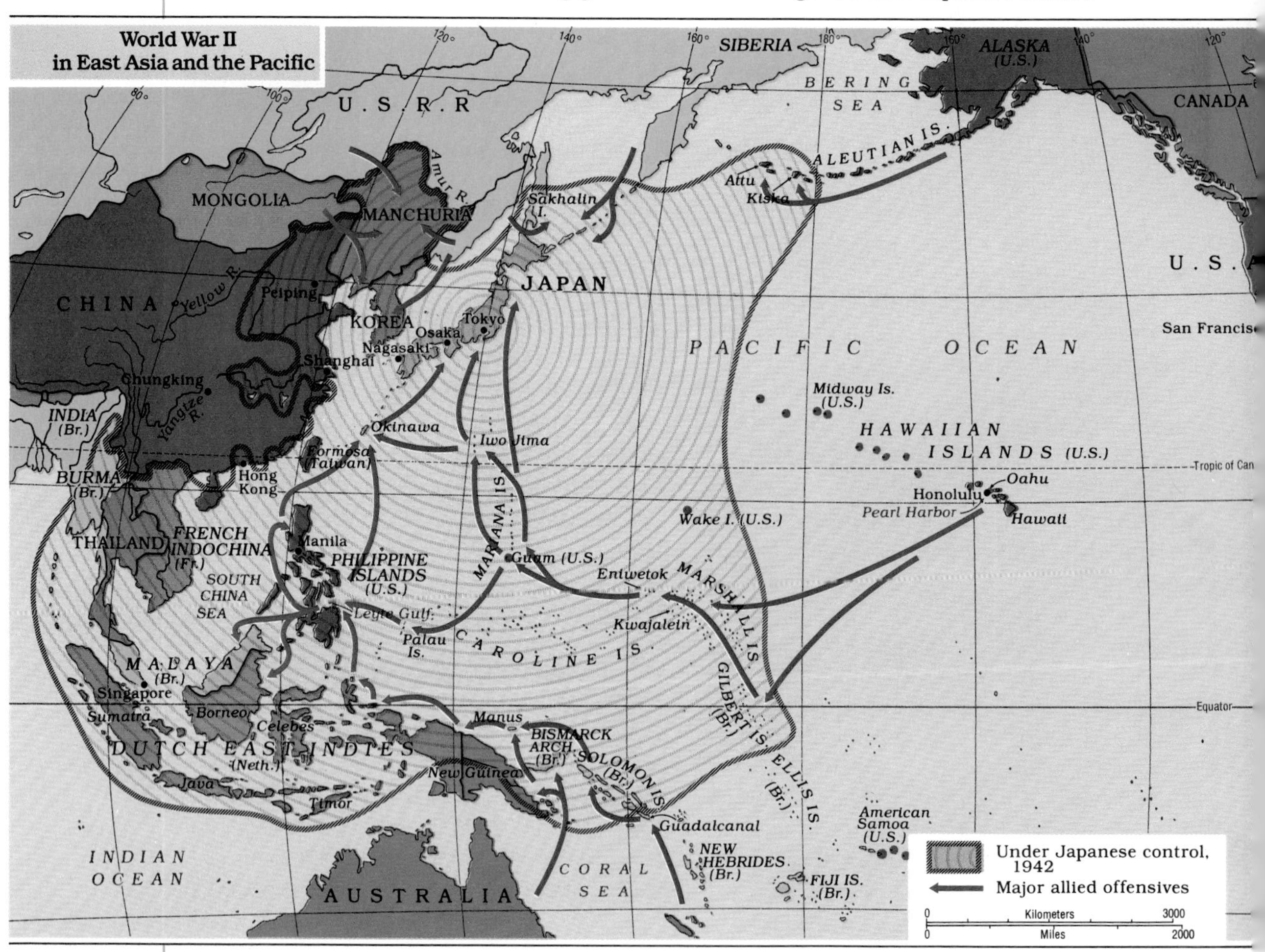

fields of the Caucasus and pushed to the banks of the Volga River, where they prepared to lay siege to the city of Stalingrad. Axis armies also crushed resistance in the Balkans. In North Africa, German General Erwin Rommel's *Afrika Korps* pushed British General Bernard Montgomery's army across the desert to the Egyptian border. There the Germans made plans to smash into Egypt and take the Suez Canal and the rich Middle East oil fields. With air bases in North Africa as well as in Italy and Greece, the Axis powers drove the British navy and shipping out of the Mediterranean Sea. In the Atlantic, German U-boats sank ships faster than the Allies could replace them. From the skies over England, German bombers rained death and destruction daily.

But in the fall of 1942, the tide began to turn. In November, Montgomery's army defeated Rommel at El Alamein and drove the Germans back across the North African desert. Four days later, a large American invasion force under the command of General Dwight Eisenhower landed in Morocco and Algeria.

Allied advances. With the British pushing westward along the North African coast and American forces driving eastward, German and Italian armies were caught in between. After bitter fighting, the Axis troops surrendered in May 1943. This made it possible once again for Allied ships to use the Mediterranean Sea.

From their North African base, the Allies invaded Sicily in the summer of 1943 and quickly took that island. In September they made their first landing in Italy. There, Italians overthrew the dictator Mussolini and imprisoned him. Though he was rescued by German paratroopers and taken behind the German lines, he was no longer the leader of the Italian people. The new Italian government not only quickly surrendered to the Allies but also joined them in the fight against Germany. Military victory in Italy was anything but easy, however. The German armies resisted stubbornly, and the rugged Italian mountains made each mile of advance costly for the Allies. They did not gain full control of Italy until almost the end of the war. At about the same time, Mussolini was caught and killed by Italian patriots.

Meanwhile, the blitzkrieg that had taken German armies deep into Russia came to a grinding halt. The Germans suffered one of their most costly defeats of the war at Stalingrad. A heroic defense by Russian soldiers and civilians and the severe Russian winter combined to defeat the Germans. German losses came to a half million men. A German summer offensive in 1943 was thrown back, and from that time on, Russian armies kept on the attack. By early 1944, the Russians had driven the Germans out of most of the Soviet Union and were ready to enter Poland.

Meanwhile, the Allies were winning the battle of the Atlantic. Improved antisubmarine techniques allowed the Allies in 1943 to cut their shipping losses, compared with those of the previous year, by more than 80 percent. Although the German submarine remained an important weapon, it no longer had the ability to cripple Allied supply lines. By mid-1943, mountains of supplies from America's factories were being shipped

Activities

1. USING A MAP Below are several map assignments relating to the study of World War II. The activity as described here is designed to involve several groups of students, each group doing a different map. However, you may find it advantageous to combine several of the maps and have the entire class do them. Or you might be able to present and discuss the material using classroom maps and then skip right to the analysis of the maps.

Divide the class into groups for the following assignments.

a. On an outline map of the world, indicate those countries that were members of the Axis, the Allies, and those that remained neutral. (See *World Book Encyclopedia,* Vol. 21, page 381.)

b. On an outline map of Europe and Africa, indicate the greatest extent of German expansion. Also note how and when the various conquests were made. (See text page 685 and *World Book,* Vol. 21, page 385.)

c. On an outline map of Asia and the Pacific, indicate the greatest extent of Japanese expansion. Show when each area was captured. (See text page 682 and *World Book,* Vol. 21, pages 403 and 384.)

d. On an outline map of Europe and Africa, show the Allied strategy for attacking Germany. Mark the places and dates of the various invasions, and use arrows to indicate the Allied progress. (See text page 685 and *World Book,* Vol. 21, page 384.)

e. On an outline map of Asia and the Pacific, show the American strategy for defeating Japan. Mark the progress by arrows, and indicate when each step was taken. (See text page 682 and *World Book*, Vol. 21, page 403.)
f. On an outline map of the world, indicate casualties for the major countries involved in the war. (See *World Book*, Vol. 21, page 411.)
g. On an outline map of Europe, indicate the occupying countries at the end of the war, and show those countries that later became Communist and those that did not.

Display the maps for all the groups to study and compare. After the groups have at least examined each other's maps, discuss what is shown on each map and how the maps are related. (Casualties were greater where most of the fighting took place; countries occupied the areas that they invaded; etc.) Some critics have said that the United States and Britain could have planned World War II strategy that would have put the Soviet Union in a less advantageous position after the war. Have the class try to design a strategy that would have prevented the Soviet Union from occupying, and thus controlling, as much land as it did. Ask: Why was such a strategy not executed? In the Far East, thousands of people were killed while executing the island-hopping strategy. Ask: Was this necessary? How else could Japan have been attacked?

across the Atlantic to the European theater of war. At the same time, British and American bombers were delivering a fearful pounding on German industrial cities. By 1944, the Allies were able to send as many as 2,000 bombers on a single raid.

Closing in on Germany. On June 6, 1944 the largest armada ever assembled crossed the English Channel to begin the invasion of France. In top command of the Allied invasion forces was General Dwight Eisenhower. In fierce fighting along the coast of Normandy, Allied troops succeeded in establishing a beachhead. Within two weeks, a million troops with tanks and field guns had put ashore. Late in July they broke out of the expanded beachhead and fanned out across France. In mid-August, another American army invaded the south of France from the Mediterranean Sea and drove northward up the Rhone Valley. On August 25, Paris fell to American and French troops.

During those same months, the Russians were pounding the German armies along a broad front from the Baltic States to Rumania. By the late autumn of 1944, Allied armies stood ready to strike into Germany from both the east and the west. A desperate German counteroffensive in Belgium in December 1944 briefly threatened to stop the advance from the west. But the Allies recovered quickly and pushed the Germans back in the battle of the Bulge.

On June 6, 1944, American troops go ashore at Utah Beach in Normandy. These troops were unopposed, but those landing farther south, at Omaha Beach, met with fierce German resistance.

World War II ended in Europe in May 1945, when Allied forces pushed deep into Germany.

Victory in Europe. The end came for Germany in the spring of 1945. Allied troops crossed the Rhine River and drove toward the heart of Germany. Russian troops entered Germany from the east and pressed toward Berlin. Hitler took his life there on May 1, only a day before the Russians entered the city. On May 8, German forces throughout Europe surrendered.

President Roosevelt did not live to see the final defeat of Germany. The President's health, weakened by the strains of wartime leadership, had been failing for many months. In 1944 he won a fourth term, defeating his Republican opponent, Governor Thomas Dewey of New York. Few realized how ill Roosevelt was. On April 12, 1945, while working on a speech at his favorite vacation

Background Information

1. PICTURE The beaches chosen for the Normandy Invasion were given code names for security and military reasons. The United States First Army landed on Utah and Omaha beaches, while the British Second Army landed on Gold, Juno, and Sword. Airborne divisions were dropped behind the German lines.

Background Information

2. DEATH CAMPS When Hitler came to power in Germany, he needed to fix the blame for the problems besetting the country after its defeat in World War I. Building on the long tradition of anti-Semitism, he used the Jews as scapegoats. He blamed them for everything from the loss of World War I to the depression of the 1920s and 1930s. The Jews were also unacceptable according to Hitler's theory of a master race. Besides the 6 million Jews who were executed in these camps, several million other political prisoners and supposed opponents of the regime were also imprisoned, made slave laborers, and/or executed.

The following is some information about several of the twenty-two camps that were established.

In **Buchenwald,** prisoners were used as slave laborers in arms factories and quarries. Over 100,000 died there, and another 21,000 prisoners were freed when the camp was taken in 1945. **Dachau** was one of the first camps built. In 1933 it became an extermination camp for Jews and political prisoners. After 1943 the prisoners were used for slave labor. Brutal, senseless medical experiments were done on about 3,500 people there. Most of the people died. Thirty-two thousand people were liberated in 1945. **Auschwitz,** in Poland, opened in 1940. Two and one-half million people were executed there, and another 500,000 starved to death. **Bergen-Belsen** was the first camp liberated by the Allies—in April 1945. The Allies found 10,000 unburied dead and 40,000 starving, dying prisoners, thereby confirming the stories they had been told about the death camps.

spot—Warm Springs, Georgia—he suffered a cerebral hemorrhage and died instantly. Vice President Harry Truman succeeded to the Presidency.

Death camps. During 1943 and 1944, stories about Nazi mass killings of Jews and political enemies had filtered out of Europe. As Allied armies drove into Poland and Germany, those stories were confirmed by the horrible scenes they came upon. At Buchenwald, Dachau, Auschwitz, Bergen-Belsen, and a dozen other places, the Nazis had built death camps—"extermination factories"—for the systematic and efficient slaughter of human beings. In Hitler's "final solution to the Jewish problem," 6 million people were killed. Only the arrival of Allied troops saved the starving survivors. Many had been scheduled for death in the gas chambers on the following day.

At the end of the war, the Allies held war crimes trials. A number of top Nazi leaders, found guilty, were given prison terms or were executed. Many others who had taken part in the atrocities of the Hitler era escaped. For more than thirty years, survivors of the experience would continue to hunt for these people to bring them to trial.

Island-hopping in the Pacific. In the Pacific, Allied forces remained on the offensive after 1942. The strategy of the Allies was called *island-hopping.* Moving from the western Pacific toward Japan, Allied naval, air, and land forces attacked certain strategic islands, bypassing and isolating others held by the Japanese. During the next two years, American forces moved in turn through the Solomon, Gilbert, and Marshall Islands. Meanwhile, General Douglas MacArthur, commander of the Allied forces in the Southwest Pacific, advanced along the New Guinea coast. In October 1944, MacArthur and American forces landed in the Philippines. A few days later, Japan engaged American naval ships in the battle of Leyte Gulf and lost most of what was left of its fleet. This was the last great naval battle of the war.

Moving ever closer to Japan, American forces took the islands of Iwo Jima and Okinawa in costly battles during the spring of 1945. From those bases, American bombers launched almost daily fire-bombing raids on Japanese cities, with their closely packed wooden buildings. One raid on Tokyo in March 1945 resulted in the destruction of 15 square miles (39 square km) of the city and took the lives of 83,000 people. Meanwhile, the American navy shelled coastal cities and set up a blockade of Japan.

By now, Japan was completely cut off. With the war in Europe over, the Allies were free to mass their armed might in the Pacific. Still, the Japanese refused to surrender, hoping to save something through negotiations. It appeared that only an invasion of the home islands would bring unconditional surrender. General MacArthur went forward with plans for an invasion in November 1945. In such an invasion, it was expected that American casualties would reach 1 million.

The atomic bomb. The dreaded invasion never took place. Since 1939, American scientists had been racing against German scientists to develop an atomic bomb. In July 1945, the Americans successfully tested a bomb in Alamogordo, New Mexico. On August 6, a lone Air Corps bomber flew over the industrial city of Hiroshima and dropped a single atomic bomb. The blast leveled 4 square miles (10.4 square km) and killed 100,000 people instantly. Another 100,000 would die of the aftereffects of the bomb. Two days later, the Soviet Union declared war on Japan. It did so in keeping with a promise to enter the Pacific war within three months after the European war ended. Then, on August 9, a second atomic bomb was dropped, this time on the city of Nagasaki. Five days later, Japan surrendered.

Truman and his advisers never doubted that the atomic bomb should be used. In their minds, that was the whole point of making the weapon. And by

American tanks equipped to operate both in water and on land move on Guam in July 1944. Through the strategy of island-hopping, the war in the Pacific was brought ever closer to Japan.

3. THE MANHATTAN PROJECT In 1939, Albert Einstein, acting for a group of scientists, wrote a letter to President Roosevelt outlining the potential military use of nuclear fission. In 1940, $6000 was provided for research. The Manhattan Engineer District was organized in 1942 to coordinate the work, called the Manhattan Project, and a concerted effort to produce an atomic bomb was under way. In December 1942, Enrico Fermi, working at the University of Chicago under the football stadium, succeeded in producing the first controlled chain reaction of nuclear fission. This made the bomb possible. Production of uranium and plutonium was expanded. The first atom bomb was tested near Los Alamos, New Mexico, on July 16, 1945.

4. ERWIN ROMMEL (1891–1944) Rommel was a person so brilliant in opposition that even his enemies respected him. He was nicknamed "The Desert Fox" because of his daring successes as the leader of the *Afrika Korps.* Only a shortage of gasoline and the dogged opposition of the British finally defeated him in North Africa. Back in Europe in 1944, he was in charge of the defenses on the French coast and was greatly improving them when D-Day came. He lost his command when he told Hitler that there was no hope of winning the war. Implicated in the unsuccessful attempt by German military leaders to assassinate Hitler, Rommel was allowed to poison himself rather than stand trial.

2. DEBATE Have the class divide itself pro and con to research and present a debate on the following topic: Resolved, That the United States was justified in dropping the atomic bomb on Japan. Be sure to judge the debate on the presentation of arguments, on the amount and accuracy of facts and opinions cited, and on skill in questioning and answering. Asking or attempting to answer questions such as "What is the only country in the world to prove conclusively that it would be willing to use atomic weapons?" or "What if your father had been one of the estimated one million casualties of an invasion of the Japanese Islands?" makes this a debate that students really become involved in.

bringing the war to an end, the use of the bomb may well have prevented a million American casualties. Yet a later generation would question the decision to use the bomb. Some scientists who worked on the bomb had recommended that the first one be exploded far from a populated area in the presence of Japanese observers to demonstrate the bomb's power. Whatever the wisdom of the final decision, the use of the bomb not only ended World War II but ushered in the Atomic Age.

A record production. America's victory could never have been achieved without the production of its factories and farms. The United States not only provided supplies for its own armed forces but it helped to feed, clothe, and arm its allies as well. As in World War I, America's peacetime industry changed over to wartime production. The government allocated raw materials and set production goals. It also mobilized science for the war effort. Scientists developed not only new weapons but also products like synthetic rubber to replace the supplies of natural rubber that had fallen into Japanese hands.

The result of these efforts was a record production of goods. When President Roosevelt set a goal of 50,000 planes a year in 1940, German General Hermann Goering had sneered, "The Americans can't build planes, only electric ice boxes and razor blades." Even many Americans doubted that Roosevelt's goal could be reached. But by 1944, America's aircraft factories had almost doubled that goal. Shipyards produced five merchant ships a day. The time needed to build an aircraft carrier was cut from thirty-five months to fifteen; the time to build a destroyer, from twelve months to five. From July 1940 to August 1945 the United States turned out 296,000 planes, 86,000 tanks, and 71,000 naval craft, plus millions of guns.

Government controls. In spite of long-held attitudes about limited government, Americans accepted sweeping new powers imposed by their government during wartime. Among them was the power to fix prices on all goods. This was done through the Office of Price Administration (OPA). The government also controlled wages and salaries, "freezing" them at the levels of September 15, 1942. Corporate profits were taxed heavily, both to help finance the war and to assure that no group profited unduly. Another form of wartime controls was *rationing*. This was needed so that scarce consumer goods could be distributed fairly. Among the goods that were rationed were fuel oil, gasoline, sugar, butter, coffee, meat, and shoes.

Wartime labor. Some 16 million men and some several hundred thousand women served in the armed forces during World War II. With so many people in uniform, there was not only full employment but also a labor shortage. Indeed, wartime demand helped to bring the nation out of the Great Depression. Workers were encouraged to take jobs in war industries by patriotic appeals, draft deferments, and the promise of good pay. Women moved into many jobs previously held by men. Many defense plants had almost as many women workers as men. Some 300,000 women worked in the aircraft industry alone.

"Rosie the Riveter" became the symbol of women workers in wartime.

Industries also dropped their bars against blacks. The first step to improving job opportunities for blacks came in 1941, before the United States had entered the war but while it was gearing up its production. A. Philip Randolph, a civil rights leader, threatened a march on Washington to protest the continued discrimination of blacks in defense industries and the armed forces. President Roosevelt responded with an executive order to end discrimination in hiring in defense plants. To enforce the order, he set up the Fair Employment Practices Commission (FEPC). This agency improved the situation for blacks seeking work, but the empty seats at factory workbenches during the war improved it even more. With jobs plentiful in Northern cities, black migration from the rural South increased. At the same time, a million black Americans served in the armed forces.

A turning point. The moment when Britain was left standing alone against the gathered might of the Nazi war machine marked a turning point in the thinking of millions of Americans. The world they now saw was far different from the world of George Washington's day. Isolation, they began to see, no longer met the needs of the nation in a shrinking world. For other Americans, the moment of change came on Pearl Harbor Day—December 7, 1941. "That day," said one of the Senate's leading isolationists later, "ended isolation for any realist." The signing of the *Declaration of the United Nations* confirmed this change in thinking.

A worker in an American factory during World War II machines a part on a lathe. Hundreds of thousands of women worked in defense plants, turning out weapons, tanks, ships, and planes.

3. INTERVIEW During World War II, 16,112,566 Americans served in the armed forces. Have the students make up a series of questions to ask veterans concerning the war. Be sure to include questions about noncombat aspects of life in the service, since the majority of the people served as support for the combat troops. Try to find women veterans (Wacs, Waves, Spars, and so on) to see how they contributed to the war effort. This was the first war that these branches were involved in. Again, if the interviews could be taped, they could serve as an oral history resource for many classes. Emphasize to those who are conducting the interviews that the big stories of the war have probably been told by many historians, but the students could do original historical work on more obscure, and often more interesting, aspects. These stories, if not recorded soon, will be lost forever when the veterans die. The local VFW or American Legion post would certainly be willing to cooperate with this project if the class runs out of willing relatives and neighbors.

Other students might be interested in doing interviews about life on the home front during the war.

4. BULLETIN-BOARD DISPLAY Most of the study of World War II is devoted to military developments. However, activities on the home front were an important aspect of America's wartime experience. People on the home front also suffered and sacrificed. Ask your students to search through old magazines and books on World War II for pictures and stories about the American home front during the war. Discuss these stories, or if possible, display the pictures for the class.

5. BOOK REPORT In 1949 the United States State Department published a volume describing the preparations for peace that had been made during the war period. *Postwar Foreign Policy Preparations, 1939–1945* (Westport, Connecticut: Greenwood Press, Inc., 1975) describes in great detail those efforts made, rather surprisingly early in the war, to establish international order at the end of the conflict. Assign several students to read and report on this book.

6. DISCUSSION In World War II, 327,716 Americans died either in combat or from other causes and 670,846 were wounded. Such numbers mean little until they are seen as individuals. Josef Stalin, the dictator of the Soviet Union during World War II, said that a single death is a tragedy but a million deaths are a statistic. Ask: Is this statement a callous remark, or does it say something about human nature? Do we tend to forget too easily or fail to grasp the enormity of such killing? What does it mean when we refer to human deaths as "body counts"? Does it weaken a country to be concerned about these questions?

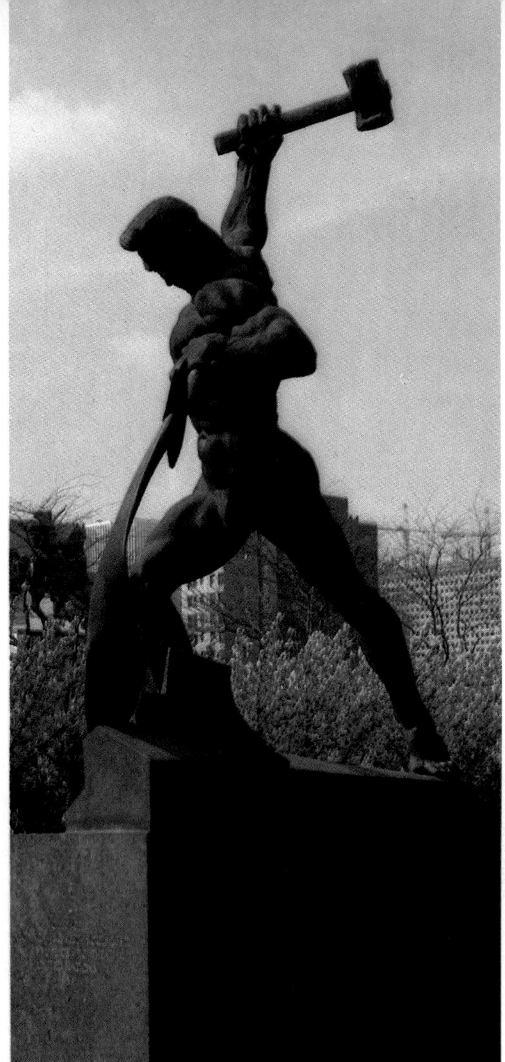

This statue at United Nations headquarters in New York stresses the UN's peacekeeping role. It recalls the Biblical prophecy that nations "shall beat their swords into plowshares."

In his fourth inaugural address, in 1945, President Roosevelt spoke the minds of a growing majority when he pledged a continuing American involvement in world affairs.

> We have learned that we cannot live alone, at peace; that our own well-being is dependent upon the well-being of other nations far away. We have learned that we must live as men and not as ostriches. . . . We have learned to be citizens of the world, members of the human community.

Planning the postwar world. Even before the United States entered the war, Roosevelt had begun to lay down the conditions for a peaceful postwar world. In August 1941 he had met with Prime Minister Churchill at sea, and they had drawn up the *Atlantic Charter.* Much of it resembled Wilson's Fourteen Points. There should be no territorial changes against the wishes of the people involved. All people should have the right to choose their own government. All nations should enjoy access to trade and raw materials, and freedom of the seas should be preserved. Above all, nations should abandon the use of force to accomplish their goals and should join in a "permanent system of general security."

During the war, President Roosevelt met with Winston Churchill of Great Britain and Joseph Stalin of Russia in two conferences. At each, the leaders of the three major Allies not only planned the war effort but looked ahead toward the postwar world. The first of these meetings was at Tehran, Iran, in 1943. After agreeing on a second front in France the next year, the three leaders also agreed that an international organization should be formed to keep the peace after the war. That same year the United States Congress, in sharp contrast to its action in 1919, voted for a resolution to create such an organization. During the summer of 1944, representatives of several nations met in Washington to begin to work out ideas for a United Nations Charter.

The next meeting of the leaders was at Yalta on the Black Sea in February 1945. Churchill, Roosevelt, and Stalin made important decisions there about postwar Germany, Eastern Europe, and Asia (see page 699). They also settled differences over a veto power and representation in a postwar international organization. The Russians also agreed to join in drafting a United Nations Charter.

Approval for the United Nations. Fifty nations met in San Francisco in April 1945 to draft the Charter. The United Nations was mainly an American idea, and the Charter reflected American ideas. It established a Security Council of eleven member nations, including five permanent members. This body, in which each of the big powers had a veto, was to make the actual decisions of the United Nations. A General Assembly, in which all nations would have a vote, would discuss questions and make recommendations to the Council.

How much the American people had changed their view of America's proper role in world affairs by 1945 can be seen in the results of a public opinion poll and in the vote of the Senate. The poll showed that 66 percent of the people favored American membership in the United Nations, with only 3 percent opposed. In the Senate, where the League of Nations Covenant had been defeated years before, the United Nations Charter was approved within one week by a vote of 89 to 2. It was clear that Americans were now ready to take on larger responsibilities for insuring world peace.

CHECKUP

1. What were the major Allied military actions that led to the defeat of the Axis powers in Europe in World War II?
2. How did the strategy that was employed in the Pacific bring about the defeat of Japan?
3. Before the war ended, what plans had Allied leaders made for the postwar world?

Key Facts from Chapter 33

1. As Hitler and Mussolini set out on a path of aggression in Europe in the 1930s, America turned away from isolationism and gave aid to Great Britain.
2. The Japanese attack on Pearl Harbor in December 1941 plunged the United States into World War II. America's major allies were Britain, France, Russia, and China. Opposing them were the Axis powers, led by Germany, Italy, and Japan.
3. In Europe, World War II ended in May 1945 as the Russian and American armies closed in on Berlin. In Asia, the war ended in August 1945 after the use of the atomic bomb against Japan had ushered in the Atomic Age.
4. Even before World War II ended, the United States had taken the lead in setting up the United Nations, an international organization for keeping the peace.

ANSWERS TO REVIEW QUESTIONS

1. The choice for the United States regarding its role in world affairs was between involvement and isolation.
2. Leaders of France and England met with Hitler and were assured that if he were allowed to annex the Sudetenland, it would be his last territorial demand. Without the support from France and England to defend its territory, Czechoslovakia had to yield, and war was averted.
3. Many Americans believed the United States should do nothing that might draw it into the war. Some of these people agreed that, though Hitler posed a menace, a well-armed America could stand alone. Other people felt that a German victory would create no threat to America; they insisted that an American agreement with Germany could maintain peace and civilization throughout the world. Another group of Americans believed that the United States must give all needed aid to Britain, even at the risk of war.
4. When Japan began to exploit military opportunities in the Pacific, the United States decided to try to halt Japanese aggression through economic pressure. It put an embargo on aviation gasoline to Japan, and it limited the sale of other goods. The United States also made a loan to China. Japan's response was to make a full-scale military alliance with Germany and Italy.
5. The Allied strategy to defeat Germany mounted invasions from both the east and the west to penetrate to the heart of the country. Allied troops crossed the Rhine River and drove west. Russian troops attacked from the east and pressed toward Berlin. On May 8, 1945, German forces throughout Europe surrendered.

6. The offensive strategy of the Allied forces in the Pacific was called island-hopping. Naval, air, and land forces moved from the western Pacific toward Japan. They attacked some islands held by the Japanese, and bypassed and isolated others. Moving closer to Japan, American bombers raided Japanese cities, and the American Navy set up a blockade of Japan.
7. Price controls were placed on consumer goods to keep prices from rising. Wages and salaries were frozen. Corporate profits were taxed heavily to help finance the war and to insure that no group profited unduly. Rationing was another form of wartime control, instituted so that scarce consumer goods could be distributed fairly.
8. Many of the plans for world peace after the war were included in the Atlantic Charter, drawn up by Churchill and Roosevelt. The Atlantic Charter stated that there should be no territorial changes against the wishes of the people involved; that all people should have the right to choose their own government; that all nations should enjoy access to trade and raw materials; that freedom of the seas should be preserved; and that all nations should abandon the use of force to reach their goals, joining in a permanent system of general security. At a later meeting, in Tehran in 1943, the leaders of Russia, America, and England met and also agreed that an international peacekeeping organization should be formed.

★ REVIEWING THE CHAPTER ★

People, Places, and Events

Adolf Hitler *P. 671*
Benito Mussolini *P. 671*
Axis Powers *P. 671*
Ludlow Resolution *P. 672*
Neville Chamberlain *P. 673*
America First Committee *P. 677*
Lend-Lease plan *P. 677*
Greer *P. 678*
Pearl Harbor *P. 680*
General Erwin Rommel *P. 683*
"Extermination factories" *P. 686*
Atlantic Charter *P. 690*
Yalta *P. 691*
United Nations Security Council *P. 691*

Review Questions

1. The United States was faced with a choice between which two policies when the Axis alliance first threatened world peace? *Pp. 671–672* Les. 1
2. How was war averted when Czechoslovakia prepared to fight Hitler on his demands for the Sudtenland? *P. 673* L. 1
3. After France fell, what opposing views were put forth in the United States about the war? *Pp. 676–677* Les.1
4. What events led Japan to make a full-scale military alliance with Germany and Italy? *P. 679* Les. 1
5. Describe the Allied strategy that brought defeat to Germany in 1945. *P. 685* Les. 2
6. What Allied strategy in the Pacific war led to the isolation and blockading of Japan? *P. 686* Les. 2
7. List some of the wartime conditions of domestic production, consumption, and employment in the United States. *Pp. 688–689* Les. 2
8. What were the plans for world peace after the war? *P. 690* Les. 2

Chapter Test

Complete the sentences below by using the vocabulary from this chapter. Write your answers on a separate sheet of paper.

1. In seizing Manchuria in 1931, Japan violated both the Nine-Power Treaty and the __Kellogg-Briand Pact__.
2. Germany violated the Treaty of __Versailles__ when Hitler sent troops into the __Rhineland__ in 1935.
3. Having become dictators themselves, __Hitler__ and __Mussolini__ aided Francisco Franco to power in __Spain__.
4. President F. D. Roosevelt's foreign policy in the Western Hemisphere was called the __Good Neighbor__ Policy.
5. When Hitler changed the sitzkrieg to a __blitzkrieg__, he conquered Norway and Denmark and pushed through the Low Countries into __France__.
6. To help cash-starved Britain pay the cost of war in 1941, President Franklin Roosevelt devised the __Lend-Lease__ plan.
7. Allied victories in the Coral Sea and at the islands of __Midway__ and __Guadalcanal__ put, and kept, Japan on the defensive in the Pacific war.
8. When Allied troops landed in Italy in 1943, the Italian people __overthrew__ Mussolini and Italy __joined__ the Allied forces.
9. Use of the __atomic bomb__ on the Japanese cities of __Hiroshima__ and __Nagasaki__ ended World War II.
10. The Allied leaders—__Churchill__, __Roosevelt__, and __Stalin__—met at Yalta in February 1945.

★ REVIEWING THE UNIT ★

1823	*Monroe Doctrine*
1867	*Purchase of Alaska*
1898	*Spanish-American War* *Hawaii annexed*
1900	*Open Door in China*
1914	*Panama Canal opened*
1917	*United States enters World War I*
1918	*World War I ends*
1928	*Kellogg-Briand Pact*
1941	*United States enters World War II*
1945	*World War II ends* *United Nations founded*

During its early years, the United States followed a policy of isolationism. In 1823, the Monroe Doctrine warned European powers to stay out of the Western Hemisphere. In the late 1800s, America's foreign policy shifted. The United States defeated Spain in the Spanish-American War and acquired possessions in the Caribbean and Pacific areas. The construction and defense of the Panama Canal led the United States to play a strong role in the Caribbean in the early 1900s.

When World War I broke out in Europe in 1914, America tried to stay out of the conflict. German submarine warfare was a major factor in drawing America into the war in 1917 on the side of the Allies. After the Allied victory, President Wilson played a major role in the peace conference. Many of his Fourteen Points were ignored, but the League of Nations he proposed was set up. However, the United States refused to join this international group.

In the 1930s, Hitler of Germany and Mussolini of Italy set out on aggressive courses in Europe. World War II broke out in 1939. In December 1941, America entered the war against the Axis after Japan attacked Pearl Harbor. After several years of deadly strife in Europe, the Pacific, and elsewhere, the war ended in 1945 with an Allied victory. America's development of the atomic bomb, which it used against Japan, ushered in the Atomic Age. The United States played a major part in setting up the United Nations, an international peacekeeping organization.

Answers to Unit Questions

1. The bird represents the Soviet Union. The doctor represents the United States Congress. The baby with the monkey wrench represents the problems that Communism would cause in Western Europe. Their goal is the cottage, representing Western Europe.
2. If the bird arrives first, Western Europe will be thrown into turmoil, perhaps eventually turning Communist.
3. The United States Congress is pictured as a doctor because United States aid could prevent these problems. The cartoonist is also playing on the old stories of the doctor racing the stork.
4. The view is favorable. The title indicates who the cartoonist wants to win.
5. Uncle Sam is holding the bucket. The bucket marked AID would help Europe bail itself out of its problems.
6. The isolationists are against aid to Europe.
7. If the United States does not aid Europe, the entire Free World boat, both Western Europe and the United States, will eventually sink (be taken over or collapse economically or politically).

★ REVIEWING THE UNIT ★

Skills Development: Interpreting Cartoons

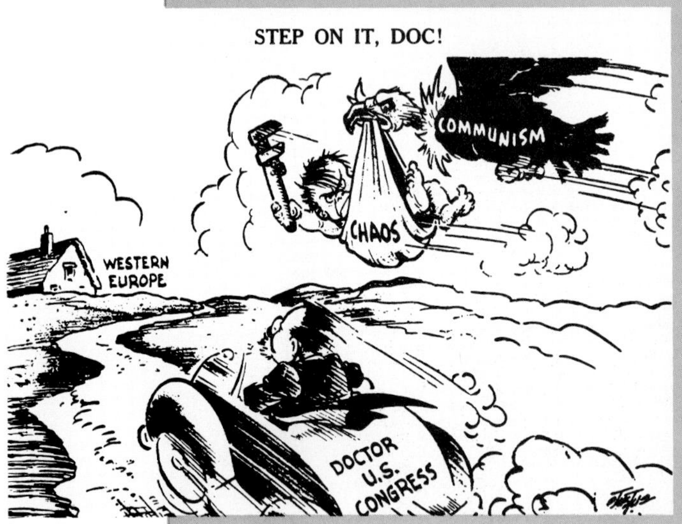
STEP ON IT, DOC!
COMMUNISM
CHAOS
WESTERN EUROPE
DOCTOR U.S. CONGRESS

Justus in Minneapolis Star

THERE ARE SUCH
WHY SHOULD WE HELP? THE LEAK IS IN HIS END OF THE BOAT!
AID
ISOLATIONISTS
EUROPE

Talburt in The World Journal Tribune

At the end of World War II, the people of many European countries were without food, shelter, or a place to work. With their economy in ruins, these nations were in danger of falling under Communist control. The United States thought that the best way to fight the Communists in Europe was to make sure the people had jobs and good homes. So it proposed a plan for giving aid to these nations to help them rebuild their economy. As soon as Congress passed the foreign aid plan, American ships began carrying food, clothing, and new machines to Europe.

The newspaper cartoons on this page show different views of American foreign aid. Study the cartoons and then answer the questions.

1. In the cartoon at the top, what do the figures in the race represent? What is the goal of their race?
2. What will happen if the bird and the baby arrive first at the cottage?
3. Why do you think the United States Congress is pictured as a doctor?
4. Does the cartoon at the top express a favorable or unfavorable view of United States aid to other nations? Explain your answer.
5. In the cartoon at the bottom, who is the figure holding the bucket marked AID? How will Europe use the bucket?
6. What do the isolationists in the United States think about helping Europe?
7. What does the cartoonist suggest will probably happen if the United States does not give aid to Europe?
8. For each cartoon, write one sentence that tells the point of view you think each cartoonist is expressing.

Unit 10

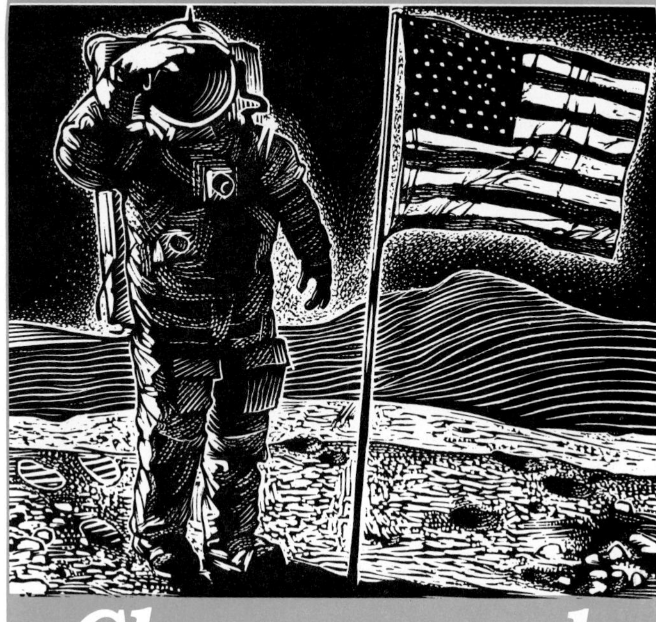

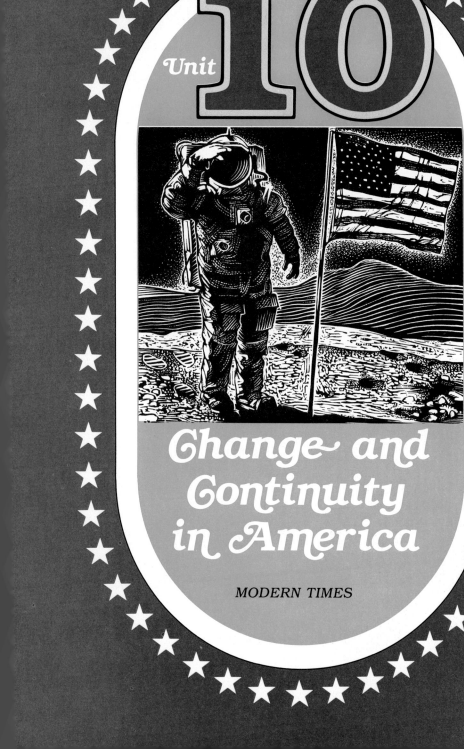

Change and Continuity in America

MODERN TIMES

Background Information

1. PRESIDENT NIXON'S CHINA TRIP In 1972, President Nixon visited China for seven days. Here he is shown at the famous Great Wall of China. The trip was historic, since it marked a dramatic reversal for the former "cold warrior." On the other hand, reporters complained that there were few substantive statements of agreement or mutual policies. In several speeches, Nixon emphasized that there were reasons and opportunities for cooperation even though the two countries were ideologically opposed. As part of the ceremonial exchange of gifts, the Chinese gave America a pair of giant pandas, the only ones in the Unites States. The trip was a highlight of Nixon's administration. It also stimulated a new interest in Chinese goods and culture. Trade with China had just reopened after about twenty-five years of Chinese isolation behind what was termed the "bamboo curtain."

THE COLD WAR AND BEYOND

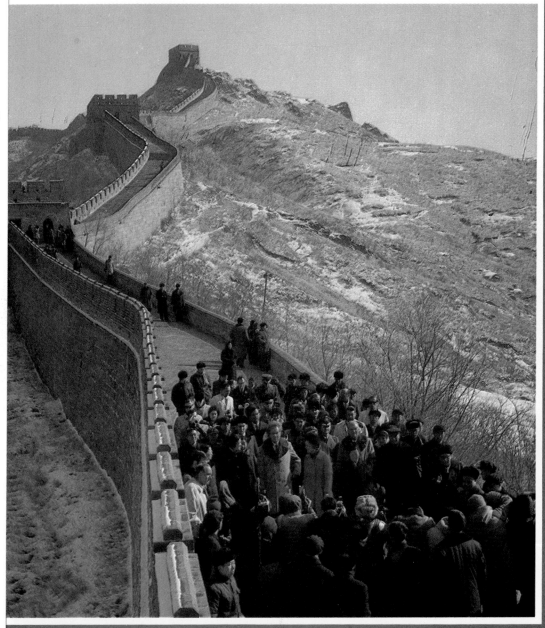

LESSON 1

THE ONLY THING that doesn't change, we are told, is change itself. Change is a law of life—for societies as well as for people. Change may come at a snail's pace, as it does in traditional societies. Or it may come with a rush, as in modern societies. But come it must.

Yet it is just as true that continuity is also a law of life. Neither societies nor people can escape their past. We are all shaped by our experiences, even by the experiences of generations long past. These continuities are the cement that holds a society together. The fact that there *are* such continuities allows the authors of this book to pose its central question: What is it that makes Americans American? What are the values, characteristics, and experiences—good and bad—that have shaped us and that bind us together as a people and, at least in some degree, make us different from other peoples?

In this book, we have singled out nine such values, characteristics, and experiences. We have presented the history of the United States in a way meant to heighten your understanding of each. A look at the unit headings in the Table of Contents will refresh your memory of these basic themes.

In this final unit, you will read about the United States in more recent times. As you do, you should ask yourself about the extent to which those values, characteristics, and experiences continue to shape our present. Ask also about the extent to which they may have become less important than they were

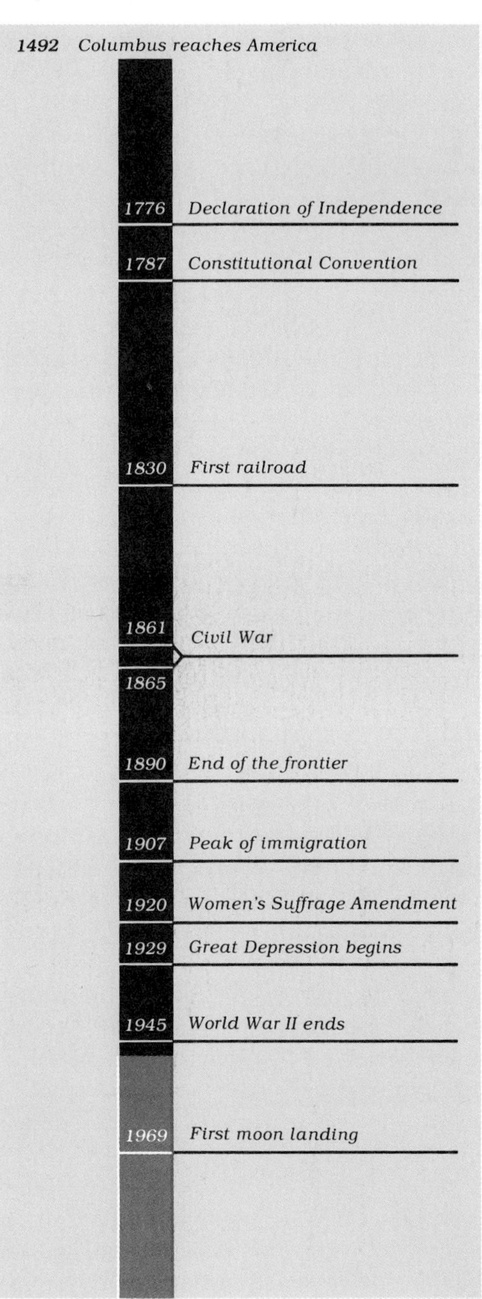

LESSON 1 *(2 to 3 days)*

Performance Objectives

1. To depict in a dramatization those points in the Yalta agreement that later caused disagreement between the United States and the Soviet Union. **2.** To identify and explain orally the United States policy toward the Soviet Union during the cold war. **3.** To explain orally or in writing how Germany came to be divided into two separate parts.

Famous People

Harry Truman, George Kennan

Vocabulary

Cold war, Yalta Conference, reparations, zones of occupation, Potsdam Conference, iron curtain, puppet government, containment, Truman Doctrine, Marshall Plan (European Recovery Program), Berlin airlift, NATO

Activities

1. INTRODUCING THE UNIT The central theme of this unit can be summed up in the phrase *continuity and change.* In earlier units, themes were developed showing how various values, characteristics, and experiences have combined to make America what it is today. In this unit as you look at the last several decades of American history, try to indicate to the class how the recent ideas and events are continuing and/or changing these themes.

As an introductory activity, review the themes of the previous units using the Table of Contents. You may also want to review, at least for yourself, the previous Introducing-the-Unit activities, since they emphasize the themes of the units. With the class, develop a discussion about the importance and influence of each theme today. Use the questions on pages 697 and 698 as guides. Try to find specific current issues that apply to the themes from the text. For example, the tax revolt of the late seventies, symbolized by Proposition 13, which made a drastic cut in the local property tax in California, can be seen as an expression of the idea of limited government.

As you go through these last chapters, try to relate the ideas and events to past themes and trends. This is especially important as you approach the present, because it is so difficult to put contemporary events in historical perspective. It is impossible to judge, for example, the long-range effects of what has been called the "post-Watergate morality" in government, but it is possible to see it as part of the reform theme in American history.

in the past. Does belief in America as Opportunity continue to shape the American present? To what extent do our traditional ideas about Revolution shape our foreign policy and our attitudes toward the rest of the world? In this age of bigness, are the old American attitudes about Limited Government merely a quaint relic of the past? Have Americans' ideas about Progress changed, and if so, in what ways? How, if at all, have older ideas about America's proper role in world affairs influenced the present? In other words, how much is Change and how much is Continuity? Someone has written that journalists tend to see everything as new, while historians tend to see nothing as new. If that is true, then the problem for the thoughtful student of American society, as well as for the leaders of government, is to pick one's way between these two mistaken tendencies.

Origins of the Cold War

As World War II drew to a close, there was reason for hope that a new age of peace and cooperation was about to begin. The United States, Great Britain, and the Soviet Union had worked together in a mighty effort to defeat the Axis powers. The new-born United Nations was off to a promising start. Further, with the dawning of the Atomic Age, there was a widespread belief that the world simply had no alternative to peace and cooperation if human society was to survive.

Yet in less than two years, the good feelings and high promise of 1945 gave way to charges and countercharges, to fear, suspicion, and mistrust. By 1947, the two great powers, the United States and the Soviet Union, were locked in a struggle known as the *cold war.*

A history of mistrust. Relations between the United States and Russia had been filled with mistrust since the Communists came to power in 1917. The Soviets had not forgotten that between 1918 and 1920 the Allies, including the United States, had sent troops into Russia to aid those who were trying to overthrow the new government. Nor had they forgotten that the United States refused to recognize Russia's Communist government until 1933.

For their part, Americans were repelled by the suppression of free thought

The presence of American troops in Russia in 1918–1919 was resented by Soviet officials.

2. **FILMS** *The Truman Years,* Presidential Administration series (19 minutes, b&w; Teaching Film Custodians). *Berlin—A Study in Two Worlds* (43 minutes, color; Teaching Films Custodians). *Germany After the Fall* (58 minutes, b&w; National Educational Television).

and free speech in the Soviet Union and by the brutalities of the Stalin regime. In 1939, Americans were shocked by Russia's treaty with Nazi Germany. The pact was soon followed by Russia's invasion of Finland and its takeover of the Baltic States—Estonia, Latvia, and Lithuania. Only war against a common enemy could have brought the United States and Russia together as allies.

During World War II, feelings between the two countries grew more friendly. Yet suspicions lingered. The chief stumbling block to better relations was Russia's demand that its allies open a Western Front—that is, invade France. Such an invasion would lessen the pressure of German armies inside Russia. The Western Allies said they could not carry out such an invasion until 1944. Stalin suspected that they were delaying in the hope that Soviet and Nazi armies would bleed each other white. Indeed, some people in America and England stated this hope quite openly.

The Yalta agreements. As you know, with victory in sight, Roosevelt, Churchill, and Stalin met in February 1945 at the Russian city of Yalta. The agreements hammered out at that conference would shape the course of events in the postwar world. At Yalta, the three leaders discussed the futures of Germany and Eastern Europe. Twice in a generation, Germany had invaded Russia, using Eastern Europe as its invasion route. Each time, millions of Russians had died. Determined that this would never happen again, Stalin wanted a peace that would end Germany's power to make war. He demanded that Germany pay heavy reparations in the form of machinery and labor. As the country that had suffered the greatest damage, the Soviet Union insisted on receiving half of the German reparations.

Churchill and Roosevelt were in general agreement with Stalin on a harsh peace for Germany, although not on the total amount of German reparations. It was also agreed that until a peace treaty was drawn up, Germany would be divided into four zones of occupation—American, British, Russian, and French. Berlin, the capital city, would be administered by these four powers, even though it was deep in the Soviet zone.

As for the countries of Eastern Europe—the string of small states bordering the Soviet Union from Poland to the boundary of Greece—Russia insisted that their governments must be "friendly." That meant they must be under Russian influence or control, lest they again serve as an invasion route to the Soviet Union. Churchill and Roosevelt appeared to agree that Eastern Europe should be within the Soviet sphere of influence. In any case, they knew there was little they could do to prevent this. Soviet troops were already occupying most of those countries. At the same time, however, Churchill and Roosevelt got Stalin to agree to free, democratic elections in Poland. The Big Three also agreed that the temporary governments in Eastern Europe would be "representative of the popular will" and that free elections would be held later.

The other important agreement at Yalta concerned the war in the Pacific. American military leaders were anxious to bring the Soviet Union into the war in the Far East. They believed this would

3. DRAMATIZATION The Yalta and Potsdam conferences at the end of World War II were crucial to the postwar world. Many of the seeds for cooperation and distrust were sown there. An interesting project would be to write and produce a play about either one of the conferences. There are many possible roles, and many other people could be involved in the research and writing of the play. Following are some books that would be helpful in this project: Clement R. Attlee's *Twilight of Empire* (New York: A.S. Barnes, 1962); James F. Byrnes's *Speaking Frankly* (Westport, Conn.: Greenwood Press, Inc., 1974); Winston Churchill's *The Second World War: Triumph and Tragedy* (Boston: Houghton Mifflin Company, 1953); John R. Deane's *The Strange Alliance* (Bloomington, Ind.: Indiana University Press, 1973); Herbert Feis's *Churchill-Roosevelt-Stalin: The War They Waged and the Peace They Sought* (Princeton, N.J.: Princeton University Press, 1967) and *Between War and Peace: The Potsdam Conference* (Princeton, N.J.: Princeton University Press, 1960; William Leahy's *I Was There* (New York: Whittlesey House, 1950); Charles L. Mee's *Meeting at Potsdam* (New York: M. Evans & Co., 1975); Robert Murphy's *Diplomat Among Warriors* (Westport, Conn.: Greenwood Press, Inc., 1976); Robert Sherwood's *Roosevelt and Hopkins* (New York: Harper & Brothers, Publishers, 1950); Edward Stettinius's *Roosevelt and the Russians: The Yalta Conference* (Westport, Conn.: Greenwood Press, Inc.); and Harry Truman's *Memoirs,* Vol. 1, *Year of Decisions* (Garden City, N.Y.: Doubleday & Company, 1955).

end the fighting more quickly and reduce American losses. At Yalta, Stalin agreed to enter the war in the Pacific in "two or three months" after the defeat of Germany. In return, the Soviet Union would regain territory and rights in the Far East that Russia had lost in its 1904–1905 war with Japan.

Within months after Yalta, cracks began to appear in Allied unity. Stalin knew that the strong anti-Russian feelings of the Poles would result in the choice of an anti-Soviet government in Poland. He therefore refused to allow free elections in that country. At the same time, Russia was tightening its grip on the other countries of Eastern Europe. In areas that they occupied, the Russians were soon stripping German factories of machinery.

By this time, Harry Truman had become President of the United States, following the death of President Roosevelt. As Vice President, Truman had not been told of any of the private discussions that lay behind the public Yalta agreements. More suspicious of the Russians than Roosevelt had been, the new President was convinced that the Soviet Union was scrapping the Yalta agreements. Truman was ready to voice his strong feelings to the Russians.

The Potsdam Conference. All of this did not make for a promising start to the next meeting of the Big Three. It took place in July 1945 in the Berlin suburb of Potsdam. The meeting lasted two weeks but ended with few agreements. By this time, the United States no longer favored heavy German reparations. It was feared that such reparations would weaken Germany so much that its recovery would be set back. Then the United States might have to replace from its zone of occupation the machinery that the Russians were removing from their zone. The final agreement was that each occupying nation would get reparations mainly from its own zone. The Russians did not like this decision, since they occupied the least industrialized part of Germany.

Truman and Stalin also differed sharply over Eastern Europe. The United States no longer accepted the idea of a Soviet sphere of influence in this region. What to Russia seemed both reasonable and necessary to protect its borders now appeared to the United States to be an attempt to expand the Russian empire. The United States hoped to see independent, democratic countries in Eastern Europe—countries whose people had the right to choose their leaders in free elections.

For a year and a half after the Potsdam Conference, relations grew worse between the Soviet Union and the United States. The two countries could not agree on the terms of a peace treaty. The United States became convinced that the Soviets wanted not cooperation but world domination. For its part, Russia believed that the Americans, negotiating "with the atom bomb on their hip," were seeking the capitalist encirclement of the Soviet Union.

The "iron curtain." Under the guns of the occupying Red army, the Soviets set up "puppet" governments in the countries of Eastern Europe. Stalin clamped an ever tighter control over the region. He tied the Eastern European countries to the Soviet Union economically, politi-

Britain's Clement Attlee, America's Harry Truman, and Russia's Joseph Stalin pose at Potsdam.

cally, and militarily and cut them off from the West. Visiting the United States in May 1946, Winston Churchill said that the Soviet Union had drawn down an *iron curtain* across the center of Europe. From behind that iron curtain came stories of killings and prison camps.

In his iron curtain speech, Churchill also urged Western unity against continued Soviet expansion. "I am convinced that there is nothing they [the Russians] admire so much as strength," he said, "and there is nothing for which they have less respect than weakness, especially military weakness."

The policy of containment. American policy makers were already thinking along the same lines. A state department official named George Kennan prepared a statement of what American policy should be. He declared that both historic Russian goals and Communist ideology were *expansionist*—that is, aimed at enlarging the territory under Russia's control. Therefore, the United States should follow a long-term policy "of firmness, patience, and understanding, designed to keep the Russians confronted with superior strength at every [point] where they might otherwise be inclined to encroach upon the vital interests of a stable and peaceful world." This would be accomplished through diplomatic and economic as well as military pressures. This policy, known as *containment,* would be America's basic foreign policy for the next thirty years.

The Truman Doctrine. One region where Russia was showing expansionist tendencies was in the northeastern Mediterranean. There the Soviets tried to pressure Turkey to give up control of

4. DISCUSSION After the students have read the lesson, have them define the term *cold war.* Identify the issues coming out of the Yalta and Potsdam conferences. Then discuss how the United States responded to the issues. Be sure to define and explain the terms from the Vocabulary section of this lesson.

5. RESEARCH / ORAL OR WRITTEN REPORT One of the most interesting figures of the World War II era was General George C. Marshall. He was described as a "Man for All Seasons." Dean Acheson said, "The moment General Marshall entered a room everyone in it felt his presence." Eisenhower said of Marshall "if he was not a perfect example of patriotism and a loyal servant of the United States, I never saw one." Have one or several of your students report to the class about this man who was general of the Army, chief of staff throughout World War II, ambassador to China, secretary of state, and secretary of defense.

6. ANALYZING SOURCE MATERIAL Have some students read and report to the class on the following documents from Commager's *Documents of American History:* 562, "The Surrender of Germany"; 563, "Military Occupation of Japan"; 564, "Truman's Statement on Fundamentals of American Foreign Policy"; 565, "United Nations Participation Act"; 574, "The Truman Doctrine"; 575, "American Aid to Greece and Turkey"; 577, "The Marshall Plan"; 587, "Universal Declaration of Human Rights"; 589, "The North Atlantic Treaty."

7. USING A MAP Provide the students with copies of an outline map of Europe today. Have them label the countries and indicate which of those nations belong to the NATO and Warsaw Pact alliances. In several days, provide copies of the outline map again for students to complete as a quiz. This quiz will easily determine which students are unfamiliar with the European countries. You may also want to review the maps from Chapter 33, Lesson 2, Activity 1. This activity showed the relationship between troop placement at the end of the war and the subsequent political ties of the countries.

the Dardanelles, a strait leading from the Black Sea to the Mediterranean Sea. In Greece, Communist-led rebels were trying to overthrow the Greek government. Should Communists win control of Greece or should Turkey yield control of the Dardanelles, Russia would realize its centuries-old ambition to become a Mediterranean power.

In early 1947, Britain, which had been giving aid to the Greek government, told the United States that it could no longer afford to do so. President Truman and his advisers decided that here was a place to apply the containment policy. On March 12, 1947, Truman went before Congress to ask for $400 million to aid Greece and Turkey. He tied this request to a statement of American policy that came to be known as the *Truman Doctrine.*

> I believe that it must be the policy of the United States to support free peoples who are resisting attempted [take-overs] by armed minorities or by outside pressures.

Congress voted the money. Russian pressure on Turkey later eased, and in 1949 the Greek government won its civil war against the rebels.

With the Truman Doctrine, the United States appeared to embark on a new role in world affairs. If the words of the Doctrine meant what they appeared to say, then the United States was offering to help any "free peoples" that were resisting communism, anywhere in the world.

The Marshall Plan. Western Europe represented an even larger problem than Greece and Turkey. The economy of Western Europe's countries, shattered by the war, had not recovered by 1947. Widespread poverty, many people believed, was a breeding ground for communism. Communist parties in France and Italy had already made large gains. In June 1947, Secretary of State George Marshall announced a plan to provide billions in aid to European countries. The *Marshall Plan* appealed to American humanitarianism. It also appealed to hardheaded self-interest. Restoring the economic health of Europe would help starving people, would check communism, and would revive America's most important trading partners.

In proposing the plan, Marshall said that it was "directed not against any country or doctrine, but against hunger, poverty, desperation, and chaos." Though the Soviet Union and its satellites were invited to take part in the plan, the Russians soon denounced it as "American imperialism." They would not permit countries under Soviet influence to take part. Debate in Congress on the plan lasted for many months. However, after Communists in Czechoslovakia seized control of the government in their country in February 1948, Congress quickly approved the plan. In the next three years the United States put $12 billion into the Marshall Plan, known officially as the *European Recovery Program.* These funds made possible an amazing recovery. By 1950, Western Europe was back on its feet.

The two Germanys. As the cold war deepened, agreement on a German peace treaty became less and less likely. Germany, lying in the heart of Europe, was the most populous and potentially the strongest country on the continent. Each side knew that control of Germany could mean control of Europe. Each would accept a peace treaty for a unified Germany only on its own terms.

In 1947 the United States, Britain, and France combined their zones into one. In the following year, they announced their intention of turning this zone into a new West German state. The Russians were strongly opposed. In June 1948, Russia halted all overland traffic into West Berlin. Its aim was to force the West either to abandon Berlin or to give up its plans for a West German state. The West did neither. The United States organized an airlift to fly supplies into Berlin. The Berlin airlift was successful, and after nearly a year the Russians yielded and ended the blockade. In October 1949, the Federal Republic of Germany (West Germany) came into being. Shortly afterward, the Soviets created the German Democratic Republic (East Germany). Thus the temporary division of Germany after the war was made permanent.

The formation of NATO. In the face of the Berlin blockade, many leaders in America and Western Europe became convinced that economic assistance to Europe would not be enough. Soviet armies posed a military threat to Western Europe. Therefore in 1949 the United States joined with nine European countries, Canada, and Iceland to form the North Atlantic Treaty Organization (NATO). Greece, Turkey, and West Germany later joined (see the map on page 704). This treaty committed American power to the defense of Europe, for it

Marshall Plan supplies reach Greece over a railroad line that was restored with Marshall Plan aid. After the war, some 250 bridges and 10 tunnels had to be rebuilt on this line.

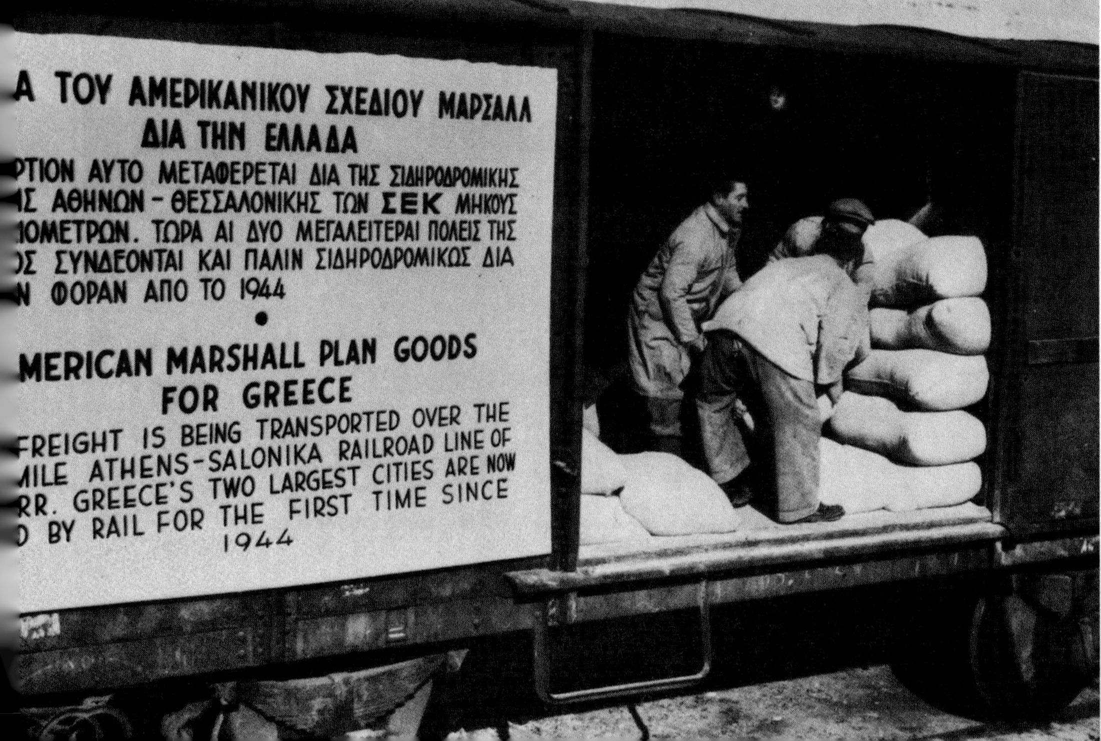

8. RESEARCH / WRITTEN REPORTS George F. Kennan, a career diplomat, was at center stage during the period under study in this unit. In an article written anonymously in *Foreign Affairs*, he first presented the argument for the policy of containment. The policy is explained in Kennan's *Memoirs, 1925–1950* (Boston: Little, Brown and Company, 1972). Have several students read this book, especially Chapter 15, "The X-Article." Other students might be interested in reading some of the contemporary criticism of his article, some of which is also described in the book. The most famous criticism was that by Walter Lippmann.

Background Information

2. BERLIN AIRLIFT During the 462 days of "Operation Vittles," the United States Air Force flew 277,000 missions to Berlin's Tempelhof Airport. At the height of the airlift, a plane was arriving every $3\frac{1}{2}$ minutes.

LESSON 2 *(1 day)*

Performance Objectives

1. To explain orally or in writing why the occupation of Japan went so much more smoothly than the occupation of Germany. 2. To describe orally or in writing the Communist takeover in China after World War II and to explain why it happened. 3. To identify orally or in writing reasons why the United States forces went to war in Korea in 1950.

Famous People

Chiang Kai-shek, Mao Tse-tung, General Douglas MacArthur

Vocabulary

Formosa, People's Republic of China, UN "police action"

Activities

1. **DISCUSSION** On August 30, 1945, General Douglas MacArthur and a small group of military aides landed at the Atsugi airfield in Japan. They were unarmed and had no military escort. They came as conquerors among 300,000 well-armed Japanese soldiers. Many people feared for MacArthur's safety. Winston Churchill remarked that this act was the most outstanding accomplishment of any commander during World War II. MacArthur felt there was no gamble involved at all. He based his opinion on his knowledge of the Japanese character. Ask: What do you think MacArthur meant? MacArthur went on to be a very successful administrator of the American occupation. Why, do you think, did the occupation go well?

provided that an attack upon one was to be considered an attack upon all. With NATO, the emphasis of containment shifted from economic aid to military defense. Meanwhile, in 1948 Congress renewed the draft.

In September 1949 the Soviet Union successfully tested an atomic bomb. With the American nuclear monopoly ended, the United States provided both more money and additional troops to NATO to make it an effective force. General Dwight Eisenhower, who had become president of Columbia University, was called back into service to take command of NATO forces.

CHECKUP

1. On what points in the Yalta agreements did Russia and the United States later disagree?
2. In dealing with Russia during the years of the cold war, what was the policy of the United States? How was it implemented?
3. How did Germany come to be divided into two parts with different governments?

The heavy line on the map marks the division between the Communist countries and the other nations of central and southeastern Europe. Churchill called this boundary the iron curtain.

LESSON 2

Peace and Another War in Asia

While the cold war in Europe took most of America's attention, events of importance were also taking place in Asia. In fact it would be in Asia rather than in Europe that a shooting war would break out only five years after World War II ended.

The occupation of Japan. At the end of World War II, American troops occupied Japan. General Douglas MacArthur, commander of the occupation forces, actually governed the country, issuing his orders through the Japanese emperor. Some important social and economic reforms were carried out. Great industrial monopolies were broken up, much in the style of American antitrust actions. Large landholdings were divided among the Japanese peasants. In 1947 a new constitution was put into effect, creating a Western type of democratic government. One of the features of the constitution was that Japan was to have no armed forces and was to renounce war.

The Japanese occupation went remarkably smoothly. One reason was the cooperativeness of the Japanese people. Another was that, unlike the situation in Germany, there was only one occupying power in Japan. The Soviet Union had no part in the postwar occupation of that Asian country.

In 1951 the United States and forty-eight other countries (but not the Soviet Union) signed a peace treaty with Japan. The treaty gave back Japan's full sovereignty. It also allowed Japan to build its armed forces once again. By this time, other events in the Far East had caused the United States to change its mind about an unarmed Japan.

Communist control of China. One of those events was the triumph of the Communists in China. Ever since 1927, the Nationalist troops of Chiang Kai-shek and the Communist forces led by Mao Tse-tung had battled for control of China. During most of that time, Chiang had the upper hand. During World War II, the two groups suspended their civil war in order to fight the invading Japanese. After the war, several American efforts to help the two sides find a compromise ended in failure. Serious mistakes by the overconfident Chiang, corruption in his government, poor morale in the army, and the loss of popular support turned the tide in favor of the Communists. By 1949, Chiang's armies, had withdrawn from mainland China to the nearby island of Formosa (Taiwan), and Mao proclaimed the People's Republic of China, a Communist state.

Mao's victory touched off a bitter debate in the United States. Only two years after the policy of containment had been adopted, another country was "lost" to communism. Although the United States had sent hundreds of millions of dollars in military aid to Chiang's government, some critics said this help had been too little and too late. Others argued that no amount of American aid could have saved the corrupt and inefficient Chiang regime. Whatever the truth of the case was, the victory of the Communists in China changed the picture in Asia.

A divided Korea. Under the wartime agreements of the Allies, Korea, on the Asian mainland, was to become free and independent. For forty years it had been under Japanese control. At the end of

2. LISTENING FOR INFORMATION Read to your students from *Modern Far Eastern International Relations* by Harley F. MacNair and Donald Lachs (New York: Octagon Books, 1976), Chapter XVII, "Japan and Korea."

3. RESEARCH / ORAL REPORTS Have several students research and report on the civil war in China and the Communist takeover. Be sure to have them tell *why* things happened as well as *what* happened. They should give some biographical information on Chiang Kai-shek and Mao Tse-tung also.

4. USING A MAP On January 12, 1950, Secretary of State Dean Acheson delivered a speech to the National Press Club entitled "Crisis in China—An Examination of United States Policy." In the speech, Acheson described the American defense perimeter in the Far East, saying: "This defensive perimeter runs along the Aleutians to Japan and then goes to the Ryukyus. We hold important defense positions in the Ryukyu Islands, and these we will continue to hold. The defensive perimeter runs from the Ryukyus to the Philippine Islands." Critics of Acheson stated that this gave a green light to the North Koreans to invade South Korea. Have a student trace Acheson's defense perimeter on a wall map. Ask: Do you think Acheson's statement was a "green light" for the invasion of South Korea? If this was the perimeter, why did the United States defend South Korea?

Background Information

PICTURE Sixteen nations sent troops to make up the United Nations forces in Korea. In addition to the United States, those nations were Australia, Belgium, Canada, Colombia, Ethiopia, France, Great Britain, Greece, Luxembourg, the Netherlands, New Zealand, the Philippines, South Africa, Thailand, and Turkey. Forty-one nations sent military equipment, food, and other supplies. At their greatest strength, the combined UN and South Korean forces numbered 1,110,000 (590,000 South Koreans, 480,000 Americans, and 39,000 from the other countries). The North Korean army had about 260,000 soldiers. The Communist Chinese supported the North Koreans with 780,000 troops, and the Russians sent equipment.

World War II, American troops accepted the surrender of Japanese forces in Korea south of 38° north latitude. The Russians accepted the surrender of the Japanese north of that line. This division, intended to be temporary, hardened during the cold war. When the two powers finally withdrew their armies in 1949, they left behind a pro-Soviet government in the North and a pro-United States government in the South. Each claimed to be the sole legal government of all of Korea, and each threatened to reunite the country by force.

On June 25, 1950, the North Korean army invaded South Korea. Until then, the United States had not considered Korea strategically important. But if the invasion had been planned and approved by the Soviet Union, as the United States believed, then it was a threat to the policy of containment. It was also a challenge to the idea of collective security on which the United Nations rested.

The Korean war. President Truman promptly ordered American naval and air forces to help South Korea. The United States also asked the United Nations to declare the invasion an act of aggression and to ask member nations to join in turning the invaders back. Because the Soviet delegate was not present to cast what surely would have been a veto, the United Nations Security Council was able to pass the resolution. (The Soviets were boycotting the United Nations because the UN refused to give China's seat to the Chinese Communist government.) The Korean war thus became a UN "police action." However, more than 90 percent of the troops in the United Nations force came from South Korea and the United States. General Douglas MacArthur was named commander of the UN forces in Korea, and American forces were quickly moved there from Japan to turn back the invading North Koreans.

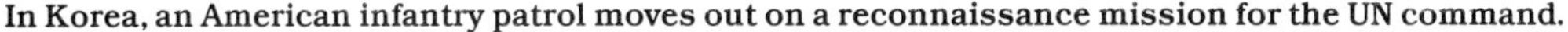

In Korea, an American infantry patrol moves out on a reconnaissance mission for the UN command.

In the early weeks of the fighting, North Korean troops nearly drove the United Nations forces off the peninsula. But the UN forces finally held the line in the southeastern corner of the country. In September, MacArthur staged a brilliant landing by sea at Inchon, behind North Korean lines. This landing, together with a UN offensive in the South, forced the North Koreans to retreat back across the 38th parallel.

The original aim of the police action had been to drive the aggressors from South Korea. With the war going so well, however, both the United States government and the United Nations now favored completely defeating the North Korean army and unifying the country. Chinese warnings not to push near the Yalu River, Korea's border with China, were ignored. In November 1950, Chinese troops streamed across the border, driving UN armies back below the 38th parallel. MacArthur's forces finally held, and a new offensive took them to about the original line dividing North and South Korea.

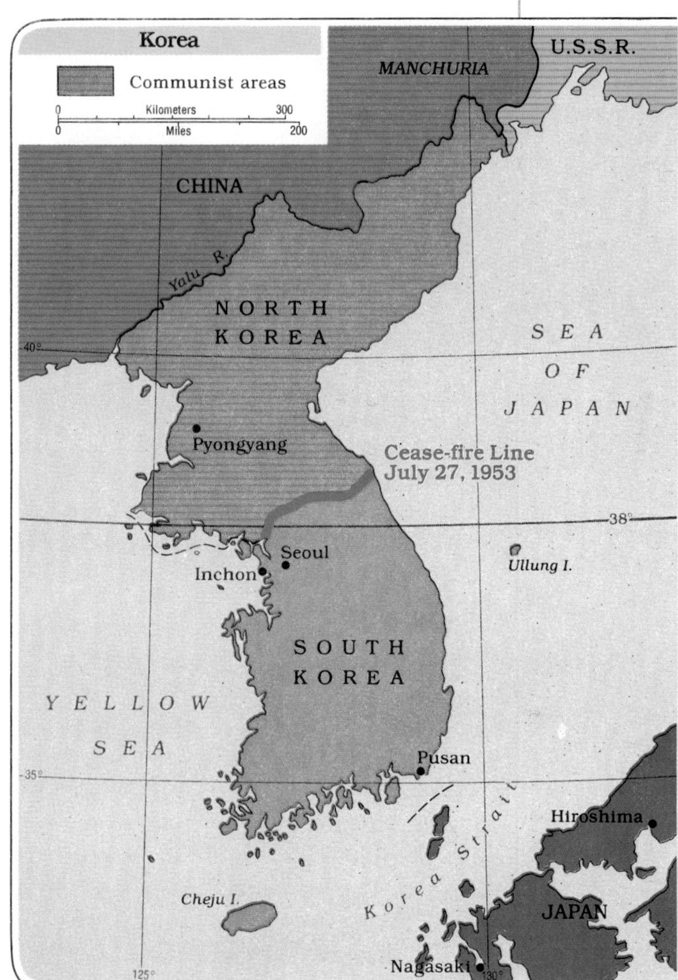

The end of the war in Korea left that country divided very much as it was at the beginning.

MacArthur and Truman. The United States and the United Nations now appeared to be willing to return to their original objective of simply defending South Korea from invasion. General MacArthur, however, was in favor of bombing bases in China, blockading China's coast, and encouraging Chiang to attack the mainland from Taiwan. President Truman and his advisers opposed this widening of the war. When MacArthur insisted on his views publicly, the President saw this as a challenge not only to his policy but to the American principle of civilian control of the military. Truman removed MacArthur from command.

Not many military or government leaders agreed with MacArthur's proposals for the conduct of the war. General Omar Bradley, chairman of the joint chiefs of staff, said MacArthur's plan

5. RESEARCH / ORAL REPORTS President Truman explained his decisions in regard to Korea in a book entitled *Plain Speaking: An Oral Biography of Harry S. Truman* (New York: G.P. Putnam's Sons, 1974) by Merle Miller. This book is a compilation of interviews that Mr. Miller had with President Truman during the 1960s. It is a no-punches-pulled view of the Truman Presidency, with open and candid comments on the people with whom Truman worked and fought. Have some of your students read about the decisions to defend Korea and to fire General MacArthur and then report to the class about the politics and people involved in those decisions.

"would involve us in the wrong war, at the wrong place, at the wrong time, and with the wrong enemy." And in the 1952 presidential campaign, neither party adopted MacArthur's proposals for expanding the war. After two years of negotiations, an armistice was finally arranged, in 1953. But no peace treaty was ever agreed upon.

CHECKUP

1. Why did the occupation of Japan following World War II go more smoothly than the occupation of Germany?
2. How did the Communists succeed in getting control of China?
3. Why did United States forces go to war in Korea in 1950?

LESSON 3

A Time of Global Tensions

The frustration of fighting a limited war had a good deal to do with the defeat of the Democrats and the election of General Dwight Eisenhower in 1952. Before and during the presidential campaign, some Republicans loudly criticized the policy of containment. They said that rather than "surrender" the people of the "captive nations of Eastern Europe" to "godless communism," the United States should "roll back the iron curtain" and "liberate" them. In the Far East, the United States should "unleash Chiang Kai-shek" upon Red China.

Some of this talk came from John Foster Dulles, the Republican party's leading expert on foreign affairs. Eisenhower appointed Dulles secretary of state. Dulles was a strong anti-Communist who viewed the struggle between the superpowers as a moral contest, a struggle between good and evil.

"Don't be Afraid—I Can Always Pull You Back"

Herblock's Special for Today (SIMON & SCHUSTER, 1958)

Containing Communist expansion. Despite such talk, however, the Eisenhower administration did not depart from the policy of containment. Short of war, there was no way in which the United States could force Russian armies out of Eastern Europe, and Americans clearly did not want war. In 1953 the people of East Berlin rose up against Communist rule. In 1956 the people of Hungary rose in armed rebellion, seeking independence from the Soviets. Soviet tanks crushed each uprising within days. On each occasion, the United States expressed sympathy, but it sent neither aid nor troops.

The Eisenhower administration did, however, change America's military program. It placed less emphasis on costly large armies and more emphasis on air power and nuclear weapons. As the secretary of defense put it, this policy would give the United States "more bang for a buck." Rather than fight costly ground wars in far-off places like Korea, Secretary Dulles warned that the United States would meet Communist expansion with "massive retaliation" and "by means and at places of our own choosing." This was interpreted as a threat of nuclear war. Dulles believed, however, that by telling the other side where the line was drawn and then being prepared to go to the very brink of war to keep it from being crossed, war would be unnecessary. Critics of Dulles called this *brinksmanship*.

American policy makers in the 1950s also favored regional treaty arrangements with friendly countries as another way of containing Communist expansion. A treaty was made with a group of nations in Southeast Asia, and another was made with a group in the Middle East. Neither treaty was a very effective barrier to communism.

A thaw in the cold war. Soon after Eisenhower took office, several events made possible a thaw in the cold war. The end of the Korean war relaxed tensions in Asia. In March 1953, Joseph Stalin, the suspicious tyrant who ruled the Soviet Union, died. After a two-year power struggle, during which several men shared power in Russia, Nikita Khrushchev became the top Soviet leader. In another development, the Soviet Union matched America's development of the hydrogen bomb with one of its own in 1953. It was now clear to both sides that nuclear war would be, as President Eisenhower had said, "race suicide." The new leaders of Russia spoke of "coexistence" and "peaceful competition."

In 1955 the leaders of the United States, the Soviet Union, Britain, and France met in Geneva, Switzerland, in the first summit meeting held in ten years. Although no agreements came out of the meeting, it became clear to each side that the other sincerely wanted to avoid nuclear war. Tensions lessened, and people spoke of the "spirit of Geneva."

The growth of nationalism. Within fifteen years after World War II, the great colonial empires broke up. As the winds of nationalism blew across Asia and Africa, former European colonies became independent countries. Most of those developing nations wished to concentrate on solving their own problems. They often sought economic aid from the big powers, but they also wanted to steer clear of falling under outside influence. On the other hand, the great powers tried to use their aid to gain influence in the new countries. Those new nations that aligned themselves with neither the Western democracies nor the Communist powers were sometimes referred to as the *third world*. From the mid-1950s on, it was increasingly in this third world that the rivalry of the superpowers would be played out.

In the Middle East, Arab nationalism was heightened and partly shaped by opposition to the new state of Israel. This country at the eastern end of the Mediterranean was created under a United Nations resolution in 1948. In Egypt, Gamal Abdel Nasser, a strong

LESSON 3 *(2 days)*

Performance Objectives

1. To identify orally or in writing the change in Soviet-American relations during the 1950s. **2.** To describe the part played by the United States in the 1956 war in the Middle East. **3.** To explain the two ways in which the United States became involved with events in Cuba during Kennedy's administration.

Famous People

John Foster Dulles, Nikita Khrushchev, Gamal Abdel Nasser, Fidel Castro, John F. Kennedy

Vocabulary

"Massive retaliation," brinksmanship, race suicide, "coexistence," "peaceful cooperation," "spirit of Geneva," third world, Eisenhower Doctrine, U-2 spy plane, Central Intelligence Agency (CIA), Bay of Pigs, Berlin Wall, Cuban missile crisis, atomic test ban, hot line, détente

Activities

1. USING A MAP On a wall map of the world, have your students locate and label each of the important places mentioned in the lesson: Korea, East Berlin, Hungary, Lebanon, Moscow, Geneva, Suez Canal, Sinai Peninsula, Camp David, Bay of Pigs, Sverdlovsk (where the U-2 was shot down), and Vienna.

2. LISTENING FOR INFORMATION Read to your students from John Kenneth Galbraith's *The Age of Uncertainty,* the section on John Foster Dulles (page 235). Encourage your students to learn more about Dulles, and ask them to decide if Galbraith was being fair to Dulles in the description of him.

nationalist, rose to power in 1952. One of his goals was to destroy Israel and another was to gain control of the Suez Canal. That waterway, owned by Britain and France, ran through Egyptian territory. Nasser also wanted to be the leader of the entire Arab world. Hoping to retain Western influence in Egypt, the United States offered to help finance the construction of the Aswan Dam on the Nile River. When it became clear that Nasser would welcome the money but not the influence, Secretary Dulles withdrew the offer. Nasser then seized the Suez Canal, saying that canal tolls would pay for the dam.

In recent years, the differences between Israel and the Arab countries and the growing demand for oil from the Middle East have made that part of the world the focus of international tensions.

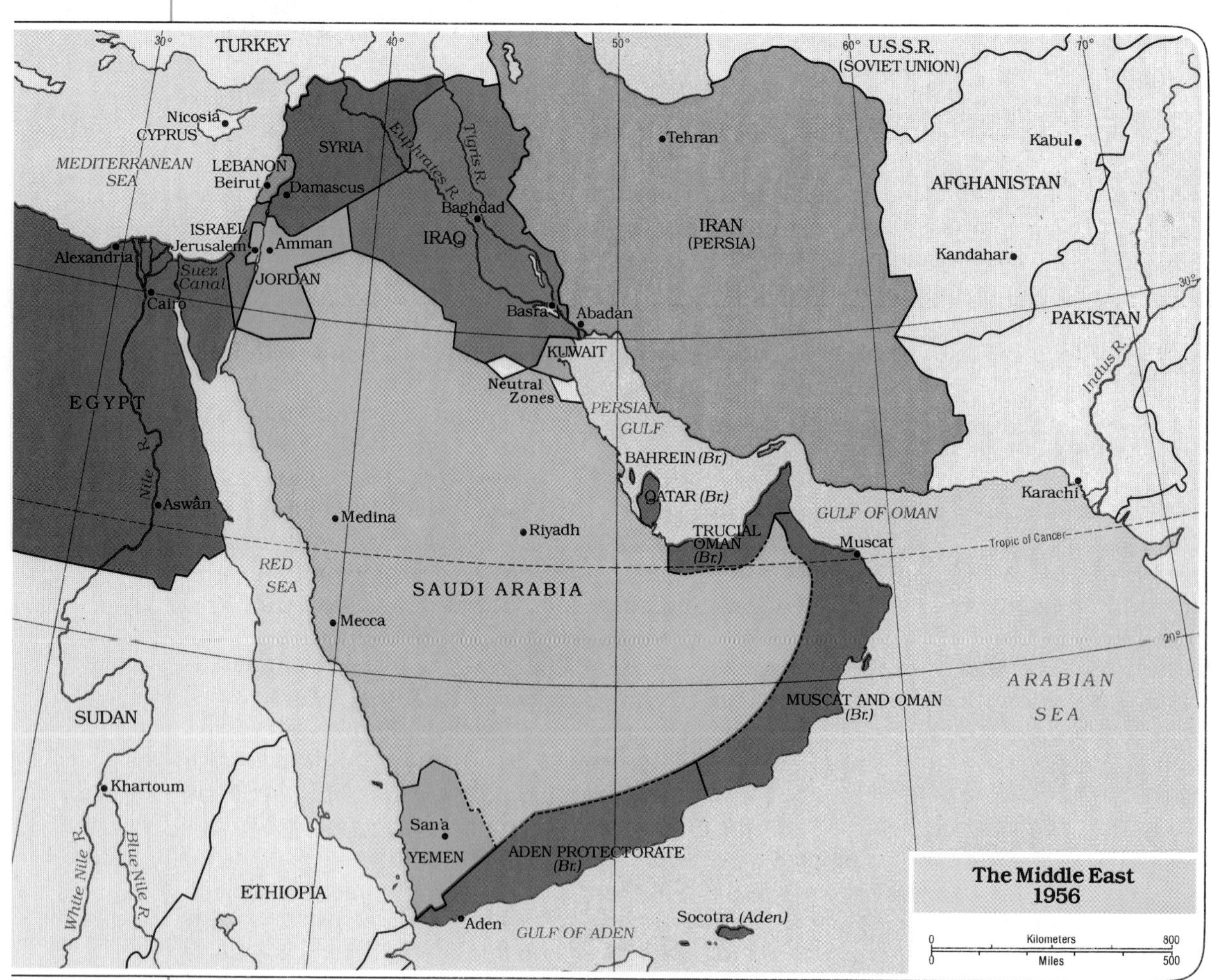

War in the Middle East. Britain and France had long considered the canal, through which Middle East oil and other goods flowed to Europe, as a lifeline. They felt they could not allow it to fall into Nasser's hands. Meanwhile, Egyptian forces had been conducting border raids on Israel for a year or more. Carrying out a secret plan, Israeli armies launched a full attack in October 1956, quickly sweeping across the Sinai Peninsula to the canal. Great Britain and France meanwhile sent troops to occupy the canal.

The United States, which had had no advance information about this action from its allies, Britain and France, demanded that the fighting end. So did the Soviet Union, which threatened to send "volunteers" to the Middle East. The United States and Russia joined in supporting a UN resolution that stopped the fighting and forced the three invading forces to withdraw from the territories they had occupied.

Fearing that the Soviets might gain influence in the Middle East in the wake of the Suez war, President Eisenhower announced an extension of the containment policy to that region. The United States, said the President, would defend countries in the Middle East "against overt armed aggression from any nation controlled by international communism." The statement became known as the *Eisenhower Doctrine*. Under this Doctrine, the United States responded to a request from the government of Lebanon in 1958 for help in putting down a revolution. Several thousand United States marines were sent to Lebanon, and the rebellion was ended.

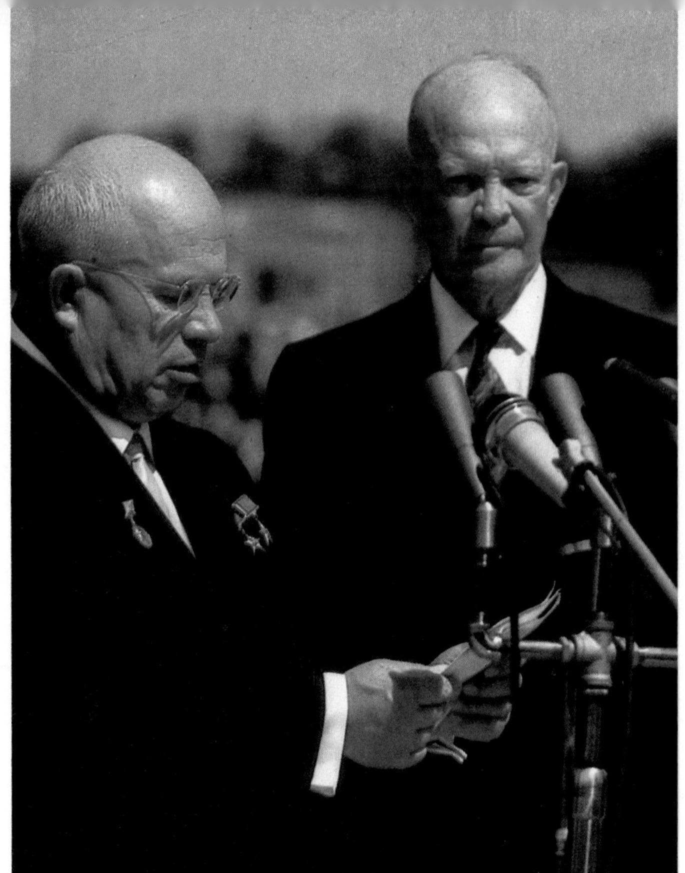

In 1959, Soviet Premier Nikita Khrushchev and President Eisenhower meet in Washington.

Relations with Russia. The four-power control of Berlin continued to raise tensions. Situated deep inside East Germany, Berlin was a thorn in the side of the Soviets. It offered an easy escape route for the thousands who wished to leave Communist rule in East Germany. From time to time, Khrushchev threatened to blockade the city again or to find some other way to get the Western powers out. However, the Western powers remained firm.

Yet even quarrels over Berlin did not stand in the way of a further easing of tension between the United States and

3. CREATING A TIME LINE
Have students make time lines showing the events from this lesson. The time period will be from about 1952 to 1963. After the students have completed their time lines, have them mark with a plus sign each event that brought the United States and the Soviet Union closer together. Then have them mark with a minus sign each event that pushed the two nations further apart. Discuss the events thus identified to see if the class understands them. Be sure that students can tie individual events to the overall picture of the period and also tie them to historical trends. (They should be able to associate Kennedy's actions in Cuba with the Monroe Doctrine or the Roosevelt Corollary, for example.)

4. RESEARCH / ORAL OR WRITTEN REPORT A good example of John Foster Dulles's interpretation of foreign policy as a moral crusade can be found in a speech Dulles delivered at his father's church in Watertown, N.Y., on October 11, 1953. *The New York Times* covered this speech. Have several of your students use a library microfilm reader to find that speech in *The Times* and report to the class on those sections that would indicate Dulles's belief in a moral crusade.

5. THOUGHT PROVOKER "When America has run its course, I know what headnote will appear in the history books. It will be: The United States—a great world power that died of a surfeit of pragmatism.' " Ask: What is meant by this statement? Were Eisenhower and Kennedy pragmatic? Is pragmatism a virtue, or is it an outward sign of cowardice?

In June of 1978, Alexander Solzhenitsyn delivered the graduation speech at Harvard University. Have one of your students find out what the exiled Russian author said that day and see if there is a connection between his words and the words quoted above.

6. FILMS *The Eisenhower Years,* Presidential Administration series (22 minutes, b&w; Teaching Film Custodians). *The Khrushchev Era,* The Red Myth series (29 minutes, b&w; National Educational Television). *Fidel Castro,* Biography series (26 minutes, b&w; McGraw-Hill Films).

the Soviet Union. In 1959, Khrushchev toured the United States. His friendly talks with the President at Camp David, Maryland, led to talk of a "spirit of Camp David." There was rising hope that a summit meeting scheduled for Geneva in May 1960 might bring real progress on arms control and possibly even German reunification. Those hopes were shot down in early May along with a U-2. This was a high-flying United States spy plane that was taking pictures over the Soviet Union. Outraged, Khrushchev cancelled the summit meeting.

Revolution in Cuba. Near the end of Eisenhower's second term, a Cuban revolution led by Fidel Castro overthrew Fulgencio Batista, Cuba's dictator. American opinion toward Castro was friendly at first. It soured rapidly, however, as Castro held public executions of a number of Batista's supporters, confiscated the property of American businesses, and made clear his wish to steer an independent course from the United States. Fidel Castro also developed close ties to the Soviet Union. The Central Intelligence Agency (CIA) secretly provided support and training for anti-Castro Cubans. Many of them had fled to Florida and other parts of the United States after Castro came to power. These Cubans were preparing for an invasion of Cuba. They and their American supporters believed that the Cuban people would then rise up against Castro.

This was the situation when President John F. Kennedy took office in 1961. Believing that most Cubans were anti-Castro and would rise against him at the first chance, Kennedy let the plan for an invasion of Cuba go forward. In April 1961 about 1,400 anti-Castro Cubans landed at the Bay of Pigs on the southern coast of Cuba. All were killed or captured within a few days. There had been no popular uprising. For its role in the affair, the United States suffered a great loss of prestige.

Kennedy's approach. The Bay of Pigs was a poor beginning for an administration that prided itself on toughness. In his inauguration address President Kennedy had said that his administration would be

> unwilling to witness or permit the slow undoing of those human rights to which this nation has always been committed, and to which we are committed today at home and around the world.

That was Kennedy's pledge to continue the policy of containment. Kennedy also said that the United States would be willing to negotiate, but that it would do so only from a position of strength.

In June 1961, President Kennedy met with Soviet Premier Nikita Khrushchev in Vienna, Austria. Kennedy hoped the meeting would lead to a further easing of the cold-war strains. The Soviet leader, however, took a hard line. He demanded a settlement on Berlin. He also made clear that his country would support revolutions in the third world. Determined to show strength, Kennedy called up army reserves, increased the draft, and encouraged civilians to build bomb shelters.

With refugees flowing out of East Germany through West Berlin by the thousands each day, the Soviets took matters into their own hands. In August

1961, workmen hastily built a wall that shut off East Berlin from West Berlin. The wall stands to this day. Since it was on the East Berlin side of the boundary, there was no way the United States could stop its construction without using force. Although there was talk of war for a while, that quickly passed. But the wall stood as a grim symbol of the continued division of Berlin. It also was an embarrassing reminder of the Soviet failure in East Germany.

The Cuban missile crisis. One year later Russia offered a more serious challenge to the United States. The Soviet Union secretly prepared to install short-range missiles in Cuba, only 90 miles (144 km) from the United States. Photographs taken from American planes in October 1962 showed missile bases being built.

On national television President Kennedy announced that the United States would not permit this plan to proceed. He announced a naval blockade of Cuba to prevent any ships carrying missiles from entering Cuba, and he demanded that the bases be dismantled.

For six days the world stood at the brink of war. No one knew whether the Soviet ships on their way to Cuba would challenge the blockade. Behind the scenes, messages passed back and forth between Kennedy and Khrushchev. American planes took to the skies with

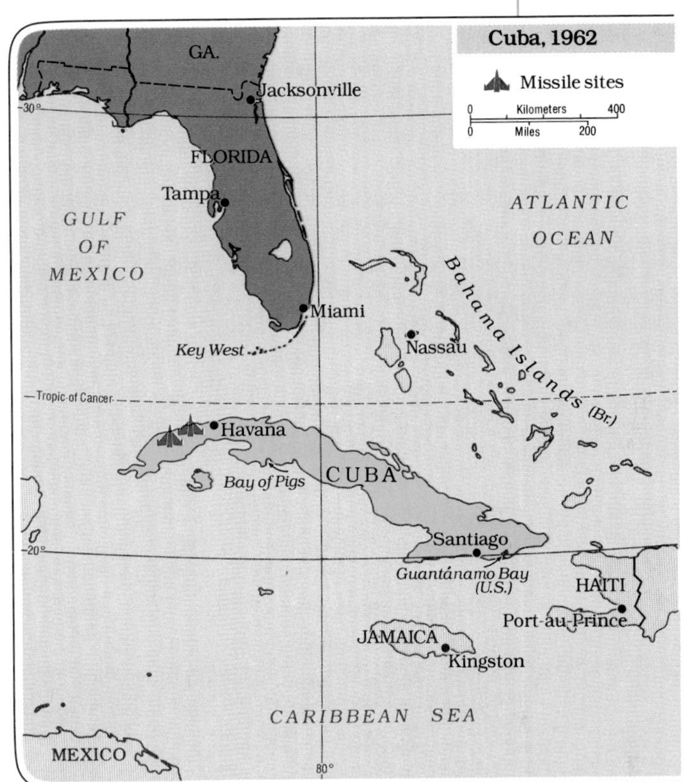

This photograph, taken as the missile crisis was coming to an end, shows a Russian freighter outbound from Cuba. The long objects on deck are presumably missiles that have been removed from the bases (located on the map above) that the Castro government had prepared.

7. USING A MAP It is important that students understand something of the continuing conflict in the Middle East. Provide them with outline maps of the area. Have them draw in the current boundaries of Israel. Then have them compare the current boundaries with those of 1956, as shown on page 710. They should also label the surrounding countries. Next have them research and label the particular areas of conflict, such as the Sinai Peninsula and the Golan Heights. Ask: Does the geography of the Middle East present any "natural" boundaries for Israel? Would the Arab nations accept these?

LESSON 4 *(2 days)*

Performance Objectives

1. To explain orally or in writing why the United States forces became involved in Vietnam. **2.** To explain orally or in writing the policies of Presidents Johnson and Nixon in the war in Vietnam. **3.** To explain orally or in writing the policies of the United States regarding the conflict between Israel and the Arab nations.

Famous People

Ho Chi Minh, Lyndon Johnson, General William Westmoreland, Henry Kissinger, Leonid Brezhnev, Anwar Sadat

Vocabulary

Indochina, National Liberation Front, Vietcong, Tonkin Gulf Resolution, Tet offensive, Vietnamization, Strategic Arms Limitation Talks (SALT), oil embargo, shuttle diplomacy

live nuclear bombs, and it seemed likely that Russian planes were doing the same. When the Russian ship carrying the missiles reached the blockade, however, it turned back. The crisis was over. In its aftermath, the missile bases were taken apart, and the United States promised not to invade Cuba.

One outcome of the Cuban missile crisis was a determination by each side to avoid such dangerous confrontations in the future. In 1963 the United States, Russia, and a number of other countries agreed to the first atomic test ban. It applied to the testing of bombs on the ground, in space, and under water. (Only underground testing was still permitted.) Also in 1963 a direct telegraph-teleprinter line called the *hot line* was installed between the White House and Moscow. Its purpose was to permit the heads of the governments to communicate with each other directly and instantly in a time of crisis that threatened war. In a speech during the summer of 1963, President Kennedy said that each side must reexamine its cold-war attitudes. The world, he said, must be made "safe for diversity." Ironically, the Cuban missile crisis led the two superpowers away from war with each other and into a period of *détente*—a relaxing of tensions.

CHECKUP

1. How did relations change between the United States and the Soviet Union during the 1950s?
2. What part did America play in the war in the Middle East in 1956?
3. In what two ways did the United States become involved with events in Cuba during Kennedy's administration?

LESSON 4

From the Vietnam War to the Present

One principle of American strategy during the cold war was to avoid a land war on the vast Asian continent. As cold-war tensions eased in the 1960s, the United States departed from this principle—with disastrous results.

The French in Indochina. The French colony of Indochina—made up of the states of Cambodia, Vietnam, and Laos—dated back to the middle of the nineteenth century. Beginning in the 1930s a Vietnamese Communist named Ho Chi Minh became the leader of an independence movement. It was directed at first against the French and then against the Japanese, who occupied Indochina during World War II. When France tried to restore colonial rule after the war, Vietnamese nationalists led by Ho set up a government in the northern part of the country and declared independence. For the next eight years, France tried to crush the independence movement but failed.

The United States had generally supported independence for Europe's colonies in Asia after World War II. Following the victory of the Communists in China, however, the Truman administration began to supply arms for the French to use against the Communist-led nationalists in Indochina. By 1954, the United States was bearing 75 percent of the cost of the war. With the French facing defeat, the United States briefly considered intervening with air and naval forces. President Eisenhower, however, went against the advice of Secretary Dulles and several military leaders, and refused to intervene.

After the French armies suffered a crushing defeat in 1954, a truce was arranged. The three Indochinese states of Vietnam, Cambodia, and Laos were to be independent and neutral. Vietnam would be temporarily divided at 17° north latitude, with the Communists controlling the northern part until the future of the country was decided by nationwide elections in 1956.

The United States in Vietnam. Soon after the agreement, the United States replaced France as the chief supporter of the anti-Communist government of South Vietnam. In 1956 the government in South Vietnam refused to allow elections. Thus the country was now divided in the familiar cold-war pattern. North Vietnam received aid from the Soviet Union and China. South Vietnam was backed by the United States.

Why did the United States become involved in Vietnam? The answer lies in the idea of containment. In explaining American support for South Vietnam, President Eisenhower agreed that the United States had no vital interest in that country itself. But he likened the countries of Southeast Asia to a row of dominoes. The fall of one would result in a chain reaction that would knock down all the others.

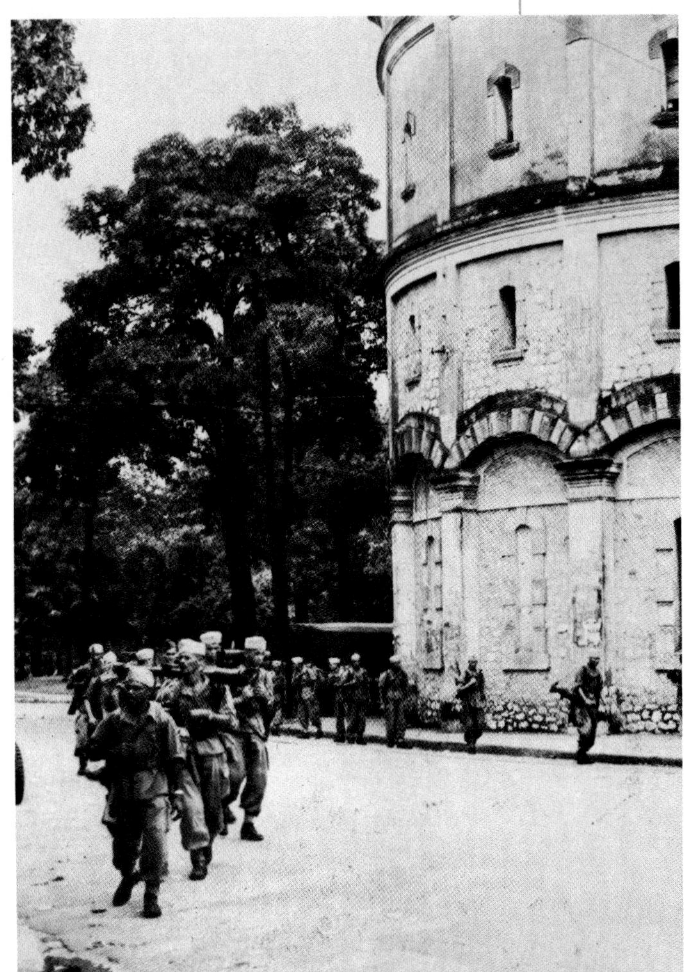

In 1954, French troops withdraw from the city of Hanoi in what for many years had been the French colony of Indochina. Hanoi later became the capital of Communist North Vietnam.

After a promising beginning, the South Vietnamese government began to lose popular support. In the late 1950s, the Communist-led National Liberation Front drew together the many groups in South Vietnam that opposed the government. By 1959, the Front's guerrilla arm, the Vietcong, was becoming successful in the countryside of South Vietnam. By the time President Eisenhower left office, he had increased economic and military aid to several hundred million dollars a year and had sent more than 600 military advisers to train South Vietnamese troops. Under President Kennedy, the number of advisers

Activities

1. **FILMS** *Last Reflections on a War* (44 minutes, b&w; National Educational Television). *Vietnam: An Historical Document* (56 minutes, color; produced by CBS News; Carousel Films).

grew to 16,000. By the time Lyndon Johnson became President, South Vietnam was almost completely dependent on American military and economic aid.

After the French withdrew, Vietnam was split into Communist and non-Communist areas.

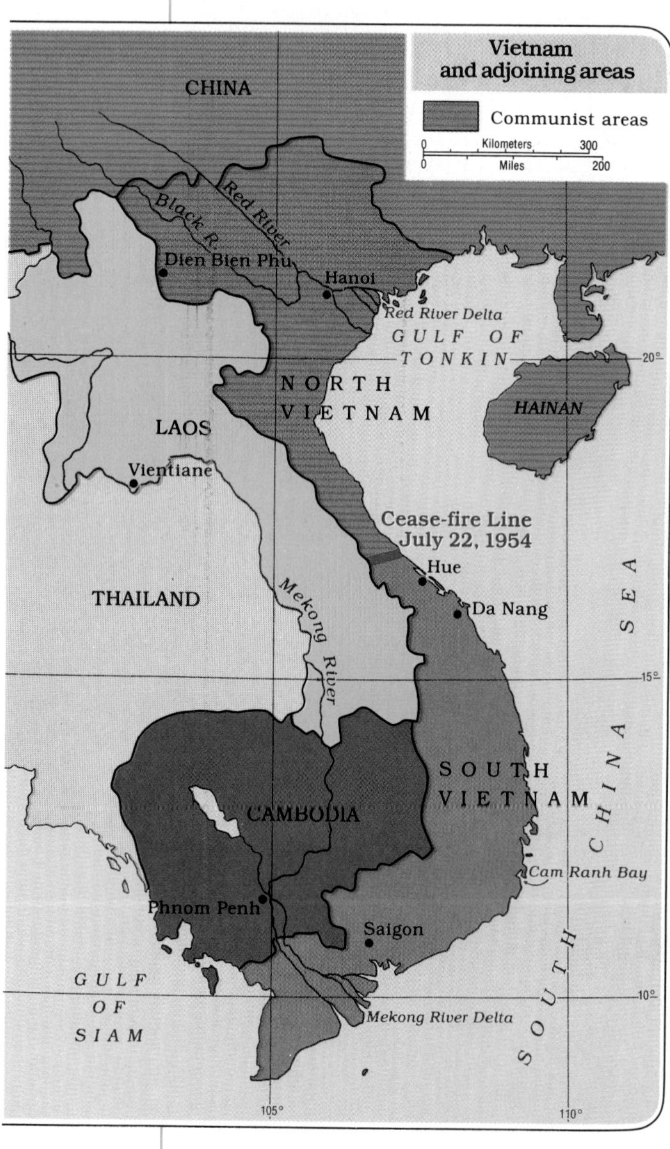

The Vietcong were being supplied and trained by North Vietnam. Some North Vietnamese troops were also involved in the warfare in South Vietnam's countryside. By 1964, the Vietcong had gained control of most of the countryside, and there was a strong possibility that the government of South Vietnam might collapse.

A mounting involvement. President Johnson was determined that South Vietnam would not fall. In the summer of 1964, North Vietnamese gunboats and a United States destroyer fired on each other in the Gulf of Tonkin, off the coast of North Vietnam. President Johnson seized upon the incident to win congressional approval of a resolution he had actually prepared some months earlier. The *Tonkin Gulf Resolution* allowed the President to take "all necessary measures to repel armed attack against the forces of the United States and to prevent further aggression." President Johnson later regarded this resolution as a blank check to widen the war.

Following his victory in the election of 1964, Johnson sent thousands of United States troops to join the fighting. The American Air Force also began heavy bombing of North Vietnam. By this time, Washington viewed the war not simply as another exercise in containment but as a test of America's will. Over the next several years there came a stream of optimistic predictions by American officials of an early end to the war. Each such prediction, however, was usually accompanied by a request for more troops. By 1968, more than a half million American soldiers were in

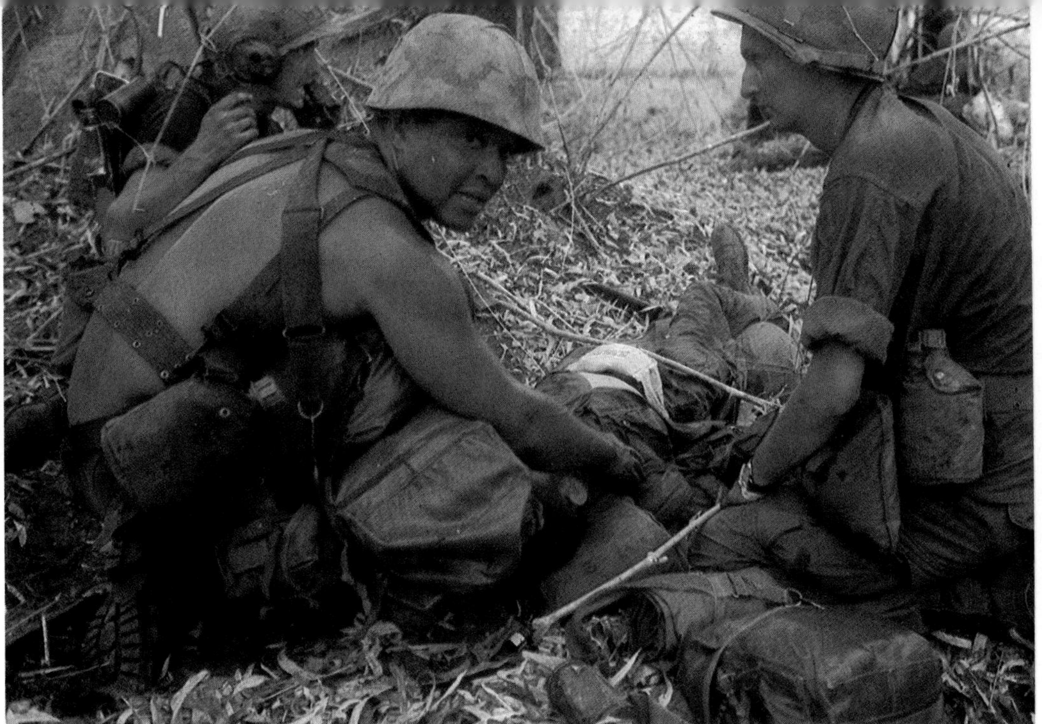

American medics tend to a wounded comrade in Vietnam. American casualties there totaled 460,000.

Vietnam. Meanwhile, each increase in American troops was met by additional troops from North Vietnam.

A reversal of policy. In January 1968 the Communists launched the Tet (New Year's) offensive. This was a coordinated attack on more than thirty major cities in South Vietnam, including the capital city of Saigon. There was even fighting at the gates of the American embassy. Most of the gains the Communists made were wiped out over the following month. The Tet offensive showed, however, that the rosy statements about an early end to the war were not realistic.

The war was becoming increasingly unpopular in the United States. When General William Westmoreland, the American commander, asked for still another 200,000 troops, President Johnson reversed his policy. He announced that the United States would end the bombing of North Vietnam and seek a negotiated settlement to end the war. He also said he would not run for reelection. Peace talks were begun in Paris, but they were still stalled when Johnson was succeeded by President Richard Nixon in 1969.

Throughout his career, Nixon had been a strong supporter of containment. He was committed to keeping South Vietnam free of Communist control. But he also promised to bring this unpopular war to an end. American efforts to win the war between 1965 and 1968 had not been successful. Nixon now tried to end American involvement through a plan he called *Vietnamization*. United States troops would be gradually withdrawn as the South Vietnamese became

2. GUEST SPEAKERS Vietnam is too recent for an unemotional study. Bias, prejudice, tears, hate, and frustration still exist, and understanding them is essential to understanding the war. In every community in America there can be found people who believe our involvement in Vietnam was the biggest mistake in our national history and other people who believe that the United States could have won the Vietnam War if it had remained strong and kept the will to fight. Invite speakers from both sides to your class, and let your students try to make judgments for themselves.

3. DISCUSSION Below are several positions about the Vietnam War. Have your students first support and then challenge each one, giving facts and logical arguments for each side.

a. South Vietnam was only a stepping stone in the Communist plan for world conquest.

b. The United States does not have the material, intellectual, or moral resources to be at once an American power, a European power, and an Asian power. This task belongs to the United Nations.

c. The United States had to be involved in Vietnam to demonstrate that aggression must not be permitted to succeed.

d. Success in Vietnam was vital to the national interests of the United States. Painful as our losses were, they were a price that had to be paid if world peace was to be achieved.

e. The war in Vietnam was primarily a civil war, and the United States had no business being there.

4. RESEARCH / ORAL OR WRITTEN REPORTS In 1971 *The New York Times* printed the Pentagon Papers. These were described as the secret history of the Vietnam War. Have several students report to the class on what these papers have to say about events described in the text, such as the Tonkin Gulf Resolution, the Tet offensive, and the decision to bomb North Vietnam in 1964.

5. RESEARCH / DISCUSSION Have your students gather and present information about conditions in Southeast Asia today. Ask: Was there a "falling-dominoes" situation as President Eisenhower warned? Have the people suffered? Are their lives better, or worse? Does this information change anyone's opinion about what the United States should have done?

6. RESEARCH Approximately 56,800 Americans were killed in the Vietnam War. Another 303,700 were wounded; 780 are still termed missing in action (MIA). Over 600 prisoners of war (POWs) were returned. Have students research the human elements of these statistics. Ask: Did local people die in Vietnam? What has happened to their families? What has happened to the permanently disabled veterans? What about the families of the MIAs today? How have the POWs adjusted to their return to a much different America? (The *Time* magazine issue of July 3, 1978, has an article concerning the POWs' five-year reunion.) The information the students discover could be told as reports or by other creative means of expression. Students might draw pictures expressing their views. Interviews with veterans or their families could be excellent but should be carefully prepared.

better trained and did more of the fighting. This would be accompanied by renewed air attacks on North Vietnam.

Winding down the war. During the next three years, the United States carried out this plan for "winding down the war." In 1970 the United States briefly widened the war with an assault into neighboring Cambodia, where North Vietnamese supply bases were believed to be. The Ho Chi Minh Trail in Laos was also bombed. By 1972, American forces had been reduced from more than a half million to 75,000.

Meanwhile, private talks between the North Vietnamese and Henry Kissinger, Nixon's adviser on foreign policy, produced an agreement for a cease-fire in January 1973. The United States would withdraw its remaining troops within sixty days. North Vietnam would return American prisoners.

As a strategy for withdrawing American troops from the war, Vietnamization was highly successful. But it could not also serve the purposes of containment. Few expected the truce between North and South Vietnam to last, and indeed, fighting was soon renewed. The end came with suddenness in the spring of 1975. In the face of a North Vietnamese offensive, South Vietnam ordered a withdrawal of its forces from certain areas. The withdrawal was badly managed, and turned into a rout. With all discipline gone, the South Vietnamese army fled to the south. Within a few weeks North Vietnam's troops were at the very gates of Saigon, South Vietnam's capital. South Vietnamese leaders fled the country. All resistance collapsed, and in April 1975, Saigon fell and the war was over. Vietnam was finally united and independent, but under Communist control. At the same time in Cambodia, Communists took control of that country.

An era of negotiation. At the time he took office, Nixon had a reputation as a hard-line cold-warrior, yet he surprised many people by his negotiations with Communist countries. None of his actions surprised people more than his reversal of the twenty-year-old policy of the United States toward the People's Republic of China.

After the victory of the Communists in China's civil war, the United States had continued to recognize the Nationalist government of Chiang Kai-shek on Formosa as the legal government of China. In 1954 America made a defense treaty with that government, assuring its defense against any attack by Mao's armies. Throughout the 1950s and 1960s, the United States regarded Mao's government as an enemy and had no dealings with it.

Meanwhile, relations between Soviet Russia and China had chilled. Mao charged the Russian leaders with not practicing "true communism," and he laid claim to the leadership of world communism. The two countries also renewed ancient quarrels over their long, common border in Asia.

In the early 1970s, President Nixon believed that the time was right to ease tensions with China. The Chinese leaders agreed. In August 1971, the President announced that he would visit China the following year. The visit produced few agreements, but it clearly improved relations. Both countries agreed to solve their differences by peaceful means.

In May 1972, President Nixon was in Moscow for talks with the Russian leader, Leonid Brezhnev. The two agreed to limit the number of defensive missile sites as well as the number of offensive missiles in the two countries. They agreed to work toward further progress in the Strategic Arms Limitation Talks (SALT). These talks and two later meetings between Nixon and Brezhnev contributed to détente.

Attention on the Middle East. During the 1970s, the Middle East occupied a great deal of America's attention in foreign affairs. In 1973 there was yet another war between Israel and its neighbors. This time Arab oil countries put an embargo on their oil—that is, prevented movement of the oil—to the United States and countries of Western Europe to force them to follow more pro-Arab policies. The embargo lasted many months. In the United States it caused shortages of gasoline and heating oil. Long lines of cars at gas stations were familiar sights.

The war itself was ended by a truce arranged by the United States and the Soviet Union after eighteen days of fighting. This time the United States took an active part in seeking both a short-term and a long-term solution in the Middle East. American policy was to try to get the two sides to the bargaining table. Henry Kissinger, now Nixon's secretary of state, played the key role in arranging that the forces on each side pull back. Through *shuttle diplomacy*—going back and forth, in this case between Israeli and Arab capitals, to work out an agreement—Kissinger reestablished American influence in the region.

Although peace efforts stalled for several years, they were revived in the fall of 1977 when Egyptian President Anwar Sadat made a dramatic trip to Israel. The Carter administration followed the role laid out by Kissinger earlier, conferring with both sides and encouraging them to settle their differences. In 1978, while hard negotiating remained, there was more reason for hope than there had been in thirty years.

The victims of the "holdup" are the leaders of West Germany, France, the United States, and Britain. This Dutch cartoon reflects widely held feelings at the time of the Arab oil embargo.

BEHRENDT—Het Parool, Amsterdam/ROTHCO

A different world. The world at the end of the 1970s had changed greatly since World War II. The time when countries were drawn as if by magnets to one of the two superpowers was gone. In Europe, strong and independent countries no longer felt they must follow the

7. ESSAY Have the students write essays in which they compare and contrast the role of the United States in Vietnam with its role in the Middle East conflict. In the opening paragraphs of their essays, students should outline the general situation and explain why the United States became involved. They should then go on to explain the policies of the various Presidents in regard to these situations. Finally, the students should make recommendations concerning lessons that the United States should have learned from both situations that could be applied to future international conflicts. Since this is the last lesson directly dealing with American foreign policy, this essay might be used partly as a summary exercise about the trends of American foreign policy. Students should describe how United States foreign policy in recent years shows the influence of past ideas and themes.

Background Information

CARTOON The leaders shown in this cartoon are (left to right) Willy Brandt, Georges Pompidou, Richard Nixon, and Edward Heath. The oil embargo stimulated efforts toward developing new forms of energy, conserving energy, and finding new oil locations. Those efforts have not as yet succeeded, however, since oil importation by the United States has increased since the embargo.

ANSWERS TO REVIEW QUESTIONS

1. Russia wanted to become a Mediterranean power and to gain a larger influence in the oil-rich and strategic Middle East. In the interest of these objectives, Russia tried to pressure Turkey to give up control of the Dardanelles, a strait from which Russia would be able to monitor traffic between the Black Sea and the Mediterranean Sea. Russia also hoped that Communist-led rebels would succeed in over-throwing the Greek government and, thereby, Russia could develop closer ties with that Mediterranean country.
2. Germany was the most populous and potentially the strongest country in Europe. Control of Germany could mean control of the continent.
3. The North Atlantic Treaty Organization was formed to provide a military defense for Western Europe to contain the threat posed by the Soviet armies. The treaty committed American power to the defense of Europe, for it provided that an attack on any NATO member would be considered an attack on all. When NATO was formed in 1949, member nations were the United States, Canada, Ireland, Great Britain, France, Belgium, Denmark, the Netherlands, Luxembourg, Norway, Italy, and Portugal. Greece and Turkey joined in 1951, and West Germany signed in 1954.
4. If the invasion had been planned by Russia, as Truman believed, it was regarded as a threat to the policy of containment and to the idea of collective security on which the United Nations rested.

lead of the United States. Communist countries were increasingly independent of Moscow. In fact, each of the two greatest Communist countries, China and the Soviet Union, regarded the other as its greatest enemy. In Southeast Asia, Communist Vietnam and Communist Cambodia fought a sharp border war in early 1978. In Africa and Asia, new nations were concerned with working out their own destinies. For its part, the United States had come to realize the limits of its power to control events around the world.

The policy of containment did not fit such a world. By the end of the Vietnam War, the United States had largely discarded it. When two opposing groups, one of them Communist, fought for control of the African country of Angola in 1975–1976, the United States did not become involved. The Carter administration announced a decision to remove the last American troops from Korea by the early 1980s. The stress in foreign affairs during the early Carter years shifted toward human rights and arms control. The United States would once again seek to be a moral leader in the world. Americans had no wish to retreat to isolationism. That was impossible. But they also decided that their nation could not be expected to police the world.

These developments in foreign affairs after World War II had a great impact upon affairs within the United States. They influenced the size and role of government, the attitudes of the people, and the shape of the economy. You will read about domestic America during the cold war in the next chapter.

CHECKUP

1. Why did the United States forces become involved in war in Vietnam?
2. What policies were followed by Presidents Johnson and Nixon in Vietnam?
3. What has been the United States policy in regard to the Arab-Israeli conflict?

Key Facts from Chapter 34

1. After World War II, the United States and the Soviet Union became locked in the cold war, a struggle for global leadership.
2. During the cold war, the basic foreign policy of the United States became one of containment—resisting Communist expansion wherever the interests of the United States and the Communist powers collided.
3. Between 1950 and 1974, the United States twice became involved in "hot wars" in Asia. The war in Korea ended in 1953 in a stalemate. The war in Vietnam ended with a Communist victory following the withdrawal of the last American troops in 1974.
4. By the mid-1970s, the United States recognized that it could not police the world. During the early years of the Carter administration, the emphasis in foreign policy was on human rights and arms control.

★ REVIEWING THE CHAPTER ★

People, Places, and Events

Cold war *P. 698*
Potsdam Conference *P. 700*
Truman Doctrine *P. 701*
Marshall Plan *P. 702*
Douglas MacArthur *P. 705*
Dwight D. Eisenhower *P. 708*
John Foster Dulles *P. 709*
Nikita Khrushchev *P. 709*
Israel *P. 709*
Eisenhower Doctrine *P. 711*
John F. Kennedy *P. 712*
Bay of Pigs *P. 712*
Indochina *P. 714*
Tonkin Gulf Resolution *P. 716*
Henry Kissinger *P. 718*

Review Questions

1. Following World War II, what were Russia's objectives in Greece and Turkey? *Pp. 701–702* Les. 1
2. Why did each side in the cold war want to control Germany? *P. 702* Les. 1
3. For what purpose was the North Atlantic Treaty Organization formed? Who were member nations? *Pp. 703–704* Les. 1
4. Why did President Truman want to help South Korea when it was invaded by North Korea in 1950? *P. 706* Les. 2
5. What new emphasis was made in America's military program by the Eisenhower administration? *Pp. 708–709* Les. 3
6. How did the growth of nationalism in the postwar years affect Africa and Asia? What is meant by the term *third world? P. 709* Les. 3
7. What important outcome of the Cuban missile crisis represented a change in Soviet-American relations? *P. 714* Les. 3
8. Why did the United States discard the policy of containment? *P. 717* Les. 4

Chapter Test

Match each description in the first section with the correct name or names in the second section. A name may match more than one description or none at all. Write your answers on a separate piece of paper.

1. President who developed a plan called Vietnamization
2. Leaders at Yalta who agreed to divide Germany
3. Led a revolution in Cuba
4. Seized the Suez Canal for Egypt
5. Led Nationalist troops in China
6. Commander of the occupation forces in Japan
7. Soviet leader who urged coexistence
8. Made the iron-curtain speech
9. Wanted to bomb bases in China during the Korean war
10. Proclaimed the People's Republic of China.

a. Winston Churchill
b. Fidel Castro
c. Dwight Eisenhower
d. Douglas MacArthur
e. Joseph Stalin
f. Richard Nixon
g. Nikita Khrushchev
h. Lyndon Johnson
i. Ho Chi Minh
j. Franklin D. Roosevelt
k. Gamal Abdel Nasser
l. Chiang Kai-shek
m. Mao Tse-tung

5. The Eisenhower administration placed less emphasis on costly large armies and more emphasis on air power and nuclear weapons. This shift was planned to give the United States more military power for less money.
6. As nationalist movements developed in Africa and Asia, former European colonies became independent countries. Most of these nations wanted to concentrate on solving their own problems and develop their countries without aligning themselves with either the Western democracies or the Communist powers. In this respect, these newly independent countries were sometimes referred to as the third world. They often sought economic aid from the big powers, but they wanted to avoid falling under outside influence. On the other hand, the great powers tried to use their aid to gain influence.
7. A period of détente developed in which the two nations tried to avoid dangerous confrontations.
8. As nations around the world became more independent of the superpowers, the United States no longer was able to control world events through the policy of containment.

ANSWERS FOR CHAPTER TEST

1. f **2.** a, e, j **3.** b **4.** k **5.** l **6.** d **7.** g **8.** a **9.** d **10.** m

Background Information

PICTURE This is a farm in the Midwest. The crop shown here is corn, the most valuable crop grown in the United States. Each year American farmers produce about $14 billion worth, or well over half of the world total. American consumption of corn is about 45 pounds (20 kg) per person every year. In addition, corn is a main source of feed for hogs and cattle and an ingredient in a wide variety of products, ranging from antifreeze and explosives to plastics and varnish.

CHAPTER 35

DOMESTIC AFFAIRS, 1945-1960

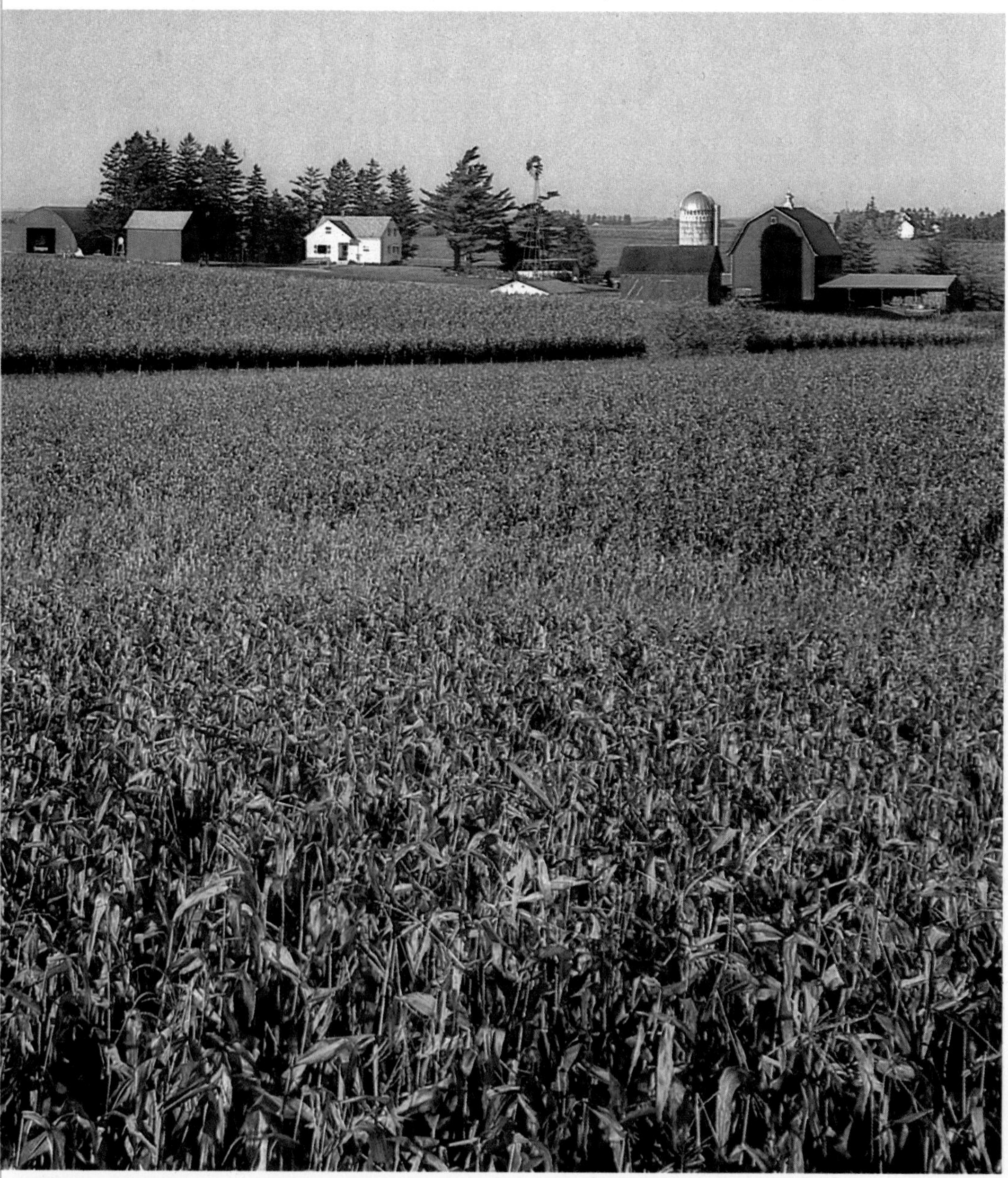

LESSON 1

EVEN AS AMERICANS celebrated victory over Japan and the end of World War II, a mood of uncertainty hung over the country. The United States had emerged from the war as the strongest power in the world. It had not been invaded, and with the exception of Pearl Harbor, it had not been bombed. Wartime demand for goods had brought on a booming economy and full employment. Yet people could not forget that just five years before, the nation had been struggling to escape from the depression. With the war over, people wondered, would the nation slide back into a depression? How lasting would the changes of the New Deal prove to be? And perhaps as important, where did the new President, Harry Truman, stand on issues?

Harry Truman had risen through local Missouri politics to a seat in the United States Senate. There he had gained a reputation for hard work and loyalty to the Democratic party. When Roosevelt sought a record-breaking fourth term in 1944, he chose Truman as his vice presidential running mate. But following the Democrats' victory, Roosevelt rarely informed the new Vice President on important matters. Truman was therefore unprepared to take over the Presidency when Roosevelt died suddenly on April 12, 1945. A stunned Truman said that he felt as if "the moon, the stars, and all the planets had fallen on me. I've got the most terribly responsible job a man ever had." During the next four months, Truman's efforts were almost entirely devoted to the war effort.

From War to Peace

The major problem facing Truman and the country at the end of the war was the building of a solid peacetime economy. Within weeks, Truman started to take action on domestic issues. He sent to Congress a twenty-one-point program that he would later call the *Fair Deal.* In it he proposed an increase in the minimum wage, extended coverage of social security, full-employment legislation, a permanent Fair Employment Practices Commission, public housing and slum clearance, and long-range planning to protect natural resources and build projects like the Tennessee Valley Authority. Over the following weeks, Truman added proposals for federal aid to education and for health insurance. He thus made clear that he wanted to consolidate and extend New Deal reform.

The President also proposed that the government regulate atomic energy. Congress did pass an atomic energy act that put control of nuclear research and production under the Atomic Energy Commission. But the lawmakers gave Truman little else of what he wanted. Since the end of the New Deal, conservatives had made gains in Congress, and in 1945 a group of conservative Democrats and Republicans held control.

Demobilization. With the war over, arms contracts were cancelled and government spending dropped from $83 billion to $31 billion. With this drop in spending, and with the returning servicemen and servicewomen looking for

LESSON 1 *(1 to 2 days)*

Performance Objectives

1. To examine by questionnaire the problems and successes of the reconversion to a peacetime economy after World War II. **2.** To identify orally or in writing the provisions and effects of the Taft-Hartley Act. **3.** To describe orally or in writing the issues, candidates, and results of the election of 1948.

Famous People

Harry Truman, Hubert H. Humphrey, J. Strom Thurmond, Henry Wallace

Vocabulary

Fair Deal, Fair Employment Practices Commission, Servicemen's Readjustment Act of 1944 (GI Bill of Rights), Taft-Hartley Act, closed shop, right-to-work laws, union shop, "cooling-off" period, "do-nothing Congress," "socialized medicine"

Activities

1. INTERVIEW Almost every family has members who lived through the postwar reconversion of the economy. Have the students make up a questionnaire to use in interviews with their family members. Questions should be directed at the problems and successes of the reconversion as seen from an individual's own point of view. The interview could also bring out interesting personal information, such as what items were most sought after as they became available again after the war. Students should also find out how the jobs of family members were affected as the economy returned to peacetime production.

2. RESEARCH / ORAL REPORTS The Taft-Hartley Act is an important labor-management law. Have your students study the act itself. Then assign several interested students to research and report to the class about various labor disputes in which the Taft-Hartley Act has been invoked. Have these students discuss with the class the importance of the "cooling-off" period.

3. LISTENING FOR INFORMATION Read to your students from *Memoirs* by Harry S. Truman (Garden City, N.Y.: Doubleday & Company, 1958). Select readings about the reconversion of the economy and the election of 1948. For a saltier version, read Merle Miller's *Plain Speaking* (New York: Berkley Publishers, 1974, paperback). Have the class decide how Truman's personality affected the election as well as the accounts of the incidents in the book.

jobs, there were predictions that 8 to 10 million people would be unemployed.

Truman hoped to convert to a peacetime economy in a rapid but orderly manner. It would take time to reconvert factories from making war goods to making civilian goods. If too many troops returned home immediately and began looking for work, industry might not have enough jobs available. But pressure from families to "bring the boys home" was so great that Truman had to yield. By April 1946, almost 7 million servicemen and servicewomen had been returned to civilian life.

The Servicemen's Readjustment Act of 1944, popularly known as the GI Bill of Rights, assisted veterans in taking up civilian life. Under this law, a grateful nation helped veterans buy homes and farms, start businesses, receive medical care, and most important, continue their education. Eventually, 8 million veterans of World War II went to college under the GI Bill.

A peacetime economy. Reconversion of the economy from war to peace went much more quickly and smoothly than anyone had expected. By the end of 1945, fully 90 percent of the war industries were back to making peacetime goods. During the war years, Americans had saved $140 billion, and they were now ready to buy the goods. Thus, instead of the glut of civilian goods that some had feared, industry found it could not produce enough to keep up with the demand. Indeed, industry would not fully satisfy this pent-up demand until 1948.

Nor was there the expected unemployment. Returning veterans found jobs readily. But those returning from the armed services did create a problem for many women who had taken jobs in wartime. Because most employers had guaranteed members of the services their old jobs on their return, those people now took jobs away from women who had held them.

Prices and wages. The big economic problem of the postwar era turned out to be not unemployment but inflation. Truman wanted to end wartime wage and price controls as soon as it was safe to do so. He hoped to prevent inflation by lifting controls gradually so that increased production could soak up spending power. Much of the public, however, resisted even temporarily continuing wartime controls. People had money to spend and were willing to pay the prices to purchase the goods they wanted.

More important, labor demanded immediate wage increases to make up for the wartime rise in living costs. Employers, on the other hand, insisted they could not raise wages unless they were allowed to raise prices. Further, business argued that price controls were holding back the very production that everyone wanted. Meanwhile, farmers joined in the complaints about price ceilings for their products. Each group wanted to end controls on itself but to keep them on the others.

Finding it impossible to keep a firm ceiling on wages and prices, Truman agreed to a formula to allow some rises in both. But this did not settle the problem. Labor was especially unhappy. In 1946 there were more than 5,000 strikes. The biggest strikes were in the important steel, auto, coal, and railroad industries. At one point, the frustrated President ordered federal troops to move the coal. He even threatened to draft striking railroaders into the Army, but Congress would not give its approval to such an action.

Truman asked Congress to extend the wartime price-control law, which was to expire on June 30, 1946. When Congress passed a greatly weakened bill, Truman vetoed it. Without controls, prices skyrocketed 25 percent in sixteen days. Near the end of July, Congress passed another weak price-control law, and this time Truman signed it.

A Republican Congress. By the fall of 1946, frustration over strikes, shortages, and rising prices was high. The people put much of the blame on the President. "To err is Truman" went a joke of the time. The Republican party capitalized on this frustration with the campaign slogan "Had Enough? Vote Republican." Americans did; and for the first time since 1930, Republicans controlled both houses of Congress. President Truman accepted the election results as an expression of the people's will. He ended price controls on everything except rent.

Truman and the Eightieth Congress cooperated on Greek-Turkish aid, the Marshall Plan, and other matters involving foreign affairs. On domestic issues, however, they were poles apart. Congress cut back federal spending, dooming any hope for Truman's programs for public housing and education. It also refused to increase social security benefits. On taxation, it passed a bill that reduced the tax on low incomes by 3 percent, but reduced the tax on incomes of more than $100,000 by 48 to 65 percent. Truman vetoed this bill.

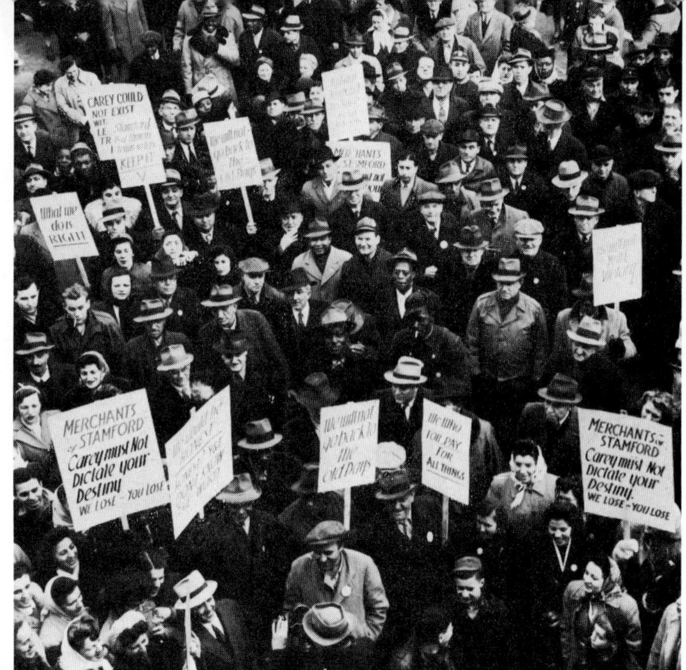

In 1946, workers in a Connecticut city demonstrate during a labor-management dispute. Rising prices at that time brought demands for wage increases, and many strikes occurred.

The most important law passed by the Eightieth Congress dealt with labor relations. Conservatives had long felt that the National Labor Relations Act of 1935 unduly favored labor. To tip the scales the other way, Congress in 1947 passed the Taft-Hartley Act. It outlawed the *closed shop*, a business that agrees to hire only union members. The law allowed states to pass *right-to-work laws* that would make *union shops* illegal. A union shop is a business in which newly hired employees must become union members and keep their membership as a condition of employment. Eighteen states promptly passed right-to-work laws. The Taft-Hartley Act also defined certain union practices as unfair and

4. RESEARCH / WRITTEN REPORTS Henry Wallace has been called many things—some kind and some unkind—but he is, nevertheless, an extremely interesting historical figure. Have some of your students report on his life, paying special attention to Wallace's role in the 1948 presidential election.

5. CREATIVE EXPRESSION
Many times one can learn much about a period in history from its music. Have several of your students gather recordings of the hit songs of the Truman postwar years. Ask them to make a tape recording in which they play excerpts of the music, showing the values and ideas of the period. Be sure the students explain what they are attempting to show.

forbade them. And it allowed the President to end some strikes for an eighty-day "cooling-off" period. With considerable exaggeration, organized labor called the bill a "slave-labor bill," and Truman vetoed it. But Congress passed it over his veto. In the long run the Taft-Hartley Act has not seriously hurt strong unions, although it has made it harder in "right-to-work" states to organize new unions.

The election of 1948. The Democrats nominated Truman again in 1948, even though many of them felt the prospect was gloomy for a Democratic victory. At the Democratic convention, liberals led by Mayor Hubert H. Humphrey of Minneapolis, Minnesota, added a strong civil rights plank to the party platform. This plank led many Southern Democrats to split from the Democratic party. They formed the States' Rights Democratic party and chose Governor J. Strom Thurmond of South Carolina as their candidate. Henry Wallace, who had been Vice President from 1937 to 1941 and had also served as secretary of agriculture under both Roosevelt and Truman, had already formed a Progressive party with himself as its presidential candidate. Thus, Truman seemed likely to lose support from both conservatives and liberals. It seemed a foregone conclusion that the Republican nominee, Governor Thomas Dewey of New York, would be the next President.

Truman, however, took his campaign to the people. He traveled 31,000 miles and made nearly 700 speeches, most of them from the back platform of his campaign train. In his speeches, he sharply attacked the Eightieth Congress, which he called the "do-nothing Congress." On election day, Truman pulled off one of the biggest upsets in American political history. He won 303 electoral votes to Dewey's 189 and Thurmond's 39.

Now President in his own right, Truman renewed his earlier proposals to update the New Deal and also added several new proposals. Yet even though both houses of Congress had a Democratic majority, Truman failed to get his major proposals enacted. The cry of "socialized medicine" killed the President's request for national health insur-

From the platform of his 1948 campaign train, President Truman speaks to California voters.

ance, and a similar charge ended Truman's plan for helping farmers more directly. Nor would Congress pass Truman's proposals on federal aid to education, a higher tax on inherited wealth, and a strengthening of civil rights.

Congress did approve a number of Truman's proposals. It increased the minimum wage, extended social security coverage to another 10 million people, and voted more funds for hospitals and flood control. It also passed a law to build more public housing. Though Truman's civil rights proposal was voted down, the President did succeed in desegregating the armed forces by executive order.

CHECKUP

1. Why did predictions that there would be large-scale unemployment after the war prove to be wrong?
2. What effect did the lifting of wage and price controls have?
3. How did the Taft-Hartley Act alter the relationship between the forces of labor and management?

LESSON 2

Cold-War Politics

The cold war in foreign affairs was accompanied at home by a demand for loyalty and a hunt for *subversives*—that is, those bent on overthrowing the government, presumably in the interest of promoting communism. In 1946 President Truman began a program of loyalty checks in all Executive departments of the government.

The search for subversives. Even earlier, the House Un-American Activities Committee (HUAC) had investigated the activities of numerous groups and the ideas and past histories of thousands of people. HUAC's investigations took it to Hollywood to search for movies with Communist messages and for writers and actors with Communist leanings. Many state legislatures had set up similar committees that had issued long lists of organizations labeled as "subversive." Such committees agreed with J. Edgar Hoover, director of the Federal Bureau of Investigation (FBI), who likened communism to a "disease that spreads like an epidemic," for which "a quarantine is necessary to keep it from infecting this whole nation." The Truman Doctrine, in defining Communist subversion as the major threat to freedom abroad, added support for this view.

The hunt for subversives resulted in two highly publicized court actions that were the subject of much controversy. In January 1950, Alger Hiss, a former State Department official who had traveled with Roosevelt to Yalta, was convicted of passing secret government information to a Communist party member in the 1930s. Later in 1950, Ethel and Julius Rosenberg were convicted as members of a spy ring that passed atomic secrets to the Soviet Union. The Rosenbergs were executed in 1953—the nation's first and only peacetime executions for treason.

United States Attorney General J. Howard McGrath warned that Communists "are everywhere—in factories, offices, butcher shops, on street corners, in private business—and each carries in himself the germs of death for society." By 1950, all levels of government, and many public and private organizations as well, were digging into the political views and personal lives of

LESSON 2 *(2 days)*

Performance Objectives

1. To explain orally or in writing how the cold war affected domestic affairs. **2.** To describe orally or in writing the domestic policies of the Eisenhower administration. **3.** To describe orally or in writing the American reaction to the launching of the Russian sputniks.

Famous People

J. Edgar Hoover, Alger Hiss, Ethel and Julius Rosenberg, J. Howard McGrath, Joseph R. McCarthy, Dwight Eisenhower, Richard Nixon, Adlai Stevenson

Vocabulary

Subversives, loyalty checks, House Un-American Activities Committee (HUAC), loyalty oaths, McCarthyism, censured, farm surplus, *Sputnik*, National Defense Education Act

Activities

1. DISCUSSION Read to your students from Merle Miller's *Plain Speaking*, Chapter 38, "The Cause and Cure of Hysteria." In this chapter, Truman describes the period under study in this lesson as one of fear and hysteria and likens it to the periods of the Salem witch trials, the alien and sedition laws, the relocation of the Japanese Americans during World War II, the persecution of the Mormons, the Palmer raids, and the "Red scare" of the 1920s. Briefly discuss with the class each of these "hysterical" periods, explaining the fear and describing the outcome. Ask: Why does this type of hysteria seem to emerge every so often in American history? Are there common characteristics in the various examples? Is the hysteria internally, or externally, caused?

2. RESEARCH / ORAL REPORTS It may be too easy to dismiss the cold war fear of subversives as little more than hysteria. Ask your students to study some of the issues mentioned in the text. Ask them to decide: Were the Rosenbergs guilty? Was Alger Hiss a Communist agent? Encourage the students to read some of the recent books on these subjects before they decide.

In a similar vein, in the late 1950s J. Edgar Hoover wrote a book called *Masters of Deceit: What Communist Bosses are Doing Now to Bring America to Its Knees* (New York: Holt, Rinehart & Winston, 1958). Have your students read this book and critique it. They should decide if Hoover was guilty of hysteria or whether he knew more than other people about what was really going on.

Born in MISSOURI
In Office 1945–1953
Party DEMOCRATIC

Approved use of atomic bomb to end World War II. Supported economic aid for war-damaged countries and mutual-defense programs. Sent troops to Korea to repel Communist invasion.

★ ★ ★ ★ ★ ★ ★ ★

employees and requiring loyalty oaths. Many citizens managed to keep a sense of balance on this subject. To others, however, anyone who favored civil liberties or questioned cold-war foreign policy was a Communist or at least a Communist sympathizer.

McCarthyism. Exploiting this climate of fear, Republican Senator Joseph R. McCarthy of Wisconsin rocketed to public attention. In February 1950, he charged that there were 205 "known Communists" in the State Department. (He later reduced the number to 81 and then to 57.) Although McCarthy did not uncover even one Soviet agent, he held the headlines for the next four years with his investigations and charges of Communist conspiracies. Thus, the name *McCarthyism* came to be used for the practice of making reckless and unsupported charges against people. In truth, the practice was widespread, and many besides McCarthy used it in those times of fear.

McCarthy had considerable support. After he helped to defeat for reelection a senator who had criticized him, many other senators feared to stand up to him. Some Republican members of Congress, while disagreeing with McCarthy, were glad to have him attack the Democrats for what the Wisconsin senator called "twenty years of treason."

McCarthy finally overreached himself when he charged the United States Army with harboring Communists. The televised hearings in 1954 on those charges let millions of people see for the first time McCarthy's bullying tactics. The senator then began to lose public support. Later that year the United States Senate censured him by a vote of 67 to 22. McCarthy sank back into obscurity almost as quickly as he had risen from it. At the time of his death in 1957, he was no longer a power in the Senate.

The election of 1952. McCarthy's charges that the Democrats were "soft on communism" added to that party's problems in the 1952 elections. Frustrations over the war in Korea and corruption among some officials in the Truman administration made a Republican victory likely. For their presidential candidate, Republicans chose the popular war hero, General Dwight Eisenhower, with Congressman Richard Nixon of California as his running mate. The Democratic nominee was Governor Adlai Stevenson of Illinois. Despite his thoughtful speeches, Stevenson had no chance against the respected "Ike" Eisenhower, the Republican formula of K, C_2 (Korea, communism, and corruption), and the feeling that it was "time for a change." Eisenhower won by more than 6 million popular votes and received 442 electoral votes to 89 for Stevenson.

The Eisenhower program. During his campaign, Eisenhower had promised to return to the states some of the power held by the federal government and to lessen the federal government's role in the economy. His appointments to cabinet positions confirmed his resolve to have a government more friendly to business. The press called the cabinet "nine millionaires and a plumber," the latter being the secretary of labor, a former union official.

One of the President's first acts was to end the price and wage controls that had been imposed during the Korean war. He also signed into law a bill that turned over the federal government's offshore oil claims to the states. Eisenhower did not propose selling off the Tennessee Valley Authority to private industry, as some supporters thought he might. But when a government atomic energy plant in Tennessee needed more electric power, he gave the contract (later cancelled) to a private electric company rather than to TVA. Similarly, under Eisenhower the Atomic Energy Commission allowed private electric companies to build atomic power plants.

Yet those who hoped that the new administration would dismantle the New Deal and Fair Deal social programs were disappointed. Eisenhower, who defeated Stevenson for a second time in 1956, accepted the welfare state. In fact, during his two terms the minimum wage was again raised, social security was widened to cover 90 percent of American workers, and money was provided for hospitals and urban renewal.

★34★

Dwight D. Eisenhower

1890–1969

Born in TEXAS
In Office 1953–1961
Party REPUBLICAN

Became President after winning military fame in World War II. Opposed price and wage controls. Favored more power for states, continued foreign aid, and strong defenses.

3. DEBATE Article I, Section 6, of the United States Constitution states: "The Senators and Representatives shall . . . in all cases, except treason, felony and breach of the peace, be privileged from arrest during their attendance at the session of their respective houses, and in going to and returning from the same; and for any speech or debate in either house, they shall not be questioned in any other place." Senator McCarthy systematically attacked many persons from the floor of the Senate but could not be sued for libel. Targets of his attacks tried to have him repeat his charges outside the Senate chambers but he refused to do so. McCarthy's downfall occured when he attacked other senators. The Senate, after an investigation, gave him a formal rebuke. Have students organize a debate on the following topic: Resolved, That senators and representatives should not be immune from libel for statements made in their respective chambers.

4. RESEARCH / ORAL REPORTS Have several students investigate the furor in the United States after the launching of the sputniks. This research should include editorials as well as magazine and newspaper stories. Students should cite the reasons that were given for the United States "falling behind" the Soviet Union. They should also describe the solutions that were proposed. Have the students decide if the writers of the articles were overreacting or whether the United States needed a severe shock to make it concentrate its efforts. The students should report their findings to the class.

LESSON 3 *(2 days)*

Performance Objectives

1. To compare and contrast orally or in writing the 1920s and the 1950s. 2. To identify orally or in writing changes in the work force after World War II. 3. To describe orally or in writing the advances made during the 1950s toward achieving racial justice.

Famous People

Chief Justice Earl Warren, Rosa Parks, Martin Luther King, Jr.

Vocabulary

"Military-industrial complex," computer, automation, Federal Highway Act of 1956, "baby boom," white-collar workers, guaranteed annual wage, NAACP, *Brown* v. *Board of Education of Topeka, Kansas,* boycott, nonviolence, Southern Christian Leadership Conference, Student Nonviolent Coordinating Committee (SNCC), "sit-in," Freedom Riders

Activities

1. **READING FOR INFORMATION** After students have read the lesson, have them take notes comparing and contrasting the 1920s and 1950s. The students could list the similarities in one column and the differences in a second column. After they have completed the assignment, discuss their answers. Have students keep their notes to use in Chapter 36, when they will compare and contrast the 1950s with the 1960s and early 1970s.

The farm problem. The Eisenhower administration's handling of the farm problem demonstrated that it would not stray too far from the path laid out in the New Deal. The demand for food during World War II had temporarily ended farm surpluses. But after the war, surpluses again piled up, and the government bought and stored them, thus supporting crop prices. By the 1950s, crop yields had increased so greatly that surpluses mounted. In 1952 the government held surpluses worth $1.4 billion; by 1956 the crop surpluses were valued at $8.3 billion. Annual storage costs totalled hundreds of millions of dollars.

The Eisenhower administration's approach to the surplus situation was twofold. It lowered the support prices to discourage farm production. And it paid farmers to take land out of production. New Dealers might have gone at the problem a bit differently, but they would have recognized the Eisenhower farm program as a child of their own. And, as in the case of the New Deal, it was not the government program but an increase in world demand some years later that eased the farm problem.

The race into space. The Space Age opened on October 4, 1957. The Soviet Union sent into orbit around the earth a three-pound (1.4-kg) ball of metal called *Sputnik*. This was the world's first artificial satellite. One month later, the Soviets launched *Sputnik II.* It weighed more than 1,000 pounds (450 kg) and carried a live dog.

The news of the launching of the sputniks jolted Americans. It appeared that the Soviet Union had beaten America at its own game—science and technology. What is more important, the United States now felt new concern about its national security. A rocket powerful enough to put a sputnik into space was plainly powerful enough to fire a missile across the ocean.

The Soviets' space success spurred the American government to action. The United States poured money into the space program to try to catch up to the Russians. Congress also passed the National Defense Education Act in 1958. This law provided grants and loans to promising college students in many fields, but especially in the sciences.

CHECKUP

1. What effect did the cold war have on domestic affairs?
2. How did the Eisenhower administration deal with the problem of farm surpluses?
3. How did Americans react to the orbiting of *Sputnik*?

LESSON 3

American Life in the 1950s

The America of the 1950s was similar in many ways to the America of the 1920s, although there were some important differences. Like the 1920s, the 1950s were prosperous years. Despite two recessions, the gross national product rose by 50 percent. Much of this increase resulted from government spending, which directly accounted for 20 percent of all goods and services bought. More than half of this spending was for military purposes. Indeed, the dependence of many industries upon such spending led President Eisenhower to warn about the dangers of a "military-industrial complex."

The benefits of heavy government spending were spread throughout the entire economy, creating jobs and buying power for many millions. Advances in science and technology made possible a great flow of goods. Americans became familiar with two new words that, they were told, would soon change their lives. One word was *computer*—a machine that handles information and solves problems with great speed. The other was *automation*—the automatic handling of steps in a manufacturing process without benefit of human labor.

Automation permits the control of machines by other machines or devices. From the control room shown above, one person can direct the manufacturing processes in an entire paper mill.

The consumer society. For the majority of Americans who identified the good life with material things, the 1950s were very good times indeed. The mass of consumer goods available in the 1950s dwarfed the amount available in the prosperous 1920s. Americans, who made up only 6 percent of the world's population, produced and consumed more than a third of the world's goods and services during the 1950s. Stereos, dishwashers, tape recorders, food freezers, and clothes washers and dryers soon became standard in American homes. Advertisers spent $10 billion each year to convince the public that happiness depended on using their products. Purchases were made easy by readily available consumer credit and the appearance of the credit card in 1950.

Many of the new goods and services were connected with leisure and entertainment, a sign that Americans had both more money and more free time. By 1960, there was one television set for every four Americans. There was a car for every three Americans, and the Federal Highway Act of 1956 promised an interstate network of 40,000 miles to travel on. New roads, cars, higher incomes, and a postwar "baby boom" fed the new American Dream of a house in the suburbs. Whole new towns sprang up, complete with shopping centers and industrial parks. Within another decade, more Americans would live and work in the suburbs than in the cities.

A large and new part of the consuming public was made up of young people. Spending billions, they shaped entire industries as they sought in styles of dress and music to put distance between themselves and an older generation. Teenagers' dollars made millionaires of such rock and roll stars as Elvis Presley, Chuck Berry, Jerry Lee Lewis, and the Everly Brothers.

Background Information

1. COMPUTERS In 1890, Herman Hollerith invented a punch-card tabulating machine, a precursor of the modern computer. The first purely electronic computer, ENIAC (Electronic Numerical Integrator and Computer), was built for the United States Army in 1946. The computer required 18,000 vacuum tubes. In 1956, Walter H. Brattain, John Bardeen, and William B. Shockley won a Nobel prize for developing the transistor. Their discovery eliminated the need for vacuum tubes. Thus the ENIAC, which required a large room for storage, was no longer viable. What the huge ENIAC could do in 1946 could be done faster in 1956 by a machine no bigger than a suitcase. In the late 1960s, silicon chips came into use, and today miniaturization is here. The information held by the ENIAC can now be stored in a space the size of the head of a pin. Ask your students to imagine what is coming.

2. BULLETIN-BOARD DISPLAY Have students identify the current changes in the work force by researching the available statistics in the latest edition of *The U.S. Fact Book* (New York: Grosset & Dunlap), which is prepared by the U.S. Bureau of the Census. Then have the students compare current statistics with those of the 1950s as shown in *Historical Statistics of the United States, Colonial Times to 1970* (Washington, D.C.: U.S. Bureau of the Census, 1975). The students should make charts of the comparisons for bulletin-board display.

3. FILMS *Computers and the Mind of Men,* a series of six films: *The Control Revolution; Engine at the Door; Logic by Machine; Managers and Models; Universal Machine;* and *Universe of Numbers* (each 29 minutes, b&w; National Educational Television). *The Warren Years: The Great Decisions* (24 minutes, b&w; National Education Television). *Segregation in Schools,* Edward R. Murrow See It Now series (28 minutes, b&w; CBS Films).

4. DISCUSSION In the late 1970s, America experienced a "fifties revival." Shows such as *Grease* on Broadway, *American Graffitti* in the movies, *Happy Days* and *LaVerne and Shirley* on television featured styles, music, and personalities of the 1950s. Rock and roll concerts featured many of the old groups. Have the class discuss what characteristics of the 1950s were depicted. Ask: If young people of the fifties generation were considered to be passive, uncommitted stick-in-the-muds, why would young people of the 1970s be so interested in them? Have your students try to explain this phenomenon.

Changes in the work force. Changes in the economy were accompanied by important changes in the work force. Most of those changes continued earlier trends. The percentage of white-collar workers, about 20 percent of the work force in 1900, reached 50 percent in the 1950s. The number of women in the work force also continued to rise. By 1960, 40 percent of American women held full-time or part-time jobs. A growing number of those working women were married. Most took jobs to add to the family income rather than to find fulfillment outside the home. Also, the effects of the GI Bill began to be felt. The doors of business and the professions began to open to hundreds of thousands who had taken advantage of free college education and vocational training.

Labor unions became stronger in the 1950s. The American Federation of Labor and the Congress of Industrial Organizations merged in 1955 after twenty years of separation and often bitter fighting. Labor-management relations in the major industries were more peaceful than in the 1930s and the postwar years. By now, management had accepted unions as a reality, and negotiations between the two sides settled into a businesslike pattern. Industry avoided long strikes that would interrupt growth and profits. The unions gained more benefits for their members. The auto workers' union was the first to win a guaranteed annual wage.

"Don't rock the boat." As in the 1920s, there was a widespread belief that the problems that had dogged Americans for a generation had been solved. Despite two recessions, Americans believed they had learned to use the powers of government to manage the economy and avoid economic depression. Business, labor, and government seemed to have learned to accept each other's roles.

American society in the 1950s was not without its critics. They expressed concern about a growing conformity in the lives of Americans. They saw a drab sameness—in clothes, in houses ("little boxes made of ticky tacky," sang folksong writer Pete Seeger), and worst of all, in thought and goals. A survey of college students showed that the goals of this generation were security and comfort—not excellence. Critics decried a generation whose motto seemed to be "Don't rock the boat."

As in the 1920s, many millions of Americans did not share in the prosperity of the 1950s. Twenty percent of Americans were below the poverty line, defined by the United States government at that time at $3,000 a year. Entire regions—for example, Appalachia, running along nearly the whole Appalachian Mountain range—were desperately poor. So also were large numbers of American Indians, blacks, and Hispanic Americans. Millions of elderly of all races found it hard to make ends meet. For many people, things had gotten worse in the 1950s, not better.

Civil rights. The fight against Nazi racism in World War II lent fresh support to the drive for racial justice in America. In the 1940s and early 1950s, federal courts struck down a number of Jim Crow laws, with the National Association for the Advancement of Colored People leading the fight. In 1954 the NAACP won its most important victory in the case of *Brown* v. *Board of Education of Topeka, Kansas.* Speaking for a unanimous Supreme Court, Chief Justice Earl Warren struck down the "separate but equal" doctrine of *Plessy* v. *Ferguson* (see page 386). Segregated schools, said the Court, are unequal by their very nature. State and local school segregation laws therefore violate the guarantee of "equal protection of the laws" of the Fourteenth Amendment, and are unconstitutional. The Court later ordered school authorities to desegregate "with all deliberate speed."

But desegregation proceeded very slowly. Segregationists resisted with every kind of roadblock and delay. In 1957 the governor of Arkansas used the National Guard to keep seven black children from entering all-white Central High School in Little Rock. President Eisenhower, who was personally cool to the Brown decision, nevertheless ordered in federal troops to uphold the authority of the federal courts. Central High was integrated. Still, as late as 1960, in four Southern states there was not a single desegregated school. In six others, 99 percent of black students were still in segregated schools.

In 1957 and 1960, Congress passed two laws dealing with the voting rights of Southern blacks. They were very limited measures, however, and were very hard to enforce. They brought little change. Nevertheless, some people took comfort in the fact that Congress had passed the first civil rights laws since Reconstruction.

Change came slowly through the courts and Congress. So blacks developed other means to bring down Jim Crow. One breakthrough grew out of a chance happening. In Montgomery, Alabama, on December 1, 1955, Rosa Parks, a black woman, refused to give up her seat on a bus to a white passenger who was standing. As Alabama law required, she was arrested. Under the leadership of a young minister named Martin Luther King, Jr., blacks then began a boycott of Montgomery's buses.

Martin Luther King, Jr. *(front row, center)* leads a civil rights demonstration in Alabama.

5. DISCUSSION / WRITTEN REPORTS Discuss with your students those cases that led up to the *Brown* v. *Board of Education of Topeka, Kansas,* decision: The Civil Rights Cases, 1883 (Supreme Court found the Civil Rights Act of 1875 unconstitutional and in effect said that the system of "white supremacy" was beyond federal control because it was a question of private human relationships and not state-made sanctions); *Plessy* v. *Ferguson,* 1896 (Supreme Court upheld the "separate but equal" concept); *Allston* v. *School Board of Norfolk,* 1940 (Federal district court ruled that Negro teachers must be paid the same as white teachers if they do the same work); *Morgan* v. *Virginia,* 1946 (Supreme Court ruled that state segregation laws were unconstitutional as applied to public transportation in interstate commerce); *Shelley* v. *Kraemer,* 1948 (Supreme Court ruled that state or federal enforcement of discrimination against Negroes violated the Fourteenth and Fifteenth amendments); *Sweatt* v. *Painter* and *McLaurin* v. *Oklahoma State Regents,* 1950 (Supreme Court ruled in both cases that equal protection under law applied, and isolation because of race was unconstitutional). Ask your students to do further research into these cases to find out how they were started, what the main issues were, and what the outcomes were.

Background Information

2. *BROWN* v. *BOARD OF EDUCATION OF TOPEKA, KANSAS* In 1951, Oliver Brown sued the city board of education, seeking the enrollment of his daughter in the all-white school in her neighborhood. Thurgood Marshall (see page 738) argued the case for Brown in the Supreme Court.

ANSWERS TO REVIEW QUESTIONS

1. Truman sent to Congress a twenty-one-point program that included the following proposals: an increase in the minimum wage; extended coverage of social security; full-employment legislation; a permanent Fair Employment Practices Commission; public housing and slum clearance; and long-range planning to protect national resources and to build projects like the TVA. He later added proposals for federal aid to education and for health insurance.
2. When the war ended, arms contracts were cancelled and government spending decreased drastically. The Truman administration feared that with this drop in spending and with returning servicemen and servicewomen looking for jobs, there would be widespread unemployment. It was also feared that it would take too much time to reconvert factories from making wartime goods to making civilian goods.
3. The House Un-American Activities Committee investigated people who were possibly Communists or who might have Communist leanings. They searched for movies with Communist messages and for writers and actors with Communist sympathies.
4. Under Eisenhower, programs were adopted to accept the welfare state, raise the minimum wage, widen social security to include over 90 percent of Americans, provide money for hospitals and urban renewal, and help farmers with their surplus produce.

The boycott lasted for more than a year. King held his followers together with his message of Christian love and nonviolence. Finally, a federal court order and large financial losses by the bus company forced the company and the city to give in. This success brought national attention and support to King. In 1957 he started the Southern Christian Leadership Conference to organize other nonviolent protests against Jim Crow laws.

In 1960, black college students, members of the Student Nonviolent Coordinating Committee (SNCC), staged a "sit-in" to desegregate a lunch counter in Greensboro, North Carolina. During the next year and a half, 70,000 students—both blacks and whites—took part in sit-ins. They held wade-ins at Jim Crow beaches and pools and kneel-ins in segregated churches. Still another group, known as Freedom Riders, rode interstate buses to integrate the buses and waiting rooms in Southern cities. By enduring verbal and physical abuse, the nonviolent Freedom Riders and those who held sit-ins won support for their cases.

These activities in the area of civil rights were about all that upset the calm of America in the middle and late 1950s. On the whole, those were tranquil years at home. Further, since 1953, no American had died on a battlefield. Few people, if any, could have guessed the shocks that were in store for American society during the next two decades. In the final chapter of this book, you will be reading about those events.

CHECKUP

1. What similarities did the 1950s in America have to the 1920s?
2. How did the work force change during the years following World War II?
3. What advances were made during the 1950s toward achieving racial justice?

Key Facts from Chapter 35

1. After World War II, the United States reconverted relatively smoothly from a wartime economy to a peacetime economy.
2. The cold war abroad was accompanied at home by a hunt for Communists. For several years in the early 1950s, charges that were often unsupported created a climate of fear.
3. The election of Harry Truman to the Presidency in 1948 was one of the biggest upsets in political history. The election of Dwight Eisenhower in 1952 brought to an end twenty years of Democratic administrations.
4. The Space Age opened in 1957 as the Soviet Union put *Sputnik* into orbit. This feat spurred the United States to set up a space program.
5. Civil rights advances during the 1950s included the Supreme Court's order to desegregate the public schools and the striking down of various Jim Crow laws through the efforts of Martin Luther King, Jr., and others.

★ REVIEWING THE CHAPTER ★

People, Places, and Events

Harry Truman *P. 723*
Fair Deal *P. 723*
Atomic Energy Commission *P. 723*
Taft-Hartley Act *P. 725*
Ethel and Julius Rosenberg *P. 727*
National Defense Education Act *P. 730*
Federal Highway Act of 1956 *P. 731*
Martin Luther King, Jr. *P. 733*
Student Nonviolent Coordinating Committee *P. 734*

Review Questions

1. What Fair Deal programs did Truman propose? *P. 723* Les. 1
2. Identify the major problems that the Truman administration feared would result from the conversion to a peacetime economy in the mid 1940s. *P. 724* Les. 1
3. What were the subjects of investigations by the House Un-American Activities Committee? *P. 727* Les. 2
4. Describe three of Eisenhower's social programs. *P. 729* Les. 2
5. What factors caused Eisenhower to be concerned about the development of a "military-industrial complex?" *P. 730* Les. 3
6. In the 1950s what groups of Americans became larger parts of the consuming public? work force? *Pp. 731–732* Les. 3
7. What were some problems with the voting-rights laws passed by Congress in 1957 and 1960? *P. 733* Les. 3

Chapter Test

For these sentences, write the letters of the correct endings. Some sentences have more than one correct ending. Use a separate sheet of paper.

1. Under Truman, Congress passed legislation to **(a)** desegregate education, **(b)** control nuclear production, **(c)** provide national health insurance.
2. The GI Bill **(a)** removed price and wage controls, **(b)** outlawed the closed shop, **(c)** assisted veterans.
3. The most important law passed by the Eightieth Congress, the Taft-Hartley Act, dealt with **(a)** farm price supports, **(b)** national unemployment, **(c)** labor relations.
4. The search for subversives in America **(a)** was supported by Senator Joseph McCarthy, **(b)** uncovered Soviet agents in the United States Army, **(c)** promoted civil liberties.
5. The election of Eisenhower in 1952 was supported by public **(a)** distrust of war heroes, **(b)** desire for a change, **(c)** fear of communism.
6. The Eisenhower administration **(a)** was friendly to business, **(b)** began the space program, **(c)** rejected the welfare state.
7. Heavy government spending during the 1950s **(a)** prevented automation, **(b)** created jobs, **(c)** aided the consumer society, **(d)** financed an interstate highway system, **(e)** created the military-industrial complex.
8. Economic prosperity in the 1950s was accompanied by **(a)** poverty for 20 percent of all Americans, **(b)** rejection of conformity, **(c)** stronger labor unions.
9. The NAACP led the fight against **(a)** the Southern Christian Leadership Conference, **(b)** Jim Crow laws, **(c)** Freedom Riders.
10. Support for civil rights during the 1950s and 1960s came from **(a)** Martin Luther King, Jr., **(b)** Rosa Parks, **(c)** *Plessy v. Ferguson*, **(d)** Congress.

5. In the 1950s the gross national product increased by 50 percent. Much of this was due to government spending for goods and services. And half of that spending was for military purposes. Eisenhower feared the dependence of so many industries on government military spending in peaceful times.
6. A large, new part of the consuming public was made up of young people from the "baby boom." Their spending power shaped entire industries as they sought new styles in hair, clothing, and music. In the 1950s the number of working women increased to 40 percent of the work force, and the number of white-collar workers increased to 50 percent.
7. The 1957 and 1960 voting-rights laws were limited and very hard to enforce. In the end, they brought little change.

ANSWERS FOR CHAPTER TEST

1. b **2.** c **3.** c **4.** a
5. b, c **6.** a, b **7.** b, c, d, e
8. a, c **9.** b **10.** a, b, d

ONLY YESTERDAY: THE '60s AND '70s

Background Information

1. SPACE SHUTTLE Scheduled to begin operating by the early 1980s, the space shuttle orbiter is designed to make more than one flight, thereby cutting the cost of space travel. Economical space travel will encourage the development of space laboratories, factories, and other commercial activities. Shown here being test-launched by a 747, the *Enterprise* orbiter is actually the second stage of the shuttle system. The first stage is made up of two booster rockets that will launch the orbiter and then fall back to earth by parachutes. The orbiter is designed to carry four passengers and, after its mission, land on a runway like an ordinary jet airplane.

LESSON 1

DWIGHT EISENHOWER was one of the best-liked men ever to serve as President. Had he not been limited to two terms by the Twenty-second Amendment (1951), there is little doubt that he could have won a third term if he had cared to run again. As it was, the 1960 presidential race was open. The Republicans chose Richard M. Nixon, the Vice President under Eisenhower, for their candidate. The Democratic nomination went to Senator John F. Kennedy of Massachusetts. With a talent for politics and with family wealth to back his campaign, Kennedy had built an efficient organization that helped him win key primary elections. Lyndon Johnson of Texas, the Senate majority leader, accepted the Democratic nomination for Vice President.

The Kennedy and Johnson Years

At the start of the 1960 campaign, polls showed Nixon with a large lead. Many people expected that Kennedy's Catholic religion would be a serious obstacle to his election. They recalled how the religious issue had hurt Al Smith in 1928. But Kennedy did much to downplay the religious issue by dealing with it openly and honestly. More important than the religious issue was Kennedy's performance in a series of four television debates with Nixon. These were the first presidential debates ever televised. The youthful, attractive Kennedy was able to convince viewers that he was a worthy presidential candidate. Lyndon Johnson's presence on the ticket held Texas and several Southern states for the Democrats. As a result, John Kennedy, at the age of forty-three, became the youngest person ever to be elected President. He received 303 electoral votes to Nixon's 219. The margin between the two in popular votes was less than two tenths of 1 percent. This difference averaged out to less than one vote per voting precinct in the country.

The New Frontier. During his campaign, Kennedy spoke of the challenges facing Americans as the *New Frontier*. The term soon became a slogan for his Presidency. During Kennedy's years in office, he sought to update and extend various programs of the welfare state. He also urged Congress to adopt a plan for medical care for the elderly, and he favored federal aid to education. To stimulate the lagging economy, Kennedy proposed a tax cut. It would encourage business owners to invest in new plants and would also put more money for buying goods into the hands of consumers.

Kennedy was determined that the United States overtake the Soviet Union in the space race. He set a goal of putting an American on the moon before 1970. He also sought a larger military budget and increased military aid to friendly countries. His most imaginative proposal in the foreign field was the Peace Corps. Under this program, thousands of Americans would take their skills as teachers, farming experts, nurses, and other vocations to the peoples of underdeveloped countries all over the world.

LESSON 1 *(2 days)*

Performance Objectives

1. To identify in writing the accomplishments of the New Frontier and the Great Society. **2.** To identify orally or in writing the major achievements in civil rights during the Kennedy and Johnson years. **3.** To explain orally or in writing how the war in Vietnam affected the Presidency of Lyndon Johnson.

Famous People

John F. Kennedy, Lyndon Johnson, Robert C. Weaver, Thurgood Marshall, James Meredith, Lee Harvey Oswald, Hubert Humphrey, Barry Goldwater, Malcolm X, Eugene McCarthy, Robert F. Kennedy, Spiro Agnew, George Wallace

Vocabulary

New Frontier, Peace Corps, Manpower Training Act, Civil Rights Act of 1964, Great Society, "war on poverty," Economic Opportunity Act of 1964, Job Corps, Volunteers in Service to America (VISTA), Project Head Start, Voting Rights Act of 1965, Twenty-fourth Amendment, black power, Black Panthers, white backlash, ghetto riots, Watts, Kerner Commission

Activities

1. READING FOR INFORMATION Have the students list the achievements and failures of President Kennedy and President Johnson, using their textbooks and any other sources. The students should then compare the two leaders to determine who the class thinks was the stronger and more effective President. After the class has discussed the comparisons, ask: Who is best remembered by the American people? Why?

2. ESSAY The Kennedy-Johnson era marked a high point in the civil rights movement. Have students write essays in which they describe and explain the various developments and personalities involved in this dramatic period. Their essays should include information about the differences between the integrationist and the black-power groups as well as the role of the government in the struggle.

3. BOOK REPORTS Assign students to read and report on the following autobiographical books by people who were directly involved in the civil rights movement of the 1960s. The books include a range of philosophies, so having the students make comparisons between them could be very useful. Eldridge Cleaver, *Soul on Ice* (New York: McGraw-Hill, 1968); Sammy Davis, Jr., with Jane and Burt Boyar, *Yes I Can* (New York: Farrar, 1965); Mrs. Medgar Evers with William Peters, *For Us the Living* (Garden City, N.Y., Doubleday, 1967); Coretta Scott King, *My Life with Martin Luther King, Jr.* (New York: Holt, Rinehart & Winston, 1969); Malcolm X with Alex Haley, *The Autobiography of Malcolm X* (New York: Grove Press, 1965).

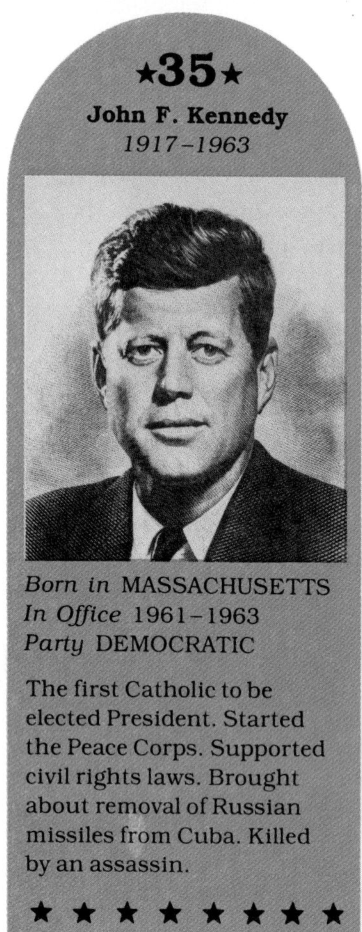
★35★
John F. Kennedy
1917–1963

Born in MASSACHUSETTS
In Office 1961–1963
Party DEMOCRATIC

The first Catholic to be elected President. Started the Peace Corps. Supported civil rights laws. Brought about removal of Russian missiles from Cuba. Killed by an assassin.

★ ★ ★ ★ ★ ★ ★ ★

Kennedy had no difficulty getting approval for his defense, space, and Peace Corps proposals. His success in social legislation was more limited. Congress voted for improvements in social security and unemployment benefits. It also spent a small amount of money to aid distressed areas and to build low-cost housing. In 1962 the Manpower Training Act helped train people for jobs. But conservative Democrats and Republicans combined to block medical care to the elderly, federal aid to education, and a civil rights bill.

Civil Rights. During his campaign, Kennedy had strongly favored the extension of civil rights. As President he appointed a number of blacks to important positions. Robert C. Weaver became the Federal Housing Administrator, and Thurgood Marshall was made a federal judge. (Under Kennedy's successor, Lyndon Johnson, Weaver became the first black to serve in the cabinet, and Marshall became the first black to serve on the Supreme Court.) Yet Kennedy at first proceeded cautiously in the civil rights area.

Nevertheless, when events called for immediate steps to protect civil rights, Kennedy acted promptly. Federal marshalls were sent into the South to protect those who were demonstrating for the integration of public facilities. In 1962 the President sent troops to Mississippi to protect James Meredith, a black Air Force veteran who had enrolled at the state university. He did the same in 1963 in Birmingham after marchers who were peacefully protesting the refusal to let blacks vote had been subjected to violence.

Soon after his action in Birmingham, Kennedy sent a strong civil rights bill to Congress. On the one hundredth anniversary of the Emancipation Proclamation, the President told the nation on television, the achievement of full civil rights by black people was long overdue. To those who said that laws could not change people's hearts, the President replied that laws were needed to check their behavior.

To win support for the bill, more than 200,000 civil rights supporters held a march on Washington. Gathered before the Lincoln Memorial, they and millions

Continued on page 740

Television and Government

Television has enabled millions of Americans to know more about how their government works. It has permitted them to see their leaders in action and has brought the process of government closer to millions of TV viewers.

The television screen first showed the investigative role of Congress in 1951. Hearings on organized crime were held by a committee headed by Senator Estes Kefauver of Tennessee. Three years later, another congressional investigation—the Army-McCarthy hearings (see page 728)—held viewers spellbound as they watched the month-long proceedings. But the largest audience for a congressional hearing occurred during the 1973 investigation of the Watergate affair. As Americans watched the hearings, they learned much about the constitutional grounds on which a President may be impeached.

Television has also focused on the executive branch of government. Since President Eisenhower first answered journalists' questions before TV cameras in 1955, there have been many other televised presidential press conferences. Television has also helped Americans decide which candidate they will support in an election. In 1960, the two major candidates for President, John F. Kennedy and Richard M. Nixon, met in a series of nationally televised debates. Many people felt that these debates turned the tide for Kennedy, making it possible for him to win that very close election. In 1976, the rival candidates, Jimmy Carter and Gerald Ford, also debated on television.

Television—like other technological developments—can be used in many different ways. It has often been criticized for its shortcomings. Yet without doubt, television has helped to make Americans more politically aware and better acquainted with the machinery of their government.

Democratic senatorial candidates in New York State meet in 1977 in a televised debate.

4. DISCUSSION After the students have read Sidelights on History, page 739, have them discuss other times that television has affected Americans' views of politicians. The discussion should touch on the effect of highly publicized demonstrations, such as those against President Johnson's Vietnam policies and the violent incidents at the Democratic Convention in 1968. Ask: Are demonstrations designed and staged for television by groups that want the exposure? Can a politician manipulate television coverage to favor himself or herself? How can television newspersons decide when they are covering news and when they are being used?

5. GUEST SPEAKER Almost every county in America had at least one resident who joined the Peace Corps. If possible, invite one of these volunteers to come to your class and tell the students about his or her experiences. Though the Peace Corps came about during the Kennedy administration, the idea of the Peace Corps belongs to the late Senator Hubert H. Humphrey. Have one of your students describe when, how, where, and why Senator Humphrey introduced this idea.

Background Information

2. PICTURE Lyndon Johnson took the oath of President at 2:39 P.M. aboard Air Force One, the presidential plane, at Love Field in Dallas. Johnson is standing between his wife, Lady Bird, and Jacqueline Kennedy. The oath was administered by Federal Judge Sarah T. Hughes, an old friend of Johnson's. The swearing-in took place one hour and thirty-nine minutes after Kennedy died.

of others watching on television heard Martin Luther King, Jr., declare:

> I have a dream that one day on the red hills of Georgia the sons of former slaves and the sons of former slaveowners will be able to sit down together at the table of brotherhood. . . . I have a dream that one day [in] the state of Alabama. . . little black boys and black girls will be able to join hands with little white boys and white girls and walk together as sisters and brothers.

The march on Washington marked the height of the integrationist phase of the civil rights movement.

Johnson succeeds Kennedy. Kennedy's civil rights bill would finally be passed, but only after Kennedy was in his grave. On November 22, 1963, the President was shot and killed in Dallas, Texas. While in the custody of the Dallas police, the assassin, Lee Harvey Oswald, was himself killed by an unbalanced man only two days later.

Lyndon Johnson takes the oath as President following John F. Kennedy's assassination.

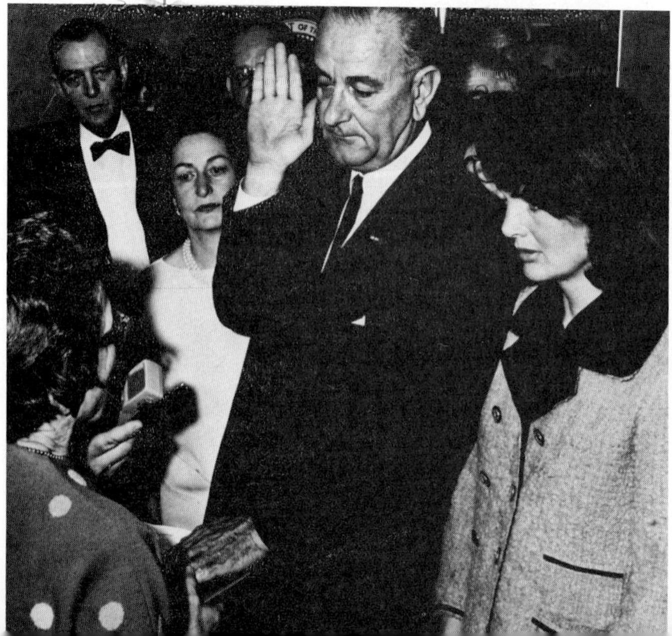

Only hours after Kennedy's death, Vice President Lyndon Johnson was sworn in as the thirty-sixth President of the United States. The son of a Populist legislator in Texas, Johnson knew what it meant to grow up poor. He was elected to Congress in 1937, and served in both the House and the Senate. He was highly regarded for his skills as a political leader. Taking advantage of the wave of emotion following Kennedy's death, Johnson skillfully pressed Congress to pass laws that the late President had supported. Congress passed Kennedy's tax bill and also his civil rights bill. The Civil Rights Act of 1964 was in fact even stronger than the one Kennedy had sought. It gave the federal government more power to protect black people's voting rights. It also helped speed up school integration; ended racial discrimination in hotels, restaurants, theaters, and other public accommodations; and prohibited race or sex discrimination in hiring. Though enforcement was often difficult, this act was the most important civil rights law since the Reconstruction era. Even as Congress debated this bill, the nation received a grim reminder of why federal protection of civil rights was needed. Three young civil rights workers were murdered in Mississippi. They were part of several hundred who were spending the summer helping blacks register for voting.

Toward the Great Society. In addition to completing the Kennedy program, Johnson was anxious to make his own mark. He declared that "we have the opportunity to move not only toward the rich society, but upward to the Great Society." In January 1964, the President announced a "war on poverty." The key measure in that war was the Economic Opportunity Act of 1964. Under this law, the Office of Economic Opportunity gave money to local communities to provide relief and jobs for the poor. It started the Job Corps to train young people for careers, and it helped poor high-school students find summer work. It also set up Volunteers in Service to America (VISTA), a kind of domestic peace corps to help people in poor areas improve their living conditions. This act was the first of several that Johnson would get Congress to pass in his quest for the Great Society.

At the Democratic convention in 1964, Johnson was the unanimous choice of his party for the Presidency. He chose Senator Hubert Humphrey of Minnesota as his running mate. Johnson swept aside the Republican contender, Senator Barry Goldwater of Arizona, in a landslide, 486 to 52. Goldwater carried only his own Arizona and four Southern states. Each house of Congress had a large Democratic majority.

The Eighty-ninth Congress that met in January 1965 was thus Lyndon Johnson's Congress, and he made the most of it. The President presented Congress with wide-ranging plans to move the country forward.

Sweeping reforms. Under Johnson's prodding, Congress passed the most sweeping reforms since New Deal days. One important program was Medicare. This act provided health care for the aged through the social security program. A second part of Johnson's program provided large-scale federal aid to schools for the first time. As a condition for this aid, school districts had to show that desegregation of students and teachers had been started. Congress also provided aid to colleges. Funds were set aside for helping low-income tenants with rent payments, for building more public housing, and for creating more jobs. The Office of Economic Opportunity was greatly expanded. New programs were begun, including Project Head Start. This was a preschool program for children whose family backgrounds had not prepared them to do well in school. A start was also made on dealing with the problems of water pollution and air pollution. And the discriminatory quota system was removed from the immigration laws (see page 437).

Great Society legislation also included the Voting Rights Act of 1965. Despite earlier laws, many Southern blacks found themselves unable to vote. One device by which they were still deprived of their voting rights was the literacy test (see page 387). Local officials who gave the test often made it easy for whites but very difficult for blacks. The Voting Rights Act of 1965 allowed federal examiners to supervise voter registration and see that the same literacy test was given to all who were seeking to vote. A second device that had kept many blacks from voting was the poll tax (see page 387). In 1964, the Twenty-fourth Amendment ended the use of a poll tax as a device to keep people from casting their votes. Within less than a year, voting registration of Southern blacks rose by 40 percent. By the end of the 1960s, black candidates were running—with considerable success—for various elective offices.

6. DISCUSSION It was thought that the religious issue would be very important in the 1960 election, but it had faded by election day. Ask: Why would there be a religious issue in Kennedy's election? How did Kennedy neutralize the issue? How was religion an issue in Jimmy Carter's election?

7. RESEARCH/WRITTEN REPORT One of the most important achievements in education in this country was the passage in 1965 of the Elementary and Secondary Education Act (ESEA). Assign some of the students to study this act in detail, learning all about its different titles. Ask them to find out how this act has helped their own school district and to determine ways in which the act might help the district in some of its current problems.

8. RESEARCH/ORAL REPORTS Have some students investigate the similarities between the Kennedy and Lincoln assassinations. Students are always fascinated by the number of coincidences that have been discovered. Other students may want to investigate and report on the conspiracy theories that have been suggested concerning the assassinations. Both of these assassinations, it seems, will never be entirely settled in people's minds.

9. INTERVIEW On November 22, 1963, a shocked nation learned of the assassination of its President. This was the first presidential assassination in sixty years. Have students interview family members and neighbors about reactions to the assassination. Almost all of them will recall exactly what they were doing when they heard the news. Many of them may have seen the actual shooting of Lee Harvey Oswald on television. They also may have observations about the President's funeral.

10. FILMS *The Age of Kennedy: The Early Years* (42 minutes, b&w; NBC Films). *The Age of Kennedy: The Presidency* (52 minutes, b&w; NBC Films). *The Presidency: Crisis in Office* (15 minutes, b&w; Universal Educational and Visual Arts).

Divisions in the civil rights movement. To those who opposed equality for blacks, Martin Luther King, Jr., wrote:

> Do what you will and we will still love you. Bomb our homes and threaten our children; send your hooded perpetrators of violence into our communities and drag us out on some wayside road, beating us and leaving us half dead, and we will still love you. But we will soon wear you down by our capacity to suffer.

Martin Luther King's victory over segregation and race hatred through love and nonviolence was recognized in 1964 with the Nobel peace prize. Yet even while King was receiving his award, there were growing divisions in the civil rights movement. They came at a time when the battle for equality was shifting from an attack upon Jim Crow to gaining jobs. Not all blacks agreed with King's goal of integration nor with his tactic of nonviolence.

One who did not agree with King's approach was Malcolm X. (The X replaced the family name of Little, which Malcolm called his "slave name.") Malcolm X was a leading Black Muslim. The Black Muslim organization was a religious group whose members believed in separation of the races. If King was the idealist appealing to people's better nature, Malcolm was the realist, reminding them of bitter experience. To Malcolm, King's march on Washington was nothing more than "a picnic, a circus" because, he declared, it had been taken over by whites. The problems of blacks, Malcolm held, would never be answered by "tripping and swaying along arm-in-arm with the very people they were supposed to be angrily revolting against. . . ." White people would never give up anything important, Malcolm believed, as long as blacks were ready to turn the other cheek. After Malcolm split from the Black Muslims to form his own group, he was killed in 1965 by several black gunmen at a public meeting.

Others, equally impatient with King's goals and methods, raised the cry of *black power.* The phrase meant different things to different people. At the least, it meant pride in race and control by blacks of their own organizations, businesses, and communities. One black-power slogan urged people to "Be Black, Buy Black." Some groups—for example, the Black Panthers—favored a black political party and resistance to white authority. As the civil rights movement of the 1950s became the Black Revolution of the 1960s many whites responded with fear and anger. The white reaction came to be known as the *white backlash.*

Ghetto riots. During the 1950s and 1960s, the flow of Southern blacks to Northern cities increased. In the 1950s alone, the black poverty-stricken neighborhoods—or *ghettos*—of the twelve largest cities gained 2 million people. During the same period, an equal number of whites left those cities. Civil rights laws did little to help the millions in the ghettos solve their problems—rat-infested housing, unemployment, drug dealers, and greedy merchants.

In July 1965, Watts, the black ghetto of Los Angeles, exploded with fire and violence. The toll included thirty-five people dead, hundreds of white-owned businesses destroyed, and many homes of black residents burned. Between 1965 and 1967, there were ghetto riots

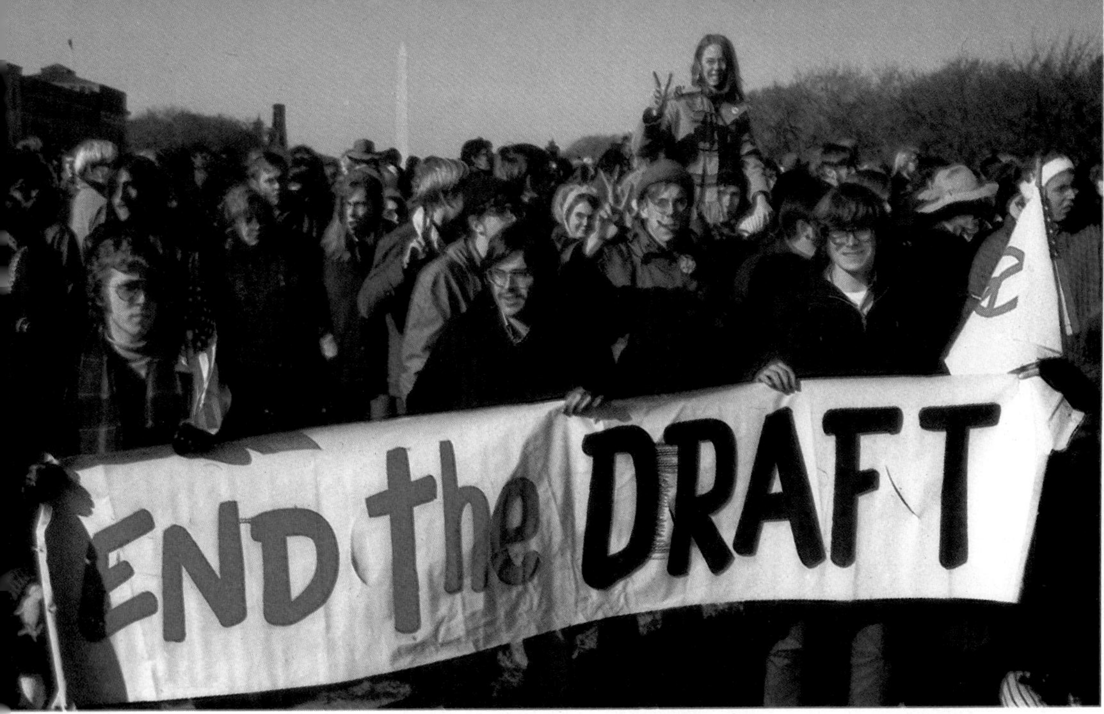

This protest against American participation in the war in Vietnam took place in Washington, D.C.

in seventy-six cities, including major riots in Newark, New Jersey, and Detroit, Michigan.

The riots bewildered many Americans. They were unable to understand the feelings of rage that could lead ghetto dwellers to destroy their own neighborhoods. President Johnson appointed a special commission to study the cause of the violence. The report of this group, the Kerner Commission, in 1968 found that the chief cause was "white racism." It also warned that the situation was getting worse, not better. "Our nation," said the report, "is moving toward two societies, one black, one white—separate and unequal."

Before the Kerner Commission reported, the nation received another shock when Dr. King was struck down by an assassin's bullet on April 4, 1968. His death touched off another round of rioting and burning in 170 cities. The worst rioting was in the nation's capital. With King's passing, most blacks regarded his program of nonviolent resistance as an idea that had run its course.

The election of 1968. Lyndon B. Johnson's Presidency was wrecked by the war in Vietnam. To many Americans, it was never clear why the United States was in Vietnam. The President's explanations made it no clearer. He talked of democracy and the free world, yet South Vietnam was hardly democratic. He spoke of honoring America's commitments, yet the United States had no treaty with South Vietnam. Several large demonstrations against sending American troops to Vietnam and against the bombing of North Vietnam took

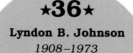

Lyndon B. Johnson
1908–1973

Born in TEXAS
In Office 1963–1969
Party DEMOCRATIC

Supported antipoverty and civil rights programs. Sent additional troops to Vietnam, but did not seek reelection because of strong American opposition to the Vietnam War.

place in 1965. As the war dragged on, protests increased. Demonstrators for peace marched, held meetings, and burned draft cards. Thousands of young men fled to Canada and elsewhere to avoid the draft. By 1968, students and police had clashed on scores of college campuses across the country. Growing numbers of older people also opposed the war.

By 1967, President Johnson had begun to limit his public appearances to military bases and other places where he would not be met by antiwar protests. But few people gave Senator Eugene McCarthy of Minnesota any chance when he announced that he would oppose President Johnson for the Democratic nomination as an antiwar candidate. In the New Hampshire presidential primary in March 1968, however, Johnson only narrowly defeated the little-known McCarthy. At this time, Robert F. Kennedy, now a senator from New York, announced that he, too, would enter the race. Faced with growing opposition, Johnson made the surprise announcement that he would not be a candidate for reelection. Soon afterward, Vice President Hubert Humphrey declared that he, too, would enter the race.

A three-way contest for the nomination took place during the spring. Then, only hours after winning the California primary in June, Robert Kennedy was shot and killed by a Jordanian immigrant. After Kennedy's death, the Democrats nominated Hubert Humphrey, who, despite personal doubts, had supported Johnson on the war. Outside the convention hall in Chicago, police and antiwar demonstrators, ranging from moderates to radicals, engaged in bloody clashes. Humphrey's campaign never recovered from the impression left by the televised scenes of violence.

By contrast, the Republican convention was a peaceful affair. Richard Nixon had lost to Kennedy in 1960 and then two years later had lost in a bid to become governor of California. His political career had seemed over. But in a remarkable comeback in 1968, he easily won the Republican nomination. Nixon chose Maryland's Governor Spiro Agnew as his running mate.

Nixon and Humphrey both had to worry about a third-party candidate. Governor George Wallace of Alabama ran on the American Independent party ticket. In 1962, he had pledged "segregation now, segregation tomorrow, segregation forever." In both North and South, Wallace appealed to those who were part of the white backlash against the civil rights movement. But his appeal was broader than that. He spoke also for many who were tired of demonstrators and were fed up with "liberals, intellectuals, and longhairs" who, Wallace said, ran the country.

Humphrey's campaign was hurt by the fact that as Vice President under Lyndon Johnson he had been connected with Johnson's unpopular war policies. Nixon was able to ride to power on discontent—over the war, student protestors and civil rights disturbances, and rising crime rates. His "law and order" campaign was meant to appeal to those he referred to as the "nonshouters, the nondemonstrators." They made up what Nixon called "the silent majority" of decent Americans. A promise to change Johnson's Vietnam policy helped Humphrey narrow Nixon's large margin near the end of the campaign, but Nixon won the election. He received 301 electoral votes to 191 for Humphrey and 46 for Wallace.

CHECKUP

1. What were some of the accomplishments of the New Frontier? of the Great Society?
2. What were the major achievements in civil rights during the Kennedy and Johnson years?
3. How did the war in Vietnam affect the Presidency of Lyndon Johnson?

LESSON 2

A Turbulent Decade

The Nixon administration relaxed pressure on school districts to desegregate, and the President himself spoke out against busing to achieve racial balance in the schools. Yet this did not result in a reversal of the dramatic gains made in desegregating Southern schools in the 1960s. Indeed, by the mid-1970s, school integration was further advanced in the South than in the North. Northern cities, where large numbers of blacks had moved in recent years, now became the main centers of resistance to school desegregation.

Nixon's approach. President Nixon was opposed to many of the social programs begun under President Johnson. Saying that social problems could not be solved by "throwing money at them," Nixon abolished the Office of Economic Opportunity and ended many of its programs. He also favored reducing federal aid to education. When Congress voted money for programs Nixon did not wish to support, he *impounded* the money—that is, refused to spend it. This raised a constitutional question of whether a President could so defy the will of Congress. The question never had a final answer in the courts.

At the same time, Nixon proposed certain positive steps. He offered a promising plan to improve the welfare program, which nearly everyone agreed was in need of reform. The bill was lost, however, in election-year politics in 1972. In his second term, Nixon did not renew the proposal. President Nixon also proposed the first large-scale federal program to deal with air and water pollution. Congress responded by providing

Continued on page 747

LESSON 2 *(2 days)*

Performance Objectives

1. To identify orally or in writing the principal achievements of the Nixon administration. **2.** To explain orally or in writing why Nixon resigned. **3.** To explain orally or in writing how Gerald Ford came to be President. **4.** To identify orally or in writing the major problems facing Jimmy Carter's administration.

Famous People

Richard Nixon, George McGovern, George Wallace, Sam Ervin, Spiro Agnew, Gerald Ford, John Mitchell, Robert Haldeman, John Ehrlichman, Nelson Rockefeller, Jimmy Carter, Walter Mondale

Vocabulary

Impounded, Environmental Protection Agency, revenue sharing, Arab oil embargo, Watergate Seven, *nolo contendere,* indictments

Background Information

APOLLO FLIGHTS
Apollo was the name chosen by NASA for the series of United States manned moon flights. They were launched from the John F. Kennedy Space Center at what was then Cape Kennedy. In 1963 President Johnson had changed the name of Cape Canaveral to Cape Kennedy. Ten years later the Floridians voted to change it back. The space center retained its name.

In order to reach the moon, a vehicle has to attain a speed of 24,300 miles (39,110 km) per hour. Between December 1968 and December 1972 there were nine flights to the moon, with six landings. On the moon, the astronauts completed many experiments, and they brought back over 400 pounds (181 kg) of soil and rock.

The Moon Landing

"Tranquility Base here. The *Eagle* has landed." The calm words of Commander Neil A. Armstrong crackled across 240,000 miles (384,000 km) of space to planet Earth. The date was July 20, 1969, the time 4:17 P.M., EDT. Some $6\frac{1}{2}$ hours later, he stepped out of the lunar module and onto the surface of the moon while a billion people on Earth watched the scene on television. The next day, Armstrong and Edwin E. "Buzz" Aldrin, Jr., explored the moon's surface, collected rocks, and performed experiments. After $21\frac{1}{2}$ hours, they rejoined astronaut Michael Collins on the orbiting spaceship, *Apollo 11*, for the return to Earth.

The voyage of the three astronauts had begun four days earlier when their rocket blasted off from Cape Kennedy, Florida. In another sense, it started forty-three years before in Auburn, Massachusetts, where Professor Robert A. Goddard of Clark University conducted experiments with rockets. It was the cold-war rivalry with the Soviet Union that gave space exploration its biggest impetus. Stung by the fact that Russia had been first with a man in space, President Kennedy, in 1961, set the goal of putting an American on the moon before 1970. During the next eight years, thousands of scientists, engineers, technicians, and other workers teamed up to turn one of humanity's oldest dreams into reality. Although the moon landing was part of the international space race, Commander Armstrong viewed the achievement in broader terms. "That's one small step for a man," he said as he first set foot on the moon, "one giant leap for mankind."

In 1971, Astronaut James Irwin prepares to explore the surface of the moon. He is standing beside the exploration vehicle called a lunar rover. At right is the landing craft of the Apollo 15 expedition.

several billion dollars to aid cities and towns in cleaning up air and water. It also created the Environmental Protection Agency to enforce acts requiring clean air and water. Another Nixon proposal adopted by Congress was *revenue sharing.* Under this plan, the federal government gave money directly to the states to use as they saw fit in dealing with a number of important problems. At the same time, however, direct federal spending on those same problems was cut back. The total of federal money available in some states turned out to be less than before. Nevertheless, the program did permit state officials more power to decide how the money should be spent.

During his campaign, Nixon had claimed that the rising crime rate was partly the result of decisions of the Supreme Court, headed by Chief Justice Earl Warren. Those decisions, he said, paid too much attention to the rights of society. He promised to appoint judges who would not "coddle" criminals. During his Presidency, Nixon was able to make four appointments of conservative judges to the Supreme Court. While the new Court did not reverse the earlier decisions of the Warren Court, it did limit somewhat the rights of the accused. During these years, Congress also provided money to strengthen local law enforcement. Nonetheless, crime rates continued to rise.

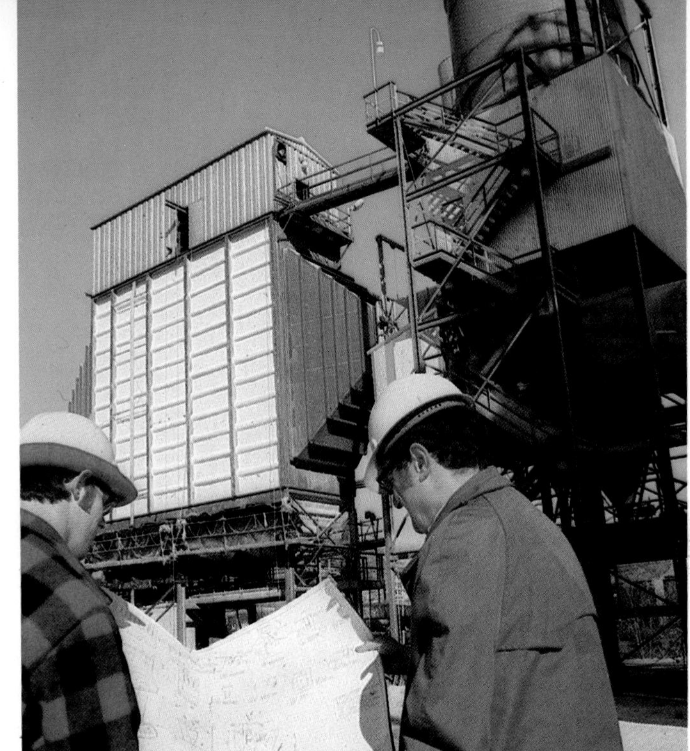

At this lime plant in Ohio, smoke depressors *(right rear)* are intended to curb air pollution. During the 1970s, Congress embarked on a major program to clean up America's air and water.

Recession and war protests. Throughout Nixon's years in office, the economy was plagued with problems. Many of them were connected with the Vietnam War. The cost of the war caused ever larger budget deficits, and the deficits contributed to inflation. Unemployment also rose during the Nixon years. An Arab oil embargo, 1973–1974, slowed the whole economy. The Arab countries were trying to pressure the United States to change its Middle East policy, following another Arab-Israeli war. When the embargo finally ended in 1974, the oil-exporting countries set prices at three to four times what they had been earlier. Between 1974 and 1976, the United States had its worst recession since the depression of the 1930s. Unemployment reached 8 percent, and inflation soared to 12 percent.

Nixon's Presidency was also plagued by continuing protests against the war.

Activities

1. DISCUSSION/ESSAY President Nixon, the only President ever to resign from office, has been blamed for many things and has been criticized perhaps more than any other President. But that is not the whole story. Ask: What did President Nixon accomplish while he was in office? Why did he resign? Have the students write essays about how they think Nixon will be judged by historians in one hundred years.

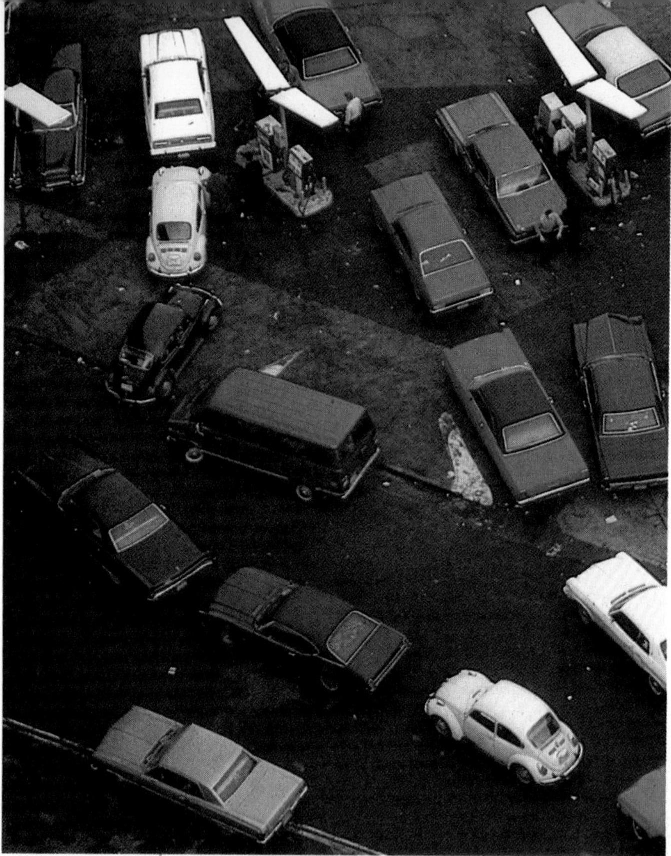

Motorists seeking gas line up at a filling station during the Arab oil embargo of 1973–1974.

2. RESEARCH/WRITTEN REPORTS At times during his first term, Nixon was a very unpopular President. And yet he defeated George McGovern by a landslide in the 1972 election. Have several students make a study of Senator McGovern and his 1972 campaign against Nixon. Have other students do a similar study of George Wallace. They should try to determine the impact of his leaving the race.

What had once been denounced as "Lyndon Johnson's war" was now called "Richard Nixon's war." The announcement in May 1970 that American troops had carried the war from Vietnam into neutral Cambodia touched off widespread demonstrations, especially on college campuses around the country. In actions stemming from demonstrations, four young antiwar protesters were killed by National Guardsmen at Kent State University in Ohio. At Jackson State College in Mississippi, police killed two students. Those events widened the gulf between many Americans and their government.

The election of 1972. In 1971, public opinion polls showed that if an election were held at that time, Richard Nixon would have lost. Yet in the fall of 1972, Nixon won reelection by one of the biggest margins in American history. A number of factors led to this reversal. One was that Nixon's policy of "winding down the war" in Vietnam seemed to be working. By election day in 1972, there were fewer than 75,000 American troops in Vietnam, down from a high of 540,000 under President Johnson. There were also reports of progress in peace negotiations. Another reason for Nixon's victory was his decision to end the draft. This took some of the steam out of the antiwar protests. And the President's visits to China and Russia in 1972 marked him as a statesman.

To run against Nixon, the Democrats chose a dark horse, Senator George McGovern of South Dakota. McGovern won the nomination by appealing for the support of peace activists, minorities, and the young. But this same support marked him with an image of a slightly radical, impractical candidate, which he could not shake during the campaign. Nixon occupied the broad middle of the road. The threat that George Wallace might again drain off votes from the major-party candidates ended when he was shot by a crazed man in May 1972. The attack left Wallace partially paralyzed and unable to campaign. Nixon carried every state except Massachusetts and rolled up almost 18 million more votes than McGovern.

The Watergate burglary. When Nixon took the oath of office to begin his second term, he stood at the height of his power. But events were soon to cast him down. On the night of June 17, 1972, five burglars had been caught looking for documents at the Democratic party headquarters at the Watergate Apartments in Washington, D.C. Investigation showed that they were working with two other men who had had ties to the White House. President Nixon denied any White House involvement and dismissed the whole matter as a "third-rate burglary." Despite charges by George McGovern and several startling stories by two reporters for *The Washington Post*, the break-in did not become an important campaign issue.

When the Watergate Seven came to trial in January 1973, however, Judge John Sirica refused to believe the story that they had acted on their own. Before being sentenced, one of the defendants admitted he had lied. He charged that White House "higher-ups" had approved of the burglary. Amid denials from the White House, a federal grand jury called several Nixon officials to testify. One of them, Presidential Counsel John Dean, told what he knew.

The Watergate investigation. In the summer of 1973, a Senate committee headed by Sam Ervin, a North Carolina Democrat, opened hearings on the Watergate affair. Testimony indicated that despite denials of many Nixon officials, the White House may have blocked an FBI investigation and paid "hush money" to the burglars. This attempt to cover up a crime, if true, was an obstruction of justice and itself a criminal act. The hearings also uncovered a tale of illegal entries, burglaries, wiretaps, talk of blackmail payoffs, illegal campaign contributions, illegal spending of campaign funds, an "enemies list," and the sabotage of opponents' campaigns. All these acts had been under the direction of people in the White House.

Was President Nixon one of these people? Exactly how much did he know about all this? Those key questions were not answered for certain in the committee hearings. But during the hearings, it was learned that the President had tape-recorded all conversations in his office. The tapes would hold the answers.

For the next year, there was a tug-of-war over the tapes. On one side were the Senate committee, the government's own special Watergate prosecutor, and Judge Sirica. On the other side was President Nixon. Claiming "executive privilege," the President refused to give the tapes up. When the Watergate special prosecutor persisted, Nixon had him dismissed. Both the attorney general and his assistant resigned in protest. This touched off such a storm of criticism that in the fall of 1973 Nixon finally turned over a few tapes to Judge Sirica. However, those tapes raised more questions than they answered. One tape had a gap of 18 1/2 minutes. Experts said the tape had been deliberately erased.

Evidence of corruption. In the midst of all those troubles, a separate investigation of corruption in Maryland turned up evidence of criminal activity against Vice President Spiro Agnew. At the time he was governor of Maryland, Agnew had taken bribes from contractors. The pay-offs had continued even after Agnew became Vice President. To avoid a long

3. RESEARCH/ORAL REPORT President Nixon's attempts to make the Supreme Court more conservative were surrounded by controversy. Have your students find out who he appointed, what their backgrounds were, and what effect they had on the philosophy of the Court. Other students could examine the reasons why some of the appointments Nixon made were not confirmed by the Senate. Did the Senate oppose the appointees because of their qualifications, or their political views?

4. RESEARCH/WRITTEN REPORTS Watergate has been the subject of award-winning movies, TV shows, and many books, starting with Bob Woodward and Carl Bernstein's *All the President's Men* (New York: Simon & Schuster, 1974). Have some of your students compile a chronology of the events in the Watergate affair, from the break-in to the resignation and pardon of Nixon. Have others compile a roster of all the Watergate "stars." More sophisticated students could gather as many books as possible about the affair and concentrate on one aspect of it; for example, the missing 18½-minute segment of tape. Have them discover each author's treatment of the particular aspect and note the similarities and differences between the authors.

In the Watergate affair, Attorney General John Mitchell testifies before a Senate committee.

5. **DISCUSSION** There has been much controversy over persons profiting from their notoriety due to involvement in the Watergate affair. ("Don't buy books by crooks" is one slogan that appeared on bumper stickers.) It is a very complex issue, involving freedom of speech, the public's right to know, and the person's right to earn a living. Ask your students to discuss their feelings on this issue. Ask: Would you feel the same way if the person profiting had committed another type of crime, such as murder?

trial, the government agreed to accept from Agnew a plea of *nolo contendere* (no contest) to a lesser charge of evading income taxes. This was accompanied by Agnew's resignation from office. Under the Twenty-fifth Amendment, President Nixon named Gerald Ford of Michigan, a veteran member of the House of Representatives, to serve as Vice President.

In the spring of 1974 a federal grand jury handed down *indictments* (that is, said there was enough evidence to justify a trial) against a number of prominent people in the Nixon administration. They included former Attorney General John Mitchell; Robert Haldeman and John Ehrlichman, formerly Nixon's two closest aides; and four other White House officials. The House Judiciary Committee then began hearings on whether Nixon should be impeached. The committee demanded forty-two more tapes. Once again, Nixon refused. The President's public support was slipping fast. Hoping to end the criticism, Nixon again denied involvement and supplied edited transcripts of the tapes. Many people believed, however, that the edited versions had not told the whole story.

The resignation of Nixon. By summer, Nixon's defenses were falling apart. In June the public learned that the grand jury that had indicted his aides also had named the President as an "unindicted co-conspirator." This meant the jury believed that he too should be charged with criminal acts but doubted that this could be done under the Constitution. On July 30, the Judiciary Committee voted to recommend that the full House impeach Nixon. A few days later, the Supreme Court ruled that Nixon must give up the tapes.

There was no way out. Nixon now admitted that the tapes would show that almost from the start he had been part of the cover-up. With impeachment and conviction certain, Nixon resigned on August 9, 1974. Gerald Ford thus became the first person in American history to become President without having been elected to that national office. He in turn appointed former New York Governor Nelson Rockefeller as the new Vice President.

The Ford administration. An honest, open man, Gerald Ford did much to restore public confidence in the government. Polls showed that after his first three weeks in office, seven out of ten Americans approved of the way he was doing his job. On the other hand, many people objected strongly when Ford granted former President Nixon a full pardon for any crimes he might have committed while in office. Ford's hope was that the pardon would allow Americans to put the "nightmare of Watergate" behind them. Many people, however, thought Nixon should have received the same treatment as the others involved in Watergate. All together, thirty-three members of the Nixon administration were found guilty of crimes related to Watergate, and a number were sent to jail. Ford's popularity slipped further as his administration proved unable to deal effectively with unemployment and inflation.

The 1976 election. Ford sought a full term in 1976 against a man who may have been the greatest dark horse in American political history. When Jimmy Carter began his quest for the Presidency in 1974, he was known by few people outside of Georgia, where he had served one term as governor. But Carter worked tirelessly. He appealed to people as an honest man, an outsider to Washington politics, and one who wanted to restore the people's faith in their government. By winning many primaries, Carter was able to capture the Democratic party nomination. He chose Senator Walter Mondale of Minnesota as his vice-presidential running mate. Carter was the first candidate from the Southeast since before the Civil War. This fact helped him carry every Southern state, and this achievement in turn resulted in his victory.

As President, Jimmy Carter would find it difficult to bring about all the changes he had hoped to make. During his first years, President Carter pressed for programs to conserve energy and to make government more efficient. His administration also tried to hold down both inflation and unemployment, and to encourage economic growth. It was clear, however, that the economic problems that had dogged America for nearly a decade would not yield to easy solutions. Furthermore, farmers during those years had been caught between rising costs and lower prices, and were

6. RESEARCH/DISCUSSION Two men are often given credit for keeping the nation together during the trying period just before and just after President Nixon resigned. General Alexander Haig served as chief of staff for Nixon prior to the resignation. Have some students research his role in maintaining the office of President. Ask: What praise and criticism did Haig receive?

Gerald Ford became President without ever being nationally elected. Have students research and report to the class about Ford's efforts to reestablish the credibility of the office of President. Discuss what could have happened to the country had Haig and Ford been different kinds of people.

7. DISPLAY Caricature is an essential part of today's political cartoons. Have students collect political cartoons of Gerald Ford when he was President. Compare these caricatures with photographs of him. Ask: Did the drawings show what he really looked like, or did they attempt to indicate some aspect of his personality? Display these caricatures along with others of famous people. Perhaps someone in the class could draw caricatures of people in the school.

8. BULLETIN-BOARD DISPLAY/DISCUSSION Have students find magazine and newspaper articles concerning the problems faced by Jimmy Carter's administration. Display these articles on the bulletin board for the class to examine. After the class has had a chance to view the display, ask: Are these problems peculiar to Carter's administration, or did he inherit them from previous ones?

LESSON 3 *(2 to 3 days)*

Performance Objectives

1. To explain orally or in writing the changes in behavior, attitudes, and beliefs exhibited during the 1960s and 1970s.
2. To identify orally or in writing the goals and achievements of the feminist movement of the 1960s and 1970s.
3. To evaluate orally or in writing the success in recent years of minority groups in achieving equal rights.

Famous People

Betty Friedan, Gloria Steinem, Cesar Chavez, Jose Gutierrez, Rudolfo Gonzales

Vocabulary

Red power, Chicano power, gray power, Women's Liberation, National Organization for Women (NOW), Affirmative Action, consciousness-raising groups, Equal Rights Amendment (ERA), *barrios,* United Farm Workers, *La Raza Unida* (United Race), Crusade for Justice, termination, Declaration of Indian Purpose

experiencing hard times. It appeared likely that the farm population, already below 10 million, might decline further.

CHECKUP

1. What were the principal achievements of the Nixon administration?
2. Why did President Richard Nixon resign?
3. What were the major problems facing Jimmy Carter as President?

LESSON 3

American Society

The 1960s and 1970s saw a breaking away from the sameness in behavior, attitudes, and beliefs that had marked the 1950s. The signs were everywhere: from changed hair styles and clothing to loud rock music; from different ideas of morality to experimenting with drugs. At least a part of this was related to the desire of the young to declare their independence from the old. But the changes were related to something more. A sizable minority of young people, and some older ones, rejected what they saw as the bigness, impersonality, and hectic pace of modern life. They also turned their backs on materialism and on the idea of success through disciplined hard work. These people experimented with different life-styles. They declared that feeling and emotion were as important paths to truth as was reason. Some talked about reshaping American society through revolutionary change. Others were content simply to "do their own thing."

Many Americans, young and old, found such changes in behavior bewildering, and the questioning of their beliefs and moral values threatening. What was remarkable, however, was the high tolerance for diversity that American society showed.

During these same years, there were important steps in the direction of greater openness and equality. The cry of *black power* was joined by cries of *red power* (by American Indians), *Chicano power* (by Mexican Americans), and *gray power* (by older citizens), among others. The most notable gains, however, were made, not by a minority, but by a majority—women.

Farm Population in the United States
(as a percentage of total population)

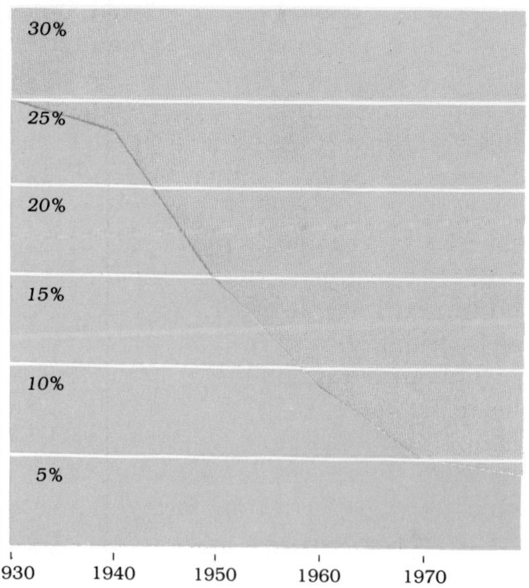

Women's Liberation. The feminist movement, quiet since the 1920s, came to life again in the 1960s. It was not just the old matter of women receiving less pay than men for the same work, although that was part of it. Nor was it only that women's opportunities for advancement were still limited, although that was part of it too. The challenge raised by feminists in the '60s and '70s

★37★

Richard M. Nixon

1913–

Born in CALIFORNIA
In Office 1969–1974
Party REPUBLICAN

Supported lowered voting age. Withdrew troops from Vietnam. Eased tensions with China. Resigned from Presidency while facing probable impeachment for role in Watergate affair.

★38★

Gerald R. Ford

1913–

Born in NEBRASKA
In Office 1974–1977
Party REPUBLICAN

The first appointed Vice President and the first to become President upon the resignation of a Chief Executive. Pardoned Nixon. Fought inflation. Pursued conservative policies.

★39★

Jimmy Carter

1924–

Born in GEORGIA
In Office 1977–
Party DEMOCRATIC

First President from Old South since the Civil War. Supported human rights at home and overseas, and sought to bring peace to Middle East. Worked for energy conservation.

dealt with the basic subject of the roles assigned to women in a male-dominated society. Females were conditioned from childhood, it was argued, to think of themselves only as wives and mothers. Males were taught to believe that they would do "man's work" and become the leaders in business and politics. Such conditioning, wrote Betty Friedan in *The Feminine Mystique* (1963), limited women's chances to achieve their full potential as human beings.

Led by Betty Friedan, a group of 300 Americans—men as well as women—formed the National Organization for Women (NOW) in 1966. This organization's aim was to eliminate sex stereotypes and to open the way to political and economic power for women. NOW and similar organizations were aided by the Civil Rights Act of 1964. This law, you will recall, forbade discrimination on the grounds of sex as well as race and religion. Another law in 1968 led businesses, schools, and universities to set *Affirmative Action* goals for bringing qualified women and minorities into the labor force.

Activities

1. ESSAY/DISCUSSION After the students have read the lesson, have them write essays in which they compare the attitudes, beliefs, and behaviors of young people in the 1950s with those of young people in the 1960s and early 1970s. The essays should explain what the young were interested in, how they viewed materialism, and how they acted. As a follow-up activity, discuss with the class the current attitudes, beliefs, and behaviors. Ask: Are today's youth more like those of the 1950s, or 1960s? Why?

2. USING A CHART The two charts included in this lesson suggest areas of further research for students. The charts also can provide a good lesson in the use—and abuse—of statistics.

a. Have the students look at the chart on page 752. Ask: Does this chart indicate a rapid decline in farm population? Have some students make a similar chart, using the actual numbers of people living on farms. Does the decline seem as dramatic? Have other students make a chart of farm production. Why has that not declined proportionally to the decline in farm population?

b. Have the students do similar work relating to the chart on page 754. Along with the actual numbers, have them find and chart the income of women as it has changed.

c. Divide the class into two groups. Have one group try to show, using statistics, that the position of women in the labor market has really improved over the last twenty years. Have the other group try to find and use statistics to show that women are really not doing that well.

3. DISCUSSION At the Harvard graduation exercises in 1978, Alexander Solzhenitsyn said: "In a society that worships material well-being, people are not ready to die for ideals. They are prepared only for concessions, attempts to gain time, betrayal." Solzhenitsyn said this in criticism of the Western world in general and the United States in particular. Yet the text says that in the 1960s, "a sizable minority of young people . . . turned their backs on materialism." Ask: Are the ideas of Solzhenitsyn and the authors in conflict? Who is right? What about materialism in the United States today? Are people victimized by it? Is materialism bad, good, or neutral? If it is bad, what can be done about it?

4. DISCUSSION Women's Liberation can be a very controversial topic. Some people joke about it, some are very serious about it, and others are bored with it. Some women are very much against Women's Liberation. Ask: Why would a woman be against her own liberation? Is there something in the word *liberation* that frightens her? Have students identify the goals and evaluate the achievements of the feminist movement in recent years.

Background Information

BARBARA JORDON A Texas Democrat, Barbara Jordan was the first black woman elected from a Southern state to serve in Congress. She was elected in 1972, having previously served in the Texas Senate for six years. In 1978 she did not seek reelection to office, leaving Congress to work with the Lyndon Johnson Foundation.

Women in the Labor Force in the United States
(as a percentage of total employed)

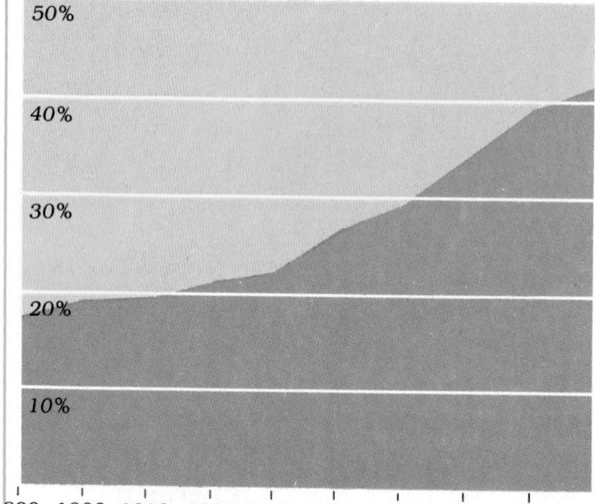

Some changes came quickly, others slowly. The number of women in politics increased dramatically. So did the numbers in the professions, and in the work force generally. As in the 1950s, the wish to add to the family income was one of the reasons. But there were additional reasons, as one mother of four explained: "I wanted some adult companionship, a feeling of accomplishment; having the cleanest floor on the block isn't the greatest thing that can happen to you." However, women still found it difficult to rise to the top of their professions. Perhaps the greatest changes came about through thousands of small *consciousness-raising groups.* Through these groups, women came to think about themselves and their place in society differently from before.

At the same time, it must be noted that not all women—indeed, not even a majority—agreed with all the goals of the Women's Liberation movement. Many said they felt entirely fulfilled as wives and mothers and did not wish to change. Supporters of the women's movement said that this was a choice all women should be free to make.

In 1972, Congress approved and sent to the states an *Equal Rights Amendment* (ERA). It reads: "Equality of rights under the law shall not be denied or abridged by the United States or by any state on account of sex." By early 1978, thirty-three of the thirty-eight states needed for adoption had approved it.

In recent years, as the graph shows, many women have taken jobs outside the home. An increasing number—like Congresswoman Barbara Jordan of Texas—have sought public office.

The minorities emerge. Encouraged by the example of the Black Revolution, other minorities demanded recognition. Mexican Americans were a group second in size only to black Americans, and they were subject to the same injustices. During the 1960s they experienced the same stirrings of ethnic pride and made the same demands for equal rights that blacks did. Mexican-American self-help groups arose in the *barrios*, or segregated neighborhoods, in which they lived. Young activists who called themselves *Chicanos* began to press for classes in the schools that would deal with their Mexican heritage. They also asked that Spanish as well as English be taught in public schools where there were large numbers of Spanish-speaking children. They noted that opportunity was closed to the Mexican-American children who could not understand English.

The best known of the Mexican-American leaders to arise during this time was Cesar Chavez. Chavez organized migrant workers into the United Farm Workers in the 1960s. He used nonviolent, direct action and a hunger strike to call attention to the cause of the migrant workers. Organizing a successful nationwide grape boycott, he forced the growers to recognize the United Farm Workers. Chavez's union lost membership to the competing Teamster's Union in the 1970s. Nonetheless, he remained perhaps the most important leader for the masses of Mexican Americans.

More controversial were two other Mexican-American leaders, Jose Gutierrez and Rudolfo Gonzales. Gutierrez organized a Chicano political party called La Raza Unida (United Race) in Texas in 1970. The party managed to elect a few officials in local elections in Texas and elsewhere, but it had little success in the cities. Gonzales founded the Crusade for Justice, an organization in Colorado to help the Mexican-American community. Gonzales talked of reclaiming the Southwest for Chicanos, but he never made clear how it could be done.

Many Mexican Americans as well as other Americans opposed Gutierrez, Gonzales, and their movements. At the same time, there is no question that, overall, the Chicano movement has helped to stir pride in and bring greater recognition to Mexican Americans.

American Indians. You will recall that in 1934 the practice of breaking up Indian reservations was stopped. Under a new law, Congress encouraged tribal landowning and tribal life. It also provided money for services on the reservations. During the next twenty years, Indians made important gains.

In the early 1950s, however, the government changed its Indian policy once more. Under the new plan, called *termination*, the reservation system would be ended. Tribal lands were to be divided among members of the tribe. The federal government would stop providing the special health and education services it had long furnished. Indians would be encouraged to move to the cities, where jobs were supposed to be plentiful. There they would enter into the mainstream of American life.

When the new plan was put into effect on several reservations, it led to disaster. Many who left the reservations for the cities could not find jobs. They also

5. RESEARCH/ORAL REPORTS American public schools must have Affirmative Action plans in force to comply with federal and state laws. Have some students investigate what is being done in their school to comply with Affirmative Action rules and regulations. Ask: How has Affirmative Action affected hiring practices in the school? How has it affected school programs, such as athletics? After students have reported to the class, discuss the following question: Is Affirmative Action good for the young people of America? Why, or why not?

6. RESEARCH/ORAL REPORTS The following Mexican-American leaders and celebrities may be familiar to your students: playwright Luis Valdez, poet Augustín Lira, novelist Richard Vásquez, the late United States Senator Joseph Montoya of New Mexico, sociologist Ernesto Galarza, quarterbacks Joe Kapp and Jim Plunkett, golfers Nancy López and Lee Trevino, tennis immortal Richard "Pancho" Gonzales, guitarist and singer Trini Lopez, pop singer Vikki Carr, two-time Academy Award winner Anthony Quinn, and folksinger Joan Baez. These are just some of the prominent Mexican Americans of the United States. Have interested students make reports to the class on these or other famous Mexican Americans. Ask them to pay special attention to any problems the people might have had because of their minority status.

7. **DISCUSSION** Have the class compile a list of jobs in your school, town, and state that are held predominantly by persons of one sex. Discuss whether each discrepancy is a result of sexist practice, or sex-role stereotyping; i.e., whether the other sex is prevented from joining the occupation, or whether people are taught that they cannot or should not want to do that job. Are there class members who are interested in nontraditional occupations? Which is more effective in keeping people out of nontraditional jobs, sexism or sex-role stereotyping?

8. **RESEARCH/ORAL REPORT** As the average age of Americans increases due to increased longevity and declining birthrates, some experts feel that the dominance of the youth culture will decline. One group that will try to hurry that day is the people who believe in gray power. Have some students investigate the goals and achievements of the gray power movement. Perhaps they could interview a member of the Gray Panthers to see what issues concern this group.

9. **CONTEST** As a culminating activity for the unit, the class might enjoy dividing into two groups for a contest. Before the contest, have the groups submit possible questions. This forces them to review the material. You might expand the contest to include other units as well. It is also entertaining to include some trivia questions from current events or even entertainment or sports.

found it hard to adjust to the "cement prairies" and to strange ways of living. Those who had sold their share of land found themselves trapped. Often those native Americans who had stayed on their land also had a difficult time. Seeing that the policy was a failure, President Eisenhower ended it in 1958.

At a meeting in Chicago in 1961, representatives from sixty-seven tribes developed their own proposals for a new Indian policy. In their Declaration of Indian Purpose, they asked that reservations be restored and that government assistance in education, health, and housing be improved. Most important, they called for the "right to choose our own way of life." During the 1960s, President Johnson's administration did provide more money for reservations as part of the War on Poverty. But funds were cut back in later years.

Over the next few years, frustrated Indian leaders took a number of direct actions to call attention to the situation of their people. In 1969 a group of Indians took over the abandoned prison on Alcatraz Island in San Francisco Bay. They held it for months before being forced off. The following year, another group occupied the building that housed the Bureau of Indian Affairs in Washington, D.C., for several days. In 1973, armed Indians took over the village of Wounded Knee, South Dakota, the site of a massacre of Indians in 1890. They held the village for more than two months to dramatize their demand for the return of Indian lands that had been taken over several hundred years. Little was gained, however, from these demonstrations. Although certain Indian tribes obtained large amounts of money by selling oil rights on their lands or by recovering lands illegally taken from them, the vast majority of Indians lived in poverty as forgotten Americans. In the prosperous 1970s, the average Indian family's income was far below the poverty line. Indians lived, on the average, twenty years less than other Americans and had a suicide rate twice as high.

At a vineyard in California, Cesar Chavez *(right)* maps strategy for striking farmworkers.

Black Americans. In 1978, on the tenth anniversary of the Kerner Commission's report on ghetto riots, a study showed important changes in the position of many black Americans. "As a whole," the study stated, "the nation's 25 million blacks have gained enormously in the last decade. . . . Many urban blacks, perhaps 30 percent, have worked their way into the middle class and have moved to the suburbs or to better housing within the cities." Larger numbers of blacks were going to colleges, entering the professions, and holding political office. Some of the nation's largest cities, including Detroit, Los Angeles, Washington, D.C., Newark, Cleveland, Atlanta, and New Orleans, had had black mayors.

The same report warned, however, that for the millions left in the ghettos, the situation had become worse. Few of the places that had urban riots in the 1960s had changed. Unemployment among black teenagers was running between 40 and 50 percent. The report cautioned that many of those left in the ghetto might never escape from it. These people and their children might become "a permanent underclass"—poor, unemployed, and without hope.

As Americans assembled their list of unfinished business for the 1980s, they did not lack for items. Equal rights and opportunity, the environment, energy, the cities, inflation, unemployment, peace—the list was a long one. Yet in preparing themselves for the task, Americans could find strength in their nation's past. Although the challenges of an earlier day were different, they had seemed no less difficult at the time. The record of Americans in meeting their challenges, though far from perfect, nonetheless gave reason for confidence as the United States entered its third century as a nation.

CHECKUP

1. Why did many changes take place during the 1960s and 1970s in behavior, attitudes, and beliefs?
2. What were the goals of the feminist movement of the 1960s and 1970s?
3. What success have Mexican Americans and American Indians had in recent years in achieving equal rights?

Key Facts from Chapter 36

1. The Black Revolution of the 1960s brought about substantial gains for many blacks. But for many others—particularly those in the ghettos—there continued to be high unemployment and widespread poverty.
2. In July 1969, American astronauts became the first human beings to set foot on the moon.
3. During the 1960s, America became increasingly involved in the war in Vietnam. As the war dragged on, discontent at home mounted, and during Richard Nixon's administration, American troops were withdrawn.
4. The investigation into the Watergate scandal revealed evidence of criminal acts under the direction of people in the White House. As a result of the investigation, Richard Nixon resigned as President in 1974.
5. The feminist movement of the 1960s and 1970s saw women gain more economic and political power and participate more fully in most areas of American life.

ANSWERS TO REVIEW QUESTIONS

1. Many people thought that Kennedy's Catholic religion would be a serious obstacle to his election.
2. As President, John Kennedy appointed a number of blacks to important positions. Robert C. Weaver, for example, was appointed Federal Housing Administrator and Thurgood Marshall became a federal judge. Kennedy also supported the efforts that were being made to end segregation in the South. He sent federal marshalls to protect those who were demonstrating for the integration of public facilities in the South. In 1962 he sent troops to protect James Meredith, a black who had enrolled at Mississippi's all-white state university. In 1963 he again sent troops into the South to protect peaceful demonstrators protesting refusals to let blacks vote. Soon after that action he sent a stirring civil rights bill to Congress. The bill was not passed during his Presidency but became law under his successor, Lyndon Johnson.
3. Under this law, the Office of Economic Opportunity gave money to local communities to provide jobs and aid for the poor. The Job Corps was started to train young people for careers, and programs were developed to help poor high school students find summer work. Under the act, VISTA, a kind of domestic peace corps, was also set up and funded. The purpose of VISTA was to help poor people improve their living conditions.

4. Congress responded to President Nixon's proposal for a federal program to handle pollution by voting billions of dollars to aid cities and towns in cleaning up their air and water. The Environmental Protection Agency was created to enforce acts that would help to fight pollution.
5. Many Americans, especially college students, were angered by the announcement in May 1970 that American troops had carried the war in Vietnam into neutral Cambodia.
6. Republicans as well as Democrats feared that Wallace would drain off votes from the major party candidates. When the assassination attempt caused Wallace to withdraw from the presidential race, most of his conservative supporters voted for Nixon.
7. Many Americans showed open resistance to the attitudes and beliefs of the 1950s in their dress, hair styles, and ideas and practices regarding morality. They rejected materialism as a goal. Many turned their backs on the pursuit of success through disciplined hard work. Some advocated the reshaping of America through revolutionary change within.
8. The goal of the National Organization for Women was to break down sex stereotypes and to open the way to political and economic power for women.
9. Some of the problems that Americans must continue to work toward solving are equal rights and opportunities, environmental pollution, energy shortages, inflation, unemployment, decaying cities, and obstacles to world peace.

★ REVIEWING THE CHAPTER ★

People, Places, and Events

Civil Rights Act of 1964 *P. 740*
The Great Society *P. 740*
Voting Rights Act of 1965 *P. 741*
The Kerner Commission *P. 743*
Revenue sharing *P. 747*
Watergate burglary *P. 749*
Betty Friedan *P. 753*
Affirmative Action *P. 753*
Cesar Chavez *P. 755*
Declaration of Indian Purpose *P. 756*

Review Questions

1. What did many people think would be a serious obstacle to the election of John F. Kennedy? *P. 737* Les. 1
2. Describe some of the steps Kennedy took to extend the civil rights of black Americans. *Pp. 738, 740* Les. 1
3. In what ways did the Economic Opportunity Act of 1964 contribute to President Johnson's "war on poverty?" *P. 741* L.1
4. What was the significance of the creation of the Environmental Protection Agency? *P. 747* Les. 2
5. What United States action in Vietnam touched off widespread demonstrations by Americans in May 1970? *P. 748* L.2
6. How did the assassination attempt on George Wallace influence the election results in 1972? *P. 748* Les. 2
7. What were some of the signs of change in attitudes of Americans in the 1960s and 1970s? *P. 752* Les. 3
8. What was the goal of the National Organization for Women? *P. 753* Les. 3
9. Identify at least seven major problems that Americans must continue to work toward solving in the 1980s. *P. 757* L.3

Chapter Test

On a separate piece of paper, write ***T*** *if the statement is true and* ***F*** *if the statement is false.*

1. John Kennedy's term for the challenges facing America in the 1960s was the New Frontier. T
2. President Kennedy easily persuaded Congress to approve his proposals for civil rights, tax reform, defense spending, space travel, and federal aid to education. F
3. Lyndon Johnson won the Democratic nomination in 1968 by explaining why United States troops were in Vietnam. F
4. President Nixon was opposed to many of the social programs begun under the Johnson administration because he believed that social problems could not be solved by "throwing money at them." T
5. The cost of the Vietnam War caused large budget deficits and contributed to national inflation. T
6. The Supreme Court ruled that the tapes proved Nixon guilty of impeachable offenses. F
7. Gerald Ford was the first President of the United States never elected to national office. T
8. During the 1960s and 1970s there were important steps in the direction of greater equality for blacks, American Indians, Chicanos, and women. T
9. The Equal Rights Amendment stated that under the law, equality of rights could not be denied or abridged on account of religion. F
10. Even in the 1970s, the income of the average American Indian family was far below the poverty line. T

★ REVIEWING THE UNIT

1948	*Marshall Plan*
1950–1953	*Korean War*
1954	*Army-McCarthy hearings*
1958	*Sputnik spurs space program*
1962	*Cuban missile crisis*
1968	*Height of involvement in Vietnam*
1969	*Astronauts land on moon*
1972	*Nixon visits China*
1973	*Arab oil embargo begins*
1974	*Nixon resigns*
1976	*Jimmy Carter elected President*

After World War II, America reconverted to a peacetime economy. In Europe, the United States and Russia became involved in a cold war. America helped European countries that were resisting communism and pursued a program of containment to halt Russian expansion. The United States also resisted communism in Asia. War in Korea from 1950 to 1953 ended inconclusively. The cold war abroad was accompanied by a hunt for Communists at home, creating a climate of fear and suspicion.

The quiet of the late 1950s gave way to turbulence and violence in the 1960s. In 1962, Russia supplied missiles for Communist Cuba, but war was averted when Russia withdrew the missles. The Black Revolution saw Martin Luther King, Jr., lead marches and rallies to promote civil rights and eliminate discrimination. During the decade, assassins killed President John Kennedy, Martin Luther King, Jr., and Robert Kennedy. The United States became deeply involved in Vietnam after Communists threatened to take over that country. The costly, drawn-out war became very unpopular at home. Under President Richard Nixon, American forces were withdrawn. In 1969, American astronauts landed on the moon.

The Watergate scandal brought about the resignation of President Nixon in 1974. He was succeeded by Vice President Gerald Ford. In 1976 Jimmy Carter was elected President. He faced difficult problems in reducing inflation and unemployment and in carrying out a program to conserve energy resources.

Answers to Unit Questions

1. a. Expansion **b.** 1845—Texas entered the Union; 1853—Gadsden Purchase; 1867—Purchase of Alaska; 1898—Hawaii annexed and Puerto Rico ceded to the United States; 1917—Purchase of the Virgin Islands
2. 1807—New Jersey abolished property-holding and taxpaying qualifications for voting; 1826—Maryland removed religious qualifications for voting and office holding; 1870—Citizens guaranteed the right to vote by Fifteenth Amendment; 1920—Women received right to vote by Nineteenth Amendment; 1965—Voting Rights Act; 1971—Voting age lowered to 18 by Twenty-sixth Amendment
3. *Civil rights movement:* 1831—Nat Turner slave uprising; 1857—Dred Scott decision; 1863—Emancipation Proclamation; 1865—Slavery prohibited by Thirteenth Amendment; 1868—Citizenship given to all persons born or naturalized in United States by Fourteenth Amendment; 1870—Citizens guaranteed the right to vote by Fifteenth Amendment; 1875—Civil Rights Act; 1896—*Plessy* v. *Ferguson*; 1954—*Brown* v. *Board of Education of Topeka, Kansas;* 1955—Dr. King led Montgomery boycott; 1965—Voting Rights Act; 1968—Affirmative Action Programs mandated by law. *Women's rights movement:* 1848—Woman's Rights Convention; 1920—Women received right to vote by Nineteenth Amendment; 1968—Affirmative Action Programs mandated by law; 1972—ERA sent to states for ratification

The event that is a part of both movements is the mandating of Affirmative Action Programs.

★ REVIEWING THE UNIT ★

Skills Development: Creating a Time Line

In your study of American history, you have learned about many of the important events that have helped to shape the nation. Some of those events are shown in the chronological listing that follows.

Use this listing to create a time line. Remember that before you draw a time line, you need to decide on the scale to be used (see page 78).

1803 Louisiana Purchase
1807 New Jersey abolished property-holding and taxpaying qualifications for voting
1819 Acquisition of Florida completed
1826 Maryland removed religious qualifications for voting and office holding
1831 Nat Turner slave uprising
1845 Texas entered the Union
1848 Woman's Rights Convention
1853 Gadsden Purchase
1857 Dred Scott decision
1863 Emancipation Proclamation
1865 Slavery prohibited
1867 Purchase of Alaska
1868 Citizenship was given to all persons born or naturalized in the United States
1870 Citizens guaranteed the right to vote regardless of race, color, or previous condition of slavery
1875 Civil Rights Act guaranteed equal rights in public places without distinction of color
1896 *Plessy* v. *Ferguson*
1898 Hawaii annexed
Puerto Rico ceded to United States
1917 Purchase of the Virgin Islands
1920 Women received right to vote
1954 *Brown* v. *Board of Education of Topeka, Kansas*
1955 Martin Luther King, Jr., led Montgomery, Alabama, boycott
1965 Voting Rights Act
1968 Affirmative Action Programs mandated by law
1971 Voting age lowered to 18
1972 Equal Rights Amendment sent to the states for ratification

From a time line, you are able to see not only the sequence of events but also certain trends or themes. Study the time line and then answer the following questions.

1. **a.** What theme of American history is suggested by the events in 1803 and 1819?
   b. Identify the six other events that relate to this theme.
2. Another theme is the growth of democracy as more Americans won the right to vote. Name the six events from the time line that specifically relate to this theme.
3. Which events are associated with the civil rights movement? the women's rights movement? Which event is a part of both movements?
4. Select one of the following themes to add to the time line: America's wars; inventions; development of the labor movement; Constitutional amendments; presidential elections; foreign policy doctrines; growth of the welfare state; development of American political parties. Using your textbook, identify at least six events associated with the theme you choose and add them to the time line. Show these events in a different color.

CREDITS

Cover: Stefan Martin   Maps: Lothar Roth
Graphs and Charts: John D. Firestone Associates
Unit Openers: Stefan Martin

All presidential portraits are from the United States Bureau of Engraving and Printing unless otherwise indicated.

CHAPTER 1: 2—Harald Sund. 5—Rare Book Division, New York Public Library, Astor, Lenox and Tilden Foundations. 6—*TL*, Ron Toelke; *TR*, Culver; *BL*. Culver; *BM*. Bettmann Archive: *BR*, Culver. 9—Bibliotheque Nationale. 13—Tiroler Landesmuseum Ferdinandeum, Innsbruck. 14—No credit. 15—Alan Band Associates, courtesy of Victoria and Albert Museum, London.

CHAPTER 2: 18—Abby Aldrich Rockefeller Folk Art Collection. 20—Virginia State Library. 21—Brown Brothers. 22—National Park Service, Jamestown. 24, 27—Culver. 31—New-York Historical Society. 33—No credit.

CHAPTER 3: 38—New York State Historical Association, Cooperstown. 40—Rare Book Division, New York Public Library, Astor, Lenox and Tilden Foundations. 42—Detail, Enoch Pratt Free Library. 45—William L. Clements Library, University of Michigan. 47, 50—Culver. 53—Massachusetts Charitable Mechanics Association, on loan to Science Museum of Boston.

CHAPTER 4: 56—Courtesy of The Henry Francis du Pont Winterthur Museum. 59—National Portrait Gallery, Smithsonian Institution. 60—American Museum of Natural History. 62—Brown Brothers. 63, 65—Culver. 67—Bettmann Archive. 69—John Work Garrett Library of Johns Hopkins University. 72—Peabody Museum of Salem, photo by Mark Sexton. 74—Culver.

CHAPTER 5: 80—Detail, courtesy of The New-York Historical Society. 83—Historical Society of Pennsylvania. 87—*L*, Emmet Collection, Manuscripts and Archives Division, New York Public Library, Astor, Lenox and Tilden Foundations. 89—Detail, Massachusetts Historical Society. 90—Bettmann Archive. 92—Rhode Island Historical Society. 95—United States Postal Service. 97—Reproduced through the courtesy of the Virginia Historical Society.

CHAPTER 6: 103—Courtesy of Fort Ticonderoga Museum. 104—Culver. 107—American Antiquarian Society. 117—Library of Congress. 118—Mike Godfrey for Silver Burdett.

CHAPTER 7: 120—Anne S. K. Brown Military Collection. 123—Bettmann Archive. 124—Culver; except *BM*, courtesy of The New-York Historical Society. 126—George Rogers Clark National Historical Park. 132—Brown Brothers. 133—New York Public Library Picture Collection.

CHAPTER 8: 138—Historical Society of Pennsylvania. 140—Historical Society of Pennsylvania. 145—Bibliotheque Nationale. 146—Culver. 147—From *History of Hungary*, picture by Stephan Pekary, Cserlpfalvi.

CHAPTER 9: 154—Independence National Historical Park. 156—Culver. 161—Bettmann Archive. 162—Courtesy of The New-York Historical Society. 164—Stokes Collection, New York Public Library. 166—Culver. 168—Courtesy of The New-York Historical Society. 169—United States Department of the Treasury. 174-197—Don Pulver.

CHAPTER 10: 198—Collection of L. L. Bean. 203—New York City Art Commission. 204—Stokes Collection, New York Public Library. 207—Giraudon, courtesy of Musée Carnavalet. 211—Courtesy of Pennsylvania Academy of Fine Arts. 212—Culver. 213—Library of Congress. 214—New York State Historical Association, Cooperstown.

CHAPTER 11: 216—Louisiana State Museum. 218—Mariners Museum. 222—Filson Club. 223—United States Supreme Court. 224—Amon Carter Museum. 226—Bettmann Archive. 227—Library of Congress. 228—Anne S. K. Brown Military Collection. 230—New-York Historical Society. 233—Culver. 235—*L*, Culver; *M*, Library of Congress.

CHAPTER 12: 242—New-York Historical Society. 245—Missouri Historical Society. 250—Culver. 253—New-York Historical Society. 256—Munson-Williams-Proctor Institute, Utica. 258—Library of Congress. 260—Culver.

CHAPTER 13: 262—J. N. Bartfield Galleries, New York. 268, 269—Culver. 273—Bettmann Archive. 277—Library of Congress. 279—New-York Historical Society. 280—Culver, 283—*L. M.* Culver.

CHAPTER 14: 286—Harald Sund. 292—Northern Natural Gas Collection, Joslyn Art Museum, Omaha, Nebraska. 295—Photo used by permission of Curator's Division, Historical Department of The Church of Jesus Christ of Latter-day Saints.

CHAPTER 15: 309, 310—Culver. 312, 316—Bettmann Archive. 319—National Portrait Gallery, Smithsonian Institution.

CHAPTER 16: 325—Hirschl and Adler Galleries. 326—Courtesy of St. John Fisher College, Rochester. 328—Bettmann Archive. 330—Louisiana State Museum. 333—Courtesy of Kenneth M. Newman, Old Print Shop, New York City. 336—Culver. 339—Kansas Historical Society. 343—Culver.

CHAPTER 17: 346—Anne S. K. Brown Military Collection. 349—Library of Congress. 350—Culver. 353—*L*, Bettmann Archive; *R*, Cook Collection, Valentine Museum, Richmond. 355—Bettmann Archive. 360—Bradley Smith from Photo Researchers. 363—Culver. 365—*TL*, Library of Congress; *TR*, Bettmann Archive; *BL*, *BR*, Culver.

CHAPTER 18: 368—Library of Congress. 370, 371—Culver. 372—Anne S. K. Brown Military Collection. 375, 377, 379, 380—Culver. 385—New-York Historical Society. 386, 388—Culver.

CHAPTER 19: 394—Brown Brothers. 397—United Press International. 402—Culver. 404—Minnesota Historical Society. 407—Birmingham Museums and Art Gallery, Birmingham, England. 408, 409—Culver.

CHAPTER 20: 412—Brown Brothers. 414—Courtesy of Newberry Library, Chicago. 423—Brown Brothers.

CHAPTER 21: 426—Prints Division, New York Public Library, Astor, Lenox and Tilden Foundations. 428—Culver. 431—Bettmann Archive. 433—George Eastman House. 435—Port Authority of New York and New Jersey. 437—Culver. 439—John Running. 440—Sybil Shelton from Monkmeyer. 442—Library of Congress. 443—United States Army photo.

CHAPTER 22: 446—Kurt Scholz from Shostal Associates. 449—Marsha Perlman. 455—Culver. 456—Peggo Cromer.

CHAPTER 23: 465—Shostal Associates. 468—I. N. Phelps Stokes Collection, New York Public Library, Astor, Lenox and Tilden Foundations. 470—Gus Johnson, courtesy Connecticut State Library. 474—Culver. 475—Bettmann Archive. 477—Print Collection, New York Public Library, Astor, Lenox and Tilden Foundations. 478—Bettmann Archive.

CHAPTER 24: 484—Wells Fargo Bank History Room. 486—Oakland Museum History Department. 488—Smithsonian Institution. 489—Pony Express Museum. 491—Smithsonian Institution. 496—Bettmann Archive. 497—Denver Public Library, Western History Collection.

CHAPTER 25: 500—National Steel Corporation. 503—Culver. 506—*T*, Culver; *B*, Pach/Bettmann Archive. 508, 510—Culver. 512—George Eastman House. 514—United States Department of Labor. 516—Edison National Historical Park. 517—Culver.

CHAPTER 26: 520—Culver. 522—Historical Society of Wisconsin. 526, 528—Culver. 529—*T*, Bettmann Archive; *B*, Wyoming State Archives and Historical Department. 531—Culver. 533—Bettmann Archive. 535—Culver. 536—Brown Brothers. 537—*T*. © New York Times Company. Reprinted by permission. 540—Culver.

CHAPTER 27: 546—Addison Gallery of American Art, Phillips Academy. 549—Franklin Delano Roosevelt Library. 551, 553—Culver. 554—Bradley Smith from Photo Researchers. 556—Culver. 557—Northern Natural Gas Collection, Joslyn Art Museum, Omaha, Nebraska.

CHAPTER 28: 560—Library of Congress. 562—Culver. 565—International Harvester Company. 567—Library of Congress. 569, 570—Culver. 571—*Judge*. 572—Culver. 575—Brown Brothers. 576; 577, *M*—Culver.

CHAPTER 29: 580—Los Angeles County Art Museum. 581—American Telephone and Telegraph Company. 585, 587—Culver. 588—Brown Brothers. 590—Jacob Riis Collection, Museum of the City of New York. 593; 594; 596; 597; 598, *L, M*—Culver.

CHAPTER 30: 602—Copyright © 1934 (renewed) 1962 by The Condé Nast Publications Inc. 604—*M*, Library of Congress. 607—United Press International. 608—Wide World. 611, 612, 613—Culver. 615—United Press International. 618—Wide World.

CHAPTER 31: 626—United States Naval Academy Museum. 629—Culver. 631—Peabody Museum of Salem, photo by Mark Sexton. 632—New York Public Library, Astor, Lenox and Tilden Foundations. 637, 639, 641—Culver.

CHAPTER 32: 653—Erich Lessing from Magnum. 655—Brown Brothers. 657, 658—Smithsonian Institution. 660—Keystone. 663—Library of Congress. 664—Culver.

CHAPTER 33: 670—United States Navy Combat Art. 678—United Press International. 680-681—United States Navy Combat Art. 684—United States Coast Guard. 687—United States Navy Combat Art. 689—National Archives. 690—Eric Carle from Shostal Associates.

CHAPTER 34: 696—Magnum. 698—Culver. 701—Brown Brothers. 703—Wide World. 706—United States Army. 711—Bill Ray from Black Star. 713—United Press International. 715—Wide World. 717—United Press International. 719—Rothco.

CHAPTER 35: 722—Grant Heilman. 725—United Press International. 726—Harry S. Truman Library. 731—Mark Godfrey from Magnum. 733—Dan Budnik from Woodfin Camp Associates.

CHAPTER 36: 736—NASA. 739—Martin Levick from Black Star. 740—Cecil Stoughton. 743—Constantine Manos from Magnum. 747—David Forbert from Shostal Associates. 748—Sepp Seitz from Magnum. 750—Dennis Brack from Black Star. 753—*R*, The White House. 754—Ginger Chih. 756—Paul Fusco from Magnum.

PRESIDENTS AND VICE PRESIDENTS OF THE UNITED STATES

President	*Birth-Death*	*State**	*Term*	*Party*	*Vice President*
George Washington	1732–1799	Va.	1789–1797	None	John Adams
John Adams	1735–1826	Mass.	1797–1801	Federalist	Thomas Jefferson
Thomas Jefferson	1743–1826	Va.	1801–1805	Democratic-Republican	Aaron Burr
			1805–1809		George Clinton
James Madison	1751–1836	Va.	1809–1813	Democratic-Republican	George Clinton
			1813–1817		Elbridge Gerry
James Monroe	1758–1831	Va.	1817–1825	Democratic-Republican	Daniel D. Tompkins
John Quincy Adams	1767–1848	Mass.	1825–1829	National Republican	John C. Calhoun
Andrew Jackson	1767–1845	Tenn.	1829–1833	Democratic	John C. Calhoun
			1833–1837		Martin Van Buren
Martin Van Buren	1782–1862	N.Y.	1837–1841	Democratic	Richard M. Johnson
William H. Harrison	1773–1841	Ohio	1841	Whig	John Tyler
John Tyler	1790–1862	Va.	1841–1845	Whig	....
James K. Polk	1795–1849	Tenn.	1845–1849	Democratic	George M. Dallas
Zachary Taylor	1784–1850	La.	1849–1850	Whig	Millard Fillmore
Millard Fillmore	1800–1874	N.Y.	1850–1853	Whig	....
Franklin Pierce	1804–1869	N.H.	1853–1857	Democratic	William R. King
James Buchanan	1791–1868	Pa.	1857–1861	Democratic	John C. Breckinridge
Abraham Lincoln	1809–1865	Ill.	1861–1865	Republican	Hannibal Hamlin
			1865		Andrew Johnson
Andrew Johnson	1808–1875	Tenn.	1865–1869	Democratic	....
Ulysses S. Grant	1822–1885	Ill.	1869–1873	Republican	Schuyler Colfax
			1873–1877		Henry Wilson
Rutherford B. Hayes	1822–1893	Ohio	1877–1881	Republican	William A. Wheeler
James A. Garfield	1831–1881	Ohio	1881	Republican	Chester A. Arthur
Chester A. Arthur	1830–1886	N.Y.	1881–1885	Republican	....
Grover Cleveland	1837–1908	N.Y.	1885–1889	Democratic	Thomas A. Hendricks
Benjamin Harrison	1833–1901	Ind.	1889–1893	Republican	Levi P. Morton
Grover Cleveland	1837–1908	N.Y.	1893–1897	Democratic	Adlai E. Stevenson
William McKinley	1843–1901	Ohio	1897–1901	Republican	Garret A. Hobart
			1901		Theodore Roosevelt
Theodore Roosevelt	1858–1919	N.Y.	1901–1905	Republican	....
			1905–1909		Charles W. Fairbanks
William H. Taft	1857–1930	Ohio	1909–1913	Republican	James S. Sherman
Woodrow Wilson	1856–1924	N.J.	1913–1921	Democratic	Thomas R. Marshall
Warren G. Harding	1865–1923	Ohio	1921–1923	Republican	Calvin Coolidge
Calvin Coolidge	1872–1933	Mass.	1923–1925	Republican	....
			1925–1929		Charles G. Dawes
Herbert C. Hoover	1874–1964	Calif.	1929–1933	Republican	Charles Curtis
Franklin D. Roosevelt	1882–1945	N.Y.	1933–1941	Democratic	John N. Garner
			1941–1945		Henry A. Wallace
			1945		Harry S. Truman
Harry S. Truman	1884–1972	Mo.	1945–1949	Democratic	....
			1949–1953		Alben W. Barkley
Dwight D. Eisenhower	1890–1969	N.Y.	1953–1961	Republican	Richard M. Nixon
John F. Kennedy	1917–1963	Mass.	1961–1963	Democratic	Lyndon B. Johnson
Lyndon B. Johnson	1908–1973	Texas	1963–1965	Democratic	....
			1965–1969		Hubert H. Humphrey
Richard M. Nixon	1913–	N.Y.	1969–1973	Republican	Spiro T. Agnew
			1973–1974		Agnew/Ford
Gerald R. Ford	1913–	Mich.	1974–1977	Republican	Nelson R. Rockefeller
Jimmy Carter	1924–	Ga.	1977–	Democratic	Walter Mondale

**State of residence at election*

FACTS ABOUT THE STATES

State	Year and order of admission*	Area in sq. mi. and rank	Population (1977) (estimated) and rank	Representatives	Capital city
Alabama	1819 (22)	51,609 (29)	3,690,000 (21)	7	Montgomery
Alaska	1959 (49)	586,400 (1)	407,000 (49)	1	Juneau
Arizona	1912 (48)	113,909 (6)	2,296,000 (32)	4	Phoenix
Arkansas	1836 (25)	53,104 (27)	2,144,000 (33)	4	Little Rock
California	1850 (31)	158,693 (3)	21,896,000 (1)	43	Sacramento
Colorado	1876 (38)	104,247 (8)	2,619,000 (28)	5	Denver
Connecticut	1788 (5)	5,009 (48)	3,108,000 (24)	6	Hartford
Delaware	1787 (1)	2,057 (49)	582,000 (47)	1	Dover
Florida	1845 (27)	58,560 (22)	8,452,000 (8)	15	Tallahassee
Georgia	1788 (4)	58,876 (21)	5,048,000 (14)	10	Atlanta
Hawaii	1959 (50)	6,424 (47)	895,000 (40)	2	Honolulu
Idaho	1890 (43)	83,557 (13)	857,000 (41)	2	Boise
Illinois	1818 (21)	56,400 (24)	11,245,000 (5)	24	Springfield
Indiana	1816 (19)	36,291 (38)	5,330,000 (12)	11	Indianapolis
Iowa	1846 (29)	56,290 (25)	2,879,000 (25)	6	Des Moines
Kansas	1861 (34)	82,264 (14)	2,326,000 (31)	5	Topeka
Kentucky	1792 (15)	40,395 (37)	3,458,000 (23)	7	Frankfort
Louisiana	1812 (18)	48,523 (31)	3,921,000 (20)	8	Baton Rouge
Maine	1820 (23)	33,215 (39)	1,085,000 (38)	2	Augusta
Maryland	1788 (7)	10,577 (42)	4,139,000 (18)	8	Annapolis
Massachusetts	1788 (6)	8,257 (45)	5,782,000 (10)	12	Boston
Michigan	1837 (26)	58,216 (23)	9,129,000 (7)	19	Lansing
Minnesota	1858 (32)	84,068 (12)	3,975,000 (19)	8	St. Paul
Mississippi	1817 (20)	47,716 (32)	2,389,000 (29)	5	Jackson
Missouri	1821 (24)	69,686 (19)	4,801,000 (15)	10	Jefferson City
Montana	1889 (41)	147,138 (4)	761,000 (43)	2	Helena
Nebraska	1867 (37)	77,227 (15)	1,561,000 (35)	3	Lincoln
Nevada	1864 (36)	110,540 (7)	633,000 (46)	1	Carson City
New Hampshire	1788 (9)	9,304 (44)	849,000 (42)	2	Concord
New Jersey	1787 (3)	7,836 (46)	7,329,000 (9)	15	Trenton
New Mexico	1912 (47)	121,666 (5)	1,190,000 (37)	2	Santa Fe
New York	1788 (11)	49,576 (30)	17,924,000 (2)	39	Albany
North Carolina	1789 (12)	52,719 (28)	5,525,000 (11)	11	Raleigh
North Dakota	1889 (39)	70,665 (17)	653,000 (45)	1	Bismarck
Ohio	1803 (17)	41,222 (35)	10,701,000 (6)	23	Columbus
Oklahoma	1907 (46)	69,919 (18)	2,811,000 (27)	6	Oklahoma City
Oregon	1859 (33)	96,981 (10)	2,376,000 (30)	4	Salem
Pennsylvania	1787 (2)	45,333 (33)	11,785,000 (4)	25	Harrisburg
Rhode Island	1790 (13)	1,214 (50)	935,000 (39)	2	Providence
South Carolina	1788 (8)	31,055 (40)	2,876,000 (26)	6	Columbia
South Dakota	1889 (40)	77,047 (16)	689,000 (44)	2	Pierre
Tennessee	1796 (16)	42,244 (34)	4,299,000 (17)	8	Nashville
Texas	1845 (28)	267,339 (2)	12,830,000 (3)	24	Austin
Utah	1896 (45)	84,916 (11)	1,268,000 (36)	2	Salt Lake City
Vermont	1791 (14)	9,609 (43)	483,000 (48)	11	Montpelier
Virginia	1788 (10)	40,815 (36)	5,135,000 (13)	10	Richmond
Washington	1889 (42)	68,192 (20)	3,658,000 (22)	7	Olympia
West Virgina	1863 (35)	24,181 (41)	1,859,000 (34)	4	Charleston
Wisconsin	1848 (30)	56,154 (26)	4,651,000 (16)	9	Madison
Wyoming	1890 (44)	97,914 (9)	406,000 (50)	1	Cheyenne

*For first 13 states, year of ratification of Constitution

Vancouver
C. Flattery
WASHINGTON
Seattle
Olympia
Tacoma
Mt. Rainier 14,410 ft.
Spokane
Portland
Columbia R.
Salem
Eugene
OREGON
C. Blanco
IDAHO
Boise
Salmon R.
Snake R.
Great Falls
Missouri R.
Helena
MONTANA
Yellowstone R.
Billings
Grand Teton 13,766 ft.
Idaho Falls
WYOMING
NORTH DAKOTA
Bismarck
Fargo
BLACK HILLS
Pierre
Cheyenne R.
SOUTH DAKOTA
Sioux Falls
C. Mendocino
Sacramento R.
Central Valley
SIERRA NEVADA
Reno
Carson City
NEVADA
Humboldt R.
Great Salt Lake
Ogden
Salt Lake City
Green R.
Cheyenne
N. Platte R.
NEBRASKA
San Francisco
Berkeley
Oakland
San Jose
Sacramento
San Joaquin R.
Fresno
Mt. Whitney
UTAH
Longs Pk. 14,256 ft.
S. Platte R.
Platte R.
Denver
COLORADO
Mt. Elbert 14,433 ft.
Pikes Pk. 14,110 ft.
Pueblo
Colorado R.
KANSAS
CALIFORNIA
Pt. Conception
Bakersfield
Las Vegas
Mojave Desert
Blanca Pk. 14,317 ft.
Arkansas R.
Glendale
Pasadena
Los Angeles
Long Beach
Anaheim
San Bernardino
Riverside
San Diego
ARIZONA
Santa Fe
Albuquerque
NEW MEXICO
OKLAHOMA
Amarillo
Phoenix
Tucson
Rio Grande
Lubbock
Llano Estacado
El Paso
Fort Worth
TEXAS
Waco
Austin
San Antonio
Laredo
Corpus Christi
MEXICO
PACIFIC OCEAN
ROCKY MOUNTAINS
COAST RANGES
GREAT PLAINS
Great Basin
Colorado Plateau
Columbia Plateau
ASIA
SOVIET UNION
Arctic Circle
Barrow
BROOKS RANGE
Bering Strait
Nome
ALASKA
St. Lawrence I.
Yukon R.
Fairbanks
St. Matthew I.
ALASKA RANGE
Mt. McKinley 20,320 ft.
CANADA
Monday
International Date Line
Sunday
BERING SEA
Nunivak I.
Anchorage
Juneau
Kenai Pen.
Gulf of Alaska
Alexander Arch.
ALEUTIAN ISLANDS
Near Is.
Rat Is.
Andreanof Is.
Unimak I.
Fox Is.
Kodiak I.
0 300 mi.
0 500 km

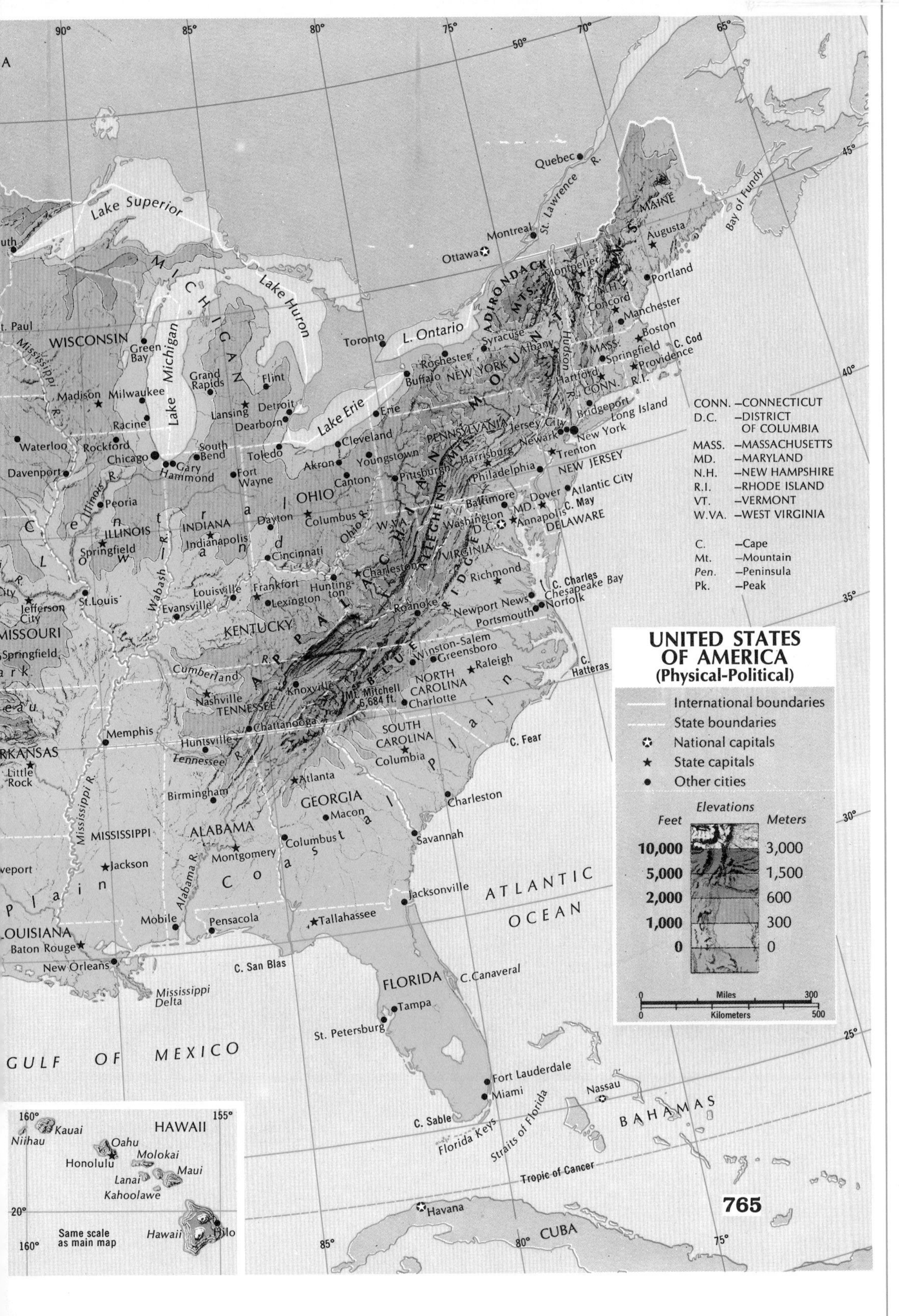

UNITED STATES OF AMERICA
(Physical-Political)
International boundaries
State boundaries
National capitals
State capitals
Other cities
Elevations
Feet
Meters
10,000
3,000
5,000
1,500
2,000
600
1,000
300
0
0
Miles
300
Kilometers
500
CONN. –CONNECTICUT
D.C. –DISTRICT OF COLUMBIA
MASS. –MASSACHUSETTS
MD. –MARYLAND
N.H. –NEW HAMPSHIRE
R.I. –RHODE ISLAND
VT. –VERMONT
W.VA. –WEST VIRGINIA
C. –Cape
Mt. –Mountain
Pen. –Peninsula
Pk. –Peak
Lake Superior
Lake Michigan
Lake Huron
Lake Erie
L. Ontario
MICHIGAN
WISCONSIN
ILLINOIS
INDIANA
OHIO
KENTUCKY
TENNESSEE
MISSISSIPPI
ALABAMA
GEORGIA
FLORIDA
SOUTH CAROLINA
NORTH CAROLINA
VIRGINIA
W.VA.
PENNSYLVANIA
NEW YORK
NEW JERSEY
DELAWARE
MD.
D.C.
CONN.
R.I.
MASS.
VT.
N.H.
MAINE
MISSOURI
LOUISIANA
ADIRONDACK MTS.
APPALACHIAN MOUNTAINS
ALLEGHENY MTS.
BLUE RIDGE
Mt. Mitchell 6,684 ft.
Central Lowland
Coastal Plain
ATLANTIC OCEAN
GULF OF MEXICO
BAHAMAS
CUBA
Havana
Nassau
Tropic of Cancer
Straits of Florida
Florida Keys
C. Sable
C. Canaveral
C. San Blas
Mississippi Delta
C. Fear
C. Hatteras
C. Charles
C. May
C. Cod
Chesapeake Bay
Long Island
Bay of Fundy
St. Lawrence R.
Hudson R.
Mississippi R.
Ohio R.
Illinois R.
Wabash R.
Tennessee R.
Cumberland R.
Alabama R.
Quebec
Montreal
Ottawa
Toronto
Augusta
Portland
Montpelier
Concord
Manchester
Boston
Providence
Springfield
Hartford
Bridgeport
Albany
Syracuse
Rochester
Buffalo
Erie
New York
Jersey City
Newark
Trenton
Philadelphia
Atlantic City
Dover
Baltimore
Annapolis
Washington
Harrisburg
Pittsburgh
Youngstown
Cleveland
Akron
Canton
Columbus
Dayton
Cincinnati
Toledo
Detroit
Dearborn
Flint
Lansing
Grand Rapids
South Bend
Fort Wayne
Gary
Hammond
Chicago
Milwaukee
Racine
Madison
Green Bay
Rockford
Waterloo
Davenport
Peoria
Springfield
Indianapolis
St. Paul
Duluth
St. Louis
Jefferson City
Springfield
Louisville
Frankfort
Lexington
Evansville
Huntington
Charleston
Richmond
Roanoke
Newport News
Norfolk
Portsmouth
Winston-Salem
Greensboro
Raleigh
Charlotte
Knoxville
Nashville
Chattanooga
Memphis
Huntsville
Birmingham
Atlanta
Columbia
Charleston
Savannah
Macon
Columbus
Montgomery
Jackson
Little Rock
Mobile
Pensacola
Tallahassee
Jacksonville
Tampa
St. Petersburg
Fort Lauderdale
Miami
Baton Rouge
New Orleans
HAWAII
Niihau
Kauai
Oahu
Honolulu
Molokai
Lanai
Maui
Kahoolawe
Hawaii
Hilo
Same scale as main map

Index

1 2 3 4 5 6 7 8 9 10 - VH - 85 84 83 82 81 80 79 78